Contents

KU-501-933

OPPOSITE MOUNT FUJI PREVIOUS PAGE WOMEN WEARING KIMONO

Introduction to
Japan

Japan intrigues in a way no other country does. It has a unique ability to embrace the present without discarding the past. From Zen Buddhism to robotics, the island country's traditions, technology and creativity are inspiring and exciting. Whether you enjoy sushi and sake, or manga and anime, the richness of the culture and the hospitality of the people make visiting the "Land of the Rising Sun" a rewarding experience.

The sheer diversity and intensity of experiences on offer to visitors in the cities or the countryside can be overwhelming. Whether browsing trendy fashion boutiques, electronics stores buzzing with the latest gadgets or a centuries-old shop, you are sure to find something strikingly unusual or innovative. Take a turn down a side street and it won't be long before you stumble upon an exquisite Buddhist temple or Shintō shrine, or perhaps a boisterous local *matsuri* parade. Head to the **countryside**, and you might glimpse a high-speed train reflected in the waters of emerald-green rice paddies.

Seeing the ancient and contemporary waltzing around hand in hand may appear incongruous, but it's important to remember the reasons behind it – few other countries have ever changed so fast in so short a period of time. **Industrialized** at lightning speed in the late nineteenth century, Japan shed its feudal trappings to become the most powerful and outwardly aggressive country in Asia in a matter of decades. After defeat in World War II, the nation transformed itself from atom-bomb victim to **economic giant**, the envy of the world. Having weathered a decade-long recession from the mid-1990s, Japan is now relishing its "**soft power**" status as the world's pre-eminent purveyor of pop culture, with the visual media of manga and anime leading the way.

The "**bubble years**" of 1980s Japan scared many international visitors away in the belief that the country was hideously expensive. The truth is that it's no more costly to travel around than Western Europe or the US, and in many ways a fair bit cheaper. Hotel rooms can be on the small side but are often reasonably priced, and food is so

ABOVE SUMO WRESTLERS **RIGHT** BULLET TRAIN, TOKYO

THE ROUGH GUIDE TO
JAPAN

This seventh edit
Paul Gray, Sal
Simon Scott,

Windsor and Maidenhead

95800000088061

ROUGH
GUIDES

cheap that many travellers find themselves eating out three times a day. Public transport in Japan's cities is surprisingly good value, while recent price-cutting means that airline tickets now rival the famed bargain rail passes as a means to get to far-flung corners of the country.

In the **cities**, you'll first be struck by the massive number of people constantly on the move. These dense, hyperactive metropolises are the places to catch the latest trend, the hippest fashions and must-have gadgets before they hit the rest of the world. Yet it's not all about modernity: Tokyo, Kyoto, Osaka and Kanazawa, for example, also provide the best opportunities to view traditional performance arts, such as kabuki and nō plays, as well as a wealth of Japanese visual arts in major museums. **Outside the cities**, there's a vast range of travel options, from the UNESCO World Heritage-listed Shiretoko National Park in Hokkaidō to the balmy subtropical islands of Okinawa.

Japan reveals numerous contradictions. The Japanese are experts at focusing on detail (the exquisite wrapping of gifts and the mouthwatering presentation of food are just two examples) but often miss the broader picture. Rampant development and sometimes appalling pollution are difficult to square with a country also renowned for cleanliness and the appreciation of nature. Part of the problem is that **natural cataclysms**, such as earthquakes and typhoons, regularly hit Japan, so few people expect things to last for long anyway. And there's no denying the pernicious impact of **tourism**, with ranks of gift shops, ugly hotels, ear-splitting announcements and crowds often ruining potentially idyllic spots.

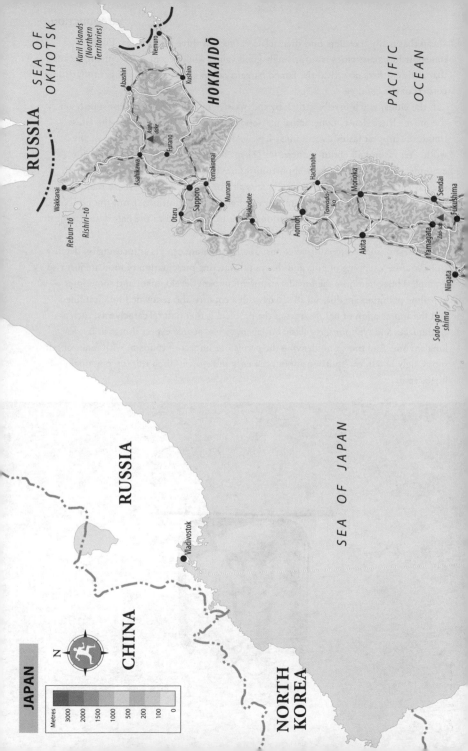

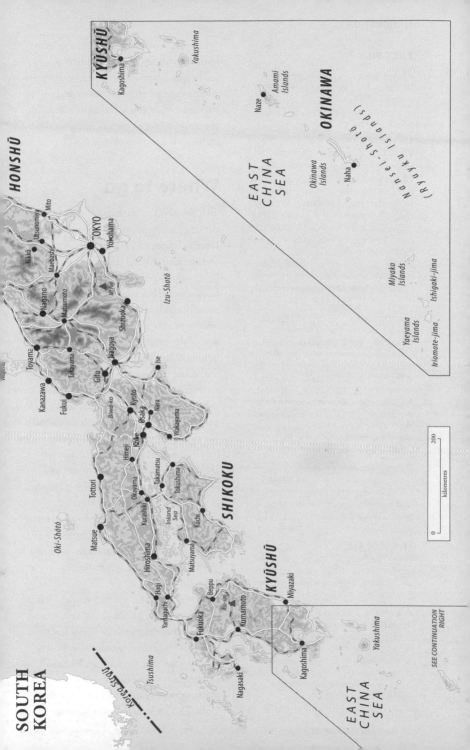

And yet, time and again, Japan redeems itself with unexpectedly beautiful landscapes, charmingly courteous people and its tangible sense of history and cherished traditions – few will be able to resist the chance to get to grips with this endlessly fascinating culture.

Where to go

Two weeks is the minimum needed to skim the surface of what Japan can offer. The capital, Tokyo, and the former imperial city and thriving cultural centre of Kyoto, will be top of most visitors' itineraries, and justifiably so, but you could avoid the cities entirely and head to the mountains or smaller islands to discover an alternative side of the country, away from the most heavily beaten tourist tracks.

It would be easy enough to spend a fortnight just in **Tokyo**. The metropolis is home to some of the world's most ambitious architecture, stylish shops and internationally celebrated restaurants and bars – as well as glimpses of traditional Japan at scores of temples, shrines and imperial gardens. Consider also taking in a couple of the city's surrounding attractions, in particular the historic towns of **Nikkō**, home to the amazing Tōshō-gū shrine complex, and **Kamakura**, with its giant Buddha statue and tranquil woodland walks.

Northern Honshū sees surprisingly few overseas visitors, but its sleepy villages and relaxed cities deserve to be better known. The Golden Hall of **Hiraizumi** more than warrants the journey, and can be easily combined with the islet-sprinkled **Matsushima Bay** or rural **Tōno**. The region is also known for its vibrant **summer**

JOURNEYS WITH FOOD

Eating is undoubtedly one of the highlights of travelling in Japan – a fair amount of domestic tourism is geared this way, with locals heading all over the country to sample subtle nuances of taste. Food not only changes by the season, but is also produced for certain activities – from train journeys to street festivals – and for maximum convenience available instantly or served quickly. Here are a few delicious recommendations to look out for as you journey around Japan:

Ekiben No major train journey in Japan is complete without an *ekiben* – a type of boxed lunch only sold at train stations. It's intended to showcase local cuisine and is often presented in interestingly quirky containers.

Kare-pan A good example of how Japan adapts foreign cuisines, *kare-pan* or curry bread is deep-fried sweet dough filled with curry. A great spicy snack if you need a break from rice and noodles.

Mitarashi dango Usually sold outside Shintō shrines, *mitarashi dango* are small pieces of grilled *mochi* (rice cake) on skewers and slathered in a delicious sweet and salty sauce. Best enjoyed with a steaming cup of green tea.

Sōmen Japan is home to a variety of noodles, but *sōmen* are the most delicate. Long, thin and white, they are best eaten cold in summer with a light dipping sauce, and preferably on a breezy river deck (see p.480), but are also available from convenience stores.

Oden Oden is a "hodgepodge" of vegetables, tofu, fishcake and boiled eggs stewed in a *dashi* broth and popular in winter. You can fish out the bits you want from the steaming trough at street stalls or convenience stores.

Sōki soba Okinawa's take on noodles is simple but truly delicious and quite possibly life-extending (see box, p.785): yellow strands of soba, served with broth and a couple of hunks of pork rib.

Taiyaki Literally "grilled sea bream" but actually a sweet fish-shaped waffle filled with *an* (red bean) but also sometimes sold with chocolate and custard cream.

Takoyaki This street-friendly food hails from Osaka but is found all over Japan. Small pieces of octopus (*tako*) are grilled (*yaki*) in balls of batter and served with a special brown sauce, mayonnaise and bonito flakes.

ABOVE SŌKI SOBA

festivals, notably those at Sendai, Aomori, Hirosaki and Akita, and for its sacred mountains, including **Dewa-sanzan**, home to a sect of ascetic mountain priests, and the eerie, remote wastelands of **Osore-zan**.

Further north, across the Tsugaru Straits, **Hokkaidō** is Japan's final frontier, with many national parks including the outstanding **Daisetsu-zan**, offering excellent hiking trails over mountain peaks and through soaring rock gorges. The lovely far northern islands of **Rebun-tō** and **Rishiri-tō** are ideal summer escapes. Hokkaidō's most historic city is **Hakodate**, with its late nineteenth-century wooden houses and churches built by expat traders, while its modern capital, **Sapporo**, is home to the raging nightlife centre of Suskino and the original Sapporo Brewery. Winter is a fantastic time to visit, when you can catch Sapporo's amazing Snow Festival and go skiing at some of Japan's top resorts, such as **Niseko**.

Skiing, mountaineering and soaking in hot springs are part of the culture of **Central Honshū**, an area dominated by the magnificent Japan Alps. **Nagano**, home to the atmospheric pilgrimage temple, Zenkō-ji, and the old castle town of **Matsumoto** can be used as a starting point for exploring the region. Highlights include the tiny mountain resort of **Kamikōchi** and the immaculately preserved Edo-cra villages of **Tsumago** and **Magome**, linked by a short hike along the remains of a 300-year-old stone-paved road. **Takayama** deservedly draws many visitors to its handsome streets lined with merchant houses and temples, built by generations of skilled carpenters. In the remote neighbouring valleys, you'll find the rare thatched houses of **Ogimachi**, **Suganuma** and **Ainokura**, remnants of a fast-disappearing rural Japan.

On the Sea of Japan coast, the historic city of **Kanazawa** is home to Kenroku-en, one of Japan's best gardens, and the stunning 21st Century Museum of Contemporary Art. **Nagoya**, on the heavily industrialized southern coast, is a more manageable city than Tokyo or Osaka, and has much to recommend it, including the fine Tokugawa Art Museum and many great places to eat. The efficient new airport nearby also makes the city a good alternative entry point. From Nagoya, it's a short hop to the pretty castle towns of **Inuyama** and **Gifu**, the latter holding summer displays of the ancient skill of *ukai*, or cormorant fishing.

South of the Japan Alps, the **Kansai** plains are scattered with ancient temples, shrines and the remnants of imperial cities. **Kyoto**, custodian of Japan's traditional culture, is home to its most refined cuisine, classy ryokan, glorious gardens, and magnificent temples and palaces. Nearby **Nara** is on a smaller scale but no less impressive when it comes to venerable monuments, notably the great bronze Buddha of Tōdai-ji and Hōryū-ji's unrivalled collection of early Japanese statuary. The surrounding region contains a number of still-thriving religious foundations, such as the highly atmospheric temples of **Hiei-zan** and **Kōya-san**, the revered Shintō shrine **Ise-jingū**, and the beautiful countryside pilgrimage routes of the UNESCO World Heritage-listed **Kumano** region.

Not all of Kansai is so rarefied, though. The slightly unconventional metropolis of **Osaka** has an easy-going atmosphere and boisterous nightlife, alongside several worthwhile sights. Further west, the port of **Kōbe** offers a gentler cosmopolitan feel, while **Himeji** is home to Japan's most fabulous castle, as well as some impressive modern gardens and buildings.

For obvious reasons, **Hiroshima** is the most visited location in **western Honshū**. On the way there, pause at **Okayama** to stroll around one of Japan's top three gardens, Kōraku-en, and the appealingly preserved Edo-era town of **Kurashiki**. The beauty of the Inland Sea, dotted with thousands of islands, is best appreciated from the idyllic fishing village of **Tomonoura**, the port of **Onomichi** and the relaxed islands of **Nao-shima**, **Ikuchi-jima** and **Miyajima**.

Crossing to the San-in coast, the castle town of **Hagi** retains some handsome samurai houses and atmospheric temples, only surpassed by even more enchanting **Tsuwano**, further inland. One of Japan's most venerable shrines, **Izumo Taisha**, lies roughly midway along the coast, near the city of **Matsue**, on a strip of land between two lagoons and home to the region's only original fort.

Shikoku is the location for Japan's most famous pilgrimage (a walking tour around 88 Buddhist temples), but also offers dramatic scenery in the **Iya valley** and along its rugged coastline. The island's largest city, **Matsuyama**, has an imperious castle and the splendidly ornate Dōgo Onsen Honkan – one of Japan's best hot springs. There's also the lovely garden Ritsurin-kōen in **Takamatsu** and the ancient Shintō shrine at **Kotohira**.

The southernmost of Japan's four main islands, **Kyūshū** is probably best known for **Nagasaki**, an attractive and cosmopolitan city that has overcome its terrible wartime history. Hikers and onsen enthusiasts should head up into the central highlands, where **Aso-san**'s smouldering peak dominates the world's largest volcanic crater, or to the more southerly meadows of **Ebino Kōgen**. So much hot water gushes out of the ground in **Beppu**, on the east coast, that it's known as Japan's hot-spring capital. **Fukuoka**, on the other hand, takes pride in its innovative modern architecture and an exceptionally lively entertainment district.

Okinawa comprises more than a hundred islands stretching in a great arc to within sight of Taiwan. An independent kingdom until the early seventeenth century, traces of the island's distinctive, separate culture still survive. The beautifully reconstructed former royal palace dominates the capital city, **Naha**, but the best of the region lies on its remoter islands. This is where you'll find Japan's most stunning white-sand beaches and its best diving, particularly around the subtropical islands of **Ishigaki**, **Taketomi** and **Iriomote**.

When to go

Average temperature and weather patterns vary enormously across Japan. The main influences on Honshū's climate are the mountains and surrounding warm seas, which bring plenty of rain and, in the colder months, snow. **Winter** weather differs greatly, however, between the western Sea of Japan and the Pacific coasts, the former suffering cold winds and heavy snow while the latter tends towards dry, clear winter days. Regular heavy snowfalls in the mountains provide ideal conditions for skiers.

QUINTESSENTIAL JAPAN

Japan has something of a reputation for being a bit off the wall when it comes to contemporary culture – the high-pressured work culture has produced an eclectic array of leisure activities. Here are a few examples of some uniquely Japanese things to seek out during your stay:

Bathhouses The ultimate relaxation for Japanese people is to soak in hot spring waters, but if you can't make it to an onsen resort then it's worth seeking out a neighbourhood *sentō* (bathhouse). Watch out for the *denkiburo* – a bath with mild electric shocks believed to reduce muscle pain.

Capsule hotels (see p.42 & p.138) No, it's not like sleeping in a coffin. But yes, the rooms at capsule hotels are pretty darn small, and there's no more characteristic Japanese sleeping experience – including ryokan.

Game centres Bash the hell out of the world's weirdest arcade machines in one of the game centres strewn liberally across the land – you'll even find them in minor towns.

Gender-bending performances In traditional Kabuki theatre men play female roles, but in twenty-first-century Japan there's also the Takarazuka Revue, an all-women musical theatre troupe where the *otoko-yaku* (male roles) are the main stars, and Visual kei rock groups, where the male musicians perform in wigs, make-up, leather corsets and lace.

Karaoke Unleash your inner rock star at a "karaoke box" where you can sing to your heart's content, in private and by the hour, as well as be served food and drinks. If you miss the last train home, it's also a great place to wait for the next one.

Pachinko parlours (see p.410) Perhaps the world's most monotonous form of gambling, these glorified pinball arcades are still worth having a gawp at, or even just a listen to – peek in the door, and you'll be amazed by the gigantic din that crashes out. Dare to step inside, and prepare to be visually assaulted by rows of LED panels, all being glared at by silent, serious-looking gamers.

Theme cafés Most big Japanese cities have a couple of interesting options for caffeine addicts: have your coffee served by costumed girls at a maid café (see box, p.144), amid thousands of comic books at a *manga kissaten* (see box, p.144) or surrounded by purring felines at a cat café.

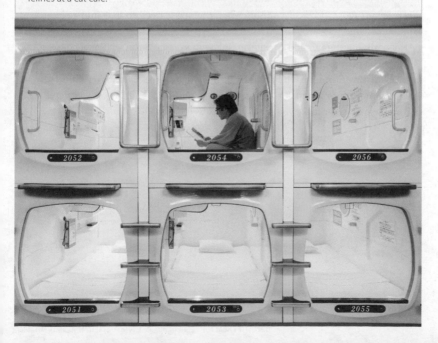

AVERAGE DAILY TEMPERATURES AND MONTHLY RAINFALL

	Jan	Feb	Mar	Apr	May	Jun	Jul	Aug	Sep	Oct	Nov	Dec
AKITA												
Max/Min ºC	2/-5	3/-5	6/-2	13/4	18/8	23/14	26/18	28/19	24/15	18/8	11/3	4/-2
rainfall mm	142	104	104	105	112	127	198	188	211	188	191	178
KŌCHI												
Max/Min ºC	12/4	12/4	15/7	19/12	22/17	24/19	28/24	29/25	28/22	23/17	19/12	14/7
rainfall mm	64	142	160	188	244	323	257	213	323	279	175	107
NAGASAKI												
Max/Min ºC	9/2	10/2	14/5	19/10	23/14	26/18	29/23	31/23	27/20	22/14	17/9	12/4
rainfall mm	71	84	125	185	170	312	257	175	249	114	94	81
SAPPORO												
Max/Min ºC	2/-10	2/-10	6/-7	13/-1	18/3	21/10	24/16	26/18	22/12	17/6	11/-1	5/-6
rainfall mm	25	43	61	84	102	160	188	155	160	147	56	38
TOKYO												
Max/Min ºC	10/1	10/1	13/4	18/10	23/15	25/18	29/22	31/24	27/20	21/14	17/8	12/3
rainfall mm	110	155	228	254	244	305	254	203	279	228	162	96

Despite frequent showers, **spring** is one of the most pleasant times to visit Japan, when the weather reports chart the steady progress of the cherry blossom from warm Kyūshū in March to colder Hokkaidō around May. A rainy season (*tsuyu*) in June ushers in the swamp-like heat of **summer**; if you don't like tropical conditions, head for the cooler hills or the northern reaches of the country. A bout of typhoons and more rain in September precede **autumn**, which lasts from October to late November; this is Japan's most spectacular season, when the maple trees explode into a plethora of brilliant colours.

Also worth bearing in mind when planning your visit are Japan's **national holidays**. During such periods, including the days around New Year, the "Golden Week" break of April 29 to May 5 and the Obon holiday of mid-August, the nation is on the move, making it difficult to secure last-minute transport and hotel bookings. Avoid travelling during these dates, or make your arrangements well in advance.

OPPOSITE FROM TOP DETAIL OF HOKUSAI PAINTING; YAEYAMA ISLANDS; MIYAJIMA

Author picks

Our authors have ventured to every corner of Japan to find the very best the country has to offer. Here are some of their personal highlights:

Hokusai in Obuse Using the name "The Old Man Mad About Art", the artist created wonderful paintings (not prints!) in this little town in his final years (see p.354).

Speed into the future For a hands-on experience of the 600kph trains of tomorrow, head to the SCMaglev and Railway Park outside Nagoya (see p.406).

Tea-picking The finest green tea in Japan has been cultivated on the low rolling hills of Wazuka-cho, near Uji, since the thirteenth century (see box, p.472).

The Yaeyama Islands Finally on the budget-airline route maps, Ishigaki-jima (see p.805) is the hub of this tantalizingly tropical slice of Japan – stunning beaches, great diving and about as laidback as Japan gets.

Outdoor adventure Journey through Hokkaidō to reach remote Rishiri-tō and Rebun-tō (see p.330), volcanic islands crisscrossed with epic hiking and cycling trails.

Cross the roof of Japan The Tateyama-Kurobe Alpine Route (see box, p.388) combines buses, funiculars and cable-cars to whisk you over the Japan Alps, with spectacular mountain views.

Kōbe Jazz This is where Japanese jazz began: the city has a number of excellent live clubs and listening lounges (see p.550).

Spectacular views The views of the Seto Ohashi bridge and the Inland Sea from Washu-zan (see p.574) are some of Japan's most spectacular.

Sumo Watch the titanic, ritualized clashes of the nation's sporting giants in the centuries-old martial art characterized by uniquely Japanese traditions (see p.58).

The maples of Miyajima There's no better place to embrace the magnificent colours of the Japanese autumn than this ancient pilgrimage island (see p.594).

Our author recommendations don't end here. We've flagged up our favourite places – a perfectly sited hotel, an atmospheric café, a special restaurant – throughout the guide, highlighted with the ★ symbol.

29

things not to miss

It's not possible to see everything that Japan has to offer in one trip – and we don't suggest you try. What follows, in no particular order, is a selective and subjective taste of the country's highlights: impressive museums, tranquil gardens, lively festivals, awe-inspiring temples and much more. All entries are colour coded to the corresponding chapter and have a page reference to take you straight into the Guide.

1

1 KYOTO
Page 420
The capital of Japan for a thousand years, endowed with an almost overwhelming legacy of temples, palaces and gardens, and also home to the country's richest traditional culture and most refined cuisine.

2 YAKUSHIMA
Page 773
Commune with millennium-old cedar trees in Kirishima-Yaku National Park, a UNESCO World Heritage Site.

3 KŌYA-SAN
Page 526
Mingle with monks and pilgrims on one of Japan's holiest mountains, home to over a hundred monasteries.

4 EARTH CELEBRATION
Page 285
Vibrant international world music festival, hosted by the drumming group Kodō on the lovely island of Sado-ga-shima.

5 CLIMB MOUNT FUJI
Page 201

Make the tough but rewarding hike up Japan's tallest peak, a long-dormant volcano of classic symmetrical beauty.

6 YUKI MATSURI
Page 295

Stare at mammoth snow and ice sculptures in Sapporo, Hokkaidō, every February.

7 STAY AT A RYOKAN
Page 44

Treat yourself to a night of luxury in a ryokan, a traditional Japanese inn, where you enter a world of elegance and meticulous service.

8 SAKE BREWERIES
Pages 358 & 382

Discover the amazing varieties of this ancient Japanese alcoholic drink at the venerable sake breweries in Obuse or Takayama.

9 SHINJUKU AND SHIBUYA
Pages 123 & 121

These neon-drenched Tokyo districts are contemporary Japan in a nutshell, and particularly spellbinding come evening time.

10 TAKETOMI-JIMA
Page 811

Bathe in the warm waters surrounding this speck of an Okinawan island, a sleepy spot whose few buildings are topped with terracotta tiles.

10

11 KAMIKŌCHI
Page 370

This busy but pretty mountain village preserves a Shangri-la atmosphere and serves as the gateway to the Northern Alps.

12 OGIMACHI
Page 384

Discover the distinctive *gasshō-zukuri* houses, whose steep-sided thatched roofs are said to recall two hands joined in prayer.

13 NIKKŌ
Page 170

This pilgrim town is home to the fabulously over-the-top Tōshō-gū shrine, one of Japan's most sumptuous buildings.

14 HIROSHIMA
Page 586

Pay your respects to the A-bomb's victims in the city of Hiroshima, impressively reborn from the ashes of World War II.

15 KABUKIZA
Page 92

This is the best place to enjoy kabuki, the most dramatic of traditional Japanese performing arts.

16 NAMETOKO GORGE
Page 681

Regarded as a natural "power spot", a mystical place where clear-blue waters cut through pristine forest and gush over mossy boulders.

17 NARA
Page 485

The ancient former capital is home to the Buddhist temple of Tōdai-ji.

11

12

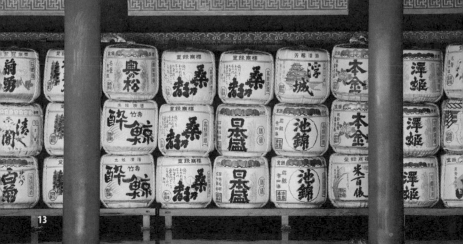

13

14

15

16

17

21

22

24 HIMEJI-JŌ
Page 554

Relive the days of the samurai at this, Japan's most impressive feudal-era fortress.

25 NAHA FISH MARKET
Page 789

The fish section of Naha's delightful market area is a truly spectacular sight – a whole rainbow of seafood to choose from and have cooked for you.

26 AWA ODORI
Page 659

Dance through the streets at the country's biggest Obon bash, held in Tokushima, Shikoku.

27 TOKYO'S ART SCENE
Page 108

Tokyo remains the most important art city in Asia – hit the Roppongi Art Triangle to see why.

28 KAISEKI-RYŌRI
Page 50

Indulge yourself with a meal of *kaiseki-ryōri*, Japan's haute cuisine, comprising of a selection of beautifully prepared morsels made from the finest seasonal ingredients.

29 ONSEN
Page 61

Take a dip at a top onsen resort town, such as Dōgo or Sukayu Onsen, or experience the exquisite warmth of a rotemburo (outdoor bath) as the snow falls.

24

25

26

THE NATIONAL ART CENTER, TOKYO

27

28

29

Itineraries

Japan may not be terribly large, but there are enough historic, natural and contemporary sights to keep you busy for months on end. Most visitors hit Tokyo and Kyoto, the capitals past and present, but the further you get from the beaten track, the more rewarding the experience. These itineraries head all over Japan's varied landscapes, and give at least an idea of what this fascinating country is all about.

THE FULL MONTY

Hitting most of Japan's main sights, this itinerary loosely follows the old Tōkaidō route that linked Tokyo with Kyoto, then moves further west to within a short ferry ride of the Korean peninsula.

❶ **Tokyo** Japan's wonderful capital has something for everyone – the only question is what to do with your time there, which will never be quite enough. **See p.78**

❷ **Mount Fuji** This emblematic volcanic cone, just west of Tokyo, is climbable through the summer, but visible from the Shinkansen trains all year round. **See p.201**

❸ **Kyoto** Contrary to the expectations of many visitors, Japan's vaunted ancient ex-capital is actually a large, modern city, albeit one brimming with compelling historical gems. **See p.420**

❹ **Nara** Just south of Kyoto, Nara is a far more rustic place – witness the deer merrily grazing around the temples and shrines. **See p.485**

❺ **Naoshima** Take a detour from the mainland route to this small island, home to swathes of fantastic modern art. **See p.650**

❻ **Hiroshima** The name of this city is etched quite firmly into the world's conscience. Dark

tourism it may be, but the gutted Hypocenter is a stark reminder of those tragic times. **See p.586**

❼ **Fukuoka** Way out west, this is perhaps the friendliest city in the land – its characteristic *yatai* stalls make perfect places in which to bond with ramen-slurping locals over a few glasses of sake. **See p.702**

WORLD HERITAGE TOUR

Japan boasts thirteen cultural and four natural UNESCO World Heritage Sites; focusing your visit on the country's ancient wonders alone could keep you well occupied for a good ten days or more.

❶ **Nikkō** One of Japan's most relaxed cities, where a clutch of dreamy temples lurks in the mountainous forests around the fabulously preposterous UNESCO-listed Tōshō-gū complex. **See p.170**

❷ **Shirakawa-gō and Gokayama** The lovingly preserved villages of Shirakawa-gō and Gokayama, with their distinctive A-frame houses, give a glimpse of Japanese rural life centuries ago. **See p.383**

❸ **Kyoto** Having functioned as capital for around one millennium, it's no surprise that over two dozen places in Kyoto have been

ABOVE FROM LEFT OTARU CANALS, HOKKAIDŌ; GEISHA IN GION DISTRICT, KYOTO

protected as World Heritage Sites; whatever you do, don't miss the phenomenal Kiyomizu-dera temple. **See p.420**

❹ **Miyajima** Close to Hiroshima, this is one of Japan's most famed attractions – a vermilion-red *torii* rising elegantly from the sea. **See p.594**

❺ **Nara** This historic city has eight sites showcasing the early development of Buddhism, as well as a Shintō shrine, a primeval forest, a park and a palace. **See p.485**

❻ **Shuri Castle** If you make it as far as Okinawa, don't miss this castle, a fantastic relic of the Ryūkyū Kingdom that once ruled this gorgeous island chain. **See p.787**

TŌHOKU–HOKKAIDŌ

You could easily spend a couple of weeks wending your way up Honshū's northern tip, full of rich heritage and timeless agricultural scenes, before making your way over into the

unspoilt, wild landscape of Hokkaidō, Japan's northernmost island, which bursts with natural phenomena and wildlife.

❶ **Sendai** Stroll the tree-lined streets of the city and take day-trips to the Yamadera temple complex and the scenic bay of Matsushima. **See p.234**

❷ **Dewa-sanzan** Spend a few days hiking up this extinct volcano along the pilgrims' route taken by the Yamabushi ascetic mountain hermits. **See p.271**

❸ **Tōno Valley** Cycle through the rural landscape of this flat valley and envelop yourself in the mysterious folk tales embedded in the region's ancient shrines and rock carvings. **See p.246**

❹ **Aomori** Stop in at Honshū's northernmost city and take excursions to the eerie landscape of Shimokita Hantō, populated by wandering souls, and Towada-ko, for a hike around a volcanic lake. **See p.254**

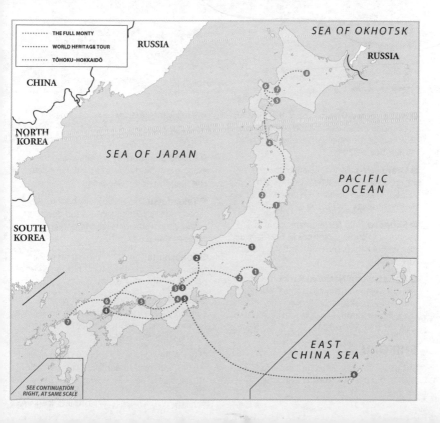

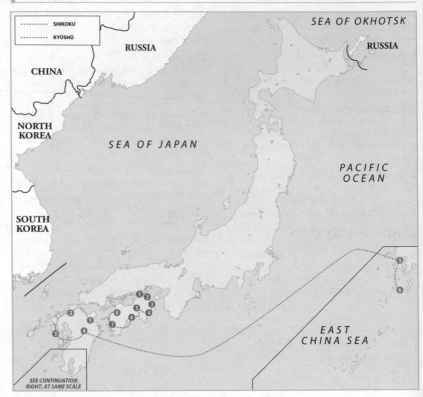

❺ Noboribetsu Onsen Explore the smoking, sulphurous volcanic landscape before a relaxing soak back at the inn and the delights of ryokan cuisine. **See p.320**

❻ Otaru Step back in time and marvel at the imposing Meiji-era public buildings and luxurious homes built on the profits of the herring industry. **See p.304**

❼ Sapporo From the ultimate summer evenings to snow sculptures in February, a visit to Hokkaidō's bustling capital is a must. **See p.295**

❽ Daisetsu-zan National Park Excellent skiing in winter, cherry blossoms in spring, endless fields of summer flowers and magnificent autumn colours – this national park has it all. **See p.324**

SHIKOKU

Shikoku is the least visited of Japan's four main islands, but it is well worth making the trip here.

The following itinerary could be done in two weeks, at a push, or at a more leisurely pace over three.

❶ Inland Sea journey Naoshima and the exciting art islands offer captivating modern art and friendly people. **See p.648**

❷ Takamatsu This amiable city has one of Japan's most beautiful gardens and dozens of *sanuki udon* restaurants serving tasty thick white noodles. **See p.637**

❸ Tokushima The city of the energetic Awa Odori dance festival also has a historic *bunraku* puppet theatre. **See p.658**

❹ Kaifu Thanks to big waves and warm Pacific currents, Shikoku's eastern coast is a great place to come if you're on the lookout for excellent surfing spots. **See p.664**

❺ Iya Valley One of the country's most hidden regions, with rustic mountain villages and the atmosphere of an older, slower Japan. **See p.666**

❻ Kōchi The hometown of Sakamoto Ryōma, one of Japan's most revered samurai heroes, the densely populated city of Kōchi has a lively night food market. **See p.669**

❼ Uwajima Visit a sex museum and watch a bloodless bullfighting match in this quiet, unassuming town. **See p.678**

❽ Matsuyama Check out the magnificent ancient castle and historic hot spring of Dōgo Onsen in Shikoku's largest city. **See p.686**

KYŪSHŪ

You could forget Tokyo and Kyoto entirely and still get a pretty accurate impression of Japan by visiting its third-largest island, home to active volcanoes, great food, friendly locals and hot springs aplenty.

❶ Beppu This is one of Japan's foremost hot-spring resorts. A small, pleasingly retro place where steam billows from the streets; there are even a couple of onsen hiding away in the forested hills above town. **See p.746**

❷ Fukuoka Start your trip in the island's main city, where you can expect tasty meals, boisterous nightlife and a thoroughly enjoyable vibe. **See p.702**

❸ Nagasaki Like Hiroshima, this city has rebounded with phenomenal gusto from the atomic blasts that left the place in tatters. Head on a trip to intriguing Battleship Island – a Bond-villain set so otherworldly that it didn't even need to be touched up for the film. **See p.718**

❹ Aso This giant volcanic crater, with sulphurous steam still shooting out from the peaks at its centre, is an easily accessible place in which to get a handle on rural Japan. **See p.738**

❺ Kagoshima Interested in seeing a volcano explode? Sakurajima erupts several times a day, just across the bay from this unique city. **See p.761**

❻ Yakushima The inspiration behind certain Studio Ghibli cartoons, the richly forested highlands on this pristine island feature trees so old, nobody has yet been able to verify their age. **See p.773**

VENDING MACHINE, TOKYO

Basics

Getting there

Tokyo's Narita International Airport (see p.130), Osaka's Kansai International Airport (see p.448) and Centrair (see p.407) near Nagoya are the main international flight gateways, while Tokyo's Haneda Airport (see p.130) has recently expanded and now offers a wider range of international connections.

Airfares are highest around the Golden Week holiday period at the beginning of May, and the Obon festival in mid-August, as well as at Christmas and New Year, when seats are at a premium. Prices drop during the "shoulder" seasons – April to June and September to October – with the best deals in the low season, January to March and November to December (excluding Christmas and New Year).

Flights from the UK and Ireland

All Nippon Airways (ANA; Ⓦ ana.co.jp), British Airways (Ⓦ britishairways.com), Japan Airlines (JAL; Ⓦ jal.com) and Virgin (Ⓦ virgin-atlantic.com) fly nonstop from **London** to Tokyo, with the trip taking about twelve hours. Return **fares** start from around £500 direct if you're very lucky, but since you can find occasional special indirect deals (usually via Russia, China or the Middle East) for as low as £400, it pays to shop around. There are no direct flights from **Dublin**; transferring in the Middle East can bring return prices as low as €600, though it's always worth considering a budget flight to London or mainland Europe if you can find a good deal from there.

Flights from the US and Canada

A number of airlines fly nonstop from **the US and Canada** to Tokyo, Osaka and Nagoya, including Air Canada (Ⓦ aircanada.ca), All Nippon Airways (ANA; Ⓦ ana.co.jp), American Airlines (Ⓦ aa.com), Japan Airlines (JAL; Ⓦ jal.com) and United (Ⓦ united.com); there are connections from virtually every US regional airport. Flying time to Tokyo is around fifteen hours from New York, thirteen hours from Chicago and ten hours from Los Angeles. Low-season return **fares** to Tokyo start at around US$700 from Chicago or New York; US$550 from Los Angeles; and Can$700 from Vancouver.

Flights from Australia, New Zealand and South Africa

Qantas (Ⓦ qantas.com.au), Japan Airlines (JAL; Ⓦ jal.com) and Air New Zealand (Ⓦ airnewzealand.com) operate nonstop flights to Tokyo from **Australia and New Zealand**. Flying time is around ten hours from Australia and twelve hours from New Zealand. Return **fares** from Australia to Tokyo can drop as low as Aus$500 with Jetstar (Ⓦ jetstar.com), who fly from Cairns, Darwin, Melbourne and the Gold Coast. From New Zealand, direct routings will cost at least NZ$1100, though again you can lop a fair bit from this by flying indirectly with Jetstar, via Australia.

Flying from **South Africa**, you'll be routed through Southeast Asia or the Middle East. Promotional fares can be as cheap as R8000, though you're more likely to be paying upwards of R11,000.

Flights from other Asian countries

If you're already in Asia, it can be quite cheap to fly to Tokyo with **low-cost regional carriers**. Air Asia (Ⓦ airasia.com) have flights from Kuala Lumpur and Bangkok; Cebu Pacific (Ⓦ cebupacificair.com) fly from Cebu and Manila; Fastar (Ⓦ eastarjet.com), Jeju Air (Ⓦ jejuair.net) and Jin (Ⓦ jinair.com) each run flights from Seoul; HK Express (Ⓦ hkexpress.com) make the run from Hong Kong; and Scoot (Ⓦ flyscoot.com) scoot over from Bangkok, Singapore and Taipei. Japanese operations include Peach (Ⓦ flypeach .com), who offer flights from Seoul, Shanghai and Taipei; and Vanilla Air (Ⓦ vanilla-air.com), who connect to Ho Chi Minh City, Hong Kong and Taipei.

Train and ferry

Adventurous travellers can take advantage of a number of alternative routes to Japan from Europe

---

A BETTER KIND OF TRAVEL

At Rough Guides we are passionately committed to travel. We believe it helps us understand the world we live in and the people we share it with – and of course tourism is vital to many developing economies. But the scale of modern tourism has also damaged some places irreparably, and climate change is accelerated by most forms of transport, especially flying. All Rough Guides' flights are carbon-offset, and every year we donate money to a variety of environmental charities.

and Asia via **train and ferry**. There are three long-distance train journeys – the Trans-Siberian, Trans-Mongolian and Trans-Manchurian – all of which will put you on the right side of Asia for a hop across to Japan. The shortest ferry route is on the hydrofoil between Busan in South Korea and Fukuoka (Hakata port) on Japan's southern island of Kyūshū.

The Trans-Siberian train and getting there from Russia

The classic overland adventure route to or from Japan is via the **Trans-Siberian** train, a seven-night journey from Moscow to Vladivostok on Russia's far-eastern coast. The cost of a one-way ticket in a four-berth sleeper compartment between **Moscow** and **Vladivostok** is around £290/US$365/Aus$490 (see W seat61.com for the latest info), on top of which you'll need to factor in costs for visas, hotels etc along the way. You'll end up saving a lot of money if you arrange your own visa and buy tickets within Russia; however, to avoid some of the inevitable hassles (tickets often sell out in summer, for example), most people choose to go through an agent. The same advice goes for the **Trans-Manchurian** train, which heads from Moscow down through northern China and terminates in Beijing, and the **Trans-Mongolian**, which runs from Moscow via Mongolia to Beijing. You can then take a train to Shanghai and pick up a ferry to Japan (see below).

Vladivostok Air (W www.vladivostokavia.ru) and S7 (W s7.ru) offer connections from Vladivostok to Narita. If you're absolutely insistent on continuing your journey without flying, you can take a weekly **ferry** (W dbsferry.com) to the Japanese port of Sakaiminato, near Matsue. These head via the Korean city of Donghae, where there's a nine-hour stopover, and take 43 hours in total. The cheapest tickets cost ¥22,000 one-way. For those planning to return from Japan to Europe on this route, you could try arranging your **visa** at the Russian Embassy in Tokyo (see p.166) or the Osaka consulate (see p.525), though in practice you may have to go through an agency in your own country.

The shortest journey from Russia to Japan is on the ferry service (May–Oct; 5hr) from **Korsakov** on the Siberian island of Sakhalin to Wakkanai in Hokkaidō.

Ferries from China and South Korea

Both the Shanghai Ferry Company (T 06 6243 6345, W shanghai-ferry.co.jp) and Japan–China

International Ferry Co (T 06 6536 6541, W shinganjin .com) ply the **Shanghai–Osaka** route (46hr; from ¥22,000); the latter heads from **Kōbe** on alternate weeks. Conditions on board are good, the berths are clean and comfortable, and facilities include swimming pools, restaurants and even discos. There have also, in the past, been services between **Qingdao** and **Shimonoseki**, though these were discontinued in late 2015 and may never return.

There are daily ferry and hydrofoil services from **Busan** in South Korea to **Fukuoka** (see p.706) and Shimonoseki (see box, p.605).

AGENTS AND OPERATORS

Artisans of Leisure US T 1 800 214 8144, W artisansofleisure .com. Luxury private tours, including ones focused on food, art, gardens and even ceramics.

IACE Travel US T 1 866 735 4223, W iace-asia.com. US-based Japan specialist with many packages and themed tours to Tokyo.

Inside Japan UK T 0117 370 9751, US T 1 303 952 0379, Aus T 07 3703 3838; W insidejapantours.com. Great range of well-designed small-group, self-guided and fully tailored trips, ranging from Tokyo stopovers to Mount Fuji climbs.

Into Japan UK T 01865 841 443, W intojapan.co.uk. Upmarket tailor-made and special-interest tours, plus off-the-peg fifteen-day Luxury Japan packages.

Japan Journeys UK T 020 7766 5267, W japanjourneys.co.uk. Tokyo options include an anime and manga-themed tour.

Japan Package Australia T 02 9264 7384, W www .japanpackage.com.au. Sydney-based agent offering a variety of Japan packages (including plenty of anime tours) as well as Japan Rail Passes.

Japan Travel Bureau (JTB) US T 1 877 798 9808, W online .jtbusa.com; Canada T 416 367 5824, W jtb.ca; Australia T 1300 739 330, W japantravel.com.au. The various wings of this Japanese operation offer tours of the capital, Fuji, Nikkō and beyond; they also handle Sunrise Tours (see box, p.36).

Japan Travel Centre UK T 020 7611 0150, W www .japantravel-centre.com. Offers flights, accommodation packages, Japan Rail Passes and guided tours.

Magical Japan UK T 0161 440 7332, W magicaljapan.co.uk. Various guided tours, all offering at least three days in and around Tokyo; customized packages possible.

Mitsui Travel Australia T 02 9232 2720, W mitsuitravel.com.au. Specializing in shorter tours, including a two-day onsen stay in Tokyo and Hakone.

Travel Japan Australia T 02 9267 0555, W traveljapan.com.au. Provides everything from flights to Tokyo to packages and customized itineraries.

Travel Wright W wrightwaytravel.org. An annual tour to Japan (usually Sept) focused around the work and legacy of architect Frank Lloyd Wright.

Visas and red tape

All visitors to Japan must have a passport valid for the duration of their stay. At the time of writing, citizens of Ireland, the UK and certain other European countries can stay in Japan for up to ninety days without a visa provided they are visiting for tourism or business purposes; this stay can be extended for another three months (see below). Citizens of Australia, Canada, New Zealand and the US can also stay for up to ninety days without a visa, though this is not extendable and you are required to be in possession of a return air ticket. Anyone from these countries wishing to stay longer will have to leave Japan and then re-enter.

Citizens of certain **other countries** must apply for a visa in advance in their own country. Visas are usually free, though in certain circumstances you may be charged a fee of around ¥3000 for a single-entry visa. The **rules** on visas do change from time to time, so check first with the nearest Japanese embassy or consulate, or on the Japanese Ministry of Foreign Affairs website Ⓦ www.mofa.go.jp.

Visa extensions

To get a **visa extension** you'll need to fill in two copies of an "Application for Extension of Stay", available from the **Tokyo Regional Immigration Bureau** at 5-5-30 Kōnan, Minato-ku (Mon–Fri 9am–noon & 1–4pm; ☎03 5796 7111, Ⓦwww .immi-moj.go.jp), a short walk from Tennōzu Isle Station. Go early in the day, since the process takes forever; also note that your application may not be confirmed for two weeks. Bring along passport photos (and your passport, of course), a letter explaining your reasons for wanting to extend your stay, and a fee of ¥4000. In addition, you may be asked to show proof of **sufficient funds** to support your stay, and a valid onward ticket out of the country.

If you're not a national of one of the few countries with six-month reciprocal visa exemptions (these include Ireland and the UK), expect a thorough grilling from the immigration officials. An easier option – and the only alternative available to nationals of those countries who are not eligible for an extension – may be a short trip out of the country, say to South Korea or Hong Kong, though

you may still have to run the gauntlet of immigration officials on your return.

Working holiday visas

Citizens of the UK, Ireland, Canada, Australia and New Zealand, among other countries, can apply for a **working holiday visa** if they are aged between 18 and 30 (officially up to 25 for Canadians and Australians, though there are often ways around this); this grants a stay of up to one year and entitles the holder to take paid employment so long as your stay is "primarily deemed to be a holiday". Full details of the scheme can be found at Ⓦ www.mofa.go.jp.

Note that if you're on any sort of working visa and you leave Japan temporarily, you must get a **re-entry visa** before you leave if you wish to continue working on your return. Re-entry visas are available from local immigration bureaux.

Volunteer visas

British nationals are eligible for the **volunteer visa scheme**, which allows holders to undertake voluntary work for charitable organizations in Japan for up to one year. Your application must include a letter from the host organization confirming details of the voluntary work to be undertaken and the treatment the volunteer will receive (pocket money and board and lodging are allowed, but formal remuneration is not). You must also be able to show evidence of sufficient funds for your stay in Japan. Contact the Japanese embassy (see below) to check the current details of the scheme.

Residency cards

Foreigners legally allowed to stay in Japan for more than ninety days – basically those with legal employment or married to a Japanese citizen – must obtain **residency status** before their first ninety days is up. **Resident cards** (Zairyū kādo; 在留 カード) can be issued, with prior arrangement, at the main international airports, though most people end up applying at their local government office. The cards include your photograph and must (legally speaking) be carried at all times, though they're rarely checked.

JAPANESE EMBASSIES AND CONSULATES

You'll find a full list on Ⓦ www.mofa.go.jp.
Australia 112 Empire Circuit, Yarralumla, Canberra ☎ 02 6273 3244, Ⓦ au.emb-japan.go.jp.

Canada 255 Sussex Drive, Ottawa ☎ 613 241 8541, ⓦ ca
.emb-japan.go.jp.

China 1 Liangmaqiao Dongjie, Chaoyang, Beijing ☎ 010 8531
9800, ⓦ cn.emb-japan.go.jp.

Ireland Nutley Building, Merrion Centre, Nutley Lane, Dublin
☎ 01 202 8300, ⓦ ie.emb-japan.go.jp.

New Zealand Level 18, Majestic Centre, 100 Willis St, Wellington
☎ 04 473 1540, ⓦ nz.emb-japan.go.jp.

Singapore 16 Nassim Rd ☎ 65 235 8855, ⓦ sg.emb-japan.go.jp.

South Africa 259 Baines St, Groenkloof, Pretoria ☎ 012 452 1500,
ⓦ japan.org.za.

South Korea Twin Tree Tower A, 6 Yulgok-ro, Jongno-gu, Seoul
☎ 02 2170 5200, ⓦ kr.emb-japan.go.jp.

UK 101–104 Piccadilly, London ☎ 020 7465 6500, ⓦ uk.emb
-japan.go.jp; 2 Melville Crescent, Edinburgh ☎ 0131 225 4777,
ⓦ edinburgh.uk.emb-japan.go.jp.

US 2520 Massachusetts Ave NW, Washington DC ☎ 202 238 6700,
ⓦ us.emb-japan.go.jp.

Getting around

**The time of year is an important factor to
consider when arranging your transport
around Japan. Peak travelling seasons are
the few days either side of New Year, the
Golden Week holidays of late April and
early May, and the mid-August Obon
holiday (see p.57). During these times, the
whole of Japan can seem on the move,
with trains, planes and ferries packed to
the gills and roads clogged with traffic.
Book well in advance and be prepared to
pay higher fares on flights, as all discounts
are suspended during peak periods.**

Domestic **travel agencies**, such as Japan Travel
Bureau (see p.32), can book all types of transport
and are also useful sources for checking travel
schedules. The staff in these agencies have access
to the **jikokuhyō timetable**, an incredible source
of information, updated monthly, on virtually every
form of public transport in Japan. There's always a
jikokuhyō available for consultation at stations, and
most hotels have a copy too.

If you're going to travel around Japan a lot, get
hold of a **Japan Railways (JR) English timetable**
for all the Shinkansen and many major express train
services, available from JNTO offices in Japan and
abroad (see p.76) and at major train stations. Also
incredibly useful is the **Hyperdia Timetable**
(ⓦ hyperdia.com), an online resource providing a
whole range of travel options, including transfers by
air, bus, train and ferry between almost any two
points in Japan; using the "from/to" function on

Google Maps will also give you most of the information you'll require.

By train

The vast majority of services on Japan's brilliant rail
network are operated by the six regional **JR (Japan
Railways)** companies: JR Hokkaidō (ⓦ www
.jrhokkaido.co.jp), JR East (ⓦ www.jreast.co.jp), JR
Central (ⓦ english.jr-central.co.jp), JR West (ⓦ www
.westjr.co.jp), JR Shikoku (ⓦ jr-shikoku.co.jp) and JR
Kyūshū (ⓦ jrkyushu.co.jp). JR is run as a single
company as far as buying tickets is concerned.
Smaller rail companies, including Hankyū, Kintetsu,
Meitetsu, Odakyū and Tōbu, are based in the major
cities and surrounding areas, but in the vast
majority of Japan it's JR services that you'll be using.

Individual **tickets** can be pricey, especially for the
fastest trains, but many discount tickets and **rail
passes** are available to cut the cost. If you plan to
travel extensively by train, the various Japan Rail
passes provide the best overall deal (see box, p.37).
If you have lots of time, and are travelling during
the main student holiday periods, the **Seishun 18
ticket** (see p.37) is also an excellent buy.

Shinkansen

For many visitors, riding the **Shinkansen** (新幹線) is
an eagerly anticipated part of a trip to Japan. Often
referred to as the "Bullet Train" because of the smooth,
rounded design of the earliest locomotives, you'll
barely notice the speed of these smooth-running
beasts, which purr along some lines at a whopping
320kph; some lines are planning to upgrade to
360kph in due course. They are also frighteningly
punctual (two seconds late on the platform and you'll
be waving goodbye to the back end of the train), not
to mention reliable (only the severest weather conditions or earthquakes stop the Shinkansen).

The busiest Shinkansen route is the **Tōkaidō–
San'yō** line, which runs south from Tokyo through

TRAVEL INFORMATION SERVICE

JR East Infoline (daily 10am–6pm;
☎ 050 2016 1603) is an information
service in English, Chinese and Korean
dealing with all train enquiries
nationwide. Train bookings cannot be
made on this service, but they will be
able to tell you about the **fastest route**
between any two points on the system
and where to make a seat reservation.

LEFT LUGGAGE

You'll usually only find **left-luggage offices** at the largest train stations in big cities, though all train stations, many subway stations, department stores and shopping centres have **coin lockers** where you can stash your bags. These come in a range of sizes, charging from ¥300 to ¥600 for a day's storage.

Nagoya, Kyoto, Osaka and Hiroshima, terminating at Hakata Station in Fukuoka (the Tōkaidō line runs from Tokyo to Shin-Osaka Station, while the San'yō line continues from there to Fukuoka).

The **Tōhoku line** is the main northern route, passing through Sendai and terminating at Shin-Aomori; an extension through the Seikan Tunnel to Hakodate opened in 2016, and this new **Hokkaidō line** will be extended to Sapporo by 2031. The **Akita line** runs from Tokyo to Akita on the north coast, while the **Yamagata line** to Shinjō, in the middle of the Tōhoku region, splits off west from the Tōhoku line at Fukushima; these are both "mini-Shinkansen" services, and are not as fast as the regular ones.

The **Jōetsu line** heads north from Tokyo, tunnelling through the mountains to Niigata along the Sea of Japan coast, with the **Nagano line** (also known as the Hokuriku line) branching off west at Takasaki to end at Nagano; an extension to Kanazawa opened in 2015. Lastly, the **Kyūshū line** connects Kagoshima with Hakata.

To travel by Shinkansen, you'll pay a hefty **surcharge** on top of the basic fare for a regular train. Three types of Shinkansen services are available: the *Kodama* (こだま), which stops at all stations; the *Hikari* (ひかり), which stops only at major stations; and the *Nozomi* (のぞみ; available on the Tōkaidō–San'yō line only), the fastest service, for which you'll have to pay an extra fee (and which you're not allowed to take if you're travelling on most types of rail pass). If you're travelling from Tokyo to Fukuoka, the *Nozomi* shaves an hour off the six-hour journey on the *Hikari*, but for shorter hops to Nagoya, Kyoto or Osaka, the time saved isn't generally worth the extra expense. Note that some lines employ alternative names for these services; for example, the Kyūshū Shinkansen has *Tsubame* (slowest), *Sakura* and *Mizuho* (fastest) services.

On the train, there are announcements and electronic signs in English telling you which stations are coming up. Get to the door in good time before the train arrives, as you'll generally only have a few seconds in which to disembark before the train shoots off again.

Other trains

Aside from the Shinkansen, the fastest services are **limited express** (*tokkyū*; 特急) trains, their misleading name deriving from the fact that they make a limited number of stops. Like Shinkansen, you have to pay a surcharge to travel on them, and there are separate classes of reserved and non-reserved seats (see box below). Less common are the **express** trains (*kyūkō*; 急行), which also only stop at larger stations but carry a lower surcharge. Oddly, the **rapid** trains (*kaisoku*; 快速) are slower still, making more stops than express ones, but with no surcharge. **Ordinary** trains (*futsū*; 普通) are local services stopping at all stations, and usually limited to routes under 100km.

TRAIN CLASSES AND RESERVATIONS

On Shinkansen trains and JR *tokkyū* (limited express) and *kyūkō* (express) services, there's a choice of ordinary (*futsū-sha*; 普通車) carriages or more expensive first-class **Green Car** (*guriin-sha*; グリーン車) carriages, where seats are two abreast either side of the aisle (as opposed to three). There may be a choice between **smoking** (*kitsuen*; 喫煙), and **non-smoking** (*kin'en*; 禁煙) cars; these days, many services are either entirely non-smoking or have smoking cabins in between certain carriages. On *Nozomi* Shinkansen, it's also possible to buy **standing-only tickets** for a small discount.

Each train also has both reserved (*shitei-seki*; 指定席), and unreserved (*jiyū-seki*; 自由席) sections. **Seat reservations** cost between ¥300 and ¥500, depending on the season; they are free if you have a rail pass. You cannot sit in the reserved section of a train without a reservation, even if it's empty and the unreserved section full, although you can buy a reservation ticket from the train conductor.

If you don't have a reservation, aim to get to the station early, locate your platform and stand in line at the marked section for the unreserved carriages; ask the platform attendants for *jiyū-seki*, and they'll point the way. If you have a reservation, platform signs will also direct you where to stand, so that you're beside the right door when the train pulls in.

SUNRISE TOURS

There are several **great-value deals** only available to overseas visitors on tourist visas offered by **Sunrise Tours**, a division of the Japan Travel Bureau (see p.32). For example, for ¥23,400 per person, Sunrise offers a two-day, one-night unaccompanied trip to Kyoto from Tokyo with reserved seats on the Shinkansen and a night's accommodation at a reasonable tourist hotel in Kyoto; for slightly more you can upgrade the hotel and go on the faster *Nozomi* trains. This is cheaper than the cost of a return Shinkansen ticket to Kyoto alone. The package is also flexible: you can stay longer than one night in Kyoto and return on any train you like (on a pre-specified day) as long as you cancel your return-seat reservation and take your chances in the unreserved section of the train (see box, p.35). There are **Shinkansen tours** starting in Osaka, Kyoto and Nagoya, too; for the latest details see ⓦjtb-sunrisetours.jp.

The above categories of train and surcharges apply to all JR services, and to some, but not all, private rail routes. To confuse matters further, you may find that if you're travelling on a JR train on one of the more remote branch lines, you may be charged an additional fare due to part of the old JR network having been sold off to another operating company.

There are several **SL (steam locomotive)** services across the country, which run from spring through to autumn, mainly at weekends and during holidays. These leisurely trains, with lovingly restored engines and carriages, are a huge hit with tourists, and you'd be well advised to book in advance. Among the most popular routes are the the JR Kamaishi line from Tōno in northern Honshū (see p.247) and the Yamaguchi line between Ogōri and Tsuwano in western Honshū (see p.616).

Buying tickets

JR **tickets** can be bought at any JR station and at many travel agencies. At major city stations, there will be a **fare map** in English beside the vending machine. Otherwise, if you're buying your ticket from the ticket counter, it's a good idea to have written down on a piece of paper the date and time you wish to travel, your destination, the number of tickets you want and whether you'll need smoking or non-smoking seats. A fallback is to buy the minimum fare ticket from the vending machine and pay any surcharges on or when leaving the train – though this may sound dodgy, it's completely kosher, and locals often do this too.

To make **advance reservations** for *tokkyū* and Shinkansen trains, or to buy special types of tickets, you'll generally need to go to the green window, or "*midori-no-madoguchi*" – sales counters marked by a green logo.

In order to swap your exchange voucher for a **Japan Rail Pass**, you'll have to go to a designated ticket office; they're listed in the booklet you'll receive with your rail pass voucher and on the rail pass website.

Japan Rail passes

If you plan to make just one long-distance train journey, such as Tokyo to Kyoto one-way, a **Japan Rail Pass** (ⓦjapanrailpass.net) will not be good value, but in all other cases it will be. At the time of writing, the full Japan Rail Pass could only be bought *outside* Japan from a travel agency (see p.32 for a few suggestions); however, JR is set to allow purchases inside Japan for a premium, so check the latest situation before you travel. For unfettered flexibility, the full Japan Rail Pass is the way to go, while **regional Japan Rail Passes** (see box opposite) are good deals if they fit with your travel itinerary; most of these can be purchased at stations inside Japan. All the prices quoted here are for ordinary rail passes – Green Car passes cost more (see box, p.35). Note that you will have to be travelling on a tourist visa to buy any of these passes.

The full **Japan Rail Pass** allows travel on virtually all JR services throughout Japan, including buses and ferries, and is valid for seven (¥29,100), fourteen (¥46,400) or twenty-one (¥59,400) consecutive days. The major service for which it is not valid is the *Nozomi* Shinkansen (see p.35); if you're caught on one of these, even unwittingly, you'll be liable for the full fare for the trip. As with all JR tickets, **children** aged between 6 and 11 years inclusive pay half-price, while those under 6 travel free.

If you buy the pass abroad, the cost in your own currency will depend on the exchange rate at the time of purchase – you might be able to save a little money by **shopping around** between agents offering the pass, because they don't all use the same exchange rate. You'll be given an **exchange voucher**, which must be swapped for a pass in Japan **within three months**. Once issued, the dates on the pass cannot be changed. Exchanges can only be made at designated JR stations; you'll be issued with a list of locations (essentially every major JR station and international airport) when you buy your pass. Note that passes can only be issued if you're

JAPAN REGIONAL RAIL PASSES

If you'll be concentrating on one or two specific parts of Japan, it may be wise to take advantage of the many regional passes on offer. Most of these can be purchased inside Japan.

All Shikoku Rail Pass JR Shikoku Ⓦ jr-shikoku.co.jp. Covers the whole island, but must be purchased outside Japan; allows travel on JR and private lines, from two days (¥7400) to five days (¥10,000).

Hokkaidō Rail Pass JR Hokkaidō Ⓦ www2.jrhokkaido.co.jp /global. Covers the whole island. ¥15,000 for a three-day ticket, ¥22,000 for five days and ¥24,000 for seven days.

Kansai Area Pass JR West Ⓦ www.westjr.co.jp. Covers the Kansai area. ¥2200 for one day, ¥4300 for two days, ¥5300 for three days and ¥6300 for four days. JR West also offer other passes covering slightly different areas, including the San'yō-San'in Pass (¥19,000 for seven days), which extends as far south as Fukuoka on Kyūshū.

Kyūshū Rail Pass JR Kyūshū Ⓦ jrkyushu.co.jp. Covers the whole island. ¥15,000 for three days, ¥18,000 for five days. The Northern Kyūshū Rail Pass covers just the north, including Nagasaki, Kumamoto, Aso, Yufuin and Beppu (¥8500 for three days, ¥10,000 for five days).

Nagano, Niigata Area Pass JR East Ⓦ www.jreast.co.jp. Covers Nagano and Niigata area of northern Honshū, including Nikkō. ¥18,000, valid for five journeys within a fourteen-day period.

Tōhoku Area Rail Pass JR East Ⓦ www.jreast.co.jp. Covers most of northern Honshū, including Aomori, Sendai and Nikko. ¥19,000, valid for five journeys within a fourteen-day period.

Tokyo Wide Pass JR East Ⓦ www.jreast.co.jp. Covers the full Greater Tokyo area. ¥10,000 for three days.

---

travelling on a **temporary visitor visa**; JR staff are very strict about this, and you'll be asked to show your passport when you present your exchange voucher for the pass or when you buy a pass directly in Japan. Also, note that if you lose your pass, it will not be replaced, so take good care of it.

JR Pass holders can get a **discount**, typically around 10 percent, at all JR Group **hotels**; check the list in the information booklet provided when you buy your pass.

Other discount tickets

The **Seishun 18 ticket** (青春18きっぷ; Ⓦ jreast.co.jp) is available to everyone regardless of age, but only valid during school vacations (roughly July 20 to September 10, and December 10 to January 10; they go on sale ten days before the school vacations start, and can be bought up to ten days before the vacations end. For ¥11,850 you get five day-tickets that can be used to travel anywhere in Japan, as long as you take only the slow *futsū* and *kaisoku* trains. The tickets can also be split and used individually by different people. If you're not in a hurry, this ticket can be the **biggest bargain** on the whole of Japan's rail system: you can, for example, use one of the day-tickets to travel from Tokyo to Nagasaki – it'll take almost 24 hours, but cost the equivalent of just over ¥2000. The tickets are also handy for touring a local area in a day, since you can get on and off trains as many times as you wish within 24 hours.

Kaisūken (回数券) are usually four or more one-way tickets to the same destination. These work out substantially cheaper than buying the tickets individually, and as such are good for groups travelling to the same destination.

Furii kippu (フリー切符) excursion-type tickets are available for various areas of Japan, usually with unlimited use of local transport for a specified period of time. The **Hakone Freepass** (see box, p.208), offered by the Odakyū railway company, covering routes from Tokyo to the lakeland area of Hakone, is particularly good value. If you plan to travel in one area, it's always worth asking the JR East Infoline (see box, p.34) or the tourist information offices if there are any other special tickets that could be of use.

By plane

The big two **domestic airlines** are All Nippon Airways (ANA; Ⓦ ana.co.jp) and Japan Airlines (JAL; Ⓦ jal.co.jp). Both carriers offer substantial **discounts** for advance bookings, with an extra discount if the booking is made entirely online. There's little difference between the two as far as prices and quality of service are concerned.

Local **low-cost airlines** have ballooned of late, providing much-needed competition to the rail; these include **Skymark** (Ⓦ skymark.co.jp), **Solaseed Air** (Ⓦ solaseedair.jp), **Peach** (Ⓦ flypeach.com), **Vanilla Air** (Ⓦ vanilla-air.com) and **Jetstar** (Ⓦ jetstar .com). Services are usually fine, though with the usual restrictions on baggage allowance.

If you're not using a rail pass, low-cost or discounted plane fares are well worth considering. For example, to travel by train to Sapporo from Tokyo costs ¥26,820 and takes over eight hours, compared with a discounted plane fare which can fall to as low as ¥9000 for a journey of an hour and a half. Discounts are generally not available during the peak travelling seasons.

DISCOUNT TICKET SHOPS

In most big cities, usually in shopping areas near stations, you can find **discount ticket shops**, or *kinken shoppu* (金券ショップ), which sell, among other things, cheap airline and Shinkansen tickets. These shops buy up discount group tickets and sell them on individually, usually at around twenty percent cheaper than the regular prices. These are legitimate operations, but you'll need to be able to read and speak some Japanese to be sure you've got the ticket you need, and there may be some days when travel isn't allowed. With the Shinkansen tickets, you can't make seat reservations at a discount shop, so you'll need to go to a JR ticket office to arrange these.

Both JAL and ANA offer **discount flight passes** to overseas visitors, which are definitely worth considering if you plan to make several plane trips. JAL (🌐 jal.co.jp/yokosojapan) offers the **oneworld Yokoso** and **Welcome to Japan** passes: the former pass, only available to those using oneworld carriers to fly into Japan (including JAL, British Airways and Qantas), allows you to purchase up to five flights at the fixed price of ¥10,800 each; the latter pass, available to anyone regardless of which airline used, is more expensive, and you need to buy a minimum of two flights. These fares are excellent value if you plan to visit far-flung destinations, such as the islands of Okinawa. These tickets are not available during peak travelling seasons such as July and August and the New Year and Golden Week holidays.

By bus

Japan has a comprehensive system of **long-distance buses** (*chōkyori basu*; 長距離バス), including **night buses** (*yakō basu;* 夜行バス), between major cities. Fares are always cheaper than the fastest trains, but the buses are usually slower and can get caught up in traffic, even on the expressways (Japan's fastest roads), especially during peak travel periods. Most bus journeys start and finish next to or near the main train station. For journeys over two hours, there is usually at least one rest stop.

Willer Express (🌐 willerexpress.com) is one of the largest long-distance bus operators and offers some great deals, including special three-, five- and seven-day bus passes for foreign visitors. A seven-hour overnight service from Tokyo to Kyoto can cost as little as ¥3200; by way of comparison, the Shinkansen costs ¥13,900, but takes just two and a quarter hours.

There are hundreds of small bus companies operating different routes, so for full details of current services, timetables and costs make enquiries with **local tourist information offices**. Buses come into their own in the more rural parts of Japan where there are few or no trains. With a handful of exceptions (mentioned in the Guide), you don't need to book tickets on such services but can pay on the bus. JR runs a number of buses, some of which are covered by the various rail passes. Other private bus companies may also offer bus passes to certain regions; again, check with local tourist offices for any deals.

By ferry

One of the most pleasant ways of travelling around this island nation is by **ferry**. Overnight journeys between Honshū and Hokkaidō in the north, and Kyūshū and Shikoku in the south, are highly recommended. If you can't spare the time, try a short hop, say to one of the islands of the Inland Sea, or from Niigata to Sado-ga-shima.

On the **overnight ferries**, the cheapest fares, which entitle you to a sleeping space on the floor of a large room with up to a hundred other passengers, can be a bargain compared with train and plane fares to the same destinations. For example, the overnight ferry fare from Ōarai, two hours north of Tokyo, to Tomakomai, around an hour south of Sapporo on Hokkaidō, can be as low as ¥8500 (🌐 sunflower.co.jp); even if you pay extra for a bed in a shared or private berth, it's still cheaper than the train, and you'll have a very comfortable cruise as part of the bargain. Ferries are also an excellent way of transporting a bicycle or motorbike (though you'll pay a small supplement for these); many also take cars.

Ferry **schedules** are subject to seasonal changes and also vary according to the weather, so for current details of times and prices, it's best to consult the local tourist information office.

CABLE-CARS AND ROPEWAYS

It's worth noting a linguistic distinction that applies to the transport at several of Japan's mountain resorts. What is known in the West as a cable-car (a capsule suspended from a cable going up a mountain) is called a **ropeway** in Japan, while the term **"cable-car"** means a funicular or rack-and-pinion railway.

By car

While it would be foolhardy to rent a car to get around Japan's big cities, **driving** is often the best way to tour the country's less populated and off-the-beaten-track areas. Japanese roads are of a very high standard, with the vast majority of signs on main routes being in *rōmaji* as well as Japanese script. Although you'll have to pay **tolls** to travel on the expressways (reckon on around ¥30 per kilometre), many other perfectly good roads are free; regular **petrol** averages around ¥140 a litre.

Car rental

For a group of people, **renting a car** to tour a rural area over a couple of days can work out much better value than taking buses. It's often possible to rent cars for less than a day, too, for short trips. There are car rental counters at all the major airports and train stations. The main Japanese companies include Mazda Rent-a-Car (**W**mazda-rentacar.co.jp); Nippon Rent-a-Car (**W**nipponrentacar.co.jp); Nissan Rent-a-Car (**W**nissan-rentacar.com); and Toyota Rent-a-Car (**W**rent.toyota.co.jp). Budget, Hertz and National also have rental operations across Japan (although not as widely spread). **Rates**, which vary little between companies and usually include unlimited mileage, start from around ¥5500 for the first 24 hours for the smallest type of car (seating four people), plus ¥1000 insurance. During the peak seasons of Golden Week, Obon and New Year, rates for all cars tend to increase.

Since you're unlikely to want to drive in any of the cities, the best rental **deals** are often through **Eki Rent-a-Car** (**W**www.ekiren.co.jp), which gives a discounted rate by combining the rental with a train ticket to the most convenient station for the area you wish to explore. Eki Rent-a-Car's offices are close to stations, as are often those of other major car rental firms. Another interesting option for getting around Japan is **Japan Campers** (**W**japancampers .com), which has a range of excellent camper vans for hire from their lot near Narita Airport.

Most cars come with a **GPS** (Global Positioning Satellite) navigation system, sometimes with an English-language mode – ask for this when you book. Input the telephone number or address for a location (the hotel you're staying at or a museum you want to visit, for example) and the GPS system will plot the course for you.

To rent a car you must have an **international driver's licence** based on the 1949 Geneva Convention (some international licences are not valid, including those issued in France, Germany and Switzerland), as well as your national licence.

Officially, if you have a French, German or Swiss licence (regular or international) you are supposed to get an official Japanese translation of the licence – contact your local Japanese embassy for further info. You may get lucky and find a car rental firm that doesn't know or ignores this rule, but don't count on it. If you've been in Japan for more than six months, you'll need to apply for a Japanese licence.

Rules of the road

Driving is on the **left**, the same as in Britain, Ireland, Australia, South Africa and most of Southeast Asia, and international traffic signals are used. The bilingual *Japan Road Atlas* (¥2890), published by Shōbunsha, includes many helpful notes, such as the dates when some roads close during winter. If you're a member of an automobile association at home, the chances are that you'll qualify for reciprocal rights with the Japan Auto Federation (**W**jaf .or.jp), which publishes the English-language *Rules of the Road* book, detailing Japan's driving code. The top **speed limit** in Japan is 80kph, which applies only on expressways, though drivers frequently exceed this and are rarely stopped by police. In cities, the limit is 40kph.

If you've drunk any **alcohol** at all, even the smallest amount, don't drive – it's illegal, as well as dumb, and if you're caught by the police you'll be in big trouble, as will anyone sharing the vehicle with you (drunk or otherwise).

Parking

There are always **car parks** close to main train stations; at some, your vehicle will be loaded onto a rotating conveyor belt and whisked off to its parking spot. Reckon on ¥500 per hour for a central city car park and ¥300 per hour elsewhere. If you manage to locate a **parking meter**, take great care not to overstay the time paid for (usually around ¥300/hour); some have mechanisms to trap cars, which will only be released once the fine has been paid directly into the meter (typically ¥10,000–15,000). In rural areas, parking is not so much of a problem and is rarely charged.

By bike

Although you're unlikely to want to **cycle** around the often traffic-clogged streets of Japan's main cities, a bike is a great way to get from A to B in the smaller towns and countryside, allowing you to see plenty en route. Cycle touring is a very popular activity with students over the long summer vacation. Hokkaidō, in particular, is a cyclist's dream, with excellent roads through often stunning scenery and a network of basic but ultra-cheap cyclists' accommodation.

In many places, you can **rent bikes** from outlets beside or near the train station; some towns even have free bikes – enquire at the tourist office. Youth hostels often rent out bikes, too, usually at the most competitive rates. You can **buy** a brand-new bike in Japan for under ¥20,000 but you wouldn't want to use it for anything more than getting around town; for sturdy touring and mountain bikes, hunt out a specialist bike shop or bring your own. Although **repair shops** can be found nationwide, for foreign models it's best to bring essential spare parts with you. And despite Japan's low crime rate, a small but significant section of the Japanese public treats bikes as common property; if you don't want to lose it, make sure your bike is well chained whenever you leave it.

If you plan to take your bike on a train or bus, ensure you have a **bike bag** in which to parcel it up; on trains, you're also supposed to pay a special **bike transport supplement**, but almost nobody does this.

If you're planning a serious cycling tour, an excellent investment is *Cycling Japan* by Brian Harrell, a handy practical guide detailing many touring routes around the country. There's also useful cycling information on the following sites: Ⓦjapancycling .org, Ⓦkancycling.com and Ⓦoutdoorjapan.com.

Hitching

There's always a risk associated with **hitching**. That said, Japan is one of the safest and easiest places in the world to hitch a ride, and in some rural areas it's just about the only way of getting around without your own transport. It's also a fantastic way to meet locals, who are often only too happy to go kilometres out of their way to give you a lift just for the novelty value (impecunious students apart, hitching is very rare in Japan), or the opportunity it provides to practise English or another foreign language.

As long as you don't look too scruffy, you'll seldom be waiting long for a ride; as is the case anywhere, it's best to pick your standing point wisely (somewhere cars can see you and stop safely, and are likely to be heading your way). It's a good idea to write your intended destination in large *kanji* characters on a piece of card to hold up. Note that in Japan, convenience stores are a godsend; almost all have toilets, and spare cardboard boxes which you can tear up and scrawl your destination on. Carry a

stock of small gifts you can leave as a thank you; postcards, sweets and small cuddly toys are usually popular. Will Ferguson's *A Hitchhiker's Guide to Japan* and his entertaining travel narrative *Hokkaidō Highway Blues* (see p.866) are useful reference books.

City transport

Japan is famed for its efficient, clean and safe public transport, and that extends to cities too, whether you're travelling by subway, bus, monorail, tram or ferry. Many cities offer useful pre-paid **transport cards**, which are listed through the Guide. For **planning journeys**, the route function on Google Maps (Ⓦmaps.google.com) usually works like a charm.

Subway

Tokyo's colourful **subway** map may look daunting, but the system is relatively easy to negotiate. This subway system, and others around the country (Fukuoka, Kōbe, Kyoto, Osaka, Nagoya, Sapporo, Sendai and Yokohama), employ simple colour-coding on trains and maps, as well as clear English-language signage. Tickets usually start at around ¥170, and increase by number of stations travelled; buy them at the vending machines beside the gates. Trains usually run daily from around 5am to midnight.

Buses

Buses are a good way of cutting across certain cities. Compared to the subway there's little information in English; you may have to get used to recognizing *kanji* place names, or memorize the numbers of useful bus routes. The final destination is listed on the front of the bus, along with the route number. In some cities you pay a flat rate on entry; in others, you take a numbered ticket on entry, and the driver uses this to calculate the final total on disembarkation (you'll see it ticking upwards on a panel above his head).

Taxis

For short hops, **taxis** are often a good, if expensive, option. The basic rate is usually up to ¥730 for the first 2km, after which the meter racks up ¥80 every 275m, plus a time charge when the taxi is moving at less than 10km per hour. Between 11pm and 5am, rates are twenty to thirty percent higher. All in all, you can easily end up spending thousands on a single short ride.

Note that there's never any need to open or close the passenger **doors**, which are operated by the taxi driver – trying to do it manually can damage the mechanism, and will get your driver seething. This is just one reason why some taxis refuse to take foreigners; **communication difficulties** are another, bigger, reason, and as such it's always a good idea to have the name and address of your destination clearly written on a piece of paper (in Japanese, if possible).

Accommodation

Japan's reputation for being an extremely expensive place to visit is a little outdated in most fields – but it's certainly justified as far as accommodation goes. The country suffers from a dearth of accommodation at more or less all budget levels, and there are few bargains. However, if you look hard you'll find plenty of affordable places. You'll often find the best value – along with plenty of atmosphere – at a traditional ryokan or a family-run minshuku, the Japanese equivalent of a B&B.

It's wise to **reserve** at least your first few nights' accommodation before arrival, especially at the cheaper hostels and minshuku in Tokyo and Kyoto, where budget places can prove elusive. If you do arrive without a reservation, make use of the free accommodation booking services in Narita and Kansai International airports (see p.130 & p.448). Once in Japan, book one or two days ahead to ensure that your selected targets aren't full. Outside peak season, however, you'll rarely be stuck for accommodation. Around major **train stations** there's usually a clutch of business hotels and a **tourist information desk** – the majority will make a booking for you.

Most large- and medium-sized hotels in big cities have English-speaking receptionists who'll take a booking over the phone. The cheaper and more rural the place, however, the more likely you are to have to **speak in Japanese**, or a mix of Japanese and English. Don't be put off: armed with the right phrases (see Language, p.869), and speaking slowly and clearly, you should be able to make yourself understood – many of the terms you'll need are actually English words pronounced in a Japanese way. If you're having difficulty, the staff at your current accommodation may be able to help. **Booking online** is an option, with the advantage that you'll often get a slightly lower room rate; major chains and places that receive a lot of foreign guests generally have an English-language page (though often on amazingly dated-looking websites).

Check-in is generally between 3pm and 7pm, and check-out by 10am. Almost without exception, **security** is not a problem, though it's never sensible to leave valuables lying around in your room. In hostels, it's advisable to use lockers, if provided, or leave important items at the reception desk. Standards of **service** and **cleanliness** vary according to the type of establishment, but are usually more than adequate.

Payment and taxes

While credit cards are becoming more widely accepted, in many cases **payment** is still expected in cash. In hostels and many cheaper business hotels, you'll be expected to pay when you check in.

While all hotel rates must include eight-percent **consumption tax** – itself set to rise (see box, p.68) –there are a couple of other taxes to look out for. Most top-end hotels add a **service charge** of ten to fifteen percent, while in Tokyo the Metropolitan Government levies a tax of ¥100 per person per night in rooms that cost over ¥10,000 per person per night (or ¥200 if the room costs over ¥15,000); check to make sure if these are included in the published room rate. In hot-spring resorts, there's a small **onsen tax** (usually ¥150), though again this may already be included in the rates. And it's always worth asking when booking if there are any **deals**, usually referred to as "plans", such as special weekend rates at business hotels.

ROUGH GUIDE ACCOMMODATION PRICES

Unless stated otherwise, **hotel** prices in this book are quoted per night for the cheapest double room in high season, excluding breakfast. **Ryokans and other traditional accommodation** always quote per person, usually with food, so for these places we give the price for two people including breakfast and dinner; exceptions are noted in the reviews. For **hostels** we quote the per-person rate for a dorm bed, as well as the price of private rooms where available; breakfast is not included unless otherwise stated. **Capsule hotel** rates are for a single "room" for one person. All necessary taxes and service charges are included in the quoted rates.

Tipping is not necessary, nor expected, in Japan. The only exception is at high-class Japanese ryokan, where it's good form to leave ¥2000 for the room attendant – put the money in an envelope and hand it over discreetly at the end of your stay.

ONLINE ACCOMMODATION RESOURCES

Japan Hotel Association Ⓦ j-hotel.or.jp. Covering most major cities, though the hotels tend to be part of big, expensive chains. Lots of information provided.

Japan Hotel Net Ⓦ japanhotel.net. Offering a good range of accommodation nationwide, with a special section on ski resorts. Lots of information, including photos.

JAPANiCAN Ⓦ japanican.com. Good deals on around 4000 hotels, ryokan and tours across the country.

Japan Ryokan Association Ⓦ ryokan.or.jp. Around 1200 ryokan and hotels offering Japanese-style accommodation, many of them with onsen baths. Links take you to the relevant homepage, and there's plenty of background information about staying in ryokan.

Japanese Guest Houses Ⓦ japaneseguesthouses.com. Over 550 ryokan – from humble to grand – across the country. Also offer cultural tours in Kyoto.

Japanese Inn Group Ⓦ japaneseinngroup.com. A long-established association of about 80 good-value ryokan and minshuku.

The Ryokan Collection Ⓦ ryokancollection.com. Book one of 32 specially selected top ryokan, grouped in six locations across Japan.

Travel Rakuten Ⓦ travel.rakuten.com. Pick of the local booking sights with great discounts on published rates and the broadest selection of properties.

Hotels

Most Western-style **hotel** rooms have en-suite bathrooms, TV, phone and air conditioning as standard; there's usually high-speed internet access too, sometimes through LAN only if there's no wi-fi. Don't expect a lot of character, however, especially among the older and cheaper business hotels, although things are slowly beginning to improve and even relatively inexpensive chains are now smartening up their act.

Rates for a double or twin room range from an average of ¥30,000 at a top-flight hotel, to ¥15,000–20,000 for a smartish establishment, which will usually have a restaurant and room service. At the lowest level, a room in a basic hotel with minimal amenities will cost ¥5000–10,000. Charges usually vary quite a bit depending upon how many people are using the room, and breakfast is usually available for an additional fee (sometimes quite substantial) or is occasionally free. Most hotels offer non-smoking rooms, and some have "ladies' floors". **Wi-fi** is still not a given, even in hotels (where you may have to head to the lobby for a connection), but most places now have it; accommodation with wi-fi is indicated in the guide with a 🛜 symbol.

Business hotels

Modest **business hotels** constitute the bulk of the middle and lower price brackets. Primarily designed for those travelling on business and usually clustered around train stations, they are perfect if all you want is a place to crash out, though at the cheapest places you may find just a box with a tiny bed, a desk and a chair crammed into the smallest possible space. While the majority of rooms are single, most places have a few twins, doubles or "semi-doubles" – a large single bed which takes two at a squeeze. Squeeze is also the operative word for the aptly named "unit baths", which business hotels specialize in; these moulded plastic units contain a shower, bathtub, toilet and washbasin but leave little room for manoeuvre.

That said, some business hotels are relatively smart, and there are a number of reliable **chains** including *Tōyoko Inn* (Ⓦ toyoko-inn.com), which has scores of hotels across the country, offering a simple breakfast and free internet connections in their room rates. More upmarket are *Washington Hotels* (Ⓦ washington-hotels.jp) and the *Solare* group (Ⓦ solarehotels.com), which encompasses *Chisun* business hotels and the smarter *Loisir* chain. Some have smoking and non-smoking floors.

Capsule hotels

Catering mainly for commuters – often in various states of inebriation – who have missed their last train home are **capsule hotels**; you'll find them mostly near major stations. Inside are rows of tube-like rooms, roughly 2m long, 1m high and 1m wide; despite their "coffin-like" reputation, they can feel surprisingly comfy, with a mattress, bedding, phone, alarm and TV built into the plastic surrounds. The "door" consists of a flimsy curtain, which won't keep out the loudest snores, and they are definitely not designed for claustrophobics. However, they're relatively cheap at ¥2500–4500

JAPANESE SCRIPT

To help you find your way around, we've included **Japanese script** for all place names and for sights, hotels, restaurants, cafés, bars and shops. Where the English name for a point of interest is very different from its Japanese name, we've also provided the *rōmaji*, so that you can easily pronounce the Japanese.

JAPANESE ADDRESSES

Japanese **addresses** are, frankly, a little bit ridiculous – when it's impossible to find the building you're looking for even when you're standing right in front of it, it's clear that there are some major system failures. This stems from the fact that in many places, including Tokyo, **few roads have names**; instead, city districts are split into numbered blocks, on which the numbers themselves are usually not visible.

Addresses start with the largest **administrative district** – in Tokyo's case it's Tōkyō-*to* (metropolis), but elsewhere most commonly it's the *ken* (prefecture) accompanied by a seven-digit postcode – for example, Saitama-ken 850-0072. Next comes the *ku* (ward; for example Shinjuku-ku), followed by the *chō* (district), then three numbers representing the *chōme* (local neighbourhood), block and individual building. Finally, there might come the building name and the floor on which the business or person is located – much like the American system, 1F is the ground floor, 2F the first floor above ground, and B1F the first floor below ground.

Japanese addresses are therefore written in **reverse order** from the Western system. However, when written in English, they usually follow the Western order; this is the system we adopt in this Guide. For example, the address 2-12-7 Roppongi, Minato-ku identifies building number 7, somewhere on block 12 of number 2 *chōme* in Roppongi district, in the Minato ward of Tokyo (this can also be written as 12-7 Roppongi, 2-chōme, Minato-ku). Where the block is entirely taken up by one building, the address will have only two numbers.

Actually **locating an address** on the ground can be frustrating – even Japanese people find it tough. The old-fashioned way is to have the address written down, preferably in Japanese, and then get to the nearest train or bus station; once in the neighbourhood, find a local police box (*kōban*), which will have a detailed local map. The modern-day solution is, inevitably, Google Maps, on which the results of address searches are usually accurate. If all else fails, don't be afraid to phone – often someone will come to meet you.

per night, and fun to try at least once, though the majority are for men only. You can't stay in the hotel during the day – not that you'd want to – but you can leave luggage in their lockers. Check-in usually starts around 4pm and often involves buying a ticket from a vending machine in the lobby. Rates generally include a *yukata* (cotton dressing gown), towel and toothbrush set, and many establishments have onsen-like communal bathing facilities. Kyoto and Osaka offer a couple of stylish modern takes on the capsule hotel that are worth trying (see p.453 & p.519), while recent years have seen a few **cabin hotels** enter the market. These are just like the capsules, but with a tiny bit of attached space for you to stand, and occasionally an internet-ready computer terminal to boot.

Love hotels

Love hotels – where you can rent rooms by the hour – are another quintessential Japanese experience. Generally located in entertainment districts, they are immediately recognizable from the sign outside quoting prices for "rest" or "stay", and many sport ornate exteriors. Some can be quite sophisticated: the main market is young people or married couples taking a break from crowded apartments. All kinds of tastes can be indulged at love hotels, with rotating beds in mirror-lined rooms now decidedly passé in comparison with some of the fantasy creations on offer. Some rooms even come equipped with video cameras so you can take home a souvenir DVD of your stay. You usually choose your room from a back-lit display indicating those still available, and then negotiate with a cashier lurking behind a tiny window (eye-to-eye contact is avoided to preserve privacy). Though "rest" rates are high (from about ¥5000 for 2hr), the price of an overnight stay can be the same as a business hotel (roughly ¥8000–10,000), although you usually can't check in until around 10pm.

Japanese-style accommodation

A night in a traditional Japanese inn, or **ryokan**, is one of the highlights of a visit to Japan. The best charge five-star hotel rates, but there are plenty where you can enjoy the full experience at affordable prices. Cheaper are **minshuku**, family-run guesthouses, and the larger government-owned **kokuminshukusha** (people's lodges) located in national parks and resort areas. In addition, some temples and shrines offer simple accommodation, or you can arrange to stay with a Japanese family through the **homestay** programme (see box, p.46).

It's advisable to **reserve** at least a day ahead and essential if you want to eat in. Though a few places

STAYING IN JAPANESE-STYLE ACCOMMODATION

Whenever you're staying in Japanese-style accommodation, you'll be expected to check in early – between 3pm and 6pm – and to follow local custom from the moment you arrive.

Just inside the front door, there's usually a row of **slippers** for you to change into, but remember to slip them off when walking on the tatami. The **bedding** is stored behind sliding doors in your room during the day and only laid out in the evening. In top-class ryokan this is done for you, but elsewhere be prepared to tackle your own. There'll be a mattress (which goes straight on the tatami) with a sheet to put over it, a soft quilt to sleep under, and a pillow stuffed with rice husks.

Most places provide a **yukata**, a loose cotton robe tied with a belt, and a short jacket (*tanzen*) in cold weather. The *yukata* can be worn in bed, during meals, when going to the bathroom and even outside – in resort areas many Japanese holiday-makers take an evening stroll in their *yukata* and wooden sandals (*geta*; also supplied by the ryokan). Wrap the left side of the *yukata* over the right; the opposite is used to dress the dead.

The traditional Japanese **bath** (*furo*) has its own set of rules (see box, p.61). It's customary to bathe in the evenings. In ryokan, there are usually separate bathrooms for men (男) and women (女), but elsewhere there will either be designated times for males and females, or you'll simply have to wait until it's vacant – it's perfectly acceptable for couples and families to bathe together, though there's not usually a lot of space.

Evening **meals** tend to be early, at 6pm or 7pm. Smarter ryokan generally serve meals in your room, while communal dining is the norm in cheaper places. **At night**, the doors are locked pretty early, so check before going out – they may let you have a key.

don't take foreigners, mainly through fear of language problems and cultural faux pas, you'll find plenty that do listed in the Guide chapters. JNTO (see p.76) also publishes useful lists of ryokan and distributes brochures of the *Japanese Inn Group* (see p.42), which specializes in inexpensive, foreigner-friendly accommodation.

Ryokan

Rooms in a typical **ryokan** are generally furnished with just a low table and floor cushions sitting on pale green rice-straw matting (tatami) and a hanging scroll – nowadays alongside a TV and phone – decorating the alcove (tokonoma) on one wall. Though you'll increasingly find a toilet and washbasin in the room, baths are generally communal. The rules of ryokan etiquette (see box above) may seem daunting, but overall these are great places to stay.

Room rates vary according to the season, the grade of room, the quality of meal you opt for and the number of people in a room; prices almost always include breakfast and an evening meal. Rates are usually quoted per person and calculated on the basis of two people sharing. One person staying in a room will pay slightly more than the advertised per-person price; three people sharing a room, slightly less. On average, a night in a basic ryokan will cost between ¥8000 and ¥10,000 per head, while a classier establishment, perhaps with meals served in the room, will cost up to ¥20,000.

Top-rank ryokan with exquisite meals and the most attentive service imaginable can cost upwards of ¥50,000 per person.

At cheaper ryokan, it's possible to ask for a room without **meals**, though this is frowned on at the more traditional places and, anyway, the delicious multicourse meals are often very good value. If you find miso soup, cold fish and rice a bit hard to tackle in the morning, you might want to opt for a Western breakfast, if available.

Minshuku and kokuminshukusha

There's a fine line between the cheapest ryokan and a **minshuku**. In general, minshuku are smaller and less formal than ryokan: more like staying in a private home, with varying degrees of comfort and cleanliness. All rooms will be Japanese-style, with communal bathrooms and dining areas. A night in a minshuku will cost from around ¥4000 per person excluding meals, or from ¥6000 with two meals; rates are calculated in the same way as for ryokan.

In country areas and popular resorts, you'll also find homely guesthouses called **pensions** – a word borrowed from the French. Though the accommodation and meals are Western-style, these are really minshuku in disguise. They're family-run – generally by young couples escaping city life – and specialize in hearty home cooking. Rates average around ¥8000 per head, including dinner and breakfast.

In the national parks, onsen resorts and other popular tourist spots, minshuku and pensions are supplemented by large, government-run **kokumin-shukusha**, which cater to family groups and tour parties. They're often quite isolated and difficult to get to without your own transport. The average cost of a night's accommodation is around ¥8000 per person, including two meals.

Temples and shrines

A few Buddhist **temples** and Shinto **shrines** take in regular guests for a small fee, and some belong to the *Japanese Inn Group* (see p.42) or the Japan Youth Hostels association (see below). By far the best places to experience temple life are at the Buddhist retreat of Kōya-san (see p.526) and in Kyoto's temple lodges (see p.452).

Though the accommodation is inevitably basic, the food can be superb, especially in temple lodgings (*shukubō*), where the monks serve up delicious vegetarian cuisine (*shōjin-ryōri*). In many temples, you'll also be welcome to attend the early-morning prayer ceremonies. Prices vary between ¥4000 and ¥10,000 per person, with no meals or perhaps just breakfast at lower rates.

Hostels

Japan has over four hundred **hostels** spread throughout the country, offering cheap accommodation. The majority of hostels are well run, clean and welcoming, with the best housed in wonderful old farmhouses or temples, often in great locations.

There are two main types of hostel in Japan. Increasing in number every year are **private establishments**, which tend to be far friendlier affairs than those run by the government or **Japan Youth Hostels** (JYH; ⓦjyh.or.jp), which is affiliated to Hostelling International (HI; ⓦhihostels.com). The JYH hostels generally impose a six-night maximum stay, evening curfews and a raft of regulations. **Membership** cards are not required at government or private hostels, but all JYH ask for a current Youth Hostel card. Non-members have to buy a "welcome stamp" (¥600) each time they stay at a JYH hostel; six stamps within a twelve-month period entitles you to the Hostelling International card. JNTO offices abroad and around Japan stock a free **map** that gives contact details of all JYH hostels.

The average **price** of hostel accommodation ranges from around ¥2000 per person for a dorm bed (or even less in Okinawa) up to ¥6000 for a private room; this means that once you've included meals, a night at a private room in a hostel may work out only slightly less expensive than staying at a minshuku, or a night at a business hotel. Rates at some hostels increase during peak holiday periods.

It's essential to make **reservations** well in advance for the big-city hostels and during school vacations: namely, New Year, March, around Golden Week (late April to mid-May), and in July and August. At other times, it's a good idea to book ahead, since hostels in prime tourist spots are always busy; some close for a day or two in the off season, and others for the whole winter. If you want an evening meal, you also need to let them know a day in advance. Hostel accommodation normally consists of either dormitory bunks or shared Japanese-style tatami rooms, with communal bathrooms and dining areas. An increasing number also have private or family rooms, but these tend to fill up quickly. **Bedding** is provided. The majority of hostels have **laundry** facilities and internet access; wi-fi is usually a given these days and almost always free, though there's occasionally a small charge for using the hostel's own computer terminals.

At the JYH and government hostels, optional **meals** are sometimes offered; these vary in quality, though can be pretty good value. Dinner will generally be Japanese-style, while breakfast frequently includes bread, jam and coffee, sometimes as part of a buffet. Some hostels have a basic kitchen.

Check-in is generally between 3pm and 8pm; you sometimes have to vacate the building during the day (usually by 10am at JYH hostels).

TO BE, OR NOT TO AIRBNB?

The combination of Japan's high accommodation prices and high occupancy rates has led many travellers to give **Airbnb** (ⓦairbnb.com) a go. In Tokyo, the bulk of apartments go for ¥10,000–20,000 per night, and private rooms ¥3000–12,000; rates are usually 20–40 percent lower around the country. The government has, of late, been put under pressure by a hotel industry haemorrhaging revenue; fears of a total crackdown on non-licensed guesthouses, known as *minpaku* (民泊) in Japan, have been allayed, but with the situation still somewhat up in the air, you're advised to check the site for updates far in advance of your visit.

HOMESTAY PROGRAMMES & WWOOF

Homestay **programmes** are a wonderful way of getting to know Japan – contact any of the local tourism associations and international exchange foundations listed in this book to see if any programmes are operating in the area you plan to visit.

It's also possible to arrange to stay at one of nearly four hundred or so organic farms and other rural properties around Japan through **WWOOF** (Willing Workers on Organic Farms; ⓦwwoof.org). Bed and board is provided for free in return for work on the farm; see Living in Japan (p.72) for more details. This is a great way to really experience how country folk live away from the big cities and the beaten tourist path. To get a list of host farms, you have to take out an annual membership, though a few examples are posted on the Japanese site (ⓦwwoofjapan.com).

Camping

There are thousands of **campsites** (*kyampu-jō*) scattered throughout Japan, with prices ranging from nothing up to ¥5000 or more to pitch a tent. In some places, you'll also pay an entry fee of a few hundred yen per person, plus charges for water and cooking gas. In general, facilities are pretty basic compared with American or European sites; many have no hot water, for example, and the camp shop may stock nothing but Pot-Noodles. Most sites only open during the summer months, when they're packed out with students and school parties.

JNTO publishes lists of selected campsites, or ask at local tourist offices. If you haven't got your own tent, you can often hire everything on site or rent simple cabins from around ¥2500 – check before you get there. The best sites are in national parks and can be both time-consuming and costly to get to unless you have your own transport. Sleeping rough in national parks is banned, but elsewhere in the countryside **camping wild** is tolerated. However, it's advisable to choose an inconspicuous spot – don't put your tent up till dusk and leave early in the morning. Pitch too early or wake too late, and don't be too surprised if worried locals alert the local police to your presence (though as long as you've got your passport handy, you should be fine).

Mountain huts

In the main hiking areas, you'll find a good network of **mountain huts** (*yama-goya*). These range from basic shelters to much fancier places with wardens and meals. Huts get pretty crowded in summer and during student holidays; count on at least ¥5000 per head, including two meals. Many places will also provide a picnic lunch. You can get information about mountain huts from local tourist offices.

Long-term accommodation

There's plenty of long-term **rental accommodation** available in Japan, making it a relatively easy and affordable country in which to set up home.

Newcomers who arrive without a job, or who are not on some sort of expat package that includes accommodation, usually start off in what's known as a **gaijin house** (foreigner house). Located in Tokyo, Kyoto and other cities with large foreign populations, these are shared apartments with a communal kitchen and bathroom, ranging from total fleapits to the almost luxurious. They're usually

JAPAN'S CHEAPEST SLEEPS

The cheapest places to stay in Japan are not sleazy love motels, capsule hotel pods or (Okinawa aside) youth hostel dormitories. No, to really hit the bottom of the barrel you have to head to an **internet café**, where you can get a night's sleep for under ¥1500. Those thinking that such places cannot count as accommodation would be wrong – while most have "regular" computer terminals lining open corridors, many have terminals in tiny, walled-off cubicles, often with a choice between a soft, reclinable chair and a cushioned floor (the latter being particularly comfortable). Many also have shower facilities (usually ¥100), snack counters, and free soft-drink vending machines. Indeed, many Japanese actually live semi-permanently in these places, if they can't afford rent elsewhere – they're known locally as the "cyber-homeless". Drawbacks include occasional loud snorers, and neighbouring couples making the most of some rare, if imperfect, privacy. You'll find such establishments in almost any large city in Japan; at some, you'll need to pay a one-off membership fee of around ¥300.

rented by the month, though if there's space, weekly or even nightly rates may be available. You'll find *gaijin* houses advertised in the English-language press, or simply ask around. Monthly rates for a shared apartment in Tokyo start at ¥30,000–40,000 per person if you share a room, and ¥50,000–60,000 for your own room. A deposit may also be required.

The alternative is a **private apartment**. These are usually rented out by real estate companies, though you'll also find places advertised in the media. Unfortunately, some landlords simply refuse to rent to non-Japanese. Some rental agencies specialize in dealing with foreigners, or you could ask a Japanese friend or colleague to act as an intermediary. When you've found a place, be prepared to pay a deposit of one to two months' rent in addition to the first month's rent, key money (usually one or two months' non-refundable rent when you move in) and a month's rent in commission to the agent. You may also be asked to provide information about your financial situation and find someone – generally a Japanese national – to act as a guarantor. The basic monthly rental in Tokyo starts at ¥50,000–60,000 per month for a one-room box, and upwards of ¥100,000 for somewhere more comfortable with a separate kitchen and bathroom.

Food and drink

One of the great pleasures of a trip to Japan is exploring the full and exotic range of Japanese food and drink. While dishes such as sushi and tempura are common the world over these days, there are hundreds of other types of local cuisine that may provide new and delicious discoveries. Regional specialities abound, and many locals seemingly holiday to different parts of the country for culinary reasons alone. It's hard to blame them, for many Japanese recipes embody a subtlety of flavour and texture rarely found in other cuisines, and the presentation is often so exquisite that it feels an insult to the chef to eat what has been so painstakingly crafted.

Picking at delicate morsels with chopsticks is only one small part of the dining experience. It's far more common to find Japanese tucking into robust and cheap dishes such as hearty bowls of **ramen noodles** or the comforting concoction **karē raisu** (curry rice) as well as burgers and fried chicken from

ubiquitous Western-style fast-food outlets. All the major cities have an extensive range of restaurants serving Western and other Asian dishes, with Tokyo, Kyoto and Osaka in particular being major destinations for foodies.

Eating out needn't cost the earth. Lunch is always the best-value meal of the day, with many restaurants – even some posh ones – offering set menus for around ¥1000. If you fuel up well for lunch, a cheap bowl of noodles for dinner could carry you through the night.

Throughout the Guide, eating and drinking places that offer **wi-fi** are indicated with a 📶 symbol.

Meals

Breakfast is generally served from around 7am to 9am at most hotels, ryokan and minshuku. At the top end and mid-range places you'll generally have a choice between a Western-style breakfast or a traditional meal consisting of miso soup, grilled fish, pickles and rice; at the cheaper minshuku and ryokan, only a Japanese-style meal will be available. Western-style breakfasts, when available, sometimes resemble what you might eat at home, but most commonly involve wedges of thick white tasteless bread and some form of eggs and salad. Most cafés also have a "morning-service" menu which means *kōhii* and *tōsuto* (coffee and toast).

Restaurants generally open for **lunch** around 11.30am and finish serving at 2pm. Lacklustre sandwiches are best passed over in favour of a full meal at a restaurant; **set menus** (called *teishoku*) are always on offer and usually cost ¥600–1200 for a couple of courses, often with a drink.

Teishoku are sometimes available at night, when you may also come across **course menus** (*kōsu menyū*), which involve a series of courses and are priced according to the number of courses and quality of ingredients used. At any time of day, you can snack in **stand-up noodle bars** – often found around train stations – and from revolving conveyor belts at cheap **sushi** shops.

Dinner, the main meal of the day, is typically served from 6pm to around 9pm; some restaurant chains, even in the countryside, stay open all night. In a traditional Japanese meal, you'll usually be served all your courses at the same time, but at more formal places, rice and soup are always served last. You are most likely to finish your meal with a piece of seasonal **fruit**, such as melon, orange, persimmon or *nashi* (a crisp type of pear), or an ice cream (if it's green, it will be flavoured with *matcha* tea).

At **tea ceremonies** (see box, p.54), small, intensely sweet *wagashi* are served – these prettily decorated sweetmeats are usually made of pounded rice, red azuki beans or chestnuts. *Wagashi* can also be bought from specialist shops and department stores and make lovely gifts.

Where to eat

A **shokudō** is a kind of canteen that serves a range of traditional and generally inexpensive dishes. Usually found near train and subway stations and in busy shopping districts, *shokudō* can be identified by the displays of plastic meals in their windows. Other restaurants (*resutoran*) usually serve just one type of food – for example **sushi-ya** serve sushi and sashimi, and **yakitori-ya** serve *yakitori* – or specialize in a particular style of cooking, such as *kaiseki* (haute cuisine) or *teppanyaki*, where food is prepared on a steel griddle, either by diners themselves or a chef.

All over Japan, but particularly in city suburbs, you'll find bright and breezy **family restaurants**, such as *Royal Host* and *Jonathan's*, American-style operations specifically geared to family dining and serving Western and Japanese dishes. The food at these places can be on the bland side, but is invariably keenly priced. They also have menus illustrated with photographs to make ordering easy. If you can't decide what to eat, head for the restaurant floors of major **department stores**, where you'll find a collection of Japanese and Western operations, often outlets of reputable local restaurants. Many will have plastic food displays in their front windows and daily special menus.

YOKOCHŌ

A trip to Japan is not complete without a night out at a **yokochō**. These market-style areas often focus on food and drink, and many are packed with dozens upon dozens of minuscule eateries. With smoke and steam rising from the open-air "kitchens" (often nothing more than a small grill), they can be hugely photogenic. English-language menus and signage are rare at these places, but many places specialize in a particular type of food, making selection and ordering a simple exercise in walking around and pointing. Almost all stalls will sell beer, as well as sake.

Western and other ethnic food restaurants proliferate in the cities, and it's seldom a problem finding popular **foreign cuisines** such as Italian (*Itaria-ryōri*), French (*Furansu-ryōri*), Korean (*Kankoku-ryōri*), Chinese (*Chūgoku-ryōri* or *Chūka-ryōri*) or Thai (*Tai ryōri*) food. However, the recipes are often adapted to suit Japanese tastes, which can mean less spicy dishes than you may be used to.

Coffee shops (*kissaten*) are something of an institution in Japan, often designed to act as a lounge or business meeting place for patrons starved of space at home or the office. Others have weird designs or specialize in certain things, such as jazz or comic books. In such places, a speciality coffee or tea will usually set you back ¥500 or more. There are also plenty of cheap and cheerful operations like *Doutor* and *Starbucks*, serving drinks and snacks at reasonable prices, as well as a recent glut of more characterful hipster-style operations; search these places out for a cheap breakfast or a quick bite.

Finally, for something different, check out **Nagomi Visit** (ⓦwww.nagomivisit.com), a site that links guests to hosts who will pick you up from the station and take you back to their home for lunch or dinner.

Where to drink

The liveliest places to **drink** are **izakaya**, pub-type restaurants which also serve an extensive menu of mainly small dishes. Traditional *izakaya* are rather rustic-looking, although in the cities you'll come across more modern, trendy operations aimed at the youth market. One type of traditional *izakaya* is the *robatayaki*, which serves charcoal-grilled food. Most *izakaya* open around 6pm and shut down around midnight, if not later; there'll usually be a cover charge of ¥200–500 per person. From mid-June to late August, outdoor **beer gardens** – some attached to existing restaurants and *izakaya*, other stand-alone operations – flourish across Japan's main cities and towns; look out for the fairy lights on the roofs of buildings, or in street-level gardens and plazas.

Regular bars, or **nomiya**, often consist of little more than a short counter and a table, and are run by a *mama-san* if female, or *papa-san* or master if male. Prices at most *nomiya* tend to be high, and although you're less likely to be ripped off if you speak some Japanese, it's no guarantee. All such bars operate a **bottle keep** system for regulars to stash a bottle of drink with their name on it behind the bar. It's generally best to go to such bars with a regular, since they tend to operate like mini-clubs,

BENTŌ: THE JAPANESE PACKED LUNCH

Every day, millions of Japanese trot off to school or work with a **bentō** stashed in their satchel or briefcase. Bentō are boxed **lunches** which are either made at home or bought from shops all over Japan. Traditional bentō include rice, pickles, grilled fish or meat and vegetables. There are thousands of permutations depending on the season and the location in Japan, with some of the best being available from department stores, where there's always a model or picture to show you what's inside the box. At their most elaborate, in classy restaurants, bentō come in beautiful multilayered lacquered boxes, each compartment containing some exquisite culinary creation. Among housewives, it's become something of a competitive sport and art form to create fun designs out of the bentō ingredients for their children's lunch. Empty bentō boxes in a huge range of designs are sold in the household section of department stores and make lovely souvenirs.

with non-regulars being given the cold shoulder. *Nomiya* stay open to the early hours, provided there are customers. A variation on the *nomiya* is the **tachinomiya**, or standing bar, which are usually cheaper and more casual. Some specialize in selling premium wines or sake, and they often serve good food alongside the drinks.

Some bars also have cover charges (for which you'll usually get some small snack with your drink), although there's plenty of choice among those that don't, so always check before buying your drink. Bars specializing in **karaoke** aren't difficult to spot (see box, p.153); if you decide to join in, there's usually a small fee to pay and songs with English lyrics to choose from. Some places also do all-you-can-drink specials, which usually work out cheaper if you'll be having three or more drinks; two hours of singing and drinking will set you back ¥2000–3000 per head.

Ordering and etiquette

On walking into most restaurants in Japan, you'll be greeted by the word *irasshaimase* ("welcome"). Indicate with your fingers how many places are needed. After being seated you'll be handed an *oshibori*, a damp, folded hand towel, usually steaming hot, but sometimes offered refreshingly cold in summer. A chilled glass of water (*mizu*) will also usually be brought automatically.

To help you decipher the menu, there's a basic glossary of essential words and phrases at the end of this book (see p.877). It's always worth asking if an English menu is available. If a restaurant has a plastic food window display, get up from your seat and use it to point out to your waiter or waitress what you want. If all else fails, look round at what your fellow diners are eating and point out what you fancy. Remember that the *teishoku* (set meal) or *kōsu* (course) meals offer the best value. The word

Baikingu (written in katakana and standing for "Viking") means a help-yourself buffet.

Don't stick **chopsticks** (*hashi*) upright in your rice – though it is an allusion to death, for most Japanese it simply just looks wrong. Also, never cross your chopsticks when you put them on the table, or use them to point at things. When it comes to eating soupy noodles, it's considered good form to slurp them up noisily; it's also fine to bring the bowl to your lips and drink directly from it.

When you want the **bill**, say *okanjō o kudasai*; the usual form is to pay at the till on the way out, not by leaving money on the table. There's no need to leave a **tip**, but it's polite to say *gochisō-sama deshita* ("That was delicious!") to the waiter or chef. Only the most upmarket Western restaurants and top hotels will add a service charge (typically ten percent).

Sushi, sashimi and seafood

Many non-Japanese falsely assume that all **sushi** is fish, but the name actually refers to the way the rice is prepared with vinegar, and you can also get sushi dishes with egg or vegetables. Fish and seafood are, of course, essential and traditional elements of Japanese cuisine, and range from the seaweed used in *miso-shiru* (soup) to the slices of tuna, salmon and squid laid across the slabs of sushi rice. Slices of raw fish and seafood on their own are called **sashimi**.

In a traditional **sushi-ya** (sushi restaurant), each plate is freshly made by a team of chefs working in full view of the customers. If you're not sure of the different types to order, point at the trays on show in the glass chiller cabinets at the counter, or go for the *nigiri-zushi mori-awase*, six or seven different types of fish and seafood on fingers of sushi rice. Other types of sushi include *maki-zushi*, rolled in a sheet of crisp seaweed, and *chirashi-zushi*, a layer of rice topped with fish, vegetables and cooked egg.

While a meal at a reputable *sushi-ya* can hit ¥5000 (or even more at a high-class joint), there are still some excellent places serving lunch sets for ¥600 and up. At **kaiten-zushi** shops, where you choose whatever sushi dish you want from the continually replenished conveyor belt, the bill will depend upon how much you order: anything from ¥600–3000 per person. In *kaiten-zushiya*, plates are colour-coded according to how much they cost, and are totted up at the end for the total cost of the meal. If you can't see what you want, you can ask the chefs to make it for you. Green tea is free, and you can usually order beer or sake.

To try **fugu**, or blowfish, go to a specialist fish restaurant, which can be easily identified by the picture or model of a balloon-like fish outside. *Fugu's* reputation derives from its potential to be fatally poisonous rather than its bland, rubbery taste. The actual risk of dropping dead at the counter is virtually nil, at least from *fugu* poisoning – you're more likely to keel over at the bill, which (cheaper, farmed *fugu* apart) will be in the ¥10,000 per-person bracket. *Fugu* is often served as part of a set-course menu including sashimi slivers, and a stew made from other parts of the fish served with rice.

A more affordable and tasty seafood speciality is **unagi**, or eel, typically basted with a thick sauce of soy and sake, sizzled over charcoal and served on a bed of rice. This dish is particularly popular in summer, when it's believed to provide strength in the face of sweltering heat.

Noodles

The three main types of **noodle** are soba, udon and ramen.

Soba are thin noodles made of brown buckwheat flour. If the noodles are green, they've been made with green-tea powder. There are two main styles of serving soba: hot and cold. It comes in a clear broth, often with added ingredients such as tofu, vegetables and chicken. Cold noodles piled on a bamboo-screen bed, with a cold sauce for dipping (which can be flavoured with chopped spring onions, seaweed flakes and *wasabi* – grated green horseradish paste), are called *zaru-soba* or *mori-soba*. In more traditional restaurants, you'll also be served a flask of the hot water (*soba-yu*) to cook the noodles, which is added to the dipping sauce to make a soup drink once you've finished the soba.

In most soba restaurants, **udon** will also be on the menu. These chunkier noodles are made with plain wheat flour and are served in the same hot or cold styles as soba. In **yakisoba** and **yakiudon** dishes the noodles are fried, often in a thick soy sauce, along with seaweed flakes, meat and vegetables.

Ramen, or yellow wheat-flour noodles, were originally imported from China but have now become part and parcel of Japanese cuisine. They're usually served in big bowls in a steaming oily soup, which typically comes in three varieties: miso (flavoured with fermented bean paste), *shio* (a salty soup) or *shōyu* (a broth made with soy sauce). The dish is often finished off with a range of garnishes, including seaweed, bamboo shoots, pink and white swirls of fish paste, and pork slices. You can usually spice it up with condiments such as minced garlic or a red pepper mixture at your table. Wherever you eat ramen, you can also usually get **gyōza**, fried half-moon-shaped dumplings filled with pork or seafood, to accompany them.

Rice dishes

A traditional meal isn't considered finished until a bowl of rice has been eaten. This Japanese staple also forms the basis of the alcoholic drink sake, as well as **mochi**, a chewy dough made from pounded glutinous rice (usually prepared and eaten during festivals such as New Year).

KAISEKI-RYŌRI: JAPANESE HAUTE CUISINE

Japan's finest style of cooking, **kaiseki-ryōri**, comprises a series of small, carefully balanced and expertly presented dishes. Described by renowned Kyoto chef Murata Yoshihiro as "eating the seasons", this style of cooking began as an accompaniment to the tea ceremony and still retains the meticulous design of that elegant ritual. At the best *kaiseki-ryōri* restaurants, the **atmosphere** of the room in which the meal is served is just as important as the food, which will invariably reflect the best of the season's produce; you'll sit on tatami, a scroll decorated with calligraphy will hang in the *tokonoma* (alcove) and a waitress in kimono will serve each course on beautiful china and lacquerware. For such a sublime experience you should expect to pay ¥10,000 or more for dinner, although a lunchtime *kaiseki* bentō (see box, p.49) is a more affordable option, typically costing around ¥5000.

THE MODERN WAY OF FOOD

Flick through the channels of your TV in Japan, and it won't be long before you hit your first **food programme**. As well as showing off the delights of Japanese cuisine, these can be rather hilarious to watch, for they all follow the same tried-and-trusted format. First of all, footage will be shown of the food being prepared, to multiple coos from the presenters (and canned ones from the studio audience). Once the food is ready, the camera zooms in on a morsel being slowly teased apart (more cooing), and then on it being held aloft with a shaky pair of chopsticks (yet more cooing). Then comes the first taste; the camera zooms in on the recipient who, predictably self-conscious, is left with only two options: **oishii** and **umai**, which both mean "delicious!".

Nobody now knows if this is life imitating art or the other way around, but Japanese almost always do this with the first bite of a meal. It'll be expected of you, too, and with sudden silence and all eyes on you there's only one thing to say… "*oishii!*"

Rice is an integral part of several cheap snack-type dishes. **Onigiri** are palm-sized triangles of rice with a filling of soy, tuna, salmon roe, or sour *umeboshi* (pickled plum), all wrapped up in a sheet of crisp *nori* (seaweed). They can be bought at convenience stores for ¥100–150 each, and are ingeniously packaged so that the *nori* stays crisp until the *onigiri* is unwrapped. **Donburi** is a bowl of rice with various toppings, such as chicken and egg (*oyako-don*, literally "parent and child"), strips of stewed beef (*gyū-don*) or *katsu-don*, which come with a *tonkatsu* (see below) pork cutlet.

A perennially popular Japanese comfort food is **curry rice** (*karē raisu* in *rōmaji*). Only mildly spicy, this bears little relation to the Indian dish: what goes into the sludgy brown sauce that makes up the curry is a mystery, and you'll probably search in vain for evidence of any beef or chicken in the so-called *biifu karē* and *chikin karē*.

Most cities now also have South Asian restaurants with actual South Asian staff; you can often get a good curry and naan to go for just ¥500, which is up there with the best value Japan has to offer.

Meat dishes

Meat is an uncommon part of traditional Japanese cuisine, but in the last century dishes using beef, pork and chicken have become a major part of the national diet. Burger outlets are ubiquitous, and expensive steak restaurants, serving up dishes like **sukiyaki** (thin beef slices cooked in a soy, sugar and sake broth) and **shabu-shabu** (beef and vegetable slices cooked at the table in a light broth and dipped in various sauces), are popular treats.

Like *sukiyaki* and *shabu-shabu*, **nabe** (the name refers to the cooking pot) stews are prepared at the table over a gas or charcoal burner by diners who throw a range of raw ingredients (meat or fish along with vegetables) into the pot to cook. As things cook, they're fished out, and the last thing to be immersed is usually some type of noodle. *Chanko-nabe* is the famous chuck-it-all-in stew used to beef up sumo wrestlers.

Other popular meat dishes include **tonkatsu**, breadcrumb-covered slabs of pork, crisply fried and usually served on a bed of shredded cabbage with a brown, semi-sweet sauce; and **yakitori**, delicious skewers of grilled chicken (and sometimes other meats and vegetables). At the cheapest *yakitori-ya*, you'll pay for each skewer individually, typically ¥100–150 per stick. **Kushiage** is a combination of *tonkatsu* and *yakitori* dishes, where skewers of meat, seafood and vegetables are coated in breadcrumbs and deep-fried.

Vegetarian dishes

Despite being the home of macrobiotic cooking, **vegetarianism** isn't a widely practised or fully understood concept in Japan. You might ask for a vegetarian (*saishoku*) dish in a restaurant and still be served something with meat or fish in it. If you're a committed vegetarian, things to watch out for include *dashi* stock, which contains *bonito* (dried tuna), and omelettes, which may contain chicken stock. To get a truly vegetarian meal, you will have to be patient and prepared to spell out exactly what you do and do not eat when you order. **Vege-Navi** (ⓦ vege-navi.jp) lists many vegetarian, vegan and macrobiotic options across the country.

If you're willing to turn a blind eye to occasionally eating meat, fish or animal fats by mistake, then tuck in because Japan has bequeathed some marvellous vegetarian foods to the world. Top of the list is **tofu**, compacted cakes of soya-bean curd, which comes in two main varieties, *momengoshi-dōfu* (cotton tofu), so-called because of its fluffy texture, and the smoother, more fragile *kinugoshi-dōfu* (silk tofu). Buddhist cuisine, *shōjin-ryōri*, concocts whole menus based around different types of tofu dishes; although they can be expensive, it's worth searching out the specialist restaurants serving this type of food, particularly in major temple cities, such as Kyoto, Nara and Nagano. Note, though, that the most popular tofu dish you'll come across in restaurants – *hiya yakko*, a small slab of chilled tofu topped with grated ginger, spring onions and soy sauce – is usually sprinkled with *bonito* flakes.

Miso (fermented bean paste) is another crucial ingredient of Japanese cooking, used in virtually every meal, if only in the soup *miso-shiru*. It often serves as a flavouring in vegetable dishes, and comes in two main varieties: the light *shiro-miso*, and the darker, stronger-tasting *aka-miso*.

Most Japanese assume that no foreigners are able to stomach the nation's favourite breakfast snack: **nattō**, a sticky, stringy treat made with fermented beans. Its strong taste, pungent aroma and unfamiliar texture can be off-putting to Western palates, and many young Japanese hate the stuff;

it's worth trying at least once, though, and is usually served in little tubs at breakfast, to be mixed with mustard and soy sauce and eaten with rice. Hawaiian Japanese eat it with raw tuna – you can do likewise by picking the components up at any supermarket, then mixing them together.

Other Japanese dishes

Said to have been introduced to Japan in the sixteenth century by Portuguese traders, **tempura** are lightly battered pieces of seafood and vegetables. Tempura are dipped in a bowl of light sauce (*ten-tsuyu*) mixed with grated *daikon* radish and sometimes ginger. At specialist tempura restaurants, you'll generally order the *teishoku* set meal, which includes whole prawns, squid, aubergines, mushrooms and the aromatic leaf *shiso*.

Oden is a warming dish, usually served in winter but available at other times too – it tastes much more delicious than it looks. Large chunks of food, usually on skewers, are simmered in a thin broth, and often served from portable carts (*yatai*) on street corners or in convenience stores from beside the till. The main ingredients are blocks of tofu, *daikon* (a giant radish), *konnyaku* (a hard jelly made

---

DINING ON THE CHEAP

Japan isn't exactly paradise for budget travellers, but as far as food goes, there are some very good ways to stretch your yen. Many head straight to chain **convenience stores** such as 7-Eleven, AM/PM and Lawson, which sell snacks and drinks round the clock. Not quite as numerous, but found in every city district, **supermarkets** sell bananas, sandwich fodder and other regular backpacker staples, as well as super-cheap fresh noodles; note that in the hours before closing (9–11pm), they tend to lop off up to half of the price of sushi and other bentō sets.

If you want to eat out, try a **standing noodle bar**; a bowl of soba or udon will cost from ¥250, though it can be tricky to operate the Japanese-only ticket machines. However, the real value is to be had at local **fast-food chains**, almost all of which supply English-language menus. All of the following can be found several times over in every single city; just ask around.

CoCo Ichiban-ya ココ壱番屋 Ⓦ ichibanya.co.jp. A quirky curry chain which allows you to piece together your meal. First, choose the type of stock you desire, then the amount of rice you want (up to a mighty 900g), then your desired level of spice (level one barely registers a hit; level ten provides a veritable spice-gasm). Then comes the fun add-your-ingredients bit: choices include beef, okra, scrambled egg, cheese, tonkatsu, *nattō* (see above) and a whole lot more. It'll end up costing ¥600–1100. **Daily 8am–midnight, often later.**

Matsuya 松屋 Ⓦ www.matsuyafoods.co.jp. Fronted by yellow, Japanese-only signs with red and blue blobs on them, this chain specializes in cheap curry (from ¥330) and *gyūdon* (beef on rice, ¥380). They chuck in a steaming-hot bowl of miso soup with whatever you order. **Daily 24hr.**

Saizeriya サイゼリヤ Ⓦ www.saizeriya.co.jp. Budget Italian food, often surprisingly good; their tasty doria (meaty rice gratin) will fill a hole for ¥299, pasta dishes and small pizzas can be had from ¥399, or have a fried burger-and-egg set for ¥399. The wine prices are also ridiculous – ¥100 per glass, or an astonishingly cheap ¥1080 for a 1.5-litre bottle. **Daily 8am–midnight, often later.**

★**Yoshinoya** 吉野屋 Ⓦ www.yoshinoya.com. You can't miss the bright orange signs marking branches of the nation's favourite fast-food chain, famed for its cheap, tasty bowls of *gyūdon* (beef on rice) from just ¥380. When they started reselling this dish after sales were choked off by a BSE scare there was a 1.5km-long queue outside their main Shinjuku branch. **Daily 24hr.**

from a root vegetable), *konbu* (seaweed), hard-boiled eggs and fish cakes. All are best eaten with a smear of fiery English-style mustard.

Japan's equivalent of the pizza is **okonomiyaki**, a fun, cheap meal that you can often assemble yourself. A pancake batter is used to bind shredded cabbage and other vegetables with either seafood or meat. If it's a DIY restaurant, you'll mix the individual ingredients and cook them on a griddle in the middle of the table. Otherwise, you can sit at the kitchen counter watching the chefs at work. Once cooked, *okonomiyaki* is coated in a sweet brown sauce and/or mayonnaise and dusted off with dried seaweed and flakes of *bonito*, which twist and curl in the rising heat. At most *okonomiyaki* restaurants, you can also get fried noodles (*yakisoba*). In addition, *okonomiyaki*, along with its near-cousin **takoyaki** (battered balls of octopus), are often served from *yatai* carts at street festivals.

Authentic Western restaurants are now commonplace across Japan, but there is also a hybrid style of cooking known as **yōshoku** ("Western food"), which developed during the Meiji era early in the twentieth century. Often served in *shokudō*, *yōshoku* dishes include omelettes with rice (*omu-raisu*), deep-fried potato croquettes (*korokke*) and hamburger steaks (*hanbāgu*) doused in a thick sauce. The contemporary version of *yōshoku* is **mukokuseki** or "no-nationality" cuisine, a mishmash of world cooking styles usually found in *izakaya*.

Drinks

The Japanese are enthusiastic social drinkers. It's not uncommon to see totally inebriated people slumped in the street, though on the whole drunkenness rarely leads to violence.

If you want a **non-alcoholic** drink, you'll never be far from a coffee shop (*kissaten*) or a *jidō hambaiki* (**vending machine**), where you can get a vast range of canned drinks, both hot and cold; note that canned coffee, and even some of the tea, is often very sweet. Soft drinks from machines typically cost ¥120 and up; hot drinks are identified by a red stripe under the display, cold drinks by a blue one. Vending machines selling beer, sake and other alcoholic drinks are rare these days; those that still exist require a Japanese ID card to function, and as such are only of use to foreigners with good powers of persuasion. Most 24-hour **convenience stores** sell alcohol around the clock; look for the *kanji* for alcohol (酒) outside.

Sake

Legend has it that the ancient deities brewed Japan's most famous alcoholic beverage – **sake**, also known as *nihonshu* – from the first rice of the new year. Although often referred to as rice wine, the drink, which comes in thousands of different brands, is actually brewed, and as such more closely related to beer (which long ago surpassed sake as Japan's most popular alcoholic drink).

Made either in **sweet** (*amakuchi*) or **dry** (*karakuchi*) varieties, sake is graded as *tokkyū* (superior), *ikkyū* (first) and *nikyū* (second), although this is mainly for tax purposes; if you're after the best quality, connoisseurs recommend going for *ginjo-zukuri* (or *ginjo-zō*), the most expensive and rare of the *junmai-shu* pure rice sake. Some types of sake are cloudier and less refined than others, and there's also the very sweet, milky and usually non-alcoholic **amazake**, often served at temple festivals and at shrines over New Year.

In restaurants and *izakaya* you'll be served sake in a small flask (*tokkuri*) so you can pour your own serving or share it with someone else. You will also be given the choice of drinking your sake **warm** (*atsukan*) or **cold** (*reishu*). The latter is usually the preferred way to enable you to taste the wine's complex flavours properly; never drink premium sake warm. When served cold, sake is sometimes presented and drunk out of a small wooden box (*masu*) with a smidgen of salt on the rim to counter the slightly sweet taste. Glasses are traditionally filled right to the brim and are sometimes placed on a saucer or in a *masu* to catch any overflow; they're generally small servings because, with an **alcohol content** of fifteen percent or more, sake is a strong drink – and it goes to your head even more quickly if drunk warm. For more on sake, check out Ⓦ sake-world.com.

Beer

American brewer William Copeland set up Japan's first **brewery** in Yokohama in 1870 to serve fellow expats streaming into the country in the wake of the Meiji Restoration. Back then the Japanese had to be bribed to drink beer, but these days they need no such encouragement, knocking back a whopping 5.5 billion litres of the stuff a year – almost 60 litres per adult. Copeland's brewery eventually became Kirin, now one of Japan's big four brewers along with Asahi, Sapporo and Suntory. All turn out a range of lagers and dark beers, as well as low-malt beers called **happōshu**, and no-malt varieties called **dai-san-no-biiru**, which are popular because of their lower price (the higher the malt content, the higher the government tax), even if they generally taste insipid. Some of the standard cans and bottles are design classics, among them Kirin Ichiban, Asahi Super Dry and a couple of the Sapporo beers; look out for seasonal additions to the designs, featuring things like snowflakes, red leaves or sakura flowers.

Standard-size cans of beer **cost** around ¥200 from a shop or vending machine, while bottles (bin-biiru) served in restaurants and bars usually start at ¥500. **Draught beer** (nama-biiru) is often available and, in beer halls, will be served in a jokki (mug-like glass), which comes in three different sizes: dai (big), chū (medium) and shō (small).

Craft beer is now a huge thing in Japan, and every city will have at least a smattering of microbreweries, as well as bars selling a selection of brews from around Japan; many craft beers have way more character than found in the products of the big four, but prices are relatively expensive, with a large glass usually costing ¥700–1000. Recommendations for **brewpubs** have been given throughout the Guide, but for more information on the craft beer scene, check out the bilingual free magazine The Japan Beer Times (Ⓦ japanbeertimes.com) and the blog Beer in Japan (Ⓦ beerinjapan.com).

Shōchū

Generally with a higher alcohol content than sake, **shōchū** is a distilled white spirit made from rice, barley, sweet potato or several other ingredients. You can get an idea of its potency (usually 15–25 percent, though sometimes higher) by its nickname: white lightning. Shōchū is typically mixed with a soft drink into a sawā (as in lemon-sour) or a chūhai highball cocktail, although purists favour

---

THE WAY OF TEA

Tea was introduced to Japan from China in the ninth century and was popularized by Zen Buddhist monks, who appreciated its caffeine kick during their long meditation sessions. Gradually, tea-drinking developed into a formal ritual known as cha-no-yu, or the "way of tea", whose purpose is to heighten the senses within a contemplative atmosphere. The most important aspect of the **tea ceremony** is the etiquette with which it is performed. Central to this is the selfless manner in which the host serves the tea and the humble manner in which the guests accept it.

The spirit of wabi, sometimes described as "rustic simplicity", pervades the Japanese tea ceremony. The traditional **teahouse** is positioned in a suitably understated garden, and naturalness is emphasized in all aspects of its architecture: in the unpainted wooden surfaces, the thatched roof, tatami-covered floors and the sliding-screen doors (fusuma) which open directly onto the garden. Colour and ostentation are avoided. Instead, the alcove, or tokonoma, becomes the focal point for a single object of adornment, a simple flower arrangement or a seasonal hanging scroll.

The **utensils** themselves also contribute to the mood of refined ritual. The roughcast tea bowls are admired for the accidental effects produced by the firing of the pottery, while the water containers, tea caddies and bamboo ladles and whisks are prized for their rustic simplicity. The guiding light behind it all was the great tea-master **Sen no Rikyū** (1521–91), whose "worship of the imperfect" has had an indelible influence on Japanese aesthetics.

Having set the tone with the choice of implements and ornamentation, the host whisks powdered green tea (**matcha**) into a thick, frothy brew and presents it to each guest in turn. They take the bowl in both hands, turn it clockwise (so the decoration on the front of the bowl is facing away) and drink it down in three slow sips. It's then customary to admire the bowl while nibbling on a dainty sweetmeat (**wagashi**), which counteracts the tea's bitter taste.

enjoying the drink straight, or with ice. There's something of a *shōchū* boom currently going on in Japan, and the best brands are very drinkable and served like sake (see p.53). The cheap stuff, however, can give you a wicked hangover.

Western alcoholic drinks

The Japanese love **whisky**, with the top brewers producing several respectable brands, often served with water and ice and called *mizu-wari*. In contrast, Japanese **wine** (*wain*), often very sweet, is a less successful product, at least to Western palates. Imported wines, however, are widely sold – not only are they becoming cheaper, but there is now a better choice and higher quality available in both shops and restaurants; most convenience stores sell bottles from ¥500.

Tea, coffee and soft drinks

Japanese cities are full of chain cafés – as often as not a *Starbucks*, although local operations such as *Doutor*, *Tully's* and *Caffè Veloce* are also common. Despite the convenience of these places, one of Tokyo's great joys is whiling away time in **non-chain cafés** (sometimes called *kissaten*), where the emphasis is on service and creating an interesting, relaxing, highly individual space. Recently, a glut of hipster-style **coffee** joints has sprung up around the country – to Western travellers, they'll feel a lot more familiar than the *kissaten*. Café menus are often in English as well as Japanese, but if that fails, choose between hot (*hotto*) or iced (*aisu*); if you want milk, ask for *miruku-kōhii* (milky coffee) or *kafe-ore* (café au lait).

You can also get regular **black tea** in all coffee shops, served either with milk, lemon or iced. If you want the slightly bitter Japanese **green tea**, *ocha* ("honourable tea"), you'll usually have to go to a traditional teahouse. Green teas, which are always served in small cups and drunk plain, are graded according to their quality. *Bancha*, the cheapest, is for everyday drinking and, in its roasted form, is used to make the smoky *hōjicha*, or mixed with popped brown rice for the nutty *genmaicha*. Medium-grade *sencha* is served in upmarket restaurants or to favoured guests, while top-ranking, slightly sweet *gyokuro* (dewdrop) is reserved for special occasions. Other types of tea you may come across are **ūron-cha** (Oolong tea), a refreshing Chinese-style brew, and **mugicha**, made from roasted barley.

As well as the international brand-name **soft drinks** and fruit juices, there are many other soft drinks unique to Japan. You'll probably want to try *Pocari Sweat* or *Calpis* for the name on the can alone.

The media

For those who can read Japanese, there are scores of daily newspapers and hundreds of magazines covering almost every subject. In the big cities, English newspapers and magazines are readily available, while on TV and radio there are some programmes presented in English or with an alternative English soundtrack, such as the main news bulletins on NHK. Throughout this Guide we list websites wherever useful (some will be in Japanese only).

Newspapers and magazines

Japan's top paper, the *Yomiuri Shimbun*, sells over nine million copies daily (combining its morning and evening editions), making it the most widely read **newspaper** in the world. Lagging behind by about one million copies a day is the *Asahi Shimbun*, seen as the intellectual's paper, with the other three national dailies, the *Mainichi Shimbun*, the right-wing *Sankei Shimbun* and the business paper the *Nihon Keizai Shimbun*, also selling respectable numbers.

The **English-language daily** newspaper you'll most commonly find on newsstands is *The Japan Times* (Ⓦ japantimes.co.jp). It has comprehensive coverage of national and international news, as well as occasionally interesting features, some culled from the world's media; it's also great for updates when there's a sumo tournament on. Other English newspapers include *The International New York Times*, formerly the *International Herald Tribune* and published in conjunction with the English-language version of the major Japanese newspaper *Asahi Shimbun*; the *Daily Yomiuri* (Ⓦ yomiuri.co.jp); and the Japan edition of the *Financial Times*.

The Tokyo listings **magazine** *Metropolis* and its website (Ⓦ metropolis.co.jp) are packed with interesting features, reviews, and listings of film, music and other events. The twice-yearly publication *KIE* (Kateigaho International Edition; Ⓦ int.kateigaho .com) is a gorgeous glossy magazine which covers cultural matters, with many travel features and in-depth profiles of areas of Tokyo and other parts of Japan. Other widely available English-language magazines include *Time* and *The Economist*.

Bookshops such as Kinokuniya and Maruzen stock extensive ranges of imported and local magazines. For those who are studying Japanese, or even just trying to pick up a bit of the language during your stay, the bilingual magazine *Hiragana Times* is good.

Television

Funded much like Britain's BBC, the state broadcaster **NHK** (Ⓦ nhk.or.jp) has two **TV channels** – the regular NHK, and NHK–Educational – as well as three satellite channels, and NHK World, an international channel which often veers towards propaganda. Many TV sets can access a bilingual soundtrack, and it's thus possible to tune into English-language commentary for NHK's nightly 7pm news; films and imported TV shows on both NHK and the commercial channels are also sometimes broadcast with an alternative English soundtrack. **Digital, satellite and cable** channels available in all top-end hotels include BBC World, CNN and MTV.

Festivals

Don't miss attending a festival (matsuri) if one happens during your visit – it will be a highlight of your stay in Japan. The more important events are listed below.

In recent years, several **non-Japanese festivals**

DATES IN JAPAN

According to the Japanese system of **numbering years**, which starts afresh with each change of emperor, 2017 is the twenty-ninth year of Heisei – Heisei being the official name of Emperor Akihito's reign. Upon his death (or abdication; see box, p.87), the number will reset to 1 for the first year of his successor's reign. This shouldn't cause you too many problems, since the "regular" calendar is more visible, though prepare for some initially confusing dates on train passes, hotel receipts and the like.

It's also important to note that Japanese dates run **year-month-day** – going from big to small, just like the time on your digital watch, it actually makes a lot of sense.

---

have caught on, with a few adaptations for local tastes. Women give men gifts of chocolate on **Valentine's Day** (February 14), while on **White Day** (March 14) men get their turn to give the object of their affection more chocolate (white, of course). Later on in the year, **Pocky Day** (November 11) is an even more overtly commercial day, even by Japanese standards – people give their loved ones boxes of Pocky, sweet breadsticks whose skinny nature vaguely resembles the date (eleven-eleven). **Christmas** is also an almost totally commercial event in Japan. Christmas Eve, rather than New Year, is *the* time to party and a big occasion for romance – you'll be hard-pressed to find a table at any fancy restaurant or a room in the top hotels.

Festival and holiday calendar

Note that if any of the following public holidays fall on a Sunday, then the following Monday is also a holiday.

JANUARY

Ganjitsu (or Gantan) Jan 1. People all over the country gather at major shrines to honour the gods with the first shrine visit of the year (a practice known as *hatsumōde*). Public holiday.

Seijin-no-hi (Adults' Day) Second Mon in Jan. Twenty-year-olds celebrate their entry into adulthood by visiting their local shrine. Many women dress in sumptuous kimono. Public holiday.

Yama-yaki Fourth Sat of Jan. The slopes of Wakakusa-yama, Nara, are set alight during a grass-burning ceremony (see box, p.494).

FEBRUARY

Setsubun Feb 3 or 4. On the last day of winter by the lunar calendar, people scatter lucky beans round their homes and at shrines or temples to drive out evil and welcome in the year's good luck. In Nara, the event is marked by a huge lantern festival on Feb 3.

Yuki Matsuri Early to mid-Feb. Sapporo's famous snow festival features giant snow sculptures (see box, p.295).

MARCH

Hina Matsuri (Doll Festival) March 3. Families with young girls display beautiful dolls (*hina ningyō*) representing the emperor, empress and their courtiers dressed in ancient costume. Department stores, hotels and museums often put on special displays at this time.

Cherry-blossom festivals Late March to early May. With the arrival of spring in late March, a pink tide of cherry blossom washes north from Kyūshū, travels up Honshū during the month of April and peters out in Hokkaidō in early May. There are cherry-blossom festivals, and the sake flows at blossom-viewing (*hanami*) parties.

MUSIC FESTIVALS

Late July and August in Japan is the time for **rock and popular music festivals**. One of the best is the **Earth Celebration** on Sado-ga-shima (see box, p.285), where the famed Kodō drummers collaborate with guests from the world music scene. If you want to catch up on the latest in Japanese rock and pop then schedule your visit to coincide with the most established event, as far as foreign bands is concerned, **Fuji Rock** (ⓦ fujirockfestival.com). This huge three-day event hosts a wide range of top-name acts covering musical genres from dance and electronica to jazz and blues, on multiple stages. It takes place at Naeba Ski Resort in Niigata prefecture, easily accessible from Tokyo via Shinkansen. It's possible to visit for a day, camp or stay in the hotels that in winter cater to the ski crowd.

Attracting an audience of well over 100,000 and simpler to get to is **Summer Sonic** (ⓦ summersonic.com), a two-day event held in Chiba, just across the Edo-gawa from Tokyo. This festival showcases a good mix of both local and overseas bands and has both indoor and outdoor performances.

Rock in Japan (ⓦ rijfes.jp), focusing on domestic bands, is usually held in August at Hitachi Seaside Park, north of Tokyo in Ibaraki-ken (accessible from Ueno Station).

APRIL

Hana Matsuri April 8. The Buddha's birthday is celebrated at all temples with parades or quieter celebrations, during which a small statue of Buddha is sprinkled with sweet tea.

Takayama Matsuri April 14–15. Parade of ornate festival floats (*yatai*), some carrying mechanical marionettes.

Kamakura Matsuri Mid-April. Kamakura's week-long festival includes traditional dances, costume parades and horseback archery.

MAY

Kodomo-no-hi (Children's Day) May 5. The original Boys' Day now includes all children, as families fly carp banners, symbolizing strength and perseverance, outside their homes. Public holiday.

Aoi Matsuri (Hollyhock Festival) May 15. Costume parade through the streets of Kyoto, with ceremonies to ward off storms and earthquakes (see box, p.463).

Kanda Matsuri Mid-May. One of Tokyo's top three *matsuri*, taking place in odd-numbered years at Kanda Myōjin, during which people in Heian-period costume escort eighty gilded *mikoshi* through the streets (see box, p.159).

Tōshō-gū Grand Matsuri May 18. Nikkō's most important festival (see box, p.175), featuring a parade of over a thousand costumed participants and horseback archery to commemorate the burial of Shogun Tokugawa Ieyasu in 1617. There's a smaller-scale repeat performance on October 17.

Sanja Matsuri Third weekend in May. Tokyo's most boisterous festival takes place in Asakusa (see box, p.159). Over a hundred *mikoshi* are jostled through the streets, accompanied by lion dancers, geisha and musicians.

JUNE

Sannō Matsuri Mid-June. In even-numbered years the last of Tokyo's big three *matsuri* (after Kanda and Sanja) takes place, focusing on colourful processions of *mikoshi* through Akasaka (see box, p.159).

JULY

Gion Yamagasa July 1–15. Fukuoka's main festival (see p.704) culminates in a 5km race, with participants carrying or pulling heavy *mikoshi*, while spectators douse them with water.

Tanabata Matsuri (Star Festival) July 7. According to legend, the only day in the year when the astral lovers, Vega and Altair, can meet across the Milky Way. Poems and prayers are hung on bamboo poles outside houses.

Gion Matsuri July 17. Kyoto's month-long festival focuses around a parade of huge floats hung with rich silks and paper lanterns (see box, p.463).

Hanabi Taikai Last Sat in July. The most spectacular of Japan's many summer firework displays takes place in Tokyo, on the Sumida River near Asakusa (see box, p.159). Some cities also hold displays in early Aug.

AUGUST

Nebuta and Neputa Matsuri Aug 1–7. Aomori and Hirosaki hold competing summer festivals, with parades of illuminated paper-covered figures (see boxes, p.255 & p.262).

Tanabata Matsuri Aug 6–8. Sendai's famous Star Festival (see box, p.234) is held a month after everyone else, so the lovers get another chance.

Obon (Festival of Souls) Aug 13–15, or July 13–15 in some areas. Families gather around the ancestral graves to welcome back the spirits of the dead and honour them with special Bon-Odori dances on the final night.

Awa Odori Aug 12–15. The most famous *Bonodori* takes place in Tokushima, when up to eighty thousand dancers take to the streets (see box, p.659).

SEPTEMBER

Yabusame Sept 16. This festival, featuring spectacular displays of horseback archery (*yabusame*) by riders in samurai armour, takes place at Tsurugaoka Hachimangū shrine in Kamakura (see p.614).

OCTOBER

Kunchi Matsuri Oct 7–9. Shinto rites mingle with Chinese- and European-inspired festivities to create Nagasaki's premier celebration (see box, p.722), incorporating dragon dances and floats in the shape of Chinese and Dutch ships.

Kawagoe Grand Matsuri Third Sat & Sun in Oct. One of the liveliest festivals in the Tokyo area, involving some 25 ornate floats and hundreds of costumed revellers (see p.181).

Jidai Matsuri Oct 22. Kyoto's famous, if rather sedate, costume parade vies with the more exciting Kurama-no-Himatsuri, a night-time fire festival which takes place in a village near Kyoto (see box, p.463).

NOVEMBER

Shichi-go-san Nov 15. Children aged 3, 5 and 7 don traditional garb to visit their local shrine.

DECEMBER

Ōmisoka Dec 31. Just before midnight on the last day of the year, temple bells ring out 108 times (the number of human frailties according to Buddhist thinking).

Sports and outdoor activities

In 1964, Tokyo became the first Asian city to host the Olympic Games; in 2020, it will become the first to do so twice (see box, p.119). Together with the World Cup that Japan co-hosted in 2002, these events hint at a surprisingly sporty scene in a country that most outsiders might associate more closely with academic performance than with athletic endeavour. Big believers in team spirit, the Japanese embrace many sports with almost religious fervour.

Spectator sports

Baseball, football and even mixed martial arts are all far more popular than home-grown sumo. Martial arts, such as aikido, judo and karate, all traditionally associated with Japan, have a much lower profile than you might expect.

Baseball

Baseball first came to Japan in the 1870s, but it wasn't until 1934 that the first professional teams were formed. Now Japan is *yakyū* (baseball) crazy, and if you're in the country from April to the end of October, during the baseball season, consider watching a professional match. Even if you're not a

fan, the buzzing atmosphere and audience enthusiasm can be infectious – Osaka's Hanshin Tigers are famed for their boisterous fans (and consistently underperforming team).

In addition to the two professional leagues, **Central** and **Pacific**, each with six teams, there's the equally (if not more) popular **All-Japan High School Baseball Championship**. You might be able to catch one of the local play-offs before the main tournament, which is held each summer at Kōshien Stadium near Osaka.

In the professional leagues, the teams are sponsored by big businesses, a fact immediately apparent from their names, such as the Yakult Swallows (named after a food company) and Yomiuri Giants (this time a newspaper conglomerate). The victors from the Central and Pacific leagues go on to battle it out for the supreme title in the seven-match **Japan Series** every autumn.

Tickets for all games are available from the stadia or at advance ticket booths. They start at ¥1500 and go on sale on the Friday two weeks prior to a game. For more information on Japan's pro-baseball leagues, check out the official professional league site (Ⓦ npb.or.jp), and the fan-site Baseball Guru (Ⓦ baseballguru.com).

Football

Generally referred to as **soccer** in Japan, **football** was introduced here in 1873 by an Englishman: Lieutenant Commander Douglas of the Royal Navy. However, it wasn't until Japan's first professional soccer league, the **J-League** (Ⓦ j-league.or.jp), was launched in 1993 that the sport captured the public's imagination. Following on from the success of the 2002 World Cup, hosted jointly by Japan and Korea, the sport is now a huge crowd puller.

Games are played between March and October, with a break in August. Eighteen clubs play in the top **J1 division**, and together with teams from lower leagues, they also participate in the **Emperor's Cup**; the best go on to play in the Asian Champions League, a contest won in the past by no fewer than five Japanese teams (Jubilo Iwata, JEF United Chiba, Tokyo Verdy, Urawa Red Diamonds and Gamba Osaka).

Sumo

There's something fascinating about Japan's national sport, **sumo**, even though the titanic clashes between the enormous, near-naked wrestlers can be blindingly brief. The age-old pomp and ceremony that surrounds sumo – from the design of the *dohyō* (the ring in which bouts take place) to the wrestler's slicked-back topknot – give the sport a gravitas completely absent from Western wrestling. The sport's aura is enhanced by the majestic size of the wrestlers themselves: the average weight is around 140kg, but they can be much larger – Konishiki, one of the sumo stars of the 1990s, for example, weighed a scale-busting 272kg.

At the start of a bout, the two **rikishi** (wrestlers) wade into the ring, wearing only *mawashi* aprons, which are essentially giant jockstraps. Salt is tossed to purify the ring, and then the *rikishi* hunker down and indulge in the time-honoured ritual of psyching each other out with menacing stares. When ready, each *rikishi* attempts to throw his opponent to the ground or out of the ring using one or more of 82 legitimate techniques. The first to touch the ground with any part of his body other than his feet, or to step out of the *dohyō*, loses.

SUMO: WHO'S WHO AND WHAT'S WHAT

Accounts of **sumo** bouts (*basho*) are related in Japan's oldest annals dating back around two thousand years when it was a Shintō rite connected with praying for a good harvest. By the Edo period, sumo had developed into a spectator sport, and really hit its stride in the post-World War II period when *basho* started to be televised. The old religious trappings remain, though: the *gyōji* (referee) wears robes similar to those of a Shintō priest and above the *dohyō* hangs a thatched roof like those found at shrines.

Sumo **tournaments** take place on odd-numbered months, running for fifteen days (see below). The day starts at 9pm with the amateur divisions, before the stadium starts to fill up around 3pm for the professional ranks. These guys fight every day; if they win eight or more they go up the rankings, if they lose eight or more they go down, and whoever gets the most wins in the top division wins the trophy. At the very top of the tree is the **yokozuna** level – a lifelong rank which does not necessarily signify the most recent champion.

SUMO CHAMPIONS

In recent years, champions have been almost exclusively **Mongolian** in origin. The Japanese veteran **Kotoshōgiku**'s victory in January 2016 came ten long years after the previous win by a Japanese-born wrestler, with Mongolian fighters scooping an incredible 57 of the 59 intervening tournaments (the other two were won by Kotoōshū from Bulgaria, and Estonia's Baruto). The Mongolian run started in 2002 with the great **Asashōryū** who, in 2005, became the first wrestler in history to win all six tournaments in a calendar year. "Asa" was something of a pantomime villain, stirring up controversy on a regular basis before being ushered out of the sport in 2010. By then he had developed a tremendous rivalry with his closest challenger, fellow-Mongolian **Hakuhō**. These two great fighters both became *yokozuna*, to be joined shortly after Asashōryū's retirement by two more Mongolians, **Harumafuji** and **Kakuryū**; at the time of writing, these two and Hakuhō were all still going strong, and Hakuhō had become the most decorated wrestler in centuries of sumo history.

THE ANNUAL SUMO TOURNAMENTS

The must-see **annual sumo tournaments** are held at the following locations, starting on the second Sunday of the month and lasting for two weeks: Kokugikan in **Tokyo** (Jan, May & Sept); Osaka Furitsu Taiiku Kaikan in **Osaka** (March); Aichi-ken Taiiku-kan in **Nagoya** (July); and the Fukuoka Kokusai Centre, **Fukuoka** (Nov).

Despite sumo's declining popularity, it's still difficult to book the prime ringside **seats** (around ¥45,000 for four seats in a tatami-mat block) but quite feasible to bag reserved seats in the balconies (starting around ¥3200). The cheapest unreserved seats (¥2200) go on sale on the door on the day of the tournament at 9am. To be assured of a ticket, you'll generally need to be there before 11am, though tickets only ever sell out on the last day of a *basho*. Matches start at 9am for the lower-ranked wrestlers, and at this time of day it's OK to sneak into any vacant ringside seats to watch the action close up; when the rightful owners turn up, play the dumb-foreigner card and return to your own seat. The sumo superstars come on around 4pm, and the day finishes at 6pm on the dot.

Full details in English about **ticket sales** can be found on the sumo association's website (ⓦ sumo.or.jp), and it's also possible to buy online at ⓦ buysumotickets.com. Also note that NHK televises each *basho* daily from 3.30pm.

Despite their formidable girth, top *rikishi* enjoy the media status of supermodels, their social calendars being documented obsessively by the media. When not fighting in tournaments, groups of *rikishi* live and train together at their **heya** (stables), the youngest wrestlers acting pretty much as the menial slaves of their older, more experienced, colleagues. If you make an advance appointment, it's possible to visit some *heya* to observe the early-morning practice sessions; contact the Tokyo tourist information centres (see p.133) for details. For all you could want to know and more on the current scene, plus how to buy tickets, check out the official website of sumo's governing body, **Nihon Sumo Kyōkai**, at Ⓦ sumo.or.jp.

Martial arts

Japan has bequeathed to the world several forms of **martial** fisticuffs, and many visit to learn or hone one of the forms. If you'd like to do likewise, it's usually best to start by contacting the relevant federation in your home country; in Tokyo, however, there are a few particularly foreigner-friendly associations (see p.166).

The martial art most closely associated with Japan is **judo**, a self-defence technique that developed out of the Edo-era fighting schools of Jūjutsu. Then there's **aikido** – half-sport, half-religion, its name translates as "the way of harmonious spirit", and the code blends elements of judo, karate and kendo into a form of non-body-contact self-defence. It's one of the newer martial arts, having only been created in Japan in the twentieth century and, as a rule, is performed without weapons. For a painfully enlightening and humorous take on the rigours of aikido training, read Robert Twigger's *Angry White Pyjamas*.

Karate has its roots in China and was only introduced into Japan via the southern islands of Okinawa in 1922. Since then, the sport has developed many different styles, several with governing bodies and federations based in Tokyo.

Lastly, there's **kendo**; meaning "the way of the sword", this is Japanese fencing where players either use a long bamboo weapon, the *shinai*, or a lethal metal *katana* blade. This martial art has the longest pedigree in Japan, dating from the Muromachi period (1392–1573); it developed as a sport during the Edo period.

Tokyo, with its many **dōjō** (practice halls), is the best place in the country in which to view or learn these ancient sports. Tokyo's Tourist Information Centres (see p.133) have a full list of *dōjō* that allow visitors to watch practice sessions for free.

Rugby

Rubgy has been something of a niche sport in Japan. The national team was famously obliterated 145–17 by New Zealand in the 1995 World Cup (a record defeat), but the game in Japan has since come on in leaps and bounds: Japan even provided the shock of the 2015 tournament – some would say the entire history of rugby – with a last-second win over South Africa. Partly as a result of said improvement, Japan is due to host the **2019 World Cup** tournament; Tokyo will host some games in the Ajinomoto Stadium out west, and some will also be held in Yokohama. On the **domestic** front, teams from around Japan compete in the national Top League, which runs from August to January (check Ⓦ en.rugby-japan.jp for schedule and venue information).

Outdoor activities

Popular **outdoor activities** include **skiing, hiking** and **mountain climbing**. The Tokyo-based Outdoor Club Japan (Ⓦ outdoorclubjapan.com), and the International Outdoor Club (IOC; Ⓦ iock ansai.com) in the Kansai region provide informal opportunities to explore the countryside in the company of like-minded people. The bilingual quarterly magazine *Outdoor Japan* (Ⓦ outdoor japan.com) is also a mine of useful information.

Skiing and snowboarding

Japan is a **ski and snowboard paradise**; even on the shortest trip to the country it's easy to arrange a day-trip to the slopes, since many major resorts on Honshū are within a couple of hours' train ride of Tokyo, Nagoya or Osaka. Serious skiers will want to head to the northern island of Hokkaidō, which has some of the country's best ski resorts.

The **cost** of a ski trip needn't be too expensive. Lift passes are typically ¥4000 per day, or less if you ski for several days in a row; equipment rental averages around ¥4000 for the skis, boots and poles per day, while accommodation at a family-run minshuku compares favourably to that of many European and American resorts.

Transport to the slopes is fast and efficient; at one resort (Gala Yuzawa in Niigata; Ⓦ galaresort.jp) you can step straight off the Shinkansen onto the ski lifts. Ski maps and signs are often in English, and you're sure to find some English-speakers and, at the major resorts, *gaijin* staff, if you run into difficulties.

Top **resorts** can get very crowded, especially at weekends and during holidays; if you don't want

TAKING A HOT-SPRING DIP

The Japanese islands boast a tremendous abundance of **hot springs**. While such waters bubble from the ground elsewhere, in Japan this natural bounty has been turned into an art form – there are thousands upon thousands of **onsen** (温泉) dotted across the country, and you'll never be too far from one. What may be viewed in the West as rather decadent or esoteric is simply a fact of life here – businessmen bathe between meetings, families drop by at weekends, pensioners pop along for a wash, and guffawing teens rinse off the stress after school. And of course, pink-skinned foreigners use them as a means of heightening their cultural experience – even if they may not, at least initially, be as comfortable as most Japanese in the company of naked strangers.

Taking a traditional Japanese **bath**, whether in an onsen, a *sentō* (a bathhouse with regular, rather than hot-spring, water) or a ryokan (see box, p.44), is a ritual that's definitely worth mastering. Everyone uses the same water, and the golden rule is to wash and rinse the soap off thoroughly before stepping into the bath – showers and bowls are provided, as well as soap and shampoo in most cases. Ryokan and the more upmarket public bathhouses provide small towels (bring your own or buy one on the door if using a cheaper *sentō*), though no one minds full nudity. Baths are typically **segregated**, so memorize the *kanji* for female (女), which looks a little like a woman; and male (男), which looks sort of like a chap with a box on his head.

Note that **tattoos** – which are associated with the *yakuza* in Japan – are a big issue when it comes to public bathing. Even if you look nothing like a member of the local mafia, you may be asked to cover up the offending image, or even denied access to the baths entirely. If you're intending to visit any particular bathing establishment, the best course of action is to get your accommodation (or a local tourist office) to call ahead for verification of their tattoo regulations.

Onsen establishments run the full gamut from small-and-cosy to theme-park. Whole books have been written about the various facilities available across Japan, but here are a few recommendations:

Beppu, Kyūshū This Kyūshū town is essentially one massive onsen, with steam billowing from the drains in the manner of a Manhattan-based film noir. There are hundreds of places to bathe here, including olde-worlde Takegawara (see p.796), but most magical are the "hidden onsen" in the forests overlooking the town (see box, p.749).

Jigokudani Monkey Park, Chūbu The home of the famed "snow monkeys", this onsen (see p.362) has a special rotemburo (outdoor hot-spring bath) in which the local macaque community pop by for a bathe. Human-friendly baths are also available.

Noboribetsu Onsen, Hokkaidō Set among the sulphurous, volcanic landscape of central Hokkaidō, this little resort (see p.320) has a bunch of appealing ryokan at which to take a dip.

Sakurajima, Kyūshū Sakurajima is a highly active volcano (see p.768), often seen belching trails of ash. There are onsen at the base of said active volcano. Enough said.

Yunomine Onsen, Kansai Dating back over 1800 years, it's obvious why this onsen (see box, p.535) has been designated a World Heritage spot.

to ski in rush-hour conditions, plan your trip for midweek. In addition, the runs are, on the whole, much shorter than in Europe and the US. Compensating factors, however, are fast ski lifts, beautiful scenery – especially in the Japan Alps – and the opportunity to soak in onsen hot springs at night.

Recommended for beginners is either Gala Yuzawa (see above) or Naeba (W princehotels .co.jp/ski/naeba), both reached in under two hours from Tokyo by Shinkansen. Nozawa Onsen (see p.358) also has good beginners' runs, but its off-the-beaten-track location makes it a better bet for more experienced skiers. Appi Kōgen and Zaō Onsen in northern Honshū (see p.231) and Hakuba in Nagano (see p.359) are considered the Holy Trinity of Japanese ski resorts. Shiga Kōgen (see p.361) is another mammoth resort in Nagano. If you're after the best powder-snow skiing without the crowds, head north to Hokkaidō, to the world-class resorts of Furano (see p.327) and Niseko (see p.308). There are also many slopes easily accessible on a day-trip from Sapporo (see box, p.299).

All the major travel agents offer **ski packages**, which are worth considering. Hakuba-based Ski Japan Holiday (W japanspecialists.com) and Niseko-based SkiJapan.com (W skijapan.com) both have plenty of experience setting up deals for the expat community. **Youth hostels** near ski areas also often have excellent-value packages, including accommodation, meals and lift passes, and can arrange competitive equipment rental.

Mountaineering and hiking

Until the twentieth century, few Japanese would have considered climbing one of their often sacred mountains for anything other than religious reasons. These days, prime highland beauty spots such as Kamikōchi are very popular with day-**hikers** and serious **mountaineers**, so much so that they risk being overrun. In addition, there are scores of national parks and other protected areas (see p.850), and exploring these and other picturesque parts of the countryside on foot is one of the great pleasures of a trip to Japan. Nevertheless, bear in mind that those areas close to cities can get very busy at weekends and during holidays. If you can, go midweek or out of season when the trails are less crowded.

Hiking trails, especially in the national parks, are well marked. Campsites and mountain huts open during the climbing season, which runs from June to the end of August. The efficient train network means that even from sprawling conurbations like Tokyo, you can be in beautiful countryside in just over an hour – top hiking destinations from the capital include the lakes, mountains and rugged coastline of the **Fuji-Hakone-Izu National Park** (see p.203) to the southwest, and **Nikkō** (see p.170) to the north. Things get even better around the country, in areas such as Hokkaidō's **Daisetsu-zan National Park** (see p.324), the **Japan Alps** (see p.353), the island of **Yakushima** off Kyūshū (see p.773), and **Aso-san** (see p.739) and **Ebino Kōgen** (see p.759) on Kyūshū itself. The website ⓦoutdoorjapan.com has useful ideas and information if you plan to go hiking or camping in Japan.

Rafting, canoeing and kayaking

All the snow that gets dumped on Japan's mountains in winter eventually melts, swelling the country's numerous rivers. Although the vast majority of these have been tamed by dams and concrete walls along the riverbanks, there are stretches that provide the ideal conditions for **whitewater rafting**, **canoeing** and **kayaking**. Prime spots for these activities are Minakami in Gunma-ken (see box, p.180), Hakuba in Nagano-ken (see p.359), the Iya Valley (see p.666) and Shimanto-gawa (see p.675), both in Shikoku, and Niseko (see p.308) in Hokkaidō. A reputable firm to contact to find out more is Canyons (ⓦcanyons.jp).

Golf

One of Japan's premier pro-golfing events is the **Japan Open Golf Championship** (ⓦwww.jga .or.jp), held each October. If you fancy a round yourself, you'll find (somewhat old, but still useful) details of 2349 courses of eighteen holes or more at **Golf in Japan** (ⓦgolf-in-japan.com); local tourist information centres will always be able to direct you to the nearest course. Course fees vary widely from ¥3000 at the cheapest places to over ¥40,000 for a round at the most exclusive links.

Beaches, surfing and diving

Given that Japan is an archipelago, you'd be forgiven for thinking that it would be blessed with some pleasant beaches. The truth is that industrialization has blighted much of the coastline and many of the country's beaches are covered with litter and/or polluted. The best **beaches** are those furthest away from the main island of Honshū, which means those on the islands of Okinawa, or the Izu and Ogasawara islands south of Tokyo.

Incredibly, Japan's market for surf goods is the world's largest, and when the surfers aren't hauling their boards off to Hawaii and Australia, they can be found braving the waves at various home locations. Top **surfing** spots include the southern coasts of Shikoku and Kyūshū (see boxes, p.664 & p.757). Closer to Tokyo, pros head for the rocky east Kujūkuri coast of the Chiba peninsula, while the beaches around Shōnan, near Kamakura, are fine for perfecting your style and hanging out with the trendiest surfers.

The best places to head for **diving** are Okinawa (see box, p.784) and the island of Sado-ga-shima, near Niigata (see p.280). Those with walrus-like hides may fancy braving ice diving in the frozen far northern reaches of Hokkaidō (see box, p.336).

Culture and etiquette

Japan is famous for its complex web of social conventions and rules of behaviour. Fortunately, allowances are made for befuddled foreigners, but it will be greatly appreciated – and even draw gasps of astonishment – if you show a grasp of the basic principles. We provide a few tips for eating and drinking etiquette which are sure to come in handy (see p.49 & box p.53), but the two main danger areas are footwear and bathing (see box, p.61), which, if you get them wrong, can cause great offence.

Some general pointers

Japan is a strictly hierarchical society where men generally take precedence, so women shouldn't expect doors to be held open or seats vacated. **Sexual discrimination** remains widespread, and foreign women working in Japan can find the predominantly male business culture hard going.

Pushing and shoving on crowded trains or buses is not uncommon. Never respond by getting angry or showing **aggression**, as this is considered a complete loss of face. By the same token, don't make your **opinions** known too forcefully or contradict people outright; it's more polite to say "maybe" than a direct "no", so if you get a vague answer to a question don't push for confirmation unless it's important.

Note that it's particularly unwise to criticize any aspect of Japanese society, however small, to a local; in a land where people tend to describe themselves as a "we", it's often taken as a personal insult.

Blowing your nose in public is also considered rude – locals keep sniffing until they find somewhere private (this can continue for hours on end, which is great fun if you're sitting next to a sniffler on a long train ride). An even more common agony for visitors is having to **sit on the floor** at people's houses and certain restaurants – excruciatingly uncomfortable for people who aren't used to it. If you're wearing trousers, sitting cross-legged is fine; otherwise, tuck your legs to one side.

Meetings and greetings

Some visitors to Japan complain that it's difficult to **meet local people** – the Japanese themselves famously have problems meeting each other, as evidenced by regular pay-for-company stories in the international press, and the legion of "snack" bars (where local men essentially pay to have their egos massaged). It's also true that many Japanese are shy of foreigners, mainly through a fear of being unable to communicate. A few words of Japanese will help enormously, and there are various opportunities for fairly formal contact, such as through the Goodwill Guides (see box, p.76). Otherwise, try popping into a local bar, a *yakitori* joint or suchlike; with everyone crammed in like sardines, and emboldened by alcohol, it's far easier to strike up a conversation.

Whenever Japanese meet, express thanks or say goodbye, there's a flurry of **bowing** – and, between friends, an energetic waving of hands. The precise depth of the bow and the length of time it's held for depend on the relative status of the two individuals; foreigners aren't expected to bow, but it's terribly infectious and you'll soon find yourself bobbing with the best of them. The usual compromise is a slight nod or a quick half-bow. Japanese more familiar with Western customs might offer you a hand to shake, in which case treat it gently – they won't be expecting a firm grip.

Japanese people tend to **dress** smartly, especially in Tokyo. Tourists don't have to go overboard, but will be better received if they look neat and tidy, while for anyone hoping to do business, a snappy suit (any colour, as long as it's black) is *de rigueur*. It's also important to be **punctual** for social and business appointments.

An essential part of any **business meeting** is the swapping of *meishi* (**name cards**); if you're doing business here, it's a very good idea to have them printed in Japanese as well as English. Always carry a copious supply, since you'll be expected to exchange a card with everyone present. *Meishi* are offered with both hands, held so that the recipient can read the writing. It's polite to read the card and then place it on the table beside you, face up. Never write on a *meishi*, at least not in the owner's presence, and never shove it in a pocket – pop it into your wallet, a dedicated card-holder, or somewhere suitably respectful.

JAPANESE NAMES

Japanese **names** are traditionally written with the family name first, followed by a given name, which is the practice used throughout this book (except where the Western version has become famous, such as Issey Miyake). When dealing with foreigners, however, they may well write their name the other way round. Check if you're not sure because, when **addressing people**, it's normal to use the family name plus *-san*: for example, Suzuki-san. *San* is an honorific term applied to others, so you do not use it when introducing yourself or your family. As a foreigner, you can choose whichever of your names you feel comfortable with; you'll usually have a *-san* tacked onto the end of your given name. You'll also often hear *-chan* or *-kun* as a form of address; these are diminutives reserved for very good friends, young children and pets. The suffix *-sama* is the most polite form of address.

Hospitality and gifts

Entertaining, whether it's business or purely social, usually takes place in bars and restaurants. The host generally orders and, if it's a Japanese-style meal, will keep passing you different things to try. You'll also find your glass continually topped up. It's polite to return the gesture but if you don't drink, or don't want any more, leave it full.

It's a rare honour to be invited to someone's home in Japan, and if this happens you should always take a **gift**, which should always be wrapped, using plenty of fancy paper and ribbon if possible. Most shops gift-wrap purchases automatically, and anything swathed in paper from a big department store has extra cachet.

Japanese people love giving gifts (in fact, they are more or less obliged to give souvenirs known as *omiyage* to friends and colleagues following any holiday), and you should never refuse one if offered, though it's good manners to protest at their generosity first. Again, it's polite to give and receive with both hands, and to belittle your humble donation while giving profuse thanks for the gift you receive. It's the custom not to open gifts in front of the donor, thus avoiding potential embarrassment.

Shoes and slippers

It's customary to change into **slippers** when entering a Japanese home or a ryokan, and not uncommon in traditional restaurants, temples and, occasionally, museums and art galleries. If you come across a slightly raised floor and a row of slippers, then use them; leave your shoes either on the lower floor (the *genkan*) or on the shelves (sometimes lockers) provided. Also try not to step on the *genkan* with bare or stockinged feet. Once inside, remove your slippers before stepping onto tatami (the rice-straw flooring), and remember to change into the special **toilet slippers** kept inside the bathroom when you go to the toilet.

Toilets

Although you'll still come across traditional Japanese squat-style **toilets** (*toire* or *otearai*; トイレ／お手洗い), Western sit-down toilets are becoming the norm. Look out for nifty enhancements such as a heated seat and those that flush automatically as you walk away. Another handy device plays the sound of flushing water to cover embarrassing noises.

Hi-tech toilets, with a control panel to one side, are very common. Finding the flush button can be a challenge – they're often tiny things on wall panels, marked with the *kanji* for large (大) or small (小), used for number twos and ones respectively.

Most public toilets now provide **paper** (often extremely thin), though not always soap for washing your hands. There are public toilets at most train and subway stations, department stores and city parks, and they're generally pretty clean.

Shopping

Even if you're not an inveterate shopper, cruising Japan's gargantuan department stores or rummaging around its vibrant discount outlets is an integral part of local life that shouldn't be missed. Japan also has some truly enticing souvenirs, from lacquered chopsticks and delicate handmade paper to the latest electronic gadgets.

All prices are fixed, except in flea markets and some discount electrical stores where bargaining is acceptable. Though it's always worth asking, surprisingly few shops take **credit cards** and fewer

---

DUTY-FREE SHOPPING

Foreigners can make purchases **duty-free** (that is, without the eight percent consumption tax – see box, p.68) in a whole bunch of shops around the country – participating outlets usually have a Duty Free sticker in the window by the entrance (look for a Rising Sun-style red circle with white flower petals). To take advantage of the scheme, you'll need a minimum total spend of ¥5000 at a single store; there's an upper limit of ¥500,000 on perishable goods such as food, drinks, tobacco, cosmetics and film, which have to be taken out of the country within 30 days. Your passport will be required on purchase, and it must have an entry stamp from customs – if you manage to enter Japan without one (such as by using the automatic gates at the airport), ask for a stamp from an immigration officer. The shop will attach a copy of the customs document (割印, *wariin*) to your passport, to be removed by customs officers when you leave Japan.

still accept cards issued abroad, so make sure you have plenty of cash.

In general, shop **opening hours** are from 10am or 11am to 7pm or 8pm. Most shops close one day a week, not always on Sunday, and smaller places tend to shut on public holidays. If you need anything **after hours**, you'll find late-opening convenience stores in even the smallest towns, and stores that are open 24 hours in most towns and cities, often near the train station.

Arts and crafts

Many of Japan's **arts** and **crafts** date back thousands of years and have been handed down from generation to generation. Though the best can be phenomenally expensive, there are plenty of items at more manageable prices that make wonderful **souvenirs**. Most department stores have at least a small crafts section, but it's far more enjoyable to trawl Japan's specialist shops. Kyoto is renowned for its traditional crafts, and in Tokyo you'll find a number of artisans still plying their trade, while most regions have a vibrant local crafts industry turning out products for the tourists.

Some of Japan's most beautiful traditional products stem from **folk crafts** (*mingei*), ranging from elegant, inexpensive bamboo-ware to woodcarvings, toys, masks, kites and a whole host of delightful dolls (*ningyō*). Peg-shaped *kokeshi* dolls from northern Honshū are among the most appealing, with their bright colours and sweet, simple faces. Look out, too, for the rotund, round-eyed *daruma* dolls, made of papier-mâché, and fine clay *Hakata-ningyō* dolls from northern Kyūshū.

Ceramics

Japan's most famous craft is its **ceramics** (*tōjiki*). Of several distinct regional styles, *Imari-ware* from Arita in Kyūshū (see box, p.715) is best known for its colourful, ornate designs, while the iron-brown unglazed *Bizen-ware* from near Okayama (see box, p.568) is satisfyingly rustic. Other famous names include *Satsuma-yaki* (from Kagoshima), *Kasama-yaki* (from Ibaraki), Kanazawa's highly elaborate *Kutani-yaki* and Kyoto's *Kyō-yaki*. Any decent department store will stock a full range of styles, or you can visit local showrooms. Traditional tea bowls, sake sets and vases are popular souvenirs.

Lacquerware

Originally devised as a means of making everyday utensils more durable, **lacquerware** (*shikki* or *urushi*) has developed over the centuries into a

ANTIQUE AND FLEA MARKETS

The regular outdoor **antique** and **flea markets** of Tokyo and Kyoto, usually held at shrines and temples (see individual city accounts for details), are great fun to attend. You need to get there early for the best deals, but you're likely to find some gorgeous secondhand kimono, satin-smooth lacquerware or rustic pottery, among a good deal of tat. Flea markets are also great for stocking up on inexpensive clothes and household items.

unique art form. Items such as trays, tables, boxes, chopsticks and bowls are typically covered with reddish-brown or black lacquer and either left plain or decorated with paintings, carvings, sprinkled with eggshell or given a dusting of gold or silver leaf. Though top-quality lacquer can be hugely expensive, you'll still find very beautiful pieces at reasonable prices. Lacquer needs a humid atmosphere, especially the cheaper pieces which are made on a base of low-quality wood that cracks in dry conditions, though inexpensive plastic bases won't be affected. Wajima is one of the most famous places for lacquerware in Japan (see box, p.398).

Paper products and woodblock prints

Traditional Japanese **paper** (*washi*), made from mulberry or other natural fibres, is fashioned into any number of tempting souvenirs. You can buy purses, boxes, fans, oiled umbrellas, lampshades and toys all made from paper, as well as wonderful stationery.

Original **woodblock prints**, *ukiyo-e*, by world-famous artists such as Utamaro, Hokusai and Hiroshige, have long been collectors' items fetching thousands of pounds. However, you can buy copies of these "pictures of the floating world", often depicting Mount Fuji, willowy geisha or lusty heroes of the kabuki stage, at tourist shops for more modest sums. Alternatively, note that some art shops specialize in originals, both modern and antique.

Textiles, metalwork and pearls

Japan has a long history of making attractive **textiles**, particularly the silks used in kimono (see box, p.66). Other interesting uses of textiles include *noren*, a split curtain hanging in the entrance to a

THE COMEBACK OF THE KIMONO

In Japan, **kimono** are still worn by both sexes on special occasions, such as weddings and festival visits to a shrine. But as the demand for high-class kimono, such as those made by the craftspeople of Kyoto, declines – a result of the falling birth rate and Japan's ageing population – the one bright spot for the industry is the trend to adapt old kimono to new uses. Increasing numbers of fashion-conscious young women have taken to wearing a kimono like a coat over Western clothes or coordinating it with coloured rather than white *tabi* (traditional split-toed socks). At the same time, fashion designers are turning to kimono fabrics and styles for contemporary creations.

BUYING KIMONO

Few visitors to Japan fail to be impressed by the beauty and variety of kimono available, and every department store has a corner devoted to ready-made or tailored kimono. **Ready-made versions** can easily cost ¥100,000, while ¥1 million for the best made-to-measure kimono is not uncommon. Much more affordable **secondhand or antique kimono** can be found in tourist shops, flea markets or in the kimono sales held by department stores, usually in spring and autumn. Prices can start as low as ¥1000, but you'll pay more for the sumptuous, highly decorated wedding kimono (they make striking wall hangings), as well as the most beautifully patterned **obi**, the broad, silk sash worn with a kimono. A cheaper, more practical alternative is the light cotton **yukata**, popular with both sexes as a dressing gown; you'll find them in all department stores and many speciality stores, along with **happi coats** – the loose jackets that just cover the upper body. To complete the outfit, you could pick up a pair of **zōri**, traditional straw sandals, or their wooden counterpart, **geta**.

DRESSING UP

If you want to try the full kimono look, you'll find that many of the big hotels have a studio where you can **dress up** and have your photo taken (typically around ¥10,000–15,000), while some guesthouses also offer the opportunity. The most popular place to don kimono is, of course, Kyoto (see p.444). Men can get in on the act, too, dressing up in what is called "samurai" style (around ¥5000), though the male kimono is much less florid in design than the female version, and is usually in muted colours such as black, greys and browns.

restaurant or bar; cotton *tenugui* (small hand towels), decorated with cute designs; and the *furoshiki*, a square, versatile wrapping cloth that comes in a variety of sizes.

While the chunky iron kettles from Morioka in northern Honshū are rather unwieldy mementos, the area also produces delicate *fūrin*, or **wind chimes**, in a variety of designs. **Damascene** is also more portable, though a bit fussy for some tastes. This metal inlay-work, with gold and silver threads on black steel, was originally used to fix the family crest on sword hilts and helmets, though nowadays you can buy all sorts of jewellery and trinket boxes decorated with birds, flowers and other intricate designs.

Pearls are undoubtedly Japan's most famous jewellery item, ever since Mikimoto Kōkichi first succeeded in growing cultured pearls in Toba in 1893. Toba (see p.541) is still the centre of production, though you'll find specialist shops in all major cities, selling pearls at fairly competitive prices.

Books

Imported foreign-language **books** are expensive and only available in major cities. However, some locally produced English-language books are cheaper here than they would be at home, if you can find them at all outside Japan. The best bookshops are Kinokuniya, Tower Books (part of Tower Records), Maruzen, Yūrindō and Junkudō, all of which stock imported newspapers and magazines as well as a variable selection of foreign-language books.

Department stores

Japan's most prestigious **department stores** are Isetan, Mitsukoshi and Takashimaya, followed by the more workaday Seibu, Tōbu and Matsuzakaya. All of these big names have branches throughout Japan, and sell almost everything, from fashion, crafts and household items to stationery and toys. One floor is usually devoted to restaurants, while bigger stores may also have an art gallery, travel bureau, ticket agent and a currency-exchange desk, as well as English-speaking staff and a duty-free service. Seasonal sales, particularly those at New Year and early July, can offer great bargains.

Electrical and electronic goods

Japan is a well-known producer of high-quality and innovative **electrical** and **electronic goods**. New designs are tested on the local market before going into export production, so this is the best place to check out the latest technological advances. The majority of high-tech goods are sold in discount stores, where prices may be up to forty percent cheaper than at a conventional store. Akihabara, in Tokyo (see p.93), is the country's foremost area for electronic goods, but in every major city you can buy audio equipment, computers, software and any number of ingenious gadgets at competitive prices.

Similarly, Japanese **cameras** and other photographic equipment are among the best in the world. Shinjuku, in Tokyo, is the main centre, where you can pick up the latest models and find discontinued and secondhand cameras at decent prices.

Before buying anything, compare prices – many shops are open to **bargaining** – and make sure the items come with the appropriate voltage switch (Japanese power supply is 100V). It's also important to check that whatever you buy will be compatible with equipment you have at home, if necessary. For English-language instructions, after-sales service and guarantees, stick to export models, which you'll find mostly in the stores' duty-free sections, but bear in mind that they may not be any cheaper than you would pay at home.

Fashion

Top **Japanese labels** such as Issey Miyake, Yohji Yamamoto, Comme des Garçons and Evisu jeans are worn by fashionistas around the world, but there are also plenty of up-and-coming designers and streetwear labels to discover in Japan. The epicentre of chic is Tokyo's Omotesandō (see p.117) and the surrounding Aoyama and Harajuku areas. If you want to check out the latest designers and labels, such as Jun Takahashi, Tsumori Chisato and Yanagawa Arashi, then head to the boutiques here and in trendy Daikanyama (see p.113) and Nakameguro (see p.113), or hit town during Tokyo Fashion Week (🌐 jfw.jp), held twice a year. Kyoto also has an interesting fashion scene (see p.465).

Finding **clothes** that fit is becoming easier as young Japanese are, on average, substantially bigger-built than their parents, and foreign chains tend to carry larger sizes. **Shoes**, however, are more of a problem. While stores stock larger sizes nowadays, the range is still pretty limited – your best bet is to try a large department store, or the ubiquitous branches of ABC Mart.

Food and drink

Edible souvenirs include various types of rice crackers (*sembei*), both sweet and savoury, vacuum-packed bags of pickles (*tsukemono*), and Japanese sweets (*okashi*) such as the eye-catching *wagashi*. Made of sweet, red-bean paste in various colours and designs, *wagashi* are the traditional accompaniment to the tea ceremony. Tea itself (*ocha*) comes in a variety of grades, often in attractive canisters, while sake (see p.53), premium *shōchū* or Japanese whisky are other great gift options, and often come in interestingly shaped bottles with beautiful labels.

Travelling with children

With high standards of health, hygiene and safety, and lots of interesting things to do, Japan is a great place to travel with children. At museums and other sights, school-age kids usually get reduced rates, which may be up to half the adult price. Children under age 6 ride free on trains, subways and buses, while those aged 6 to 11 pay half fare.

It's a good idea to bring a lightweight, easily collapsible **pushchair**. You'll find yourself walking long distances in cities and, while many subway and train stations now have lifts, there are still plenty of stairs.

Finding **hotels** offering **family rooms** that fit more than three people is tough: international chain hotels are your best bet. A great alternative is a Japanese-style ryokan or minshuku where you can share a big tatami room. Only at the more upmarket Western-style hotels will you be able to arrange **babysitting**.

All the products you need – such as **nappies** and **baby food** – are easily available in shops and

---

THE BEST OF JAPAN FOR KIDS

Tokyo Whether shopping for the latest teenager fashions or checking out the fabulous Ghibli Museum, kids of all ages will love Japan's high-octane capital (see box, p.106).

Taketomi, Okinawa Hop on a bike, or board a buffalo-drawn carriage, to explore the beautiful star-sand beaches of this tiny, car-free island (see p.811).

Sumo A visit to the sumo will make children the envy of their school pals (see p.58).

Snow monkeys, Honshū See the world-famous snow monkeys bathe at the Jigokudani Monkey Park (see p.362).

Amusement parks Strap yourself into some white-knuckle rides at Universal Studios in Osaka (see p.514), Tokyo Dome City or Disneyland in Tokyo (see p.108) or Fujikyū Highland in Fuji-Yoshida (see p.199).

Ryokan Kids will love the ritual of staying overnight in a ryokan (see p.44).

The Great Outdoors, Hokkaidō Explore spectacular lakes, steaming valleys and active volcanoes. In winter, there's great skiing and ice festivals (see box, p.295).

Bullet trains The thought of travelling at speeds faster than a racing car may well put paid to the "are we there yet?" cliché (see p.34).

Kyoto Follow the path up the mountain at the Fushimi-Inari shrine (see p.432), spotting the stone foxes and counting the *torii* as you go (all 10,000 of them); explore the magnificent castle of Nijō-jō (see p.427) with its squeaky, intruder-repelling "nightingale floors"; or take a day-trip to the monkey park and towering bamboo grove of Arashiyama (see p.467).

Karaoke While adult crooners tend to use karaoke parlours (see box, p.153) as a means of getting drunk cheaply, venues are open through the day, and most are private-room affairs – fun places for kids to enjoy belting out their favourite hits.

---

department stores, though not necessarily imported varieties. If you need a particular brand, it would be wise to bring it with you. Although **breastfeeding** in public is generally accepted, it's best to be as discreet as possible. Most Japanese women who breastfeed use the private rooms provided in department stores, public buildings and in many shops, or find a quiet corner.

The hazy situation with regard to smoking in Japanese **restaurants** (most still allow it), combined with uncommon dishes and Japanese-language menus, will provide parents trying to feed fussy kids with certain challenges. One solution is to ask your hotel to point you in the direction of the nearest **"family restaurant" chain**, such as *Royal Host* or *Jonathan's*; all have children's menus including Western and Japanese dishes with pictures of each dish, as well as non-smoking sections.

Travel essentials

Costs

Despite its reputation as being an outrageously expensive country, prices in Japan have dropped, or at least stabilized, in recent years. With a little planning, it is a manageable destination even for those on an absolute minimum **daily budget** of ¥4000–7000. By the time you've added in some transport costs, a few entry tickets, meals in classier restaurants and one or two nights in a ryokan or business hotel, ¥10,000–15,000 per day is more realistic.

Holders of the **International Student Identity Card** (ISIC; Ⓦ isiccard.com) are eligible for discounts on some transport and admission fees, as are children. A **Hostelling International card** (Ⓦ hihostels.com) qualifies you for a reduction of ¥600 on the rates of official youth hostels, though these days most of the best establishments are privately run (see p.45).

As well as checking out our tips on how to make your yen go further (see box opposite), take a look at JNTO's website (Ⓦ jnto.go.jp) for further ideas on

---

CONSUMPTION TAX

A **consumption tax** (*shōhizei*) is levied on virtually all goods and services in Japan, including restaurant meals and accommodation. At the time of writing, the rate was eight percent, though it's set to rise to ten percent from October 2019. Tax is supposed to be included in the advertised price, though you'll come across plenty of shops, hotels, restaurants and bars which haven't quite got around to it; double-check to be on the safe side.

SAVING YOUR YEN

No two ways about it – Japan is an expensive place to visit. However, there are plenty of ways in which to make your trip affordable.

Getting there A number of low-cost airlines, both Japanese and international, now fly to Japan, meaning that you can enter or leave the country very cheaply if travelling to and from destinations such as South Korea, China, Taiwan, Malaysia or even Australia (see p.31).

Getting around Most travellers are savvy enough to organize a Japan Rail Pass before their trip (see box, p.37); alternatively, other discount train passes are available, including the crazy-cheap Seishun 18 ticket (see p.37). Don't forget other forms of transport, too: taking a bus (see p.38) is often the cheapest way from A to B, and you can pick up some good fares on the budget airlines. Overnight ferries and buses are an economical way of getting around (see p.38).

Sights Most of the country's temples and shrines are absolutely free, as is taking in the banks of eye-popping neon in Tokyo's Shinjuku or Akihabara. Hot-spring bathing can also be very cheap (see box, p.61).

Sleeping Japan has a whole bunch of cheap hostels (see p.45) and less-cheap business hotels (see p.42) and minshuku (see p.44). To really scrape the bottom of the barrel, try sleeping in an internet café (see box, p.46).

Eating This is one area in which Japan is actually very affordable by developed-country standards. However, if you want to cut costs even further, you can get super-cheap meals from restaurant chains (see box, p.52) or standing noodle bars.

Drinking Bars and *izakaya* are expensive – and that's before you include the cover charges which can make bar-crawls a very costly proposition. The solution – convenience stores. Public drinking is quite legal in Japan, and many an expat regularly pops down to the 7-Eleven for a "*kombini* Martini".

saving money. **Welcome Card** schemes, for example, operate in some areas of the country, which entitle you to discounts at certain museums, sights, shops, restaurants and transport services. At the time of writing, there were ten Welcome Card schemes in operation, including in the Tōhoku area (see p.222) and the Tokyo museum pass (see box, p.136).

Crime and personal safety

Japan boasts one of the lowest crime rates in the world. On the whole, the Japanese are honest and law-abiding, there's little theft, and drug-related crimes are relatively rare. Nonetheless, it always pays to be careful in crowds, and to keep money and important documents stowed in an inside pocket or money belt, or in your hotel safe.

The presence of **police boxes** (*kōban*) in every neighbourhood helps to discourage petty crime, and the local police seem to spend the majority of their time dealing with stolen bikes and helping bemused visitors – Japanese and foreigners – find addresses. In theory, you should carry your **passport** or ID at all times; the police have the right to arrest anyone who fails to do so. In practice they rarely stop foreigners, but if you're found without ID, you'll most likely be escorted back to your hotel or apartment to collect it. Anyone found

with **drugs** will be treated less leniently; if you're lucky, you'll simply be fined and deported, rather than sent to prison.

The generally low status of women in Japan is reflected in the amount of **groping** that goes on in crowded commuter trains. If you do have the misfortune to be groped, the best solution is to grab the offending hand, yank it high in the air and embarrass the guy as much as possible. Fortunately, more violent **sexual attacks** are rare, though harassment, stalking and rape are seriously under-reported. Women should exercise the same caution about being alone with a man as they would anywhere – violent crimes against women are rare, but they do occur.

The Tokyo Metropolitan Police run an **English-language hotline** (☎03 3501 0110; Mon–Fri 8.30am–5.15pm). Another useful option is **Tokyo English Language Lifeline** (TELL; ☎03 5774 0992, ⓦ telljp.com; daily 9am–11pm). Each prefecture also has a Foreign Advisory Service, with a variety of foreign-language speakers who can be contacted as a last resort.

Earthquakes

Japan is home to one-tenth of the world's active volcanoes; it's also the site of one-tenth of its major

EARTHQUAKE SAFETY PROCEDURES

If you do have the misfortune to experience more than a minor rumble, follow the safety procedures listed below:

- Extinguish any **fires** and turn off **electrical appliances**.
- Open any **doors** leading out of the room you're in, as they often get jammed shut, blocking your exit.
- Stay away from **windows** because of splintering glass. If you have time, draw the curtains to contain the glass.
- Don't rush outside (many people are injured by falling masonry), but get under something solid, such as a ground-floor **doorway**, or a **desk**.
- If you are outside when the quake hits, head for the nearest **park** or other **open space**.
- If the earthquake occurs at night, make sure you've got a **torch** (all hotels, ryokan, etc provide flashlights in the rooms).
- When the tremors have died down, go to the nearest open space, taking your documents and other valuables with you. It's also a good idea to take a cushion or pillow to protect your head against **falling glass**.
- Eventually, make your way to the designated **neighbourhood emergency centre** and get in touch with your **embassy**.

earthquakes (over magnitude 7 on the Richter scale). At least one quake is recorded every day somewhere in the country (see Ⓦ www.jma .go.jp/en/quake for details of the most recent), though fortunately the vast majority consist of **minor tremors** that you probably won't even notice. One that the whole world noticed occurred off the country's east coast in March 2011 (see box, p.225). The fifth most powerful earthquake in recorded history, it unleashed a **tsunami** of prodigious force; the combined effect killed almost 16,000 people, and caused a meltdown at the nuclear power plant in Fukushima, where the effects will be felt for decades.

Earthquakes are notoriously difficult to predict, and it's worth taking note of a few basic **safety procedures** (see box above). Aftershocks may go on for a long time, and can topple structures that are already weakened. Do note, however, that since the 1980s buildings have been designed to withstand even the most powerful quakes. Japan is equipped with some of the world's most **sophisticated sensors**, and architects employ mind-boggling techniques to try to ensure the country's high-rises remain upright. Most casualties are caused by fire and traffic accidents, rather than collapsing buildings.

Electricity

The **electrical current** is 100v, 50Hz AC in Japan east of Mt Fuji, including Tokyo; and 100v, 60Hz AC in western Japan, including Nagoya, Kyoto and Osaka. Japanese plugs have either two flat pins or, less commonly, three pins (two flat and one rounded, earth, pin). If you are coming from North America, Canada, the UK or Europe, the voltage difference should cause no problems with computers, digital cameras, mobile phones and the like, most of which can handle between 100V and 240V. Larger appliances such as hairdryers, curling irons and travel kettles should work, but not quite as efficiently, in which case you may need a converter. And, while Japanese plugs look identical to North American plugs, there are subtle differences, so you may also need an adaptor; you certainly will if coming from the UK or Europe.

Health

Japan has high standards of health and hygiene, and there are no significant diseases worth worrying about. There are no immunizations or health certificates needed to enter the country.

Medical treatment and **drugs** are of a high quality, but can be expensive – if possible, you should bring any medicines you might need with you, especially prescription drugs. Also bring a copy of your prescription and make sure you know what the generic name of the drug is, rather than its brand name. Some common drugs widely available throughout the US and Europe are generally not available in Japan, and some are actually **illegal** to bring into the country – prominent prescription drugs on the no-no list are codeine and some ADHD medication, for which you may need advance permission to bring into Japan. The Health Ministry website (Ⓦwww.mhlw.go.jp) has more specific details on these, and the forms you'll need to fill in to bring this medication into Japan legally. Also note that the contraceptive pill is only available on prescription.

Although mosquitoes buzz across Japan in the warmer months, **malaria** is not endemic, so there's no need to take any tablets. It's a good idea to pack mosquito repellent, however, and to burn coils in your room at night, or to use a plug-in repellent.

Tap **water** is safe to drink throughout Japan, but you should avoid drinking directly from streams or rivers. It's also not a good idea to walk barefoot through flooded paddy fields, due to the danger of water-borne parasites. Food-wise, you should have no fears about eating raw seafood or sea fish, including the notorious *fugu* (blowfish). However, raw meat and river fish are best avoided.

Emergencies and medical help

In the case of an **emergency**, the first port of call should be to ask your hotel to phone for a doctor or ambulance. You could also head for, or call, the nearest tourist information office or international centre (in major cities only), which should be able to provide a list of local doctors and hospitals with English-speaking staff. Alternatively, you could call the toll-free 24-hour Japan Helpline (Ⓣ0570 000 911, Ⓦjhelp.com).

If you need to call an **ambulance** on your own, dial Ⓞ119 and speak slowly when you're asked to give an address. Ambulance staff are not trained paramedics, but will take you to the nearest appropriate hospital. Unless you're dangerously ill when you go to hospital, you'll have to wait your turn in a clinic before you see a doctor, and you'll need to be persistent if you want to get full details of your condition: some doctors are notorious for withholding information from patients.

For minor ailments and advice, you can go to a **pharmacy**, which you'll find in most shopping areas. There are also numerous smaller **private clinics**, where you'll pay in the region of ¥10,000 to see a doctor. You could also try **Asian medical remedies**, such as acupuncture (*hari*) and pressure point massage (*shiatsu*), though it's worth trying to get a personal recommendation to find a reputable practitioner.

Insurance

It's essential to take out a good **travel insurance** policy, particularly one with comprehensive medical coverage, due to the high cost of hospital treatment in Japan (see box below).

Internet

Many visitors soon realize that Japan doesn't quite live up to its tech-savvy reputation. A fair few local websites (including those of some expensive hotels and restaurants) are laughably bad; with italicized Times New Roman fonts and copious Clipart characters, many seem to have been imported directly from the mid-1990s.

However, things are finally starting to improve, and **wi-fi** access is becoming more widespread. Most big-city **cafés** offer it for free (though at some you have to register), and it's par for the course at privately run **hostels**, though at **hotels** you still can't be sure; at the top end, you may well have to pay a daily fee (typically ¥1000). Some hotels also offer free broadband in the rooms, and should be able to supply a cable if necessary. Others may provide at least one terminal for guests travelling without their own computer, generally also for free.

Wi-fi has now been rolled out in most **convenience stores** – you have to register once, then log in each time. At the time of writing, Lawson stores were by far the easiest at which to get online, with 7-Eleven not far behind, and Family Mart at the bottom of the queue. **Subway stations** in Tokyo, Kyoto and some other cities are also now wired for wi-fi. Accommodation, restaurants and bars with wi-fi are indicated in the Guide with the ⬥ symbol.

Taking a small step back in time, **cybercafés** can be found across Japan, often as part of a 24-hour computer-game and manga centre. Free access is sometimes available (usually in cultural exchange centres, or regular cafés looking to boost business); otherwise, expect to pay around ¥200–400 per hour.

Laundry

All hotels provide either a **laundry service** or, at the lower end, **coin-operated machines**. These typically cost ¥200–300 for a wash (powder ¥30–50) and ¥100 for ten minutes in the drier. You'll also find coin-operated laundries (*koin randorii*) in nearly all Japanese neighbourhoods, often open long hours. Virtually all Japanese washing machines use cold water.

LGBT travellers

Gay travellers should have few concerns about visiting Japan. The country has no laws against homosexual activity and outward discrimination is very rare, including at hotels and ryokan where two people of the same sex sharing a room will hardly raise an eyebrow.

That said, marriage remains an almost essential step on the career ladder, keeping many Japanese gays in the closet, often leading double lives and/or being apathetic about concepts of gay liberation and rights. General codes of behaviour mean that public displays of affection between any couple, gay or straight, are very rare – so don't expect a warm welcome if you walk down the street hand in hand or kiss in public. In recent times being gay has come to be seen as more acceptable – and among young people it's rarely an issue – but Japan has a long way to go before it can be considered truly gay-friendly.

Useful online English sources of information on the city's gay life include Fridae (ⓦfridae.com), Utopia (ⓦutopia-asia.com) and the tri-lingual lesbian-focused Tokyo Wrestling (ⓦtokyowrestling.com).

Living in Japan

Employment opportunities for foreigners have shrunk since the Japanese economy took a nosedive, though finding employment is far from impossible, especially if you have the right qualifications (a degree is essential) and appropriate visa.

Unless you take part in the **working holiday visa** programme (see p.33), foreigners working in Japan must apply for a **work visa** *outside* the country, for which the proper sponsorship papers from your prospective employer will be necessary. Work visas do not need to be obtained in your home country, so if you get offered a job, it's possible to sort out the paperwork in South Korea, for example. A few employers may be willing to hire you before the proper papers are sorted, but you shouldn't rely on this, and if you arrive without a job make sure you have plenty of funds to live on until you find one. Anyone staying in Japan more than ninety days must also apply for residency status (see p.33).

Teaching English

The most common job available to foreigners is **teaching English**. Some of the smaller schools are far from professional operations (and even the big ones get lots of complaints), so before signing any contract it's a good idea to talk to other teachers and, if possible, attend a class and find out what will be expected of you. If you have a professional teaching qualification, plus experience, or if you also speak another language such as French or Italian, your chances of getting one of the better jobs will be higher.

Another option is to get a place on the government-run **Japan Exchange and Teaching Programme** (JET; ⓦjetprogramme.org), aimed at improving foreign-language teaching in schools and promoting international understanding. The scheme is open to graduates aged 40 and under, preferably holding some sort of language-teaching qualification. Benefits include a generous salary, help with accommodation, return air travel to Japan and paid holidays. Applying for the JET programme is a lengthy process for which you need to be well prepared. Application forms for the following year's quota are available from late September, and the deadline for submission is early December. Interviews are held in January and February, with decisions made in March. After health checks and orientation meetings, JETs head off to their posts in late July on year-long contracts, which can be renewed for up to two more years by mutual consent.

Other jobs

A much more limited job option for *gaijin* is **rewriting** or **editing** English **translations** of Japanese text for technical documents, manuals, magazines and so on. For such jobs, it's a great help if you know at least a little Japanese. These days, there are also good opportunities for *gaijin* with **ski instructor** or **adventure sports** experience to work on the ski slopes, particularly in resorts such as Niseko, Furano and Hakuba which target overseas visitors. Other options include **modelling**, for which it will be an asset to have a professional portfolio of photographs, and **bar work** and **hostessing**, with the usual warnings about the dangers inherent in this type of work. Whatever work you're looking for – or if you're doing any sort of business in Japan – a smart set of clothes will give you an advantage, as will following other general rules of social etiquette (see p.62).

EMPLOYMENT RESOURCES

Daijob Ⓦ daijob.com. Japan's largest bilingual jobs website – and a great pun to boot (*daijobu* means "no problem").

GaijinPot Ⓦ gaijinpot.com. Classifieds focused on English-language teaching.

Japan Association for Working Holiday Makers Ⓦ jawhm .or.jp. Job referrals for people on working holiday visas.

Jobs in Japan Ⓦ jobsinjapan.com. Broad range of classified ads.

WWOOF (Willing Workers on Organic Farms) Ⓦ wwoofjapan.com. Opportunities to work and live on organic farms across Japan, plus a few hotels and resorts.

Studying Japanese language and culture

There are all sorts of opportunities to study Japanese language and culture. In order to get a **student** or **cultural visa**, you'll need various documents from the institution where you plan to study and proof that you have sufficient funds to support yourself, among other things. Full-time courses are expensive, but once you have your visa, you may be allowed to undertake a minimal amount of paid work.

Japan's Ministry of Education, Culture, Sports, Science and Technology (MEXT; Ⓦ mext.go.jp) offers various **scholarships** to foreign students wishing to further their knowledge of Japanese or Japanese studies, undertake an undergraduate degree, or become a research student at a Japanese university. You'll find further information on the informative Study in Japan website (Ⓦ studyjapan.go.jp), run by the Ministry of Foreign Affairs, or by contacting your nearest Japanese embassy or consulate.

Tokyo, Osaka, Kyoto and other major cities have numerous **Japanese language schools** offering intensive and part-time courses. Among the most established are Berlitz (Ⓦ berlitz.co.jp), with branches nationwide, and Tokyo Kogakuin Japanese Language School (5-30-16 Sendagaya, Shibuya-ku; ☎03 3352 3851, Ⓦ technos-jpschool .ac.jp). The monthly bilingual magazine *Hiragana Times* (Ⓦ hiraganatimes.com) and the listings magazines *Metropolis* and *Tokyo Journal* also carry adverts for schools, or check out the Association for the Promotion of Japanese Language Education (2F Ishiyama Building, 1-58-1 Yoyogi, Shinjuku-ku; ☎03 4304 7815, Ⓦ nisshinkyo.org), whose website lists accredited institutions.

Maps

The Japan National Tourist Organization (JNTO) **tourist maps** cover Tokyo, Kansai, Kyoto and the whole country. These are available for free at JNTO offices abroad (see p.76) and at Tourist Information Centres (TIC) in Japan (see p.133), and are fine for most purposes. Tourist offices in other areas usually provide local maps, often dual-language. If you need anything more detailed, note that most bookshops sell maps, though you'll only find English-language maps in the big cities. If you're **hiking**, the best maps are those in the *Yama-to-kōgen* series, published by Shōbunsha but in Japanese only.

Note that **maps on signboards** in Japan, such as a map of footpaths in a national park, are usually oriented the way you are facing. So, if you're facing southeast, for example, as you look at the map, the top will be southeast and the bottom northwest.

There are also decent maps **online**. Google's are typically excellent, while with a little hunting you'll be able to find apps offering offline-friendly maps (Ⓦ maps.me is a good one). Perhaps equally useful are maps portraying the subway networks in Tokyo, Osaka and other major cities, since such maps are sometimes not visible anywhere once you're on the trains themselves.

Money

The **Japanese currency** is the **yen** (*en* in Japanese). Notes are available in denominations of ¥1000, ¥2000, ¥5000 and ¥10,000, while coins come in

---

EXCHANGE RATES

Exchange rates at the time of writing are as follows:

£1 = ¥144
€1 = ¥123
US$1 = ¥117
Can$1 = ¥88
Aus$1 = ¥85
NZ$1 = ¥81

For current exchange rates see Ⓦ xe.com

CREDIT CARD EMERGENCY NUMBERS

If you lose a credit or debit card, call the following toll-free numbers, available 24 hours:

American Express ☎ 03 3220 6100
MasterCard ☎ 00531 113886
Visa International ☎ 00531 440022

values of ¥1, ¥5, ¥10, ¥50, ¥100 and ¥500. Apart from the ¥5 piece, a copper-coloured coin with a hole in the centre, all other notes and coins indicate their value in Western numerals.

Though **credit and debit cards** are far more widely accepted than they were a few years ago, Japan is still very much a cash society. The most useful cards to carry are Visa and American Express, followed closely by MasterCard, then Diners Club; you should be able to use these in hotels, restaurants, shops and travel agencies accustomed to serving foreigners. However, many retailers only accept locally issued cards.

ATMs

The simplest way of obtaining cash in Japan is by making an **ATM** withdrawal on a credit or debit card. Both the **post office** and Seven Bank (whose machines are located in **7-Eleven** stores) operate ATMs that accept foreign-issued cards. Post office machines accept Visa, PLUS, MasterCard, Maestro, Cirrus and American Express, with instructions provided in English; 7-Eleven ATMs accept all of these, too, except overseas-issued MasterCard brand cash cards and credit cards (including Cirrus and Maestro cards). Withdrawal limits will depend on the card issuer and your credit limit. If the machine doesn't allow you to withdraw money in the first instance, try again with a smaller amount.

Seven Bank ATMs are often accessible 24 hours. You'll also find post office ATMs not only in post offices, but also In stations, department stores and the like throughout the city – they're identified with a sticker saying "International ATM Service". Their ATMs have more **restricted hours** than the Seven Bank machines, but the ones in major post offices can be accessed at weekends and after the counters have closed, though none is open round the clock.

Changing money

You can change cash at the **exchange counters** (ryōgae-jo; 両替所) of main post offices and certain banks – the bigger branches of Tokyo-Mitsubishi UFJ (ⓦ bk.mufg.jp/english) and SMBC (Sumitomo Mitsubishi Banking Corporation; ⓦ www.smbcgroup .com) are your best bet. The post office handles cash in six major currencies, including American, Canadian and Australian dollars, sterling and euros. **Hotels** are only supposed to change money for guests, but some might be persuaded to help in an emergency. Remember to take your passport along in case it's needed, and allow plenty of time, since even a simple transaction can take twenty minutes or more. Banks or exchange counters are listed throughout the Guide in destinations where there are no ATMS accepting foreign cards, or where obtaining money is particularly difficult.

Opening hours and public holidays

Business hours are generally Monday to Friday 9am–5pm, though private companies often close much later in the evening and may also open on Saturday mornings. Department stores and bigger **shops** tend to open around 10am and shut at 7pm or 8pm. Local shops, however, will generally stay open later, while many convenience stores are open 24 hours. Most shops take one day off a week, not necessarily on a Sunday.

The majority of **museums** close on a Monday, but stay open on Sundays and national holidays (closing the following day instead); last entry is normally thirty minutes before closing. However, during the New Year festival (January 1–3), Golden

PUBLIC HOLIDAYS

If one of the holidays listed below falls on a Sunday, then the following Monday is also a holiday.

New Year's Day Jan 1
Coming of Age Day Second Mon in Jan
National Foundation Day Feb 11
Spring Equinox March 20/21
Shōwa Day April 29
Constitution Memorial Day May 3
Greenery Day May 4
Children's Day May 5
Marine Day Third Mon in July
Respect the Aged Day Third Mon in Sept
Autumn Equinox Sept 23/24
Health and Sports Day Second Mon in Oct
Culture Day Nov 3
Labour Thanksgiving Day Nov 23
Emperor's Birthday Dec 23

CALLING HOME FROM ABROAD

The main companies in Japan offering **international phone calls** are KDDI (☎001), Softbank Telecom (☎0041), Cable & Wireless IDC (☎0061) and NTT (☎0033). If you want to call abroad from Japan from any type of phone, choose a company (there's little difference between them all as far as rates are concerned) and dial the relevant access code (see below), then the destination's country code, before the rest of the number. Note that the initial zero is omitted from the area code when dialling the UK, Ireland, Australia and New Zealand from abroad. For operator assistance for overseas calls, dial ☎0051.

Australia international access code + 61
New Zealand international access code + 64
UK international access code + 44
US and Canada international access code + 1
Ireland international access code + 353
South Africa international access code + 27

Week (April 29–May 5) and Obon (the week around August 15), almost everything shuts down. Around these periods, all transport and accommodation is booked out weeks in advance, and all major tourist spots get overrun.

Phones

You're rarely far from a payphone in Japan. The vast majority of payphones take both coins (¥10 and ¥100) and **phonecards**.; they don't give change, but do return unused coins, so for local calls use ¥10 rather than ¥100 coins.

Everywhere in Japan has an **area code**, which can be omitted if the call is a local one. Area codes are given for all telephone numbers throughout this Guide. Toll-free numbers begin with either ☎0120 or 0088; in a few cases you may come across codes such as 0570, which are non-geographical and should always be included with the main number wherever you're calling from. Numbers starting with 080 or 090 are to mobile phones.

Mobile phones

Practically everyone in Japan has a **mobile phone** (*keitai-denwa*, sometimes shortened to *keitai*), many of which can be used like a prepaid travel card on trains, subways and in shops.

Most foreign **3G models** will work in Japan – contact your mobile phone service provider before leaving your home country. Visitors can **buy data-only SIM cards** easily, as long as their phones are unlocked; you can get a 30-day card for ¥2650 at Yodobashi Camera, which has branches nationwide. Another solution for short-term visitors is to **rent** a phone (buying a prepaid phone in Japan generally requires you to show proof of local residency) at the airport, in Tokyo or online; options

include PuPuRu (ⓦwww.pupuru.com/en) and B-Mobile (ⓦwww.bmobile.ne.jp/english), who both also rent out data cards for Internet access on your laptop. Other mobile phone operators include the predominant **DoCoMo** (ⓦwww.nttdocomo.co.jp), and **Softbank** (ⓦsoftbank.jp/en), both of which have rental booths at the major airports.

Post

Japan's **mail** service is highly efficient and fast, with **post offices** (*yūbinkyoku*) all over the country, easily identified by their red-and-white signs – a T with a parallel bar across the top, the same symbol that you'll find on the red letterboxes. All post can be addressed in Western script (*rōmaji*), provided it's clearly printed.

In urban post offices there are separate counters, with English signs, for postal and banking services. If you need to send bulkier items or **parcels** back home, you can get reasonably priced special envelopes and boxes for packaging from any post office. The maximum weight for an overseas parcel is 30kg (less for some destinations). A good compromise between expensive airmail and slow sea mail is Surface Air Lifted (SAL) mail, which takes around three weeks to reach most destinations, and costs somewhere between the two. For English-language information about postal services, including postal fees, see the Post Office website (ⓦpost.japanpost.jp).

Central post offices generally **open** Monday–Friday 9am–7pm, Saturday 9am–5pm and Sunday 9am–12.30pm, with most other branches opening Monday–Friday 9am–5pm only. A few larger branches may also open on a Saturday from 9am to 3pm, and may operate after-hours services for parcels and express mail.

For sending parcels and baggage around Japan, take advantage of the excellent, inexpensive *takuhaibin* (or *takkyūbin*, as it's more commonly known) or **courier delivery services**, which can be arranged at most convenience stores, hotels and some youth hostels. These services – which typically cost under ¥2000 – are especially handy if you want to send luggage (usually up to 20kg) on to places where you'll be staying later in your journey or to the airport to be picked up prior to your departure.

Smoking

Many visitors to Japan are quite taken aback by how much smoke they're forced to inhale on a daily basis – notoriously conservative at the best of times, the country has, so far, failed to move with developed-nation norms in such regards. **Smoking** is banned on nearly all public transport (you'll find smoking rooms and carriages on some trains, though) and in most public buildings, shops and offices; in restaurants, bars, *izakaya*, cafés and even some hotel lobbies, however, you're likely to be inhaling smoke. An increasing number of cities are clamping down on smoking in the street, though smokers can light up in designated areas – look for the smoke-swathed huddle around the pavement ashtrays. Fines for smoking where it's prohibited typically start at ¥2000, though at the moment you are more likely to get away with a warning.

Time

The whole of Japan is nine hours ahead of Greenwich Mean Time, so at noon in London it's 9pm in Tokyo. Japan is fourteen hours ahead of Eastern Standard Time in the US. There is no daylight saving, so during British Summer Time, for example, the difference drops to eight hours.

Tipping

Tipping is not expected in Japan (the exception being upmarket Western restaurants and top hotels, which may add a service charge, typically ten percent). If someone's been particularly helpful, the best approach is to give a small present, or offer some money discreetly in an envelope.

Tourist information

The **Japan National Tourism Organization** (JNTO; ⓦ jnto.go.jp) maintains a number of overseas offices (see below). Within Japan, JNTO operates **Tourist Information Centres** (TIC), all of which have English-speaking staff, in central Tokyo (see p.133), Tokyo's Narita and Haneda airports (see p.130) and Kansai International Airport (see p.448). Though staff will help sort out routes and timetables, they can't make travel reservations or usually sell tickets to theatres, cinemas and so on; instead, they'll direct you to the nearest appropriate outlet.

There is a network of government-run **tourist information offices** (観光案内所; *kankō annaijo*), many with English-speaking staff, in all major towns and cities and in the prime tourist destinations; you'll find a full list on the JNTO website. These offices are usually located in or close to the main train station or in the city centre; look out for the signs. In practice, the amount of English information available – whether written or spoken – is a bit hit and miss, but staff should be able to assist with local maps, hotel reservations and simple queries. There are also ordinary local tourist information offices: practically every town has these, though there's only a slim chance of getting English-language assistance.

JNTO OFFICES ABROAD

Australia Suite 1, Level 4, 56 Clarence St, Sydney (☎ 02 9279 2177, ⓦ jnto.org.au).

GOODWILL GUIDES

A useful source of English-language information is the **Goodwill Guides**, groups of volunteer guides, mostly in central and western Japan, who offer their services free – although you're expected to pay for their transport, entry tickets and any meals you have together. Their language abilities vary, but they do provide a great opportunity to learn more about Japanese culture and to visit local restaurants, shops and so forth with a Japanese-speaker. You'll find the groups listed on the JNTO website, ⓦ jnto.go.jp. Otherwise, tourist information offices can usually provide contact details of local groups and may be willing to help with arrangements; try to give at least two days' notice.

Canada 481 University Ave, Suite 306, Toronto (☎ 416 366 7140, ⓦ ilovejapan.ca).

UK 5th Floor, 12/13 Nicholas Lane, London (☎ 020 7398 5670, ⓦ seejapan.co.uk).

US 11 West 42nd St, 19th Floor, New York (☎ 212 757 5640, ⓦ japantravelinfo.com); 340 E. 2nd St, Little Tokyo Plaza, Suite 302, Los Angeles (☎ 213 623 1952).

Travellers with disabilities

Disability has always been something of an uncomfortable topic in Japan, with disabled people generally hidden from public view. In recent years, however, there has been a certain shift in public opinion, particularly in the wake of the bestseller *No One's Perfect* by Ototake Hirotada (2003), the upbeat, forthright autobiography of a 23-year-old student born without arms or legs.

The government is spearheading a drive to provide more accessible hotels and other facilities (referred to as "barrier-free" in Japan). Most train and subway **stations** now have an extra-wide manned ticket gate and an increasing number have escalators or lifts. Some **trains**, such as the Narita Express from Narita International Airport into Tokyo, have spaces for wheelchair users, but you should reserve well in advance. For travelling short distances, **taxis** are an obvious solution, though none is specially adapted and few drivers will offer passengers help getting in or out of the car.

New **hotels** are required to provide accessible facilities and several older ones are making them available, too. Your best bet is one of the international chains or modern Western-style business hotels, which are most likely to provide fully adapted rooms, ramps and lifts; check ahead to ensure the facilities meet your requirements. Similarly, most modern shopping complexes, museums and other public buildings are equipped with ramps, wide doors and accessible toilets.

But although things are improving, Japan is not an easy place to get around for anyone using a wheelchair, or for those who find it difficult to negotiate stairs or walk long distances. In cities, the sheer crush of people can also be a problem at times. Although it's usually possible to organize assistance at stations, you'll need a Japanese-speaker to phone ahead and make the arrangements. For further information and help, contact the **Japanese Red Cross Language Service Volunteers** (c/o Volunteers Division, Japanese Red Cross Society, 1-1-3 Shiba Daimon, Minato-ku, Tokyo 105-8521). You'll find useful, if slightly outdated, information on their website, ⓦ accessible.jp.org.

Tokyo

東京

TOKYO SKYTREE AND THE SUMIDA-GAWA

1

Tokyo

With its sushi and sumo, geisha and gardens, neon and noodles, it may seem that Tokyo is in danger of collapsing under the weight of its own stereotypes. Yet ticking off a bunch of travel clichés is rarely this much fun, and as you might expect of the planet's largest metropolis, there's also enough nuance here to keep you entertained for a lifetime. Ordered yet bewildering, Japan's pulsating capital will lead you a merry dance: this is Asia at its weirdest, straightest, prettiest, sleaziest and coolest, all at the same time.

Caught up in an untidy web of overhead cables, plagued by seemingly incessant noise, the concrete and steel conurbation may seem the stereotypical urban nightmare. Yet step back from the frenetic main roads and chances are you'll find yourself in tranquil backstreets, where dinky **wooden houses** are fronted by neatly clipped bonsai trees. Wander beyond the hi-tech emporia, and you'll discover charming fragments of the old city such as **temples** and **shrines** wreathed in wisps of smoking incense.

Centuries of organizing itself around the daily demands of millions of inhabitants have made Tokyo something of a **model metropolitan environment**. Trains run on time and to practically every corner of the city, **crime** is hardly worth worrying about, and shops and vending machines provide everything you could need (and many things you never thought you did) 24 hours a day.

With so much going on, just walking the streets of this hyperactive city can be an energizing experience. It need not be an expensive one, either. You'll be pleasantly surprised by how **affordable** many things are. Cheap-and-cheerful *izakaya* – bars that serve food – and casual cafés serving noodles and rice dishes are plentiful, the metro is a bargain, and tickets for a sumo tournament or a kabuki play can be bought for the price of a few drinks.

Browsing the **shops** and marvelling at the passing parade is mesmerizing – the next best thing to having a ringside seat at the hippest of catwalk shows. The city's great

KABUKICHŌ, SHINJUKU

Highlights

❶ Asakusa Bustling Sensō-ji temple is at the heart of Tokyo's most colourful and evocative district, packed with craft shops, traditional inns and restaurants. **See p.99**

❷ Roppongi Art Triangle Tokyo's art scene is the envy of the rest of Asia – for a primer, make a hop between the three major galleries constituting the "Art Triangle". **See p.108**

❸ Meiji-jingū Escape the urban clamour amid the verdant grounds of the city's most venerable Shintō shrine. **See p.117**

❹ Harajuku Packed with boutiques, cafés and trendy brunch spots, this youthful area is a breeding ground for the Japanese fashions of

tomorrow – and those too strange ever to hit the mainstream. **See p.117**

❺ Shinjuku Tokyo in microcosm, from the tiny bars of Golden Gai to the Gotham City-like Tokyo Metropolitan Government Building. **See p.123**

❻ Ghibli Museum Most visitors will have seen at least one Studio Ghibli anime – get behind the scenes at this imaginative museum. **See box, p.126**

❼ Sky restaurants Many of Tokyo's tallest towers are topped with restaurants: head to Hibiki or Hokkaidō for prime views of this famously high-rise city. **See p.142 & p.147**

HIGHLIGHTS ARE MARKED ON THE MAP ON PP.82–83

1

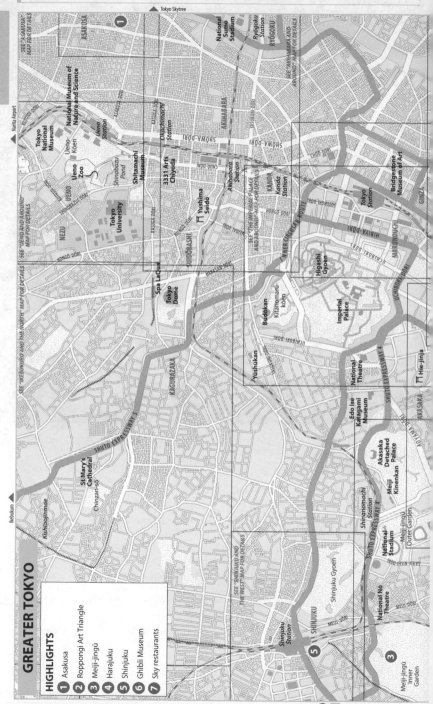

Tokyo Skytree

GREATER TOKYO

HIGHLIGHTS

1 Asakusa
2 Roppongi Art Triangle
3 Meiji-jingū
4 Harajuku
5 Shinjuku
6 Ghibli Museum
7 Sky restaurants

Narita Airport

Ikebukuro

SEE "ASAKUSA" MAP FOR DETAILS

ASAKUSA

National Sumo Stadium

Ryōgoku Station

RYŌGOKU

SEE "AKIHABARA AND AROUND" MAP FOR DETAILS

National Museum of Nature and Science

Tokyo National Museum

Ueno-Kōen

Ueno Station

Ueno Zoo

Shinobazu Pond

Shitamachi Museum

3331 Arts Chiyoda

Okachimachi Station

AKIHABARA

SHOWA-DORI

SHOWA-DORI

Akihabara Station

Bridgestone Museum of Art

GINZA

SEE "UENO AND AROUND" MAP FOR DETAILS

NEZU

UENO

Tokyo University

Yushima Seidō

KANDA

Kanda Station

Tokyo Station

MARUNOUCHI

HIBIYA-DORI

SEE "IKEBUKURO AND THE NORTH" MAP FOR DETAILS

Spa LaQua

SUIDŌBASHI

SEE "THE IMPERIAL PALACE AND AROUND" MAP FOR DETAILS

INNER CIRCULAR ROUTE

Higashi Gyoen

Tokyo Dome

Budōkan

Kitanomaru-kōen

Imperial Palace

UCHIBORI-DORI

KAGURAZAKA

Yūshūkan

National Theatre

Hie-jinja

AKASAKA

SHUTO EXPRESSWAY 4

St Mary's Cathedral

Chinzan-sō

SHUTO EXPRESSWAY

Edo Isei Kataçami Museum

Akasaka Detached Palace

Kishibojinmae

Meiji Kinenkan

Shinanomachi Station

Meiji-jingū Outer Garden

National Stadium

GAIEN-NISHI-DORI

SEE "SHINJUKU AND THE WEST" MAP FOR DETAILS

Shinjuku Gyoen

SHINJUKU

National Nō Theatre

MEIJI-DORI

Shinjuku Station

5

MEIJI-DORI

3

Meiji-jingū Inner Garden

9

1

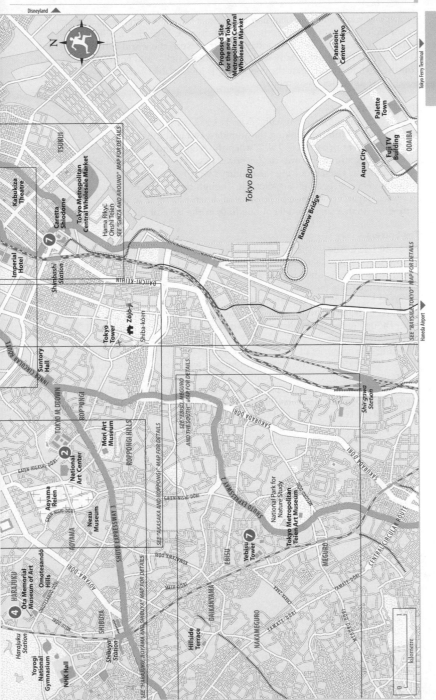

Disneyland ▲

N

Proposed Site for the new Tokyo Metropolitan Central Wholesale Market

Panasonic Center Tokyo

Tokyo Ferry Terminal ▶

Palette Town

Aqua City

Fuji TV Building

ODAIBA

Tokyo Bay

Rainbow Bridge

TSUKIJI

Kabukiza Theatre

Caretta Shiodome

Tokyo Metropolitan Central Wholesale Market

Hama Rikyū Onshi Teien
SEE "GINZA AND AROUND" MAP FOR DETAILS

Imperial Hotel

Shimbashi Station

DAIICHI-KEIHIN

SEE "BAYSIDE TOKYO" MAP FOR DETAILS ▶

Haneda Airport ▶

Suntory Hall

Zōjō-ji

Tokyo Tower

Shiba-kōen

SOTO CIRCULAR ROUTE

TOKYO MIDTOWN

ROPPONGI

Mori Art Museum

National Art Center

ROPPONGI HILLS

GAIEN-HIGASHI-DŌRI

SEE "EBISU, MEGURO AND THE SOUTH" MAP FOR DETAILS

SAKURADA-DŌRI

Shirokawa Station

Aoyama Reien

Nezu Museum

AOYAMA

GAIEN-NISHI-DŌRI

SHUTO EXPRESSWAY 3

SEE "AKASAKA AND ROPPONGI" MAP FOR DETAILS

KOMAZAWA-DŌRI

National Park for Nature Study

Tokyo Metropolitan Teien Art Museum

MEGURO

SAKURADA-DŌRI

HARAJUKU

Ota Memorial Museum of Art

Omotesandō Hills

OMOTESANDŌ-DŌRI

AOYAMA-DŌRI

MEIJI-DŌRI

SEE "HARAJUKU, AOYAMA AND SHIBUYA" MAP FOR DETAILS

EBISU

Yebisu Tower

DAIKANYAMA

MEIJI-DŌRI

NAKAMEGURO

YAMATE-DŌRI

MEGURO-DŌRI

CENTRAL CIRCULAR ROUTE

Harajuku Station

Yoyogi National Gymnasium

NHK Hall

Shibuya Station

SHIBUYA

Hillside Terrace

YAMATE-DŌRI

0   kilometre   1

1

wealth and relative lack of planning restrictions have given **architects** almost unparalleled freedom to realize their wildest dreams. Likewise, in über-chic bars, restaurants and clubs you'll see today what the rest of the world will get tomorrow. You may not figure out exactly what makes Tokyo tick – and you're sure to get a little confused while trying – but the conclusion is inescapable: Japan's powerhouse capital is a seductive and addictive experience.

Brief history

The city's founding date is usually given as 1457, when minor lord Ōta Dōkan built his castle on a bluff overlooking the Sumida-gawa and the bay. However, a far more significant event occurred in 1590, when the feudal lord **Tokugawa Ieyasu** (see p.825) chose the obscure castle town for his power base. He seized control of the whole of Japan ten years later, reuniting the country's warring clans and taking the title of **shogun** – effectively a military dictator. Though the emperor continued to hold court in Kyoto, Japan's real centre of power would henceforth lie in Edo, at this point still little more than a small huddle of buildings at the edge of the Hibiya inlet.

The Edo era

By 1640 **Edo Castle** was the most imposing in all Japan, complete with a five-storey central keep, a double moat and a spiralling network of canals. The *daimyō* (feudal lords), who were required by the shogun to spend part of each year in Edo, were granted large plots for their estates on the higher ground to the west of the castle, an area that became known as **Yamanote**. Artisans, merchants and other lower classes were confined to **Shitamachi** (literally, "low town"), a low-lying, overcrowded region to the east. Though growing less distinct, this division between the "high" and "low" city is still apparent today.

During two centuries of peace, when Edo grew to be the most populous city in the world, life down in the Shitamachi buzzed with a wealthy merchant class and a vigorous, often bawdy, subculture of geisha and kabuki, of summer days on the Sumida-gawa, moon-viewing parties and picnics under the spring blossom. Inevitably, there was also squalor, poverty and violence, as well as frequent fires; in January 1657, the **Fire of the Long Sleeves** laid waste to three-quarters of the city's buildings and killed an estimated 100,000 people. This came just after Japan adopted a policy of national seclusion, which was to last for over 200 years.

The Meiji era

In 1853, Commodore Matthew Perry of the US Navy landed just west of Tokyo with a small fleet of **"Black Ships"**, demanding that Japan open at least some of its ports to foreigners. A year after the subsequent **Meiji Restoration**, in 1868 (see p.827), the emperor took up permanent residence in the city, now renamed **Tokyo** (Eastern Capital) in recognition of its proper status. As Japan quickly embraced Western technologies, the face of Tokyo gradually changed: the castle lost much of its grounds, canals were filled in or built over, and Shitamachi's wealthier merchants decamped to more desirable Yamanote. In addition, brick buildings, electric lights, trams, trains and then cars all made their first appearance in Tokyo around this time.

The twentieth century

The city remained disaster-prone: in 1923 the **Great Kantō Earthquake** devastated half of Tokyo and 100,000 people perished. More trauma was to come during **World War II**. In just three days of sustained incendiary bombing in March 1945, hundreds of thousands were killed and great swathes of the city burnt down, including Meiji-jingū, Sensō-ji, Edo Castle and most of Shitamachi. From a prewar population of nearly seven million, Tokyo was reduced to around three million people in a state of near-starvation. This time, regeneration was fuelled by an influx of American dollars

TOKYO ORIENTATION

Tokyo is even bigger than you might think – technically, it spreads from the mountains in the north and west to a chain of tropical islands some 1300km away in the south. However, as a visitor you're unlikely to stray beyond its most central municipalities, or wards (*ku* in Japanese); a useful reference point is the **Yamanote line**, an overland train loop that encloses the city centre and connects most places of interest to visitors.

At the very centre of Tokyo sits the **Imperial Palace** (see p.85), the city's spiritual heart. East of here, the wider **Ginza** district (see p.90) forms the heart of downtown Tokyo, functioning as its main shopping and financial centre. Just to the north lies **Akihabara** (see p.93), a tech-lover's paradise and home to most of the city's famed maid cafés; north again, the parks, museums and zoo in **Ueno** (see p.96) make for a great day out. East towards the river, spellbinding **Asakusa** (see p.99) is Tokyo's most traditional district, with temples and craft shops at every turn. A boat ride down the Sumida-gawa will bring you to **Bayside Tokyo** (see p.102), where skyscraper-filled islands rise from the sea. Back inland are the neighbouring disticts of **Akasaka** (see p.108) and **Roppongi** (see p.108), the latter particularly notable for its galleries and nightlife. South of central Tokyo, **Ebisu** (see p.113) is home to some of the city's main hipster hangouts; north of here the action takes a turn for the hectic in **Harajuku**, **Aoyama** and **Shibuya** (see p.116), before going all *Blade Runner* in **Shinjuku** (see p.123), the very epitome of rushed-off-its-feet Tokyo. Lastly, north of the centre is the busy **Ikebukuro** district (see p.127), with some diverting nearby sights.

and food aid under the Allied Occupation, plus a manufacturing boom sparked by the Korean War in 1950.

By the time Emperor Hirohito opened the Tokyo **Olympic Games** in October 1964, Tokyo was truly back on its feet and visitors were wowed by the stunning new Shinkansen trains running west to Osaka. The economy boomed well into the late 1980s, when Tokyo land prices reached dizzying heights, matched by excesses of every conceivable sort.

In 1991, **the financial bubble** burst. This, along with revelations of political corruption, financial mismanagement and the release of deadly Sarin gas on Tokyo commuter trains by the AUM cult in 1995 (see p.831), led to a more sober Tokyo in the late 1990s.

Tokyo today

In the new millennium, as the economy recovered, so did the city's vitality. Events such as the 2002 World Cup, growing interest in Japanese **pop culture** and the thriving food scene have contributed to more curious overseas visitors heading to Tokyo, with some staying on, making the capital feel more cosmopolitan than ever before. District after district has undergone a structural makeover, starting with Roppongi and Shiodome back in 2003. One of the latest mega-developments is at Oshiage east of the Sumida-gawa, where the **Tokyo Skytree** (see p.102) is Japan's tallest structure; expect another great glut of building in the run-up to the **2020 Olympic Games**.

The Imperial Palace and around

A vast chunk of central Tokyo is occupied by the **Imperial Palace**, home to the emperor and his family. The surrounding public **gardens** provide a gentle introduction to the city, giving a glimpse of its origins as a castle town. The most attractive of these is **Higashi Gyoen**, where remnants of the seventeenth-century Edo Castle still stand amid formal gardens, while to its north **Kitanomaru-kōen** is a more natural park containing the excellent **National Museum of Modern Art**. Just outside the park's northern perimeter, the nation's war dead are remembered at the controversial shrine of **Yasukuni-jinja**.

1

East of the palace, **Marunouchi** has enjoyed a stylish reinvention of late, with the opening of several new shopping and restaurant complexes, and the recent redevelopment of **Tokyo Station** and its environs. To the south is **Yūrakuchō**, which – like Marunouchi – is home to theatres, airline offices, banks and corporate headquarters; and the adjoining district of **Hibiya**, centred around a Western-style park.

The Imperial Palace

皇居, Kōkyo • Entrance off Uchibori-dōri • Access to grounds by official tour only; apply online and bring your passport • Mon–Fri 10am & 1.30pm • 75min • Free • ☎ 03 3213 1111, ⓦ sankan.kunaicho.go.jp • Sakuradamon or Nijūbashimae stations

Huge and windswept, the Imperial Plaza forms a protective island in front of the modern **Imperial Palace**, the site of which is as old as Tokyo itself. Edo Castle was built here by Ōta Dōkan in 1457 (see p.825), and its boundaries fluctuated through the following centuries; at its greatest extent, the castle walls also surrounded what is now Tokyo Station, as well as parts of present-day Marunouchi.

Follow the groups of local tourists straggling across the broad avenues to **Nijūbashi**, one of the palace's most photogenic corners, where two bridges span the moat and a

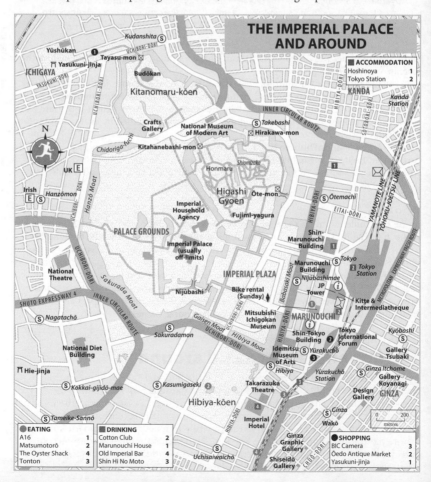

THE IMPERIAL PALACE AND AROUND

DESCENDANTS OF THE SUN GODDESS

Emperor Akihito, the 125th incumbent of the Chrysanthemum Throne, traces his ancestry back to 660 BC and Emperor Jimmu, great-great-grandson of the mythological Sun Goddess Amaterasu. Most scholars, however, acknowledge that the first emperor for whom there is any historical evidence is the fifth-century Emperor Ojin.

Until the twentieth century, emperors were regarded as living deities whom ordinary folk were forbidden to set eyes on, or even hear. Japan's defeat in World War II ended all that and today the emperor is a symbolic figure, a head of state with no governmental power. While he was crown prince, **Emperor Akihito** had an American tutor and studied at Tokyo's elite Gakushūin University, followed by a stint at Oxford University. In 1959 he broke further with tradition by marrying a commoner, **Shōda Michiko**.

Following in his father's footsteps, **Crown Prince Naruhito** married high-flying Harvard-educated diplomat Owada Masako in 1993. The intense press scrutiny that the couple came under when they failed to produce a male heir (current laws prohibit a female succession) has been cited as one of the reasons for the princess's miscarriage in 1999. Two years later the crown princess gave birth to a baby girl, **Aiko**, but has barely been seen in public since, suffering from a variety of stress-related illnesses. One piece of good news for the royal succession is that Princess Kiko, wife of Naruhito's younger brother, gave birth to a boy, Hisahito, in 2006; the young prince is third in line for the throne after his uncle and father, though he may, in fact become second in line before too long – in August 2016, Akihito gave only his second-ever televised address, mentioning his health problems and advancing age, and hinting at an extremely rare Japanese abdication.

jaunty little watchtower perches on its grey stone pedestal beyond. Though this double bridge is a late nineteenth-century embellishment, the tower dates back to the seventeenth century and is one of the castle's few original structures.

Except for the two days a year when Nijūbashi can be crossed (on December 23 – the emperor's birthday – and on January 2), admission to the **palace grounds** is possible only on pre-arranged **official tours**, conducted in Japanese but with English-language brochures and audio guides available. The present-day incarnation of the palace is a long, sleek, 1960s structure, built to replace the nineteenth-century Meiji palace building, which burnt down in the 1945 bombing raids.

Higashi Gyoen

東御苑 • East entrance off Uchibori-dōri, north entrance opposite National Museum of Modern Art • Tues–Thurs, Sat & Sun 9am–4pm (closed occasionally for court functions) • Free token available at park entrance; hand back on exit • Ōtemachi or Takebashi stations

Though there's little to evoke the former glory of the shogunate's castle beyond some formidable gates and towering granite walls, **Higashi Gyoen** (East Garden) is a good place for a stroll. You'll likely enter via **Ōte-mon**, the eastern gate to the garden – and formerly to Edo Castle itself. At the southern end of the garden lies its finest remaining watchtower, the three-tiered **Fujimi-yagura**, built in 1659 to protect the citadel's southern flank. From here, a path winds gently up, beneath the walls of the main citadel, and then climbs more steeply towards **Shiomizaka**, the "Tide-Viewing Slope", from where it was once possible to gaze out over Edo Bay. You emerge on a flat grassy area, empty apart from the stone foundations of **Honmaru** (the "inner citadel"), with fine views from the top.

Kitanomaru-kōen

北の丸公園 • North entrance off Yasukuni-dōri • 24hr • Free • Kudanshita or Takebashi stations

Edo Castle's old northern citadel is now occupied by the park of **Kitanomaru-kōen**. With its ninety-odd cherry trees, it's a popular viewing spot come *hanami* time, while rowing boats can be rented in warmer months on **Chidoriga-fuchi**, an ancient pond

1

once incorporated into Edo Castle's moat. These natural pleasures aside, the park is also home to a couple of interesting museums and the Budōkan arena (see p.166).

National Museum of Modern Art

国立近代美術館, Kokuritsu Kindai Bijutsukan • Tues–Sun 10am–5pm, Fri until 8pm • ¥1000; extra fees apply for special exhibitions • ☎ 03 5777 8600, ⓦ www.momat.go.jp

Located on the southern perimeter of the park is the **National Museum of Modern Art**. Strewn over three large levels, its excellent permanent collection showcases Japanese art since 1900, as well as a few pieces of work from overseas; the former includes Gyokudo Kawai's magnificent screen painting *Parting Spring* and works by Kishida Ryūsei, Fujita Tsuguharu and postwar artists such as Yoshihara Jirō. On the fourth floor you'll find the earliest works, as well as a resting area with fantastic views over the moat and palace grounds.

Crafts Gallery

工芸館, Kōgeikan • Daily 10am–5pm • ¥210; usually ¥550 for special exhibitions • ☎ 03 5777 8600, ⓦ www.momat.go.jp

Tucked away on the west side of Kitanomaru-kōen, the **Crafts Gallery** exhibits a selection of top-quality traditional Japanese craft works, many by modern masters. Erected in 1910 as the headquarters of the Imperial Guards, this neo-Gothic red-brick pile is one of very few Tokyo buildings dating from before the Great Earthquake of 1923 – it looks like the kind of place Harry Potter would have gone to school, had he been Japanese.

Yasukuni-jinja

靖国神社 • Entrance off Yasukuni-dōri • Daily 6am–6pm • Free • ⓦ www.yasukuni.or.jp • Kudanshita or Ichigaya stations

A monumental red steel *torii*, claimed to be Japan's tallest, marks the entrance to **Yasukuni-jinja**. This shrine, whose name means "for the repose of the country", was founded in 1869 to worship supporters of the emperor killed in the run-up to the Meiji Restoration. Since then it has expanded to include the legions sacrificed in subsequent wars, in total nearly 2.5 million souls, of whom some two million died in the Pacific War alone; the parting words of kamikaze pilots were said to be "see you at Yasukuni". Every year some eight million Japanese visit this shrine, which controversially includes several war criminals (see box below).

Standing at the end of a long avenue lined with cherry and ginkgo trees and accessed through a simple wooden gate, the architecture is classic Shintō styling, solid and unadorned except for two gold imperial chrysanthemums embossed on the main doors.

THE PROBLEM WITH YASUKUNI

Ever since its foundation as part of a Shintō revival promoting the new emperor, **Yasukuni-jinja** has been a place of high controversy. In its early years the shrine became a natural focus for the increasingly aggressive nationalism that ultimately took Japan to war in 1941. Then, in 1978, General Tōjō, prime minister during World War II, and thirteen other "Class A" **war criminals** were enshrined here, to be honoured along with all the other military dead. Japan's neighbours, still smarting from their treatment by the Japanese during the war, were outraged.

This has not stopped top politicians from visiting Yasukuni on the anniversary of Japan's defeat in World War II (August 15). Because Japan's postwar constitution requires the separation of state and religion, ministers have usually maintained that they attend as private individuals, but in 1985 Nakasone, in typically uncompromising mood, caused uproar when he signed the visitors' book as "Prime Minister". Recent PMs have continued to visit Yasukuni – always in an "unofficial" capacity – despite continued protests both at home and abroad.

Yūshūkan

遊就館 • Daily 9am–5pm • ¥800 • ☎ 03 3261 8326

To the right of the inner shrine you'll find the **Yūshūkan**, a military museum established in 1882. The displays are well presented, but the intrigue lies as much in what is left out as in what is included. Events such as the Nanking Massacre ("Incident" in Japanese) and other atrocities by Japanese troops are glossed over, while the Pacific War is presented as a war of liberation, freeing the peoples of Southeast Asia from Western colonialism. The most moving displays are the ranks of faded photographs and the "bride dolls" donated by the families of young soldiers who died before they were married. You exit through a hall full of military hardware, including a replica of the glider used by kamikaze pilots on their suicide missions, its nose elongated to carry a 1200kg bomb, while a spine-chilling, black *kaiten* (manned torpedo) lours to one side.

Marunouchi

丸の内

Due north of Ginza, the business-focused **MARUNOUCHI** district has lately been transformed from a dull stretch of offices to a dynamic, tourist-friendly location. A major programme of construction and development – including the restoration of Tokyo Station's original handsome red-brick structure, has added swish shopping plazas, restaurants and cafés to the area.

Mitsubishi Ichigōkan Museum

三菱一号館美術館, Mitsubishi Ichigōkan Bijutsukan • 2-6-2 Marunouchi, Chiyoda-ku • Daily 10am–6pm, Fri until 8pm • Price depends on exhibition – usually ¥1600, with ¥200 discount to foreign tourists with ID • ☎ 03 5405 8686, ⓦ mimt.jp • Tokyo or Nijūbashimae stations

Worth a look for its design as much as its contents, the **Mitsubishi Ichigōkan Museum** is housed in a meticulous reconstruction of a red-brick office block designed by British architect Josiah Conder; the original was erected on the same site in 1894, only to be demolished in 1968. Exhibitions rotate every four months or so, and almost exclusively focus on nineteenth-century European art, usually of a pretty high calibre.

Intermediatheque

インターメディアテク • 2-3F Kitte Building, 2-7-2 Marunouchi, Chiyoda-ku • Mon–Thurs & Sun 11am–6pm, Fri & Sat 11am–8pm; closed a few days per month • Free • ☎ 03 5777 8600, ⓦ intermediatheque.jp • Tokyo Station

The double-level **Intermediatheque** is, without doubt, one of the most intriguing museum spaces in the city, hosting exhibitions that are sharply curated and pieced together with a rare attention to aesthetic detail. The permanent exhibition is a well-presented mishmash of various objects of scientific and cultural heritage accumulated by the University of Tokyo; the animal skeletons are the most eye-catching exhibits, but poke around and you'll find everything from Central American headwear to objects damaged by the nuclear explosions in Nagasaki.

Yūrakuchō and Hibiya

有楽町・日比谷

South of Marunouchi lies **Yūrakuchō**, a high-rise district that's home to yet more giant pieces of urban furniture. Most notable is the arresting **Tokyo International Forum**, a stunning creation by American architect Rafael Viñoly, which hosts concerts and conventions. Head south from Yūrakuchō and you'll soon be in the **Hibiya** district, highlight of which is Tokyo's first European-style park, **Hibiya-kōen** (日比谷公園), a refreshing oasis of greenery.

1 **Idemitsu Museum of Arts**

出光美術館, Idemitsu Bijutsukan • 9F Teigeki Building, 3-1-1 Marunouchi, Chiyoda-ku • Tues–Sun 10am–5pm, Fri until 7pm • ¥1000 • ☎ 03 5777 8600, ⓦ idemitsu.com/museum • Hibiya or Yūrakuchō stations

Sitting above the Imperial Theatre, the **Idemitsu Museum of Arts** houses a magnificent collection of mostly Japanese art, though only a tiny proportion is on show at any one time. Its historically important pieces range from early Jōmon (10,000 BC–300 BC) pottery to late seventeenth-century *ukiyo-e* paintings.

Ginza and around

Although now a couple of decades past its heyday, **Ginza**'s glut of luxury malls and flagship stores remains the envy of Tokyo; umpteen bars, restaurants and cafés still reverberate with distinct echoes of the "bubble period", a time in which Tokyo itself was the envy of the rest of the world. Factor in a sprinkling of great museums and galleries, and the sights of the neighbouring districts of **Nihombashi** and **Shiodome**, and you're set for the day.

Ginza

銀座

GINZA, the "place where silver is minted", took its name after Shogun Tokugawa Ieyasu started making coins here in the early 1600s. It was a happy association – one street, Chūō-dōri, grew to become Tokyo's most stylish shopping thoroughfare. Though some of its shine has faded and cutting-edge fashion has moved elsewhere, Ginza still retains much of its elegance and undoubted snob appeal. Here you'll find the greatest concentration of exclusive shops and restaurants in the city, the most theatres and cinemas, branches of major department stores and a fair number of art galleries (see box below).

Chūō-dōri is the main shopping street, while **Harumi-dōri** cuts across the centre from the east. The two roads meet at a famed intersection known as **Ginza Yon-chōme crossing**, which marks the heart of Ginza: awesome at rush hour, this spot often features in films and documentaries as the epitome of this overcrowded yet totally efficient city.

ON THE ART TRAIL IN GINZA

Though a little short on tourist sights, Ginza is the bastion of Tokyo's commercial galleries – there are enough of them here to keep you busy for a full day.

Design Gallery 3-6-1 Ginza, Chūō-ku ☎ 03 3571 5206; Ginza Station. Hidden up on the seventh floor of the Matsuya Ginza department store, this gallery may be tiny, but shows are usually curated by Japan's top designers. The adjacent Design Collection retail area stocks the very best in product design. Mon & Tues 10am–7.30pm, Thurs–Sun 10am–8pm.

Ginza Graphic Gallery 7-7-2 Ginza, Chūō-ku ☎ 03 3571 5206; ⓦ www.dnp.co.jp/gallery/ggg; Ginza Station. Single-room space hosting monthly exhibitions that cover – for the most part – graphic design work from the best of Japan's creators. Closes for a few days between shows. Mon–Fri 11am–7pm, Sat 11am–6pm.

Maison Hermès 8F 5-4-1 Ginza, Chūō-ku ☎ 03 3569 3611; Ginza Station. Possibly the most charming gallery space in all Tokyo, set at the top of the Renzo Piano-designed "bubble-wrap" building that's home to Hermès' Tokyo boutique. Worth a look whatever the exhibit – the gallery usually hosts themed shows of Japanese and international art. Daily 11am–7pm.

Shiseidō Gallery B1F 8-8-3 Ginza, Chūō-ku ☎ 03 3572 3901, ⓦ group.shiseido.co.jp/gallery; Shimbashi or Ginza stations. Located in the distinctive red showroom of the eponymous Japanese cosmetics giant, this small basement gallery hosts group and solo shows – some well worth a look, others merely so-so. Tues–Sat 11am–7pm, Sun 11am–6pm.

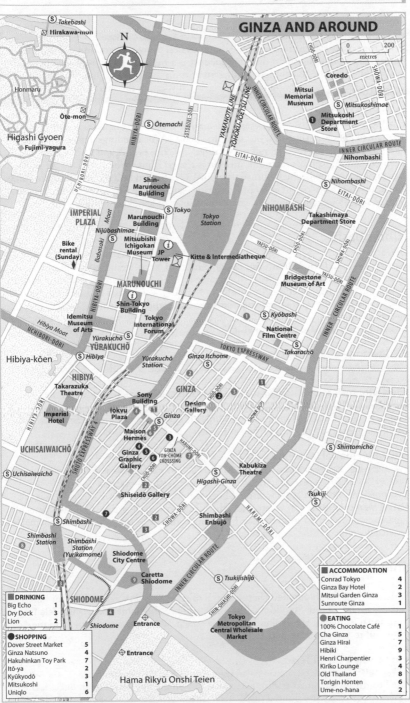

GINZA AND AROUND

Takebashi
Hirakawa-mon

Honmaru

Higashi Gyoen
Fujimi-yagura

Ōte-mon

Ōtemachi

Coredo

Mitsui Memorial Museum

Mitsukoshimae

Mitsukoshi Department Store

Nihombashi

Nihombashi

NIHOMBASHI

Shin-Marunouchi Building

IMPERIAL PLAZA

Nijūbashimae

Bike rental (Sunday)

Marunouchi Building

Mitsubishi Ichigokan Museum

Babasaki

Moat

Tokyo

Tokyo Station

JP Tower

Kitte & Intermediatheque

Takashimaya Department Store

Bridgestone Museum of Art

MARUNOUCHI

Idemitsu Museum of Arts

Shin-Tokyo Building

Tokyo International Forum

Kyōbashi

National Film Centre

Takarachō

Hibiya Moat

UCHIBORI-DŌRI

Yūrakuchō

YŪRAKUCHŌ

Hibiya

Yūrakuchō Station

TOKYO EXPRESSWAY

Ginza Itchome

Hibiya-kōen

HIBIYA

Takarazuka Theatre

GINZA

Sony Building

Imperial Hotel

Tōkyū Plaza

Design Gallery

Ginza

UCHISAIWAICHŌ

Maison Hermès

Ginza Graphic Gallery

GINZA YON-CHŌME CROSSSING

Shintomicho

Uchisaiwaichō

Shiseidō Gallery

Higashi-Ginza

Kabukiza Theatre

Tsukiji

Shimbashi

Shimbashi Station

Shimbashi Station (Yurikamome)

Shimbashi Enbujō

SHOWA-DŌRI

HARUMI-DŌRI

Shiodome City Centre

SHIODOME

Caretta Shiodome

Tsukijishijō

Shiodome

Entrance

Tokyo Metropolitan Central Wholesale Market

Entrance

Hama Rikyū Onshi Teien

DRINKING
Big Echo	1
Dry Dock	3
Lion	2

SHOPPING
Dover Street Market	5
Ginza Natsuno	4
Hakuhinkan Toy Park	7
Itō-ya	2
Kyūkyodō	3
Mitsukoshi	1
Uniqlo	6

ACCOMMODATION
Conrad Tokyo	4
Ginza Bay Hotel	2
Mitsui Garden Ginza	3
Sunroute Ginza	1

EATING
100% Chocolate Café	1
Cha Ginza	5
Ginza Hirai	7
Hibiki	9
Henri Charpentier	3
Kiriko Lounge	4
Old Thailand	8
Torigin Honten	6
Ume-no-hana	2

0   200
metres

N

1

Sony Building

ソニービル • 5-3-1 Ginza, Chūō-ku • Daily 11am–7pm • Free • Ⓦ www.sonybuilding.jp • Ginza Station

With four of its eleven storeys showcasing the latest Sony gadgets, and any number of products in development, the **Sony Building** is a must for techno-freaks. There's a tax-free shop on the fourth floor and restaurants on most levels, but even if you're a technophobe it's worth popping along to see just what all the fuss is about.

Kabukiza Theatre

歌舞伎座 • 4-12-15 Ginza, Chūō-ku • Gallery open daily 11am–7pm • Free • Ⓦ kabuki-za.co.jp • Higashi-Ginza Station

The famed **Kabukiza Theatre** is one of Ginza's most iconic buildings. First opened in 1889, the theatre has been rebuilt several times, a victim of fires and war damage. The architect behind its most recent incarnation is Kengo Kuma, who reinstated the elaborate facade of the original, which burned down in 1921; backed by a modern 29-storey office block, this is classic "city of contrasts" territory. Catch a play (see p.157) or simply check out the fifth-floor gallery, with its wonderful display of kabuki costumes.

Nihombashi

日本橋

North of Ginza, **NIHOMBASHI** was once the heart of Edo's teeming Shitamachi (see p.84), growing from a cluster of riverside markets in the early seventeenth century to become the city's chief financial district. The early warehouses and moneylenders subsequently evolved into the banks, brokers and trading companies that line the streets today. Other than the **bridge** at its heart – Japan's kilometre zero – the area's museums are the main reason to visit.

Bridgestone Museum of Art

ブリヂストン美術館, Burijisuton Bijutsukan • 1-10-1 Kyōbashi, Chūō-ku • ☎ 03 3563 0241, Ⓦ bridgestone-museum.gr.jp • Tokyo, Kyōbashi or Nihombashi stations

Closed for major renovation at the time of writing, and expected to reopen in 2019, the superb **Bridgestone Museum of Art** has an impressive collection of paintings by Van Gogh, Renoir, Degas, Monet, Manet, Miró, Picasso and other heavyweights, as well as Meiji-era Japanese paintings in Western style.

Mitsui Memorial Museum

三井記念美術館, Mitsui Kinen Bijutsukan • 7F Mitsui Main Building, 2-1-1 Nihombashi Muromachi, Chūō-ku • Tues–Sun 10am–5pm • ¥1000, or ¥1300 for special exhibitions • ☎ 03 5777 8600, Ⓦ mitsui-museum.jp • Mitsukoshimae Station

Just north of the main branch of the Mitsukoshi department store (see p.163) is the **Mitsui Memorial Museum**, where a superb collection spanning three hundred years of Japanese and Asian art is on display. Changing exhibitions follow a seasonal theme, but are usually aimed at the connoisseur.

Shiodome

汐留

South of Ginza is **Shiodome**, where a clutch of sparkling skyscrapers harbour hotels and restaurants. From Shiodome, it's an easy walk to the **Hama Rikyū Onshi Teien** traditional garden or the Tsukiji fish market (see p.103); you can also pick up the monorail to Odaiba from here (see p.104).

Hama Rikyū Onshi Teien

浜離宮恩賜庭園 • 1-1 Hamarikyūteien, Chūō-ku • Daily 9am–4.30pm • ¥300; tea ¥510 • Shiodome Station

The beautifully designed traditional garden of **Hama Rikyū Onshi Teien** once belonged to the shogunate, who hunted ducks here. These days the ducks are protected inside the garden's nature reserve, and no longer used for target practice. Next to the entrance is a sprawling, 300-year-old pine tree and a manicured lawn dotted with sculpted, stunted trees. There are three ponds, the largest spanned by a trellis-covered bridge that leads to a floating teahouse, *Nakajima-no-Chaya*; in early spring lilac wisteria hangs in fluffy bunches from trellises around the central pond. From the Tokyo Bay side of the garden, there's a view across to the Rainbow Bridge (see p.108), and you can see the floodgate which regulates how much sea water flows in and out of the ponds with the tides.

By far the nicest way of approaching the gardens is to take a ferry from Asakusa, down the Sumida-gawa (see box, p.99); often the entry price is included with the ticket.

Akihabara and around

秋葉原

Up the tracks from the Ginza area, a blaze of adverts and a cacophony of competing audio systems announce **AKIHABARA**. Akiba, as it's popularly known, is renowned as Tokyo's foremost discount shopping area for electrical and electronic goods of all kinds; but it's also a hotspot for fans of anime and manga and is famed as the spawning ground for the decidedly surreal "maid cafés" (see box, p.144). Though Akiba's buzzing, neon-lit streets are almost entirely dedicated to technological wizardry and pop culture, there are sights to the west, including the lively Shintō shrine of **Kanda Myōjin**, and an austere monument to Confucius at **Yushima Seidō**. Across the Sumida-gawa to the east lies sumo central, **Ryōgoku**.

TAKING THE PULSE OF AKIHABARA

There are few other Tokyo districts in which so many travellers actually avoid the sights: instead, **contemporary culture** is Akihabara's main, or even exclusive, drawcard. Here are a few ways in which to enjoy the more modern delights of Akiba.

Anime Part of the UDX Building, a mainstay of the local IT industry, the **Tokyo Anime Center** (東京アニメセンター; 4F UDX Building, 4-14-1 Sotokanda; Tues–Sun 11am–7pm; ☏ 03 5298 1188, ⓦ animecenter.jp) features small displays on recent anime, and hosts regular events that can be a lot of fun.

Electronics Akihabara's electronic stores are descendants of a postwar black market in radios and radio parts that took place beneath the train tracks around Akihabara Station. You can recapture some of the atmosphere in the **Tōkyō Radio Depāto** (東京ラジオデパート; 1-10-11 Sotokanda; daily 11am–7pm) – four floors stuffed with plugs, wires, boards and tools for making or repairing audiovisual equipment.

Maid cafés The whole area is riddled with maid cafés (see box, p.144), with said maids clamouring for custom on the road outside *Super Potato* (see below); two safe bets are *Mai:lish* (see p.143) and *Maidreamin* (see p.143) – the latter is on the second floor of the Zeniya building, which boasts seven full levels of maid cafés, and nothing else.

Robots You'd have to bring quite a bit of cash to purchase the equipment necessary to put together a full robot at **Technologia** (テクノロジア; 4-12-9 Sotokanda; daily 10am–7pm), but this store carries a large amount of such goodies, and is well worth a peek even if you're not a roboteer.

Video games Head on up to the fifth floor of **Super Potato** (スーパーポテト; 1-11-2 Sotokanda; daily 11am–8pm), which has a whole bunch of old-school arcade games including Bomberman, Mario (the NES version) and several iterations of Street Fighter II. If that sounds a little Nintendo-focused, try **Club Sega** (クラブセガ; 1-11-1 Sotokanda; daily 10am–11.30pm), which has two floors of arcade games and one of interactive music machines atop its six levels.

1

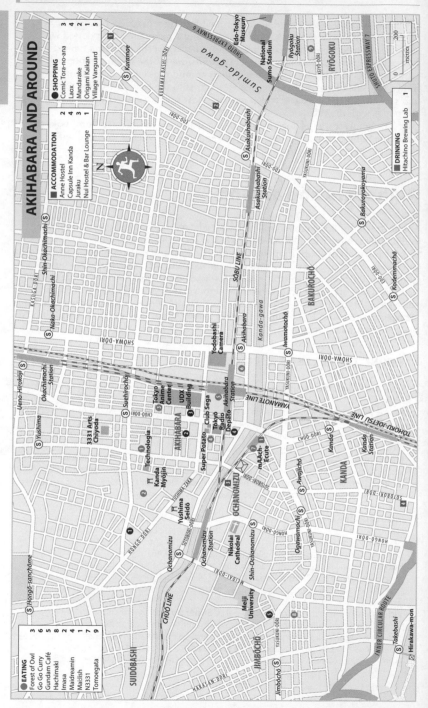

AKIHABARA AND AROUND

■ ACCOMMODATION
Anne Hostel	2
Capsule Inn Kanda	4
Juraku	3
Nui Hostel & Bar Lounge	1

● SHOPPING
Comic Tora-no-ana	3
Laox	4
Mandarake	2
Origami Kaikan	1
Village Vanguard	5

■ DRINKING
Hitachino Brewing Lab	1

● EATING
Forest of Owl	3
Go Go Curry	6
Gundam Café	5
Hachimaki	8
Imasa	2
Maidreamin	4
Mai1ish	1
N3331	7
Tomoegata	9

3331 Arts Chiyoda

3331アーツ千代田 • 6-11-14 Sotokanda, Chiyoda-ku • Noon–7pm; closed Tues • Usually free, though charges apply for some special exhibitions • ☎ 03 6803 2441, ⓦ 3331.jp • Suehirochō Station

Down a side street a little north of Suehirochō Station is the landscaped entrance to the **3331 Arts Chiyoda** complex. Based inside a renovated school, the centre hosts close to twenty galleries, where you'll find a revolving mix of exhibitions, interactive installations and workshops.

Kanda Myōjin

神田明神 • 2-16-2 Sotokanda, Chiyoda-ku • Daily 9am–4pm • Free • Ochanomizu and Marunouchi stations

A vermilion gate marks the entrance to **Kanda Myōjin**, one of the city's oldest shrines and host to one of its top three festivals, the **Kanda Matsuri** (see p.159). Founded in 730 AD, the shrine originally stood in front of Edo Castle, where it was dedicated to the gods of farming and fishing (Daikoku and Ebisu). Later, the tenth-century rebel Taira no Masakado – who was beheaded after declaring himself emperor – was also enshrined here. When Shogun Tokugawa Ieyasu was strengthening the castle's fortifications in 1616, he took the opportunity to move the shrine, but mollified Masakado's supporters by declaring him a guardian deity of the city. Poke around to the west of the main shrine, and you'll find *Imasa*, a charming and almost otherworldly café (see p.143).

Yushima Seidō

湯島聖堂 • 1-4-25 Yushima, Bunkyō-ku • Daily: May–Oct 9.30am–5pm; Nov–April 9.30am–4pm • Free • Ochanomizu Station

A copse of woodland hides **Yushima Seidō**, which was founded in 1632 as an academy for the study of the ancient classics. Today, the quiet compound contains an eighteenth-century wooden gate and, at the top of broad steps, the imposing, black-lacquered Taisen-den, or "Hall of Accomplishments", where a shrine to Confucius is located; look up to see panther-like guardians poised on the roof tiles.

Ryōgoku

両国

The **RYŌGOKU** area has just two sights – and one of those is only in action for six weeks of the year. For a fortnight each January, May and September, major **sumo tournaments** fill the National Sumo Stadium (see p.166) with a pageant of thigh-slapping, foot-stamping and arcane ritual. But even if your visit doesn't coincide with a tournament, it's still worth heading to Ryōguku to see the fantastic **Edo-Tokyo Museum**, or to take a stroll down the banks of the Sumida-gawa.

Edo-Tokyo Museum

江戸東京博物館, Edo-Tōkyō Hakubutsukan • 1-4-1 Yokoami, Sumida-ku • Tues–Fri & Sun 9.30am–5.30pm, Sat 9.30am–7.30pm • ¥600 • ☎ 03 3626 9974, ⓦ edo-tokyo-museum.or.jp • Ryōgoku Station

You'll need plenty of stamina for the extensive **Edo-Tokyo Museum**, housed in a colossal building behind the Sumo Stadium; the ticket lasts a whole day, so you can come and go. The museum tells the history of Tokyo from the days of the Tokugawa shogunate to postwar reconstruction, using life-sized replicas, models and holograms, as well as more conventional screen paintings, ancient maps and documents, with plenty of information in English, including a free audio guide. The display about life in Edo's Shitamachi, with its pleasure quarters, festivals and vibrant popular culture, is particularly good.

1

Ueno and around

上野

Most people visit **UENO** for its park, **Ueno Kōen**, which is home to a host of good museums, including the prestigious **Tokyo National Museum**, plus a few relics from Kan'ei-ji, a vast temple complex that once occupied this hilltop. But Ueno also has proletarian, Shitamachi roots (see p.84), and much of its eastern district has a rough-and-ready feel, which is best experienced in the market area of **Ameyokochō** (see box below). The west side of central Ueno, just southeast of Tokyo University, is home to the appealing **Kyū Iwasaki-tei Gardens**.

Ueno Kōen

上野公園 • Various entrances; information desk by east gate • Ueno Station

Although it's far from being the city's most attractive park, **Ueno Kōen** is where all Tokyo seems to flock during spring's cherry blossom season. Outside this brief period, however, the park only gets busy at weekends, and during the week it can be a pleasant place for a stroll, particularly around Shinobazu Pond.

Shitamachi Museum

下町風俗資料館, Shitamachi Fūzoku Shiryōkan • 2-1 Ueno Kōen, Taitō-ku • Tues–Sun 9.30am–5.30pm • ¥300 • ☎ 03 3823 7451,
Ⓦ www.taitocity.net/taito/shitamachi • Ueno or Ueno-Hirokōji stations

At the southern end of the park, the **Shitamachi Museum** occupies a partly traditional-style building beside Shinobazu Pond. A reconstructed merchant's shophouse and a 1920s tenement row, complete with sweet shop and coppersmith's workroom, fill the ground floor. The upper floor is devoted to rotating exhibitions focusing on articles of daily life. All the museum's exhibits – most of which you can handle – have been donated by local residents; take your shoes off to explore the shop interiors.

Shinobazu Pond

不忍池, Shinobazu-no Ike • Ueno Station

Glorious **Shinobazu Pond**, once an inlet of Tokyo Bay, is now a wildlife protection area hosting a permanent colony of wild black cormorants as well as temporary populations of migrating waterfowl. A causeway leads out across its reeds and lotus beds to a small, leafy island occupied by an octagonal-roofed temple, **Benten-dō**, dedicated to the goddess of good fortune, water and music (among other things); inside, the ceiling sports a snarling dragon. **Boats** can be hired to take out on the pond (daily 10am–6pm; row-boats ¥700, pedaloes ¥600–700).

AMEYOKOCHŌ

The bustling **market** area south of Ueno Station, **Ameyokochō** (アメ横丁), extends nearly half a kilometre along the west side of the elevated JR train lines down to Okachimachi Station. The name – an abbreviation of "Ameya Yokochō", or "Candy Sellers' Alley" – dates from the immediate postwar days when sweets were a luxury and the hundreds of stalls here mostly peddled sweet potatoes coated in sugar syrup (*daigakuimo*). Since **rationing** was in force, blackmarketeers joined the candy sellers, dealing in rice and other foodstuffs, household goods and personal items. Later, American imports found their way from army stores onto the streets here, especially during the Korean War in the early 1950s, which is also when the market was legalized. Ameyokochō still retains a flavour of those early days: stalls specializing in everything from bulk tea and coffee to jewellery and fish line the street, gruff men with sandpaper voices shout out their wares, and there's a clutch of *yakitori* bars under the arches.

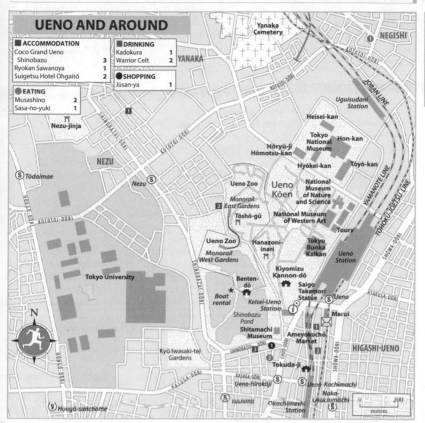

UENO AND AROUND

■ ACCOMMODATION		■ DRINKING	
Coco Grand Ueno		Kadokura	1
Shinobazu	3	Warrior Celt	2
Ryokan Sawanoya	1	● SHOPPING	
Suigetsu Hotel Ohgaisō	2	Jūsan-ya	1
● EATING			
Musashino	2		
Sasa-no-yuki	1		

Kiyomizu Kannon-dō

清水観音堂 • 24hr • Free

The red-lacquered **Kiyomizu Kannon-dō** sits to the east of the Shinobazu Pond. Built out over the hillside, this temple is a smaller, less impressive version of Kyoto's Kiyomizu-dera (see p.435), but has the rare distinction of being one of Kan'ei-ji's few existing remnants, dating from 1631.

Tōshō-gū

東照宮 • 9-88 Ueno, Taitō-ku • Daily 9am–sunset • ¥200 • Nezu or Ueno stations

A tree-lined avenue marks the approach to Tokugawa Ieyasu's shrine, **Tōshō-gū**. Ieyasu died in 1616 and is buried in Nikkō (see box, p.175), but this was his main shrine in Tokyo, founded in 1627 and rebuilt on a grander scale in 1651. For once it's possible to penetrate beyond the screened entrance and enclosing walls to take a closer look inside, where the highlight is Ieyasu's shrine room, resplendent in burnished black and gold.

Ueno Zoo

上野動物園, Ueno Dōbutsuen • 9-83 Ueno Kōen, Taitō-ku • Tues–Sun 9.30am–4pm • ¥600, free for children 12 and under; monorail ¥150 • ☎ 03 3828 5171, ⓦ www.tokyo-zoo.net

Considering the fact that **Ueno Zoo** is over a century old, it's less depressing than might be feared. Yet while the macaques seem to have a whale of a time on the rocky crag

1

they call home, the same cannot be said of the bears and big cats, which tend to pace around small corners of their pens. Other animals include rare gorillas and pygmy hippos, as well as a couple of pandas. The east and west parts of the zoo are connected by monorail, though a walking path plies the same route.

National Museum of Western Art

国立西洋美術館, Kokuritsu Seiyō Bijutsukan • 7-7 Ueno Kōen, Taitō-ku • Tues–Sun 9.30am–5.30pm, Fri until 8pm • ¥430, or more for special exhibitions • ☎ 03 3828 5131, ⓦ www.nmwa.go.jp • Ueno Station

The **National Museum of Western Art** is instantly recognizable from the Rodin statues on the forecourt. The museum, designed by Le Corbusier, was erected in 1959 to house the mostly French Impressionist paintings left to the nation by Kawasaki shipping magnate Matsukata Kōjirō. Since then, works by Rubens, Tintoretto, Max Ernst and Jackson Pollock have broadened the scope of this impressive collection.

National Museum of Science and Nature

国立科学博物館, Kokuritsu Kagaku Hakubutsukan • 7-20 Ueno Kōen, Taitō-ku • Tues–Sun 9am–5pm, Fri until 8pm • ¥600 • ☎ 03 5777 8600, ⓦ www.kahaku.go.jp • Ueno Station

The **National Museum of Science and Nature** offers lots of videos and interactive displays, though sadly very little is labelled in English. Six floors of displays cover natural history as well as science and technology. In the "exploration space" on the second floor, pendulums, magnets, mirrors and hand-powered generators provide entertainment for the mainly school-age audience, while down in the basement there's an aquarium. The highlight, however, is on the second floor: sitting amid other stuffed animals, with surprisingly little fanfare, is Hachikō, Japan's canine hero (see box, p.122). Almost all visitors, even the locals, walk past without a second glance – a rather sad end for the country's most famous hound.

Tokyo National Museum

東京国立博物, Tokyo Kokuritsu Hakubutsukan • 13-9 Ueno Kōen, Taitō-ku • Tues–Sun 9.30am–5pm, though often later (see website) • ¥620 • ☎ 03 5405 8686, ⓦ www.tnm.jp • Ueno Station

Dominating the northern reaches of Ueno Park is the **Tokyo National Museum**, containing the world's largest collection of Japanese art, plus an extensive collection of Oriental antiquities. The museum style tends towards old-fashioned reverential dryness, but among such a vast collection there's something to excite everyone's imagination. Displays are rotated every few months from a collection of 110,000 pieces, and the special exhibitions are usually also worth seeing if you can stand the crowds.

Hon-kan

The **Hon-kan**, the museum's central building, presents the sweep of Japanese art, from Jōmon-period pottery (pre-fourth century BC) to early twentieth-century painting, via theatrical costume for kabuki, nō and *bunraku*, colourful Buddhist mandalas, *ukiyo-e* prints, exquisite lacquerware and even seventeenth-century Christian art from southern Japan.

Heisei-kan

In the **Heisei-kan**, you'll find the splendid Japanese Archeology Gallery, containing important recent finds. Highlights include the chunky, flame-shaped Jōmon pots and a collection of super-heated Sue stoneware, made using a technique introduced from Korea in the fifth century.

Hōryū-ji Hōmotsu-kan

In the southwest corner of the compound lurks the **Hōryū-ji Hōmotsu-kan**, containing a selection of priceless treasures donated over the centuries to Nara's Hōryū-ji temple (see p.496). The most eye-catching display comprises 48 gilt-bronze Buddhist statues in various poses, each an island of light in the inky darkness, while there's also an eighth-century inkstand, water container and other items said to have been used by Prince Shōtoku (see p.820) when annotating the Lotus Sutra.

Tōyō-kan

The museum's final gallery is the **Tōyō-kan**, housing a delightful hotchpotch of Asian antiquities: Javanese textiles and nineteenth-century Indian prints rub shoulders with Egyptian mummies and a wonderful collection of Southeast Asian bronze Buddhas.

Kyū Iwasaki-tei Gardens

旧岩崎邸庭園, Kyū Iwasaki-tei Teien • 1-3-45 Ikenohata, Taitō-ku • Daily 9am–5pm • ¥400; tea ¥500 • ☎ 03 3823 8340 • Yushima Station

The west side of central Ueno is dominated by seedy love hotels and dubious bars. Take a short walk past Yushima Station, however, and you'll discover a remnant of a much more genteel past. The **Kyū Iwasaki-tei Gardens** date from 1896 and surround an elegant **house**, designed by British architect Josiah Conder, which combines a Western-style two-storey mansion with a traditional single-storey Japanese residence. The wooden Jacobean and Moorish-style arabesque interiors of the Western-style mansion are in fantastic condition – in stark contrast to the severely faded screen paintings of the Japanese rooms. The lack of furniture in both houses makes them a little lifeless, but it's nonetheless an impressive artefact in a city where such buildings are increasingly rare. You can take tea in the Japanese section, or sit outside and admire the gardens, which also combine Eastern and Western influences.

Asakusa and around

浅草

ASAKUSA is best known as the site of Tokyo's most venerable Buddhist temple, Sensō-ji, whose towering worship hall is filled with a continual throng of petitioners and holiday-makers. Stalls before the temple cater to the crowds, peddling trinkets and keepsakes as they have done for centuries; old-fashioned craftshops display exquisite hair combs, paper fans and calligraphy brushes; and all around is the inevitable array of restaurants, drinking places and fast-food stands. It's the infectious carnival atmosphere that makes Asakusa so appealing. The biggest festival here is the Sanja Matsuri (see box, p.159), but there are numerous smaller celebrations; ask at the information centre (see p.133) in front of Sensō-ji's main gate if there's anything on.

A more futuristic side of Tokyo is on view across the Sumida-gawa to the east, where the soaring **Tokyo Skytree** dominates the skyline; you also can't miss the Philippe Starck-designed Asahi Beer Hall, which is replete with what's supposed to be a stylized flame, but is known to all and sundry as the "Golden Turd" (金のうんこ, kin-no-unko). The river itself defines Asakusa almost as much as the temple, and ferries (see box below) are a lovely way to get in or out of the area.

ASAKUSA FERRIES

Though you can easily reach Asakusa by subway, a more pleasant way of getting here – or away – is **by river**. The **Sumida-gawa service** runs from Hinode Pier on Tokyo Bay (see p.133) to the jetty at Asakusa, under Azuma-bashi (every 30–50min, 10am–6.30pm; 40min; ¥780); some boats call at the Hama Rikyū Onshi Teien (see p.92) en route. Alternatively, the space-age Himoko and Hotaruna ferries connect Odaiba with Asakusa, usually via Hinode (6 daily; ¥1560).

1

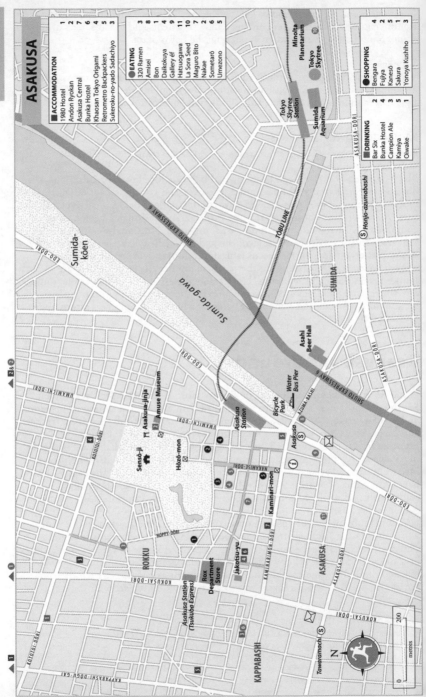

ASAKUSA

ACCOMMODATION
1980 Hostel	1
Andon Ryokan	2
Asakusa Central	7
Bunka Hostel	6
Khaosan Tokyo Origami	4
Retrometro Backpackers	5
Sukeroku-no-yado Sadachiyo	3

EATING
320 Ramen	3
Amisei	8
Bon	1
Daikokuya	4
Gallery éf	9
Hatsuogawa	11
La Sora Seed	10
Maguro Bito	7
Nakae	2
Sometarō	6
Umezono	5

SHOPPING
Bengara	4
Fujiya	2
Kanesō	5
Sakura	1
Yonoya Kushiho	3

DRINKING
Bar Six	2
Bunka Hostel	4
Campion Ale	3
Kamiya	5
Oiwake	1

PLAYING DRESS-UP

Asakusa has plenty of shops selling kimono, both new and used, and these can make for fantastic souvenirs. However, if you're not sure that you'll ever need one again, you can make use of the many **kimono rental spots** dotted around the area – there seems to be one on almost every street (there are also a few in Harajuku, Shibuya and other areas). Figure on ¥3000 for the day, and ¥1500 to have your hair done.

Sensō-ji

浅草寺 • North end of Nakamise-dōri • 24hr • Free • Asakusa Station

The great **Kaminari-mon**, or "Thunder Gate", named after its two vigorous guardian gods of thunder and wind (Raijin and Fūjin), marks the southern entrance to **Sensō-ji**. This magnificent temple, also known as Asakusa Kannon, was founded in the mid-seventh century to enshrine a tiny golden image of Kannon, the goddess of mercy, which, legend has it, was ensnared in the nets of two local fishermen. The main temple approach starts under **Kaminari-mon**, or "Thunder Gate", which boasts a gigantic red paper lantern – 4m in height, it weighs in at a whopping 670kg.

The main hall

There's a great sense of atmosphere as you approach the main hall, with its sweeping, tiled roofs, from **Nakamise-dōri**, a colourful parade of small shops selling all manner of souvenirs. The double-storeyed treasure gate, **Hōzō-mon**, stands astride the entrance to the main temple complex; the treasures, fourteenth-century Chinese sutras, are locked away on the upper floor. The two protective gods – *Niō*, the traditional guardians of Buddhist temples – are even more imposing than those at Kaminari-mon. Beyond, the crowd clustered around a large, bronze incense bowl waft the pungent smoke – breath of the gods – over themselves for its supposed curative powers before approaching the temple's inner sanctum where the little Kannon is a *hibutsu*, a hidden image considered too holy to be on view. Three times a day, drums echo through the hall into the courtyard as priests chant sutras beneath the altar's gilded canopy.

Asakusa-jinja

浅草神社

Like many Buddhist temples, Sensō-ji accommodates Shintō shrines in its grounds, the most important being **Asakusa-jinja**, dedicated to the two fishermen brothers who netted the Kannon image, and their overlord. More popularly known as Sanja-sama, "Shrine of the Three Guardians", this is the focus of the tumultuous **Sanja Matsuri**, Tokyo's biggest festival (see box, p.159).

Amuse Museum

アミューズミュージアム • 2-34-3 Asakusa, Taitō-ku • Tues–Sun 10am–6pm • ¥1080 • ☎ 03 5806 1181, ⓦ amusemuseum.com • Asakusa Station

Just outside the east gate of Sensō-ji is the **Amuse Museum**, a six-storey complex incorporating a café, shop and bar, bridging the gap between old and new with a few quirky exhibition spaces dedicated to Japan's cultural past. It's mostly filled by a rotating showcase of items from private collector Tanaka Chuzaburo's collection of more than 30,000 items, displayed with stylish panache – the permanent collection of traditional patched clothing (*boro*) looks more like the interior of a trendy boutique. The building's rooftop terrace, home to *Bar Six* (see p.151), offers amazing views of Sensō-ji and the Tokyo Skytree.

1

Tokyo Skytree

東京スカイツリー • 1-1-2 Oshiage, Sumida-ku • ☎ 03 6658 8012, ⓦ tokyo-skytree.jp • Oshiage or Tokyo Skytree stations

Across the river, the **Tokyo Skytree** is the city's newest star attraction, and the world's tallest tower at 634m in height – the only structure to beat it, at the time of writing, is Dubai's mighty Burj Khalifa (830m). The main rationale behind the project was to replace the comparatively puny Tokyo Tower (see p.112) as the city's digital broadcasting beacon, although the sightseeing potential of the structure is being fully exploited, with the Skytree offering the city's highest public observatory – a dizzying 450m above the ground – as well as an aquarium and planetarium at its base, plus tourist shops, restaurants and landscaped public spaces.

The observation decks

Daily 8am–10pm • 350m deck ¥2060, or ¥2570 booked online (currently in Japanese only) with time assigned; 450m deck ¥1030 extra, no advance purchase possible • Foreign visitors with ID can also purchase a special "Fast Skytree" ticket, which beats the queues: 350m deck ¥3000, both decks ¥4000

On sunny days and weekends, prepare for mammoth queues for the **observation decks** – first for the tickets, then for the lifts, and then for the return trip. The wait, however, is just about worthwhile, and there's a certain tingly excitement to be had in watching the numbers on the lift panel getting higher and higher. Even the views from the **lower deck** (350m) are fantastic, with giant touch-screen displays showing precisely what you're looking at. Mount Fuji is, in theory, within visible range, but mist often blocks the view even in sunny weather, and it's usually only visible a couple of times per month. Those who choose to head on to the **upper deck** (450m) will see more or less the same thing, although its space-age interior design is rather lovely – the inclined walkway wraps around the building, giving you the impression that you're climbing to the top. Note that foreign visitors with valid ID can beat the queues for a small premium, and most find it worth the extra investment.

Sumida Aquarium

すみだ水族館, Sumida Suizokukan • 5F and 6F Tokyo Solamachi West Yard • Daily 9am–9pm • ¥2050 • ☎ 03 5619 1821, ⓦ sumida-aquarium.com

Every major tower in Tokyo seems to have an **aquarium** attached, and the Skytree is no exception. It's a pretty good one, though, with a 350,000-litre tank (the largest in Japan) at its centre; clever design of the glass walls mean that you can see the whole tank from almost any angle.

Konica Minolta Planetarium

コニカミノルタプラネタリウム • 7F Tokyo Solamachi East Yard • Hourly shows daily 11am–9pm • ¥1200 • ☎ 03 5610 3043

At the **Konica Minolta Planetarium** – part planetarium, part 4D cinema – the delights of the cosmos are relayed, for the sake of superfluous technology, in glorious smell-o-vision. Science has yet to capture the true scent of the stars, and though it's probably fair to assume that Finnish forests and Asian aromatherapy oils might be a bit wide of the mark, it's a fun experience nonetheless.

Bayside Tokyo

Several of the city's prime attractions are to be found around Tokyo Bay, not least the teeming fish market of **Tsukiji**, whose proposed relocation has been a major controversy of late. Across the Rainbow Bridge lies the modern waterfront suburb of **Odaiba**, built on vast islands of reclaimed land and home to **Miraikan**, Tokyo's best science museum, as well as huge shopping malls.

On the north side of the bay, **Kasai Rinkai-kōen** is a good place to catch the sea breeze and has a fine **aquarium**. From the park, the Cinderella spires of **Tokyo Disneyland** are clearly visible to the west.

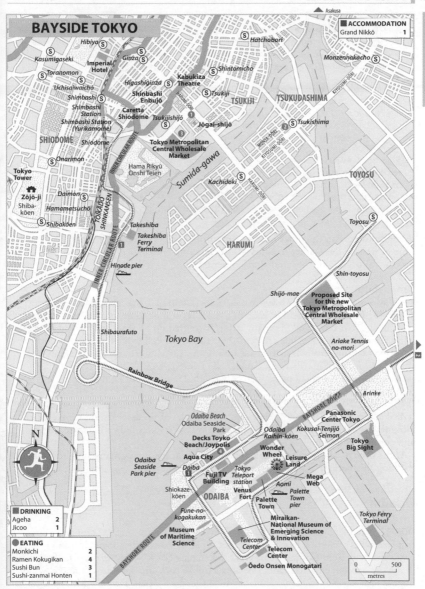

BAYSIDE TOKYO

Asakusa

■ **DRINKING**
Ageha   2
Jicoo   1

● **EATING**
Monkichi   2
Ramen Kokugikan   4
Sushi Bun   3
Sushi-zanmai Honten   1

Tsukiji

築地

A dawn visit to the vast **Tokyo Metropolitan Central Wholesale Market**, more popularly referred to by the name of its surrounding area, **Tsukiji**, has long been one of Tokyo's undisputed highlights. The site on which the market is located dates back to 1657, when the Tokugawa shogunate (see p.825) had the debris from the Furisode (Long Sleeves) Fire shovelled into the marshes at the edge of Ginza, thus creating "reclaimed land", or "*tsukiji*". Proposals have long been afoot to shift the market east to Toyosu,

1

TSUKIJI TROUBLES

It's been dubbed the "fish market at the centre of the world" for its influence on world seafood prices. Generating almost **¥2 billion** (£14m/US$17.5m) in sales daily, Tsukiji is undoubtedly big business, but during recent years the market's volume of trade has been dropping, along with the number of wholesalers and middlemen who work there.

Uppermost on merchants' minds is the Tokyo Metropolitan Government's plan to shift the market to **Toyosu**, 2km across the bay. The site was previously used by Tokyo Gas, and the highly toxic ground was cleaned up before construction started on the new complex, which cost around ¥590bn (£4.2bn/US$5.2bn) to build. The stalls were all supposed to move out to Toyosu in November 2016, but surveys conducted in the months before that showed that the new site's levels of mercury, benzene, arsenic and cyanide – slightly worrying substances, even away from raw fish – were all above government standards. Because of these concerns over **toxins**, ones echoed by many of the marketfolk themselves, Tokyo governor Yuriko Koike brought a sudden halt to proceedings just before the move.

At the time of writing, everything remained up in the air, with market life going on as normal at the old site, and the new building waiting for tenants who may never arrive.

though progress on the move has been anything but smooth (see box above) and at the time of writing the market remains at its original site – contact one of the city's tourist offices (see p.113) for the latest developments.

Jōnai-shijō

場内市場 • Mon–Sat 4am–2pm; check website for occasional holidays • ⓦ tsukiji-market.or.jp • Tsukiji or Tsukiji-Shijō stations

While the future of the market is up in the air, it's still possible that nothing at all will change. For now, Tsukiji's main action is centred on its **jōnai-shijō** (main market), lying closest to the water in a crescent-shaped hangar. Eels from Taiwan, salmon from Santiago and tuna from Tasmania are among the 480 different types of seafood – two thousand tonnes of it – that come under the hammer here daily.

The headline **tuna auctions** happen between 5.25am and 6.15am. Though viewing tours had been suspended at the time of writing, they'll hopefully recommence whether the market stays here or moves to Toyosu – many a traveller has ended up waxing lyrical about getting up before dawn to witness sales of these rock-solid frozen fish, looking like steel torpedoes, all labelled with yellow stickers indicating their weight and country of origin.

At the time of writing, it was still possible to eat at the many, many **sushi restaurants** flanking the market; *Sushi Bun* (see p.145) is recommended.

Odaiba

お台場

ODAIBA is an island of reclaimed land in Tokyo Bay. The name means "cannon emplacements", referring to the defences set up in the bay by the shogun in 1853 to protect the city from Commodore Perry's threatening Black Ships (see p.826). The remains of the two cannon emplacements, one now a public park, are these days dwarfed by the huge landfill site Rinkai Fukutoshin, of which Odaiba is a part. Here the Metropolitan Government set about constructing a brand-new urban development, fit for the twenty-first century, in 1988. The subsequent economic slump and spiralling development costs slowed the project down and, when the **Rainbow Bridge** linking Odaiba to the city opened in 1993, the area was still a series of empty lots. Odaiba has since filled out and is most appreciated by locals for its seaside location and sense of space – so rare in Tokyo. At night, the illuminated Rainbow Bridge, giant technicolour Ferris wheel and twinkling towers of the Tokyo skyline make Odaiba a romantic date location.

While you're here, consider going for a dip at Ōedo Onsen Monogatari (see box, p.165), one of Tokyo's largest hot-spring resorts.

GETTING TO AND FROM ODAIBA

The simplest way of reaching Odaiba is to hop on the **Yurikamome monorail** (ⓦ yurikamome.co.jp), which starts at Shimbashi Station and arcs up to the Rainbow Bridge on a splendid circular line, stopping at all the area's major sites before terminating at Toyosu, also a subway stop; single tickets here from the "mainland" are around ¥320. In addition, **trains** on the Rinkai line, linked with the JR Saikyō line and the Yūrakuchō subway line, run to the central Tokyo-Teleport Station on Odaiba; if you're coming to the area on JR trains, this usually works out cheaper than the monorail, and there are direct services from Ikebukuro, Shinjuku, Shibuya and Ebisu, among other places.

   Buses from Shinagawa Station, southwest of the bay, cross the Rainbow Bridge and run as far as the Maritime Museum (see map, pp.82–83), stopping at Odaiba Kaihin-kōen on the way. There is also a variety of bus services (some free) to the Ōedo Onsen Monogatari. Once you're on Odaiba, you can make use of the free Tokyo Bay Shuttle bus services, which depart on a loop every 20min or so.

   Finally, **ferries** shuttle from the pier at Hinode (日の出) to Odaiba Seaside Park or Palette Town; some also stop next to the Tokyo Big Sight exhibition centre – the journey costs from just ¥480 and doubles as a Tokyo Bay cruise. The space-age *Himoko* and *Hotaruna* ferries also connect Odaiba with Asakusa, sometimes via Hinode (6 daily; ¥1560), and there are also ferries to Kasai Rinkai-kōen (see p.108).

Panasonic Center Tokyo

パナソニックセンター東京 • 3-5-1 Ariake, Kōtō-ku • Tues–Sun 10am–6pm • Free; Risupia ¥500 • ☎ 03 3599 2600, ⓦ panasonic.net/center/tokyo • Ariake or Kokusai Tenjijō Seimon monorail stations

At the **Panasonic Center Tokyo**, the electronics group's showcase, you can try out the latest Nintendo games on a large-screen plasma display or high-resolution projector, as well as check out the company's technologies of tomorrow. The centre includes the fun "digital network museum" **Risupia**, at which you're issued with an electronic tag upon entering the hi-tech display hall; as you learn about science and mathematics from the computer games and simulations within, the tag keeps track of how well you're doing.

Palette Town

パレットタウン • 1-3-15 Aomi, Kōtō-ku • Aomi monorail station

Aomi Station is the stop for the vast **Palette Town** shopping and entertainment complex, which offers something for almost everyone: test-drive a Toyota, go for a spin on a giant Ferris wheel, or see Tokyo at its wackiest in Tokyo Leisureland. Outside Harajuku and Akihabara, this is the most popular place in Tokyo for *cosplay* costume-wearing youngsters.

Mega Web

メガウェブ • Daily 11am–9pm • Entry and simulations free, vehicle rental at Ride Studio ¥200–300 • ☎ 03 3599 0808, ⓦ megaweb.gr.jp

On Palette Town's east side, **Mega Web** is a design showcase for Toyota's range of cars. For the casual visitor, it's most interesting as a glimpse into the future of the company, and by extension the automotive industry in general. It's often possible to pilot some kind of futuristic electric vehicle along the pleasing blue track that swoops around the building; consult the website for information, and note that you'll probably need to show an international driving licence.

Wonder Wheel

ワンダーウィール • Daily 10am–10pm • ¥920

Just behind the Mega Web showroom are some more hi-tech diversions, the best of which is the **Wonder Wheel**, a candy-coloured, 115m-diameter Ferris wheel, which takes sixteen minutes to make a full circuit. If heights hold no fear then plump for one of the wheel's four fully transparent gondolas, which enable you to see down through the floor; they cost no extra, though you may have to queue.

TOKYO FOR KIDS

Tokyo is a fantastic city for **kids**. For starters, there's a whole swathe of **museums**, the best ones being Miraikan (see below), the National Museum of Science and Nature (see p.98) and Edo-Tokyo Museum (see p.95). For animal lovers, there's the fabulous Tokyo Sea Life Park at Kasai Rinkai-kōen (see p.108) and Ueno Zoo (see p.97).

The city also boasts Tokyo Disneyland (see p.108), of course, and the thrill of the rides at Tokyo Dome (see p.128) as well as the wonderful Ghibli Museum (see p.126), based on the popular anime films produced by the Ghibli studio.

Don't forget the myriad **shops** (see p.160) featuring the latest hit toys and crazes. For older, tech-savvy kids, the electronic emporia of Akihabara will be a must (see p.93).

Venus Fort

ヴィナスフォート • Daily 11am–9pm • ⓦ www.venusfort.co.jp

The west side of Palette Town is dominated by **Venus Fort**, one of Tokyo's most original shopping and factory outlet malls. It's partly designed as a mock Italian city, complete with piazza, fountains and Roman-style statues – even the ceiling is painted and lit to resemble a perfect Mediterranean sky from dawn to dusk.

Miraikan

日本科学未来館, Nihon Kagaku Miraikan • 2-3-6 Aomi, Kōtō-ku • 10am–5pm; closed Tues • ¥620, Dome Theater ¥300 • ☏ 03 3570 9151, ⓦ www.miraikan.jst.go.jp • Telecom Center monorail station

West of Palette Town is Tokyo's best science museum, the **National Museum of Emerging Science and Innovation**, also known as the **Miraikan**. Here you can learn about the latest in robot technology, superconductivity (including Maglev trains), space exploration, earthquakes and much more, as well as check out the weather around the world by looking up at a giant sphere covered with one million light-emitting diodes showing the globe as it appears from space that day. For an extra fee you can catch a science flick in the spherical Dome Theater.

Odaiba beach

お台場浜, Odaiba-hama • Daiba monorail station

On the north side of the island, Odaiba's man-made **beach** – part of **Odaiba Seaside Park** – boasts a fantastic view of the Rainbow Bridge (see p.108), as well as an unexpected scale copy of the Statue of Liberty. It's a wonderful place to be in the evening, looking at the bridge and twinkly lights beyond, especially if you take off your shoes and dip your feet into the water.

Joypolis

ジョイポリス • 1-6-1 Daiba, Minato-ku • Daily 10am–10pm • Adult ¥800, child aged 7–17 ¥500; passport for unlimited rides (day/evening) adult ¥4300/3300, child ¥3300/2300 • ☏ 03 5500 1801, ⓦ tokyo-joypolis.com • Odaiba-Kaihin-kōen monorail station

Fronting the beach are a couple of linked shopping malls, **Aqua City** and **Decks Tokyo Beach**. Apart from plenty of shops and restaurants (see p.145), the former includes the Mediage multiplex cinema, while the latter has **Joypolis**, a multistorey arcade filled with Sega's interactive entertainment technology.

Fuji TV Building

富士テレビビル, Fuji Terebi Biru • 2-4-8 Daiba, Minato-ku • Viewing platform Tues–Sun 10am–6pm • ¥550 • Daiba monorail

A surreal, sci-fi aura hangs over Tange Kenzō's **Fuji TV Building** – with a huge metal sphere suspended in its middle, it looks as if it's been made from a giant Meccano set. You can pay to head up to the 25th-floor **viewing platform**, or save the cash for a drink in the *Sky Lounge* at the top of the neighbouring *Grand Pacific Le Daiba* hotel, where the view is thrown in for free.

CLOCKWISE FROM TOP LEFT OMOIDE YOKOCHŌ, SHINJUKU (P.123); MAID CAFÉ (BOX, P.144); HIE-JINJA, AKASAKA (P.108) >

1

Rainbow Bridge

レインボーブリッジ • Observation rooms and promenade daily: Jan–March, Nov & Dec 10am–6pm; April–Oct 9am–9pm • Free • Shibaura Futō monorail station

From Odaiba you can cross back to mainland Tokyo along the **Rainbow Bridge**, a 918m-long, single-span suspension bridge in two levels: the lower bears the waterfront road and the monorail, the upper the Metropolitan Expressway. On both sides is a pedestrian **promenade** linking the **observation rooms** in the anchorages at either end of the bridge. The walk along the bridge takes about half an hour and provides good views across the bay, even as far as Mount Fuji if the sky is clear.

East of Odaiba

An enjoyable way to experience Tokyo Bay is to head out to **Kasai Rinkai-kōen** (葛西臨海公園), some 7km east of Odaiba. The park's biggest draw is its superb aquarium, the **Tokyo Sea Life Park**, but it's also a favourite weekend spot for many families who visit to picnic, cycle or paddle off its small, crescent-shaped beach. Bird enthusiasts also come to ogle water birds and waders in the well-designed sanctuary. Just to the east is Tokyo's own take on the **Disney** mega-park theme.

Tokyo Sea Life Park

葛西臨海水族館, Kasai Rinkai Suizokukan • 6-2-3 Rinkai-chō, Edogawa-ku • 9.30am–5pm; last entry 4pm; closed Wed • ¥700, children free • ☎ 03 3869 5152, Ⓦ www.tokyo-zoo.net • Ferry from Odaiba Seaside Park; 50min; ¥1130 one-way, ¥1650 return; last boat back around 5pm • Kasai Rinkai-kōen Station; from Odaiba, take the Rinkai line and transfer to JR Keiyō line at Shin-Kiba

The highlight of the **Tokyo Sea Life Park**, set under a glass-and-steel dome overlooking the sea, is a pair of vast tanks filled with tuna and sharks, where silver shoals race round you at dizzying speeds. Smaller tanks elsewhere showcase sea life from around the world, from flashy tropical butterfly fish and paper-thin sea horses to the lumpy mudskippers of Tokyo Bay.

Tokyo Disney Resort

東京ディズニーリゾート • 1-1 Maihama, Urayasu-shi, Chiba • Generally open 8/9am–10pm; call to check times beforehand • One-day passport for Tokyo Disneyland or Tokyo DisneySea adult ¥7400, child aged 12–17 ¥6400, child aged 4–11 ¥4800; two-day passport for both parks ¥13,200/11,600/8600 respectively; discount passports available from 3pm • ☎ 0570 008632, Ⓦ www.tokyodisneyresort.co.jp • Maihama Station

This big daddy of Tokyo's theme parks, **Tokyo Disney Resort**, is made up of two main sections: **Tokyo Disneyland**, a close copy of the Californian original; and **Tokyo DisneySea**, a water- and world travel-themed area. With an average of over 30,000 visitors per day (many more over weekends and holidays), expect queues.

Akasaka and Roppongi

AKASAKA and **ROPPONGI** are famed nightlife zones, but both also have sights worth visiting during the daytime. In the former you'll find **Hie-jinja**, one of Tokyo's most historic shrines, while in the latter an "Art Triangle" has been formed by the **Suntory Museum of Art** in the huge **Tokyo Midtown** complex, the **National Art Center** and the **Mori Art Museum** in the equally enormous **Roppongi Hills** development. **Tokyo Tower** remains the area's retro landmark, and nearby is the venerable temple **Zōjō-ji**.

Hie-jinja

日枝神社 • 2-10-15 Nagatachō, Chiyoda-ku • 24hr • Free • Akasaka, Akasaka-mitsuke or Tameike-sannō stations

At the southern end of Akasaka's main thoroughfare, Sotobori-dōri, stands a huge stone *torii*, beyond which is a picturesque avenue of red *torii* leading up the hill to **Hie-jinja**, a

Shintō shrine dedicated to the god Ōyamakui-no-kami, who is believed to protect against evil. Hie-jinja's history stretches back to 830 AD, when it was first established on the outskirts of what would become Edo. The shrine's location shifted a couple more times before Shogun Tokugawa Ietsuna placed it here in the seventeenth century as a source of protection for his castle (now the site of the Imperial Palace); the current buildings date from the 1950s.

From the main entrance through the large stone *torii* on the east side of the hill, 51 steps lead up to a spacious enclosed courtyard. To the left of the main shrine, look for the carving of a female monkey cradling her baby, a symbol that has come to signify protection for pregnant women. In June, Hie-jinja hosts one of Tokyo's most important festivals, the **Sannō Matsuri** (see box, p.159).

Tokyo Midtown

東京ミッドタウン・9-7-1 Akasaka, Minato-ku・Ⓦ www.tokyo-midtown.com・Roppongi or Nogizaka stations

Tokyo Midtown is an enormous mixed-use complex of offices, shops, apartments, a convention centre, two museums and other public facilities, plus the small park Hinokichō-kōen, all revolving around the 248m-high **Midtown Tower**. The complex's design and visual influences come from traditional Japanese architecture and art: look out for the *torii* in the rectangular archway entrance to the Galleria shopping mall.

Suntory Museum of Art

サントリー美術館, Santorii Bijutsukan・3F Galleria, Tokyo Midtown・Mon & Sun 10am 6pm, Wed Sat 10am 8pm・Entry price varies by exhibition, usually around ¥1000・❶ 03 3470 1073, Ⓦ www.suntory.co.jp/sma

Landscaped gardens planted with 140 trees nestle behind and along the west side of the complex, where you'll find the **Suntory Museum of Art**. This elegant Kengo Kuma-designed building hosts changing exhibitions of ceramics, lacquerware, paintings and textiles. There's also an on-site café serving tasty nibbles from Kanazawa, the capital of Ishikawa prefecture.

21_21 Design Sight

21_21デザインサイト・9-7-6 Akasaka, Minato-ku・Daily 10am–7pm・¥1100・❶ 03 3475 2121, Ⓦ 2121designsight.jp

Two giant triangular planes of steel, concrete and glass peeking out of a green lawn are part of the **21_21 Design Sight**, a fascinating collaboration between architect Andō Tadao and fashion designer Issey Miyake. The building's seamless shape was inspired by Miyake's A-POC ("A Piece Of Cloth") line, and the main gallery digs one floor into the ground to provide an elevated, airy space in which to view the various design exhibitions.

National Art Center

国立新美術館, Kokuritsu Shin Bijutsukan・7-22-2 Roppongi, Minato-ku・10am–6pm, until 8pm on Fri; closed Tues・Entrance fee varies with exhibition・❶ 03 6812 9900, Ⓦ www.nact.jp・Nogizaka or Roppongi stations

A billowing wave of pale-green glass ripples across the facade of the Kurokawa Kisha-designed **National Art Center** which, at 48,000 square metres, is Japan's largest such museum, the huge halls allowing for some very ambitious works to be displayed. Of the twelve exhibition rooms, two are devoted to shows curated by the museum (the centre has no collection of its own); the rest of the rooms are organized by various art associations from across Japan, making for a very eclectic mix. While you are here, linger in the main atrium to admire the conical pods that soar up three storeys, and explore the excellent museum shop.

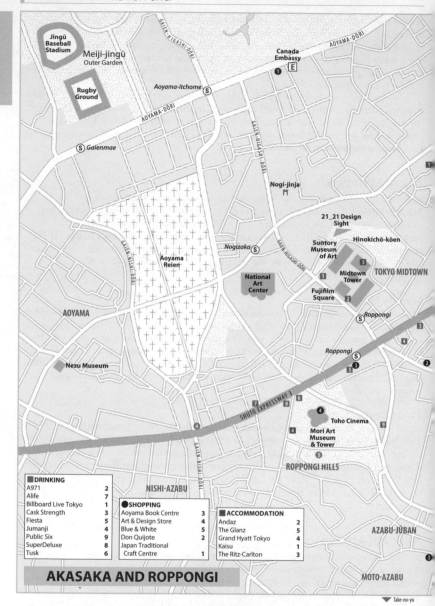

Jingū Baseball Stadium

Meiji-jingū
Outer Garden

Rugby Ground

Aoyama-itchome Ⓢ

Canada Embassy
Ⓔ

AOYAMA-DŌRI

GAIEN-HIGASHI-DŌRI

Ⓢ Gaienmae

AOYAMA-DŌRI

GAIEN-HIGASHI-DŌRI

Nogi-jinja

21_21 Design Sight

Suntory Museum of Art

Hinokichō-kōen

Nogizaka Ⓢ

Aoyama Reien

GAIEN-NISHI-DŌRI

GAIEN-HIGASHI-DŌRI

National Art Center

Midtown Tower

TOKYO MIDTOWN

AOYAMA

Fujifilm Square

Ⓢ Roppongi

Nezu Museum

Roppongi Ⓢ

SHUTO EXPRESSWAY 3

Toho Cinema

Mori Art Museum & Tower

GAIEN-NISHI-DŌRI

ROPPONGI HILLS

■ DRINKING
A971 — 2
Alife — 7
Billboard Live Tokyo — 1
Cask Strength — 3
Fiesta — 5
Jumanji — 4
Public Six — 9
SuperDeluxe — 8
Tusk — 6

NISHI-AZABU

● SHOPPING
Aoyama Book Centre — 3
Art & Design Store — 4
Blue & White — 5
Don Quijote — 2
Japan Traditional
Craft Centre — 1

■ ACCOMMODATION
Andaz — 2
The Glanz — 5
Grand Hyatt Tokyo — 4
Kaisu — 1
The Ritz-Carlton — 3

AZABU-JŪBAN

AKASAKA AND ROPPONGI

MOTO-AZABU

▼ Take-no-yu

Roppongi Hills

六本木ヒルズ • 8-11-27 Akasaka, Minato-ku • ⓦ roppongihills.com • Roppongi Station

Roppongi's metamorphosis was jump-started by the success of the **Roppongi Hills** development where, amid the shops, offices and residences, you'll also find a traditional Japanese garden and pond, a liberal sprinkling of funky street sculptures and an open-air arena for free performances. If you approach Roppongi Hills through the main Metro Hat entrance from Roppongi Station, at the top of the

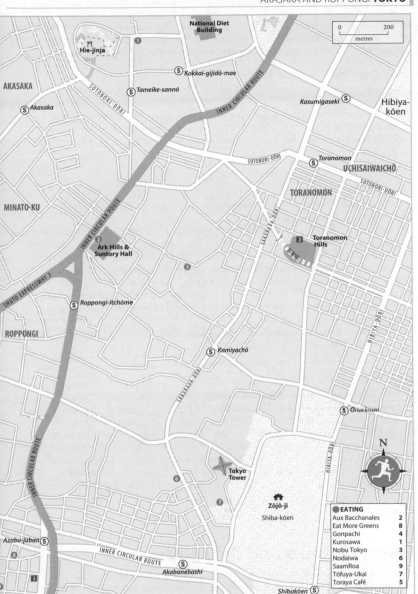

escalators you'll see Louise Bourgeois' **Maman**, a giant bronze, stainless-steel and marble spider.

Mori Art Museum

森美術館, Mori Bijutsukan • 53F Mori Tower, Roppongi Hills • Daily 10am–10pm, Tues closes 5pm • ¥1600 • ☎ 03 6406 6100, ⓦ mori.art.museum

The "Museum Cone", a glass structure enclosing a swirling staircase, forms the entrance to the **Mori Art Museum**, more than fifty storeys overhead. This large gallery space,

1

which occupies the prime top floors of the Mori Tower, puts on large and adventurous exhibitions, with a particular focus on Asian artists – they're generally extremely well-curated affairs, even down to themed menu items at the on-site café.

Tokyo City View

東京シティビュー • 54F Mori Tower, Roppongi Hills • Daily 9am–1am, last entry midnight • ¥1800; Skydeck ¥500 extra • ⓦ www.roppongihills.com/tcv/en

In the same tower as the Mori Art Museum, one floor up, the **Tokyo City View** observation deck is one of the best viewpoints in the city. If the weather is fine, it's possible to get out on to the rooftop **Skydeck** for an alfresco view that's particularly enchanting during and after sunset.

Tokyo Tower

東京タワー • 4-2-8 Shiba-kōen • Daily 9am–11pm • Main observatory ¥900, top observatory ¥700 extra • ☎ 03 3433 5111, ⓦ tokyotower.co.jp • Akabanebashi or Kamiyachō stations

You can't miss **Tokyo Tower**, a distinctive red-and-white structure rising high above the wider Roppongi area. Built during an era when Japan was becoming famous for producing cheap copies of foreign goods, this 333m-high replica of the Eiffel Tower, opened in 1958, manages to top its Parisian role model by several metres. At the tower's base a plethora of the usual souvenir shops, restaurants and other minor attractions has been added over the years, most incurring additional fees and none really worth seeing in their own right. There are good views of Tokyo Bay from the uppermost observation deck, but, at 250m, it's no longer the city's highest viewpoint – you can get 20m higher at the nearby Tokyo City View (see above), while the Tokyo Skytree (see p.102) rises to a vertiginous 450m.

Zōjō-ji

増上寺 • 4-7-35 Shiba-kōen • 24hr • Free • Akabanebashi, Onarimon or Shiba-kōen stations

The main point of interest at **Shiba-kōen** park (芝公園) is **Zōjō-ji**, the family temple of the Tokugawa clan. Dating from 1393, Zōjō-ji was moved to this site in 1598 by Tokugawa Ieyasu (the first Tokugawa shogun) in order to protect southeast Edo spiritually and provide a waystation for pilgrims approaching the capital from the Tōkaidō road. This was once the city's largest holy site, with 48 sub-temples and over a hundred other buildings. Since the fall of the Tokugawa, however, Zōjō-ji has been razed to the ground by fire three times, and virtually all the current buildings date from the mid-1970s; some find it all rather lacking in charm.

Ebisu, Meguro and the south

Named after the Shintō god of good fortune, **Ebisu** is home to hundreds of buzzing bars, many stylish restaurants and the huge, multipurpose **Yebisu Garden Place** development. Uphill to the west of Ebisu lies **Daikanyama**, one of Tokyo's classiest districts, and a great place to chill out at a pavement café or cruise boutiques. Dip downhill again to browse a rather earthier version of the same in **Nakameguro**, whose cherry-tree-lined riverbanks are prime strolling territory. **Meguro**, south along the river from here, is home to the tranquil **National Park for Nature Study**. Lastly, in the transport and hotel hub of **Shinagawa** you'll find the historic temple **Sengaku-ji**, a key location in Tokyo's bloodiest true-life samurai saga, and the wide-ranging **Hara Museum of Contemporary Art**.

Ebisu

恵比寿 • Ebisu Station

The focus of **EBISU** is **Yebisu Garden Place** (恵比寿ガーデンプレイス), a shopping, office and entertainment complex built on the site of the nineteenth-century brewery that was the source of the area's fortunes. For visitors, the main draw here is the excellent **Tokyo Photographic Art Museum**.

Tokyo Photographic Art Museum

東京都写真美術館, Tōkyō-to Shashin Bijutsukan • Yebisu Garden Place • Tues–Sun 10am–6pm, Thurs & Fri until 8pm • Admission charges vary • ☎ 03 3280 0031, ⊛ topmuseum.jp • Ebisu Station

The best sight in the Ebisu area is the **Tokyo Photographic Museum** – also known as the **TOP Museum** – which was fully remodelled in 2016 and hosts excellent exhibitions by major Japanese and Western photographers. There are three full floors of exhibitions (two above ground, one below), with a café on the entrance; exhibitions can last anything from two weeks to three months, but there's usually a good spread of themes at any one time.

Daikanyama

代官山 • Daikanyama Station

A ten-minute stroll west along Komazawa-dōri from Ebisu Station, or one stop from Shibuya on the Tōkyū Tōyoko line, is **DAIKANYAMA**. Home to some of the city's classiest homes, shops and watering holes, the village-like, laidback vibe makes a refreshing break from the frenzy of nearby Shibuya. The area is most notable for its many boutiques and cafés, but even if you're not in the market for clothing or caffeine it's worth a visit for the relaxed atmosphere. Major developments here include **Hillside Terrace**, a one-stop area for drinking, dining and shopping; and the even newer **Log Road** complex, a relatively small affair bookended by craft-beer pubs.

Nakameguro

中目黒 • Nakameguro Station

Immediately southwest of Daikanyama is bohemian **NAKAMEGURO**, one of Tokyo's trendiest areas, with a laidback, boho feel and a liberal sprinkling of eclectic boutiques and small cafés and bars. The district hugs the banks of the Meguro-gawa, a particularly lovely spot to head during cherry-blossom season and in the height of summer, when the waterway provides some natural air conditioning.

Meguro

目黒 • Meguro Station

Within walking distance of Nakameguro or Ebisu, **MEGURO** is decidedly less appealing than its neighbouring areas – the atmosphere here is more city than village. Nevertheless, there are a few interesting things to see, even if they're frustratingly spread out.

Tokyo Metropolitan Teien Art Museum

東京都庭園美術館, Tōkyō-to Teien Bijutsukan • 5-21-9 Shirokanedai, Meguro-ku • **Museum** Daily 10am–6pm, closed second & fourth Wed of the month • Entry varies by exhibitions, usually ¥1000 • **Garden** Daily 10am–9pm • Entry included with museum ticket, otherwise ¥100 • ☎ 03 3443 0201, ⊛ www.teien-art-museum.ne.jp • Meguro or Shirokanedai stations

The Art Deco building housing the elegant **Tokyo Metropolitan Teien Art Museum** is the former home of Prince Asaka Yasuhiko, Emperor Hirohito's uncle, who lived in Paris for three years during the 1920s, where he developed a taste for the European style. It's worth popping in to admire the gorgeous interior decoration (particularly in the octagonal study room upstairs) and tranquil surrounding Japanese gardens; the exhibitions themselves tend to be curated along similarly genteel lines.

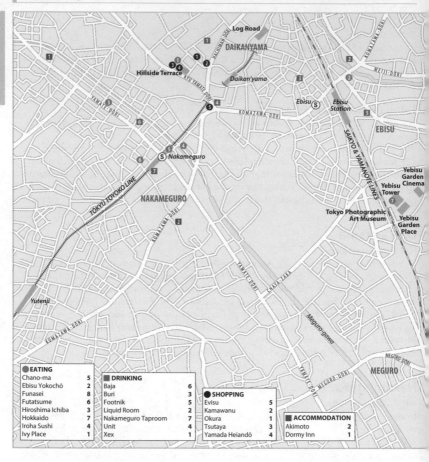

●EATING		■ DRINKING		●SHOPPING		■ ACCOMMODATION	
Chano-ma	5	Baja	6	Evisu	5	Akimoto	2
Ebisu Yokochō	2	Buri	3	Kamawanu	2	Dormy Inn	1
Funasei	8	Footnik	5	Okura	1		
Futatsume	6	Liquid Room	2	Tsutaya	3		
Hiroshima Ichiba	3	Nakameguro Taproom	7	Yamada Heiandō	4		
Hokkaido	7	Unit	4				
Iroha Sushi	4	Xex	1				
Ivy Place	1						

National Park for Nature Study

自然教育園, Shizen Kyōiku-en • 5-21-5 Shirokanedai, Meguro-ku • Tues–Sun 9am–4.30pm, May–Aug until 5pm • ¥310 •
Ⓦ www.ins.kahaku.go.jp • Meguro or Shirokanedai stations

The spacious **National Park for Nature Study** is a worthy attempt to preserve the original natural features of the countryside before Edo was settled and developed into Tokyo. Among the eight thousand trees in the park are some that have been growing for five hundred years, while frogs can be heard croaking amid the grass beside the marshy ponds. The whole place is a bird-spotter's paradise, and it's also one of the few areas in Tokyo where you can really escape the crowds.

Happōen

八芳園 • 1-1-1 Shirokanedai, Meguro-ku • **Garden** Daily 10am–5pm • Free • **Teahouse** Daily 11am–5pm • ¥800 •
Shirokanedai Station

The lovely **Happōen** garden's name means "beautiful from any angle" and, despite the addition of a modern wedding hall on one side, this is still true. Most of the garden's design dates from the early twentieth century, when a business tycoon bought up the land, built a classical Japanese villa (still standing by the garden's entrance) and gave it the name Happōen. The garden harbours ancient bonsai trees, a stone lantern said to

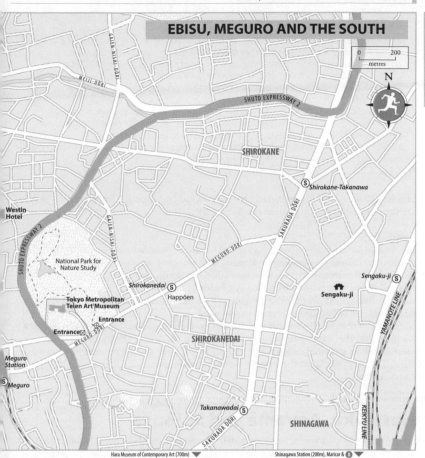

Hara Museum of Contemporary Art (700m) ▼   Shinagawa Station (200m), Maricar & ⑧ ▼

have been carved eight hundred years ago by the Heike warrior Taira-no Munekiyo, and a central pond. Nestling amid the trees is a delightful **teahouse**.

Shinagawa and around

品川 • Shinagawa Station

The transport and hotel hub of **SHINAGAWA** was once the location of one of the original checkpoints on the Tōkaidō, the major highway into Edo during the reign of the shoguns. These days, most travellers who find themselves in Shinagawa are merely changing trains or travelling on one of the many train lines snaking through the area, but those with a little time to spare should visit the eclectic **Hara Museum of Contemporary Art**.

Hara Museum of Contemporary Art

原美術館, Hara Bijutsukan • 4-7-25 Kitashinagawa, Shinagawa-ku • Tues–Sun 11am–5pm, Wed until 8pm • ¥1100 • ☎ 03 3445 0651, ⓦ www.haramuseum.or.jp • Shinagawa Station

In a quiet residential area around 800m south of Shinagawa Station, the **Hara Museum of Contemporary Art** has a small permanent collection including quirky installations, such as *Rondo*, by Morimura Yasumasa, whose self-portrait occupies the downstairs toilet. The

1

REAL-LIFE MARIO KART

If you're in Tokyo for any length of time, you may well see Mario, Luigi, Toad, Yoshi and other characters from the classic game **Super Mario Kart** dashing around the city streets in tiny go-karts. This is no mere marketing stunt, but an activity that you can actually take part in yourself. Whizzing about in a costume, and most likely unable to remove the cartoonish grin from your face, this is about the best fun you can have in Tokyo, whether you're a fan of the game or not.

The **Maricar** team (☎03 6712 8275, ⊛maricar.com) run three separate courses from their office in Shinagawa; all of them take in Tokyo Tower and Roppongi, with Shibuya and Odaiba also options, and prices start at ¥8000. You'll need to be in possession of a foreign or international driving licence (full details are on the website). Note that you'll be driving on real roads, and, unlike in the game, you only have one life.

---

building itself, a 1938 Bauhaus-style house designed by Watanabe Jin, is worth a look, as are the tranquil sculpture gardens overlooked by the museum's pleasant café.

Sengaku-ji

泉岳寺 • 2-11-1 Akanawa, Minato-ku • **Temple** Daily: April–Sept 7am–6pm; Oct–March 7am–5pm • Free • ☎03 3441 5560, ⊛sengakuji.or.jp • **Museum** Daily: April–Sept 9am–4.30pm; Oct–March 9am–4pm • ¥500 • Sengaku-ji Station

Around a kilometre north of Shinagawa is **Sengaku-ji**, home to the graves of **Asano Takumi** and his **47 rōnin** (see box below). Most of what you see now was rebuilt after World War II, but a striking gate decorated with a metalwork dragon dates back to 1836. The graves of the 47 *rōnin* are in the temple grounds (it's hard to resist the temptation to count them all), as well as the statue and grave of **Oishi Kuranosuke**, their avenging leader; a **museum** to the left of the main building contains their personal belongings, as well as a receipt for the severed head of Kira. The entrance is on the eastern side of the complex, which is a little tricky to track down.

Harajuku, Aoyama and Shibuya

If it's "wacky" Japan you're after, **Harajuku** should be neighbourhood number one on your list – indeed, in terms of human traffic, there can be few more fascinating districts on the whole planet. Streets here often resemble densely populated catwalks, complete with zany clothing, hairstyles and accessories. **Shibuya**, just south of

---

THE 47 RŌNIN

Celebrated in kabuki and *bunraku* plays, as well as on film, *Chūshingura* is a true story of honour, revenge and loyalty. In 1701, a young *daimyō*, Asano Takumi, became embroiled in a fatal argument in the shogun's court with his teacher and fellow lord Kira Yoshinaka. Asano had lost face in his performance of court rituals and, blaming his mentor for his lax tuition, drew his sword within the castle walls and attacked Kira. Although Kira survived, the shogun, on hearing of this breach of etiquette, ordered Asano to commit *seppuku*, the traditional form of suicide, which he did.

Their lord having been disgraced, Asano's loyal retainers, the **rōnin** – or masterless samurai – vowed revenge. On December 14, 1702, the 47 *rōnin*, lead by **Oishi Kuranosuke**, stormed Kira's villa, cut off his head and paraded it through Edo in triumph before placing it on Asano's grave in Sengaku-ji. The shogun ordered the *rōnin's* deaths, but instead all 47 committed *seppuku* on February 14, 1703, including Oishi's 15-year-old son. They were buried with Asano in Sengaku-ji, and today their graves are still wreathed in the smoke from the bundles of incense placed by their gravestones.

Harajuku, is almost absurdly busy – a neon-drenched, *Kanji*-splattered, high-rise jungle second only to Shinjuku for sheer eye-popping madness. East of Harajuku, those with gilt-edged credit cards will feel more at home among the big-brand boutiques of **Aoyama**.

Harajuku

原宿

As well as the wooded grounds of **Meiji-jingū Inner Garden**, **HARAJUKU** is also blessed with Tokyo's largest park, **Yoyogi-kōen**. However, ask Tokyoites what Harajuku means to them and they won't be talking about trees or shrines – the neighbourhood is one of the city's most important fashion centres (see box, p.120), and there are reams of appealing places in which to reflect on your purchases over a coffee.

Elegant **Omotesandō** (表参道) bisects the neighbourhood, flanked on either side by dense networks of streets, packed with funky little boutiques, restaurants and bars. The hip, independent Harajuku style is very much in evidence south of Omotesandō on **Cat Street**, a curvy pathway lined with cafés, small restaurants and eclectic emporia. By contrast, the Andō Tadao-designed **Omotesandō Hills** is a glitzy complex of upmarket designer shops, restaurants and residences. Meanwhile, the **Takeshita-dōri** (竹下通り) shopping alley provides an intriguing window on Japanese teen fashion, with shops selling every kind of tat imaginable.

Meiji-jingū

明治神宮 • Daily sunrise–sunset • Free • ⓦ meijijingu.or.jp

Covering parts of both Aoyama and Harajuku are the grounds of **Meiji-jingū**, Tokyo's premier Shintō shrine, a memorial to Emperor Meiji and his empress Shōken. Together with the neighbouring shrines to General Nogi and Admiral Tōgō, Meiji-jingū was created as a symbol of imperial power and Japanese racial superiority. Rebuilt in 1958 after being destroyed during World War II, the shrine is the focus of several annual **festivals** (see box, p.159). Apart from the festivals, Meiji-jingū is best visited midweek, when its calm serenity can be appreciated without the crowds.

The shrine's grounds are split into two distinct parts. The **Inner Garden**, beside Harajuku Station, includes the emperor's shrine, the empress's iris gardens, the Treasure House and extensive wooded grounds. The less important **Outer Garden**, 1km east, south of Sendagaya and Shinanomachi stations, contains several sporting arenas, including the National Stadium – centrepiece of the 2020 Olympics (see box, p.119).

Inner Garden

御苑 • **Inner Garden** Daily sunrise–sunset • Free • **Jingū Naien** Daily 8.30am–5pm • ¥500 • Harajuku or Meiji-jingūmae stations

The most impressive way to approach the **Inner Garden** is through the southern gate next to Jingū-bashi, the bridge across from Harajuku's mock-Tudor station building. From the gateway, a wide gravel path runs through densely forested grounds to the 12m-high **Ō-torii**, the largest Myōjin-style gate in Japan, made from 1500-year-old cypress pine trees from Taiwan.

To the left of the Ō-torii is one entrance to the **Jingū Naien** (神宮内苑), a traditional garden said to have been designed by the Emperor Meiji for his wife. The garden is at its most beautiful (and most crowded) in June, when over one hundred varieties of **irises**, the empress's favourite flowers, pepper the lush greenery with their purple and white blooms. From the garden's main entrance, the gravel path turns right and passes through a second wooden *torii*, **Kita-mon** (north gate), leading to the impressive **Honden** (central hall). With their Japanese cypress wood and green copper roofs, the Honden and its surrounding buildings are a fine example of how Shintō architecture can blend seamlessly with nature.

1

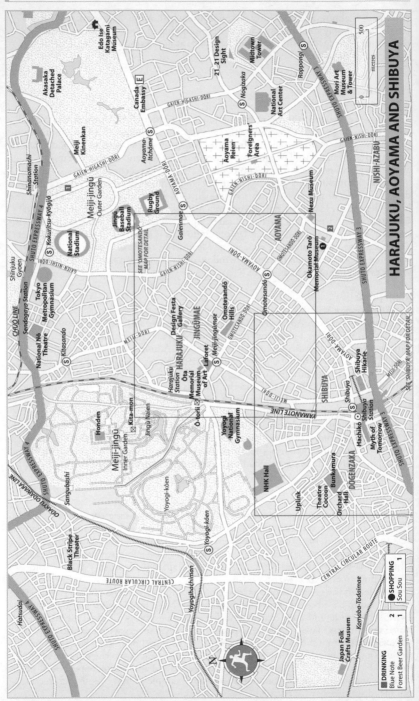

HARAJUKU, AOYAMA AND SHIBUYA

Akasaka Detached Palace

Edo Ise Katagami Museum

Meiji Kinenkan

Canada Embassy

21-21 Design Sight

Midtown Tower

Roppongi Ⓢ

Mori Art Museum & Tower

Nogizaka Ⓢ

National Art Center

GAIEN-HIGASHI-DŌRI

Aoyama Itchōme Ⓢ

Aoyama Reien

Foreigners' Area

GAIEN-NISHI-DŌRI

NISHI-AZABU

Shinanomachi Station

GAIEN-HIGASHI-DŌRI

Meiji-jingū Outer Garden

Jingū Baseball Stadium

Rugby Ground

Galenmae Ⓢ

AOYAMA-DŌRI

Nezu Museum

AOYAMA

Kokuritsu-Kyōgijō

National Stadium

SEE 'OMOTESANDŌ' MAP FOR DETAIL

GAIEN-NISHI-DŌRI

OMOTESANDŌ-DŌRI

Omotesandō Ⓢ

Okamoto Tarō Memorial Museum

CHŪŌ LINE

Shinjuku Gyoen

Sendagaya Station

Tokyo Metropolitan Gymnasium

MEIJI-DŌRI

Design Festa Gallery

HARAJUKU

JINGŪMAE

Omotesandō Hills

OMOTESANDŌ-DŌRI

AOYAMA-DŌRI

National Nō Theatre

Kitasandō Ⓢ

Harajuku Station

Ōta Memorial Museum of Art

Laforet

Meiji-jingūmae Ⓢ

SHIBUYA

Shibuya Hikarie

Shibuya Ⓢ

SEE 'SHIBUYA' MAP FOR DETAIL

Honden

Meiji-jingū Inner Garden

Kita-mon

Ō-torii

Jingū Naien

YAMANOTE LINE

Yoyogi National Gymnasium

Hachikō Shibuya Station

Myth of Tomorrow

AOYAMA-DŌRI

MEIJI-DŌRI

Sangūbashi Ⓢ

Yoyogi-kōen

NHK Hall

DŌGENZAKA

Bunkamura

Uplink

Theatre Cocoon

Orchard Hall

Black Stripe Theater

Yoyogi-kōen Ⓢ

Yoyogihachiman Ⓢ

CENTRAL CIRCULAR ROUTE

Hatsudai

Komaba-Tōdaimae

SHUTO EXPRESSWAY 4

ODAKYŪ ODAWARA LINE

CENTRAL CIRCULAR ROUTE

N

0   nietres   500

■ DRINKING	
Blue Note	2
Forest Beer Garden	1

● SHOPPING	
Sou Sou	1

Japan Folk Crafts Musuem   2

Ⓔ

THE 2020 OLYMPICS

In 2020 Tokyo will host the **Olympic and Paralympic Games** (Ⓦtokyo2020.jp), becoming the first Asian city to host the Games twice. The opening ceremony will get under way on 24 July, 2020, at the **National Stadium** in Meiji-jingū Outer Garden. The original stadium, built for the 1964 Olympics, was demolished in 2015 as part of preparations for the Games, and it's safe to say that even clockwork-efficient Japan has failed to escape the Olympic curses of funding and planning. In late 2012, it was announced that a design by the late British-Iraqi architect **Zaha Hadid** had been selected by the Sport Council, but her plans drew a raft of criticism, notably from Japanese architects ("turtle-like" and "rather vaginal" were among the most cutting descriptions), and city politicians worried about the cost. Said costs started to spiral, with Hadid's team blaming a lack of competition among contractors; by the time her plans were finally ditched in 2015, the estimates had risen to ¥252 billion (£1.82bn/$2.43bn). A cheaper design by **Kengo Kuma** was selected as the alternative, and is set to be completed by November 2019. All being well, the stadium will host the opening ceremony, the athletics events and the football final.

Mercifully, two of Tokyo's most iconic venues are due to change little for the 2020 Games: the superlative **Tokyo Metropolitan Gymnasium**, just north of Meiji-jingū Outer Garden, and the **Yoyogi National Gymnasium** in Yoyogi-kōen (see below), each a design classic built for the 1964 event, and respectively set to host the table tennis and handball. Other notable venues will include the **Budōkan** (see p.166), to be used for judo; the **Tokyo International Forum** (see p.159), scheduled to host the weightlifting; and the **National Sumo Stadium** (see p.166), which for sixteen days will have to put up with boxers' punches instead of sumo slaps. In addition, the **Imperial Palace gardens** (see p.86) will form an incredibly photogenic backdrop to the road cycling events. The rest of the action will take place around Tokyo Bay, or in arenas outside the city centre. Knowing Tokyo, and following Prime Minister Shinzō Abe's humble-yet-hilarious Super Mario impression at the closing ceremony of the Rio Games in 2016, it's going to be quite a party.

Yoyogi-kōen

代々木公園 • Daily 24hr • Free • Harajuku, Yoyogi-kōen or Meiji-jingūmae stations

Tokyo's largest park, **Yoyogi-kōen**, is a favourite spot for joggers and bonneted groups of kindergarten kids with their minders. Once an imperial army training ground, the park was dubbed "Washington Heights" after World War II, when it housed US military personnel. In 1964 the land was given over to the Olympic athletes' village, after which it became Yoyogi-kōen. Two of the stadia, built for those Olympics and also due to host events in the 2020 edition (see box above), remain the area's most famous architectural features: the boat-shaped steel suspension roof of Tange Kenzō's **Yoyogi National Gymnasium** was a structural engineering marvel at the time; the smaller stadium, in the shape of a giant swirling seashell, is used for basketball.

Ōta Memorial Museum of Art

太田記念美術館, Ōta Kinen Bijutsukan • 1-10-10 Jingūmae, Shibuya-ku • Tues–Sun 10.30am–5.30pm • Usually ¥700 for regular exhibitions, ¥1000 for special exhibitions • ☏ 03 3403 0880, Ⓦukiyoe-ota-muse.jp • Harajuku or Meiji-jingūmae stations

Near the crossing of Omotesandō and Meiji-dōri, look out for **Laforet**, a trendy boutique complex behind which is the excellent **Ōta Memorial Museum of Art**. Put on slippers to wander the small galleries, set over on two levels, which feature *ukiyo-e* paintings and prints from the private collection of the late Ōta Seizō, an insurance tycoon. The art displayed comes from a collection of twelve thousand pieces, including masterpieces by Utamaro, Hokusai and Hiroshige.

1

HARAJUKU STYLE

With its name immortalized in several Western songs, Harajuku is better known abroad for its zany **youth culture** than it is for shopping, and with very good reason. Swing by the Harajuku Station area on a weekend and you'll see crowds of youngsters, mainly female, dressed up to the nines in a series of bizarre costumes; the epicentre is Jingū-bashi, a small bridge heading towards Meiji-jingū shrine (see p.117) from Harajuku Station.

Of the styles to look out for, **Cosplay** is probably the most familiar to outsiders: it involves dressing up as an anime, manga or game character, with occasionally startling results. Also easy to spot is **Gothic Lolita**, a mix of the gothic and the girlie; this itself is split into subgenres including punk, black, white (as in the hues) and country style. There are plenty more, including a whole host of smaller genres: **Visual Kei** adherents go for crazy make-up and hairstyles; **Decora** is a bright, flamboyant style often featuring myriad toys, pieces of jewellery and other accessories; **Kawaii**, which means "cute" in Japanese, usually involves clothing more appropriate to children. More styles are born every year, of course.

Design Festa Gallery

デザイン・フェスタ・ギャラリー • 3-20-18 Jingūmae, Shibuya-ku • Daily 11am–8pm • Free • ☏ 03 3479 1442, ☒ designfesta.com • Harajuku or Meiji-jingūmae stations

An anything-goes arts space sprouting out of Harajuku's backstreets, the **Design Festa Gallery** is an offshoot of the Design Festa, Japan's biggest art and design event. Behind the Day-Glo paintings, graffiti, sculptures and red scaffolding swarming over the building's front like some alien metal creeper, the interior features eclectic displays

OMOTESANDŌ

● EATING	
Aoyama Flower Market	8
Bepokah	1
Commune 246	7
Crisscross	10
Harajuku Gyōzaro	5
La Fée Délice	6
Las Chicas	9
Maisen	3
Sakuratei	2
Tokyo Snake Center	4

● SHOPPING	
6% Dokidoki	3
Bapexclusive	13
Chicago	2
Comme des Garçons	11
Gallery Kawano	7
Hysterics	12
Issey Miyake	10
Kiddyland	5
Kura Chika Yoshida	9
Musubi	1
Onitsuka Tiger	4
Oriental Bazaar	6
Ragtag	8
Yohji Yamamoto	14

■ ACCOMMODATION	
Caravan Tokyo	1

0   200
metres

ranging from quirky sculpture to video installations – even the toilet is plastered from floor to ceiling with artwork.

Aoyama

青山

Harajuku's chaotic creativity finally gives way to **AOYAMA**'s sleek sophistication, as Omotesandō crosses Aoyama-dōri and narrows to a two-lane street lined with the boutiques of many of Japan's top designers (see p.163).

Okamoto Tarō Memorial Museum

岡本太郎記念館, Okamoto Tarō Kinenkan • 6-1-19 Minami-aoyama, Minato-ku • 10am–5.30pm; closed Tues • ¥600 • Ⓦ taro-okamoto.or.jp • Omotesandō Station

The quirky **Okamoto Tarō Memorial Museum** once functioned as the studio of the avant-garde artist; it now houses examples of his intriguing, often whimsical work, as well as a pleasant café. If this has whetted your appetite, you might consider heading to the larger Okamoto Taro Museum of Art in Kawasaki, between Tokyo and Yokohama (Ⓦwww.taromuseum.jp).

Nezu Museum

根津美術館, Nezu Bijutsukan • 6-5-1 Minami-aoyama, Minato-ku • Tues–Sun 10am–5pm • ¥1100 • ☎ 03 3400 2536, Ⓦ www.nezu-muse.or.jp • Omotesandō or Nogizaka stations

The prestigious **Nezu Museum** sits at the far eastern end of Omotesandō, in an elegant building designed by Kengo Kuma. The museum houses a classy collection of Oriental treasures, including the celebrated *Irises* screens, traditionally displayed for a month from the end of each April – expect big crowds for this popular exhibition. The museum's best feature, enjoyable any time of year and fully justifying the entrance fee, is its extensive garden, which slopes gently away around an ornamental pond. Dotted through it are several traditional teahouses, and mossy stone and bronze sculptures.

Aoyama Reien

青山霊園 • 2-32-2 Minami-aoyama, Minato-ku • Aoyama-itchōme, Gaienmae or Nogizaka stations

Tokyo's most important graveyard is officially entitled **Aoyama Reien**, but most know it as **Aoyama Bochi**. Everyone who was anyone is buried here, and the graves, many decorated with elaborate calligraphy, are interesting to browse. Look out for the section where foreigners are buried: their tombstones provide a history of early *gaijin* involvement in Japan. Many locals enjoy partying here during the *hanami* season, under the candyfloss bunches of pink cherry blossoms.

Shibuya

渋谷

It's hard to beat **SHIBUYA**, birthplace of a million-and-one consumer crazes, as a mind-blowing introduction to contemporary Tokyo. Teens and twenty-somethings throng **Centre Gai** (センター街), the shopping precinct that runs between the district's massive department stores. Centre Gai is bookended to the south by Shibuya Station, visible across the hordes of people navigating the famously busy Shibuya crossing – one of the most famous **pedestrian crossings** in the world. One perch from which to view the crowds of people swarming across is the bridge corridor linking the JR station with Shibuya Mark City complex. This space has been put to excellent use as the gallery for Okamoto Tarō's 1969 fourteen-panel painting **Myth of Tomorrow** (*Asu-no-shinwa*), a 30m-long mural created in 1969 depicting the moment the atomic bomb exploded in Hiroshima. Although there are a few interesting sights in the area, Shibuya, with a wealth of bars and clubs (see p.152 & p.154), is primarily an after-dark destination.

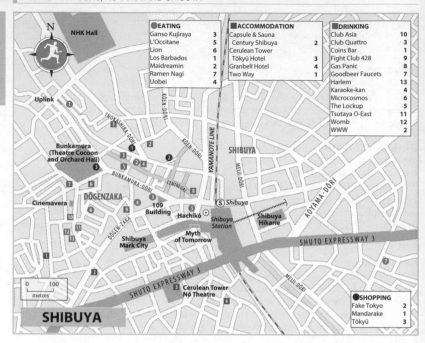

■EATING	
Ganso Kujiraya	3
L'Occitane	5
Lion	6
Los Barbados	1
Maidreamin	2
Ramen Nagi	7
Uobei	4

■ACCOMMODATION	
Capsule & Sauna	
Century Shibuya	2
Cerulean Tower	
Tōkyū Hotel	3
Granbell Hotel	4
Two Way	1

■DRINKING	
Club Asia	10
Club Quattro	3
Coins Bar	1
Fight Club 428	9
Gas Panic	8
Goodbeer Faucets	7
Harlem	13
Karaoke-kan	4
Microcosmos	6
The Lockup	5
Tsutaya O-East	11
Womb	12
WWW	2

●SHOPPING	
Fake Tokyo	2
Mandarake	1
Tōkyū	3

SHIBUYA

Shibuya Hikarie Building

渋谷ヒカリエ • 2-21-1 Shibuya, Shibuya-ku • **Creative Space** 8 daily 11am–8pm • Ⓦ hikarie.jp • Shibuya Station

A 34-storey tower rising just east of Shibuya Station, the **Shibuya Hikarie** complex contains offices, shops, restaurants and various cultural facilities, including a 2000-seat theatre whose lobby provides a sweeping view of the skyline. For regular visitors, the prime attraction is **Creative Space 8** on the eighth floor, a mix of gallery space and shops.

Japan Folk Crafts Museum

日本民芸館, Nihon Mingeikan • Tues–Sun 10am–5pm • ¥1100 • ☎ 03 3467 4527, Ⓦ mingeikan.or.jp • Komaba-Tōdaimae Station

Just two stops down the Keiō Inokashira line from Shibuya Station is the excellent **Japan Folk Crafts Museum**, a must-see for lovers of handcrafted pottery, textiles and lacquerware. The gift shop is a fine source of souvenirs. Opposite the museum stands a nineteenth-century **nagayamon** (long gate house), brought here from Tochigi-ken by the museum's founder, Yanagi Sōetsu (see p.841).

HACHIKŌ

A statue outside Shibuya Station marks the waiting spot of **Hachikō** (1923–35), an Akita dog who would come to greet his master every day as he returned home from work – a practice that continued for almost a decade after the professor's death, with the dog arriving on time every day to greet the train. Locals were so touched by Hachikō's devotion that a **bronze statue** was cast of the dog. During World War II, the original Hachikō statue was melted down for weapons, but a replacement was reinstated beside the station in 1948 – it remains one of Tokyo's most famous rendezvous spots. You can see the real Hachikō in the National Museum of Science and Nature, where he lives on in stuffed form (see p.98), and there's a memorial by his master's grave in Aoyama Cemetery (see p.121).

Shinjuku and the west

Some 4km due west of the Imperial Palace, **SHINJUKU** (新宿) is the modern heart of Tokyo. From the love hotels and hostess bars of **Kabukichō** to shop-till-you-drop department stores and hi-tech towers, the district offers a tantalizing microcosm of the city. Vast **Shinjuku Station**, a messy combination of three train terminals and connecting subway lines, splits the area into two. There's also the separate **Seibu-Shinjuku Station**, north of the JR Station. At least two million commuters are fed into these stations every day and spun out of sixty exits. If you get lost here (it's easily done), head immediately for street level and get your bearings by looking out for the skyscrapers of the **Nishi-Shinjuku** (西新宿) area to the west.

West of Shinjuku, the JR Chūō line will transport you to a must-see sight for anime fans: the **Ghibli Museum** at Mitaka. Also out this way is **Shimokitazawa**, dubbed one of the world's coolest neighbourhoods by *Vogue* in 2014.

Tokyo Metropolitan Government Building

東京都庁, Tōkyō Tochō • 2-8-1 Nishi-shinjuku, Shinjuku-ku; both observation rooms 45F • South observation room daily 9.30am–5.30pm; north observation room daily 9am–11pm; each observation room is closed a couple of days per month • Free • Free tours Mon–Fri 10am–3pm • Tochōmae Station

Some 13,000 city bureaucrats clock in each day at the Gotham City-like **Tokyo Metropolitan Government Building** (TMGB), a 400,000-square-metre complex designed by Tange Kenzō. The complex includes twin 48-storey towers, an adjacent tower block, the Metropolitan Assembly Hall (where the city's councillors meet) and a sweeping, statue-lined and colonnaded plaza.

On the ground floor of the north tower you'll find the excellent Tokyo Tourist Information Centre (see p.133); free **tours** of the complex depart from here. Both the towers have **observation rooms**; the southern one is quieter and has a pleasant café, while the northern one is usually open later, and features a shopping area and (overpriced) restaurant. It's worth timing your visit for dusk, so you can see the multicoloured lights of Shinjuku spark into action.

Omoide Yokochō

思い出横丁

Squashed up against the train tracks running north from the Odakyū department store is **Omoide Yokochō**, commonly known as Memories Alley. Lit by hundreds of *akachochin* (red lanterns), it's also known as Shomben Yokochō (しょんべん横丁, Piss Alley), a reference to the time when patrons of the area's many cramped *yakitori* joints and bars relieved themselves in the street, for want of other facilities. Don't be put off: the alley remains a cheap and atmospheric place to eat and drink (and there are toilets these days). Enjoy it while you can, too, as there's regular talk of redeveloping the area. A pedestrian tunnel at the southern end of the alleys, just to the right of the cheap clothes outlets, provides a short cut to the east side of Shinjuku Station.

Kabukichō

歌舞伎町 • Northeast of Shinjuku Station

Red-light district **KABUKICHŌ** is named after a kabuki theatre that was planned for the area in the aftermath of World War II, but never built. For casual wanderers it's all pretty safe thanks to street security cameras, but at heart it's still one of the seediest corners of the city. In its grid of streets you'll see self-consciously primped and preening touts who fish women into the male host bars; the *yakuza* who run the show are there, too, though generally keeping a much lower profile.

1

SHINJUKU AND THE WEST

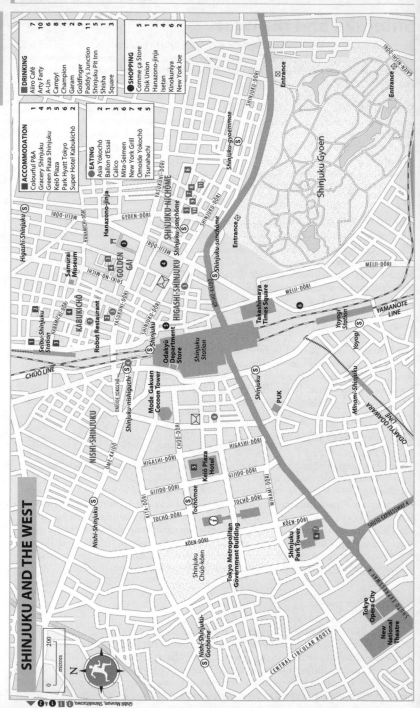

■ ACCOMMODATION

Colourful P&A	1
Gracery Shinjuku	4
Green Plaza Shinjuku	3
Keiō Plaza	5
Park Hyatt Tokyo	6
Super Hotel Kabukichō	2

■ EATING

Asia Yokochō	2
Ballon d'Essai	1
Calico	3
Mita-Seimen	6
New York Grill	7
Omoide Yokochō	4
Tsunahachi	5

■ DRINKING

Aiiro Café	7
Arty Farty	10
A-Un	6
Campy!	8
Champion	4
Garam	2
Goldfinger	9
Paddy's Junction	11
Shinjuku Pit Inn	5
Shisha	1
Square	3

● SHOPPING

Comme ça Store	5
Disk Union	1
Hanazono-jinja	3
Isetan	4
Kinokuniya	6
New York Joe	2

Ghibli Museum, Shimokitazawa, ▼

Higashi-Shinjuku Ⓢ
Seibu-Shinjuku Station
MEIJI-DŌRI
HANAMICHI-DŌRI
KABUKICHŌ
Samurai Museum
SHIKI-ON-MICHI
GOLDEN GAI
Hanazono-jinja
GYOEN-DŌRI
Robot Restaurant
YASUKUNI-DŌRI
MEIJI-DŌRI
YASUKUNI-DŌRI
SHINJUKU-DŌRI
HIGASHI-SHINJUKU
Shinjuku-sanchōme
Shinjuku Ⓢ
Odakyū Department Store
Shinjuku Station
CHŪŌ LINE
OMOIDE YOKOCHŌ
Shinjuku-nishiguchi Ⓢ
Mode Gakuen Cocoon Tower
OME-KAIDO
NISHI-SHINJUKU
Nishi-Shinjuku Ⓢ
HIGASHI-DŌRI
Keiō Plaza Hotel
GIJIDO-DŌRI
KITA-DŌRI
Tochōmae Ⓢ
TOCHŌ-DŌRI
KŌEN-DŌRI
Shinjuku Chūō-kōen
Tokyo Metropolitan Government Building
Nishi-Shinjuku-Gochōme Ⓢ
Tokyo Opera City
New National Theatre
SHUTO EXPRESSWAY 4
CENTRAL CIRCULAR ROUTE
Shinjuku Park Tower
KŌEN-DŌRI
MINAMI-DŌRI
TOCHŌ-DŌRI
CHŪŌ-DŌRI
PUK
Shinjuku Ⓢ
Yoyogi Ⓢ
Yoyogi Station
YAMANOTE LINE
MEIJI-DŌRI
Takashimaya Times Square
Shinjuku-gyoenmae
Shinjuku-sanchōme Ⓢ
KOSHŪ-KAIDO
Entrance
Entrance
Entrance
SHINJUKU-DŌRI
MEIJI-DŌRI
GAIEN-NISHI-DŌRI
Shinjuku Gyoen
SHINJUKU-NICHŌME
MEIJI-DŌRI
TSUKIJI-DŌRI
ŌKUBO-DŌRI
Minami-Shinjuku
ODAKYŪ ODAWARA LINE
ODAKYŪ LINE

N

metres
0   200

Golden Gai

ゴールデン街

Just west of the Hanazono-jinja is **Golden Gai**, one of Tokyo's most atmospheric (and seedy) bar quarters. Since just after World War II, intellectuals and artists have rubbed shoulders with Kabukichō's demimonde in the tiny bars here. For decades this hugely atmospheric warren of around 150 drinking dens was teetering on the brink of oblivion, the cinderblock buildings under threat from both property developers and from their own shoddy construction. However, Golden Gai has since undergone a mini-renaissance, with a younger generation of bar masters and mistresses taking over – or at least presiding over – some of the shoebox establishments. Many bars continue to welcome regulars only (and charge exorbitant prices to newcomers), but *gaijin* visitors no longer risk being fleeced rotten, since most places now post their table and drink charges outside the door.

Samurai Museum

サムライミュージアム • 2-25-6 Kabukichō, Shinjuku-ku • Daily 10.30am–9pm • ¥1800, plus ¥500 to dress up in samurai clothing • ☎ 03 6457 6411, ⓦ samuraimuseum.jp • Shinjuku or Seibu-Shinjuku stations

The **Samurai Museum** is a funky new addition to the Shinjuku area. Here you can check out displays of samurai costumes and helmets, and if you're willing to shell out more on top of the already-hefty ticket price you can don similar togs yourself. If you time it right, there are four daily "shows" in which a genuine samurai actor comes by to show off his sword-wielding prowess.

Hanazono-jinja

花園神社 • 5-17-3 Shinjuku, Shinjuku-ku • 24hr • Free • Shinjuku, Seibu-Shinjuku, Higashi-shinjuku or Shinjuku-sanchōme stations

Set in grounds studded with vermillion *torii*, the attractive **Hanazono-jinja** shrine predates the founding of Edo by the Tokugawa, but the current granite buildings are modern re-creations – the shrine was originally sited where the department store Isetan now is. At night spotlights give the shrine a special ambience, and every Sunday there's a flea market in its grounds (see p.160).

Shinjuku Gyoen

新宿御苑 • 11 Naitomachi, Shinjuku-ku • **Garden** Tues–Sun 9am–4.30pm, last entry 4pm; villa second & fourth Sat of month 10am–3pm • ¥200 • **Rakū-tei** Tues–Sun 10am–4pm • Tea ¥700 • Main entrance Shinjuku-gyoenmae Station; west gate Sendagaya Station

The largest and arguably the most beautiful garden in Tokyo is **Shinjuku Gyoen**. The grounds, which once held the mansion of Lord Naitō, the *daimyō* of Tsuruga on the coast of the Sea of Japan, were opened to the public after World War II. Apart from spaciousness, the gardens' most notable feature is the variety of design. The southern half is traditionally Japanese, with winding paths, stone lanterns, artificial hills, and islands in ponds linked by zigzag bridges, and is home to *Rakū-tei*, a pleasant **teahouse**. At the northern end of the park are formal, French-style gardens, with neat rows of tall birch trees and hedge-lined flowerbeds. Clipped, broad lawns dominate the middle of the park, which is modelled on English landscape design.

Western Tokyo

Tokyo sprawls for quite some way west of Shinjuku, and there are some very fashionable neighbourhoods dotted around this densely populated but relatively low-level jigsaw of suburbs. By far the most interesting for shorter-term visitors to

1

Japan is **Shimokitazawa**, Tokyo's own little hipster paradise. Heading even further out, but still easily accessible by train, the **Suginami** area has long been associated with the animation industry; it's the location for several production houses, and home to many key artists, but of more interest to the traveller is the immensely popular **Ghibli Museum**.

Shimokitazawa

下北沢 • Shimokitazawa Station, 4 stops west of Shibuya on the Keio-Inokashira line, or 6 stops southwest of Shinjuku on the Odakyū line

Small, cute and quirky, **Shimokitazawa** – known as **Shimokita** for short – is a prime draw for young, bohemian sorts, and a nice escape from "regular" Tokyo; gone are the high-rise blocks and incessant noise of Shinjuku, just 5km to the east, replaced here with narrow, relatively traffic-free lanes, and a general air of calm. The charms of Shimokita are essentially the same as most hipster areas around the world: vintage clothing stores, record shops, galleries, live music bars, and independent cafés serving flat whites to people writing blogs on their Macs. There's not all that much in the way of sights here, bar a couple of tucked-away shrines, but you'll find plenty of shops, cafés and bars at which to while away the time.

Suginami Animation Museum

杉並アニメーションミュージアム • 3-29-5 Kamiogi, Suginami-ku • Tues–Sun 10am–6pm • Free • W sam.or.jp • 20min walk or 5min bus ride (platform 0 or 1; ¥220) from Ogikubo Station on the JR lines or Marunouchi subway line

Astroboy, Gundam and many other anime characters are all present and correct at the well-organized **Suginami Animation Museum**, situated atop a retro-looking function hall. Colourful displays trace the development of animation in Japan, from the simple black-and-white 1917 feature *Genkanban-no-maki* (The Gatekeepers) to digital escapades such as *Blood: The Last Vampire*. Videos with English subtitles explain how anime are made, while interactive computer games allow you to create your own animations. You can watch anime screenings in the small theatre, and there's also a library packed with manga and DVDs (some with English subtitles).

Ghibli Museum

ジブリ美術館, Jiburi Bijutsukan • 1-1-83 Shimorenjaku, Mitaka-ku • 10am–6pm; closed Tues • ¥1000; advance bookings only (museum can be booked out for weeks at a time); 2400 tickets per day are available and can be bought online or from Lawson convenience stores • T 0570 055777, W ghibli-museum.jp • Short walk (follow signs) or bus ride (¥210) from south exit of Mitaka Station, on JR Chūō line; or walkable from Kichijōji Station, also on JR Chūō line

The utterly beguiling **Ghibli Museum** is one of Tokyo's top draws for international visitors – and an essential one for those interested in anime. It's very popular, so reserve tickets well ahead of time. Though it needs little introduction, the Ghibli animation studio was responsible for blockbuster movies including *My Neighbour Totoro*, *Princess Mononoke* and the Oscar-winning *Spirited Away*. Visiting the museum is a little like climbing inside the mind of famed Ghibli director Hayao Miyazaki: walls are plastered with initial sketches of the characters that would eventually garner worldwide fame; a giant clock is bisected by a winding staircase; and – of course – there's the grinning cat-bus from *Totoro*. There's also a small movie theatre where original short animated features, exclusive to the museum, are screened. All in all, it's a guaranteed fun day out for all that will probably have you scurrying to watch the films later.

Ghibli Museum sits inside pretty **Inokashira Park** (井の頭公園, Inokashira Kōen); from Kichijoji Station, it's a pleasant fifteen-minute stroll through the park's tree-shaded walks to the museum, past a pleasant carp-filled lake and a small zoo. A favourite haunt of courting couples, the park is mobbed by everyone during *hanami* season, when it explodes in a profusion of pink blossoms.

Ikebukuro and the north

Northern Tokyo's main commercial hub is **IKEBUKURO** (池袋). Cheap accommodation and good transport links have attracted an increasing number of expatriates, typically Chinese and Taiwanese, but including a broad sweep of other nationalities, which lends Ikebukuro a faintly cosmopolitan air. Either side of the hectic station (around one million passengers pass through each day), the massive department stores Tōbu and Seibu – two of the largest in Japan – square off against each other. Bar the Frank Lloyd Wright-designed **Myōnichikan** there's not all that much to see in the area; Ikebukuro is, however, useful as a springboard to interesting sights such as **Rikugi-en**, a wonderful old stroll-garden.

Myōnichikan

明日館 • 2-31-3 Nishi-Ikebukuro, Toshima-ku • Tues–Sun 10am–4pm, closed during functions • ¥400, or ¥600 including coffee or Japanese tea and sweets • ⓣ 03 3971 7535, ⓦ jiyu.jp • Ikebukuro Station

The distinctive **Myōnichikan** ("House of Tomorrow") is a former school designed by Frank Lloyd Wright and his assistant Endō Arata. The geometric windows and low-slung roofs are trademark Wright features, but the buildings are best appreciated from inside, where you get the full effect of the clean, bold lines, echoed in the hexagonal chairs, light fittings and other original furnishings.

Rikugi-en

六義園 • 6 Honkomagome, Bunkyō-ku • Daily 9am–5pm • ¥300 • Entrance on Hongō-dōri, 5min south of Komagome Station

Rikugi-en was designed in the early eighteenth century by high-ranking feudal lord **Yanagisawa Yoshiyasu**, who took seven years to create this celebrated garden – with its 88 allusions to famous scenes, real or imaginary, from ancient Japanese poetry – and then named it Rikugi-en, "garden of the six principles of poetry", in reference to the rules for composing *waka* (poems of 31 syllables). Few of the 88 landscapes have survived – the guide map issued at the entrance identifies a mere eighteen – but Rikugi-en still retains its rhythm and beauty, beginning as you enter with an ancient, spreading cherry tree, then slowly unfolding along paths that meander past secluded arbours and around the indented shoreline of an islet-speckled lake.

Suidōbashi

水道橋

East of Ikebukuro and west of Akihabara lies the district of **SUIDŌBASHI**, where the stadium, shopping centres and amusement-park thrill rides of **Tokyo Dome City** punctuate the skyline. The centrepiece is the plump, white-roofed **Tokyo Dome** (東京ドーム), popularly known as the "Big Egg", Tokyo's major baseball venue (see p.165). Also part of the Dome City complex is the upmarket **Spa LaQua** onsen (see box, p.165).

TOKYO'S LAST TRAMLINE

Early twentieth-century Tokyo boasted a number of tramlines; now only the 12km-long **Toden-Arakawa Line** (都電荒川線) remains, running north from Waseda to Minowa-bashi. The most interesting section lies along a short stretch from **Kōshinzuka Station**, a fifteen-minute walk northwest of Sugamo Station, from where the line heads southwest towards Higashi-Ikebukuro, rocking and rolling along narrow streets and through Tokyo backyards.

Pre-paid cards can be used on the system, as can Toei day-tickets (see box, p.132). Ordinary tickets cost ¥170, however far you travel; pay as you enter.

1

Tokyo Dome City Attractions

東京ドームシティ アトラクションズ 1-3-61 Kōraku, Bunkyō-ku • Daily 10am–10pm • Passport with unlimited rides adult ¥4200, child aged 13–17 ¥3700, child aged 3–12 ¥3100; after 5pm ¥3000/2700/2500 respectively • ☎ 03 5800 9999, Ⓦ www.laqua.jp • Suidōbashi or Kōrakuen stations

The best rides at the large **Tokyo Dome City Attractions** amusement park are those in the LaQua section, where the highlight is Thunder Dolphin, a high-speed roller coaster guaranteed to get you screaming (for ages 8 and older). If you haven't got the stomach for that, try the Big O, the world's first hub-less and spoke-less Ferris wheel.

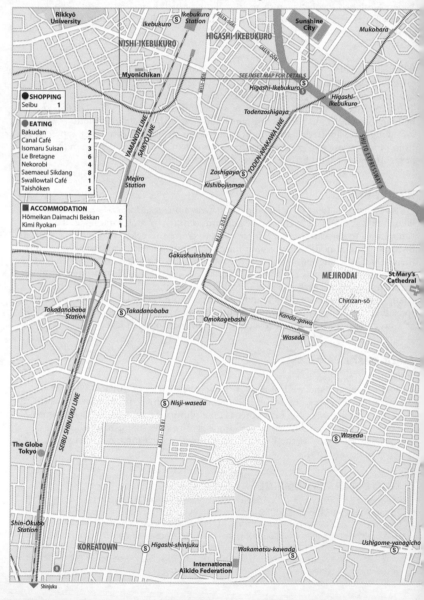

Kagurazaka

神楽坂

Just west of Iidabashi Station, the district of **Kagurazaka** has become a popular spot of late with Tokyoites young and old. Chic restaurants, cafés and shops line Kagarazaka-dōri, the area's main drag, and there are plenty more dotting the genteel alleyways to the north. If you're in luck, you'll spot a geisha or two tripping along the lanes – some still work hereabouts, remnants of the area's history as an entertainment quarter.

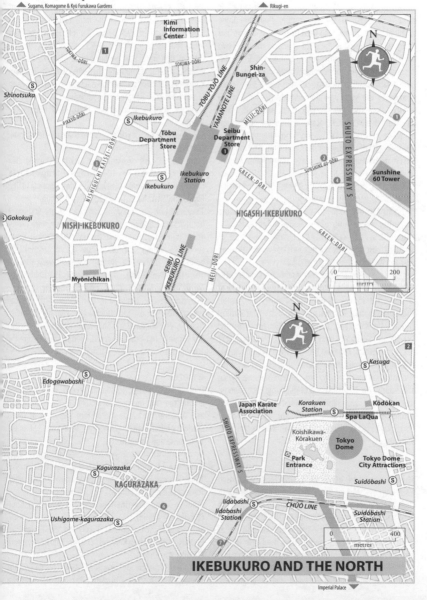

IKEBUKURO AND THE NORTH

1

ARRIVAL AND DEPARTURE   TOKYO

If you're **arriving** in Tokyo from abroad, you'll touch down at Narita International Airport or Haneda Airport. If you're coming to the capital from elsewhere in Japan, it's more likely that you'll arrive at one of the main train stations (Tokyo, Ueno, Shinagawa or Shinjuku) or the long-distance bus terminals, the main ones being at Tokyo and Shinjuku stations.

BY PLANE

Narita International Airport (成田国際空港), better known as Narita (📞0476 348000, 🌐narita-airport.jp), is some 66km east of the city centre. There are three terminals; T3 is a new wing used by low-cost carriers and designed with a nod to the 2020 Olympics; the other two terminals both have tourist information and Welcome Inn Reservation Centres for accommodation bookings. If you have a Japan Rail Pass exchange order (see p.36) you can arrange to use your pass immediately (it's valid on JR services from the airport); pick it up at the JR travel agencies – not the ticket offices – in the basement, though be aware the queues can be very long. Alternatively, you can collect it later from any major JR station.

Destinations Hiroshima (1 daily; 1hr 40min); Nagoya (6 daily; 1hr 10min); Naha (4 daily; 3hr 20min); Niigata (1 daily; 1hr); Osaka (6 daily; 1hr 20min); Sapporo (6 daily; 1hr 45min).

Haneda Airport Located on a spit of land jutting into Tokyo Bay 20km south of the Imperial Palace, Haneda Airport (羽田空港; 📞03 5757 8111, 🌐haneda-airport.jp) is where most domestic flights touch down, as well as an ever-increasing roster of international services.

Destinations Akita (7 daily; 1hr); Asahikawa (13 daily; 1hr 35min); Fukuoka (2–4 hourly; 1hr 45min–2hr); Hakodate (9 daily; 1hr 15min); Hiroshima (14 daily; 1hr 25min); Kagoshima (hourly; 1hr 50min); Kōchi (8 daily; 1hr 50min); Komatsu (for Kanazawa; 11 daily; 1hr); Kumamoto (hourly; 1hr 50min); Kushiro (5 daily; 1hr 35min); Matsuyama (11 daily; 1hr 15min); Miyazaki (hourly; 1hr 45min); Nagasaki (16 daily; 1hr 55min); Noto (2 daily; 1hr); Ōita (11 daily; 1hr 30min); Okayama (4 daily; 1hr 20min); Okinawa (Naha; 1–4 hourly; 2hr 30min); Osaka (2–3 hourly; 1hr); Sapporo (every 30min; 1hr 30min); Takamatsu (10 daily; 1hr 10min); Tokushima (6 daily; 1hr 15min); Toyama (6 daily; 1hr); Wakkanai (2 daily; 1hr 45min); Yamagata (daily; 55min).

BY TRAIN

Shinkansen and other JR trains Most Shinkansen train journeys start or finish at Tokyo Station (東京駅), close to the Imperial Palace. Those heading to or from the west also call at Shinagawa Station (品川駅), around 6km southwest, while trains travelling north will also call at Ueno Station (上野駅), some 4km northeast of the Imperial Palace. All three stations are on the Yamanote line and are connected to several subway lines. Other long-distance JR services stop at Tokyo and Ueno stations,

Shinjuku Station (新宿駅) on Tokyo's west side and Ikebukuro Station (池袋駅) in the city's northwest corner.

Non-JR trains Non-JR trains terminate at different stations: the Tōkyū Tōyoko line from Yokohama ends at Shibuya Station (渋谷駅); the Tōbu Nikkō line runs from Nikkō to Asakusa Station (浅草駅), east of Ueno, and the Odakyū line from Hakone finishes at Shinjuku Station, which is also the terminus for the Seibu-Shinjuku line from Kawagoe. All these stations have subway connections and (apart from Asakusa) are on the Yamanote rail line.

Asakusa Station destinations Nikkō (1–2 hourly; 1hr 55min).

Shibuya Station destinations Yokohama (every 5min; 30min).

Shinjuku Station destinations Hakone (hourly; 1hr 30min); Kamakura (every 10–20min; 1hr); Matsumoto (18 daily; 2hr 35min); Nikkō (daily; 1hr 55min); Shimoda (daily; 2hr 45min); Yokohama (every 20–30min; 30min).

Tokyo Station destinations Fukuoka (Hakata Station; 2 hourly; 5hr); Hiroshima (hourly; 4–5hr); Kamakura (every 10–20min; 1hr); Karuizawa (hourly; 1hr 20min); Kyoto (every 15–30min; 2hr 15min–3hr 40min); Morioka (3 hourly; 2hr 20min–3hr 30min); Nagano (every 30min–1hr; 1hr 40min–2hr); Nagoya (every 15–30min; 1hr 40min–3hr); Niigata (1–3 hourly; 2hr–2hr 20min); Okayama (every 30min–1hr; 3hr 15min–4hr); Sendai (every 10–15min; 1hr 40min–2hr 20min); Shimoda (hourly; 2hr 40min–3hr); Shin-Kōbe (every 30min–1hr; 3hr 15min); Shin-Osaka (every 15–30min; 2hr 30min–4hr 10min); Yokohama (every 5–10min; 40min).

BY BUS

Long-distance buses pull in at several major stations around the city. The main overnight services from Kyoto and Osaka arrive beside the eastern Yaesu exit of Tokyo Station; other buses arrive at Ikebukuro, Shibuya, Shinagawa and Shinjuku.

Ikebukuro Station destinations Ise (3 daily; 8hr); Kanazawa (4 daily; 7hr 30min); Nagano (4 daily; 4hr 10min); Niigata (hourly; 5hr 30min); Osaka (1 daily; 8hr); Toyama (3 daily; 6hr 50min).

Shibuya Station destinations Himeji (1 daily; 9hr); Kōbe (1 daily; 8hr 40min).

Shinagawa Station Hirosaki (1 daily; 9hr 15min); Imabari (1 daily; 12hr 10min); Kurashiki (1 daily; 11hr); Tokushima (1 daily; 9hr 20min).

Shinjuku Station destinations Akita (1 daily; 8hr 30min); Fuji Yoshida (14 daily; 1hr 50min); Fukuoka

TRANSPORT BETWEEN THE CITY AND AIRPORTS

Whether you're landing at Narita or Haneda, the number of options for transport into central Tokyo can be somewhat bewildering.

NARITA AIRPORT

Keisei trains The fastest way into Tokyo from Narita is on the Skyliner express train (1–3 hourly, 7.30am–10.30pm; 41min to Ueno; ¥2470) operated by Keisei (🆆 keisei.co.jp), who also offer the cheapest train connection into town in the form of the *tokkyū* (limited express) service (every 30min; 6am–11pm; 1hr 11min to Ueno; ¥1030). Both services stop at Nippori, where it's easy to transfer to the Yamanote or the Keihin Tōhoku lines.

JR trains JR's Narita Express, also known as the N'EX (🆆 www.jreast.co.jp/e/nex), runs to several city stations. The cheapest fare is ¥3020 to Tokyo Station (every 30min, 7.45am–9.45pm; 1hr), and there are also frequent direct N'EX services to Shinjuku (hourly; 1hr 20min; ¥3190). N'EX services to Ikebukuro (1hr 20min; ¥3190) and Yokohama (1hr 30min; ¥4290) via Shinagawa are much less frequent. JR usually run some kind of discount scheme for foreign passport holders; at the time of writing, return tickets valid for two weeks were available to all stations (even Yokohama) for ¥4000. You can save some money by taking the slightly slower, but far less comfortable, JR *kaisoku* (rapid) train to Tokyo Station (hourly; 1hr 25min; ¥1320).

Buses The cheapest way into Tokyo is on the Access Narita buses (🆆 accessnarita.jp), which head to Ginza and Tokyo stations, and cost just ¥1000; they depart every fifteen minutes at peak times, and even have toilets on board, but they can be prone to traffic delays. You can pay with cash on the bus. Alternatively, the more costly Airport Limousine buses (☎ 03 3665 7220, 🆆 www.limousinebus.co.jp) can be useful if you're weighed down by luggage and staying at or near a major hotel; journeys to central Tokyo typically cost ¥3100, and take at least ninety minutes. The ¥3400 Limousine & Metro Pass combines a one-way bus trip from Narita to central Tokyo and a 24-hour metro pass valid on nine of Tokyo's thirteen subway lines.

Taxis Taxis to the city centre cost around ¥30,000, and are little faster than going by bus.

HANEDA AIRPORT

Monorail From Haneda Airport, it's a short monorail journey (every 5–10min, 5.20am–11.15pm; 13–19min; ¥490) to Hamamatsuchō Station on the Yamanote line.

Train Alternatively, you can board a Keihin Kūkō-line train to Shinagawa (every 10min; 24min; ¥410) or Sengakuji, and connect directly with other rail and subway lines.

Buses Limousine bus (☎ 03 3665 7220, 🆆 www.limousinebus.co.jp) to the city centre will set you back ¥1030–1230, depending upon your destination, and take around an hour; the same goes for the Haneda Airport Express services (🆆 hnd-bus.com).

Taxis A taxi from Haneda to central Tokyo costs ¥4000–8000.

(1 daily; 14hr 20min); Hakone-Tōgendai (14 daily; 2hr 10min); Kawaguchi-ko (14 daily; 1hr 45min); Kurashiki (2 daily; 11hr); Matsumoto (16 daily; 3hr 10min); Nagano (4 daily; 3hr 40min); Nagoya (2 daily; 7hr 10min); Okayama (2 daily; 10hr 30min); Osaka (4 daily; 7hr 40min); Sendai (8 daily; 5hr 30min–6hr 30min); Takayama (2 daily; 5hr 30min).

Tokyo Station destinations Aomori (2 daily; 9hr 30min); Fukui (1 daily; 8hr); Hiroshima (1 daily; 12hr); Kōbe (1 daily; 8hr 45min); Kōchi (1 daily; 11hr 35min); Kyoto (hourly; 8hr); Matsuyama (2 daily; 11hr 55min); Morioka (2 daily; 7hr 30min); Nagoya (16 daily; 5hr 20min); Nara (1 daily; 9hr 30min); Osaka (hourly; 8hr 20min); Sendai (1 daily; 5hr 30min); Shimonoseki (2 daily; 14hr 20min); Takamatsu (1 daily; 10hr 15min); Yamagata (4 daily; 5hr 30min–8hr).

BY FERRY

Takeshiba Ferry Terminal (竹芝フェリーターミナル) Jetfoils (2 daily; 1hr 45min–2hr 10min) and ferries (6–7 weekly; 4hr 20min–8hr) to Ōshima (see p.217) run from Tokyo's Takeshiba Ferry Terminal (see map, p.103), two stops from Shimbashi on the Yurikamome monorail. They are operated by Tōkai Kisen (☎ 03 5472 9999, 🆆 tokaikisen.co.jp).

Tokyo Ferry Terminal (東京フェリーターミナル) Long-distance ferries to and from Tokushima in Shikoku (1 daily; 19hr) and Kita-Kyūshū in Kyūshū (1 daily; 35hr) run from Tokyo Ferry Terminal at Ariake, on the man-made island of Odaiba (see map, p.103) in Tokyo Bay; for details, see Ocean Tōkyū Ferry (☎ 03 3528 1011, 🆆 www.otf.jp). Buses run from the port to Shin-Kiba Station, from which you can catch the metro or the overland JR Keiyō line. A taxi from the port to central Tokyo costs around ¥2000.

1

GETTING AROUND

Getting around Tokyo is easy thanks to the city's super-efficient **trains** and **subways**, and there are also a couple of monorails, one tramline – the Toden-Arakawa Line (see box, p.127) – and many buses. Walking and cycling are great ways to explore.

SUBWAY

Its colourful map (see pp.134–135) may look daunting, but Tokyo's subway is relatively easy to negotiate: the simple colour coding on trains and maps, as well as clear signposts (many also in English), directional arrows and alpha-numeric station codes, make this by far the most *gaijin*-friendly form of transport. You'll have a much less crowded journey if you avoid travelling at rush hour (7.30–9am & 5.30–7.30pm).

Subway network There are two systems, the nine-line Tokyo Metro (ⓦ www.tokyometro.jp) and the four-line Toei (ⓦ www.kotsu.metro.tokyo.jp). The systems share some stations, but unless you buy a special ticket from the vending machines that specifies your route from one system to the other, or you have a pass (see box below), you cannot switch mid-journey between the two sets of lines without paying extra at the ticket barrier; the fare is deducted automatically if you're using a card. Subways also connect to overland train lines, such as the Yamanote.

Tickets Most travel is now done by card (see box below), but paper tickets can be bought at the vending machines beside the electronic ticket gates (ticket sales windows are only found at major stations). Most trips across central Tokyo cost no more than ¥200. Ticket machines generally have multi-language functions, but if you're fazed by the wide range of price buttons, buy the cheapest ticket (usually ¥170) and sort out the difference with the gatekeeper at the other end.

Running times Trains run from around 5am to just after midnight, and during peak daytime hours as frequently as every 5min (and at least every 15min at other times).

Station exits Leaving a station can be complicated by the number of exits, but there are maps close to the ticket barriers and on the platforms indicating where the exits emerge, and strips of yellow tiles on the floor mark the routes to the ticket barriers.

TRAINS

JR East trains (ⓦ jreast.co.jp) are another handy way of getting around the city. The various JR lines all have their own colour coding on maps – take care not to confuse these with those of the subway network. The main lines you'll find useful are the circular Yamanote (coloured lime green on the transport map); the Chūō line (orange), which starts at Tokyo Station and runs west to Shinjuku and the suburbs beyond; the Sōbu line (yellow) from Chiba in the east to Mitaka in the west, which runs parallel to the Chūō line in the centre of Tokyo; and the Keihin Tōhoku line (blue) from Ōmiya in the north, through Tokyo Station, to Yokohama and beyond. It's fine to transfer between JR lines on the same ticket, but you'll have to buy a new ticket if you transfer to a subway line, unless you have a PASMO or Suica card (see box below).

Tickets and passes The lowest fare on JR lines is ¥140. Ticket machines are easy to operate if buying single tickets, if you can find your destination on the network maps. Both Pasmo and JR Suica prepaid cards (see box below) work at the ticket gates, while JR also run their own one-day Tokunai Pass (¥750), which gives unlimited travel within the Tokyo Metropolitan District Area.

BUSES

Once you've got a feel for the city, buses can be a good way of cutting across the few areas not served by a subway or train line. Only a small number of the buses or routes are labelled in English. The final destination is listed on the front of the bus, along with the route number. You pay on entry, by dropping the flat rate (¥210) into the fare box by the driver (there's a machine in the box for changing notes).

MONORAIL

Tokyo has a couple of monorail systems: the Tokyo monorail, which runs from Hamamatsuchō to Haneda Airport (see

---

TOKYO TRANSPORT PASSES

Although they don't save you any money, the most convenient way to travel is to use a **Pasmo** (ⓦ pasmo.co.jp) or JR **Suica** stored-value card. Both can be used on all subways, many buses and both JR and private trains in the wider Tokyo area. The card can be recharged at ticket machines and ticket offices. To get either card (available from ticket machines in metro and JR stations), you have to spend a minimum of ¥2000, of which ¥500 is a deposit, which will be returned to you, plus any remaining value (minus a small processing fee) when you cash in the card before leaving Tokyo.

If you need to ride Tokyo's metro and trains a lot in the space of a day, you'll find both Tokyo Metro and Toei have **day tickets** for use exclusively on their own subway systems (¥600 and ¥700 respectively); the Toei pass also covers the city's buses and single tramline. However, it's usually more convenient to get a one-day **economy pass** covering both systems for ¥1000.

p.130); and the Yurikamome monorail, which connects Shimbashi with Toyosu via Odaiba (see p.104). These services operate like the city's private rail lines – you buy separate tickets for journeys on them or travel using the various stored-value cards, such as Pasmo and Suica (see box opposite).

BIKE

As well as the options listed below, check out the bike rental outfits listed on ⓦ cycle-tokyo.cycling.jp; the website also contains lots of useful information about cycling in the city.

Community Cycle One of the easiest means of getting hold of a bike is the Community Cycle (ⓦ docomo-cycle.jp) scheme, which has cycle docks across the city; after registering online (you pay with your bank card) and receiving a pass code, it's ¥150 for the first half-hour, then ¥100 for each subsequent one.

Imperial Palace free rental Every Sunday, 150 bikes are made available for free rental (10am–3pm; ⓦ jbpi.or.jp), at the police box by exit 2 of Nijūbashimae Station – it's first come, first served, and you're only allowed to ride on the designated paths flanking the east side of the palace.

Sumida Park Bicycle Parking In an underground space beside the bridge in Asakusa (daily 6am–8pm; ¥200 for 4hr, ¥300 for a day, ¥1200 for the week; ☏ 03 5246 1305); note that they only have a limited number of bikes available.

FERRIES

The Tokyo Cruise Ship Company (ⓦ suijobus.co.jp) runs several ferry services, known as *suijō basu* (water buses), in and around Tokyo Bay. Many depart from or pass through Hinode Pier on Tokyo Bay (see map, p.103); it's close by Hinode Station on the Yurikamome monorail, or a 10min walk from Hamamatsuchō Station on the Yamanote line.

Sumida-gawa service Regular boats ply the route between Hinode Pier and Asakusa to the northeast of the city centre (every 30–50min, 10am–6.30pm; 40min;

¥780); some boats call at the Hama Rikyū Teien (see p.92), entry to which is often included with the ticket price. The ferries' large picture windows give a completely different view of the city from the one you'll get on the streets – reason enough for hopping aboard.

Himiko and Hotaluna For a few yen more you can travel on the *Himiko* or the *Hotaluna*, near-identical space-age ferries designed by Matsumoto Reiji, a famous manga artist. Both run from Asakusa to Odaiba (6 daily; ¥1560), sometimes via Hinode Pier. At night, the *Himiko* changes its name to *Jicoo* and morphs into a floating bar (see p.152).

Ferries to Odaiba Hinode Pier is the jumping-off point for regular ferries to various points around the island of Odaiba (20min; from ¥480), operated by the Tokyo Cruise Ship Company.

Cruises Several good cruises around Tokyo Bay depart from Hinode Pier daily; the most interesting are those including eat-all-you-can buffets (see box, p.146).

TAXIS

For short hops, taxis are often the best option. The basic rate is ¥730 for the first 2km, after which the meter racks up ¥80 every 275m, plus a time charge when the taxi is moving at less than 10km per hour. Between 11pm and 5am, rates are twenty to thirty percent higher. When flagging down a taxi, note that a red light next to the driver means the cab is free; green means it's occupied. There are designated stands in the busiest parts of town, but be prepared for long queues after the trains stop at night, especially in areas such as Roppongi and Shinjuku.

Taxi firms Major taxi firms include Hinomaru Limousine (☏ 03 3212 0505, ⓦ hinomaru.co.jp) and Nippon Kōtsū (☏ 03 3799 9220, ⓦ www.nihon-kotsu.co.jp/en). Uber (ⓦ uber .com) is functional in Tokyo, though it's still not in common use among locals, and is not all that much cheaper than the regular cabs (and, in fact, quite often more expensive).

INFORMATION AND TOURS

TOURIST INFORMATION CENTRES (TICS)

Tokyo City i B1F Kitte Building, 2-7-2 Marunouchi ⓦ en.tokyocity-i.jp; Tokyo Station; map p.86. The city's best tourist information centre, with multilingual staff, accommodation- and tour-booking facilities, and good general advice. There are also information kiosks in the arrivals halls at Narita and Haneda airports. Daily 8am–8pm.

Japan National Tourism Organization (JNTO) 2F Shin-Tokyo Building, 3-3-1 Marunouchi ☏ 03 3201 3331, ⓦ jnto.go.jp; Yūrakuchō Station; map p.86. The main Tokyo office of the JNTO has multilingual staff, a desk for booking accommodation across Japan, and a notice board with information on upcoming events. Daily 9am–5pm.

Asakusa Culture and Sightseeing Centre In front of Sensō-ji's main gate, Kaminari-mon ☏ 03 3842 5566;

Asakusa Station; map p.100. Provides English-language information on local festivals, tours, ferries and places to eat. The office almost counts as a sight in itself – designed by Kengo Kuma, the interior is rather striking, and it's also possible to take the lift up to the eighth floor for spectacular views. Daily 9am–8pm.

Tokyo Tourist Information Centre 1F Tokyo Metropolitan Government No. 1 Building, 2-8-1 Nishi-Shinjuku ☏ 03 5321 3077, ⓦ gotokyo.org; Tochō-mae Station; map p.124. Another excellent tourist information centre, though it's a little bit out of the way. Daily 9.30am–6.30pm.

OTHER INFORMATION

Websites and apps The official online sources for Tokyo information are the excellent websites of the Tokyo

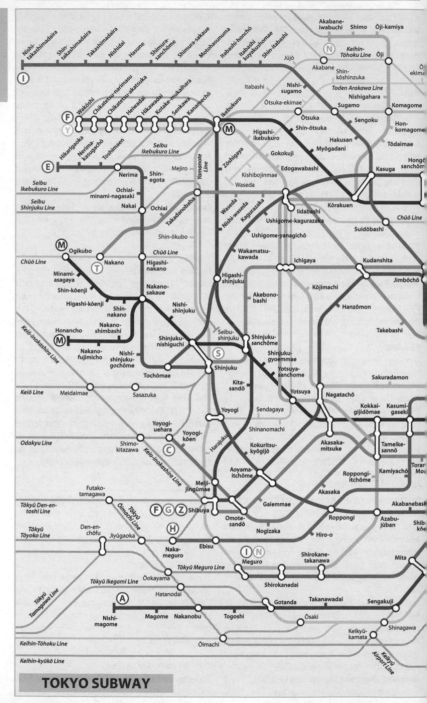

TOKYO SUBWAY

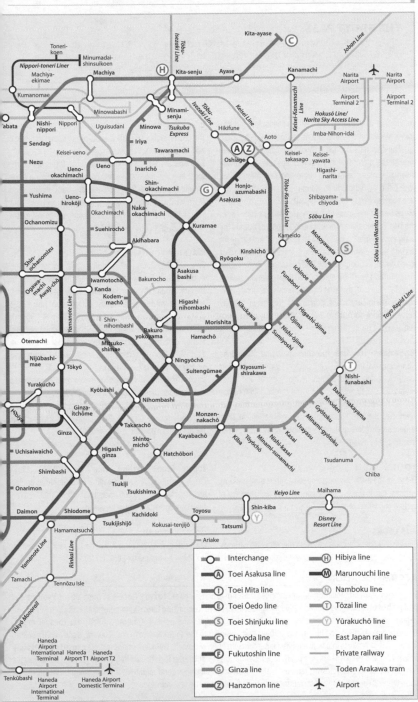

1

THE GRUTT PASS

One of the best deals on offer in Tokyo is the **Grutt Pass**. For ¥2000 you get a ticket booklet which allows free or discounted entry to seventy attractions, including all major museums. Valid for two months after first being used, the ticket can be bought at participating venues and the Tokyo Tourist Information Centre in Shinjuku (see p.133), among other outlets.

Convention and Visitors Bureau (⌨tcvb.or.jp) and the Tokyo Metropolitan Government (⌨tourism.metro.tokyo.jp). Those with smartphones should consider downloading one of the many free city subway apps, which provide invaluable maps, as well as route and fare information, with many working offline. A Japanese-language app can also come in handy when dining out.

Maps Decent free maps of the city are available from any of the TICs. Bilingual maps on public notice boards outside the main exits to most subway and train stations are handy for getting your immediate bearings. There are also decent maps online – Google's is typically excellent, while with a little hunting you'll be able to find apps offering offline-friendly maps of the city (⌨maps.me is a good one). Equally useful are maps portraying the Tokyo subway network, since such maps are not visible anywhere once you're on the trains themselves – there is, of course, one in this Guide (see pp.134–135).

Magazines The free monthly magazine *Metropolis* (⌨metropolisjapan.com) is packed with interesting features, reviews, and listings of films, music and other events, as is their website; the same can be said for *Time Out* (⌨timeout.com/tokyo), whose magazine comes out every two months. You'll find these publications at TICs, larger hotels, foreign-language bookshops and places frequented by *gaijin*.

TOURS

There are the usual bus tours and some interesting walking options, but if these are not your cup of tea, then try a cycling or go-Kart tour.

BUS TOURS

Established operations such as Hato Bus Tours (⌨hatobus.com) and Japan Grey Line (⌨www.jgl.co.jp/inbound) offer a wide variety of tours, from half-day jaunts around the central sights (¥5000) to visits out to Kamakura, Nikkō and Hakone (from ¥14,000).

Sky Bus ☎03 3215 0008, ⌨skybus.jp. Offers four tours, most in open-top double-decker buses, including a route around the Imperial Palace grounds and through Ginza and Marunouchi (50min; ¥1600), and an Odaiba night tour (2hr; ¥2100). They also have three hop-on, hop-off routes (¥3500), with tickets valid for 24hr.

WALKING TOURS

Free walking tours with English-speaking guides are available on selected days of the week in various parts of the city: around the Imperial Palace (Wed, Sat & Sun 1pm), starting from the JNTO tourist information office (see p.133); around Ueno (Wed, Fri & Sun 10.30am & 1.30pm), starting from Green Salon, on the park-side exit of Ueno Station (see map, p.97); and around Asakusa (Sat & Sun 11am & 1.15pm), starting from the Asakusa Culture and Sightseeing Centre (see p.133).

Eyexplore Tokyo ⌨eyexploretokyo.com. Small outfit running a few photo-tours of the city (¥9900).

Haunted Tokyo ⌨hauntedtokyotours.com. Interesting English-language tours focusing on the spookier parts of Tokyo's history (usually 2–3hr; ¥4500).

CYCLING TOURS

Tokyo Great Cycling Tour ☎03 4590 2995, ⌨tokyocycling.jp. See the capital on a couple of guided bike tours (6hr; ¥10,000 including lunch) that run on Tuesdays, Thursdays and at weekends.

GO-KART TOURS

Maricar ⌨maricar.com. A fun go-kart tour inspired by the *Mario Kart* game (see box, p.116).

ACCOMMODATION

The choice of accommodation in Tokyo ranges from no-expense-spared **luxury hotels** to atmospheric **ryokan** and budget **hostels** charging around ¥2500 a night. Central Tokyo (comprising Ginza, Nihombashi, Akasaka and Roppongi) is largely the domain of expensive, world-class establishments and upmarket business hotels. For cheaper rooms, there's a greater choice in Shinagawa, Shibuya and Shinjuku to the south and east, and Asakusa, Ueno and Ikebukuro in the north – Asakusa in particular has a large concentration of hostels. Quirkier options include **capsule hotels** (see box, p.138) and **love hotels** (see p.43); recommendations for the latter include *Two Way* (see p.139) and *Colourful P&A* (see p.140). Wherever you stay, remember that trains stop running around midnight; if you're a night animal, opt for somewhere near one of the entertainment districts to avoid costly taxi journeys.

ESSENTIALS

Reservations Whatever your budget, it's wise to reserve your first few nights' accommodation before arrival. A good local booking site is ⓦ travel.rakuten.com (you'll need to register first), while ⓦ ryokan.or.jp also has a list of good places to stay (mostly ryokan) in Tokyo and beyond. Otherwise, the international standbys have plenty of Tokyo options: try ⓦ trivago.com for hotels or ⓦ hostelworld.com for hostels.

Taxes In addition to the standard hotel taxes (see p.41) there's an extra charge of ¥100 per person per night on rooms costing over ¥10,000 per night, and ¥200 for those costing ¥15,000 or above.

THE IMPERIAL PALACE AND AROUND

★**Hoshinoya** 星のや 1-9-1 Ōtemachi, Chiyoda-ku ☎ 050 3786 1144, ⓦ hoshinoyatokyo.com; Ōtemachi Station; map p.86. Tokyo has been crying out for a place like this, and finally it's here: a top-end hotel with ryokan-like elements to its decor and service. As such, despite being seventeen floors high, it all feels rather intimate, with the scent of flowers and incense wafting through the common areas. 🛜 **¥72,000**

Tokyo Station 東京ステーションホテル 1-9-1 Marunouchi, Chiyoda-ku ☎ 03 5220 1111, ⓦ thetokyo stationhotel.jp; Tokyo Station; see p.86. It has been great to see this grand old dame back in business – this hotel, set within Tokyo station itself, first opened for business in 1915, but was closed throughout the station's mammoth refurb. Designers have plumped for dainty Euro-chic in the rooms, and there are chandeliers all over the place. 🛜 **¥47,000**

GINZA AND AROUND

★**Conrad Tokyo** コンラッド東京 1-9-1 Higashi-Shinbashi, Minato-ku ☎ 03 6388 8000, ⓦ conradtokyo .co.jp; Shiodome Station; map p.91. This luxury hotel easily holds its own when it comes to cutting-edge contemporary design and five-star facilities. But it's the views that really steal the show – from the lobby and bayside rooms feast your eyes on what are arguably the best vistas in Tokyo, taking in Hama Rikyū Gardens, Odaiba and the Rainbow Bridge. It's absolutely magical at night. 🛜 **¥60,000**

Mitsui Garden Ginza 三井ガーデンホテル銀座 8-13-1 Ginza, Chūō-ku ☎ 03 3543 1131, ⓦ www.gardenhotels .co.jp; Shimbashi Station; map p.91. Italian designer Piero Rissoni's chic design for Mitsui's flagship hotel helps it stand out from the crowd. Rooms are decorated in earthy tones with great attention to detail, but it's the bird's-eye views of the city and bay that grab the attention – quite spectacular from each and every room. 🛜 **¥25,000**

Sunroute Ginza ホテルサンルート銀座 1-15-11 Ginza, Chūō-ku ☎ 03 5579 9733, ⓦ sunroute.jp;

TOKYO'S BEST PLACES TO STAY

Best for views Conrad Tokyo (see below)
Best modern-style ryokan Andon Ryokan (see p.138)
Best for luxury Hoshinoya (see below)
Best old-school ryokan Sukeroku-no-yado Sadachiyo (see p.138)
Best love hotel Two Way (see p.139)
Best hostel Bunka Hostel (see p.138)

Ginza-itchōme Station; map p.91. This business hotel is one of the cheaper options in fancy Ginza (especially if you book online), and just a few minutes' walk from several metro stations. Rooms are stylish and well equipped, and surprisingly large for the price and location. 🛜 **¥15,000**

AKIHABARA AND AROUND

Anne Hostel 庵ホステル 2-21-14 Yanagibashi, Taitō-ku ☎ 03 5829 9090, ⓦ j-hostel.com; Asakusabashi or Kuramae stations; map p.94. A lovely little place: part hostel, part traditional minshuku (see p.44), it's tremendously popular with international guests. Most rooms, even a couple of the dorms, boast tatami flooring, and prices include a decent little breakfast. 🛜 Dorms **¥2600**, twins **¥6800**

Juraku ホテルジュラク 2-9 Kanda-Awajichō, Chiyoda-ku ☎ 03 3271 7222, ⓦ hotel-juraku.co.jp/ocha; Ochanomizu or Akihabara stations; map p.94. On entry, this super little place comes across as something like a four-star, with a quirky, faux-industrial facade and a smart, honey-toned lobby. The rooms (some female-only) are superbly designed too. Throw in a convenient location and cheery staff, and you can't really go wrong. 🛜 **¥17,000**

Nui Hostel & Bar Lounge ヌイホステルバーラウンジ 2-14-13 Kuramae, Taitō-ku ☎ 03 6240 9854, ⓦ backpackersjapan.co.jp/nui; Kuramae Station; map p.94. Just 15min on foot from Asakusa, this hostel is an excellent choice. The funky common area features a bar that's hugely popular with locals, and a great mingling spot; the pine beds in the dorms aren't quite as fancy, but they do the job. 🛜 Dorms **¥3000**, doubles **¥7400**

UENO AND AROUND

Coco Grand Ueno Shinobazu ココグラン上野不忍ホテル 2-12-14 Ueno, Taitō-ku ☎ 03 3834 6221, ⓦ cocogrand.co.jp/uenoshinobazu; Yushima Station; map p.97. Reliable hotel with friendly staff and a choice of Western- or Japanese-style accommodation, the latter quite spacious but a bit more expensive. Many rooms have great views across Shinobazu pond. 🛜 **¥19,000**

★**Ryokan Sawanoya** 旅館澤の屋 2-3-11 Yanaka, Taitō-ku ☎ 03 3822 2251, ⓦ sawanoya.com; Nezu

1

CAPSULE HOTELS

A real Tokyo treat, **capsule hotels** (see p.92) are generally clustered around major train stations, and cost ¥3000–4000. The majority are for men only, but some are female-friendly.

Capsule & Sauna Century Shibuya カプセル＆サウナセンチュリー渋谷 1-19-14 Dōgenzaka, Shibuya-ku ☎03 3464 1777; Shibuya or Shinsen stations; map p.122. Right in the heart of Shibuya's prime sleaze quarter, this is a decent enough capsule hotel to use if you're too tired to wait for the first train of the morning; rates for daytime use are also reasonable at just ¥1200. Male only. 🛜 ¥3700

Capsule Inn Kanda カプセルイン神田 1-8-9 Uchikanda, Chiyoda-ku ☎03 3295 9000, ⓦ capsuleinn.com; Kanda Station; map p.94. Just two minutes' walk from the west exit of the Kanda JR station, this ten-storey inn features 144 rooms, with separate levels for women and men. 🛜 ¥4200

Ginza Bay Hotel 銀座ベイホテル 7-13-15 Ginza, Chūō-ku ☎03 6226 1078, ⓦ bay-hotel.jp; Higashi-Ginza Station; map p.91. More expensive than most capsule hotels, but designed with far more care too, with little flourishes such as gorgeous pine fittings in the bathing areas, and USB ports in the pods. It's also the cheapest place to stay in the Ginza area, and has a female-only floor. 🛜 ¥5000

Green Plaza Shinjuku グリーンプラザ新宿 1-29-2 Kabukichō, Shinjuku-ku ☎03 3207 4923, ⓦ hgpshinjuku.jp; Shinjuku Station; map p.124. Giant capsule hotel with 630 rooms (making it the largest such facility in Japan), friendly staff and a good fitness and sauna area; the rooftop spa baths cost extra, as do rooms with wi-fi. Male only. 🛜 ¥4500

Station, map p.97. This welcoming family-run inn is a real home from home. Though nothing fancy, it offers good-value tatami rooms, all with washbasin, TV, telephone and a/c. Few are en suite, but the two lovely Japanese-style baths more than compensate. No meals. 🛜 ¥10,200

Suigetsu Hotel Ohgaisō 水月ホテル鴎外荘 3-3-21 Ikenohata, Taitō-ku ☎03 3822 4611, ⓦ ohgai.co.jp; Nezu Station; map p.97. A rare example of a mid-range hotel with a Japanese flavour, this place is built around the Meiji-period house and traditional garden of novelist Mori Ōgai. The three wings contain a mix of Western and tatami rooms; the latter offer more atmosphere, but at double the price. Rates with or without meals available. 🛜 ¥15,000

ASAKUSA

1980 Hotel 1泊1980円ホテル 3-10-10 Shitaya, Taitō-ku ☎03 6240 6027, ⓦ 1980stay.com; Inya Station; map p.100. The numbers in the name are the price, not the year – this is basically the cheapest hostel in Tokyo, and its capsule-like beds are just fine. 🛜 Dorms ¥1980

★**Andon Ryokan** 行燈旅館 2-34-10 Nihonzutsumi, Taitō-ku ☎03 3873 8611, ⓦ andon.co.jp; Minowa Station; map p.100. At this architectural gem, traditional ryokan design is fused with modern materials. The dimly lit tatami rooms share bathrooms and are tiny, but come with DVD players and very comfortable futons. Other plus points include a top-floor jacuzzi spa you can book for private dips. Breakfast included. 🛜 ¥8100

Asakusa Central 浅草セントラルホテル 1-5-3 Asakusa, Taitō-ku ☎03 3847 2222, ⓦ pelican.co.jp /asakusacentralhotel; Asakusa Station; map p.100. Modest business hotel which, despite a recent price hike, still rises above the competition thanks to the winning combination of English-speaking staff, a convenient location on Asakusa's main street, and small but well-appointed rooms, all of which come with TV and telephone. 🛜 ¥13,000

★**Bunka Hostel** ブンカホステル 1-13-5 Asakusa, Taitō-ku ☎03 5806 3444, ⓦ bunkahostel.jp; Asakusa Station; map p.100. A remarkably stylish addition to the Asakusa hostel scene, with comfy, curtained-off berths adding some rare privacy to the dorm experience – a true bargain, as far as Tokyo accommodation goes. The lobby bar is a real winner, too (see p.151). 🛜 Dorms ¥3000

Khaosan Tokyo Origami カオサン東京オリガミ 3-4-12 Asakusa, Taitō-ku ☎03 3871 6678, ⓦ khaosan-tokyo .com; Asakusa Station; map p.100. Part of the *Khaosan* chain, but a far more appealing option than the unfriendly original – rooms have been given Japanese stylings, and you'll see a fair few paper cranes around the place. There are grand views of Asakusa from the lounge, and the location can't be sniffed at. 🛜 Dorms ¥3200, doubles ¥7200

Retrometro Backpackers レトロメトロバックパッカーズ 2-19-1 Nishi-Asakusa, Taitō-ku ☎03 6322 7447, ⓦ retrometrobackpackers.com; Asakusa or Tawaramachi stations; map p.100. As far as backpackers go, it takes one to know one, and the owner of this tiny, two-dorm hostel (one dorm is female-only) certainly knows her stuff. Balinese and Thai stylings betray her favourite former travel destinations, and there's a sense of cosiness here absent from some of Tokyo's larger hostels. 🛜 Dorms ¥2600

★**Sukeroku-no-yado Sadachiyo** 助六の宿 貞千代 2-20-1 Asakusa, Taitō-ku ☎03 3842 6431, ⓦ sadachiyo .co.jp; Asakusa or Tawaramachi stations; map p.100. Step back into Edo-era Asakusa in this delightful old inn marked by a willow tree and stone lanterns, northwest of Sensō-ji temple. The elegant tatami rooms are all en suite, though you can also use the traditional Japanese-style baths. Dinner and breakfast are included, and they can also arrange performances of traditional arts, including geisha dances. 🛜 **¥21,600**

BAYSIDE TOKYO

Grand Nikkō ホテルグランド日航 2-6-1 Daiba, Minato-ku ☎ 03 5500 6711, ⊛ tokyo.grand-nikko.com; Daiba monorail; map p.103. Rising up over the bay, the most luxurious of Odaiba's hotels has a light-filled lobby, walls peppered with contemporary art and, from all but the lower levels, great views of the Rainbow Bridge and the city across Tokyo Bay. Rooms are spacious (you'll pay a bit more for bridge views), and staff are helpful to a tee. 🛜 **¥47,500**

AKASAKA AND ROPPONGI

Andaz アンダズ 1-23-4 Toranomon, Minato-ku ☎ 03 6830 1234, ⊛ tokyo.andaz.hyatt.com; Toranomon Station; map pp.110–111. Japan's first branch of Hyatt's luxury *Andaz* offshoot has touched down in Tokyo, taking up the upper section of the new Toranomon Hills complex. No attention to detail has been spared, from the perfumed lobby to the immaculate rooms, all decorated with Japanese-style flourishes from award-winning interior designers. 🛜 **¥45,000**

The Glanz ホテルザグランツ 2-21-3 Azabu-jūban, Minato-ku ☎ 03 3455 7770, ⊛ theglanz.jp; Azabu-Jūban Station; map pp.110–111. Highly appealing option with sleek, designer-style rooms including spa-style bathrooms and glimpses of Tokyo Tower. There are reduced rates if you check in after 10pm, and all rates include breakfast. 🛜 **¥15,000**

★**Grand Hyatt Tokyo** グランドハイアットホテル東京 6-10-3 Roppongi, Minato-ku ☎ 03 4333 1234, ⊛ tokyo .grand.hyatt.jp; Roppongi Station; map pp.110–111. Glamour is the order of the day at the *Grand Hyatt*. The rooms' appealing design uses wood and earthy-toned fabrics, and restaurants and bars are all very chic, particularly *The Oak Door* and the slick sushi bar *Roku Roku*. 🛜 **¥59,000**

★**Kaisu** カイス 6-13-5 Akasaka, Minato-ku ☎ 03 5797 7711, ⊛ kaisu.jp; Akasaka Station; map pp.110–111. This is one of the few hostels in the club-heavy Roppongi area – it's not cheap, but being able to stagger home at 4am certainly saves money over a long cab ride. This is no party hostel, however, but a beautiful place set into an old geisha house. 🛜 Dorms **¥4300**

The Ritz-Carlton リッツカールトン東京 Tokyo Midtown, 9-7-1 Akasaka, Minato-ku ☎ 03 6434 8100, ⊛ ritzcarlton.com; Roppongi Station; map p.110–111. Occupying the top nine floors of the 53-floor Midtown Tower, this ultra-luxury hotel has a more contemporary look than usual for a *Ritz-Carlton*. The choice is between

deluxe rooms or suites – both offering the height of comfort. 🛜 **¥81,000**

EBISU, MEGURO AND THE SOUTH

Akimoto 旅荘秋元 3-2-8 Nakameguro, Meguro-ku ☎ 03 3711 4553; Naka-Meguro Station; map pp.114–115. This minshuku is a super little find in fashionable Nakameguro, an area which is pricey at the best of times. There are a few floors of small tatami rooms (not en-suite), a general air of calm and an extremely relaxed manager. No meals. **¥4000**

Dormy Inn ドーミーイン目黒青葉台 3-21-8 Aobadai, Meguro-ku ☎ 03 3760 2211; Naka-Meguro Station; map pp.114–115. Within walking distance of trendy Nakameguro and a stone's throw from the banks of the delightful Meguro-gawa (see p.113), this functional business hotel is a good deal. Each room has a hotplate and small fridge, so it's feasible to self-cater. There's also a large communal bathroom and sauna, plus free bike rental. 🛜 **¥13,000**

HARAJUKU, AOYAMA AND SHIBUYA

Caravan Tokyo キャラバントウキョウ 3-13 Minami-Aoyama, Minato-ku ☎ 080 4145 3422, ⊛ caravan tokyo.com; Omotesandō Station; map p.120. Glamping in Tokyo? Yep, it's quite possible, at this custom-built caravan located in the *Commune 246* snack-courtyard complex (see p.148); mod cons include a/c, heating, a shower and a real bed. Not quite the great outdoors, but pretty great nonetheless. Book on Airbnb. 🛜 **¥20,000**

Cerulean Tower Tōkyū Hotel セルリアンタワー東急ホテル 26-1 Sakuragaoka-chō, Shibuya-ku ☎ 03 3476 3000, ⊛ ceruleantower-hotel.com; Shibuya Station; map p.122. Shibuya's ritziest accommodation, with a range of intriguingly designed rooms, some featuring bathrooms with glittering views of the city. Also on site are a pool and gym (free to guests on the executive floor), several restaurants, a jazz club and even a nō theatre in the basement (see p.157). 🛜 **¥55,000**

Granbell Hotel グランベルホテル 15-17 Sakuragaoka-chō, Shibuya-ku ☎ 03 5457 2681, ⊛ granbellhotel.jp; Shibuya Station; map p.122. This boutique hotel has a hip feel, courtesy of curtains with Lichtenstein-style prints, kettles and TVs from the trendy local electronics range Plus Minus Zero, and a neutral palette of greys, crisp whites and natural colours. 🛜 **¥22,000**

Two Way ホテルツーウェイ 15-2 Maruyama-chō, Shibuya-ku ☎ 03 3476 2020, ⊛ hote-twoway.com; Shibuya Station; map p.122. Of Tokyo's hundreds upon hundreds of love hotels, this place in Shibuya, with decor that veers towards Southeast Asian in style, is one of the best value. There's even a "group" room, the infamous #405: goodness only knows what might occasionally go on in here, but on more innocent evenings it's home to groups of

1

uni students having a boozy party, or even bunches of local lads watching a Premier League football game. ☞ "Rest" from **¥3600**, "stay" from **¥5700**

SHINJUKU AND THE WEST

Colourful P&A ホテルカラフルP&A 2-45-10 Kabukichō, Shinjuku-ku ☎03 5155 5544, ⓦpaplaza.com; Seibu-Shinjuku Station; map p.124. Quirky Shinjuku love hotel with colour-coded floors – take your pick from the pink rooms of the second floor to the purple of the seventh. The "VIP" eighth floor has pricier themed rooms, including "Aqua Fantasy", "Oriental World" and the zebra-print-infested "Designer Home". ☞ "Rest" from **¥5500**, "stay" from **¥9900**

★Gracery Shinjuku ホテルグレイスリー 1-19-1 Kabukichō, Shinjuku-ku ☎03 6833 2489, ⓦshinjuku .gracery.com; Seibu-Shinjuku Station; map p.124. Yes, this is the "Godzilla hotel" that you may have spotted on your walk around Shinjuku. Despite the presence of the hulking beast by the upper-level lobby (he looks particularly fine when guarding you over breakfast), and the stylish rooms, it's not all that expensive a place to stay. ☞ **¥19,000**

Keiō Plaza 京王プラザホテル 2-2-1 Nishi-Shinjuku, Shinjuku-ku ☎03 3344 0111, ⓦkeioplaza.co.jp; Tochōmae Station; map p.124. Though it's long since been knocked off its perch as the tallest, most glamorous hotel in Shinjuku, this enormous place nevertheless retains some of its original cachet. The premier rooms, in grey and brown tones, are very stylish, and those on the west side have sweeping views across to the Tokyo Metropolitan Government Building; there are also garish Hello Kitty rooms available. An outdoor pool opens up in summer. ☞ **¥32,500**

★Park Hyatt Tokyo パークハイアット東京 3-7-1-2 Nishi-Shinjuku, Shinjuku-ku ☎03 5322 1234, ⓦtokyo .park.hyatt.jp; Tochōmae Station; map p.124.

Occupying the upper section of Tange Kenzō's Shinjuku Park Tower, this is the epitome of sophistication and holding up very well to newer rivals. All the huge rooms have breathtaking views, as do the restaurants and spa, pool and fitness centre at the pinnacle of the tower. ☞ **¥64,000**

Super Hotel Kabukichō スーパーホテル歌舞伎町 2-39-9 Kabukichō, Shinjuku-ku ☎03 6855 9000, ⓦsuperhoteljapan.co.jp; Higashi-Shinjuku Station; map p.124. A budget treat, with small but comfortable en-suite rooms, rather beautiful communal bathing areas, well-trained staff, and a surprisingly generous free breakfast. Rates for a double room occasionally drop below ¥10,000. ☞ **¥12,000**

IKEBUKURO AND THE NORTH

★Hōmeikan Daimachi Bekkan 鳳明館台町別館 5-12-9 Hongō, Bunkyō-ku ☎03 3811 1187, ⓦhomeikan.com; Hongō San-chōme or Kasuga stations; see map pp.128–129. Of the three ryokan under the *Hōmeikan* name, this one is the real looker, with its ancient carpentry and traditional design. There are no en-suite bathrooms, but all rooms have tatami mats and look out on an exquisite little Japanese garden. Service is impeccable, too. The sister establishment across the road, the Meiji-era *Honkan*, is the only inn in the city that's a listed cultural property. No meals. ☞ **¥12,000**

Kimi Ryokan 貴美旅館 2-36-8 Ikebukuro, Toshima-ku ☎03 3971 3766, ⓦkimi-ryokan.jp; Ikebukuro Station; see map pp.128–129. A great-value institution on Tokyo's budget scene, and a good place to meet fellow travellers – make sure you book well ahead. Rooms are compact but clean, access to a kitchen helps keep eating costs down and staff are friendly and speak English. There is a 1am curfew, and the place is a bit tricky to find, in the backstreets of west Ikebukuro. ☞ **¥7200**

EATING

When it comes to **gastronomic experiences**, few places can compare to Tokyo. The number, range and quality of restaurants are breathtaking, with practically any world cuisine you can think of available alongside all the usual (and many unusual) Japanese dishes. There are fantastic choices all over the city, but in general the most exciting places are found around Ginza, Shibuya, Shinjuku and Harajuku. Don't leave without visiting one of Tokyo's famous **open-air food markets** (known as *yokochō*); such places are inevitably cramped and highly photogenic, and you'll find a good example in most neighbourhoods. Also of note are a number of "**sky restaurants**" – many of the city's tallest towers are topped with restaurant levels, with prices that aren't necessarily sky-high.

ESSENTIALS

Prices There's no need to panic. Even Michelin-starred restaurants offer good-value set-meal specials, particularly for lunch. There's also an abundance of fast-food options, and many cafés also offer light meals. Many *Izakaya* (see p.48) serve decent food, too.

Listings For up-to-date information on Tokyo's restaurant scene, check out *Metropolis* (ⓦmetropolis.co.jp), *Time Out* (ⓦtimeout.com/tokyo), Bento.com (ⓦbento.com), and

the rather more homespun Tokyo Belly (ⓦtokyobelly.com) and Tokyo Cheapo (ⓦtokyocheapo.com).

Cooking courses Learning to cook is currently very popular in Tokyo, but you'll usually need to book well in advance. Try Buddha Bellies (☎03 5716 5751, ⓦbuddhabelliestokyo.jimdo.com) for lessons in making sushi, bentō or udon; Mayuko's Little Kitchen (☎080 3502 2005, ⓦmayukoslittlekitchen.com) for Japanese home-cooking; Elizabeth Andoh (☎03 5716 5751,

1

@tasteofculture.com) for cooking workshops; and Arigato Japan (@090 6484 9577, @arigatojapan.co.jp) for highly popular market dining tours.

THE IMPERIAL PALACE AND AROUND
RESTAURANTS

A16 Brick Square, 2-6-1 Marunouchi, Chiyoda-ku @03 3212 5215, @www.giraud.co.jp/a16; Tokyo Station; map p.86. One of the most pleasantly located restaurants in the boutique-heavy Marunouchi area, serving Californian-Italian cuisine at indoor and outdoor tables facing the lovely garden at Brick Square – a great place to chill over a glass of wine and a crisp pizza (try the *funghi*; ¥2050). Mon–Sat 11am–11pm, Sun 11am–10pm.

Matsumotorō 松本楼 1-2 Hibiya-kōen, Chiyoda-ku @03 3503 1451, @matsumotoro.co.jp; Hibiya Station; map p.86. On a sunny day it's a pleasure to sit on the terrace of this venerable restaurant in Hibiya-kōen, Tokyo's first Western-style park. The food is pretty standard, along the lines of *omu-raisu* (rice-filled omelette; ¥1200), hamburgers and other Western "favourites". Daily 10am–9pm.

The Oyster Shack かき小屋 1-6-1 Uchisaiwai-chō, Chiyoda-ku @03 6205 4328, @kakigoya.jimdo.com; Shimbashi Station; map p.86. One of the city's most atmospheric oyster bars, snuggled under the train track arches north of Shimbashi Station. Oysters cost from ¥300 (with occasional all-you-can-eat specials for ¥3000); alternatively, there's a whole aquarium's worth of scallops, turban shells, garlic calamari and other stuff to slurp down. Mon–Fri 4–11.30pm, Sat & Sun noon–11pm.

Tonton 登運とん 2-1-10 Yurakuchō, Chiyoda-ku, @03 3508 9454; Hibiya Station; map p.86. One of the most famous under-the-tracks restaurants in all Tokyo – not entirely on account of its food, most of which is served in grilled-skewer form (offal being the speciality), but more due to its superb location, and an atmospheric, ever-present cloud of smoke which can make the chefs hard to see. Daily 11.30am–10.30pm.

TOKYO'S BEST RESTAURANTS

Best okonomiyaki *Sometarō* (see p.145) or *Sakuratei* (see p.148)

Best ramen *Ramen Nagi* (see p.148) or *Ramen Kokugikan* (see p.145)

Best views *Hibiki* (see below) or *Hokkaidō* (see p.147)

Best soba *Kurosawa* (see p.146)

Best sushi *Sushi Bun* (see p.145) or *Iroha* (see p.147)

Best tempura *Hachimaki* (see opposite)

Best tofu *Sasa-no-yuki* (see p.144) or *Ume-no-hana* (see below)

Best yakitori *Omoide Yokochō* (see p.149)

GINZA AND AROUND
RESTAURANTS

Ginza Hirai 銀座ひらい 5-9-5 Ginza, Chūō-ku @03 6280 6933; Higashi-Ginza Station; map p.91. About as old-school Ginza as you can get: mustard-yellow walls and dark-wood furnishings make it an atmospheric venue to tuck into conger eel on rice – ¥1800 will get you a bowl of the stuff, plus pickles and miso soup. Daily 11.30am–2.30pm & 5.30–10pm.

Hibiki 響 46F Caretta Shiodome Building, 1-8-1 Higashi-Shinbashi, Minato-ku @03 6215 8051, @www.dynac-japan.com/hibiki; Shiodome Station; map p.91. This modern *izakaya* boasts some of Tokyo's best views, high up on the 46th floor with large windows facing out over Tokyo Bay. The cuisine is contemporary Japanese, and lunch sets (¥1300 for the daily special, ¥1200 for a fried fish set) are particularly good value; count on around ¥6000 a head in the evening. Mon–Fri 11am–3pm & 5–11.30pm, Sat & Sun 11am–4pm & 5–11pm.

Old Thailand オールドタイランド 2-15-3 Shimbashi, Minato-ku @03 6206 1532; Shimbashi Station; map p.91. Lively Thai restaurant whose menu eschews the regular rundown, instead offering unusual creations such as specialities from the northeastern Isaan region, and delectable Chiang Mai curry noodles (¥1100). Mon–Sat 11.30am–3pm & 5pm–11pm.

★Torigin Honten 鳥ぎん本店 5-5-7 Ginza, Chūō-ku @03 3571 3333, @torigin-ginza.co.jp; Ginza Station; map p.91. Bright, popular restaurant hidden away on a side street – look for the red sign. They serve snacks such as *yakitori* (from ¥170 per stick) and *kamameshi* (kettle-cooked rice with a choice of toppings; from ¥880). Their ¥750 weekday *toridon* (chicken on rice) lunch sets are a real bargain. Daily 11.30am–10pm.

Ume-no-hana 梅の花 5F 2-3-6 Ginza, Chūō-ku @03 3538 2226, @www.umenohana.co.jp; Ginza-Itchōme Station; map p.91. Trickling streams and bamboo screens set the mood in this elegant restaurant specializing in melt-in-the-mouth tofu creations. The tofu comes natural, deep-fried, boiled, grilled or sweetened for dessert; sets change by the season, but lunch courses generally go from ¥2100, while dinner sets start at ¥3560. Daily 11am–4pm & 5–10pm.

CAFÉS

100% Chocolate Café 100%チョコレートカフェー 2-4-16 Kyōbashi, Chūō-ku @03 3273 3184, @choco-cafe.jp; Kyōbashi Station; map p.91. You've got to admire the sheer style of this place: its chocolate-bar-styled ceiling, as well as the "chocolate library" lining one wall, were dreamed up by Masamichi Katayama, one of Tokyo's hottest designers. While you can just pop in to buy a selection of small chocolates (¥440 for two, from a selection of 56), it would be a sin not to indulge in a hot chocolate (¥430), or their wonderful range of slurp-worthy desserts. Mon–Fri 8am–8pm, Sat & Sun 11am–7pm.

Henri Charpentier アンリシャルペンティエール 2-8-20 Ginza, Chūō-ku ☎03 3562 2721, ⓦhenri-charpentier .com; Ginza-Itchōme Station; map p.91. This deep-pink boutique offers the ultimate in Tokyo patisseries on the ground floor and a *salon de thé* below. Here you can enjoy crêpe suzette (¥1725), flambéed at your table, as well as a range of gold-flecked chocolate morsels and seasonal specialities, to go with a choice of coffees, teas and infusions (¥860 or so). Don't leave before checking out the cleverly hidden toilets. Daily 11am–9pm.

Kiriko Lounge キリコラウンジ 6F Tokyo Tokyu Plaza 5-2-1 Ginza, Chūō-ku ☎03 6264 5590; Ginza Station; map p.91. Set in Tokyu Plaza, one of central Tokyo's newest large developments, this swanky place allows you to drain coffee (from ¥650) with a superlative view of Ginza's high-rise, through some truly gigantic windows. You can save a few hundred yen by taking it in a paper cup, and sitting in the common area. Mon–Sat 11am–11pm, Sun 11am–9pm.

AKIHABARA AND AROUND

RESTAURANTS

Go Go Curry ゴーゴーカレー 1-16-1 Kanda-Sakumachō, Chiyoda-ku ☎03 5256 5525, ⓦwww.gogocurry.com; Akihabara Station; map p.94. No doubt about it, the official meal of Akihabara regulars is *tonkatsu* curry (fried pork cutlet on rice, smothered in curry sauce), and one of the heartiest you'll find is at this chain, whose main branch – complete with gorilla logo – is in Akihabara. Plates start at ¥700, and in keeping with the rather odd opening hours ("go" is Japanese for the number five), you get ¥100 off before 5.55pm. Daily 9.55am–9.55pm.

★**Hachimaki** はちまき 1-19 Kanda-Jimbōchō, Chiyoda-ku ☎03 3291 6222; Jimbōchō Station; map p.94. Dating back to 1931, this tempura specialist is one of Tokyo's best time-warp restaurants: black-and-white photos abound, yellowing wallpaper makes it feel like the whole place has been dunked in tea, and there's nary a sign that you're in the twenty-first century. Have a crack at their delectable *tendon*, which gets you four freshly made tempura on rice (¥1000). Daily 11am–9pm.

Tomoegata 巴潟 2-17-6 Ryōgoku, Sumida-ku ☎03 3632 5600, ⓦtomoegata.com; Ryōgoku Station; map p.94. In the heart of sumo territory, and a grand place to head if you're off to a tournament, this is a good place to sample *chanko-nabe*, the wrestlers' protein-packed meat, seafood and vegetable stew. Their sets (¥860–4860) come in sizes named after the various levels of sumo – the *yokozuna* course would fill a whale, but even the cheapest one is pretty hearty. Daily 11.30am–2pm & 5–11pm.

CAFÉS

★**Forest of Owl** アウルの森 5F 4-5-8 Soto-Kanda, Chiyoda-ku ☎03 3254 6366, ⓦ2960.tokyo; Akihabara Station; map p.94. One of the newest additions to Akiba's swarm of quirky cafés – and Tokyo's ever-increasing roster of animal-related ones (see box, p.144) – this place allows you to sip a vending-machine beverage (included in the ¥890 entrance fee) amid a "forest" featuring a few dozen owls. You're likely to see one flashing past your face or feet quite regularly, and can even pop one onto your hand (staff will assist and give you a kitchen glove for protection). Mon & Tues, Thurs–Sun noon–10pm, Wed noon–4pm.

Gundam Café ガンダムカフェー 1-1 Kanda-Hanaokachō, Chiyoda-ku ☎03 3251 0078, ⓦg-cafe.jp; Akihabara Station; map p.94. In the suitably sci-fi interior of this café you can experience what a pilot from the incredibly popular anime series *Mobile Suit Gundam* would eat – or at least our terrestrial equivalent. Café time and bar time (from 5pm) have different menus. Coffee from ¥400. Mon–Fri 10am–10pm, Sat 8.30am–11pm, Sun 8.30am–9.20pm.

★**Imasa** 井政 2-16-9 Sotokanda, Chiyoda-ku ☎03 3258 0059; Ochanomizu Station; map p.94. This café is something of a treat: essentially forming part of the Kanda Myōjin complex (see p.95), it's set in a wooden building dating from the 1920s, fringed with gardens and boasting a mix of traditional and modern fittings. The coffee's great, too (from ¥600) – though even if it were awful this place would still be worth a visit. Mon–Fri 11am–4.30pm.

Maidreamin メイドリーミング 2F 1-8-10 Soto-Kanda, Chiyoda-ku ☎03 6252 3263, ⓦmaidreamin.com; Akihabara Station; map p.94. The spangly, anime-like Akiba branch of the *Maidreamin* maid café chain (see box, p.144) draws a small stream of foreigners thanks to English-speaking staff – they'll let you know exactly which cute poses to make, which cute sounds to mimic and so on. It's all rather fun, and charged at ¥500 per person per hour, with an order from the menu mandatory: drinks cost ¥600–1000, with meals a little more expensive. Each of the seven levels of this building also host maid cafés, and there's another good branch of *Maidreamin* in Shibuya (see p.149). Daily 10am–11pm.

Mai:lish マイリッシ 2F FH Kowa Square, 3-6-2 Soto-Kanda, Chiyoda-ku ☎03 5289 7310, ⓦmailish.jp; Suehirochō Station; map p.94. Akiba's famed maid cafés (see box, p.144) come in all sorts of shapes, sizes and styles; this is one of the originals, a relaxed venue in which costumed girls pander to their customers' every whim. It's ¥500 per hour, and you're obliged to order something from the menu: drinks cost from ¥550. Daily 11am–10pm.

N3331 mAAch-Ecute Building, 1-25-4 Kanda-Sudachō, Chiyoda-ku ☎03 5295 2788, ⓦn3331.com; Akihabara Station; map p.94. Fun even if you're not a trainspotter,

1

this inventively located café pokes up over the rails near Akihabara – there'll be a JR service whizzing past the floor-to-ceiling windows every minute or two. As well as passable coffee (from ¥480), they serve a range of alcoholic drinks. Mon–Sat 11am–11pm, Sun 11am–9pm.

UENO AND AROUND

RESTAURANTS

Musashino 武蔵野 2-8-1 Ueno, Taitō-ku ☏ 03 3831 1672; Ueno-Hirokōji Station; map p.97. One of Ueno's few remaining old-style restaurants serving *tonkatsu*, for which the area was once famed. They come in big, thick, melt-in-the-mouth slabs; choose between standard *rōsu* (fatty belly meat) and the leaner *hire* (loin fillet), both costing ¥1000 including soup, rice and pickles. Daily 11.30am–9pm.

★**Sasa-no-yuki** 笹乃雪 2-15-10 Negishi, Taitō-ku ☏ 03 3873 1145, ⓦ sasanoyuki.com; Uguisudani Station; map p.97. Three centuries ago, the chef here was said to make tofu like "snow lying on bamboo leaves", and both the name and the quality have survived, though the old wooden house is now marooned among flyovers. Calm prevails over the tatami mats as you feast on delicately flavoured silk-strained tofu. Prices are reasonable, with most tofu plates priced at around ¥750, and full courses

starting at ¥5000 (or ¥2200 for lunch). Tues–Sun 11.30am–9pm.

ASAKUSA

RESTAURANTS

320 Ramen ３２０ラーメン 2-15-1 Asakusa, Taitō-ku, no phone; Asakusa Station map p.100. Don't expect any culinary fireworks at this spit-and-sawdust ramen bar, but the bowls – at just ¥320 – are excellent backpacker fare, and they don't taste too bad at all. 10am–7.30pm; closed Sat.

★**Bon** 梵 1-2-11 Ryusen, Taitō-ku ☏ 03 3872 0375, ⓦ fuchabon.co.jp; Iriya Station; map p.100. A rare chance to sample *fucha ryōri*, a distinctive style of Zen Buddhist cuisine in which each of the ornately presented vegetable dishes is traditionally served from one large bowl, and the meal begins and ends with tea. The setting, a charming old Japanese house, and the calm service, make it an experience not to be missed. Reservations essential, with courses starting at ¥5400. Mon & Tues, Thurs & Fri noon–1.30pm & 5–7pm, Sat noon–7pm, Sun noon–6pm.

Daikokuya 大黒家 1-38-10 Asakusa, Taitō-ku ☏ 03 3844 1111; 1-31-9 Asakusa ☏ 03 3844 2222, ⓦ tempura.co.jp; Asakusa Station; map p.100. There's always a lunchtime queue at this venerable tempura

---

MAIDS, BUTLERS AND CATS: TOKYO'S QUIRKY CAFÉS

Japan is famed for appropriating Western cultural standards, and Tokyo's various quirky takes on the humble café are all worth sampling – some would say that you haven't really visited Tokyo if you haven't tried at least one.

MAID AND BUTLER CAFÉS

The weird and wonderful **maid cafés** range in style from seedy to sci-fi via the unashamedly kitsch. Most are clustered among the electronics outlets to the west of Akihabara Station; head there after sunset and you'll see lines of girls clamouring for custom. The deal is usually the same: costumed girls (and sometimes guys) serve up food and drink in an excruciatingly "cute" manner, their voices screeching a full two octaves above their natural pitch. There's usually an hourly fee, and you're also expected to order some food or drink from the menu. Recommended places to try include *Mai:lish* (see p.143), and the *Maidreamin* branches in Akihabara (see p.143) and Shibuya (see p.149).

The success of maid cafés spawned a male equivalent: the equally interesting **butler cafés**, where handsome, dressed-up young chaps (often Westerners) serve coffee, cake and wine to an exclusively female clientele. Though the format is essentially the same as that for the maid café, butler cafés tend to be fancier and are often rather more expensive. A good one to try is *Swallowtail Café* in Ikebukuro (see p.150).

ANIMAL CAFÉS

The current hit formula in Tokyo's polymorphous *kissaten* culture is the **animal café**. The craze started relatively tamely with cat cafés, but in recent years, others have popped up offering experiences with different animals – rabbits, hedgehogs, snakes, owls and even penguins. Some establishments are clearly putting profit over animal welfare; if you do visit an animal café, things to look out for are whether or not the animals are allowed "off-time" away from visitors and whether they have enough space to wander. Recommended establishments listed in this Guide include the *Calico* (see p.149) and *Nekorobi* (see p.150) cat cafés, *Tokyo Snake Center* (see p.149) and *Forest of Owl* (see p.143), all of which treat their animals well.

restaurant, set in an attractive old building. The speciality is *tendon* – shrimp, fish and prawn fritters on a bowl of rice (from ¥1550). If the main branch is too busy, head for the annexe around the corner. Mon–Fri & Sun 11.10am–8.30pm, Sat 11.10am–9pm.

Hatsuogawa 初小川 2-8-4 Kaminarimon, Taitō-ku ☎03 3844 2723; Asakusa Station; map p.100. Look for the profusion of potted plants outside this tiny, rustic eel restaurant. It's very foreigner-friendly and a lovely place to experience one of Japan's most delectable fish dishes (eel sets from ¥1500). Mon–Sat noon–1.30pm & 5–7.30pm, Sun 5–7.30pm.

La Sora Seed ラソラシド 31F Solamachi, 1-1-2 Oshiage, Sumida-ku ☎03 5414 0581, ⓦkurkku.jp; Oshiage Station; map p.100. Ecologically sound operation boasting one of the best possible views of the huge Skytree tower (see p.102). The company leans on European flavours, including great meatballs made with organic pork. Lunch sets go from ¥3100, dinner for almost three times that. Daily 11am–4pm & 6–11pm.

Maguro Bito まぐろ人 1-21-8 Asakusa, Taitō-ku ☎03 3844 8736, ⓦmagurobito.com; Asakusa Station; map p.100. Fuji TV viewers once voted this the top *kaiten-zushiya* in Japan, and it's easy to see why: the quality of fish and other ingredients is excellent, the turnover fast and the decor on the ritzy side. Expect a queue (but it moves fast). Electronically price-coded plates range from ¥170 to ¥530. Mon–Fri 11.30am–9.30pm, Sat & Sun 11am–10pm.

Nakae 中江 1-9-2 Nihonzutsumi, Taitō-ku ☎03 3872 5398, ⓦsakuranabe.com; Minowa Station; map p.100. This venerable restaurant specializes in dishes made with horse meat, including *sukiyaki* (hotpot). The interior, decorated with beautiful ink paintings of horses, looks pretty much like it did a century ago when the whole area was a thriving red-light district. Small one-pot dishes start at ¥1700, and full courses will run you close to ¥10,000. Tues–Fri 5–10pm, Sat & Sun 11.30am–9pm.

★**Sometarō** 染太郎 2-2-2 Nishi-Asakusa, Taitō-ku ☎03 3844 9502; Tawaramachi Station; map p.100. This rambling, wooden restaurant specializes in *okonomiyaki*, but also offers some quirky house creations such as *osomeyaki* (a variation of *okonomiyaki*, made with Worcester sauce), all costing from ¥800. There are English instructions on the menu, and staff are pleased to help out with your on-the-table creations. Daily noon–10.30pm.

CAFÉ

★**Gallery éf** ガラリーエフ 2-19-18 Kaminarimon, Taitō-ku ☎03 3841 0442, ⓦgallery-ef.com; Asakusa Station; map p.100. The *kura* (traditional storehouse) at the back of this appealing café provides an intimate venue for an eclectic mix of concerts, performance art, and exhibitions that cover most of the space – the rest is taken up by the café's collection of retro goods. Drinks, meals

(mostly Western-style, such as chilli beans and spaghetti) and desserts are served using vintage tableware, and they carry a few import beers as well. Choose from four different types of blended coffee (¥550), or plump for a tasty fruit juice (¥630). Café and gallery 11am–7pm, bar 6pm–midnight; closed Tues.

BAYSIDE TOKYO
RESTAURANTS

Monkichi もん吉 3-8-10 Tsukushima, Chūō-ku ☎03 3531 2380; Tsukishima Station; map p.103. As patronized by no less a luminary than Brad Pitt (whose photo is on the wall), this friendly place is a classic *monjayaki* restaurant on an alley just off Monja-dōri. Try their speciality, *omuraisu monja*, for ¥1080. Daily 11am–10pm.

★**Ramen Kokugikan** ラーメン国技館 5F Aqua City, 1-7-1 Daiba, Minato-ku ☎03 3599 4700; Odaiba Kaihin-kōen monorail; map p.103. Six top ramen noodle chefs from around Japan square off against each other in this section of Aqua City's restaurant floor. A bowl will cost you from ¥800 (the Hakata variety, from Fukuoka city, is well worth trying). The outdoor balcony, when it's open, boasts fantastic views across the bay towards Tokyo's twinkling lights. 📶 Daily 11am–11pm.

★**Sushi Bun** 鮨文 5 Tsukiji, Chūō-ku ☎03 3541 3860; Tsukijishijō Station; map p.103. One of the most *gaijin*-friendly options among the rows of sushi stalls within the old Tsukiji fish market. They have an English menu with sets at ¥2800, though you won't regret spending ¥1000 more for their top quality ten-piece selection including creamy *uni* (sea urchin). Mon–Sat 6am–2.30pm, but closed during occasional market holidays.

Sushi-zanmai Honten すしざんまい本店 4-11-9 Tsukiji Chūō-ku ☎03 3541 1117; Tsukiji Station; map p.103. This pleasantly noisy place is the main, and best, branch of a popular chain of sushi restaurants run by Kimura Kiyoshi, the self-proclaimed "King of Tuna". Filling sushi sets go from ¥1620. Daily 24hr.

AKASAKA AND ROPPONGI
RESTAURANTS

Aux Bacchanales オーバッカナル 2F Ark Mori Building, 1-12-32 Akasaka, Minato-ku ☎03 3582 2225, ⓦauxbacchanales.com; Roppongi-Itchōme Station; map pp.110–111. Tucked away in the Ark Hills complex, this is one of Tokyo's most authentic Parisian-style brasseries – their steak frites (¥2580) is the real thing – and it's a pleasant spot to hang out sipping coffee or red wine. Pastries start at ¥210, while daily lunch specials of both meat and fish dishes go for under ¥1300. Daily 10am–midnight.

Gonpachi 権八 1-13-11 Nishi-Azabu, Minato-ku ☎03 5771 0170, ⓦgonpachi.jp; Roppongi Station; map

1

DINING ON THE WATER

Lunch and dinner cruises on **yakatabune**, low-slung traditional boats lit up with paper lanterns, are a charming Tokyo eating institution, dating back to the Edo period. The boats accommodate anything from sixteen to a hundred people on trips along the Sumida-gawa and out on Tokyo Bay. For a bar-like alternative, see *Jicoo* (see p.152).

Amisei あみ清 ☎ 03 3844 1869, �🌐 amisei.com; Asakusa Station; map p.100. Cruises set off down the Sumida-gawa from the southwest side of Azumabashi, Asakusa. Two-hour evening trips cost ¥8640, including all the tempura you can eat. More lavish menus can be ordered and, naturally, prices skyrocket for cruises on the night when Asakusa

holds its annual fireworks extravaganza in July.
Funasei 船清 ☎ 03 5479 2731, �🌐 www.funasei .com; map pp.114–115. Bay cruises, lasting two-and-a-half hours, run out of Shinagawa and offer a choice of Japanese- and Western-style menus, with unlimited bar access, for around ¥10,800 per person.

---

pp.110–111. A faux-Edo-period storehouse is home to this atmospheric Japanese restaurant. Take your pick between reasonably priced soba (from ¥800) and grilled items (from ¥180) on the ground and second floors, or sushi on the third floor – a full meal will set you back around ¥3000. There's a wonderful samurai drama atmosphere, and it's easy to see how the place inspired the climactic scenes of Quentin Tarantino's *Kill Bill Vol. 1*. Daily 11.30am–3.30am.

★**Kurosawa** 黒澤 2-7-9 Nagatachō, Chiyoda-ku ☎ 03 3580 9638, �🌐 9638.net/nagata; Tameike-sannō Station; map pp.110–111. The design of this atmospheric restaurant was inspired by the sets from Akira Kurosawa's movies *Yojimbo* and *Red Beard*, and a meal here is a superb experience. Given the quality, the lunch prices are a real steal. On entry you'll be asked whether you want to sit in the downstairs soba section (bowls from under ¥800) or head on to the refined upstairs rooms, where you'll have to remove your shoes, for juicy *tonkatsu* cutlet (sets around ¥1300). 📶 Mon–Fri 11.30am–3pm & 5–10pm, Sat noon–9pm.

Nobu Tokyo 東京 Toranomon Towers Office, 4-1-28 Toranomon, Minato-ku ☎ 03 5733 0070, �🌐 nobu restaurants.com; Kamiyachō Station; map pp.110–111. There's a dramatic Japanese-style design for Nobu Matsuhisa's Tokyo operation, where you can sample the famous black-cod dinner (Robert de Niro's favourite) for around ¥4600. For something a bit different, try *tiradito*, *Nobu*'s South American twist on sashimi. Mon–Fri 11.30am–2pm & 6–10.30pm, Sat & Sun 6–10.30pm.

★**Nodaiwa** 野田岩 1-5-4 Higashi-Azabu, Minato-ku ☎ 03 3583 7852, ⑩ nodaiwa.co.jp; Kamiyachō Station; map pp.110–111. Kimono-clad waitresses shuffle around this 160-year-old *kura* (storehouse), converted into one of Tokyo's best eel restaurants; a set meal will cost around ¥5000. The private rooms upstairs can only be booked by parties of four or more; if it's busy, they may guide you to the annexe around the corner, which has an almost identical interior. Mon–Sat 11am–1.30pm & 5–8pm.

SaamRoa サムロア 2-12-9 Azabu-Jūban, Minato-ku ☎ 03 5484 3388, ⑩ saamroa.com; Azabu-Jūban Station; map pp.110–111. A fine and tempting range of authentic Thai dishes is served at this casual place bedecked with colourful, ethnic trinkets. The set lunches are great value (around ¥1000), though also consider the *laab* (a dryish curry made with pork, basil and water spinach; ¥1490). Daily 11.30am–2pm & 5–11pm.

★**Tōfuya-Ukai** とうふ屋うかい 4-4-13 Shiba-kōen, Minato-ku ☎ 03 3436 1028, ⑩ ukai.co.jp; Akabanebashi Station; map pp.110–111. At the foot of Tokyo Tower, this stunning re-creation of an Edo-era mansion, incorporating huge beams from an old sake brewery, serves unforgettable tofu-based *kaiseki*-style cuisine. Book well ahead, especially for dinner (at least a month in advance). Set meals only, with lunch from ¥5940 on weekdays, and dinner from ¥10,800. Daily 11am–10pm.

CAFÉ
Eat More Greens イートモアグリーンズ 2-2-5 Azabu-Jūban, Minato-ku ☎ 03 3798 3191, ⑩ eatmoregreens .jp; Azabu-Jūban Station; map pp.110–111. Taking its inspiration from urban US vegetarian cafés and bakeries, this appealing place mixes random pieces of wood furniture, good organic food (¥1000 for a set meal) and a street-side terrace, along with seriously good doughnuts (from ¥220). Quality has dropped slightly since a change of ownership, however, and there are fewer vegan-friendly choices on the menu. Mon–Fri 11am–11pm, Sat & Sun 9am–11pm.

EBISU, MEGURO AND THE SOUTH
RESTAURANTS
Chano-ma チャノマ 6F Naka-Meguro Kangyō Building, 1-22-4 Kami-Meguro, Meguro-ku ☎ 03 3792 9898; Naka-Meguro Station; map pp.114–115. Dining while seated on the floor is not exactly uncommon in Tokyo, but at this casual eatery the dining space is actually a padded, bed-like platform – this is

true lounging. (They do also have regular tables.) Overlooking the river in swanky Nakameguro, they serve some very tasty rustic-style Japanese fusion dishes (lunch sets from ¥1000), as well as a great selection of teas and flavoured lattes. Mon–Thurs & Sun noon–2am, Fri & Sat noon–4am.

Ebisu Yokochō 千恵比寿横丁 Ebisu, Minato-ku; Ebisu Station; map pp.114–115. Not a restaurant, but a whole clutch of them, crammed into a hugely atmospheric covered arcade east of Ebisu Station. Come in the evening and take your pick – there's a curry stand, several noodle joints, places specializing in seafood, and even a miniature karaoke bar. In addition, the venues and the tables in them are arranged in a way that lends itself to mingling. Daily 5pm–late.

Futatsume ふたつめ 3-9-5 Kami-Meguro, Meguro-ku ⓣ03 3712 2022; Naka-Meguro Station; map pp.114–115. Grand little *kushiage* (deep-fried sticks) place, selling skewered snacks from just ¥100; choices include breaded camembert, shiitake and salmon, and they're all best washed down with a gigantic highball (¥980). Mon–Sat 6pm–3am.

★Hiroshima Ichiba 広島市場 1-29-12 Aobadai, Meguro-ku ⓣ03 3760 7147; Naka-Meguro Station; map pp.114–115. This chain sells the best *tantan-men* (ramen with a spicy, oily sauce and minced pork; ¥850) in the city, and their delectable *gyōza* (¥310) aren't far¡ off. The attractive Nakameguro branch basically does the simple things really, really well, and every customer walks out rubbing their belly. Daily 11am–2am.

Hokkaidō 北海道 39F Ebisu Garden Place Tower, 4-20-3 Ebisu, Shibuya-ku ⓣ03 5448 9521; Ebisu Station; map pp.114–115. One of the best views in Tokyo, looking out west from the highest tower in Ebisu – Fuji is visible on a clear day. The food is cheap, considering, with the seafood *yakisoba* a steal at ¥890, and rice dishes blanketed with roe for a little more. The ¥500 cocktails make this a surprisingly romantic sunset spot. Daily 11.30am–2.30pm & 4.30–9.30pm.

★Iroha Sushi いろは寿司 1-5-13 Kami-Meguro, Meguro-ku ⓣ03 5722 3560, ⓦirohasushi.com; Naka-Meguro Station; map pp.114–115. Relaxed sushi den that's the diametric opposite of most restaurants in this fancy part of town – you won't see any hipsters or bohos here, just salary-folk and older locals. Every single piece is freshly made, yet the place remains cheaper than any *kaiten-zushiya*, especially at lunchtime, when huge sets go from just ¥680; the largest is just ¥1050, and will fill almost any belly. Daily 11.30am–2.30pm & 5–10.30pm.

Ivy Place アイヴィプレイス 16-15 Sarugakuchō, Shibuya-ku ⓣ03 6415 3232, ⓦtysons.jp; Daikanyama Station; map pp.114–115. This large, attractive venue is *so* Daikanyama – always full at brunchtime with shopping-bag-toting folk, tucking into buttermilk pancakes (¥1300), eggs with chorizo and potatoes (¥1400) and more. Good coffee, too. Daily 7am–11pm.

TOKYO TEAHOUSES

Tokyo's **teahouses** are becoming more popular as the health benefits of tea are promoted. There are also teahouses with pretty settings in Hama Rikyū Onshi Teien (see p.92), Shinjuku Gyoen (see p.125) and Happōen (see p.114).

★Aoyama Flower Market 青山フラワーマーケット B1 5-1-2 Aoyama, Minato-ku ⓣ03 3400 0887, ⓦafm-teahouse; Omotesandō Station; map p.120. Yes, it's a flower shop – but one whose heady aromas also permeate a fantastic tea-space, tucked away through a door at the back. They've a good range of herbal and green-tea concoctions on offer in the ¥750 range, though prepare for a half-hour queue at weekends. Daily 11am–8pm.

Cha Ginza 茶銀座 5-5-6 Ginza, Chiyoda-ku ⓣ03 3571 1211; Ginza Station; map p.91. This teahouse, run by a tea wholesaler, offers a modern take on the business of sipping *sencha*. Iron walls add a contemporary touch, and the rooftop area, where they serve *matcha*, is the place to hang out with those Tokyo ladies who make shopping a career. ¥800 gets you two different cups of the refreshing green stuff, plus a traditional sweet. Tues–Sun 11am–6pm.

Toraya Café トラヤカフェ Keyakizaka-dōri, 6-12-2 Roppongi, Minato-ku ⓣ03 5789 9811; Roppongi Station; map pp.110–111. Stylish café specializing in Japanese teas and sweets made from azuki beans; figure on over ¥1000 for both the former and the latter. It's usually busy with ladies lunching or sipping tea between boutique visits. Daily 10am–10pm.

Umezono 梅園 1-31-12 Asakusa, Taitō-ku ⓣ03 3841 7580; Asakusa Station; map p.100. This traditional tea shop in the heart of Asakusa is famous for its *awa-zenzai*, millet flour cakes wrapped in sweet azuki bean paste, served with seeds of Japanese basil for contrast. Alternatively, choose a bowl of *anmitsu* from the window display: a colourful concoction of agar jelly, azuki beans and sticky rice topped with a variety of fruits (and, if you're really hungry, whipped cream or ice cream; from ¥800). 10am–8pm; closed Wed.

HARAJUKU, AOYAMA AND SHIBUYA

RESTAURANTS

Bepokah ベポカ 2-17-6 Jingūmae, Shibuya-ku ☎03 6804 1377, ⓦbepocah.com; Meiji-jingūmae Station; map p.120. Given their mutual adoration of raw fish, you'd think that Peruvian cuisine would have a bigger impact in Japan. This is one of the few places in Tokyo in which you'll find quality *ceviche* (dishes from ¥1800), as well as Andean staples such as *lomo saltado* (stir-fried beef on rice; ¥1600) and *ají de gallina* (chicken in an almost curry-like yellow cream; ¥1600). Pricey, but just about worth it. Mon–Fri 6pm–1am, Sat 5pm–midnight.

Commune 246 コミューン246 3-13 Minami-Aoyama, Minato-ku; no phone, ⓦcommune246.com; Omotesandō Station; map p.120. This open-air courtyard space is almost like a boho slice of London, San Francisco or Melbourne – a clutch of small snack shacks selling all sorts, from gourmet hot dogs and burgers to Thai food and ramen. It's also a good drinking spot. Daily 11am–10pm; closed Dec–Feb.

Ganso Kujiraya 元祖くじら屋 2-9-22 Dōgenzaka, Shibuya-ku ☎03 3461 9145, ⓦwww.kujiraya.co.jp; Shibuya Station; map p.122. Like it or not, the Japanese have eaten whale meat for centuries, and this smart, surprisingly cheap venue is a good option if you'd like to see – and taste – what the fuss is about. Most dishes are ¥780–980, but it's best visited at lunch when you'll get a hearty set from ¥1000. Mon–Fri 11am–2pm & 5–10.30pm, Sat & Sun 11.30am–11.30pm.

Harajuku Gyōzaro 原宿餃子楼 6-2-4 Jingūmae, Shibuya-ku ☎03 3406 4743; Meiji-jingūmae Station; map p.120. Though there are few Japanese customers at this atmospheric dumpling spot, the fare on offer is cheap and tasty – just ¥290 for a round of succulent *gyōza*, and ¥250 for cucumber in miso paste (mix some chilli oil into the latter and you'll draw some funny looks, but it tastes great). Mon–Sat 11.30am–4am, Sun 11.30am–11pm.

La Fée Délice ラフェデリース 5-11-13 Jingūmae, Shibuya-ku ☎03 5766 4084, ⓦlafeedelice.com; Meiji-jingūmae Station; map p.120. The best of Harajuku's many creperies – most of them just plonk a mini Fuji of whipped cream on their creations, but the chefs here have actually trained in France. Sweet and savoury crepes go for ¥1000 and up. Mon–Sat 11.30am–11pm, Sun 11am–10pm.

Las Chicas ラスチカス 5-47-6 Jingūmae, Shibuya-ku ☎03 3407 6865, ⓦlaschicas.jp; Omotesandō Station; map p.120. A green oasis in the backstreets of Harajuku that's always been a winner for its fairy-lit, relaxed ambience. Safest are the burgers and chunky sandwiches (around ¥1400) or eggs Benedict (¥1400); more interesting choices include *feijoada*, a black-bean stew originating in Rio de Janeiro. Daily 11.30am–11pm, Fri & Sat until 11.30pm.

★**Los Barbados** ロスバルバドス 41-26 Udagawachō, Shibuya-ku ☎03 3496 7157; Shibuya Station; map p.122. This little *izakaya* is a little different from the norm: under a large map of the Congo, the Africa-phile owner whips up great food from across the African continent, including Tunisian *brik* (an eggy, flash-fried pastry; ¥850) and Senegambian rice-and-meat staples such as *maafe* and *yassa*. Wash it all down with some Kenya Cane. Mon–Sat noon–11pm.

Maisen まい泉 4-8-5 Jingūmae, Shibuya-ku ☎03 3470 0071, ⓦmai-sen.com; Omotesandō Station; map p.120. Located in an old bathhouse, this long-running *tonkatsu* restaurant serves up great-value set meals from ¥1580; prices dip under ¥1000 for lunch. The actual bathhouse bit is the smoking section of the restaurant. Daily 11am–10pm.

★**Ramen Nagi** ラーメン凪 1-3-1 Higashi, Shibuya-ku ☎03 3499 0390, ⓦn-nagi.com; Shibuya Station; map p.122. At this crazy-busy gourmet ramen joint, the waiter will give you a choice of how soft or hard you'd like your (superb) noodles cooked. There are a few interesting selections available on the fun cross-section menu, including the "Midorio", made with basil and cheese – weird, but it works. More regular varieties are served in a rich broth, topped with delicious pork slices and a heap of chopped spring onions – a bargain at ¥890 a bowl. Mon–Sat 11.30am–4pm & 5pm–4am, Sun noon–2am.

★**Sakuratei** さくら亭 3-20-1 Jingūmae, Shibuya-ku ☎03 3479 0039, ⓦsakuratei.co.jp/en; Meiji-jingūmae Station; map p.120. Funky, cook-your-own *okonomiyaki*, *monjayaki* and *yakisoba* joint behind the weird and wonderful Design Festa gallery (see p.120). Dishes start at ¥950, and feature some quirky options such as curry or Okinawan ingredients. A good drinks selection means it's a fun place at night. ⓦ Daily 11am–11pm.

Uobei 魚べい 2-29-1 Dōgenzaka, Shibuya-ku ☎03 3462 0241; Shibuya Station; map p.122. Searingly bright restaurant in which your sushi is ordered by touch screen, then delivered by rail on automated plates – the only humans you see are those who point you to your table and take your cash. Gimmicky, yes, but it's a lot of fun – not to mention cheap, since most plates are ¥108 for two sushi. Daily 11am–midnight.

CAFÉS

Crisscross クリスクロス 5-7-28 Minami-Aoyama, Minato-ku ☎03 6434 1266; Omotesandō Station; map p.120. One of Aoyama's "it" places at the time of writing, selling good coffee (from ¥600) and dessert dishes such as buttermilk pancakes (¥1600). For cheaper eats, pick up something from the adjoining Breadworks bakery. Daily 8am–10pm.

★**Lion** ライオン 2-19-13 Dōgenzaka, Shibuya-ku ✆03 3461 6858; Shibuya Station; map p.122. Not the place for animated conversations, this *Addams Family*-style institution set amid the love hotels of Dōgenzaka is where businessmen bunking off work come to appreciate classical music with their coffee (¥500 and up). Seats are arranged to face a pair of enormous speakers. Daily 11am–10.30pm.

L'Occitane 2F Likes Bldg, 2-3-1 Dōgenzaka, Shibuya-ku ✆03 5428 1564; Shibuya Station; map p.122. This café above the eponymous cosmetics store has one huge draw – it's a prime viewing spot for Shibuya crossing. Thankfully, the coffee's fine. Daily 10am–9pm.

★**Maidreamin** メイドリーミング B1 30-1 Udagawachō, Shibuya-ku ✆03 6427 8938, ⓦmaidreamin.com; Shibuya Station; map p.122. This sci-fi-style maid café (see box, p.144) is an all-out cuteness assault, its glammed-up staff sporting inch-long fake eyelashes and umpteen petticoat layers. Entry ¥500 per hour, plus you have to make one order from the menu. Mon–Thurs & Sun 1–11pm, Fri & Sat 1pm–5am.

Tokyo Snake Center 東京スネークセンター 8F Sanpo-Sogo Building, 6-5-6 Jingūmae, Shibuya-ku ✆03 6427 9912, ⓦsnakecenter.jp; Meiji-jingūmae Station; map p.120. One of the better "weird-animal" cafés in Tokyo, and decently priced at ¥1000 entry, including a drink; it's ¥540 more to pet a small snake. 11am–8pm; closed Tues.

SHINJUKU AND THE WEST
RESTAURANTS

Asia Yokochō アジア横丁 1-21-1 Kabukichō, Shinjuku-ku, no phone; Seibu-Shinjuku Station; map p.124. Chefs and customers from all over Asia gather at this quirky open-air spot, on the rooftop of the Maruhan building. The atmosphere can be raucous, and a poke around the various stalls will reveal everything from Korean meat to Indian curries, via Filipino food and Turkish shishas. Daily noon–late.

Mita-Seimen 三田製麵 1-13-3 Nishi-Shinjuku, Shinjuku-ku ✆03 5909 3832; Shinjuku Station; map p.124. Illuminated by faux-paper windows, this attractive joint sells cheap, tasty *tsukemen* (¥730) from its winning location in Nishi-Shinjuku. Daily 11am–2am.

New York Grill 52F Park Hyatt Tower, 3-7-1-2 Nishi-Shinjuku ✆03 5323 3458, ⓦtokyo.park.hyatt.jp; Tochōmae Station; map p.124. Sitting pretty on the 52nd floor of the *Park Hyatt*, the *New York Grill* offers great views and Stateside-sized portions – after the ¥6200 buffet lunch you won't need to eat much else all day. Bookings essential. Daily 11.30am–2.30pm & 5.30–10.30pm.

★**Omoide Yokochō** 思い出横丁 1-2-7 Nishi-Shinjuku, Shinjuku-ku; Shinjuku Station; map p.124. It's almost pointless recommending specific establishments on this hugely atmospheric *yokochō* alley – just stroll along a few times, until you've spied both the food you desire, and a free seat. Most places daily 4pm–midnight.

★**Tsunahachi** つな八 3-31-8 Shinjuku, Shinjuku-ku ✆03 3352 1012, ⓦtunahachi.co.jp; Shinjuku Station; map p.124. The main branch of the famous tempura restaurant almost always has a queue outside, though you're likely to get seated quickly if you settle for the upstairs rooms away from the frying action (or ask for the non-smoking section). Everything is freshly made, and even the smallest set (¥1500, including soup, rice and pickles) will fill you up. Daily 11am–10pm.

CAFÉS

Ballon d'Essai バロンデッセ 2-30-11 Kitazawa, Setagaya-ku ✆03 6407 0511, ⓦballondessai.com; Shimokitazawa Station; map p.124. This little hidey-hole in Shimokitazawa, 5km west of Shinjuku, makes coffee from a blend of five types of bean – at least take a photo of the artwork before downing your flat white (¥360). 🛜 Mon–Fri 11.30am–9pm, Sat & Sun 10.30am–9pm.

Calico きゃりこ 6F, 1-16-2 Kabukichō, Shinjuku-ku, ✆03 6457 6387, ⓦcatcafe.jp; Shinjuku Station; map p.124. A great place to experience the cat café phenomenon (see box, p.144); ¥600 gets you thirty minutes of quality time with around fifty gorgeous kitties. With instructions and menu in English, it's very foreigner friendly, and offers inexpensive drinks and food. No kids under 12 are allowed. Daily 11am–10pm.

IKEBUKURO AND THE NORTH
RESTAURANTS

Bakudan ばくだん 1-21-1 Higashi-Ikebukuro, Toshima-ku, no phone; Ikebukuro Station; map pp.128–129. Most *takoyaki* booths are much of a muchness, but the name of this place – "bomb" – hints at its super-sized servings. One of its *takoyaki* (octopus balls – ball-shaped snacks of batter filled with minced or diced octopus; from ¥370) is as large as a whole tray of normal-sized octopus balls. A long queue is inevitable, giving you time to choose from toppings such as *yakitori* sauce, *kimchi* and lavered seaweed. Daily 10am–11pm.

★**Isomaru Suisan** 磯丸水産 3-25-10 Nishi-Ikebukuro, Toshima-ku ✆03 5953 2585; Ikebukuro Station; map pp.128–129. This fantastic seafood *izakaya* is heaving all evening, every evening – in fact, it's so popular that it never shuts. There's no English menu, but there are plenty of pictures and live sea creatures to point at – try their colossal *sazae* (sea snails), or the splendid-value eel on rice (*unadon*; ¥980). Daily 24hr.

Le Bretagne ルブルターニュ 4-2 Kagurazaka, Shinjuku-ku ✆03 3235 3500, ⓦle-bretagne.com;

1

Iidabashi Station; map pp.128–129. Attractive French-run restaurant down a little side-street in Kagurazaka, offering authentic crepes (both sweet and savoury) and buckwheat *galettes* from ¥1080, as well as home-made Breton-style cider. Also serves good coffee. Tues–Sat 11.30am–10.30pm, Sun 11.30am–9pm.

★**Saemaeul Sikdang** セマウル食堂 1-1-4 Hyakuninchō, Shinjuku-ku ☎03 6205 6226; Shin-Ōkubo Station; map pp.128–129. This outpost of an authentic Korean chain is by far the best *yakiniku* restaurant in Koreatown. Order some *yeoltan bulgogi* (the meat from *shabu-shabu* without the soup, mixed with spicy paste; ¥880 per portion) and a boiling *doenjang jjigae* (a spicier, chunkier miso soup served with rice; a ¥780 portion will feed two), and watch as the ethnic-Korean staff nonchalantly blanket the rest of your table with free side dishes. To make things feel even more like Seoul, order a bottle of flavoured *soju* to wash everything down with. Daily 11.30am–2am.

Taishōken 大勝軒 2-42-8 Minami-Ikebukuro, Toshima-ku ☎03 3981 9360; Higashi-Ikebukuro Station; map pp.128–129. Diners at this noodle restaurant are arranged almost as if they're praying to the chefs at work in the centre – and, in a sense, they are here to worship. This is the *honten* (head branch) of the eponymous noodle behemoth, and the very birthplace of *tsukemen* – try a bowl here (from ¥700) and you'll notice that the original taste is somewhat more subtle than the fatty broths in vogue these days. 11am–10pm; closed Wed.

CAFÉS

Canal Café カナルカフェー 1-9 Kagurazaka, Shinjuku-ku ☎03 3260 8068, ⓦcanalcafe.jp; Iidabashi Station; map pp.128–129. This is a surprisingly tranquil and appealing waterside spot, particularly romantic at night when the old clapperboard boathouses sparkle with fairy lights, or during the blossom-heavy *sakura* season. The café-restaurant has decent-value pasta and pizza meals (sets from ¥1300); for coffee alone, you can head to the outdoor section, though annoyingly they only serve in paper cups. Tues–Fri 11.30am–11pm, Sat & Sun 11.30am–9.30pm.

Nekorobi ねころび 3F Tact TO Bldg, 1-28-1 Higashi-Ikebukuro, Toshima-ku ☎03 6228 0646, ⓦnekorobi.jp; Ikebukuro Station; map pp.128–129. This cat café (see box, p.144) has a minimum ¥1100 cover charge for the first hour (¥1300 at weekends), which gets you unlimited drinks and use of internet, Wii or DVD terminals – though most go straight for the cat toys, and a play with their favourite felines. Daily 11am–10pm.

Swallowtail Café スヲローテール B1F 3-12-12 Higashi-Ikebukuro, Toshima-ku ⓦbutlers-cafe.jp; Ikebukuro Station; map pp.128–129. A "butler café" (see box, p.144) where young guys dressed like Jeeves are the solicitous waiters in a room hung with chandeliers and antique-style furniture. Booking through the (mostly Japanese) website is essential. Expect to spend at least ¥2500 per head. Daily 10.30am–9pm.

DRINKING AND NIGHTLIFE

Tokyo's **nightlife** options run the gamut from *izakaya* to live music venues (known as "live houses"). The distinction between restaurants, bars and clubs in the city's *sakariba* ("lively places"), such as Ginza, Shibuya or Shinjuku, is hazy, with many places offering a range of entertainment depending on the evening or customers' spirits.

BARS AND IZAKAYA

Tokyo is a drinkers' paradise with a vast range of venues serving practically any brand of booze from around the world as well as local tipples such as sake, *shōchū* (a vodka-like spirit) and award-winning Japanese whisky. Roppongi easily has Tokyo's greatest concentration of foreigner-friendly *gaijin* bars, but note that many are closed on Sunday. If there's live music anywhere you'll often pay for it through higher drinks prices or a cover charge. Some regular bars also have cover charges and *izakaya* (bars that serve food) almost always do, though you'll usually get a small snack served with your first drink. There's plenty of choice among those that don't, though, so always check the deal before buying your drink.

THE IMPERIAL PALACE AND AROUND

Marunouchi House 丸の内ハウス 7F Shin-Marunouchi Bldg, 1-5-1 Maranouchi, Chiyoda-ku ☎03 5218 5100; Tokyo Station; map p.86. The best thing about the open-plan space here, with its seven different restaurants and

bars, is that you can take your drinks out on to the broad wraparound terrace for great views of Tokyo Station and towards the Imperial Palace. Cover charges may apply at night. Mon–Sat 11am–4am, Sun 11am–11pm.

Old Imperial Bar Imperial Hotel, 1-1-1 Uchisaiwaichō, Chiyoda-ku ☎03 3539 8088, ⓦwww.imperialhotel .co.jp; Hibiya Station; map p.86. All that remains in Tokyo of Frank Lloyd Wright's Art Deco *Imperial Hotel* is this re-created bar. Try its signature Mount Fuji cocktail (¥1630), a wickedly sweet blend of gin, cream, egg white and sugar syrup with a cherry on top, which was invented here in 1924. While you sip it, ask to see the photo albums of how the hotel once looked. Smart attire recommended. 🛜 Daily 11.30am–midnight.

★**Shin Hi No Moto** 新日の基 2-4-4 Yūrakuchō, Chiyoda-ku ☎03 3214 8021; Yūrakuchō or Hibiya stations; map p.86. Known to all and sundry as "Andy's", this is a lively English-owned *izakaya* under the tracks just south of Yūrakuchō Station. Reservations essential. Mon–Sat 5pm–midnight.

TOKYO'S TOP PLACES TO DRINK

Best for cheapskates *Coins Bar* and *Gas Panic* (see p.152 & p.154)

Best for Art Deco stylings *Old Imperial Bar* (see opposite)

Best for a sake education *Bunka Hostel* (see p.138) and *Buri* (see p.152)

Best for views *Bar Six* (see below)

Best for events *SuperDeluxe* (see p.154)

Best for microbrewed beer *Nakameguro Taproom* (see p.152) and *Campion Ale* (see below)

Best for Japanese whisky *Cask Strength* (see p.152)

Best for weirdness value *The Lockup* (see p.153)

Best club *Ageha* (see p.154)

Best gay venue *Arty Farty* (see p.155)

GINZA AND AROUND

Dry Dock ドライドック 3-25-10 Shimbashi, Minato-ku ☎03 5777 4755; Shimbashi Station; map p.91. Cosy craft-beer bar with a nautical theme nestling beneath the train tracks. Its no-smoking policy is a welcome change, and patrons often spill outside to enjoy the regularly changing menu of Japanese and overseas microbrews. Note there's no food served on Saturday. Mon–Fri 5pm–midnight, Sat 5pm–10pm.

Lion ライオン 7-9-20 Ginza, Chūō-ku ☎03 3571 2590; Ginza Station; map p.91. Opened in 1934, this flagship beer hall of the Sapporo chain is a rather baronial place, with dark tiles and mock wood panelling. As well as good draught beer (giant ones ¥1080), there are sausages, sauerkraut and other German snacks on offer alongside international pub grub, and a restaurant upstairs. You'll find other branches scattered around Tokyo, all using the same formula. 🛜 Mon–Sat 11.30am–11pm, Sun 11.30am–10.30pm.

AKIHABARA AND AROUND

Hitachino Brewing Lab 常陸野ブルーイングラボ mAAch-Ecute Building, 1-25-4 Kanda-Sudachō, Chiyoda-ku ☎03 3254 3434, ⓦhitachino.cc; Akihabara Station; map p.94. One of Tokyo's most attractive microbreweries, serving Hitachino's famous Nest ale and another eight varieties on tap, as displayed in a beer-rainbow array of test tubes. Try a taster set for ¥880. Mon–Sat 11am–11pm, Sun 11am–9pm.

UENO AND AROUND

★**Kadokura** カドクラ 6-13-1 Ueno, Taitō-ku ☎03 3832 5335; Ueno Station; map p.97. Bustling *tachinomiya* that usually gets boisterous even before office kicking-out time – a great place to make new friends over a freezing beer or highball (from ¥400). Daily 10am–11pm.

Warrior Celt ウオリアーケルト 3F Ito Building, 6-9-22 Ueno ☎03 3836 8588, ⓦwarriorcelt.jp; Ueno Station; map p.97. Occasionally wild bar whose regulars are led on by a veritable United Nations of bar staff. Key ingredients include a fine range of beers, good food, a nightly happy hour (5–7pm), live bands and, last but not least, "Ladies' Night" on Thursdays (cocktails ¥500 for female customers). 🛜 Mon–Thurs 5pm–midnight, Fri & Sat 5pm–5am.

ASAKUSA

Bar Six バー6 6F 2-34-3 Asakusa, Taitō-ku ☎03 5806 5106; Asakusa Station; map p.100. Sophisticated watering hole on the sixth floor of the Amuse Museum complex (see p.101), surrounded by a standing-only outdoor terrace. The Asakusa views are amazing, especially of Sensō-ji, which is illuminated at night. Give the "Asakusa" mojitos a whizz. Tues–Sun 6pm–2am.

★**Bunka Hostel** ブンカホステル 1-13-5 Asakusa, Taitō-ku ☎03 5806 3444, ⓦbunkahostel.jp; Asakusa Station; map p.100. The lobby of this excellent hostel (see p.138) doubles as a bar, as stylish as any in the area – the wall of Bunka-labelled sake jars behind the bar is extremely photogenic. They've more than thirty varieties of sake on offer, with the type (dry, sweet, strong, etc) explained on the English-language menu – a perfect place in which to get acquainted with Japan's most traditional drink. 🛜 Tues–Sun 6pm–2am.

Campion Ale カンピオンエール 2-2-2 Nishi-Asakusa, Taitō-ku ☎03 6231 6554, ⓦcampionale.com; Tawaramachi Station; map p.100. Brew-pubs are ten-a-penny in Tokyo these days, but this one stands out from the pack: not only is it ideally located for the Asakusa

SUMMER BEER GARDENS

Helping to mitigate Tokyo's sticky summers are the **outdoor beer gardens** that sprout around the city from late May through to early September, typically on the roofs of department stores such as Tobu in Ikebukuro, or in street-level gardens and plazas. One of the best beer gardens is *Forest Beer Garden* (see p.153) in Meiji-jingū's Outer Garden, close to Shinanomachi Station. **Rooftop bars** are also very pleasing places to drink in warm months; *Xex* (see p.152) is a good option.

1

backpacker and tourist crowds, it's British-owned, and serves suitably authentic ales (usually 15 on tap) and hearty pub dishes. Mon–Fri 5–11.30pm, Sat & Sun noon–11.30pm.

Kamiya 神谷 1-1-1 Asakusa, Taitō-ku ☎ 03 3841 5400; Asakusa Station; map p.100. Established in 1880, this was Tokyo's first Western-style bar. It's famous for its Denki Bran ("electric brandy" – a mix of gin, wine, Curaçao and brandy), invented in 1883. It's a potent tipple (and just ¥270 a shot), though they also make a "weaker" version. 11.30am–10pm; closed Tues.

BAYSIDE TOKYO

Jicoo ジコー ☎ 0120 049490, ⓦ jicoofloatingbar.com; Hinode Station; map p.103. This night-time persona of the futuristic ferry *Himiko* (see p.133) shuttles between Hinode, under the Rainbow Bridge, and Odaiba. To board costs ¥2600 (it takes half an hour from point to point, but you can stay on as long as you like), drinks cost from ¥700 and there's a DJ playing so you can take to the illuminated dancefloor and show off your best John Travolta moves. Daily 8am–11pm.

AKASAKA AND ROPPONGI

A971 Tokyo Midtown, 9-7-3 Akasaka, Minato-ku ☎ 03 5413 3210; Roppongi Station; map pp.110–111. This relaxed café-bar and restaurant at the front of the Midtown complex, with mid-twentieth-century modernist furnishings, has proved itself a popular hangout with the area's many expats. ⓦ Mon–Thurs 10am–2am, Fri & Sat 10am–5am, Sun 10am–midnight.

★**Cask Strength** B1 3-9-11 Roppongi, Minato-ku ☎ 03 6432 9772, ⓦ cask-s.com; Roppongi Station; map pp.110–111. Attractive basement venue with one of Tokyo's best selections of whisky, including some rare Japanese choices – those with a nose for Karuizawa or Yamazaki Single Malt will be in paradise. Daily 6pm–late.

Public Six 6-8-22 Roppongi, Minato-ku ☎ 03 5413 3182, ⓦ bagus-99.com; Roppongi Station; map pp.110–111. This new gastropub boasts a truly zany exterior, and has become popular as a place to watch sports over some good food and drink. Food is generally Western in nature, though often with Japanese flourishes; drinks-wise, they have at least six craft beers on tap, as well as house cocktails, and plenty of varieties of sake. Mon–Sat 5pm–5am, Sun 5pm–3am.

Tusk タスク 1F Roppongi Hills West Walk, 6-10-1 Roppongi, Minato-ku ☎ 03 3478 9991, ⓦ tuskbar.jp; Roppongi Station; map pp.110–111. One of Roppongi's most popular hang-out spots, this swanky DJ bar isn't all that pricey, considering the location. Order your cocktail or tequila (all around ¥1500) from the 10m-long bar, and throw it back under the gaze of two whopping paintings. ⓦ Mon–Sat 5pm–5am, Sun 5pm–midnight.

EBISU, MEGURO AND THE SOUTH

Baja バハ 1-16-12 Kami-Meguro, Meguro-ku, no phone; Naka-Meguro Station; map pp.114–115. Seemingly decorated with everything the owner could find in his garage, this is one of the most entertaining bars in the Nakameguro area, with a good mix of foreigners and oddball Japanese. Drinks (including cocktails) cost ¥500; no tax, no table charge, cool music, and they also whip up yummy tacos – a winner. Daily 5pm–5am.

★**Buri** ぶり 1-14-1 Ebisu-nishi, Shibuya-ku ☎ 03 3496 7744; Ebisu Station; map pp.114–115. A great range of chilled "one-cup sake" (a sealed glass, the size of a small can, already filled with sake, that you just pull the top off; ¥800) is the speciality at this trendy *tachinomiya* that's one of the best in town. Good *yakitori*, too, and just wait until you see the toilet door. Daily 3pm–midnight.

Footnik フットニック 1F Asahi Building, 1-11-2 Ebisu, Shibuya-ku ☎ 03 5795 0144, ⓦ footnik.net; Ebisu Station; map pp.114–115. A bar devoted to soccer, with a game or two on the big screen every night, pints of imported beer for ¥1000 or so, and reasonable food. For popular matches you'll have to pay an entry charge. ⓦ Daily 3pm–1am, later at weekends.

★**Nakameguro Taproom** 中目黒タップルーム GT Plaza C-Block 2F, 2-1-3 Kami-Meguro, Meguro-ku ☎ 03 5768 3025, ⓦ bairdbeer.com; Naka-Meguro Station; map pp.114–115. This sleek real-ale nirvana serves beers (¥1000) from Baird Brewing Company, which started life out west in Numazu, on the Izu Peninsula (see p.211). It also serves good food, and gets nice and busy at weekends. ⓦ Mon–Fri 5pm–midnight, Sat & Sun noon–midnight.

Xex ゼックス 3F La Fuente, 11-1 Sarugaku-chō, Shibuya-ku ☎ 03 3476 065, ⓦ xexgroup.jp; Daikanyama Station; map pp.114–115. This sleek rooftop bar is more like something you'd expect to find in Southeast Asia than Tokyo, with loungey seating dotted around a small pool. Pizza and sushi are on offer to augment the wine selection, and there's occasional live jazz. Mon–Fri 5.30pm–4am, Sat & Sun 5.30pm–midnight.

HARAJUKU, AOYAMA AND SHIBUYA

Coins Bar コインズバー B1 Noa Shibuya Building, 36-2 Udagawa-chō, Shibuya-ku ☎ 03 3463 3039; Shibuya Station; map p.122. This cool little basement bar offers most drinks for ¥320, making it a top choice if you're on a budget. Music is usually hip-hop and R&B, despite the soul vinyl covers dotting the place; they also bring in DJs most weekends, when there's a ¥300 entry fee. Daily 4pm–12.30am, later at weekends.

★**Fight Club 428** ファイトクラブ428 2-27-2 Dōgenzaka, Shibuya-ku ☎ 03 3464 1799; Shibuya

KARAOKE BARS AND BOXES

You'll find branches of the biggest **karaoke** chains – *Karaoke-kan*, *Shidax* and *Big Echo* – all over the city; the charge is typically ¥800 per person per hour, but some independent bars are cheaper, and you'll almost always have a private room for your group, rather than a stage visible to all. There are always plenty of English-language songs to butcher, although it certainly helps to have a Japanese-speaker on hand to operate the karaoke system. Almost all venues serve alcohol, and many have drink-all-you-can (*nomi-hōdai*) specials; two hours of booze costs ¥3000 or so, plus the actual singing fee, and as a rule of thumb these deals usually work out cheaper if you're planning to have four or more drinks. If you're a first-timer, alcohol certainly helps to ease things along – those who are too shy to sing at the beginning of a session often end up hogging the microphone all night long.

Big Echo ビッグエコ 4-2-14 Ginza, Chūō-ku ☎03 3563 5100; Ginza Station; map p.91. The most appealing branch of this major chain, with a few interesting themed rooms, including a Hello Kitty one. From ¥850 per person, with a minimum order of one drink. Daily 24hr.

Fiesta フィエスタ B1 6-2-35 Roppongi, Minato-ku ☎03 5410 3008, ⓦfiesta-roppongi.com; Roppongi Station; map pp.110–111. A particularly good karaoke bar for newbie *gaijin*, offering thousands of songs in English, as well as several other languages – 26,000 hits, in all. ¥3500 including three drinks. Mon 7pm–midnight, Tues–Sat 7pm–5am.

Karaoke-kan カラオケ館 30-8 Udagawachō, Shibuya-ku ☎03 3462 0785; Shibuya Station; map p.122. Japan's premier karaoke-box operator has branches liberally peppered across the capital. Rooms 601 and 602 in their Udagawachō branch were featured in the movie *Lost in Translation*. An hour of karaoke here costs from ¥900 per person, with a minimum order of one drink. Daily 24hr.

Station; map p.122. Of Shibuya's array of weird bars, this is one of the oddest – part of a fitness centre, the bar itself is set right next to a functional kickboxing cage. You can spar there yourself for ¥1000, though staff will only allow you to do this before your drink (most priced at ¥500). Mon–Thurs 6pm–midnight, Fri & Sat 6pm–5am, Sun noon–6pm.

Forest Beer Garden 森のビアガーデン 14 13 Kasumigaoka-machi, Minato-ku ☎03 5411 3715; Shinanomachi Station; map p.118. This open-air beer garden, fronting the Meiji Kinenkan wedding hall, offers an eat-and-drink-all-you-can deal (*tabi-nomi-hōdai*) for men (¥4200) and women (¥3900). June–Sept only: Mon–Fri 5–10pm, Sat & Sun noon–10pm.

Goodbeer Faucets グッドビアフォーセツ 2F 1-29-1 Shoto, Shibuya-ku ☎03 3770 5544, ⓦgoodbeer faucets.jp; Shibuya Station; map p.122. An excellent place for craft beer, selling over forty varieties on draught – some made by the Goodbeer brewery, others from across Japan and abroad. Large glasses of the good stuff cost ¥750–1300, with ¥200 off during happy hour (Mon–Thurs 5–8pm, Sun 1–7pm). 🛜 Mon–Thurs 5pm–midnight, Fri 5pm–3am, Sat & Sun 1pm–midnight.

★**The Lockup** ザロックアップ B1 33-1 Udagawachō, Shibuya-ku ☎03 5728 7731; Shibuya Station; map p.122. The house-of-horrors-style entrance is so dark it's a trip merely walking into this bar, the best of a small chain of prison-themed establishments. Make it through and you'll be handcuffed then led to a cell-like room where you can take your pick of weird cocktails: some arrive in test tubes; others have fake eyeballs inside. Periodically, the lights dim and staff try their best to terrify customers – brilliant fun, believe it or not. Mon–Thurs 5pm–1am, Fri & Sat 5pm–5am, Sun 5pm–midnight.

SHINJUKU AND THE WEST

Champion チャンピオン Golden Gai, off Shiki-no-michi; Shinjuku-sanchōme Station; map p.124. At the western entrance to the Golden Gai stretch (see p.125), this is the largest bar in the area. There's no cover charge and most drinks are a bargain ¥500 – some even less. The catch? You have to endure tone-deaf patrons crooning karaoke for ¥100 a song. Mon–Sat 6pm–6am.

★**Shisha** シーシャ 3-30-3 Kitazawa, Setagaya-ku ☎03 3468 0601; Shimokitazawa Station; map p.124. This tiny, loungey bar in Shimokitazawa, 5km west of Shinjuku, has perhaps the city's cheapest shisha (from ¥800 per person), with a wide range of flavours to choose from. Drop by before 5pm and you can have a drink for an extra ¥100 – they're usually affordable at ¥400, in any case. Daily 2pm–3am or so.

Square スクエーア 2F 3rd Street, Golden Gai; Shinjuku-sanchōme Station; map p.124. Cute, squashed little upper-floor bar in Golden Gai (see p.125) with cheery staff, cheery customers, decent drinks, and some dangerous-looking bras on the wall. Look out for the blue sign, which is, ironically, a circle. Cover charge ¥500. Mon–Sat 6pm–4am.

CLUBS

The Tokyo clubbing scene took a turn for the better in 2016, when a Footloose-like law forbidding dancing was

1

finally repealed; the law, on the books since 1948, banned dancing in licensed premises after midnight (and in unlicensed premises at all), though in practice it was ignored for much of the twentieth century and only enforced occasionally since 2001, so not all that much has changed, especially in the main clubbing regions, Roppongi and Shibuya. Local DJs to look out for are Satoshi Tomiie, a house legend since the early 1990s; Ken Ishii, well known for his techno sets; the hard-house-loving Ko Kimura; and rising star Xonora, a ball of energy who has spun her smooth beats at most of Tokyo's top clubs.

BAYSIDE TOKYO

Ageha アゲハ Studio Coast, 2-2-10 Shin-Kiba, Kōtō-ku ☎ 03 5534 2525, ⓦ ageha.com; Shin-Kiba Station; map p.103. Ultra-cool mega-club with an outdoor pool, body-trembling sound system and roster of high-profile events. It's out by Tokyo Bay, but there's a free shuttle bus here from Shibuya – check the website for details and make sure you turn up at least half an hour before you want to depart to get a ticket to board the bus. Entry usually ¥3000. Usually Fri & Sat only.

AKASAKA AND ROPPONGI

Alife 1-7-2 Nishi-Azabu, Minato-ku ☎ 03 5785 2531, ⓦ e-alife.net; Roppongi Station; map pp.110–111. Closed for a while, this famed venue reopened in 2016, and is setting about reclaiming its mantle as one of Roppongi's top spots. As with the earlier incarnations, the second-floor lounge area is a good place to chill out after you've worked up a sweat to the house and techno being spun on the large dancefloor below. The cost of entry varies, but expect to pay more at weekends, even more after 11pm, and yet more again if you're a guy. Events most nights except Sun.

Jumanji ジュマンジ Marina Building 3-10-5 Roppongi, Minato-ku ☎ 03 5410 5455, ⓦ jumanji55.com; Roppongi Station; map pp.110–111. Aptly, considering its name, *Jumanji* can be a bit of a zoo: with the ¥1000 early-entry fee often including a couple of drinks (and sometimes, particularly for women, unlimited trips to the bar within a certain time window), there's essentially no entry charge, meaning that at weekends there's barely any wiggle-room. Great fun, though, and a hugely popular pick-up spot. Open most nights.

★ **SuperDeluxe** スーパーデラックス B1F 3-1-25 Nishi-Azabu, Minato-ku ☎ 03 5412 0515, ⓦ super-deluxe .com; Roppongi Station; map pp.110–111. Billing itself as a place for "thinking, drinking people", this club hosts a brilliant range of arty events – anything from live music performances and album launches to the monthly PechaKucha nights (see box below), a showcase for Tokyo's creative community. Events most nights.

EBISU, MEGURO AND THE SOUTH

★ **Unit** ユーニット Za-House Bldg, 1-34-17 Ebisu-Nishi, Shibuya-ku ☎ 03 5459 8630, ⓦ unit-tokyo.com; Ebisu or Daikanyama stations; map pp.114–115. DJ events and gigs from an interesting mix of artists and bands at this cool three-floor club, café and lounge bar. Events most nights.

HARAJUKU, AOYAMA AND SHIBUYA

Club Asia クラブアシア 1-8 Maruyamachō, Shibuya-ku ☎ 03 5458 2551, ⓦ clubasia.co.jp; Shibuya Station; map p.122. A mainstay of the clubbing scene, with the emphasis on techno and trance nights, though they occasionally wander into other territories such as reggae and new wave. It's in the heart of the Dōgenzaka love hotel district, and a popular place for one-off gigs by visiting DJs. Entry usually ¥3000 plus a drink. Open Fri & Sat, and sometimes Sun & Thurs.

Gas Panic ガスパニック B1 21-7 Udagawachō, Shibuya-ku ☎ 03 3462 9099, ⓦ gaspanic.co.jp; Shibuya Station; map p.122. For many a year, the various *Gas Panic* clubs have, between them, constituted Tokyo's meat markets, with this one now the biggie. Free entry, cheap

---

PECHAKUCHA NIGHT

It started in 2003 as an idea to bring people to a new "creative art" basement venue called *SuperDeluxe* in the then pre-Roppongi Art Triangle days, but in a few short years **PechaKucha Night** (ⓦ pechakucha.org) became a worldwide **phenomenon** – it has now spread to over 700 cities and counting. Co-created by Tokyo-based architects Astrid Klein and Mark Dytham (KDa), the presentation format – 20 images shown for 20 seconds each, with the exhibitor talking along in time – keeps participants on their toes, often forcing funny ad-lib moments due to the high pace. More importantly, it acts as a platform for these creators to share their ideas. PechaKucha ("chit-chat") has ended up being the perfect platform for Tokyo's **young, up-and-coming creators** who would never previously have had a place to share their works in front of a large audience.

PechaKucha usually takes place at *SuperDeluxe* (see above) once a month, and there are occasional events held at Shibuya's Hikarie Building (see p.122).

drinks, and lots of youngsters (both Japanese and foreign) doing things their parents wouldn't be proud of. Free entry. Daily 6pm–late.

★**Harlem** ハーレム 2-4 Maruyama-chō, Shibuya-ku ☎03 3461 8806, ⓦwww.harlem.co.jp; Shibuya Station; map p.122. The city's prime hip-hop venue for two full decades, keeping abreast of the genre's undulations with a roster of young, energetic DJs. The crowd are almost all dressed to the nines – do likewise or you might as well not be here. Usually ¥3000 with a drink. Events most nights; sometimes closed Sun or Mon.

Microcosmos ミックロコスモス 2-23-12 Dōgenzaka, Shibuya-ku ☎03 5784 5496, ⓦmicrocosmos-tokyo .com; Shibuya Station; map p.122. A good example of the new breed of Tokyo club, this chic dance space has a relaxed vibe, and tends to draw a sophisticated crowd. Music ranges across the spectrum from reggae and hip-hop to electro and techno. Usually ¥2500 with a drink. Events Fri & Sat.

★**Womb** ウーム 2-16 Maruyama-chō, Shibuya-ku ☎03 5459 0039, ⓦwomb.co.jp; Shibuya Station; map p.122. Mega-club with a spacious dancefloor, enormous glitter ball (reputedly the largest in Asia) and a pleasant chill-out space. Top DJs work the decks, but be warned that at big events it can get ridiculously crowded. Usually ¥3000 with a drink; discount before midnight. Events most nights.

SHINJUKU AND THE WEST

Garam ガラム 7F Dai-Roku Polestar Bldg, 1-16-6 Kabukichō, Shinjuku-ku ☎03 3205 8668; Shinjuku Station; map p.124. This tiny, Jamaican-style dancehall is very friendly, and the place to head if you're into reggae. The cover charge is unusually reasonable, and includes one drink. Entry ¥1000–1500. Daily 9pm–6am.

LGBT BARS

With over 150 bars and clubs, Shinjuku-Nichōme is the most densely packed area of gay and lesbian venues in Japan, but clubbing events are held around the city. Check websites for regular monthly standbys such as Shangri-la at *Ageha* (see opposite), Goldfinger (ⓦgoldfingerparty .com) and Diamond Cutter (ⓦdiamondcutter.jp), all of which will have a cover charge of around ¥3000. The "Basics" section of this book has more general advice on Tokyo's gay and lesbian scene (see p.72).

SHINJUKU AND THE WEST

Aiiro Café アイイロカフェ Tenka Building 7, 2-18-1 Shinjuku, Shinjuku-ku ☎03 3358 3988, ⓦaliving.net; Shinjuku-sanchōme Station; map p.124. Many a night in Nichōme starts with a drink at this place, and quite a few finish here too. The bar itself is tiny, which is why scores of

patrons hang out on the street corner outside, creating a block party atmosphere at weekends. Mon–Sat 6pm–4am, Sun 6pm–1am.

★**Arty Farty** アーティファーティ 2F Dai 33 Kyutei Building, 2-11-7 Shinjuku, Shinjuku-ku ☎03 5362 9720, ⓦarty-farty.net; Shinjuku-sanchōme Station; map p.124. As the night draws on, this pumping bar with a small dancefloor gets packed with an up-for-fun crowd. Their annexe bar, within staggering distance, hits its stride later in the evening and draws a younger clientele. Daily 6pm–1am.

A-Un 阿吽 3F 2-14-16 Shinjuku, Shinjuku-ku ☎070 6612 9014; Shinjuku-sanchōme Station; map p.124. A quirky bar in many ways: it's lesbian-friendly but doesn't mind fellas coming in; the sound system is unusually good; and you can bring your own booze for ¥500. Entry is usually ¥1000 including a free drink. The bar's name represents the first and last letters of the Sanskrit alphabet. Daily 6pm–2am, Fri & Sat until 4am.

Campy! キャンピー 2-13-10 Shinjuku, Shinjuku-ku ☎03 6273 2154; Shinjuku-sanchōme Station; map p.124. This highly colourful venue is perhaps the tiniest of the area's many minuscule gay bars, but what it lacks in size it makes up for in pizzazz – the drag queen staff sure help. One of the better local venues for straight folk. Daily 6pm–2am (Fri & Sat until 4am).

Goldfinger ゴールドフィンガー 2-12-11 Shinjuku, Shinjuku-ku ☎03 6383 4649; Shinjuku-sanchōme Station; map p.124. This fun, female-only bar is famed for the regular wild parties it runs (ⓦgoldfingerparty.com), and though these are actually held elsewhere, the bar itself is a fun drinking hole, styled something like an old motel and presided over by glamourpuss DJs. Daily 6pm–2am, Fri & Sat until 4am.

★**Paddy's Junction** パッディーズジャンクション 2-13-16, Shinjuku, Shinjuku-ku ☎03 3355 7833, ⓦpaddys-junction.com; Shinjuku-sanchōme Station; map p.124. With its foreign and English-speaking staff, this Irish-style pub offers the area something a wee bit different. There's cheap food (including excellent fish and chips), lots of imported beers, and cocktails are just ¥300 during the 5–7pm happy hour – a great starting or meet-up point for a night on the tiles. Daily 5pm–1am.

LIVE MUSIC

Pop and rock acts usually play in "live houses", many of which are little more than a pub with a small stage, although some clubs such as *SuperDeluxe* (see opposite) and *Unit* (see opposite) also have live music events. Jazz and blues are also incredibly popular in Tokyo, with scores of clubs across the city. There are several larger venues where top local and international acts do their thing, most notably the cavernous Tokyo

1

GAY FESTIVALS

Out-and-proud gay life in Tokyo is still somewhat coming out of its shell, and until recently there were no concrete annual events. However, there are now at least a couple of established fixtures on the calendar.

Rainbow Reel Late July ⓦ rainbowreeltokyo.com. This annual film festival is now a permanent fixture of Tokyo's gay calendar, showing films from around the world with English subtitles. A dance party typically rounds things off.

Tokyo Pride Parade Two days in May ⓦ tokyorainbowpride.com. The city's Pride Parade failed, for years, to establish itself as a regular "thing". Now it seems to be here to stay, acting as the hub of a full-on Rainbow Week. However, the dates have been in flux – check the website for details.

Dome (see p.165) and the Budōkan (see p.166). Tickets for concerts can be bought through ticket agencies (see p.167).

ROCK AND POP

Billboard Live Tokyo ビルボードライブ東京 4F Tokyo Midtown 9-7-4 Akasaka, Minato-ku ☎03 3405 1133, ⓦ billboard-live.com; Roppongi Station; map pp.110–111. A relatively intimate space at which everyone on the three levels gets a great view of the stage. Acts tend to appeal to an older crowd, with everything from jazz to bossa nova (Sergio Mendes has performed here a few times), and from R&B to funk. Tickets usually from ¥5800, but can be much higher for the big names. Events most nights.

Club Quattro クラブクアットロ 5F Quattro Building, 32-13 Udagawa-chō, Shibuya-ku ☎03 3477 8750, ⓦ club-quattro.com; Shibuya Station; map p.122. Intimate rock music venue which tends to showcase up-and-coming bands and artists, though it also plays host to well-known local and international acts. Tickets ¥2000–4500. Events most nights.

Liquid Room リキッドルーム 3-16-6 Higashi, Shibuya-ku ☎03 5464 0800, ⓦ liquidroom.net; Ebisu Station; map pp.114–115. Live-music venue hosting some pretty prominent bands; they also throw DJ events from time to time in their *Liquid Loft* space. Tickets ¥2800–5800. Events most nights.

Tsutaya O-East 2-14-8 Dōgenzaka, Shibuya-ku ☎03 5458 4681, ⓦ shibuya-o.com; Shibuya Station; map p.122. This complex has several venues, all hosting live-music events, ranging from J-pop to hard rock. International bands also play here. Tickets from ¥2500. Events most nights.

★**WWW** B1F Rise Bldg, 13-17 Udagawachō, Shibuya-ku ☎03 5458 7685, ⓦ www-shibuya.jp; Shibuya Station; map p.122. Former cinema hall which now works well as a place to stand and tap your feet. Acts are a mixed bag of genres, from shoegaze

to electronica, but they're all pretty high quality; all-night events sometimes take place in the upper level, and they sell out fast. Tickets from ¥2500. Events most nights.

JAZZ AND BLUES

Blue Note ブルーノート 6-3-16 Minami-Aoyama, Minato-ku ☎03 5485 0088, ⓦ bluenote.co.jp; Omotesandō Station; map p.118. Tokyo's premier jazz venue, part of the international chain, attracts world-class performers. Entry for shows is ¥6000–10,000 (including one drink) depending on the acts, though prices hit the stratosphere for the global stars. Events most evenings.

Cotton Club コットンクラブ 2F Tokia Building, 2-7-3 Marunouchi ☎03 3215 1555, ⓦ cottonclubjapan .co.jp; Tokyo Station; map p.86. Ritzy jazz club with top-class performers, from the same stable as the *Blue Note* (see above). It's run as a supper club with two shows a night; ticket prices vary (¥5000–12,000), depending on where you sit and who's on. Two shows per evening.

Shinjuku Pit Inn 新宿ピットイン B1F Accord Shinjuku Building, 2-12-4 Shinjuku, Shinjuku-ku ☎03 3354 2024, ⓦ pit-inn.com; Shinjuku Station; map p.124. Serious, long-standing jazz club which has been the launch platform for many top Japanese performers. Tickets ¥3000. Shows most evenings from 7.30pm.

TRADITIONAL JAPANESE MUSIC

★**Oiwake** 追分 3-28-11 Nishi-Asakusa, Taitō-ku ☎03 3844 6283, ⓦ oiwake.info; Iriya Station; map p.100. A fantastic *izakaya*, especially if you're into traditional Japanese music: three times a night, a clutch of musicians appear armed with *shamisen* (Japanese lutes), *shakuhachi* (flute) and the like, and pour their wonderful tunes out while visitors down their sake. Music charge ¥2000, plus one food-and-drink order per customer. Tues–Sat Mon 6pm–midnight.

ENTERTAINMENT AND THE ARTS

Tokyo has all the entertainment options you'd expect of a major city, plus a couple of local ones. Here you can sample all of Japan's major performing arts, from **theatre** to **contemporary dance** (see p.844). Grab any chance you have to see a concert of **traditional Japanese music** (see p.845). **Information** about performances is available in the English-language press and from the tourist information centres; **tickets** can be bought from the venue or through a ticket agency (see p.167).

TRADITIONAL THEATRE

The easiest of Japan's traditional performance arts for foreigners to enjoy are kabuki and the puppet theatre of *bunraku*, which predates kabuki but whose plays share many of the same storylines. If you don't want to sit through a full performance, which can last up to four hours, note that single-act tickets are often available. With its highly stylized, painfully slow movements and archaic language, nô, the country's oldest form of theatre, isn't as appealing, though some find the rarefied style incredibly powerful. Take advantage of hiring recorded commentaries in English at the theatre to gain a better understanding of what's happening on stage. Subtitles displayed on a screen beside the performers (or, at the National Theatre, on the back of each seat) are also sometimes used.

Cerulean Tower Nô Theatre セルリアンタワー能楽堂 26-1 Sakuragaoka-chô, Shibuya-ku ☎03 3477 6412, ⓦwww.ceruleantower-noh.com; Shibuya Station; map p.122. In the basement of the luxury *Cerulean Tower* hotel (see p.139), this theatre provides an elegant setting for both professional and amateur nô and *kyôgen* performances (tickets typically ¥3500 and up).

★**Kabukiza** 歌舞伎座 6-18-2 Ginza, Chûô-ku ☎03 3541 2600, ⓦkabuki-bito.jp; Higashi-Ginza Station; map p.91. Tokyo's oldest and largest kabuki theatre, this is the best place to head if you're at all interested in catching a performance. Getting a ticket (¥4000–22,000), on the other hand, can be tricky; they usually become easier to buy after the fifteenth of each month. Single-act tickets

(¥800–2000) are available on the door for those who don't want to commit to a whole performance.

National Nô Theatre 国立能楽堂 4-18-1 Sendagaya, Shibuya-ku ☎03 3230 3000, ⓦwww.ntj.jac.go.jp; Sendagaya Station; map p.118. Hosts nô performances several times a month, with tickets starting at around ¥2700. Printed English explanations of the plot help make some sense of what's going on.

National Theatre 国立劇場 4-1 Hayabusachô, Chiyoda-ku ☎03 3230 3000, ⓦwww.ntj.jac.go.jp; Hanzômon Station; map p.86. In its two auditoria, Tokyo's National Theatre puts on a varied programme of traditional theatre and music, including kabuki, *bunraku*, court music and dance. English-language earphones and programmes are available. Tickets start at around ¥1500 for kabuki and ¥4500 for *bunraku*.

Shimbashi Embujô 新橋演舞場 6-18-2 Ginza, Chûô-ku ☎03 3541 2600, ⓦshinbashi-enbujo.co.jp; Higashi-Ginza Station; map p.91. This large theatre stages a range of traditional dance, music and theatre, including the "Super-kabuki" (kabuki with all the bells and whistles of modern musical theatre). Single-act tickets for regular kabuki performances range from ¥800 to ¥1500 depending on the length of the act.

CONTEMPORARY AND INTERNATIONAL THEATRE

Camp as a row of tents, the most unique theatrical experience you can have in Tokyo is Takarazuka (see box, p.158), the all-singing, all-dancing, all-female revue which

DINING WITH ROBOTS

Opened in 2012, the **Robot Restaurant** (ロボットレストラン; 1-7-1 Kabukichô, Shinjuku-ku ☎03 3200 5500, ⓦshinjuku-robot.com; Shinjuku Station) is perhaps Tokyo's zaniest attraction, and provides a little trip back to the wild days before Japan's financial bubble burst. It all starts at the entrance foyer, where there's nary an inch of regular, boring space – everything glistens, shines, flashes or reflects. There's far more of the same heading down the stairs to the trippy, video-screen-lined hall where you'll be seated with other excited tourists and locals. Though the website, and plenty of YouTube clips, will give you a great idea of what to expect, the performances are far more fun if you have no idea what's coming – for now, it should suffice to say that dozens of robots, scantily dressed girls, more LEDs than anyone could ever count, and a wall of roaring music are on the cards. Most visitors enjoy it, but a fair few leave grumbling about the price – a recent hike raised tickets to ¥8000 per head (plus ¥1000 for a light bentô meal). Performances run daily at 5.55pm, 7.50pm & 9.45pm, and sometimes also 4pm.

1

appears occasionally at the Takarazuka Theatre (see below). If your Japanese is up to it, there are plenty of modern Japanese dramas to enjoy: look out for productions by chelfitsch (see below), or anything by the director Ninogawa Yukio who's famous for his reinterpretations of Shakespeare. Overseas theatre companies often appear at the Tokyo Globe or Shinjuku's New National Theatre, though seats sell out months in advance for the bigger names.

Black Stripe Theater B1 Sangubashi Guesthouse, 4-50-8 Yoyogi, Shibuya-ku ☏080 4184 0848, ⓦblackstripetheater.com; Sangubashi Station; map p.118. A relatively recent addition to the expat theatre scene, this company has staged plays by Harold Pinter and David Mamet. Tickets ¥4000.

chelfitsch ⓦchelfitsch.net. Founded by award-winning writer Okada Toshiki, this internationally acclaimed group put on excellent shows in Tokyo when they're not busy touring the globe (which is most of the time). They can usually be relied on for one new performance each year, although the venues and prices vary.

★**The Globe Tokyo** 東京グローブ座 3-1-2 Hyakunin-chō, Shinjuku-ku ☏03 3366 4020, ⓦwww.tglobe.net; Shin-Ōkubo Station; map pp.128–129. A variety of works, including Shakespearean plays and Western-style operas, are performed in this modern-day replica of the famous Elizabethan stage in London. Tickets from ¥4500.

New National Theatre 新国立劇場 1-20 Honmachi, Shinjuku-ku ☏03 5352 9999, ⓦnntt.jac.go.jp; Hatsudai Station; map p.124. Just behind Tokyo Opera City, the New National Theatre comprises three stages specially designed for Western performing arts, including opera, ballet, dance and drama. Discount tickets (under ¥2000) for restricted-view seats are sold from 10am on the day; you'll otherwise pay at least double that.

★**PUK** 2-12-3 Yoyogi, Shibuya-ku ☏03 3370 5128, ⓦpuppettheatrepuk.wordpress.com; Shinjuku Station; map p.124. This charming puppet theatre was founded in 1929 as La Pupa Klubo, and survived a government witch-hunt during the war. It's home to a resident group of puppeteers, as well as visiting troupes, and puts on shows that both young and old can enjoy.

★**Takarazuka Theatre** 宝塚劇場 1-1-3 Yūrakuchō, Chūō-ku ☏03 5251 2001, ⓦkageki.hankyu.co.jp; Hibiya Station; map p.86. Mostly stages musicals, punched out by a huge cast in fabulous costumes. The theatre, immediately north of the *Imperial Hotel* (see p.150), also stages regular Takarazuka performances (see box, p.158). Tickets start at ¥3500; performances run most days except Wed at either 11am or 1pm, and at 3pm.

Theatre Cocoon シアターコクーン 2-24-1 Dōgenzaka, Shibuya-ku ☏03 3477 9999, ⓦwww.bunkamura.co.jp; Shibuya Station; map p.122. Part of Shibuya's

Bunkamura arts centre, this modern theatre hosts some of Tokyo's more accessible fringe productions.

Za Kōenji 座高円寺 2-1-2 Kōenji-Kita, Suginami-ku ☏03 3223 7300, ⓦza-koenji.jp; Kōenji Station. Managed by the non-profit Creative Theater Network, and set in a suitably dramatic building designed by leading architect Itō Toyō, this venue (around 5km west of Shinjuku) presents a high-quality programme of drama, dance and music performances.

BUTŌ

The highly expressive avant-garde dance form of butō (or butoh), which originates from Japan, shouldn't be missed if you're interested in modern dance. It can be minimalist, introspective, and often violent or sexually explicit.

Dairakudakan Kochūten 大駱駝艦壺中天 B1 2-1-18 Kichijōji-Kitamachi, Musashinoshi ☏0422 214982, ⓦdairakudakan.com; Kichijōji Station. The studio of legendary butō troupe Dairakudakan; sometimes there are joint productions here with visiting foreign dancers. It's a little way out west – 16min by JR train from Shinjuku.

CLASSICAL MUSIC & OPERA

The city is well stocked with Western classical music venues, and there are usually one or two concerts every week, either by one of Tokyo's several resident symphony orchestras or by a visiting group, as well as occasional performances of opera. Concerts of traditional Japanese music, played on instruments such as the *shakuhachi* (flute), the *shamisen* (a kind of lute that is laid on the ground) and the *taiko* (drum), are much rarer.

NHK Hall NHKホール 2-2-1 Jinnan, Shibuya-ku ☏03 3465 1751, ⓦwww.nhk-sc.or.jp/nhk_hall; Harajuku or Shibuya stations; map p.122. One of Tokyo's older auditoria for classical concerts, but still well thought of and home to the highly rated NHK Symphony Orchestra. It's next to the NHK Broadcasting Centre, south of Yoyogi-kōen. Tickets cost from ¥2000 to ¥10,000, depending upon the performance.

Orchard Hall オーチャドホール 2-24-1 Dōgenzaka, Shibuya-ku ☏03 3477 9111, ⓦwww.bunkamura.co.jp; Shibuya Station; map p.122. Part of the Bunkamura arts centre, this large concert hall hosts a wide range of classical music performances throughout the year, and has very good acoustics.

★**Suntory Hall** Ark Hills サントリーホール 1-13-1 Akasaka, Minato-ku ☏03 3505 1001, ⓦwww.suntory.co.jp/suntoryhall; Roppongi-Itchōme Station; map pp.110–111. Reputed to have the best acoustics in the city, this elegant concert hall has one of the world's largest pipe organs, which is sometimes used for free lunchtime recitals; check the website for details of this and other events. Prices vary by performance.

Tokyo Bunka Kaikan 東京文化会館 5-45 Ueno, Taitō-ku ☏ 03 3828 2111, ⓦ t-bunka.jp; Ueno Station; map p.97. Tokyo's largest classical music venue, with an extravagantly designed main hall that seats over 2300. It has a busy and varied schedule of performances and a marvellous interior dating back to the 1960s, while ticket prices tend to be cheap.

Tokyo International Forum 東京国際フォーラム 3-5-1 Marunouchi, Chiyoda-ku ☏ 03 5221 9000, ⓦ www.t-i-forum.co.jp; Yūrakuchō Station; map p.91.

The Forum's four multipurpose halls (including one of the world's largest auditoria, with over five thousand seats) host an eclectic mix of performing arts, including classical music and opera.

Tokyo Opera City 東京オペラシティ 3-20-2 Nishi-Shinjuku, Shinjuku-ku ☏ 03 5353 9999, ⓦ operacity.jp; Hatsudai Station; map p.124. This stunningly designed concert hall, with a giant pipe organ, seats over 1600 and has excellent acoustics – though despite its name it hosts only music concerts, not full-blown opera. There's a more intimate recital hall too.

MAJOR TOKYO FESTIVALS

Whenever you visit Tokyo, the chances are there'll be a **festival** (*matsuri*) taking place somewhere in the city. The tourist information centres can provide comprehensive lists of events in and around Tokyo, or check in the English press for what's on. Below is a review of the city's biggest festivals. Note that dates may change, so be sure to double-check before setting out.

January 1: Ganjitsu (or Gantan) The first shrine visit of the year (*hatsu-mōde*) draws the crowds to Meiji-jingū, Hie-jinja, Kanda Myōjin and other city shrines. Performances of traditional dance and music take place at Yasukuni-jinja. National holiday.

January 6: Dezomeshiki At Tokyo Big Sight in Odaiba, firemen in Edo-period costume pull off dazzling stunts atop long bamboo ladders.

Second Monday in January: Momoteshiki Archery contest and other ancient rituals at Meiji-jingū to celebrate "Coming-of-Age Day". It's a good time to spot colourful kimono, here and at other shrines.

February 3 or 4: Setsubun The last day of winter is celebrated with a bean-scattering ceremony to drive away evil. The liveliest festivities take place at Sensō-ji, Kanda Myōjin, Zōjō-ji and Hie-jinja.

March: AnimeJapan Taking place at Tokyo Big Sight, this is one of the world's largest animation events; as well as screenings and presentations, there's a fun area for cosplay enthusiasts.

Early April: Hanami Cherry-blossom-viewing parties get into their stride. The best displays are at Chidoriga-fuchi Park and nearby Yasukuni-jinja, Aoyama Cemetery, Ueno-kōen and Sumida-kōen.

Mid-May: Kanda Matsuri One of Tokyo's top three festivals, taking place in odd-numbered years at Kanda Myōjin, during which people in Heian-period costume escort eighty gilded *mikoshi* (portable shrines) through the streets.

Third weekend in May: Sanja Matsuri Tokyo's most rumbustious annual bash, when over one hundred *mikoshi* are jostled through the streets of Asakusa, accompanied by lion dancers, geisha and musicians.

Mid-June: Sannō Matsuri The last of the big three festivals (after Kanda and Sanja), this takes place in even-numbered years, focusing on colourful processions of *mikoshi* through Akasaka.

Early July: Yasukuni Matsuri The four-night summer festival at Tokyo's most controversial shrine is well worth attending for its jovial parades, Obon dances and festoons of lanterns.

Late July and August: Hanabi Taikai The summer skies explode with thousands of fireworks, harking back to traditional "river opening" ceremonies. The Sumida-gawa display is the most spectacular (view it from riverboats or Asakusa's Sumida-kōen on the last Sat in July), but those in Edogawa, Tamagawa, Arakawa and Harumi come close.

Mid-August: Fukagawa Matsuri Every three years Tomioka Hachiman-gū, a shrine in Fukagawa, east across the Sumida-gawa from central Tokyo, hosts the city's wettest festival, when spectators throw buckets of water over a hundred *mikoshi* being carried through the streets.

November 15: Shichi-go-san Children aged 3, 5 and 7 don traditional garb to visit the shrines, particularly Meiji-jingū, Hie-jinja and Yasukuni-jinja.

Late November: Tokyo International Film Festival One of the world's top competitive film festivals (ⓦ tiff-jp.net), with a focus on Japanese and Asian releases. The main venues for the week-long event are the cinemas in Roppongi Hills and Shibuya's Bunkamura (map p.122), though screenings take place at halls and cinemas throughout the city.

December 17–19: Hagoita-ichi The build-up to New Year begins with a battledore fair outside Asakusa's Sensō-ji temple.

1

CINEMA

On "First Day" (in other words the first day of the month, though some chains have their own monthly "Cinema Day" on different dates), tickets cost ¥1100, as opposed to the regular price of around ¥1800, or ¥2500 for a reserved seat (*shitei-seki*). Women can also get discounted tickets (¥1000) on Ladies' Day, usually Wednesday. Otherwise, you can buy slightly reduced tickets in advance from a ticket agency (see p.167). Listings are published on Friday in *The Japan Times*, and can also be found on online sources such as *Metropolis* (ⓦ metropolisjapan.com) and *Time Out* (ⓦ timeout.com/tokyo).

★**Cinema Vera** シネマヴェーラ 4F Kinohaus, 1-5 Maruyama-chō, Shibuya-ku ☎03 3461 7703, ⓦ cinemavera.com; Shibuya Station; map p.122. The vast majority of films here are Japanese-language only; however, they're mainly black-and-white or Technicolor classics dating from the 1950s to the 1970s, and the location in the heart of Shibuya's raucous love-motel district makes this a good date spot.

National Film Centre 東京国立近代美術館フィルムセンター 3-7-6 Kyōbashi, Chūō-ku ☎03 3272 8600, ⓦ www.momat.go.jp; Kyōbashi Station; map p.91. A treasure trove for cinephiles, with a small gallery on the seventh floor for film-related exhibitions and two small cinemas screening retrospectives from their vast movie archive. Most are Japanese classics, though they occasionally dust off their collection of foreign films.

Toho Cinemas Roppongi Hills TOHOシネマズ六本木ヒレズ Roppongi Hills, Roppongi, Minato-ku ☎03 5775 6090; Roppongi Station; map pp.110–111. Ultra-modern multiplex cinema with bookable seats, late-night screenings and popular Japanese films with English subtitles.

Uplink アップリンク 37-18 Udagawachō, Shibuya-ku ☎03 6825 5502, ⓦ uplink.co.jp; Shibuya Station; map p.122. World cinema is a staple at this arts centre, which combines a couple of cinemas with a gallery, live music, bar and various workshops.

Yebisu Garden Cinema 恵比寿ガーデンシネマ Yebisu Garden Place, 4-20 Ebisu, Shibuya-ku ☎03 5420 6161; Ebisu Station; map pp.114–115. There are two screens at this modern cinema, with numbered seating, showing an interesting range of non-mainstream US and British releases.

SHOPPING

Cruising the boutiques and fashion malls while toting a couple of designer-label carrier bags is such a part of Tokyo life that it's hard not to get caught up in the general enthusiasm. There are shops to suit every taste and budget, from funky **fashion boutiques** and swanky **department stores** to some great **crafts shops** and wonderfully quirky **souvenir** and **novelty stores**. Antique and bargain hunters shouldn't miss out on a visit to one of the city's **flea markets**, which if nothing else can turn up some unusual curios. More information can be found at ⓦ tokyo-bazaar.com.

ANIME AND MANGA

Manga (see p.842) are available just about everywhere, from train station kiosks to bookshops – at the latter and in CD shops (see p.162) you'll also find anime DVDs. Akihabara is the key shopping area for anime, manga and associated character goods, though with some time on your hands you could also give Ikebukuro or Nakano a try. Apart from the places listed below, devoted fans should schedule time at the shops in the Ghibli Museum (see p.126).

Comic Tora-no-ana コミックとらのあな 4-3-1 Soto-Kanda, Chiyoda-ku ☎03 3526 5330; Akihabara Station; map p.94. Seven floors of manga and related products, including self-published works and secondhand comics on the top floor. There are several other branches across the city. Daily 10am–10pm.

Mandarake まんだらけ 31-2 Udagawachō, Shibuya-ku ☎03 3477 0777, ⓦ mandarake.co.jp; Shibuya Station; map p.94. If you're into character dolls and plastic figures based on anime and manga, this subterranean operation is the place to head. They also have a wide range of secondhand manga as well as posters, cards and even costumes. There's another branch in Akihabara (see map, p.122). Daily noon–8pm.

ANTIQUE AND FLEA MARKETS

There's at least one flea market in Tokyo every weekend, though you'll need to arrive early for any bargains.

Hanazono-jinja 花園神社 5-17-3 Shinjuku, Shinjuku-ku; Shinjuku-sanchōme Station; map p.124. You're more likely to find junk than real antiques at this market, but its setting in the grounds of a shrine, on the east side of Shinjuku (see p.125), is highly attractive. Most Sun 6am–3pm.

★**Ōedo Antique Market** 大江戸骨董市 Tokyo International Forum, 3-5-1 Marunouchi, Chiyoda-ku ⓦ antique-market.jp; Yūrakuchō Station; map p.86. One of the largest regular flea markets in Tokyo, with some 250 vendors offering real antiques and interesting curios. Don't expect any bargains, though. Usually first and third Sun of month 9am–4pm.

Yasukuni-jinja 靖国神社 3-1-1 Kudankita, Chiyoda-ku; Kudanshita or Ichigaya stations; map p.86. One of the few temple flea markets which actually takes place every week; the goods on offer here aren't always particularly impressive, but the dramatic setting (see p.88) makes it a great visit anyway. Sun dawn–dusk.

ARTS AND CRAFTS

Tokyo has a wealth of specialist arts and crafts shops, with the largest concentration in and around Asakusa. All the following outlets are good places to hunt for souvenirs, including paper products, satin-smooth lacquerware and sumptuous textiles. Also check out the splendid gift shop at the Japan Folk Crafts Museum (see p.122) for folk craft items, and the ones in the basement of the National Art Center (see p.109) for great contemporary gifts.

GINZA AND AROUND

★**Ginza Natsuno** 銀座夏野 6-7-4 Ginza, Chūō-ku ☎ 03 3569 0952, ⓦ www.e-ohashi.com; Ginza Station; map p.91. Stuffed to the rafters with an incredible collection of over 1000 types of chopstick, plus chopstick rests and rice bowls. Prices range from ¥200 up. Several other branches around the city. Mon–Sat 10am–8pm, Sun 10am–7pm.

Itō-ya 伊東屋 2-7-15 Ginza, Chūō-ku ☎ 03 3561 8311, ⓦ ito-ya.co.jp; Shibuya Station; map p.91. This fabulous stationery store, comprising 11 floors and two annexes (Itō-ya 2 & 3), is a treasure trove full of packable souvenirs such as traditional *washi* paper, calligraphy brushes, inks and so on. There are several other branches around the city, including one in Ginza Station. Mon–Sat 10.30am–8pm, Sun 10.30am–7pm.

★**Kyūkyodō** 鳩居堂 5-7-4 Ginza, Chūō-ku ☎ 03 3571 4429; Ginza Station; map p.91. Filled with the dusty smell of *sumi-e* ink, this venerable shop has been selling traditional paper, calligraphy brushes and inkstones since 1800. During Edo times, they provided incense to the emperor, but the shop's history actually goes back even further – it was first founded in Kyoto in 1663 and, amazingly, the same family still runs it. Daily 10am–7pm.

AKIHABARA AND AROUND

★**Origami Kaikan** おりがみ会館 1-7-14 Yushima, Bunkyō-ku ☎ 03 3811 4025, ⓦ origamikaikan.co.jp; Ochanomizu Station; map p.94. This outpost for the production and dyeing of *washi* (Japanese paper) was founded in 1858, and to this day they continue to sell it on the premises – there's also an exhibition hall on the second floor. It's possible to take lessons (some free) in the art of paper folding here. Mon–Sat 9.30am–6pm.

UENO AND AROUND

★**Jūsan-ya** 十三や 2-12-21 Ueno, Taitō-ku ☎ 03 3831 3238; Ueno-Hirokōji Station; map p.94. Tiny shop across the road from Shinobazu Pond, where a craftsman sits making beautiful boxwood combs – just as successive generations have done since 1736. A truly beautiful place to visit, even if you're not buying. Mon–Sat 10am–6.30pm.

ASAKUSA AND AROUND

Bengara べんがら 1-35-6 Asakusa, Taitō-ku ☎ 03 3841 6613; Asakusa Station; map p.100. This tiny store is crammed with a wide variety of *noren*, the split curtain seen hanging outside every traditional shop or restaurant. Even if you don't own a shop or restaurant, there'll be somewhere suitable in your own home for one of these – the toilet door is a (surprisingly) popular choice. Daily 10am–6pm; closed third Sun of month.

Fujiya ふじ屋 2-2-15 Asakusa, Taitō-ku ☎ 03 3841 2283; Asakusa Station; map p.100. Hand-printed cotton towels (*tenugui*) designed by the Kawakami family; some end up becoming collectors' items, so choose carefully. 10am–6pm; closed Thurs.

Kanesō かね惣 1-18-12 Asakusa, Taitō-ku ☎ 03 3844 1379; Asakusa Station; map p.100. A mind-boggling array of knives, scissors, shears and files, crafted by the Hirano family over five generations. Daily 11am–7pm.

Yonoya Kushiho よのや櫛舗 1-37-10 Asakusa, Taitō-ku ☎ 03 3844 1755; Asakusa Station; map p.100. Tokyo's finest hand-crafted boxwood combs and hair decorations; much of the wood used here is sourced from forest land south of Kagoshima, and it's reputed to be particularly suitable for hair. 10.30am–6pm; closed Wed.

AKASAKA AND ROPPONGI

Art & Design Store 3F Roppongi Hills Mori Tower, 6-10-1 Roppongi, Minato-ku ☎ 03 6406 6654; Roppongi Station; map pp.110–111. A wonderful store near the entrance to Roppongi Hills' City View. The selection is ever-changing, but often features products from some of Japan's most famous contemporary designers; look out for the polka-dot-splashed produce of Yayoi Kusama. There's also a small gallery space here. Daily 11am–9pm.

★**Blue & White** ブルーアンドホワイト 2-9-2 Azabu-Jūban, Minato-ku ☎ 03 3451 0537; Azabu-Jūban Station; map pp.110–111. Small store that sells exclusively blue-and-white-coloured products made in Japan; though the concept may sound contrived, the goods have been selected with care, and include *yukata*, *furoshiki* (textile wrapping cloths), quilts, pottery and traditional decorations. Mon–Sat 10am–6pm, Sun 11am–6pm.

Japan Traditional Craft Centre 伝統工芸青山スクエア 1F Akasaka Ouji Building, 8-1-22 Akasaka, Minato-ku ☎ 03 5785 1001, ⓦ kougeihin.jp; Aoyama-Itchōme Station; map pp.110–111. This centre showcases the works of craft associations across the nation – everything from finely crafted chopsticks to elegant lacquerware and metalwork. Daily 10am–7pm.

EBISU, MEGURO AND THE SOUTH

Kamawanu かまわぬ 1-19-23 Sarugaku-chō, Shibuya-ku ☎ 03 3797 4788; Daikanyama Station; map

1

pp.114–115. Small shop selling excellent *tenugui* cloths in a variety of styles which, although modern, also make use of Japanese motifs. They also have a very nice-looking range of traditional fans. Daily 11am–7pm.

Yamada Heiandō 山田平安堂 2F Hillside Terrace, 18-12 Sarugaku-chō, Shibuya-ku ☎03 3464 5541, ⓦheiando.com; Daikanyama Station; map pp.114–115. Hunt down this store for lacquerware – both traditional and contemporary – found on tables no less distinguished than those of the imperial household and Japan's embassies. Mon–Sat 10.30am–7pm, Sun 10.30am–6.30pm.

HARAJUKU, AOYAMA AND SHIBUYA

Musubi むす美 2-31-8 Jingūmae, Shibuya-ku ☎03 5414 5678; Meiji-jingūmae Station; map p.120. Pick up beautifully printed fabric *furoshiki* here to use instead of wrapping paper – they're also great gifts in themselves. Their origami design prints are particularly unusual. Note that there's no obvious sign on the shop – look for the dangling handbags on the ground level of a silver building. 11am–7pm; closed Wed.

Oriental Bazaar オリエンタルバザアー 5-9-13 Jingūmae, Shibuya-ku ☎03 3400 3933, ⓦorientalbazaar.co.jp; Meiji-jingūmae Station; map p.120. Although it may seem like a tourist trap, this very popular, one-stop souvenir emporium, selling everything from secondhand kimono to origami paper and top-class antiques, offers great deals and an almost unbeatable selection. 10am–7pm; closed Thurs.

BOOKS AND MUSIC

Most big hotels have a shop stocking English-language books on Japan, as well as imported newspapers and magazines. In an age of digital downloads, Tokyo bucks the trend by sustaining many CD and record shops. The range of music on offer is impressively eclectic, with a huge selection of foreign imports boosting an already mammoth local output of cheesy J-pop.

Aoyama Book Centre 青山本屋 6-1-20 Roppongi, Minato-ku ☎03 5485 5511, ⓦaoyamabc.jp; Roppongi Station; map pp.110–111. Innovative bookshop with a fine collection of titles related to design, architecture and photography. Also carries lots of foreign magazines. Daily 10am–10pm.

Disk Union ディスクユニオン 1-40-7 Kitazawa, Setagaya-ku ☎03 3467 3231; Shimokitazawa Station; map p.124. Of the twenty-odd *Disk Union* branches scattered around Tokyo, the Shimokitazawa one is by far the most notable – a huge venue with pretty much every major genre and sub-genre covered, and one of Tokyo's best vinyl collections. Daily 11.30am–9pm.

★**Kinokuniya** 紀伊國屋 Takashimaya Times Square, Annex Building, 5-24-2 Sendagaya, Shinjuku-ku ☎03 5361 3301; Shinjuku Station; map p.124. The sixth floor of Kinokuniya's seven-storey Shinjuku outlet offers Tokyo's widest selection of foreign-language books and magazines, including loads of Rough Guides. Daily 10am–8pm; closed one Wed each month.

★**Tsutaya** 蔦屋 17-5 Sarugaku-chō, Shibuya-ku ☎03 3770 2525, ⓦtsite.jp; Daikanyama Station; map pp.114–115. The design of this bookshop, whose exterior weaves together a lattice of white letter Ts, has scooped architects Klein Dytham a bunch of awards. Filled all day, every day with a preening young crowd, it's now the fulcrum of the whole Daikanyama area. They've a tremendous selection of English-language books, as well as a *Starbucks* (good luck finding a seat) and lounge bar. Daily 7am–2am.

CAMERAS AND ELECTRONIC GOODS

Akihabara boasts Tokyo's biggest concentration of stores selling electronic goods. Shinjuku is Tokyo's prime area for cameras and photographic equipment, though Ikebukuro also has a solid reputation for new and secondhand deals at reasonable prices. Compare prices – many shops are open to bargaining – and make sure there's the appropriate voltage switch (the Japanese power supply is 100V). It's also important to check that whatever you buy will be compatible with equipment you have at home.

BIC Camera ビックカメラ 1-11-1 Yūrakuchō, Chiyoda-ku ☎03 5221 1111; Yūrakuchō Station; map p.86. The main branch of BIC offers hard-to-beat prices for cameras and audio and electronic goods – practically any gizmo you want can be found here. You'll find other branches scattered around Tokyo's main shopping centres, including several in Ikebukuro, Shinjuku and Shibuya. Daily 10am–10pm.

Laox ラオクス 1-2-9 Soto-Kanda, Chiyoda-ku ☎03 3255 9041; Akihabara Station; map p.94. One of the most prominent names in Akiba and probably the best place to start browsing: they have a well-established duty-free section with English-speaking staff, and nine stores where you can buy everything from pocket calculators to plasma screen TVs. Mon–Fri 10am–8pm, Fri & Sat 10am–9pm.

DEPARTMENT STORES

Although they're not as popular as they once were, Tokyo's massive department stores are likely to have almost anything you're looking for. They're also more likely to have English-speaking staff and a duty-free service than smaller shops, though prices tend to be slightly above average. Seasonal sales can offer great bargains.

★**Isetan** 伊勢丹 3-14-1 Shinjuku, Shinjuku-ku ☎03 3352 1111, ⓦisetan.co.jp; Shinjuku-sanchōme Station; map p.124. One of the city's best department stores, with an emphasis on well-designed local goods and a reputation for promoting up-and-coming fashion designers. Their annexe, housing men's clothing and accessories, is particularly chic. The daily opening ceremony, with all staff bowing as you walk through the store, is worth attending. Daily 10am–8pm.

Mitsukoshi 三越 1-4-1 Nihombashi-Muromachi, Chūō-ku ☎03 3241 3311; Mitsukoshimae Station; map p.91. Tokyo's most prestigious and oldest department store – dating back to 1673 – is elegant, spacious and renowned for its high-quality merchandise. Designer boutiques and more contemporary fashions are concentrated in the southerly *shin-kan* ("new building"). Daily 10.30am–7.30pm.

Seibu 西武 1-28-1 Minami-Ikebukuro, Toshima-ku ☎03 3981 0111; Ikebukuro Station; map pp.128–129. Sprawling department store with a reputation for innovation, especially in its homeware store Loft, and its clothing and lifestyle offshoot Parco. There's a great chill-out area on the rooftop. Mon–Sat 10am–9pm, Sun 10am–8pm.

Tōkyū 東急 2-24-1 Dōgenzaka, Shibuya-ku ☎03 3477 3111; Shibuya Station; map p.122. Top dog in the Shibuya department store stakes, with branches all over the area, particularly around the train station. This main store specializes in designer fashions and interior goods. Daily 11am–7pm.

FASHION

The city's epicentre of clothing chic is Omotesandō, where dazzlingly designed boutiques for famed brands such as Chanel, Ralph Lauren and Louis Vuitton vie to outdo each other in extravagance, alongside top Japanese labels such as Issey Miyake and Comme des Garçons. Daikanyama, Nakameguro and Shimokitazawa are also worth browsing around – the fashion shops in the last two areas are slightly cheaper. For shoes, ubiquitous ABC-Mart stores are usually your best bet.

GINZA AND AROUND

★ **Dover Street Market** 6-9-6 Ginza, Chūō-ku ☎03 6228 5080, ⊛ginza.doverstreetmarket.com; Ginza Station; map p.91. This large new complex has started to draw young fashionistas back to Ginza from the west, and with good reason – the several floors here feature clothing from pretty much every major Japanese designer, plus a few of the Antwerp Six, without the department-store atmosphere that usually goes with such choice. Mon–Sat 11am–8pm.

Uniqlo ユニクロ 5-7-7 Ginza, Chūō-ku ☎03 3569 6781 ⊛www.uniqlo.co.jp; Ginza Station; map p.91. Inexpensive but still cool, this local brand has found mammoth success overseas. This is their flagship Tokyo store, designed by Klein Dytham, also responsible for the Tsutaya bookshop in Daikanyama (see opposite). Other branches all over the city. Daily 11am–9pm.

EBISU, MEGURO AND THE SOUTH

Evisu エヴィス 1-1-5 Kami-Meguro, Meguro-ku ☎03 3710 1999, ⊛evisu.com; Nakameguro Station; map pp.114–115. Main branch of the ultra-trendy – and ultra-pricey – Japanese jeans designer. Stock up here on shirts,

KIMONO AND YUKATA

Japan's national costume, the **kimono**, is still worn by both sexes for special occasions, such as weddings and festival visits to a shrine. Ready-made kimono can easily cost ¥100,000, while ¥1 million is not uncommon for the best made-to-measure garments. Secondhand or antique kimono, with prices as low as ¥1000, can be found at tourist shops, flea markets or in the kimono sales held by department stores, usually in spring and autumn; Oriental Bazaar (see opposite) also offers a good selection of pre-loved kimono. You'll pay more for the highly decorated wedding kimono (they make striking wall hangings), as well as for the most beautifully patterned *obi*, the broad, silk sash worn with a kimono. Light cotton **yukata** are popular with both sexes as dressing gowns; you'll find them in all department stores and many speciality stores, along with *happi* coats – the loose jackets that just cover the upper body. To complete the outfit, pick up a pair of traditional **wooden sandals** (*geta*).

Chicago シカゴ 4-26-26 Jingūmae, Shibuya-ku ☎03 5414 5107, ⊛www.chicago.co.jp; Meiji-jingūmae Station; map p.120. There's a fine selection of kimono, *obi* and so on at this Harajuku thrift store, as well as rack upon rack of good used clothes. Daily 11am–8pm.

Gallery Kawano ギャラリー 川野 102 Flats-Omotesandō, 4-4-9 Jingūmae, Shibuya-ku ☎03 3470 3305; Omotesandō Station; map p.120.

Excellent selection of vintage kimono, *yukata* and *obi*, with swatches of gorgeous kimono fabric available too. Daily 11am–6pm.

Sakura 桜 2-41-8 Asakusa, Taitō-ku ☎03 5826 5622; Asakusa Station; map p.100. Not your regular kimono shop – this tiny store sells Gothic-style clothing made with patches of old kimono fabric. Their pantaloons, which morph from skirt to trousers by way of hidden buttons, are fantastic. Daily 12.30–9.30pm.

1

T-shirts, sweatshirts and a full range of accessories. Daily noon–8pm.

★**Okura** オクラ 20-11 Sarugaku-chō, Shibuya-ku ☎03 3461 8511; Daikanyama Station; map pp.114–115. Youthful boutique specializing in indigo-dyed traditional and contemporary Japanese fashions, from jeans and T-shirts to kimono and *tabi* socks. No English sign – look for a low, wooden-style building, usually with some form of indigo fabric hanging outside. Daily 11am–8pm.

HARAJUKU, AOYAMA AND SHIBUYA

6% Dokidoki ロクパーセントドキドキ 2F 4-28-16 Jingūmae, Shibuya-ku ☎03 3479 6116, ⊚dokidoki6 .com; Meiji-jingūmae Station; map p.120. Focusing on the "Kawaii" clothing genre (see box, p.120), this second-floor store is as loud as it gets: loud clothing, loud decor, loud music. Daily noon–8pm.

★**Bapexclusive** 5-5-8 Minami-Aoyama, Minato-ku ☎03 3407 2145, ⊚bape.com; Omotesandō Station; map p.120. A Bathing Ape, the streetwear brand of designer Nigo, has a string of boutiques all over Aoyama and Harajuku, of which this is the main showroom. One of their T-shirts will set you back at least ¥6000; poking around the swanky store is, mercifully, free. Daily 11am–8pm.

Comme des Garçons 5-2-1 Minami-Aoyama, Minato-ku ☎03 3406 3951, ⊚comme-des-garcons .com; Omotesandō Station; map p.120. More like an art gallery than a clothes shop, this beautiful store is a suitable setting for the high fashion menswear and womenswear by renowned designer Rei Kawakubo. Daily 11am–8pm.

Fake Tokyo フェーク東京 18-4 Udagawa-chō, Shibuya-ku ☎03 5456 9892, ⊚www.faketokyo.com; Shibuya Station; map p.122. Hidden away on a back-street near the Loft mall, this two-level store is great for contemporary female fashion. Candy, on the ground level, caters to younger tastes, while Sister up above is a fair bit more elegant. Daily noon–2am.

★**Hysterics** 5-5-3 Minami-Aoyama, Minato-ku ☎03 6419 3899, ⊚hystericglamour.jp; Omotesandō Station; map p.120. The premier outlet for Hysteric Glamour, a fun, retro-kitsch Americana label which is one of Japan's leading youth brands. Daily noon–8pm.

Issey Miyake 三宅一生 3-18-11 Minami-Aoyama, Minato-ku ☎03 3423 1407, ⊚isseymiyake.co.jp; Omotesandō Station; map p.120. One of the top names in world fashion, famous for his elegant, eminently wearable designs. This flagship store, a pink building with Art Deco touches, is suitably fancy. Daily 11am–8pm.

★**Kura Chika Yoshida** クラチカヨシダ 5-6-8 Jingūmae, Shibuya-ku ☎03 5464 1766, ⊚www .yoshidakaban.com; Omotesandō Station; map p.120. Access the full range of bags, wallets and luggage at this

shrine to the hip Japanese brand Porter. It's just off Omotesandō, behind Tokyo Union Church. noon–8pm; closed Wed.

Onitsuka Tiger おにつかタイガー 4-24-14 Jingūmae, Shibuya-ku ☎03 3405 6671, ⊚onitsukatiger.com; Meiji-jingūmae Station; map p.120. Selling trainers as seen on the most fashionable feet, this Japanese brand started business back in 1949. Other branches across the city. Daily 11am–8pm.

★**Ragtag** ラグタグ 6-14-2 Jingūmae, Shibuya-ku ☎03 6419 3770, ⊚ragtag.jp; Meiji-jingūmae Station; map p.120. A great place selling secondhand goods from selected designers, including local uber-brands Comme des Garçons, Yohji Yamamoto and United Arrows. Daily 11am–8pm.

★**Sou Sou** そうそう 5-4-24 Minami-Aoyama, Minato-ku ☎03 3407 7877, ⊚sousou.co.jp; Omotesandō Station; map p.118. After the Japanese saying "sō sō", meaning "I agree with you", this range of modern design shoes and clothes based on traditional forms, such as split-toe *tabi* (socks), is eminently agreeable. Their plimsolls are an ideal match for jeans. There's also an outlet in Venus Fort (see p.106). Daily 11am–8pm.

Yohji Yamamoto 山本耀司 5-3-6 Minami-Aoyama, Shibuya-ku ☎03 3409 6006, ⊚yohjiyamamoto.co.jp; Omotesandō Station; map p.120. Flagship store of Japanese fashion icon Yohji Yamamoto, famed for his edgy, single-colour designs. Daily 11am–8pm.

SHINJUKU AND THE WEST

Comme ça Store 3-26-6 Shinjuku, Shinjuku-ku ☎03 5367 5551; Shinjuku Station; map p.124. Stylish, multi-level showcase for Comme Ça du Mode, a bright and affordable unisex clothing brand; also has a good café up top. Mon–Sat 11am–11pm, Sun 11am–8pm.

New York Joe ニューヨークジョー 3-26-4 Kitazawa, Setagaya-ku ☎03 5738 2077; Shimokitazawa Station; map p.124. Set in what was once a bathhouse, this is the best of the Shimokitakawa area's many vintage clothing stores, selling a wide range of first-rate secondhand goods. All items are under ¥10,000, and you can get a big discount if taking suitable goods to swap. Daily noon–8pm.

TOYS, GAMES AND NOVELTIES

The land that gave the world Super Mario Brothers, the Tamagotchi and Hello Kitty is forever throwing up new must-have toys, games and novelties. Tokyo's top toy and novelty stores are prime hunting grounds for the next big craze before it hits the world market. For more traditional playthings, poke around the craft stalls of Asakusa's Nakamise-dōri. Also keep an eye out for the ubiquitous "¥100 Shops" (everything at ¥108, including tax), which can yield a crop of bargain souvenirs.

Don Quijote ドンキホーテ 3-14-10 Roppongi, Minato-ku ☎03 5786 811, ⓦdonki.com; Roppongi Station; map pp.110–111. Fancy some sushi-print socks? A mind-boggling array of stuff is piled high and sold cheap here – everything from liquor to sex toys, as well as gadgets galore. A national institution, it's worth visiting just for the gawp factor. Several branches around the city. Daily 24hr.

Hakuhinkan Toy Park 博品館 8-8-11 Ginza, Chūō-ku ☎03 3571 8008, ⓦhakuhinkan.co.jp; Shimbashi Station; map p.91. This huge toy shop also houses a theatre, staging Japanese-language shows which might entertain little ones – or at least distract them from

spending up a storm on your behalf. Daily 11am–8pm.

Kiddyland キッディランド 6-1-9 Jingūmae, Shibuya-ku ☎03 3409 3431, ⓦwww.kiddyland.co.jp; Meiji-jingūmae Station; map p.120. Flagship store boasting six full floors of toys, stationery, sweets and other souvenirs. Daily 10am–8pm, closed every third Tues.

Village Vanguard ヴィレッジヴァンガード B1F 3-14 Kanda-Ogawamachi, Chiyoda-ku ☎03 5281 5535; Jimbōchō or Ogawamachi stations; map p.94. This "exciting bookstore" stocks an amazing hotchpotch of toys and novelties, from inflatable bananas to Batman accessories – and a few fun books and CDs. You'll find quite a few branches around the city. Daily 10am–11pm.

SPORTS AND ACTIVITIES

In 1964, Tokyo became the first Asian city to host the **Olympic Games**; in 2020, it will become the first to do so twice (see box, p.120). Together with the World Cup that Japan co-hosted in 2002, these events hint at a surprisingly sporty scene in a country that most outsiders might associate more closely with academic performance than with athletic endeavour. **Baseball** is the city's premier sporting obsession, but **football** is hot on its heels. Japan's national sport, **sumo**, also has a high profile, although its popularity has slipped in recent decades.

BASEBALL

The baseball season runs from April to October. Tokyo's big teams are the Yomiuri Giants and the Yakult Swallows. Tickets start at under ¥2000, and go on sale on the Friday two weeks prior to a game.

Jingū Baseball Stadium 神宮球場 13 Kasumigaoka, Shinjuku-ku ☎03 3404 8999, ⓦwww.jingu-stadium .com; Gaienmae Station; map p.118. One of the stadia grouped in Meiji-jingū's Outer Gardens, this is the base of the Yakult Swallows.

Tokyo Dome 東京ドーム 1-3 Koraku, Bunkyō-ku ☎03 5800 9999, ⓦwww.tokyo-dome.co.jp; Suidōbashi

Station; map pp.128–129. This huge covered arena is home to the Yomiuri Giants, and is a great place to take in a night game.

FOOTBALL

Professional J-League (ⓦjleague.jp) games are held from March to October, with a break in August. Eighteen clubs play in the top J1 division, and together with teams from lower leagues, they also participate in the Emperor's Cup; primarily a winter event, its final takes place on New Year's Day.

Ajinomoto Stadium 味の素スタジアム 376-3 Nishimachi, Chōfu ☎0424 400555; Tobitakyū Station.

PUBLIC BATHS AND ONSEN

Until a few decades ago life in Tokyo's residential neighbourhoods focused round the **sentō**, the public bath. A surprising number of *sentō* survive, many fed by natural onsen waters, and these are supplemented by larger hot-spring resorts, some of which truck curative water in from elsewhere. Wherever you head, note that it's hugely important to observe local bathing etiquette (see box, p.61).

Jakotsu-yu 蛇骨湯 1-11-11 Asakusa, Taitō-ku; Asakusa Station; map p.100. Located down a back alley just south of Rox department store, "black", mineral-rich hot-spring water is the thing here. One bath is designed to give you a mild but stimulating electric shock, and it also offers a small open-air bath (rotemburo). ¥460. 1pm–midnight; closed Tues.

Ōedo Onsen Monogatari 大江戸温泉物語 2-6-3 Aomi, Kōtō-ku; free shuttle buses from Shinagawa and Tokyo stations. More of a theme park than a bathhouse, this giant onsen goes in for nostalgic kitsch in a big way. Extra fees are charged for massages, hot

sand and stone baths and a separate footbath in which tiny fish nibble the dead skin from your feet – more pleasant than it sounds. Mon–Fri ¥2610 (¥2070 after 6pm), Sat & Sun ¥2830 (¥2290 after 6pm), ¥2160 surcharge 1am–6am. Daily 11am–9am.

Spa LaQua 6F 1-1-1 Kasuga, Bunkyō-ku; Suidōbashi or Korakuen stations; map pp.128–129. Spread over five floors, this is by far the most sophisticated of Tokyo's bathing complexes, and is fed by onsen water pumped from 1700m underground. Mon–Fri ¥2630, Sat & Sun ¥2960; ¥1940 surcharge 1am–6am. Daily 11am–9am.

1

Head west on the Keiō line to reach this stadium, home to FC Tokyo (ⓦfctokyo.co.jp) and Tokyo Verdy (ⓦwww .verdy.co.jp).

MARTIAL ARTS

From judo and karate to aikido and kendo (see p.60), Tokyo is the best place in Japan to sate any martial arts cravings you may have. The tourist information centres (see p.133) can provide a list of *dōjō* that allow visitors to watch practice sessions for free.

All-Japan Kendo Federation 全日本剣道連盟 Nippon Budōkan, 2-3 Kitanomaru-kōen, Chiyoda-ku ☎03 3211 5804; Kudanshita Station; map p.86. The Budōkan is the venue for the All-Japan Championships each autumn, and the children's kendo competition in the summer.

International Aikido Federation 全日本合気道連盟 17-18 Wakamatsuchō, Shinjuku-ku ☎03 3203 9236, ⓦaikikai.or.jp; Wakamatsu-Kawada Station; map pp.128–129. You can learn more about the sport by heading here – if you like what you see and are in Tokyo for a while, it's quite possible to participate in their classes.

Japan Karate Association 日本空手協会 2-23-15 Kōraku, Bunkyō-ku ☎03 5800 3091, ⓦjka.or.jp; Iidabashi or Kōrakuen stations; map pp.128–129. Home of the world's largest karate association teaching the Shokotan tradition. You can apply to train here, but it's best to call or email first.

Kōdokan 講道館 1-16-30 Kasuga, Bunkyō-ku ☎03 3818 4172, ⓦkodokan.org; Kasuga or Kōrakuen stations; map pp.128–129. This *dōjō* has an upper-floor spectators' gallery open to visitors free of charge, with classes held most evenings. There's also a hostel here where you can stay if you have an introduction from an authorized judo body or an approved Japanese sponsor. Classes Mon–Fri 5–8pm, Sat 5–7.30pm.

Nippon Budōkan 日本武道館 2-3 Kitanomaru-kōen, Chiyoda-ku ☎03 3216 5143, ⓦnipponbudokan.or.jp; Kudanshita Station; map p.86. Around fifty free martial-arts exhibition matches are held annually at this large, octagonal arena, an important centre for all martial arts, including judo.

SUMO

Sumo has declined substantially in popularity since the turn of the millennium, but is currently undergoing something of a renaissance, and if you're in Tokyo at tournament (*basho*) time, it's certainly worth popping along. Dates of tournaments, as well as other useful information, are posted on the Nihon Sumō Kyōkai website (ⓦsumo.or.jp).

National Sumo Stadium 国技館 1-3-28 Yokoami, Kōtō-ku ☎03 3622 1100, ⓦsumo.or.jp; Ryōgoku Station; map p.94. The National Sumo Stadium in Ryōgoku is the venue for Tokyo's three *basho* during the middle fortnights of January, May and September, with tickets going on sale a month before each tournament. They're available from ticket agencies (see opposite), but the cheapest ones (up in the gods) are only sold on the day (¥2200); come before midday and you should be fine, but tickets sometimes sell out on the first and last days of the 15-day tournament, at which times you should be there by 8am.

DIRECTORY

Banks As with the rest of Japan, the ATMs with the best chance of accepting foreign cards (see p.74) are in post offices and 7-Eleven stores.

Embassies Australia, 2-1-14 Mita, Minato-ku ☎03 5232 4111, ⓦjapan.embassy.gov.au; Canada, 7-3-38 Akasaka, Minato-ku ☎03 5412 6200, ⓦjapan.gc.ca; China, 3-4-33 Moto-Azabu, Minato-ku ☎03 3403 3064, ⓦwww.china -embassy.or.jp; Ireland, 2-10-7 Kōjimachi, Chiyoda-ku ☎03 3263 0695, ⓦirishembassy.jp; New Zealand, 20-40 Kamiyamachō, Shibuya-ku ☎03 3467 2271, ⓦnzembassy .com/japan; Russian Federation, 2-1-1 Azabudai, Minato-ku ☎03 3583 4224, ⓦrussia-emb.jp; South Africa, 4F 1-4 Kojimachi, Chiyoda-ku ☎03 3265 3366, ⓦsajapan .org; South Korea, 1-2-5 Minami-Azabu, Minato-ku ☎03 3452 7611; UK, 1 Ichibanchō, Chiyoda-ku ☎03 5211 1100, ⓦukinjapan.fco.gov.uk; USA, 1-10-5 Akasaka, Minato-ku ☎03 3224 5000, ⓦjapan.usembassy.gov.

Emergencies The Tokyo Metropolitan Police has an English-language hotline on ☎03 3501 0110 (Mon–Fri 8.30am–5.15pm). Japan Helpline (☎0570 000911, ⓦjhelp.com/en/jhlp.html) provides 24hr advice in English.

Tokyo English Life Line (☎03 5774 0992, ⓦteljp.com) provides telephone counselling (daily 9am–11pm). Numbers for the emergency services are listed in Basics (see p.71).

Hospitals and clinics To find an English-speaking doctor and the hospital or clinic best suited to your needs, phone the Tokyo Medical Information Service (Mon–Fri 9am–8pm; ☎03 5285 8181, ⓦwww.himawari.metro.tokyo.jp); they can also provide emergency medical translation services over the phone. Two major hospitals with English-speaking doctors are St Luke's International Hospital at 9-1 Akashichō, Chūō-ku (☎03 3541 5151, ⓦhospital.luke.or.jp), and Tokyo Adventist Hospital at 3-17-3 Amanuma, Suginami-ku (☎03 3392 6151); their reception desks are open Monday to Friday 8.30–11am for non-emergency cases. Among several private clinics with English-speaking staff, try Tokyo Medical and Surgical Clinic at 32 Shiba-kōen Building, 3-4-30 Shiba-kōen, Minato-ku (by appointment only Mon–Fri 8.30am–5.30pm, Sat 8.30am–noon; ☎03 3436 3028, ⓦtmsc.jp).

Immigration To renew visas, apply to the Tokyo Regional Immigration Bureau at 5-5-30 Konan, Minato-ku (Mon–Fri

9am–noon & 1–4pm; ☎03 5796 7112, ⓦwww.immi-moj.go.jp). To reach it, take the Konan exit from Shinagawa Station and then bus #99 from bus stop 8. Go early in the day since the process takes forever.

Left luggage Most hotels will keep luggage for a few days. The baggage room (daily 7.30am–8.30pm) at Tokyo Station can hold bags for the day for ¥600; the station information desks will point the way. Coin lockers can be found in many metro stations (¥300–800 depending on size), and can only be used for a maximum of three days.

Lost property If you've lost something, try the local police box (*kōban*). Alternatively, ask your hotel to help call the following offices to reclaim lost property: taxis ☎03 3648 0300; JR ☎03 3231 1880; Tokyo Metro ☎03 3834 5577; Toei bus and subway ☎03 3812 2011. If all else fails, contact the Metropolitan Police Lost and Found Office on ☎03 3501 0110.

Pharmacies The American Pharmacy in the Marunouchi Building at 2-4-1 Marunouchi, Chiyoda-ku (Mon–Fri 9am–9pm, Sat 10am–9pm, Sun 10am 8pm; ☎03 5220 7716), has English-speaking pharmacists and a good range of drugs and general medical supplies. Alternatively, try the National Azabu Pharmacy (☎03 3442 3495), above the National Azabu supermarket (nearest subway Station Hiro-o). Major hotels usually stock a limited array of common medicines.

Post offices Tokyo's Central Post Office is on the west side of Tokyo Station. Major post offices that are open daily 24 hours can be found in Shinjuku and Shibuya, among other city areas.

Ticket agencies To buy tickets for theatre performances, concerts and sporting events, use one of the major advance ticket agencies: Ticket Pia (ⓦt.pia.co.jp), branches of which can be found in all main city areas; Lawson (ⓦl-tike.com), which has thousands of convenience stores across the city; or CN Playguide (ⓦcnplayguide.com). Major events sell out quickly; don't expect to be able to buy tickets at the venue door.

Around Tokyo

YŌMEI-MON, TŌSHŌ-GŪ SHRINE

Around Tokyo

Tokyo has more than enough sights to keep you busy, but it doesn't take long to get to some great places from the capital, and it's well worth the effort. The single best reason for venturing out is Nikkō, around 130km to the north, famed for its World Heritage-listed, mountain-based shrine complex. West of Tokyo there's the scenic Fuji Five Lakes area, from where you'll be able to tackle Japan's highest and most majestic peak, or simply relax in the beautiful countryside; and Hakone, a mix of sulphur-seeping moonscapes, thrilling cable-car rides and hot springs.

The temple complex of **Naritasan Shinshō-ji**, with its lovely pagoda, extensive gardens, woods and ornamental ponds, is the highlight of the pilgrim town of **Narita**, some 60km northeast of Tokyo. Around 40km north of Tokyo, meanwhile, is **Kawagoe**, a great place to wander through nostalgic nineteenth-century streetscapes, poke around ancient temples and shrines, and indulge in some serious souvenir shopping.

Sacred **Mount Takao**, just an hour west of the capital, provides a more verdant escape for the casual walker and is the starting point for serious hikes northwest to the **Chichibu-Tama National Park**. Further west lie the inviting landscapes of the **Fuji-Hakone-Izu National Park**, particularly beautiful around **Hakone** and south through **Izu Hantō**, which warrant a couple of days' exploration. Off the coast here, **Ōshima** pokes its smouldering head out of the ocean, its laidback way of life providing a beguiling excursion for those on a more leisurely schedule.

Closer to Tokyo, **Kamakura** is one of Japan's major historical sights, home to several imposing Zen temples and the country's second-largest bronze Buddha, the magnificent **Daibutsu**. There are also hiking trails through the surrounding hills, and an enjoyable train ride further along the coast to the sacred island of **Enoshima**. Just north of Kamakura you're back into the urban sprawl where Tokyo merges with **Yokohama**, Japan's second-largest and most cosmopolitan city.

Nikkō and around

日光

"**NIKKŌ** is Nippon", goes the town's slogan. It's only half-correct, though: visitors to Japan come expecting a mix of the ancient and the modern, but this town, 128km north of the capital, is up there with the most traditional in the country. In fact, it's what a lot of people expect of Kyoto, the vaunted dynastic capital way out west, before they see the traffic jams, factories and high-rise buildings.

OWAKUDANI, HAKONE

Highlights

❶ Nikkō The dazzling shrine Tōshō-gū is the star turn of this cosy mountain town, and is surrounded by a beautiful national park and lakes. **See p.170**

❷ Chinatown, Yokohama Yokohama's Chinatown – the largest in Japan – is a blast of bright colours, pungent smells and frenetic commercial life, all focused around the lively Kantei-byō shrine. **See p.185**

❸ Kamakura Japan's ancient seaside capital offers woodland walks between peaceful temples and bustling shrines, not to mention a giant bronze Buddha with a secretive smile. **See p.188**

❹ Mount Fuji You don't need to climb Fuji to admire its snowcapped form, but reaching the summit is a rewarding, once-in-a-lifetime challenge. **See p.201**

❺ Hakone This premier onsen resort has traditional ryokan, a funicular and ropeway ride, plus a lovely lake you can sail across in a seventeenth-century-style galleon. **See p.203**

❻ Shimoda Take a ride in a replica of one of the Black Ships that finally connected an isolationist Japan to the wider world. **See p.211**

HIGHLIGHTS ARE MARKED ON THE MAP ON P.172

NIIGATA

FUKUSHIMA

NIKKŌ
NATIONAL PARK

Yudanaka
Onsen

Obuse

Minakami

Yumoto **Kegon**
Falls
Ryuzu Falls
Chuzenji-ko Chuzenji

Nikkō
Imaichi

TOCHIGI

GUNMA

Asama-yama
(2568m)

NAGANO SHINKANSEN

Maebashi

Karuizawa

Takasaki

Utsunomiya

Mashiko

Mito

Oyama
Shimodate

TŌHOKU SHINKANSEN

KASHIMA
NADA
SEA

NAGANO

Chichibu

SAITAMA

CHICHIBU-TAMA
NATIONAL PARK

Kawagoe

Ōmiya

IBARAKI

Kasumiga-ura
Lake

YAMANASHI

Kōfu

Mitake

TŌKYŌ-TO

Mt Takao

Ghibli
Museum

Mitaka

Narita

Narita
Airport

Kawaguchi-
ko

Ōtsuki

Shōji-ko

Fuji-Yoshida

Sai-ko

Motosu-ko

Yamanaka-ko

4 *Mt Fuji*

Gotemba

HAKONE

TOMEI EXPRESSWAY

KANAGAWA

Kawasaki

TŌKYŌ

Disneyland

Haneda
Airport

2
Yokohama

Ichihara

Tōkyō-
wan

Kamakura

Enoshima

3 Yokosuka

Kisarazu

CHIBA

Ōhara

FUJI-HAKONE-IZU
NATIONAL PARK

Fuji

5
Odawara

Hakone-
Yumoto

Ashino-ko

Mishima

Sagami-
wan

Miura

Katsuura

Numazu

Atami

Shūzen-ji

Shizuoka

Itō

SHIZUOKA

Suruga-wan

Izu-hantō

6 Shimoda

Irō-zaki

Okata

Ōshima

Motomachi

Habu

Kamogawa

Tateyama

Bōsō-hantō

Kujūkuri-hama Coast

PACIFIC OCEAN

N

To-shima

Nii-jima

Shikine-jima

Izu Shotō Islands

Kōzu-shima

Miyake-jima

Mikura-jima

0   50
kilometres

ROUND TOKYO

HIGHLIGHTS

1 Nikkō
2 Chinatown, Yokohama
3 Kamakura
4 Mount Fuji
5 Hakone
6 Shimoda

Most visit Nikkō to see the World Heritage-listed **Tōshō-gū** shrine complex, which sits at the base of mountains crisscrossed by the outstanding hiking trails of **Nikkō National Park**. It's also worth investigating the far less crowded **Tōshō-gū Museum of Art**, and the **Tamozawa Imperial Villa Memorial Park**, before crossing the Daiya-gawa to explore the dramatically named **Ganman-ga-fuchi abyss** – in fact a modest gorge flanked by a tranquil walking path. The most beautiful parts of the aforementioned national park are around **Chūzenji-ko** lake, some 17km west of Nikkō, and the quieter resort of **Yumoto**, higher up in the mountains.

Outside the peak summer and autumn seasons, and with a very early start, it's possible to see both Tōshō-gū and Chūzenji-ko in a long day-trip from Tokyo, but to get the most out of the journey it's best to stay **overnight**. In contrast to most Japanese urban areas, the town is refreshingly quiet after dark: very little is open after 8pm, bar a couple of renegade bars and two convenience stores, allowing you to wander the town's lanes unmolested by traffic or flashing lights, drinking in the fresh air which remains clement all through the summer.

Brief history

Although Nikkō has been a holy place in both the Buddhist and Shintō religions for over a thousand years, its fortunes only took off with the death of **Tokugawa Ieyasu** in 1616. In his will, the shogun requested that a shrine be built here in his honour. However, the complex, completed in 1617, was deemed not nearly impressive enough by Ieyasu's grandson, **Tokugawa Iemitsu**, who ordered work to begin on the elaborate decorative mausoleum seen today.

Iemitsu's dazzling vision had an underlying purpose. The shogun wanted to stop rival lords amassing money of their own, so he ordered the *daimyō* to supply the materials for the shrine, and to pay the thousands of craftsmen. The mausoleum, Tōshō-gū, was completed in 1634 and the jury has been out on its over-the-top design ever since. Whatever you make of it, Tōshō-gū – along with the slightly more restrained Taiyūin-byō mausoleum of Iemitsu – is entirely successful at conveying the immense power and wealth of the Tokugawa dynasty.

Despite its popularity as a tourist destination today, barely a century ago Nikkō, in the wake of the Meiji Restoration, was running to seed. It was foreign diplomats and business people who began to favour it as a highland retreat from the heat of the Tokyo summer in the 1870s; the inevitable railway tethering to the capital was completed in 1890. Since then, thankfully, little has changed.

Shin-kyō

神橋 • Off Nihon Romantic Highway • Daily: April–Sept 8am–5pm; Oct to mid-Nov 8am–4pm; mid-Nov to March 9am–4pm • ¥300

At the top of Nikkō's main street is the red-lacquered **Shin-kyō**, a bridge that is one of the town's most famous landmarks. Legend has it that when the Buddhist priest Shōdō Shōnin visited Nikkō in the eighth century, he was helped across the Daiya-gawa at this very spot by the timely appearance of two snakes, which formed a bridge and then vanished. The original arched wooden structure first went up in 1636, but has been reconstructed many times since, most recently in 2005. There's no need to pay the entrance fee, since the structure is cleary visible (and more photogenic) from the road.

Rinnō-ji

輪王寺 • Daily: April–Oct 8am–5pm; Nov–March 8am–4pm • ¥400, or ¥900 including Taiyūin Reibyō (see p.176); Treasure House ¥300

North of Shin-kyō, an uphill pedestrian path works through gorgeous woodland; follow it up and you'll soon emerge in front of the main compound of **Rinnō-ji**, a Tendai Buddhist temple founded in 766 by Shōdō Shōnin, whose statue stands on a

NIKKŌ

rock at the entrance. The large, red-painted hall, **Sanbutsu-dō**, houses three giant gilded statues: the thousand-handed Kannon, the Amida Buddha and the fearsome horse-headed Kannon. It's worth the entry fee to view these awe-inspiring figures from directly beneath their lotus-flower perches. Note that this hall will remain under protective housing until 2020, as part of a mammoth restoration programme. Rinnō-ji's **Treasure House** (宝物殿, Hōmotsuden), opposite the Sanbutsu-dō, has some interesting items on display, but its nicest feature is the attached Shōyō-en, an elegant garden with a strolling route around a small pond.

Tōshō-gū

東照宮 • Daily: April–Oct 8am–5pm; Nov–March 8am–4pm • ¥1300

Broad, tree-lined Omotesandō leads up to the main entrance to **Tōshō-gū**, just to the west of Rinnō-ji. You'll pass under a giant stone *torii* (one of the few remaining features of the original 1617 shrine), while on the left is an impressive red and green five-storey pagoda, an 1819 reconstruction of a 1650 original, which burned down. Ahead is the Omote-mon gate, the entrance to the main shrine precincts.

Once inside, turn left to reach the **Three Sacred Storehouses** (*Sanjinko*) on the right and the **Sacred Stables** (*Shinkyūsha*) on the left, where you'll spot Tōshō-gū's most famous painted woodcarvings – the "hear no evil, see no evil, speak no evil" **monkeys**, which represent the three major principles of Tendai Buddhism. The route leads to the steps up to the dazzling **Yōmei-mon** (Sun Blaze Gate), with its wildly ornate carvings, gilt and intricate decoration. A belfry and drum tower stand alone in front of the gate. Behind the drum tower is the **Honji-dō**. This small hall is part of

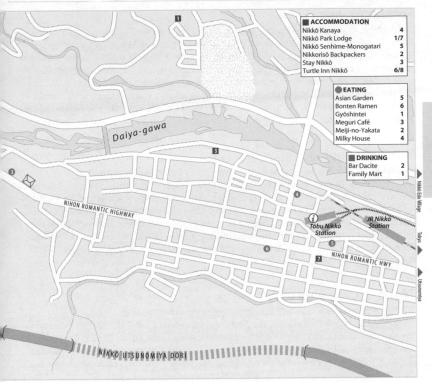

Rinnō-ji temple and contains a ceiling painting of a "roaring dragon"; a priest will demonstrate how to make the dragon roar by standing beneath its head and clapping to create an echo.

Beyond the Yōmei-mon, just above the Sakashita-mon gate to the right of the inner precinct, the temple's famed **sleeping cat** (*nemuri neko*) is usually accompanied by gawping crowds – you'd otherwise easily miss this minute, underwhelming carving. Two hundred stone steps lead uphill from the gate to the surprisingly unostentatious **tomb of Ieyasu**, which is set amid a glade of pines, and about the only corner of the shrine where tourists are generally absent.

Directly in front of the Yōmei-mon is the serene white and gold gate of **Kara-mon**, beyond which is the **Haiden**, or hall of worship. The side entrance to the hall is to the right of the gate; you'll need to remove your shoes and stop taking photographs. Inside, you can walk down into the Honden, the shrine's central hall, which is still decorated with its beautiful original paintwork.

NIKKŌ FESTIVALS

Every year, on May 18, the **Grand Festival** re-stages the spectacular burial of Ieyasu at Tōshō-gū, with a cast of over one thousand costumed priests and warriors taking part in a colourful procession through the shrine grounds, topped off with horseback archery. It's well worth attending, as is its smaller-scale cousin (also called the Grand Festival) on October 17, which doesn't have the archery and only lasts half a day, and the "**Light Up Nikkō**" event (end of Oct/beginning of Nov), during which the major temple buildings are illuminated at night to great effect.

Futarasan-jinja

二荒山神社 • Daily: April–Oct 8am–4.30pm; Nov–March 9am–3.30pm • Free; garden ¥200

After Tōshō-gū, the simple design of **Futarasan-jinja** comes as a relief to the senses. This shrine, originally established by the priest Shōdō Shōnin in 782, is the main one dedicated to the deity of Mount Nantai, the volcano whose eruption created nearby Chūzenji-ko. There are some good paintings of animals and birds on votive plaques in the shrine's main hall, while the attached garden offers a quiet retreat, with a small teahouse serving *matcha* green tea and sweets. You can also inspect the *bakemono tōrō*, a "phantom lantern" made of bronze in 1292 and said to be possessed by demons.

Taiyūin Reibyō

大猷院霊廟 • Daily: April–Oct 8am–5pm; Nov–March 8am–4pm • ¥550, or ¥900 including Rinnō-ji (see p.173)

The charming **Taiyūin Reibyō** contains the mausoleum of the third shogun, Tokugawa Iemitsu, who died in 1651. This complex, hidden away on a hillside and surrounded by lofty pines, was deliberately designed to be less ostentatious than Tōshō-gū. Look out for the green god of wind and the red god of thunder in the alcoves behind the Futatsuten-no-mon gate, and the beautiful Kara-mon (Chinese-style gate) and fence surrounding the gold and black lacquer inner precincts – extremely photogenic, especially when dusk begins to encroach.

Tōshō-gū Museum of Art

東照宮美術館, Tōshō-gū Bijutsukan • Daily: April–Oct 8am–5pm; Nov–March 8am–4pm • ¥800

Tucked away behind Tōshō-gū, the **Tōshō-gū Museum of Art** – the former head office of the shrine – is set in a huge wooden mansion dating from 1928. Inside, the collection features an array of sliding doors and screens decorated by the top Japanese painters of the day; together, they constitute one of Japan's most beautiful collections of such art.

Meiji-no-Yakata

明治の館 • Daily 24hr • Free

The pretty gardens of **Meiji-no-Yakata** were formerly the grounds of American trade representative F.W. Horne's early twentieth-century holiday home. The various houses amid the trees are now fancy restaurants (see p.178), but even if you don't eat here, it's worth wandering around to take in the sylvan setting.

Tamozawa Imperial Villa

田母沢御用邸記念公園, Tamozawa Goyōtei Kinen Kōen • Off Nihon Romantic Highway • 9am–4.30pm; closed Tues • ¥500

In stark contrast to Nikkō's temples and shrines is the Zen-like simplicity of the beautifully restored **Tamozawa Imperial Villa**. This 106-room residence, surrounded by manicured gardens (including a 400-year-old weeping cherry tree), combines buildings of widely different heritage, some parts dating back to 1632. Three emperors have lived in it, including Akihito, who was evacuated here during World War II. As you stroll the corridors, take time to appreciate the intricate details and the gorgeous screen paintings.

Ganman-ga-fuchi abyss

含満ヶ淵 • Daily 24hr • Free

The wonderfully named **Ganman-ga-fuchi abyss** is a rocky little gorge cut through by a river that, while crystal-clear, can be a roaring beast after the rains. Accessed via a small path from the road, a delightful, easy-to-walk **trail** hugs the south side of the rocky river valley. Part of the walk is lined by the **Narabi-jizō**, a few dozen decaying stone statues of Jizō, the Buddhist saint of travellers and children. Sporting scarlet bibs and woven caps, and backed by forest, they make for an enchanting sight.

Yashio Onsen

やしおの湯, Yashio-no-Yu • 1726-4 Kiyotakiwanoshiro-machi • 10am–9pm; closed Thurs • ¥300 • ☎ 0288 53 6611

Nikkō's municipal onsen, **Yashio**, is set a little way west of the town, and offers large communal baths and rotemburo (outdoor baths). It's possible to walk here from central Nikkō if you have an hour to spare; the most pleasant route is via the Ganman-ga-fuchi abyss, after which you turn right onto the main road, then look for the signs.

2

ARRIVAL AND DEPARTURE

NIKKŌ

Nikkō is accessible on two lines from Tokyo, which serve stations sitting almost side by side in the east of the town. The JR station is a real beauty, a historic wooden building designed by Frank Lloyd Wright; however, unless you've got a JR pass, the Tōbu line will generally be more convenient.

BY TŌBU TRAIN

The Tōbu-Nikkō line (ⓦ www.tobu.co.jp) runs from Tōbu-Asakusa Station, connected by tunnel to Asakusa subway station; an alternative access point for this line is Kita-Senju Station, at the end of the Hibiya line. Note that on some trains you'll need to change at Shimo-Imaichi, while some direct trains split on the way, so be sure to board the right carriage. There are two types of train to choose from: the regular "Kaisoku" ones (2hr 20min; ¥1360), or the fancier limited express "Spacia" (1hr 50min; ¥2700); most people

end up travelling with a travel pass (see box below).

BY JR TRAIN

You can also reach Nikkō on JR trains but the fares are far higher (¥5380 each way if travelling with Shinkansen), so travelling this way only makes sense if you have a JR pass (see p.36). The fastest route (around 2hr total) is by Shinkansen from either Tokyo or Ueno to Utsunomiya (宇都宮), where you change to the JR Nikkō line for a local train to the JR Nikkō terminus, just east of the Tōbu station.

INFORMATION

Tourist information The main tourist office, the Nikkō Kyōdo Centre, is on the main road from the station to the Tōshō-gū complex (daily 9am–5pm; ☎0288 54 2496, ⓦ nikko-jp.org). If you're planning on walking in the area, you can pick up the free *Tourist Guide of Nikkō*, which shows you all the hiking trails found within Nikkō National Park. There's also an excellent information desk at the Tōbu-

Nikkō station (daily 8.30am–5pm; ☎0288 53 4511).

ATMs The main post office (Mon–Thurs 8.45am–6pm, Fri 8.45am–7pm, Sat & Sun 9am–5pm) on the approach road to Tōshō-gū has an ATM which accepts foreign-issued cards, as do the ones in the post offices opposite Tōbu Station and up at Chūzenji; otherwise, it's near impossible to use credit cards in the town.

ACCOMMODATION

Nikkō has plenty of accommodation, and is the best base for the area. If you're looking for a quieter environment, consider staying up at Chūzenji-ko or Yumoto (see p.179). Rates at virtually all places are slightly higher in the **peak seasons**: August, from October to early November, and during major holidays. During these periods reservations are essential.

Nikkō Kanaya 日光金谷ホテル 1300 Kami-hatsuishi-machi ☎0288 54 0001, ⓦkanayahotel.co.jp. This

charming heritage property, practically a museum piece, remains Nikkō's top Western-style hotel, harking back to

---

TŌBU TRAVEL PASSES

Tōbu offers **travel passes** to foreigners, covering the return trip from Tokyo and transport around the Nikkō area. These tickets, which can only be bought at Tōbu stations, include the fare from Asakusa to Nikkō (express train surcharges of ¥830–1160 for the Spacia still apply), unlimited use of local buses, and discounts on entrance charges at many of the area's attractions. If you're planning a trip out to Chūzenji-ko (see p.179), the most useful ticket is the **four-day All Nikkō Pass** (¥4520 April–Nov, ¥4150 Dec–March). The **two-day pass** (¥2670) is a similar price to the standard return train fare from Tokyo to Nikkō, so basically only saves you the local bus fares around Nikkō.

2

the glamorous days of early twentieth-century travel. There are some cheaper rooms with en-suite shower or just a toilet (the hotel has a communal bath) but for the full effect, splash out on the deluxe grade. Note that there's another *Kanaya* up in Chuzenji-kō (see p.180). 🛜 **¥17,820**

Nikkō Park Lodge 日光パークロッジ 11-6 Matsubara-chō & 2828-5 Tokorono ☎ 0288 53 1201, 🌐 nikkoparklodge.com. This hostel has two locations in town: one right by the Tōbu station, and the other in a lovely spot high up on the north bank of the river – not terribly convenient, but it makes for a memorable stay. Vegan dinners are available. 🛜 Dorms **¥2800**, doubles **¥8980**

Nikkō Senhime-Monogatari 日光千姫物語 6-48 Yasukawa-chō ☎ 0288 54 1010, 🌐 senhime.co.jp. Large, highly comfortable option in the calm western side of town, boasting a mix of tatami and Western-style rooms, and charming bathing facilities. Their meals are also quite superb. 🛜 **¥18,360**

★ Nikkorisō Backpackers にっこり荘バックパカーズ 1107 Naka-hatsuishi-machi ☎ 0288 54 0535, 🌐 nikkorisou.com. Housed in a building which looks like a giant school carpentry experiment, this amiable hostel has a delightful location near the river, and small but cosy rooms. Discounts kick in if you're staying more than one night. 🛜 Dorms **¥3000**, twins **¥6900**

★ Stay Nikkō ステーイ日光ゲストハウス 2-360-13 Inari-machi ☎ 0288 25 5303, 🌐 staynikko.com. A relatively recent addition to the town's accommodation scene, this place is a real winner – presided over by a super-friendly (and English-speaking) Japanese-Thai couple, it only has four rooms, all with shared facilities, making for an atmosphere halfway between a guesthouse and a homestay. The breakfasts (¥800) go down very well, and the peaceful riverside location is another bonus. 🛜 **¥7900**

Turtle Inn Nikkō タートルイン日光 2-16 Takumi-chō ☎ 0288 53 3168, 🌐 turtle-nikko.com. Popular pension run by an English-speaking family, in a quiet location next to the river. There are small, plain tatami rooms with common bathrooms, and en-suite Western-style rooms, plus a cosy lounge. Add ¥1080 for breakfast, and ¥2160 for the evening meal. They also run a fancier, slightly more expensive annexe, the *Hotori-an*, down the road beside the path to the Ganman-ga-fuchi abyss; it boasts a pottery shop on site, as well as a bath with forest views, and meals are taken at the *Turtle Inn*. 🛜 **¥9600**

EATING

The Nikkō area's culinary speciality is **yuba-ryōri** – milky, thin strips of tofu, usually rolled into tubes and cooked in various stews; this can be enjoyed at many local restaurants, but you may well be served it as part of meals at your accommodation. Note that most **restaurants** in town shut at around 8pm.

Asian Garden アジアン ガーデン Opposite Tobu Nikkō Station ☎ 0288 542801. Indian restaurant with a good vegetarian set menu (¥950) and reasonably priced meat-based set meals from ¥1200. Lunch sets are also a bargain, at ¥800 and up. 🛜 Daily 10am–11pm.

★ Bonten Ramen 梵天ラーメン 264-1 Matsubara-chō ☎ 0288 53 6095. This ramen bar is one of very few places in Nikkō open for a late-ish dinner. You'll find miso, burnt soy and salt soup varieties on the English-language menu (all ¥500–960); they're all pretty darn good, but those made with springy thicker noodles tend to be best. Daily 11am–9.30pm.

Gyōshintei 堯心亭 2339-1 Sannai ☎ 0288 53 3751. Sample exquisitely prepared *shōjin-ryōri* (Buddhist vegetarian cuisine) in a traditional tatami room, served by kimono-clad waitresses: bentō lunches cost from ¥2200, dinner from ¥4500, and some sets include fish. It's part of the charming Meiji-no-Yakata complex (see p.176), so you can gaze out on a lovely garden as you eat, then walk off the calories in and around the surrounding sights. 11.30am–7pm; closed Thurs.

Meguri Café Cafe 廻 909-1 Naka-hatsuishi-machi ☎ 0288 25 3122. Run by a husband-and-wife team, this true vegan café has a great laidback atmosphere. Meals use vegetables grown in their own garden, as well as local organic produce. You'll also find some yummy dessert choices, mostly Western style (such as cakes), and plenty of fresh fruits. Daily 11.30am–6pm.

★ Meiji-no-Yakata 明治の館 2339-1 Sannai ☎ 0288 53 3751. If you get to this charmingly nostalgic stone villa (once a Meiji-era holiday home) at around 10am, you can make a table reservation, then go sightseeing; come back when it opens at 11am, and treat yourself to the best coffee this side of Tokyo, plus some cheesecake (¥1080 will get you both), possibly after some clam chowder (¥700). With everything served by starched-shirted sorts, with fancy bowls and utensils, it's a small price to pay for some luxury. Otherwise, go the whole hog with their mix of Japanese and Western staples – mains start at ¥1500. 🛜 Daily 11am–7.30pm.

Milky House ミルキーハウス 2-2-3 Inari-machi ☎ 0288 53 4166. A short walk from the train stations, this friendly local spot is a good place to sample *yuba-ryōri*; sets including it as a main cost ¥1650, but better for most people are the small "sampler sets" featuring the tofu (which is particularly fresh here) and some mushroom tempura for just ¥500. They've also a full roster of tasty soba and udon bowls. 11am–3pm; closed Wed.

DRINKING

Bar Dacite バー「デイサイト」 1300 Kami-hatsuishi-machi ☎0288 54 0001, ⓦkanayahotel.co.jp. The dark and cosy hotel bar at the swanky *Nikkō Kanaya* (see p.177) is the town's best spot for a nightcap – not that there's much competition. Cocktails suit the elegant atmosphere best, and the menu features some house specials. Daily 6–10.30pm.

Family Mart ファミリーマート 1-16 Yasukawa-chō, no phone. This convenience store may be a left-field drinking

recommendation, but there are a few sound reasons behind it: first, its location – from the outdoor tables you'll be able to hear the rushing river, and see the dark mountains behind; second, it has a splendid selection of boutique cup sake, including an exceedingly tasty local brown-glass number, long served by appointment to Tōshō-gū; and finally, after a certain hour, it's the only place in Nikkō you can go for a drink. 📶 Daily 24hr.

Chūzenji-ko and Yumoto

中禅寺湖・湯元

Some 10km west of Nikkō lies the tranquil lake of **Chūzenji-ko**, most famed for the dramatic **Kegon Falls** that flow from it. Buses from Nikkō run east along Route 120 and up the twisting, one-way road to reach **CHŪZENJI**, the lakeside resort. Both the lake and waterfalls were created thousands of years ago, when nearby **Mount Nantai** (男体山, Nantai-san; 2486m) erupted, its lava plugging the valley.

Many buses from Nikkō continue northwest of Chūzenji to terminate 45 minutes later at the onsen village of **YUMOTO**, which nestles cosily at the base of the mountains on the northern shore of lake **Yuno-ko**.

Kegon Falls

華厳の滝, Kegon-no-taki • Daily: Jan, Feb & Dec 9am–4.30pm; March, April & Nov 8am–5pm; May–Sept 7.30am–6pm; Oct 7.30am–5pm • Lift ¥550 • ⓦkegon.jp

The best view of the **Kegon Falls** can be had from the viewing platform at their base. The lift to this vantage point lies east across the car park behind the Chūzenji bus station; don't be put off by the queues of tour groups – a shorter line is reserved for independent travellers. The lift drops 100m through the rock to the base of the falls, from where you can see over a tonne of water per second cascading from the Ojiri River, which flows from the Chūzenji-ko lake.

Futarasan-jinja

二荒山神社 • Off Nihon Romantic Highway • 24hr • Temples free; Mount Nantai ¥500

This colourful shrine, around 1km west of the Kegon Falls along the shore of Chūzenji-ko, is the second **Futarasan-jinja** of the Nikkō area (the first is in Nikkō itself). The shrine, which once bore the name Chūzenji, has a pretty view of the lake, but is nothing extraordinary. There's also a third Futarasan-jinja, on the actual summit of Mount Nantai; to reach it you'll have to pay to climb the volcanic peak, which is owned by the shrine. The hike up is beautiful but takes around four hours, and should only be attempted in good weather; the tourist offices in Nikkō (see p.177) can provide maps.

Ryūzu Falls

竜頭の滝, Ryūzu -no-taki • Daily 24hr • Free • ☎0288 55 0388

Heading 6km west around Chūzenji-ko from Futarasan-jinja, on a gorgeous lakeside path, you'll eventually spot the spectacular, 60m-high **Ryūzu Falls**, which boast clear views of the lake. At the base of the falls are several gift shops and noodle bars, one of which has a superb location overlooking the water as it gushes into the lake. Note that there's also a great hiking route from here to Yumoto (see below).

Yumoto

The village of **YUMOTO** nestles cosily at the base of the mountains on the northern shore of lake **Yuno-ko**, 15km northwest of Chūzenji-ko. A lovely way to take in the scenery is to rent a rowing boat at the lakeside *Yumoto Rest House* (¥1000 for 50min; May–Oct only). Alternatively, you could walk around the lake in about an hour.

Onsen-ji

温泉寺 • At the back of the village, 5min walk from the bus terminal • April–Nov daily 10am–2pm • ¥500

The small temple of **Onsen-ji** is notable for its onsen bath, which you can use. Nearby is **Yu-no-daira**, a field where bubbling water breaks through the ground – this is the source of the sulphur smell that hangs so pungently in the air. There's a free footbath, great for soaking weary feet, near the *Yumoto Hillside Inn* (see below).

Senjōgahara marshland plateau

戦場ヶ原

If you're feeling energetic, it's worth embarking on the easy and enjoyable 10km **hike** from Yumoto across the **Senjōgahara marshland plateau**, past two spectacular waterfalls and back to Chūzenji-ko. First, follow the west bank of Yuno-ko around to the steps down to the picturesque Yudaki Falls (湯滝). The trail continues along the Yu-gawa through shady woods before emerging beside the Izumiyado, a large pond and the start of a two-hour tramp across the raised walkways above the Senjōgahara marshland, which blooms with wild flowers during the summer. Roughly one hour further on, at the Akanuma junction, you can branch off back to the main road, or continue along the riverside path for thirty minutes to the main road and bridge overlooking the **Ryūzu Falls** (see p.179).

ARRIVAL AND DEPARTURE	CHŪZENJI-KO AND YUMOTO

By bus Buses up to Chūzenji-ko (¥1100 one-way) and on to Yumoto (¥1700) run at fairly frequent intervals from outside both of Nikkō's train stations between 6am and 6pm, and usually take 45min, though travelling times can easily double – or even triple – during *kōyō* in mid-October, the prime time for viewing the changing autumn leaves, when traffic is bumper to bumper. If you haven't bought a Tōbu pass (see box, p.177), it's still possible to save money on transport by buying a two-day bus pass at either train station; for unlimited return trips to Chūzenji-ko the cost is ¥2000, while to Yumoto it's ¥3000.

ACCOMMODATION

Chūzenji Kanaya Hotel 中禅寺金谷ホテル 2482 Chugushi ☎ 0288 51 0001, ⓦ kanayahotel.co.jp. The most luxurious place to stay on the lake, and affiliated to the eponymous hotel in Nikkō (see p.177). It's a couple of kilometres away from the tourist village, en route to the Ryūzu Falls, and has been especially designed to blend in with the woodland surroundings. 📶 **¥24,000**

Yumoto Hillside Inn 湯元ヒルサイドイン 2536 Yumoto ☎ 0288 62 2434, ⓦ hillsideinn.jp. A Western-style hotel in a wooden chalet with an outdoor deck, English-speaking owners, a small heated swimming pool and indoor and outdoor onsen. Rates include two meals. 📶 **¥20,000**

MINAKAMI AND ADVENTURE SPORTS

The sprawling township of **Minakami** (水上), buried deep in the mountains of Gunma-ken, about 65km west of Nikkō, has become one of the hottest spots in Japan for adventure sports. No fewer than ten whitewater rafting companies, including **Canyons** (☎ 0278 72 2811, ⓦ canyons.jp), offer trips down the Tone-gawa. Other activities include paragliding, canyoning, abseiling, rock-climbing and a wide variety of treks, including the ascent to the summit of **Tanigawa-dake** (谷川岳; 1977m). To relax after all this, you can head to **Takaragawa onsen** (宝川温泉; daily 9am–5pm; ¥1500 before 4pm, ¥1000 after 4pm; ⓦ takaragawa.com), famous for its mixed-sex bathing (though it also has separated baths) and its four huge rotemburo.

To reach Minakami, take the Shinkansen (1hr; ¥5900) to **Jōmō-Kōgen** (上毛高原), from where the town is a 20min bus ride. The **tourist office** (daily 9am–5.15pm; ☎ 0278 72 2611, ⓦ enjoy-minakami.com) is opposite the station. **Places to stay** include the Canyons-run *Alpine Lodge* (from ¥4000 per person), which offers private rooms plus a lively bar; and the aforementioned **Takaragawa onsen** (from ¥21,600 per person).

Narita

成田

Thanks to its international airport, **NARITA** is the first place most people hit when arriving in Japan. While the overwhelming majority of visitors scoot straight off to Tokyo without a second glance, Narita is actually a nice little town, a temporary or permanent home to many flight crews. For the casual visitor, there's one fantastic sight: the enormous temple complex of **Naritasan Shinshō-ji**, which attracts more than ten million pilgrims each year.

2

Naritasan Shinshō-ji

成田山新勝寺 · Located at the end of Omotesandō · Daily 24hr · Free

The thousand-year-old temple of **Naritasan Shinshō-ji** is an important landmark in the Shingon sect of Buddhism. As long as you're not here on one of the main festival days (New Year, and Setsubun on February 3 or 4), you'll find that it doesn't get crowded, such is its vast size. The colourful three-storey pagoda in front of the Great Main Hall dates from the eighteenth century and is decorated with fearsome gilded dragon heads snarling from under brightly painted rafters. Behind the main hall, the temple's pretty gardens include a calligraphy museum, small forests and ornamental ponds.

ARRIVAL AND INFORMATION   NARITA

By train Narita is connected both to Ueno in Tokyo (every 30min; 1hr) and the airport (every 15min; 7min) by JR and Keisei trains, which arrive at separate stations a minute's walk from each other and around a 15min walk from the temple.

Tourist information There's a tourist information desk next to the JR station and at the Narita Tourist Pavilion on Omotesandō, the town's main shopping street (Tues–Sun: Jan–May & Oct–Dec 9am–5pm; June–Sept 10am–6pm; ⓦ www.nrtk.jp).

ACCOMMODATION

9 Hours ナインアワーズ成田空港 Narita Airport, Terminal 2 ☏ 0476 33 5109, ⓦ ninehours.co.jp. If you've a late arrival or early departure, this airport capsule hotel can save you heaps on a cab ride. ⓦ Overnight ¥4900, "nap" ¥1500 for first 2hr then ¥500 for each 1hr.

★**Azure Guesthouse** ゲストハウス アズール 10min walk southwest of the train stations ☏ 0476 91 5708, ⓦ azure-guesthouse.com. A friendly, surprisingly stylish place with English-speaking staff and good facilities. Book online for the best rates. Dorms ¥2900, doubles ¥7900

EATING AND DRINKING

Jet Lag Club ジェットラッグクラブ 508 Kami-chō ☏ 0476 22 0280. Lively British-style pub popular with local expats and visiting flight crews. Cocktails are just ¥400 during the 3–8pm happy hour. Daily 10am–2am.
Kikuya 菊屋 385 Naka-machi, opposite the Tourist

Pavilion. Moderately fancy-looking restaurant, serving reasonably priced *unagi* (eel); at around ¥2400 per portion, it's far costlier than regular fish, though pretty standard for eel. Daily 10am–9pm.

Kawagoe

川越

The interesting old castle town of **KAWAGOE** lies just 40km north of Tokyo. Although it doesn't look promising on arrival, Kawagoe's compact area of sights, around 1km north of the main station, is aptly described as a "Little Edo", and once you've browsed the many traditional craft shops and paused to sample the town's culinary delights, you'll probably find the day has flown by. On the third Saturday and Sunday of October Kawagoe hold its grand **matsuri**, one of the most lively festivals in the Tokyo area, involving some 25 ornate floats (called *dashi*) and hundreds of costumed celebrants.

2

KURAZUKURI

Kawagoe's fortunes owe everything to its strategic position on the Shingashi River and Kawagoe-kaidō, the ancient highway to the capital. If you wanted to get goods to Tokyo – then called Edo – they more than likely had to go via Kawagoe, and the town's merchants prospered as a result, accumulating the cash to build fireproof **kurazukuri**, the black, two-storey shophouses for which the town is now famous. At one time there were over two hundred of these houses, but their earthen walls didn't prove quite so effective against fire as hoped (nor were they much use in the face of Japan's headlong rush to modernization). Even so, some thirty remain, with sixteen prime examples clustered together along Chūō-dōri, around 1km north of the JR and Tōbu stations.

Kita-in

喜多院 • Around 500m east of Hon-Kawagoe Station • Palace daily 9am–4.30pm • Palace and Gohyaku Rakan ¥400 • ☎ 049 222 0859

Kawagoe's major highlight is **Kita-in**, the main temple complex of the Tendai Buddhist sect. There's been a temple on these grounds since 830, and it gained fame when the first Tokugawa shogun, Ieyasu, declared the head priest Tenkai Sōjō a "living Buddha". Such was the reverence in which the priests here were held that, when the temple burnt down in 1638, the third shogun, Iemitsu, donated a secondary palace from Edo Castle (on the site of Tokyo's present-day Imperial Palace) as a replacement building. This was dismantled and moved here piece by piece, and is now the only remaining structure from Edo Castle which survives anywhere. You have to pay an entry fee to view the palace part of the temple, but it's well worth it. Serene gardens surround the palace and a covered wooden bridge leads across into the temple's inner sanctum.

The entry fee also includes access to the **Gohyaku Rakan**, a remarkable grove of stone statues. Although the name translates as "500 Rakans", there are actually 538 of these enigmatic dwarf disciples of Buddha, and no two are alike.

Yamazaki Art Museum

山崎美術館, Yamazaki Bijutsuken • 9.30am–5pm; closed Wed & last 2 days of the month • ¥500 • ☎ 049 224 7114

Housed in the old Kameya *okashi* (sweet) shop, warehouse and factory, the **Yamazaki Art Museum** is dedicated to the works of Meiji-era artist Hashimoto Gahō. Some of his elegant screen paintings hang in the main gallery, while there are examples of the *okashi* once made here in the converted storehouses; entry includes tea and *okashi*.

ARRIVAL AND INFORMATION   KAWAGOE

By train Of the three train lines to Kawagoe, the fastest is the express on the Tōbu line from Ikebukuro (32min; ¥470); you can get off either at Kawagoe Station (which is also on the slower JR Saikyō line) or at Tōbu Kawagoe-shi, which is marginally closer to the town's main road, Chūō-dōri. Trains also run on the Seibu Shinjuku line from Shinjuku to Hon-Kawagoe Station; fastest and most direct are the Redarrow

services (45min; ¥1000), while slow trains take 1hr (¥500).
Tourist office The staff at Kawagoe Station's tourist office (daily 9am–4.30pm; ☎ 049 222 5556) can provide you with a map of the town and an English pamphlet on the sights.
Bike rental The Shimo bicycle store (daily 10am–7pm), immediately northwest of the main square, in front of the Seibu line terminus, rents out bikes (¥700/day).

EATING

Cafe Elevato カフェエレバートと Chūō-dōri. The most appealing of the town's cafés, set in a rather imposing building that's nevertheless very swish-looking on the inside. Coffees cost from ¥500, and they also sell bottles of Coedo beer – Kawagoe's very own brew – for ¥750. Daily 11am–9pm.
Ichinoya いちのや 1-18-10 Matsue-chō. Local gourmands flock to Kawagoe for eel, most famously sampled at this venerable restaurant, where there are two

floors of tatami rooms in which to scoff set courses; cheapest is the *unadon* eel-on-rice bowl (¥2160). Daily 9am–7pm.
★Kotobukian 寿庵 Beside Kita-in. Entered under an easy-to-spot wooden tower near the temple, this is a great place for soba. The green *seirosoba* variety is particularly notable; try it served in a delightful stack of three plates (¥1080), or mixed with okra, *nattō*, seaweed and tempura shavings (¥1050). 9am–1pm & 4–8pm; closed Wed.

Yokohama

横浜

On its southern borders Tokyo merges with **YOKOHAMA**, Japan's second most populous city (home to 3.6 million people) and a major international port. Though essentially part of the same mega-conurbation, central Yokohama feels far more spacious and airy than central Tokyo, thanks to its open harbour frontage and generally low-rise skyline, and though it can't claim any outstanding sights, the place has enough of interest to justify a day's outing from Tokyo.

Locals are proud of their city's international heritage, and there's definitely a cosmopolitan flavour to the place, with its scattering of Western-style buildings, Chinese temples and world cuisines, and its sizeable foreign community. The upmarket suburb of **Yamate** (also known as "the Bluff") is one of the city's highlights and boasts a splendid museum; the area forms a pleasant contrast with the vibrant alleys, trinket shops and bustling restaurants of nearby **Chinatown**, the city's other big draw.

2

Brief history

When Commodore Perry sailed his "Black Ships" into Tokyo Bay in 1853, Yokohama was a mere fishing village of some eighty houses on the distant shore. But it was this harbour, well out of harm's way as far as the Japanese were concerned, that the shogun designated one of the five **treaty ports** open to foreign trade in 1858.

From the early 1860s until the first decades of the twentieth century, Yokohama flourished on the back of raw silk exports, a trade dominated by British merchants. During this period the city provided the main conduit for new ideas and inventions into Japan: the first bakery, photographers', ice-cream shop, brewery and – perhaps most importantly – the first railway line, which linked today's Sakuragi-chō with Shimbashi in central Tokyo in 1872. The **Great Earthquake** levelled the city in 1923, and it was devastated again in air raids at the end of World War II; the rebuilt city is, however, among the world's largest ports.

Motomachi and Yamate

元町・山手

The narrow, semi-pedestrianized shopping street of **Motomachi** exudes a faint retro flavour with its European facades. You'll get more of the old Motomachi feel in the two streets to either side, particularly Naka-dōri (仲通), to the south, with its funky cafés and galleries.

At the northeast end of Motomachi, a wooded promontory marks the beginning of the **Yamate** district. The panoramic view from **Harbour View Park** is particularly beautiful at night; if you look really hard, just left of the double chimney stacks, you'll see the Tokyo Skytree blinking away.

Yokohama Foreign General Cemetery

外国人墓地, Gaikokujin Bochi • 96 Yamate-chō • March–Dec Sat & Sun noon–4pm • ¥200 donation • ☎ 045 622 1311, ⓦ yfgc-japan.com

Just a few minutes' walk south of the Harbour View Park, you'll likely happen upon the **Yokohama Foreign General Cemetery**, which sits on a west-facing hillside. Over 4500 people from more than forty countries are buried here, the vast majority either British or American.

Yamate Museum

山手博物館, Yamate Hakubutsukan • 254 Yamate-chō • Daily 11am–4pm • ¥200 • ☎ 045 622 1188

The tiny **Yamate Museum** is housed in the city's oldest wooden building, erected in 1909. Exhibits focus on life in the area during the foreign-settlement period, and include a collection of cartoons from *Japan Punch*, a satirical magazine published here in the late nineteenth century. However, it's the stunning building itself that's the main draw.

2

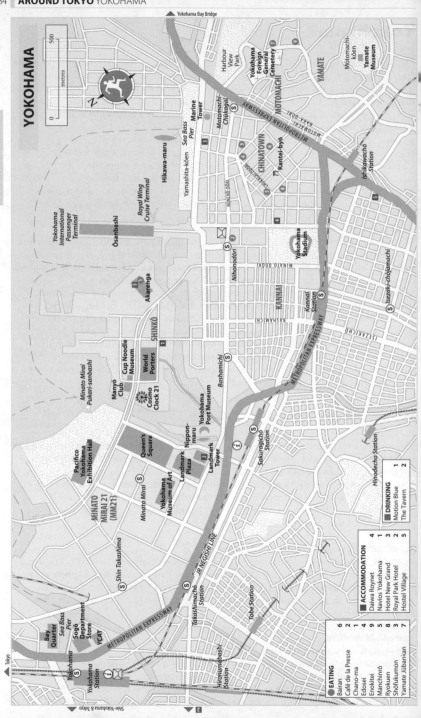

YOKOHAMA

0 — 500 metres

Yokohama Bay Bridge

Yokohama International Passenger Terminal

Osanbashi

Royal Wing Cruise Terminal

Hikawa-maru

Sea Bass Pier

Marine Tower

Yamashita-kōen

Harbour View Park

Yokohama Foreign General Cemetery

Motomachi-Chūkagai (S)

MOTOMACHI

Motomachi-kōen

Yamate Museum

YAMATE

MOTOMACHI EXPRESSWAY

NAKA-DŌRI

CHINATOWN

Kantei-byō

Ishikawachō Station

Akarenga

SHINKŌ

Cup Noodle Museum

World Porters

Manyō Club

Cosmo Clock 21

Yokohama Port Museum

Bashamichi

Nihonōdori (S)

HONCHŌ-DŌRI

MINATO ŌDŌRI

Yokohama Stadium

KANNAI

BASHAMICHI

Kannai Station (S)

Isezaki-chōjamachi (S)

ISEZAKICHŌ

Minato Mirai Pukari-sanbashi

Pacífico Yokohama Exhibition Hall

Queen's Square

Minato Mirai (S)

Yokohama Museum of Art

Landmark Plaza

Nippon-maru

Landmark Tower

MINATO MIRAI 21 (MM21)

Shin Takashima (S)

Sakuragichō Station (S)

METROPOLITAN EXPRESSWAY

Hinodechō Station

JR NEGISHI LINE

Takashimachō Station (S)

Tobe Station

Bay Quarter

Sea Bass Pier

Sōgō Department Store

YCAT

Shin Takashima (S)

METROPOLITAN EXPRESSWAY

Yokohama Station (S)

Hiranumabashi Station

Tokyo

Shin-Yokohama & Tokyo

ACCOMMODATION

Daiwa Roynet	4
Navios Yokohama	1
Hotel New Grand	3
Royal Park Hotel	2
Hostel Village	5

● EATING

Bairan	6
Café de la Presse	2
Chano-ma	1
Edosei	4
Enokitei	9
Manchinrō	5
Ryokuen	8
Shōfukumon	3
Yamate Jūbankan	7

■ DRINKING

Motion Blue	1
The Tavern	2

Chinatown

中華街, Chūka-gai

Founded in 1863, Yokohama's **Chinatown** is the largest in Japan: its streets contain roughly two hundred restaurants and over three hundred shops, while some eighteen million tourists pass through its narrow alleyways every year; few leave without tasting what's on offer, from steaming savoury dumplings to a full-blown meal in one of the famous speciality restaurants (see p.188).

Kantei-byō

関帝廟 · 140 Yamashita-chō · Daily 9am–7pm · Free; ¥500 to see main altar

The focus of community life is **Kantei-byō**, a shrine dedicated to Guan Yu, a former general and guardian deity of Chinatown. The building is a bit cramped, but impressive nonetheless, with a colourful ornamental gateway and writhing dragons wherever you look. You can pay to enter the main building to see the red-faced, long-haired Guan Yu, but it's not really worth it.

The harbour

From the eastern edge of Chinatown it's a short hop down to the harbour, which is fronted by **Yamashita-kōen**, a pleasant park created as a memorial to victims of the Great Earthquake. Here you can pick up a *Sea Bass* ferry (see p.187) or take a harbour cruise (see box below) from the pier beside the **Hikawa-maru** (see below). The 106m-high **Marine Tower**, built in 1961, is still the focal point of the area after all these years, but it's better to save your money for the Landmark Tower's much higher observation deck (see p.186). Cruise ships pull up at **Ōsanbashi** pier to berth at the International Passenger Terminal, a beautifully fluid design inspired by ocean waves.

Hikawa-maru Museum

日本郵船氷川丸, Nikon Yūsen Hikowe maru · Off Yamashita-kōen · Tues–Sun 10am–5pm · ¥200 · ☎ 045 641 4362, ⓦ nyk.com/rekishi

The *Hikawa-maru*, a retired passenger liner also known as the *Queen of the Pacific*, was built in 1930 for the NYK line Yokohama–Seattle service, though it was later commandeered as a hospital ship during World War II. It now serves as the **Hikawa-maru Museum**, with the ship done up to look as it did in its prime.

Minato Mirai 21 (MM21)

みなとみらい21 · ⓦ www.minatomirai21.com

Occupying over two square kilometres of reclaimed land and disused dockyards, **Minato Mirai 21**, or MM21, is an ever-expanding mini-city of apartment blocks, offices, recreational and cultural facilities.

Yokohama Port Museum

横浜みなと博物館, Yokohama Minato Hakubutsukan · 2-1-1 Minatomirai · Tues–Sun 10am–5pm · ¥600 March–Nov, ¥400 Dec–Feb · ⓦ nippon-maru.or.jp

Built in 1930, the **Nippon-maru** training sail ship saw service up until 1984 (during which time she sailed the equivalent of 45 times round the world) and now forms part

---

YOKOHAMA SIGHTSEEING CRUISES

From Yamashita-kōen you can join the *Marine Shuttle* or *Marine Rouge* for a variety of **sightseeing cruises** around the harbour (from ¥1000 for 40min; ⓦ yokohama-cruising.jp); the *Marine Rouge* also offers lunch and dinner cruises (¥2520 plus ¥5500–11,000 for food). In addition, the bigger and more luxurious *Royal Wing* cruise ship (☎ 045 662 6125, ⓦ royalwing.co.jp) runs lunch, tea and dinner cruises from Ōsanbashi pier (¥1500–2500 plus ¥1500–5400 for food).

of the enjoyable **Yokohama Port Museum**. You can explore the entire vessel, which has plenty of English labelling throughout.

Landmark Tower

横浜ランドマークタワー • 2-2-1 Minatomirai • **Observation deck** Daily 10am–9pm (Sat until 10pm) • ¥1000 • ⓦ yokohama-landmark.jp

You can't miss the awesome, 296m-tall **Landmark Tower** – Yokohama's tallest building by far, and still ranked second countrywide. The **Sky Garden observation deck** is on its 69th floor, and on clear days, when Fuji is flaunting her beauty, the superb views more than justify the entry fee. You can also enjoy a coffee for about the same price in the opulent *Sirius Sky Lounge*, another floor up in the *Royal Park Hotel*, or splash out on an early evening cocktail as the city lights spread their magic.

Yokohama Museum of Art

横浜美術館, Yokohama Bijutsukan • 3-4-1 Minatomirai • 10am–6pm; closed Thurs • ¥500; varying prices for special exhibitions • ☎ 045 221 0300, ⓦ yokohama.art.museum

The highlight of the MM21 area is the splendid **Yokohama Museum of Art**, which is filled with mostly twentieth-century works of Japanese and Western art. Such refinement is set off to fine effect by designer Tange Kenzō's cool, grey space, which grabs your attention as much as the exhibits.

Shinkō island

新港

Between MM21 and Ōsanbashi is **Shinkō** island, which was reclaimed about a hundred years ago as part of Yokohama's then state-of-the-art port facilities. There are a few interesting things to see here, including a huge Ferris wheel, and an even huger spa complex; on the eastern side of the island, two handsome red-brick warehouses dating from 1911 now form the attractive **Akarenga** shopping, dining and entertainment complex.

Cosmo Clock 21

コスモクロック21 • 2-8-1 Shinkō • Mon–Fri 11am–9pm, Sat & Sun 11am–10pm; occasionally closed on Thurs • ¥700

The slowly revolving **Cosmo Clock 21** is one of the world's largest Ferris wheels, with a diameter of 112m; one circuit takes around fifteen minutes, allowing plenty of time to enjoy the view, which is particularly spectacular at night. The clock's changing colours provide a night-time spectacle in their own right.

Manyō Club

万葉倶楽部, Manyō Kaiabu • 2-7-1 Shinkō • Daily 10am–9pm • ¥2700 • ☎ 045 663 4126

Spread over five floors, the **Manyō Club** spa complex offers a variety of hot-spring baths – the water is trucked in from Atami onsen down the coast – in addition to massages and treatments, restaurants and relaxation rooms. The rooftop is one of the best places from which to admire the night-time colour display of the Cosmo Clock.

Cup Noodle Museum

カップヌードルミュージアム • 2-3-4 Shinkō • 10am–6pm; closed Tues • ¥500 • ☎ 045 345 0825, ⓦ cupnoodles-museum.jp

Instant noodles are one of Asia's most important snacks, and the contribution made since 1971 by the Japanese Cup Noodle brand is traced in the fun, beautifully designed **Cup Noodle Museum**. There are all sorts of interactive displays, though for many the main sources of enjoyment are sampling some of the many Cup Noodle varieties, and purchasing quirky branded souvenirs.

ARRIVAL AND DEPARTURE **YOKOHAMA**

Located on the northwest side of town, **Yokohama Station** functions as the city's main transport hub, offering train, subway, bus and even ferry connections, and featuring several gargantuan department stores.

BY TRAIN

From Shibuya The fast Tōkyū-Tōyoko line (every 5–10min; 30min; ¥270) runs via Naka-Meguro, calling at Yokohama Station before heading off underground to Minato Mirai and terminating at Motomachi-Chūkagai Station. Some services actually start life way back in Saitama prefecture as Fukutoshin metro trains, stopping at Ikebukuro and Shinjuku-sanchōme stations before switching identity in Shibuya. JR's Shōnan-Shinjuku line runs into Yokohama Station from Shibuya and Shinjuku (every 20–30min; 24min; ¥390).

From Tokyo Station You can choose from the Tōkaidō or Yokosuka lines (both every 5–10min; 30min; ¥470), or the Keihin-Tōhoku line (every 5–10min; 40min; ¥470). All three are JR lines; the first two terminate at Yokohama Station, while the latter continues to Sakuragichō, Kannai and Ishikawachō.

From Narita Airport A few services on JR's Narita Express (N'EX) run to Yokohama Station (hourly; 1hr 30min; ¥4290), but some of these divide at Tokyo Station, so check before you get on. Otherwise, you can take the cheaper JR rapid train (2hr; ¥1940).

From Haneda Airport Keihin-Kyūkō line trains run frequently to Yokohama Station (every 10min; 30min; ¥450), or there are limousine buses (every 10min; 30min; ¥720).

From Shin-Yokohama Shinkansen trains pause briefly at Shin-Yokohama, 5km north of the centre. From here there's a subway link to the main Yokohama Station (11min; ¥240), Sakuragichō and Kannai, but it's cheaper and usually quicker to get the first passing JR Yokohama-line train (¥170).

BY FERRY

Ferries to and from Ōshima (departing 11.20pm Fri & Sat, returning 2.30pm Sat & Sun; 6hr 30min out, 3hr 30min back) call at Ōsanbashi pier, a short walk from the city centre.

BY BUS

Services head around the country from the depot at Yokohama train station.

Destinations Hirosaki (1 daily; 9hr 45min); Hiroshima (1 daily; 12hr); Kyoto (2 daily; 6hr 30min–9hr); Nagoya (1 daily; 6hr 30min); Nara (1 daily; 8hr); Osaka (3 daily; 7hr 15min–8hr).

GETTING AROUND

By train Getting around central Yokohama is easy on either the Tōkyū-Tōyoko line or the JR Negishi line (the local name for Keihin-Tōhoku trains). Trains on both lines run every 5min.

By subway A single subway line connects Kannai and stations north to Shin-Yokohama, on the Shinkansen line; services run every 5–15min.

By Akai Kutsu sightseeing bus A retro-style sightseeing bus runs from outside Sakuragichō Station's east exit via Minato Mirai, the Akarenga complex, Chinatown and Yamashita-kōen to Harbour View Park, then loops back via Ōsanbashi pier. Services run every 10–15min (¥100 per hop, or ¥300 for a day-pass).

By ferry Perhaps the most enjoyable way of getting about the city is on the *Sea Bass* ferries (Ⓦ yokohama-cruising.jp) that shuttle between Yokohama Station (from a pier in the Bay Quarter shopping complex) and southerly Yamashita-kōen, with some services stopping at Minato Mirai and Akarenga en route. There are departures every 15min (daily 10am–7.30pm; ¥350–700).

INFORMATION

Tourist information The most useful centre (daily: April–Nov 9am–6pm; Dec–March 9am–7pm; ☏ 045 211 0111) is immediately outside Sakuragichō Station's east entrance, but there's another in the harbourfront Sanbo Centre (Mon–Fri 9am–5pm; ☏ 045 641 4759), east of Kannai Station. There's also a booth in the underground concourse at Yokohama Station (daily 9am–7pm; ☏ 045 441 7300).

ACCOMMODATION

★**Daiwa Roynet** ダイワロイネットホテル 204-1 Yamashita-chō, Naka-ku ☏ 045 664 3745, Ⓦ daiwaroynet .jp. Secure, clean and in a good location, this is a good-value business hotel, where rooms are both cheaper and more stylish than anything else in this category. 📶 **¥10,300**

Navios Yokohama ナヴィオス横浜 Shinkō-chō, Naka-ku ☏ 045 633 6000, Ⓦ navios-yokohama.com. One of the best-value options in Yokohama; ask for a room facing the Landmark Tower for terrific night-time views. Western-style doubles **¥15,000**, Japanese-style doubles **¥19,000**

Hotel New Grand ホテルニューグランド 10 Yamashita-chō, Naka-ku ☏ 045 681 1841, Ⓦ hotel-newgrand .co.jp/english. Built in the late 1920s in European style, the main building of this upmarket hotel retains some of its original elegance, while many rooms in the newer tower offer bay views. **¥39,000**

Royal Park Hotel ローヤルパークホテル 2-2-1-3 Minato Mirai, Nishi-ku ☏ 045 221 1111, Ⓦ yrph.com. This hotel occupies the 52nd to 67th floors of the Landmark Tower, so spectacular views are guaranteed. Rooms are fairly spacious and come with good-sized bathrooms. As well as a fitness club and swimming pool (extra charges apply), facilities include a tea ceremony room and the *Sirius Sky Lounge*. 📶 **¥30,000**

Hostel Village ホステルヴィレッジ 3-11-2 Matsukage-chō, Naka-ku ☏ 045 663 3696, Ⓦ yokohama .hostelvillage.com. As the name suggests, this hostel is spread across various buildings; the main location is nice and clean, has a fun rooftop area, and holds regular parties and other themed nights. They also do good weekly and monthly deals for those who'll be in Yokohama a while. 🛜 Dorms **¥2400**, doubles **¥4700**

EATING

One of Yokohama's highlights is sampling the enormous variety of restaurants and snack-food outlets cramming the streets of **Chinatown**; most are much of a muchness, selling the same food in all-you-can-eat form. In fine weather, the casual little eating places on the ground floor of **Akarenga** (see p.186) are a good option.

CHINATOWN

Bairan 梅蘭 133-10 Yamashita-chō ☎045 651 6695, ⓦbairan.jp. Small, unpretentious restaurant tucked in the backstreets and known for its Bairan *yakisoba*, stir-fried noodles served like a sort of pie, crispy on the outside and with various varieties of juicy stuffing (from ¥940). Mon–Fri 11.30am–3pm & 5–10pm, Sat & Sun 11am–10pm.

Edosei 江戸清 192 Yamashita-chō ☎045 681 3133. Mega-size steamed dumplings are the speciality here, stuffed with interesting ingredients including black bean and walnut, onion and seafood, shrimp and chilli, plus the usual barbecued pork. Prices vary, but one dumpling can be as much as ¥500. Mon–Fri 9am–8pm, Sat & Sun 9am–9pm.

Manchinrō 萬珍樓 153 Yamashita-chō ☎045 681 4004, ⓦmanchinro.com. This famous restaurant has been serving tasty Cantonese cuisine since 1892. Though prices are on the high side, the portions are generous; noodle and fried-rice dishes start at around ¥1200, lunch sets at ¥2200, and evening course menus at ¥5000. The branch behind serves a full range of dim sum. Daily 11am–10pm.

Ryokuen 緑苑 220 Yamashita-chō ☎045 651 5651. Simple, stylish Chinese teashop with some thirty types of tea on the menu, from ¥800 for a pot. 11.30am–6.30pm; closed Thurs.

Shōfukumon 招福門 81-3 Yamashita-chō ☎045 664 4141. Multistorey restaurant offering all-you-can-eat dim sum deals for ¥3000, plus fried rice and soup. Mon–Fri 11.30am–10pm, Sat & Sun 11am–10pm.

THE REST OF THE CITY

★**Café de la Presse** カフェードゥラプレス 2F Media Centre Building, 11 Nihon-dōri ☎045 222 3348. Viennese-style café in the corner of one of Yokohama's grand old buildings. Go for a coffee or tea (from ¥480), with a dessert such as macaroons or their utterly delectable crème brûlée (¥600). They also serve croques monsieur (¥800), and other sandwiches and light meals. Tues–Sun 10am–8pm.

Chano-ma チャノマ 3F Akarenga 2, 1-1-2 Shinkō, Naka-ku ☎045 650 8228. Sit back with a cocktail and nibble modern Japanese dishes at this large, relaxed restaurant-cum-tearoom – a sister of the one in Tokyo (see p.146) – with a very contemporary vibe. Lunch sets from ¥1400. Mon–Thurs & Sun 11am–11pm, Fri & Sat 11am–5am.

Enokitei えの木てい 89-6 Yamate-chō ☎045 623 2288. Set in a venerable Yamate former residence, this cute English-style café serves dainty sandwiches and home-made cakes. Tues–Fri 11am–7pm.

Yamate Jūbankan 山手十番館 247 Yamate-chō ☎045 621 4466. Pleasant French restaurant in a pretty clapboard house opposite the Foreigners' Cemetery. Although the upstairs is on the formal side (set lunches from ¥3500), the more casual ground floor offers sandwiches and *croques* (¥800), as well as a more filling lunch platter (¥2000). In July and August the restaurant runs a popular beer garden. Daily 11am–9pm.

DRINKING AND NIGHTLIFE

Motion Blue モーションブルー 3F Akarenga 2, 1-1-2 Shinkō, Naka-ku ☎045 226 1919. This cool jazz club attracts top acts – for which you'll usually pay top prices (though there are regular free performances, too). There's no charge, though, to park yourself at the attached *Bar Tune*'s long counter and soak up the ambience. Mon–Fri 5pm–midnight, Sat & Sun 11am–1.30pm & 5pm–midnight.

The Tavern ザタヴァーン B1F 2-14 Minami Saiwai-chō ☎045 322 9727, ⓦthe-tavern.com. British-style pub popular with local expats. It serves the sort of bar food that will appeal to homesick Brits, including good fish and chips (¥1240). Mon & Tues 6pm–midnight, Wed & Thurs 6pm–1am, Fri 6pm–5am, Sat 5pm–5am, Sun noon–midnight.

Kamakura and around

鎌倉

The small, relaxed town of **KAMAKURA** lies an hour's train ride south of Tokyo, trapped between the sea and a circle of wooded hills. The town is steeped in history, and many of its 65 temples and 19 shrines date back some eight centuries, when, for a brief and tumultuous period, it was Japan's political and military centre. Its most famous sight is the **Daibutsu**, a glorious bronze Buddha surrounded by trees, but the town's ancient **Zen temples** are equally compelling. Kamakura's prime sights can be covered on a day-trip from Tokyo, but the town more than justifies a two-day visit, allowing you time to explore the enchanting temples of **east Kamakura** and follow one of the gentle "hiking courses" up into the hills, or head out west to **Enoshima** and its own clutch of appealing sights.

Brief history

In 1185 the warlord **Minamoto Yoritomo** became the first permanent shogun and the effective ruler of Japan. Seven years later he established his military government – known as the *bakufu*, or "tent government" – in Kamakura. Over the next century, dozens of grand monuments were built here, notably the great Zen temples founded by monks fleeing Song-dynasty China. Zen Buddhism flourished under the patronage of a warrior class who shared similar ideals of devotion to duty and rigorous self-discipline.

The Minamoto rule was brief and violent. Almost immediately, Yoritomo turned against his valiant younger brother, **Yoshitsune**, who had led the clan's armies, and hounded him until Yoshitsune committed ritual suicide (*seppuku*) – a favourite tale of kabuki theatre. Both the second and third Minamoto shoguns were murdered, and in 1219 power passed to the Hōjō clan, who ruled as fairly able regents behind puppet shoguns. Their downfall followed the Mongol invasions in the late thirteenth century, and in 1333 Emperor Go-Daigo wrested power back to Kyoto; as the imperial armies

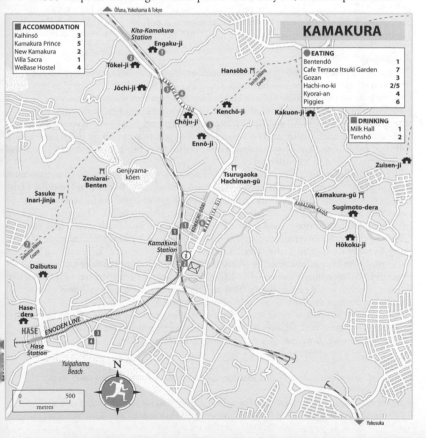

> ## KAMAKURA THROUGH THE YEAR
>
> The town's biggest **festivals** take place in early April (second Sun to third or fourth Sun) and mid-September, including displays of horseback archery and costume parades, though the summer fireworks display (second Tues in Aug) over Sugami Bay is the most spectacular event.
>
> Kamakura is also well known for its **spring blossoms** and **autumn colours**, while many temple gardens are famous for a particular flower – for example, Japanese apricot at Zuisen-ji and Tōkei-ji (Feb) and hydrangea at Meigetsu-in (mid-June).

2

approached Kamakura, the last Hōjō regent and an estimated eight hundred retainers committed *seppuku*. Kamakura remained an important military centre before fading into obscurity in the late fifteenth century. Its **temples**, however, continued to attract religious pilgrims until Kamakura was "rediscovered" in the last century as a tourist destination and a desirable residential area within commuting distance of Tokyo.

Kita-Kamakura

北鎌倉

As the Tokyo train nears **Kita-Kamakura** Station, urban sprawl gradually gives way to gentle, forested hills which provide the backdrop for some of Kamakura's greatest Zen temples. Chief among these are **Kenchō-ji** and the wonderfully atmospheric **Engaku-ji**. It takes over an hour to cover the prime sights, walking south along the main road, the Kamakura-kaidō, to the edge of central Kamakura. If you have more time, follow the Daibutsu Hiking Course (see box, p.192) up into the western hills.

Engaku-ji

円覚寺 • 409 Yama-no-uchi • Daily: April–Oct 8am–5pm; Nov–March 8am–4pm • ¥300; Butsunichi-an ¥100, or ¥500 including tea

The second most important – but most satisfying – of Kamakura's major Zen temples, **Engaku-ji** lies buried among ancient cedars just two minutes' walk east of Kita-Kamakura Station. It was founded in 1282 to honour victims (on both sides) of the ultimately unsuccessful Mongolian invasions in 1274 and 1281. The layout follows a traditional Chinese Zen formula – a pond and bridge (now cut off by the train tracks), followed by a succession of somewhat austere buildings – but the encroaching trees and secretive gardens add a gentler touch.

The first building inside the compound is Engaku-ji's two-storey main gate, **San-mon**, a magnificent structure rebuilt in 1783. Beyond, the modern **Butsu-den** (Buddha Hall) houses the temple's primary Buddha image, haloed in soft light, while behind it the charming **Shari-den** lies tucked off to the left past an oblong pond. This small reliquary, usually closed to visitors, is said to contain a tooth of the Buddha brought here from China in the early thirteenth century. It's also considered Japan's finest example of Song-dynasty Zen architecture, albeit a sixteenth-century replica. The main path continues gently uphill to another pretty thatched building, **Butsunichi-an**, where regent Hōjō Tokimune was buried in 1284; in fine weather tea is served in its attractive garden. Finally, you'll come to tiny **Ōbai-in**, which enshrines a pale yellow Kannon statue, but its best attribute is a nicely informal garden.

On the way out, follow signs up a steep flight of steps to the left of San-mon to find Kamakura's biggest bell, **Ōgane**, forged in 1301 and an impressive 2.5m tall; the adjacent teahouse, *Bentendō* (see p.198), is a great place to relax.

Tōkei-ji

東慶寺 • 1367 Yama-no-uchi • Daily: March–Oct 8.30am–5pm; Nov–Feb 8.30am–4pm • ¥100 • **Treasure House** Tues–Sun 9.30am–3.30pm • ¥300 • ⓦ tokeiji.com

A short walk along the main road from Engaku-ji, **Tōkei-ji** was founded as a nunnery in 1285 by the young widow of Hōjō Tokimune. The intimate temple boasts a pleasing

ZAZEN

Zazen, or sitting meditation, is a crucial aspect of Zen Buddhist training, particularly among followers of the Rinzai sect. Several temples in Kamakura hold public *zazen* sessions at various levels, of which the most accessible are those at Engaku-ji (April–Oct daily 5.30am; Nov–March daily 6am; plus second and fourth Sun of month at 10am; ☎0467 22 0478) and Kenchō-ji (Fri & Sat 5pm in the Hōjō; ☎0467 22 0981). These hour-long sessions are free and no reservations are required, though it's best to check the current schedule with the temple or Kamakura tourist office (see p.197) before setting out, and you should get there at least fifteen minutes early. Though non-Japanese speakers are welcome, you'll get much more out of it if you have someone with you who can translate.

cluster of buildings and a profusion of flowers at almost any time of year: Japanese apricot in February, magnolia and peach in late March, followed by peonies and then irises in early June; September is the season for cascades of bush clover. There's an elegant café just downhill from the entrance, and the start of the wonderful Daibutsu Hiking Course (see box, p.192) is also nearby.

Tōkei-ji is more popularly known as the **"Divorce Temple"**. Up until the mid-nineteenth century, when women were given the legal right to seek divorce, this was one of the few places where wives could escape domestic ill-treatment. If they reached the sanctuary, which many didn't, they automatically received a divorce after three years according to traditional temple law. Husbands could be summoned to resolve the dispute or, ultimately, sign the divorce papers. Some of these documents are preserved in the **Treasure House**, including two books detailing the women's reasons for seeking sanctuary – unfortunately, not translated.

Kenchō-ji

建長寺 • 8 Yama-no-uchi • Daily 8.30am–4.30pm • ¥300 • ⓦ kenchoji.com

The greatest of Kamakura's Zen temples is **Kenchō-ji**, headquarters of the Rinzai sect and Japan's oldest Zen training monastery. More formal than Engaku-ji and a lot less peaceful, largely because of the neighbouring high school, Kenchō-ji contains several important buildings, most of which have been relocated here from Tokyo and Kyoto to replace those lost since the temple's foundation in 1253. The design of the layout shows a strong Chinese influence; the founding abbot was another Song Chinese émigré, in this case working under the patronage of Hōjō Tokiyori, the devout fifth regent and father of Engaku-ji's Tokimune.

The main complex

The **main complex** begins with the towering, copper-roofed **San-mon**, an eighteenth-century reconstruction, to the right of which hangs the original temple bell, cast in 1255 and considered one of Japan's most beautiful. Beyond San-mon, a grove of gnarled and twisted juniper trees hides the dainty, nicely dilapidated **Butsu-den**. The main image is, unusually, of Jizō (the guardian deity of children) seated on a lotus throne, his bright, half-closed eyes piercing the gloom. Behind is the **Hattō**, or lecture hall, one of Japan's largest wooden Buddhist buildings. The curvaceous Chinese-style gate, **Kara-mon**, and the **Hōjō** hall beyond are much more attractive structures. Walk round the latter's balcony to find a **pond-garden** generally attributed to a thirteenth-century monk, making it Japan's oldest-surviving Zen garden.

Central Kamakura

Modern Kamakura revolves around the central **Kamakura Station** and a couple of touristy streets leading to the town's most important shrine, **Tsurugaoka Hachiman-gū**. The traditional approach to this grand edifice lies along **Wakamiya-ōji**, which runs straight from the sea to the shrine entrance. Shops here peddle a motley collection of

2

KAMAKURA HIKING COURSES

There are two extremely pleasant **hiking courses** to tackle in central Kamakura, both giving you the chance to enjoy some lovely wooded scenery. The hikes, while a decent workout, are both pretty straightforward and quite possible to do in flip-flops (though trickier if it has been raining).

DAIBUTSU HIKING COURSE

Past **Tōkei-ji** (東慶寺) and along the main valley is Jōchi-ji (浄智寺), beside which you'll find steps which mark the start of the **Daibutsu Hiking Course** (大仏ハイキングコース). This meandering 2.2km-long ridgetop path makes an enjoyable approach to the **Daibutsu**, Hase's Great Buddha (see p.194). Even if you're not walking the whole route it's well worth going as far as the captivating cave-shrine dedicated to the goddess **Zeniarai Benten** (銭洗弁天), the "Money-Washing Benten", an incarnation of the goddess of good fortune, music and water. To find it, follow the somewhat erratic signs from **Genjiyama-kōen** (源氏山公園), a pleasant park, which lead you along a trail heading vaguely south through the park to a road junction where the main trail turns right; here, you'll pick up signs pointing steeply downhill to where a *torii* and banners mark the Zeniarai Benten shrine entrance. Duck under the tunnel to emerge in a natural amphitheatre filled with a forest of *torii* wreathed in incense and candle smoke. According to tradition, money washed in the spring, which gushes out of a cave on the opposite side from the entrance, is guaranteed to double at the very least, though not immediately.

If you're following the Daibutsu Hiking Course all the way to **Hase**, then rather than retracing your steps, take the path heading south under a tunnel of tightly packed *torii*, zigzagging down to the valley bottom. Turn right at a T-junction to find another avenue of vermilion *torii* leading uphill deep into the cryptomeria forest. At the end lies a simple shrine, **Sasuke Inari-jinja** (佐助稲荷神社), which dates from before the twelfth century and is dedicated to the god of harvests. His messenger is the fox; as you head up the steep path behind, to the left of the shrine buildings, climbing over tangled roots, you'll find fox statues of all shapes and sizes peering out of the surrounding gloom. At the top, turn right and then left at a white signboard to pick up the hiking course for the final 1.5km to the Daibutsu (see p.194).

TEN'EN HIKING COURSE

The **Ten'en Hiking Course** (天園ハイキングコース) begins just behind the Hōjō in Kenchō-ji (see p.191); the path heads up the steep steps past **Hansōbō**, a shrine guarded by statues of long-nosed, mythical *tengu*. It takes roughly one and a half hours to complete the 5km trail, which loops round the town's northeast outskirts to Zuisen-ji (see p.194); for a shorter walk (2.5km), you can cut down earlier to Kamakura-gū (see opposite). This trail is less busy than the Daibutsu course, and even on a sunny weekend, it's quite possible to find yourself alone in the forest for decent periods of time.

souvenirs and crafts, the most famous of which is *kamakura-bori*, an 800-year-old method of laying lacquer over carved wood. More popular, however, is *hato*, a French-style biscuit first made by Toshimaya bakers a century ago. Shadowing Wakamiya-ōji to the west is **Komachi-dōri**, a narrow, pedestrian-only shopping street, packed with more souvenir shops, restaurants and, increasingly, trendy boutiques.

Tsurugaoka Hachiman-gū

鶴岡八幡宮 • 2-1-31 Yuki-no-shita • Daily 6am–8.30pm • Free

A majestic, vermilion-lacquered *torii* marks the front entrance to **Tsurugaoka Hachiman-gū**, the Minamoto clan's guardian shrine since 1063. Hachiman-gū, as it's popularly known, was moved to its present site in 1191, since when it has witnessed some of the more unsavoury episodes of Kamakura history. Most of the present buildings date from the early nineteenth century, and their striking red paintwork, combined with the parade of souvenir stalls and the constant bustle of people, creates a festive atmosphere in sharp contrast to that of Kamakura's more secluded Zen temples.

Three humpback bridges lead into the shrine compound between two connected ponds known as **Genpei-ike**. These were designed by Minamoto Yoritomo's wife, Hōjō

Masako, and are full of heavy, complicated symbolism, anticipating the longed-for victory of her husband's clan over their bitter enemies, the Taira; strangely, the bloodthirsty Masako was of Taira stock.

The Mai-den

The **Mai-den**, an open-sided stage at the end of a broad avenue, was the scene of an unhappy event in 1186, when Yoritomo forced his brother's mistress, Shizuka, to dance for the assembled samurai. Yoritomo wanted his popular brother, Yoshitsune, killed, and was holding Shizuka prisoner in the hope of discovering his whereabouts; instead, she made a defiant declaration of love and only narrowly escaped death herself, though her newborn son was murdered soon after. Her bravery is commemorated with classical dances and nō plays during the shrine **festival** (Sept 14–16), which also features demonstrations of horseback archery on the final day.

The main shrine

Beyond the Mai-den, a long flight of steps leads up beside a knobbly, ancient ginkgo tree, reputedly 1000 years old and scene of the third shogun's murder by his vengeful nephew, to the **main shrine**. It's an attractive collection of buildings set among trees, though, as with all Shintō shrines, you can only peer in. Appropriately, the principal deity, Hachiman, is the God of War.

East Kamakura

The eastern side of Kamakura contains a scattering of less-visited shrines and temples, including two of the town's most enchanting corners. It's possible to cover the area on foot in a half-day, or less if you hop on a bus for the return journey.

Hōkoku-ji

報国寺 • 2-7-4 Jomyoji • Daily 9am–4pm • Bamboo gardens ¥200

The well-tended gardens and simple wooden buildings of **Hōkoku-ji**, or Take-dera – the "Bamboo Temple" – are attractive in themselves, but the temple is best known for a grove of evergreen bamboo protected by the encircling cliffs. This dappled forest of thick, gently curved stems, where tinkling water spouts and the soft creaking of the wind-rocked canes muffle the outside world, would seem the perfect place for the monks' meditation. Too soon, though, the path emerges beside the manicured rear garden, which was created by the temple's founding priest in the thirteenth century.

Sugimoto-dera

杉本寺 • 903 Nikaido • Daily 8am–4.30pm • ¥200

One of Kamakura's oldest temples, **Sugimoto-dera** is set at the top of a steep, foot-worn staircase lined with fluttering white flags. Standing in a woodland clearing, the small, thatched temple, founded in 734, exudes a real sense of history. Inside its smoke-blackened hall, spattered with pilgrims' prayer stickers, you can slip off your shoes and take a look behind the altar at the three wooden statues of Jūichimen Kannon, the eleven-faced Goddess of Mercy. The images were carved at different times by famous monks, but all three are at least 1000 years old. According to legend, they survived a devastating fire in 1189 by taking shelter – all by themselves – behind a giant tree; since then the temple has been known as Sugimoto ("Under the Cedar").

Kamakura-gū

鎌倉宮 • 154 Nikaido • Daily 9am–4pm • ¥300

Mainly of interest for its history and torchlight nō dramas in early October, **Kamakura-gū** was founded by Emperor Meiji in 1869 to encourage support for his new imperial regime. The shrine is dedicated to Prince Morinaga, a forgotten fourteenth-century hero who helped briefly restore his father, Emperor Go-Daigo, to the throne. The prince was soon denounced, however, by power-hungry rivals and held for nine months in a Kamakura cave before being executed. The small cave and a desultory treasure house lie to the rear of the classically styled shrine, but don't really justify the entry fee.

A road heading north from Kamakura-gū marks the beginning – or end – of the short cut to the Ten'en Hiking Course (see box, p.192).

Zuisen-ji

瑞泉寺 • 710 Nikaido • Daily 9am–4.30pm • ¥200

Starting point of the main trail of the Ten'en Hiking Course (see box, p.192), **Zuisen-ji**'s quiet, wooded location and luxuriant gardens make it an attractive spot, though the temple's fourteenth-century Zen garden, to the rear of the main building, is rather dilapidated.

Hase

長谷

The west side of Kamakura, an area known as **Hase**, is home to the town's most famous sight, the **Daibutsu** (Great Buddha), cast in bronze nearly 750 years ago. On the way, it's worth visiting **Hase-dera** to see an image of Kannon, the Goddess of Mercy, which is said to be Japan's largest wooden statue. Both these sights are within walking distance of Hase Station, three stops from Kamakura Station on the private Enoden line.

Hase-dera

長谷寺 • Daily: March–Sept 8am–5pm; Oct–Feb 8am–4.30pm • ¥300 • ⓦ hasedera.jp • Hase Station

Hase-dera stands high on the hillside a few minutes' walk north of Hase Station, with good views of Kamakura and across Yuigahama beach to the Miura peninsula beyond. Though the temple's present layout dates from the mid-thirteenth century, according to legend it was founded in 736, when a wooden eleven-faced Kannon was washed ashore nearby. The statue is supposedly one of a pair carved from a single camphor tree in 721 by a monk in the original Hase, near Nara; he placed one Kannon in a local temple and pushed the other out to sea.

Nowadays the **Kamakura Kannon** – just over 9m tall and gleaming with gold leaf (a fourteenth-century embellishment) – resides in an attractive, chocolate-brown and cream building at the top of the temple steps. This central hall is flanked by two smaller buildings: the right hall houses a large Amidha Buddha carved in 1189 for Minamoto Yoritomo's 42nd birthday to ward off the bad luck traditionally associated with that age; the one on the left shelters a copy of an early fifteenth-century statue of Daikoku-ten, the cheerful God of Wealth. The real statue is in the small **treasure hall** immediately behind, alongside the original temple bell, cast in 1264. The next building along is the **Sutra Repository**, where a revolving drum contains a complete set of Buddhist scriptures – one turn of the wheel is equivalent to reading the whole lot. In the far northern corner of the complex, a **cave** contains statues of the goddess Benten and her sixteen children, or disciples, though it can't compete with the atmospheric setting of the Zeniarai Benten cave-shrine (see box, p.192).

Ranks of **jizō statues** are a common sight in Hase-dera, some clutching sweets or "windmills" and wrapped in tiny woollen mufflers; these sad little figures commemorate stillborn or aborted children.

The Daibutsu

大仏 • 4-2-28 Hase • Daily: April–Sept 7am–6pm; Oct–March 7am–5.30pm • ¥200 • **Entering statue** Daily 8am–4.30pm • ¥20

After all the hype, the **Daibutsu**, in the grounds of Kōtoku-in temple, can seem a little disappointing at first sight. But as you approach, and the Great Buddha's serene, rather

2

aloof face comes more clearly into view, the magic begins to take hold. He sits on a stone pedestal, a broad-shouldered figure lost in deep meditation, with his head slightly bowed, his face and robes streaked grey-green by centuries of sun, wind and rain. The 13m-tall image represents Amida Nyorai, the future Buddha who receives souls into the Western Paradise, and was built under the orders of Minamoto Yoritomo to rival the larger Nara Buddha, near Kyoto. Completed in 1252, the statue is constructed of bronze plates bolted together around a hollow frame – you can climb inside for a fee – and evidence suggests that, at some time, it was covered in gold leaf. Amazingly, it has withstood fires, typhoons, the tsunami of 1495 which washed away its surrounding hall, and even the Great Earthquake of 1923.

Enoshima

江の島

Tied to the mainland by a 600m-long bridge, and easily reached from Kamakura, the tiny, sacred island of **Enoshima** – less than 1km from end to end and largely covered with woods – has a few sights, including some shrines and a botanical garden, but the prime appeal is wandering its network of well-marked paths.

The private Enoden-line train rattles from Kamakura to Enoshima Station, from where it's roughly a fifteen-minute walk southwest to the island, via a bridge constructed over the original sand spit. Once over the bridge, walk straight ahead under the bronze *torii* and uphill past restaurants and souvenir shops to where the steps to the main shrine begin; though the climb's easy enough, there are three **escalators** tunnelled through the hillside (¥350 for all three).

Enoshima-jinja

江の島神社 • Daily 9am–4.30pm • ¥150

The island features a wide-ranging shrine area – **Enoshima-jinja** – with three separate components, founded in the thirteenth century and dedicated to the guardian of sailors and fisherfolk. Inside one, Hatsu-no-miya, sits Enoshima's most famous relic – a naked **statue of Benten**, housed in an octagonal hall halfway up the hill. The statue has been here since the days of Minamoto Yoritomo (1147–99) of the Kamakura Shogunate, who prayed to it for victory over the contemporary Fujiwara clan. Although ranked among Japan's top three Benten images, it's a little hard to see what all the fuss is about.

Samuel Cocking Park

サムエル・コッキング苑, Samyueru Cokkingu-en • April–June, Sept & Oct Mon–Fri 9am–6pm, Sat & Sun 9am–8pm; July & Aug daily 9am–8pm; Nov–March Mon–Fri 9am–5pm, Sat & Sun 9am–8pm • Park ¥200, lighthouse ¥300

This nicely laid-out botanical garden is known as the **Samuel Cocking Park** after the English merchant and horticulturalist who built Japan's first greenhouse here in 1880. If it's a clear day, you'll get good views south to Ōshima's (occasionally smoking) volcano, and west to Fuji from the lighthouse inside the garden.

ARRIVAL AND DEPARTURE	KAMAKURA AND AROUND

KAMAKURA

By train You can take either the JR Yokosuka line from Tokyo Station via Yokohama, or the JR Shōnan-Shinjuku line from Shinjuku via Shibuya and Yokohama (both 1hr; ¥920); from Tokyo Station, make sure you board a Yokosuka- or Kurihama-bound train to avoid changing at Ōfuna. Trains stop at Kita-Kamakura Station before pulling into the main Kamakura Station a few minutes later.

ENOSHIMA

By train If you're visiting Enoshima after Kamakura, you can hop onto the Enoden line (ⓦenoden.co.jp) at Kamakura Station (every 12min; 25min; ¥260); trains pull in to Enoshima Station, from where it's roughly a 15min walk southwest to the island, over the bridge. Alternatively, if you're heading straight to Enoshima from Tokyo, the most straightforward route is the Odakyū-Enoshima line direct from Shinjuku to Katase-Enoshima Station (片瀬江ノ島

駅), which lies just north of the bridge, on the western side of the river; a helpful travel pass (see below) is available for this route.

Travel pass If you're planning to visit Enoshima, it's worth considering the Odakyū Enoshima-Kamakura Freepass, a one-day discount ticket (¥1470) covering a return trip to Katase-Enoshima Station on the Odakyū line from Shinjuku, and unlimited travel on the Enoden line; it means that you'll have to hit Enoshima first and last, while visiting Kamakura on a loop trip, but it's feasible.

GETTING AROUND

By train Given the narrow roads and amount of traffic, it's usually quickest to use the trains as far as possible and then walk. On the west side of Kamakura Station are ticket machines and platforms for the private Enoden line (ⓦ enoden.co.jp) to Hase and Enoshima (every 12min; daily 6am–11pm); Kamakura to Hase costs ¥190, to Enoshima ¥260. If you plan to hop on and off the Enoden line a lot and haven't got any other form of discount ticket, it's worth investing in the Kamakura-Enoshima Pass (¥700), which entitles you to unlimited travel on this line, plus JR services.

By bus The only time a bus might come in handy is for the more far-flung restaurants or the eastern shrines and temples. Local buses depart from the main station concourse; for the eastern shrines you want stand 4 for Kamakura-gū and stand 5 for Sugimoto-dera (¥200 minimum fare). To make three or more journeys by bus, you'll save money by buying a Kamakura Free Kippu day pass (¥550), which is available from the JR ticket office. The pass also covers JR trains from Kamakura to Kita-Kamakura and Enoden line services as far as Hase.

INFORMATION

Kamakura tourist office Outside the main, eastern exit of Kamakura Station, immediately to the right, there's a small tourist information window (daily: April–Sept 9am–5.30pm; Oct–March 9am–5pm; ☏ 0467 23 3050), with English-speaking staff.

Enoshima tourist office You can pick up an English-language map of the island at the small tourist office, which is on your left as you come off the bridge (daily 10am–5pm; ☏ 0466 26 9544, ⓦ fujisawa-kanko.jp).

Services There's an international ATM (Mon–Fri 8am–9pm, Sat & Sun 8am–7pm) at the post office on Wakamiya-ōji.

ACCOMMODATION

Most people visit Kamakura on a day-trip from Tokyo, but if you do want to stay over note that many places charge more at weekends and during peak holiday periods, when it can be tough to get a room. Central Kamakura offers little budget accommodation, but has a fair choice of mid-range hotels.

Kaihinso かいひん荘 4-8-14 Yuigahama ☏ 0467 22 0960, ⓦ kaihinso.jp. Nestled by the beach, this hotel is one for the romantics, with elegant rooms and a peaceful setting. The building went up in 1924; though added to since, the Western-style section is now protected property. You can stay in one of the two rooms here, or in tatami rooms in the newer Japanese section; some of the latter have views onto the garden. ☏ **¥26,000**

★**Kamakura Prince** ホテル鎌倉プリンス 1-2-18 Shichirigahama-higashi ☏ 0467 32 1111, ⓦ princehotels.com/kamakura. Located by the beach, just a couple of stops west of Hase Station on the Enoden line, this hotel is a real winner, and great value at this price range. Guest rooms surround a delightful pool, while floor-to-ceiling windows offer generous ocean views (from some rooms you can see Mt Fuji, too); a golf range and excellent *teppanyaki* restaurant round things off. ☏ **¥12,500**

New Kamakura ホテルニューカマクラ 13-2 Onari-machi ☏ 0467 22 2230, ⓦ newkamakura.com. One of the best-value places to stay in Kamakura is this early twentieth-century, Western-style building by Kamakura Station. It's a little bit worn, but most rooms are light and airy, with a choice of Western or Japanese style. ☏ **¥7000**

★**Villa Sacra** ヴィラサクラ 13-29 Onari-machi ☏ 0467 22 5311, ⓦ villasacra.com. For something a bit different, give this modern ryokan a whirl. It's situated in an old Japanese house, renovated with funky artistic flourishes. Staff are switched on, and the common room is a nice place to hang out with other guests. No meals; breakfast available for an extra fee. ☏ **¥8500**

★**WeBase Hostel** ウィーベースホステル 4-10-7 Yuigahama ☏ 0467 22 1221, ⓦ we-base.jp. Superbly convenient hostel, just over 15min on foot from Kamakura Station, and 2min from the beach. Brand new at the time of writing, it's a large place which feels rather more modern than you'd expect in Kamakura – features include a couple of outdoor showers, a large veranda for coffee and chit-chat, and even a yoga studio. ☏ Dorms **¥3800**, doubles **¥9600**

EATING

Kamakura is famous for its beautifully presented **Buddhist vegetarian cuisine**, known as *shōjin ryōri*, though there's plenty more casual dining on offer at local restaurants. You can have a stab at creating some Japanese food yourself with

2

the **cooking classes** on offer from Mariko, a friendly local (from ¥7000 for 2–3hr; various options available, in English; ⓦjapanese-cooking-class-kamakura.com).

KAMAKURA

Bentendō 弁天堂 1-7-6 Ko-machi ☎0467 25 3500. At this wonderful teahouse in the grounds of Engaku-ji temple (see p.190), you can enjoy a cup of *matcha* (¥600) while admiring the view across the valley to Tōkei-ji (see p.190). Daily 11am–4pm.

Cafe Terrace Itsuki Garden カフェテラス樹ガーデン On Daibutsu Hiking Course. A fantastic place to get your breath back if you're panting your way along the Daibutsu Hiking Course (see box, p.192). There are seats inside, but in warmer months everyone's out on the steeply arrayed outdoor terraces. Coffees and teas cost around ¥600, alcoholic drinks a little more. Daily 10am–7pm.

Gozan 五山 1435-1 Yamanouchi ☎0467 25 1476. A homely restaurant that's one of the few cheaper places to eat near Kita-Kamakura Station. Their soba and udon dishes (from ¥800) are tasty enough, though if you want a real feed, go for the all-day lunch sets (¥1100). Daily 10am–8pm.

Hachi-no-ki 鉢の木 7 Yamanouchi ☎0467 22 8719; Kita-Kamakura branch ☎046 723 3722. Reservations are recommended for this famous *shōjin ryōri* restaurant beside the entrance to Kenchō-ji, though it's easier to get a table at their newer Kita-Kamakura branches. Whichever you opt for, prices start at around ¥3500. Kenchō-ji branch Tues–Fri 11.30am–2.30pm, Sat & Sun 11am–3pm; main Kita-Kamakura branch 11am–2.30pm & 5–7pm, closed Wed.

Kyorai-an 去来庵 157 Yamanouchi ☎0467 24 9835. Beef stew prepared in a demi-glace sauce has a long history in Japan, and *Kyorai-an* has one of the tastiest around; the set (¥2800) served with toast or rice, salad and coffee is the best value. The restaurant itself is inside a traditional Shōwa-era Japanese house. Mon–Thurs 11am–3pm, Sat & Sun 11am–5pm.

★**Piggies** ピギーズ 1-6-28 Yuki-no-shita ☎0467 95 9063. This small Peruvian-run place certainly stands out from the tourist-trap restaurants in central Kamakura. The Andean soul food includes hearty meat sandwiches (¥800) and *choripapas* (a plate of fries and chunks of chorizo, smothered in sauce; ¥600), plus Peruvian drinks such as luminous-yellow Inca Cola (¥300) and a full range of Cusqueña beer (¥600; the red one's best). At the time of writing, they were also set to introduce ceviche to the menu. Mon–Fri 11am–6pm, Sat & Sun 10am–8pm.

ENOSHIMA

Kinokuniya 紀伊国屋 1-3-16 Tasegaikan ☎0466 22 4247; Enoshima Station. Heading towards Enoshima from the station, you'll pass this simple ryokan-cum-restaurant on your right. It's highly popular with locals on account of the cheap sets; try the *kin-me-dai* (a delicious local red fish, served in soy) set, which goes for ¥1000, including coffee. Daily 11am–4pm.

Shonan Burger 湘南バーガー Enoshima ☎0466 29 0688. Fun little burger bar, just over the Enoshima bridge on the right. Their eponymous burger (¥400) is a real treat: a fishcake patty served with ground radish, perilla leaf and a miniature shoal of tiny sardines – look inside before you bite. Daily 11am–7pm.

DRINKING

Milk Hall ミルクホール 2-3-8 Ko-machi ☎0467 22 1179, ⓦmilkhall.co.jp. Dimly lit, jazz-playing coffee house-cum-antique shop buried in the backstreets west of Komachi-dōri. Best for an evening beer, wine or cocktail (all from ¥700), rather than as a place to eat. Occasional live music. Daily 11am–10.30pm.

★**Tenshō** 天昇 1-3-4 Ko-machi ☎0467 22 6099. Get away from the tourists and down with the locals at this *tachinomiya*, whose raucous nature is the very antithesis of the regular genteel Kamakura atmosphere. *Yakitori* sticks go from ¥130, and sets of Hoppy (a type of fake beer with added alcohol) from ¥400. 3–10pm; closed Mon.

Fuji Five Lakes

The best reason for heading 100km west from Tokyo towards the area known as **FUJI FIVE LAKES** is to climb **Mount Fuji** (富士山), Japan's most sacred volcano and, at 3776m, its highest mountain. Fuji-san, as it's respectfully known by the Japanese, has long been worshipped for its latent power (it last erupted in 1707) and near-perfect symmetry; it is most beautiful from October to May, when the summit is crowned with snow. The climbing season is basically July and August; even if you don't fancy the rather daunting ascent, just getting up close to Japan's most famous national symbol is a memorable experience. Apart from Mount Fuji, don't miss the wonderfully atmospheric shrine **Fuji Sengen-jinja**, in the area's transport hub of **Fuji-Yoshida**.

2

MOUNT TAKAO

An hour west of Shinjuku, **Mount Takao** (高尾山; 600m; ⓦtakaotozan.co.jp), also referred to as Takao-san, is a particularly pleasant place for a quick escape from Tokyo, and is a starting point for longer trails into the mountains in the **Chichibu-Tama National Park** (秩父多摩国立公園). The Keiō line from Shinjuku provides the simplest and cheapest way of reaching the terminus of Takao-san-guchi (1hr; ¥390). After a hike up or a ride on the cable-car or chairlifts (both ¥470 one-way, ¥900 return), you'll get to **Yakuo-in** (薬王院; ⓦtakaosan.or.jp/index .html), a temple founded in the eighth century and notable for the ornate polychromatic carvings that decorate its main hall. It hosts the spectacular **Hiwatarisai** fire ritual on the second Sunday in March back in Takao-san-guchi, where you can watch priests and pilgrims march across hot coals – and even follow them yourself. From the temple, it's a relatively short walk to Takao's summit.

During the summer, the **five lakes** in the area are packed with urbanites fleeing the city. **Kawaguchi-ko** is not only a popular starting point for climbing Mount Fuji, but also features a kimono museum and the easily climbable Mount Tenjō, which has outstanding views of Mount Fuji and the surrounding lakes. The smallest of the other four lakes, horseshoe-shaped **Shōji-ko** (精進湖), 2km west of Kawaguchi-ko, is by far the prettiest. The largest lake, **Yamanaka-ko** (山中湖), southeast of Fuji-Yoshida, is just as developed as Kawaguchi-ko and has fewer attractions, while **Motosu-ko** (本栖湖) and **Sai-ko** (西湖) – the best for swimming and camping – are fine, but not so extraordinary that they're worth the trouble of visiting if you're on a short trip.

Fuji-Yoshida

富士吉田

FUJI-YOSHIDA, some 100km west of Tokyo, lies so close to Mount Fuji that when the dormant volcano eventually blows her top the local residents will be toast. For the time being, however, this small, friendly town acts as an efficient transport hub for the area, as well as the traditional departure point for journeys up the volcano, with frequent buses leaving for Mount Fuji's fifth station (see p.201) from outside the train station. If you're in town in late August, you'll find the main thoroughfare illuminated spectacularly, when seventy bonfires are lit along its length at night-time during the **Yoshida Fire Festival** (August 26 & 27).

Fuji Sengen-jinja

富士浅間神社 • Off Fuji Panorama Line road • 24hr • Free • Head uphill from the station along the main street towards Fuji; turn left where the road hits a junction and walk 200m

The volcano aside, Fuji-Yoshida's main attraction is its large, colourful Shintō shrine, **Fuji Sengen-jinja**, set in a small patch of forest. Sengen shrines, dedicated to the worship of volcanoes, encircle Fuji, and this is the most important, dating right back to 788. The beautiful main shrine was built in 1615. Look around the back for the jolly, brightly painted wooden carvings of the deities Ebisu the fisherman and Daikoku, the god of wealth, good humour and happiness.

Fujikyū Highland

富士急ハイランド • Mon–Fri 9am–5pm, Sat & Sun 9am–6pm; closed second Tues of month • Entry ¥1500; one-day ride pass including entry ¥5700 • ⓦ www.fujiq.jp • One train stop west of Mount Fuji Station

An appealingly ramshackle amusement park, **Fujikyū Highland** features a handful of hair-raising roller coasters, including the Takabisha, which claims to have the world's steepest drop – 121 degrees of terror. Avoid coming at weekends or during holidays unless you enjoy standing in long queues.

2

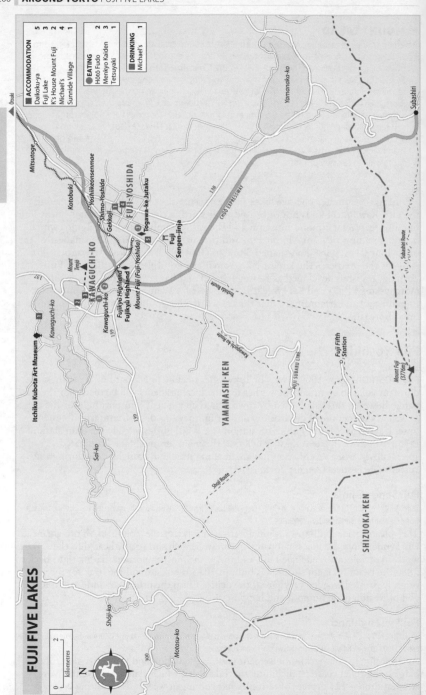

FUJI FIVE LAKES

N

0   kilometres   2

ACCOMMODATION
Daikoku-ya   5
Fuji Lake   3
K's House Mount Fuji   2
Michael's   4
Sunnide Village   1

● **EATING**
Hōtō Fudō   2
Menkyo Kaiden   3
Tetsuyaki   1

■ **DRINKING**
Michael's   1

Ōtsuki

Mitsutoge

Kotobuki

Yoshikeonsennae

Shimo-Yoshida

FUJI-YOSHIDA

Gekkōji

Togawa-ke Jutaku

Fuji
Sengen-jinja

138

CHUŌ EXPRESSWAY

Subashiri

Subashiri Route

Mount
Tenjō

KAWAGUCHI-KO

Kawaguchi-ko

Fujikyu Highland
Fujikyū Highland
Mount Fuji (Fuji-Yoshida)

137

139

Kawaguchi-ko

Itchiku Kubota Art Museum

Yoshida Route

Kawaguchi-ko Route

YAMANASHI-KEN

FUJI SUBARU LINE

Fuji Fifth
Station

Mount Fuji
(3776m)

Sai-ko

Shōji Route

SHIZUOKA-KEN

Shōji-ko

300

Motosu-ko

Yamanaka-ko

Kawaguchi-ko

河口湖

The small lakeside resort of **KAWAGUCHI-KO** lies a couple of kilometres west of Fuji-Yoshida, and makes a more appealing place to stay. With its cruise boats and souvenir shops, it's the tourist hub of the area, and is often choked with traffic during the holiday season. However, the lake is placid and strikingly beautiful.

Tenjō-zan

天上山 • Off Misaka-michi • **Cable-car** Daily 9am–5pm • ¥450 one-way, ¥800 return

The fabulous view of Mount Fuji from the top of **Tenjō-zan** is probably the highlight of a trip to Kawaguchi-ko; of course, you'll also get a great view of the lake from here, since it's right next door. You can either take a cable-car ride up to the lookout, or get some exercise by hiking up, which takes 45 minutes.

Itchiku Kubota Art Museum

久保田一竹美術館, Kubota Itchiku Bijutsukan • 2255 Guchiko, 4km northwest of Kawaguchi-ko • April–Nov daily 9.30am–5.30pm; Dec–March 10am–4.30pm, closed Wed • ¥1300 • ☎ 0555 76 8811, ⊛ itchiku-museum.com • Bus from Kawaguchi-ko Station (25min)

One of the highlights of Kawaguchi-ko is the **Itchiku Kubota Art Museum**, on the northern shore of the lake. This small museum, housed in a Gaudí-esque building, showcases the work of Itchiku Kubota, who refined the traditional *tsujigahana* textile-patterning technique and applied it to kimono. Inside the pyramid-shaped building are pieces from the artist's *Symphony of Light* series, a continuous mountain landscape through the seasons, formed when the kimono are placed side by side.

Mount Fuji

富士山

"A wise man climbs Fuji once. A fool climbs it twice", says the Japanese proverb. Don't let the sight of children and grannies trudging up lull you into a false sense of security: at 3776m in height – more than enough for altitude sickness to take hold – this is a tough climb. There are several **routes** up the volcano, with the ascent on each divided into sections known as **stations**; the summit is the tenth station. Most people take a bus to the fifth station (*go-gōme*) on the **Kawaguchi-ko route**, about halfway up the volcano, where a Swiss-chalet-style gift shop marks the end of the road; for most people, it's four or five hours from here to the summit. The traditional hike, though, begins down at Fuji-Yoshida and ascends via the **Yoshida route**; it takes around five hours to walk up to this route's fifth station, and another six hours to reach the summit. The shortest route (around four hours from the fifth station) is the **Fujinomiya-guchi** to the south, accessible by bus from Shin-Fuji Station, on the Shinkansen route; these buses also pass Fujinomiya JR Station en route. Many climbers choose to ascend the mountain at **night** in order to reach the summit by dawn; during the season, the lights of climbers' torches resemble a line of fireflies trailing up the volcanic scree.

Essential items to carry include at least one litre of water and some food, a torch and batteries, a raincoat and extra clothes. However hot it might be at the start of the climb, the closer you get to the summit the colder it becomes, with temperatures dropping to well below freezing. Sudden rain and lightning strikes are not uncommon.

Mount Fuji's official **climbing season**, when all the facilities on the mountain are open, including lodging huts (see box, p.202) and phones at the summit, runs from July 1 to the end of August. You can climb outside these dates, but don't expect all, or indeed any, of the facilities to be in operation, and be prepared for snow and extreme cold towards the summit. Once you're at the summit, it will take around an hour to make a circuit of the crater.

2

ARRIVAL AND DEPARTURE

By bus The easiest way to reach the Fuji Five Lakes area is to take the bus (¥1800; 1hr 45min in good traffic) from the Shinjuku bus terminal in Tokyo, on the west side of the train station; there are also services from Tokyo Station and Shibuya. During the climbing season there are frequent services, including at least three a day that run directly to the fifth station on the Kawaguchi-ko route, halfway up Mount Fuji (¥1540 one-way, ¥2100 return; 1hr 15min). If you're planning on visiting the Hakone area, the regular bus to Gotemba costs ¥1510

(hourly; 2hr); alternatively, the Fuji Hakone Pass allows you to combine the Fuji Five Lakes area with a trip around Hakone (see box, p.208).

By train The train journey from Shinjuku Station involves transferring from the JR Chūō line to the Fuji Kyūkō line at Ōtsuki, from where local trains (some with Thomas the Tank Engine decoration) chug first to Mount Fuji Station (the old name, Fuji-Yoshida, is still commonly used) and then on to Kawaguchi-ko; the whole process will take at least 2hr (¥4310).

GETTING AROUND

By bus A comprehensive system of buses will help you get around once you've arrived at either Fuji-Yoshida or Kawaguchi-ko. The two-day Retrobus pass (¥1200 or ¥1500, depending on the route) allows travel around the Fuji Five Lakes area.

On foot It's easy enough to walk from Kawaguchi-ko Station down to the lake in 15min or so, and those without

too much luggage can access most of its surrounding hotels on foot.

By bicycle You'll see plenty of tourists pedalling around the Kawaguchi-ko area. Most rent bikes from their accommodation, though there are plenty of other rental outlets around, including one just opposite the train station, on the left (¥500/hr, ¥1500/day).

INFORMATION

Fuji-Yoshida tourist office On the left as you exit Mount Fuji Station (daily 9am–5pm; ☎ 0555 22 7000, ⓦ www.city.fujiyoshida.yamanashi.jp), with tons of information in English. If you're here to climb Fuji, pick up a free copy of the various maps on offer (also available at the

Kawaguchi-ko tourist office – see below); there's similar information on the tourist office website.

Kawaguchi-ko tourist office Outside Kawaguchi-ko Station, this branch (daily 8.30am–5.30pm; ☎ 0555 72 6700) is just as useful as its counterpart in Fuji-Yoshida.

ACCOMMODATION

FUJI-YOSHIDA

Daikoku-ya 大国屋 Honchō-dōri, Fuji-Yoshida ☎ 0555 22 3778. This original pilgrims' inn on the main road still takes guests in its very traditional and beautifully decorated tatami rooms (though the owner prefers guests who can speak some Japanese). Rate includes two meals. Closed Oct–April. **¥14,000**

Michael's マイケルズ 3-21-37 Shimo-yoshida ☎ 0555 72 9139, ⓦ mtfujihostel.com. American-run hostel with spick-and-span rooms, a quiet backstreet location – though one very close to the train station – and a lively bar (see opposite). Private rooms are a particularly good deal for single travellers. 🛜 Dorms **¥3000**, private rooms (per person) **¥3600**

KAWAGUCHI-KO

★**Fuji Lake** 富士レーク 1 Funatsu, Kawaguchi-ko-machi ☎ 0555 72 2209, ⓦ fujilake.co.jp. Large lakeside

hotel that dates back to the 1930s, making it one of Japan's oldest such facilities. Its rooms are all large and very stylish, and feature charming wash-rooms into which onsen water is piped. There's another fantastic onsen downstairs. 🛜 **¥14,700**

★**K's House Mount Fuji** ケイズハウス富士山 6713-108 Funatsu, Kawaguchi-ko-machi ☎ 0555 83 5556, ⓦ kshouse.jp. Super-friendly hostel with a choice of either bunk-bed dorms or private tatami-style rooms, some en suite. Also on offer are a well-equipped kitchen, comfy lounge, internet access, laundry and bike rental, as well as a small bar. They'll even pick up from the station for free (8am–7.30pm). Their new hostel, *Fuji View*, further up the slopes, is a similar operation. 🛜 Dorms **¥2500**, doubles **¥7200**

Sunnide Village サニーデビレッジ Kawaguchi-ko-machi ☎ 0555 76 6004, ⓦ www.sunnide.com. This attractive complex of hotel and holiday cottages offers

---

ACCOMMODATION ON MOUNT FUJI

There are seventeen **huts** on Fuji, most of which provide dorm accommodation from around ¥5300 per night (add ¥1000 on weekends) for just a bed (no need for a sleeping bag), with an option to add meals for ¥1000 each. It's essential to book in advance during the official climbing season (July & Aug). The huts also sell snacks and stamina-building dishes, such as curry rice. For a full list of the huts, with contact numbers, see the Fuji-Yoshida city website (ⓦ www.city.fujiyoshida.yamanashi.jp).

FUJI-NOODLES

Both Fuji-Yoshida and Kawaguchi-ko are renowned for their thick *teuchi* (handmade) **udon noodles**. *Fuji-Yoshida udon* comes topped with shredded cabbage and carrot, and is usually prepared and served in people's homes at lunchtime only; the tourist offices can provide a Japanese list and map of the best places serving it. Most of these will serve just three types of dishes: *yumori*, noodles in a soup; *zaru*, cold noodles; and *sara*, warm noodles dipped in hot soup. In Kawaguchi-ko, be sure to try **hōtō**, a hearty broth served piping hot; ingredients vary, and some places serve it with exotic meats such as venison and bear, but sweet pumpkin is the local favourite.

2

---

spectacular views across the lake towards Mount Fuji, and has lovely public baths, too. It's on the north side of the lake, towards the Itchiku Kubota Art Museum. 🛜 Doubles **¥12,600**, cottages **¥16,000**

EATING

FUJI-YOSHIDA

★**Menkyo Kaiden** 麺許皆伝 849-1 Kami-Yoshida ☎0555 23 8806. This is the undisputed udon favourite with lunching locals; you may have to wait for a seat. The menu can be a little confusing, but staff recommend the *yokubari*, which comes in a miso-base soup (¥550). Mon–Sat 11am–2pm.

KAWAGUCHI-KO

★**Hōtō Fudo** ほうとう不動 Train station plaza ☎0120 41 0457. Right in front of the train station in a building with a

wood-panelled exterior, this small restaurant serves decent *hōtō* (see box above) for ¥1080, as well as *basashi* (raw horse meat; ¥1080) and a range of other tasty Japanese food. Daily 11am–9pm.

Tetsuyaki 鉄焼き 3486-5 Kawaguchiko-chō, no phone. This *teppanyaki* spot is frequently the only place in town open after 8pm. Mains go from ¥800, and include steak, *okonomiyaki* (pancake-like batter dish with various fillings) and rice dishes; mercifully, since few bars around the lake stay open too long after sundown, they also sell alcoholic drinks. Daily noon–10pm.

DRINKING

Michael's マイケルズ 3-21-37 Shimo-yoshida ☎0555 72 9139, ⓦmtfujihostel.com. Even if you're not staying overnight at this Fuji-Yoshida hostel (see opposite), it's worth swinging by the bar if you're in the area – the

atmosphere can be surprisingly raucous for provincial Japan. Simple pub snacks are on offer alongside a modest range of drinks. 🛜 Daily 11.30am–4pm & 7pm–2am; closed Sat lunch & Thurs eve.

Hakone

箱根

South of Mount Fuji and 90km west of Tokyo is the lakeland, mountain and onsen area known as **HAKONE**, always busy at weekends and during holidays. Most visitors follow the well-established day-trip route, which is good fun and combines rides on several trains or buses, a funicular, a cable-car and a sightseeing ship across the Ashino lake. However, the scenery is so pretty, and there's so much else to see and do – including some great **art museums** and numerous **onsen** – that an overnight stay is encouraged. Weather permitting, you'll also get great views of nearby Mount Fuji.

The traditional day-trip itinerary, described below, runs anticlockwise from **Hakone-Yumoto**, gateway to the **Fuji-Hakone-Izu National Park**, then over the peaks of **Sōun-zan**, across the length of **Ashino-ko** to **Moto-Hakone**, and back to the start. Approaching Hakone from the west, you can follow a similar route clockwise from Hakone-machi, on the southern shore of Ashino-ko, to Hakone-Yumoto.

Hakone-Yumoto

箱根湯元

HAKONE-YUMOTO, the small town nestling in the valley at the gateway to the national park, is marred by scores of concrete-block hotels and *bessō*, vacation villas for company workers – not to mention the usual cacophony of souvenir shops. It does, however, have some good **onsen** (see box, p.206), which are ideal for unwinding after a day's sightseeing around the park.

Miyanoshita
宮ノ下

Rising up into the mountains, the Hakone-Tozan **switchback railway** zigzags for nearly 9km alongside a ravine from Hakone-Yumoto to the village of Gōra. There are small traditional inns and temples at several of the stations along the way, but the single best place to alight is the village onsen resort of **MIYANOSHITA**. Interesting antique and craft shops are dotted along its main road, and there are several hiking routes up **Mount Sengen** (804m) on the eastern flank of the railway – one path begins just beside the station. At the top (an hour's walk or so) you'll get a great view of the gorge below. After the walk you can relax in the appealing day-onsen **Tenoyu** (see box, p.206). Miyanoshita's real draw, however, is its handful of splendid **hotels**, the most historic of which is the *Fujiya* (see p.210), which opened for business in 1878; it's well worth a look even if you're not staying, and its *Orchid Lounge* is great for afternoon tea.

Hakone Open-Air Museum
彫刻の森美術館, Chōkoku no Mori Bijutsukan · 1121 Ninotaira · Daily 9am–5pm · ¥1600 · ⓦ hakone-oam.or.jp

Travelling two stops uphill from Miyanoshita on the Hakone-Tozan railway brings you to Chōkoku no Mori (彫刻の森), where you should alight if you want to visit the nearby **Hakone Open-Air Museum**. This worthwhile museum is packed with sculptures, ranging from works by Rodin and Giacometti to Michelangelo reproductions and bizarre modern formations scattered across the landscaped grounds, which have lovely views across the mountains to the sea. You can rest between galleries at several restaurants or cafés, and there's also a traditional Japanese teahouse here.

Gōra to Ashino-ko
Funicular tram Every 10–15min · ¥420 one-way · **Cable-car** Every 1–2min · ¥1370 one-way to Ashino-ko

The Hakone-Tozan railway terminates at **GŌRA** (強羅), where you can stop for lunch, or overnight. Continuing west on the day-trip route, you'll transfer to a **funicular tram**, which takes ten minutes to cover the short but steep distance to **Sōunzan**, the start of the cable-car ride. From here, the **cable-car** floats like a balloon on its thirty-minute journey high above the mountain to the Tōgendai terminal beside **Ashino-ko**, stopping at a couple of points along the way.

Hakone Museum of Art
箱根美術館, Hakone Bijutsukan · 1300 Gōra · 9am–4pm; closed Thurs · ¥900 · ⓦ moaart.or.jp/hakone

En route to Sōunzan, you might want to stop at Kōen-kami (公園上), a couple of stops from Gōra, for the **Hakone Museum of Art**. Its collection of ancient ceramics – some of which date back as far as the Jōmon period – is likely to appeal to experts only, but the delicate moss gardens and the view from the traditional teahouse across the verdant hills are captivating.

Ōwakudani
大涌谷

If the weather is playing ball, you should get a good glimpse of Mount Fuji in the distance as you pop over the hill at the first cable-car stop, **ŌWAKUDANI**. This is the site of a constantly bubbling and steaming valley formed by a volcanic eruption three thousand years ago. A series of tectonic belches in recent years saw the cable-car station and surrounding area fully closed down, with visitors unable to get off and explore;

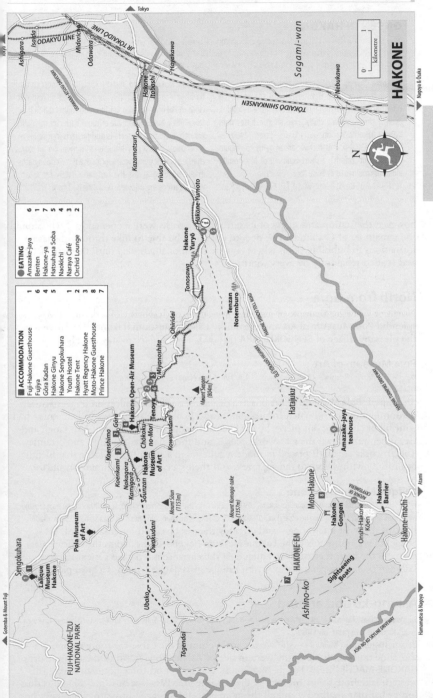

HAKONE

2

ACCOMMODATION	
Fuji-Hakone Guesthouse	1
Fujiya	6
Gōra Kadan	4
Hakone Ginyu	5
Hakone Sengokuhara Youth Hostel	1
Hakone Tent	2
Hyatt Regency Hakone	3
Moto-Hakone Guesthouse	8
Prince Hakone	7

● EATING	
Amazake-jaya	6
Benten	1
Hakone-ya	7
Hatsuhana Soba	5
Naokichi	4
Naraya Café	3
Orchid Lounge	2

Tokyo

ODAKYU LINE

JR TOKAIDO LINE

Isata

Ashigara

Midorichō

Odawara

Hakone Itabashi

Hayakawa

TOKAIDO SHINKANSEN

Sagami-wan

Nebukawa

Nagoya & Osaka

Kazamatsuri

Iriuda

Hakone-Yumoto

Hakone Yuryō

Tonosawa

Tenzan Notemburo

HAKONE TOZAN RAILWAY

Ohiradai

Miyanoshita

Mount Sengen (804m)

OLD TOKAIDO HIGHWAY

Hatajuku

NISEI TURNPIKE TOLL ROAD

Hakone Open-Air Museum

Tenoyu

Chōkoku-no-Mori

Hakone Museum of Art

Kowakudani

Kōenkami

Nakagora

Kamigora

Sōunzan

Gōra

Kōenshimo

Pola Museum of Art

Lalique Museum Hakone

Sengokuhara

FUJI-HAKONE-IZU NATIONAL PARK

Gotemba & Mount Fuji

Ubako

Ōwakudani

Mount Sōun (1153m)

Mount Komaga-take (1357m)

HAKONE-EN

Togendai

Ashino-ko

Sightseeing Boats

Hakone Gongen

Moto-Hakone

Amazake-jaya teahouse

Hakone Barrier

AVENUE OF CRYPTOMERIA

Onshi-Hakone Kōen

Hakone-machi

Atami

Hamamatsu & Nagoya

HAKONE-IZU SKYLINE DRIVEWAY

N

0 — 1 kilometre

2

ONSEN IN HAKONE

The sulphuric steam rising from the mountain of Sōun-zan makes it clear that something is going on beneath the surface of Hakone. As with any such place in Japan, this volcanic activity also makes it a prime spot for a soak in mineral-heavy **onsen** water.

Hakone Yuryō 箱根湯寮 ⓦhakoneyuryo.jp. Set back in the forest near Hakone-Yumoto, this onsen is a good option; bathing out by the trees is quite delightful, even if the weather's chilly. Free shuttle buses from Hakone-Yumoto Station. Daily 10am–8pm; ¥1400.
Tenoyu てのゆ. Attractive onsen with rotemburo (outdoor hot springs), a short walk out of Miyanoshita along the main road to Gōra. Mon–Fri 11am–7pm, Sat & Sun 11am–8pm; ¥1600 Mon–Fri, ¥2100 Sat & Sun.

Tenzan Notemburo 天山野天風呂. The most stylish bathhouse in the area is this luxurious riverside complex close to Hakone-Yumoto Station, and connected to it by free shuttle buses. There are outdoor baths for men and women, including waterfalls and jacuzzis in a series of rocky pools, plus a clay-hut sauna for men. For an extra charge both men and women can use the wooden baths in the building across the car park. Rarely for Japan, visible tattoos are allowed. Daily 9am–11pm; ¥1300.

---

however, the station and many of its surrounding paths were reopened in 2016. Should the remainder of Ōwakudani be opened up, you'll be able to hike through the lava formations to bubbling pools where eggs are traditionally boiled until they are black and scoffed religiously by every tourist.

North from Gōra

North of Gōra are a couple of excellent museums, both worthy of a detour: the splendid **Pola Museum of Art** and the quirky **Lalique Museum Hakone**. The latter is in the pleasant village of **SENGOKUHARA** (仙石原), a good place to stay the night.

Pola Museum of Art

ポーラ美術館, Pōra Bijutsukan • 1285 Sengokuhara • Daily 9am–5pm • ¥1800 • ⓦ polamuseum.or.jp • Bus from Gōra Station (15min; ¥300)

The superb **Pola Museum of Art** boasts a diverse and eclectic collection of Western art, predominantly from French Impressionists and École de Paris artists. When you've had your fill of checking out pieces by the likes of Renoir, Monet, Picasso, Van Gogh and Cézanne, hunt down the glasswork section, and the Japanese paintings and ceramics. The artworks are all displayed in modern galleries in a stunning building that blends beautifully with the surrounding forest, and there's a café and restaurant on site too.

Lalique Museum Hakone

箱根ラリック美術館, Hakone Rarikku Bijutsukan • 186-1 Sengokuhara • Daily 9am–5pm • ¥1500, or ¥2100 including train carriage with drinks and dessert (reservation necessary) • ☎ 0406 84 2225, ⓦ lalique-museum.com • Bus from Gōra Station (25min; ¥420)

Perhaps the most interesting – and certainly the most beautifully situated – of Sengokuhara's museums is the **Lalique Museum Hakone**, dedicated to the delicate glass pieces of the French artist René Lalique. At the entrance is a parked Orient Express Pullman train carriage, kitted out with Lalique glass panels, which is a great place for tea.

Ashino-ko and around

Sightseeing boats Tōgendai to Moto-Hakone or Hakone-machi ¥1000 • Daily 9.30am–5pm, every 30–40min • ⓦ hakone-kankosen .co.jp • **Komaga-take cable-car** ¥1080

From **Tōgendai** (桃原台) – the westernmost point of the cable-car route from Gōra – a shoreline trail winds along the western side of **Ashino-ko** (芦ノ湖) to the small resort of **HAKONE-MACHI** (箱根町) some 8km south, taking around three hours to cover. This western lakeshore is not covered by the Hakone Free Pass (see box, p.208) and is thus somewhat marginalized – and all the more peaceful for it. Most visitors, however, hop straight from the cable-car on to one of the colourful **sightseeing ships**, modelled after the seventeenth-century man o' war *The Sovereign of the Seas*, that regularly sail the length of the lake in around thirty minutes; you can see Fuji's peak reflected in the waters from the northern end of Ashino-ko. A cluster of upmarket hotels and ryokan can be found at Hakone-machi, where the sightseeing boats dock before or after hitting Moto-Hakone.

Boats also run from Tōgendai to the *Prince* hotel resort at **Hakone-en** (箱根園), midway down the east side of the lake. A cable-car here glides up the 1357m **Komagatake** (駒ヶ岳), from where there's a fabulous view.

Hakone Barrier

箱根関所, Hakone Sekisho • Daily: March–Nov 9am–5pm; Dec–Feb 9am–4.30pm • ¥500

The southern end of the lake is the location of the **Hakone Barrier**, a gateway through which all traffic on the **Tōkaidō**, the ancient road linking Kyoto and Edo, once had to pass (see box below). What stands here today is a reproduction, enlivened by waxwork displays which provide the historical background, and there's nothing much to keep you.

Onshi-Hakone Kōen

恩賜箱根公園 • Daily 9am–4.30pm • Free

North of the Hakone Barrier, the wooded promontory between Hakone and Moto-Hakone, **Onshi-Hakone Kōen**, is an easily accessible Fuji-viewing spot. After panting your way up 200-odd steps, you'll come to a garden area and an observation point; despite the hordes of tourists pouring off the ferries to the south, and padding their way through Moto-Hakone to the north, this place is usually pretty quiet.

Moto-Hakone

元箱根

Part of the **Tōkaidō ancient road** – shaded by 420 lofty cryptomeria trees planted in 1618, and now designated "Natural Treasures" – runs for around 1km beside the road leading from the Hakone Barrier to the lakeside **MOTO-HAKONE** tourist village. The prettiest spot around here is the vermilion *torii* (gate), standing in the water just north of Moto-Hakone – a scene celebrated in many an *ukiyo-e* print and modern postcard. The gate belongs to the **Hakone Gongen** (箱根権現) and is the best thing about this small Shintō shrine, set back in the trees, where samurai once came to pray.

Ashino-ko to Hakone-Yumoto

From either Hakone-machi or Moto-Hakone you can take a **bus** back to Hakone-Yumoto or Odawara (see p.208). Far more rewarding, however, is the 11km **hike** along part of the **Tōkaidō ancient road**, which begins five minutes up the hill from the Hakone-Tozan bus station in Moto-Hakone; to find the start of the route, watch for

---

THE HAKONE BARRIER

In 1618 the second shogun, Tokugawa Hidetada, put up the **Hakone Barrier** (Sekisho) – actually more of a large compound than a single gate – which stood at Hakone-machi until 1869. The shogun decreed that all his lords' wives and their families live in Edo (now Tokyo) and that the lords themselves make expensive formal visits to the capital every other year, a strategy designed to ensure no one attempted a rebellion. The Tōkaidō, on which the barrier stands, was one of the major routes in and out of the capital, and it was here that travellers were carefully checked to see how many guns they were taking into the Edo area; the barrier also ensured that the lords' families were prevented from escaping. Any man caught trying to dodge the barrier was crucified and then beheaded, while accompanying women had their heads shaved and were, according to contemporary statute, "given to anyone who wants them".

2

the spot where large paving stones are laid through the shady forests. After the first 2km the route is all downhill and takes around four hours.

When the path comes out of the trees and hits the main road, you'll see the **Amazake-jaya Teahouse** (see p.210). From here, the path shadows the main road to the small village of **HATAJUKU** (畑宿), where since the ninth century craftsmen have perfected the art of *yosegi-zaiku*, or marquetry. The wooden boxes, toys and other objects inlaid with elaborate mosaic patterns make great souvenirs; there are workshops throughout the village, including one right where the path emerges onto the main road. Hatajuku is a good place to pick up the bus the rest of the way to Hakone-Yumoto if you don't fancy hiking any further.

ARRIVAL AND INFORMATION   HAKONE

By train Most people visit Hakone aboard the Odakyū-line train from Shinjuku, using one of the company's excellent-value travel passes (see box below). To get to Hakone-Yumoto – at the end of the line – on the basic trains (2hr; ¥1190), you may have to change in Odawara (小田原); for an extra fee you can take the more comfortable "Romance Car" (hourly; 1hr 30min; ¥2080) all the way. If you're using a JR Pass (see p.36), the fastest route is to take a Shinkansen to Odawara, from where you can transfer to an Odakyū train or bus into the national park area.

By bus The Odakyū express bus (hourly; ¥1950) from Shinjuku bus terminal will get you to Hakone in a couple of

hours. Buses stop first at Hakone-Yumoto, followed by Moto-Hakone, the *Prince* hotel at Hakone-en (see p.210) and finally Tōgendai. It's also possible to visit by bus from the Fuji Five Lakes area, in which case you'll enter Hakone through Sengokuhara to the north, passing through the major town of Gotemba; passes will save you money (see box below), as well as hassle on the local buses, which don't give any change.

Tourist information You can pick up a map of the area and plenty of other information at the very friendly Hakone tourist office (daily 9am–5.45pm; ☎0460 85 5700, ⓦ hakone.or.jp), situated in the buildings at the bus terminal, across the street from Hakone-Yumoto Station.

ACCOMMODATION

Excellent transportation links mean you can stay pretty much anywhere in the national park and get everywhere else easily. There's a good range of budget options and some top-grade ryokan; a profusion of offerings on Airbnb has seen prices decrease slightly at the lower end of the spectrum.

ASHINO-KO

Moto-Hakone Guesthouse 元箱根ゲストハウス 103 Moto-Hakone ☎0460 83 7880, ⓦ motohakone.com.

Simple guesthouse a short bus ride (get off at Ōshiba) or stiff 10min walk uphill from Moto-Hakone village. The reward for the journey is spotless Japanese-style rooms

---

HAKONE TRAVEL PASSES

Touring the Hakone area is great fun, but the various train, funicular, cable-car and boat tickets can add up quickly. One way to prevent this, and save a bundle of cash, is to invest in one of the many **travel passes** covering the area. As well as covering almost all transport, they can be used to lop a little off entry prices to some sights. You can buy passes at the **Odakyū Sightseeing Service Centre** at the west exit of Shinjuku Station (daily 8am–6pm; ☎03 5321 7887, ⓦ www.odakyu.jp /english); the English-speaking staff here can also make reservations for tours and hotels.

Hakone Freepass If you plan to follow the traditional Hakone route, invest in this pass, which comes in either two- or three-day versions; from Shinjuku, it costs ¥5140/¥5640 (2/3 days); from Odawara or Gotemba it costs ¥4000/¥4500 (2/3 days). The pass covers a return journey on the Odakyū line from Shinjuku to Odawara, and unlimited use of the Hakone-Tozan line, Hakone-Tozan funicular railway, cable-car, boats across the lake and most local buses.

Hakone One-day Pass If you're already in Odawara

or Gotemba you can buy a special one-day pass for ¥2000. It doesn't cover the journeys to or from Tokyo, nor the cable-car and boat.

Fuji Hakone Pass If you're going directly from Hakone to the neighbouring Fuji Five Lakes area (or vice versa) then the three-day Fuji Hakone Pass (¥8000 from Shinjuku, ¥5650 from Odawara) is the way to go. This offers the same deal as a Hakone Freepass but also covers a one-way express bus trip between the Hakone area and Kawaguchi-ko.

2

and extremely friendly service – a cup of coffee will be plonked in front of you in no time at all. Surcharge of ¥1000 at weekends. 📶 **¥4860** per person

Prince Hakone プリンス箱根 144 Moto-hakone ☎ 0460 83 1111, ⓦ princehotels.com. This hotel boasts a prime location on the eastern shore of Ashino-ko and a multitude of facilities, including access to an outdoor hot bath with a view of the lake. 📶 **¥20,000**

GORA

Gōra Kadan 強羅花壇 1300 Gōra ☎ 0460 82 3331, ⓦ gorakadan.com. One of Hakone's most exclusive ryokans is the stuff of legend, which means you might have to wait an eternity to secure a reservation. Expect beautiful tatami rooms, antiques, exquisite meals and a serene atmosphere. Rates include two meals. 📶 **¥100,000**

★**Hakone Tent** 箱根テント 1320-257 Gōra ☎ 0460 83 8021, ⓦ hakonetent.com. Created from an old ryokan, this striking, modern guesthouse has been a fantastic recent budget addition to the area. The on-site onsen is a delight, and travellers usually end up having a natter over sake or beer at the welcoming bar before collapsing onto their futons. The single room is great value at ¥4000. 📶 Dorms **¥3500**, doubles **¥9000**

Hyatt Regency Hakone ハイアット リージェンシー箱根 1320 Gōra ☎ 0460 82 2000, ⓦ hakone.regency .hyatt.com. This slickly designed hotel is a treat, offering some of the largest rooms in Hakone and elegant facilities, including a lounge, two restaurants and the Izumi onsen spa. For those who can't bear to be parted from their pooch, there are even dog-friendly stone-floored rooms. 📶 **¥30,000**

MIYANOSHITA

Fujiya 富士屋ホテル 359 Miyanoshita ☎ 0460 82 2211, ⓦ fujiyahotel.jp. The first Western-style hotel in Japan, this place is a living monument to a more glamorous era of travel, and boasts lots of Japanese touches, including traditional gardens and decorative gables like those found in temples. The plush 1950s-style decor is retro-chic, the rooms are good value, and there are a couple of great on-site places to eat and drink. 📶 **¥14,000**

Hakone Ginyu 箱根吟遊 100-1 Miyanoshita ☎ 0460 82 3355, ⓦ hakoneginyu.co.jp. Outstanding luxury ryokan, where guests are assured maximum comfort. The views across the valley are stunning and the interiors are a tasteful blend of old and new. Huge *hinoki* wood tubs on private verandas are a major plus. Rates include two meals. 📶 **¥66,000**

SENGOKUHARA

Fuji-Hakone Guesthouse 富士箱根ゲストハウス 912 Sengokuhara ☎ 0460 84 6577, ⓦ fujihakone.com. Tucked into a pleasingly secluded spot, this convivial guesthouse – run by the friendly, English-speaking Takahashi-san and his family – has comfortable tatami rooms, though the defining feature is the onsen water piped into no fewer than four separate baths. Breakfast available. 📶 **¥10,800**

Hakone Sengokuhara Youth Hostel 箱根仙石原ユースホステル 912 Sengokuhara ☎ 0460 84 8966, ⓦ jyh .or.jp. Directly behind the *Fuji-Hakone Guesthouse*, and run by the same family, this hostel offers good dorm accommodation in a lovely wooden building. The on-site hot spring is a nice bonus if you've been hiking. 📶 Dorms **¥3550**

EATING

ASHINO-KO

Hakone-ya 箱根屋 45 Moto-Hakone ☎ 0460 83 6107. This is the best of the rather motley bunch of tourist restaurants in Moto-Hakone, serving dishes such as extremely filling *katsu-don* (¥1080) and cheaper bowls of soba or udon, with pretty views out over the lake. Daily 10am–7pm.

HAKONE-YUMOTO

Hakone-Yumoto is stacked with good places to eat. There are also three good-value restaurants at the nearby Tenzan Notemburo bathhouse (see box, p.206) serving rice, *shabu-shabu* (hotpot) and *yakiniku* (grilled meat) dishes.

Hatsuhana Soba はつ花そば 635 Hakone-Yumoto ☎ 0460 85 8287. The Hakone area is famed for its soba, on account of the purity of the local water, and this restaurant is the best place to try it. Several options are available, including tempura and curry bowls, but you can't go wrong with the *teijo soba*, served with grated yam and raw egg (¥1000). To get here from the station, follow the riverbank into town, then turn left at the first bridge – it's right on the

other side, overlooking the river. Daily 10am–7pm.

★**Naokichi** 直吉 696 Hakone-Yumoto ☎ 0460 85 5148. Excellent, elegant restaurant serving the scrumptious local speciality, *yubadon* – soy milk skin in fish broth served on rice (¥980). Not sold yet? There's also a free onsen footbath just outside. To find it, head up the river path from the station; you'll soon spot the place on your right. 11am–6pm; closed Tues.

HATAJUKU

Amazake-jaya 甘酒茶屋 Hatajuku. Rest at this charming teahouse, just as travellers did hundreds of years ago, and sip a restorative cup of the milky, sweet rice drink *amazake*, with some pickles, for ¥400. Daily 7am–5.30pm.

MIYANOSHITA

★**Naraya Café** ならやカフェー 404-13 Miyanoshita. There's one major draw at this lovely café, just down the road from Miyanoshita Station – a footbath that runs under the table in the outdoor section, making it possible to bathe your toes while sipping a latte (¥400), or perhaps even a cocktail. Hot dogs and other snacks are available, and there's a gallery on the top level. 🛜 10.30am–6pm; closed Wed. **Orchid Lounge** 359 Miyanoshita ☎ 0460 82 2211, ⓦ fujiyahotel.co.jp. The tea lounge at the wonderful *Fujiya* hotel (see opposite) is a grand spot for coffee (¥1500 with cake) or afternoon tea (¥1000); it's a pleasure to sit down and relax with a view over the garden and carp-filled pond. Daily 9am–9pm.

SENGOKUHARA

Benten 弁天 226 Sengokuhara. If you're staying in the Sengokuhara area, this simple *izakaya* is a good bet for dinner and a drink – it's one of the few places around in which the majority of customers are locals. It serves simple bowls of ramen from ¥450, plus fried seafood, and a range of local drinks. Daily 2–9pm.

Izu Hantō

伊豆半島

Formed by Mount Fuji's ancient lava flows, **Izu Hantō** protrudes like an arrowhead into the ocean southwest of Tokyo, a mountainous spine whose tortured coastline features some superb scenery and a couple of decent beaches. Direct train services from Tokyo run down Izu's more developed east coast to the harbour town of **Shimoda**, a good base for exploring southern Izu. The only settlement of any size in central Izu is **Shuzenji**, whose nearby **onsen** resort has long been associated with novelists such as Kawabata Yasunari and Sōseki Natsume (see p.867). Izu's mild climate makes it a possible excursion even in winter, though it's close enough to Tokyo to be crowded at weekends, and is best avoided during the summer holidays.

Shimoda and around

下田

Trains peel off down the east coast of Izu at Atami, cutting through craggy headlands and running high above bays ringed with fishing villages or resort hotels. Nearly halfway down the peninsula is **Itō** (伊東), the port where Will Adams launched Japan's first Western-style sailing ships (see box, p.213), but there's nothing really to stop for until you reach **SHIMODA**. Off season, this small, amiable town, with its attractive scenery and sprinkling of temples and museums, makes a good base for a couple of days' exploring. Shimoda was one of the places Commodore Perry parked his "Black Ships" in 1854, making it one of Japan's first ports to open to foreign trade. The people of Shimoda are immensely proud of their part in Japanese history and you'll find Black Ships everywhere; there's even a **Black Ships Festival** (around the third Friday to Sunday in May), which sees American and Japanese naval bands parade through the streets, followed by the inevitable fireworks.

Central Shimoda lies on the northwestern shore of a well-sheltered harbour, surrounded by steep hills. Most of its sights are in the older, southerly district, where you'll find a number of attractive grey-and-white latticed walls near the original fishing harbour; this style of architecture (known as *namako-kabe*), found throughout Izu, is resistant to fire, earthquakes and corrosive sea air. Tourist boats run from Shimoda to Izu's southern cape, **Irō-zaki**, while a few kilometres north of town there are onsen baths at **Rengaiji Onsen**.

Brief history

Having signed an initial treaty in Yokohama, which granted America trading rights in Shimoda and Hakodate (on Hokkaidō) and consular representation, Commodore Perry sailed his Black Ships (*Kurofune*) down to Izu. Here, in Shimoda's Ryōsen-ji, he concluded a supplementary **Treaty of Friendship** in 1854. Russian, British and Dutch merchants were granted similar rights soon after, and in 1856 **Townsend Harris** arrived in Shimoda as the first American Consul. By now, however, it was obvious Shimoda was too isolated as a trading post and Harris began negotiating for a revised treaty,

2

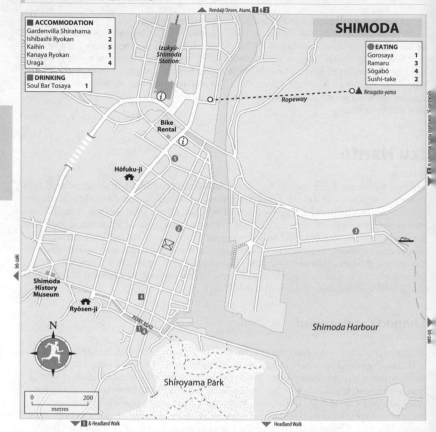

SHIMODA

ACCOMMODATION
Gardenvilla Shirahama	3
Ishibashi Ryokan	2
Kaihin	5
Kanaya Ryokan	1
Uraga	4

DRINKING
Soul Bar Tosaya	1

EATING
Gorosaya	1
Ramaru	3
Sōgabō	4
Sushi-take	2

which was eventually signed (again in Shimoda) in July 1858. Kanagawa replaced Shimoda as an open port, and the burgeoning foreign community decamped north to Yokohama.

Ryōsen-ji

了仙寺 · **Museum** Daily 8.30am–5pm · ¥500 · ⓦ www.izu.co.jp/~ryosenji

Your first stop in Shimoda should be **Ryōsen-ji**, where Commodore Perry signed the Treaty of Friendship in 1854 (see p.211), though this small but elaborate temple, founded in 1635, is less interesting than its attached **museum**, which is full of fascinating historical documents and wood-block prints, many of them original, from the 1850s. Delightful portraits of Perry and his devilish crew, penned by Japanese artists, contrast with the European view of Japan – embellished with Chinese touches – from contemporary editions of the *Illustrated London News* and other European journals. Many exhibits relate to the tragic Saitō Okichi, the servant girl of Consul Harris, who earned the nickname of Tōjin ("foreigner's concubine"), while a second room contains a somewhat incongruous display of sex in religious art, including some beautiful pieces from India, Nepal and Japan's Shintō shrines.

From Ryōsen-ji, **Perry Road** leads east along a small river lined with willows and picturesque old houses, some now converted into cafés and antique shops.

WILL ADAMS

In 1600 a Dutch ship washed up on east Kyūshū, the sole survivor of five vessels that had set sail from Europe two years previously; three-quarters of the crew had perished from starvation and the remaining 24 were close to death. One of those rescued was the navigator, an Englishman called **Will Adams** (1564–1620). He was summoned by **Tokugawa Ieyasu**, the future shogun, who quizzed Adams about European affairs, religion and various scientific matters. Ieyasu liked what he heard and made Adams his personal adviser on mathematics, navigation and armaments. Adams, known locally as Anjin ("pilot"), later served as the shogun's interpreter and as a diplomat, brokering trade treaties with both Holland and Britain. In return he was granted **samurai status** – the first and last foreigner to be so honoured – along with a Japanese wife and an estate near Yokosuka on the Miura Peninsula.

Adams' main task, however, was to oversee the construction of Japan's first Western-style sailing ships. In 1605 he set up a shipyard at **Itō**, on the east coast of Izu, where he built at least two ocean-going vessels over the next five years. His fascinating life story is told in Giles Milton's *Samurai William* and also forms the basis for James Clavell's novel, *Shogun*. Each August, Itō's Anjin Matsuri celebrates Adams.

Shimoda History Museum

下田開国博物館, Shimoda Kaikoku Hakubutsukan • Daily 8.30am–5.30pm • ¥1000

Heading west from Ryōsen-ji, you'll soon come to the **Shimoda History Museum**, housed in two *namako-kabe* buildings on opposite sides of the street. Consul Harris and Saitō Okichi feature prominently, alongside caricatures of big-nosed foreigners. The museum also includes plenty of information, much of it in English, about local life, including the area's distinctive architecture and festivals.

Hōfuku-ji

宝福寺 • **Temple museum** Daily 8am–5pm • ¥300

When Saitō Okichi (see opposite) died in 1890, none of her family came forward to claim her body, so it was left to a local priest to bring her back to the family temple for burial. Her **grave** now lies behind the otherwise unremarkable **Hōfuku-ji**, where there's another small museum dedicated to her memory.

Nesugata-yama

寝姿山 • Ropeway daily 9am–5pm, departures every 10–15min • ¥1000 return

The east side of Shimoda is dominated by the 200m-high peak of **Nesugata-yama**. On a clear day it's worth taking the ropeway from beside the train station up to the summit for dramatic views of the harbour and out to the Izu islands on the eastern horizon.

Gyokusen-ji

玉泉寺 • **Museum** Daily 8am–5pm • ¥300

Along the promenade at the far, eastern, side of Shimoda Harbour is **Gyokusen-ji**, where Townsend Harris established Japan's first American consulate in 1856 – he lived and worked there for about fifteen months, accompanied by his Dutch interpreter, Chinese servants and, possibly, his servant girl Saitō Okichi. On entering the **Townsend Harris Museum**, to the right of the temple, you're greeted by a startling, life-size model of Harris, complete with splendid handlebar moustache, relaxing in his rocking chair in full evening dress while Okichi offers him a glass of milk.

Rendaiji Onsen

蓮台寺温泉 • **Trains** run from Shimoda to Rendaiji Station (2–3 hourly; 3–4min; ¥170), from where it's a short walk west across the river and highway to the village • Most local **buses** drop you on the main street (1–2 hourly; 10min; ¥170)

Set in a narrow valley 3km north of Shimoda, just west of National Highway 414, **RENDAIJI ONSEN** is a quiet, one-street village consisting mostly of exclusive ryokan (see p.215) that tap into the area's abundant supply of hot water. You can visit these **onsen baths** even if you're not staying overnight. There are also a few meandering back lanes to explore.

Irō-zaki

石廊崎 • Bus from Izukyū-Shimoda Station roughly every 30min (1–2 hourly; 40min) • Tourist boats from Shimoda (usually 1–2 hourly; 25min; ¥1400)

From Shimoda, Highway 136 sets off southwest towards Izu's southern cape, **Irō-zaki**, 17km away. Arriving by road, you'll be greeted by an expanse of car parks, but Irō-Zaki improves dramatically as you walk out along the promontory for about 500m, past souvenir shops and a lighthouse, to a minuscule **shrine** balanced on the cliff edge. The views here are superb: on either side the sea has cut deep-blue gashes into the coastline, leaving behind a sprinkling of rocky islets between which colourful tourist boats bob and weave.

ARRIVAL AND DEPARTURE   SHIMODA AND AROUND

By train *Super View Odoriko* express trains (hourly; 2hr 40min–3hr; ¥6440), which have extra-wide windows to take in the spectacular coastal views, run direct from Tokyo Station to Izukyū-Shimoda Station on the north side of Shimoda town; some services divide at Atami for Shuzenji, so check you're in the right section. There are also "normal" services, which involve a change: you can take a Shinkansen as far as Atami and change (2hr 45min in total; ¥5940), or go on a slow service to Itō and change there (4hr in total; ¥3890). Note that JR passes are not valid beyond Itō, so you'll need to pay a supplement or buy another ticket.

By bus There are buses from in front of Shimoda Station to Izu locations unreachable by train; these include Irō-zaki (1–2 hourly; 40min) and Shuzenji (1 daily; 2hr).

GETTING AROUND

By car Car rental is available from Nippon Rent-a-Car (☎0558 22 5711), Nissan (☎0558 23 4123) and Toyota (☎0558 27 0100), all with outlets close to the station.

By bike You can rent bikes at Noguchi Rentacycle (daily 9.30am–6pm; ¥500/hr, ¥2000/day; ☎0558 22 1099), one block south of the station.

By boat Tourist boats run to Irō-zaki (usually 1–2 hourly; 25min; ¥1400), departing from the tourist wharf on the east side of Shimoda.

INFORMATION AND ACTIVITIES

Tourist information There's an information desk inside the front exit of the station (daily 9am–5pm; ☎0558 22 3200); they usually sell discounted tickets to the town's sights. The Shimoda Tourist Association (daily 10am–5pm; ☎0558 23 5593, ⬡shimoda-city.info) is southeast of the station beside the main crossroads; both places can help with town maps and accommodation.

Harbour cruises From the tourist wharf you can take a short 20min harbour cruise on a replica Black Ship (daily 9.10am–4pm; every 30min–1hr; ¥1200).

ACCOMMODATION

Much of the town's accommodation consists of either pricey resort **hotels** on the harbourfront or rather run-down minshuku. However, there are a few appealing options around the station and among the older streets to the south. Other possibilities in the area include the more stylish ryokan in **Rendaiji**, 3km north of Shimoda, and a series of beach-side hotels and guesthouses lining the Shirahama coast, starting a few kilometres east of Shimoda.

CITY CENTRE

Kaihin 下田海浜ホテル 3-26-7 Shimoda-shi, a 10min walk from Perry Rd ☎0558 22 2065, ⬡itoenhotel.com. Not the prettiest building, but the location on a quiet bay and the reasonable rates (including two meals) are a plus. Rooms are mostly Japanese-style, with balconies and sea views, and there are two onsen baths, one with sea views, plus a rotemburo. **¥18,000**

Uraga ホテルウラガ 3-3-10 Shimoda-shi ☎0558 23 6600. Clean, bright business hotel in the south part of town. It's worth paying a little extra for the larger twins, but all rooms are comfortable, and the coffee shop serves Japanese and Western breakfasts. Some English spoken. **¥10,500**

SHIRAHAMA

★**Gardenvilla Shirahama** ガーデンヴィラ白浜 2644-1 Shirahama ☎0558 22 8080, ⬡gardenvilla.jp. The best of the many new (and new-ish) options in Shirahama. Its rooms are cosy enough, but to get the most out of the place you'll have to visit in the warmer months, when you can make use of the swimming pool (July–Sept) and properly appreciate the outdoor rotemburo and ocean-view balcony – the latter is a great place to eat their excellent Western-style breakfasts (¥1000). **¥10,500**

RENDAIJI ONSEN

Kanaya Ryokan 金谷旅館 ☎0558 22 0325. Set in a beautiful, traditional building, this ryokan features the most appealing of Rendaiji's many onsen – a big wooden public bath (non-guests ¥700) in a cavernous hall. There are several other pools here too, including a rotemburo, where many of your fellow bathers will be local families. The ryokan also has an observatory for stargazing, and a tea ceremony room. It's located on the main highway, just north of the village turning. Rates include two meals. **¥23,000**

Ishibashi Ryokan 石橋旅館 ☎0558 22 2222, ⓦkur-ishibashi.com. Also known as the *Kur Hotel*, this beautiful and welcoming place has several attractive baths (non-guests ¥1050), including a little rotemburo. It's in Rendaiji proper, tucked under a small hill on the right as you walk from the highway. Rates include two meals. **¥28,000**

EATING

Shimoda has a number of affordable *izakaya* and sushi **restaurants**. As with the rest of Izu, the town is justly proud of its *kin-me-dai*, a red-scaled fish with a silver, coin-like eye, and the rather magnificent English name of "Splendid Alfonsino". There are also a few good **coffee shops** scattered around town and along Perry Road, some of which double as antiques showrooms.

Gorosaya ごろさや 1-5-25 Shimoda-shi ☎0558 23 5638. Relaxed and popular fish restaurant which apparently predates the arrival of the Black Ships. Their standard *teishoku* (around ¥1700) includes a choice of sashimi, tempura or grilled *kin-me-dai* – almost everyone's here for the latter, and rightly so. 11.30am–2pm & 5–9pm; closed Thurs.

★**Ramaru** ラーマル 1-1 Shimoda-shi ☎0558 27 2510. This retro-style American burger bar was nothing special until they started selling their now-famous Shimoda burger (¥1000), a real beast filled with a giant slab of *kin-me-dai*, topped with a chunk of brie and drizzled with a tangy soy sauce. Absolutely wonderful, and quite possibly the best burger on offer in all Japan – worth the ten-minute walk from central Shimoda. Daily 10am–5pm.

Sōgabō 草画房 3-14-6 Shimoda-shi ☎0558 27 1123. The best and most attractive of Perry Road's many cafés, its tatami interior boasting a mix of seating styles, from wooden to cushioned to floor mats; most go for the tables with views out over the stream. Try a coffee or green-tea latte; it'll set you back around ¥650. Daily 10am–5pm.

Sushi-take 寿司竹 2-4-6 Shimoda-shi ☎0558 22 2026. Choose from the picture menu or counter display at this sushi outlet, or simply opt for one of the well-priced sushi sets (from ¥1500). They also serve *donburi* dishes, including *aji-don* (local horse mackerel). 11.30am–3pm & 5–11pm; closed Thurs.

DRINKING

Soul Bar Tosaya 3-14-30 Shimoda-shi ☎0558 27 0587. One of a few quirky places to drink in the Perry Road area, selling drinks from ¥500. The music's pretty cool, and generally in keeping with the establishment's name. Daily 6pm–midnight.

Shūzen-ji Onsen

修善寺 温泉

Not to be confused with the modern town of **Shuzenji**, 3km to the northwest, **SHŪZEN-JI ONSEN** consists of little more than one road and a string of riverside hotels and souvenir shops along a narrow valley. Follow the main street west and you'll soon reach an open area with some pleasant older buildings and a succession of red-lacquered bridges over the tumbling Katsura-gawa. Here, on a rocky outcrop beside the river, is **Tokko-no-yu**, Shūzen-ji's first and most famous **onsen**. According to legend, the onsen was "created" in

SHŪZEN-JI'S SHOGUNS

During the Kamakura period (1185–1333), Shūzen-ji was a favourite place of exile for the shoguns' potential rivals. In 1193 **Minamoto Noriyori**, the younger brother of Shogun Yoritomo, committed suicide – some say he was murdered – after being banished here on suspicion of treason. A more famous death occurred soon after when **Minamoto Yoriie** was murdered in the bath. Yoriie was the son of Yoritomo and had succeeded to the title of Shogun in 1199, aged only 18. Four years later his mother, Hōjō Masako, and grandfather seized power and sent Yoriie packing to Shūzen-ji, where he started planning his revenge. His plot, however, was discovered in 1204, and not long afterwards Yoriie was found dead, supposedly killed by bathing in poisoned water.

2

ONSEN IN SHŪZEN-JI

The town's most famous *onsen*, **Tokko-no-yu**, is now considered too public to be used for bathing, though you can soak your feet here. There are, however, other onsen just a short walk away.

Hako-yu 筥湯. This old-style building with a watchtower near *Tokko-no-yu* offers a lovely cedarwood onsen bath. Daily noon–9pm; ¥350.

Yu-no-sato-mura 湯の郷村. Follow the path west from *Tokko-no-yu* along the river, meandering across pretty bridges and through bamboo groves, and 400m later you'll emerge near this modern bathhouse, complete with both rotemburo and sauna. Daily 9am–10pm; ¥700 for 1hr, ¥950 no time limit.

---

807 by Kōbō Daishi, the founder of Shingon Buddhism (see p.527), when he found a boy washing his ailing father in the river; the priest struck the rock with his *tokko* (the short, metal rod carried by Shingon priests), and out gushed hot water with curative powers.

Shūzen-ji

修善寺 • **Museum** Daily: April–Sept 8.30am–4.30pm; Oct–March 8.30am–4pm • ¥300

As well as founding Shūzen-ji's first onsen, Kōbō Daishi is also credited with founding the nearby temple, **Shūzen-ji**, from which the town gets its name. The present temple, which stands at the top of the steps on the river's north bank, was rebuilt in 1883 and its now quiet halls belie a violent history (see box, p.215).

Opposite the Shūzen-ji temple office you'll find a small **museum** full of temple treasures, including possessions allegedly belonging to Kōbō Daishi and Minamoto Yoriie, and what is said to be Yoriie's death mask, all red and swollen. There's also information, some of it in English, about the many novels and plays inspired by these dramatic events, including Okamoto Kidō's famous modern kabuki play *Shūzen-ji Monogatari*, written in 1911.

Shigetsu-den

指月殿

The unassuming grave of Minamoto Yoriie (see box, p.215) lies on the hillside directly across the valley from Shūzen-ji, beside a smaller temple, **Shigetsu-den**, which Yoriie's repentant mother, Hōjō Masako, built to appease the soul of her son. Though not a dramatic building, it's the oldest in Shuzenji and has a fine Buddha statue inside accompanied by two guardians. Also on this side of the river, you'll find a delightful path snaking its way through a copse of bamboo.

ARRIVAL AND INFORMATION
SHŪZEN-JI ONSEN

By train Travelling to Shūzenji from Tokyo, the best option is a *Super View Odoriko* train direct from Tokyo Station to Shūzenji Station (2 daily; 2hr 10min); the trains divide at Atami, so make sure you're in the right carriage. Alternatively, hop on any of the regular Shinkansen services to Mishima (every 30min; 40min), from where the private Izu-Hakone Railway runs south to Shūzenji (¥500).

By bus Buses depart from outside Shūzenji Station to Shūzen-ji Onsen (every 10–20min; ¥210), dropping you at a terminal east of the village centre. Buses also depart from here to Shimoda and other destinations around the peninsula.

Tourist information Shūzenji's tourist information office (daily 9am–5pm; ☎ 0558 72 2501, ⊚ shuzenji.info) is in the city hall, on the main road coming into Shūzen-ji Onsen, a short walk east of the bus terminus.

Car rental Try Nissan (☎ 0558 72 2332) or Toyota (☎ 0558 74 0100) – both have branches near Shūzenji Station.

ACCOMMODATION AND EATING

Fukui 民宿福井 ☎ 0558 72 0558. This minshuku, one of a group on the northern hillside, welcomes non-Japanese speakers. None of the rooms has its own bathroom, but there is a lovely little rotemburo perched on the hillside. Rates include two meals. **¥13,000**, or **¥10,000** without meals

Goyōkan 五葉館 ☎ 0558 72 2066, ⊚ goyokan.co.jp. The lack of en-suite facilities at this comfortable ryokan is compensated for by large onsen baths, an affable, English-speaking owner, and cool, colour-coded rooms which are surprisingly modern for such a far-flung town. It's located a few doors down to the east of *Yukairō Kikuya* (see below), and behind a latticework facade. **¥17,000**

Nanaban なゝ番 On the main road east of the Shūzen-ji Onsen bus terminal ☎0558 72 0007. You'll find plenty of atmosphere at this rustic soba restaurant. Though they serve reasonably priced rice and noodle dishes, their speciality is *Zen-dera* soba, in which you dip cold soba in an eye-watering, do-it-yourself sauce of sesame and freshly grated horseradish – it's said to bring you the blessings of Buddha, so is surely a bargain at ¥1350. 10am–4pm; closed Thurs.

Okura おくら On the main road east of the Shūzen-ji Onsen bus terminal ☎0558 73 2266. In the evening, head to this friendly little *izakaya*, opposite *Nanaban* (see above), with an English menu and well-priced set meals from around ¥1300. Tues–Sun 11.30am–2pm & 5.30–9pm.

Yukairō Kikuya 湯回廊菊屋 ☎0558 72 2000. One of the nicest places to stay hereabouts, this elegant ryokan – patronized most famously by the writer Natsume Sōseki (see p.867) – sits under a high-peaked roof immediately opposite the bus station. Two meals included. **¥36,000**

Izu-Ōshima

伊豆大島

Some 110km south of Tokyo, **IZU-ŌSHIMA**, or simply Ōshima, is the nearest and largest of the **Izu-Shotō**, a chain of seven volcanic islands (see box, p.219) stretching over 300km of ocean. While the other volcanoes are now dormant, Ōshima's **Mihara-yama** (764m) does occasionally smoulder; its most recent major eruption took place in 1986, when the island was evacuated, but fortunately for much of the time it simply steams away. Mihara-yama found fame as the location for the *Godzilla* films (see p.856), for which the barren lava fields provided a fittingly apocalyptic backdrop. Other than the volcano, Ōshima's main draw is its forests of **camellia**. Things get pretty busy with visitors on summer weekends; for the forests, springtime is best, since the blossoms of an estimated three million trees colour the lower slopes a dusky red, an event celebrated with a month-long **festival** (Feb–March) of folk dances and other events. Whenever you visit, try to stay at least one night, to experience the slow pace of island life.

ARRIVAL AND DEPARTURE IZU-ŌSHIMA

By plane At the time of writing, JAL was scheduled to get its daily morning flight to Ōshima back up and running from Haneda Airport, though by the time you've included travelling to the airport and check-in time, the jetfoils are just as quick.

By jetfoil The best way of getting to Ōshima is on one of the jetfoils (2 daily; 1hr 45min–2hr 10min; ¥6830) operated by Tōkai Kisen (☎03 5472 9999, ⓦtokaikisen.co.jp) from Tokyo's Takeshiba pier, two stops from Shimbashi on the Yurikamome monorail. They dock either at Motomachi or at the tiny port of Okata (岡田), 7km away on the more sheltered north coast, depending on the weather.

Remember to check which port it's leaving from for the return journey, either by going to the port terminal in Motomachi or asking at your accommodation. Tōkai Kisen also operate jetfoils from Atami (2–3 daily; 45min; ¥4400).

By ferry Tōkai Kisen also runs a ferry service (1 daily July & Aug; 1 daily except Tues Sept–June; 4hr 20min–8hr; from ¥4280), occasionally via Yokohama. Outward sailings leave from Tokyo's Takeshiba pier at 10pm or 11pm, arriving in Motomachi or Okata early the next morning, while the return boat departs early afternoon, getting back to Tokyo the same evening; times vary, so check locally for the current schedule.

GETTING AROUND

By bus There are at least nine services daily on the main route running north from Motomachi to Okata (20min; ¥360) and Ōshima Park (35min; ¥550) via the airport. The second main route takes you south from Motomachi to Habu (9–11 daily; 35min; ¥670) on the island's southeastern tip. Buses also head up Mihara-yama from Motomachi (5 daily; 25min; ¥860) and Ōshima-kōen (2 daily; 25min; ¥840).

By car By far the best way of getting around the island is with your own transport. There are a number of car rental outfits, including Toyota (☎04992 21611) and local company Ōshima Rent-a-Car (☎04992 21043). Rates start

at around ¥5500 for the smallest car for up to six hours, and the car will be delivered to the port if you book in advance.

By bike and scooter You can rent bicycles (¥1500/day), mountain bikes (¥2500/day) and scooters (¥5000/day) from three outlets on the road heading inland and uphill from Motomachi ferry terminal; they're all on the right. Cyclists usually have a stab at a circuit of the island (44km; 4–6hr), which is best tackled anticlockwise.

Taxis A taxi from Motomachi to Okata will cost around ¥3000, to the airport around ¥1500; call Ōshima Kankō Jidōsha on ☎04992 21051.

INFORMATION

Tourist information The tourist office (daily 8.30am–5pm; ☎04992 22177, ⊚izu-oshima.or.jp) is across the road from the ferry terminal. They provide maps, bus timetables and a wealth of other information, though very little in English. You can also pick up basic maps at the ferry terminal in Okata.

Opening hours The island is essentially closed for business by 8pm, including almost all shops. A couple of

eating places in Motomachi stay open until 11pm or so.

Wi-Fi The island is an almost entirely wifi-free zone, though there is a hotspot at a secondary information office (daily 9.30am–4pm) just uphill from Motomachi ferry terminal, on your left.

Money There's a post office with ATM on the main road in Motomachi, though you're advised to bring along enough cash to cover your stay.

Motomachi

元町

Ōshima's main town, **MOTOMACHI**, is generally a sleepy little place which only springs into action when a ferry docks. It is, however, the hub of island life, where you'll find most of the facilities, and it makes a good base for exploring the island. There's a very nice black-sand beach, **Kobō-hama** (弘法浜), a short walk to the south – a grand spot for a sunset swim or an evening drink.

Museum of Volcanoes

火山博物館, Kazan Hakubutsukan • Around 600m from the port, on the town's southern outskirts • Daily 9am–5pm • ¥500 • ☎04992 24103

The rather grand **Museum of Volcanoes** was built after the 1986 eruption partly to lure tourists back to the island. Nothing much is labelled in English, though few things – lumps of volcanic rocks, video footage of eruptions, and the like – really need explaining.

Hama-no-yu

浜の湯 • 300m north of the ferry terminal • Daily: July & Aug 11am–7pm; Sept–June 1–7pm • ¥300

The best of Motomachi's several **onsen** baths is **Hama-no-yu**, a big public rotemburo on the cliff edge. It's the perfect spot for watching the sun go down – particularly on clear days, when Mount Fuji's silhouette adds a poetic touch. Note that the bathing is mixed; you'll need to bring a swimming costume.

ACCOMMODATION AND EATING   MOTOMACHI

Akamon ホテル赤門 ☎04992 21213, ⊚ooshima -akamon.com. The most luxurious accommodation hereabouts, with a choice of tatami or Western-style rooms (the latter in separate chalet-style cottages), an attractive rotemburo and onsen bath, and excellent seafood meals. To find it, walk up the road heading inland from the ferry terminal, then take the first left where you'll see its distinctive red gates at the end of the lane. Rates include two meals. 🛜 **¥28,000**

Mandarin Island マンダリンアイランドホテル ☎04992 20600, ⊚mandarin.a-asia.net. About as cheap a place to stay as you'll get in Motomachi, and nothing to write home about, though there's an outdoor pool for summer use, and the secluded location (a short walk east of the town centre) means that you'll most likely get a good sleep. **¥10,000**

★**Otomodachi** おともだち ☎04992 20061. The most

reliable of the row of little eating places opposite the port, serving a broad range of reasonably priced set meals; ¥1000 will buy you a generous meal, though you'll have to pay double that for one featuring *kin-me-dai*, a tasty local fish (see p.198). Daily 7am–3pm & 5–10pm.

Sushikō 寿し光 ☎04992 20888. This moderately swanky restaurant has sushi and sashimi sets from ¥1000, as well as pizzas, salads, *donburi* and the like. It's upstairs in a modern building just south of the ferry terminal, on the left. Daily 11am–2pm & 5–11pm.

Yocchan よっちゃん, no phone. Open later than most places in town, and with views over the ocean from its tables out back, this tiny snack hut is a good evening target – most customers here are salty sea dogs knocking back beer (¥350) and *yakitori* (¥150 and up), or some fried *yakionigiri* rice-balls (¥500). Mon–Sat 5–11pm.

THE IZU ISLANDS

Ōshima is merely the first, and – at 52km in circumference – the largest, of the **Izu Islands** (伊豆諸島, Izu-shotō), which dot the ocean in a skinny line stretching for more than 1000km. Given that they're all officially part of Tokyo, this makes the Japanese capital the longest city on earth, at least in an administrative sense. Most of these islands see very few international visitors, but if you don't mind spending hours (even days) on a ferry, you can reach these remote parts of Japan quite easily. Each of the main islands has its own distinctive draw:

Nii-jima (2hr 20min from Tokyo by jetfoil; 9hr on overnight ferry). Famed for its beaches, this island has developed a reputation for (occasionally debauched) summer weekend parties. Maehama beach, out west, is popular for windsurfing, though most scenic is the long, cliff-backed Habishi beach, over on the east side.

Miyake-jima (6hr 30min from Tokyo on overnight ferry). Like a little Fuji jutting out of the sea, this volcano-island has been active in recent times – due to belches of sulphuric gas it was completely evacuated in 2000, with its residents only returning in 2005. It boasts great hiking trails through camellia and hydrangea, and beaches next to lava flows.

Mikura-jima (45min from Miyake-jima on fishing boat). A little south of Miyake-jima, this small island is famed for its dolphins, with tours operating March–Oct.

Ogasawara Islands (25hr from Tokyo by ferry). As far south as Okinawa's main island, the subtropical islands of Chichi-jima and Haha-jima take more than a day to get to by ferry. Never having been connected to a continental landmass, their unique flora and fauna has seen them dubbed the "Galapagos of the Orient".

2

Okata

岡田

There's a fifty-fifty chance that your ferry or jetfoil will arrive in **OKATA**, rather than Motomachi. In many ways, it's a more characterful place than its bigger brother, a salty sort of village backed by steep hills, which feels cut off from the rest of the island, giving a genuine sense of remoteness to those who choose to stay here. There are plenty of accommodation options and a few places to eat (most stop serving after 7pm), although not all that much to actually do.

ACCOMMODATION — OKATA

Kichiyō 吉陽 **T 04992 75871, W to-on.info.** Tucked into a charming alley just opposite the ferry terminal, this friendly backpacker venue (the only one on the island) has room for twenty in its four tatami rooms. **¥3500** per person

Mihara-yama

三原山 • Bus from Motomachi (5 daily; 25min; ¥860) or Ōshima-kōen (2 daily; 25min; ¥840)

From Motomachi the road climbs steeply up the mostly grassy slopes of **Mihara-yama**, affording good views over Motomachi and the island's west coast and, if you're lucky, northwest across Izu Hantō to Mount Fuji. At the top, a clutch of souvenir shops sits on the rim of a much older crater, from where you get your first sight of the smouldering new summit, its flanks streaked with black ribbons left by the 1986 lava flows. A path leads 2.2km across the floor of the old crater, where grasses are gradually recolonizing the black, volcanic soils, and up to the new summit, from where you can peek down into the new crater's sulphurous pit.

From here, you can continue for another 2.5km round the rim and either return to the car park or walk down the northern slopes to rejoin the road 3km further down, but still 500m above sea level, near the *Ōshima Onsen Hotel* (大島温泉ホテル). The hotel itself is rather dilapidated and overpriced, but its **rotemburo** (daily 1–9pm; ¥800) offers a great view of the volcano.

Northern Honshū

MATSUSHIMA BAY

Northern Honshū

When the poet Matsuo Bashō set out to travel along the "narrow road to the deep north" in 1689, he commented, somewhat despondently, "I might as well be going to the ends of the earth." Even today, many urban Japanese regard the harsh mountainous provinces of northern Honshū as irredeemably backward. Not that the region is all thatched farmhouses and timeless agricultural vistas, but certainly rural traditions have survived here longer than in many other parts of the country. However, it doesn't take long to encounter the huge array of festivals, and nor do you have to delve deep to discover the rich heritage of folk tales and traces of ancient religious practices that give northern Honshū a deliciously mysterious tang.

Northern Honshū, or **Tōhoku** as much of the area is known, was the last part of Japan's main island to be brought under central control. As such, it boasts more in the way of military sights – ruined castles, samurai towns and aristocratic tombs – than great temples or religious foundations. The one glorious exception comes north of **Sendai** at the otherwise insignificant town of **Hiraizumi**, where the opulent Golden Hall (Konjiki-dō) has to be seen to be believed. In contrast, the archetypal north-country town lies not far away at **Tōno**, often referred to as the birthplace of Japanese folklore, where goblin-like *kappa* inhabit local rivers, fairy children scamper through old farmhouses, and secretive shrines hark back to primitive cults. Darker forces are also at work further north, where souls in purgatory haunt the volcanic wasteland of **Osore-zan**, on the hammerhead peninsula of **Shimokita Hantō**. In summer, pilgrims come here to consult blind mediums, while further west, the holy mountain range of **Dewa-sanzan** is home to *yamabushi*, ascetic priests endowed with mystical powers.

Apart from during festival season in summer, Tōhoku's **cities** tend to be less exciting than elsewhere in Japan. **Sendai**, though, which is by far the largest, is a dynamic urban centre that's home to a dramatic hilltop mausoleum, while the lanes and backstreets of **Morioka** abound in charm, and **Aomori** in the far north is thriving, thanks to its new Shinkansen link with Hokkaidō, and also holds a magnificent ancient relic, the so-called Sannai-Maruyama Site. Smaller towns not be missed include **Kakunodate**, inland between Morioka and Akita, with its samurai mansions and riverside cherry-tree "tunnel".

Tōhoku's splendid scenery ranges from prolific rice fields and cosseted orchards to wild rugged coastlines and the pine-studded islands of **Matsushima Bay**. Its central

YAMABUSHI WATERFALL PURIFICATION, DEWA-SANZAN

Highlights

❶ Matsushima Bay Studded with temple-topped islands, celebrated by poets, and home to succulent oysters, this stunning bay makes a wonderful day-trip from Sendai. **See p.238**

❷ Hiraizumi A tiny but extraordinary golden shrine bears witness to this sleepy riverside town's role as a Buddhist powerhouse, almost a thousand years ago. **See p.243**

❸ Cycling in the Tōno valley Pedal your way through a lush valley, nestling between wooded hills, where every rice paddy and old farmhouse seems to have its own intriguing legend. **See p.246**

❹ Sannai-Maruyama Site Showcasing the hillside homes and mysterious artefacts of the ancient Jōmon people, this verdant archeological site is a true-life treasure-trove. **See p.256**

❺ Kakunodate Discover the samurai heritage of this appealing town, including streets of gloriously preserved grand houses with extensive, impeccably maintained gardens. **See p.268**

❻ Dewa-sanzan Visit one of Japan's most sacred mountains and spend a day or two with the legendary *yamabushi* priests. **See p.271**

❼ Sado-ga-shima Dance to the rhythmic global beat at the annual Earth Celebration, hosted by international drumming sensation Kodo. **See p.280**

HIGHLIGHTS ARE MARKED ON THE MAP ON P.224

spine of soaring mountains provides excellent opportunities for hiking and skiing, notably around **Zaō Onsen** in **Yamagata-ken** and the more northerly **Towada-Hachimantai** area. Both are noted for their flora and fauna, including black bears in remoter districts, while **Towada-ko** itself is a massive crater lake accessed via the picturesque **Oirase valley**. The World Heritage-listed **Shirakami-Sanchi** mountains, on the border between Aomori and Akita prefectures, are equally beautiful, and remote enough to remain undeveloped. On **Sado-ga-shima**, a large island lying off Niigata,

NORTHERN HONSHŪ

HIGHLIGHTS

1 Matsushima Bay
2 Hiraizumi
3 Cycling in the Tōno valley
4 Sannai-Murayama Site
5 Kakunodate
6 Dewa-sanzan
7 Sado-ga-shima

THE GREAT EAST JAPAN EARTHQUAKE

The **Great East Japan Earthquake** of March 11, 2011, was at magnitude 9.0 the largest ever recorded in Japan. It triggered a **tsunami** that devastated the eastern coast of Tōhoku; some waves exceeded 40m in height. With the region's cities located safely inland, it was the smaller towns, fishing villages and industrial sites strung along the shoreline that bore the brunt of the onslaught. The worst affected areas were those closest to the epicentre, around 70km east of the Oshika Hantō peninsula and 130km east of Sendai. Almost 19,000 people died, with the highest casualties occurring in such places as **Ishinomaki** (see p.242) and the steel manufacturing centre of **Kamaishi**.

Tōhoku, like all Japan, has a long history of earthquakes. One of similar strength is known to have occurred in 869 AD, while the Sanriku Earthquake of 1896 claimed 27,000 victims. Past experience did not prevent the construction of four **nuclear power plants** along the coast, however. While none was damaged by the earthquake itself, the tsunami knocked out all power at the **Fukushima Daiichi (Number One) Plant**, 110km south of Sendai, causing its cooling systems to fail. Within three days, all three of its functioning reactors went into **meltdown**, in the worst nuclear disaster since Chernobyl. As of 2017, radiation leaks from the plant have stopped, but one reactor is still not under control, and an exclusion zone of 20km remains in force.

Meanwhile, thanks to a colossal reconstruction programme that incorporates stronger defences against any future tsunami, normal life has returned to Tōhoku. Radiation levels in the region – in agricultural products and seafood as well as in the air and the ocean – are now officially deemed to be entirely safe, and with all transport connections once more fully operational, there's no reason for tourists to stay away.

The city of **Fukushima** itself, 90km northwest of the eponymous nuclear power station, is not described in this book for the simple reason that it's an unassuming prefectural capital that holds little of interest to visitors. If you do pass through, you can pick up information on the disaster and ongoing recovery from the tourist office at the station, or at the Decontamination Information Plaza, 400m north at 1-31 Sakae-machi (Mon–Fri 9am–5pm; ☎024 529 5668, ⓦjosen-plaza.env.go.jp).

dramatic mountain and coastal scenery provides the backdrop for a surprisingly rich culture – a legacy of its isolation as well as the infamous characters once exiled here.

The ideal **time to visit** is either spring or autumn, when the scenery is at its finest, and before the coastal plans start to swelter and everything gets too busy. In early August, thousands of visitors flock to Tōhoku's big four **festivals** in Sendai, Aomori, Hirosaki and Akita. If you're travelling at this time, make sure to sort out transport and accommodation well in advance. Apart from ski resorts, many tourist facilities outside the major cities shut down from early November to late April.

GETTING AROUND   NORTHERN HONSHŪ

By plane Northern Honshū has several international flight connections, with services from China, Russia, South Korea and Taiwan coming into Aomori, Fukushima, Niigata and Sendai airports. These airports, along with those at Akita, Iwate Hanamaki, Shōnai near Tsuruoka, and Yamagata, are also served by flights to and from domestic destinations all over Japan.

By train The Tōhoku Shinkansen runs the full length of northern Honshū, parallel to but well inland from the east coast, and passing through such cities as Sendai and Morioka, all the way to Aomori. Since 2016 the line has even continued beyond, burrowing beneath the sea via the new Seikan Tunnel to reach Hokkaidō. Spur lines also branch west, to Shinjō via Yamagata and to Akita via Kakunodate, while a separate cross-country Shinkansen connects Tokyo and Niigata. In addition, smaller JR and private lines thread through the region. The JR East (Tōhoku Area) rail pass (ⓦjapanrailpass.net), valid for five journeys within a fourteen-day period (¥19,000 for foreign visitors), covers an area stretching from Tokyo to every destination in this chapter apart from Niigata.

By bus Public buses can be sporadic at the best of times, with many services stopping completely in winter, when heavy snowfalls close the mountain roads. Check timetables and connections with local tourist offices before you set off.

By car As public transport is limited, especially in rural areas, car rental is definitely worth considering.

Aizu-Wakamatsu

会津若松

Centuries ago, **AIZU-WAKAMATSU**, in the heart of southern Tōhoku 300km from Tokyo, was an important castle town on the main trunk road north. Set in the middle of a wide valley near one of Japan's largest lakes, Inawashiro-ko, it's rather off the beaten track these days, but its history is sufficiently dramatic to attract tourists and pilgrims alike. Most come on day-trips, to tour such sights as its reconstructed castle keep, an attractive samurai house, and the graves of nineteen young casualties of the Boshin War. Be warned, though, that Aizu-Wakamatsu sprawls across a considerable area, making it much too large to explore comfortably on foot.

Iimori-yama

飯盛山 • Daily 9am–5pm • Free; escalator ¥250 • ⓦ iimoriyama.jp

From Aizu-Wakamatsu Station, at the northwest corner of the city, **Byakko-dōri** heads to the foothills 2.5km east, to reach the **Iimori-yama**, famous as the spot where a group of young soldiers killed themselves during one of the final battles of the Meiji Restoration in 1868. The warriors of Aizu-Wakamatsu were among the few clans to put up serious opposition to the imperial armies during the so-called Boshin War, and the **Byakkotai** (White Tigers) were one of several bands of young fanatics who joined the fighting. Twenty of them, all aged sixteen and seventeen, were cut off from their comrades. Trying to reach the safety of the castle, they climbed Iimori-yama, only to think they saw Tsuruga-jō in flames. Assuming the battle to be lost, they committed *seppuku*, ritual suicide by disembowelment. Although in fact the castle was not burning, the boys are still revered as heroes.

Scaling the hill's steep staircases takes roughly 10min; alternatively, there's a handy escalator. At the top, an imperial eagle – a gift from the Italian Fascist Party in 1928, and supported on a Roman pillar from Pompeii – dominates the small clearing, and underlines the disturbing aspects of the story. Apart from one boy who was saved before he bled to death, the rest lie buried in the row of graves to the left. Twice each year, on April 24 and Sept 24, proud parents watch as local schoolboys of the same age re-enact the suicides. The whole site is heavily commercialized, including various displays and exhibitions as well as cafés and souvenir shops.

Sazae-dō

さざえ堂 • Daily 8.15am–sunset; ¥400

Sazae-dō, just downhill from Iimori-yama, is an elegant and extraordinary octagonal wooden building erected in 1796 as part of a larger temple complex. Resembling a pagoda, it's a unique structure, in which two external ramped walkways spiral around a central column, inside which are sealed 33 statues of Kannon, the Goddess of Mercy.

Buke-yashiki

武家屋敷 • Daily: April–Nov 8.30am–5pm, Dec–March 9am–4.30pm • ¥870 • ☎ 024 228 2525, ⓦ bukeyashiki.com • On Haikara-san and Akabe bus routes from station

Buke-yashiki, a magnificent reproduction of a nineteenth-century **samurai residence**, nestles against the foothills 4km southeast of the station; with time to spare, it's fun to walk along the demanding and hard-to-find footpath that winds along the hillside here from Iimori-yama, 2km north. This spacious compound once belonged to **Saigō Tanomo**, a chief retainer of the Aizu clan, and its 38 rooms range from a sand-box toilet and cypress bathtub to a "classy reception room" reserved for the Lord of Aizu.

When Saigō went off to fight in the Boshin War in 1868, he left his wife and daughters, aged between 2 and 16, at home. As the imperial army closed in, the family decided to commit suicide rather than be taken prisoner. The 16-year-old failed to die immediately but was killed soon after by an enemy soldier – mannequins in the relevant room re-enact the scene – and the house was set on fire.

The complex also includes several original buildings brought from surrounding villages, including what's labelled as a "feudal clan style rice polishing area" and a thatched shrine.

Tsuruga-jō

鶴ヶ城 • 1-1 Ōte-machi • Daily 8.30am–5pm • ¥410, ¥510 with tea • ☎ 024 227 4005, ⦿ tsurugajo.com

The large park that surrounds the original site of Aizu-Wakamatsu's castle, **Tsuruga-jō**, is 2.7km south of the station, on the far side of downtown. Set between massive stone ramparts and looming over a moat, the castle's imposing entrance rather dwarfs the dainty white keep inside.

Originally built in 1384, Tsuruga-jō was besieged by Meiji troops for several months in 1868, before the Aizu clan finally surrendered. The new government ordered it to be demolished and it lay in ruins until 1965, when the central keep was rebuilt – it now houses an uninteresting local history museum – and the gardens landscaped.

The castle is the focus of the city's main **festival** (Sept 22–24), which includes a procession of samurai and ceremonies for the Byakkotai.

Fukushima Museum

福島県立博物館, Fukushima Kenritsu Hakubutsukan • 1-25 Jōtō-machi • Tues–Sun 9.30am–5pm • ¥270 • ☎ 024 228 6000, ⦿ www.general-museum.fks.ed.jp

The ultra-modern **Fukushima Museum**, outside the east gate of Tsuruga-jō but still within the castle park, covers local history from mock-ups of Jōmon-period huts (2000 BC) to a charcoal-driven bus from the 1930s. The displays are well presented, with sufficient English for non-Japanese speakers to get the gist of what's going on.

ARRIVAL AND DEPARTURE
AIZU-WAKAMATSU

By train Aizu-Wakamatsu Station is on the northern edge of the city. Trains on the scenic JR Ban'etsu line run east to the nearest Shinkansen station, Kōriyama, one stop south of Fukushima on the Tōhoku line. Ban'etsu trains also head northwest towards the coast; one daily goes all the way to Niigata, but for west-coast destinations it's more usual to have to change at Niitsu, 20km inland from Niigata. The

most attractive approach to Aizu-Wakamatsu is via the private Tōbu and Aizu lines, which provide connections, and one daily direct service, all the way to Nikkō.

Destinations Kitakata (8 daily; 15min); Kōriyama (hourly; 1hr); Niigata (1 daily; 2hr 40min); Niitsu (5 daily; 2hr 30min); Nikkō (1 daily; 3hr).

INFORMATION AND GETTING AROUND

Tourist information Aizu-Wakamatsu has two helpful tourist offices, one in the train station (daily 9am–5.30pm; ☎ 024 232 0688, ⦿ aizukanko.com) and the other inside the castle's north gate (daily 8.30am–5pm; ☎ 024 227 4005). Both have English-speaking staff, and give out excellent English-language hand-drawn maps to the city.

By bus City buses depart from outside the train station every 20min for Buke-yashiki (Akabe; platform 4), or you

can catch the splendid vintage Haikara-san loop-line buses (clockwise or anticlockwise) from platform 6 to Tsuruga-jō, Buke-yashiki and Iimori-yama. Single journeys cost ¥210, or you can buy an all-day pass for ¥500.

By bike Ask at the station tourist office for details of the city's bike-rental scheme (¥500/day).

By car Eki Rent-a-Car have an office in the station building (☎ 024 224 5171, ⦿ www.ekiren.co.jp).

ACCOMMODATION

Aizuno Youth Hostel 会津野ユースホステル 88 Kakiyashiki, Terasaki Aizu-Takada-chō ☎ 024 255 1020, ⦿ aizuno.com. Neat, scrupulously maintained little hostel, amid the rice fields 12km west of Aizu-Wakamatsu, which offers bunk beds in shared rooms, as well as singles, twins

and family rooms, plus good food (breakfast ¥400, dinner ¥800) and bike rental. To get here, take the JR Tadami line to Aizu-Takada Station (20min from Aizu-Wakamatsu Station), then walk for just over 2km northwest, first heading straight ahead from the station, then turning right at the second intersection. 🛜 Dorms ¥3900, rooms ¥8800

Ekimae Fuji Grand Hotel 駅前フジグランドホテル
5-25 Ekimae-machi ☎024 224 1111, Ⓦ fujigrandhotel
.co.jp. Big, busy and rather monolithic red-brick business
hotel, right outside Aizu Wakamatsu station. Guests have
free admission to the adjoining onsen. Some of the older
rooms are a tad careworn, but it's really not bad value.
Rates include breakfast. 🛜 ¥8800

Washington Hotel 会津若松ワシントンホテル 201
Byakko-machi ☎024 222 6111, Ⓦ aizu-wh.com
/washington-hotels.jp/aizuwakamatsu. Large, reliable
chain hotel, less than a 5min walk straight ahead (east) of
Aizu-Wakamatsu Station along Byakko-dōri, and offering
comfortable rooms, a coffee lounge, a bar and a tenth-floor
restaurant, serving Japanese and Western meals. Rates
include breakfast. 🛜 ¥9000

EATING

Mitsutaya 満田屋 1-1-25 Ōmachi ☎024 227 1345,
Ⓦ www.mitsutaya.jp. This striking historic structure, on
the western edge of downtown 1.3km south of the station,
started life almost two centuries ago as a bean-paste mill.
It's now a local foodie favourite thanks to its *dengaku*,
charcoal-grilled skewers of rice, tofu and/or vegetables.
You can eat a good lunch here for under ¥1500. Mon, Tues
& Thurs–Sun 10am–5pm.

Takino 田季野 5-31 Sakae-machi ☎024 225 0808,

Ⓦ www.takino.jp. Tucked into the downtown
backstreets, southeast of where Chūō-dōri meets
Nanokomachi-dōri junction, the beautiful old building is a
little tricky to find, but it's worth it to sample tasty food
such as the house speciality *wappa-meshi*, a wooden box
of steamed rice with various toppings such as flowering
fern (*zenmai*), mushrooms (*kinoko*), fish or seafood.
Expect to pay around ¥1500, including pickles and soup.
🛜 Daily 11am–9pm.

Kitakata

喜多方

With its mountain climate and abundant supplies of pure water, the area surrounding
Aizu-Wakamatsu is famous for making high-quality **sake**. On a day-trip to the centre
of production, **KITAKATA**, 17km north of Aizu-Wakamatsu, you can visit a sake brewery
as well as several distinctive **kura** (traditional storehouses). At some point, such a craze
for constructing these fireproof storehouses, encased in thick mud walls, swept through
Kitakata that the town is now said to hold more than two thousand *kura*. Including the
more recent brick versions, they're built in an extraordinary range of styles, and today
even the post office and other public offices hide behind *kura* facades. To see plenty of
prime examples, there's no need to venture beyond the compact central district into the
sprawling modern town beyond.

Yamatogawa Sake Brewing Museum

大和川酒造北方風土館, Yamatogawa Shuzō Kitakata Fūdokan • 4761 Tera-machi • Daily 9am–4.30pm • Free • ☎012 060 2233,
Ⓦ bit.ly/yamatogawa

The **Yamatogawa Sake Brewing Museum**, 1km north of the station, occupies an
attractive collection of seven *kura*. Sake was made here from 1790 to 1990, before
production moved to a new automated plant. After a guided tour – aided by a brief
English pamphlet – you'll get the opportunity to taste a few samples, with no obligation
to buy. Note the globe of cedar fronds hanging in the entrance hall. Traditionally,
breweries hang a green cedar ball outside in March, when the freshly brewed sake is put
in vats to age; by September the browned fronds indicate that it's ready to drink.

ARRIVAL AND INFORMATION   KITAKATA

By train Kitakata Station, on the south side of town, is
on the Ban'etsu West line from Aizu-Wakamatsu (8 daily;
15min), as it heads towards the Sea of Japan. Walk
straight ahead, north, for around 10min to reach the
historic core.

Tourist information Kitakata's main tourist office is at

the station (daily 8.30am–5.15pm; ☎024 124 2633,
Ⓦ kitakata-kanko.jp). Their website includes a detailed
English-language map and guide.

Bike rental Rental bikes are available at the Satō and
Akugawa shops, opposite the station (both daily
8am–6pm; from ¥250/hr, ¥1000/day).

EATING

Kitakata is renowned for its **ramen**, and holds nearly a hundred outlets from which to choose.

Makoto Shokudō まこと食堂 7116 Odazuki-michishita ☎ 024 122 0232. Kitakata's most famous old ramen place, in the backstreets east of the main shopping street, Chūō-dōri, has atmospheric old tatami rooms. As well as noodles for under ¥1000, they serve other, similarly inexpensive, dishes. Tues–Sun 7.30am–3pm.

Yamagata

山形

Few tourists make it to the large workaday city of **YAMAGATA**, ringed by high mountains 65km west of Sendai. Apart from a couple of engaging museums, its main attraction is as a base for visiting nearby **Yamadera**'s atmospheric temples, and **Zaō Onsen**, an excellent spot for summer hiking and winter skiing, known for its beguiling "snow monsters" (*juhyō*) – fir trees engulfed in wind-sculpted ice and snow. The one time of year when it's really worth staying longer is in early August, when the major **Hanagasa Matsuri** festival engulfs the city in colour and activity.

Central Yamagata occupies a grid of streets immediately northeast of the train station. Its southern boundary is **Ekimae-dōri**, the broad avenue that leads straight ahead from the station as far as the *Castle* hotel, where it's intersected by the main shopping street, **Nanokamachi-dōri**.

Kajō-kōen

霞城公園

The one district of Yamagata that holds much interest for sightseers is the city's largest park, **Kajō-kōen**, which starts 700m northwest of the station. Originally home to a long-vanished castle, of which only the beautifully restored **East Gate** now survives, it's still almost entirely encircled by a moat, and now holds a couple of absorbing museums as well as various municipal sports facilities.

Yamagata Prefectural History Museum

山形県立博物館, Yamagata Kenritsu Hakubutsukan • 1-8 Kajō-machi • Tues–Sun 9am–4.30pm • ¥300 • ☎ 023 645 1111, ⓦ www.yamagata-museum.jp

A hulking concrete building on the eastern side of Kajō-kōen is home to the **Yamagata Prefectural History Museum**, an entertaining hotch-potch that covers natural history and geology as well as the region's human story. Displays kick off with fossils and stuffed birds, move on to some

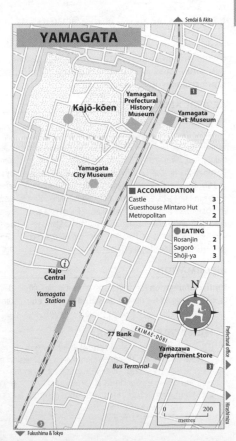

YAMAGATA

▲ Sendai & Akita

Kajō-kōen

Yamagata Prefectural History Museum

Yamagata Art Museum

Yamagata City Museum

ACCOMMODATION
Castle	3
Guesthouse Mintaro Hut	1
Metropolitan	2

EATING
Rosanjin	2
Sagorō	1
Shōji-ya	3

Kajo Central

Yamagata Station

N

EKIMAE-DŌRI

77 Bank

Yamazawa Department Store

Bus Terminal

0   200
metres

Prefectural office

Hirashimizu

▼ Fukushima & Tokyo

3

THE KILNS OF HIRASHIMIZU

The pretty pottery village of **Hirashimizu** (平清水) has a surprisingly rural atmosphere, despite its location in Yamagata's southeastern outskirts. There's just one main street and a small river running down from the surrounding hills, providing local potters with their distinctive speckled clay. If you explore a little, you'll find several family **potteries** with showrooms (generally daily 9am–5pm; open until 6pm in high season). To reach Hirashimizu, take a bus from Yamagata Station (hourly; 15min; ¥300).

POTTERIES

Shichiemon-gama 七右衛門窯 153 Hirashimizu ☎023 642 7777. The largest pottery in the area, Shichiemon-gama offers visitors the chance to throw a pot or two. A 1hr 30min lesson costs ¥2160, while pots are on sale for ¥1000 upwards. Daily 9am–5pm.

Seiryū-gama 精龍窯 50-1 Hirashimizu ☎023 631 2828. One of the best local workshops, offering assorted short courses from ¥2000. Daily 9am–5pm.

---

dramatic Jomon artefacts from two thousand years ago, then swing through Yamagata's period as a castle town before ending with exhibits of local crafts.

Yamagata City Museum

山形市郷土館, Yamagata-shi Kyōdo-kan • 1-1 Kajō-machi • Tues–Sun 9am–4.30pm • Free • ☎ 023 644 0253, Ⓦ bit.ly /yamagata-folklore

For visitors, the appeal of the **Yamagata City Museum**, in the southeast corner of Kajō-kōen, lies as much in the rather extraordinary pink octagonal clapboard building in which it's housed as it does in the museum itself. Built in 1878 as the town's principal hospital, it now holds a gruesome collection of early medical equipment and anatomical drawings, including, notably, a pregnancy guide rendered as woodblock prints.

ARRIVAL AND DEPARTURE   YAMAGATA

By plane Yamagata Airport serves domestic routes only (Ⓦ yamagata-airport.co.jp). Shuttle buses, timed to coincide with flights, connect it with Yamagata's bus terminal and train station, 20km south (7 daily; 35min; ¥980).
Destinations Nagoya (2 daily; 1hr 15min); Osaka Itami (3 daily; 1hr 25min); Tokyo Haneda (2 daily; 1hr 5min).
By train Yamagata is on a spur of the Tōhoku Shinkansen that branches north from the main line at Fukushima and dead-ends north of Yamagata at Shinjō. In addition, the very scenic east–west Senzan line provides direct connections with Sendai, via Yamadera.

Destinations Fukushima (hourly; 1hr 10min); Sendai (hourly; 1hr 20min); Shinjō (hourly; 1hr 10min); Tokyo (hourly; 2hr 30min–3hr 15min); Yamadera (hourly; 20min).
By bus All long-distance buses use Yamagata's central bus terminal, in the Yamakō building (山交ビル) behind Ekimae-dōri's Yamazawa department store. Most city buses stop outside the station's east exit.
Destinations Niigata (2 daily; 3hr 40min); Sendai (every 30min; 1hr); Tokyo (4 daily; 7hr 15min); Toyama (1 daily; 7hr); Tsuruoka (9 daily; 1hr 50min).

INFORMATION

Tourist information The main tourist office is in the Kajō Central Building, to the right of the station's western exit

(daily 9am–5.30pm; ☎023 647 2333, Ⓦ yamagatakanko .com).

HANAGASA MATSURI

During Yamagata's main **festival**, held annually from August 5 to 7, this normally sedate city bursts into life. The event involves a procession of more than ten thousand **dancers** accompanied by brightly decorated floats and Taiko drums. Traditionally, *yukata*-clad women wearing flowery hats perform slow, graceful dances in unison, but in recent years there has been a much greater variety of dance groups. Members of the crowd can also join in during several circle-dancing sessions.

GETTING AROUND

By bus A sightseeing bus loops every 10min between the station and the major sights (daily 9.30am–6.30pm; ¥100 flat fare).

By bike Free rental bikes can be picked up (and dropped off) at seven locations around Yamagata, including the tourist office.

Car rental Car rental companies clustered around the station include Eki Rent-a-Car (☎023 646 6322, ⓦwww .ekiren.co.jp) and Toyota (☎023 625 0100, ⓦrent.toyota .co.jp).

ACCOMMODATION

Castle ホテルキャッスル 4-2-7 Tōka-machi ☎023 631 3311, ⓦhotelcastle.co.jp. Just over a 5min walk along Ekimae-dōri from the station, this large hotel offers well-sized, contemporary Western-style rooms as well as reasonably priced Chinese, Japanese and Mediterranean restaurants. Breakfast costs ¥1200 per person. ☞ **¥8400**

Guesthouse Mintaro Hut ゲストハウス ミンタロハット 5–13 Ōte-machi ☎090 2797 1687, ⓦmintarohut.com. Welcoming budget option, near the northeast corner of Kajō-kōen park 1.5km north of the station, and named for an eponymous hut on New Zealand's Milford Track. The four simple Western-style guest rooms share use of a cosy lounge and communal kitchen, plus free bikes. ☞ Doubles **¥6000**

Metropolitan ホテルメトロポリタン 1-1-1 Kasumi-chō ☎023 628 1111, ⓦwww.yamagatametropolitan.jp. Smart, modern hotel conveniently located right above the station, with large and comfortable rooms in both Japanese and Western styles, and a Japanese restaurant that's open for all meals. If you're travelling on a JR rail pass, you can enjoy substantial discounts. ☞ **¥11,200**

EATING

Yamagata's **speciality foods** include marbled Yonezawa beef, similar to the more famous Matsuzaka variety, and *imoni*, a warming winter stew of potato, meat, onions and *konnyaku* (a jelly-like food made from the root of the devil's tongue plant), served in a slightly sweet sauce.

Louisiana Hurricane ルイジアナハリケーン 1-3-1 Kasumi-chō ☎023 631 5012. Despite the transatlantic name, this lively place, just along from the station, styles itself a British pub and devotes much of its energies and wall space to celebrating the Beatles. Besides cocktails and the company of expats, it also offers hearty plates of Western-style food for around ¥800. ☞ Daily 6pm–7am

Rosanjin ロサンジン 2-2-34 Ekimae-dōri ☎023 615 2650. Cosy restaurant, serving authentic pizzas (from ¥1180) fresh from its wood-burning oven, along with similarly priced pasta and other Italian specialities. The owner speaks an idiosyncratic mix of French and Italian. ☞ Mon–Sat noon–2.30pm & 5.30–11pm, Sun noon–2.30pm & 5.30–10pm.

Sagorō 佐五郎 1-6-10 Kasumi-chō ☎023 631 3560, ⓦwww.sagoro.jp. Refined restaurant, poised on the second floor above its own butcher store, which makes an ideal spot to sample the local beef *sukiyaki* and *shabu-shabu*. Set dinner menus start from ¥4860, but you can get a good lunch for ¥1500. Mon–Sat 11.30am–3pm & 5–10pm.

★Shōji-ya 庄司屋 14-28 Sawai-machi ☎023 622 1380, ⓦshojiya.jp. Turn right out of the station and head south for around 800m until you come to a level crossing; turn left, away from the tracks, and you'll come to Yamagata's oldest soba restaurant 50m along on the left. No one speaks English and there's no English menu, but it's easy enough to sample handmade soba (¥790–1640) in any form you fancy – with hot duck soup and vegetables, for example – at the smart, spotless shared tables. ☞ Tues–Sun 11am–8.30pm.

Zaō Onsen

蔵王温泉

Up in the mountains 20km southeast of Yamagata city, **ZAŌ ONSEN** is the main focus of activity in the Zaō Quasi National Park, an attractive region of volcanoes, crater lakes and hot springs. In winter, from December to late March, the resort offers some of Japan's finest **skiing**, with more than a dozen runs to choose from, as well as night skiing and onsen baths to soak away the aches and pains. Non-skiers can enjoy the ropeway (cable-car) ride over the plateau known as **Juhyō Kōgen**, where a thick covering of snow and hoarfrost transforms the trees into giant "snow monsters" (*juhyō*).

Juhyō Kōgen

Zaō Sanroku Ropeway (蔵王山麓ロープウェイ) Daily: April to mid-Dec 8.30am–5pm, mid-Dec to March 8.15am–4.45pm, every 10min **Sancho Ropeway** (サンチョロープウェイ) Daily: April to mid-Dec 8.30am–5pm, mid-Dec to March 8.30am–4.30pm • One-way: Zaō Sanroku only ¥800, both ¥1500; return: Zaō Sanroku only ¥1500, both ¥2600 • ☎ 023 694 9518, ⓦ zaoropeway.co.jp

The Zaō Sanroku Ropeway (cable-car) takes visitors up to the mountains to see the **Juhyō Kōgen**, or "Snow Monster Plateau", where the eerie frozen firs are at their most spectacular in February. At the base station, ten minutes' walk southeast of the bus station, the **Juhyō Museum** displays photos of the ghostly frozen formations (same opening hours as lifts; free).

From the Juhyō Kōgen station at the upper end of the Sanroku Ropeway, the separate Sanchō Ropeway climbs in turn to the Zaō Jizō Sanchō Station. At 1661m, this top station lies between Sampō Kōjin-san (1703m) and Jizō-san (1736m), just two of the peaks that make up the ragged profile of **Zaō-san**.

During the summer hiking season (May–Oct), you can follow the right-hand (southeasterly) path over Jizō-san and Kumano-dake (1841m) for spectacular views and a fairly rugged hour's walk to the desolate, chemical-blue **Okama crater lake** (御釜火口湖, Okama Kakōko).

Dai-rotemburo onsen

大露天風呂 • Daily: April & Nov 9am–sunset; May–Oct 6am–7pm • ¥470 • ☎ 023 694 9417 • Many ryokan offer a bus shuttle for guests

Zaō Onsen village has plenty of public baths where you can recover from skiing or hiking with a good, long soak. The pick of the bunch, the unforgettable outdoor **Dai-rotemburo onsen**, and open in summer only, is twenty minutes' walk uphill from the bus station, Fed by hot springs, surrounded by discoloured rock and overflowing with steamy sulphur-laden water, it can accommodate up to two hundred bathers.

ARRIVAL AND INFORMATION   ZAŌ ONSEN

By bus Regular buses run from Yamagata Station to the Zaō Onsen bus terminal (hourly; 40min; ¥1000), at the bottom of the village; in summer, one bus each day continues all the way to Okama lake (May–Oct; 1hr 30min; one-way Yamagata–Okama ¥2050, Okama–Yamagata ¥1490). During ski season, buses also run between Zaō Onsen and Sendai (daily, late Dec to mid-March; departs Sendai 8am, Zaō Onsen 4.30pm; 1hr 40min; ¥1600

one-way; reservations advisable; ☎ 022 261 5333, ⓦ https://japanbusonline.com, and from Sendai Airport to Zaō Onsen (4 daily, mid-Dec to early April; 1hr 50min; ¥1800; ☎ 022 323 4737).

Tourist information The tourist office, which hands out English-language resort information and ski maps, is at the bus terminal (daily 9am–6pm; ☎ 023 694 9328, ⓦ zao -spa.or.jp).

ACCOMMODATION AND EATING

Gokan-no-yu Tsuruya 五感の湯つるや 710 Zaō Onsen ☎ 023 694 9112, ⓦ www.tsuruyahotel.co.jp. High-end option, opposite the bus station, where the authentic ryokan experience includes lavish *kaiseki* meals and a choice of stylish indoor, open-air and private hot-spring baths. Guests get discounts on lift passes and equipment rental. Two meals a day cost an extra ¥5150 per person. ☏ **¥11,100**

Izakaya Robata 居酒屋炉端 42-7 Zaō Onsen ☎ 023 694 9565. There's usually a good atmosphere at this small, popular *izakaya* near the river, well known for its lamb barbecue skewers and other flame-grilled dishes, with full dinners starting at ¥2000. Mon–Wed & Fri–Sun: Jan–March & late Dec 11am–midnight, April to mid-Dec 11am–11pm.

SKIING IN ZAŌ ONSEN

Zaō is one of Japan's largest **ski areas**, covering 750 acres and equipped with 41 lifts to access slopes suited to all levels. Its northerly position ensures a large annual snowfall of dry, high-quality, powder snow. A shuttle bus (mid-Dec to late March; ¥100) moves skiers and snowboarders between the base lifts. Lift passes cost ¥4000 for 4hr, ¥5000 per day, ¥21,600 for seven days (plus ¥500 pass deposit); equipment and clothing rental is available from shops near the base stations (ski set around ¥3000 per day, clothing ¥3000).

Lodge Chitoseya ロッジちとせや 954 Zaō Onsen ☎ 023 694 9145, ⓦ lodge-chitoseya.com. Located after the first bridge as you head right from the station, this reasonable and comfortable lodging has a hostel-like atmosphere and an English-speaking manager. Rates include breakfast; dinner costs an extra ¥1475 per person. ≋ **¥10,500**

Yamadera

山寺 • ☎ 023 695 2843, ⓦ rissyakuji.jp

The temple complex of Risshaku-ji, or **YAMADERA** as it's more popularly known, is one of Tōhoku's most holy places. Set on a steep, rocky hillside, 14km northeast of Yamagata and 75km west of Sendai, it was founded in 860 by a Zen priest of the Tendai sect, and reached its peak during the Kamakura period (1185–1333). Today around forty temple buildings still stand scattered among the ancient cedars.

Kompon Chūdō

根本中堂 • Daily 8am–5pm • ¥200

Yamadera's main hall, the magnificent **Kompon Chūdō**, stands at the foot of the mountain temple complex. To get there from the station, cross the river and follow the road to the right, passing a row of shops selling souvenirs and snacks.

Dating from 1356, Kompon Chūdō shelters a flame that was brought 1100 years ago from Enryaku-ji, the centre of Tendai Buddhism near Kyoto (see p.474), and which is said to have been burning ever since. Peer inside, and you should see the lantern hanging on the left-hand side.

Risshaku-ji temple walk

立石寺 • Daily 6am–6pm • ¥300

Entering Yamadera's **San-mon gate** (山門) brings you to the start of the **Risshaku-ji temple walk**. Over 1100 steps weave their way up past moss-covered *Jizō* statues, lanterns and prayer wheels, and squeeze between looming rocks carved with prayers and pitted with caves. At the highest temple, **Okuno in**, breathless pilgrims tie prayer papers around a mammoth lantern and light small bunches of incense sticks. Before you set off back downhill, don't miss the views over Yamadera from the terrace of **Godai-dō**, perched on the cliff-face just beyond the distinctive red **Nōkyō-dō** pavilion.

Yamadera Bashō Memorial Museum

山寺芭蕉記念館, Yamadera Bashō Kinenkar • 4223 Nanin • Daily 9am–4.30pm • ¥400 • ☎ 023 695 2221, ⓦ yamadera-basho.jp

Located on a hilltop behind Yamadera Station, with a panoramic view of the Risshaku-ji temple, the modern **Yamadera Bashō Memorial Museum** commemorates the visit of the famous poet Bashō to Yamadera. Travelling before the days of coach parties, he penned a characteristically pithy ode to Yamadera: "In the utter silence of a temple, a cicada's voice alone penetrates the rocks." Exhibits include original haiku poems and Edo-period artworks.

ARRIVAL AND DEPARTURE

YAMADERA

By train Yamadera Station, across the river 400m southwest of the temple, is on the JR Senzan line between Yamagata and Sendai.

Destinations Sendai (hourly; 1hr); Yamagata (hourly; 20min).

ACCOMMODATION AND EATING

Yamadera village consists mainly of expensive **ryokan** and souvenir shops; some of the latter set up boiling vats of **konnyaku balls** outside, good for a warming snack (¥100 skewer).

Yamadera Pension 山寺ペンション 4273-1 Yamadera ☎023 695 2134. The most attractive accommodation option in town, in a traditional half-timbered building facing the station. The Western-style rooms are comfortable and tastefully decorated. Rates include two meals in the restaurant *Onoya* downstairs, also open to non-guests and specializing in tasty handmade soba dishes costing from ¥1000. **¥17,800**

Sendai

仙台

The largest city in the Tōhoku region, **SENDAI** is a sprawling but pleasant place, with broad tree-lined avenues and a lively downtown district. Though often regarded as little more than a staging post on the way to Matsushima Bay (see p.238), the city's **castle ruins** and associated history museum, and the ornate mausoleum of its revered founder, the *daimyō* **Date Masamune**, are worth a brief stop.

Though central Sendai had to be rebuilt after World War II, its streets follow the original grid pattern laid out by Masamune in the seventeenth century. The main downtown area, a high-rise district of offices, banks and shopping malls, lies on the east bank of the **Hirose-gawa**. Its principal thoroughfare, **Aoba-dōri**, runs west from the train station to the far side of the river, where the main historic sights are located. Roughly halfway along, it's crossed by bustling **Ichiban-chō**, which together with the covered **Chūō-dōri** forms the heart of a bustling nightlife and shopping neighbourhood.

Sendai also hosts some colourful festivals, including the **Tanabata** or Star Festival in August, and the **Jorenji Street Jazz Festival** (second weekend in Sept; ⓦj-streetjazz.com) a month later, which sees the city-centre streets transformed into an urban music venue.

Aoba-jō

青葉城 • 1 Kawauchi-ku • ☎022 214 8259, ⓦwww.sendaijyo.com • Free • Buses from stop #9 at Sendai Station run to Aobajōshi-mae (20min), at the foot of the hill beneath the castle

The wooded hilltop park, **Aobayama-kōen** (青葉山公園), across the river 2.7km west of Sendai Station, was the original site of the magnificent **Sendai Castle**, popularly known as **Aoba-jō**. In the wake of wartime bombing and subsequent US occupation, only a few stretches of wall and a reconstructed gateway remain, but the setting itself is superb, protected by the river to the east and a deep ravine on its south side. At the top of the hill, an equestrian statue of local warlord **Date Masamune** surveys the city below.

You can get a good idea of the castle's former glory at the **Aoba-jō Exhibition Hall** (青葉城資料展示館; daily 9am–5pm; ¥700; ☎022 222 0218), above the park's souvenir shops, where a short film simulates a trip "inside" the castle.

Sendai City Museum

仙台市博物館, Sendai-shi Hakubutsukan • 26 Kawauchi, Aoba-ku • Tues–Sun 9am–4.45pm • ¥460 • ☎022 225 3074, ⓦbit.ly/sendai-museum

The modern, well-laid-out **Sendai City Museum**, just north of Aobayama-kōen, traces the city's history from the early Stone Age to the present day. The main emphasis,

---

SENDAI'S STAR FESTIVAL

In early August each year, over two million people cram into Sendai for the three-day festival of **Sendai Tanabata** (仙台七夕祭; Star Festival; Aug 6–8; ⓦsendaitanabata.com), which celebrates the one occasion in the year when – weather permitting – the two astral lovers, Vega the weaver, and Altair the cowherd, can meet. The city centre is awash with thousands of bamboo poles festooned with colourful paper tassels, poems and prayers, and there's an impressive fireworks display over the Hirose-gawa.

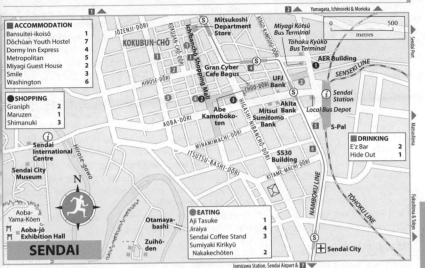

however, is on the glory days under Date Masamune, the "One-Eyed Dragon", and his successors. Pretty much everything of importance is up on the second floor, including displays of Masamune's armour, with the distinctive crescent moon on the helmet, his sword and various portraits – always diplomatically shown as having two eyes.

Zuihō-den mausoleum

瑞鳳殿 • 23-2 Otamayashita, Aoba-ku • Mausoleum and museum daily: Feb–Nov 9am–4.30pm, Dec & Jan 9am–4pm • ¥550, including entry to museum • ☎ 022 262 6250, ⓦ zuihoden.com • From Sendai Station, walk 25min, or catch a bus from stop #11 to Otamaya-bashi

When Date died in 1636, aged 70, he was buried atop a separate wooded hill not far east along the river from Aoba-jō. In due course his two immediate successors joined him, and their three **mausoleums** – Masamune's is **Zuihō-den**, while his son Tadamune and grandson Tsunamune are in Kansen-den and Zenno-den respectively – can be reached by climbing a broad stone staircase through the trees. The opulent, Momoyama-style tombs, with vivid polychrome carvings glittering against the plain dark wood and overhanging eaves, were destroyed during the war, so what you see today are 1980s reconstructions, the result of a five-year project during which researchers exhumed the actual graves. You can see the treasures they unearthed, as well as fascinating footage of the excavations, in a one-room **museum** alongside Zuihō-den.

ARRIVAL AND DEPARTURE   SENDAI

By plane Sendai's airport, 25km south of the centre (ⓦ sendai-airport.co.jp), is used by international as well as domestic services; direct trains run to Sendai Station

(25min; ¥650), while buses serve Sendai and other regional cities (ⓦ www.aizubus.com).
Destinations Fukuoka (6 daily; 2hr 10min); Hiroshima

DATE MASAMUNE

Known as the "One-Eyed Dragon", the fearsome warrior **Date Masamune** (1567–1636) lost an eye to smallpox in childhood. Heir to a long line of powerful *daimyō* in the Tōhoku region, he established Sendai after he was granted the fiefdom in return for helping bring Tokugawa Ieyasu to power in 1603. His Date clan constructed a castle in a highly ornate Momoyama style that made it more like a luxurious palace than a fortress, with painted ceilings and huge rooms divided by glorious screens, and ruled the city for the next 270 years.

(2 daily; 1hr 40min; Kanazawa (2 daily; 1 hr); Nagoya (6 daily; 1hr 15min); Okinawa Naha (daily; 3hr 15min); Osaka Itami (16 daily; 1hr 25min); Osaka Kansai (4 daily; 1hr 40min); Sapporo (13 daily; 1hr 10min); Tokyo Narita (2 daily; 1hr).

By train The main JR station on the eastern side of Sendai is linked by the Tōhoku Shinkansen line with Tokyo to the south and Morioka and Aomori to the north. Local JR lines run west to Yamagata and east to Matsushima.

Destinations Hon-Shiogama (every 15–30min; 30min); Ichinoseki (hourly; 35min); Ishinomaki (every 30min; 50min–1hr 30min); Matsushima-kaigan (every 30min; 30–40min); Morioka (every 30min; 40min); Tokyo (every 20min; 1hr 30min–2hr 25min); Yamadera (hourly; 1hr); Yamagata (hourly; 1hr 20min).

By bus Most local and long-distance buses stop on the west side of Sendai Station, though JR buses (ⓦ jrbustohoku .co.jp) bound for Niigata and Tokyo (Shinjuku) leave from

the east side. Express buses go to Kyoto, Osaka, Nagoya and destinations around Tōhoku from the Miyagi Kōtsū bus terminal (ⓦ miyakou.co.jp) at the west end of Hirose-dōri, as does the JR bus to Akita, while buses for Tokyo Station also leave from Tōhoku Kyūkō, across the road.

Destinations Akita (3 daily; 5hr); Aomori (6 daily; 4hr 50min); Hirosaki (9 daily; 4hr 20min); Morioka (hourly; 2hr 40min); Nagoya (daily; 10hr 30min); Niigata (8 daily; 4hr); Osaka (daily; 12hr 15min); Tokyo (daily; 6hr 30min); Tokyo Shinjuku (3 daily; 5hr 30min); Tsuruoka (10 daily; 2hr 20min); Yamagata (every 30min; 1hr).

By ferry Ferries from Nagoya and Hokkaidō (ⓦ taiheiyo -ferry.co.jp) dock at Sendai Port, 12km west of the city, which is served by local buses from the main station (40min; ¥490).

Destinations Nagoya (3–4 weekly; 21hr); Tomakomai (Hokkaidō; 6 weekly; 15hr).

INFORMATION

Tourist information Sendai's main tourist office (daily 8.30am–7pm; ☎ 022 222 4069, ⓦ sendai-travel.jp) is on

the JR station's second floor; the helpful English-speaking staff can help with hotel bookings.

GETTING AROUND

By train Sendai has one subway line, running north–south. To reach the subway from Sendai's JR station, follow the signs through the basement of the Seibu store.

By bus The easiest way to get around Sendai is by the local tourist bus, Loople Sendai, which stops at most of the city's sights. A one-day pass, sold at the station, the various sights, and on buses, costs ¥620, or you can simply pay the driver ¥260, for each trip. A one-day bus and subway pass costs ¥900, while the two-day Marugoto Pass (¥2670) also

covers the JR lines that service Yamadera, Matsushima and Sendai Airport.

By car Rental outlets at the east exit of Sendai Station include Eki Rent-a-Car (☎ 022 292 6501, ⓦ www.ekiren .co.jp) and Nippon (☎ 022 297 1919, ⓦ www.nrgroup -global.com).

Taxis There are plenty of taxis outside the main station exit, or call Inari (☎ 022 241 1122) or Teisan Cabs (☎ 022 231 5151).

ACCOMMODATION

There are plenty of mid-range and expensive **business hotels** within walking distance of the train station, with branches of most of the large chains in the streets to the east and south. **Budget accommodation** is more limited, though a few options are available further from the centre.

★ **Bansuitei-ikoisō** 晩翠亭いこい荘 1-8-31 Kimachi-dōri, Aoba-ku ☎ 022 222 7885, ⓦ ikoisouryokan.co.jp. An excellent ryokan just outside the downtown area but easily accessible by city bus #1 or #2, and subway (stop: Kita-Yonbanchō). Rooms are impeccably clean and nicely decorated, with fine wooden floors, and there are separate male and female onsen. Two meals will cost an extra ¥2750 per person. 🛜 **¥11,400**

★ **Dōchūan Youth Hostel** 道中庵ユースホステル 2-3-7 Onoda, Taihaku-ku ☎ 022 247 0511, ⓦ bit.ly/dochuan -hostel. The pick of Sendai's three youth hostels, built in traditional farmhouse style amid the trees. Accommodation is in small tatami rooms, laid out as dorms or private doubles. There's also a cedar bath and excellent food – the English-speaking warden grows his own rice and vegetables. The one drawback is the location, 6km south of the city centre; catch a

JR train to Taishidō and walk 6min south, or take the subway to Tomizawa and walk 10min east. Breakfast ¥600 extra. Closed 2 wks in Nov. 🛜 Dorms **¥3888**, doubles **¥9288**

Dormy Inn Express ドーミーインEXPRESS 2-10-17 Chūō, Aoba-ku ☎ 022 715 7077, ⓦ bit.ly/dormy-sendai. Budget business hotel, near Hirose-dōri subway station, a 5min walk northwest of the station towards the city centre, with ageing but adequate en-suite rooms. A major plus is that they offer thirty free dinners nightly (first-come, first-served), as well as free ramen. 🛜 **¥11,000**

Metropolitan ホテルメトロポリタン 1-1-1 Chūō-dōri, Aoba-ku ☎ 022 268 2525, ⓦ www.sendaimetropolitan .jp. Large, very comfortable high-rise hotel adjoining Sendai Station – turn left from the west exit – with decent-sized Western- and Japanese-style rooms. Facilities include Japanese and Chinese restaurants, bar, café, gym and indoor pool. 🛜 **¥19,000**

Miyagi Guest House 宮城ゲストハウス 2-1-35 Kakyō-in, Aoba-ku ☎022 393 5133, 🌐bit.ly /sendaimiyagi. Friendly hostel, a 10min walk north of the JR station – print their online map if you can – with clean but small dorms and a communal tatami lounge space, plus one private tatami double. Rates drop after two nights. 🛜 Dorm **¥2500**, double **¥6500**

Smile スマイルホテル 3F, 4-3-22 Ichiban-chō, Aoba-ku ☎022 261 7711, 🌐smile-hotels.com. Simple but modern and perfectly acceptable business hotel, 1.5km from the station but right in the thick of things if you want to shop or dine in the busy Ichiban-chō mall. 🛜 **¥8000**

Washington Hotel 仙台ワシントンホテル 4-10-8 Chūō-dōri, Aoba-ku ☎022 745 2222, 🌐sendai .washington-hotels.jp. Smart, friendly business hotel, across from Sendai Station; follow the raised pedestrian walkway to the left from the west exit. Stylish modern rooms, including some singles specifically for women, plus buffet breakfasts for ¥900. 🛜 **¥12,240**

EATING

Sendai's best-known speciality is **gyū-tan** – grilled, smoked or salted calf's tongue – though locals rejoice when **oysters** from Matsushima Bay become available in winter (Dec–March). Be sure to call in at *Abe Kamaboko-ten*, a famous shop in the Chūō-dōri mall, to try the popular snack *sasa-kamaboko*, a leaf-shaped cake of rather rubbery white-fish paste. Otherwise, **Chūō-dōri** and the connecting **Ichiban-chō** arcades are good places to look for restaurants and cafés, as is the immediate vicinity of Sendai Station.

Aji Tasuke 味太助 4-4-13 Ichiban-chō ☎022 225 4641, 🌐aji-tasuke.co.jp. At Sendai's best-known *gyū-tan* restaurant, you can sit at the counter and watch expert chefs prepare beef tongue in all its forms. A bowl of "tail soup" costs ¥500, a simple plate of tongue ¥1200, and set meals from ¥1700. Mon & Wed–Sun 11.30am–10pm.

Jiraiya 地雷也 2-1-15 Kokubun-chō, Aoba-ku ☎022 261 2164, 🌐jiraiya.com. Welcoming little *izakaya* in the heart of the shopping and dining district, where to go with your sake you can order all sorts of seafood delights, from tasty little fish balls for ¥900 to whole fried rockfish or sashimi platters, both costing ¥3500. Mon–Sat 5–11.30pm, Sun 5–10.30pm.

Sendai Coffee Stand 仙台コーヒースタンド 1-3-12 Kokubun-chō, Aoba-ku ☎022 797 1015, 🌐coffee-stand.com. Hip little coffee roasters one block west of the central arcade, where appetizing aromas lure passing pedestrians inside, and you can linger over a cup at a handful of outdoor tables. 🛜 Tues–Sat 11am–8pm, Sun 11am–7pm.

Sumiyaki Kirikyū Nakakechōten 炭焼 利久 名掛丁 店 1-8-29 Chūō-dōri, Aoba-ku ☎022 713 9677. Always assuming you're up for popping a cow's tongue in your mouth, the ¥1782 beef set dinner at this outlet of a busy and wildly popular local chain, in the final easternmost stretch of the Chūō-dōri covered mall, lets you sample Sendai's favourite delicacy *gyū-tan* in four ways – thinly sliced with salad; in a peppery broth; stewed with tomato or curry; and charcoal grilled. Daily 11.30am–11pm.

DRINKING

Kokubun-chō, just west of the Ichiban-chō shopping mall, is Sendai's main entertainment district, filled with bars, clubs and nightspots.

E'z Bar 日記 B1 2-12-19 Kokubun-chō, Aoba-ku ☎022 399 8439, 🌐ezbar.jp. A small and convivial shot bar in the basement of the Daisankyouritsu building, *E'z* offers a good range of drinks, small art exhibitions and also sells the owner's handmade candles. Tues–Sun 8pm–4am.

Hide Out ハイドアウト 2F 2-8-11 Kokubun-chō, Aoba-ku ☎022 268 6776. This small second-floor bar and "information exchange centre" is a shrine to bourbon, whisky, football and blues. Its genial host, late opening times and the contents of the thousand-plus bottles of spirits covering every surface will ensure you exchange information till the small, or even not so small, hours. ¥600 cover, drinks from ¥600. 🛜 Daily 8pm–8am, irregular closures.

ENTERTAINMENT

Gran Cyber Cafe Bagus グランサイバーカフェバグース 2-4-5 Chūō-dōri, Aoba-ku ☎022 217 7051, 🌐bagus-99 .com. Covering three floors, this huge arcade is primarily focused on gaming, though it also features non-digital attractions like pool tables, darts, a massage room and a space to read manga. 🛜 24hr.

SHOPPING

As well as the covered malls of Chūō-dōri and Ichiban-chō, be sure to check out the small alleys that run off Ichiban-chō, including Toichi Ichiba and Iroha Yokochō, which hold assorted independent **curio shops** and small bars and restaurants.

Graniph グラニフ 3-3-26 Ichiban-chō ☎ 022 212 5565, ⓦ graniph.com. In the heart of the shopping arcade, this shop sells limited edition T-shirts (from ¥2000) and clothes with fun designs from leading contemporary artists. Daily 11am–8pm.

Maruzen 丸善 1-3-1 Chūō-dōri ☎ 022 264 0151. The best place in town for foreign-language books and magazines; you'll find it across from the station, on the first floor of the AER Building. Daily 10am–9pm.

Shimanuki しまぬき 1-1-1 Chūō-dōri ☎ 022 267 4021, ⓦ shimanuki.co.jp. Towards the west end of Chūō-dōri, this traditional crafts shop sells a lovely array of *kokeshi* dolls, wooden toys, *ittōbori* carved birds, fabrics, ironware and lacquer goods. There's another branch in Sendai station. Daily 10.30am–8.30pm.

Matsushima Bay

松島湾, Matsushima-wan

A magnificent watery maze of wooded, temple-topped islands, threaded through with mysterious channels and scattered with secret inlets, **Matsushima Bay** is officially designated one of Japan's top three scenic areas, along with Miyajima (see p.594) and Amanohashidate (see p.480). Measuring roughly 12km by 14km and a short train ride northeast of Sendai, the bay holds over 260 **islands** of every conceivable shape and size, many said to bear such resemblances as tortoises, whales, or human profiles, and each with scraggy fringes of contorted pine trees protruding out of its white rock faces. There are so many, in fact, that they're credited with acting as a natural barrier against tsunamis, and thus sparing Matsushima from devastation during the disaster of 2011; it has even been suggested that similar artificial islands should be constructed all along the Tōhoku coastline.

Bashō, travelling through in 1689, commented that "much praise had already been lavished upon the wonders of the islands of Matsushima". Some modern visitors find the bay too commercialized to live up to such high expectations, but a **boat trip** among the islands still makes an enjoyable outing, especially if you can manage to avoid the often overcrowded weekends and holidays. **Matsushima town** itself holds several picturesque spots, as well as an impressive temple, **Zuigan-ji**, that's home to an impressive collection of art treasures. Although most tourists simply come on a day-trip from Sendai, if you're planning to continue north along the coast, some reasonable accommodation options make an overnight stop in Matsushima worth considering.

Matsushima

松島

On first impression, the modern town of **MATSUSHIMA** appears to amount to little more than a strip of resort hotels and souvenir shops. As soon as you explore away from that coastal ribbon, however, you'll start to appreciate this spot's venerable history. Matsushima's roots date back as far as 828, when the Zen priest Jikaku Daishi Enrin founded **Zuigan-ji**. That temple, together with associated shrines scattered in the woods nearby as well as on readily accessible islets just offshore, provides the focus for a hugely rewarding half-day stroll.

Zuigan-ji

瑞巌寺 • 91 Matsushima Chōnai • Daily: Feb & Nov 8am–4pm, March & Oct 8am–4.30pm, April–Sept 8am–5pm, Dec–Jan 8am–3.30pm • ¥700, including Seiryū-den • ☎ 022 354 2023, ⓦ zuiganji.or.jp

Set well back from the bay, five minutes' walk either north of Matsushima-kaigan Station or west of the central boat pier, Zuigan-ji is approached via an imposing grove of 400-year-old cedar trees. As well as walking up that central avenue, be sure to detour north to explore the many cave shrines hollowed into the rocks alongside.

This ancient temple has been rebuilt many times since its foundation, and had to be restored to its original splendour following damage during the 2011 tsunami, but retains a compelling sense of history. Though deceptively plain from the outside, the buildings bear the unmistakeable stamp of **Date Masamune** (see box, p.235), the first lord of Sendai, who oversaw the reconstruction of Zuigan-ji in the early seventeenth century. He employed the best craftsmen and the highest-quality materials to create a splendid monument of intricately carved doors and transoms, wood-panelled ceilings and gilded screens lavishly painted with hawks, chrysanthemums, peacocks and pines.

As well as the customary array of temple treasures, the modern **Seiryū-den** museum nearby holds a statue of a squinting Masamune in full armour and uncompromising mood – for once, it's clear that his right eye is missing – plus effigies of his angelic-looking wife and eldest daughter.

Entsū-in

円通院 • 67 Matsushima Chōnai • Daily: April–Nov 8.30am–5pm, Dec–March 9am–4pm • ¥300 • ☏ 022 354 3206, ⓦ entuuin.or.jp

In a separate precinct next door to Zuigan-ji, south towards Matsushima-kaigan Station, **Entsū-in** is dedicated to the glory of the Date clan. There's an exquisite raked-gravel garden to your left as you enter, and yet more cave shrines amid the mossy hillside rocks at the far end, but its central feature, also known as **Sankeiden**, is the mausoleum of **Date Mitsumune**, Date Masamune's grandson, who died aged 19, allegedly of poisoning, in 1645.

Godai-dō

五大堂 • 111 Matsushima Chōnai • Daily dawn–dusk • Free • ☏ 022 354 2618, ⓦ bit.ly/godai-do

Two tiny islands, just north of Matsushima's central ferry pier, are linked to the mainland and each other via vermilion footbridges. No one knows why the planks of the bridges are separated by precarious gaps, but it has been suggested that it kept women – who were forbidden access – from crossing and sullying the sacred ground, because of their awkward traditional shoes and kimono. The object of their curiosity was the **Godai-dō**, a picturesque pavilion built by order of Masamune in the early 1600s. It houses statues of five Buddhist deities, which can only be seen every 33 years. Until the next viewing, scheduled for 2039, visitors have to make do with admiring the charming carvings of the twelve animals of the zodiac that decorate the eaves.

Fukūra-jima

福浦島 • Daily 8am–5pm • ¥200

Not far north of Godai-dō, a 252m-long footbridge spans the oyster beds to reach the island of **Fukūra-jima**. A natural botanical garden, it's home to more than 250 native plant species, and even on the busiest tourist days it offers the chance to escape and enjoy some peaceful time in nature. Walking around the island, which is filled with great picnic spots and also holds a simple café/snack bar, takes about an hour.

Ojima

雄島 • Daily 24hr • Free

If you turn right as you come out of Matsushima-kaigan Station, away from the town centre, and follow the coastal footpath south for around 500m, you'll come to the slim vermilion footbridge that crosses to the tiny island of **Ojima**. Centuries ago, the soft volcanic rock here was hollowed into over a hundred little caves, half of which still hold

---

MATSUSHIMA PANORAMAS

The hills that surround Matsushima town offer abundant panoramic views of the bay. Of the four main lookout points, southerly **Sōkanzan** (双観山) is deemed to provide the best all-round views, encompassing both Shiogama and Matsushima itself; take a taxi (¥2500 return fare) to avoid the thirty-minute climb on a busy road. Alternatively, **Saigyō Modoshi-no-matsu** (西行戻しの松) is a more pleasant fifteen-minute scramble west of the station.

weatherbeaten statues and *itabi* (carved votary tablets). Come early enough in the day, and you may well find you have the whole island to yourself.

ARRIVAL AND INFORMATION
MATSUSHIMA

By train The JR Senseki line runs direct to Matsushima from the lower level of Sendai Station; get off the train at Matsushima Kaigan Station (松島海岸駅) rather than Matsushima Station, which is further from the main sights. Destinations Hon-Shiogama (every 30min; 10min); Ishinomaki (hourly; 45min); Sendai (every 30min; 40min).

By boat As one or both legs of a day-trip from Sendai, it's straightforward to make the scenic crossing of Matsushima Bay by boat, between Shiogama (塩釜), 16km northeast of Sendai, and Matsushima town. Regular trains connect Sendai with Hon-shiogama Station, 700m west of Shiogama's Marine Gate ferry pier (マリンゲート). The boats typically leave every hour, on the hour, in either

direction, though more frequent services operate during peak periods (daily: departures from Shiogama 9am–3pm, from Matsushima 10am–3pm; 50min; ¥1500, or ¥2900 for the top deck; ☎ 022 354 3453, ⓦ marubun-kisen.com).

Sightseeing cruises Regular boats set off from Matsushima tourist pier to make 50min cruises around the bay (daily: April–Oct 9am–4pm; Nov–March 9am–3pm; 50min; ¥1500; ☎ 022 354 2233, ⓦ matsushima.or.jp).

Information The tourist office outside Matsushima Kaigan Station is well stocked with brochures and leaflets (Mon–Fri 9.30am–4.30pm, Sat & Sun 9am–5pm; ☎ 022 354 2263, ⓦ matsushima-kanko.com). Be wary of their town map, though – it's not drawn to scale.

ACCOMMODATION

While Matsushima is a very easy day-trip from Sendai, it does hold a crop of smart but generally expensive hotels.

Century Hotel センチュリーホテル 8 Senzui ☎ 022 354 4111, ⓦ centuryhotel.co.jp. Modern waterfront hotel, near the bridge to Fukūra-jima, where the more expensive of the Western and tatami en-suite rooms have sea-view balconies, and the huge onsen has panoramic windows looking over the bay. Having breakfast and dinner costs around ¥6000 extra per person. **¥15,850**

Ryotei Unseian 旅亭 云静庵 17 Sanjukari ☎ 022 355 0888. Formerly the *Resort Inn Matsushima*, this bright modern hotel has Western-style en-suite rooms. To reach it, turn right from the station and follow the road leading under the tracks and up the hill for around 700m. Rates include breakfast and dinner. **¥17,200**

EATING

Busy with visitors every lunchtime, Matsushima offers a fine array of reasonably priced seafood restaurants, especially along the seafront as you approach Fukūra-jima, and also some appealing little snack places and noodle shops in the temple district. This region is especially renowned for its **oysters**, which have been farmed in the shallower parts of Matsushima Bay for around three hundred years.

Donjiki Chaya どんじき茶屋 89 Chōnai ☎ 022 354 5855. In a thatched building surrounded by gardens in the woods south of Zuigan-ji, this restaurant is great for lunch or a light snack. The menu offers soba, *dango* (rice dumplings) and drinks. Bowls of noodles start at around ¥450. Daily 9am–4.30pm.

Osakana Project お魚プロジェクト 13-32 Fugendō ☎ 022 353 3166. Also known as "Fish Project", this small canteen, the first in a row of similar, vociferously competing outfits at the point where you turn off the main road to

follow the waterfront to the Fukūra-jima bridge, sells seafood delights including rich oyster stews for ¥1500 or a bowl of eel and rice for ¥1800. Pay by buying a ticket from the machine outside the front door. Daily 9am–5pm.

Santori Chaya さんとり茶屋 24-4-1 Senzui ☎ 505 796 4571. A small, simple restaurant on the waterfront north of the Godai-dō, serving reasonable *teishoku* (traditional set menu) as well as sashimi, sushi and rice dishes. Head upstairs for great sea views. Main dishes cost around ¥1000. Mon, Tues & Thurs–Sun 11.30am–3pm & 5.30–10pm.

Oshika Hantō

牡鹿半島

North of Sendai, Honshū's coastal plain gives way to a fractured shoreline characterized by deep bays and knobbly peninsulas. The first such is the **Oshika Hantō**, a rugged spine on the eastern edge of Sendai Bay, whose broken tip forms the tiny island of **Kinkazan**.

This has been a sacred place since ancient times, but its prime attractions these days are its isolation and the hiking trails through forests inhabited by semi-wild deer and monkeys.

As the closest point on land to the epicentre of the **2011 earthquake**, this area was devastated by the ensuing tsunami. The destruction left a permanent scar on the physical landscape as well as on the psyche of the local population. Understandably, dealing with foreign tourists has not been the priority, but there are signs of a rebirth.

Ishinomaki

石巻

The principal town in the Oshika Hantō, and its major gateway, **Ishinomaki** stands 30km east of Matsushima at the mouth of northern Japan's largest river, the Kitakami. Its generally forlorn air is hardly surprising: around 3600 people died here during the tsunami, and a total of 57,000 buildings were either wholly or partially destroyed. The districts closest to the sea were inundated to a depth of 8.6m – the deepest recorded anywhere – and are destined to become a memorial park rather than being rebuilt.

Ishinomori Mangattan Museum

石ノ森萬画館, Ishinomori Manga-kan • 2-7 Nakaze, Ishinomaki • March–Nov daily 9am–6pm, closed third Tues of each month; Dec–Feb Mon & Wed–Sun 9am–5pm • ¥800 • ☎ 022 596 5055, ⓦ man-bow.com/manga

Housed in a rather extraordinary flying-saucer-shaped building, propped up on stilts, the futuristic **Ishinomori Mangattan Museum** somehow survived the tsunami, and served as a centre for relief efforts. It's now reverted to its original function, to celebrate the locally born **Shōtarō Ishinomori** (1928–98), said to be the most prolific **manga artist** of all time. Trains from Sendai are decorated with "cyborg warriors" and other characters he created, while colourful mannequins line the twenty-minute walk from Ishinomaki Station, along the main commercial strip and across the river, all the way to the museum. For manga-lovers, its displays of books, images and superhero effigies are an absolute delight, though with almost all the captions in Japanese only, it's the TV screens showing old episodes of Ishinomori's 1970s hit series *Kamen Rider* that are most likely to hold the attention of casual visitors.

ARRIVAL AND INFORMATION   ISHINOMAKI

By train Ishinomaki Station, at the west end of the centre, had to be entirely rebuilt after the tsunami, as indeed did the local sections of the JR Senseki train line, which connects the town with Sendai and now passes through some eerily desolate, treeless swathes of coastal flatlands.
Destinations Kogota (10 daily; 40min); Sendai (every 30min; 1hr–1hr 25min).

By bus The main bus stops are directly in front of Ishinomaki Station.
Destinations Ayukawa (7 daily; 1hr 30min); Sendai (hourly; 1hr 20min); Tokyo Shinjuku (2 daily; 7hr 10min).

Information The Ishinomaki Community & Info Center, at 2-8-11 Chūō on the main road just west of the river, doubles as both the tourist office and the place to learn about the tsunami and the ongoing process of reconstruction (Mon & Wed–Sun 9.30am–6pm; ☎ 022 598 4425).

Kinkazan

金華山

The conical island of **KINKAZAN** ("Mountain of the Gold Flowers"), 1km off the tip of Oshika Hantō, makes an interesting day-trip, though its ferry connection usually operates on Sundays only. Its first recorded inhabitants were gold prospectors, and although the seams were exhausted long ago, it's still associated with wealth and good fortune. The prime sight, the shrine of **Koganeyama-jinja** (黄金山神社), is dedicated to the twin gods of prosperity, Ebisu and Daikoku, and stands in a clearing, cropped by hungry deer, on the island's west slope of Kinkazan, fifteen minutes' uphill walk from the ferry pier. From behind the shrine buildings, a rough path leads to a stiff 2km hike up the 445m peak, an effort rewarded with truly magnificent views along the peninsula and west towards distant Matsushima.

ARRIVAL AND DEPARTURE   KINKAZAN

By bus Buses connect the nearest train station, Ishinomaki, with Ayukawa (鮎川), a former whaling port with intermittent ferry service to Kinkazan.

By boat Seadream offers an occasional service between Ayukawa and Kinkazan, typically on Sunday mornings only (¥3000 round-trip; ☎022 544 1955, ⓦbit.ly/seadream -kinkazan); see website for current schedules.

Hiraizumi and around

For a brief period, almost a thousand years ago, the temples of **Hiraizumi**, now a quiet backwater 100km north of Sendai, rivalled even Kyoto in their magnificence. Though the majority of monasteries and palaces are long vanished, the gloriously extravagant **Konjiki-dō** and the other treasures of **Chūson-ji** bear witness to the area's former wealth and artistic accomplishment. Hiraizumi also boasts one of Japan's best-preserved Heian-period gardens at **Mōtsū-ji**, while a boat ride between the towering cliffs of the nearby **Geibikei** or **Gembikei** gorges (see box, p.246) provides a scenic contrast and offers especially spectacular views in autumn.

Hiraizumi

平泉

Nowadays it's hard to picture **HIRAIZUMI** as the resplendent capital of the **Fujiwara** clan, who chose this spot on the banks of the Kitakami-gawa for their "paradise on earth." At first sight it's a rather dozy little town on a busy main road, but the low western hills conceal the breathtaking gilded **Konjiki-dō**, which has somehow survived war, fire and natural decay for nearly nine centuries. You can easily cover this and the nearby gardens of **Mōtsū-ji** in a day, staying in either Hiraizumi or Ichinoseki, or even as a half-day stopover while travelling between Sendai and Morioka.

Brief history

Early in the twelfth century, **Fujiwara Kiyohira**, the first lord of the Fujiwara clan, set about building a vast complex of Buddhist temples and palaces, lavishly decorated with gold from the local mines, in what is now Hiraizumi. Eventually, the clan's wealth and military might alarmed the southern warlord **Minamoto Yoritomo** (see p.189), who was in the throes of establishing the Kamakura shogunate. Yoritomo's valiant brother, **Yoshitsune**, had previously trained with the warrior monks of Hiraizumi, so when Yoritomo turned against him, Yoshitsune fled north. At first the Fujiwara protected him, but they soon betrayed him on the promise of a sizeable reward, and in 1189 Yoshitsune committed suicide (although according to one legend he escaped to Mongolia, where he resurfaced as Genghis Khan). Meanwhile, Yoritomo attacked the Fujiwara, destroying their temples and leaving the town to crumble into ruin. Passing through Hiraizumi five hundred years after Yoshitsune's death, **Bashō** caught the mood in one of his famous haiku: "The summer grass, 'tis all that's left of ancient warriors' dreams."

> ### HIRAIZUMI FESTIVALS
>
> The flight of Yoshitsune to Hiraizumi (see above) is commemorated with a costume parade during the town's main spring **festival** (May 1–5), which also features open-air nō performances at Chūson-ji. Other important annual events include an ancient **sacred dance**, Ennen-no-Mai, held by torchlight at Mōtsū-ji on January 20, May 5 and during the autumn festival (Nov 1–3).

3

Chūson-ji

中尊寺 • 202 Koromonoseki • Daily: April–Oct 8am–5pm; Nov–March 8.30am–4.30pm • ¥800 including Konjiki-dō, Kyōzō and Sankōzō • ☎ 019 146 2211

The Fujiwara's initial construction work concentrated on the temple of **Chūson-ji**, which had been founded by a Tendai priest from Kyoto halfway through the ninth century. Of the forty original buildings that were built on the forested hillside, only two remain: Konjiki-dō (the Golden Hall) and the nearby sutra repository, Kyōzō. From the main road, a broad avenue leads uphill past minor temples sheltering under towering cryptomeria trees, until you reach the first building of any size, the Hondō, on the right-hand side. Chūson-ji's greatest treasure, the Konjiki-dō, is a little further up on the left in a concrete hall.

Konjiki-dō

金色堂

Although the **Konjiki-dō** is tiny – only 5.5 square metres – and protected behind plate glass, it still makes an extraordinary sight. The whole structure gleams with thick gold leaf, while the altar inside is smothered in mother-of-pearl inlay and delicate gilded copper friezes set against dark burnished lacquer. The altar's central image depicts Amida Nyorai, flanked by a host of Buddhas, bodhisattvas and guardian kings, all swathed in gold. Unveiled in 1124, this extravagant gesture of faith and power took fifteen years to complete and the bodies of all four generations of the Fujiwara lords still rest under its altar.

Kyōzō

恭三

Set behind the Konjiki-dō, Chūson-ji's other original building, the **Kyōzō**, is not nearly so dramatic. This small plain hall, erected in 1108, used to house more than five thousand Buddhist sutras written in gold or silver characters on rich indigo paper. The hall next door was built in 1288 to shelter the Konjiki-dō – and now houses an eclectic collection of oil paintings – while, across the way, there's a much more recent nō stage where outdoor performances are held in summer by firelight (Aug 14), and during Hiraizumi's major spring and autumn festivals.

Sankōzō

讃衡蔵

The road beside the entrance to the Konjiki-dō leads to the modern **Sankōzō**, a museum containing what remains of Chūson-ji's treasures. The most valuable items are a statue of the Senju Kannon (Thousand-Armed Goddess of Mercy), a number of sutra scrolls, and a unique collection of lacy metalwork decorations (*kalavinkas*), which originally hung in the Konjiki-dō.

Mōtsū-ji

毛越寺 • Aza Osawa 58 • Daily: April–Oct 8am–5pm; Nov–March 8.30am–4.30pm • ¥500, including museum • ☎ 019 146 2331

The Heian-period temple complex of **Mōtsū-ji**, a delightful spot for a stroll, lies less than ten minutes' walk west from Hiraizumi Station. In the twelfth century, the Fujiwara added to the temple itself, originally founded in 850, until it was the largest in northern Honshū. Only a few foundation stones of the original temple remain, along with Japan's best-preserved Heian garden, the **Jōdo-teien**, whose main feature is a large lake, speckled with symbolic "islands", in the midst of velvet lawns. You'll find flowers in bloom almost every season, including cherry blossom, lotus, bush clover and azaleas, but the most spectacular display comes in late June, when thirty thousand irises burst into colour. The small **museum** to the left of the entrance displays photos of Mōtsū-ji's colourful festivals.

The garden's annual **poetry competition**, held on the last Sunday in May, re-creates a pastime from a bygone era. Participants, dressed in traditional clothes, sit writing by a stream, under umbrellas. As they compose their poems, cups of sake are floated to them on the water and their completed works are read aloud by a master of ceremonies.

ARRIVAL AND INFORMATION

HIRAIZUMI

By train Hiraizumi is on the Tōhoku main line; change at Ichinoseki, the nearest Shinkansen station, for connections to and from Sendai.

Destinations Hanamaki (hourly; 40min); Ichinoseki (hourly; 10min); Kitakami (hourly; 30min); Morioka (hourly; 1hr 20min).

Tourist information The tourist office at the station has English maps and leaflets (daily 8.30am–5pm; ☎ 019 146 2110, ⓦ hiraizumi.or.jp).

GETTING AROUND

By bus Regular buses connect the station with Mōtsū-ji and Chūson-ji on the Run Run loop line (both ¥140), and also with Ichinoseki (¥310).

By bike Swallow Tours, facing the station, rent bikes (April–Nov 8am–5pm, Dec–March 9am–4pm; ¥500/2hr, ¥1000/day; ☎ 019 146 5086).

ACCOMMODATION

Hiraizumi doesn't have many accommodation options, but there are a few onsen hotels and small inns.

Daimonjiyama Camp-jō Nagashima 大文字山キャンプ場 51-661 Yamada ☎ 019 146 5564. This campsite, attractively located on lush slopes 7km east of the station, across the river and best reached by taxi, is an appealing deal in spring and summer. Pitch ¥200, plus tent rental per person ¥300

Hiraizumi Hotel Masashi-bō 平泉ホテル武蔵坊 15 Osawa ☎ 019 146 2241, ⓦ www.musasibou.co.jp. Admittedly this massive concrete hotel, on the hillside 850m northwest of the station towards Chūson-ji, has seen better days, but even if its tatami rooms are a bit rundown, the food is good, and its large onsen baths enjoy panoramic views. Rates include two meals. 🌐 **¥21,000**

Shirayama Ryokan 志羅山旅館 139-5 Shirayama ☎ 019 146 2883. A clean and comfortable traditional inn, in the side streets west of the station. You'll need to call ahead to let them know when you plan to arrive. Rates include two meals. **¥16,000**

EATING

As well as a couple of small restaurants lining the road from the station to Mōtsū-ji temple, several more near Chūson-ji serve noodles and classic dishes, albeit at slightly inflated prices. If you fancy a picnic, head for the small supermarket on the road to Mōtsū-ji.

Izumi Sobaya 泉そば屋 75 Izumiya ☎ 019 146 2038. On the north side of the station, just before the crossroads, this small and simple place serves good-value *soba teishoku* (traditional set menu) from ¥570. Mon, Tues & Thurs–Sun 9am–5pm.

Seoul Shokudō ソウル食堂 115-6 Shirayama ☎ 019 146 5199. A *yakiniku* (Korean barbecue) restaurant that has set meals, an English menu and a good range of vegetarian choices, with individual dishes starting at ¥670. Tues–Fri 5pm–midnight, Sat & Sun 10am–2pm & 5pm–midnight.

Ichinoseki

一関

There's nothing especially distinguished about the small town of **ICHINOSEKI**, other than the fact that it holds the closest Shinkansen station to Hiraizumi, 8km north. Its good transport connections, however, coupled with the assortment of business hotels, bars and restaurants clustered near the station, make it a convenient overnight base for visiting not only Hiraizumi itself, but also the Geibikei and Genbikei gorges.

ARRIVAL AND INFORMATION

ICHINOSEKI

By train Ichinoseki is on the Tōhoku Shinkansen and Tōhoku main JR lines, and is the terminal for Geibikei trains.

Destinations Geibikei (9 daily; 30min); Hiraizumi (hourly; 10min); Kogota (hourly; 50min); Morioka (every 30min; 40min–1hr 30min); Sendai (hourly; 35min); Shin-Hanamaki (every 30min; 25min).

By bus Frequent buses run to local destinations from Ichinoseki Station.

GEIBIKEI GORGE

The Hiraizumi area boasts two river **gorges** with confusingly similar names. **Geibikei** (猊鼻渓) – the more impressive of the two, as opposed to **Genbikei** (厳美渓) – is a narrow defile, 20km east of Hiraizumi and best viewed by boat. You can get there by bus (stop #7; 45min; ¥1000 all-day pass) or train (JR Ōfunato line to Geibikei Station; 9 daily; 30min; ¥500) from Ichinoseki Station – an attractive ride either way. To reach the dock from the bus stop, turn left at the main road, then take the first right; from the train station, turn right and walk for five minutes, following the road under the tracks.

The Geibikei **boat trip** is a lot of fun (7–10 departures daily: April–Aug 8.30–4.30pm, Sept to mid-Nov 8.30–4pm, mid-Nov to March 9.30am–3pm; 90min; ¥1600; ☎ 019 147 2341, ⓦ geibikei .co.jp). Despite poling fairly sizeable wooden punts upstream for 2km, the boatmen still find breath to regale their passengers with local legends, details of the passing flora and endless statistics about the gorge. It's all in Japanese, of course, but the general mirth is infectious.

Destinations Chūson-ji (every 15–20min; 25min); Geibikei (9–11 daily; 30–40min); Hiraizumi (every 15–20min; 20min; last bus Mon–Sat 7pm, Sun 6.30pm).

Tourist information The tourist office at Ichinoseki Station has English maps and brochures (daily 9am–5.30pm; ☎ 019 123 2350, ⓦ ichitabi.jp).

The Tōno valley

遠野バレー, Tōno bērē

Set in a bowl of low mountains in the heart of one of Japan's poorest regions, the town of **Tōno** is surrounded by the flat **Tōno valley**. The people of Tōno and the farmers of the valley take pride in their living legacy of farming and folk traditions, embodied by the district's **magariya** – large, L-shaped farmhouses – and the focus of several museums devoted to the old ways. This area is most famous for its **folk tales**, known as *Tōno Monogatari* (see box, p.248); references to these legends and traces of primitive cults are everywhere you look, along with ancient shrines and rock carvings, all serving to permeate the valley with a mysterious undercurrent. Allow a couple of days to do it all justice.

Flat, peaceful roads and a slow rural pace of life make this region especially suited to explorations by **bike**. Cycle paths and routes lead to and around the main sights and can easily be covered in a day's leisurely riding. The valley's eastern portion is especially lovely, and in many areas you really feel as though you've stepped back in time.

Tōno

遠野

TŌNO itself is a small town set among flat rice lands, with orchards and pine forests cloaking the surrounding hills. Although it's mainly useful for its hotels, banks and other facilities, it does hold a couple of museums worth seeing before you set off around the valley.

Tōno Municipal Museum

遠野市立博物館, Tōno Shiritsu Hakubutsukan • 3-9 Higashidate-chō • May–Oct daily 9am–5pm, Nov–April Tues–Sun 9am–5pm; also closed last day of every month • ¥310 • ☎ 019 862 2340

Just over 500m south of the station, across a small stream, you'll find the **Tōno Municipal Museum** at the back of a modern red-brick building that doubles as the town library. Along with a thorough overview of Tōno's festivals, crafts and agricultural traditions, its entertaining exhibitions and videos provide information about the local environment.

Tōno Folktale and Storytelling Centre

とおの昔話村, Tōno Mukashi-banashi mura • 2-11 Chūō-dōri • Daily 9am–5pm • ¥500 with Castle Town Materials Museum •
☎ 019 862 7887

The **Tōno Folktale and Storytelling Centre**, five minutes' walk south of the station (turn right just before the stream), dedicates itself to bringing Tōno's folk tales alive. Its interactive multimedia displays are entertaining enough to hold your interest even if you don't understand the captions and commentary, which are largely in Japanese, though the live storytelling sessions are way beyond the grasp of non-native speakers. The various buildings in the on-site "village" include the inn where Yanagita Kunio stayed while researching local legends (see box, p.248).

Tickets also include admission to the **Tōno Castle Town Materials Museum** (遠野城下町資料館; same hours), just on the restored pedestrian street that starts across the road, which exhibits historical artefacts including armour, weapons, tableware, textiles and paintings.

ARRIVAL AND INFORMATION TŌNO

By train To reach Tōno by train, change off the Shinkansen line at Shin-Hanamaki, or the north–south JR Tōhoku line at Hanamaki, and catch the JR Kamaishi line for the scenic journey east to Tōno Station, in the heart of town. Very infrequently, the route is served by an extraordinary deluxe steam train, themed in honour of Kenji Miyazama's celebrated 1927 novel *Night on the Galactic Railroad* and named the SL *Ginga*; for details and schedules, visit ⓦ bit.ly /sl-ginga. In addition, a few trains on the Kamaishi line each day come all the way from Morioka to Tōno, via Hanamaki. Destinations Hanamaki (9 daily; 50min–1hr 15min); Morioka (3 daily; 1hr 25min); Shin-Hanamaki (9 daily; 45min–1hr).

Tourist information Tōno's tourist office, at the station, hands out maps and brochures covering both town and valley, some in English (daily 8.30am–5.30pm; ☎ 019 862 1333, ⓦ tonojikan.jp). The attached shop stocks *The Legends of Tōno*.

GETTING AROUND

By bus By far the most useful of the local buses that run from outside Tōno Station are those that head northeast to Denshō-en and Furusato-mura, and pass close to the *Tōno Youth Hostel* (see p.248). Check with the tourist office for schedules.

By bike The tourist office and other outlets on the station concourse rent bicycles (¥500/2hr; up to ¥1000/ day). Tōno maps show three recommended cycling routes of around 4hr each, which cover the main sights – also possible by car, they're reasonably well signposted, though not always in English.

ACCOMMODATION

Kuranoya くら乃屋 45-136 Sanchiwari, Kōkōji, Matsuzaki-chō ☎ 019 860 1360, ⓦ kuranoya-tono.com. Rural B&B, run by a welcoming and very helpful English-speaking (and cat-loving) couple, across the river 3km northwest of the station, on the valley's western slopes. Three of the five en-suite Japanese-style rooms are eight-tatami, the others twelve-tatami. Rates include breakfast, while dinner is available for ¥1000. 🛜 **¥12,000**

Minshuku Tōno 民宿とおの 2-17 Zaimoku-chō ☎ 019 862 4395, ⓦ minshuku-tono.com. Friendly family-run minshuku, just north of the railway tracks 5min from the station. The eleven rooms have seen better days, and share bathroom facilities, but the dining room, with its open hearth and excellent rustic food, compensates. Rates include two meals, and single rooms are available. 🛜 **¥19,900**

3

THE LEGENDS OF TŌNO

When the far-sighted folklorist **Yanagita Kunio** visited Tōno in 1909, he found a world that was still populated by the shadowy figures of demons and other generally malevolent spirits, whom the farmers strove to placate using ancient rituals. The following year, he published the first book to tap the rich oral traditions of rural Japan, **Tōno Monogatari** (rendered into English as *The Legends of Tōno*). He heard the 118 tales from Kyōseki Sasaki (or Kizen), the educated son of a Tōno peasant, to whom goblins, ghosts and gods were part of everyday life.

People in Tōno still talk about **Zashiki Warashi**, a mischievous child spirit (either male or female) who can be heard running at night and is said to bring prosperity to the household. Another popular tale tells of a farmer's beautiful daughter who fell in love with the family horse. When the farmer heard that his child had married the horse, he hanged it from a mulberry tree, only for his grieving daughter to be whisked off to heaven clinging to her lover.

Probably the most popular character from the legends is the **kappa**, an ugly water creature who, although not unique to Tōno, seems to exist here in large numbers. You'll find *kappa* images everywhere in town, including postboxes and outside the station; even the police box is *kappa*-esque. The traditional *kappa* has long skinny limbs, webbed hands and feet, a sharp beak, and a hollow on the top of his head that has to be kept full of water. He's usually green, sometimes with a red face, and his principal pastime is pulling young children into ponds and rivers. Should you happen to meet a real *kappa*, remember to bow – on returning your bow, the water will flow out of the hollow on his head, and he'll have to hurry off to replenish it.

Tōno Youth Hostel 遠野ユースホステル 13-39-5 Tsuchibuchi-chō ☎019 862 8736, ⓦtono-yh.com. Delightful little hostel, set amid the rice fields 5km northeast of central Tōno; catch a bus from Tōno station to Nitagai, then walk for 10min. The two four-bed dorms, which share indoor and outdoor baths, can also be rented as private rooms, while the genial manager speaks good English and has basic bikes for rent. The home cooking is excellent, which is just as well as there no restaurants nearby; breakfast costs ¥600, dinner ¥1200. ⓦ Dorms ¥3400

EATING

Local **speciality foods** to sample in the area's restaurants and minshuku include *hitsuko soba*, small bowls of rough, handmade noodles eaten with a mix of chicken, raw egg, onion and mushrooms, and the regional dish, *nambu hitssumi* (or *suiton*), a soup laced with seasonal vegetables and dumplings. Restaurants in the folk villages (and open the same hours) also serve delicacies such as *ayu* (river fish) and *jingisukan* (barbecued lamb). The **Tōno shopping mall**, a block southeast of the station in the Topia Department Store, holds a well-stocked **supermarket** plus a small **farmers' market** selling fresh fruit and vegetables.

Itō-ke 伊藤家 2-11 Chūō-dōri ☎019 860 1110. Simple high-quality noodle place, adjoining the Folktale Centre 500m south of the station and open for lunch only. Soba dishes, including their chicken-based *hitssumi*, cost from ¥700. Daily 11am–5pm.

Taigetsu 待月 3-1 Shinkoku-chō ☎019 862 4933. This cosy café, 100m straight down the main street from the station, serves good cake and coffee (¥450) along with slightly pricier small dishes like cheese on toast, pizza, curry and ramen. Daily 10am–10pm.

Ume-no-ya うめのや 2-2 Shinkoku-chō ☎019 862 2622. Opposite *Taigetsu*, a minute's walk south of the station, this simple restaurant offers decent portions of curry rice, *ebi-fry* (fried prawns), omelettes from ¥600 and set meals from ¥100. Mon & Wed–Sun 11.30am–8pm.

West of Tōno

The main valley narrows **west of Tōno**, funnelling the road and railway along beside the Sarugaishi-gawa. The wooded southern hillside hides some unusual **shrines** and an appealing group of **Buddha images**, which makes one of the best short trips out of Tōno. Note that the imposing **Chiba Magariya**, however, a celebrated *magariya* farmhouse 11km up the valley, is closed for restoration, and is not expected to reopen until at least 2023.

Unedori-jinja

卯子酉神社 • 2.5km southwest of Tōno Station • Accessible during daylight hours • Free

Head west out of Tōno on the south side of the river for 2.5km, on the old Route 283, and look out for a stone staircase on the left. At the bottom of the steps, past the house, you'll find a pine tree festooned with red and white ribbons. Behind it lies **Unedori-jinja**, a tiny shrine dedicated to the god in charge of matrimonial affairs; if you want to get married, tie a red ribbon onto the tree with your left hand.

Gohyaku Rakan

五百羅漢 • 2.8km southwest of Tōno Station

To reach the **Gohyaku Rakan**, climb the stone staircase alongside Unedori-jinja, cross a lane and follow the path into a narrow, wooded valley filled with mossy stones. Keep looking closely at the stones: at first you won't see anything, but gradually faint outlines appear, then full faces and rounded bodies, until you're seeing little figures everywhere. There are supposedly five hundred of these Buddhist "disciples", which were carved by a local monk in the late eighteenth century to pacify the spirits of the victims of a terrible famine in 1754.

Northeast of Tōno

The broad valley **northeast of Tōno** holds several somewhat touristy "folk villages" aimed at preserving the old crafts. The best one to visit is **Furusato-mura**, though the smaller **Denshō-en** and **Sui-kōen** are slightly more accessible. Other sights to aim for include a *kappa* pool, an old watermill and a temple housing Japan's tallest Kannon statue. However, the chief highlight hereabouts is the scenery of rice fields and rolling hills, dotted with the occasional thatched farmhouse.

Denshō-en

伝承園 • 6-5-1 Tsuchibuchi, 5km northeast of Tōno Station • Daily 9am–5pm, last entry 4pm; closed 4th Mon of every month • ¥320 • ☎ 019 862 8655, ⓦ densyoen.jp • hourly buses on route 340 from Tōno stop at either end of the village (15–20min; ¥310)

The museum village of **Denshō-en** preserves buildings relocated from around Tōno, including a waterwheel, storehouses and a *magariya* (see p.246), where local folk demonstrate weaving, rope-making and other crafts. A small shrine room at the back of the *magariya* is filled with brightly dressed dolls, which represent **Oshira-sama**, an agricultural deity worshipped throughout northern Honshū. According to legend, Tōno's original Oshira-sama came from the same tree on which the horse-husband died (see box opposite). The deities, often used by blind mediums, are also supposed to predict the future – hence all the prayer papers tied around the shrine.

Jōken-ji

常堅寺 • 7-50 Tsuchibuchi, 5.4km northeast of Tōno Station • 24hr • Free

Immediately east of Denshō-en, a signposted turn to the right leads in around 400m to the **Jōken-ji** temple. Founded in 1490, the temple is mainly of interest for its statue of **Obinzuru-sama**, a little figure in a cloak and hat with a very shiny anatomy – the deity is supposed to cure illnesses if rubbed in the appropriate place. Behind the temple there's a **kappa pool**, home to a particularly helpful *kappa* credited with dousing a fire in Jōken-ji. An eccentric local has also built a small shrine to himself beside the pool; if he's around, he'll probably regale you with incomprehensible but good-natured stories.

Fukusen-ji

福泉寺 • 7-57 Matsuzaki-chō, Komagi, 7km north of Tōno Station • April–Dec daily 8am–5pm • ¥300 • ☎ 019 862 3822

Coming from Tōno, a road branches north just before Denshō-en, and follows the main valley for another 2km to **Fukusen-ji**, a temple founded in 1912 and renowned for its 17m-tall image of **Kannon**, the Goddess of Mercy. Completed in 1963, the slender gilded statue has a blue hairdo and is claimed to be the largest wooden statue in Japan; carving it from a single tree trunk took twelve years. It stands in an attractive temple at the top of the hill, where the artist's tools, and photos of the huge tree being brought to Tōno by train, are also on display.

To cycle to Tōno from Fukusen-ji, take the road back towards Denshō-en for about a minute, then turn onto the Tōno-Towa Bicycle Path indicated by the happy *kappa* sign to the right. This 8km-long cycleway winds through rice fields and along streams before joining Route 396 for the final two kilometres.

Furusato-mura

ふるさと村 • Tukimoushi-chō, Kamitukimoushi 5-89-1, 10km north of Tōno Station • Daily: March–Oct 9am–5pm, Nov–Feb 9am–4pm, last entry 1hr before closing • ¥540, workshops ¥600–1000 • ☎ 019 864 2300, ⓦ tono-furusato.jp • Some Denshō-en buses continue up the valley (every 1–2hr; 25min; ¥500)

The largest and most attractive of Tōno's folk museums, **Furusato-mura**, stands 3km northwest of Denshō-en. It's a close approximation to a working village, complete with rice fields, vegetable plots and duck ponds. The five refurbished *magariya* on the hillside date from the eighteenth and nineteenth centuries; pensioners sit beside smoking hearths, busily making souvenirs such as straw slippers, wooden *kappa* and bamboo baskets. The old folk also run a number of workshops, including how to make straw horses and bamboo dragonflies, as well as soba making and *mocha*-pounding, should you want to have a go. You can also buy their handiwork in the museum shop, where a small restaurant serves good-value lunch sets.

East of Denshō-en

たかむろ水光園, Takamuro Sui-kōen • 7-175-2 Tsuchibuchi-chō, 8km northeast of Tōno Station • Daily 10am–4pm; closed 4th Mon of every month • admission ¥320, bath, open until 9pm nightly, ¥540 • ☎ 019 862 2834, ⓦ tono-suikouen.jp

Although the most beautiful part of the Tōno valley lies **east of Denshō-en**, to appreciate it you'll have to get off onto the side roads. One attractive ride leads out to an old watermill then loops back past the third folk village. To find the turning, follow Route 340 for 3km east from Denshō-en, then fork right immediately after crossing a red-lacquered bridge. The lane climbs gently uphill, heading beyond some old farms to a small thatched **watermill** (山口の水車). En route, you pass the **house of Kyōseki Sasaki** (see box, p.248), opposite which there's a path signed to **Dan-no-hana** (ダンノハナ), a place where, in the not-so-distant past, anyone aged over sixty was sent to die. Here, however, the elderly residents got bored of waiting, so they came down to work the fields during the day and returned to their hill at night.

When you head back down to the main road, look out on the left for a turning signed to **Denderano** (デンデラ野). Follow this lane west for nearly 2km and you'll come to the last of the folk villages, **Takamuro Sui-kōen**, which has a *magariya*, a *kappa* pool and displays of antique farm implements, as well as a solar-powered sauna and steam bath.

Morioka

盛岡

A former castle town set at the confluence of three rivers, the small, congenial city of **MORIOKA** has few outstanding attractions beyond wandering through its older neighbourhoods and around the ruins of the castle itself. With its attractive setting, well-priced accommodation, interesting local cuisine and entertainment, though, Morioka makes a good stop on the journey through northern Honshū, and provides access to hikes around the nearby **Hachimantai plateau**.

Iwate-kōen

岩手公園 • 1-37 Uchimaru • 24hr • Free

Iwate-kōen, Morioka castle park, was once the seat of the Nambu lords. As so often, the castle itself, which took 36 years to complete (1597–1633), stood at the highest point in the city, atop a hill overlooking the river confluence that's now a twenty-minute walk east of the station. Although only a small monument now commemorates the site of the fortress, destroyed during the Meiji Restoration, some of the mighty, maze-like walls and ramparts that once encircled it still remain. With its plants, trees, shrines and water features, however, the park makes a peaceful space for a stroll. Along its eastern edge, a pleasant riverside path follows the bank of **Nakatsu-gawa**.

One block north of the park, a 300-year-old cherry tree, celebrated locally as the **Ishiwari Sakura** (石割桜) or "rock-splitting cherry", emerges from a fissure in a rounded granite boulder. No one knows whether it really broke the rock open, but it's a startling sight, especially when it blossoms in spring.

Morioka History and Culture Museum

もりおか歴史文化館, Morioka Rekishi Bunkakan • 1-50 Uchimaru, Iwate-kōen • Daily: April–Oct 9am–7pm, Nov–March 9am–6pm; closed 3rd Tues of each month • ¥300 • ☎ 019 681 2100, ⓦ morireki.jp

There's no faulting the high quality of the displays in the **Morioka History and Culture Museum**, a modern building within the castle park. Large-scale models plus illuminated maps and scrolls in the upstairs galleries trace the development of the city, while the sumptuous family treasures of the Nanbu clan are given pride of place. The one snag is the paucity of English captions, which means you're likely to race through a bit faster than it deserves.

3

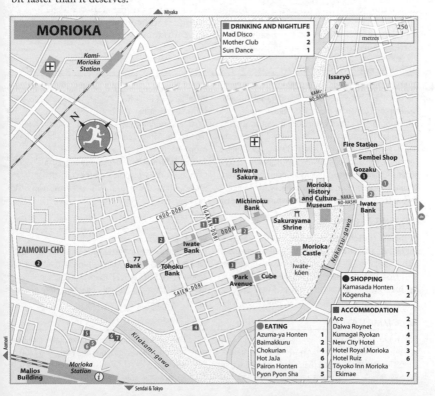

3

MORIOKA FESTIVALS

Morioka plays host to two major **summer festivals**. At the end of the rice-planting season, the **Chagu-Chagu Umakko** (チャグチャグ馬コ; second Sat in June) features a 15km procession of a hundred richly caparisoned horses, ending at the city's Hachiman-gū shrine. Then, in early August, thousands of dancers and drummers parade through town during the **Sansa Odori** (さんさ踊り; Aug 1–4), accompanied by flutes and followed by a general knees-up.

Gozaku
こざ九

Cross the Nakatsu-gawa from the northeast corner of the castle park, via the **Naka-no-hashi** (中ノ橋), then turn immediately left, and you'll come to a row of traditional Meiji-era buildings known as **Gozaku** (こざ九). These now house stores selling simple local products such as brushes, straw and wicker goods, while fancier boutiques opposite specialize in the region's most famous crafts, including heavy iron kettles and eye-catching cotton textiles dyed with intricate patterns. Appetizing odours greet you at the top of the street, where a *sembei* shop turns out local-style rice crackers sprinkled with sesame seeds or nuts; walk round the side and you can see the bakers hard at work.

Zaimoku-chō
材木町 盛岡

A traditional shopping street runs parallel to the Kitakami-gawa through the small **Zaimoku-chō** neighbourhood, a five-minute walk northeast of the station on the opposite bank of the river. Several attractive boutiques and craft shops sell local specialities, including pottery, heavy iron kettles, cotton textiles dyed with intricate patterns and colourful hand-painted paper kites.

ARRIVAL AND INFORMATION

By train Morioka Station is west of the city centre; beyond the city, the Tōhoku Shinkansen line from Tokyo splits, heading north to Aomori and west to Akita.

Destinations Akita (hourly; 1hr 30min); Aomori (hourly; 1hr 20min); Hanamaki (every 30min; 30min); Kakunodate (hourly; 45min); Kitakami (every 30min; 15–50min); Sendai (every 30min; 40min); Shin-Hanamaki (every 30min; 10min); Tazawako (hourly; 35min); Tokyo (every 30min; 2hr 15min); Towada-Minami (4 daily; 2hr 15min).

By bus Local and long-distance buses depart from the east side of Morioka Station, with seasonal regional services including those to the Hachimantai plateau and Towada-ko (ⓦ iwate-kenpokubus.co.jp).

Destinations Aomori (4 daily; 3hr 30min); Hirosaki (hourly; 2hr 15min); Sendai (hourly; 2hr 40min); Tokyo (daily; 7hr 30min).

Tourist information Morioka's city and regional tourist office is on the second floor of the train station (daily 9am–5.30pm; ☎019 625 2090, ⓦ www.japan-iwate .info).

GETTING AROUND

By bus The City Centre Loop Bus, also known as "Denden-mushi", runs a 35min loop between the station and various central locations (all-day pass ¥300, or ¥100 per ride; ☎019 654 2141, ⓦ iwatekenkotsu.co.jp).

By bike Cycle rental outlets include Saseki Bicycles, beside the river near *Hotel Ruiz* (¥200/hr, ¥1000/day;

☎019 624 2692).

By car Rental offices at the station include Nippon Rent-a-Car (☎019 635 6605, ⓦ nrgroup-global.com) and Eki Rent-a-Car (☎019 624 5212, ⓦ www.ekiren.co.jp).

By taxi Morioka's central booking office is on ☎019 622 5240.

ACCOMMODATION

Ace ホテルエース 2-11-35 Chūō-dōri ☎019 654 3811, ⓦ www.hotel-ace.co.jp. A 10min walk from the station, across the river, this is a good choice if you want to stay in the downtown area. The rooms are small but comfortable,

and a little sprucer in the newer annexe. Rates include a large Japanese and Western buffet breakfast. ☎ **¥7200**

Daiwa Roynet ダイワロイネット 1-8-10 Ōdōri ☎019 604 2155, ⓦ daiwaroynet.jp. Good-value business hotel, with bright, reasonably sized rooms, on the loop bus route 1.2km northeast of the station, near Morioka's main shopping and dining arcade as well as the principal sights. ☎ **¥9900**

★Kumagai Ryokan 熊ヶ井旅館 3-2-5 Ōsawakawara ☎019 651 3020, ⓦ kumagairyokan.com. A short walk from the station over the river, this cosy old-fashioned ryokan is one of the best options in town, with a welcoming English-speaking owner, attractive tatami rooms, private and communal baths, and well-priced meals available (breakfast ¥1000, dinner ¥2000, Mon–Sat only). ☎ **¥9000**

New City Hotel ニューシティホテル 13-10 Ekimae-dōri ☎019 651 5161, ⓦ moriokacityhotel.co.jp. Handily tucked away close to the river, in a quiet spot just 350m from the station, this eight-storey brick-coloured block holds snug modern rooms aimed at business travellers. Rates include a rather pitiful breakfast. ☎ **¥8500**

Hotel Royal Morioka ホテルロイヤル盛岡 1-11-11 Saien-dōri ☎019 653 1331, ⓦ hotelroyalmorioka.co.jp. High-end hotel in the heart of the entertainment district, with spacious and elegantly furnished Western-style rooms. The two in-house restaurants, serving *shabu-shabu* and Korean barbecue, are complemented by a Starbucks on the ground floor. Breakfast available for ¥1350. ☎ **¥13,200**

Hotel Ruiz ホテルルイズ 7-15 Ekimae-dōri ☎019 625 2611, ⓦ hotel-ruiz.jp. A short walk from the station, just before the main bridge across the river, this mid-range business hotel offers a choice of Western- or Japanese-style rooms plus rather ordinary French, Japanese and Chinese restaurants. Rates include breakfast. ☎ **¥9000**

Tōyoko Inn Morioka Ekimae 東横INN盛岡駅前 14-5 Ekimae-dōri ☎019 625 1045, ⓦ toyoko-inn.com. Chain hotel, facing the station, with smart and clean rooms, very much targeted at Japanese business travellers. Rates include a light Japanese breakfast. ☎ **¥7640**

EATING

Azuma-ya Honten 東家本店 1-8-3 Nakanohashi-dōri ☎019 622 2252, ⓦ wankosoba-azumaya.co.jp. This fine old restaurant, east across the Nakatsu-gawa from the castle park, is a good place to head to for *wanko-soba*, traditionally served in multiple tiny bowls. Unadorned noodles start at ¥540, with lunch sets from ¥1080 and *wanko* course menus from ¥2700. This local chain also has outlets near the station and in the entertainment district. ☎ Daily 11am–8pm.

Baimakkuru バイマックルー 1-4-22 Nakanohashi-dōri ☎019 622 8109. Against a soundtrack of unrelenting Thai pop, the chef at this welcoming and popular restaurant whips up great curries at lunch (set menus from ¥860) and all sorts of Thai specialities at night. Daily 11.30am–3pm & 6–11pm.

Chokurian 直利庵 1-12-13 Nakanohashi-dōri ☎019 624 0441. Opened in 1884, this is the best-known restaurant in town for *wanko-soba*. Expect to pay around ¥3000 for a full all-you-can-eat blow-out, although they also serve reasonably priced standard noodle dishes in an adjoining room. Mon, Tues & Thurs–Sun 11am–9pm.

Hot JaJa ホットジャジャ 9-5 Ekimae-dōri ☎019 606 1068, ⓦ pyonpyonsya.co.jp. Convenient and very popular *ja-ja men* place near the station, run by the same people as the neighbouring *Pyon Pyon Sha*. As well as good noodles – servings start at ¥500, with sets from ¥800 – they also offer the excellent local Baeren Beer, inspired by German brewing traditions. ☎ Daily 10am–midnight.

★Pairon Honten 白龍本店 5-15 Uchimaru ☎019 624 2247. One of the most popular places for *ja-ja men*, just off Ōdōri, across from Iwate-kōen; walk under the big *torii*, and it's on your left. The huge, cheap portions are so filling that staff advise first-time customers to try the regular (*futsū*;

THE NOODLES OF MORIOKA

One highlight of visiting Morioka is its cuisine. The city's most famous speciality is **wanko-soba**, named after the small bowls in which the thin, flat buckwheat noodles are served. They're often eaten as a contest, during which diners don an apron and shovel down as many bowls as possible while a waitress relentlessly dishes up more; to stop, you have to get the top on to your emptied bowl – easier said than done.

Another rather odd Morioka concoction, **reimen**, was originally a summer dish, though you can easily find it year-round here as well as in other parts of Japan. It consists of a large bowl of cold, semi-transparent, slightly chewy egg noodles eaten with Korean *kimchi* (spicy pickled vegetables) plus assorted garnishes that might include boiled egg, sesame seeds and slices of apple or cold meat.

One last local speciality is another unusual noodle dish: **ja-ja men**, a bowl of thick, white noodles (a bit like udon) that comes with a few slices of cucumber, red pickles and a slab of brown miso paste. Many local noodle shops serve *ja-ja men*; mix up the miso paste and noodles once you are served and, if you're still hungry when you've finished, crack open and beat up a raw egg in your bowl and hand it to your server, who will pour broth over it to make *chii tantan*, a palate-cleansing soup. It's a little bland if eaten straight, so most locals add either grated ginger or miso paste to give it a bit more flavour.

3

HIKES AROUND MORIOKA

The highest peak in Tōhoku, **Iwate-san** (岩手山; 2041m), dominates Morioka's northern horizon. It marks the eastern edge of the **Hachimantai plateau**, a beautiful area for hiking among marshes and pine forests. While the actual summit of the volcano is an immensely challenging trek, and tends in any case to be off limits to visitors, you can spend a wonderful day walking around the plateau to the north of Iwate-san, from where it's an easy stroll to the less daunting summit of **Hachimantai** (八幡平; 1613m). From the Hachimantai Chōjō bus stop, a well-marked path leads to the summit (40min), across Hachiman-numa marshes. Afterwards, you can wander assorted tracks across the plateau, enjoying views south to the barren slopes of Iwate-san.

A couple of infrequent summer-only bus routes connect Morioka with Hachimantai Chōjō, taking between two and two and a half hours (one-way around ¥1300; ⓦ iwate-kenpokubus .co.jp). Precise timetables change each year; ask at Morioka's tourist office for the latest details.

¥500) size first; an egg to drop in your soup costs another ¥50. Expect queues during peak lunch and dinner hours. Mon–Sat 11.30am–9pm.

Pyon Pyon Sha ぴょんぴょん舎 9-3 Ekimae-dōri ☎ 019 606 1067, ⓦ pyonpyonsya.co.jp. *Reimen* specialist, on the main road a very short walk ahead from the station's east exit. A helping of cold noodles with beef costs ¥900; the "original style" is the least spicy, but they also serve all sorts of hotter Korean pickles and soups. 🛜 Daily 11am–midnight.

DRINKING AND NIGHTLIFE

For a small city, Morioka has a surprisingly bustling nightlife with a thriving **club** scene and plenty of lively **bars**. The main areas for drinking and entertainment are in the streets on either side of the covered Ōdori shopping arcade.

Mad Disco マッド・ディスコー B1 1-6-3 Hinoshita ☎ 019 681 6660, ⓦ maddisco2010.com. The place to go for Japanese-style R&B and hip-hop, with the cream of the region's DJs and MCs providing the tunes. Cover charge ¥1000–2000, usually including two drinks; women get in free on some nights. Tues–Sun 10pm–late.

Mother Club モザー・クラブ 3F Plaza Tiger Bld, 1-6-17 Ōdōri ☎ 019 651 0530, ⓦ mother-morioka.com. This small and friendly club has earned a big reputation for its eclectic mix of music, and attracts top Japanese and international DJs. Check website for current schedule. Tues–Sat 10pm–4am, occasionally open Sun & Mon.

Sun Dance サンダンス 2-4-22 Ōdōri ☎ 019 652 6526. This busy Irish bar is popular with expats and serves Tex-Mex dishes and other pub grub. It has a good range of imported beers, including Guinness on tap, as well as specials on jugs of cocktails. Mon–Thurs 5pm–midnight, Fri & Sat 5pm–2am.

SHOPPING

Ōdōri and Saien-dōri are Morioka's two major **shopping streets**, with a good selection of large department stores including Park Avenue and Cube II, as well as smaller independent retailers. Regional crafts to look out for include Nambu ironware, dyed cotton textiles and plain wooden *kokeshi* dolls.

Kamasada Honten 釜定 本店 2-5 Konya-chō ☎ 019 622 3911. Fine old store in the Gozaku merchants' neighbourhood, specializing in heavyweight traditional cast-iron kettles and the like. Mon–Sat 9am–5.30pm.

Kōgensha 光原社 2-18 Zaimoku-chō ☎ 019 622 2894, ⓦ morioka-kogensya.sakura.ne.jp. Centred around a lovely courtyard, this craftshop sells modern and traditional pottery, ironware, paper and bamboo designs. It also has a café at the back. Daily 10am–6pm.

Aomori

青森

Honshū's northernmost city, **AOMORI**, sits at the inland end of Mutsu Bay, sheltered by the twin claws of the Tsugaru and Shimokita peninsulas. Long-serving as a port for travellers heading northwards, it was boosted in 2016 when the opening of the 46km **Seikan Tunnel** instigated a direct Shinkansen link under the sea to Hokkaidō.

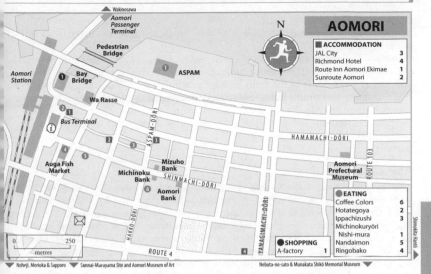

The area around Aomori Station and the adjacent **harbourside** in particular have been extensively redeveloped to create a bright modern cityscape equipped with attractive waterfront promenades, busy cafés and a colourful museum. Aomori, though, also offers a glimpse of Japan's remote past, in the shape of the extraordinary **Sannai-Maruyama Site**, southwest of the centre. To experience the city at its very best, aim to come during August's raucous **Nebuta Matsuri** festival, when Aomori really comes to life.

Wa Rasse

ワ・ラッセ • 1-1-1 Yasukata • Daily: May–Aug 9am–7pm, Sept–April 9am–6pm, closed Aug 9 & 10 • ¥600 • ☎ 017 752 1311, ⓦ www.nebuta.jp/warasse

A bizarre, angular and highly conspicuous edifice, cloaked in **strips** of red and black metal and just a minute's walk from the station towards the harbourfront, was built to house **Wa Rasse**, a museum and cultural centre that celebrates the Nebuta Matsuri festival. Its darkened central hall displays five huge illuminated floats that took part in the most recent festival, each a dramatic explosion of colour bursting with menacing figures. There are regular screenings of the event, while live dance and drumming performances are staged three times daily at weekends and during holidays, when you can try on masks and play drums or other instruments.

NEBUTA MATSURI

One of the biggest and rowdiest festivals in the entire country, the **Nebuta Matsuri** (Aug 2–7; ⓦ www.nebuta.jp) takes its name from *nebuta*, meaning **lanterns**. These days, though, it's not so much "lanterns" that are paraded through the night-time streets of Aomori as gigantic bamboo-framed paper sculptures, mounted on enormous floats and illuminated from within by electricity rather than candles. Taking the form of kabuki actors, samurai or even sumo wrestlers in dramatic poses, they're painted by well-known local artists, and their progress through the city is accompanied by much energetic dancing and enthusiastic disorder. According to local legend, the tradition originated in 800, when a band of rebels was lured out of hiding by an imaginative general who had his men construct an eye-catching lantern and play festive music.

Auga fish market

アウガ新鮮市場, Auga Shinshen Ichiba • 1-3-7 Shinmachi-dōri • Mon–Sat 5am–6.30pm (closed some Wed) • ☎ 017 721 8000, Ⓦ auga.co.jp/shinsen.html

A short walk from the station, at the west end of Aomori's main shopping street, the old-fashioned **Auga fish market** occupies the basement of the multipurpose Auga building (アウガ). Most of the stalls here are piled high with iridescent fish, hairy crabs, scallops and squid, but a few display neat pyramids of Aomori's other staple product: juicy, oversized **apples**. At the end nearest the street, the recommended *Ringobako* **restaurant** (see p.258) sells well-priced seafood meals long after the market itself is closed.

ASPAM

青森県観光物産館, Aomori-kan Kankō Bussan-kan • 1-1-40 Yasukata • Daily: building open 9am–10pm; Panorama Movie Theatre and Observation Platform April–Oct 9am–7pm, Sept–March 9am–6pm; shops and restaurants hours vary • Building free; Panorama Movie Theatre ¥600, Observation Platform ¥400, combination ticket ¥800 • ☎ 017 735 5311, Ⓦ aomori-kanko.or.jp

The futuristic fifteen-storey glass wedge on the waterfront, ten minutes' walk west of the harbour and station and glowing a spectacular green after dark, is **ASPAM**. Designed as a showcase for regional tourism and industry, it's actually a huge letter "A" (for Aomori). The ground floor holds assorted souvenir and craft shops, with lots of local seafood on sale, while the second floor is home to the Panorama Movie Theatre, which screens 360° films about the prefecture. Up on the thirteenth floor, the Observation Platform looks out across the city and the bay. While none of this really amounts to a must-see attraction, it's worth dropping in to pick up tourist information or gifts. Come at 11.30am or 2pm daily, and you can enjoy live *shamisen* music performances.

Sannai-Maruyama Site

三内丸山遺跡, Sannai-Maruyama Iseki • 305 Aza-Maruyama • Daily: June–Sept 9am–6pm; Oct–May 9am–5pm • Free • ☎ 017 781 6078, Ⓦ sannaimaruyama.pref.aomori.jp • Nebtan-Go shuttle bus (¥200 per trip, ¥500 all day) from either Aomori Station (25min) or Shin-Aomori Station (15min), or local bus #6 from Aomori Station (¥330)

The **Sannai-Maruyama Site**, in a rural setting 5km southwest of Aomori Station or 3km south of Shin-Aomori Station, centres on one of Japan's most remarkable ancient settlements. Between around 3500 BC and 2000 BC, an era known to archeologists as the Early and Middle **Jōmon** periods, these hillside meadows were occupied by a substantial **village**. Its inhabitants lived by fishing in the sea, and hunting with dogs, and buried their dead in large ceramic jars.

Start your visit by wandering for half an hour or so through the actual village. As well as reconstructed pithouses – small, hobbit-like dwellings roofed with turf and/or thatch – you'll see a rather extraordinary three-level structure supported on huge tree-trunk pillars. Only its timber skeleton has been rebuilt, as no one knows exactly what it looked like, let alone how it was used. Then return to the superb modern **museum** that adjoins the main entrance, which displays the pick of the artefacts that have been excavated here, ranging from pottery needles and spearheads to enigmatic ceramic effigies. Note that in winter, when the site is covered by snow, it's harder to get a sense of the settlement itself – it still looks magnificent, though.

Aomori Museum of Art

青森県立美術館, Aomori Kenritsu Bijutsukan • 185 Chikano, Yasuta • Daily: June–Sept 9am–6pm; Oct–May 9.30am–5pm, closed 2nd and 4th Mon of each month • ¥510; temporary exhibitions extra • ☎ 017 783 3000, Ⓦ aomori-museum.jp • Nebtan-Go shuttle bus (¥200 per trip, ¥500 all day) from either Aomori Station (20min) or Shin-Aomori Station (20min), or local bus #6 from Aomori Station (¥310)

A short walk from the Sannai-Maruyama Site (though slightly more circuitous by road), the stark, white, low-lying and labyrinthine **Aomori Museum of Art** seems an extension of the snowy landscape that surrounds it for much of the year. As well as hosting stimulating temporary exhibitions, it holds a fine permanent collection. The highlight is more than 120 works by the Hirosaki-born artist **Nara Yoshimoto**, famous for his depictions of grumpy, defiant girls and sculptures of white dogs, the largest of which, the colossal 8.5m-tall Aomori Ken, was commissioned for the museum, and stands dolefully outdoors, staring at his similarly enormous bowl. One gallery is devoted to three huge backdrops by **Marc Chagall**, painted in 1942 for a production of the ballet *Aleko*.

Aomori Prefectural Museum

青森県立郷土館, Aomori Kenritsu Kyōdo-kan • 2-8-14 Honcho • Tues–Sun: May–Oct 9am–6pm; Nov–April 9am–5pm • ¥310 • ☎ 017 777 1585, ⓦ kyodokan.com • Nebtan-Go shuttle bus (¥200 per trip, ¥500 all day) from either Aomori Station (20min) or Shin-Aomori Station (20min)

Housed in an imposing former downtown bank, 1.3km east of the station, the **Aomori Prefectural Museum** takes a look at the region's history, culture and natural environment. As well as Jōmon-era earthenware pots and beautiful, insect-eyed *dogū* figurines of unknown ritualistic purpose, excavated near Tsugaru (50km west), it includes fascinating displays on local folk culture. Vine-woven baskets and rice-straw raincoats rub shoulders with fertility dolls and the distinctive agricultural deity Oshira-sama (see p.249).

Munakata Shikō Memorial Museum

棟方志功記念館, Munakata Shikō Kinenkan • 2-1-2 Matsubara • Tues–Sun: April–Oct 9am–5pm, Nov–March 9.30am–5pm • ¥500 • ☎ 017 777 4567, ⓦ munakatashiko-museum.jp • Bus 3 from Aomori Station (15min; ¥190)

The small **Munakata Shikō Memorial Museum**, 3km southeast of the station, honours the Aomori-born woodblock artist Munakata Shikō (1903–75). Rotating exhibitions celebrate Shikō's bold, almost abstract, scenes of local festivals and Aomori people. Though best known for his black-and-white prints, he also dabbled in oils, painted screens and calligraphy.

ARRIVAL AND DEPARTURE

AOMORI

By plane Aomori Airport (☎ 017 773 2135, ⓦ aomori-airport.co.jp), 13km south of the centre, has regular JR bus connections with Aomori Station (15 daily; 35min; ¥700). Destinations Nagoya (3 daily; 1hr 30min); Osaka Itami (6 daily; 1hr 40min); Sapporo (5 daily; 50min); Tokyo Haneda (6 daily; 1hr 25min).

By train Aomori Station lies just west of the city centre, immediately inland from the Bay Bridge and Aomori passenger terminal. Trains on the Tōhoku Shinkansen line from Tokyo via Sendai, however, come no closer to the centre than Shin-Aomori Station, 5km west, where you need to change onto the JR Ōu line to reach Aomori Station (5min). Destinations Akita (3 daily; 3hr 5min); Hakodate (hourly; 2hr); Hirosaki (hourly; 30–45min); Morioka (hourly; 1hr 20min); Noheji (6 daily; 30–45min); Sendai (hourly; 2–3hr); Tokyo (hourly; 3hr 30min–5hr).

By bus Long-distance buses (ⓦ konanbus.com) terminate by the train station. Destinations Morioka (4 daily; 2hr 45min); Sendai (6 daily; 4hr 50min); Tokyo (2 daily; 9hr 30min); Towada-ko (April–Oct, 6–8 daily; 3hr 15min).

By ferry Tsugaru Kaikyo (☎ 017 766 4673, ⓦ www.tsugarukaikyo.co.jp) operates frequent ferries that carry cars and foot passengers to Hokkaidō (Hakodate; 8 daily; 3hr 40min) from Aomori Ferry terminal, 5km west of Aomori Station (20min by bus; ¥300).

INFORMATION AND GETTING AROUND

Tourist information Aomori's most useful tourist office is immediately outside the station, adjoining the JR Bus terminal (daily 8.30am–7pm; ☎ 017 723 4670, ⓦ atca.info). You can also pick up regional information at ASPAM.

By bus Central Aomori is small enough to explore on foot, but you'll need local buses to reach the southern sights. The Nebtan-Go shuttle bus, which departs from both Aomori and Shin-Aomori stations, links all the main attractions, including Sannai-Maruyama, for ¥200 per trip or ¥500 all day; at weekends and during public holidays, the ¥500 all-day pass also covers all other local buses.

By car Toyota (☎ 017 734 0100, ⓦ rent.toyota.co.jp) and

Nippon (☎017 722 2369, ⊛nipponrentacar.co.jp) have rental outlets near the station. For cabs, call Asahi Taxi (☎017 711 0451) or Miyago Kankō Taxi (☎017 743 0385).

By bike You can rent fixed-gear bikes (May–Oct daily 10am–5pm) for ¥300 a day from the bicycle parking lot to the left of the station.

ACCOMMODATION

Though it has plenty of central chain hotels, Aomori is short of budget options and ryokan. Be sure to book ahead, especially if you're coming for Nebuta Matsuri (Aug 2–7).

JAL City ホテルJALシティ 2-4-12 Yasukata ☎017 732 2580, ⊛aomori-jalcity.co.jp. The smart rooms at this popular business hotel, just south of ASPAM 600m east of the station, are well priced, and there's a decent in-house restaurant. The seafood-heavy Japanese buffet breakfast costs ¥1500. 🛜 **¥13,000**

Richmond Hotel リッチモンドホテル青森 1-6-6 Nagashima ☎017 732 7655, ⊛aomori.richmondhotel. jp. This modern high-rise hotel, at a major intersection 1.3km east of the station, is particularly convenient for those travelling by car. Rooms are comfortable and spacious, and a buffet breakfast costs ¥1100 extra. 🛜 **¥16,000**

Route Inn Aomori Ekimae ルート イン 青森駅前 1-1-24 Shinmachi-dōri ☎017 731 3611, ⊛route-inn .co.jp. Though not readily conspicuous, this veteran business hotel stands directly across from the station. That handy location and the bargain rates are the strongest plus factors, while the one drawback is the phenomenally hard mattresses. There's also an onsen, and rates include a decent buffet breakfast. 🛜 **¥7050**

Sunroute Aomori ホテルサンルート 1-9-8 Shinmachi-dōri ☎017 775 2321, ⊛sunroute.jp. Well-priced business hotel, a 5min walk from the station, with large, en-suite Western-style rooms and a couple of decent Japanese restaurants. Breakfast costs ¥1300 extra. 🛜 **¥7500**

EATING

Seafood, apples and apple products fill Aomori's food halls and souvenir shops. Local specialities worth sampling include **hotate kai-yaki**, fresh scallops from Mutsu Bay grilled in their shells and served with a dash of miso sauce, and **jappa-jiru**, a cod-fish stew that's available in winter.

Coffee Colors コーヒーカラーズ 2-2-21 Hakko-dōri ☎017 752 6251, ⊛coffee-colors.com. Stylish and popular downtown coffee roasters, with a few in-house tables where customers can appreciate their espresso and drip coffees, as well as speciality teas. 🛜 Daily 9am–6pm.

★**Hotategoya** 帆立小屋 1-3-2 Yasukata ☎017 752 9454, ⊛aomori-den.jp/hotategoya.htm. The gimmick at this simple seafood place, in the small arcade to the left of the station's east exit, is that for ¥500 you can "fish" for scallops, using a rod and hook in an open aquarium, and eat whatever you catch within three minutes – they guarantee you at least two. Alternatively, you can get a plate of grilled fish for ¥680, assorted sashimi for ¥550, or barbecue prawns, mackerel or octopus at your table for around ¥600 per serving. Daily 10am–10pm.

Ippachizushi 一八寿し 1-10-1 Shinmachi-dōri ☎017 722 2639. Behind its simple white facade, this little back-alley restaurant serves some of Aomori's best sushi and sashimi. There's no English menu; just sit at the counter and point to whatever takes your fancy. Individual portions start at around ¥750, with sushi sets from ¥2200 and sashimi from ¥2500 in the evening. Mon–Sat 11.30am–9.45pm, Sun 11.30am–8.45pm.

★**Michinokuryōri Nishi-mura** みちのく料理 西むら 10F ASPAM, 1-1-40 Yasukata ☎017 734 5353, ⊛michinokunishimura.com. For a real treat, head up to the tenth floor of the landmark waterfront ASPAM building, and sample the finest local cuisine, including *hotate* and *jappa-jiru*, at reasonable prices. Individual dishes from ¥360, set meals from ¥1340 for lunch, ¥2570 in the evening. Reserve ahead in summer. 🛜 April–Oct Mon–Sat 11am–10pm, Sun 11am–8.30pm; Nov–March Mon–Fri 11am–4pm & 5–8pm, Sat & Sun 11am–8pm.

Nandaimon 南大門 1-8-3 Shinmachi-dōri ☎017 777 2377, ⊛nandaimon.tv. Cheap and cheerful Chinese-Korean restaurant, a short walk from the station, that serves good-value *yakiniku* (Korean BBQ) and grilled *hotate*, with plenty of meat options. Lunch sets start at ¥880, with *bibimbap* at ¥980 and an all-you-can-eat meat blowout for ¥4500. English menus available. 🛜 Daily 11am–11pm.

★**Ringobako** りんご箱 B1 Auga Bldg, 1-8-3 Shinmachi-dōri ☎017 763 5255, ⊛auga-ringobako .com. Large, lively, canteen-like restaurant, attached to the market in the basement of the Auga building, and a great place to sample the local seafood. Find an empty chair at one of the wooden-crate tables, and order from an enticing picture menu that ranges through tempura fish with rice for ¥900, via mixed sushi for ¥1500 or a substantial sashimi bowl costs ¥1700, up to full set dinners for around ¥3000. The central stage hosts *shamisen* music performances, daily at 12.45pm & 7pm. 🛜 Mon–Fri 10am–3pm & 4.30–11pm, Sat & Sun 10am–11pm.

SHOPPING

Aomori is a great place to pick up souvenirs. As well as *nebuta* paper **lanterns** and seafood, look out for regional products ranging from kites and embroidery to lacquerware, brightly painted horses, and *Tsugaru kokeshi* dolls. ASPAM and the JR station both hold crafts shops, while the main shopping street, **Shinmachi-dōri**, offers good browsing.

A-Factory A-工場 1-4-2 Yanagigawa ☏ 017 752 1890. This bright, modern gallery, right by the station and all but underneath the huge suspension bridge, is the centrepiece of Aomori's redeveloped harbourfront. As well as cider brewed on site, it sells all sorts of regional foodstuffs, and holds snack bars and cafés. 📶 Daily 9am–8pm.

Shimokita Hantō

The **Shimokita Hantō** peninsula protrudes into the ocean northeast of Aomori like a great axe-head. The jagged "blade" at its northern end is covered with low, forested peaks, of which the most notorious is **Osore-zan**, the "terrible mountain" where Buddhists believe the spirits of the dead linger on their way to paradise. Despite the mountain's growing commercialization, Osore-zan's bleak crater lake, surrounded by a sulphurous desert where pathetic statues huddle against the bitter winds, is a compelling, slightly spine-tingling place; an eerie wasteland where souls hover between life and death.

Osorezan-bodaiji

恐山菩提寺 • May–Oct daily 6am–6pm; festival July 20–24 • ¥500 • ☏ 017 522 3825, ⊛ bit.ly/osorezan-bodaiji

The main focus of **Osore-zan** (恐山), an extinct volcano consisting of several peaks, lies about halfway up its eastern slopes, where the fearsome **Osorezan-bodaiji** temple sits on the shore of a silvery crater lake. Though the temple was founded in the ninth century, Osore-zan was already revered in ancient folk religion as a place where dead souls gather. It's easy to see why – the desolate volcanic landscape, with its yellow- and red-stained soil, multicoloured pools and bubbling, malodorous streams, makes for an unearthly scene. The temple also receives a steady trickle of non-spectral visitors, while during the summer **festival** in July, people arrive in force to contact their ancestors or the recently deceased through the mediation of *itako*, usually blind, elderly women who turn a profitable trade.

Roughly 110km along the curving coastline northeast of Aomori, Osorezan-bodaiji stands 14km west of the workaday town of **Mutsu** (むつ), on the southern edge of Shimokita Hantō. The winding road up from there climbs through pine forests, passing a succession of stone monuments and a spring where it's customary to stop for a sip of purifying water. You eventually reach a large **lake**, beside which a small humped bridge represents the journey souls make between this world and the next; those who led an evil life are said to find it impossible to cross over. After a quick look round the temple, take any path leading over the hummock towards the lake's barren foreshore. The little heaps of **stones** all around are said to be the work of children who died before their parents. They have to wait here, building stupas, which demons gleefully knock over during the night – most people add a pebble or two in passing. Sad little statues, touchingly wrapped in towels and bibs, add an even more melancholy note to the scene. Many have offerings piled in front of them: bunches of flowers, furry toys – faded and rain-sodden by the end of summer – and plastic windmills whispering to each other in the wind.

ARRIVAL AND INFORMATION   SHIMOKITA HANTŌ

By train from Aomori Nine daily trains on the private Aomori Tetsudō line from Aomori – for which JR passes are valid – take 45min to reach Noheji (野辺駅), from where another nine daily trains on the JR Ōminato line make the 45min run to two stations in the southern suburbs of Mutsu: Shimokita Station and Ōminato Station.

By train from Hachinohe If you're heading to or from the south, travel via the Shinkansen station at Hachinohe, 85km southeast of Aomori and 100km northeast of Morioka. From there, the private Aomori Tetsudō line makes fifteen daily 45min trips to Noheji, connected as above with Shimokita and Ōminato stations.

By bus Buses run from Shimokita Station to Osore-zan (May–Oct, 3–5 daily; 45min; ¥800 each way), passing via the central Mutsu bus terminal en route, so you can go up the mountain straight off the JR train then get off in the centre of Mutsu on the way back down if you plan to stay the night. Alternatively, blue-and-white JR buses (for which rail passes are valid) run from Ōminato Station to Mutsu's JR bus terminal, east of the town centre and confusingly called Tanabu Station (田名部駅).

Tourist information Mutsu's tourist office (daily 10am–5pm; ☏ 017 522 0909) is in the ground-floor lobby of Masakari Plaza (まさかりプラザ), a pink building northwest of the JR bus terminal.

ACCOMMODATION

Murai Ryokan むら井旅館 9-30 Tanabe-chō, Mutsu ☏ 017 522 5581. Just in front of Masakari Plaza, this is one of the nicest places to stay in Mutsu. Although none of the tatami rooms is en suite, everything's extremely clean, there's a nice onsen and the food is great. Rates include two meals; room only is available for ¥4300 per person. **¥14,000**

Hotel New Green ホテルニューグリーン 1-4 Honmachi, Mutsu ☏ 017 522 6121. With a choice of Western- or Japanese-style rooms, this business hotel is reasonably priced and convenient for the station and restaurants. It's a 5min walk west from the JR bus terminal; keep going past the private bus terminal and Matsukiya department store, then turn left at the T-junction. **¥9500**

EATING

Masakari Plaza マサカリプラザ 2-46 Shimokita-chō, Mutsu ☏ 017 523 7111, ⓦ ph-m.jp. Japanese restaurant up on the second floor of the somewhat faded *Plaza* hotel, serving a decent range of set meals from ¥1600, and noodle dishes for as little as ¥500. 🛜 Daily noon–2pm & 5–11pm.

Shuyu Kaikyō Zen 酒遊海峡善 3-29 Tanabe-chō, Mutsu ☏ 017 522 7233. Welcoming little *izakaya* in the heart of Mutsu, tucked in an alleyway parallel to the river, and offering daily sashimi specials for ¥500, more substantial meat and fish dishes for around ¥2000, plus the pick of local sake. Mon–Sat 5pm–midnight.

Hirosaki

弘前

Behind its modern facade, **HIROSAKI**, former seat of the Tsugaru clan, still retains remnants of its feudal past. Its older and more interesting districts lie around 3km west of the station, across the Tsuchibuchi-gawa, which runs through the city centre. Resplendent at cherry-blossom time, the **Hirosaki-kōen** park here holds the picturesque turrets of Hirosaki-jō, the town's original castle, still surrounded by moats. To the north is a neighbourhood of traditional samurai houses, while to the south you'll find a well-preserved Japanese garden, **Fujita Kinen Teien**, and a collection of Meiji-era Western-style buildings.

Hirosaki's summer lantern festival, the **Neputa Matsuri** (Aug 1–7), has its own museum, and there's also a district of dignified **Zen temples** in the west of town. You can pretty much see all the sights in a day-trip from Aomori, but Hirosaki is a pleasant place to stay for a night or two.

Hirosaki-jō

弘前城 • Shimoshirogane-chō • Castle April to late Nov daily 9am–5pm • ¥310, ¥510 with botanical garden • ☏ 017 233 8739, ⓦ hirosakipark.jp

The large landscaped park **Hirosaki-kōen** (弘前公園) is celebrated for its 2600 **cherry trees**, at their most spectacular between April and early May, when they form the centrepiece of the annual Cherry Blossom Festival. It holds the site of the **Hirosaki-jō** castle, which when originally completed by the Tsugaru lords in 1611 stood five storeys tall. After being razed by lightning a mere sixteen years later, however, it was not rebuilt until 1810, and then only in a much smaller three-storey form, on a different spot.

What you see today is that abbreviated version, itself much rebuilt since it and other surrounding structures were largely destroyed during the Meiji Restoration.

The park itself is a real pleasure to stroll though at any time of year, large enough that from whichever side you enter it takes around ten minutes to zigzag your way between its broad concentric **moats**, mighty **walls** and imposing wooden **gateways**. Having first admired the actual castle from a purpose-built viewing platform that neatly frames it with the imposing volcanic peak of **Mount Iwaki** on the western horizon, you can then enter the three-storey **donjon**, which has costumes for visitors to try on and a scale model of the castle in its heyday. There's also a small **botanical garden** on the east side of the park.

Neputa Mura

ねぷた村 • 61 Kamenokō-machi • Daily: April–Nov 9am–5pm, Dec–March 9am–4pm • ¥500 • ☏ 017 239 1511, ⓦ neputamura.com

The **Neputa Mura** museum, devoted to Hirosaki's lantern festival, **Neputa Matsuri**, stands just outside the northeast corner of Hirosaki-kōen. Like the festival itself, the museum gets off to a rousing start with a demonstration of energetic **drumming** (which you can try yourself). Afterwards, you can admire the collection of impressive floats, with the giant lanterns painted with scenes from ancient Chinese scrolls and the faces of scowling samurai. Local crafts are also on display, and the shop is a good spot to pick up such souvenirs as ingenious spinning tops, cotton embroideries or black-and-white Tsugaru pottery.

Ishiba

石破 • 88 Kamenokō-machi • Daily 8.30am–7.30pm, closed irregularly • Tour ¥100 • ☏ 017 232 1488

The old **Ishiba** shop and residence, opposite Kita-mon, the northern gate of Hirosaki-kōen, was built 250 years ago to sell rice baskets and other household goods to the Tsugaru lords. The family (now selling sake) still lives here, so you can only get a glimpse of the warehouse behind. However, you can visit several other houses from this era in the smart residential street behind the shop.

Fujita Kinen Teien

藤田記念庭園 • 8-1 Kamishirogane-chō • Mid-April to mid-Nov Tues–Sun 9am–5pm; also open Mon during Cherry Blossom and Autumn festivals, and first 3 wks of Aug • ¥310 • ☏ 017 237 5525, ⓦ hirosakipark.or.jp

A beautiful and unusually varied Japanese garden, across the main road at the southwest corner of the castle park, **Fujita Kinen Teien** was commissioned in 1919 by

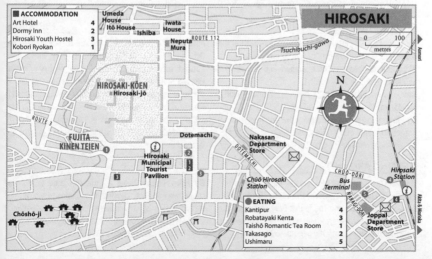

HIROSAKI FESTIVALS

CHERRY BLOSSOM FESTIVAL (桜まつり)

Between April 23 and May 5, the little white turret of Hirosaki-jō, floodlit and framed in **pink blossom**, is the focus of the Cherry Blossom Festival, as Hirosaki-kōen's two-thousand-odd trees signal the end of the harsh northern winter.

NEPUTA MATSURI (弘前ねぷたまつり)

The centrepiece of the Hirosaki Neputa festival, which lasts from August 1 to 7, is a parade of large, illuminated three-dimensional **paper lanterns** accompanied by energetic **drumming** and **dancing** through the streets. It's similar in style to the Aomori Nebuta Matsuri (see box, p.255), but here the lanterns are fan-shaped, and illustrate scenes from the heroic legends of Sangokushi ("Three Kingdom Saga") and Suikoden ("Outlaws of the Marsh"), both originally from China.

local entrepreneur Ken'ichi Fujita. It consists of three distinct sections, spreading down and across a steep hillside. At the highest point, closest to the park and alongside Fujita's elegant residence – be sure to drop into the tearoom up here (see opposite) – dark pines frame the distant peak of Iwaki-san, in a definitive example of "borrowed scenery". Paths head downward to a tumbling waterfall, from where a perfect red-lacquer bridge leads to another flat area of lawns and ponds at the bottom.

Chōshō-ji

長勝寺 • 23-8 Nishishige-mori • Jan–March, Nov & Dec by appointment only; April–Oct daily 9am–4.30pm • ☎ 017 232 0813 • ¥310 • Bus #3 for Shigemori (¥200); get off at the Chōshō-ji Iriguchi stop

In the seventeenth century, around thirty temples were relocated to create a "temple town" district in Hirosaki. The most striking of these, **Chōshō-ji**, stands roughly 1.5km southwest of the castle, and is the family temple and burial place of the Tsugaru clan. Excavations in 1954 revealed the mummified body of **Prince Tsugutomi**, son and heir of the eleventh lord, whose death at the age of 17 in 1855 was variously blamed on assassination, poisoning or eating peaches with imported sugar. During the Cherry Blossom Festival, the **mummy** is on display; otherwise you'll have to make do with a photo in the mortuary room behind the main altar, where it's rather overshadowed by a life-like statue of **Tsugaru Tamenobu**, the founder of the clan.

ARRIVAL AND INFORMATION

HIROSAKI

By train Hirosaki Station, a 25min walk southeast of the castle area, is on the JR Ōu line, which runs southwest to Akita and northeast to both Aomori and the nearest Shinkansen station, Shin-Aomori.
Destinations Akita (3 daily; 2hr 5min); Aomori (hourly; 30–45min).

By bus Long-distance buses arrive at the terminal immediately west of the train station (ⓦ konanbus.com).
Destinations Morioka (hourly; 2hr 15min); Sendai (9 daily;

4hr 20min); Tokyo (daily; 9hr); Towada-ko (late April to late Oct 3 daily; 3hr 15min–4hr); Yokohama (daily; 9hr 15min).

Tourist information There's a large tourist office in Hirosaki Station (daily 8.45am–6pm; ☎ 017 226 3600, ⓦ hirosaki-kanko.or.jp), and another in the Hirosaki Municipal Tourist Pavilion, at 2-1 Shimoshirogane-chō just south of the castle park (daily 9am–6pm; ☎ 017 237 5501), which also displays *neputa* floats and exhibits on local culture.

GETTING AROUND

By bus Local buses that stop outside the station include the "¥100 loop bus", which makes frequent circuits between the station and the Tourist Pavilion outside the castle parks (daily, every 10min, April–Nov 10am–6pm, Dec–March 10am–5pm; ¥100 per trip, ¥500 all day).

By bike Hirosaki being a little too large to explore comfortably on foot, bicycles are available to rent at the station, the Tourist Pavilion and a handful of other locations (mid-May to mid-Nov only, daily 8.45am–4pm; regular bikes ¥500/day; electric bikes ¥1000).

ACCOMMODATION

Art Hotel アートホテル 1-1-2 Ōmachi ☎017 237 0700, ⓦart-hirosaki-city.com. Large but stylish modern hotel, immediately to the left across the station forecourt and formerly known as the *Naqua City*, with small but comfortable business-style rooms and a buffet restaurant serving Japanese and international cuisines. Rates include breakfast. 📶 **¥8000**

Dormy Inn ドーミーイン弘前 71-1 Hon-chō ☎017 232 4151, ⓦbit.ly/dormy-hirosaki. Crisp chain hotel, a couple of blocks southwest of the castle park, with good-value a/c rooms and a partially open-air rooftop onsen; every 30min, a free shuttle runs to and from the station. Rates include breakfast, and free noodles are offered nightly. 📶 **¥9100**

Hirosaki Youth Hostel 弘前ユースホステル 11 Mori-machi ☎017 233 7066, ⓦbit.ly/hirosaki-hostel. An old but welcoming hostel, open May–Nov only, in a central location a couple of minutes' walk south of the Fujita garden. Coming from the station, catch the loop bus to Daigaku Byōin-mae. Accommodation is in six-bed dorms, with breakfast available for ¥680, and dinner for ¥2000. 📶 Dorms **¥3840**

Kobori Ryokan 小掘旅館 89 Hon-chō ☎017 232 5111, ⓦkobori-ryokan.com. Run by two friendly women (and supervised by their cat), this old wooden ryokan near the castle offers a choice of smart tatami rooms as well as two Western-style rooms. En-suite rooms cost ¥1080 extra, as does breakfast, while dinner is ¥2160. 📶 **¥9720**

EATING

Like Aomori, Hirosaki has a fine tradition of **folk music**, played on the *Tsugaru jamisen*, which has a thicker neck than the ordinary *shamisen* stringed instrument and is struck harder. Look out for restaurants offering dinner concerts.

Kantipur カンティプル 1-1-1 Ekimae-chō ☎017 255 0371. Friendly restaurant, to the right as you exit the station on the ground floor of the *Tōyoko Inn* building, serving tasty Indian and Thai curries and other dishes. Set lunch menus start at ¥800, while dinner will cost around ¥2000. 📶 Daily 11am–3pm & 5pm–midnight.

Robatayaki Kenta ろばた焼 3 Okeya-machi ☎017 235 9514. This cheap and popular *izakaya*, a favourite downtown rendezvous for locals, specializes in grilled food such as *yakitori*; prices for individual dishes start at ¥600. It fills up quickly at the weekends – if you can't get a seat here, try the branch around the corner. Daily 5pm–2am.

Taishō Romantic Tea Room 大正浪漫喫茶室 Fujita Kinen Teien, 8 Uehaka Banko ☎017 237 5690, ⓦbit.ly/taishotearoom. This charming little Art Deco café, in the "Western House" of the Fujita garden but open even on days when the garden itself is closed, is like something you might find in an English country house. While most customers come for tea and cakes – ¥720 buys a "sweet set" with an apple pie or turnover or other pastry plus tea or coffee – the café also offers daily lunch specials, ranging from curry or pasta to salad, for ¥975. 📶 Daily 9am–5pm.

Takasago 高砂 1-2 Oyakata-machi. You may have to wait in line to enjoy lunch at this inexpensive soba restaurant, set in an attractive old wooden house in the lanes southeast of the castle grounds. The limited menu includes tempura soba, *zaru* soba and curry soba; expect to pay around ¥1000 for a full meal. Tues–Sun 11am–6pm.

Ushimaru ウシマル 10-1 Oaza Ekimae-chō ☎017 288 6070, ⓦushimaru2015.com. Busy but very efficient Japanese diner, 200m along the modern pedestrianized mall directly ahead of the station. The speciality is charcoal-grilled meat and fish, with individual table-top braziers if you want to prepare your own food; single items cost under ¥500, while full meals for two start at ¥4000. They also prepare good-value lunch specials such as a ¥600 beef curry. 📶 Mon–Sat 11am–2pm & 5–11pm.

South to Towada-ko

十和田湖

Japan's third-deepest lake, the steep-sided, crystal-clear **Towada-ko**, fills a 300m-deep volcanic crater in the northern portion of the Towada-Hachimantai National Park. While the lake itself is of course a major tourist destination, for many visitors the true highlight is the approach over high passes and along deep wooded valleys. Of the four main access roads, the most attractive route is to head south from Aomori via the Hakkōda mountains, Sukayu Onsen and the picturesque **Oirase valley**. For this last stretch it's the done thing to walk the final few kilometres alongside the tumbling Oirase-gawa, and then hop on a cruise boat across to the lake's main tourist centre, **Yasumiya**. Note that many roads around Towada-ko are closed in winter, and public buses only operate between April and November.

Hakkōda-san

八甲田さん • Ropeway: daily, March to mid-Nov 9am–4.20pm, mid-Nov to Feb 9am–3.40pm • ¥1180 one-way, ¥1850 round-trip • ☏ 017 738 0343, ⓦ hakkoda-ropeway.jp

South of Aomori, Route 103 climbs steeply onto the Kayano plateau before reaching the flanks of **Hakkōda-san**. Every winter, up to 8m of snow falls on these mountains, transforming the fir trees into "snow monsters" (*juhyō*) and maintaining a flourishing ski industry. In summer, this beautiful spot offers excellent walking among Hakkōda-san's old volcanic peaks, the tallest of which is Ōdake (1584m). To ease the climb, the **Hakkōda Ropeway** (cable-car) can whisk you to the top of nearby Tamoyachi-dake (1326m), from where you can walk down to Sukayu Onsen; both places are stops on the bus route from Aomori to Towada-ko.

Sukayu Onsen

酸ヶ湯温泉 • 50 Sukayuzawa • Bath 7am–6pm • ¥600 • ☏ 017 738 6400, ⓦ sukayu.jp • Take a bus from Aomori, direction Towada-ko

The most famous of the many onsen resorts in the Aomori region, **Sukayu Onsen** consists of just one single **ryokan**, which boasts a "thousand-person" cedar-wood bath. Heavy with sulphur, Sukayu's healing waters have been popular since the late seventeenth century, and this is one of very few onsen left in Japan that is not segregated.

ACCOMMODATION

SUKAYU ONSEN

Sukayu Onsen Ryokan 酸ヶ湯温泉旅館 50 Sukayuzawa, Minami Arakawasan Kokuyurin ☏ 017 738 6400, ⓦ sukayu.jp. The only ryokan in the resort, in business for over three hundred years, offers assorted traditional tatami rooms in the large building, the most expensive of which have private baths. Rates depend on whether you choose a six-, eight or ten-mat room; those shown here include two meals, though you can also book a room without food, starting at ¥3500 per person. **¥11,880**

The Oirase valley

奥入瀬渓流, Oirase Keiryu

South of Sukayu, the road crosses another pass and then descends through pretty deciduous woodlands – spectacular in autumn – to reach the village of **YAKEYAMA** (焼山). That's the start of the **Oirase valley** walk, but you'd do better to join the path at **ISHIGEDO** (石ヶ戸), 5km further down the road. From there, it takes less than three hours to walk the 9km to Towada-ko, following a well-trodden path that heads gently upstream. Although the experience is slightly marred by the need to join the fairly busy main road for short stretches, for the most part you're walking beside the Oirase-gawa as it tumbles among ferns and moss-covered rocks, through a narrow tree-filled valley punctuated by ice-white waterfalls. When you finally emerge at lakeside **NENOKUCHI** (子ノ口), you can either pick up a passing bus or take a scenic cruise across Towada-ko to Yasumiya.

Towada-ko

十和田湖

A massive crater lake, roughly 44km in circumference, **Towada-ko** lies trapped within a rim of pine-forested hills within the Towada-Hachimantai National Park. Famous for its spectacularly clear water, with visibility to a depth of 17m, the lake is best appreciated on a **boat trip**. The westerly of the two knobbly peninsulas that break its regular outline on the southern side shelters the only major settlement up here, **YASUMIYA** (休屋), which is itself also known somewhat confusingly as Towada-ko. Though this small town consists almost entirely of hotels and souvenir shops, its shady lakeside setting makes it a pleasant overnight stop.

The Maidens by the Lake
おとめの像, Otome no Zō

Once you've navigated the lake, the other thing everyone does in Towada-ko is pay a visit to the famous statue of the **Maidens by the Lake**, which stands on the shore fifteen minutes' walk north of central Yasumiya. The two identical bronze women, roughcast and naked, appear to be circling each other with hands almost touching. Created in 1953 by the poet and sculptor **Takamura Kōtarō**, then 70 years old, they are said to represent his wife, a native of Tōhoku, who suffered from schizophrenia and died tragically young.

ARRIVAL AND DEPARTURE
TOWADA-KO

By train The closest rail station to the lake is 33km southwest. Towada-minami Station (十和田南), which is connected by bus with Yasumiya between April and mid-Nov only, is on the JR Hanawa line between Morioka and Ōdate (大館). Ōdate in turn is on the main JR line between Aomori and Akita. Reserve tickets in advance if at all possible.
Destinations Morioka (7 daily; 2hr 15min); Ōdate (7 daily; 40min).
By bus Public buses only travel to and from Towada-ko between mid-April and mid-November. Yasumiya's town centre is dominated by two bus terminals, standing

opposite each other on a T-junction just inland from the boat pier. The more northerly is for JR buses (ⓦbit.ly /towadakobus), and is used by services to Towada-minami and Aomori; buses to Hirosaki and Hachimantai use the Towada-ko terminal, opposite (ⓦbit.ly/hirosakibus). To get to Akita, catch a bus south to Towada-minami, then take a local train to Ōdate.
Destinations All services mid-April to mid-Nov only: Aomori (6–8 daily; 3hr 15min); Hachimantai (daily; 2hr 30min); Hirosaki (2 buses Sat & Sun only; 3hr 15min); Ōdate (daily; 1hr 30min); Towada-minami (4 daily; 1hr).

INFORMATION AND TOURS

Tourist information The local tourist office is immediately north of the Yasumiya JR bus terminal (daily 8am–5pm; ☎017 675 2425, ⓦtowadako.or.jp).
Boat trips Sightseeing cruises (ⓦtoutetsu.co.jp/ship .html) operate on the lake from mid-April until the end of January, with the most interesting route being the circuit

between Yasumiya and Nenokuchi (mid-April to early Nov; hourly; 50min; ¥1440). In winter, when there are far fewer sailings, boats tend to make shorter loop trips from Yasumiya (¥1120).
Bike rental You can rent bicycles (¥700/2hr) at Yasumiya and drop them off at Nenokuchi (or vice versa).

ACCOMMODATION

Kohan No Yado Minshuku Nagomi 湖畔の宿　民宿 和み 37 Towada-ko Yasumitai, Kazuno-gun ☎017 675 2932, ⓦkohannoyado-nagomi.com. Simple but very well kept modern minshuku, across the road from the lake and a few minutes' walk south of the centre, and offering a choice of Japanese- and Western-style rooms. The owner speaks English, and the rates include two good meals. 📶 **¥13,360**
Lake Towada Lodge Campsite 十和田湖 生出キャン プ場 486 Yasumiya ☎017 675 2368, ⓦbit.ly /towadacamp. In summer, the patches of flat land around Towada-ko fill with tents; this is the closest campsite to Yasumiya, 3km southwest of town. A shop on site sells food and rents a range of camping equipment. Late April to Oct. Two-person site **¥800**

Syunzan-sō 春山荘　5-1 Towada-ko Hanyasumiya, Okuse ☎017 675 2607, ⓦsyunzansou.com. Traditional inn in a charming old building, just a few minutes' walk from the pier, with tatami rooms sharing a communal bathroom. Rates include two meals, room only costs ¥4420 per person. 📶 **¥12,960**
Towada-ko Grand Hotel 十和田湖グランドホテル 486 Towada-ko Hanyasumiya, Okuse ☎017 670 6001, ⓦtowadako-gh.com. Large resort hotel, facing the lake and located south of the ferry pier, and which is often filled with Japanese seniors. As well as large and luxurious tatami rooms and several onsen baths, amenities include a bar, café and souvenir shop. Rates include breakfast and dinner. 📶 **¥15,600**

Kirisuto No Haka
キリストの墓 • 33-1 Nozuki, Shingō • Museum Mon, Tues & Thurs–Sun 9am–5pm • ¥200 • ☎017 878 3741

Just outside the town of **SHINGŌ**, 30km east of Towada-ko along Route 454, **Kirisuto No Haka** – Christ's Grave – is a mound of earth, topped with a wooden cross, which was erected in 1935 to commemorate an unusual local myth. The story goes that Jesus came to Japan as a 21-year-old and learned from a great master, before returning to Judea to spread the wonders of "sacred Japan". Supposedly, these revolutionary teachings were what led Jesus to the cross, but in another twist it was Jesus's brother Isukiri who was crucified, while Christ himself escaped to Shingō, where he married, had several children and lived until the age of 106. A small **museum** nearby, run under the auspices of the local yoghurt factory, displays a scripture corroborating the story, though it doesn't give much detail about the nationalist historian, Banzan Toya, who "discovered" the tale in the 1930s – a time when Japan was funnelling substantial resources into demonstrating Japanese racial superiority.

Ōishigami Pyramids

大石神ピラミッド

The two **Ōishigami Pyramids**, 6km west of Kirisuto No Haka, were, like Christ's Grave, identified during the 1930s by Banzan Toya. He claimed to have unearthed ancient writings that proved that the Japanese built pyramids tens of thousands of years before the Egyptians and Mexicans. To the untrained eye, neither pyramid amounts to anything more than a pile of huge boulders, but the top of the higher one makes a great picnic spot.

Akita

秋田

One of the few large cities on the northwest coast of Japan, **AKITA** was founded in the eighth century, but almost nothing of the old city remains. These days, thanks to its access to some of the country's few domestic oil reserves, it's an important port and industrial centre. The few central sites – three contrasting museums – can easily be covered on foot in half a day, but with its airport and Shinkansen services, Akita makes a convenient regional base.

Senshū-kōen

千秋公園 • 1-1 Senshū-kōen • ☎ 018 832 5893

The centre of modern Akita is bounded to the east by its smart train station, and to the north by the willow-lined moats of its former castle, **Kubota-jō**. This was Akita's second castle, founded in 1604 by the Satake clan who, unusually for northerners, backed the emperor rather than the shogun during the Meiji Restoration. Despite their loyalty, the castle was abandoned by the late nineteenth century and the site is now a park, **Senshū-kōen**.

Akita Museum of Art

秋田県立美術館, Akita Kenritsu Bijutsukan • 1-4-2 Naka-dōri • Daily 10am–6pm • ¥300 • ☎ 018 853 8686, ⓦ www.akita-museum-of-art.jp

A striking wedge-shaped building, facing Senshū-kōen from the south, the **Akita Museum of Art** was unveiled in 2013. It displays the collection of the Masakichi Hirano art foundation, and especially works by local artist Tsuguharu Foujita. The most memorable, *Events in Akita*, is a 20m-long canvas depicting Akita's annual festivals that takes up an entire wall. It was completed in an incredible fifteen days in 1937, after which the wall of Foujita's studio had to be knocked down to get it out.

Kantō Festival Centre

ねぶり流し館, Neburi-Nagashi-kan • 1-3-30 Omachi • Daily 9.30am–4.30pm • ¥100, or ¥250 with Aka-renga Kyōdo-kan • ☎ 018 866 7091

The **Kantō Festival Centre**, across a small river west of Senshū-kōen, is devoted to informing visitors about local festivals in general, and in particular the **Kantō Matsuri** (see box opposite). Videos show the most recent celebrations, which take place during

> ## KANTŌ MATSURI
>
> The city of Akita is home to one of the great Tōhoku summer festivals, the **Kantō Matsuri** (Aug 3–6; ⓦ www.kantou.gr.jp) – though it's a pleasantly low-key affair compared to events in Sendai (see box, p.234) and Aomori (see box, p.255). During the festival, around two hundred teams of men and young boys parade through the streets, toting hefty *kantō* – bamboo poles. Each pole measures up to 12m long, weighs perhaps 60kg, and is strung with dozens of brightly coloured **paper lanterns**. Endlessly, rhythmically, exuberantly transferring the swaying, top-heavy structures from hip to head, hand or shoulder, participants compete to demonstrate their skills in managing to keep them upright throughout.

the first week of every August, in honour of the coming harvest. You're encouraged to have a go with a *kantō* yourself.

Aka-renga Kyōdo-kan

赤れんが郷土館 • 3-3-21 Omachi • Daily 9.30am–4.30pm • ¥200, or ¥250 with Kantō Festival Centre • ☎ 018 864 6851

A red-and-white-brick Western-style building 500m south of the festival centre, formerly the headquarters of Akita Bank, is home to the **Aka-renga Kyōdo-kan**. The well-preserved banking hall and offices are worth a quick look, while the modern extension behind it houses a series of woodcuts by **Katsuhira Tokushi**, a self-taught local artist acclaimed for his bold, colourful depictions of rural life.

ARRIVAL AND INFORMATION   AKITA

By plane Akita's airport (☎ 018 886 3366, ⓦ akita-airport.com) is 20km southeast of the city. A limousine bus carries passengers to and from the train station (every 30min; 35min; ¥930; ⓦ akita-chuoukotsu.co.jp).
Destinations Nagoya (2 daily; 1hr 30min); Osaka Itami (6 daily; 1hr 25min); Sapporo (4 daily; 1hr 5min); Tokyo Haneda (9 daily; 1hr 15min).

By train Akita's JR station is on the east side of town. Destinations Aomori (3 daily; 3hr 5min); Hirosaki (3 daily; 2hr 5min); Kakunodate (hourly; 45min); Morioka (hourly; 1hr 35min); Niigata (3 daily; 3hr 40min); Tokyo (hourly; 3hr 50min); Tsuruoka (4 daily; 1hr 50min).
By bus Long-distance buses stop outside Akita Station. Destinations Sendai (3 daily; 5hr); Tokyo (3 daily; 9–12hr).

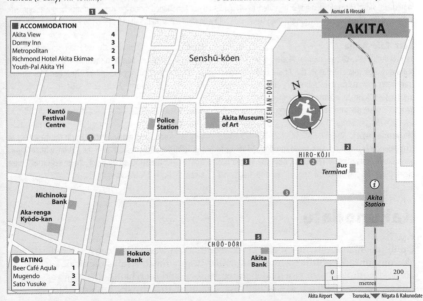

ACCOMMODATION
Akita View	4
Dormy Inn	3
Metropolitan	2
Richmond Hotel Akita Ekimae	5
Youth-Pal Akita YH	1

Senshū-kōen

Kantō Festival Centre

Police Station

Akita Museum of Art

OTEMAN-DŌRI

AKITA

Aomari & Hirosaki

HIRO-KŌJI

Bus Terminal

Akita Station

Michinoku Bank

Aka-renga Kyōdo-kan

CHŪŌ-DŌRI

Hokuto Bank

Akita Bank

EATING
Beer Café Aqula	1
Mugendo	3
Sato Yusuke	2

0   200
metres

Akita Airport   Tsuruoka, Niigata & Kakunodate

By car Eki Rent-a-Car (☎018 833 9308, ⚲www.ekiren.co.jp), Nissan Rent-a-Car (☎018 824 4123, ⚲nissan-rentacar.com) and Toyota Rentals (☎018 833 0100, ⚲rent.toyota.co.jp) have offices near the JR station.

By ferry Shin-Nihonkai Ferry (☎018 880 2600, ⚲snf.jp) sails to Tomakomai, the main port on Hokkaidō, from Akita's ferry terminal, 8km northwest of the station and served by connecting buses (30min; ¥400). The ferry also offers connections southwest along the Honshū coast, to Niigata and Tsuruga.

Destinations Niigata (daily; 7hr 45min); Tomakomai, Hokkaidō (6 weekly; 11hr 20min); Tsuruga (daily; 21hr).

Tourist information Akita's tourist office is at the JR station (daily: April–Oct 9am–7pm, Nov–March 9am–6pm; ☎018 832 7941, ⚲akita-yulala.jp). Ten free bicycles are lent to visitors each day, first-come, first-served.

ACCOMMODATION

Akita View 秋田ビューホテル 6-1-2 Naka-dōri ☎018 832 1111, ⚲viewhotels.co.jp/akita. Large business hotel in the heart of the shopping and nightlife district, a short walk west of the station. The rooms are slightly faded but comfortable, the restaurant serves both Chinese and French cuisine, and there's a gym with sauna. Rates include a substantial buffet breakfast. ⚲ **¥11,700**

Dormy Inn ドーミーイン 2-3-1 Naka-dōri ☎018 835 6777, ⚲bit.ly/dormy-akita. This business hotel has contemporary monochrome interiors, spacious singles and a good range of facilities, including a nice public bath on the eleventh floor. ⚲ **¥10,500**

Metropolitan ホテルメトロポリタン 7-2-1 Naka-dōri ☎018 831 2222, ⚲metro-akita.jp. Classy hotel, immediately outside the station, which belongs to JR East and therefore offers JR Pass holders discounts of around twenty percent. The rooms are tastefully decorated, and there's a stylish cocktail bar and elegant Japanese restaurant. Breakfast costs ¥1600. ⚲ **¥22,000**

Richmond Hotel Akita Ekimae リッチモンドホテル秋田駅前 2-2-26 Naka-dōri ☎018 884 0055, ⚲richmondhotel.jp. A straightforward 5min walk west of the station, this smart modern business hotel offers decent-sized rooms and good service. The Japanese buffet breakfast costs ¥1100 extra. ⚲ **¥9000**

Youth-Pal Akita YH ユースパルあきた 3-1 Kamiyashiki ☎018 880 2303, ⚲youthpal-akita.la.coocan.jp. This large municipal hostel-cum-conference centre, 5km west of the station, is a good bargain, with spacious Japanese- and Western-style rooms plus decent meals. To get here, take a bus to the Akita Seishōnen Center (bus stop #6; 30min; ¥160), then walk west for 5min and it's on the right. Breakfast costs ¥760, and dinner from ¥1080. ⚲ Dorms **¥3350**, rooms **¥8640**

EATING AND DRINKING

Akita's main bar and restaurant area is one block southeast of the Aka-renga Kyōdo-kan museum. The most famous local speciality is **kiritampo**, a substantial stew of chicken, mushrooms, onions, glass noodles, seasonal vegetables and the key ingredient, *mochi* (rice cakes), made of pounded, newly harvested rice and shaped round a cedar-wood stick before grilling over a charcoal fire. **Shottsuru** – a strong-tasting stew made with a broth of fermented, salted fish – is more of an acquired taste.

Beer Cafe Aqula アックーウーラー 1-2-40 Omachi ☎018 864 0141, ⚲aqula.co.jp. Modelled on a German brauhaus, this modern bar in the Aqula building serves craft beers from its own microbrewery and hearty, largely meat-based food to accompany them, such as tongue, generous spare ribs and German sausage. Individual dishes start at ¥750. ⚲ Daily 11.30am–2pm & 5–11pm.

Mugendo 無限堂 2-4-12 Naka-dōri ☎018 825 0800, ⚲mugendo.jp. With its dark-wood interior and stained-glass lamps, this popular restaurant near the station is a great place to sample local specialities and traditional regional dishes. Look for the red curtain around the wooden entrance. Lunch dishes such as noodles start at ¥800; expect to pay around ¥3500 a head for dinner. ⚲ Mon–Fri 11am–2pm & 5–10pm, Sat & Sun 11am–10pm.

Sato Yosuke 佐藤洋介 2-6-1 Naka-dōri ☎018 834 1720, ⚲sato-yoske.co.jp/akitaten.htm. Very reasonable, very tasty udon and inaiwa restaurant in the basement of the Seibu department store, near the station, with set meals from ¥1240. The attached shop sells choice delicacies to take away. ⚲ Daily 11am–9pm.

Kakunodate

角館

Up in the inland hills, 50km east of Akita and 60km west of Morioka, the rather glorious, unspoiled little town of **KAKUNODATE** very much retains the air of a feudal outpost, complete with strictly delineated samurai and merchants' quarters. Kakunodate was laid out as a military settlement in 1620 by the lords of Akita, with a castle on a hill to the north, a **samurai town** of around eighty residences, and 350 merchants' homes in a cramped district to the south.

   Kakunodate never having grown to become a city, its original layout has survived the years, still incorporating a cluster of spacious 200-year-old samurai mansions. You'll find them, set behind neatly fenced gardens, lining the wide avenues of the samurai quarter, which stands immediately north of the more modern and somewhat run-down central commercial district. An even more attractive vestige of the past is the weeping **cherry trees**, brought here from Kyoto three centuries ago. Several hundred survive, most spectacularly in the 2km "tunnel" of trees along the raised eastern embankment of the Hinokinai-gawa.

   All in all, Kakunodate is an enchanting place, well worth an overnight stay in its own right despite being easy to visit on a day-trip from Akita or Morioka alike.

Aoyagi-ke

青柳家 • 3 Omote-machi • Daily: April–Nov 9am–5pm, Dec–March 9am–4pm • ¥500 • ☎ 018 755 3257, ⓦ samuraiworld.com

If you're at all constrained by time or budget, the samurai house to prioritize visiting is **Aoyagi-ke**. A large thatched structure towards the northern end of the quarter, readily identifiable thanks to its unusually grand entrance gate, it was built in 1890 and remained inhabited until 1985. The compound now contains an eclectic mix of galleries, displaying everything from samurai armour and agricultural implements to beautiful painted screens and memorabilia from the Sino-Japanese and Pacific wars. One building, designated the Akita Folk Art Museum, showcases local crafts, with demonstrations of techniques, and holds a wonderful array of vintage gramophones and cameras.

Denshōkan

伝承館 • 10-1 Omote-machi • Daily: April–Nov 9am–4.30pm, Dec–March 9am–4pm • ¥300, or ¥520 with Hirafuku Memorial Art Museum • ☎ 018 754 1700

Housed in an attractive red-brick building in the heart of the samurai district, the **Denshōkan** museum, also called the **Heritage Centre**, holds various Satake-clan treasures. It doubles as a training school for *kaba-zaiku*, the local craft in which boxes, tables and tea caddies are coated with a thin veneer of **cherry bark**. Developed in the late eighteenth century to supplement the income of impoverished samurai, *kaba-zaiku* is now Kakunodate's trademark souvenir. You don't have to pay for admission to access the museum's large gift shop, well stocked with examples, or the little café on its second floor.

Hirafuku Memorial Art Museum

平福記念美術館, Hirafuku Kinen Bijutsukan • 4-4 Omote-machi • Daily: April–Nov 9am–4.30pm, Dec–March 9am–4pm • ¥300, or ¥520 with Denshōkan • ☎ 018 754 3888

Behind its sterile concrete exterior, the **Hirafuku Memorial Art Museum** houses a small but decent collection of traditional Japanese art. Built in honour of father and son Hirafuku Suian and Hirafuku Hiyasui, the museum spotlights the work of Naotake Odano and other painters from Kakunodate.

Ishiguro-ke

石黒家 • 1 Omote-machi • Daily 9am–5pm • ¥300 • ☎ 018 755 1496

Dating back to 1809, the impressive **Ishiguro-ke** is one of Kakunodate's oldest samurai houses. Part of the building is still occupied by a descendant of the Ishiguro family – the original occupant was financial adviser to the *daimyō*. After a brief guided tour of the main house, you're left to admire exhibits including armour, weapons and old maps in the adjoining fireproof warehouse (*kura*), once used for storing rice, miso and other valuables.

ARRIVAL AND INFORMATION

By train Kakunodate Station, on the southeastern edge of town, is a stop on the Shinkansen spur that connects Morioka with Akita, and is also linked by the scenic private Akita Nairiku Jūkan Railway to Takanosu, 100km north through the mountains.

Destinations Akita (hourly; 45min); Morioka (hourly; 45min); Takanosu (3 daily; 2hr).

Tourist information The main tourist office is in a *kura*-style building at the station (daily 9am–6pm; 018 754 2700, kakunodate-kanko.jp). They stock excellent English-language brochures, and will also look after your bags for ¥300/day, significantly cheaper than the station lockers.

ACCOMMODATION

Folkloro Kakunodate フォルクローロ角館 14 Nakasuga-zawa 018 753 2070, www.folkloro-kakunodate.com. Located right beside the station, this business hotel is your best bet for a simple, modern Western-style room. JR Pass holders get a ten percent discount, and rates include a buffet breakfast in the decent second-floor restaurant. **¥13,600**

Machiyado Neko No Suzo 町宿 ねこの鈴 28 Shitachu-chō 018 742 8105, oogiri.co.jp/nekonosuzu. Most of the dozen guest rooms in this small central inn are Japanese-style, but there are also a few rather chintzy Western-style alternatives, as well as a spacious hot-spring bath. The breakfast spread costs ¥1300 per person. **¥13,000**

Tamachi Bukeyashiki Hotel 田町武家屋敷ホテル 23 Tamachi Shimo-chō 018 752 1700, bukeyashiki.jp. Housed in a stunning Meiji-style building on the southern edge of the commercial district, 800m west of the station, this traditional inn provides attractive and luxurious tatami rooms as well as smart Western-style rooms with Art Deco touches. Rates include breakfast; the exquisite dinners cost from ¥5000 per person. **¥20,500**

EATING AND DRINKING

Aoyagi-ke 青柳家 3 Omote-machi 018 754 3257, samuraiworld.com. Kakunodate's most interesting samurai house (see p.269) holds two restaurants, including this noodle specialist in the gatehouse, where the *inaniwa udon* – long, slippery noodles in a thin soup of mushrooms, onion and bamboo shoots, costing ¥1080 – is especially recommended. Daily 9am–5pm.

Inaho 食堂いなほ 4-1 Tamachikami-chō 018 754 3311, inaho.pepper.jp. This elegant restaurant, where the road in from the station reaches the centre, serves great-value Japanese food in its upstairs dining room, with simple noodle dishes starting at ¥700 and nine-dish *kaiseki* meals from ¥1500. Daily 11.30am–1.30pm & 5.30–9pm.

Kosendō 古泉洞 9 Higashi-Katsuraku-chō 018 753 2902. Set in an attractive former schoolhouse in the southerly half of the samurai quarter, this is a popular lunch spot. Speciality dishes include soba noodles served with bamboo, with prices starting at around ¥1000. Daily 9am–4.30pm.

Sakuramaru Coffee 櫻丸珈琲 24-1 Machiokachi-machi 018 749 7339. The open timber deck of this bright modern coffee shop, on the short road between the main riverside car park and the samurai quarter, makes an ideal place to take a break from sightseeing, over an espresso coffee or Japanese tea (both around ¥400). They also serve ¥400–500 pastries, cheesecake and the like, as well as cold beer. Daily 10am–6pm.

Nyūtō Onsen

乳頭温泉

As well as several ski resorts, the Towada Hachimantai National Park, northeast of Kakunodate, is home to a hot-spring area known as **Nyūtō Onsen**. Set roughly 15km beyond the magnificent lake Tazawa-ko, the deepest in all Japan, this comprises eight separate onsen along with their adjoining ryokan. The most famous and attractive of the bunch is the **Tsurunoyu Onsen**, a 350-year-old establishment with eight separate baths and three rotemburo, each fed by a different source (non-guests daily 9am–5pm; ¥600).

A fifteen-minute walk east from Tsurunoyu, the rotemburo at **Ganiba Onsen** nestles quietly next to a small brook and forest – the perfect spot to shuck away the cares of travelling (non-guests Tues–Sun 9am–5pm; ¥500).

ARRIVAL AND DEPARTURE

By train The nearest train station for Nyūtō Onsen is Tazawako, 20km northeast of Kakunodate on the Shinkansen line between Morioka (hourly; 40min) and Akita (hourly; 1hr). From the station, catch a bus bound for the Tazawa Kōgen Ski-jō (every 70–90min; 50min) and get off at Tazawa Kōgen Onsen. With advance notice, both *Tsurunoyu* or *Ganiba* onsen will pick up guests from here.

ACCOMMODATION

Ganiba Onsen 蟹場温泉 Sendatsu ☎018 746 2021, ⓦ nyuto-onsenkyo.com. In a peaceful setting surrounded by nature, this traditional ryokan offers a choice of spacious Western or well-kept tatami rooms. All look out onto the surrounding woods, while some adjoin the wraparound veranda. The big draw, though, is the wonderful outdoor bath set in natural rocks amid the forest. Rates include two meals. 📶 **¥19,700**

Tsurunoyu Onsen 鶴の湯温泉 50 Sendatsu ☎018 746 2139, ⓦ tsurunoyu.com. Although the ancient wooden building of this ryokan abounds in picturesque rustic charm, it has to be said that amenities are on the basic side. The cosy tatami rooms come with a small *irori* or fire pit, and there's a choice of mixed- and single-sex onsen. Rates include two meals. **¥17,100**

Yamanoyado Inn 山の宿 1-1 Sawayunotai ☎018 746 2100, ⓦ tsurunoyu.com. Housed in a newer building, the slightly less traditional sister of *Tsurunoyu* has more spacious rooms with modern amenities. Rates include two meals. 📶 **¥27,600**

Dewa-sanzan

出羽三山

A lumpy extinct volcano with three separate peaks, **Dewa-sanzan** faces the Sea of Japan across the prolific rice fields of the Shōnai plain. Also known as **Dewa-san**, this is one of Japan's most sacred mountains; **pilgrims** have been arriving to trek up its slopes for more than a thousand years. The arduous climb takes in ancient cedar woods, alpine meadows and three intriguing shrines, where *yamabushi* (mountain ascetics) continue to practise ancient rites that combine Tendai Buddhism with elements of Taoism and Shintō.

Though it's possible to complete the circuit in one long day, it's more enjoyable to spread it over two or three days, and spend a couple of nights in the *shukubō* (temple lodgings) scattered over the mountain. Potential stop-overs before or after you hike the trail include the village of **Haguro-machi** (羽黒町), the traditional start of the pilgrimage, or the larger town of **Tsuruoka** (鶴岡), a short bus ride northwest, which holds a few moderately interesting sights.

DEWA-SAN AND THE YAMABUSHI

Although these days Dewa-san and its three shrines fall under the banner of Shintō, the mountain was originally home to one of the colourful offshoots of Esoteric Buddhism, later unified as **Shugendō**. The worship of Dewa-san dates from the seventh century, when an imperial prince fled to this area following the death of his father. In a vision, a three-legged crow led him to Haguro-san (Black Wing Mountain), where he lived to the ripe old age of 90, developing his unique blend of Shintō, Buddhism and ancient folk religion. Later, the **yamabushi**, the sect's itinerant mountain priests – literally, "the ones who sleep in the mountains" – became famous for their mystic powers and extreme asceticism. One route to enlightenment consisted of living in caves off a diet of nuts and wild garlic. Once fairly widespread, the sect dwindled after the mid-nineteenth century, when Shintō reclaimed Japan's mountains for its own. Nevertheless, you'll still find a flourishing community of *yamabushi* around Dewa-san, kitted out in natty checked jackets, white knickerbockers and tiny black pillbox hats. Each also carries a huge conch-shell horn, the haunting cry of which summons the gods.

The best time to see *yamabushi* in action is during the area's various **festivals**. During the biggest annual bash, the Hassaku Matsuri (Aug 24–31), pilgrims take part in a fire festival on Haguro-san to ensure a bountiful harvest. At New Year, Haguro-san is also the venue for a festival of purification, known as the Shōreisai, which combines fire and acrobatic dancing with ascetic rituals.

If you'd like to try your hand at being a *yamabushi*, several two- and three-day taster **courses** are available, in which participants get to stand under waterfalls, leap over fires and take part in a pilgrimage. Prices start from around ¥25,000; contact Tsuruoka's tourist office for information (see p.275).

The Dewa-san circuit

Precisely how you tackle Dewa-san will depend on when you visit and how much walking you want to do. Ideally, the aim is to pay your respects at all three shrines, each set on its own peak. That's only possible in midsummer, however, as only the thatch-roofed **Gōsaiden** shrine, at the summit of Haguro-san, remains open all year; **Gassan-jinja** on Gassan is open from July to mid-September, while **Yudonosan-jinja** on Yudono-san is open from May to early November. Just to complicate matters, the path itself stays open longer.

The traditionally recommended **route**, starting from Haguro-machi, is to climb Haguro-san on the first day, and then continue via Gassan to Yudono-jinja on the second. Once there, you can either head straight to Tsuruoka or spend the night in a *shukubō* and visit the temples in tiny **Ōami**, home to so-called "living Buddhas", the next day.

Ideha Bunka Kinenkan

いでは文化記念館 • 72 Injuminami, Haguro-machi • Mon & Wed–Sun: April–Nov 9am–4.30pm, Dec–March 9.30am–4pm • ¥400 • ☎ 023 562 4729 • Buses from Tsuruoka (8–15 daily; 40min) serve Haguro-machi – get off at the Haguro Centre stop

The village of **HAGURO-MACHI** (羽黒町) is set at the foot of the Dewa-san hike. Before heading off, anyone interested in the *yamabushi* should take a look at the **Ideha Bunka Kinenkan** museum, where remarkably hi-tech exhibitions contain examples of *yamabushi* clothes and foodstuffs, as well as holograms of various rituals.

The Haguro-san route

羽黒山ルート

Starting from a weather-beaten, red-lacquered gate in Haguro-machi, the trail up the 414m peak of **Haguro-san** (羽黒山) incorporates the 2446 well-worn steps of three long staircases that were constructed by a monk in the early seventeenth century. The climb is only 1.7km long, but takes most visitors around an hour to complete. It begins with a deceptively gentle amble beside a river among stately cedar trees, where pilgrims purify themselves. After passing a magnificent five-storey pagoda, last rebuilt in the fourteenth century, it's uphill all the way, past a little **teashop** (late April to early Nov daily 8.30am–5pm) that affords superb views, until a large red *torii* indicates you've made it.

Gōsaiden shrine

三神合祭殿, San-jin Gōsaiden • Museum: mid-April to late Nov daily 8.30am–4pm • ¥300 • Buses from the Haguro-sanchō bus stop, set amid a cluster of restaurants and souvenir shops, connect the shrine with Tsuruoka (50min) via Haguro-machi (15min), and also with Gassan Hachigōme

The **Gōsaiden shrine** compound, at the top of the Haguro-san trail, holds several unmistakably Buddhist buildings. In the **Gōsaiden** itself, the monumental vermilion hall at the centre, the mountain's three deities are enshrined behind gilded doors, and beneath an immaculate thatch. Immediately in front, the lily-covered **Kagami-ike** is said to mirror the spirits of the gods, but is better known for its treasure hoard of over five hundred antique polished-metal hand mirrors. In the days before women were allowed onto Dewa-san, their male relatives would consign one of their mirrors into the pond. The finest such mirrors are now proudly displayed in the shrine **museum**, which also holds a useful relief map of Dewa-san.

Gassan

月山 • Buses to Gassan only run daily in July & Aug, and at weekends in Sept, from both Tsuruoka via Haguro-machi (1hr 20min), and from Haguro-san (4 daily; 55min)

Beyond Haguro-san, the trail follows a high ridge all the way to Dewa-san's middle shrine, perched atop **Gassan** (月山; 1984m), the highest peak in the range. It's a long 20km walk, though, so given the choice all but the most dedicated hikers might prefer to catch a bus as far as the "Eighth Station", **Gassan Hachigōme**. Even from there it takes over two hours to cover the final 5km to Gassan (1900m), on a beautiful section of the ridgetop path that crosses the marshy Mida-ga-hara meadows, renowned for the explosion of rare alpine plants in late June.

Gassan-jinja

月山神社 • July to mid-Sept daily 6am–5pm • ¥500

The final few metres of the ridge walk to Gassan consist of a scramble to reach the rocky peak, where the **Gassan-jinja** shrine huddles behind stout stone walls. The view, in clear weather at least, is magnificent, but the shrine itself is the least interesting of Dewa-san's trio. Nonetheless, you have to be purified before venturing inside. Bow your head while a priest waves his paper wand over you and chants a quick prayer; then rub the paper cut-out person (which he gives you) over your head and shoulders before placing it in the water.

Yudonosan-jinja

湯殿山神社 • May to early Nov daily 8am–5pm • ¥500 • A shuttle bus runs from the *torii* in Yudono-san to Yudono-jinja (5min; ¥100), or it's a steep 20min walk; between May and early Nov there's a bus from Tsuruoka (3 daily; 1hr 20min)

On the far side of Gassan, the trail drops steeply for 9km, to reach the final shrine, **Yudonosan-jinja** (湯殿山神社), an ochre-coloured rock washed by a hot spring in a narrow valley on the mountain's west flank. During the final descent, you have to negotiate a series of iron ladders strapped to the valley side where the path has been washed away. Once at the river, it's only a short walk to the inner sanctum of Dewa-san, which occupies another walled area. Inside, take off your shoes and socks before receiving another purification, and then enter the second compound. Having bowed to the steaming orange boulder, you can then haul yourself over it using ropes to reach another little shrine on the far side. A ten-minute trot down the road from there will bring you to the **Yudono-san** (湯殿山) bus stop.

Ōami

大網 • All buses from Yudono-san to Tsuruoka stop at Ōami (every 2hr; 30min)

The hamlet of **ŌAMI**, 20km northwest of Yudonosan-jinja on the road to Tsuruoka, is worth a stop for its two **"living Buddhas"**, the naturally mummified bodies of ascetic Buddhist monks who starved themselves to death. You'll find the mummies, or *miira*, on display in two rival temples, **Dainichibō** and **Chūren-ji**, on either side of the village.

Dainichibō

大日坊 • Daily 8am–5pm • ¥500 • ☎ 023 554 6301, ⓦ dainichibou.or.jp • From Ōami bus stop, follow red signs of a little bowing monk, then turn left at the post office and walk for 10min

Dainichibō, the more accessible of Ōami's two temples, is on the east side of the village, and is thought to have been founded in 807 by Kōbō Daishi (see box, p.527). After a brief purification ceremony and introductory talk, the head priest shows you the hard-working saint's staff, a handprint of Tokugawa Ieyasu, and other temple treasures, before taking you to the **mummy**. The tiny figure sits slumped on an altar, dressed in rich red brocades from which his hands and skull protrude, sheathed in a dark, glossy, parchment-thin layer of skin. He's said to have died in 1782 at the age of 96, having lived merely on a diet of nuts, seeds and water. As the end drew closer, the monk took himself off to a cave to meditate and eventually stopped eating altogether. Finally, he was buried alive with a breathing straw until he expired completely. This process of self-mummification as a path to enlightenment, known as **sokushimbutsu**, was relatively common prior to the nineteenth century, when the practice was banned.

Chūren-ji

注連寺 • Daily 8am–5pm • ¥500 • 2km from Ōami bus stop; head north on a country road and follow the signs until you reach a fork, at which you turn left and walk past a graveyard

Though it's a bit of a walk from Ōami, **Chūren-ji** is slightly less commercialized and more atmospheric than Dainichibō. As usual, visitors receive a short talk and a purification ceremony before entering the side hall, where the *miira* rests in a glass case. This particular living Buddha, Hommyokai Shonin, is said to have been a criminal before he saw the error of his ways and devoted himself to the ascetic life.

ARRIVAL AND INFORMATION
DEWA-SANZAN

By bus Two bus services connect Tsuruoka with Dewa-Sanzan. One runs around ten times daily via the Zuishinmon stop (瑞信門) in Haguro-machi to the Haguro-sanchō stop at the top of Haguro-san, with onward services continuing to Gassan Hachigōme between July and Sept. The second runs four times daily, from late April to early Nov only, between Tsuruoka and Yudonosan-jinja. For current schedules, visit ⓦ bit.ly/dewa-sanzan.

Tourist information Maps and bus timetables are available at Tsuruoka's information centre (see opposite), while useful online resources include ⓦ hagurokanko.jp, ⓦ bit.ly/dewa-sanzan and ⓦ dewasanzan.jp.

ACCOMMODATION

If possible, try to spend at least one night while visiting Dewa-sanzan at a **shukubō** (temple lodging). There are over thirty in Haguro-machi's Tōge district, including several traditional thatch-roofed inns, each run by a *yamabushi*; you may well be invited to attend a prayer service, involving a lot of conch-blowing and a ritual fire. Prices don't vary much (typically ¥7000–7500 per person, with meals), and all serve the exquisitely prepared *shōjin-ryōri* (Buddhist vegetarian cuisine) favoured by *yamabushi*.

Saikan 斎館 Haguro-san ☎ 023 562 2357, ⓦ bit.ly/saikan. This impressive old *shukubō*, up on the mountain at the end of a mossy path that leads left from the top of the Haguro-san route, just before you duck under the *torii*, enjoys fabulous views over the Shōnai plain. As well as simple accommodation, they also offer excellent vegetarian lunches, available to non-residents as well (from ¥1620; reservations recommended). Rates include breakfast and dinner. **¥15,120**

Sankō-in 羽黒山三光院 92 Tōge, Haguro-machi ☎ 023 562 2302. A lovely old thatched place near the centre of Haguro-machi, this authentic temple lodging serves vegetarian cuisine. Rates include breakfast and dinner. **¥15,200**

Tamon-Kan 多聞館 115 Tōge, Haguro-machi ☎ 023 562 2201, ⓦ www.tamonkan.net. This attractive traditional ryokan, in an impressive 300-year-old building in the heart of Haguro-machi, stays open all year round, offers more comfortable accommodation than the various *shukubō*, and serves excellent *shōjin-ryōri* cuisine. Rates include breakfast and dinner. 🛜 **¥16,200**

Yudono-san Sanrōjo 湯殿山参籠所 7 Rokujuri-yama, Tamugimata ☎ 023 554 6131. This summer-only mountain inn (open April–Nov) occupies a wonderful setting beside the Yudonosan-jinja bus terminal. As well as attractive rooms and a great onsen, it offers delicious lunches to both residents and non-residents (from ¥1575; reservations recommended). Rates include breakfast and dinner. **¥15,120**

Tsuruoka

鶴岡

The former castle town of **TSURUOKA** is mainly useful for visitors as a staging post on the pilgrimage to Dewa-sanzan. Its historic core, on the banks of the Uchi-gawa, consists of a handful of attractive willow-lined streets, and stands 2km south of the station, which as ever is surrounded by business hotels, department stores and bus terminals. The principal sights of interest are clustered in and around **Tsuruoka-kōen**, the park where the castle once stood, and include an eclectic local museum and an unusual Edo-period school for samurai.

Chidō Hakubutsukan

致道博物館 • 10-18 Kachū-Shin-machi • March–Nov daily 9am–5pm; Dec–Feb Mon, Tues & Thurs–Sun 9am–4.30pm • ¥700 • ☎ 023 522 1199

Around half an hour's walk southwest of the station, just beyond the southwest corner of Tsuruoka-kōen, the **Chidō Hakubutsukan** originally served as a retirement home for lords of the ruling Sakai clan. Various striking buildings stand within the compound, including the conspicuous **Nishitagawa District Office**, built in 1881 in Western style. The **Goinden**, the lords' residence, was constructed only two decades earlier, but in a classic Japanese design, and now houses Sakai family heirlooms as well as a beautiful collection of bamboo fishing rods made by trainee samurai. Local folk culture is well represented in a massive thatched farmhouse and in a modern building packed with old fishing tackle, sake barrels, lacquerware and huge wooden mortars.

Chidō-kan

致道館 • 11-45 Baba-chō • Mon, Tues & Thurs–Sun 9am–4.30pm • Free • ☏ 023 523 4672

Tsuruoka's Confucian school, **Chidō-kan**, immediately outside the southeast corner of Tsuruoka-kōen, was founded in 1805 by the ninth Sakai lord, who wanted to restore order among his restless clan and educate young samurai. Although it closed its doors in 1873, a few of the original buildings remain intact, including a shrine to Confucius, and the main auditorium, where you can see the old textbooks and printing blocks as well as some marvellous photos of the school when still in use.

ARRIVAL AND DEPARTURE

TSURUOKA

By plane The only scheduled flights that use Shōnai Airport (ⓦ www.shonai-airport.co.jp), 12km northwest of Tsuruoka, fly to and from Tokyo Haneda (4 daily; 1hr 5min). Limousine buses to and from Tsuruoka train station connect with every flight (25min; ¥780).

By train Tsuruoka Station is 2km north of the town centre. Destinations Akita (4 daily; 1hr 50min); Niigata (4 daily; 1hr 45min).

By bus Most buses stop in front of the train station;

long-distance buses use the Shōkō Mall bus centre, a few minutes' walk west, under the *Dai-ichi* hotel.

Destinations Sendai (10 daily; 2hr 20min); Tokyo (2 daily; 8–9hr); Yamagata (9 daily, 1hr 50min).

Tourist information Tsuruoka's tourist office is outside the station (daily: March–Oct 9.30am–5.30pm, Nov–Feb 10am–5pm; ⓦ www.tsuruokakanko.com).

Car rental Toyota Rent-a-Car, alongside the station at 8-01 Suehiro-machi (☏ 023 528 0100, ⓦ rent.toyota.co.jp).

ACCOMMODATION

Narakan 会良館 2-35 Hiyoshi-chō ☏ 023 522 1202, ⓦ narakan.seesaa.net. Small, friendly modern inn, equipped with good-value tatami rooms and serving traditional food. Go left from the station for 5min, then turn right at *Hotel Alpha One*, walk another 5min and it's on the left after the traffic lights. Rates include two meals; various meal plans are available. 🛜 **¥10,600**

Tokyo Dai-ichi Hotel 東京第一ホテル 2-10 Nishiki-machi ☏ 023 524 7611, ⓦ tdh-tsuruoka.co.jp. Large, modern and very yellow business hotel, in the heart of the shopping district 400m southwest of the station, offering

sizeable, comfortable rooms plus a very impressive rooftop bath. Rates include two meals. 🛜 **¥13,500**

Tsuruoka Youth Hostel 鶴岡ユースホステル 1-1 Miyanomae, Sanze ☏ 501 510 8243, ⓦ bit.ly /tsuruoka-hostel. Well off the beaten track, up in the woods on a hillside in a seaside village 20km southwest of Tsuruoka, this splendid old hostel makes for a welcoming rest if you fancy a day off from your travels, and the idea of macrobiotic vegetarian food and 1950s jazz appeals. It's a 15min walk from Sanze Station, three stops out of town on the JR Uetsu line. 🛜 Dorms **¥2800**

EATING

Well-priced restaurants and fast-food outlets, serving staples such as soba, udon and *izakaya* dishes, are clustered around the station.

Shonaihan Shiruketchiano 庄内藩しるけっちあーの 10-18 Kachushin-machi ☏ 023 524 3632, ⓦ bit.ly /shonaihan. Cheery little café/restaurant, next to the Chidō Hakubutsukan, which serves all sorts of healthy meals and snacks using choice local produce, including vegetable soups and stews and fresh juices. Set meals start at around ¥1000, while you can also just drop in for a coffee. 🛜 Mon–Wed & Fri–Sun 11am–5pm.

Shonai Sakaba Mitaba 荘内酒場 三鷹 12-30 Nishiki-machi ☏ 023 524 4572. Friendly Japanese restaurant, open in the evenings only and just 250m from the station – turn right at the first intersection, and it's on your left on the second block. The food, ranging from tempura mushrooms to sashimi and oysters, is uniformly delicious, and a full meal is likely to cost upwards of ¥2500. Mon–Sat 5pm–2am.

Niigata

新潟

Most visitors to **NIIGATA**, the largest port-city on the Sea of Japan coast, are either heading to Sado-ga-shima (see p.280) or making use of the ferry and air connections to Korea, China and Russia. Sitting on the banks of Shinano-gawa, at the point where it reaches the sea, Niigata itself is a likeable but unexciting city, with few specific sights apart from a well-presented local history museum. Although a tsunami devastated much of the eastern city in 1964, its historic downtown core, west of the river, retains some attractive streets of older houses.

Niigata's main thoroughfare starts from the station as **Higashi-dōri**, and runs through the Bandai City district, which is home to large department stores, cinemas and restaurants, until it reaches the Shinano-gawa after 1km. It then crosses the river via the Bandai-bashi bridge, to become **Masaya-kōji** as it continues through downtown's **Furu-machi** (古町) shopping district on the far side. Centring on the covered shopping mall of Furumachi-dōri, this area extends north to Hiro-kōji and south to Niitsuya-kōji, with the **Hon-chō** market on its eastern edge.

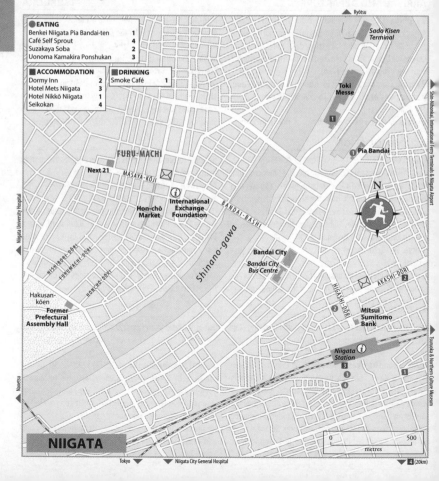

Hakusan-kōen

白山公園 • 1-2 Ichiban Hori-dōri-chō, Chūō-ku • **Park** 24hr • Free • **Enkikan teahouse** (燕喜館) Daily 9am–5pm, closed first & third Mon of each month • Tea ¥400 • ☎ 025 224 6081 • Catch a bus for Irefune-chō and get off at the Assembly Hall

On the southwestern edge of downtown, across the river 2.5km west of the station, the pleasant park of **Hakusan-kōen** contains a shrine to the God of Marriage as well as various stone monuments, including one dedicated to the happiness of pine trees. There are also a couple of manicured lily-pad-covered ponds around which wisteria trellises bloom into life in late spring.

Enkikan, a Meiji-era teahouse in the park's northwest corner, was transplanted here from Kyoto. Its pristine tatami rooms, overlooking a peaceful garden, provide a delightful opportunity for a rest; tea (or coffee) is served in the room of your choice.

Former Prefectural Assembly Hall

新潟県記念館, Niigata-ken Kinenkan • 3-3 Ichiban Hori-dōri-chō, Chūō-ku • Jan & Feb Wed–Sun 9am–4.30pm; March–June & Sept–Dec Tues–Sun 9am–4.30pm; July & Aug Tues–Sun 9am–5pm • Free • ☎ 025 228 3607, Ⓦ bit.ly/niigata-hall

The highly conspicuous gingerbread building on the eastern edge of Hakusan-kōen is the **Former Prefectural Assembly Hall**, which was built in 1883. Local representatives continued to meet here until 1932, but it now holds an exhibition that tells the story of Japan's young democracy in action, and includes a fascinating array of archive sepia photos.

Hon-chō Market

本町市場, Hon-chō Ichiba • Daily 8am–5pm, closed three days a month, usually on Sun • Ⓦ honcho6.com

Spreading through a few pedestrianized streets south of Masaya-kōji, around 700m west of the river, the lively **Hon-chō Market** is the perfect spot to recapture the flavour of old Niigata. A true relic of the past, this fresh-produce and seafood market offers the chance to mix with locals, find cheap places to eat, and try out your bargaining skills.

Northern Culture Museum

北方文化博物館, Happō Binka Hakubutsukan • 2-15-25 Somi, Yokogoshi • Daily: April–Nov 9am–5pm, Dec–March 9am–4.30pm • ¥800 • ☎ 025 385 2001, Ⓦ hoppou-bunka.com • Express bus from Bandai City or Eki-mae terminal (10 daily; ¥500 one-way); last bus back leaves at 5pm

The fertile plains around Niigata used to support a number of wealthy landowners, who lived in considerable luxury until they were forced by the Land Reform Act of 1946 to sell all rice land above 7.5 acres per household. One such family was the Itō, whose superb mansion is now the centrepiece of the **Northern Culture Museum**, 12km southeast of the city centre in the village of Yokogoshi. Their huge house was erected in 1887 and comprises sixty rooms filled with family heirlooms, but it's the classic **garden** that steals the show. Viewed from inside, it forms a magnificent frieze along one side of the principal guest room.

ARRIVAL AND DEPARTURE　　　　　　　　　　　　　**NIIGATA**

By plane Niigata Airport (☎ 025 275 2633, Ⓦ niigata -airport.gr.jp) is 8km northeast of Niigata's train station, to which it's connected by regular buses (every 20–30min; 30min; ¥410).
Destinations Centrair (2 daily; 55min); Fukuoka (3 daily; 2hr); Harbin (1 weekly; 2hr 10min); Nagoya (1 daily; 1hr); Okinawa (1 daily; 3hr 5min); Osaka Itami (10 daily; 1hr 10min); Sapporo (5 daily; 1hr 10min); Tokyo Narita (1 daily; 1hr 10min).
By train Niigata Station, in the city centre, is the northern terminus for trains on the Jōetsu Shinkansen line from

Tokyo. Local JR lines run north along the Sea of Japan coast to Akita, and west along the coast to Jōetsumyōkō, where it meets the Shinkansen line to Kanazawa.
Destinations Akita (3 daily; 3hr 40min); Jōetsumyōkō (5 daily; 2hr); Tokyo (1–2 hourly; 1hr 40min–2hr 20min); Toyama (2 daily; 3hr 50min); Tsuruoka (4 daily; 1hr 45min); Yamagata (2 daily; 3hr 40min).
By bus Most express buses use the Niigata Kōtsu Bus Centre, also known as Bandai City Bus Centre, 800m northwest of Niigata Station, though some also stop

3

ECHIGO-TSUMARI

Every three years, the mountainous, rural and relatively unspoiled Echigo-Tsumari region of Niigata-ken, roughly 100km south of Niigata itself, hosts a spectacular international art festival. The **Echigo-Tsumari Art Triennial** takes place between late July and mid-September, with the next event at the time of writing due in 2018. Artists from all over the world are invited to exhibit their work, with previous standouts including Cai Guo Qiang from China, who reconstructed an old Chinese climbing kiln, and Rina Banerjee, who, inspired by the Taj Mahal, converted a school gymnasium into a giant bird cage. For more details, check out ⓦechigo -tsumari.jp.

Even if you can't coincide with the festival, this region is still hugely rewarding to visit. The main places to head for are **Tokamachi**, **Matsudai** and **Matsunoyama**, all of which have fascinating permanent exhibition facilities built for past triennials, as well as plenty of sculptures and other artworks sited in paddy fields and on hillsides.

The best way to **get around** is to rent a car, although during the festival free bikes are available at all the main sites. You can travel here by local train from either Echigo-Yuzawa on the Niigata Shinkansen route or Saigata on the Joetsu line.

ACCOMMODATION

Thanks to the Triennial, Echigo-Tsumari offers some truly extraordinary lodging opportunities. If you're lucky enough to be visiting during the relatively limited opening periods, and reserve long enough in advance, it's possible to spend a night in one of six **artworks**, which are either newly commissioned structures or renovated abandoned buildings such as old farms or schools. Both those listed below can be visited during the day as well as accommodating overnight guests. Precise opening dates vary each year; check individual websites for current details, or see ⓦbit.ly/echigo-stay.

★**Dream House** 夢の家 642 Matsunoyama Yumoto ☎025 596 3134, ⓦtsumari-artfield.com /dreamhouse. Serbian performance artist Marina Abramovic's refurbished century-old farmhouse, near a hot spring 4km south of Matsunoyama, merges tradition and modern elements in a simple and elegant building. Guests are expected to sleep in "dream suits", and record their dreams in a Dream Book. Breakfast costs ¥500; dinner is not available. 📶 **¥25,200**

★**House of Light** 光の館 2891 Ueno-ko, Tokamachi ☎025 761 1090, ⓦhikarinoyakata.com. This meditation house, a pavilion raised on stilts on a hillside 9km northwest of Tokamachi, was designed by James Turrell in traditional local style. It features a retractable roof, a slick modern interior, and media installations, and combines natural and artificial light to stunning effect. The house sleeps up to twelve, with the express aim of holding three family groups; smaller parties are expected to share with others. Breakfast is not available; dinner can be ordered for ¥2000 and up. 📶 **¥20,000**, plus **¥4000** per person

outside the train station. For current timetables, visit ⓦwww.niigata-kotsu.co.jp.

Destinations Kanazawa (2 daily; 4hr 40min); Kyoto (daily; 8hr 10min); Nagano (4 daily; 3hr 30min); Osaka (daily; 9hr 30min); Sendai (8 daily; 4hr); Tokyo Ikebukuro (14 daily; 5hr 20min); Yamagata (2 daily; 3hr 40min).

By ferry As detailed on p.280, the Sado Kisen Terminal, on the east bank of the Shinano-gawa 2.3km northeast of the station, is the base for ferries and jetfoil services to Ryōtsu on Sado Island, operated by Sado Kisen (☎025 245 1234, ⓦsadokisen.co.jp). The Shin-Nihonkai Ferry Terminal, also on the east bank and 1km further downstream, is used by direct ferries to Otaru (Hokkaidō), and by a ferry that hops along the Honshū coast, heading north to Akita and on to Tomakomai on Hokkaidō, and also west to Tsuruga; all are operated by Shin-Nihonkai (☎025 273 2171, ⓦsnf.jp). Both terminals are linked by local buses, costing ¥210, to Niigata Station. The Sado Kisen terminal has its own special bus (15min); for Shin-Nihonkai, catch a bus for Rinkō Nichōme and get off at Suehiro-bashi (20min).

Destinations Akita (daily; 7hr 45min); Otaru, Hokkaidō (daily; 16–20hr); Ryōtsu, Sado (10–16 daily; 1hr 5min–2hr 30min); Tomakomai, Hokkaidō (daily; 16hr); Tsuruga (daily; 13hr).

INFORMATION

Tourist information The city's helpful tourist office, well stocked with English brochures, is outside the central, Bandai, exit of Niigata Station (daily 9am–7pm; ☎025 241 7914, ⓦnvcb.or.jp). Other useful online resources include ⓦenjoyniigata.com and ⓦvisit-niigata.com.

GETTING AROUND

By bus Local buses depart from the station terminal; most make their first stop outside the Bandai City Bus Centre. The most useful routes for visitors are the City Loop Bus, which makes a circuit around the central attractions, and the special bus to the Sado Kisen ferry terminal, which leaves from platform 3 outside the station. Both charge ¥210 per trip, which is the flat fare for all bus journeys within the city centre; a one-day pass costs ¥500. Timetables are available on ⓦ www.niigata-kotsu.co.jp.

By bike Ask at the tourist office about Niigata's great bike rental system; bikes cost from ¥200/3hr, and can be picked up and dropped off at several locations, including the station.

By car Outlets include Eki Rent-a-Car (☎ 025 245 4292, ⓦ www.ekiren.co.jp) and Nissan (☎ 025 243 5523, ⓦ nissan-rentacar.com).

ACCOMMODATION

Dormy Inn ドーミーイン新潟 1-7-14 Akashi-dōri ☎ 025 247 7755, ⓦ bit.ly/dormy-niigata. Modern, distinctly yellow business hotel, 600m northeast of the station, with Japanese and Western-style rooms and a pleasant onsen. As well as free noodles nightly, there's a good ¥1200 breakfast buffet, and a free shuttle to the station. 📶 **¥8000**

Hotel Mets Niigata ホテルメッツ新潟 1-96-47 Hanazono ☎ 025 246 2100, ⓦ www.hotelmets.jp/niigata. This stylish new JR-owned hotel could hardly be more convenient – guest access is from inside the station, though the comfortable rooms are high enough to be noise-free. They offer a good Japanese breakfast buffet, and there are plenty of cafés and restaurants located close by. 📶 **¥16,000**

Hotel Nikkō Niigata ホテル日航新潟 5-1 Bandai-jima ☎ 025 240 1888, ⓦ www.hotelnikkoniigata.jp. This towering high-rise hotel, 1.7km north of the station, is the tallest building on the Sea of Japan coast, and ideally located both for the adjoining Toki Messe convention centre, and the Sado Island ferry terminal a few hundred metres along the riverside. Rooms are Western-style – all have great views, being on the 22nd floor and above – and there are two restaurants, a café and a bar. Breakfast costs ¥2000 extra per person. 📶 **¥18,000**

★ Seikokan 清廣館 802 Deyu Agano-shi, Deyu Onsen ☎ 025 062 3833, ⓦ seikokan.jp. This wonderful old family-run inn in the hamlet of Deyu Onsen, 25km southeast of Niigata, is perfect for a relaxing ryokan experience. The rooms in the wooden building are spacious and comfortable, there's an atmospheric 100-year-old bath, and the public areas include tasteful modern design touches. Rates include two meals, with vegetables fresh from the garden. To get here, catch a train from Niigata to Shibata or Suibara (20min–1hr); the friendly English-speaking owners will usually be happy to pick you up. 📶 **¥22,000**

EATING

Niigata is widely known for its fresh fish and fragrant rice, which means excellent **sushi**. Glutinous rice is used to make *sasa-dango*, a sweet snack of bean paste and rice wrapped in bamboo leaves, while in winter, *noppe* combines taro, ginkgo nuts, salmon roe and vegetables in a colourful stew that's commonly served as a side dish. Niigata-ken's most famous product, however, is its sake, available all over town.

★ Benkei Niigata Pia Bandai-ten 弁慶 新ピア万代店 2-4 Bandai-jima ☎ 025 255 6000, ⓦ sado-benkei.com. The Pia Bandai fish market, 15min walk north of the station – or a simple bus ride – towards the Sado ferry terminal, holds a number of good seafood restaurants, but if you don't speak Japanese this conveyor-belt sushi place is much the easiest option. Ultra-fresh dishes cost ¥130–520, while you can order off-menu by pointing to whichever daily special your neighbours seem to be enjoying. There's another branch on the Furumachi-dōri mall downtown. Mon, Tues & Thurs–Sun 10.30am–9.30pm.

Café Self Sprout 自分発芽 1-8-26 Yoneyama ☎ 025 246 9395, ⓦ kasuri-nishida.com. Quirky, very friendly little vegetarian café, not far from the station, serving ¥1100 set lunches such as brown rice with salad and mushroom bakes, or sweet potato and soybean curry, as well as coffee drinks. Daily 10am–5pm.

Suzakaya Soba 須坂屋そば 1-4-29 Benten-chō ☎ 025 241 7705, ⓦ suzakaya.web.fc2.com. Sizeable soba restaurant, a short walk north of the station, that's especially useful for a cheap lunch or after-hours meal. Tasty fresh soba noodles, topped perhaps with breaded pork cutlets or tempura prawn, cost from ¥1000, while full set meals start at ¥3000. Ten percent discount for holders of one-day bus passes. Mon–Sat 11am–1am, Sun 11am–midnight.

Uonoma Kamakura Ponshukan 魚沼釜蔵 ぽんしゅ館 1-96-47 Hanazono ☎ 025 240 0792. All-day restaurant, immediately across from the south exit of the station, specializing in local delicacies, and seafood in particular, with lunchtime rice bowls, noodles or stews for around ¥1000, and full dinners from ¥3000. Daily 6.30–10am & 11am–11pm.

DRINKING

Smoke Café スモークカフェ 1-18-4 Sasaguchi ☎025 246 0250, ⓦsmokecafe.jp. Friendly, trendy bar, in the backstreets just south of the station on the second floor of a modern building behind the *Chisun Hotel*, where the wide array of international beers includes Guinness and Belgian Trappist brew (pints from ¥800), and they also serve good pizza and pasta. Tues–Thurs & Sun 6pm–2am, Fri & Sat 6pm–3am.

Sado-ga-shima

佐渡島

For centuries, the rugged, S-shaped island of **SADO-GA-SHIMA**, out to sea 35km off Honshū, was a place of exile for criminals and political undesirables. Even today, it still exudes a unique atmosphere born of its isolation, while its distinct cultural heritage encompasses haunting folk songs, nō theatre and puppetry, as well as the more recently established Kodō drummers.

Measuring roughly 60km north to south, and thus much too large to think of as a day-trip destination, Sado consists of two parallel mountain chains, linked by a fertile central plain that shelters most of its historic sites, including several important **temples**, such as Kompon-ji, founded by the exiled Buddhist monk Nichiren. The Edo-period gold mines of **Aikawa**, on the northwest coast, make another interesting excursion, but the island's greatest appeal lies in its **coastal scenery**, and the glimpses it affords of an older Japan.

Sado is becoming increasingly popular as a location for trekking, biking, canoeing and other **outdoor activities**. It hosts a number of international competitions, including a gruelling annual triathlon each September (ⓦbit.ly/sado-triathlon).

Brief history

From ancient times onwards, the powers-that-be viewed Sado as a suitably remote place to banish their enemies and unwanted elements of society. The most illustrious exile was the former emperor **Juntoku** (reigned 1211–21) who, after trying to wrest power back from Kamakura, was condemned to spend his final years here, and survived another twenty years. A few decades later, **Nichiren**, the founder of the eponymous Buddhist sect (see p.836), found himself on the island for a couple of years; he wasted no time in erecting temples and converting the local populace. Then there was **Zeami**, a famous actor and playwright credited with formalizing nō theatre, who was sent here in 1434 and spent eight years in exile at the end of his life.

In 1601, rich seams of gold and silver were discovered in the mountains above Aikawa. From then on, criminals were sent to work in Japan's most productive **gold mine**, supplemented by supposedly "homeless" workers forcibly removed from Edo (now Tokyo), who dug some 400km of tunnels down to 600m below sea level – all by hand. In 1896, Mitsubishi took the mines over from the imperial household, and they're now owned by the Sado Gold Mining Co, which continued to extract small quantities of gold until 1989.

ARRIVAL AND DEPARTURE   SADO-GA-SHIMA

BY FERRY
All ferries to Sado are operated by Sado Kisen (Niigata ☎025 245 1234, Ryōtsu ☎025 927 5614, Naoetsu ☎025 544 1234, Teradomari ☎025 875 3294, ⓦsadokisen.co.jp).

SADO FESTIVALS

Sado has a packed calendar of festivals from April to November. Many of these involve *okesa* folk songs and the demon-drumming known as *ondeko* (or *oni-daiko*), both of which are performed nightly during the tourist season in Ogi and Aikawa. Nō groups perform in shrines around the central plain all through June, while the island's biggest event of all is the Kodō drummers' International Earth Celebration, held in Ogi (see box, p.285).

From Niigata Sado's main gateway, Ryōtsu on the east coast, is served by jetfoils (5–9 daily; 1hr 5min; one-way ¥6260, 5-day return ¥11,300) and much slower car ferries (5–7 daily; 2hr 30min; ¥2120 each way) to and from Niigata's Sado Kisen Terminal (see p.278). Reservations are required for the jetfoil and recommended for all crossings in summer. It is possible to buy a ¥9460 day return ticket for the jetfoil, but Sado isn't geared up for day-trippers, and it's not recommended.

From Naoetsu Seasonal car ferries connect Naoetsu port, 125km southwest of Niigata (and 20min by bus from Naoetsu Station), with Ogi on Sado's south coast (March–Oct 3–4 daily, plus 1 daily for a few days around New Year; 1hr 40min; one-way ¥3650, 5-day return ¥6610).

From Teradomari Summer-only car ferries sail between Teradomari (寺泊), 50km southwest of Niigata, and Akadomari (赤泊) on Sado's southeast coast (late April to early Oct 2 daily; 1hr 5min; one-way ¥2700, 5-day return ¥4890).

INFORMATION

Tourist information Maps, bus timetables and other information, including excellent cycling and walking guides, are available at ferry terminals and the various tourist offices on the island. The best overall source of information is Sado's official website, ⓦ visitsado.com.

Look out for the excellent English tourist map, detailing hotels, restaurants, shops and attractions, that's published annually by MIJ International; their website, ⓦ mijintl.com, also carries up-to-date ferry information.

GETTING AROUND

By bus It's possible to get around most of the island by bus, if you allow plenty of time (around three days is recommended). However, in winter some services only operate at weekends or stop completely. And even at the best of times, a number of routes have only two or three buses per day, so check current timetables (available in English from tourist offices, or online at ⓦ visitsado.com). One-day (¥1500), two-day (¥2500) and three-day (¥1500) passes, covering all public transport, are sold at ferry terminals and tourist offices.

By car By far the most flexible option for exploring Sado is to rent a car, which costs from around ¥6000/day; you'll find outlets including Sado Kisen Rent-a-Car (☎ 025 927 5195) at all three ferry terminals.

By bike Several outlets in Ryōtsu and elsewhere, detailed on the tourist office website and including some hostels and hotels, rent out bikes for around ¥1500 a day, with electric-assist bikes available. Don't underestimate the sheer scale of Sado; you'll only be able to see a small proportion of the island in a day's excursion from Ryōtsu.

Ryōtsu

両津

Part fishing village, part ferry port, sitting on a huge horseshoe bay with the mountains of Sado rising behind, **RYŌTSU** is a somewhat run-down little place that still has an appealingly "authentic" – as in, uncommercialized – edge. These days, most activity

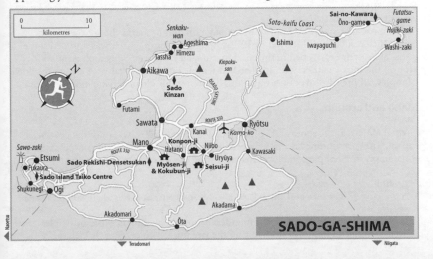

focuses on the ferry pier (両津埠頭) at its southern end, but there's still a flavour of the original fishing community among the rickety wooden houses with their coiled nets and fishy odours in the older backstreets to the north. Much of the town occupies a thin strip of land between the sea and a large salt-water lake, **Kamo-ko**, which is now used for oyster farming.

INFORMATION
RYŌTSU

Tourist information Sado's main tourist office is in the ferry terminal (daily 7am–6pm; ☎ 025 927 5000, ⓦ visitsado

.com). Buses depart from the bus terminal below the ferry building, where you'll also find car rental agencies and taxis.

ACCOMMODATION

Minshuku Tōkaen 民宿桃華園 1636-1 Kanai Shinbo ☎ 025 963 2221, ⓦ bit.ly/sado-tokaen. Tranquil guesthouse, 9km southwest of Ryōtsu, offering sizeable apartment-like suites, an onsen, and excellent food. Staff can advise on and arrange all sorts of outdoor activities, from hiking to fishing and diving. Guests are strongly advised to rent a car or bike; it's 3km from the nearest bus stop. Rates include breakfast and dinner. 🛜 **¥17,600**

Yoshidaya 吉田家 261-1 Ryōtsu-Ebisu ☎ 025 927 2151, ⓦ yosidaya.com. Large ryokan, facing the lake around a 10min walk from the ferry terminal. Most of its spacious tatami rooms have balconies with stunning views over the water. You can have a Western-style bed if you'd rather, and there's an outdoor rotemburo bath on the rooftop. Rates include two meals; deduct around ¥2600 per head for room only. 🛜 **¥21,600**

EATING

Tenkuni 天国 206 Ryōtsu-Minato ☎ 025 923 2714. This popular local restaurant, 400m southwest of the ferry terminal, specializes in fresh seafood, offering moderately

priced sashimi, tempura and *donburi* dishes, typically costing around ¥1000. **Daily 11am–3pm & 6–10pm.**

Central Sado
国仲佐渡

Sado's **central plain** is the most heavily populated part of the island, home to the majority of its sixty thousand inhabitants. A flat, fertile landscape filled with rice fields, the region also holds several impressive temples, dating back in some instances as far as the eighth century, and visibly benefiting from the wealth brought in during Sado's boom periods from the gold and rice trades.

Kompon-ji

根本寺 • 1837 Niibo-ono • Daily: April–Oct 8am–4.30pm, Nov–March 8am–3.30pm • ¥300 • ☎ 025 922 3751, ⓦ www.sado-konponji .com • On Minamisen bus line from Ryōtsu

Sado's most accessible and important temple, **Kompon-ji**, marks the spot where the exiled **Nichiren** (see p.280) lived in 1271, though the temple itself was founded some years later. Arrive early, before the coach parties, and you can enjoy a pleasant stroll around the mossy garden with its thatched temple buildings filled with elaborate gilded canopies, all presided over by a statue of Nichiren in his characteristic monk's robes.

Mano and around
真野

Coastal **MANO**, at the southwest corner of Sado's central valley, was once the provincial capital. The surrounding area holds several historic sites worth checking out, including some impressive temple complexes erected during the island's era of prosperity.

Myōsen-ji

妙宣寺 • 29 Abutsubō • Daily dawn–dusk • Free • ☎ 025 955 2061 • 3min walk from the Takeda-bashi bus stop, on the Kuninaka and Kanamarusen lines

The **Myōsen-ji** temple complex was founded by one of Nichiren's earliest disciples, the retired Samurai Tamemori Endo, during the late thirteenth century. It includes a graceful five-storey wooden pagoda that took over thirty years to build, as well as a large thatched-roof building and elegantly sculptured gardens.

Kokubun-ji

国分寺 • 113 Kokubun-ji • Daily dawn–dusk • Free • ☎ 025 955 2059 • Buses on the Minamisen line stop outside on Sat & Sun only; otherwise a 35min walk from the Takeda-bashi bus stop

Sado's oldest temple, **Kokubun-ji**, is said to date from 764, though the temple's present buildings were constructed in the late seventeenth century. Dotted around the site, a few remains, including foundation stones and the central and south gates, give you an idea how vast the original complex once was.

Sado Rekishi-Densetsukan

佐渡歴史伝説館 • 655 Mano • Daily: April–Nov 8.30am–5pm, Nov–March 9am–4.30pm • ¥800 • ☎ 025 955 2525, ⓦ sado-rekishi.jp • 30min walk southeast from central Mano; 10min from the nearest bus stop, Mano goryō-iriguchi, on bus #4 from Sawata south to Ogi

The intriguing, entertaining **Sado Rekishi-Densetsukan**, next door to a simple shrine dedicated to Emperor Juntoku, is a modern waterside museum where multimedia displays including full-sized robots and holograms bring local history and folk tales to life. Local crafts and souvenirs are also on sale, and a good restaurant offers set meals for ¥1000.

Sawata

佐和田

Half a dozen kilometres north along the coast from Mano, **SAWATA** serves as Sado's main administrative centre. There's really very little here to detain you, though its old commercial street, parallel to the seafront one block inland, holds a handful of time-forgotten old shops.

ARRIVAL AND INFORMATION

CENTRAL SADO

By bus Sawata's bus terminal is on the north side of town. Sawata destinations Aikawa (lines 1 & 10; very frequent; 20min); Ogi (lines 10 & 16; 13 daily; 1hr); Ryōtsu (lines 1 & 2; very frequent; 35–55min).

Tourist information Mano's tourist office is at 488-8

Mano-shin-machi, just south of the main junction between Route 350 and the Niibo road (April–Oct Mon, Tues & Thurs–Sat 8.30am–5.30pm, Nov–March Mon–Fri 8.30am–5.30pm; ☎ 025 955 3589, ⓦ visitsado.com).

GETTING AROUND

By bus Two roads cross Sado's central plain to link Ryōtsu with towns on the west coast: the main highway cuts southwest from Kamo-ko to Sado Airport and on to Sawata, served by buses on the Hon-sen route (line 1),

while the quieter, southerly route takes you through Niibo (新穂), Hatano (畑野) and Mano along the Minamisen bus route (line 2).

ACCOMMODATION

★ Green Village Patio House グリーンヴィレッジパティオハウス 750-4 Niibo-Uryūya ☎ 025 922 2719, ⓦ bit .ly/sado-greenvillage. Charming guesthouse with a homely 1950s feel, just east of Niibo village 9km south of Ryōtsu – drivers on the Ogi Port Minamisen line will drop you off at the turning. As well as good-value meals – having breakfast and dinner costs ¥2376 per head – the friendly owners have laundry facilities and rental bikes, and can suggest cycling routes. ☎ Dorms **¥3780**

Ryokan Urashima 浦島 978-3 Kubota, Mano ☎ 025 957 3751, ⓦ urasima.com. Ultra-modern inn, facing the beach at Mano bay just west of Sawata and designed by architect Kitayama Koh. Accommodation is in stylishly minimalist Western- and Japanese-style rooms, while French and Japanese cuisine are available in its two separate buildings, with the emphasis firmly on seafood; breakfast and dinner cost ¥4980 per person. ☎ **¥12,560**

EATING

Shimafūmi シマフウミ 105-4 Daishō, Mano ☎ 025 955 4545, ⓦ www.primosado.jp/shimafumi.html. Make the trip to this chic seafront café, and you'll be rewarded with

stunning coastal views from its outside deck, as well as great bread, pastry and sandwiches from its on-site bakery. ☎ Mon, Tues & Fri–Sun 10am–5pm.

Sushiya Maruishi すしやまるいし **1031-1 Izumi, Kanai** ⓣ 025 963 3066, ⓦ ishiharasuisan.com. Conveyor-belt sushi restaurant, on the main cross-island road 3km northeast of Sawata and 12km southwest of Ryōtsu. Run by Sado's major seafood company, it serves superbly fresh fish at very reasonable prices, with portions from ¥200. Mon–Wed & Fri–Sun 11am–9pm.

Ogi

小木

Tiny **OGI**, Sado's second port, is close to the island's southern tip, 43km southwest of Ryōtsu. A sleepy fishing town, it's split in two by a small headland, with the original harbour to the west and the modern ferry terminal on its east side. Ogi is best known for its **tub boats**, formerly fishing craft, which now bob around in the harbour for tourists, and the annual **Earth Celebration** that's hosted by the locally based Kodō drummers, during which the village's population almost doubles. This region's principal attraction, however, is the picturesque indented coastline west of town. You can explore the headland on a bike, take boat trips around it, or cycle over the top to **Shukunegi**, a traditional fishing village huddled behind a wooden palisade.

3

ARRIVAL AND INFORMATION — OGI

By bus Buses use the station behind Ogi post office, just inland from the tourist-boat pier.

Destinations Aikawa (line 10; 2 daily; 1hr 30min); Etsumi (line 11; 4 daily; 40min); Sawata (lines 10 & 16; 13 daily; 1hr).

By ferry Seasonal car ferries connect Ogi with Naoetsu on the mainland (see p.281).

Tourist information Ogi's tourist office is in the Marine Plaza building at 1935-26 Ogi-machi (Mon–Sat 8.30am–5.30pm; ⓣ 025 986 3200, ⓦ visitsado.com). On summer evenings, this building hosts performances of *okesa odori* folk singing (April–Oct; ¥500).

GETTING AROUND

By bike The ideal way to explore the headland is to rent an electric bicycle from the tourist office (¥500/2hr, ¥200 each extra hour or ¥2000/24hr).

ACCOMMODATION

Hananoki 花の木 **78-1 Shukunegi** ⓣ **025 986 2331**, ⓦ sado-hananoki.com. Set in a 150-year-old house that was transplanted to this spot, this traditional inn features a beautiful dining room complete with open hearth and organically shaped tree-trunk tables. Five of the seven tranquil, en-suite guest rooms are set in a pretty traditional garden, in a row of separate cabins with views over the surrounding paddy fields. Two meals a day, with exclusively vegetarian dishes on request, are available for ¥5400 per person. **¥12,960**

Minshuku Sakaya 民宿さかや **1991 Ogi-machi** ⓣ 025 986 2535. Popular seafront inn in central Ogi, a 5min walk east of the ferry terminal. It offers clean tatami rooms and tasty food, but unfortunately its sea views are blocked by the harbour wall. Rates include two meals. **¥14,600**

Ogi Sakuma-sō Youth Hostel 小木佐久間荘ユースホステル **1562 Ogi-machi** ⓣ **025 986 2565**, ⓦ **bit.ly/sado-ogi-hostel**. Basic and rather run-down hostel in the countryside 2km west of central Ogi, a 20min walk uphill from the ferry; take the road heading west for Shukunegi, then turn right beside the Shell fuel station. Dorms **¥3880**, rooms **¥9940**

BOAT TRIPS FROM OGI

Ogi's **tub boats**, or *tarai-bune*, were originally used for collecting seaweed, abalone and other shellfish from the rocky coves. Today they're made of fibreglass, but still resemble the cutaway wooden barrels from which they were traditionally made. If you fancy a shot at rowing one of these awkward vessels, go to the small jetty west of the ferry pier, where women will take you out for a ten-minute spin around the harbour (daily: March to mid-Oct 8.20am–5pm, mid-Oct to Nov 8.20am–4.30pm, Dec–Feb 9am–4pm; ¥500 per person; ⓣ 025 986 3153, ⓦ bit.ly/ogi-boats).

Sightseeing boats also set off from the jetty, to sail along the coast past caves and dainty islets as far as Sawa-zaki lighthouse (mid-March to mid-Nov 6–18 daily; 40min; ¥1500; ⓣ 025 975 2311).

CHILDREN OF THE DRUM

During the early 1970s, a group of students sought seclusion on Sado-ga-shima, to pursue their study of traditional *Taiko* drumming and to experiment with its potent music. A decade later, the **Kodō Drummers** unleashed their primal rhythms on the world, and they have continued ever since to stun audiences with their electrifying performances. The name Kodō can mean both "heartbeat" and "children of the drum" – despite its crashing sound, the beat of their trademark giant *Ōdaiko* is said to resemble the heart as heard from inside the womb.

The drummers are based in Kodō village, a few kilometres north of Ogi, where they have set up the **Sado Island Taiko Centre**, offering workshops for tourists (see below) and a two-year apprenticeship programme. Every year, they also host the three-day **Earth Celebration** arts festival in late August, when percussionists from all over the world and a friendly multinational audience of several thousand stir up the sleepy air of Ogi. Details of Kodō scheduled tours and the next Earth Celebration are posted on their website (ⓦ kodo.or.jp).

EATING

Shichiemon 七右衛門 643-1 Ogi-machi ☏ 025 986 2046. At the top of the shopping street curving behind the western harbour, near the Anryū-ji temple, this restaurant dishes up just one variety of delicious, handmade soba (¥480). Mon–Wed & Fri–Sun 11am–2pm.

Around Ogi

In the southwest corner of Sado, the coastline west of Ogi is perfect to explore by bike, with rocky inlets, isolated fishing villages and quiet, undulating roads. After a tough uphill pedal out of the port on the road west to Shukunegi, turn right towards a concrete *jizō* standing above the trees. From here, continue another 300m along this side road and you'll find a short flight of steps leading up to the **Iwaya cave** – the old trees and tiny, crumbling temple surrounded by *jizō* statues make a good place to catch your breath. Return to the coast and follow the road around the peninsula for stunning sea views.

Sadokoku Ogi Folk Culture Museum

佐渡国小木民俗博物館, Sadokoku Ogi Minzoku Hakubutsukan • 290-2 Shukunegi • April–Oct daily 8.30am–5pm, Nov–March Tues–Sun 8.30am–5pm • ¥500 • ☏ 025 986 2604, ⓦ bit.ly/sadokoku

On the road from Ogi to Shukunegi, next to a still-functioning boatyard, the **Sadokoku Ogi Folk Culture Museum** contains a delightful, dusty jumble of old photos, paper-cuts, tofu presses, straw raincoats and other remnants of local life. Behind, in a newer building, there's a relief map of the area and beautiful examples of the ingenious traps used by Ogi fisherfolk.

Shukunegi

宿根木

Tucked in a fold of the hills beside a little harbour full of jagged black rocks, the fishing village of **SHUKUNEGI** is a registered national historic site. As the home of skilful shipbuilders, it was an important port at the peak of Sado's gold trade between the seventeenth and nineteenth centuries. The village itself is hardly visible behind its high wooden fence – protection against the fierce winds – where its old wooden houses, three of which are open to the public in summer (June–Aug daily 10am–5pm; ¥500 each), are jumbled together, in a tangle of odd-shaped corners and narrow, stone-flagged alleys.

Sado Island Taiko Centre

佐渡太鼓体験交流館, Tatakōkan • 150-3 Ogikaneta Shinden, Kodō • Tues–Sun 9am–5pm • ¥2000 for 1hr 30min drumming lesson, available Sat & Sun 10am, 1.30pm & 3pm, and on weekdays with advance reservations; see website for details of occasional longer workshops • ☏ 025 986 2320, ⓦ sadotaiken.jp

The smart **Sado Island Taiko Centre** stands atop a hill above the Kodō village, commanding stunning views over and along the coast. You can learn drumming from Kodō drummers in fun and energetic lessons in the spacious practice room on the ground floor. The drums come in all sorts of sizes, up to giant ones that measure 3m in diameter, and you use sticks weighing up to 5kg, so come prepared for a workout.

North Sado

北佐渡

Sado's northern promontory contains the island's highest mountains and some of its finest coastal scenery. **Aikawa**, the only settlement of any size, was once a lively mining town whose gold and silver ores filled the shoguns' coffers. The mines are no longer working, but they now serve as an industrial museum, **Sado Kinzan**, where computerized robots demonstrate how things were done in days of yore.

North of Aikawa, the rather overrated **Senkaku-wan** (尖閣湾) is a small stretch of picturesque cliffs; it's better to head on up the wild Soto-kaifu coast to **Hajiki-zaki** (弾崎) on the island's northern tip. Not surprisingly, this area isn't well served by public transport, particularly in winter when snow blocks the mountain passes; to explore this part of the island you need to rent a car or be prepared for hard cycling.

Aikawa

相川

After gold and silver were discovered in 1601, the population of **AIKAWA** rocketed from a hamlet of just ten families to 100,000 people, including many brought here as convict labourers. Now less than a tenth of that size, Aikawa is primarily of interest for its **mine museum** not far inland. That said, once you get off the main road, and delve among the temples, shrines and wooden houses pressed up against the hillside, it's surprisingly attractive.

Sado Kinzan

日本最大の金銀山 • 1305 Shimo-Aikawa • Daily: April–Oct 8am–5.30pm; Nov–March 8.30am–5pm • ¥900 each mine, or ¥1400 for both • ☎ 025 974 2389, ⓦ sado-kinzan.com • Bus line 6, the Nanaura-kaigan line, connects the mine with Aikawa on the Sado Kinzan (4 daily; 10min); with connections or through service for Sawata and Ryōtsu

A steep winding road climbs 2.5km inland from Aikawa, up a narrow valley, to reach the source of the town's ancient wealth – the old gold mines of **Sado Kinzan**. Of the two underground passageways that can be explored on self-guided tours – each takes around half an hour – the most interesting and enjoyable is the **Sōdayū Tunnel**, dug by hand during the **Edo** era, from the early seventeenth century onwards, to access one of the mine's richest veins. With life-size animatronic miners hard at work in its inner recesses, visits provide a real taste of the appalling conditions here centuries ago, while a modern museum in the main building provides the full historic and geological background.

The separate **Dōyū Tunnel**, which burrows away from beside the site's ticket office, was created during the **Meiji** era, using mechanized tools. It's longer, deeper and emptier, but the highlight comes halfway along, when you emerge outdoors to be confronted by stunning views of Sado's major physical landmark, a mountain peak that was literally **split in two** by mining operations.

There's a large café and gift store up at the mine, while, given the intermittent bus service down the hillside, it's well worth **walking** back to Aikawa. Parallel to, but invisible from, the main road, a delightful footpath runs through a centuries-old **merchants' quarter**, scattered with temples and shrines.

ARRIVAL AND INFORMATION   **AIKAWA**

By bus Aikawa's bus terminal is close to the sea in the heart of town.

Destinations Ogi (line 10; 2 daily; 1hr 30min); Ryōtsu (lines 1 & 2; very frequent; 55min–1hr 30min); Sawata (lines 1 & 10; very frequent; 20min).

Tourist information Aikawa's tourist office is in the bus terminal (daily 8.30am–5.30pm; ☎ 025 974 2220, ⓦ visitsado.com).

WALKING THE CEDAR FORESTS

Sado's northern Ōsado mountain range contains primeval forests of gigantic ancient **cedar trees**. Although these are protected areas, a **walkway** near Ishina, midway along the northern coast, takes you into prime wooded areas. The circuit is fairly gentle and takes around an hour, but, given the elevation of more than 900m, high winds and temperatures 5°C below those at the coast, come prepared for changeable weather. **Trekkers** wanting to go further afield need to hire a guide, as access is strictly limited.

ACCOMMODATION AND EATING

Dōyū Ryokan 道遊旅館 333-1 Aikawa-Kabuse ☎025 974 3381, ⓦdouyuu.com. Small modern inn on a quiet street one block inland from the bus terminal, offering traditional tatami rooms, an ocean-view onsen, and excellent seafood-based cuisine – local crab is a speciality. Rates include two meals. 🛜 **¥17,400**

Hotel Ōsado ホテル大佐渡 288-1 Aikawa-Kabuse ☎025 974 3300, ⓦoosado.com. This large and luxurious seafront hotel, on the Kasugazaki headland 2km west of the town centre, offers both Japanese- and Western-style rooms. Onsen addicts will love its glorious large rotemburo. Rates include two meals. 🛜 **¥19,440**

The northern cape

Five kilometres north of Aikawa, the road skirts around the edge of a bay where jagged cliffs crumble away into clusters of **little islands**. There's a pretty good view of the bay of **Senkaku-wan** from the road itself or from the observatory in **Ageshima-yūen** (揚島遊園; 1561 Kitabisu; daily: March, April & Nov 8.30am–5pm, May–Oct 8am–5.30pm, Dec–Feb 8.30am–4.30pm; ¥550; ☎025 975 2311), a park on the bay's north side. It's possible to get even closer on the **tour boats** that make regular trips in summer (April–Nov) from **Tassha** village (達者), 2km south; expect to pay around ¥800 for a thirty-minute trip in either a glass-bottomed "shark" boat or ordinary sightseeing (*yūransen*) boats.

As you continue north, the settlements gradually peter out and the scenery becomes wilder as you approach **Ōno-game** (大野亀), a 167m rock rising up from the ocean. From here, a pretty coastal pathway leads around to the island of **Futatsu-game** (二つ亀), linked to the mainland by a thin strip of black-sand beach. An intriguing cave along the path, **Sai-no-Kawara** (賽の河原), houses hundreds of *jizō* statues. In summer this area is popular for swimming and camping, but it's worth coming at any time of year for the journey alone, especially if you return to Ryōtsu down the east coast, where you're treated to further precariously twisting roads that cling to the base of the mountains as they plummet into the sea.

ARRIVAL AND DEPARTURE   THE NORTHERN CAPE

By bus Tassha and Ageshima-Yūen are on the Kaifu bus route (line 9) from Aikawa to Iwayaguchi; services roughly hourly.

ACCOMMODATION

Sado Belle Mer Hostel 佐渡ベルメールユースホステル 369-4 Himezu ☎025 975 2011, ⓦsado.bellemer.jp. In a modern building on the hilltop near Ageshima-yūen, 9km north of Aikawa, this fine, family-run youth hostel has stunning views out over Senkaku Bay, and offers basic dorm rooms that can serve as private doubles for an extra ¥500 per person. Breakfast and dinner are available for ¥2180 per person. 🛜 Dorms **¥3672**

Sotokaifu Youth Hostel 外海府ユースホステル 131 Iwayaguchi ☎025 978 2911, ⓦsotokaifu.jp. Far-flung hostel, in a typical village house in the fishing community of Iwayaguchi, 11km south of the cape and 36km north of Aikawa; the local bus will bring you right to the front door. Simple Japanese-style dorm rooms, plus, for ¥2060 per person per day, hearty local breakfasts and dinners. 🛜 Dorms **¥4320**

Hokkaidō

北海道

SAPPORO SNOW FESTIVAL, YUKI MATSURI

Hokkaidō

An unspoiled frontier, an escape from industrialized Japan and a chance to connect with nature – although this vision of Hokkaidō is rose-tinted, Japan's main northern island certainly has an untamed and remote quality. Over seventy percent of it is covered by forest, and wildlife is ubiquitous, both in and out of the enormous national parks, where you'll also find snow-covered slopes, active volcanoes and bubbling onsen. This is Japan's second-largest island, with 22 percent of the nation's landmass, yet a mere five percent of the population lives here. Even so, cities such as the stylish capital Sapporo and historically important Hakodate are just as sophisticated and packed with facilities as their southern cousins. And now that the Shinkansen connects Japan's main island with Hokkaidō, access to this nature lover's haven is more accessible than ever.

Only colonized by the Japanese in the last 150 years, Hokkaidō is devoid of ancient temples, shrines and monuments over 200 years old. What it does have is a fascinating cultural history, defined by its dwindling **Ainu** population (see box, p.294). From spring till autumn is the ideal time to explore the island's six major national parks and countryside. Apart from the listed highlights (see opposite), other attractions include **Shikotsu-Tōya National Park**, which has two beautiful lakes and a volcano that only started sprouting in 1943, and the countryside around **Furano**, which bursts in colour with fields of lavender and other flowers. Come winter, Hokkaidō takes on a special quality; you can ski at some of Japan's best – and least crowded – ski resorts or view many snow and ice festivals, of which Sapporo's giant **Yuki Matsuri** (see box, p.295) is the most famous.

ARRIVAL AND DEPARTURE   HOKKAIDŌ

By plane Hokkaidō's main gateway is New Chitose Airport, 40km south of Sapporo, where you can pick up connecting flights to other places on the island. Several low-cost carriers, including Peach and Vanilla Air, now operate to New Chitose and around Hokkaidō.

By train Sapporo is now accessible by Shinkansen, with direct trains running from Tokyo to Shin-Hakodate-Hokuto Station (13 daily; 4hr; reserved seats only).

CRABS AT A HAKODATE MARKET STALL

Highlights

❶ Sapporo Hokkaidō's fun capital city is home to Japan's largest Snow Festival, a park designed by the artist and landscape architect Noguchi Isamu and the eponymous freshly brewed beer. **See p.295**

❷ Niseko Superb powder snow, great scenery and chic accommodation and dining add up to Japan's best ski resort. **See p.308**

❸ Hakodate Travel by rickety old trams around this historic port, newly accessible by Shinkansen, which has a gentrified harbourside district and is deservedly famous for its seafood. **See p.311**

❹ Noboribetsu Onsen Explore the steaming, sulphurous volcanic landscape, then enjoy a traditional ryokan experience complete with relaxing onsen. **See p.320**

❺ Daisetsu-zan National Park Home to Asahi-dake, Hokkaidō's highest mountain, the spectacular Sōunkyō Gorge and a choice of onsen. **See p.324**

❻ Rishiri-tō and Rebun-tō Off the beaten path, these beautiful, far northern islands are sprinkled with wild flowers and perfect for hiking and cycling. **See p.330**

❼ Shiretoko National Park Nature is in all her glory at this UNESCO World Heritage Site, which offers challenging treks and abundant wildlife – including bears. **See p.335**

HIGHLIGHTS ARE MARKED ON THE MAP ON PP.292–293

HOKKAIDO

Rebun-tō

RISHIRI-REBUN-SAROBETSU NATIONAL PARK

Korsakov (Sakhalin)

Sōya Misaki

Wakkanai

6 Kafuka
Rishiri-tō Airport

Oshidomari

Wakkanai Airport

Kutsugata

▲ *Rishiri-zan*

Rishiri-tō

6 Sarobetsu Natural Flower Garden

SŌYA LINE

SEA OF JAPAN

Kamik

Sōunky

Asahikawa

Asahikawa Airport

Biei

Asahi-dake Onsen

Shakotan Peninsula

Bibaushi

Ten 0

Takikawa

Tokachi-dake DA

Furano

NA

Furano-dake

Sahoro-dake S

Yoichi

Otaru

Okadama Airport

H o k k

Sapporo **1**

Niseko Annupuri

▲ *Yōtei-zan*

Shikotsu Kohan

Niseko

Shikotsu-ko

Furenai

2

Rusutsu

SHIKOTSU-TŌYA NATIONAL PARK

▲ *Tarumae-zan*

New Chitose Airport

Nibutani

Tōya-ko

Noboribetsu Onsen

Shiraoi

HID SANMYAKU-EF QUASI-NATIC

Usu-zan ▲

▲ *Shōwa Shin-zan*

4

Tomakomai

Tōya ○

MURORAN LINE

Oshamambe

○ Noboribetsu

HIDAKA LINE

Uchiura-wan Bay

Muroran

HAKODATE LINE

▲ *Komaga-take*

ŌNUMA QUASI-NATIONAL PARK

Ōnuma

Shin-Hakodate-Hokuto ○

3 *Hakodate Airport*

HOKKAIDŌ SHINKANSEN

Hakodate

TSUGARU-KAIKYŌ LINE

Fukushima

Seikan Tunnel

Ōma

▼ Niigata & Maizuru

▼ Akita, Niigata & Tsuruga

▼ Aomori

▼ Oarai, Akita, Niigata & Tsuruga

SEA OF OKHOTSK

Shiretoko Peninsula

SHIRETOKO NATIONAL PARK

Iwaobetsu ▲ *Iō-zan*
Utoro ▲ *Rausu-dake*
Rausu

Abashiri

Shari

✈ *Memanbetsu Airport*

AKAN NATIONAL PARK

Kawayu Onsen

Kussharo-ko

Mashū-ko

Ō-Akan-dake ▲

Akan-ko

▲ Akan Kohan

Me-Akan-dake

Teshikaga

Tsurui

KUSHIRO SHITSUGEN NATIONAL PARK

✈ *Kushiro Airport*

Kushiro

AKKESHI PREFECTURAL NATURE PARK

Chanai

Kiritappu Cape

Kiritappu Marsh

Kunashiri-tō

(DISPUTED NORTHERN TERRITORIES)

Habomai Islands

Notsuke Peninsula (Cape)

Nemuro

Nemuro Peninsula

dō

Tokachigawa Onsen

Ikeda

✈ *Tokachi-Obihiro Airport*

Hirō

PACIFIC OCEAN

rimo-Misaki

▼ *Tokyo*

SEKIHOKU LINE

SENMO LINE

NEMURO LINE

N

0 ⸺ 50
kilometres

HIGHLIGHTS

1 Sapporo
2 Niseko
3 Hakodate
4 Noboribetsu Onsen
5 Daisetsu-zan National Park
6 Rishiri-tō and Rebun-tō
7 Shiretoko National Park

THE AINU

…they are uncivilizable and altogether irreclaimable savages, yet they are attractive … I hope I shall never forget the music of their low sweet voices, the soft light of their mild, brown eyes and the wonderful sweetness of their smile.

Isabella Bird, Unbeaten Tracks in Japan, 1880

Victorian traveller Isabella Bird had some misconceived notions about the **Ainu**, but anyone who has ever listened to their hauntingly beautiful music will agree that they are a people not easily forgotten. The roots of the Ainu, who live on Hokkaidō, the Kuril Islands, Sakhalin and northern Honshū, are uncertain – some believe they come from Siberia or Central Asia, moving to their current territories in the seventh century. The early Ainu were hairy, wide-eyed and lived a hunter-gatherer existence, but their culture – revolving around powerful **animist** beliefs – was sophisticated, as shown by their unique clothing and epic songs and stories in a language quite unlike Japanese.

Up until the Meiji Restoration, Japanese contact with the Ainu in Hokkaidō, then called Ezochi, was limited to trade, and the people were largely left alone in the north of the island. However, when the Japanese sought to **colonize** Hokkaidō fully, the impact on the Ainu was disastrous. Their culture was suppressed, they were kicked off ancestral lands, saw forests cleared where they had hunted and suffered epidemics of diseases from which they had no natural immunity. Their way of life went into seemingly terminal decline and assimilation seemed inevitable after a law of 1899 labelled the Ainu as former aborigines, obliging them to take on Japanese citizenship.

Over a century later, against all odds, fragments of Ainu culture and society remain. Around 25,000 people admit to being full- or part-blooded Ainu (although the actual number is thought to be closer to 200,000). A tiny piece of political power was gained when Kayano Shigeru (1926–2006), an Ainu, was elected to the House of Councillors – the second house of Japan's parliament – in 1994. A landmark legal verdict in 1997 recognized Ainu rights over the land and led to the New Ainu Law of 1997, which aimed to protect what was left of Ainu culture and ensure it is passed on to generations to come. And in 2008, Japan's Diet also passed a resolution recognizing Ainu, for the first time in 140 years, as "an indigenous people with a distinct language, religion and culture". Generally, there is now genuine interest in and sensitivity towards this ethnic group among the Japanese who visit tourist villages such as **Akan Kohan** (see p.338), though the best place to get an accurate idea of how Ainu live today is at **Nibutani** (see box, p.320). Also worth seeking out, for a broader understanding of the Ainu and their relationship to similar ethnic groups, are the **museums** of Northern Peoples in Hakodate (see p.313) and Abashiri (see p.334).

By ferry There are overnight ferry services from Honshū. MOL Ferry Co (ⓦsunflower.co.jp) offers a service from Tokyo to Sapporo via the ports of Oarai (for Tokyo) and Tomakomai (for Sapporo), from ¥8740 (see p.300); local buses enable city transfer at either end. Shin Nihonkai Ferry (ⓦsnf.jp) runs services from Otaru to Niigata and Maizuru, north of Kyoto (see p.278). They also run overnight services from Tomakomai to Akita, Niigata and Tsuruga in Fukui-ken. For journey times and frequencies see Sapporo "Getting around" (p.301).

GETTING AROUND

By train The Hokkaidō Rail Pass (ⓦwww2.jrhokkaido .co.jp/global), costing ¥15,000 for a three-day ticket, ¥22,000 for five days and ¥24,000 for seven days, is well worth considering.

By car To reach more remote corners of the island, renting a car is best. Useful websites for general and driving information include ⓦen.visit-hokkaido.jp and ⓦnorthern-road.jp/navi.

By bike Cycling is very popular on Hokkaidō (see individual accounts for rental info).

Hitching Due to the limited train services around Hokkaidō, hitchhiking is fairly widespread (see p.40).

Sapporo

札幌

With a population of nearly two million, Hokkaidō's vibrant capital **SAPPORO** is the fifth-largest city in Japan, and as it's the transport hub of the island you're almost bound to pass through here. It's worth lingering, as Sapporo is generously endowed with parks and gardens. The mountains that attract skiers and snowboarders rise up to its south, and the dramatic coastline around the Shakotan Peninsula is less than thirty minutes away.

Sapporo is also synonymous with its beer, which has been brewed here since 1891; a visit to the handsome, late nineteenth-century **Sapporo Beer Museum and Bier Garten** is a must, as is a stroll through the grounds and museums of the **Hokkaidō University Botanical Gardens**, which date from the same era. Seeing central Sapporo's main sights will fill a day; after dark, the bars and restaurants of **Susukino** spark to life, and you'd be hard-pressed to find a livelier nightlife district outside of Tokyo or Osaka.

Head out of the city centre to see the **Historical Village of Hokkaidō**, a huge landscaped park featuring more than sixty restored buildings from the island's frontier days. **Moerenuma**, a park designed by the late Japanese-American sculptor Noguchi Isamu, also makes for a pleasant half-day trip, as do the entertaining **Sapporo Winter Sports Museum** and the interactive pleasures of **Shiroi Koibito Park**.

Pleasantly cool temperatures tempt many visitors to Sapporo's **Summer Festival** (late July to late Aug), which features outdoor beer gardens and other events in **Ōdōri-kōen**, the swathe of parkland that cuts through the city centre. This park is also the focus of activity during the fabulous **Yuki Matsuri**, a snow festival held every February (see box below).

Brief history

Sapporo's name comes from the Ainu word for the area, *Sari-poro-betsu*, meaning "a river which runs along a plain filled with reeds". The city's easy-to-follow grid-plan layout was designed in the 1870s by a team of European and American experts engaged by the government to advise on Hokkaidō's development. Statues of these advisers can be found around Sapporo; the most famous (overlooking the city from atop Hitsujigaoka hill in the south) is the one of the American **Dr William S. Clark**, who set up Hokkaidō University and whose invocation to his students – "Boys, be ambitious!" – has been adopted as the city's motto.

THE YUKI MATSURI AND OTHER SNOW FESTIVALS

Sapporo's famous snow festival, the **Yuki Matsuri** (ⓦ snowfes.com), has its origins in the winter of 1950, when six small snow statues were created by high-school children in Ōdōri-kōen, the city's main park. The idea caught on, and by 1955 the Self Defence Force (the Japanese military) was pitching in to help build gigantic **snow sculptures**, which included intricately detailed copies of world landmarks such as the Taj Mahal.

Running from early to mid-February and spread across three sites (Ōdōri-kōen, Susukino and Sapporo Tsudome), the festival now includes an international snow sculpture competition and many other events, such as snowboard jumping and nightly music performances in the park. Arrive one week in advance and you'll be able to see the statues being made, as well as take part in the construction, since at least one giant statue in Ōdōri-kōen is a community effort – all you need do is turn up and offer your services. Book **transport and accommodation** well ahead of time: with two million visitors flooding into Sapporo during the *matsuri*, finding last-minute options for both can be a challenge.

If you don't make it to Sapporo's snow festival, note that there are several other similar events around Hokkaidō that take place in January and February, including at **Abashiri** (see box, p.336), Obihiro (see box, p.342), **Asahikawa** (see box, p.323), **Otaru** (see p.304), **Shikotsu-ko** (see p.321) and Sōunkyō (see p.326).

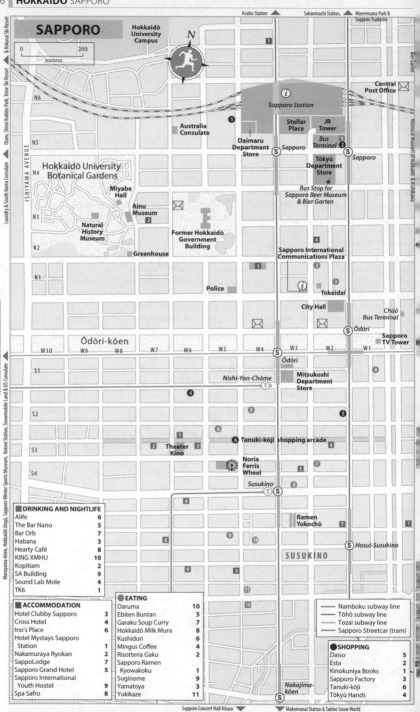

SAPPORO

0   200
metres

N

Asabu Station   Sakaemachi Station,   Moerenuma Park &
Sapporo Tsudome

Hokkaidō University Campus

Sapporo Station

Central Post Office

Australia Consulate

Daimaru Department Store

Sapporo

Stellar Place

JR Tower

Bus Terminal

Sapporo

Tōkyū Department Store

Bus Stop for Sapporo Beer Museum & Bier Garten

Hokkaidō University Botanical Gardens

Miyabe Hall

Ainu Museum

Natural History Museum

Greenhouse

Former Hokkaidō Government Building

Sapporo International Communications Plaza

Tokeidai

Police

City Hall

Chūō Bus Terminal

Ōdōri

Sapporo TV Tower

Ōdōri-kōen

W10 W9 W8 W7 W6 W5 W4 W3 W2 W1

Ōdōri

Nishi-Yon-Chōme

Mitsukoshi Department Store

S1

S2

Theater Kino

Tanuki-kōji shopping arcade

S3

Noria Ferris Wheel

S4

Susukino

Ramen Yokochō

SUSUKINO

Hosui-Susukino

Nakajima-kōen

DRINKING AND NIGHTLIFE
Alife	6
The Bar Nano	5
Bar Orb	7
Habana	3
Hearty Café	8
KING XMHU	10
Kopitiam	2
SA Building	9
Sound Lab Mole	4
TK6	1

ACCOMMODATION
Hotel Clubby Sapporo	3
Cross Hotel	4
Ino's Place	6
Hotel Mystays Sapporo Station	1
Nakamuraya Ryokan	2
SappoLodge	7
Sapporo Grand Hotel	5
Sapporo International Youth Hostel	9
Spa Safro	8

EATING
Daruma	10
Ebiten Buntan	5
Garaku Soup Curry	7
Hokkaidō Milk Mura	8
Kushidori	6
Mingus Coffee	4
Risotteria Gaku	2
Sapporo Ramen Kyowakoku	1
Suginome	9
Yamatoya	3
Yukikaze	11

SHOPPING
Daiso	5
Esta	2
Kinokuniya Books	1
Sapporo Factory	3
Tanuki-kōji	6
Tōkyū Hands	4

——	Namboku subway line
——	Tōhō subway line
——	Tozai subway line
——	Sapporo Streetcar (tram)

Sapporo Concert Hall Kitara   Makomanai Station & Takino Snow World

& Kokusai Ski Resort

Otaru, Shiroi Koibito Park, Teine Ski Resort

Laundry & South Korea Consulate

ISHIYAMA AVENUE

Historical Museum of Hokkaidō & Asahikawa

Bier Garten

Maruyama-kōen, Hokkaidō Jingū, Sapporo Winter Sports Museum, Kotoni Station, Snowmobile Land & US Consulate

Asahi University, mini university, Okudōri, Shiroi Koibito Park

Hokkaidō University Botanical Gardens

北海道大学植物園, Hokkaidō Daigaku Shokubutsu-en • Kita 3, Nishi 8 • **Gardens and museums** Tues–Sun: April–Sept 9am–4.30pm; Oct & Nov 9am–4pm • ¥420 • **Greenhouse** Nov–April Mon–Fri 10am–3.30pm, Sat 10am–12.30pm • ¥120 • ☎ 0117 06 2584, ⓦ www.hokudai.ac.jp/fsc/bg

The compact and pretty **Hokkaidō University Botanical Gardens** are the oldest in Japan. Immediately to the right as you enter is the small but absorbing **Ainu Museum**, housing a collection of around 2500 Ainu artefacts (though only a fraction are displayed at any time), ranging from clothes made of bird skins from the Kuril Islands to a sacred altar for performing the ritual slaughter of a bear cub; there are English-language captions. The **gardens** themselves feature a long pond, a greenhouse, a rockery, shaded forest walks and neat flower gardens, including a collection which shows the plants and flowers used by the Ainu in their daily lives. In the centre of it all stands the **Natural History Museum**, housed in a pale green wooden building dating from 1882. Inside is a staggering collection of bizarre stuffed animals, such as snarling wolves and huge sea lions, as well as other curiosities including a dog sled from Sakhalin. Following the red-gravel pathway around to the right of the museum leads you to **Miyabe Hall**, where you'll find intriguing displays of letters and journals belonging to Professor Miyabe Kingo, the first director of Hokkaidō University, who established the gardens in 1886. Miyabe's descriptions of his travels abroad, written in English and illustrated with photographs, make fascinating reading.

Former Hokkaidō Government Building

北海道庁旧本庁舎, Hokkaido-chō Kyū Honchōsha • Kita 3, Nishi 6 • Daily 8.45am–6pm • Free

The palatial red brick **Former Hokkaidō Government Building** (nicknamed *akarenga*, or "red-brick building"), dating to 1888, is worth a visit on your way to or from the Botanical Gardens. The building is a fine example of the local architecture that fused the late nineteenth-century European and New World influences flooding into the country with Japanese traditions. Inside, the wood-panelled interiors have been nicely maintained and hung with large-scale historical paintings.

4

Tokeidai

時計台 • Kita 1, Nishi 2 • Daily 8.45am–5pm; closed Jan 1–3 • ¥200 • ☎ 0112 31 0838, ⓦ sapporoshi-tokeidai.jp

Five blocks south of Sapporo Station, opposite the Sapporo International Communication Plaza, is the **Tokeidai**, a wooden clock tower that's one of the city's key landmarks. You'd be right in thinking that this wood-clad building would look more at home somewhere like Boston, because that's where it was made in 1878; inside is an uninspiring exhibition on the building's history.

Sapporo TV Tower

さっぽろテレビ塔, Sapporo Terebi-tō • Ōdōri Nishi 1 • Daily: May–Oct 9am–10pm; Nov–April 9.30am–9.30pm • ¥720 • ☎ 0112 41 1131, ⓦ tv-tower.co.jp

One block south of the Tokeidai lies Ōdōri kōen and the contrasting 147m red steel **Sapporo TV Tower**. During the snow festival, the viewing platform provides a lovely vista down the park, particularly at night. On a clear day, you can see the surrounding mountains and even the sea.

Susukino

すすきの

The neon-illuminated excess of **Susukino**, the largest area of bars, restaurants and nightclubs north of Tokyo, begins on the southern side of Ōdōri-kōen, and is best

---

SAPPORO'S BREWERIES

Apart from Sapporo Beer Museum you can also try the tours at **Asahi Breweries** (アサヒビール北海道工場, Asahi Biiru Hokkaidō Kōjō; daily 9am–3pm; ⓦ asahibeer.co.jp/brewery) or **Kirin Breweries** (キリンビール北海道千歳工場, Kirin Biiru Hokkaidō Chitose Kōjō; Tues–Sat 9.30–11.30am & 1–3.30pm; ⓦ www.kirin.co.jp/entertainment/factory/chitose). Reservations are required at each.

---

explored at night. This is where Sapporo goes to play, and to eat ramen (see p.302). If you're here during the day, you could window-shop the covered shopping arcade **Tanuki-kōji Shōtengai** (狸小路商店街).

Sapporo Beer Museum and Bier Garten

サッポロビール博物館, Sapporo Biiru Hakubutsukan • サッポロビール園, Sapporo Biiru-en • サッポロビール博物館, Sapporo Biiru Hakubutsukan • Kita 7 Higashi 9 • Museum: daily 11.30am–8pm; Free; beer sample ¥200 or ¥300 depending on beer, three for ¥600 • ☎ 0117 48 1876, ⓦ sapporobeer.jp • Bus #88 runs every 20min directly to the complex (¥210) from behind Tōkyū department store, near Sapporo Station, or take subway to Higashi-Kuyakusho-Mae on the Tōhō line and walk for about 1km

Just east of the city centre stands the hugely popular **Sapporo Beer Museum and Bier Garten**. It was an American adviser to Hokkaidō who noted the hops growing locally and realized that, with its abundant winter ice, Sapporo was the ideal location for a commercial **brewery**. When the first brewery opened in 1876, locals didn't touch beer, so for years Sapporo exported to the foreign community in Tokyo, which is where the company's headquarters are now.

Built in 1891, this grand red-brick complex was originally the factory of the Sapporo Sugar Company; it's now Sapporo's smallest brewery, since much of the building has been turned over to an **exhibition** on the brewing process and the history of the company, not to mention several restaurants, pubs and souvenir shops. At the end of the exhibition, while sipping beer samples, you can admire a wall coated with a century's worth of colourful ad posters. After you've learned all about the making of the beer, you can enjoy it at your leisure, along with a huge plate of Genghis Khan barbecued lamb, in the Bier Garten next door (see box, p.302).

Hokkaidō Jingū

北海道神宮 • 474 Miyagaoka, Chuo-ku • Seasonal hours but generally 7am–4.30pm • Free • ☎ 0116 11 0264, ⓦ hokkaidojingu.or.jp • 15min from Maruyama-kōen Station on the Tōzai line

The affluent suburb of Maruyama-kōen is where you'll find the island's principal Shintō shrine, **Hokkaidō Jingū**, amid a leafy park where 1400 cherry trees break into spectacular blossom each May. See the website for details of annual major **festivals**, including the main festival (June 14–16), when four *mikoshi*, or portable shrines, are paraded through the streets of Sapporo.

Sapporo Winter Sports Museum

札幌ウィンタースポーツミュージアム, Sapporo Uintā Supōtsu Myūjiamu • Daily: May–Oct 9am–6pm (June–Sept Fri & Sat till 9pm); Nov–April 9.30am–5pm • ¥600; ski jump lift ¥500 return • ☎ 0116 41 8585, ⓦ sapporowintersportsmuseum.com • Bus #14 from Maruyama-kōen subway station to Ōkurayama Kyōgijō Iriguchi bus stop (10min), and then a 10min walk uphill; a taxi from Maruyama-kōen station is around ¥1000

The highlight of the fun **Sapporo Winter Sports Museum** – which occupies the Ski Jump Stadium at Ōkurayama (大倉山), built for the 1972 Winter Olympics – is a ski jump simulator that gives you an idea of what it's like to participate in this daring winter sport. There are also simulations for bobsleighing, cross-country skiing and speed skating, among other things – it's all a hoot, and afterwards you can ride the passenger lift to the top of the ski jump to see the view for real.

WINTER SPORTS IN SAPPORO

As you'd expect for the location of the 1972 Winter Olympics, there are several good ski hills within easy reach of Sapporo, including **Teine** (ⓦ sapporo-teine.com; 10–15min from Sapporo Station to Teine Station, then 15min by bus), **Kokusai** (ⓦ sapporo-kokusai.jp; 1hr 30min from Sapporo Station by bus) and **Takino Snow World** (ⓦ takinopark.com; subway to Makomanai Station on the Namboku line, then 35min on the bus to Suzuran-kōen Higashi-guchi), which offers six cross-country ski courses from 1km to 16km long, in addition to ski and snowboard slopes, snowshoe treks and sledding.

At **Snowmobile Land** (☎ 0116 61 5355, ⓦ snowmobileland.jp), you can take a ride on one of the eponymous machines over a 90km course that winds through the forests to viewpoints looking out over the city and, most dramatically, into the base of a quarry. Rates start at ¥10,000 for 60 minutes, or ¥13,500 for 90 minutes, including all protective gear. Women riders may drive single-seaters, but not the heavier double-seaters, which they may only ride pillion. To reach the course (usually open Dec–March), take the subway to Hassamu Minami Station on the Tōzai line, then bus #41 to Fukui Entei-mae, which is the final stop.

Historical Village of Hokkaidō

北海道開拓の村, Hokkaidō Kaitaku no Mura • 50-1 Konoppuro, Atsubetsu-chō • May–Sept daily 9am–5pm; Oct–April Tues–Sun 9am–4.30pm • May–Sept ¥800, Oct–April ¥680; horse-drawn trolley car ¥250; combined ticket with Historical Museum (see below) ¥1200 • ☎ 0118 98 2694, ⓦ kaitaku.or.jp • Buses (9 daily) from platform 10 beneath Shin-Sapporo Station; train from Sapporo Station to Shinrin-kōen Station (¥260; 15min), then bus (¥210; 12min)

Some 15km from the city centre, the **Historical Village of Hokkaidō** is one of Hokkaidō's highlights. Laid out across spacious grounds in Nopporo Forest Park, this impressive outdoor museum contains some sixty buildings constructed between the mid-nineteenth and early twentieth centuries, as large-scale immigration from Honshū cranked up. Wandering around the village's four main areas, representing town, farm, mountain and fishing communities, will give you a strong impression of what Hokkaidō looked like before prefabricated buildings and concrete expressways became the norm. The buildings have been restored as beautifully inside as out and spruced up with displays related to their former use, be it sweet shop, silkworm house or woodcutter's shanty. There are guides in some houses (Japanese-speaking only) and written English explanations in all. It's a good idea to wear slip-on shoes, as you'll be taking them off a lot to explore the interiors. In summer, you can hop aboard the horse-drawn trolley car that plies the main street – in winter this is replaced by a sleigh, when some houses are shut, but the village is worth visiting even then for its special atmosphere when blanketed in snow.

To cover the whole site will take you at least half a day; either bring a picnic or try one of the inexpensive **restaurants** or refreshment stops within the village.

Historical Museum of Hokkaidō

北海道開拓記念館, Hokkaidō Kaitaku Kinenkan • 53-2 Konoppuro, Atsubetsu-chō • Tues–Sat: May–Sept 9.30am–6pm; Oct–April 9.30am–4.30pm • ¥600; combined ticket with Historical Village (see above) ¥1200 • ☎ 0118 98 0466, ⓦ www.hm .pref.hokkaido.lg.jp • Same travel details as for Historical Village of Hokkaidō (see above), but get off the bus one stop earlier at Kinenkan Iriguchi

As well as the Historical Village of Hokkaidō, the grounds of Nopporo Forest Park are also home to the mildly interesting **Historical Museum of Hokkaidō**, which contains over four thousand items showing the history of Hokkaidō from a million years ago to the present day. There are separate displays on the island's ancient times, Ainu history, colonization, the postwar period and the Hokkaidō of tomorrow.

Moerenuma Park

モエレ沼公園, Moerenuma-kōen • Park daily 7am–10pm; beach early June to early Sept 10am–4pm, closed Thurs • Free •
☎ 0117 90 1231, ⓦ sapporo-park.or.jp/moere • Subway to Kanjō-Dōri-Higashi Station on the Tōhō line, then from bus terminal above
station take bus #69 or #79 (¥210); get off at Moere-kōen Higashiguchi (combined journey around 40min), then walk 5min

About 10km northeast of the city centre, **Moerenuma Park** is part playground, part
sculpture garden displaying the works of internationally renowned artist and landscape
architect **Noguchi Isamu**. In the giant glass pyramid, which has observation decks and a
library/lounge, you can peruse English-language books about the artist, who died
shortly after completing the masterplan for the park in 1988. With its massed plantings
of cherry trees, wide lawns, the spectacular Sea Fountain water sculpture and a shallow
pebbled bathing beach, the park is popular with local families and is a convivial spot
for a picnic.

Shiroi Koibito Park

白い恋人パーク, Shiroi Kobito-kōen • 2-2-11-36 Miyanosawa • Daily 9am–7pm • Factory tour ¥600 to Miyanō-sawa Station on
the Tōzai line, then walk; or bus from JR Sapporo Bus terminal in the direction of Otaru and get off at the Nishi-machi kita 20-chome
bus stop

It may be overrun with tourists and screaming children, but **Shiroi Koibito Park**
produces Hokkaidō's most sought-after confectionery, a white-chocolate-filled cookie.
Take the tour of its European-style factory to see the cookies being made or test out
your own skills by making Hokkaidō-shaped cookies in the Cookiecraft Studio. If
you're interested in antiques, make sure to scour the vintage toy collection inside the
main building, full of gems from the Taisha and Shōwa periods; and during the
summer, walk around the beautiful rose gardens while snacking on the park's signature
ice cream. Don't miss the clock striking on the hour, presenting a ten-minute
"chocolate parade" high on the tower.

ARRIVAL AND DEPARTURE   SAPPORO

BY PLANE

New Chitose Airport (新千歳空港; ☎ 0123 23 0111,
ⓦ new-chitose-airport.jp/en) is 40km southeast of
Sapporo. From here, the fastest way to Sapporo is on the
frequent JR train (every 15min; 50min; ¥1070); the bus is
marginally cheaper (¥1030) but takes at least twice as long
to arrive at the same point.

Destinations Akita (4 daily; 1hr 5min); Aomori (5 daily;
50min); Fukuoka (4 daily; 2hr 20min); Hakodate (2 daily;
35min); Hiroshima (2 daily); Kansai International (13 daily;
2hr 10min); Kushiro (3 daily; 45min); Memanbetsu (7 daily;
45min); Nagoya (21 daily; 1hr 50min); Naha (daily; 4hr);
Osaka (12 daily; 1hr 55min); Sendai (13 daily; 1hr 10min);
Tokyo (67 daily; 1hr 30min); Wakkanai (2 daily; 55min).

Okadama Airport (札幌丘珠空港; ☎ 0117 85 7871,
ⓦ okadama-airport.co.jp), 8km northeast of Sapporo, is
mainly used for services within Hokkaidō.

Destinations Hakodate (6 daily; 45min); Kushiro (3 daily;
45min); Rishiri (daily; 1hr); Misawa (1 daily; 1hr).

BY TRAIN

Arriving by train, you'll pull in at busy JR Sapporo Station,
six blocks north of Ōdōri-kōen, the park that bisects
Sapporo from east to west.

Destinations Abashiri (4 daily; 5hr 30min); Asahikawa

(30 daily; 1hr 30min); Hakodate (15 daily; 4hr); Kushiro
(6 daily; 4hr); Noboribetsu (17 daily; 1hr 10min); Otaru
(every 10min; 30min); Tokyo (9 daily; 8hr; change to
Shinkansen at Shin-Hakodate-Hokuto Station); Tomakomai
(18 daily; 45min); Wakkanai (3 daily; 5hr 30min).

BY BUS

Long-distance buses terminate at Chūō Bus Terminal just
northeast of Ōdōri-kōen and Sapporo Station Bus Terminal
on the south side of the train station beneath the Esta
shopping complex.

Destinations Abashiri (9 daily; 6hr); Furano (10 daily; 2hr
25min); Kushiro (5 daily; 5hr 30min); Niseko (2 daily; 3hr);
Noboribetsu (daily; 1hr 40min); Tōya-ko (4 daily; 3hr);
Wakkanai (6 daily; 6–7hr).

BY FERRY

The closest ferry port to Sapporo is Otaru (see p.307), 40km
to the northwest; ferries arrive here from Maizuru (1 daily;
21hr) and Niigata (1 daily except Mon; 19hr). Ferries from
Tokyo (Oarai port) arrive at Tomakomai, 70km to the south
(1–2 daily, 19hr), as do ferries from Akita (daily; 10hr);
Hachinohe (4 daily; 7–8hr); Nagoya (every other day;
40hr); Niigata (daily; 18hr); Sendai (daily; 15hr); and
Tsuruga (daily; 19hr or 32hr depending on company).

SAPPORO ADDRESSES

Finding your way around central Sapporo is easy compared to many other Japanese cities because every address has a precise location within the city's **grid plan**. The city blocks are named and numbered according to the compass points, the apex being the **TV Tower** in Ōdōri-kōen. Sapporo Station, for example, is six blocks north of the TV Tower and three blocks west, so its address is Kita 6 (North Six), Nishi 3 (West Three), while **Nijō Fish Market** is Minami 3 (South Three), Higashi 1-2 (East One-Two).

INFORMATION

Tourist information Sapporo has several excellent tourist information facilities, all staffed by English-speakers. The Hokkaidō-Sapporo Food and Tourism Information Centre (daily 8.30am–8pm; ☎0112 13 5088, ⟨w⟩www.city.sapporo.jp) is inside Sapporo Station; you can sort out train tickets and rail passes here. Another option is the Sapporo International Communications Plaza "i" (Mon–Sat 9am–5.30pm; ☎0112 11 3678, ⟨w⟩plaza-sapporo.or.jp), on the 3rd floor of the MN Building, opposite the Tokeidai, the city's famous clock tower. Check out ⟨w⟩welcome.city.sapporo.jp and ⟨w⟩bit.ly/sapporo-guide for up-to-date information on local sites and festivals.

GETTING AROUND

Most of Sapporo's sights are within easy **walking distance** of each other, but the efficient network of **subway**, **trams** and **buses** can be useful if you get tired. Public transport stops running at around 11.30pm, after which you can hail one of the many taxis that roam Sapporo's streets.

Passes All-day passes for the subway cost ¥830 weekday; ¥520 on Sat, Sun and holidays.

By subway There are three subway lines: the green Namboku line (南北線) and the blue Tōhō line (東豊線) run from north to south through Sapporo Station, while the orange Tōzai line (東西線) intersects them both, running east to west under Ōdōri-kōen. The lowest fare is ¥200, which covers all the stops in the city centre between Sapporo Station in the north and Nakajima-kōen in the south, and Maruyama-kōen in the west and Higashi Sapporo in the east.

By tram The Sapporo Streetcar has a single line and a flat fare of ¥170. It runs from Nishi-Yon-chōme, just south of Ōdōri-kōen, out to Mount Moiwa, south of the city, and back to Susukino.

By bus Buses depart from in front of the Esta building next to Sapporo Station, or nearby; fares start at ¥210.

By car Car rental companies include: Eki Rent-a-Car (☎0117 42 8211, ⟨w⟩www.ekiren.co.jp); Nippon Rent-a-Car (☎0112 32 0921, ⟨w⟩www.nrgroup-global.com); and Orix Rent-a-Car (☎0117 26 0543, ⟨w⟩car.orix.co.jp).

By taxi Call the Taxi Association (☎0115 61 1171; Japanese only) to book a cab.

By bike Bikes can be rented from the city-wide rent-a-cycle service Porocle. A day's rental costs ¥1080. Locations and more can be found at ⟨w⟩porocle.jp.

ACCOMMODATION

Even though Sapporo has plenty of accommodation, places get booked up well in advance of the summer season and the snow festival in February. There can be great bargains to be had at the upmarket hotels in winter.

Hotel Clubby Sapporo ホテルクラビーサッポロ Kita 2, Higashi 3 ☎0112 42 1111, ⟨w⟩sapporofactory.jp/clubby. This smart hotel is part of the Sapporo Factory redevelopment. Leather and wood fittings lend an old-fashioned air to the lobby and restaurant, but the rooms are modern, spacious and elegantly decorated. ☎ **¥14,000**

★**Cross Hotel** クロスホテル札幌 2-23 Kita, Nishi 2 ☎0112 72 0010, ⟨w⟩crosshotel.com. The city's best boutique-style hotel offers rooms in three appealing decorative styles (natural, urban and hip), a relaxing rooftop pool and bath, and a cool lounge bar. ☎ **¥19,000**

Ino's Place イノーズプレイス 4-6-5 3-Higashi-Sapporo, Shiroishi-ku ☎0118 32 1828, ⟨w⟩inos-place.com. Few hostels have a juggling shop, but there's one at this cosy, welcoming place run by the wonderfully friendly Eiji and Miwa (who both speak fluent English). It's a 5min walk

NORIA FERRIS WHEEL

A popular date spot in Sapporo is the fluorescent multicoloured **Noria Ferris wheel** (Mon–Thurs & Sun 11am–11pm, Fri & Sat 11am–3am; ¥600), atop the Norbesa shopping mall at Minami 3, Nishi 5. There's a wonderful view of the city lights from the top.

from Shiroishi subway station on the Tōzai line. 🛜 Dorms **¥3400**, doubles **¥8600**

Hotel Mystays Sapporo Station ホテルマイステイズ 札幌駅北口 Kita 8, Nishi 4-15 ☎0117 29 4055, 🌐sapporo.bwhotels.jp. The stylish design in a natural palette of colours helps this business hotel stand out from the crowd around the station. Bathrooms include massage showers, and there's a pleasant café next to the lobby where the buffet breakfast is served. 🛜 **¥18,900**

★**Nakamuraya Ryokan** 中村屋旅館 Kita 3, Nishi 7 ☎0112 41 2111, 🌐nakamura-ya.com. This high-quality Japanese inn is a wonderful choice. The tatami rooms are spacious, the maids wear kimono, and there's a café in the lobby serving beautifully presented traditional meals. 🛜 **¥15,700**

★**SappoLodge** サッポロッジ Minami 5, Higashi 1-4 ☎0112 11 4314, 🌐sappolodge.com. Located a 5min walk from busy Susukino, this beautiful wood-decorated hostel offers both Japanese- and Western-style rooms. There's also a shared lounge, café/bar and bike rental. 🛜 Dorms **¥3000**, doubles **¥8000**

Sapporo Grand Hotel 札幌グランドホテル Kita 1, Nishi 4 ☎0112 61 3311, 🌐grand1934.com. Dating back to 1934, the city's first European-style hotel has some very nicely remodelled rooms, and there's an unbeatable range of facilities, including a spa and small display area on the hotel and the city's history. 🛜 **¥22,000**

Sapporo International Youth Hostel 札幌国際ユースホステル Toyohira 6-5-35 6jō ☎0118 25 3120, 🌐youthhostel.or.jp/kokusai. Just east of Exit 2 of Gakuen-mae Station on the Tōhō line, this large modern hostel has dorm rooms, tatami rooms for families, and twins for married couples. English is spoken. Breakfast ¥680. 🛜 Dorms **¥3200**, doubles **¥7600**

Spa Safro スパ サフロ Minami 6, Nishi 5 ☎0115 31 2233, 🌐www.safro.org. Amazingly luxurious and excellent-value capsule hotel in the heart of Susukino. Facilities include ornamental baths, massage and treatments and a mini-cinema. There's also a floor of capsules for women. Check-in is from 5pm. Add ¥500 to prices at weekends. Women **¥4350**, men **¥4050**

EATING

Sapporo is renowned for its **ramen** – try the version called *batā-kon*, which is a noodle broth laden with butter and corn. Another local speciality is the lamb *jingisukan* BBQ (see box below). In Susukino, **Rāmen Yoko-chō** (ラーメン横丁; daily 11am–2am) is a busy alley full of ramen joints mostly popular with tourists.

Daruma だるま Minami 5, Nishi 4 ☎0115 52 6013. This is the original cosy fifteen-seater branch of the *jingisukan* chain, tucked away on a narrow street in the midst of Susukino; look for the red lantern and scowling bald Genghis on the sign outside. One plate of meat costs ¥735. If it's full, you could try the larger places at Minami 6, Nishi 4 and Minami 4, Nishi 4. Daily 5pm–3am.

Ebiten Bunten 蛯天分店 Minami 2, Nishi 4 ☎0112 71 2867, 🌐ebiten.co.jp. Great-value tempura restaurant, with a stuffed brown bear for decoration. You can get a meal of rice topped by plump batter-covered prawns for under ¥1000. Daily 11.30am–10pm.

Garaku Soup Curry スープカレー GARAKU Minami 3, Nishi 2 ☎0112 33 5568, 🌐s-garaku.com. Soup curry is a Hokkaidō speciality, and *Garaku* is a great place to

try a soft pork variety (¥1200). Pick your spice level (between 1 and 10), but proceed with caution above 6. Tasty lassis available too. Mon–Sat 11.30am–3.30pm & 5–11.30pm, Sun 11.30–10pm.

Hokkaidō Milk Mura 北海道ミルク村 6F New Hokusai Building, Minami 4, Nishi 3 ☎0112 19 6455. Hokkaidō is famous in Japan for the quality of its milk products, and in this quirkily decorated bar, ice cream is paired with alcohol to create original concoctions. A set comes with ice cream (and one free refill), three liqueur shots from a staggering list, coffee and cookie (¥1360). Tues–Sun noon–11pm.

Kushidori 串鳥 Minami 2, Nishi 5 ☎0112 22 1231. A row of red lanterns dangles from the front of this busy *yakitori* joint. Sit at the counter to take in the full atmosphere. An English menu eases ordering from a wide

---

MEAL FIT FOR A KHAN

It's rare to find lamb on most Japanese menus, but not in Sapporo, home of the **jingisukan**, or "Genghis Khan" barbecue. This delicious feast of flame-grilled meat and vegetables gets its name from the convex table grill on which it's cooked, said to resemble the Mongolian warrior's helmet. All the restaurants at the **Sapporo Bier Garten** next to the Sapporo Beer Museum (see p.298) offer the dish, as does the rival beer garden *Kirin Biiru-en* (see box, p.298). At either, you can pig out on as much barbecue and beer as you can within one hundred minutes, for a set price of around ¥3700. You'll be provided with a plastic bib to protect against dribbles from the dipping sauce, but it's still best to dress down, since the smell of sizzled mutton lingers long after you've left. The big beer gardens, packed with tourists, have a boisterous Germanic quality; for a more intimate *jingisukan* experience, try *Daruma* (see above).

range of skewered delights, starting at around ¥130 a serving. 📶 Daily 4.30pm–12.30am.

Mingus Coffee ミンガスコーヒー Minami 1, Nishi 1 📞 0112 71 0500. With a view of Sapporo TV Tower from its sunny terrace, this hip and jazzy seventh-floor coffee shop serves delicious concoctions like orange café au lait (¥700), plus desserts and toast. Feel free to add a shot of liquor to your choice of brew. Mon–Sat 9am–midnight, Sun noon–midnight.

Risotteria Gaku リゾッテリア ガク Minami 2, Nishi 2 📞 0112 19 6004, 🌐 risotteria-gaku.net. The most central of four branches in Sapporo, serving around eighty different types of risotto, with all ingredients sourced from Hokkaidō and most for under ¥1000. Expect large portions and superb Italian desserts. Daily 11.30am–10pm.

Sapporo Ramen Kyowakoku 札幌ら〜めん共和国 Kita 5, Nishi 2 📞 0112 09 5031, 🌐 www.sapporo-esta .jp/ramen. On the tenth floor of the Esta shopping building (see p.304), this ramen bonanza features eight ramen restaurants from all over Japan (about ¥850 a bowl). 📶 Daily 11am–10pm.

Suginome 杉ノ目 Minami 5, Nishi 5 📞 0115 21 0888, 🌐 suginome.jp. Housed in a historic stone building, this traditionally decorated place is a good spot in which to sample *kaiseki*-style course meals made using local produce from ¥7560. Mon–Sat 5–11pm.

Yamatoya 大和家 Kita 1, Nishi 2 📞 0112 41 6353. Reasonably priced, unassuming sushi and tempura shop behind the clock tower that gets the nod from local foodies. A tempura-*teishoku* set lunch costs ¥1250. Mon–Sat 11am–3pm & 5–10pm.

Yukikaze 雪風 Minami 7, Nishi 4 📞 0115 12 3022. Customers eagerly wait in line at this convivial, late-night ramen shop where the noodle dishes (about ¥900) are made with loving care and better-than-average ingredients. Mon–Sat 6pm–3am, Sun 6pm–midnight.

DRINKING AND NIGHTLIFE

Amid the myriad hostess clubs and sex joints of the neon-drenched party district of **Susukino**, there are plenty of reputable bars and restaurants, making it easy to avoid the sleazy places. The covered shopping arcade **Tanuki-kōji** also has a good selection of bars. In the summer, outdoor **beer gardens** sprout across the city, including in Ōdōri-kōen.

4

BARS

The Bar Nano ザ・バー・ナノ Minami 3, Nishi 3 📞 0112 31 2668, 🌐 bit.ly/BarNanoHokkaido. Creative cocktails in a beautiful and intimate setting in the midst of Suskino. There's a ¥700 charge after 8pm. Mon–Thurs 5pm–2am, Fri & Sat 5pm–3am.

Habana ハバナ Minami 3, Nishi 6 📞 0112 19 8870, 🌐 mi -salsa.com/habana.html. On the second and third floors of the Tanuki-kōji shopping arcade, this Cuban-styled café-bar offers spicy chicken, rice entrées and lively Latin American music, plus occasional salsa parties. Daily 5.30pm–3am.

Kopitiam コピティアム Minami 3, Nishi 7 📞 0112 19 7773. Take an instant holiday from Japan at this fairly authentic Singaporean café-bar at the far west end of Tanuki-kōji shopping arcade. It's a relaxed place for a drink or light bite to eat. Mon & Wed–Fri 5.30pm–2am (Sat & Sun till 3am).

TK6 ティ・ケイ・シックス Minami 2, Nishi 6 📞 0112 72 6665, 🌐 tk6.jp. At the western end of the Tanuki-kōji arcade, this spacious and relaxed *gaijin*-run café-bar serves Aussie meat pies, salads and hefty burgers (around ¥1000), plus draught and craft beer. 📶 Daily 4pm–2am.

CLUBS

Alife エーライフ Minami 4, Nishi 6 📞 0115 33 0804, 🌐 alife.jp. One of the larger clubs in Sapporo, with a variety of DJ events, theme parties and special shows. Price varies depending on the night; Fri & Sat women pay ¥2000, men pay ¥3000; there's one drink included in entry. Daily 9pm–5am.

LGBT NIGHTLIFE IN SAPPORO

Sapporo has Japan's most visible gay and lesbian bar scene. Most bars are situated in the Susukino area, and Sound Lab Mole (see p.304) and Alife (see p.303) sometimes host gay dance nights. Like other places in Japan, Sapporo is currently fighting for official recognition of same-sex partnerships, and may be granted it soon.

Bar Orb バー オーブ 4F Shakō Kaikan Building, Minami 5, Nishi 2 📞 0902 42 7070, 🌐 www.barorb .com. On the scene since 2007, and run by English-speaker Kae, this cosy bar is great for meeting locals. Women only on Sat. Cover ¥300. Mon–Sat 6pm–2am.

Hearty Café ハーティ・カフェ 2F Dai-ichi Family Building, Minami 5, Nishi 7 📞 0115 30 6022. A relatively spacious bar where *gaijin* should receive a friendly welcome. Admission of ¥1500 includes one drink. Daily 8pm–3am, Fri & Sat till 4am. Closes randomly.

SA Building SAビル Minami 6, Nishi 6. The SA Building is home to more than twenty tiny gay bars, seating ten to twenty people in each. Most of the bars cater to men. Opening hours vary.

KING XMHU キングム Minami 7, Nishi 6 ☏0112 52 9912, ⓦkingxmhu.com. Reopened in 2016, this hugely popular nightclub has three floors decorated like a tribal temple, crazy entrance and all. Big names tend to play here and elaborate costumes are the norm. Keep tattoos covered and no flip-flops. Tickets up to ¥3500, depending on the show, but women usually get in for free. Mon–Sat 7pm–late.

Sound Lab Mole Sound Lab モール Nikō Building Basement, Minami 3, Nishi 4-24-10 ⓦmole-sapporo .jp. Basement club off the Tanuki-kōji arcade. It's open most days, either for live bands or club nights. Entry prices and hours vary depending on event.

ENTERTAINMENT

Sapporo Concert Hall Kitara 札幌コンサートホール Kitara 1-15 Nakajima-kōen ☏0115 20 2000, ⓦkitara -sapporo.or.jp. This concert hall in Nakajima Park hosts regular classical and other popular music concerts by Japanese and visiting overseas musicians.

Theater Kino シアターキノ 2F Grand Building, Minami 2, Nishi 6 ☏0112 31 9355, ⓦtheaterkino.net. A two-screen cinema showing mainly art-house films, with subtitles.

SHOPPING

Daiso ダイソ Minami 2, Nishi 2 ☏0112 21 5273, ⓦdaiso-sangyo.co.jp. Find everything you forgot to pack at this popular ¥100 store across five floors. Close to Ōdōri-kōen. Daily 10am–9pm.

Esta エスタ Kita 5, Nishi 2 ☏0112 13 2111, ⓦwww .sapporo-esta.jp. Another shopping complex next to Sapporo station; this one has Bic Camera, Uniqlo, a decent supermarket, and Jupiter, an import food store. *Ramen Kyowakoku* is on the tenth floor as well (see p.303). Daily 10am–9pm.

Kinokuniya Books 紀伊國屋 Kita 5, Nishi 5 ☏0112 31 2131, ⓦkinokuniya.co.jp. Just west of Sapporo Station, this has the best selection of English-language books and magazines. Daily 10am–9pm.

Sapporo Factory サッポロファクトリー Kita 2, Higashi 4 ☏0112 07 5000, ⓦsapporofactory.jp. This was the first brewery in the city, converted in 1993 into a shopping and entertainment complex. It now has dozens of outlets, with a huge selection of outdoor clothing and camping gear in the block furthest back from the street. Daily 10am–10pm.

Tanuki-kōji 狸小路商店街 Minami 3 ⓦtanukikoji .or.jp. The oldest shopping street in Hokkaidō, this covered shopping arcade, named after the beloved raccoon dog character, stretches for six blocks across Minami 3 and is well worth exploring.

Tōkyū Hands 東急ハンズ Minami 1, Nishi 6 ☏0112 18 6111, ⓦtokyu-hands.co.jp. A great place for souvenir shopping, with seven floors of hobby, DIY and lifestyle products. Daily 10am–8pm.

DIRECTORY

Consulates Australia (Kita 5, Nishi 6; ☏0112 42 4381); China (Minami 13, Nishi 23; ☏0115 63 5563); South Korea (Kita 2, Nishi 12; ☏0116 21 0288); Russia (Minami 14, Nishi 12; ☏0115 61 3171); US (Kita 1, Nishi 28; ☏0116 41 1115).
Hospital Sapporo City General Hospital, Kita 11, Nishi 13 (☏0117 26 2211).
Laundry Sukatto (コインランドリー スカット) Kita 4, Nishi 12-1.

Police The main police station is at Kita 1, Nishi 5 (☏0112 42 0110).
Post office The Central Post Office is at Kita 6, Higashi 1 (Mon–Fri 9am–8pm, Sat till 7pm, Sun till 5pm). There's also a branch in the Paseo shopping centre in the JR Sapporo Station complex (daily 10am–7pm, Sat & Sun till 5pm).

Otaru and around

小樽

The attractive port of **OTARU**, some 40km northwest of Sapporo, grew rich at the turn of the nineteenth century on the back of herring fishing and as a base for the modern development of Hokkaidō. Reminders of this wealth remain in the shape of scores of handsome, heritage-listed Meiji-era buildings. Parts of town are touristy, but to escape the crowds just hop on a bus to **Shukutsu**, where you'll find a couple of the best architectural examples from Otaru's glory days. In summer, take a **canal cruise** from Asakusa-bashi bridge to see the town from the water (see p.307). In February, Otaru hosts its **Snow Light Path Festival** at the same time as Sapporo, though on a much smaller scale, with small snow sculptures and lanterns running along the canal and the old train line.

If you have trouble finding somewhere to stay in Sapporo, Otaru makes an easy base for excursions back to Sapporo, or on to **Yoichi** if you're interested in the whisky distillery. However, it's also a pleasant place to spend a day or two in its own right. Otaru's romantic, antique atmosphere is best experienced beside the **Otaru Unga** (小樽運河), the portside canal lined with brick warehouses, particularly the section between Chūō-dōri, the main street heading towards the harbour from the train station, and parallel Nichigin-dōri.

Bank of Japan Otaru Museum

日本銀行旧小樽支店金融資料館, Nihon Ginkō Kū-Otaru Shiten Kinyū Shiryōkan • Nichigin-dōri, 1-11-16 Ironai ☎ 0134 21 1111, Ⓦ www3.boj.or.jp/otaru-m • Wed April–Nov 9.30am–5pm, Dec–Feb 10am–5pm; closed Wed • Free

The **Bank of Japan Otaru Museum**, a stone and brick structure dating from 1912 and in business till 2002, was designed by Kingo Tatsuno, the architect of the original red-brick Tokyo Station. Look for the striped owl keystones decorating the exterior – the birds are guardian deities of the Ainu. Inside, the 10.5m-high ceiling of the main banking hall looks as impressive today as it must have to Otaru's citizens back in the early twentieth century.

Tenguyama

天狗山 • **Ropeway** Daily 9am–9pm • Return ¥1140 • **Ski lift** Daily Dec–Feb 9am–8pm; March 9am–5pm • One-day rentals ¥3500 • ☎ 0134 33 7381, Ⓦ bit.ly/tenguyama-ropeway • Buses (¥220) run to the cable-car from platform #4 outside Otaru Station (18min)

For a wonderful view of Otaru and the bay, ride the ropeway (cable-car) up **Tenguyama**, southwest of the station, where the panoramic view has been designated one of the top three in Hokkaidō. There's a restaurant, chipmunk-feeding zone, an

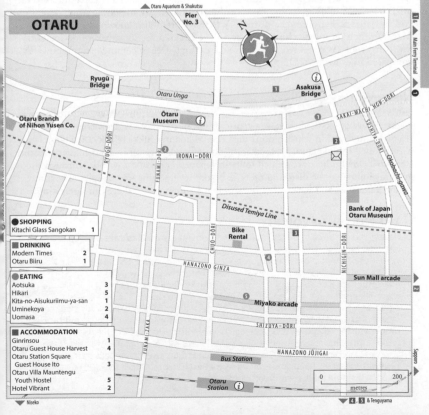

OTARU

Otaru Aquarium & Shukutsu

Pier No. 3

Ryugū Bridge

Otaru Unga

Otaru Branch of Nihon Yusen Co.

Ōtaru Museum

Asakusa Bridge

SAKAI-MACHI HON-DŌRI

SUSHIYA-DŌRI

Okobachi-gawa

RYUGŪ-DŌRI

FUNAMI-DŌRI

IRONAI-DŌRI

Main Ferry Terminal

Disused Temiya Line

Bank of Japan Otaru Museum

NICHIGIN-DŌRI

● SHOPPING	
Kitachi Glass Sangokan	1

■ DRINKING	
Modern Times	2
Otaru Biiru	1

● EATING	
Aotsuka	3
Hikari	5
Kita-no-Aisukuriimu-ya-san	1
Uminekoya	2
Uomasa	4

■ ACCOMMODATION	
Ginrinsou	1
Otaru Guest House Harvest	4
Otaru Station Square Guest House Ito	3
Otaru Villa Mauntengu Youth Hostel	5
Hotel Vibrant	2

CHŪO-DŌRI

Bike Rental

HANAZONO GINZA

Sun Mall arcade

Miyako arcade

SHIZUYA-DŌRI

FUNAMI-ZAKA

HANAZONO JŪJIGAI

Bus Station

Otaru Station

Sapporo

0   200
metres

Niseko

& Tenguyama

interesting archive outlining the history of ski materials and a free exhibition of more than seven hundred Tengu masks from all over Japan (Tengu is the long-nosed goblin after whom the mountain is named). There's also good skiing in winter with half a dozen runs varying in difficulty.

Nishin Goten Otaru Kihinkan Villa

にしん御殿小樽貴賓館 • 3-63 Shukutsu • Daily: 9am–5pm, Jan–March till 4pm • ¥1080 • ☎ 0134 61 7007, ⓦ otaru-kihinkan.jp • Bus #11 from Otaru Station heads to Shukutsu (20min); during April to mid-Oct, can be reached by Otaru Aquarium-bound boats from Otaru's Pier no. 3

From Otaru, it's about 5km to **Shukutsu** (祝津), home of the area's best historical site: the spectacular traditional Japanese villa **Nishin Goten Otaru Kihinkan Villa** (also known as Former Aoyama Villa). The Aoyama family, herring tycoons of the early twentieth century, spared little expense when they commissioned this beautiful wooden building, which is surrounded by ornamental gardens and contains exquisite screen paintings and antique pieces.

Nishin Goten

鰊御殿 • 3-228 Shukutsu • Daily: April–Oct 9am–5pm; late Oct–Nov 9am–4pm • ¥300 • ☎ 0134 22 1038, ⓦ bit.ly/herring-mansion • Bus #10 or #11 from Otaru Station heads to Shukutsu (20min); in summer (April to mid-Oct), you can hop on the Otaru Aquarium-bound boats from Otaru's Pier no. 3

By Shukutsu Harbour, a ten-minute walk from the Kihinkan Villa, you'll find several other heritage buildings dating from the herring boom era, including stone warehouses and the large-scale fishermen's dormitory **Nishin Goten** (also known as Herring Mansion) in a prominent hillside position overlooking the small harbour – look out for its red roof. As you'll see, this area is refreshingly free of commercial trappings compared to downtown Otaru.

Nikka Whisky Distillery

余市蒸溜所, Yoichi Jōryūsho • 7-6 Kurokawa-chō, Yoichi • Daily 9am–5pm; regular tours (1hr) • ¥300 • ☎ 0135 23 3131, ⓦ nikka.com/eng/distilleries • Yoichi is one stop west of Otaru on the train line; distillery is 1min walk from station

If you're interested in whisky, don't miss the fascinating **Nikka Whisky Distillery**. This was founded by **Taketsuru Masataka**, the son of a sake brewer in Hiroshima prefecture (see box below). There are guided **tours** in Japanese, or you can wander through the grounds following the distilling process, before trying some free samples. The film telling Taketsuru and Rita's story is particularly moving, and there's an interesting

---

THE WHISKY OF YOICHI

Having studied the painstaking art of sake brewing, **Taketsuru Masataka** developed a passion for Scotch whisky, and went to study the techniques of whisky-making in Scotland in 1918. While there, he met and married a young Scottish girl, Rita Cowan, despite the objections of her parents, and took her back with him when he returned to Japan two years later.

Taketsuru and Rita eventually established a **whisky distillery** (see above) in 1934 in Yoichi, which Taketsuru rightly realized had the necessary climate and conditions for whisky production. The distillery came under the control of the military in 1940, shortly after the release of its first distilled whisky, and for the duration of the war it made cheap **military ration whisky**. After the war, the company's investors insisted he focus the distillery's efforts on producing cheap, low-quality whisky, believing the Japanese population couldn't afford the luxury of high-class spirits. But Taketsuru continued to improve his methods on the side, and in 1964 was able to sell three grades of whisky for the first time. In 2008, Yoichi 20 Year Old was voted best **single malt** at the World Whisky Awards.

display of their personal possessions and Nikka advertising materials through the ages featuring, among others, Rod Stewart and Orson Welles.

ARRIVAL AND DEPARTURE

By train Limited express trains (¥1160) from Sapporo take 30–45min to reach Otaru JR Station. Local trains are slightly cheaper (¥640, roughly every 15min).

By ferry Ferries (☎0134 22 6191) from Niigata (see p.278) and Maizuru (north of Kyoto) dock at the ferry

OTARU AND AROUND

terminal, some 5km east of the train station. Regular buses run between the ferry terminal and the train station; a taxi will cost around ¥1000.

Destinations Maizuru (1 daily; 21hr); Niigata (1 daily except Mon; 19hr).

INFORMATION AND GETTING AROUND

Tourist information There's a helpful tourist office inside the train station (daily 9am–6pm; ☎0134 29 1333, ⓦcity.otaru.lg.jp), plus a couple of other tourist offices up by the canal – a larger one next to the Otaru Museum (daily 9am–6pm; 8pm in summer ☎0134 33 1661), and a tiny one by Asakusa Bridge (daily 9am–6pm; ☎0134 23 7740).

Canal cruise In the warmer months, you can get a good perspective of the town on a cruise from Asakusa-bashi bridge (40min loop; day cruise ¥1500, night cruise ¥1800; ☎0134 31 1733).

Bike rental You can rent bikes by the hour (¥400) or day (¥1500) at Charinko Otaru, a few minutes' walk from the train station. Luggage storage is free with bike rental.

ACCOMMODATION

★Ginrinsou 銀鱗荘 1-1 Sakura ☎0134 54 7010, ⓦginrinsou.com. Overlooking the bay, this beautiful Japanese-style ryokan offers eighteen luxurious tatami rooms, most with in-room onsen. Their outdoor open-air onsen is atop Cape Hiraiso, and a French restaurant, bar, and spa are on site. ☏ Half board **¥90,000**

Otaru Guest House Harvest 小樽ゲストハウスハーベスト 1-2-3 Nagahasi ☎0134 27 9736, ⓦotaru-harvest.com. This hospitable guesthouse is an easy 15min walk from the canal and offers a sun roof and terrace, shared kitchen and both Japanese-style rooms and bunk beds. ☏ Dorms **¥7500**, doubles **¥7000**

Otaru Station Square Guest House Ito 小樽駅前ゲストハウス Ito 2-3-13 Inaho ☎0134 61 1569, ⓦotaruito.com. This new budget hostel is just 5min from the JR station and very close to all the famous tourist sites. The

staff are very accommodating and have lots of suggestions for where to eat. Shared kitchen with free coffee and tea. ☏ Dorms **¥2800**, doubles **¥6600**

Otaru Villa Mauntengu Youth Hostel 小樽ヴィラ・マウンテングYH 2-13-1 Mogami ☎0134 33 7080, ⓦtengu.co.jp. You get great views of Otaru from this pleasant pension-style hostel near the cable-car up Tenguyama – take bus #9 from the station to the final stop. ☏ Breakfast and dinner extra (¥1680). Dorms **¥3350**, doubles **¥7600**

Hotel Vibrant ホテル ヴィブラント 1-3-1 Ironai ☎0134 31 3939, ⓦvibrant-otaru.jp. Occupying a former bank, the *Vibrant* offers good-value rooms with wooden floors. Rates include breakfast served in the soaring ex-banking hall. ☏ **¥6500**

EATING

Otaru is renowned for its **sushi and sashimi restaurants**. If unusual ice-cream flavours are more your thing, then Otaru may offer your only chance to tick off such flavours as sea urchin and *nattō* (fermented soyabeans), among others. Most of the restaurants on Sakai-machi Hon-dōri are overpriced, so aim for a side street.

Aotsuka 青塚 Opposite the harbour, Shukutsu ☎0134 22 8034, ⓦwww2.odn.ne.jp/aotuka. Drop by this simple waterside café, below the fishermen's dormitory, for

super-fresh fish dishes (around ¥1000). Herring, the fish that made the area's fortunes, are grilled outside. Daily 10am–7pm.

SAPPORO-OTARU WELCOME PASS

JR Hokkaidō's good-value **Sapporo-Otaru Welcome Pass** (¥1700), available to overseas visitors, includes a return train ticket and a one-day Sapporo subway ticket. Buy in Sapporo. Otaru itself offers the Otaru City Bus One-day Pass (¥750), which allows for unlimited rides on the regular bus lines and Otaru Stroller's Bus. This is sold at the bus terminal, Canal Plaza and tourist offices.

Hikari 光 Miyako-dōri Arcade ☎0134 22 0933. Good for a cup of coffee and cake for under ¥1000, this hushed café, open since 1933 and packed to the rafters with antique glass lamps and old ship steering wheels, is a rare treat and generally unmobbed by the tourist throng. 11am–6pm; closed Sat.

Kita-no-Aisukuriimu-ya-san 北のアイスクリーム屋さん 1-2-18 Ironai ☎0134 23 8983. Ice-cream parlour offering unique flavours such as squid, sea urchin and *nattō*, alongside more common ones. ¥300 for a single scoop, ¥500 for a double. Daily 9.30am–7pm (Oct–April till 4pm).

Uminekoya 海猫屋 2-2-14 Ironai ☎0134 34 8222, ⓦuminekoya.com. In an old warehouse covered in ivy, one block back from the canal, an enticing place for a drink or a light meal of Western or Japanese food. Pasta dishes are under ¥2000 and clam chowder soup is ¥650. 🛜 11.30am–2pm & 5.30–9pm; closed Tues.

★**Uomasa** 魚真 2-5-11 Inaho ☎0134 29 0259. You'll find scores of touristy sushi restaurants on Sakai-machi Hon-dōri, but this one on a side street closer to Otaru Station is a winner. Their fifteen-piece sushi set is great value at ¥2700, as are their various sashimi rice bowls. Mon–Sat noon–2pm & 4–9.30pm.

DRINKING

Modern Times モダンタイムス 1-9-6 Hanazono ☎0134 33 2025. Extremely hip and popular New York-style bar with a beautiful range of cocktails; it's easy to feel transported to a jazzier time. Mon–Thurs 7pm–1am, Fri–Sat 7pm–2am.

Otaru Biiru 小樽ビール 5-4 Minato-machi ☎0134 21 2323, ⓦotarubeer.com. A microbrewery beside the Otaru Canal turning out quaffable German-style ales; you can take a free 20min guided tour in English to see behind the scenes. Wurst sausage plates are ¥500, and pizzas are less than ¥1000. Daily 11am–11pm.

SHOPPING

Sakai-machi Hon-dōri (堺町本通り), which shadows the canal to the south, is an extremely touristy street but worth exploring, particularly for its many cut- and blown-glass shops.

Kitaichi Glass Sangokan 北一硝子三号館 7-26 Sakaimachi ☎0134 33 1993, ⓦkitaichiglass.co.jp. A good place to shop for the glass souvenirs for which Otaru is famous. Daily 9am–6pm.

Niseko

ニセコ

Around 70km south of Otaru is **NISEKO**, Japan's premier **winter resort**, with impressive amounts of perfect powder snow and top-class, interlinked ski fields. The resort hugs Mount Niseko Annupuri and faces the dormant volcano Mount Yōtei-san (also known as the Ezo Fuji for its resemblance to its more famous southern cousin). The village of **Hirafu** (比羅夫), close to the area's main town of **Kutchan** (倶知安), has seen the brunt of development, much of it through foreign investment. During the ski season (Dec–April) Hirafu booms as skiers jet in from as far afield as Melbourne, Hong Kong and London to take advantage of a fantastic range of facilities, including stylish accommodation and dining options. With the highest international population ratio in Japan, Niseko has become a foodie paradise, enticing visitors to return outside of the ski season.

Situated within the Niseko-Shakotan-Otaru Quasi National Park, the area makes an amazing **summer base** when it's far less crowded and becomes the focal point for many **adventure sports** including whitewater rafting, mountain biking and kayaking. Hiking is also a great summer option, as the trails on Yōtei-san and Annupuri offer spectacular panoramic views of the valleys below. Ask the tourist offices (see opposite) for hiking maps and accessible routes. For a fun cultural experience full of international food, dancing, and fireworks, check out the Kutchan Jaga Matsuri (potato festival) in early August.

ARRIVAL AND GETTING AROUND   NISEKO

In summer, public transport is scaled back and it gets a whole lot trickier (but not impossible) to get here – and to get around – without your own **car**.

SKIING IN NISEKO

Niseko United (@niseko.ne.jp) is the umbrella name for four separate ski resorts: **Niseko Annupuri** (ニセコアンヌプリ), **Niseko Village** (ニセコ町), **Niseko Grand Hirafu** (ニセコ グラン・ヒラフ) and **Niseko Hanazono** (花園). You can buy individual lift tickets from each of the resorts, but the smartest deal is to go for one of the All Mountain Passes (from ¥6300 for an 8hr ticket in season), which is issued as an electronic tag – you'll need to wave it at the barrier by each of the lifts – with a ¥1000 refundable deposit. Pass holders can ride the shuttle bus for free between all the resorts.

If you're looking to ski Niseko's **backcountry**, then hire a guide from either Niseko Adventure Centre (NAC; ☎0136 23 2093, @nac-web.com) or Niseko Outdoor Adventure Sports Club (NOASC; ☎0136 23 1688, @noasc.com), both in Hirafu; each employs English-speaking guides and also offers snowboarding, Telemark skiing and ice climbing in winter, and activities such as kayaking and whitewater rafting in summer. Other reputable and local ski tour operators include Black Diamond Tours (☎0136 55 5953, @blackdiamondtours.com) and Ski Japan (☎0136 22 4611, @skijapan.com).

Soaking in an **onsen** is a fine way to wind down after a day on the slopes. Try the baths at *Hirafutei* (daily 1–11pm; ¥800) on Hirafu-zaka Street, or *Yukoro* (ゆころ; daily 2–10pm; ¥700) at the southeastern end of Hirafu village.

For an excellent day option away from the tourist crowds, head to Rutsusu, considered Japan's largest ski resort with its steep slopes and tree coverage. By car, it's only 45 minutes from Niseko, but shuttle buses and tour operators run day-trips from Hirafu Welcome Centre.

By train Alight from the train at Kutchan and connect to Hirafu by bus (15min; free). Various return packages offered by JR from either Sapporo or Otaru make things really simple and can be unbeatable deals: for example, train, bus, ski-lift ticket and ski or snowboard rental for ¥5500 for the day – check with tourist information in Sapporo (see p.301) for what's available.

By bus Many buses run directly to the ski slopes from Sapporo and New Chitose Airport from around ¥2470 one-way (hourly; 2hr 30min). Good access information

is available at @nisekotourism.com. Shuttle buses crisscross the area during the tourist seasons, some of them free.

By car Peak Niseko Car Rental in Kutchan (@nisekocarrental.com) rent out 4WDs and can deliver to your accommodation.

By bike You can rent bikes from the main train stations, The Bicycle Corner in Niseko (@the-bicycle-corner.com) and Rhythm Niseko in Kutchan (@rhythmjapan.com), who can arrange tours and provide advice on your cycling plans.

INFORMATION

Tourist information Both Kutchan (daily 9am–6pm; ☎0136 22 3344) and Niseko stations (daily 9am–6pm; ☎0136 44 2468) have small tourist information booths where you might find English-speaking assistants. There's

also a welcome centre at the Grand Hirafu Parking Lot No. 1 (8.30am–6pm), where the bus from Kutchan terminates, but it's only open in the winter for skiing advice.

ACCOMMODATION

Niseko's best selection of **hotels** and **pensions** is clustered in Hirafu village. If you're looking for somewhere more peaceful, consider the options at nearby Annupuri and Niseko Village. There are plenty of **self-catering** apartments and chalets; apart from those listed below, try Hokkaidō Tracks (☎0136 21 6960, @hokkaidotracksaccommodation.com). Unless otherwise mentioned, all rates below are during high season in winter and include breakfast.

HIRAFU

Grand Papa グランパパ 163 Aza-Yamada ☎0136 23 2244, @niseko-grandpapa.com. Largish, convivial pension with an alpine theme: they even offer fondue dinners and karaoke. Free pick-up and shuttle to the slopes. 📶 **¥17,000**

Kimamaya by Odin ペンション気まま舎 170-248 Aza-Yamada ☎0136 23 2603, @kimamaya.com. French expat Nicolas Gontard has created a charming, modern

pension from the bones of an old minshuku, preserving the beams and cosy atmosphere. Meals are taken in the glass-sided *Barn* restaurant next door, which looks spectacular when lit up at night. On-site spa. 📶 **¥26,000**

★**Ki Niseko** 木ニセコ 183-43 Yamada ☎0136 21 2565, @kiniseko.com. With ski-in, ski-out access to the slopes, this is one of the newest hotels in Niseko, offering excellent views of Yōtei-san, on-site spa and beautiful onsen. It also hosts *An Dining*, a year-round restaurant

4

serving "modern Japanese" cuisine by an award-winning chef, and one of the few places that serves three meals per day. Trails or gondola for hiking Annupuri start from behind the hotel. ☞ ¥55,000

Niseko Tabi-Tsumugi Backpackers ニセコ宿たびつむぎ・アンヌプリ 44 Asahi Kutchan ☎ 0136 22 0539, ⓦ tabi-tsumugi.net/en. One of the few budget locations in the Niseko area, this peaceful hostel is close to Kutchan station. It has a fireplace and view of Mt. Yotei from the dining room. Breakfast extra ¥700. ☞ Dorms ¥3000, tatami rooms ¥10,000

The Vale Niseko ザ・ヴェール・ニセコ 166-9 Yamada ☎ 0136 22 0038, ⓦ thevaleniseko.com. Ski-in, ski-out self-catering apartments and hotel rooms are available at this well-designed contemporary complex with a lively restaurant/bar, relaxing onsen and tiny lap pool. ☞ ¥26,400

ANNUPURI, HANAZONO AND NISEKO VILLAGE

Black Diamond Lodge ブラックダイヤモンドロッジ 24-3 Niseko Village ☎ 0136 44 1144, ⓦ bdlodge.com. One of Niseko's best backpacker lodges, this comfortable place has a lively restaurant and bar. They also arrange various ski tours and packages as well as equipment rental

and car rental. ☞ Dorms ¥7500, tatami rooms ¥15,800

Hotel Kanro no Mori ホテル甘露の森 415 Aza-Niseko ☎ 0136 58 3800, ⓦ kanronomori.com. A 10min walk from the Annupuri Kokusai ski lifts, and surrounded by greenery, this appealing 78-room ryokan combines Japanese- and Western-style rooms. There's a large rotemburo, gym, and rates include two meals. ☞ ¥15,600

★The Lodge Moiwa 834 ロッジモイワ834 447-5 Aza-Niseko ☎ 050 3171 5688, ⓦ thelodgebytnf.com. Newly opened and partnered with North Face, this lodge offers "modern capsules" and ski-in, ski-out access to Moiwa Ski Resort. Breakfast and dinner are included in the price in winter only. ☞ Capsules ¥14,000

Niseko Annupuri Youth Hostel ニセコアンヌプリYH 479-4 Aza-Niseko ☎ 0136 58 2084, ⓦ youthhostel .or.jp. This charming European-style log-cabin pension with a roaring fire is the most convenient youth hostel for the slopes, located at Annupuri. Closed mid-Oct to early Dec. Bike rental available (¥1000). ☞ Dorms ¥5400

Niseko Weiss ニセコワイスホテル 79-2 Hanazono ☎ 0136 23 3311, ⓦ niseko-weiss.com. Discover the quieter side of Niseko resort before Hanazono gets overdeveloped with a stay at this stylish boutique hotel. There are both Japanese- and Western-style rooms, and a great set of onsen baths. ☞ ¥17,000

EATING

All of Niseko's hotels and pensions offer meals, but the area has such a good range of **restaurants**, **cafés** and **bars** that you can easily opt for a room only. Most restaurants tend to be open in the summer and winter tourist season only. At busier times at either time, it's a good idea to book, particularly at weekends. Check out Niseko Wine & Dine for more listings (ⓦ winedineniseko.com).

Abucha 2 阿武茶 2 191-29 Yamada ☎ 0136 22 5620, ⓦ abucha.net. At the main intersection in the village, this popular bakery, café and bar is a good option for breakfast or lunch away from the slopes. It can get extremely busy in the evenings, when a good range of standard Japanese dishes, including *nabe* stews (around ¥3500), is offered. ☞ Tues–Sun 8am–4pm & 6pm–1am.

Bang-Bang バンバン 188-24 Yamada ☎ 0136 22 4292, ⓦ niseko.or.jp/bangbang. Set back from the main drag, this convivial restaurant specializes in local fish dishes and *yakitori* (over thirty different types; ¥160–450). It's one of the few places where you're likely to be surrounded by more Japanese than *gaijin*. ☞ 5.30–11pm; closed Wed.

★Graubünden グラウビュンデン 132-26 Yamada ☎ 0136 23 3371, ⓦ graubunden.jp. This fantastic bakery-café is located on the way out of Hirafu towards Kutchan. They do a scrumptious selection of breakfasts, sandwiches and cakes (all for under ¥1200), with leaf tea served in tea cosy-covered pots. ☞ 8am–7pm; closed Thurs.

Kamimura 上村 Shiki Hotel, 190-4 Yamada ☎ 0136 21 2288, ⓦ kamimura-niseko.com. The full white tablecloth experience from the eponymous Michelin-starred chef who brings out the best from local produce. Set menus, which

may include dishes such as a snow crab and avocado salad and roasted *wagyu* beef with puréed local potato, kick off at ¥6500. Reservations essential. Winter Mon–Sat 6–11pm; check website for summer hours.

L'ocanda ロカンダ 76-12 Yamada ☎ 0136 55 8625. Family-run Italian restaurant offering delicious cakes and authentic Italian cuisine, including budget-friendly lunch sets. 11.30am–2pm, 6–10pm; closed Tues and some Wed.

Niseko Pizza ニセコピザ 167-3 Yamada ☎ 0136 55 5553, ⓦ nisekopizza.jp. In the basement of the J-Sekka complex, offering over twenty types of pizza and beautifully prepared home-made pasta – try the lasagne at ¥1800. Mon, Thurs & Fri 5–11pm, Sat & Sun 11am–11pm.

Saika 彩華 Kutchan ☎ 0136 22 0607. This cosy but extremely popular *yakitori* place is close to Kutchan station and an affordable option for dinner. Be sure to order some buttery *edamame*. Daily 6–11pm.

Tsubara Tsubara つばらつばら 132-14 Yamada ☎ 0136 23 1116. The soup curry at this friendly, relaxed bistro has a heat rating that runs from a bland zero to an on-fire twenty. It's good value too, with a meal under ¥1500. ☞ 11.30am–3pm, Sat & Sun 6–10pm; closed Wed.

DRINKING

Gyu+Bar ギュータス 167-21 Yamada ☎ 0136 23 1432, ⓦ gyubar.com. On the right, heading downhill from the main intersection, you'll find the entrance to this funky DJ bar as you go through a Coca-Cola vending-machine-turned door. Daily mid-Dec to March 5pm–midnight.

Niseko Brewing ニセコビール 4 Hon-dōri, Niseko ☎ 0136 55 5664, ⓦ nisekobeer.co.jp. This new microbrewery close to Niseko Station offers five excellent Niseko selections and lovely outdoor seating. Beer from ¥600. 4.30–10.30pm; closed Wed.

Toshiro's Bar トシローズバー 167-3 Yamada ☎ 0136 23 3377, ⓦ bit.ly/toshiros-bar. Original cocktails and over 250 bottles of liquor to chose from. 🛜 Daily April–Nov 6pm–1am; Mon–Sat Dec–March 5pm–2am.

Hakodate

函館

The first city on Hokkaidō for train travellers arriving through the Seikan Tunnel from Honshū is **HAKODATE**, 260km southwest of Sapporo. This attractive port was one of the first to open to foreign traders following the Japan–US amity treaty of 1854. Over the next few years, ten countries including Britain, Russia and the US established consulates in Hakodate, with both foreigners and rich Japanese building fancy wooden homes and elaborate churches on the steep hillsides. Many of these late nineteenth- and early twentieth-century buildings have been preserved, particularly in the **Motomachi** area, Hakodate's highlight.

Among the city's other draws are the lively fish and fresh produce market **Asa-ichi**; an outstanding exhibition on **Ainu** culture at the Hakodate City Museum of Northern Peoples; and the night view from the top of **Hakodate-yama**.

4

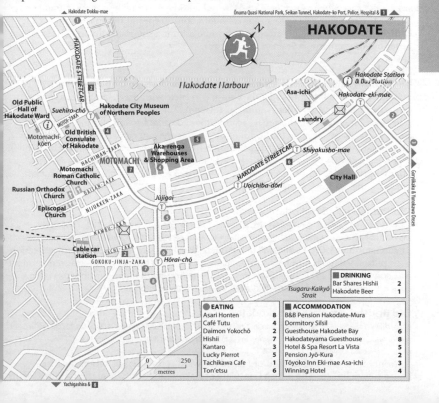

● EATING		■ ACCOMMODATION	
Asari Honten	8	B&B Pension Hakodate-Mura	7
Café Tutu	4	Dormitory Silsil	1
Daimon Yokochō	2	Guesthouse Hakodate Bay	6
Hishii	7	Hakodateyama Guesthouse	8
Kantaro	3	Hotel & Spa Resort La Vista	5
Lucky Pierrot	5	Pension Jyō-Kura	2
Tachikawa Cafe	1	Tōyoko Inn Eki-mae Asa-ichi	3
Ton'etsu	6	Winning Hotel	4

■ DRINKING	
Bar Shares Hishii	2
Hakodate Beer	1

HAKODATE PORT FESTIVAL

It's worth timing your visit to Hakodate for the **Hakodate Port Festival** (Aug 1–5; evenings), when the town revels in fireworks, food stalls, and its never-ending parade. The highlight is when twenty thousand people parade through town performing the "squid dance", an entertaining and easy jig where spectators are free to join in on the fun.

Hakodate-yama

函館山 • **Trails** May–Oct • Free • **Ropeway** (函館山ロープウェイ) Daily 10am–10pm, operating every 15min, April 24–Oct 16 till 9pm • ¥780 one-way, ¥1280 return • ☎ 0138 23 3105, ⊚ 334.co.jp • 10min uphill walk to ropeway from Jūjigai tram stop; direct buses to top of mountain from Hakodate Station (mid-April to early Nov daily 6–9pm, Sat & Sun also 1pm; 30min; ¥400); serpentine toll road open mid-April to mid-Nov, but closed to private vehicles 5–10pm

Looming over Hakodate is the 334m **Hakodate-yama**. On a clear day, the view from the summit is spectacular, but best of all is the night-time panorama. Rated as one of Japan's best night views, the twinkling lights of the port and the boats fishing for squid just off the coast create a magical scene. The energetic can climb to the summit along various trails, but most people opt for the **ropeway** (cable-car). Prepare to fight for a standing spot from sunset on.

Motomachi

元町

Heading downhill from Hakodate-yama, you'll find yourself in **Motomachi**. With its Western-style, late nineteenth-century architecture, combined with the steeply raked streets, it's easy when you're here to see why Hakodate is known as the San Francisco of Japan. The best thing to do is simply wander about, stopping to explore some of the **churches**, which are mainly free, though some ask for a suggested donation (few of the other buildings merit their entrance charges).

Churches

The most striking church in Motomachi is the white **Russian Orthodox Church** of 1916, a 700m walk uphill from Jūjigai tram stop, complete with green copper-clad onion domes and spires (daily 10am–5pm, Sat till 4pm, Sun 1–4pm; suggested donation ¥200). Inside, there's an impressive icon-festooned carved-wood altarpiece, and piped Russian choral music adds to the atmosphere. Nearby, you can admire the unusual modern architecture of the **Episcopal Church** from the outside (not open to the public), while, slightly downhill, the Gothic-style **Motomachi Roman Catholic Church** (daily 10am–4pm, Sat & Sun from noon; free) is worth a look for its decoration, which is based on the Stations of the Cross.

Old Public Hall of Hakodate Ward

旧函館区公会堂, Kyū Hakodate-ku Kōkaidō • 11-13 Motomachi • Daily 9am–5pm, April–Oct till 7pm • ¥300, or ¥720 including the Old British Consulate of Hakodate and Hakodate City Museum of Northern Peoples • ☎ 0138 22 1001, ⊚ www.zaidan-hakodate.com/koukaido

The extraordinary **Old Public Hall of Hakodate Ward** is a sky-blue and lemon confection with pillars, verandas and fancy wrought-iron and plaster decoration. This replacement was completed in 1910 after a fire destroyed the original hall, and is now used as a concert hall. A list of concerts is posted on the outside gate.

Old British Consulate of Hakodate

函館市旧イギリス領事館, Hakodate-shi Kyū Igirisu Ryōjikan • 33-14 Motomachi • Daily 9am–5pm, April–Oct till 7pm • ¥300, or ¥720 including the Old Public Hall of Hakodate Ward and Hakodate City Museum of Northern Peoples • ☎ 0138 27 8159, ⊚ hakodate-kankou.com/british

In front of the Old Public Hall of Hakodate Ward is the small Motomachi Park, beneath which is the **Old British Consulate of Hakodate**, from where the Empire's affairs in Hokkaidō were looked after from 1859 to 1934. The cream-and-blue building now houses a ho-hum museum, the twee *Victorian Rose Tea Restaurant* and a gift shop.

Hakodate City Museum of Northern Peoples

函館市北方民族資料館, Hakodate-shi Hoppō Minzoku Shiryōkan • 21-7 Suehiro-chō • Daily 9am–5pm, April–Oct till 7pm • ¥300, or ¥720 including the Old Public Hall of Hakodate Ward and the Old British Consulate of Hakodate • ☎ 0138 22 4128, ⓦ www.zaidan-hakodate.com/hoppominzoku

The **Hakodate City Museum of Northern Peoples** is in an old bank down Motoi-zaka, which leads away from the consulate. The museum's superb collection of artefacts relating to the **Ainu** and other races across Eastern Siberia and the Alaskan islands has clear, English captioning and is well worth the entrance fee. Some of the clothes on display are astonishing – look out for the Chinese silk robe embroidered with dragons, an example of the types of items traded between China, the islanders of Sakhalin and the Ainu.

Asa-ichi

朝市 • Daily 6am–noon, May–Dec from 5am • ⓦ hakodate-asaichi.com

No visit to Hakodate is complete without dropping by the atmospheric but touristy **Asa-ichi**, the morning market immediately to the west of the train station. Even if you arrive at the relatively late hour of 9am, there's still plenty to see at the hundreds of tightly packed stalls lining the streets. Old ladies in headscarves squat amid piles of vegetables and flowers in the central hall, and huge, alien-like red crabs, squid, sea urchin and musk melons are the local specialities. If you're keen, line up to catch your own squid from a huge tank to then be cut up for sashimi. Be sure to sample seafood atop a bowl of ramen or rice before you leave (see p.315). Some stores stay open till 3pm.

Goryōkaku

五稜郭 • 43-9 Goryōkaku-chō • **Viewing tower** Daily: April 21–Oct 20 8am–7pm; Oct 21–April 20 9am–6pm • ¥840 • ☎ 0138 51 4785, ⓦ goryokaku-tower.co.jp • **Open-air theatre** Late July to mid-Aug • Check website for performance schedules and tickets • ¥1000 donation • ⓦ yaqaiqeki.com • 10min walk north of the Goryōkaku-kōen-mae tram stop

The remains of **Goryōkaku**, a late nineteenth-century Western-style fort, lie some 3km northeast of the station. The star-shaped fort was built to protect Hokkaidō against attack from Russia. In the event, however, it was used by Tokugawa Yoshinobu's naval forces in a last-ditch battle to uphold the shogun against the emperor in the short-lived civil war that ushered in the Meiji Restoration of 1869. The Emperor's victory is celebrated each year in mid-May with a period costume **parade**.

What's left of the fort today – a leafy park planted with 1600 cherry trees, the moat and outer walls – looks best 90m up, from the inelegant **viewing tower** by the main entrance. On weekend evenings in the summer, open-air plays about Hakodate's history are performed enthusiastically by various amateur groups.

Yunokawa

湯の川 • 16-5 Yunokawa-chō • **Yunokawa** Onsen prices from ¥400 up • ☎ 0138 57 8988, ⓦ hakodate-yunokawa.jp/lan/en.html • **Hakodate Tropical Garden** 函館市熱帯植物園 • 1-15 Yunokawa-chō • Daily: April–Oct 9.30am–6pm; Nov–March 9.30am–4.30pm • ¥300 • ☎ 0138 57 7833, ⓦ hako-eco.com

While most locals head to Yachigashira for their onsen fix, **Yunokawa** is one of the largest in Hokkaidō, with about seventeen hot spring facilities. Several hotels offer onsen in smart settings, but for a more traditional Japanese experience, try the baths at Kappo Ryokan Wakamatsu. Yunokawa's proximity to the airport makes it a convenient stopover, if anything for a rest at the free footbath directly in front of the tram station. Surprisingly, the real draw of Yunokawa is its residential monkeys, occupying a space at Hakodate Tropical Botanical Gardens. Just like in Nagano, it is

4

here that Japanese macaque monkeys enjoy their own onsen in winter, much to the delight of gawking spectators.

ARRIVAL AND INFORMATION

By plane Hakodate's airport (☎0138 57 8881) lies 8km east of the city; buses (¥410) take roughly 20min from there to Hakodate Station.

Destinations Kansai International (3 daily; 1hr 45min); Nagoya (3 daily; 1hr 35min); Okadama (14 daily; 40min); Okushiri (2 daily; 30min); Sapporo New Chitose (2 daily; 40min); Sapporo Ikadama (6 daily; 45min); Tokyo (11 daily; 1hr 25min).

By train The Shinkansen now connects mainland Japan with Shin-Hakodate Hokuto Station. Local and express trains then connect on to the central Hakodate Station, located on the eastern side of the harbour and where trains terminate.

Destinations Aomori (hourly; 2hr); Hachinohe (hourly; 2hr); Ōnuma-kōen (9 daily; 20min); Sapporo (15 daily; 4hr); Tokyo (10 daily; 4hr).

HAKODATE

By bus The bus station is in front of the train station. Ask at the tourist office for reservations.

Destinations Ōnuma-kōen (3 daily; 1hr 10min); Sapporo (14 daily; 5hr 30min).

By ferry Ferries dock at Hakodate-kō Port, some 4km north of Hakodate Station. A shuttle bus runs from No. 11 bus stop to the Tsugaru Kaikyō Ferry Terminal (5 daily) for ¥310; Bus lines #101, #122 and #123 run by the terminals (¥240 or ¥260, depending on which ferry you alight from); A taxi from the port to the city centre is around ¥2000.

Destinations Aomori (8 daily; 3hr 40min); Ōma (3 daily; 1hr 30min).

Tourist information The helpful Hakodate tourist office (daily 9am–7pm, Nov–March till 5pm; ☎0138 23 5440, ⊛hakodate-kankou.com, ⊛hakodate.travel) is inside Hakodate Station.

GETTING AROUND

By tram There are two lines, both starting at the onsen resort of Yunokawa (湯の川), east of the city. Each runs past Goryōkaku and the train station before diverging at the Jūjigai stop in Motomachi. From here, tram #5 heads west to Hakodate Dokku-mae (函館どっく前), while tram #2 continues further south to Yachigashira (谷地頭) on the eastern side of Hakodate-yama. Trams run from about 7am–10pm.

By bus Useful buses include the shuttle bus from Hakodate Station to the Hakodate-yama ropeway and the Goryōkaku Tower; and the "LCSA (Lexa) Motomachi" bus, which operates on a continuous loop between Hakodate Station and the Bay Area/Motomachi.

Tickets One-day (¥1000) and two-day passes (¥1700) can be bought from the tourist office for unlimited use of both the trams and most city buses. These passes, only worth buying if you plan to tour extensively around town, also cover the bus service up Hakodate-yama. The ¥600 all-day tram ticket is better value; individual tram trips cost ¥210–250.

Car rental Eki Rent-a-Car (☎0138 22 7864, ⊛www.ekiren.co.jp) is next to Hakodate Station.

ACCOMMODATION

Hotels are busiest during the summer, when you'll need to book ahead. **Prices** at most places drop considerably in winter, and many have good deals for online bookings, so it's worth shopping around.

B&B Pension Hakodate-Mura B&B ペンション はこだて村 16-12 Suehiro-chō ☎0138 22 8105, ⊛bb-hakodatemura.com. Appealing B&B just off the waterfront at the start of Motomachi, offering both Western- and Japanese-style rooms, with most sharing a common bathroom. Western breakfast is ¥840. 🛜 <u>¥9500</u>

Dormitory Silsil ドミトリーシルシル 20-34 Hon-dori ☎0138 54 7773, ⊛silsiru346.web.fc2.com. Probably the cheapest accommodation in town, this hostel is a bit out of town but within easy access to the Goryōkaku area. It's nothing fancy, but there's a communal kitchen and bike rental available. 🛜 Dorms <u>¥2100</u>

Guesthouse Hakodate Bay ゲストハウス函館ベイ 12-5 Ōte-machi ☎0138 76 7667. Friendly budget accommodation located a minute from Shiyakushomae tram station. Communal kitchen. 🛜 Dorms <u>¥3240</u>, doubles <u>¥7000</u>

Hakodateyama Guesthouse 函館山ゲストハウス 17-5 Sumiyoshi-chō ☎080 4503 9044, ⊛hakog-e.cloud-line.com. This guesthouse, located at the foot of Hakodate-yama, offers a nice mix of Western and Japanese standards, with its own onsen, cosy lounge and even a record-listening space. It's within walking distance of Yachigashira tram station and Yachigashira Onsen. 🛜 Dorms <u>¥2980</u>, doubles <u>¥6800</u>

★**Hotel & Spa Resort La Vista** ラビスタ函館ベイ 12-6 Toyokawa-chō ☎0138 23 6111, ⊛bit.ly/hotelspa-lavista. With great views of the harbour and Hakodate-yama, Hakodate's luxury hotel offers elegantly designed rooms and a fantastic set of rooftop baths. Good internet deals and very affordable rates out of season. 🛜 <u>¥22,000</u>

Pension Jyō-Kura じょう蔵 9-8 Ō-machi ☎0138 27 6453, ⊛j-kura.com. Despite one or two slightly twee overtones, this pension is more than compensated by very obliging owners. It has a homely common area with a wood-burning stove where breakfast is served (¥800), and a choice of Western- or Japanese-style rooms. 🛜 **¥11,000**

Tōyoko Inn Hakodate Eki-mae Asa-ichi 東横INN函館駅前朝市 22-7 Ōte-machi ☎0138 23 1045, 🌐 toyoko-inn.com. Only a 2min walk from the station,

this branch of the handy chain is right next to the Asa-ichi morning market. 🛜 **¥8800**

Winning Hotel ウイニングホテル 22-11 Suehiro-chō ☎0138 26 1111, 🌐 hotel-winning.jp. Located in a modern but Art Deco-styled building facing the harbour; the rooms are pleasantly decorated, large, and some have lovely views. 🛜 **¥15,000**

EATING

The best places to feast on fresh **seafood** are the sushi and *donburi* restaurants in the morning market's Donbori Yokochō or the ones scattered near Hakodate Station. **Local specialities** include crab (*kani*), squid (*ika*) and ramen noodles in a salty soup topped with seafood.

★**Asari Honten** 阿さ利本店 10-11 Hōrai-chō ☎0138 23 0421. The old wooden building and tatami-floor dining rooms of this restaurant are just part of the pleasure – the rest is in the quality of the *sukiyaki*, their speciality dish, using meat fresh from the butcher downstairs and cooked in front of you. Lunch is a bargain at ¥1400–1600; set menus at other times start at ¥2200. Reservations recommended. 11am–9.30pm; closed Wed.

Café Tutu カフェトウトウ 13-5 Suehiro-chō ☎0138 27 9199. This trendy café-bar and live music space, behind one of the renovated brick warehouses by the harbour, is a quiet place to relax over gourmet coffee and cake. 🛜 Mon–Wed, Fri–Sun 11.30am–10pm.

Daimon Yokochō 大門横丁 7-5 Matsukaze-chō. ☎0138 243 0033, 🌐 hakodate-yatai.com. Choose from 26 *yatai* (stalls) serving everything from *oden* and sushi to ramen and *yakitori*. It's an atmospheric place and a good spot to drop by for a beer and a small plate of food. 🛜 Daily 5pm–midnight.

Hishii ひし伊 9-4 Hōrai-chō ☎0138 27 3300, 🌐 hishii .info. Near the Hōrai-chō tram stop, this elegant ivy-draped 1920s wooden building houses a serene teashop and antique kimono shop, plus there's a tatami area on the

second floor. They also run the nearby *Bar Shares Hishii* (see below). 🛜 Daily 10am–6pm.

Kantaro 函太郎 25-17 Goryōkaku-chō ☎0138 522 5522, 🌐 kantaro-hakodate.com. A conveyor-belt sushi restaurant chain known for their "gourmet" sushi; conveniently priced, and the fish is caught the same morning. Most plates cost ¥200–500. Daily 11am–10pm.

Lucky Pierrot ラッキーピエロ 8-11 Suehiro-chō ☎0138 23 2300, 🌐 luckypierrot.jp. One of seventeen branches of the hamburger and curry chain, this one just west of the Jūjigai tram stop is heavily Christmas-themed. Try the Chinese chicken burger (¥350), which has been voted as "Japan's best burger." Daily 10.30am–midnight (Sat till 1.30am).

★**Tachikawa Café** とん悦 15-15 Benten-chō ☎0138 22 0340, 🌐 tachikawacafe.com. Close to the Motomachi area, this nearly 200-year-old building houses an elegant café serving up artisan drinks, desserts, as well as seafood and venison fare. Wood accents and open-air seating add to the ambience. 🛜 Tues–Sun 10am–6pm.

Ton'etsu とん悦 22-2 ☎0138 22 2448, 🌐 tonetsu.com. Convivial *tonkatsu* restaurant with tatami seating and a good range of reasonably priced set meals from ¥1100, including free coffee. Daily 11.30am–9pm.

DRINKING

Goryōkaku is the city's main **drinking** area, although you'll also find several bars around the converted warehouses in Motomachi.

Bar Shares Hishii バーシェアーズヒシイ 27-1 Motomachi ☎0138 22 5584. Brought to you by the same owners as *Hishii*, this small but elegant bar is a relaxing place for an evening drink. Mon–Sat 8pm–2am.

Hakodate Beer はこだてビール 5-22 Ōte-machi

☎0138 23 8000, 🌐 hakodate-factory.com/beer. This cavernous brewery pub/restaurant, where there's sometimes live music, serves the local *ji-biiru* – sample four of their brews for ¥1300. 11am–3pm & 5–10pm; closed Wed.

DIRECTORY

Hospital Hakodate City Hospital, 1-10-1 Minato-chō (☎0138 43 2000).

Laundry Aqua Garden Hotel, 19-13 Ōtemachi, 5min walk south of the station, has a coin laundry (daily 7am–midnight).

Police The main police station is on the western side of

Goryōkaku-kōen. For emergency numbers, see p.71.

Post office The closest post office to the station, 7-18 Wakamatsu-chō, is open Mon–Fri 9am–5pm. The Central Post Office, 1-6 Shinkawa-chō, is a 10min walk east of Hakodate Station (Mon–Fri 9am–7pm, Sat & Sun 9am–5pm).

4

Ōnuma Quasi National Park

大沼国定公園, Ōnuma Kokutei Kōen

Just 29km north of Hakodate, the serene **Ōnuma Quasi National Park** can easily be visited in a day but is worth considering as an overnight stop. Of the park's three **lakes**, the largest and most beautiful is **Ōnuma**, carpeted with water lilies and containing more than one hundred tiny islands, many linked by humpback bridges. The view from the lake towards the 1133m jagged peak of the dormant volcano of **Komaga-take** (駒ヶ岳) is one of the most breathtaking scenes in Japan.

Ōnuma is popular with tour groups, but they are usually herded into sightseeing boats, leaving the walking paths around the lake and islands quiet for strolls. **Cycling** is another good way of exploring; it takes just over an hour to circumnavigate the lake. **Hikers** can also tackle the **volcano**, which has two main routes, both taking around two and a half hours to complete. The Ōnuma area is scattered with numerous **cafés**, including on the bike path, but some of the best food can be found at nearby farm restaurants.

ARRIVAL AND INFORMATION   ŌNUMA QUASI NATIONAL PARK

By train Local trains from Hakodate to Ōnuma-kōen Station take 50min, while limited express trains take 30min.

By bus There are daily buses from Hakodate despite the train being faster (3 daily; 1hr 10min).

Tourist information Information is available from

Ōnuma International Communication Plaza (daily 8.30am–5.30pm; ☎ 0138 67 2170, ⓦ onumakouen.com) next to the train station.

Bike rental Bikes can be rented (around ¥500/hr or ¥1000/day) from numerous shops around the station.

ACCOMMODATION

Higashi-Ōnuma Yaeijō campsite 東大沼野営場 Higashi-Ōnuma ☎ 0138 67 3477. On the eastern shore of Ōnuma Lake, with toilets, running water and firepits. A small café and bike rental are across the street. The nearest station is Chōshi-guchi, around 6km east of Ōnuma-kōen Station. Open late April–Oct. <u>Free</u>

Ōnuma Kōen Youth Hostel 大沼公園YH   4-3

Ikusa-gawa ☎ 0138 67 4126, ⓦ youthhostel.or.jp. This friendly hostel, a 3min walk from Ikedaen Station, offers bunk-bed dorms, good breakfasts and dinners (extra ¥1950), and activities such as canoeing, cross-country skiing and ice fishing, depending on the season. ⓦ Dorms <u>¥4050</u>, singles <u>¥5130</u>

Shikotsu-Tōya National Park

支笏洞爺国立公園, Shikotsu-Tōya Kokuritsu Kōen

Follow the picturesque coastal road or rail line around Uchiura Bay from Hakodate and you'll reach the eastern side of the **SHIKOTSU-TŌYA NATIONAL PARK**, one of Hokkaidō's prettiest lakeland and mountain areas, but also the most developed, thanks to its proximity to Sapporo, some 80km to the north. Both the park's two main caldera lakes – **Tōya-ko** to the west and **Shikotsu-ko** to the east – are active volcanoes and surrounded by excellent hiking trails. Between the two lakes lies **Noboribetsu Onsen**, Hokkaidō's largest hot-spring resort, worth visiting to soak up the otherworldly landscape of bubbling and steaming **Jigokudani** (Hell Valley).

Tōya-ko

洞爺湖

The beautiful caldera lake of **Tōya-ko** is punctuated dead centre by the conical island of **Nakajima**. Its southern shore is home to the tired-looking resort **Tōya-ko Onsen** (洞爺湖温泉), where you'll find most accommodation and local transport connections. Between late April and October, spectacular fireworks (nightly 8.45–9.05pm) illuminate the lake. Otherwise, the area has myriad shore-side areas perfect for barbecues and impromptu camping. Pretty as the location is, the best reason for visiting Tōya-ko is to see the nearby active volcano **Usu-zan**, around 2km south, and its steaming "parasite volcano" **Shōwa Shin-zan** (昭和新山; see box, p.318).

Usu-zan

有珠山 • Ropeway (有珠山ロープウェイ) daily: check website for ropeway times • ¥1500 return • ☎ 0142 75 3113, ⓦ wakasaresort .com • The ropeway station is at the end of the row of tourist shops by Shōwa Shin-zan; buses run from the bus station at Tōya-ko Onsen to Shōwa Shin-zan (4/day; 15min; ¥340 one-way)

Usu-zan remains frighteningly active; the last eruption, on March 31, 2000, coated Tōya-ko Onsen with volcanic dust and forced a three-month evacuation. To look directly into the beast, ride the ropeway to a viewing platform 300m from the crater, which also provides stunning vistas over Shōwa Shin-zan, Tōya-ko and out to sea.

Tōyako Visitor Centre and Volcanic Science Museum

洞爺湖ビジターセンター, Tōya-ko Bijitā Sentā • 火山科学館, Kazan Kagaku-kan • 142-5 Tōyako Onsen • Daily 9am–5pm; till 6pm late April–Oct • Visitor centre free; museum ¥600 • ☎ 0142 75 2555, ⓦ toyako-vc.jp • Buses for Nishiyama from Tōya-ko Onsen bus station (every 20min; 3min; ¥160 one-way)

The area damaged by the eruptions – known as the **Konpira Promenade** (daily mid-April to mid-Nov; free) – is nerve-shreddingly close to town. In front of it, in the **Tōyako Visitor Centre** building, which houses the **Volcanic Science Museum**, you can watch a seat-tremblingly loud film about that eruption and other explosions on the mountain. You can also take a bus to the **Nishiyama Crater Promenade** (西山火口散策路洞爺; daily mid-April to mid-Nov; free), a 1.3km boardwalk across the recent break in the earth's crust that ends at an eerily abandoned elementary school.

Onsen

The best way to enjoy the positive side of volcanic activity is to take an **onsen** dip. In addition to the twelve free footbaths around town, most of the lakeside hotels allow

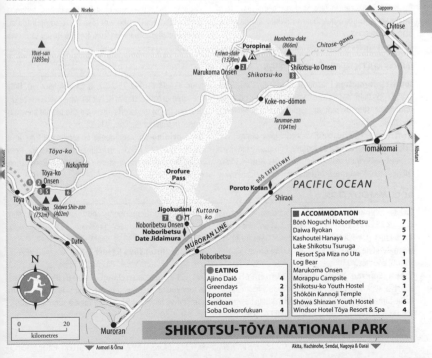

● EATING	
Ajino Daiō	4
Greendays	2
Ippontei	3
Sendoan	1
Soba Dokorofukuan	4

■ ACCOMMODATION	
Bōrō Noguchi Noboribetsu	7
Daiwa Ryokan	5
Kashoutei Hanaya	7
Lake Shikotsu Tsuruga Resort Spa Miza no Uta	1
Log Bear	1
Marukoma Onsen	2
Morappu Campsite	3
Shikotsu-ko Youth Hostel	1
Shōkōin Kannoji Temple	7
Shōwa Shinzan Youth Hostel	6
Windsor Hotel Tōya Resort & Spa	4

SHIKOTSU-TŌYA NATIONAL PARK

BIRTH OF A VOLCANO

On December 28, 1943, severe earthquakes began shaking the area around Usu-zan and continued to do so until September 1945. In the intervening period, a new lava dome rose out of the ground, sometimes at the rate of 1.5m a day. By the time it had stopped growing, **Shōwa Shin-zan**, the "new mountain" named after the reigning emperor, stood 405m above sea level. The wartime authorities were desperate to hush up this extraordinary event for fear that the fledgling mountain would serve as a beacon for US bomber planes.

Fortunately, Shōwa Shin-zan's daily growth was carefully documented by local postmaster and amateur volcanologist **Mimatsu Masao**. After the war, Mimatsu bought the land on which the mountain stood, declaring, "I purchased the volcano to continue my research uninterrupted. I did not buy it to make money. Nor did I buy it for tourists to gawk at." His efforts were rewarded in 1958 when Shōwa Shin-zan was made a Special Natural Treasure by the government.

Nevertheless, Mimatsu never turned away tourists – but nor did he charge them admission, a practice still upheld. The **Mimatsu Masao Memorial Hall** (三松正夫記念館; daily 8am–5pm; ¥300), tucked behind the ghastly row of gift shops at the base of the volcano, contains an interesting collection of exhibits on the history of the fledgling volcano.

day visitors – try the *Tōya Sun Palace* (洞爺サンパレス; 7-1 Tōyako-onsen; daily 10am–3pm; ¥800), which features two floors with more than twenty different soaking pools, some with lake views, and a large swimming pool with artificial waves and a water slide, for which you'll need your bathing costume. There are also nice rooftop baths at the *Tōya-kohantei* (daily 11am–5pm for indoor view bath and 1.30–5pm for open-air bath; ¥800), which is closer to the bus station.

ARRIVAL AND DEPARTURE   TŌYA-KO

By train Trains run to Tōya Station, on the coast, from where you can get a bus (hourly; 20min) up the hill to Tōya-ko Onsen.

By bus There are buses to Tōya-ko Onsen from Sapporo (4 daily; 3hr). Buses pull in at the Dōnan bus station, a 2min walk from the shore of Tōya-ko. From April to Oct, buses (4 daily; 15min) run from Tōya-ko Onsen to Shōwa Shin-zan.

INFORMATION AND ACTIVITIES

Tourist information The tourist office (daily 9am–5pm; ☎0142 75 2446, ⊛laketoya.com) is in front of the bus station. Be sure to pick up some onsen-cooked eggs sold there.

Wi-fi Free wi-fi is available in the entire town centre.

Lake cruises For a cruise on the lake, hop aboard the kitsch castle-styled ferry *Espoir* (daily: April–Oct 8am–4.30pm, sailings every 30min; Nov–March 9am–4pm, sailings every hour; ¥1420; ☎0142 75 2137, ⊛toyakokisen.com). Only the summer cruises stop at Nakajima, where you can see Ezo deer grazing in the forests. There are also nightly fireworks cruises in summer (8.30pm; ¥1600).

Horseriding You can arrange horseriding at Lake Toya Ranch (☎0142 73 2455, ⊛jphorseriding.com/toya; from ¥4860/40min) on the west side of the lake. Reservation required.

ACCOMMODATION

Daiwa Ryokan 大和旅館 105 Tōya-ko Onsen ☎0142 75 2415, ⊛daiwa-ryokan.jp. A popular choice for budget travellers, this traditional ryokan offers Japanese-style breakfast and has its own onsen. Singles **¥5200**, doubles **¥9200**

Shōwa Shinzan Youth Hostel 昭和新山YH 103 Sōbetsu-onsen ☎0142 75 2283, ⊛youthhostel.or.jp. At the turn-off to Shōwa Shin-zan, and a 10min bus or taxi ride (¥1300) from Tōya-ko Onsen, a hostel with bunk-bed dorms, shared tatami rooms and their own onsen, plus rental bikes (¥1000/day). Breakfast and dinner extra (¥2100). ⊛ Dorms **¥3800**, doubles **¥8600**

Windsor Hotel Tōya Resort & Spa ザ・ウィンザーホテル洞爺リゾート&スパ Shimizu Tōyako-chō ☎0142 73 1111, ⊛windsor-hotels.co.jp. If it's unfettered luxury you're after, head to the west side of the lake to this stylish hotel, which hosted the G8 summit in 2008. ⊛ **¥36,960**

EATING

Greendays グリーンディズ 40 Tōya-ko Onsen ☎ 0142 82 6553. For a coffee break on an outdoor terrace, stop by this café/bar located in front of *Nonokaze Resort*. Mon–Sat 11am–11pm.

Ippontei 一本亭 78 Tōya-ko Onsen ☎ 0142 75 3475, ⓦ 43yg.net/ippontei. Beloved ramen shop to the locals, so be sure to get here early enough as it sometimes sells out of their speciality: black soy sauce

ramen. Tues–Sun 11.30am–2pm, 6–8pm.

Sendoan 仙堂庵 144 Tōya-ko Onsen ☎ 0142 75 4111. This restaurant has standard Japanese food but fantastic lake views – try the *sansai-soba* (mountain vegetable noodles) for ¥850. Afterwards, sample their various baked goods in the shop downstairs for dessert or takeaway presents. Daily 11am–7pm.

Noboribetsu Onsen

登別温泉

East around the coast from Tōya-ko, and nestling amid lush green mountain slopes ripped through by a bubbling cauldron of volcanic activity, is **NOBORIBETSU ONSEN**. Hokkaidō's top hot-spring resort may be peppered with lumpen hotel buildings and devil-themed souvenir shops, but its dramatic landscape is definitely worth seeing, and there's ample opportunity for some serious onsen relaxation.

Jigokudani

地獄谷 • Hell Valley • A 10min walk from the bus station up Gokuraku-dōri

Noboribetsu's main street leads up to a roadside **shrine** guarded by two brightly painted statues of demons. A bit further up the street, you will find the entrance to **Jigokudani**, a steaming, lunar-like valley created by an ancient volcanic eruption. It takes one or two hours to explore the area, wandering along wooden pathways through a landscape of rusty red rocks, streaked green and white by mineral deposits, ending up at **Ōyu-numa** (大湯沼), a malevolent-looking hot-water lake. Afterwards, you can soothe your feet in a natural footbath. Bring good footwear, as the paths can be slippery.

All the hotels draw water from Jigokudani (ten thousand tonnes are pumped out daily), and many have built elaborate **baths** so that guests can enjoy the water's therapeutic benefits. The tourist offices (see opposite) provide a list of the baths open to the public. One exceptional facility is at *Dai-ichi Takimoto-kan* hotel, which has thirty indoor and outdoor baths (daily: 9am–4pm, ¥2000; 4–6pm, ¥1500).

Noboribetsu Date Jidai-mura

登別伊達時代村 • 53-1 Naka Noboribetsu-chō • Daily: April–Oct 9am–5pm; Nov–March 10am–4pm • ¥2900 • ☎ 0143 83 3434, ⓦ edo-trip.jp

If you have time, skip the village's deplorable bear park and visit the whacky Edo-era theme park **Noboribetsu Date Jidai-mura** to step back in time and watch costumed *oiran* (top-ranked courtesans), theatre shows, ninja performances and samurai shows.

DISCOVERING THE AINU

For an idea of how Ainu live today, head to **Nibutani** (二風谷), some 50km due east of the port of Tomakomai on Route 237 – the only place in Japan where they form a majority of the community. A fascinating personal collection of Ainu artefacts is on display in the charming **Kayano Shigeru Nibutani Ainu Museum** (萱野茂二風谷アイヌ資料館; 61 Nibutani; April–Nov daily 9am–5pm; Dec–March by appointment only; ☎ 0145 72 3215; ¥400, or ¥700 with the **Nibutani Ainu Culture Museum** (二風谷アイヌ文化博物館; 79 Nibutani; daily 9am–4.30pm; ¥400 or ¥700 with the Kayano Shigeru Ainu Memorial Museum), on the opposite side of the village main road, is also worth a look. To reach Nibutani, take a train south from Tomakomai to Tomikawa Station (富川), from where buses run to the village.

ARRIVAL AND INFORMATION

By train Trains run to Noboribetsu Station from where the resort is a 12min bus ride.

By bus There are direct buses to Noboribetsu Onsen from Sapporo's New Chitose Airport (2 daily; 1hr) and Tōya-ko (2 daily; 1hr 25min). Local buses connect from Tomakomai

(5 daily; 1hr 45min) and Shiraoi (5 daily; 45min) to the north, and from Muroran (15 daily; 1hr 15min) to the south.

Tourist information At the resort's bus terminal you'll find one of Noboribetsu's trio of tourist offices (daily 9am–6pm; ☎ 0143 84 3311, ⓦ noboribetsu-spa.jp).

ACCOMMODATION

Rates at all the onsen hotels typically include two meals. The town makes a good place to treat yourself to the full ryokan experience, where you're served course upon course of immaculately presented delicacies, each as beautiful to look at as to taste, before relaxing in the healing baths.

Bōrō Noguchi Noboribetsu 望楼NOGUCHI登別 203 Noboribetsu Onsen-chō ☎ 0143 84 3939, ⓦ bourou.com. A masterclass in contemporary chic, featuring Western-style suites, each with their own private spa bath. **¥66,300**

★Kashoutei Hanaya 花鐘亭はなや 134 Noboribetsu Onsen-chō ☎ 0143 84 2521, ⓦ kashoutei-hanaya.co.jp. Just below the Kōseinenkin Byōin-mae bus stop, or a 5min walk downhill from the main bus terminal, a modest-sized,

modern ryokan making an excellent choice, with exquisite meals, Japanese-style rooms and a lovely rotemburo. **¥25,500**

Shōkōin Kannoji Temple 観音山聖光院 119 Noboribetsu Onsen-chō ☎ 0143 84 2359. One of the few budget accommodations in town, this temple offers tatami rooms and their own onsen. No reservations accepted, as the temple may be unable to host during funeral ceremonies. ☎ **¥3400**

EATING

Ajino Daiō 味の大王 Gokuraku-dōri ☎ 0143 84 2415. A great little noodle shop a couple of doors up from *Soba Dokorofukuan* – try the spicy *jigoku ramen* (¥850), but pick your level carefully. 11.30am–3pm & 9pm–midnight; closed Tues.

Soba Dokorofukuan そば処福庵 30 Noboribetsu Onsen-chō ☎ 0143 84 2758. Serves delicious buckwheat noodles and set meals for under ¥1000. Daily 11.30am–2pm & 6.30–10pm.

Shikotsu-ko

支笏湖

Tourist development around the beautiful lake of **Shikotsu-ko** is remarkably low-key, despite this being the closest part of the park to Sapporo. At 363m, this is Japan's second-deepest lake (after Tazawa-ko in Akita-ken), and its blue waters never freeze over. All buses stop at the tiny village of **SHIKOTSU-KO ONSEN** (支笏湖温泉), nestled in the woods beside the mouth of the Chitose-gawa on the east side of the lake, and mercifully free of the multistorey hotels present at Tōya-ko.

SHIKOTSU-KO HIKING ROUTES

One of the easiest trails starts at the northern end of the village and leads up **Monbestu-dake** (紋別岳; 866m), which takes around one hour and twenty minutes to climb. The hike up **Eniwa-dake** (恵庭岳; 1320m), on the north side of the lake above the *Poropinai* campsite, is more challenging and takes about half a day; staff at the visitors' centre advise only climbing to the Miharashi-dai, beneath the summit, because the trail to the top can be dangerous. After this climb, you could unwind beside the lake at the foot of the mountain in the lovely rotemburo at **Marukoma Onsen** (see p.322).

Most people, however, opt to climb **Tarumae-zan** (樽前山; 1041m), an active volcano (the last eruption was in 1981) south of the lake. The hike begins at the seventh "station", three-quarters of the way up the volcano at the end of a dirt road; the easiest way of reaching the start is to hitch a ride from Shikotsu-ko. The walk from the seventh station up to the summit shouldn't take more than an hour. At the top, the pungent aroma from the steaming crater discourages lingering. Following the northwest trail down from Tarumae-zan towards the lake leads, after a couple of hours, to the moss-covered gorge of **Koke-no-dōmon** (苔の洞門); sadly, erosion at this site means that you'll only be able to view the soft green velvet rock walls from a distance. From here it's a 14km hike back to Shikotsu-ko Onsen.

Just behind the visitor centre, the **Chitose-Shikotsu-ko Ice Festival** is held from the end of January to the third week of February – it's well worth coming to see the ice sculptures and caves, which are particularly dramatic when illuminated at night.

ARRIVAL AND INFORMATION   SHIKOTSU-KO

By train If you're coming from Sapporo, take a train to Chitose (the town, not the airport; 30min, ¥1360), then take the bus from the station (4–6 daily; 45min).

By bus Daily buses run to Shikotsu-ko Onsen from New Chitose Airport (4–6 daily; 1hr), via Chitose Station.

Tourist information The visitor centre (April–Nov daily 9am–5.30pm; Dec–March Mon & Wed–Sun 9.30am–4.30pm; ☏0123 25 2404), next to the bus terminal, has displays in Japanese on the area's nature and geology, and puts on a good slide show of the lake through the seasons – you can also pick up a free area map here or rent a bike.

GETTING AROUND AND ACTIVITIES

Bike rental Getting around the lake is best with your own transport, as there are no local buses. You can rent a bike from the visitor centre or youth hostel in Shikotsu-ko Onsen.

Boat rides The usual boat rides are available on the lake (30min; ¥1200).

Walks You can opt for a gentle, self-guided nature walk if hiking uphill isn't your thing (see box, p.321), lasting about 2hr, over the old red-painted railway bridge across the Chitose-gawa and along the lakeshore to the campsite at Morappu (モラップ), 7km south.

ACCOMMODATION

★ **Lake Shikotsu Tsuruga Resort Spa Mizu no Uta** しこつ湖鶴雅リゾートスパ水の謌 Shikotsu-ko onsen ☏0123 25 2211, ⓦmizunouta.com. A gorgeous contemporary-styled ryokan where the most expensive rooms have their own private onsen baths. Two meals included. 📶 **¥42,000**

Log Bear ログベアー Shikotsu-ko onsen ☏0123 25 2738, ⓦlogbear.moto-nari.com/shikotsu. This charming log cabin and coffee house amid the tourist shops next to the bus terminal is a cosy budget option, where the owner speaks English. All rooms have shared bathrooms, and the rate includes breakfast. 📶 **¥10,000**

Marukoma Onsen 丸駒温泉 7 Poropinai ☏0123 25 2341, ⓦmarukoma.co.jp. On the west side of the lake is this plush ryokan with wonderful rotemburo (open to non-residents daily 10am–3pm; ¥1000) and stunning views across Shikotsu-ko to Tarumae-zan. Rates include two meals. **¥30,000**

Morappu Campsite モラップキャンプ場 Morappu ☏0123 25 2201. About 7km south of Shikotsu-ko Onsen, the largest campsite on the lake and attractively located. Late April to mid-Oct. Per person **¥800**

Shikotsu-ko Youth Hostel 支笏湖ユースホステル Shikotsu-ko onsen ☏0123 25 2311, ⓦyouthhostel .or.jp. This youth hostel has reasonable bunk-bed and tatami rooms and friendly management; they offer bike rental, too. Breakfast and dinner ¥2100 extra. 📶 **¥3700**

Asahikawa

旭川

Mainly a place for business and shopping, **ASAHIKAWA**, 136km northeast of Sapporo, straddles the confluence of the Ishikari, Biei, Chubetsu and Ushibetsu rivers and is surrounded by mountains. It's the access point for the Daisetsu-zan National Park (see p.324), some 40km east, and worth considering as a base for park activities or, in winter, the various nearby ski slopes, including Furano (see p.327). Asahikawa's February **Winter Festival** (see box opposite) is as impressive as Sapporo's Yuki Matsuri (see box, p.295).

Asahiyama Zoo

旭山動物園, Asahiyama Dōbutsuen • Higashi Asahikawa-chō Kuranuma • Daily: late April–Oct 9.30am–5.15pm; Nov to mid-April 10.30am–3.30pm • ¥820 • ☏0166 36 1104, ⓦbit.ly/asa-zoo • Buses leave from stop 6 In front of the JR station (40min; ¥440)

Most locals will recommend that you visit **Asahiyama Zoo**, about 10km east of the city centre. The penguins, polar bears, seals, amur leopards and others that live here appear well cared for at what, thanks to skilful marketing, is Japan's most popular zoo. A "Night Zoo" takes places for one week in August.

Hokkaidō Folk Arts and Crafts Village

北海道伝統美術工芸村, Hokkaidō Dentō Bijutsu Kogei-mura • 3-1-1 Minamigaoka • International Dyeing and Weaving Art Museum ¥600, Yukara Ori Folk Craft Museum ¥500, Snow Crystals Museum ¥700, joint entry all three ¥1300 • Daily 9am–5pm • ☎0166 62 8811, ⓦ yukaraori.com • Buses from platforms 11, 22 and 23 in front of JR station; phone for free shuttle (3 times per day)

West of the city centre is a trio of museums that make up the **Hokkaidō Folk Arts and Crafts Village**. The most interesting is the **International Dyeing and Weaving Art Museum**, which exhibits a diverse collection of handwoven fabrics from around the world, from sixteenth-century Belgian tapestries to beautiful kimono. The **Yukara Ori Folk Craft Museum** displays the colourful local style of textile, and you can watch weavers at work. Least appealing is the kitsch "Frozen"-like **Snow Crystals Museum**; the displays on the myriad shapes of snow crystals are pretty but dwarfed by the castle-like complex with turrets, an ice corridor and a two-hundred-seat concert hall with a sky-painted ceiling.

Kawamura Kaneto Ainu Memorial Hall

川村カ子トアイヌ記念館 • Hokumon-chō 11 chome • Daily 9am–5pm; ☎0166 51 2461 • ¥500 • Buses #24 and #23 run to the hall from platform 14 in front of the JR station

Asahikawa was once a major Ainu settlement. There's a modest collection of Ainu-related artefacts on display at the **Kawamura Kaneto Ainu Memorial Hall**, which celebrates the Ainu chief Kaneto who worked as a surveyor with Hokkaidō's railways. Occasionally, Ainu dance performances and events take place – call ahead to check. The **Ainu Kotan Matsuri** (アイヌコタン祭), an Ainu festival, is held each September, beside the Ishikari-gawa, around 10km south of Asahikawa.

ARRIVAL AND DEPARTURE
ASAHIKAWA

By plane Asahikawa Airport (☎0166 83 3939, ⓦ aapb .co.jp) is 18km to the east of the city, towards Biei (see p.327); buses head into town from here (8 daily; 40min).
Destinations Kansai International (daily; 2hr); Nagoya (daily; 1hr 50min); Tokyo Haneda (7 daily; 1hr 45min).
By train Trains arrive at the JR station, at the southern end of Heiwa-dōri, the city's main shopping street.

Destinations Abashiri (4 daily; 3hr 45min); Furano (15 daily in summer, 12 in winter; 1hr 10min); Sapporo (30 daily; 1hr 30min); Wakkanai (3 daily; 4hr).
By bus Buses leave from in front of the train station.
Destinations Asahi-dake Onsen (3 daily; 1hr 30min); Furano (8 daily; 2hr); Kushiro via Akan ko (2 daily; 6hr 30min); Sapporo (every 20–40min; 2hr); Sōunkyō Onsen (7 daily; 1hr 50min).

GETTING AROUND

By bus Asahikawa's main tourist attractions are spread out, and getting to them by public transport involves shuttling from the city centre on a variety of buses, all leaving from around the JR station.

INFORMATION

Tourist information There's a helpful tourist office (daily 8.30am–7pm, from 9am in winter; ☎0166 26 6665, ⓦ www.asahikawa-daisetsu.jp) inside the train station, to the right as you exit the ticket barrier. Bike rental available for ¥500 or ¥1000 depending on the type of bike.

ACCOMMODATION

Arts Hotel Asahikawa ロワジールホテル旭川 6-7 Jo-dōri ☎0166 25 8811, ⓦ solarehotels.com. Right outside the station, with good online discounts, this classy hotel has a spa/gym in the basement. ☞ **¥10,000**

ASAHIKAWA'S WINTER FESTIVAL

The spectacular Winter Festival takes place over five days in the second week of February. The giant stage for the festival's opening and closing events holds the world record for the **largest snow sculpture**. The festival's many other snow and ice sculptures are displayed in Tokiwa-kōen, a fifteen-minute walk north of the station, and along pedestrianized Shōwa-dōri, among other places.

4

ASAHIKAWA'S SAKE BREWERIES

The pure waters flowing off Daisetsu-zan are one reason that Asahikawa has long had a flourishing sake industry. To sample some of the local product, head to the **Takasago Sake Brewery** (高砂酒造; Miyashita-dōri 17-chōme; daily 9am–5.30pm; ☎0166 23 2251, ⓦtakasagoshuzo.com), set in a traditional wooden building around ten minutes' walk east of Asahikawa Station. They've been making sake here since 1899, and from late January to early March they have a tradition of building an ice dome in which some of their sakes are fermented. If you have more time, head 6km north of the city centre to the **Otokoyama Sake Brewery and Museum** (男山酒造り資料館; 2-7 Nagayama; daily 9am–5pm; ☎0166 47 7080, ⓦotokoyama.com), where there's a fascinating history of Otokoyama sake told through *ukiyo-e* woodblock prints, and you can also taste the highly rated rice wines for free. Buses #67, #70, #71, #630, #667 and #669 from platform 18 in front of the JR station will get you here.

Guest House Asahikawa ゲストハウス旭川 31-10-7, 6 Jo-dōri 2nd floor ☎0166 73 8269, ⓦguesthouse asahikawa.jp. Super-friendly hosts at a clean hostel about a 15min walk from the train station. ⓦ Dorm **¥3000**

Tōyoko Inn Asahikawa Ekimae Miyashita-dōri 東 横INN旭川駅前宮下通 11-176, Miyashita-dōri, ☎0166 25 2045, ⓦtoyoko-inn.com. This branch of the *Tōyoko Inn* is a few blocks east of the station, and marginally cheaper than the other branch in town. Breakfast included. ⓦ **¥8960**

EATING AND DRINKING

There are plenty of places to **eat** around Heiwa-dōri and, one block west, the Sanroku entertainment district, where you'll find lively *izakaya* and sushi bars.

Baikōken 梅光軒 8-chōme, 2-jo-dōri ☎0166 24 4575, ⓦbit.ly/baikoken-asahikawa. Asahikawa is renowned for its *shōyu*-style ramen: sample it at this basement restaurant a few blocks down from the station, where a large bowl will set you back about ¥1000. Daily 11am–8.30pm.

Coffee Stand Container コーヒー・スタンド・コンテナ 8-chōme, 38-19-7-jo-dōri ☎0909 751 7117, ⓦbit.ly /coffee-stand-container. Close to the *Guest House* (see above), an artsy coffee shop with comfy sofas, serving exceptional lattes and muffins. The friendly owner and barista Hiroki speaks a little English. ⓦ Mon & Wed–Sun 10am–7pm.

Hachiya ラーメンの蜂屋 7 chōme, 5-jo-dōri ☎0166 23 3729. One of several good ramen shops on the atmospheric alleyway Furariito (ふらりーと), a 10min walk from the station. You'll get a large bowl of ramen for less than ¥1000. Daily 11am–11pm.

Machibar マチバル Heiwa-dōri, 8 chōme, 2-jo-dōri ☎0166 23 5977, ⓦmomendoki.co.jp/machibar. This stylish café-bar runs over two floors and serves okay pasta, pizza and gratin for about ¥1000. Fresh fruit cocktails are ¥850. Daily 11.30am–midnight, Fri and Sat till 1am.

Taisetsu Ji Beer 大雪地ビール館 11-1604 Miyashita-dōri ☎0166 25 0400, ⓦji-beer.com. Asahikawa has a couple of *gaijin* bars, but they're lacklustre; instead, sample the local beer here, a couple of blocks east of the JR station along Miyashita-dōri in a beautiful red-brick complex. The food menu includes a *jingisukan* lunch for ¥1100 and hamburgers for ¥890. Daily 11.30am–10pm.

Daisetsu-zan National Park

大雪山国立公園, Daisetsuzan Kokuritsukōen

The 2268-square-kilometre **Daisetsu-zan National Park**, Hokkaidō's largest, offers a spectacular range of gorges, hot springs and mountains – including **Asahi-dake**, the island's tallest peak – crisscrossed by hiking trails which could keep you happily occupied for days (see box, p.326). Tourism in the park is generally low-key, especially at the wooded and remote **Asahi-dake Onsen**. **Sōunkyō Onsen**, on the northeast edge of the park, hosts the bulk of tourists, though a tasteful redevelopment has made it much more attractive than most hot-spring resorts. The highlight here is the **gorge**, a 20km corridor of jagged cliffs, 150m high in places. In July, the mountain slopes are covered with alpine flowers, while September and October see the landscape painted in vivid autumnal colours; these are the best months for hiking. During the winter, both Asahi-dake and **Kuro-dake** in Sōunkyō are popular skiing spots, enjoying the longest ski season in Japan (usually Oct–June).

Asahi-dake Onsen

旭岳温泉

Quiet and uncommercialized, **ASAHI-DAKE ONSEN** is little more than a handful of hotels and pensions dotted along a road that snakes up to the cable-car station, from where hikers in the summer and skiers in the winter are whisked to within striking distance of the 2291m summit of **Asahi-dake** (旭岳). The area's remoteness means that it remains a delightful and relatively little-visited destination. Cross-country skiers in particular will appreciate the kilometres of groomed trails, some of the best in Japan, which wind through beautiful forests of white birch and Hokkaidō spruce.

Asahi-dake

旭岳 • Ropeway daily: check the website for detailed running times, as they vary greatly by month • High season one-way ¥1800, return ¥2900; low season one-way ¥1200, return ¥1800 • ☎ 0166 68 9111, ⓦ asahidake.hokkaido.jp

It's a fifteen-minute **ropeway** (cable-car) ride to **Asahi-dake**'s top station, worth visiting for its ethereal landscape of steaming pools and rocky outcrops, even if you're not planning to hike to the top of Asahi-dake. There's a 2km strolling course from the ropeway station which takes around an hour. Food and refreshments are available at the cable-car station at the top. You can also walk to the top station; this may be necessary as the weather on Asahi-dake is temperamental and the cable-car doesn't operate during strong winds.

Asahi-dake's peak is an arduous ninety-minute to two-hour slog over slippery volcanic rock from the ropeway station, but the view from the summit is well worth the effort. From here you can hike across to Sōunkyō (see p.326).

ARRIVAL AND INFORMATION   ASAHI-DAKE ONSEN

By bus Buses run from Asahikawa Station (platform 10) to Asahi-dake Onsen (3 daily; 1hr 30min); check with the tourist office at Asahikawa Station for the timetable. The same bus leaves from Asahikawa Airport (50min).

Tourist information Near the ropeway station, the tourist office (daily: 9am–5pm; ☎ 0166 97 2153, ⓦ welcome-higashikawa.jp) has nature displays (all in Japanese), information on weather conditions on the mountain, and hiking maps. Boot rental available (¥200).

ACCOMMODATION

Asahi-dake Seishōnen Yaeijō Camp Area 旭岳青少年野営場 Yukomanbetsu ☎ 0166 97 2544. Daisetsuzan's campsite is open June 20–Sept 20; tent rental (¥550), and other camping equipment is available. Per person **¥500**

Hotel Bearmonte ホテルベアモンテ Asahi-dake Onsen ☎ 0166 97 2321, ⓦ bearmonte.jp. These upmarket but unremarkable lodgings, opposite the visitor centre, offer mainly Western-style rooms. In its favour are the nicely designed onsen baths, including rotemburo, and small gym. ☎ **¥20,000**

★**Daisetsuzan Shirakaba-sō Hotel and Youth Hostel** 大雪山白樺荘 Asahi-dake Onsen ☎ 0166 97 2246, ⓦ shirakabasou.com. There's both hotel and hostel-style lodgings at this lovely wooden building, opposite the campsite bus stop and next to a running stream; the attached log house has a convivial communal lounge and there's a rotemburo (¥500 for non-guests). The food is excellent (¥2020 surcharge for dinner and breakfast), and the hostel staff can provide all you need to climb Asahi-dake, including a bell to warn off bears. ☎ Dorms **¥6890**, doubles **¥13,860**

La Vista Daisetsuzan ラビスタ大雪山 Asahi-dake Onsen ☎ 0166 97 2323, ⓦ bit.ly/lavista-dai. In the style of a large alpine chalet, the resort's newest hotel offers pleasant, spacious accommodation, lovely views and well-designed onsen baths. Free pick-up service from Asahikawa Airport available (3 days in advance). ☎ **¥24,000**

Lodge Nutapu-Kaushipe ロッジヌタプカウシペ Asahi-dake Onsen ☎ 0166 97 2150. Next to the youth hostel (see above) and equally appealing is this attractive wooden cabin with six comfortable, Japanese-style rooms – all non-smoking. Two meals are included. Cash only. ☎ **¥16,000**

4

Sōunkyō Onsen

層雲峡温泉

On the northeastern edge of Daisetsu-zan, 70km east of Asahikawa, is **SŌUNKYŌ ONSEN**, the park's main resort and an ideal base for viewing the astonishing **Sōunkyō gorge**, its jagged rock walls carved out by the Ishikari-gawa.

The village's main street is lined with small hotels, shops and a large bathing complex, **Kurodake-no-yu** (黒岳の湯; daily 10am–9pm, Nov–Jan closed Wed; ¥600). From January to the end of March, it's also possible to enjoy the **Hyōbaku Matsuri** (Ice Waterfall Festival; ¥300), a park of giant ice sculptures which are lit spectacularly every night from 5pm to 10pm. Ice mazes, snow tubing and fireworks provide plenty of entertainment.

Sōunkyō gorge

層雲峡, Sōunkyō

About 3km east of the resort lies **Sōunkyō gorge**, with the **Ginga** ("Milky Way") and **Ryūsei** ("Shooting Star") waterfalls. A twenty-minute climb up the opposite hill will lead to a viewpoint from where you'll get a fabulous view of the two cascades of white water tumbling down the cliffs. Continuing along the road for another 5km, you'll eventually arrive at **Ōbako** ("Big Box"), a touristy spot where visitors line up to be photographed in front of the river that gushes through the narrow gap in the perpendicular cliffs. To reach the falls, a bus leaves Sōunkyō Onsen at 10am and 12.50pm each day, returning about an hour later (¥440 return). It's also possible to rent a bike from *Northern Lodge* (see opposite) and follow the main highway to the sites.

ARRIVAL AND INFORMATION

By train The nearest train station to Sōunkyō Onsen is Kamikawa (上川), 20km north; buses (¥870) take 30min from here to reach the resort.

By bus Some buses passing through Kamikawa and on to Sōunkyō originate in Asahikawa (7 daily; 1hr 50min); some also go on to Akan Kohan. See ⓦ dohokubus.com for the schedule.

Tourist information There's a small tourist office (daily 10am–5.30pm; ☎ 0165 85 3350, ⓦ sounkyo.net) in the bus terminal building, while the Sōunkyō Visitor Centre next to the cable-car station (daily June–Oct 8am–5.30pm; Nov–May 9am–5pm; ☎ 0165 89 4400) has excellent nature displays with multilingual exhibit guides and English-speakers.

ACCOMMODATION AND EATING

Beer Grill Canyon ビアグリル・キャニオン ☎ 0165 85 3361, ⓦ bg-canyon.com. In the same complex as Kurodake-no-yu (see above), this place serves tasty thin-crust pizza, regional vegetables, pasta and creative dishes such as Ezo venison stroganoff (¥1500). 📶 Daily 11.30am–3.30pm & 5.30–8.30pm; Nov–April closed Wed.

HIKING ACROSS THE PARK

You can start the **Daisetsu-zan hike** across the park's central mountain range either from the top of the ropeway (cable-car) at Asahi-dake Onsen (see p.325) or from Sōunkyō Onsen where there's also a **ropeway** (☎ 0165 85 3031, ⓦ rinyu.co.jp; one-way/return ¥1100/1950), followed by a **chairlift** (one-way/return ¥400/600) up to within one hour's hike of the 1984m **Kuro-dake** (Black Mountain); check the website for running times, which vary month by month. From the summit, capped by a small shrine and giving marvellous views of the park, there's a choice of two trails to **Asahi-dake** – the southern route via Hokkai-dake (2149m) is the more scenic.

By the time you reach Asahi-dake's summit, you'll have spent around six hours walking, so returning on foot to Sōunkyō Onsen the same day is only possible if you set out at the crack of dawn. There are **overnight huts** on the mountain, but the more comfortable option is to continue down to Asahi-dake Onsen and rest there for the night. If you don't want to backtrack for your luggage, consider having it sent on by *takkyūbin* (see p.76). Make sure you're well prepared for the hike with food, topographical maps, and bells to scare away the odd bear, even though they're not that common (see box, p.339).

Northern Lodge ホテル・ノーザンロッジ ☎0165 85 3231, ⓦh-northernlodge.com. If you crave a bit of luxury, this is a good choice, offering both tatami and Western-style rooms, with two meals included and their own onsen. Bikes are available to rent for ¥1000 per day. ⓦ **¥20,000**

Sōunkyō Auto Camping Ground 層雲峡オートキャンプ場 ☎0165 85 3368. Located 6km west of Sōunkyō, this campsite offers tent spots and rentable bungalows. Coin-operated showers and washing machine/dryers are also on site. Closed Nov–May. Campsite **¥500**, car **¥500**, bungalow 2–3 people **¥3000**, 4–6 people **¥4000**

Sōunkyō Youth Hostel 層雲峡YH ☎0165 85 3418, ⓦyouthhostel.or.jp/sounkyo. A budget hostel 10min walk uphill from the bus terminal, near the *Prince Hotel*. Dorms have bunk beds, meals are served in a rustic lounge area (there's a ¥1750 surcharge for dinner and breakfast) and you can get information – mainly in Japanese – on hiking in the park. Closed Nov–May. ⓦ Dorms **¥3800**, doubles **¥11,000**

Furano and around

富良野

Surrounded by beautiful countryside, **FURANO** is famous in Japan as the location of a popular soap opera *Kita no Kuni Kara* (*From the Northern Country*), about a Tokyo family adapting to life in Hokkaidō. The landscape evokes Provençal France, with bales of hay lying around and lone poplars etched against the peaks of Daisetsu-zan National Park. The busiest season is June and July, when vast fields of lavender and other flowers bloom, drawing visitors to the gently undulating countryside – ideal for walks, cycling and photography; the most scenic farmlands surround the tranquil settlements of **Kami-Furano** (上富良野), **Biei** (美瑛) and **Bibaushi** (美馬牛), each with its own train station. Most visitors head to the specific farms of Tomita (ファーム富田) or Flower Land Kamifurano (フラワーランドかみふらの), known for their stripes of flowers.

Biei makes for a pleasant side-trip because of its improbably blue pond, Aoiike (青い池), which once featured as a stock wallpaper for Apple. It's accessible via a bus from Biei station (5 daily; 20min; ¥540; free admission).

In winter, Furano is a centre for **skiing**. Other places to head to are Kami-Furano where the **Goto Sumio Museum of Art** (後藤純男美術館; Higashi 4-sen Kita 26-go; daily 9am–5pm, Nov–March till 4pm; ¥1000; ⓦgotosumiomuseum.com) contains dreamy landscape paintings from one of Japan's major contemporary artists, and Furano's **wine and cheese factories** (see box, p.328). Furano and the outlying towns in the area can also be used as a base for a hike up the 2077m active volcano of **Tokachi-dake**, some 20km southwest and within the Daisetsu-zan National Park.

ARRIVAL AND INFORMATION

By train In summer, and sometimes in winter, there are direct trains from Sapporo (2 daily; 2hr), but usually the fastest way is by limited express to Takikawa then change to the local train along the Furano line. From Asahikawa, the train (hourly; 1hr 10min) passes through Biei, Bibaushi and Kami-Furano.

By bus Furano is connected by direct Chuo bus with Sapporo (around 2hr 30min; ¥2260); if you're coming to ski, ask to be dropped at Kitanomine-iriguchi (the hub of the ski village), rather than getting off in the centre of town. The Lavender Bus also runs from Asahikawa Station via the airport, Furano train station, and various other stations en route, to the *New Furano Prince Hotel* (8 daily; 2hr); a taxi to the hotel from Furano Station costs around ¥2300.

Tourist information The Furano tourist office (daily 9am–6pm; ☎0167 23 3388, ⓦfuranotourism.com/en) has operations next to Furano Station and at the Kitanomine gondola station.

FURANO CULTURAL PERFORMANCES

The local tourism office is working hard to ensure that the Japanese character and charm of the Furano area aren't lost or overlooked by visiting *gaijin*. During the ski season, a free **cultural performance** is held every Sunday night at the restaurant at the Kitanomine gondola station. This includes a presentation of the town's "belly button dance", the highlight of Furano's **Heso Matsuri** (Navel Festival), held every July 28–29 and celebrating the town's position at the centre of Hokkaidō.

FERTILE FURANO

It's not just flowers that thrive in Furano's fertile soil. The area is also known for its melons, potatoes, onions, milk and grapes. At **Furano Winery** (ふらのワイン; Shimizuyama; daily 9am–4.30pm, June & Aug till 6pm; free; T 0167 22 3242, W furanowine.jp), around 4km northwest of Furano Station, you can sip from a range of eighteen different wines; some of them are quite delicious. The obvious accompaniment is cheese, and this can be sampled at the **Furano Cheese Factory** (富良野チーズ工房; Nakagoku; daily 9am–5pm, Nov–March till 4pm; free; T 0167 23 1156, W www.furano.ne.jp/furano-cheese), about 1km east of the *New Furano Prince Hotel* (see below). Apart from selling concoctions such as a brie turned black with squid ink, this fun facility also allows you to practise milking a fake cow (¥100) and sign up for bread-, butter-, cheese- and ice-cream-making workshops (¥700–880): ring ahead or email to book.

ACCOMMODATION

If you've come to ski, it's most convenient to stay in either the *Prince* hotels or at Kitanomine village, from where you can walk to the lifts. Furano town itself isn't too far away and is connected to the slopes by regular buses. In summer, the countryside around Bibaushi and Biei draws visitors with its displays of lavender, tulips, iris, cosmos and sunflowers, among others.

4

Alpine Backpackers アルパインバックパッカーズ 14-6 Kitanomine-chō T 0167 22 1311, W alpn.co.jp. A 5min walk from the Kitanomine ski lifts, this great lodge has bunk-bed dorms and twins, a kitchen, a bakery-café, and young, enthusiastic staff. They also organize balloon trips year-round, plus fishing and adventure sports such as rafting, mountain biking and horseriding in summer. Breakfast extra (¥800). Dorms **¥2800**, twins **¥5600**

Bibaushi Liberty Youth Hostel 美馬牛リバティYH Bibaushi-shigaichi T 0166 95 2141, W biei.org/liberty. Next to the Bibaushi JR station, a stylish hostel offering comfy bunk-bed dorms and private rooms; excellent, inexpensive meals are also available. Dorms **¥4700**, twins **¥11,800**

Furano Fresh Powder フレッシュパウダー・アパートメント 14-26 Kitanomine-chō T 0167 23 4738, W freshpowder.com. Six well-equipped self-catering units opposite the Kitanomine ski slopes, and sleeping between four and eight people. Five- to seven-day minimum during ski season. **¥26,000**

Natulux Hotel ナチュラクスホテル 1-35 Asahi-chō T 0167 22 1777, W natulux.com. Next to Furano Station, this tasteful boutique property sports a minimalist design contrasting concrete walls with black or brown wooden fixtures. The English-speaking management are very obliging and guests can use the neighbouring sports complex with swimming pool for free. **¥15,700**

New Furano Prince Hotel 新富良野プリンスホテル Nakagoryō T 0167 22 1111, W princehotels.co.jp/newfurano. A few kilometres south of Kitanomine village, a 400-bed oval-shaped tower block that's a world unto itself, featuring everything from several restaurants and bars, ski rental and a coin laundry, to a sophisticated onsen (guests/non-guests ¥800/¥1540) and a twee log-cabin shopping village. Families will love their Snow Land winter amusement park. In winter there are package deals with meals and ski-lift tickets. The *Prince* group has a second smaller hotel in Furano that's mainly used by groups. **¥36,400**

★**Phytoncide Mori no Kaori** フィトンチッド森の香り 17-2 Kitanomine-chō T 0167 39 1551, W woodlandfarm.co.jp. One of Furano's most original accommodation options. The charming owners, who bake their own bread and serve foods grown on their organic farm, have an amazing collection of antique cash registers. Each of the six Western-style rooms has its own bathroom, and one is wheelchair-accessible. Rates include breakfast. **¥30,700**

EATING AND DRINKING

Furano Brewery Yama no Doxon 山の独尊 20-29 Kitanomine-chō T 0167 22 5599. A rustic microbrewery where they make their own very palatable beers, sausages, smoked meats and curries. Tues–Sun noon–2.30pm, 5.30–11pm.

Kuma Gera くまげら 3-22 Hinode-machi T 0167 39 2345, W www.furano.ne.jp/kumagera. A lively place in the midst of Furano town where they serve the meat-laden *sanzoku nabe* (bandits' stew), full of duck, venison and chicken – a pot for two costs ¥3300. Daily 11.30am–11pm.

Soh's Bar ソーズ・バー Nakagoryo T 0167 22 1111. A good place for a nightcap, in a log-and-stone cabin in the forest near the *New Furano Prince Hotel* (see above), where you can admire the collection of cigarette packets. On the way there, you can go gift shopping in the attractive log-house complex, Ningle Terrace. Daily 7pm–midnight.

★**Yuigadokuson** 唯我独尊 11-8 Hinode-machi T 0167 23 4784. This local favourite is in a rustic cabin set back from the main street and is popular for its amazing curry and home-made venison sausages (¥1110). Extra curry sauce is available only if you say the secret phrase to the counter (hint: it's on the menu). Tues–Sun 11am–9pm.

Wakkanai

稚内

The windswept port of **WAKKANAI**, 320km from Sapporo and near the northern tip of Hokkaidō, is the gateway to the **Rishiri-Rebun-Sarobetsu National Park** (see p.330) and, in particular, the lovely islands of Rebun-tō and Rishiri-tō. There's little reason to linger in town apart from shopping for sports clothing, but there are a few places of minor interest in the area, should you find yourself killing time waiting for a ferry. One reason for heading here out of season is to attend the **Japan Cup National Dogsled Races**, held during the last weekend of February.

A five-minute stroll from Wakkanai Station is the impressive **North Breakwater Dome**, a 427m-long arched corridor supported by seventy concrete pillars, inspired by the arches of Rome's Colosseum. For a longer walk (around 1hr, round-trip), head west of the train station to **Wakkanai-kōen** (稚内公園), a grassy park from where, on a clear day, you can see the island of **Sakhalin**, some 60km northwest; it's now part of Russia, but before World War II it was occupied by the Japanese. Closer to the port, squid boats linger around in August.

Wakkanai is the access point for the desolate cape **Sōya Misaki** (宗谷岬), 32km east of Wakkanai and the northernmost point of Japan (7 buses daily; 50min; ¥2430 return). A couple of monuments, including "Tower of Prayer", a memorial to the Korean Airlines plane shot down by the Soviet Union just north of the cape, mark this dull spot.

ARRIVAL, DEPARTURE AND INFORMATION WAKKANAI

By plane A bus from Wakkanai's airport (☏ 0162 27 2121), 10km east of the port, costs ¥600 for the 30min journey, and a taxi ¥3890.
Destinations Sapporo (2 daily; 55min); Tokyo (2 daily; 1hr 55min).

By train Wakkanai Station (the northernmost train station on Hokkaidō) is close to both the ferry terminal and the new combined bus terminal and cinema.
Destinations Asahikawa (3 daily; 4hr); Sapporo (3 daily; 5hr 30min).

By bus There are buses to/from Sapporo, including one overnight (7 daily; 6–7hr).

By ferry Wakkanai is the jumping-off point for the islands of Rebun-tō and Rishiri-tō.
Destinations Rebun-tō (2–4 daily; 1hr 40min); Rishiri-tō (2–4 daily; 1hr 45min).

Tourist information Inside the train station is a helpful tourist office (daily 10am–6pm; ☏ 0162 22 2384, ⓦ welcome.wakkanai.hokkaido.jp/en).

ACCOMMODATION

Crowne Plaza ANA Wakkanai ANAクラウンプラザホテル稚内 1-2-2 Kaiun ☏ 0162 23 8111, ⓦ anacp wakkanai.com. One of the most luxurious options in Wakkanai, directly in front of the ferry terminal. Prices here drop dramatically in the off-season. **¥21,000**

Dormy Inn Wakkanai ドーミーイン稚内 Chūō 2-7-13 ☏ 0162 24 5489, ⓦ hotespa.net. A few minutes' walk from the station, this budget hotel offers a good seafood

breakfast buffet and onsen with harbour view. 🛜 **¥12,000**

Wakkanai Moshiripa Youth Hostel 稚内モシリパユースホステル Chūō 2-9-5 ☏ 0162 24 0180, ⓦ youthhostel .or.jp. This cute youth hostel is a 5min walk north from the train station and east of the ferry terminal; guests must check in before 8pm. Lots of space to relax and enjoy a beer. Breakfast extra (¥750). Closed mid-Oct to mid-Dec. 🛜 Dorms **¥4050**

EATING

A 15min walk south of the JR station in the Edo-style market at **Wakkanai Fukukō Ichiba** (稚内副港市場 1-6-28 Minato; 10am–10pm), you can combine a seafood or Russian meal at several inexpensive restaurants with a dip (¥750 plus ¥150 for towels) in the spacious onsen baths of Minato no Yu (港のゆ).

> ### THE RUSSIAN CONNECTION
>
> There's a monument in Wakkanai-kōen to nine female **telephone operators** who committed suicide in Sakhalin's post office at the end of World War II, rather than be captured by the Russians. Russo-Japanese relations are now much improved, and traces of Wakkanai's now defunct ferry connection with Russia remain in the tourist signs and in the stacking dolls in shops.

North Gate Hall 北門館 Chūō 3-8 ☎ 0162 22 0486. If you find yourself in need of caffeine before taking the trip on the ferry, then you might like to seek out to this quaint, old-fashioned café serving excellent siphon-style coffee. Daily 8am–9pm.

Takechan 竹ちゃん Chūō 2-8 ☎ 0162 22 7130, ⓦ take -chan.co.jp. Be sure to sample some seafood while you're in town; this place is particularly convivial, specializing in sushi and *tako-shabu* (octopus stew; ¥1575). Daily 11am–11pm.

Rishiri-Rebun-Sarobetsu National Park

利尻礼文サロベツ国立公園, Rishiri-Rebun-Sarobetsu Kokuritsu Kōen

Off the northern tip of Hokkaidō, the two islands that make up the bulk of the **Rishiri-Rebun-Sarobetsu National Park** are quite different: slender **Rebun-tō** is low-lying, its gentle hills sprinkled with alpine flowers, while **Rishiri-tō** is a Fuji-like volcano rising from the sea. Offering lush scenery and mild weather, both islands are exceptionally popular with Japanese tourists from June to September, when accommodation should be booked well in advance. At other times you're likely to have the islands to yourself, although they pretty much close down entirely between November and March. In order to get the most out of a stay here it's worth scheduling a couple of nights on each island.

Rishiri-tō

利尻島

Most people come to **RISHIRI-TŌ** to hike up the central 1721m volcano **Rishiri-zan** (利尻山). The island is sometimes called Rishiri-Fuji because its shape is said to resemble the famous southern volcano; in reality, it's spikier and a lot less symmetrical. Even if the weather is unpromising, it's still worth making the ascent (which takes 10–12hr) to break through the clouds on the upper slopes and be rewarded with panoramic views from the summit, which is crowned with a small shrine.

The most straightforward ascent of Rishiri-zan starts some 4km south of the main port of **Oshidomari** (鴛泊), at the Rishiri Hokuroku Forest Park Campsite. Information and maps for the climb are available from the island's tourist office (see below). Around fifteen minutes' climb from the peak of Chōkan-zan (長官山), the eighth station up the volcano, there's a basic hut where you can take shelter en route in an emergency. Take plenty of water, as there's none available on the mountain. Be careful of the loose rock near the summit.

The island provides a mostly vehicle-free road to circumnavigate the island at 60.2km, 20km of it exclusively for bikes. It takes about six hours at a leisurely pace, with ample opportunities to enjoy short breaks at scenic outlooks and quaint fishing villages.

As the island is famous for its *konbu* (seaweed) and *uni* (sea urchin), stop by Kamui Coast Park (神居海岸パーク; June to Sept daily 9am–11am, 1–4pm; ☎ 0163 84 3622; ¥1500). Here you can catch and open your own *uni* to eat, as well as gather your own *konbu* to package up for a unique souvenir.

ARRIVAL AND DEPARTURE
RISHIRI-TŌ

By plane There's a daily flight to Rishiri-tō from New Chitose and Okadama; the airport (☎ 0163 82 1269) is a few kilometres west of Oshidomari.

By ferry Most visitors come by ferry from Wakkanai to Oshidomari (1hr 40min); from mid-April to Oct there are three or four services daily, dropping to two during Nov–March. Unless your tickets are arranged through a tour company, ferry tickets can only be purchased on the day of travel.

INFORMATION

Tourist information The tourist office (daily 8am–6.30pm, earlier in the off season; ☎ 0163 82 2201, ⓦ www.town.rishiri.hokkaido.jp), inside the ferry terminal at Oshidomari, has maps and English notes on the hikes to Rishiri-zan and Himenuma. They also sell "mobile restrooms" (¥400 per set), which hikers are asked to use and drop off at a collection point.

GETTING AROUND

By bus Five to six buses per day run in both directions around the island (a circuit which takes 1hr 55min; starts at ¥150). If you arrive by ferry at Kutsugata on the western side of Rishiri, you'll need to get a bus north to Oshidomari (30min; ¥750).

Bus tours If time is limited, consider taking one of the three daily bus tours (¥3100–3300), which cover all the scenic highlights and are timed to connect with the ferries; details from the tourist office.

By bike Bicycles are a good way to get around and can be rented from near the ferry terminal for around ¥2000 a day.

ACCOMMODATION

Island Inn Rishiri アイランド・イン・リシリ Kutsugata ☎0163 84 3002. Located in Kutsugata on the island's west coast; the large, modern Western-style rooms here have views of either the port or the mountains. There's a public bath; rates include two meals. 📶 **¥18,000**

Rishiri Green Hill Inn 利尻ぐりーんひる inn Oshidomari ☎0163 82 2507, ⊛rishiri-greenhill.net. Just on the outskirts of Oshidomari, this clean hostel has Japanese-style rooms and large shared spaces. Hiking treks can be organized here. There's a public bath, shared kitchen, and mountain bike rental (¥1300/day). **Open April to Oct.** 📶 Dorms **¥3800**

Rishiri Hokuroku Forest Park campsite 利尻北麓野営場 Sakae-machi Oshidomari-aza ☎0163 82 2394. This campsite is 3km south of the port and on the main route up the volcano. **Open mid-May to mid-Oct.** Camping **¥500** per person; cabin for four people **¥5000**

Rishiri Island Family Camping Yu-ni 利尻島ファミリーキャンプ場ゆ～に Oshidomari ☎0163 82 2166. The most popular campsite on the island, as it's very family-friendly and usefully located close to the ferry. **Open May–Oct.** Camping **¥500** per person, cabins (sleeps 4) **¥5000**, cottages (sleeps 5) **¥16,000**

EATING

Grand Spot グランスポット Oshidomari ☎0163 86 2130. Set back from the main road, this small but popular restaurant serves excellent ramen and *hotatefurai kare* (fried scallop curry; ¥1300). Daily 11am–6pm.

Tsuki Café ツキカフェ Oshidomari ☎0163 83 1514, ⊛bit.ly/tsuki-cafe. Serving good, single-origin organic coffee, this small coffee shop is located within the ferry terminal with views of the harbour. Mid-May to Oct, daily except Wed 7.30am–3.30pm.

4

RISHIRI-REBUN-SAROBETSU NATIONAL PARK

●EATING	
Chidori	1
Grand Spot	2
Tsuki Café	3

▲ACCOMMODATION	
Hana Rebun	3
Island Inn Rishiri	7
Kushu-kohan Campground	1
Momo-iwa-sō Youth Hostel	2
Rishiri Green Hill Inn	4
Rishiri Hokuroku Forest Park Campsite	6
Rishiri Island Family Camping Yu-ni	5

Rebun-tō

礼文島

Shaped like a crab's claw adrift in the Sea of Japan, **REBUN-TŌ** is most famous for its wild flowers – from May to September the island's rolling green slopes are said to bloom with three hundred different types of alpine plants. At the island's southern end is its main port, the small settlement of **Kafuka** (香深), which spreads uphill from the coast. In the north is the small fishing village of **Funadomari** (船泊), which makes a good base for hikes out to the northern cape, Sukoton Misaki (スコトン岬). Seals can sometimes be seen resting on the rocks nearby. The whole island is fabulous **hiking** territory. The longest and most popular hike is the 32km **Hachi-jikan** (8hr) down the west coast from Sukoton Misaki, the island's northernmost point, to Motochi (元地) in the south. The cliffs at the end of this hike can be slippery and sometimes dangerous; easier is the **Cape Tour** (4hr) course, which omits the difficult coastal section of the Hachi-jikan course from Uennai to Motochi but still delivers fantastic cape views. It's best to wear trousers for either course, as parts of the path are overgrown. The youth hostel (see opposite) arranges walking groups for the two hikes and holds briefings the night before. Stock up on food and drink before you start, as there are no refreshment stops along the way. When you're all done, go for a dip at Usuyuki Onsen (うすゆきの湯) close to the ferry terminal (¥800 with towels; noon–10pm, 9pm in off season; ☎0163 86 2345, ⊛usuyuki.jp).

The island has a few less energertic options. You can join a kayaking trip with Rebun Tours to see the coastline from a unique angle (¥10,000; daily 10am–3pm; lunch included; ☎0908 428 4474, ⊛rebun.jimdo.com). Or you can stop by the Unimuki Taiken Katsugyo Centre (うにむき体験活魚センター) and open up your own fresh sea urchin to taste, as in Rishiri (¥500; Mon–Sat 8am–4pm; ☎0163 87 2506, ⊛bit.ly/rebun-to-fishery).

ARRIVAL AND DEPARTURE

By ferry Rebun-tō is only accessible by ferry from Wakkanai to Kafuka (4 daily mid-April to Oct, 2 daily Nov to mid-April; 1hr 55min). Ferries also sail between Kafuka on Rebun-tō and Oshidomari and Kutsugata on Rishiri-tō (daily; 40min).

Just like Rishiri, tickets can only be purchased on the day of travel. Hostels and most minshuku will pick you up from the ferry terminals, if you book in advance. For full details of the ferries, go to ⊛heartlandferry.jp.

INFORMATION AND TOURS

Tourist information Rebun's tourist office (April–Oct daily 8am–5pm; ☎0163 86 2655, ⊛www.rebun-island.jp/en), in the ferry terminal at Kafuka, has a good map of the island, marked with the main hiking routes including ones up Rebun-dake and to the Momo-iwa ("Peach-Shaped Rock") on the west coast. Staff can also help with booking accommodation.
Bus A local bus runs from the ferry terminal to Sukoton

Misaki and back five times a day (¥1200).
Bike rental Bike rental is available from several shops near the ferry terminal for ¥500/hr, or ¥2000/day.
Bus tours If time is limited, consider taking one of the two bus tours (¥3100–3300), which cover all the scenic highlights and are timed to connect with the ferries; details are available from the tourist office.

ACCOMMODATION

Hana Rebun 花れぶん Kafuka ☎0163 86 1177, ⊛hanarebun.com/hanarebun.html. Next to the ferry terminal, this is the luxury option, with its appealing

traditional-style rooms combining Western and Japanese interior design. The most expensive suites sport outdoor tubs on balconies. Rates include two meals. 🛜 **¥32,000**

THE ROAD TO HIMENUMA

A less strenuous alternative to climbing Rishiri-zan is the three-hour hiking trail which starts at pretty **Himenuma** pond (姫沼) and continues across the slopes of two smaller mountains making up **Pon-zan**, to the *Rishiri Hokuroku Forest Park Campsite* (see p.331). Note that the trail could be closed at times due to the weather. To get to Himenuma from Oshidomari, follow the coastal road 1km or so west until you reach a junction going up into the hills. The walk to the pond at that point is quite steep – you might be able to hitch a lift – and takes around 20min.

Kushu-kohan   Campsite   久種湖畔キャンプ場
Funadomari ☎0163 87 3110. Accessible by bus and on
the northern part of the island on the shore of Kushu Lake.
Shower and washing machine facilities. Open May to Oct.
Per person **¥600**, bungalows **¥2000**
Momo-iwa-sō Youth Hostel 桃岩荘ユースホステル
Aza Motochi, Kafuka ☎0163 86 1421, ⓦyouthhostel

.or.jp. Occupying a dramatic location on the rocky western
coast south of Motochi in a 150-year-old building, making
a good base for the Hachi-jikan hiking course; it's situated
at the end of the walk, but staff can organize transport to
the start. It gets packed in peak season and the atmosphere
becomes akin to a summer camp. Closed Oct–May. Dorms
with breakfast and dinner **¥5616**

EATING

Chidori ちどり Kafuka 1115-3 ☎0163 86 2130. Rebun is
known for a dish called *chan chan yaki*, locally caught *hokke*
(a type of mackerel) grilled and slathered with miso paste.

Sample this as a lunch set for ¥1400 at this favourite spot
near the terminal. Daily 11am–10pm.

Eastern Hokkaidō

With three major national parks, **eastern Hokkaidō** will be a high priority for those
interested in Japan's natural environment. **Abashiri** is known throughout Japan for
its old maximum-security **prison** (now a museum), and for winter boat tours
through the drift ice on the Sea of Okhotsk. Jutting into these inhospitable waters
northeast of Abashiri is **Shiretoko National Park**, a UNESCO World Heritage Site
and one of Japan's most naturally unspoiled areas. Inland, south of the peninsula, is
the **Akan National Park**, which is also stunning, with hot springs and three scenic
lakes. More eco-tourist delights await at **Kushiro Shitsugen National Park** and
Kiritappu Marsh, where you can spot regal red-crested white cranes among many
other fauna and flora.

GETTING AROUND   EASTERN HOKKAIDŌ

By car Public transport is sparse, so consider renting a
car to get around. Nippon Rent-a-Car has offices
throughout Hokkaidō, a user-friendly website and an

English phone line open Mon–Fri 9am–5pm (☎03 6859
6234, ⓦnipponrentacar.co.jp).

Abashiri

網走
Bordered by a couple of pretty lakes, the fishing port of **ABASHIRI**, 350km from
Sapporo, is best visited in the dead of winter, when snow covers the less appealing
modern parts of the town, whooper swans fly in to stay for the winter at Lake Tofutsu,
a few kilometres east of the harbour, and drift ice (*ryūhyō*) floats across the Sea of
Okhotsk (see box, p.335).

   An excellent vantage point from which to take in Abashiri's coastal location is the
summit of **Tento-zan**, directly behind the train station, where you'll also find several
enjoyable **museums**. Check with the tourist office (see p.334) for coupons to get
discounted entry to all these museums and for information on a bus service that runs
a circuit around them.

Abashiri Prison Museum

博物館 網走監獄, Hakubutsukan Abashiri Kangoku • 1-1 Yobito • Daily: May–Sept 8.30am–6pm; Oct–April 9am–5.00pm • ¥1080 •
☎0152 45 2411, ⓦkangoku.jp/world
A prison building constructed in the 1890s, **Abashiri Prison Museum** occupies the site
that was home to over 1000 hardened criminals. Now an open-air museum, learn
about the prison's cruel history and visit the main building housing five radially
constructed wings. Make sure to check out the adjoining cafeteria where you can dine
on the same daily meals eaten by prisoners at Abashiri's working prison, 3km away.

Okhotsk Ryūhyō Museum

オホーツク流氷館, Ohōtsuku Ryūhyō-kan • 245-1 Tentozan • Daily: May–Oct 8.30am–6pm; Nov–April 9am–4.30pm • ¥750 • ☎ 0152 43 5951, ⓦ ryuhyokan.com

At the informative and newly renovated **Okhotsk Ryūhyō Museum**, you can touch huge lumps of ice in a room where the temperature is kept at -15°C; coats are provided for warmth. A panoramic film of the drift ice is screened regularly throughout the day, and the observatory provides a 360° view of the Sea of Okhotsk.

Hokkaidō Museum of Northern Peoples

北海道立北方民族博物館, Hokkaidō-ritsu Hoppō Minzoku Hakubutsukan • 309-1 Shiomi • July–Sept 9.30am–4.30pm; Oct–June 9.30am–5pm, closed Mondays during low season • ¥550 • ☎ 0152 45 3889, ⓦ hoppohm.org

The **Hokkaidō Museum of Northern Peoples** has interesting displays on the native peoples of northern Eurasia and America, prompting comparisons between the different cultures. A colour-coded chart at the start of the exhibition will help you identify which artefacts belong to which races; look out for the Inuit cagoules, fascinating garments made of seal intestines.

ARRIVAL AND DEPARTURE   ABASHIRI

By plane Memanbetsu (女満別) Airport (☎ 0152 74 3115, ⓦ mmb-airport.co.jp) is 20km south of Abashiri and 35min from town by bus (¥910).
Destinations Kansai (daily; 2hr 10min); Nagoya (daily; 2hr); Sapporo (7 daily; 50min); Tokyo Haneda (5 daily; 1hr 40min).
By train By train, the fastest option is the Okhotsk limited express from Sapporo. There's also a plodding local train on the

Senmō line from the port of Kushiro, 146km south.
Destinations Asahikawa (4 daily; 3hr 45min); Kushiro (4 daily; 3hr); Sapporo (4 daily; 5hr 30min); Shiretoko-Shari (9 daily; 45min).
By bus Buses from Sapporo (ⓦ j-bus.co.jp) to Abashiri take 6hr.
Destinations Sapporo (9 daily; 6hr); Shari (5 daily; 1hr).

INFORMATION

Tourist information Inside the JR station is the helpful tourist office (Mon–Fri noon–5pm, Sat & Sun 9am–5pm;

☎ 0152 44 5849, ⓦ www.city.abashiri.hokkaido.jp).

ACCOMMODATION

Abashiri Central Hotel 網走セントラルホテル Minami 2 Nishi 3 ☎ 0152 44 5151, ⓦ abashirich.com. One of the town's top overnight choices offers a classy selection of rooms, a good restaurant (serving a buffet lunch for ¥1234) and is convenient for the shopping district. 🛜 **¥15,750**
Abashiri Ryūhyō-no-Oka Youth Hostel 網走流氷の

丘ユースホステル Aza Meiji 22-6 ☎ 0152 43 8558, ⓦ youthhostel.or.jp. A modern hostel overlooking the Sea of Okhotsk. It's a long, steep walk up here, so catch a taxi (around ¥1000), or request the station pick-up service. Bike rental is available. Breakfast and dinner for ¥1680. 🛜 Dorms **¥3850**

CRANES, SWANS AND EAGLES

Birdwatchers will be thrilled by eastern Hokkaidō. The area is home to three of Japan's top four ornithological spectacles: red-crested white cranes (*tanchō-zuru*) in the Kushiro and Kiritappu regions; whooper swans, also in the Kushiro region, and near Abashiri and Odaito towards the Notsuke Peninsula; and Steller's sea eagles at Rausu on the Shiretoko Peninsula. The fourth must-see is the cranes at Arasaki in Kyūshū. The best months to view all of these are January, February and March.

The **red-crested white cranes**, commonly called *tanchō*, are a symbol of Japan and were once found all over the country. However, they became so rare in the twentieth century that they were thought to be almost extinct. Fortunately, the birds – designated a "Special Natural Monument" in 1952 – have survived, and their population, living exclusively in eastern Hokkaidō, now numbers about one thousand. Thanks to feeding programmes at several sites around the Kushiro Shitsugen National Park (see p.341), it's possible to see these grand but shy birds; with a 2m wingspan, they are the largest in Japan.

VIEWING THE DRIFT ICE

Global warming has impacted on the drift ice off the coast of Abashiri and the Shiretoko Peninsula, and both its volume and the season for its sighting – typically February to late March – are shrinking. Should the conditions be right, the ideal way to witness this astonishing phenomenon is to hop aboard the *Aurora*, an **ice-breaking sightseeing boat**, for a one-hour tour (late Jan to end March, daily; ¥3300; ☎0152 43 6000, ⓦms-aurora.com), which departs from Abashiri two to six times a day, depending on the month and weather. The boat cracks through the ice sheets, throwing up huge chunks, some more than 1m thick. An alternative is to take the slow-moving sightseeing train **Ryūhyō Norokko-go** (流氷ノロッコ号; ¥840), which chugs along the coast between Abashiri and Shiretoko-Shari twice a day between the end of January and mid-March; there's also the regular *futsū* train that runs into Akan National Park (see p.338). **Gojiraiwa-Kankō** (ゴジラ岩観光; ☎0152 24 3060, ⓦkamuiwakka.jp/driftice) in Utoro (see p.337) offers walking trips across the ice and the chance to get in the frozen water, comfortably attired in a dry suit (¥5000).

Memanbetsu Kohan 女満別湖畔キャンプ場 Aza Meiji 22-6 ☎0152 74 4252. Outside of town but minutes from Memanbetsu Station, this camping area resides on beautiful Lake Abashiri. Communal kitchen and local onsen nearby. Open July–Sept. **¥300**

Hotel Shinbashi ホテルしんばし Shin-machi 1-2-12 ☎0152 43 4307, ⓦbit.ly/hotel-shinbashi. This old-style hotel, directly opposite the JR station, has decent tatami and Western-style rooms. Its restaurant serves good-value set meals and cheap noodle dishes. **¥6300**

Tōyoko Inn Okhotsk Abashiri Ekimae 東横INNオホーツク・網走駅前 1-3-3 Shin-machi ☎0152 45 1043, ⓦtoyoko-inn.com. This branch of the dependable hotel chain is handily located directly opposite the station. **¥7980**

EATING AND DRINKING

Abashiri specializes in fresh **seafood** – don't leave town without trying some of the freshly caught, succulent crabs. It's also home to a microbrewery, which is worth a visit to sample the local infusion.

Café & Cake Fuka カフェアンドケーキ風花 Yohito 121-7 ☎0152 48 2006, ⓦabashiri-fuka.com. A little outside of town but worth the visit, Fuka delivers with outstanding desserts and beautiful outdoor seating. Daily 10am–7pm; closed Wed.

Sushiyasu 寿し安 Minami 5 Nishi 2 ☎0152 43 4121. Reliable and inexpensive, this place is a couple of blocks behind the *Abashiri Central Hotel* (see opposite): sushi sets cost as little as ¥800 for lunch and ¥1550 for dinner. Tues–Sun 11am–2pm, 5–10pm.

Yakiniku Abashiri Biirukan Yakiniku 網走ビール館 Minami 2 Nishi 4 ☎0152 41 0008, ⓦbit.ly/yakiniku-abashiri. Sample locally brewed Abashiri beer and grilled beef here, a 5min walk from the station towards the port; the *yakiniku* set menu costs from ¥2500. Mon–Thurs & Sun 5–11pm, Fri & Sat 5pm–midnight.

Shiretoko National Park

知床国立公園, Shiretoko Kokuritsu Kōen

Since 176,000 acres of the Shiretoko Peninsula, including the **SHIRETOKO NATIONAL PARK**, gained UNESCO World Heritage Site status in 2005, there's been an increasing amount of investment in, as well as visitors to, this magnificent ecosystem, 42km east of Abashiri. Even so, by any standards the park, which covers about half the 70km-long peninsula thrusting into the Sea of Okhotsk, remains virtually untouched by signs of human development: there are few roads or tourist facilities, and **wildlife** is abundant – you're almost guaranteed to encounter wild deer, foxes and even brown bears (see box, p.339). Peak season is from June to September, the best period for hiking and viewing the five small lakes at Shiretoko Go-ko, most easily reached from the peninsula's main town, **Utoro**. In the winter, drift ice litters the shore, and some two thousand Steller's sea eagles can be observed near **RAUSU** (羅臼; ⓦrausu-shiretoko.com) on the peninsula's southeast coast. This remote fishing village can be used as a base for the park and is the only place offering winter cruises (see p.337).

ABASHIRI-KO WINTER ACTIVITIES

From late January to early March, fun winter activities take place on frozen Abashiri-ko, on the town's western flank. You can take a **snowmobile** for a spin around a 7km course over the lake (daily 9am–4.30pm; ¥3000), or be dragged around the ice sitting inside a raft or astride an inflatable banana. This site, along with the quay at Abashiri Port, is also the location for the town's mini **snow festival**, which takes place in the second week of February each year. Buses run to the lake from outside Abashiri Station. If none of that feels cold enough, then try **diving beneath the ice** (¥30,000 for two dives; ☎0152 61 5102). Book far in advance.

Utoro

ウトロ

Roads stop halfway up both sides of the Shiretoko Peninsula, so the only way you'll get to see the rocky cape, with its unmanned lighthouse and waterfalls plunging over sheer cliffs into the sea, is to take one of the sightseeing boats from **UTORO** (see opposite). Near the town's tiny harbour are several large rocks, one of which is nicknamed "Godzilla", for reasons that become obvious when you see it.

Shiretoko World Heritage Conservation Centre

知床世界遺産センター, Shiretoko Seikaiisan Sentā • 186-10 Utoro Nishi • Summer 8.30am–5.30pm; winter 9am–4.30pm; closed Tues • Free • ⓦ shiretoko-whc.jp

While in Utoro, drop by the excellent Shiretoko **World Heritage Conservation Centre** to learn about Shiretoko National Park and its vegetation and wildlife. They have separate displays on the animals of the mountain, forest, river and sea, and a scale relief map of the area.

Shiretoko Shizen Centre

知床自然センター, Shiretoko Sekai Isan Sentā • 531 Iwaobetsu, Shari-chō • Daily: summer 8am–5.30pm, winter 9am–4pm • Free; film ¥500 • ⓦ center.shiretoko.or.jp

Based outside Utoro, en route to the Five Lakes, is the **Shiretoko Shizen Centre**, which shows a twenty-minute giant-screen film throughout the day, with swooping aerial shots of the mountains and rugged coastline. Behind the centre, a few well-marked nature trails lead through forests and heathland to cliffs, down which a waterfall cascades.

Shiretoko Go-ko

知床五湖 • Late April to late Nov daily 7.30am–6pm • Short route: free; long route: ¥5000 with mandatory guide in Active Bear Season (May 10–July 31), ¥250 in Ecosystem Aware Season (late April–May 9 & Aug 1–Oct 20), free late Oct to early Nov • ⓦ goko.go.jp • Bus from Utoro (6 times daily; 25min; ¥700)

Fourteen kilometres north of Utoro, past the *Iwaobetsu Youth Hostel* (see p.338), lies the **Shiretoko Go-ko**, where five jewel-like lakes are linked by wooden walkways and sinuous forest paths. In fine weather, some of the lakes reflect the mountains, and a lookout point west of the car park provides a sweeping view across the heathland to the sea. The further you walk around the 3km circuit, the more serene the landscape becomes. Note that in the Active Bear Season, you're only able to walk the full route as part of a guided tour. There is a shorter elevated walkway which is free throughout the park's open months, and you may even see bears from that walkway. Allow at least an hour to see all five lakes.

Kamuiwakka-no-taki

カムイワッカの滝

Coming from Utoro, just before the turn-off to the Shiretoko Go-ko lakes, a dirt road continues up the peninsula. Following this track for about twenty minutes by car, as it rises uphill, will bring you to **Kamuiwakka-no-taki**, a cascading warm-water river and series of waterfalls, creating three levels of natural rotemburo, although these days only the lowest pool is accessible, due to the risk of falling rocks. To reach the bathing pool (bring your bathing costume) you'll have to climb up the river – be careful on the slippery rocks. The water is mildly acidic, so be warned that if you have any cuts it's going to sting, and bring a water bottle to rinse off with afterwards. Access by car is not allowed during the busy season (Aug and mid-Sept), thus shuttle buses run from Utoro to the site and back (¥1980; 1hr).

ARRIVAL AND DEPARTURE   SHIRETOKO NATIONAL PARK

By train The gateway to the Shiretoko Peninsula is Shari (斜里), where there's a JR station (Shiretoko-Shari) on the Senmō line.

Destinations Abashiri (7 daily; 45min); Kushiro (5 daily; 2hr 30min).

By bus From the bus terminal opposite the station, services run to Utoro (7 daily; 50min; ¥1650) and to Rausu (4 daily; 1hr; ¥1600). Between May and October, buses continue up to Iwaobetsu for the youth hostel (see p.338). In the same time period you can travel to Rausu (¥2660) via the Shiretoko Pass; note this road is closed to traffic Nov to late April. For more details check ⓦ sharibus.co.jp.

INFORMATION AND TOURS

Tourist information There's a tourist office in the road station on the way into Utoro (daily 8.30am–6.30pm; ☎0152 24 2639, ⓦ town.shari.hokkaido.jp), and, on the other side of the peninsula, there's the Rausu Visitor Centre (羅臼ビジターセンター; 6-27 Yunosawa, Rausu-chō; May–Oct 9am–5pm; Nov–April 10am–4pm; closed Mon; ☎0153 87 2828, ⓦ rausu-vc.jp) about 1km or so out of Rausu, near the Kuma-no-yu hot springs.

Cruises There are several sightseeing boats that leave from Utoro. Trips on the largest boat, the *Aurora* (☎0152 24 2147, ⓦ ms-aurora.com), run to Kamuiwakka-no-taki

waterfall and Mount Iō (end April–Oct daily, 1hr 30min; ¥3100) and out to the cape (June–Sept daily, 3hr 45min; ¥6500); you'll get closer to the coastline on one of the smaller boats run by several different operators. Gojiraiwa-Kankō (ゴジラ岩観光; ☎0152 24 3060, ⓦ kamuiwakka .jp) run cruises out to the cape (3hr–3hr 30min; ¥8000), shorter cruises up to Kamuiwakka-no-taki and Mount Iō (1hr; ¥3300); and the popular brown bear sightseeing cruise (2hr; ¥5500). Rausu is the place to go for spring and winter cruises – Gojiraiwa-Kankō also runs trips there (from ¥4000/person).

ACCOMMODATION AND EATING

Utoro has the best range of accommodation and good access to the peninsula. The more remote **Rausu** is another option if you have more time.

Café Fox カフェ・フォックス 96 Utoro-higashi ☎0152 24 2656. For some superb fish and chips, made with local fresh fish, seek out this small café, which also runs boat tours. 📶 Daily 8am–5pm, hours may change

depending on the boat schedule.

Ikkyuya 一休屋 13 Utoro-higashi ☎0152 24 2557. Just north of the bus station, there's a varied menu here, with a delicious salmon *oyako-don* ("parent-child" rice bowl, with

---

HIKING IN THE SHIRETOKO NATIONAL PARK

The peak of **Rausu-dake** (羅臼岳), the tallest mountain in Shiretoko at 1661m, can be reached in around four-and-a-half hours from the *Iwaobetsu Youth Hostel* (see p.338), passing a natural rotemburo on the way. From the summit, there are spectacular views along the whole peninsula, and to the east you should be able to see Kunashiri-tō, one of the disputed Kuril Islands, or "Northern Territories" as they are known in Japan (see box, p.338). It takes a full day to continue across Rausu-dake to Rausu.

Iō-zan (硫黄山), the active volcano that produces hot water for the Kamuiwakka-no-taki waterfalls, is a more difficult climb. The trail begins beside the Shiretoko Ōhashi, the bridge just beyond the entrance to the falls. A hike to the 1562m summit and back takes at least eight hours and can be combined with a visit to the hot waterfall.

You'll need to be a serious mountaineer to tackle the difficult ridge trail linking Iō-zan and Rausu-dake; bring a topographical map, take precautions against bears (see box, p.339) and plan to stay one or two nights at the campsites along the way. The **Rusa Field House** (ルサフィールドハウス; closed Tues; summer 9am–5pm; winter 10am–4pm; ☎0153 89 2722), about 10km north along the coast from Rausu, can provide rules and current information to mountaineers and sea kayakers.

salmon sashimi and roe) for about ¥1000. Daily 11am–6pm.

Iwaobetsu Youth Hostel 知床岩尾別ユースホステル Aza Iwaobetsu ☎ 0152 24 2311, ⊛ youthhostel.or.jp. Nestling in a valley beside the Iwaobetsu-gawa, this hostel is large and well managed, with welcoming staff and good food. Closed early Nov–late June. Rental bikes available. Meals extra (¥2200). Dorms **¥3900**

Mine-no-yu 峰の湯 Yunosawa-chō 7-3, Rausu ☎ 0153 87 3001, ⊛ rausu-minenoyu.com. The least shabby of Rausu's three large onsen hotels, the majority of rooms here are Japanese-style but have attached Western-style toilets and baths. Meals included. ☞ **¥18,000**

Shiretoko Grand Hotel 知床グランドホテル 172 Utoro-higashi ☎ 0152 24 2021, ⊛ shiretoko.co.jp. This opulent hotel has both Western- and Japanese-style rooms, as well as a rooftop onsen bath and rotemburo with views across the harbour. Meals included. ☞ **¥47,600**

Shiretoko Yaei-jō 知床野営場 Utoro-kagawa ☎ 0152 24 2722. On the hill overlooking Utoro, this well-maintained campsite is open June–Sept. Onsen nearby. Camping per person **¥400**, cabins for four people **¥3200**

Akan National Park

阿寒国立公園, Akan Kokuritsu Kōen

Some 50km south of the Shiretoko Peninsula is the densely forested **AKAN NATIONAL PARK**, its 905 square kilometres harbouring three major **lakes** – Mashū-ko, Kussharo-ko and Akan-ko – and the **volcanic peaks** of Me-Akan (female mountain) and Ō-Akan (male mountain), which formed Akan-ko. Patchy public transport makes this a difficult area to tour unless you have your own car or don't mind hitching. Nevertheless, the park is a haven for birdwatchers and walkers and has some pleasant lakeside onsen, while in **Akan Kohan** you can see traditional Ainu dancing, as well as the rare balls of algae known as *marimo*. A great way to see the lakes and some natural *marimo* is to jump on one of the sightseeing cruises. These include a stop at the Marimo Exhibition and Observation Centre on Churui-jima in the middle of Akan-ko (85min; leaves every hour; ¥1900).

ARRIVAL AND INFORMATION

AKAN NATIONAL PARK

By bus Buses run to Akan Kohan (see below) from Asahikawa (2 daily; 5hr) via Sōunkyō (see p.326; 3hr 30min). There are also tourist buses that do a loop from Kushiro Station, taking in the sites at Akan-ko, Mashū-ko and Kussharo-ko; check ⊛ akanbus.co.jp for the latest schedule.

Tourist information There's wi-fi and plenty of information on local activities, including hiking trails, at the tourist office (daily 9am–6pm; ☎ 0154 67 3200, ⊛ lake -akan.com, ⊛ kam-kankouken.jp), opposite the *New Akan Hotel Shangrila* about a 5min walk from the bus terminal towards the lake. You can rent bikes from here for ¥500/day.

Akan Kohan

阿寒湖畔

The compact onsen resort of **AKAN KOHAN** on the southern shore of the lake is the most commercialized part of the Akan National Park, with no shortage of tacky gift shops down its main street. However, it can be used as a base for hikes up the nearby peaks of **Me-Akan-dake** (雌阿寒岳; 1499m) and **Ō-Akan-dake** (雄阿寒岳; 1371m). Many of the hotels allow day visitors into their onsen baths, usually between 11am and 3pm, for around ¥1500.

THE DISPUTED KURIL ISLANDS

A protracted territorial dispute over the **Kuril Islands**, some of which can be seen clearly from the Shiretoko Peninsula, means that technically Japan and Russia are still fighting World War II. A peace accord has yet to be signed because of Russia's continued occupation of these volcanic islands, which are strung across the Sea of Okhotsk between the Kamchatka Peninsula and northeastern Hokkaidō.

Known in Japan as the **Northern Territories**, or Thousand Islands, and in Russia as the Kurils, only eight of the 56 volcanic islands are permanently inhabited. Japan demands the return of the four southernmost islands, the closest of which is less than 20km off Hokkaidō's coast. The islands themselves are fairly desolate; it is their strategic importance, **rich mineral resources** and the surrounding fishing grounds that make them so desirable.

Ainu Kotan Village

アイヌコタン • **Folklore Museum** Daily 10am–10pm • ¥300 • **Ikor dance and music performances** Evenings; times vary •
☎ 0154 67 2727, ⓦ akanainu.jp • ¥1080

At the western end of town is the **Ainu Kotan**, a contrived Ainu "village" which is little
more than a short road of gift shops selling identical carved-wood figures. Some two
hundred Ainu are said to live in the town. Traditional dance and music performances
are staged in the thatched *chise* (house) at the top of the shopping parade, and there's a
tiny **folklore museum** in a hut beside the *chise* with some traditional Ainu costumes.
There are also regular evening performances of puppet plays and traditional Ainu
dancing in the impressive Ainu Theatre Ikor (イコロ).

Akan Kohan Eco Museum Centre

阿寒湖畔エコミュージアムセンター • 1-1 Akanko Onsen 1-chōme • 9am–5pm; closed Tues • Free • ☎ 0154 67 4100,
ⓦ bit.ly/akan-kohan

At the eastern end of Akan Kohan is the **Akan Kohan Eco Museum Centre**, where you
can find out how the Akan caldera was formed and view *marimo* up close. These
velvety green balls of algae are native to Akan-ko, which is one of the few places in the
world where you'll find this nationally designated "special natural treasure". Despite
their rarity and the fact that it can take two hundred years for the *marimo* to grow to
the size of baseballs, it's possible to buy bottled baby *marimo* in all of Akan's gift shops –
although, in recent years, these souvenirs are more likely to be hand-rolled algae from
other lakes. From the Eco Museum, pleasant woodland trails lead to the **Bokke** (ボッケ),
a small area of bubbling mud pools beside the lake.

ACCOMMODATION	AKAN KOHAN

Akan-kohan Campsite 阿寒湖畔キャンプ場 5-1 Akanko Onsen ☎ 0154 67 3263, ⓦ bes.or.jp/akanko /camp.html. This decent wooded campsite is a 5min walk beyond the Ainu Kotan village (see above). Open June– Sept. Per person **¥630**

Hinanoza 鄙の座 2-8-1 Akanko Onsen ☎ 0154 67 5500, ⓦ hinanoza.com. To see how amazing Ainu carving can be, take a peek – or better yet stay – at this beautifully designed hotel, the most luxurious of the Tsuruga group's three properties by the lake. Rooms have terraces with private onsen baths. 🛜 **¥69,300**

Kiri 桐 4-3-26 Akanko Onsen ☎ 0154 67 2755, ⓦ bit.ly /kiri-akan. Meals aren't included at this good-value minshuku above a souvenir shop, but you can bathe in a beautiful handmade Sakhalin fir bathtub. **¥9000**

Mashū-ko

摩周湖

Some 35km east of Akan-ko, just outside the Akan National Park boundaries, is the
famed lake **MASHŪ-KO**, lying at the bottom of sheer cliffs that keep tourists at bay and

---

BEWARE BEARS

The **brown bear** (*ezo higuma*) is common to wilderness areas of Hokkaidō, with around two
hundred thought to be living in the Shiretoko-hantō (see p.335). The bears, which can grow to a
height of 2m and weigh up to 400kg, can be dangerous if surprised. In 2016, bear sightings in
northern Japan increased dramatically, and four people were killed in Akita and Aomori prefecture
while foraging in the forest. If you're planning a **hiking** trip in these parts, it is important to be alert
for bears and take appropriate precautions so you don't disturb them. Carrying a **bell** that jangles
as you walk is a good idea as this will warn bears of your approach and hopefully keep them away.
It's also vital, if carrying **food**, that you take great care to keep this away from bears. Don't discard
food scraps around where you camp – leave them until you reach a river or stream where they
can be washed away. If you do encounter a bear, don't run away – this will be an invitation for
them to chase you – and don't make any sudden movements or look them directly in the eyes.
Try to remain as still as possible until the bear gets bored and moves on.

the waters pristine. There are three lookout points over the 212m-deep caldera lake, which on rare occasions sparkles a brilliant blue. Usually, though, the view is obscured by swirling mists and thick cloud, creating a mysterious atmosphere which led the Ainu to christen Mashū-ko "The Devil's Lake".

ARRIVAL AND DEPARTURE MASHŪ-KO

By bus Between mid-July and mid-Oct, the "Teshikaga Eco-Passport" is offered, a hop-on hop-off bus pass serving both Mashū-ko and Kussharo-ko. It also entitles holders to free bike rental from several train stations and other various discounts. A two-day pass is ¥1500 and can be bought at both JR Mashū and Kawayu Onsen stations. Four buses leave daily from JR Mashū for their loop, and three buses leave daily from JR Kawayu Onsen for theirs; both include Mashū-ko and Kussharo-ko on their routes. See ⓦ eco-passport.net for details.

ACCOMMODATION AND EATING

The Great Bear ザ・グレートベア Genya 883, Teshikaga-chō ☎0154 82 3830, ⓦgreatbear.sakura .ne.jp. Next door to *Mashū-ko Youth Hostel*, this restaurant serves delicious meals using local ingredients – set menus range from ¥1620 to steak at ¥14,500, less if you're staying at the hostel. Daily 7.30am–9pm.

Mashū-ko Youth Hostel 摩周湖ユースホステル Genya 883, Teshikaga-chō ☎0154 82 3098, ⓦyouthhostel .or.jp. This large and modern hostel halfway to the lake from Teshikaga runs a number of reasonably priced guided tours of the area. Meals are served next door in the good-value *Great Bear* restaurant. 🛜 Dorms ¥4700, doubles ¥9800

Kussharo-ko
屈斜路湖

West of Mashū-ko is Akan National Park's largest lake, picturesque **Kussharo-ko**, at eighty square kilometres the biggest **crater lake** in Japan. It's also said to be the home of Kusshi, Japan's answer to the Loch Ness Monster. Whether it has a monster or not, Kussharo-ko is special because it is fed by onsen below, creating a warm temperature and several natural rotemburo around its edge, such as the piping-hot pools at **Wakoto Hantō** (和琴半島), a mini-promontory on the lake's southern shore. You can hop into another lakeside rotemburo at **Kotan Onsen** (コタン温泉), an easy cycle ride from the *Kussharo-Gen'ya Youth Guesthouse* (see below).

A strong whiff of sulphur from the hot springs drifts over the area's main village, **KAWAYU ONSEN** (川湯温泉), 3km from the lake, where there are several hotels and minshuku and free *ashiyu* (footbaths). The bus terminal is located here, which makes the village a good base for touring the park.

ARRIVAL AND INFORMATION KUSSHARO-KO

By train Kawayu Onsen's train station is on the Senmō line and is a 10min bus journey (¥290) south of the village; buses are timed to meet the trains, with the last bus to the onsen leaving at 6.30pm.

Tourist information There's a good tourist office (daily 9am–5pm; ☎0154 83 2670) with lots of information. The free Kawayu Eco-Museum Centre (川湯エコミュージアムセンター; 2-2-6 Kawayu Onsen; April–Oct 8am–5pm, closed Wed in April; Nov–March 9am–4pm, closed Wed) has plenty of information on the park, but it's virtually all in Japanese.

Tours The Kawayu Eco-Museum Centre (see above) can provide information on the several hiking trails around the village, one of which is wheelchair-accessible, and rent out cross-country skis and snowshoes in winter. Contact River & Field (☎080 6648 4288) if you're interested in taking a guided canoe tour of the Kushiro River (from ¥6000/person, min two people).

Bike rental You can rent bikes from Sun Energy near the Sumo Memorial Hall (April–Oct daily 8am–5pm; ¥500 for first hour, ¥100 for every additional hour).

ACCOMMODATION AND EATING

Hotel Kitafukurou ホテルきたふくろう 1-9-15 Kawayu-onsen ☎0154 83 2960, ⓦkitafukuro.com. The nicest place to stay in Kawayu Onsen, with both pleasant Japanese- and Western-style rooms and onsen baths (open to non-guests noon–6pm; ¥600). Two meals included. 🛜 ¥17,000

★**Kussharo-Gen'ya Youth Guesthouse** 屈斜路原野 ユースホステル 443-1 Kussharo-genya ☎0154 84 2609, ⓦwww.gogogenya.com. In a tent-like wooden building some 30min walk from the southern shore of Kussharo-ko, the rooms here are Western-style, and superb Japanese meals are available. You can rent mountain bikes (¥1500/

day) or take advantage of the various tours on offer, which include cross-country skiing in winter. In the evening, the staff will also take you to a natural rotemburo beside the lake. 🛜 Dorms **¥3300**, doubles **¥9800**

Orchard Grass オーチャードグラス 1-1-18 Kawayu-eki-mae ☎0154 83 3787. This nicely unchanged café, opened in 1936, is located at JR Kawayu Station and serves well-prepared curry rice. Oct–June 10am–6pm, closed Tues.

San San Go Go 三三五五 1-4-10 Kawayu-onsen ☎0154 83 3355, 🌐sansangogo.com. On the main shopping street in Kawayu Onsen, this friendly establishment serves tasty set meals, including their speciality, fried chicken, or *jingisukan* (barbecued mutton), for around ¥1300. Tues–Sat 11.30am–2pm & 6pm–midnight.

Wakoto-Hantō Kohan Camp Area 和琴半島湖畔キャンプ場 🌐akoto-hantō ☎0154 84 2350. At the Wakoto Hantō Peninsula on the southern shores of Kussharo-ko, where you can enjoy canoeing, fishing and the natural rotemburo by the lake. Open April–Oct. Per person **¥450**

Kushiro Shitsugen National Park

釧路湿原国立公園, Kushiro Shitsugen Kokuritsu Kōen

Japan's largest protected wetland, at 45,200 acres, is the **Kushiro Shitsugen National Park**. Birdwatchers flock here in winter to see **tanchō cranes** (see box, p.334), but the wetlands are home to many other birds and animals, including deer, grey herons, whooper swans and eagles. One of the best places to observe the cranes is actually just north of the park, in the fields near the village of **TSURUI** (鶴居), an hour's drive north of Kushiro, at the **Tsurui Itō Japanese Crane Sanctuary** (鶴居・伊藤タンチョウサンクチュアリ; Aza Nakasetsuri Minami; Nov–March Mon & Thurs–Sun 9am–4.30pm; ☎0154 64 2620). Half an hour further north of here towards Akan is the **Akan International Crane Centre** (daily 9am–5pm, April–Oct closed Mon; ¥400) at **GRUS**, which has breeding facilities and an exhibition hall.

ARRIVAL AND INFORMATION   KUSHIRO SHITSUGEN NATIONAL PARK

By plane Tanchō Kushiro Airport たんちょう釧路空港 (☎0154 57 8304, 🌐kushiro-airport.co.jp) is 20km west of Kushiro and 45min from town by bus (¥910). Destinations Sapporo (6 daily; 45min); Tokyo Haneda (6 daily; 1hr 50min).

By bus The industrial port of Kushiro (釧路) is the southern gateway to the park, which is best toured by car, but the Akan Kohan-bound bus from Kushiro Station also passes several of the facilities; get details from Kushiro's tourist office.

Tourist information There's a helpful tourist office (daily 9am–5.30pm; ☎0154 22 8294, 🌐kushiro-kankou.or.jp) in Kushiro Station; ask for the useful *Kushiro Wetland Teku-Teku Map* or download it from their website.

ACCOMMODATION

Hickory Wind ヒッコリーウィンド Tsurui ☎0154 64 2956, 🌐hickorywind.jp. There's excellent accommodation and a friendly welcome in this rustic location overlooking the crane sanctuary. Call ahead to be picked up at the airport or Tsurui bus station. Birdwatching tours also available. Rates include two meals. **¥22,000**

Kushiro Shitsugen Tōro Youth Hostel 釧路湿原とうろユースホステル Tōro 7, Shibecha-chō ☎0154 87 2510, 🌐tohro.net. At Tōro, on the east side of the park, a cosy hostel only moments from the train station. Dorms **¥4752**, doubles **¥9000**

Obihiro

帯広

Directly 200km east of Sapporo lies **OBIHIRO**, often considered a stopover destination en route to the eastern parts of Akan National Park and Kushiro. Though it may not be Hokkaidō's most picturesque city, it compensates with some outstanding festivals, tempting shopping opportunities and memorable cultural experiences. It's also surrounded by rich farmland; you may consider stopping by Kamishihorochō Naitaikōgen Farm (上士幌町ナイタイ高原牧場, 10am–5pm, closed Wed), Japan's largest public pasture, to enjoy fresh ice cream or climb Naitai-zan (ナイタイ山).

Obihiro Racecourse

帯広競馬場, Obihiro Keiba-jō • Nishi 13 Minami 9 • Mid-April to late-Nov, Sat–Mon 1–8.30pm • ¥100 • ☎ 0155 34 0825,
Ⓦ banei-keiba.or.jp • 20min on foot from JR Obihiro or 10min by local Tokachi bus; alight at Keiba-jō Mae bus stop

Though **Obihiro Racecourse** opened in 1932, it's only since 2007 that this officially became the only place in the world to continue to practise the sport of **Banei**. This involves one-tonne draught horses pulling sleighs across a 200m course for spectators, who often run alongside the track cheering on their favourite. Originally the races took place to display the strength of Hokkaidō's farm horses, but now it's a local betting extravaganza. When the gigantic horses aren't racing, you can visit them at the on-site stables and even offer a carrot. A small free museum dedicated to the racing tradition is next to the track.

Ikeda Wine Castle

池田ワイン城, Ikeda Wain-jō • Ikeda, Kiyomi 83-3 • Daily 11am–5pm; tours three times daily, reservation required • Free •
☎ 0157 72 2467, Ⓦ www.tokachi-wine.com • Take limited express or local train to Ikeda Station and walk 10min

Perched on top of a hill and completely out of place sits the European-looking **Ikeda Wine Castle**. Though Japan is not known for wine, and despite Hokkaidō being less than ideal for cultivating grapes, Tokachi wine is considered some of the best in Japan and has won numerous awards. A free wine tour is offered, though unmonitored wine tasting takes place throughout. In October, the castle hosts a wine festival, where participants can indulge in all-you-can-drink wine and all-you-can-eat Hokkaidō beef on the castle grounds.

Tokachigawa Onsen

十勝川温泉 • Hokumon-chō 11 chōme • Daily 11am–5pm • Free • ☎ 0155 32 6633, Ⓦ tokachigawa.net • Tokachi bus #45 from Obihiro Station toward Ecology Park to Tokachigawa Onsen stop

One of the more popular onsen resorts in Hokkaidō, **Tokachigawa Onsen** has drawn people to bathe in its golden-brown waters since 1900. Unlike other onsen that are fed by sulphuric volcanic springs, this one is a low-alkaline moor spring. Its source is ancient plants deep underground, emitting heat and copious amounts of organic matter that are said to make the skin smoother and to have beautifying effects. About twenty hotels offer one-day onsen passes in the area for ¥350–1000 (see Ⓦ tokachigawa .net for locations).

ARRIVAL AND INFORMATION   OBIHIRO

By plane Tokachi-Obihiro airport (とかち帯広空港, ☎ 0162 27 2121) is 10km east of the city; a bus costs ¥1000 (7 daily; 40min), and a taxi ¥7000. There are flights to and from Tokyo Haneda (7 daily; 1hr 30min).

By train Limited express trains from Sapporo to Obihiro take 2hr 50min.

By bus Buses leave in front of the train station.

Destinations Asahikawa via Sōunkyō (daily; 3hr 45min); Asahikawa via Furano (3 daily; 4hr); Sapporo via the Potato Liner (10 daily; 3hr 40min).

Tourist information The tourist office (daily 9am–6pm; ☎ 0155 23 6403, Ⓦ obikan.jp) is inside the JR terminal. Bike rental available.

ACCOMMODATION AND EATING

Café Green カフェグリーン Higashi 3, Minami 3 ☎ 0155 27 3751, Ⓦ bit.ly/café-green-obihiro. This cosy café serves reasonably priced drinks and smoothies, desserts and lunch sets. One of the few places open early for

breakfast. Daily 8am–1am.

Hotel Nupka ホテルヌプカ Nishi 10-20-3, Minami 2 ☎ 0155 20 2600, Ⓦ nupka.jp. Located minutes from JR Obihiro, an attractively modern hotel with a café/bar with

---

OBIHIRO'S FESTIVALS

In the winter, Obihiro hosts yet another Snow Festival, lacking the crowds of its sister Yuki Matsuri in Sapporo. In the summer during the Obon holidays, Obihiro holds one of the most impressive fireworks displays in Japan at the **Kachimai Hanabi Taikai** (勝毎花火大会).

CRISSCROSSING POROSHIRI-DAKE

Known as one of Japan's best hikes, **Poroshiri-dake** (幌尻岳) lies deep within the Hidaka mountains and is often called the "backbone" of Hokkaidō. It's a demanding hike; at 2052m, the beautiful alpine trail snakes along flowing rivers, requiring about 25 crossings, some waist-deep. Ten hours is recommended for the hike, and a hut is open mid-July to late Sept for overnight trekkers. Climbing is not recommended after heavy rainfalls because the crossings become more treacherous.

The only way to reach Poroshiri-dake without your own transport is either to hitch or take a bus to Furenai (振内) from Sapporo or Tomakomai (⦿donanbus.co.jp). From there, take a taxi to reach the starting point.

gourmet coffee and its own craft beer. Wooden bunk-bed dorms and comfortable private rooms. ⦿ Dorms ¥3400, doubles ¥21,300

Panchou ぱんちょう Nishi 1, Minami 11-19-1 ⦿0155 22 1974. Obihiro's claim to culinary fame is its *buta don*, char-grilled pork seasoned with soy sauce served over rice. Wait in line here to taste the delicious original (¥900). 11am–7pm; closed Mon and some Tues.

Toipirka Kitaobihiro Youth Hostel トイピルカ北帯広ユースホステル Higashi 52-8, Kita 4 ⦿0155 30 4165, ⦿bit.ly/toipirka-hostel. The wood-furnished hostel is the closest hostel option to Obihiro, and nearby to Tokachigawa Onsen. Its friendly owners serve up tasty organic meals. Free pick-up from Obihiro Station and free bike rental. ⦿ Dorms ¥4752, doubles ¥8200

SHOPPING

Ryugetsu Sweetpia Garden 柳月スイートピア・ガーデン Kita 9, Nishi 18 ⦿0120 25 5566, ⦿ryugetsu .co.jp/sweetpia. Renowned sweets producer Ryugetsu operates giant Tokachi Sweetpia Garden close to the city centre, and offers sugar-infused shopping, factory tours, snacking and hands-on workshops (¥700 and up). Daily 9am–6pm; early Nov to early April 9.30am–5.30pm.

4

Central Honshū

本州中部

MERCHANT HOUSE, TAKAYAMA

5

Central Honshū

Dominated by the magnificent Japan Alps, peppered with top onsen and ski resorts, time-honoured castle- and temple-towns and quaint old-fashioned villages in remote valleys, Central Honshū offers a fantastic choice of terrain and travel possibilities. If you just want to admire the grand scenery – even for a day – you can zip on the Shinkansen from Tokyo to the chief town, Nagano, home to the venerable Zenkō-ji temple.

Known locally as Chūbu, the region also boasts the summer resort of **Karuizawa** and the charming village of **Nozawa Onsen**, northeast of Nagano, where you'll find excellent ski slopes and free hot-spring baths. **Hakuba** is another popular skiing and outdoor activities destination, while in the southern half of Nagano-ken you can explore the immaculately preserved post towns that line the old Nakasendō route from Kyoto to Tokyo, even hiking for a day between the best of them – **Tsumago** and **Magome**.

The western side of the Alps holds the convivial town of **Takayama** and the unusual A-frame thatched houses of the **Shirakawa-gō** and **Gokayama** valleys. This area can also be accessed from the Sea of Japan, where the elegant, historic city of **Kanazawa**, now reached by direct Shinkansen from Tokyo, makes an ideal base. Off to the northeast, the tranquil fishing villages dotted around the rugged coastline of the **Noto Hantō** peninsula offer glimpses of a Japan far removed from the modern metropolises.

Along the southern coast of Chūbu, the main expressways and train lines between Tokyo and the Kansai region parallel the Pacific, amid ugly vistas of rampant industrialization. Even here there are places worth stopping to see, including Japan's fourth main city, **Nagoya**, an enjoyable and easily negotiated metropolis that offers day-trips to the attractive castle town of **Inuyama**, where the ancient skill of *ukai* (cormorant fishing) is still practised, or to **Meiji Mura**, an impressive outdoor museum of early twentieth-century architecture.

GETTING AROUND
CENTRAL HONSHŪ

By train and bus Since the Shinkansen was extended as far as Kanazawa in 2015, transport connections have been faster than ever. However, even though a couple of train lines cut across from coast to coast, many places in the mountains are only served by buses, which can be infrequent and pricey.

By car Renting a car will sometimes be your best bet, although several scenic routes, including the Skyline Drive across the Alps from Gifu-ken to Nagano-ken, are closed by deep snow in winter. The mountain resort of Kamikōchi and the Tateyama-Kurobe Alpine Route are similarly off limits Nov–April.

HIKING FROM KAMIKŌCHI TO YARI-GA-TAKE'S PEAK

Highlights

❶ Obuse Idyllic rural town where you can enjoy gourmet treats, sake, traditional architecture and a healthy dose of Hokusai. **See p.354**

❷ Japan Alps skiing Ride Japan's legendary powder snow at the ski resorts dotted around Nagano. **See p.358**

❸ Matsumoto Survey the mountains surrounding this friendly city from the donjon of Japan's oldest wooden castle. **See p.365**

❹ Kamikōchi Climb Japan's magnificent Alps from this beguiling alpine resort, only accessible from April to November. **See p.370**

❺ Kiso Valley Follow in the footsteps of the samurai with a hike through the picturesque post towns of the old Nakasendō route. **See p.373**

❻ Takayama A delightful town renowned for its skilled carpenters, whose craftsmanship adorns its attractive merchant houses, shrines and temples. **See p.376**

❼ Kanazawa Refined city that's home to verdant Kenroku-en and the cutting-edge vision of the 21st Century Museum of Contemporary Art. **See p.389**

❽ Gujō Hachiman August's Obon holidays offer an irresistible opportunity to dance the night away in this charming castle town. **See p.414**

HIGHLIGHTS ARE MARKED ON THE MAP ON P.348

5

Nagano

長野

The compact modern city of **NAGANO** stands at the heart of a broad and very fertile valley a little over 200km northwest of Tokyo. Capital of its own prefecture, it's best known internationally for having hosted the Winter Olympics back in 1998, courtesy of the world-class ski resorts nestled below the surrounding snowcapped peaks. Nagano

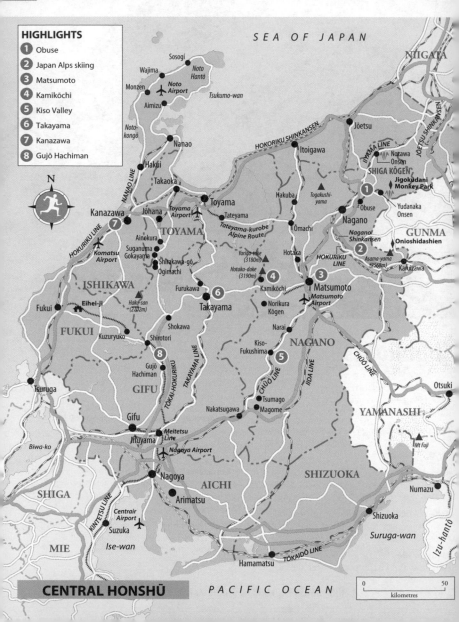

HIGHLIGHTS

1. Obuse
2. Japan Alps skiing
3. Matsumoto
4. Kamikōchi
5. Kiso Valley
6. Takayama
7. Kanazawa
8. Gujō Hachiman

SEA OF JAPAN

NIIGATA

Sosogi
Wajima
Noto Hantō
Monzen
Noto Airport
Aimizu
Tsukumo-wan

Noto-kongō
Nanao
Hakui
Takaoka
Toyama
Tateyama

HOKURIKU SHINKANSEN
Itoigawa
Jōetsu

IIYAMA LINE
JOETSU SHINKANSEN
Nozawa Onsen
SHIGA KŌGEN
Jigokudani Monkey Park

Hakuba
Togakushi-yama
Obuse
Yudanaka Onsen

Kanazawa
Jōhana
Toyama Airport
Ainokura
Suganuma
Gokayama
Shirakawa-gō
Ogimachi

TOYAMA
Tateyama-kurobe Alpine Route
Ōmachi
Nagano
Nagano Shinkansen
Onioshidashien

GUNMA
Asama-yama (2568m)
Karuizawa

Yariga-take (3180m)
Hotaka-dake (3190m)
Hotaka
HOKURIKU LINE

Komatsu Airport

ISHIKAWA
Haku-san (2702m)
Furukawa
Takayama
Kamikōchi
Matsumoto
Matsumoto Airport

Fukui
Eihei-ji
Shokawa
Norikura Kōgen
Narai

FUKUI
Kuzuryuko
Shirotori
Gujō Hachiman

GIFU
Kiso-Fukushima
NAGANO
CHŪŌ LINE
CHŪŌ LINE

Tsuruga
Gifu
Nakatsugawa
Tsumago
Magome
YAMANASHI
Otsuki

Biwa-ko
Inuyama
Meitetsu Line
Nagoya Airport

SHIGA
Nagoya
Arimatsu
AICHI
SHIZUOKA
Mt Fuji

Centrair Airport
Suzuka
Ise-wan
Numazu
Shizuoka

MIE
Hamamatsu
TŌKAIDŌ LINE
Suruga-wan
Izu-hantō

CENTRAL HONSHŪ
PACIFIC OCEAN

0 _____ 50
kilometres

SHŌRYŪDŌ WELCOME CARD

The **Shōryūdō Welcome Card**, a discount scheme for overseas tourists that covers hundreds of hotels, restaurants, transport and sightseeing facilities, is valid in the nine prefectures in central Japan: Aichi, Fukui, Gifu, Ishikawa, Mie, Nagano, Shiga, Shizuoka and Toyama. Ask at the main tourist offices for details or go to: ⓦ bit.ly/shoryudowelcome.

has been attracting Japanese visitors for centuries, however, thanks to the millions of pilgrims who flock to pay homage at the **Zenkō-ji** temple complex.

For tourists, Nagano makes an easy and rewarding stopover. Other than the temple itself, silhouetted against a splendid mountain backdrop at the top of the die-straight main street, there are few specific sights. With hotels and restaurants in abundant supply, though, it's a handy base for trips to nearby destinations such as Karuizawa, Togakushi, Obuse, Nozawa Onsen, Hakuba, and Kanbayashi Onsen, home to the famed snow monkeys.

Zenkō-ji

善光寺 • 491 Motoyoshi-chō, 2km north of JR station • Daily from 1hr before sunrise until 4.30pm April–Oct, 4.15pm March & Nov, 4pm Dec–Feb • precinct access free; inner sanctuary ¥500, with San-Mon & History Museum ¥1000 • ☎ 026 234 3591, ⓦ zenkoji.jp

Still very much the focal point of Nagano, **Zenkō-ji** was established in 642 AD to hold a remarkable treasure – a Buddhist statue that may have been the first such image ever to reach Japan, and which has remained unseen by anyone for almost fourteen centuries. Factors explaining the temple's abiding popularity include that it has traditionally welcomed adherents of all Buddhist sects, has never barred women, and is run alternately by an abbot of the Tendai sect and an abbess of the Jōdo sect. You can join the hundreds of daily petitioners searching for the "key to paradise" that lies beneath the main temple building; find it, and you'll have earned eternal salvation.

Approaching Zenkō-ji

Assuming you approach Zenkō-ji on foot, following the traditional pilgrim route up Nagano's gently sloping main street, Chūō-dōri, you'll come first to a short, narrow pedestrian precinct that's lined with stalls selling snacks and souvenirs. The building to your left is the **Daihongan** (大本願), the nunnery and residence of the high priestess of

5

Zenkō-ji, who is usually a member of the imperial family. Look out for the courtyard fountain with a statue of Mizuko Jizō, the patron saint of aborted and stillborn babies – little dolls and toys are left as offerings around the base.

The walking route then passes through an impressive 13.6m-tall gate, **Niō-mon** (仁王門). Beyond that, on the right, the **Rokujizō** (六地蔵) is a row of six large metal statues that symbolize the guardians of the six worlds through which the soul must pass: hell, starvation, beasts, carnage, human beings and heavenly beings. **Daikanjin** (大勧進) to the left, reached by crossing an attractive arched bridge, is the home of the high priest.

San-mon and the Zenkō-ji History Museum

Both daily 9am–4pm • Combined ticket including Zenkō-ji inner sanctuary ¥1000 • ☎ 026 234 3591, ⓦ zenkoji.jp

Visitors pass freely through a towering wooden gateway, the **San-mon** (山門), to reach Zenkō-ji's central courtyard. Paying ¥500 entitles you to climb a steep stairway up to its second storey, which offers sweeping views back down over Nagano. The same ticket also gives access to the **Zenkō-ji History Museum**, a pagoda off to the left of the main temple, where the statues and paintings on show date largely from the eighteenth century, and are labelled in Japanese only.

A large metal cauldron, adorned with a lion whose mouth exhales the perfumed smoke of incense sticks, stands in the centre of the temple courtyard. Pilgrims waft the smoke around their bodies before moving on to the main hall.

Hondō

本堂

The vast, imposing main hall of Zenkō-ji, the **Hondō**, dates from 1707. Once inside, the first thing you encounter is a worn-out statue of Binzuru, a physician and fallen follower of Buddha; devotees with specific ailments rub the relevant body part in the hope of finding a cure. In the awe-inspiring space beyond, where golden ornaments dangle from the high ceiling, pilgrims would formerly bed down for the night.

Make the effort to attend the **morning service** at Zenkō-ji, which typically starts around 5.30am, and you'll witness the temple at its most mystical, with the priests wailing, drums pounding and hundreds of pilgrims joined in fervent prayer. It's immediately followed by the **O-juzu Chōdai** ceremony. Dressed in colourful robes, and shaded by a giant red paper umbrella, the high priest or priestess rustles past pilgrims kneeling in the courtyard outside, blessing them by tapping them on the head with prayer beads.

O-kaidan

お戒壇 • ¥500; buy tickets from the machines to the right of Binzuru's statue

A pitch-black passage, known as the **O-kaidan** and said to house the revered **Ikkō Sanzon Amida Nyorai** (see box below), runs beneath the innermost sanctum of the

---

THE IKKŌ SANZON AMIDA NYORAI

The most sacred object in Zenkō-ji, the **Ikkō Sanzon Amida Nyorai**, is a golden statue that depicts a triad of Amida Buddha images, sharing a single halo. Believed to have been made by Buddha himself in the sixth century BC, it's said to have arrived in Japan in 552 AD, as a gift to the emperor from Korea. Originally kept in a purpose-built temple near Osaka, it swiftly became the focus of a clan feud, in which the temple was destroyed. The statue was dumped in a nearby canal, only to be rescued in 642 by **Honda Yoshimitsu**, a poor man who was passing by and apparently heard Buddha call. Honda brought the image back to his home in Nagano (then called Shinano). When news of its recovery reached Empress Kōgyoku, she ordered a temple to be built in its honour, which she named Zenkō-ji after the Chinese reading of Honda's name. The empress also ordered that the image should never be seen again, so a copy was made. Known as the **Meidachi Honzon**, this is displayed every six years in the grand **Gokaichō festival**, held between early April and late May, most recently in 2015.

Hondō. Pilgrims queue to descend the steep staircase, and grope through the dark tunnel – said to symbolize the darkness of death – seeking the metaphorical "key to paradise". Once you're in, keep your right hand on the wall, and chances are you'll find the key (which actually feels more like a door knob) towards the end of the passage.

Nagano Prefectural Shinano Art Museum

長野県信濃美術館, Nagano-ken Shinano Bijutsukan • 1-4-4 Hakoshimizu • Mon, Tues & Thurs–Sun 9am–5pm • Permanent collection ¥700, usually ¥1000 with current temporary exhibition • ☎ 026 232 0052, ⊛ npsam.com

A short walk east of Zenkō-ji, across Joyama-kōen, a city park holds the **Nagano Prefectural Shinano Art Museum**, a modernist structure built in 1966 and now showing its age. It's divided into two sections; the main gallery holds changing short-term exhibitions, while a newer wing is devoted to the vivid, dreamy landscape paintings of celebrated local artist Higashiyama Kaii (1908–99).

Saikō-ji

西光寺 • 1398-1 Kitaishido-chō • Daily sunrise–sunset • Free; guided tours from ¥300 • ☎ 026 226 8436

Not far north of the JR station, the small **Saikō-ji** temple is tucked away in a quiet courtyard just off Chūō-dōri. Also known as Karukaya-san, after the Buddhist saint who founded it in 1199, the main temple building contains two wooden statues of Jizō, the guardian of children, one carved by Karukaya, and the other by his son Ishidō.

ARRIVAL AND INFORMATION

NAGANO

By train Nagano's JR station is a major stop for trains on the Hokuriku Shinkansen line, which connects Tokyo with Kanazawa. It is also connected with Nagoya via Matsumoto, and is a hub for local services around the prefecture. The private Nagano Dentetsu runs trains to Obuse and Yudanaka from its own terminus beneath the JR station complex.

Destinations Kanazawa (every 30min; 1hr 10min); Matsumoto (hourly; 50min); Nagoya (hourly; 3hr); Obuse (hourly; 24min); Tokyo (every 30min; 1hr 30min); Yudanaka (8 daily; 45min).

By bus Long-distance buses pull in at the Nagano Bus Terminal on Basu Tāminaru-dōri, west of the JR station.

Destinations Hakuba (10 daily; 1hr); Kyoto (1 daily; 8hr); Matsumoto (hourly; 1hr 20min); Niigata (4 daily; 3hr 30min); Nozawa Onsen (5 daily; 1hr 15min); Shinano-Ōmachi (5 daily; 1hr 45min); Togakushi (5 daily; 1hr 30min); Tokyo (hourly; 3hr 40min).

Tourist information Nagano operates an excellent tourist information centre in the station's main concourse (daily: April–Oct 8am–7pm, Nov–March 9am–6pm; ☎ 026 226 5626, ⊛ nagano-cvb.or.jp). Also check out Go! Nagano (⊛ go-nagano.net), which covers the whole prefecture.

Services The Central Post Office is at 1085-4 Minami-Agata (daily 9am–7pm).

GETTING AROUND

By bus Gururin-go city buses, leaving from platform one on the west side of the JR station, run up the main street, Chūō-dōri, to Zenkō-ji (one-way ¥150).

By car Car rental is available from Eki Rent-a-Car

(☎ 026 227 8500), beside the Zenkō-ji exit of the JR station.

On foot Nagano is easy to explore on foot; walking the 2km up Chūō-dōri from the station to Zenkō-ji makes a great way to get to know the city.

ACCOMMODATION

Nagano has plenty of **accommodation**, with the many business hotels clustered close to the station including a branch of *Tōyoko Inn*. For a better ambience, or if you want to join the early morning service, it's best to stay near Zenkō-ji.

1166 Backpackers 1166 バックパッカーズ 1048 Nishimachi ☎ 026 217 2816, ⊛ 1166bp.com. Just west of the main street, a 5min walk south of Zenkō-ji, this sociable hostel has a retro design vibe, with a comfortable lounge centred around a large dining/work table. Most of the rooms are dorms, though a private double room is also

available; a snack breakfast costs ¥500, as does a bike for the day. Staff are happy to share their local knowledge. 🛜 Dorms <u>¥2800</u>, doubles <u>¥6000</u>

Chisun Grand チサングランド長野 2-17-1 Minami-Chitose ☎ 026 264 6000, ⊛ solarehotels.com. Five minutes' walk northeast of the station, and offering large

5

rooms geared towards foreign visitors, plus helpful staff, free tea and coffee in the lobby, and good-value ¥1200 buffet breakfasts in the panoramic twelfth-floor restaurant. 📶 **¥10,700**

Kokusai 21 ホテル国際21 576 Agata-machi ☎ 026 234 1111, ⓦ kokusai21.jp. This contemporary business hotel, around a 15min walk up from the station, makes a rather anonymous place to stay, but its well-appointed rooms are surprisingly spacious, and it has a good selection of restaurants, plus great views from the sixteenth-floor bar. 📶 **¥17,200**

Matsuya Ryokan 松屋旅館 Zenkō-ji Kannai ☎ 026 232 2811. Charming traditional ryokan within the Zenkō-ji precinct, offering air-conditioned, paper-screened tatami rooms with and without private bathrooms. The staff speak little English, but cheerfully serve ¥1400 Japanese breakfasts and ¥3000 dinners on request. 📶 **¥12,600**

Metropolitan Nagano メトロポリタン長野 1346 Minami-Ishido-chō ☎ 026 291 7000, ⓦ metro-n.co.jp. This good-value upmarket hotel, conveniently close to the JR station's west exit, offers comfortable high-standard Western-style rooms, plus a stylish lobby and chic restaurants. Breakfast costs an additional ¥1700. 📶 **¥10,800**

Shimizuya Ryokan 清水屋旅館 49 Daimon-chō ☎ 026 232 2580, ⓦ chuoukan-shimizuya.com. Serviceable foreigner-friendly ryokan in a very handy location on the approach to Zenkō-ji. The sizeable tatami rooms don't have en-suite bathrooms, but they share a pleasant bathing area, and there's also a laundry room. Breakfast is available for ¥880, dinner for ¥2200. 📶 **¥13,800**

World Trek Guesthouse Pise ワールドトレックゲストハウスピセ 2-1 Higashigo-chō ☎ 026 214 5656, ⓦ nagano guesthouse.com. Budget accommodation on the main street, in the form of very basic capsule-style dormitory beds and no-frills private rooms, at the back of a hip postmodern bar/restaurant that even has its own climbing wall. Rates include one free beer, while rental bicycles cost ¥1000 per day. 📶 Mixed dorms **¥3000**, female dorms **¥3200**, private doubles **¥7000**, family rooms **¥9000**

EATING

Chūō-dōri holds plenty of places to **eat**, with handmade soba as the most conspicuous local dish. To sample *shōjin ryōri*, the vegetarian cuisine prepared for the monks, head for the area around Zenkō-ji, while smaller take-out places are scattered along the long, covered Gondō arcade, which runs east of Chūō-dōri.

★**Fujiya Gohonjin** 藤屋御本陳 80 Daimon-chō ☎ 026 232 1241. This elegant Meiji-era hotel has been spruced up with a snazzy contemporary design and turned into a very sophisticated Italian restaurant, serving authentic Mediterranean food including *al dente* pasta and rustic meat and fish dishes. Set dinner menus cost from ¥1200 at lunchtime, and ¥5000 or ¥7500 for dinner. Their café-bar overlooking traditional gardens is a lovely place to relax with a drink. Mon–Fri 11.30am–3pm & 6–10pm, Sat & Sun 7–10pm.

Hakata Yatai 博多屋台 9-1 Higashigo-chō ☎ 026 219 2969. Bright, friendly youth-oriented noodle joint, facing the main street at the corner of the Gondō arcade and open long into the night; roast-pork in ramen in a substantial pork-bone broth costs ¥980. 📶 Mon–Sat 11.30am–5am, Sun 11.30am–9.30pm.

Ichiryū Manpei 一粒万平 52 Daimon-chō ☎ 026 234 8255. Fresh local vegetables – especially mushrooms – abound in the wholesome meals prepared at this main-street restaurant, popular with locals and tourists. The lunchtime buffet clocks in at a reasonable ¥1500. Mon & Wed–Sun 11.30am–6.30pm.

Mankatei 萬佳亭 2502 Higashinomon-chō ☎ 026 232 2326. Enjoy the fine dishes, including sashimi, tempura, delicate noodles, the waitresses in kimono, and the twinkling cityscape views at this classy restaurant east of Zenkō-ji, on the edge of Joyama-kōen, overlooking the downtown area. Set menus start at ¥1575 for lunch, ¥5000 for dinner. Daily 11am–2pm & 5–9pm.

Patio Daimon ぱてぃお大門 54 Daimon-chō ⓦ patio -daimon.com. Complex of restaurants and shops, all styled like traditional white-walled *kura* (storehouses), where Chūō-dōri meets Route 406. Most tastes and budgets are catered for, from a cheerful café specializing in tofu-based sweets to the private dining room (Fri & Sat only; ¥15,000 per head), while the central courtyard is often used for concerts. Hours vary.

Yamajaya やま茶屋 1315 Tsuruga Toigo-shōmachi ☎ 026 233 3900, ⓦ yama39.com. Tasteful traditional restaurant, serving delicious mountain cuisine one block south of the Gondō pedestrian arcade, and 600m south of Zenkō-ji temple. A meaty duck hotpot, rich in local mushrooms, costs ¥2000; set meals start at ¥1000 for lunch, ¥3000 in the evening. Mon–Sat 11.30am–2pm & 6–9pm, Sun 11.30am–2pm & 6–8pm.

DRINKING AND NIGHTLIFE

Nagano's nightlife is concentrated in two main areas: the tangle of lanes that connect the JR station with Chūō-dōri, and around Gondō, with small **bars** clustered at the eastern end of the arcade, and a summer-only beer garden atop Gondō's Dentetsu-line station.

India Za Supaisu INDIA ザすぱいす 1418 Minamiishido-chō ☎026 226 6136. Crammed with clocks, keepsakes and conversation pieces, this quirky, lively café-pub, just off the southern end of Chūō-dōri, is

better seen as a drinking den than a place to eat, despite its menu of curries and omelettes. Beer's half-price during the generous 4.30–8.30pm happy "hour". Daily noon–midnight.

Around Nagano

In the heart of the Japan Alps, and often dubbed "the rooftop of Japan", the area around Nagano boasts dramatic scenery which provides a perfect location for nature-based activities. It is also worth taking time to visit some of the area's small towns for their distinctive attractions. **Togakushi**, the training ground for the legendary ninja warriors, makes an enjoyable trip, while the lovely little town of **Obuse** is a centre for refined culture and cuisine.

Togakushi

戸隠

The alpine area of **Togakushi**, 20km northwest of Nagano and famous for its role in ninja history, lies within the jagged ridge of Togakushi-yama and Iizuna-Yama. As well as great scenery, there's a worthwhile **museum** and a legendary **shrine**. In winter, there's good **skiing**.

Togakushi Minzoku-kan

戸隠民族館 • 3688-12 Togakushi • Late April to mid-Nov daily 9am–5pm • ¥500 • ☎026 254 2395

The **Togakushi Minzoku-kan** is a museum complex of traditional farm buildings, some of which have exhibits on the **Ninja warriors** who once trained here (see box below). Within the complex, the Togakure-ryū Ninpō Shiryōkan displays amazing photographs of the stealthy fighters in action and examples of their lethal weapons. The Ninja House next door is great fun, with a maze of hidden doors and staircases that is fiendishly difficult to find your way out of.

Togakushi Okusha

戸隠奥社 • 3690 Togakushi • Daily 9.30am–5pm • Free • ☎026 254 2001

The entrance to **Togakushi Okusha**, the innermost of the three main sanctuaries of the **Togakushi Shrine**, faces Togakushi Minzoku-kan. According to ancient Shintō belief,

---

NINJA: THE SHADOW WARRIORS

Long before their ancient martial art was nabbed by a bunch of cartoon turtles, the **Ninja** were Japan's most feared warriors, employed by lords as assassins and spies. They practised **Ninjutsu**, "the art of stealth", which emphasized non-confrontational methods of combat. Dressed in black, Ninja moved like fleeting shadows and used weapons such as *shuriken* (projectile metal stars) and *kusarikama* (a missile with a razor-sharp sickle on one end of a chain), examples of which are displayed in the Togakushi Minzoku-kan (see above).

According to legend, Ninjutsu was developed in the twelfth century, when the warrior Togakure Daisuke retreated to the mountain forests of Iga, near Nara, and met Kain Dōshi, a monk on the run from political upheaval in China. Togakure studied Dōshi's fighting ways, and his descendants developed them into the **Togakure-ryū school** of Ninjutsu. By the fifteenth century, there were some fifty family-based Ninjutsu schools across Japan, each jealously guarding their techniques.

Although the need for Ninja declined while Japan was under the peaceful rule of the Shogunate, the Tokugawa had their own force of Ninjutsu-trained warriors for protection. One Ninja, Sawamura Yasusuke, even sneaked into the "black ship" of Commodore Perry in 1853 to spy on the foreign barbarians. Today, the Togakure-ryū school of Ninjutsu, emphasizing defence rather than offence, is taught by the 34th master, **Hatsumi Masaaki**, in Noda, Chiba-ken, just north of Tokyo.

5

Togakushi-yama was created when the god Ame-no-Tajikarao tossed away the rock door of the cave where the Sun Goddess Amaterasu had been hiding (see box, p.744). A 2km-long corridor of soaring **cedar trees** takes you to the shrine – a collection of small wooden and stone buildings under the rocks. The adventurous can continue up the sharp ridge to the summit; it's a strenuous route, so take food, water and appropriate clothing, and log your name in the book at the start of the trail.

Chūsha
中社

Head downhill from Togakushi Okusha along pleasant woodland trails through the Togakushi Ōmine Recreational Forest, and you'll come to the attractive village of **CHŪSHA**, a good base for skiing in winter (information on ⓦtogakusi.com). The outer sanctuary of the **Hōkōsha** shrine here (宝光社; 24hr; free) is decorated with intricate wooden carvings, while shops sell baskets and woven bamboo goods: the best one (where you can watch basket weavers at work) is downhill, opposite the Spar store.

ARRIVAL AND DEPARTURE   TOGAKUSHI

By bus Buses (hourly, 1hr 10min; ¥2400 return; ⓦalpico .co.jp) leave from outside the Alpico bus office, opposite Nagano train station, and run along the vertiginous Bird-line Driveway, giving panoramic city views as they wind up hairpin bends around the mountain. Stay on the bus through Chūsha, an hour from Nagano, and get off a couple of stops later at the Togakushi Okusha.

ACCOMMODATION

Togakushi Kōgen Yokokura Youth Hostel 戸隠高原 横倉ユースホステル 3347 Nakayashiro ☏026 254 2030, ⓦbit.ly/togakushihostel. This excellent-value hostel, a 5min walk south of the shrine near Chūsha, offers tatami dorms in a thatched, 150-year-old pilgrim's lodge. There's a quaint log-cabin café, with breakfast costing ¥760 and dinner ¥1260, and the owner is a hospitable woman who speaks some English. 🛜 Dorms ¥3645

EATING

Uzuraya うずらや 3229 Togakushi ☏026 254 2219. Chūsha's top restaurant for freshly made soba and tempura, occupying a thatched farmhouse and located opposite the Hōkōsha shrine on the main road. It offers a range of dishes starting around ¥600. Mon, Tues & Thurs–Sun 10.30am–4pm.

Yamabōshi やまぼうし 3511-18 Togakushi ☏026 254 2624. The excellent Italian cuisine (main dishes ¥1250 and up) and home-made desserts at this cosy restaurant, on the way up to the Hōkōsha shrine, are almost worth making the journey for on their own. Mon, Tues & Thurs–Sun 10.30am–8.30pm.

Obuse
小布施

Famous for its connection with the artist **Hokusai** and for its production of chestnuts, **OBUSE**, 16km northeast of Nagano, ranks among the most attractive small towns in Japan. Its central streets especially, around the venerable **Masuichi-Ichimura** estate and brewery, have been beautified, their pavements relaid with blocks of chestnut wood. Old buildings have been spruced up to hold excellent restaurants, bars and a super-stylish hotel, and many residents take part in an open garden scheme.

Exploring Obuse, which is surrounded by **orchards and vineyards** and dotted with traditional houses, temples, small museums and craft galleries, can make the focus of wonderful day-trip. Be wary during prime chestnut season, though, in September and October, when Obuse is often heaving with coach parties during the day. Ideally, you'd stay overnight, and perhaps use Obuse as a base for trips around the area, including to the nearby Jigokudani Monkey Park (see p.362).

FROM TOP A BABY SNOW MONKEY AT JIGOKUDANI MONKEY PARK (P.362); SHIROYONE NO SENMAIDA RICE FIELDS NEAR WAJIMA (P.399) >

5

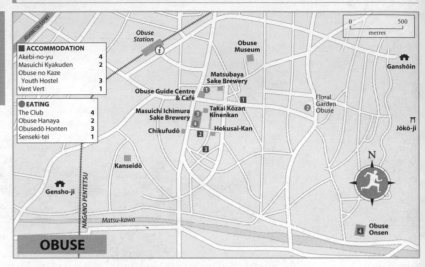

ACCOMMODATION
Akebi-no-yu	4
Masuichi Kyakuden	2
Obuse no Kaze Youth Hostel	3
Vent Vert	1

EATING
The Club	4
Obuse Hanaya	2
Obusedō Honten	3
Senseki-tei	1

OBUSE

Hokusai-kan

北斎館 • 485 Obuse • Daily: May–Aug 9am–6pm, Sept & Oct 9am–5.30pm, Nov–April 9am–5pm • ¥500 • ☎ 026 247 5206, ⓦ hokusai-kan.com

The **Hokusai-kan** museum, tucked away in a slightly confusing pedestrianized area just off Obuse's main street, is devoted to the great master of *ukiyo-e* woodblock prints, **Katsushika Hokusai**. In 1842, by which time he was well into his eighties, the artist was invited to live and work in Obuse by Takai Kōzan, the town's leading merchant and art lover. In a thatch-roofed studio especially built to suit his needs, Hokusai completed four paintings for the ceilings of two breathtaking festival floats that are now preserved in the museum. One is decorated with a dragon and a phoenix, the other with "masculine" and "feminine" variations of Hokusai's familiar wave motif. The museum's remaining galleries display other works by Hokusai, including painted scrolls, delicate watercolours and woodblock prints, along with changing exhibitions by other artists.

Takai Kōzan Kinenkan

高井鴻山記念館 • 805-1 Ōaza • Daily: April–Sept 9am–6pm, Oct–March 9am–5pm • ¥300 • ☎ 026 247 4049

The **Takai Kōzan Kinenkan**, the atmospheric home of Hokusai's patron, stands in the Masuichi-Ichimura compound, near the Hokusai-kan. Takai Kōzan was himself an accomplished artist and calligrapher, and his intriguing drawings of ghosts and goblins were intended as ironic comments on the turbulent early Meiji-era years. One room holds long banners inscribed with *kanji* characters, as well as the 2.5m-long brush used to paint them.

Obuse Museum

おぶせミュージアム • 595 Obuse • Daily: April–Sept 9am–6pm, Oct–March 9am–5pm • ¥500 • ☎ 026 247 6111

The highlight of the delightful **Obuse Museum** is the gallery devoted to a changing but ongoing exhibition of the colourful works of contemporary artist **Nakajima Chinami** (born 1945). Five of the town's traditional festival floats are also on show, complemented by successive temporary art exhibitions.

Ganshōin

岩松院 • 615 Karida • Daily 9am–5pm • ¥300 • ☎ 026 247 5504

During his years in Obuse, Hokusai painted a giant mural of a phoenix for the ceiling of the red-roofed **Ganshōin**, which occupies a superbly verdant location at the foot of the mountains 2km east of the centre. Towards the end of his life, Hokusai dedicated his energies towards creating paintings rather than prints, and it's well worth walking out here to admire this dramatic and little-known masterpiece.

Follow the well-marked footpath that wends its way south from Ganshōin, between the fields and the foothills, and after ten minutes you'll reach the wonderfully ancient **Jōkō-ji** (浄光寺; daily 9am–5pm). Built in 1408, this dark, thatched shrine stands high in the woods, atop a steep cobbled stairway.

ARRIVAL AND INFORMATION   OBUSE

By train Trains from Nagano, on the Nagano Dentetsu line, stop at Obuse station (hourly, 24min; ¥650–750), 5min walk from the centre.

Tourist information Obuse's visitor centre, at the station (daily 9am–5pm; ☎026 214 6300, ⓦobusekanko.jp),

distributes an excellent English-language map and guide, and doubles as a café. You can also pick up information at the Obuse Guide Centre & Café, at the central crossroads (April–Nov daily 9am–5pm, Dec–March Mon & Wed–Sun 9am–4pm; ☎026 247 5050).

GETTING AROUND

By bus From mid-April to Nov, an hourly shuttle bus makes a circuit of the town's sights – an all-day ticket costs ¥300.

By bike The town centre is small enough to walk around,

but rental bicycles, available at the station, the youth hostel (see below) and several other outlets, and costing around ¥400 per day, make a great way to reach the outlying temples and countryside.

ACCOMMODATION

Akebi-no-yu あけびの湯 1311 Obuse-chō ☎026 247 4800, ⓦobuse-akebinoyu.co.jp. Thanks to its hillside location, 2km southeast of the centre, rooms in this modern ryokan enjoy splendid mountain views. Guests can relax in the adjoining onsen baths for free (daily 6–8.30am & 10am–10pm; ¥500 for non-guests). Rates include two meals. 📶 **¥22,000**

★**Masuichi Kyakuden** 桝一客殿 815 Obuse-machi ☎026 247 1111, ⓦkyakuden.jp. This luxury hotel, which incorporates three kura moved from Nagano city and a central koi-filled pond, owes its chic contemporary style to John Morford, the interior designer of Tokyo's celebrated *Park Hyatt*. As well as twelve sublimely peaceful modern rooms, several of which have terraces, it holds great

restaurants and bars. Rates include breakfast. 📶 **¥37,800**

Obuse no Kaze Youth Hostel おぶせの風ユースホステル 475-2 Higashimachi ☎026 247 4489, ⓦobuse nokaze.travel.coocan.jp. Run by a hospitable family, this youth hostel makes a great budget choice; it's close to the Hokusai-kan, and offers guests a choice between Western-style dorms or tatami rooms, as well as private rooms. 📶 Dorms **¥3700**, doubles **¥7400**

Vent Vert ヴァンヴェール 34-8 Obuse-chō ☎026 247 5512, ⓦobusenoyado.com. Located above a cute French brasserie, which serves all meals daily, on an outdoor terrace when weather permits, this small hotel holds four nicely designed en-suite Western-style rooms. Rates rise by ¥1100 at weekends and during public hols. 📶 **¥13,000**

EATING

Obuse being such a popular day-trip destination, **lunch** is the most important meal for local restaurants; book ahead if you can, or at least call in earlier in the morning to reserve a table.

The Club 蔵部 815 Obuse-machi ☎026 247 5300, ⓦkyakuden.jp. The most animated and convivial of the three restaurants at *Masuichi Kyakuden*, open for lunch only, has an open kitchen where you can watch the chefs at work preparing a good range of local meat and fish dishes to complement their sakes. Expect to pay around ¥3500 per head, including drinks. 📶 Daily 11.30am–2.30pm.

Obuse Hanaya 花屋 506-1 Obuse-chō ☎026 247 1187. Delightful restaurant and café, on the east side of town beside the Floral Garden, using fresh local produce to prepare Western-style meals (lunch from ¥1000, dinner from ¥3000). 📶 Mon–Wed & Fri–Sun 11am–4pm & 6–9pm; second and fourth Wed of month, 11am–4pm only.

Obusedō Honten 小布施堂本店 815 Obuse-machi

☎026 247 2027, ⓦkyakuden.jp. Part of the *Masuichi Kyakuden* business, and behind the confectionery shop of the same name, this Zen-calm restaurant offers a *kaiseki ryōri*-style menu, from ¥2750, which changes monthly but always centres on local delicacies, especially chestnuts. Dinner is only available for *Masuichi Kyakuden* guests, by reservation only, but during the day, anyone can drop by the café section for drinks and chestnut sweets. 📶 Daily 10am–4pm & 6–8pm.

Senseki-tei 泉石亭 779 Obuse-chō ☎026 247 5166, ⓦkanseido.co.jp. Appealing restaurant, overlooking an exquisite ornamental garden, where chestnuts figure large in the wide range of set menus, starting around ¥1000. 📶 Mon & Wed–Sun 10.30am–6pm.

5

SAKE AND CHESTNUTS

You can sample the four excellent **sakes** brewed by Masuichi-Ichimura (桝一市村), and a few others, at the *teppa* counter in the brewery's shop (807 Obuse; daily 9am–6pm; ¥150–320; ☎026 247 7511, ⓦmasuichi.com). Try *Hakkin*, the only Japanese sake that's still brewed in huge cedar barrels the old-fashioned, labour-intensive way – hence its high price at ¥10,800 per bottle. Around the corner, you can sip award-winning sake for free in Obuse's other brewery, Matsubaya (松葉屋本店; 778 Nakamachi; daily 9am–6pm; ☎026 247 2019, ⓦmatsubaya-honten.co.jp).

Masuichi's sister company, Obusedō (小布施堂; 808 Obuse; daily 9am–7pm; ⓦobusedo.com), is just one of several **chestnut confectioners** in town battling it out for the public's sweet tooth. Others are Chikufudō (竹風堂; 973 Obuse; daily, May–Oct 8am–7pm, Nov–April 8am–6pm; ☎026 247 2569, ⓦchikufudo.com) and Kanseidō (桜井甘精堂; 2460 Obuse; daily 8.30am–6pm; ☎026 247 1088, ⓦkanseido.co.jp), both of which have restaurants, open shorter hours, that serve meals featuring the sweet nut.

The Nagano-ken mountains

The mountains of **Nagano-ken** are home to several ski resorts and onsen villages, including the delightful **Nozawa Onsen**, self-proclaimed home of Japanese skiing; **Hakuba**, a valley with seven different ski resorts; and **Shiga Kōgen**, Japan's largest skiing area, which lies within the Jōshinetsu Kōgen National Park. The park is also home to **Jigokudani Monkey Park**, famous for its snow monkeys, which splash about in their own rotemburo.

Nozawa Onsen

野沢温泉

Even though international word is out on how great the skiing is at **NOZAWA ONSEN**, this village of four thousand people maintains a traditional atmosphere. It has nestled at the base of Kenashi-yama (1650m), 50km northeast of Nagano, for over a thousand years. The **ski resort** (late Nov to early May; one-day lift pass ¥4900; ⓦnozawaski.com) is family-friendly, has lots of English signs and offers varied terrain that will put all levels through their paces. If at all possible, time your visit to coincide with the spectacular **Dōso-jin fire festival**, held on January 15.

Ō-yu bathhouse

大湯 • 9328 Toyosato • Daily: April–Nov 5am–11pm, Dec–March 6am–11pm • Free

Thirteen free **bathhouses**, all lovingly tended by the locals, are dotted along the narrow, twisting streets of Nozawa. The most impressive, **Ō-yu**, is housed in a temple-like wooden building in the centre of the village, complete with a trio of statues of the Buddha of Healing and his two attendant bodhisattvas. Each side of the building has two pools, one of which is so hot that it's almost impossible to get into.

Japan Ski Museum

日本スキー博物館, Nihon Sukii Hakubutsukan • 8270 Toyosato • Mon–Wed & Fri–Sun 9am–4pm • ¥300 • ☎026 985 3418

Nozawa claims to be the birthplace of Japanese skiing, as the spot where, in 1930, Hannes Schneider – an Austrian who popularized the two-pole technique – gave skiing demonstrations to awestruck crowds. One of the resort's most tricky runs is named after Schneider, and photos of the man in action, impeccably dressed in suit and tie, can be seen in the interesting little **Japan Ski Museum**, a white, church-like building at the bottom of the Hikage slope. Other exhibits include pre-war skiing equipment, and medals and memorabilia from the 1998 Winter Olympics.

ARRIVAL AND INFORMATION

By train JR Iiyama line runs from Nagano to Togari-Nozawa-Onsen station (1hr; ¥710, a 20min bus (¥310) or taxi ride (¥3000) from Nozawa Onsen itself. Shinkansen between Tokyo and Kanazawa stop at Iiyama Station, just 11min north of Nagano, with onwards connections on the Nozawa Onsen Liner Bus (20min, ¥600).

By bus Direct buses run from Nagano (1hr 15min; ¥1400) and, in ski season only, from Tokyo's Narita Airport (5hr 30min; ¥10,500).

Tourist information Nozawa Onsen's tourist information centre (daily 7.30am–6pm; ☎ 026 985 3155, ⓦ nozawa kanko.jp) is opposite the central bus terminal. English information on skiing is available at ⓦ nozawaski.com.

Bathhouses All public baths are free and open daily April–Nov 5am–11pm, Dec–March 6am–11pm.

ACCOMMODATION

In addition to the individual options listed below, it's well worth checking out foreigner-friendly local operators **Nozawa Holidays** (☎ 026 985 3272, ⓦ nozawaholidays.com), who can arrange all forms of accommodation, from self-catering apartments and cottages to traditional inns.

Haus St Anton ハウスセントアントン 9515 Toyosato ☎ 026 985 3597, ⓦ st-anton.jp. A cute little piece of Switzerland, right in the heart of the village action, with en-suite and shared-bath rooms. Hotel facilities range from its own restaurant and bar to onsen baths and ski rental, and they even offer their own home-made jams. Rates include breakfast and dinner, with the fine cuisine blending European and Japanese cooking. 🛜 **¥26,800**

Pension Schnee ペンションシュネー 8276 Toyosato ☎ 026 985 2012, ⓦ pensionschnee.com. Pretty European-style chalet in a superb ski-in, ski-out location on the mountainside. It's run by a friendly couple who were Olympic competitors, and rooms are named after resorts that have hosted the winter games. Rates include breakfast and dinner. 🛜 **¥25,000**

Ryokan Sakaya 旅館さかや 9329 Toyosato ☎ 026 985 3119, ⓦ ryokan-sakaya.co.jp. This elegant luxury ryokan, behind the Ōyu bathhouse, has its own spacious indoor and outdoor baths and a choice of Western- or Japanese-style rooms. The service is attentive and warm. Rates include breakfast only. 🛜 **¥31,200**

Sumiyosiya Nozawaonsen 住吉屋野沢温泉 8713 Toyosato ☎ 026 985 2005, ⓦ sumiyosiya.com. Gorgeous historic ryokan, updated with contemporary furnishings and offering immaculate, tasteful Japanese-style rooms in gleaming wood, some fully en suite, plus its own fully traditional bathhouse in classic style. Rates include breakfast and dinner. 🛜 **¥17,800**

EATING AND DRINKING

For a **snack**, try the local speciality *onsen manjū*, deliciously plump dumplings with different fillings; buy them from the street vendors with wooden steam-boxes. Nozawa Onsen has more in the way of **après-ski** than many Japanese ski resorts, with a few decent laidback bars, but don't expect Euro-style nightlife.

Foot フット Ō-yu ☎ 026 985 4004. Sports bar, on the main street, that makes a great rendezvous for an après-ski drink, with friendly staff and table football. 🛜 Daily 3–11.30pm.

Panorama House Buna パノラマハウスぶな Shimotakai-gun ☎ 026 985 3894. As well as great panoramic views, this slope-side restaurant serves a ¥950 curry udon that makes it worth going up the mountain even if you don't ski. Daily when lifts are running.

Yoshimi Shokudō 良味食堂 8757 Toyosato ☎ 026 985 2497. A fine place to sample the local noodles; the menu is replete with hearty stews and curries to build you up for another day on the slopes. Most dishes cost around ¥1000. Daily 11am–3pm & 5–10pm.

Hakuba
白馬

Situated in the dramatic northern Japan Alps, 45km west of Nagano, **HAKUBA** is one of Japan's top ski destinations, with assorted terrain spread across the valley in seven main ski areas and plenty of fun après-ski. The largest and most popular is **Happō-one** (八方尾根; ⓦ hakuba-happo.or.jp), site of the 1998 Nagano Olympics downhill course. **Hakuba 47** (ⓦ hakuba47.co.jp), on the other hand, which links to the **Goryū** (五竜; ⓦ hakubagoryu.com) and **Limori** (飯森) areas, is good for snowboarding and freestyle skiing with a terrain park, halfpipe and tree-skiing zone.

5

With two very pretty **lakes** – Aoki and Kizaki – the Hakuba valley also makes a fine base for rafting, biking and other outdoor pursuits in summer.

ARRIVAL AND DEPARTURE HAKUBA

By train There's no direct rail line from Nagano; express trains along the JR Ōito line from Matsumoto take around an hour.

By bus Frequent buses connect Nagano with Hakuba (1hr 10min; ¥1800; ⍵ alpico.co.jp) as well as up to four daily direct buses from Shinjuku, Tokyo (5hr; ¥8700). In winter, the ski resort sometimes runs a free bus service from Nagano (check ⍵ www.hakuba47.co.jp), while a shuttle service runs to Hakuba from Narita and Haneda airports via Shinjuku (¥9200; ⍵ naganosnowshuttle.com).

INFORMATION AND ACTIVITIES

Tourist information The tourist office (daily 8.30am–5pm; ☏ 026 172 2279, ⍵ hakubavalley.com), on the left as you exit JR Hakuba Station, will look after your bags for ¥300. The Hakuba Connect website, ⍵ hakubaconnect.com, offers good English-language information on ski areas, accommodation, nightlife and more.

Activities Ski Japan Holidays (☏ 026 172 6663, ⍵ japanspecialists.com) can arrange ski trips and tours to nearby attractions. The reliable Evergreen Outdoor Center (☏ 026 172 5150, ⍵ evergreen-outdoors.com) offers rafting and mountain biking in summer, and backcountry ski expeditions in winter.

ACCOMMODATION

New places to stay seem to appear every year. In addition to those listed below, check out the chalets and backpacker lodge deals offered by **Snowbeds Travel** (☏ 039 555 4839, ⍵ skijapantravel.com).

Azekura Sansō あぜくら山荘 Wadano ☏ 026 172 5238, ⍵ en.azekura.com. Smart, modern log house, in the Happō ski area, offering a calm, comfortable retreat and its own rotemburo, a few kilometres from the base station. Work for five hours at the lodge, and your day's lodging and meals are covered. Breakfast is ¥1200, dinner ¥3500; discounts are available for long stays. 📶 **¥15,600**

Hakuba Alps Backpackers 白馬アルプスバックパッカーズ 22407-4 Kamishiro ☏ 026 175 4038, ⍵ hakubabackpackers.com. Relaxed hostel, topped by a windmill and run by a very friendly Kiwi–Japanese couple, in Kamishiro, two stops down the train line from Hakuba. It's a little scruffy, but the price and location are ideal for the Goryū ski field. They also have some larger rental cottages. 📶 Dorms **¥2500**, doubles **¥6000**

K's House Hakuba Alps ケイズハウス白馬アルプス 22201-36 Kamishiro ☏ 026 175 4445, ⍵ kshouse.jp /hakuba. This appealing Kamishiro budget option, less than a 10min walk from Goryū, replicates the successful formula of the Kyoto and Tokyo hostel operations. As well as mixed six-bed dorms, they offer Western- and Japanese-style private doubles, with en-suite facilities, and there's a full kitchen. Closed June. 📶 Dorms **¥2900**, doubles **¥8200**

★**Maison de Sasagawa** めぞん・ど・ささがわ 4620 Hokujo Hakubamura ☏ 261 72 2386, ⍵ maisonde sasagawa.net. You become part of the family at this friendly lodge in the woods of Wadano, a 4min walk from the Happō-one base station. The owners, locals who grew up skiing hereabouts, make you very welcome, and will pick you up from the station and take you to the supermarket. Basic but comfortable Japanese or Western-style rooms, plus cosy communal dining and lounge areas, and a well-equipped kitchen. Discounts for long stays. 📶 Dorms **¥3400**, doubles **¥8400**

Morino Lodge 森のロッヂ 4692-3 Wadano ☏ 026 185 9098, ⍵ morinolodge.com. Smart lodge in Wadano, run by Scottish and Canadian owners and a 15min walk from the Happō-one base station, with stylish, modern Western rooms, dormitories, and a large open-plan lounge complete with sofas and pleasing design touches. This clued-up operation also runs several other lodges and self-contained chalets; check the website. Rates rise during the peak season, in Jan & Feb. 📶 Dorms **¥4000**, doubles **¥16,000**

Phoenix Hotel フェニックスホテル 4690-2 Hokujo ☏ 026 172 4060, ⍵ phoenixhotel.jp. Elegant boutique-style hotel, 1km from the Happō-one base station alongside the *Hakuba Tōkyū Hotel*. Both Japanese- and Western-style rooms are available, with the cheapest sharing showers (there's also an onsen). The hotel proper only operates during winter, as does *Mimi's*, its excellent fine-dining restaurant, but its opulent and much more expensive detached chalets remain open all year. Discounts for longer stays. Rooms **¥24,200**, chalets **¥120,000**

EATING

Restaurants and cafés are scattered along the valley; in high ski season, the Genki-go night shuttle-bus makes it easy to reach whichever strikes your fancy (late Dec to mid-Feb; ¥300).

Bamboo Café バンブーコーヒーバー Hakuba Station ☎026 185 4548, ⓦbamboocafehakuba.com. Hakuba is blessed with appealing coffee bars, but for sheer convenience you can't beat this friendly little café, on the left side of the station square, where you can enjoy fine coffee along with pastries, wraps and sandwiches. ☞ Daily 7am–5pm.

Gravity Worx グラヴィティー ワークス 6305 Hokujo ☎026 172 5434. In a big log cabin, a minute's walk right from Hakuba Station, this long-running café-bar is run by welcoming English-speaking staff and serves excellent home-made pizza starting under ¥1000, plus pasta, salads and desserts. Jan daily 10am–8pm, Feb–Dec Mon & Wed–Sun 10am–8pm.

Pizzakaya Country Road カントリーロード 22404-1

Kamishiro ☎026 175 2889. Near Kamishiro Station, this friendly, relaxed place offers tasty pasta and pizzas for around ¥1000, incorporating local ingredients such as mountain vegetables, seaweed and spicy cod roe. Tues–Sun 6–11pm.

Shouya Maruhachi 庄屋丸八 11032-1 Hokujo ☎026 175 1008, ⓦshouya-maruhachi.jp. Handsome merchant's house, built in 1854 and a short walk from Shinano Morue Station towards the Hakuba Iwatake ski area, which serves traditional Japanese dishes at reasonable prices during the ski season. Set meals cost ¥2000 at lunch, ¥5500 for dinner. You can take free Japanese culture courses, including how to make soba. An on-site café serves coffee and cake. ☞ Mon & Wed–Sun 11.30am–2pm & 5–9pm.

DRINKING AND NIGHTLIFE

For après-ski and evening drinks, the Echoland strip between Hakuba Ski Jumping Stadium and Hakuba 47 is the most popular area.

Hakuba Brewery Pub 白馬ビールのパブ 11420-1 Hokujo ☎026 185 2414, ⓦhakubabrewery.com. Convivial brewpub at the base of the Iwatake ski area, brewing the very epitome of local beer, using spring water that originally fell as snow on the slopes. They also serve bottled craft beers from around the world, along with standard pub grub. They're on the night-time bus route, though they also offer a free local shuttle service. ☞ Mon–Wed 3.30pm–midnight, Thurs–Sun 11am–midnight.

Master Braster マスターブラスター B1 3020-351 Echoland ☎026 172 2679, ⓦmasterbraster .homepagelife.jp. A basement reggae bar that can get lively, with suitably chilled music and bongo playing encouraged. The menu includes all kinds of Caribbean-flavoured dishes, from jerk chicken to ackee and salt fish, for around ¥1000, while you can get imported Red Stripe as well as Japanese draught beers. ☞ Daily 8pm–2am.

Shiga Kōgen

志賀高原

The often-heard complaint that Japanese ski resorts are too small certainly doesn't apply to mammoth **SHIGA KŌGEN**, active in winter only and consisting of eighteen resorts strung out along the Shiga plateau in the Jōshinetsu Kōgen National Park, 20km northeast of Nagano. The huge variety of terrain makes the one-day lift pass (¥5000), which covers the entire lift network, terrific value. It takes several days to ski the whole area; if you're short of time, head for the northern end of the mountain range to the resorts at **Okushiga-kōgen** (奥志賀高原) and **Yakebitai-yama** (焼額山), which hosted the slalom events during the 1998 Olympics.

ARRIVAL AND INFORMATION   SHIGA KŌGEN

By train From Yudanaka Station (湯田中; frequent, 40min; ¥1260), on the Nagano Dentetsu line, connecting buses head up to the Shiga Kōgen ski resorts, via a stunning mountain pass (hourly; 30min), and pass Jigokudani Monkey Park en route (see p.362).

By bus Direct buses run to Shiga Kōgen from the east exit of Nagano Station (3 daily; 1hr 15min; ¥1900; ⓦwww .nagadenbus.co.jp).

Tourist information Shiga Kōgen Tourism Association (☎026 934 2404, ⓦshigakogen.gr.jp).

ACCOMMODATION

Okushiga Kōgen Hotel 奥志賀高原ホテル ☎026 934 2034, ⓦokushiga-kougen.com. Sizeable hotel, in front of the ski slopes, which offers Western-style rooms along with amenities including a restaurant serving a buffet dinner and breakfast, cocktail lounge with an open

fireplace, big public baths and on-site ski rental. Rates include breakfast. ☞ **¥29,160**

Shiga Kōgen Prince Hotel 志賀高原プリンスホテル Yakebitai-yama ☎026 934 3111, ⓦprincehotels.com /en/shiga. Large resort hotel, at the foot of

5

Yakebitai-yama, with three separate wings: the eastern part sports retro 1980s glamour, while the slightly cheaper west wing, with its big outdoor bath, is geared to families and groups. Breakfast is included. **¥23,760**

Jigokudani Monkey Park

地獄谷野猿公苑, Jigokudani Yaen-kōen • 6845 Yamanouchi-machi • Daily: April–Oct 8.30am–5pm, Nov–March 9am–4pm • ¥500 • T 026 933 4379, W jigokudani-yaenkoen.co.jp

Famous internationally since appearing on the cover of *Life* magazine back in 1970, Japan's iconic "**snow monkeys**" are based in **Jigokudani Monkey Park**, 32km northeast of Nagano. They're actually a troupe of around two hundred Japanese long-tailed monkeys (*nihon-zaru*) that have acquired the understandable habit of bathing in hot pools located just uphill from **KANBAYASHI ONSEN** (上林温泉). Compellingly photogenic, utterly indifferent to the human commotion that surrounds them, they first started taking dips here during the 1960s, when a local ryokan owner took pity on them and left food out in winter. These days, a special rotemburo is devoted to their exclusive use; naturally they spend most time in it in winter, but they live beside the onsen year-round.

Jigokudani Monkey Park makes an easy day-trip from Nagano – with an early enough start, you can even visit Obuse (see p.354) on the way home – or, in winter, a stop-off en route to or from Shiga Kōgen (see p.361). It's hardly a wilderness destination, with the onsen resort so nearby, but there's a real sense of rural adventure to the half-hour walk up through the woods from the nearest road.

GETTING THERE — JIGOKUDANI MONKEY PARK

By train Frequent trains on the Nagano Dentetsu line from Nagano terminate in Yudanaka (湯田中; express 40min, ¥1260; local 1hr, ¥1160; Japan Rail Pass not valid), where passengers are steered onto buses up to Kanbayashi Onsen (hourly; 15min; (¥210). The park itself is a 2km uphill walk from the bus stop; set off and you'll soon spot signs. One-day passes, covering all trains and buses as well as park admission, are sold for ¥2900 at Nagano and Gondō stations.

By bus Direct buses run from Nagano to Kanbayashi Onsen (3 daily; 40min; ¥1400).

ACCOMMODATION AND EATING

Enza Café 円座町カフェ 1421-1 Hirao, Yamanouchi T 026 938 1736, W bit.ly/enzacafe. Large modern café, open to the breezes in summer, at the start of the trail up to the monkey park. As well as espresso coffees and fresh juices, they serve full meals, include chicken-broth noodles for under ¥1000. Daily 9.30am–5pm.

Kanbayashi Hotel Senjukaku 上林ホテル仙壽閣 1410 Hirao, Yamanouchi T 026 933 3551, W senjukaku.com. Elegant, traditional inn, amid the trees in Kanbayashi Onsen, that's a great place to indulge yourself. The tatami rooms are spacious and luxurious, and the outdoor baths set amid bamboo and rocks. Rates include two meals; local produce, including Shinshu beef from apple-fed cows, features high on the menu. **¥51,200**

Kōrakukan 後楽館 Yamanouchi T 026 933 4376, W www.kanbayashi-onsen.com/kourakukan.htm. Rambling wooden ryokan, set on the hillside just below the monkey park, and offering homely Japanese-style accommodation, with rates including two meals. There's a selection of indoor and outdoor onsen, including private family baths; non-residents can take a dip in the rotemburo for ¥500. **¥20,000**

Togura Kamiyamada Onsen

戸倉上山田温泉

In the heart of the mountains 20km south of Nagano, **TOGURA KAMIYAMADA ONSEN** stretches languidly along either side of the Chikuma River. Although these days the town has become somewhat urbanized, as an agglomeration of the workaday little city of **Chikuma** (千曲), it was traditionally a target for pilgrims en route from Nagano's Zenkō-ji temple, and continues to boast a strong geisha heritage. Home to a busy bar and restaurant district, along with unusual shops and easy access to surrounding nature, Togura Kamiyamada offers a wider range of diversions than the average onsen resort, and makes a great place to spend a night.

ARRIVAL AND DEPARTURE

TOGURA KAMIYAMADA ONSEN

By train Togura Station is served by trains to and from Nagano (every 30min; 25min) on the local Shinano railway. Travellers approaching from Matsumoto and points south should change from the JR line at Shinonoi, for the final 12min ride on the Shinano line. The Onsen district is 2km southwest of the station, across the river. Most hotels run their own shuttles; otherwise, hop in a taxi (¥1000).

ACCOMMODATION AND EATING

With so many **ryokan** to choose from, it's worth steering clear of the larger, old-style government options in favour of more characterful alternatives. There's a similarly broad range of places to eat and drink, with local specialities including *oshibori udon*, noodles with a spicy *daikon* radish sauce.

Daikokuya 大黒屋 2-24-1 Kamiyamada Onsen ☏ 026 275 0768. This small noodle shop is a local institution – there's often a queue at lunchtimes, but it's worth the wait. *Nintare tonkatsu*, a breaded pork fillet with garlic sauce, is a local favourite. Bowls of noodles start at ¥700. Daily 11.30am–4.30pm.

Kamesei 亀清 2-15-1 Kamiyamada Onsen ☏ 026 275 1032, ⓦ kamesei.jp. An excellent small ryokan run by a very friendly Japanese–American couple. The passageways of the old building wind around small inner gardens and ponds, tatami rooms feature modern en-suite bathrooms, and there's a "100-year-old" outdoor bath as well as a private family onsen. Breakfast and dinner cost an additional ¥5000 per person. 🛜 **¥11,000**

Karuizawa and around

軽井沢

It was on the tennis courts of the ritzy resort of **KARUIZAWA**, on the slopes of the Asama-yama volcano at the eastern edge of Nagako-ken, that Crown Prince Akihito (now the emperor) met his future wife, Michiko, in the 1950s. Later, in the late 1960s and 1970s, John Lennon and Yoko Ono spent vacations here. Thanks to decades of superstar patronage, this small town can get very hectic in summer, with Tokyoites descending to relax in the cooler mountain air and spend up a storm at the giant outlet mall and tacky tourist-shop strip to either side of the main station. However, it's straightforward enough to escape this commercial frenzy, and head into the forested hills along the network of easy local hiking and cycling routes.

Kyū-Karuizawa

旧軽井沢 • 1km north of Karuizawa Station

Karuizawa turns scenic in the **Kyū-Karuizawa** district, around a kilometre from the station. Work your way past the tourists who are jamming the pedestrianized, rather tacky, shopping street dubbed "Little Ginza", to emerge into a forest. Here you'll find the quaint wooden **Anglican Chapel** (daily 9am–5pm; free), fronted by a bust of Alexander Croft Shaw (1846–1902), a Canadian missionary who helped to popularize the area. A short walk southeast, the historic *Mampei Hotel* (see p.364) holds a small museum of memorabilia.

North of Karuizawa

Head northwest along the main road, Mikasa-dōri, and a pleasant 2km cycle ride or hike will bring you to the secluded **Old Mikasa Hotel** (旧三笠ホテル; daily 9am–5pm; ¥400), an elegant wooden building built in 1906 and which closed in 1970; it is now a national monument. Follow the road past the camping ground to **Kose** (小瀬), where a 10km hike leads in turn to the scenic **Shiraito Falls** (白糸の滝). Afterwards, head west to **Mine-no-chaya** (峰の茶屋), from where buses head back to Karuizawa.

5

Hoshino Resort

星野リゾート • **Onsen** Daily 10am–11pm • ¥1300 • **Nature tours** Daily 10am & 1.30pm; night tours available at varying times – call
☎ 026 745 7777 for rates and reservations • ☎ 026 745 5853, ⓦ hoshino-area.jp • Free buses from the south side of Karuizawa Station

Naka-Karuizawa (中軽井沢), 6km west of Karuizawa and served by free buses, is another beautiful area for cycling, hiking and relaxing. Its principal focus is the **Hoshino Resort**, where you'll find the luxury hotel *Hoshinoya Karuizawa* (see below); an excellent onsen, **Tonbo-no-yu** (トンボの湯); a forest of chestnut and larch trees where you can take guided nature tours; and a stylish, low-key shopping and dining complex, **Harunire Terrace**.

Onioshidashien

鬼押出し園 • 21km northwest of Karuizawa • Mid-March to early Dec daily 8am–5pm • ¥650 • 2–4 daily buses from Karuizawa Station
(50min; ¥1210)

Japan's highest triple-cratered **active volcano** – the 2568m **Asama-yama** (浅間山), which last erupted in 2004 – looms ominously over Karuizawa. The closest you can get to the crater is on its north side at **Onioshidashien**. This was the scene of a cataclysmic eruption on August 5, 1783, when ash from the blowout was said to have darkened the sky as far as Europe, and a 7km-wide lava flow swept away Kanbara village. When the lava cooled, it solidified into an extraordinary landscape of black boulders and bizarre rock shapes, where alpine plants now sprout and across which twisting pathways have been laid. To get a sense of the scale of the place, head up to the observation floor in the gift shop and restaurant complex at the entrance. Most of the crowds head for the central temple, **Kannon-dō**, which stands on a raised red platform amid the black rocks; for a more peaceful experience keep going to the quieter area behind.

ARRIVAL AND INFORMATION

KARUIZAWA

By train Shinkansen trains run to Karuizawa Station from Tokyo (every 30min; 1hr 5min) or Nagano (every 30min; 31min).

By bus Direct buses run to Karuizawa from Ikebukuro in Tokyo, as well as Osaka and Kyoto.

Tourist information Karuizawa's tourist information office, at the station (daily 9am–5.30pm; ☎ 026 742 2491, ⓦ karuizawa-kankokyokai.jp), hands out a good English map of the area.

GETTING AROUND

By bus While local buses from outside Karuizawa Station connect with nearby attractions, services tend to be frustratingly infrequent.

By bike The most enjoyable way to explore is using a rental bicycle from the many outlets near the station (around ¥1000 a day).

ACCOMMODATION

Karuizawa is not a cheap place to **stay**, so if you are on a budget a day-trip is probably best. The room rates shown below are for the summer high season; low-season rates tend to be much lower.

APA Hotel Karuizawa-Ekimae ホテル軽井沢駅前 1178-1135 Karuizawa ☎ 026 742 0665, ⓦ bit.ly /APAkaruizawa. Handily located beside the JR station, this dependable business hotel chain charges reasonable rates (by local standards) for functional rooms. A bonus is their restaurant's open-air terrace, where you eat breakfast. ☞ **¥20,250**

★Hoshinoya Karuizawa 星のや軽井沢 Hoshino, Karuizawa-machi ☎ 057 007 3066, ⓦ hoshinoya karuizawa.com. Outstandingly beautiful and luxurious onsen hotel, which blends with the forest and has its own hydro-power generators. Choose between garden, river and mountainside villas, each equally gorgeous and all

sporting cypress-wood bathtubs. The property holds Japanese and French fine-dining restaurants, and has a two-night minimum stay. For ¥1300, non-guests can use their wonderful hot spring. ☞ **¥59,400**

Karuizawa Prince Hotel East 軽井沢プリンスホテルイースト Kitasaku-gun ☎ 026 742 1111, ⓦ princehotels .co.jp/karuizawa-east. The best value of several *Prince* properties located on a sprawling site a few minutes' walk south of the station. It offers a mammoth shopping plaza, spa and onsen, tennis, golf and, in winter, direct access to a small ski field. Choose between stylish, large hotel rooms or log cabins. ☞ **¥45,000**

Mampei Hotel 万平ホテル 925 Kitasaku-gun

026 742 1234, ⓦ mampei.co.jp. This hotel, the area's grand dame, established in 1894, is where John and Yoko used to stay. Surrounded by the forest, it has a quirky, rambling elegance, although the cheapest rooms are a little dowdy. **¥39,000**

Hotel Wellies ホテル・ウェリーズ 2350-160 Nagakura 026 746 1670, ⓦ hotelwellies.jp. Run by a British–Japanese couple, this small hotel is one of the most affordable options in town. Named after the Duke of Wellington, it's a little patch of England in the East, with quirky design features and an eclectic mix of decor combining the modern and traditional. Rates include breakfast, which may even feature kippers; British dinners cost ¥3500 per person. There's a lovely granite-tiled family bathroom as well as an indoor garden. 🛜 **¥19,000**

EATING

As well as the individual options listed below, it's worth exploring the **Harinure Terrace** dining and shopping area in the Hoshino district, which holds several good-value restaurants and fast-food options.

Kastanie カスターニエ 2-3-2 Karaizawa-higashi 026 742 3081, ⓦ kastanie.co.jp. This local institution, a 7min walk north of Karuizawa Station, is best known for its slow-roasted chicken, but it also serves other Western dishes including fine pizzas and grilled meats. Set lunch menus with half a chicken cost ¥1580. Mon & Wed–Sun 11.30am–3.30pm & 5.30–9.30pm.

Kawakami-an 川上庵 6-10 Kyū-Karuizawa 026 742 0009, ⓦ kawakamian.com. Smart place, near the foot of Ginza street, with a fantastic terrace that comes into its own on sunny days. Handmade soba and tempura set meals cost from around ¥1800, while more unusual appetizers include oysters in oil. Daily 11am–10pm.

Sekireibashi Kawakami-an せきれい橋川上庵 2145-5 Nagakura-asa, Yokobuki 026 731 0266, ⓦ kawakamian.com. This outlet of *Kawakami-an* (see above) serves up great-value soba noodles for around ¥1000 in a lovely setting overlooking a babbling river in Hoshino's Harunire Terrace, close to several other appealing dining options. 🛜 Daily 11am–10pm.

Matsumoto

松本

The delightful city of **MATSUMOTO** spreads to either side of the Metoba River, 70km southwest of Nagano across the Hijiri Kōgen mountains. As the primary gateway to the Japan Alps, it's long been a popular tourist destination, and is famous in its own right for having retained a splendid castle, **Matsumoto-jō**. In addition, art lovers can enjoy traditional prints at the **Japan Ukiyo-e Museum** and the contemporary work of native-child Yayoi Kusama at the **Matsumoto City Museum of Art**.

Thanks to its manageable size, slower pace of life and superb natural setting, Matsumoto has attracted many former urbanites to relocate and open their own businesses, and many of the traditional white-walled houses in its appealing riverside neighbourhoods now hold ryokan, cafés, bars and small, artsy shops. The ideal time to visit is the last weekend in May, for the **Crafts Fair Matsumoto** (ⓦ matsumoto-crafts.com).

Matsumoto-jō

松本城 • 4-1 Marunouchi • Daily 8.30am–5pm • ¥610 • 026 332 0133, ⓦ matsumoto-castle.jp

Still almost entirely surrounded by its broad protective moat – there's no hill hereabouts – the magnificent fortress known as **Matsumoto-jō** is only visible once you enter its outer grounds. Nicknamed Karasu-jō – Crow Castle – thanks to its brooding black facade, it's one of only five medieval wooden castles to remain intact in Japan, and as such is an official National Treasure. It's a superb spectacle, if anything even more dramatic after dark, when spotlights emphasize its stark silhouette.

Construction of the castle started in 1592; over the centuries, it belonged to six different families, but it was never taken by force. Neither, unlike the residential palaces that originally stood alongside, did it succumb to fire, a survival credited to the small shrine at its very pinnacle. You can follow steep staircases all the way up to the sixth storey (it has the traditional hidden floor of most Japanese castles), to enjoy views of

5

the town and of the mountains that line the horizon. On your way up, display cases hold all sorts of weaponry and other artefacts.

Matsumoto City Museum

松本市立博物館, Matsumoto Shiritsu Hakubutsukan • Daily 8.30am–5pm • ¥610; same ticket as Matsumoto-jō • ☎ 026 339 7400, Ⓦ matsumoto-artmuse.jp

Admission to the castle also includes access to the quirky **Matsumoto City Museum**, which stands within the castle grounds, slightly to the right of the entrance. Displays tell the story of the city from its beginnings along with eclectic objects from Japanese folk culture and a good model of how Matsumoto looked in feudal times.

Metoba-gawa

The narrow streets that run parallel to either bank of the **Metoba-gawa** through the heart of Matsumoto are well worth exploring. **Nakamachi-dōri**, a block south of the river, is lined with attractive black-and-white-walled inns, antique and craft shops and restaurants. Prominent among them is the **Nakamachi Kura-no-Kaikan** (中町蔵の会館;

MATSUMOTO

0 — 200 metres

◼ ACCOMMODATION	
Buena Vista	7
Marumo	2
Matsumoto Back Packers	4
Matsumoto Hotel Kagetsu	1
Hotel New Station	6
Nunoya	3
Richmond Hotel	5

● EATING	
Amijok	3
Chikufudō	4
Hikariya	2
Sakura	5
Sakuraya	1
Temaezaru Shun	6

◼ DRINKING AND NIGHTLIFE	
Elbow Room	1
Give me little more	2
Hop Frog Café	4
Main Bar Coat	3

Matsumoto-jō

Matsumoto City Museum

Yohashira-jinja

Nawate-Dōri

Geiyukan

NAKAMACHI-DŌRI

Nakamachi Kura-no-kaikan

NAKAMACHI

Parco Department Store

ISEMACHI-DŌRI

KOEN-DŌRI

Metoba-gama

ROKKU-DŌRI

DAIMYO-CHŌ-DŌRI

HIGASHI-MACHI-DŌRI

EKIMAE-DŌRI

Matsumoto City Museum of Art

Matsumoto Performing Arts Centre

NHK Radio & TV Station

Suzuki Shin'ichi Talent Education Hall

Fukoshi-jinja

Matsumoto Station

Matsuden Bus Terminal

HONMACHI-DŌRI

SHIRAKABA-DŌRI

Matsumoto Electric Railway

Hotaka & Hakuba

Japan Ukiyo-e Museum & Kamikōchi

Matsumoto Folkcraft Museum

Shinjuku, Tokyo, Kiso Valley & Matsumoto Airport

daily 9am–4.30pm; free), a beautifully restored sake brewery with a soaring black-beam interior and traditional cross-hatching plasterwork outside.

Meandering beside the river on the northern side, **Nawate-dōri** is a lively pedestrian lane dotted with cafés, snack stalls and souvenir shops, and which opens onto the large **Yohoshira Jinja**.

Matsumoto City Museum of Art

松本市美術館, Matsumoto-shi Bijutsukan • 4-2-22 Chūō, 1km east of the station • Tues–Sun 9am–5pm • ¥410 • ☎ 026 339 7400, ⓦ matsumoto-artmuse.jp

Yayoi Kusama's *The Visionary Flowers* – giant technicolour tulips crossed with triffids, looming over a streetfront plaza – ensure you can't fail to spot the **Matsumoto City Museum of Art**. Inside, you'll find a fascinating gallery inside devoted to this famous Matsumoto-born contemporary artist, as well as others devoted to the calligrapher Shinzan Kamijyo and the landscape artist Tamura Kazuo.

Japan Ukiyo-e Museum

日本浮世絵美術館, Nihon Ukiyo-e Bijutsukan • 2206-1 Shimadate Koshiba • Tues–Sun 10am–5pm • ¥1200 • ☎ 026 347 4440, ⓦ japan-ukiyoe-museum.com • 15min walk from "Government Building" stop on Town Sneaker bus Western Route

Housed in an impressive modern gallery in a rather isolated spot 3km west of the station, the **Japan Ukiyo-e Museum** holds woodblock prints by the great masters, including Utagawa Hiroshige and Katsushika Hokusai. Only a fraction of its splendid collection of 100,000 prints can ever be on display, but the amiable curator will often give personally narrated slide shows.

Matsumoto Folkcraft Museum

松本民芸館, Matsumoto Mingai-Kan • Tues–Sun 9am–5pm • ¥300 • ☎ 026 333 1569 • 15min bus ride, towards Utsukushigahara Onsen

For anyone interested in Japanese crafts, **Matsumoto Folkcraft Museum**, set in a traditional-style building on the city's northeastern outskirts, makes a worthwhile stop. Exquisite objects on display include giant pottery urns, lacquerware inlaid with mother-of-pearl, and wooden chests.

ARRIVAL AND DEPARTURE   MATSUMOTO

By plane Fuji Dream Airlines fly to the small Shinshū-Matsumoto airport (☎ 026 357 8818, matsumoto-airport .co.jp), 9km southwest of the city centre; connecting buses meet all flights (25min; ¥600).
Destinations Fukuoka (2 daily; 1hr 50min); Sapporo (daily; 1hr 30min).

By train Matsumoto's station, a 20min walk southwest of the castle, has direct connections with Nagano, Nagoya and Tokyo.

Destinations Hakuba (4 daily; 1hr); Nagano (hourly; 50min); Nagoya (hourly; 2hr 10min); Nakatsugawa (hourly; 1hr 15min); Narai (10 daily; 50min); Shinano-Ōmachi (hourly; 1hr); Tokyo (1 daily; 3hr).

By bus Long-distance buses stop in front of the train station.

Destinations Kamikōchi (16 daily; 1hr 50min); Nagano (hourly; 1hr 20min); Nagoya (8 daily; 3hr 30min); Osaka (3 daily; 5hr 30min); Takayama (4 daily; 2hr 30min).

INFORMATION

Tourist information Matsumoto runs helpful information offices inside the station (daily 9am–5.45pm; ☎ 026 332 2814, ⓦ welcome.city.matsumoto.nagano.jp),

and on Daimyō-chō-dōri, one block south of the castle (daily 9am–5.45pm; ☎ 026 339 7176).

GETTING AROUND

By bus Convenient Town Sneaker minibuses follow four loop routes from the JR station; pick up a map from the tourist office (¥200 per ride, one-day pass ¥500). Regular

buses leave from the Matsuden Bus Terminal, under the ESPA department store opposite Matsumoto Station.

By bike Free bikes are available from eight sites around the city, including the City and Art museums but not the castle or station – ask the tourist office for details.

On foot The main sights are within easy walking distance of the train station.

ACCOMMODATION

Buena Vista ブエナ・ビスタ 1-2-1 Honjo ☎ 026 337 0111, ⓦ buena-vista.co.jp. Stylish Western-style hotel, a 10min walk from the station but connected by free shuttle vans. The cheapest rooms are pretty cramped, so pay extra for a premier room if you need to spread out. It holds four restaurants, with the ¥1950 breakfast buffet, up on the panoramic fourteenth floor, being the best value. 🛜 **¥13,500**

Marumo まるも 3-3-10 Chūō ☎ 026 332 0115, ⓦ www .avis.ne.jp/~marumo. In a whitewashed house and Meiji-era wooden building on the banks of the Metoba River, this small ryokan is an appealing mix of old and new, with tatami rooms, a wooden bath, a small enclosed bamboo garden and a nice café serving ¥1000 Japanese breakfasts to classical music. Note the 11pm curfew. 🛜 Per person **¥5000**, doubles **¥10,000**

★Matsumoto Back Packers 松本バックパッカーズ 1-1-6 Shiraita ☎ 026 331 5848, ⓦ matsumotobp.com. To reach this small, very friendly hostel, owned by an Irish–Japanese couple eager to share their local knowledge, head right from the station's western exit, walk for 5min, and you'll see it on the far side of the river. The tatami dorms, shared bathrooms and small kitchen are immaculately clean, and the communal lounge is very sociable. Single rooms and twins are also available. 🛜 Dorms **¥3000**, doubles **¥7000**

Matsumoto Hotel Kagetsu 松本ホテル花月 4-8-9 Ōte ☎ 026 332 0114, ⓦ hotel-kagetsu.jp. This handsome old-fashioned hotel, near the castle, may be showing a little wear and tear, but it retains some stylish touches, and boasts attractive dark-wood furniture. The tasteful tatami rooms are the same price as the larger-than-average Western-style ones. 🛜 **¥15,500**

Hotel New Station ホテルニューステーション 1-1-11 Chūō ☎ 026 335 3850, ⓦ hotel-ns.com. Welcoming, good-value business hotel, immediately left of the station's main eastern exit, with small rooms but an excellent top-floor public bath and a men-only sauna, plus free bicycle use. The lively ground-floor *izakaya* serves local specialities including *basashi* (raw horsemeat). 🛜 **¥8000**

Nunoya ぬのや 3-5-7 Chūō ☎ 026 332 0545, ⓦ bit.ly /matsumotonunoya. Delightful ryokan, in a charming wooden building in the middle of Nakamachi-dōri, with a friendly English-speaking owner. All the attractive tatami rooms share a communal Japanese-style bathroom, and there's a pleasant lounge and dining room. Breakfast is not served, but there are plenty of cafés nearby. Cash only. Per person **¥4500**, doubles **¥9000**

Richmond Hotel リッチモンドホテル松本 1-10-7 Chūō ☎ 026 337 5000, ⓦ matsumoto.richmondhotel.jp. Modern, well maintained high-rise hotel, a 5min walk from the station towards the centre of town, with decent-size rooms and mountains views from the upper storeys. Breakfast is available in the 24hr Western-style café, Gusto, on the ground floor. 🛜 **¥11,000**

EATING

The narrow lanes around the station are packed with cheap, lively **restaurants**, while the streets closer to the river and the castle hold a wider range of more upmarket options. Local **specialities** include soba, best eaten cold (ask for *zaru-soba*); *sanzuko yaki*, spicy fried chicken; and *sasa mushi*, eel steamed inside rice wrapped in bamboo leaves. You'll also spot restaurants serving horsemeat in all sorts of ways, even raw (*basashi*). **Stalls** along Nawate-dōri sell all sorts of intriguing snacks, from little fish-shaped waffles to fried octopus balls, while that same street also holds several spacious Western-style cafés.

Amijok アミジョク 3-4-14 Chūō ☎ 026 388 6238. Cute, friendly café, just off the eastern end of Nakamachi-dōri, with a retro vibe. As well as baking five different kinds of muffin each day, they serve home-made cakes, breads and savoury snacks, put on exhibitions by local artists, and sell modern crafts. Expect coffee and cake to cost around ¥600. 🛜 Mon–Wed & Fri–Sun 10am–8pm.

Chikufudō 竹風堂 3-4-20 Nakamachi-dōri ☎ 026 336 1102, ⓦ chikufudo.com. Head to the peaceful and attractive traditional dining room behind this Nakamachi-dōri shop, run by Obuse-based chestnut growers, to enjoy delicious chestnut sweets, ice creams or soup. Set lunches, featuring rice with local vegetables or, naturally, chestnuts, start at ¥1188. 🛜 Daily 10am–6pm, closed Wed in Jan & Feb.

Hikariya ヒカリヤ 4-7-14 Ōte ☎ 026 338 0186, ⓦ hikari-ya.com. Elegant 120-year-old *machiya* (townhouse) that has been beautifully converted into a very stylish complex of two restaurants: *Higashi*, serving an austere but masterful *kaiseki* menu, and *Nishi*, specializing in French cuisine. Lunch starts at ¥2800, dinner ¥6000. Mon, Tues & Thurs–Sun 11.30am–2.30pm & 5.30–10pm.

Sakura 佐蔵 1-20-26 Chūō ☎ 026 334 1050. This solitary stand-alone townhouse on an otherwise modernized city street – look out for the green "Box Oak" sign next door – holds a true local favourite; a tiny seven-seater noodle restaurant, where you pay at the ticket machine then tuck into ramen noodles for ¥800, or crisp *gyōza* dumplings for ¥500. Mon & Wed–Sun 11.30am–3pm & 5.30–10pm.

★Sakuraya 桜家 4-9-1 Ōte ☎ 026 333 2660, ⓦ sakuraya.ne.jp. Formal traditional restaurant, with

CLASSICAL MUSIC IN MATSUMOTO

Matsumoto has a reputation as a centre for classical music. It was here that **Dr Suzuki Shin'ichi**, an internationally famous music teacher, encouraged children to learn to play instruments using their natural gift for mimicry. His "Suzuki Method" is taught in the Suzuki Shin'ichi Talent Education Hall, 1km east of Matsumoto Station. The city's annual classical music festival, held between early August and early September each year, is now known as the **Seiji Ozawa Matsumoto Festival** (Ⓦ ozawa-festival.com) in honour of its current director, but may be more familiar under its previous name, the Saitō Kinene, which commemorates its founder, conductor Saitō Hideo.

For many years, Geiyūkan, a small hall on Nakamachi-dōri, has hosted weekly performances of the classical Japanese string instrument, the *shamisen*. Geiyūkan was undergoing renovation as this edition went to press, but the concerts are expected to resume at some point (芸游館; Sun 1.30pm & 3pm; ¥700 including tea and cake; Ⓣ 026 332 1107).

waitresses in kimono, which specializes in sumptuous, smoky eel dishes, Little English is spoken, but an English photo menu details set meals starting at around ¥2000. Be sure to try *sasa mushi*, bamboo-leaf parcels of steamed rice with eel. Tues–Sun 11am–2pm & 5–9pm.

Temaezaru Shun 手前ざる俊 1-4-6 Chūo Ⓣ 026 336 3036. Lively, quick-fire noodle joint, in the thick of the nightlife district a block from the station, that's a good bet for a late-night meal. A bowl of soba, abounding in local vegetables such as succulent mushrooms, costs around ¥1000. Mon–Sat 11.30am–2.30pm & 5pm–1am, Sun 5–11pm.

DRINKING AND NIGHTLIFE

★ **Elbow Room** エルボー・ルーム 4-3-3 Nawate Yokochō Ⓣ 026 339 3017. Tiny, hole-in-the-wall drinking den in a hard-to-spot lane off Nawate-dōri, which gets lively at weekends, with an eclectic mix of electronic and psychedelic sounds attracting a young crowd of skaters and partiers. Drinks around ¥500, with a range of cocktails and daily food specials for ¥600. Mon–Sat 8pm–2.30am.

Give me little more ギブミーリトルモア 3-11-7 Chūo Ⓣ 080 5117 0059, Ⓦ givemelittlemore.blogspot.jp. Attracting an arty crowd, this friendly pocket-sized wooden bar beside the river hosts DIY art exhibitions, film screenings and music performances (often featuring the owner's band) in its adjoining event space. It also offers daily food specials, usually curry (¥600). Drinks from ¥500. Tues–Sat 7pm–1.30am.

Hop Frog Café ホップカエルカフェ 3-8-28 Chūo Ⓣ 906 022 5760. This bright, friendly modern place, not far west of the art museum, has hit on a winning formula, serving both the city's best coffee and a wide range of craft beers, along with bar snacks like ¥600 sharing platters of nuts, cheese and honey, ¥800 sandwiches, and ¥1000 meat specials. Tues 5–10pm, Wed–Fri 2–10pm, Sat & Sun noon–10pm.

Main Bar Coat イン・バー・コート Miwa Bldg, 2-3-5 Chūo Ⓣ 026 334 7133, Ⓦ mainbarcoat.com. Stylish speakeasy-style bar that serves a wide range of cocktails (from ¥800) and has a good collection of whiskies too (from ¥1200). There's also an ¥800 cover charge. 🛜 Tues–Sun 6pm–1am.

Around Matsumoto

It's all about the mountains around Matsumoto. To the north is the ski centre of **Hakuba** (see p.359), while to the west is the serene lake and mountain resort of **Kamikōchi**, which gets so much snow that it is inaccessible all winter. The nearby onsen and ski resort of **Norikura Kōgen** generally makes a less crowded alternative base.

GETTING AROUND

By car The fabulous Skyline Road runs through the mountainous area around Matsumoto, crossing the "roof of Japan" to Takayama in neighbouring Gifu-ken (see p.376).

By bus The Alpico bus company offers various good-value

regional multi-day passes (Matsumoto/Kamikōchi/Norikura region 2-day pass ¥6000, 3-day pass ¥7200; 4-day pass covering Hida area as well, April–Nov ¥10,290, Dec–March ¥8800; Ⓦ alpico.co.jp).

5

Hotaka
穂高

The quiet country town of **Hotaka**, 16km north of Matsumoto, is best known for its production of the *wasabi* paste which accompanies sushi and sashimi. The ideal way to explore this tranquil area is to rent a bicycle from one of the many local outlets. Keep an eye open along the country roads for *dōsojin*, small stones on which guardian deity couples have been carved.

Dai-ō Wasabi Farm

大王わさび農場, Dai-ō Wasabi Nōjō • 1692 Hotaka • Daily: March–Oct 9am–5.20pm, Nov–Feb 9am–4.30pm • Free • ☎ 026 382 2118, Ⓦ www.daiowasabi.co.jp • 3km east of Hotaka Station; 15min by bike

Set in pleasant countryside, the enjoyably touristy **Dai-ō Wasabi Farm**, one of the largest in Japan, consists of vast fields of the fiery green horseradish growing in wide, waterlogged gravel trenches. Visitors can sample all types of *wasabi*-flavoured food, including surprisingly tasty ice cream and even beer.

Rokuzan Art Museum

碌山美術館, Rokuzan Bijutsukan • 5095-1 Hotaka • May–Oct daily 9am–5.10pm, Nov–Feb Tues–Sun 9am–4.10pm • ¥700 • ☎ 026 382 2094, Ⓦ rokuzan.jp • 700m north of Hotaka Station

The serene **Rokuzan Art Museum**, housed in an ivy-covered, church-like building and a couple of modern galleries, houses the sculptures of **Ogiwara Rokuzan** (1879–1911). Known in Japan as the "Rodin of the Orient", Rokuzan pioneered a contemporary style of portraiture with works like *The Miner*, but his career was abruptly cut short when he died of tuberculosis at the age of 32.

ARRIVAL AND INFORMATION　　　　　　　　　　　　　　　　　　　　　　　　HOTAKA

By train Direct trains on the JR Ōito line connect Hotaka with Matsumoto (every 30min; 30min; ¥320).

Tourist information Hotaka's tourist office, on the left as you exit the station, has English-speaking staff (daily: April–Nov 9am–5pm, Dec–March 10am–4pm; ☎ 026 382 9363, Ⓦ azumino-e-tabi.net).

Kamikōchi
上高地

The beautiful mountaineering and hiking resort of **KAMIKŌCHI** is hidden away high in the Azusa valley, 50km west of Matsumoto at an altitude of 1500m. In itself it amounts to little more than a bus station and a handful of hotels, scattered along the Azusa-gawa, but Kamikōchi boasts some stunning alpine scenery. The area can only be visited between late April and mid-November, before the narrow roads are blocked by heavy snow, and

---

WALTER WESTON

Born in Derbyshire, England, in 1861, the missionary **Walter Weston** was 29 years old when he first set foot in the mountains of Nagano-ken. Although the phrase "Japan Alps" was coined by another Englishman, William Gowland, whose *Japan Guide* was published in 1888, it took the appearance of Weston's *Climbing and Exploring in the Japan Alps* eight years later for the peaks really to register with mountaineers. Until then, these mountains, considered **sacred**, had only been climbed by Shintō and Buddhist priests, but now alpinism caught on as a **sport** in fast-modernizing Japan. Weston, who became its acknowledged guru, favoured Kamikōchi as a base from which to climb what he called "the grandest mountains in Japan", and frequently visited the tiny village from his home in Kōbe. Although he is honoured in Kamikōchi with a monument and a festival in his name on the first Sunday in June (the start of the climbing season), Weston is said to have wept at the prospect of mass tourism ruining his beloved mountains. His ghost can take comfort from the fact that, despite Kamikōchi's popularity, the area's beauty remains largely intact.

the resort shuts down for winter. In season, though, the place is buzzing with tourists, and the prices at its hotels and restaurants can be as steep as the surrounding mountains.

Kamikōchi owes its fortunes to the late nineteenth-century British missionary **Walter Weston** (see box opposite), who helped popularize the area as a base for climbing the Northern Alps. Both its two highest mountains – the 3190m **Hotaka-dake**, also known as Oku-Hotaka-dake, and the 3180m **Yari-ga-take** – are extremely popular climbs. One trail up Yari-ga-take has been dubbed the Ginza Jūsō ("Ginza Traverse") after Tokyo's busy shopping area. However, the congestion on the mountain is nothing compared to that at its base, where high season sees thousands of day-trippers tramping along the well-marked trails along the **Azusa valley**. With an early start, the scenic spots of the valley can be covered in a day's hike, but the best way to appreciate Kamikōchi is to stay overnight. Alternatively, visit in June, when frequent showers deter fair-weather walkers.

Azusa valley
梓川谷

At the entrance to the **Azusa valley**, 5km southwest of Kamikōchi's bus terminal, a glass-like pond reflects the snowcapped peaks. Known as the **Taishō-ike** (大正池), it formed when the Azusa-gawa was naturally dammed by a 1915 eruption of the nearby volcano, Yake-dake – dead tree trunks still poke out of the water. Rowing boats can be rented from the *Taishō-ike Hotel* (¥800/30min).

An hour-long amble sets off along the pebbly riverbank from the **Taishō-ike**. It splits after the Tashiro bridge, with one leg continuing beside the Azusa-gawa while the other follows a nature trail along wooden walkways, over chocolatey marshes. Returning the way you came, cross the Tashiro bridge to the opposite bank of the river, where the path leads past some of Kamikōchi's hotels and a rock-embedded relief statue of Walter Weston. In the centre of the village, a very photogenic wooden suspension bridge, **Kappa-bashi** (河童橋), crosses the river. A few minutes' walk from here, a good **visitor centre** (see p.372) run by the Chūbu-Sangaku National Park displays stunning photographs of the mountains.

The crowds fall away on the hike **north** from the visitor centre to the picturesque pond, **Myōjin-ike** (明神池; ¥300), with its tiny shrine and mallard ducks; the 7km return trip will take you around two hours at a leisurely pace. On October 8, Myōjin-ike hosts a festival in which two boats, their prows decorated with the head of a dragon and a legendary bird, float on the sacred pond.

The hike to Yari-ga-take

Keen hikers can follow an additional six-hour course up the valley from the **Myōjin-ike** to the **Tokusawa campsite** (徳沢) and the Shinmura suspension bridge, named after a famous climber, Shinmura Shōichi. Beyond Tokusawa, the serious hiking begins. The steep hike up the "Matterhorn of Japan" (so-called because of its craggy appearance) to the mountain huts at Ichinomata on the lower slopes of **Yari-ga-take** (槍ヶ岳) takes around five hours, and can be done in a long day from Kamikōchi. Basic huts on the mountain enable overnight stays; a futon and two meals cost around ¥8000 per person, but it can get very crowded.

Reaching the summit of Yari-ga-take may well give you a taste for mountaineering. The most popular route heads due south across the alpine ridge to **Hotaka-dake** (穂高岳), the third-highest peak in Japan, on a three-day loop that will bring you back to Kamikōchi.

ARRIVAL AND DEPARTURE | KAMIKŌCHI

By train To reach Kamikōchi by train from Matsumoto, take the Matsumoto Dentetsu line 15km west to Shinshimashima (新島々; every 30min; 30min; ¥700), then catch a connecting bus to Kamikōchi (1hr 15min; ¥2100).

By bus Direct buses run from Matsumoto bus terminal to Kamikōchi (16 daily; 1hr 50min; ¥2700 one-way, ¥4800

return). Takayama also has direct buses to Kamikōchi (11 daily; 1hr 25min; ¥2250), as well as more frequent buses to Hirayu Onsen (every 30min; 1hr; ¥1580), which has more frequent connections to Kamikōchi (every 30min; 30min; ¥1150). Daily buses also connect Norikura Kōgen (see p.372) and Kamikōchi. Once in Kamikōchi, be sure to

5

reserve your seat on a bus out again – high demand often leaves visitors at the mercy of the taxi drivers.

By car Private vehicles are banned from the valley. Drivers can park in the village of Naka-no-yu (中の湯), 12km

southwest of Kamikōchi via succesive narrow rock tunnels, and continue by bus (¥1000 one-way, ¥1800 return) or taxi (¥4500 for up to four passengers).

INFORMATION AND ACTIVITIES

Tourist information Kamikōchi's information centre, at the bus terminal (daily 8am–5pm; ☎026 395 2433, ⓦ kamikochi.or.jp), hands out a good English map that shows the main hiking trails. The staff don't speak much English, though, so if you need more information or want to arrange accommodation, you're better off seeking help at the Matsumoto tourist office (see p.367).

Hiking Be sure to pack warm, waterproof clothing even for

day walks, as the weather can change rapidly. At the height of summer, temperatures on the peaks can be freezing, especially in early morning. The staff at the Chūbu-Sangaku National Park visitor centre (daily 8am–5pm; ☎026 395 2606), just past Kappa-bashi, can provide English description of the local flora and fauna.

Services Kamikōchi has neither ATM nor bank, so bring plenty of cash.

ACCOMMODATION

Kamikōchi is not a cheap place to stay. If the options listed below are beyond your budget, consider basing yourself at the youth hostel in *Norikura Kōgen* (see opposite), and making a day-trip from there.

Kamikōchi Gosenjaku Lodge 五千尺ロッヂ ☎026 395 2221, ⓦ gosenjaku.co.jp. The less expensive of the two very comfortable *Gosenjaku* properties on the main village, with a skiers' dorm as well as private tatami rooms. Rates include two meals. 🕸 Dorms **¥10,000**, doubles **¥35,000**

Kamikōchi Imperial Hotel 上高地帝国ホテル ☎026 395 2001, ⓦ www.imperialhotel.co.jp/e/kamikochi. Built in 1933, this historic top-end hotel has the delightful spookiness of a grand old hotel in a wilderness setting. The Western-style rooms, restaurant and bar ooze quality, as does the attentive service of the staff. 🕸 **¥41,400**

Konashidaira 小梨平 ☎026 395 2321, ⓦ nihonal pskankou.co.jp. Campsite set in a serene location just a few

minutes' walk beyond Kappa-bashi and the visitor centre. Showers are available, as are self-catering cabins. Camping per person **¥800**, two-person cabins **¥9000**

Nishi-itoya Sansō 西糸屋山荘 ☎026 395 2206, ⓦ www.nishiitoya.com. The best budget option in Kamikōchi, with both bunk beds and shared tatami areas. The rates shown here include two meals, which is good value for the area. 🕸 Dorms **¥8600**, doubles **¥9900**

Yamanohidaya 山のひだや ☎026 395 2211, ⓦ i-sks .com/yh. To escape the crowds, head for this delightfully rustic lodge next to Myōjin-ike (see p.371), complete with stuffed animals as decoration. Two meals, cooked on an ancient iron range, are included in the rates. 🕸 **¥20,000**

EATING AND DRINKING

Eating options include standard soba and curry rice at inflated prices from the hotels, which also serve fancier set meals. If you're visiting for the day or planning a hike into the mountains, bring a picnic.

Kamonjigoya 嘉門次小屋 ☎026 395 2418, ⓦ kamonjigoya.wordpress.com. This attractive rustic lodge, beside Myōjin-ike (see p.371), is renowned for its

¥1600 *iwana* (river trout) lunch. The fish are roasted on sticks beside an *irori* (charcoal fire), making this an ideal refuge if the weather turns nasty. 🕸 Daily 8.30am–4.30pm.

Norikura Kōgen

乗鞍高原

Much like Kamikōchi, **NORIKURA KŌGEN**, an alpine village 30km southwest of Matsumoto, offers splendid mountain scenery, hiking trails and onsen. The closest thing to a centre in this straggle of a village is the modern onsen complex, **Yukemurikan** (湯けむり館; Mon & Wed–Sun 9.30am–9pm; ¥700), which has both indoor wooden baths and a rotemburo with mountain views.

In winter, ski lifts shoot up the lower slopes of **Norikura-dake**, while in summer the hike to the peak can be done in ninety minutes from the car park, an hour's drive from Norikura Kōgen, where the Echo Line road leaves Nagano-ken and becomes the **Skyline Road** in Gifu-ken. This is the highest road in Japan, providing splendid mountain-top views; its upper section, though, is closed from November until the end of May.

Walks around Norikura Kōgen

From the ski lifts near Yukemurikan onsen, an hour-long trail heads east to **Sanbon-daki** (三本滝), where three waterfalls converge in one pool. An alternative hiking route runs south from the ski lifts for twenty minutes, following a clearly marked nature trail with signs in English, to reach another beautiful waterfall, **Zengorō-no-taki** (善五郎の滝), where a rainbow often forms in the spray in the morning. Twenty minutes' walk further south of Zengorō, a small reflecting pond, **Ushidome-ike** (牛留池), provides a perfect view of the mountains. Continuing downhill from the pond, you can walk towards another small water hole, **Azami-ike** (あざみ池), or to the main picnic area, **Ichinose** (一の瀬), a picturesque spot at the confluence of two streams.

ARRIVAL AND INFORMATION

NORIKURA KŌGEN

By bus Norikura Kōgen can be reached by infrequent buses from both Shin-Shimashima train station, on the Matsumoto Dentetsu line, and Takayama (see p.380), changing buses at Tatamidaira and Hirayu Onsen. From June to Oct one daily bus also runs between Norikura Kōgen and Kamikōchi.

Tourist information The tourist office is opposite the Yukemurikan onsen complex (daily 9.30am–4.30pm; ☎ 026 393 2147, ⓦ norikura.gr.jp).

ACCOMMODATION

BELL Suzurangoya 鈴蘭小屋 4284-1 Azumi ☎ 026 393 2001, ⓦ bit.ly/suzurangoya. Large and friendly European-style chalet near the tourist office which features cosy rooms, large onsen baths and tasty home-cooked food. Rates include breakfast and dinner. **¥10,850**

Kyūkamura Norikura Kōgen 休暇村乗鞍高原 4307 Azumi ☎ 026 393 2304, ⓦ qkamura.or.jp/en/norikura. This modern hotel near the Ushidome pond has fine tatami rooms or fairly standard Western ones. There are

large outdoor and indoor onsen and rates that include two buffet meals; an extra heating charge applies in winter. **¥18,280**

Norikura Kōgen Youth Hostel 乗鞍高原ユースホステル 4275 Azumi Suzuran ☎ 026 393 2748. Just a 10min walk north from the bus stop, next to the ski lifts, this hostel is ideally placed for quick access to the slopes. The young, friendly staff can arrange ski rental and point out the most interesting summer hikes. Dorms **¥4280**

The Kiso valley

木曽谷

The densely forested river valley of **Kiso**, southwest of Matsumoto between the Central and Northern Alps, provides a glimpse of how Japan looked before concrete and neon became the norm. Part of the route for the 550km **Nakasendō**, one of the five main highways that spanned out from Edo (present-day Tokyo), ran through this valley. Connecting Edo with Kyoto, it reached its heyday between the seventeenth and nineteenth centuries.

Three of the eleven post towns (*juku*) that lined the Kiso-ji (Kiso road) section of the Nakasendō – **Narai**, **Tsumago** and **Magome** – have been preserved as virtual museums of the feudal past, and the latter two are linked by an easy two-hour **hiking trail** along the Nakasendō route which has deservedly become one of the most popular day-hikes in all Japan. Another *juku*, **Kiso-Fukushima**, looks less like a samurai film set than the others, but still has attractive areas and is useful as a transport hub.

Narai

奈良井

Attractive **NARAI**, 30km southwest of Matsumoto, was the most prosperous of the Kiso-ji *juku*. That fact remains evident in the village's beautifully preserved wooden buildings, with their overhanging second floors and *renji-gōshi* latticework. It can easily be visited in half a day, and is free from the tour groups that can clog Tsumago and Magome. In the conservation area, which runs for 1km south from the train station, only the occasional vehicle reminds you which century you're in.

5

In the Kamimachi area, **Nakamura House** (中村邸; April–Nov daily 9am–5pm, Dec–March Tues–Sun 9am–4pm; ¥300) dates from the 1830s, and was once home to a merchant who made his fortune in combs, still a local speciality. Side streets branch off to pretty temples and shrines in the foothills, while **Kiso-no-Ōhashi**, an arched wooden bridge, leads to the rocky banks of the Narai-gawa.

Look out for the shop selling *kashira ningyō*, colourfully painted traditional dolls and toys made of wood and plaster, as well as the sake brewery Sugi-no-Mori (杉の森), both in the Nakamachi area of town.

ARRIVAL AND INFORMATION
NARAI

By train Narai is served by local trains on the Chūō line from Matsumoto (10 daily, 50min; ¥580).
Tourist information The tourist office is in the

Nakamachi area (daily 10am–5pm; ☏ 026 434 3048, ⓦ naraijyuku.com). For historical background, visit ⓦ nakasendoway.com.

ACCOMMODATION AND EATING

Iseya 伊勢屋 388 Narai ☏ 026 434 3051, ⓦ oyado -iseya.jp. A lovely minshuku, in one of the traditional wooden post inns on the main street, with cosy tatami rooms and a peaceful inner garden. Rates include two meals. ☏ **¥21,000**

Kokoro-ne こころ音 368 Narai ☏ 026 434 3345. On the main street, with soaring wooden-beamed ceilings and an *irori* (a central charcoal fire), this appealing café serves soba noodles and other local dishes. Expect to pay around ¥1350 for a bowl of soba. Mon, Tues & Thurs–Sun 11am–3pm.

Kiso-Fukushima

木曽福島

The town of **KISO-FUKUSHIMA**, 20km southwest of Narai, is much more developed than the other *juku*. Pick up a map at the tourist office to point you towards the hilltop **Ue-no-dan** (上の段) conservation area and the serene temple **Kōzen-ji** (興禅寺).

ARRIVAL AND INFORMATION
KISO-FUKUSHIMA

By train Kiso-Fukushima is a stop for express trains on the JR Shinano line between Matsumoto (hourly; 40min) and Nagoya (hourly; 1hr 30min). Services finish quite early, so check your return journey carefully.
By bus Highway buses run from Tokyo Shinjuku (2 daily;

4hr 15min).
Tourist information The tourist office is opposite the train station (daily 9am–5pm; ☏ 026 422 4000, ⓦ www .kankou-kiso.com).

ACCOMMODATION

Tsutaya つたや 2012-4 Fukushima ☏ 026 422 2145, ⓦ kisoji-tutaya.com. A pleasant ryokan, opposite the station, combining traditional decor with modern design

touches, and with a choice of Japanese- or Western-style rooms. Rates include two meals. ☏ **¥30,240**

Magome

馬籠

The delightful old *juku* (post town) of **MAGOME** stands 800m high, in the hills above the Kiso valley, 100km southwest of Matsumoto. Its name means "horse basket", because travellers were forced to leave their nags here before tackling the mountainous stretch of road ahead. A magnificent array of black-and-white wood-and-plaster structures, their wooden roofs still held down by stone, lines up to either side of the ancient stone-flagged footpath that climbs the steep slope through the village. Several hold shops, restaurants, and small museums or galleries. Despite appearances, most date from the twentieth century; Magome has suffered a history of fires, the most recent being in 1915, when 42 houses burned down.

HIKING THE KISO-JI

The historic, enjoyable and easy-to-access hike along the Kiso-ji segment of the Nakasendō route is normally done south–north, from Magome to Tsumago. Supposedly that's to experience the tough initial climb into the mountains from Magome, though it's actually not that hard, and if anything it would be more difficult to walk in the opposite direction. The 7.7km footpath is signposted in English, and good maps are available from local tourist offices. While the hike itself takes around two hours, it's worth setting aside a whole day to explore both post towns as well. You'll enjoy the experience all the more if you stay in either Tsumago or Magome overnight.

To start the hike **from Magome**, simply keep walking uphill out of the village, past the *kōsatsu*, the old noticeboard on which the shogunate would post rules and regulations, including the death penalty for anyone found illegally logging in the forest. It's not quite as rural as you may be expecting, passing through residential districts and crisscrossing the paved road. The steepest part of the trail ends at the Magome-tōge (pass), where there's an old teahouse beside the road and a stone monument engraved with a lyrical verse by the haiku master Masaoka Shiki (see box, p.687). If you prefer not to walk uphill, catch a local bus to this point. The path then drops into a pretty stretch of forest, passing another appealing teahouse as well as two **waterfalls**, O-dake and Me-dake.

A **baggage-forwarding** service operates between mid-March and November. Hand in your bag before 11.30am at the so-called Magome Museum souvenir shop near the bus stop in Magome, or the tourist office in Tsumago, and for ¥500 it'll be delivered at the other end by 5pm.

Tōson Kinenkan

藤村記念館 • 4256-1 Magome • April–Nov daily 9am–5pm, Dec–March Mon, Tues & Thurs–Sun 9am–4pm • ¥500 • ☎ 057 369 2047, ⓦ toson.jp

The most interesting of Magome's various museums, the **Tōson Kinenkan** in the village centre is dedicated to native son **Shimazaki Tōson** (1872–1943), who put Magome on Japan's literary map with his historical novel *Yoake Mae* (*Before the Dawn*). Artefacts are labelled in Japanese only.

ARRIVAL AND INFORMATION   MAGOME

By train The closest train station to Magome, 9km west in the workaday town of Nakatsugawa (中津川), is served by direct trains from Matsumoto (hourly; 1hr 15min–2hr 30min; ¥1940) and Nagoya (hourly; 55min; ¥1320). Regular buses to Magome run from platform three outside the station (hourly; 25min; ¥560).

By bus Five buses daily connect Magome with Tsumago,

and continue to the JR station at Nagiso.

Tourist information Magome's tourist office (daily 8.30am–5pm; ☎ 026 459 2336, ⓦ kiso-magome.com), opposite the Tōson Kinenkan, stocks some good English maps and brochures; the staff speak Japanese only and can make accommodation bookings.

ACCOMMODATION

Magome-chaya Guesthouse 馬籠茶屋 4296 Magome ☎ 026 459 2038, ⓦ en.magomechaya.com. The friendly Japanese-Filipino owners of this well-maintained but relatively basic old ryokan, near the tourist office, speak some English. They also run the restaurant opposite, open for breakfast and dinner only at an additional cost of ¥4320 per person. **¥8424**

Tajimaya 但馬屋 4266 Magome ☎ 026 459 2048, ⓦ kiso-tajimaya.com. Charming inn, which has been in the same family for eight generations, downhill from the tourist office. Accommodation is in tatami rooms, while the toilets and the rather glorious wooden baths are shared. Dinner, included with breakfast in the rate, is served around an *irori* fireplace. **¥17,280**

Tsumago

妻籠

Given the number of tourists it now attracts, it's hard to believe that, back in the 1960s, **TSUMAGO**, 8km north of Magome, was virtually a ghost town, with most of its traditional Edo-era houses on the verge of collapse. The locals banded together to restore the village's buildings, earning Tsumago protected status and helping to spark the idea of cultural preservation across Japan. Telegraph poles and TV aerials are banished from sight, so that the scene that greets you on the pedestrian-only main street must be very similar to that encountered by lords and their retinues passing through here hundreds of years ago.

You can get a bird's-eye view of Tsumago from the former site of **Tsumago castle**, destroyed in the late sixteenth century. The route up is signposted off the hiking path that heads north out of the village towards Nagiso.

Nagiso-machi Museum

南木曽町博物館, Nagiso-machi Hakubutsukan • 2190 Azuma • Daily 9am–5pm • ¥600 • ☎ 026 457 3322

The main section of the two-part **Nagiso-machi Museum**, the **Waki Honjin Okuya** (脇本陣奥谷), is a finely constructed two-storey mansion that dates from 1877 and was a designated post inn for government officials. Photographs in the **Historical Museum** opposite (歴史博物館, Rekishi Hakubutsukan) show just how dilapidated Tsumago had become before restoration.

ARRIVAL AND INFORMATION TSUMAGO

By train The nearest station to Tsumago, 3.5km north at Nagiso (南木曽), serves both Matsumoto (hourly; 1hr 10min–2hr 15min; ¥1490) and Nagoya (hourly; 1hr 5min; ¥1660). Five buses daily connect Nagiso with Tsumago (7min) and Magome (35min), or you can simply walk the very pleasant rural stretch of the Nakasendo path between Nagiso and Tsumago in under an hour.

Tourist information Tsumago's helpful tourist office is in the village centre (daily 8.30am–5pm; ☎ 026 457 3123, ⓦ tumago.jp/english).

ACCOMMODATION AND EATING

Although Tsumago holds several lunchtime restaurants and cafés, evening **eating** options are limited; overnight visitors should expect to eat in their lodgings. **Local specialities** include *sansai soba* (buckwheat noodles with mountain vegetables) and *gohei-mochi* (balls of pounded rice coated in a sweet nut sauce).

Daikichi 大吉 902-1 Nagiso-chō ☎ 026 457 2595. Small minshuku at the northern end of the village, serving authentic local mountain dishes – which can include horse sashimi – and wines. **¥18,000**

Fujioto 藤乙 Nagiso-machi ☎ 026 457 3009, ⓦ tsumago-fujioto.jp. This charming traditional inn, with friendly English-speaking owners, is set in a beautiful Japanese garden. **¥21,600**

Matsushiro-ya 松代屋 807 Nagiso-chō ☎ 026 457 3022, ⓦ matsushiroya.sakura.ne.jp. Upmarket, 140-year-old ryokan that has been run by the same family for nine generations. Speciality dishes include carp sashimi, grilled river fish, and *tora soba* (soba noodles with yams). Closed Thurs. **¥21,600**

Rikyu 琉球 803-1 Nagiso-chō ☎ 026 457 2682. This traditional restaurant, towards the north end of the village, has tatami and Western-style seating, and is a great place to sample both *sansai soba* (from ¥900) and *gohei-mochi* (¥250 each). Mon & Wed–Sun 9am–4.30pm.

Takayama

高山

An absolute must-see destination, little touched by wartime bombs or modern development, the deservedly popular tourist town of **TAKAYAMA**, on the Gifu-ken side of the Central Alps 110km northeast of Nagoya, was once an enclave of skilled carpenters employed by the emperors to build palaces and temples in Kyoto and Nara. This area is known as **Hida**, so you'll also see the town referred to as "Hida Takayama", or simply "Hida".

Takayama is a delight to stroll around. It started out as a castle town, ruled by six generations of the Kanamori family between 1586 and 1692. Their long-vanished castle stood atop a conical hill to the south, with Takayama itself ranged along the east bank of the Miya-gawa, fringed by a row of shrines and temples on the forested slopes

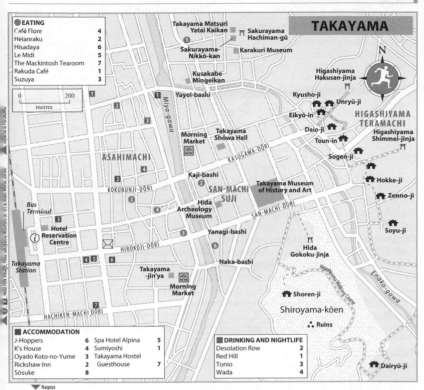

TAKAYAMA

to the east. The town's compact original core, now home to the picturesque **San-machi Suji** neighbourhood, remains its most appealing quarter, peppered with old merchant houses and small museums, and complemented by cafés and restaurants.

Takayama-jin'ya

高山陣屋 • 1-5 Hachiken-machi • Daily: April–July, Sept & Oct 8.45am–5pm, Aug 8.45am–6pm, Nov–March 8.45am–4.30pm • ¥430; English-language tours free • ☎ 057 732 0643

The administrative complex from which Takayama was ruled during the feudal era, **Takayama-jin'ya**, on the west bank of the river, makes an absorbing first stop for history-minded visitors. Built in 1615, this small-scale palace was the seat of power for the governor of the Hida area, and is the only such building to survive in Japan.

All visits follow a set course through the complex; the best way to understand what you're seeing is to join one of the regular guided tours in English. The first half of the route leads through the main building, reconstructed in 1996. You then move on to a rice storehouse dating from 1816, where only a few of the remarkable old maps and documents have been translated into English.

San-machi Suji

三町筋

The **San-machi Suji** area, on the east bank of the Miya-gawa, occupies the site of Takayama's original settlement, even if the dark wooden merchant houses that fill it date largely from the mid-nineteenth century. The quarter's three principal narrow

5

FLOATS AND FESTIVALS OF TAKAYAMA

In Takayama's two spectacular festivals, the **Sannō Matsuri** (April 14–15) and the **Hachiman Matsuri** (Oct 9–10), eleven huge elaborate *yatai* (floats), adorned with mechanical dolls (*karakuri*), are paraded around town. If you're not in town during the festivals, which attract hundreds of thousands of visitors, you can still view four of the *yatai* at the **Takayama Matsuri Yatai Kaikan** (高山祭屋台会館; daily: March–Nov 8.30am–5.30pm, Dec–Feb 9am–4.30pm; ¥820; ☎ 057 732 5100), a large exhibition hall within the grounds of the **Sakurayama Hachiman-gū** shrine. At any one time, four out of the eleven floats and the golden *mikoshi* (portable shrine) are displayed inside a huge glass case, around which visitors wind their way at different levels, in order to see all of the decoration closely. Many of the floats date from the seventeenth century; those that aren't currently on show are stored in tall storehouses (*yatai-gura*) scattered around Takayama.

streets are most evocative at dusk, when the crowds have thinned. During the day, you'll have to negotiate your way through rickshaws and tourists pottering in and out of craft shops, cafés and sake breweries (see p.382).

Takayama Museum of History and Art

飛驒高山まちの博物館, Hida-Takayama Machi no Hakubutsukan • 75 Kamiichino-machi • Daily 9am–7pm • Free • ☎ 057 732 1205

Although the large **Takayama Museum of History and Art**, in the heart of San-machi Suji, is housed in several centuries-old storehouses, their original appearance is now barely discernible. Instead the museum consists of bright modern galleries that do a great job of tracing the town's history and its former rulers, as well as providing a good introduction to local traditions and festivals. Pick up a detailed English-language brochure when you enter; few of the actual captions have been translated.

Hida Archeology Museum

飛驒みんぞくココ館, Hida Minzoku Koko-kan • 82 Kamisanno-machi • Daily: March–Oct 9.30am–4.30pm, Nov–Feb 9.30am–4.30pm • ¥500 • ☎ 057 732 1980

The former home of a doctor who was also a ninja now holds the intriguing **Hida Archeology Museum**. The ramshackle house itself is bursting with tricks and secrets, including a false ceiling in one room, which is suspended on ropes and thus could be sent crashing down on intruders, while adjoining storerooms hold assorted ancient arrowheads, pottery and carvings. There's no sign outside; look for a small but undeniably fearsome suit of samurai armour displayed in a glass case outside.

Takayama Shōwa Hall

高山昭和館, Takayama Shōwa-kan • 6 Shimoichinomachi • Daily: April–Oct 9am–6pm, Nov–March 9am–5pm • ¥800 • ☎ 057 733 7836

An idiosyncratic labour of love, hidden away behind a (free) sweets-and-souvenirs shop, the **Takayama Shōwa Hall** celebrates everyday life during the boom years of the mid-twentieth-century Shōwa era. All sorts of artefacts and domestic treasures are tucked into re-created shops and homes, laid out in a vast warren-like warehouse. For Japanese visitors, it's a real nostalgia-fest; foreigners tend to scoot through in half an hour or so, though you can linger over a movie in the eleven-seat cinema, or play Nintendo games dating from 1983 onwards.

Sakurayama Hachiman-gū

桜山八幡宮 • 178 Sakura-machi • **Shrine precincts** open 24hr, free; **Takayama Matsuri Yatai Kaikan** and **Sakurayama-Nikkō-kan** daily: March–Nov 8.30am–5.30pm, Dec–Feb 9am–4.30pm • ¥820 • ☎ 057 732 0240

Set on the slopes a short walk northeast of San-machi Suji, Takayama's main shrine, **Sakurayama Hachiman-gū**, was founded during the fourth century. The temple precincts are well worth exploring in their own right, while immediately below you'll find two modern museums, both covered by the same ticket. The **Takayama Yatai**

Kaikan holds floats from the town's major festivals (see box opposite), and the **Sakurayama-Nikkō-kan** displays a dazzling one-tenth scale replica of 28 buildings from Nikkō's Tōshōgū shrine, with lighting that fluctuates to reproduce sunrise and sunset.

Karakuri Museum

獅子会館 • 53-1 Sakura-machi • Daily 9.05am–4.25pm • ¥600 • ☎ 057 7320 881

Just south of the Sakurayama Hachiman-gū, the **Karakuri Museum** offers enjoyable demonstrations of the automated *karakuri* puppets that enliven Takayama's great festivals. A video of a *shishi* (mythical lion) dance is screened at regular intervals during the day, and you can admire masks and musical instruments used in the dances. The museum also has an excellent gift shop.

Higashiyama Teramachi and Shiroyama-kōen

A very pleasant walk along the hillside southeast of the Sakurayama Hachiman-gū, initially following the narrow Enako-gawa, leads you through the tranquil **Higashiyama Teramachi** (東山寺町) area, where thirteen temples and five shrines are dotted among the soaring pine trees. Signposted footpaths then cross the river and continue to **Shiroyama-kōen** (城山公園), a wooded park that stands on the remains of Lord Kanamori's castle, destroyed over three hundred years ago. Climb to the top of the hill, and it's still possible to trace the foundations of the donjon.

Hida Folk Village

飛騨民俗村, Hida Minzoku-mura • 1-590 Kamiokamoto-chō • Daily 8.30am–5pm • ¥700 • ☎ 057 734 4711, ⓦ bit.ly/hidafolk • 2.2km southwest of the station; 30min walk, or bus #1 (¥200 one-way, or ¥900 return ticket including admission)

In a lovely hillside location, overlooking the mountains west of town, the **Hida Folk Village** is an outdoor showcase for more than twenty traditional buildings gathered from the Hida area.

You can explore inside the houses, which include *gasshō-zukuri* thatched dwellings from the Shirakawa-gō and Gokayama districts (see p 383). Many hold displays of the farm implements and folk crafts of their original owners, while in the four old houses next to the ticket gate you can watch real artists working at traditional crafts such as lacquering and woodcarving.

Hida Takayama Museum of Art

飛騨高山美術館, Hida Takayama Bijutsukan • 1-124-1 Kamiokamoto-chō, 1.7km southwest of the station • Daily 9am–5pm • ¥1300 • ☎ 057 735 3535, ⓦ htm-museum.co.jp

The bright, modern **Hida Takayama Museum of Art**, perched on a small hill en route towards the Hida Folk Village, focuses on wonderful Art Nouveau and Art Deco artefacts. A beautiful glass fountain by René Lalique, which once stood in the Paris Lido, greets you at the entrance; further on, you'll find lustrous objets d'art by Gallé, Tiffany glass lamps, and the interior designs of Charles Rennie Mackintosh and the Vienna Secessionists.

TAKAYAMA'S MORNING MARKETS

Every day, starting at 6am in summer and 7am in winter, and lasting until around noon, Takayama has two **morning markets** (*asa ichi*). The fruit and veg market is held in front of the *jin'ya* (see p.377), while the larger, more tourist-orientated market stretches along the east bank of the Miya-gawa, between the Kaji-bashi and Yayoi-bashi. Here, apart from pickles and flowers, you can buy local handicrafts, (including *sarubobo*, the little fabric baby monkeys seen all over Takayama), grab a coffee or locally brewed beer, or sample the sweet marshmallow snack *tamaten*.

ARRIVAL AND INFORMATION

By train Takayama Station, on the western edge of downtown, is linked by the scenic, cross-country JR Takayama line with Toyama to the north and Gifu and Nagoya to the south.

Destinations Gifu (5 daily; 2hr 5min); Nagoya (5 daily; 2hr 25min); Toyama (4 daily; 1hr 25min).

By bus The long-distance bus terminal (ⓦ www .nouhibus.co.jp) is next to the train station.

Destinations Gifu (6 daily; 2hr); Gujō Hachiman (5 daily; 1hr 10min); Hirayu Onsen (every 30min; 1hr); Kamikōchi

(11 daily; 1hr 25min); Kanazawa (4 daily; 3hr); Kyoto (5 daily; 4hr 15min); Matsumoto (4 daily; 2hr 30min); Nagoya (12 daily; 2hr 40min); Ogimachi, in Shirakawa-gō region (hourly; 50min); Osaka (5 daily; 5hr 30min); Tokyo (6 daily; 5hr 30min); Toyama (4 daily; 2hr 30min).

Tourist information The Hida tourist information office, in front of the station, has clued-up, English-speaking staff (daily: April–Oct 8.30am–7pm, Nov–March 8.30am–5pm; ☎ 057 732 5328, ⓦ www.hida.jp). Online information on the broader Hida area can also be found at ⓦ hida-kankou.jp.

GETTING AROUND

By bike Bicycles can be rented from the car park to the right of the station (¥200/hr, ¥1200/day), or from the many local hostels and bike shops.

By car If you fancy renting a car to explore the region, drop in to Toyota Rent-a-Car opposite the station (daily

8am–8pm; ☎ 057 736 6110, ⓦ rent.toyota.co.jp).

Tours Two daily half-day bus tours head up to different villages in the Shirakawa-gō region (¥6690; ⓦ www .nouhibus.co.jp).

ACCOMMODATION

If you're hoping to visit Takayama during its festivals (see box, p.378), be sure to book well ahead. In addition to the places listed below, there are several inexpensive **business hotels** near the train station.

J-Hoppers ジェイ・ホパーズ 5-52 Nada-machi ☎ 057 732 3278, ⓦ takayama.j-hoppers.com. Converted from a former hotel, this friendly hostel is a slick affair. They offer dorms and private rooms (with and without private bathrooms), provide bike rental at ¥700 per day, organize inexpensive trips to destinations like Shirakawa-gō and Kamikōchi, and even provide wellies for sloshing through the winter snow. ☞ Dorms **¥2700**, doubles **¥6400**

★**K's House** ケイズ・ハウス 4-45-1 Tenman-chō ☎ 057 734 4410, ⓦ kshouse.jp. This modern backpackers' hostel, a 3min walk east of the station, features clean bunk dormitories or tatami private rooms, each with its own bathroom. There's a comfortable lounge downstairs with beanbags and internet terminals and a newly fitted kitchen to prepare meals. Bikes are available for ¥150 per hour, and the friendly English-speaking staff are happy to help. Since 2016, the same company has also run the similarly recommended *K's House Takayama Oasis*, nearby. ☞ Dorms **¥2900**, doubles **¥7200**

★**Oyado Koto-no-Yume** 古都の夢 6-11 Hanasato-chō ☎ 057 732 0427, ⓦ kotoyume.com. Small-scale ryokan, close to the station, which blends traditional style with contemporary design touches; guests get to wear their choice of colourful modern *yukata*. Both indoor and outdoor onsen are available. Rates include two meals. ☞ **¥32,000**

★**Rickshaw Inn** 旅籠 力車イン 54 Suehiro-chō ☎ 057 732 2890, ⓦ rickshawinn.com. As well as friendly English-speaking owners, this relaxing place has well-furnished tatami (shared or private bathrooms) or Western rooms (private bathrooms only). There's a comfy lounge with sofas, English newspapers, magazines and art books as well as a small kitchen for self-catering. The stylish ground-floor

suite, sleeping up to six, is great value for a family or group. Breakfast costs ¥700 extra per person. **¥8900**

Sōsuke 惣助 1-64 Okamoto-machi ☎ 057 732 0818, ⓦ irori-sosuke.com. Good-value traditional minshuku, a 10min walk west of the station, opposite the *Takayama Green Hotel*. The building is 170 years old and has a traditional *irori* hearth; the thirteen Japanese guest rooms share two single-sex bathrooms. Rates include breakfast; dinner is not served. **¥11,880**

Spa Hotel Alpina スパホテルアルピナ 5-41 Nada-machi ☎ 057 733 0033, ⓦ spa-hotel-alpina.com. Efficient modern hotel where the hundred-plus pleasant, smallish rooms offer slightly more contemporary design than your average business option. It also has the advantage of rooftop spa baths with a decent view. ☞ **¥11,300**

Sumiyoshi 寿美吉 4-21 Honmachi ☎ 057 732 0228, ⓦ sumiyoshi-ryokan.com. Delightful *gaijin*-friendly ryokan, offering en-suite or shared-bath Japanese-style rooms in a century-old building that enjoys a great riverside location. The staff are very friendly and the place is chock-full of interesting antiques and knick-knacks. Breakfast costs an additional ¥1080, and dinner ¥3240. ☞ **¥15,120**

Takayama Hostel Guesthouse Zenkō-ji 高山ホステル ゲストハウス善光寺 4-3 Tenman-chō ☎ 057 732 8470, ⓦ takayamahostelzenkoji.com. Attached to the imposing Zenkō-ji temple, on the hillside east of town, this appealing hostel offers visitors a true only-in-Japan experience. With their polished floors and graceful screens, the tatami-mat rooms, used as dorms or private rooms, are an absolute bargain; some open onto a pleasant rock garden. Like its Nagano namesake, Zenkō-ji holds a dark underground corridor that hides the "key to paradise". As this book went to press, the hostel was about to close for renovations, but it should be open again by the time you read this. Recommended donation per person **¥3000**

EATING

The best dishes to sample at Takayama's numerous **restaurants** are local specialities such as *sansai ryōri*, consisting of mountain vegetables, ferns and wild plants, or the renowned **Hida beef**. Also look out for *sansai soba*, buckwheat noodles topped with greens, and *hōba miso*, vegetables mixed with miso paste and roasted on a magnolia leaf above a charcoal brazier (a beef version is also served). One delicious snack sold around town is *mitarashi-dango* – pounded rice balls dipped in soy sauce and roasted on skewers. Note that many of the San-machi Suji tourist restaurants are only open at lunch, when they can get very busy.

RESTAURANTS

Heianraku 平安楽 6-7-2 Tenman-chō ☎ 057 732 3078. Small, friendly restaurant, a short walk from the station, with room for just a dozen diners, seated either on tatami mats or at the counter. The menu takes in both Chinese and Japanese cuisine, with favourites like pork dumplings and deep-fried chicken, and a particular emphasis on vegetarian options, including tofu and local wild vegetables. A simple dish with rice and soup costs well under ¥1000, while a set meal for two is ¥2700. Mon & Wed–Sun 11.30am–1pm & 5–9pm.

Hisadaya 久田屋 11-3 Kamisanno-machi ☎ 057 732 0216. Delightful traditional restaurant, laid out in the antique-filled rooms of a former merchant's house in the San-machi Suji neighbourhood. It's open for lunch only, serving excellent set meals of *sansai ryōri* from ¥1450 per person. Mon, Tues & Thurs–Sun 10.30am–3pm.

Le Midi ル・ミディ 2-85 Honmachi ☎ 057 736 6386, ⓦle-midi.jp. This sophisticated bistro, which feels like a slice of Paris with its red-and-white checked curtains, makes a great place to sample top-quality Hida beef and other local meat and fish dishes. A steak will set you back at least ¥4800, while lunch menus start at ¥1800 and dinner at ¥4800. Another branch, across the road, specializes in French cuisine, and there's also a takeaway booth selling its speciality pumpkin pudding. Mon–Wed & Fri 11.30am–3pm & 6–9.30pm, Sat & Sun 11.30am–3.30pm & 5–9.30pm.

★Suzuya 寿々や 24 Hanakawa-machi ☎ 057 732 2484, ⓦ suzuyatakayama.ec-net.jp. This beamed, family-run restaurant has acquired such a reputation for its Hida beef that the Western-style tables nearer the front seem always to be filled with foreign tourists. Don't let that put you off, though – the food really is good, with plates of beef to grill yourself starting at just under ¥2000, as well as local specialities including *sansai ryōri* for ¥1620 and *hōba miso* for ¥1188. There's an English menu with pictures, friendly waitresses, and the tatami rooms at the back offer a quieter ambience. Mon & Wed–Sun 11am–2.30pm & 5–8pm.

CAFÉS

Café Flore カフェフロール 37 Aioi-chō ☎ 057 735 0099. Small French café with a laidback jazz soundtrack, serving excellent coffee plus a short menu of European favourites such as pasta dishes and crêpes, costing ¥1000 or less and including vegetarian options. Mon, Tues & Thurs–Sun 11am–4.30pm & 6.30–10pm.

The Mackintosh Tearoom マッキントシュ・ティールーム 1-124-1 Kamiokamoto-cho ☎ 057 735 3535, ⓦ htm-museum.co.jp. Attached to the Museum of Art (see p.379), *The Mackintosh* is modelled on Charles Rennie Mackintosh's design of the celebrated Willow Tearooms in Glasgow, and offers specially blended tea and cakes, as well as light, low-cal Mediterranean lunches, with an emphasis on organic ingredients, from ¥1300. The view across the mountains is lovely, and you can eat outside. ☎ Mon & Wed–Sun 9am–5pm.

Rakuda Café 駱駝 1-94 Oshim-machi ☎ 057 734 5574. Bright, welcoming café in a prime people-watching location near the Sakurayama Hachiman-gū temple. As well as ¥600 snacks like apple toast, open sandwiches, small pizzas and sponge cakes, and a few larger meals like Thai green curry for ¥1000, they have a wide range of teas, coffees, and smoothies, and a refreshing home-made ginger beer. ☎ Daily 10am–5pm.

DRINKING AND NIGHTLIFE

Takayama abounds in small **bars**, especially in the Asahimachi area between the station and the Miya-gawa.

Desolation Row デゾレーション ロウ 30 Asahimachi ☎ 908 077 5699. Named after the Dylan song, this cosy little bar is not surprisingly owned and run by a major fan of 1960s rock music, who's delighted to discuss his vinyl collection – no requests, though – over whisky, sake or beer. Daily 8pm–late.

Red Hill レッド・ヒル 2-4 Sowa-chō ☎ 057 733 8139. You'll get a warm welcome from the English-speaking owner of this small bar, which serves a good range of bottled beers from around the world and appealing food drawn from a global palette. Tues–Sun 7pm–midnight.

Tonio トニオ 4-65 Honmachi ☎ 057 732 1677. Festooned with old film posters and similar memorabilia, this wood-panelled "Western bar" is a quiet place for a beer and a snack, with European-style pub-grub dishes costing around ¥1000. Daily 5pm–1am.

5

★ **Wada** 和田 Ichiban-gai • ☎ 057 733 4850. If you find yourself wondering where the locals choose to drink and nibble on snacks in this touristy town, look no further. Don't be put off by the menu items like fried chicken bowels with miso, or grilled pig's trotters – there are plenty of other things to try, and they're all good value. Dishes start at ¥500. Daily 5pm–1am.

Furukawa

古川

With its old white-walled storehouses ranged alongside a canal, sake breweries, and temples decorated with intricate woodcarvings, charming **FURUKAWA**, in the Hida province, is like a compact version of Takayama, minus the crowds. The sleepy riverside town makes an easy day-trip from Takayama, and comes alive during its annual spring *matsuri* festival.

Hida Furukawa Matsuri Kaikan

飛騨古川まつり会館 • 14-5 Ichino-machi • Daily: March–Nov 9am–5pm, Dec–Feb 9am–4.30pm • ¥800, or ¥1000 combined with Hida Crafts Museum • ☎ 057 773 3511, ⓦ okosidaiko.com

To get a taste of what Furukawa's Matsuri festival is all about, drop in at the **Hida Furukawa Matsuri Kaikan**, five minutes' walk west of the station. Here you can inspect three of the nine *yatai*, as well as watch a 3-D film of the festival and a computer-controlled performance by one of the puppets that adorn the *yatai*. Local craftsmen work here, too. Drums used in the festival are on show in an open hall on the square in front of the main hall.

Hida Crafts Museum

飛騨の匠文化館, Hida No Takumi Bunkakan • 10-1 Ichino-machi • Mon–Wed & Fri–Sun: March–Nov 9am–5pm, Dec–Feb 9am–4.30pm • ¥300, or ¥1000 with Hida Furukawa Matsuri Kaikan • ☎ 057 773 3321

Long revered for their skills, Hida craftsmen were recruited to build many of Japan's most famous temples, especially in Kyoto and Nara. The **Hida Crafts Museum** highlights local woodworkers' traditional tools and techniques, with displays showing how buildings – including the museum itself – are constructed using wooden beams without using nails. You can try for yourself on scale models.

Shirakabe-dozō

白壁土蔵

In the **Shirakabe-dozō** district, which begins south of the square at Matsuri Kaikan, a row of traditional storehouses stands beside a narrow, gently flowing canal packed with carp. Walk for five minutes southeast along the canal from here until you reach the river, and one block to the west you'll find **Honkō-ji** (本光寺), an attractive temple decorated with the intricate carving and carpentry for which the town is famous. Return to the town centre along Ichino-machi-dōri and you'll come to the 240-year-old **candle shop**

> **FURUKAWA MATSURI**
>
> The **Furukawa Matsuri** festival (April 19 & 20) celebrates the arrival of spring with grand parades of wonderfully decorated floats (*yatai*). The highlight is the **Okoshi Daiko** procession, which starts at 9pm on April 19 and runs until around 2am. Hundreds of men, clad only in baggy white underpants and belly bands and led by over a thousand people carrying lanterns, compete to place small drums (tied to long poles) atop a portable stage that bears the huge main drum, which is all the while being solemnly thumped. The men also balance atop poles and spin around on their stomachs. Extra late-night trains and buses run on festival days between Takayama and Furukawa. The *yatai* and *mikoshi* processions happen during the day. For more information see ⓦ bit.ly/furukawamatsuri.

Mishima, where a candle-maker gives regular demonstrations (三嶋; 3-12 Ichino-machi; Mon, Tues & Thurs–Sun 9am–5pm; ☎057 773 4109). The same street also holds Furukawa's two remaining **sake breweries** – Kaba (蒲; 6-6 Ichino-machi; daily 9am–5pm) and Watanabe (渡辺; 7-7 Ichino-machi; daily 9am–5pm) – both of which will gladly let you sample their products whether you buy or not.

ARRIVAL AND INFORMATION · FURUKAWA

By train Frequent local trains connect Furukawa's JR station – officially called Hida-Furukawa (飛騨古川) – with Takayama (15min; ¥240).

By bus Buses link Furukawa with Takayama (6 daily; up to 30min; ¥380).

Tourist information Helpful staff in the Kita-Hida tourist information booth, just outside Hida-Furukawa Station

(daily 9am–5pm; ☎057 773 3180, ⓦ hida-kankou.jp), can assist with finding accommodation.

Tours Satoyama Experience offer highly recommended half-day cycling and walking tours in and around Furukawa (cycling ¥4700–7300, walking ¥4700; ☎057 773 5715, ⓦ satoyama-experience.com).

ACCOMMODATION

With Takayama so close, the only strong reason to **stay** in Furukawa itself is if you're planning to hike in the surrounding mountains.

Hida Furukawa Youth Hostel 飛騨古川ユースホステル 180 Nobuka ☎057 775 2979, ⓦ bit.ly/furukawa hostel. A good base for hikers, this modern hostel is housed in a homely wooden cabin amid rice fields. Take a

bus to Shinrin-koen from Hida-Furukawa Station (15min); check times at the information booth. Rates include breakfast and dinner. Dorms **¥5500**

EATING

Katsumi 克己 5-19 Furukawa-cho ☎057 773 7888. A great spot for lunch, in a grey building a minute's walk west of the station. The lunchtime *wagamama teishoku* (¥980) is a feast of delicious vegetable, tofu and fish dishes, while in the evening you can try their fish specialities (¥2000/ head). Mon–Sat 11.30am–1pm & 5.30–10pm.

Maeda まえだ 11-10 Furukawa-chō ☎057 773 2852. On the right-hand corner of the junction with the road from the station, this friendly place has set meals starting at ¥2100 and beef curry for under ¥1000. Mon–Wed & Fri–Sun 11.30am–9pm.

Shirakawa-gō and Gokayama

白川郷・五箇山

Thanks to their thatched A-frame houses – a rare form of architecture called **gasshō-zukuri** – three picturesque villages in the **Shirakawa-gō** and **Gokayama** areas, northwest of Takayama, were jointly designated a World Heritage Site in 1995. Among the many fabled bolt holes of the Taira clan after their defeat at the battle of Dannoura (see box, p.603), these communities were until the mid-twentieth century almost entirely cut off from fast-modernizing Japan. Then, when the damming of the

5

> ### PRAYING-HANDS HOUSES
>
> **Gasshō-zukuri** means "praying hands", because the sixty-degree slope of the thatched gable roofs is said to recall two hands joined in prayer. The sharp angle is designed to cope with the heavy snowfall hereabouts, while the size of the houses is the result of multi-generational family living. The upper storeys of the home were used for industries such as making gunpowder and cultivating silkworms. The **thatched roofs** – many of which have a surface area of around six hundred square metres – are made of *susuki* grass, native to the northern part of the Hida region (wooden shingles were used in the south), and have to be replaced every 25 to 35 years.
>
> Since it can cost ¥20 million to re-thatch an entire roof, many of the houses fell into disrepair until the government stepped in with grants in 1976. Now the local preservation society decides which buildings are most in need of repair each year and helps organize the **yui**, a two-hundred-strong team who work together to re-thatch a roof within a single day. Despite these initiatives, however, fewer than 200 *gasshō-zukuri* houses now survive.

Shō-kawa in the 1960s, together with the drift of population away from the countryside, threatened their survival, local residents began a preservation movement. They have been so successful that the three villages – **Ogimachi** in Gifu-ken, and **Suganuma** and **Ainokura** in neighbouring Toyama-ken – are now in danger of being swamped by visitors. It is still worth braving the crowds to see these extraordinary buildings, set in idyllic valleys surrounded by forests and mountains. To feel the full magic of the place, arrange to stay overnight in a minshuku in a *gasshō-zukuri* house.

Ogimachi

荻町

In the shadow of the sacred mountain Hakusan, **OGIMACHI** is home to 114 **gasshō-zukuri** houses, the largest collection within the Shirakawa-gō area of the Shō-kawa valley. Many of the thatched houses were moved here when threatened by the damming of the Shō-kawa, creating a landscape that looks somewhat contrived, Matters aren't helped by the fact that the main road slices right through the village centre; it's closed to traffic between 9am and 6pm each day, but remains responsible for a massive daily influx of tourists. Even so, this is a real working village, where most of the houses are still populated by families who farm rice in the surrounding fields. Start your explorations by hiking up to the Shirakawa lookout (*tenbōdai*) at the north end of the village, which offers a bird's-eye view of Ogimachi's layout.

Wada-ke

和田家 • 997 Ogimachi • Daily 9am–5pm • ¥300 • ☎ 057 696 1058

The thatch-roofed **Wada-ke**, a prime example of local architecture which has a lily pond in front, is one of several "museum" houses. Home to generations of the wealthy Wada family, it contains fine lacquerware, decorations and furniture passed down for over two hundred years.

Myōzen-ji Temple Museum

明善寺郷土館, Myōzen-ji Kyodo-Kan • 679 Ogimachi • Daily: April–Nov 8.30am–5pm, Dec–March 9am–4pm • ¥300 • ☎ 057 696 1009

The huge five-storey **Myōzen-ji Temple Museum** was once the living quarters for the priests and monks from the adjoining temple; on its upper floors you can see where over a tonne of silk cocoons was cultivated each year. Gaps in the floorboards allowed the smoke from the *irori* fire to permeate the whole building, preserving the wood and thatch. A narrow passageway connects the main house to the thatched temple next door.

5

Doburoku Matsuri Exhibition Hall

どぶろく祭りの館, Doburoku Matsuri no Kan • April to mid-Oct & Nov daily 9am–5pm • ¥300 • ☎ 057 696 1655

The **Doburoku Matsuri Exhibition Hall** stands next to the village's main shrine, **Shirakawa Hachiman-jinja** (白川八幡神社). The exhibition itself – devoted to the annual festival (Oct 14–19), which involves the making of a rough, milky sake known as *doburoku* – is small, but you can watch a good video in Japanese about life in the village, and sample a drop of the potent alcohol.

Gasshō-zukuri Folklore Park

合掌造り民家園, Gasshō-zukuri Minka-en • 2499 Ogimachi • April–July & Sept–Nov, Mon–Wed & Fri–Sun 8.40am–5pm; Aug daily 8am–5.30pm; Dec–March Mon–Wed & Fri–Sun 9am–4pm • ¥500 • ☎ 057 696 1231

On the west side of the Shō-kawa, reached by a footbridge, the **Gasshō-zukuri Folklore Park** is an open-air museum that holds some 25 buildings gathered from around the region. Enjoy a rest and a free cup of tea in the Nakano Chōjirō family house near the entrance. In the village hall, just outside the park, you can learn how to make soba noodles (April–Oct daily 10am & 1.30pm; advance booking recommended; ¥1800).

ARRIVAL AND INFORMATION

OGIMACHI

By bus Regular buses connect Takayama to Ogimachi (hourly, 50min; ¥2470), with two daily continuing to Kanazawa (1hr 15min; ¥1850), and four daily to Toyama (1hr 25min; ¥1750); reserve seats in advance. The same bus company also runs daily tours from Takayama (¥6690; ⓦ www.nouhibus.co.jp). Direct buses from Takaoka (6 daily, 2hr 10min; ¥1800; ⓦ kaetsunou.co.jp), which is a stop on the JR Hokuriku line, stop en route at Suganuma

(¥800) and Ainokura (¥1300).

By car Touring the region by car is recommended; car rental is available in Takayama (see p.380).

Tourist information The main tourist information office (daily 9am–5pm; ☎ 057 696 1013, ⓦ shirakawa-go.gr.jp) is in the car park beside the Gasshō-zukuri Folklore Park, where the buses stop. There's a second, smaller office in the village centre.

ACCOMMODATION

The only way to see Ogimachi without the crowds is to stay overnight. Several of the thatch-roofed houses hold hugely romantic minshuku.

Furusato ふるさと 588 Ogimachi ☎ 057 696 1033. Just south of Myōzen-ji, this thatched farmhouse has endearing decorative touches throughout its tatami rooms. Rates include two meals. **¥17,600**

Kōemon 幸ェ門 456 Ogimachi ☎ 057 696 1446. A short walk from the bus terminal, this 200-year-old thatched farmhouse is redolent of times gone by, and has a friendly English-speaking owner. The modern bathrooms are shared. Rates include two meals. **¥16,800**

★**Magōemon** 孫右ェ門 360 Ogimachi ☎ 057 696 1167. Spacious traditional accommodation, sharing bathrooms, in a particularly charming thatched house that dates back three centuries. The riverside garden is a delight, while good food is served in the large communal dining room. Rates include two meals. **¥20,520**

EATING

Chūbe 忠兵衛 3065 Ogimachi ☎ 057 696 1818, ⓦ chubee.info. You'll eat well in this picturesque spot, overlooking the river at Ogimachi's south end, whether you opt for a feast of mountain vegetable cuisine, *sansai ryōri*, or prefer beef or even bear meat. Dishes cost around ¥1400,

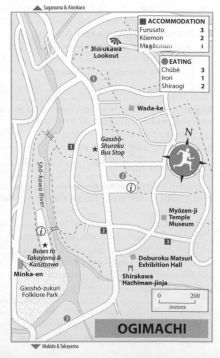

ACCOMMODATION	
Furusato	3
Kōemon	2
Magōemon	1

EATING	
Chūbe	3
Irori	1
Shiraogi	2

OGIMACHI

5

while set meals start at ¥2160. Daily 10.30am–3pm.

Irori いろり 374-1 Ogimachi ☎ 057 696 1737. You can eat around the raised hearth at this busy restaurant on the main road, at the north end of the village. Good-value set lunches, including fish, noodles or tofu, cost ¥1000, or you can simply drop in for coffee. Daily 10am–4pm.

Shiraogi しらおぎ 155 Ogimachi ☎ 057 696 1106, ⓦ j47.jp/shiraogi. In the village centre opposite the tourist office, this traditional building with lots of painted wooden signs outside has an English menu and offers a set menu of local delicacies (ask for the *shiraogi-setto*), including trout and miso bean paste, for ¥2100 a head. Daily 10am–4pm.

Suganuma

菅沼

Route 156, along the Shō-kawa valley, tunnels through the mountains, running for the most part alongside the frequently dammed river as it meanders north. Some 10km from Ogimachi, at a sharp bend in the river, the road passes the quaint hamlet of **SUGANUMA**, which holds nine *gasshō-zukuri*.

Gokayama Minzoku-kan

五箇山民俗館 • 436 Suganuma • Daily 9am–4.30pm • ¥300 • ☎ 076 367 3652

It's well worth dropping into the **Gokayama Minzoku-kan**, a folklore museum made up of two houses. One displays artefacts from daily life, the other details the production of gunpowder, manufactured here because Suganuma's remote location allowed the ruling Kaga clan to keep it secret.

Ainokura

相倉 • ⓦ g-ainokura.com

The last of the three World Heritage Site villages, and arguably the loveliest, is **AINOKURA**, 10km northeast of Suganama. Buses drop visitors on the main road, a five-minute walk from the village, which nestles on a hillside and takes roughly an hour to explore. Hike up the hill behind the main car park for a great view, and look in at the **Ainokura Minzoku-kan** (相倉民俗館; daily 8.30am–5pm; ¥200; ☎ 076 366 2732), a tiny museum of daily life that includes examples of the area's handmade paper and toys. Ainokura's charm can be all but obscured as you battle past yet another group of camera-toting day-trippers: to experience the village at its best, stay overnight.

ARRIVAL AND DEPARTURE

AINOKURA

By train If you're heading to Ainokura from the Sea of Japan coast, take a train as far as Jōhana (城端), which has direct connections to Takaoka (hourly, 53min; ¥580).

By bus Buses stop at Ainokura en route between Ogimachi (6 daily; 45min; ¥1300), Jōhana (23min; ¥600) and Takaoka (1hr 25min; ¥1000). There are four buses a day from Ogimachi to Ainokura.

ACCOMMODATION

Be sure to reserve **accommodation** well in advance – they don't like people just showing up. Seven *gasshō-zukuri* offer lodging, and it's advisable to take dinner in-house, as there are few other evening options.

Goyomon 五ヨヱ門 438 Ainokura ☎ 076 366 2154, ⓦ www.goyomon.burari.biz. A recommended *gasshō*, which has been run by the same family for several generations. The food is hearty and plentiful. 🛜 Room only, per person ¥5000, double with two meals ¥17,600

Nakaya なかや 231 Ainokura ☎ 076 366 2555, ⓦ bit .ly/nakayaainokura. The friendly owners speak a little English at this tranquil *gasshō*, which offers very tasty home-cooked traditional meals around the *irori* fireplace. Rates include two meals. 🛜 ¥17,600

EATING

Matsuya まつや 445 Ainokura ☎ 076 366 2631, ⓦ gokayama-matuya.com. Serving soba, tempura and sweets, this restaurant-cum-souvenir shop is a friendly place for lunch. They'll even look after your bags while you wander around. Dishes start at around ¥750, with set meals at ¥1650. 🛜 Daily 8am–5pm.

5

Murakami-ke

村上家 • 742 Kaminashi • Mon, Tues & Thurs–Sun: Jan–March 9am–4pm, April–Dec 8.30am–5pm • ¥300 • ☎ 076 366 2711, ⓦ murakamike.jp

The modern village of **KAMINASHI**, halfway between Ainokura and Suganuma, is home to the **Murakami-ke**, one of the oldest houses in the valley, dating from 1578. The owner gives guided tours around its tatami rooms, pointing out the sunken pit beside the entrance where gunpowder was once made, and finishing with spirited singing of folk tunes accompanied by a performance of the *bin-zasara*, a rattle made of wooden strips.

Toyama

富山

Northeast of the Gokayama valley, neither the coastal city of **Takaoka** nor the prefectural capital of **TOYAMA** (富山), further west, particularly warrants an overnight stop, and you might well do better to press on south along the coast to Kanazawa and the more scenic Noto Hantō peninsula (see p.397). That said, Toyama holds some worthwhile sights, and makes a good start or finish for excursions along the renowned Alpine Route (see box, p.388) to Nagano-ken.

Toyama Municipal Folkcraft Village

富山市民俗民芸村, Toyama Minzoku Mingei Mura • 1118-8, Anyobo • Daily 9am–5pm • ¥100 per building • ☎ 076 433 8270 • Free shuttle buses run from the Excel Tokyo hotel opposite the station

Gathered together at the foot of the Kureha hills, across the river 3km west of the station, the **Toyama Municipal Folkcraft Village** consists of nine separate museums and galleries that highlight local arts, crafts and industries. A short stroll up the hillside brings you to the atmospheric temple **Chōkei-ji** (長慶寺), where the Gohyaku Rakan terraces contain over five hundred miniature stone statues of the Buddha's disciples.

ARRIVAL AND DEPARTURE · TOYAMA

By plane Toyama Airport (☎ 076 495 3101, ⓦ toyama -airport.co.jp), used by international and domestic flights, stands 15km south of the city centre, to which it's connected by regular shuttle buses.
Destinations Dalian (2 weekly; 1hr 35min); Sapporo (1 daily; 1hr 30min); Shanghai (2 weekly; 2hr 35min); Seoul (4 weekly; 2hr); Taipei (4 weekly; 2hr 20min); Tokyo Haneda (4 daily; 1hr 5min).

By train Toyama Station, in the centre of the city, is now on the Shinkansen line between Kanazawa and Tokyo, and is also connected with Takayama and Nagoya to the south. The private Chihō line runs from the separate but adjoining

Dentetsu station to Tateyama, the western terminus of the Alpine Route.
Destinations Kanazawa (every 30min; 20min); Nagano (every 30min; 1hr 30min); Nagoya (3 daily; 4hr); Takayama (4 daily; 1hr 30min); Tateyama (hourly; 50min); Tokyo (hourly; 2hr 20min).

By bus Long-distance buses arrive at Toyama Station (ⓦ chitetsu.co.jp).
Destinations Kanazawa (18 daily; 1hr 15min); Kyoto (1 daily; 5hr); Nagoya (14 daily; 4hr); Niigata (2 daily; 3hr 50min); Osaka (4 daily; 6hr); Takayama via Shirakawa-gō (4 daily; 3hr 25min); Tokyo (Ikebukuro, 4 daily; 6hr 30min).

INFORMATION AND GETTING AROUND

Tourist information There's an information booth at Toyama Station (daily 8.30am–8pm; ☎ 076 432 9751, ⓦ visit-toyama.com). Free bike rental is available March–Nov.

Light rail An easy-to-use light rail system makes it simple to get around central Toyama.
Services The post office, main banks and shops are close to the station.

ACCOMMODATION

Toyama Manten 富山マンテンホテル 2-17 Honmachi ☎ 076 439 0100, ⓦ toyama.manten-hotel.com. This modern business hotel, on the light rail network 1km south

of the station, offers decent-sized rooms, and stands close to a lively nightlife area that's filled with restaurants. 🛜 **¥9360**

5

TATEYAMA–KUROBE ALPINE ROUTE

Perhaps the most dramatic and memorable way to travel from the Sea of Japan across the Alps to Nagano-ken – or vice versa – is to follow the spectacular **Tateyama–Kurobe Alpine Route** (立山黒部アルペンルート; ⓦ alpen-route.com). The 90km route, which traverses the roof of Japan in roughly six hours, via a quick-fire succession of buses, trains, funicular and cable-cars, only operates between mid-April and mid-November, depending on the snow.

Most visitors are day-trippers making round trips from one side or other; coming from the west, the most popular destination is **Murodō**, while from the east it's **Daikanbō**. You can pay for each segment as you come to it, but you can save money by buying either a return ticket to and from your chosen destination or a one-way ticket for the entire route, costing ¥10,850. Whichever you choose, start early, to allow time for some **hiking**.

Passengers on the Alpine Route can arrange to have their luggage transferred from Toyama Dentesu station or Tateyama to Shinano-Ōmachi station, or, if you're travelling the other way, from Shinano-Ōmachi to Toyama or Tateyama stations, or direct to any hotel in Toyama (¥1300–1800).

TATEYAMA TO MURODŌ

To reach the start of the route from Toyama, take the Chihō line to the village of **Tateyama** (立山) at the base of Mount Tateyama, one of the most sacred mountains in Japan. There you board the Tateyama Cable Railway for the seven-minute journey up to the small resort of **Bijo-daira** (美女平), meaning "beautiful lady plateau". One of the most memorable parts of the journey follows, taking the Tateyama Highland bus up the twisting alpine road, with a potential stop to hike along a boardwalk through the wetlands at **Midagahara** (弥陀ケ原), as far as **Murodō** (室堂). Early in the season, snow is piled far higher than the buses to either side of the road, giving the feel of a deep canyon. There's a decent canteen in the bus terminal at Murodō, and several places to stay nearby, while five minutes' walk north brings you to the **Mikuriga-ike** (みくりが池), an alpine lake set in a 15m-deep volcanic crater. Longer hikes in the vicinity include continuing to **Jigokudani** (地獄谷; Hell Valley), an area of boiling hot springs twenty minutes beyond the lake.

Tateyama Murodō Sansō 立山室堂山荘 14 Ashikuraji, Murodō ⓣ 076 463 1228. Not surprisingly, considering the altitude, the accommodation at this mountain hotel is rather basic, but it is comfortable and clean, and holds public baths, including one with a great panoramic view over the mountains. This is also a good place to head for lunch; the curry dishes are tasty. Rates include two meals. **¥19,800**

MURODŌ TO KUROBE-KO

From Murodō, the next section of the journey is a ten-minute bus ride along a tunnel that cuts right through Mount Tateyama to reach **Daikanbō** (大観峰). The view across the mountains from up here is spectacular, and you'll be able to admire it further as you take the Tateyama Ropeway cable-car down to **Kurobe-daira** (黒部平). From there in turn you're carried by the Kurobe Cable Railway down a subterranean terminus five minutes' walk from the edge of the Kurobe lake. This is the most likely section of the route to get congested in busy periods; between August and October especially, you may have to wait a while for a spot on the ropeway and/or cable railway. The lake was formed by the huge **Kurobe dam** (黒部ダム; ⓦ www.kurobe-dam.com), which was completed in 1963 and has an iconic status for Japanese visitors similar to that of the Hoover Dam in the US. Several tunnels and roadways now used by the Alpine Route were originally constructed to aid work on the dam. Boat trips venture out across the lake (30min; ¥1080), and there are excellent hiking trails. An easy thirty-minute walk south gets you to a campsite; bring the right gear and the Tateyama topographical map, and you can hike for days.

KUROBE-KO TO SHINANO-ŌMACHI

From the cable railway, you'll have to walk 800m to the far side of the dam to catch the trolley bus for a sixteen-minute journey through tunnels under Harinoki-dake to the end of the route proper, in the village of **Ōgizawa** (扇沢), across in Nagano-ken. Buses from here run direct to Nagano (5 daily; 1hr 45min; ¥2600; ⓦ alpico.co.jp), or down to the JR station at **Shinano-Ōmachi** (信濃大町; 40min; ¥1360), where you can catch trains to Matsumoto or Hakuba.

Tōyoko Inn Toyama Ekimae Takaramachi 東横INN 富山駅前宝町 5-1 Takaramachi ☎076 405 1045, ⓦtoyoko-inn.com. Dependable chain hotel in a busy neighbourhood 500m west of the station, targeted at business travellers but offering good-sized rooms; rates include a free Japanese breakfast. There's another Tōyoko Inn right outside the station, at 4-5 Sakuramachi. 🛜 **¥6630**

EATING

Minamoto Masu-no Sushi Museum 源ますのすしミュ ージアム 37-6 Nano-chō ☎076 429 7400, ⓦwww .minamoto.co.jp. In this 130-year-old restaurant and sushi factory, a 10min walk from Anjoji bus stop en route to Chitetsu from Toyama Station, the house speciality trout sushi comes wrapped in bamboo leaves. You can see traditional and modern sushi manufacturing processes and take part in workshops. Daily: museum 9am–5pm, dining room 11.30am–2pm.

★**Sharaku** 写楽 5-13 Otemachi ☎076 491 0700, ⓦsushi-toyama.jimdo.com. The friendly staff at this very traditional Japanese restaurant, beyond the castle park 1km south of the station, take huge pride in showing off the famed local seafood, including specialities like Japanese glass shrimp. Everything is detailed in English on their website, which they'll show you on an iPad. Sushi and sashimi set meals start at ¥1180, or you can order individual dishes from around ¥500. Mon–Fri 11.30am–1pm & 5–9pm, Sat 5–9pm.

Sushitama すし玉 5-8 Kakeosakaemachi ☎076 491 1897, ⓦsushitama.com. This high-quality *kaitenzushi* (conveyor-belt) sushi restaurant, a 15min bus or taxi ride south of the station, provides a wonderful opportunity to sample seafood from the bay; the handmade rolls are the best. Daily 11am–9pm.

Kanazawa

金沢

Back in the nineteenth century **KANAZAWA**, meaning "golden marsh", was Japan's fourth-largest city, built around a grand castle and the beautiful garden **Kenroku-en**. Only a city park now remains of the castle, but the garden is ranked among the most exquisite in the entire country, and, freshly connected to the **Shinkansen** network since 2015, Kanazawa is surging on a new wave of confidence. Abounding in attractive historic areas, and renowned for its arts and crafts, the capital of Ishikawa-ken is known to the Japanese as "little Kyoto", being the only city other than Kyoto where **geisha** still train. With its modern face ably represented by the impressive **21st Century Museum of Contemporary Art**, this is the one place on the Sea of Japan coast that you really shouldn't miss.

Kanazawa is a city that rewards a leisurely pace, so set aside at least a couple of days. Having escaped bombing during World War II, traditional inner-city areas, such as **Nagamachi**, with its samurai houses, and the charming geisha teahouse district of **Higashi Chaya**, remain intact and are a joy to wander around.

Brief history

Kanazawa had its heyday in the late fifteenth century, when a collective of farmers and Buddhist monks overthrew the ruling Togashi family, and the area, known as **Kaga** (a name that's still applied to the city's magnificent crafts, such as silk dyeing and lacquerware, and its refined cuisine), became Japan's only independent Buddhist state. Autonomy ended in 1583, when the *daimyō* Maeda Toshiie was installed as ruler by the warlord Oda Nobunaga, but Kanazawa continued to thrive as the richest province in Japan, churning out five million bushels of rice a year.

Kenroku-en

兼六園 • Kenroku-machi • Daily: March to mid-Oct 7am–6pm, mid-Oct to Feb 8am–5pm • ¥310, or ¥500 with Kanazawa-jō • ☎076 234 3800, ⓦbit.ly/kenroku-en

Originally the outer grounds of Kanazawa castle, and thus the private garden of the ruling Maeda clan, the magnificent **Kenroku-en** officially ranks in the top three gardens in Japan (the others are Kairaku-en in Mito and Kōrakuen in Okayama; see p.564). Laid out over

5

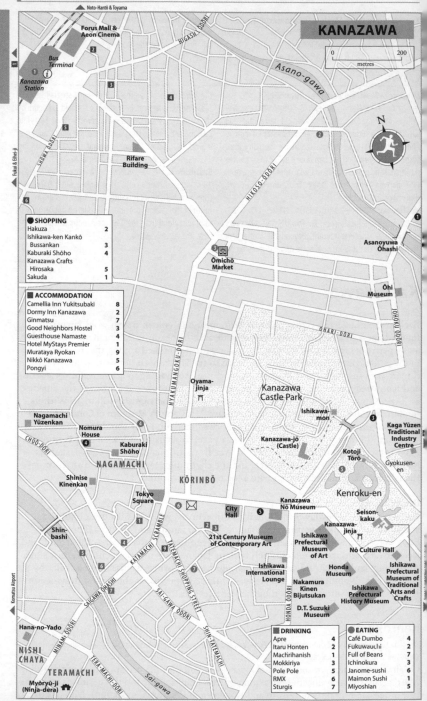

Noto-Hantō & Toyama

KANAZAWA

0 ——— 200
metres

N

Forus Mall &
Aeon Cinema

Bus
Terminal

Kanazawa
Station

Fukui & Eihei-ji

Rifare
Building

SUWA-DORI

HIGASHI-ODORI

Asano-gawa

HIKOSO-ODORI

Asanoyuwa
Ōhashi

Ōmichō
Market

Ōhi
Museum

JŌHOKU-DORI

● **SHOPPING**
Hakuza	2
Ishikawa-ken Kankō	
Bussankan	3
Kaburaki Shōho	4
Kanazawa Crafts	
Hirosaka	5
Sakuda	1

■ **ACCOMMODATION**
Camellia Inn Yukitsubaki	8
Dormy Inn Kanazawa	2
Ginmatsu	7
Good Neighbors Hostel	3
Guesthouse Namaste	4
Hotel MyStays Premier	1
Murataya Ryokan	9
Nikkō Kanazawa	5
Pongyi	6

HYAKUMANGOKU-DORI

Oyama-
jinja

ŌHARI-DORI

Kanazawa
Castle Park

Ishikawa-
mon

Kaga Yūzen
Traditional
Industry
Centre

Gyokusen-
en

Nagamachi
Yūzenkan

Nomura
House

CHŪŌ-DORI

Kaburaki
Shōho

NAGAMACHI

Shinise
Kinenkan

Shin-
bashi

Tokyo
Square

KATAMACHI SCRAMBLE

KŌRINBŌ

Kanazawa-jō
(Castle)

Kotoji
Tōrō

Kenroku-en

Kanazawa
Nō Museum

Seison-
kaku

City
Hall

21st Century Museum
of Contemporary Art

Ishikawa
International
Lounge

Ishikawa
Prefectural
Museum
of Art

Kanazawa-
jinja

Nō Culture Hall

Honda
Museum

Ishikawa
Prefectural
Museum of
Traditional
Arts and
Crafts

TATEMACHI SHOPPING STREET

Nakamura
Kinen
Bijutsukan

Ishikawa
Prefectural
History Museum

SAI-GAWA ODORI

D.T. Suzuki
Museum

HONDA-DORI

Komatsu Airport

Hana-no-Yado

**NISHI
CHAYA**

TERAMACHI

Myōryū-ji
(Ninja-dera)

SAIGAWA OMASHI

MINAMI-DORI

TERA-MACHI-DORI

SHIN-TATEMACHI

Sai-gawa

■ **DRINKING**
Apre	4
Itaru Honten	2
Machirihanish	1
Mokkiriya	3
Pole Pole	5
RMX	6
Sturgis	7

○ **EATING**
Café Dumbo	4
Fukuwauchi	2
Full of Beans	7
Ichinokura	3
Janome-sushi	6
Maimon Sushi	1
Miyoshian	5

two centuries from the 1670s onwards, it opened to the public in 1871. The name, "combined six garden", refers to the six horticultural graces it embraces: spaciousness, seclusion, artificiality, antiquity, water and panoramic views. It's a delightful place to stroll around, with an ingenious pumping system that keeps the hillside pools full of water and the fountains working. Carefully pruned and sculpted pine trees adorn the crafted landscape, and sweeping vistas gaze towards Kanazawa's geisha district, Higashi Chaya.

To experience Kenroku-en at its most tranquil, and spare yourself the likelihood of being disturbed by megaphone-toting guides and coach parties, come if you can in early morning or late afternoon.

Seison-kaku

成巽閣 • Mon, Tues & Thurs–Sun 9am–5pm • ¥700 • ☎ 076 221 0580, ⊛ seisonkaku.com

The *daimyō* Maeda Nariyasu built **Seison-kaku**, an elegant two-storey shingle-roofed villa at the southern end of Kenroku-en, in 1863, as a retirement home for his mother. Look out for paintings of fish, shellfish and turtles on the wainscots of the *shōji* sliding screens in the formal guest rooms downstairs. The view from the Tsukushi-no-rōka (Horsetail Corridor) across the mansion's own raked-gravel garden is particularly enchanting, while upstairs the decorative style is more adventurous, using striking colours and materials. Unusually for a traditional Japanese house, it has glass windows, imported from the Netherlands and installed so that the occupants could look out at falling snow in winter.

Ishikawa Prefectural Museum of Traditional Arts and Crafts

石川県立伝統産業工芸館, Ishikawa Kenritsu Dentō Sangyō Kōgeikan • 1-1 Kenroku-machi • April–Nov daily 9am–5pm, closed third Thurs of month; Dec–March Mon–Wed & Fri–Sun 9am–5pm • ¥260 • ☎ 076 262 2020

Directly accessible from Kenroku-en, the **Ishikawa Prefectural Museum of Traditional Arts and Crafts** is a showcase for contemporary expressions of the rich local craft heritage, including lacquerware, dyed silk, pottery, musical instruments and fireworks, for which Kanizawa is renowned. Although the exhibits in the upstairs galleries are not for sale, each has a price tag; a gold leaf and lacquer Buddhist family altar, for example, would set you back ¥4.5 million. The shop downstairs sells a limited array of less prized items.

Gyokusen-en

玉泉園 • 8-3 Kosho-machi • April–Nov daily 10.30am–4pm • ¥700, tea ¥1000 • ☎ 076 221 0181

Across the main road on Kenroku-en's northeastern flank, the much smaller sixteenth-century garden **Gyokusen-en** was laid out on two levels on a steep slope. Its many lovely features include mossy stone paths that lead past two ponds and a mini waterfall. A tearoom serves green tea and sweets.

Kaga Yūzen Traditional Industry Centre

加賀友禅伝統産業会館, Kaga Yūzen Dentō Sangyō Kaikan • 8-8 Kosho-machi • Mon, Tues & Thurs–Sun 9am–5pm • ¥300, silk dyeing ¥1575, kimono fittings ¥2000 (reservations required) • ☎ 076 224 5511, ⊛ kagayuzen.or.jp

At the **Kaga Yūzen Traditional Industry Centre**, next to Gyokusen-en, visitors can watch artists painting sumptuous designs on silk, following a 500-year-old dyeing method. You can then try your own hand at this traditional Kanazawa craft, or dress in a kimono made from the dyed material.

Kanazawa-jō

金沢城 • Marunouchi • Daily: March to mid-Oct 7am–6pm, mid-Oct to Feb 8am–5pm • Grounds free, castle buildings ¥310, or ¥500 with Kenroku-en • ☎ 076 234 3800, ⊛ bit.ly/kanazawa-jo

The craggy hill at the heart of Kanazawa was first fortified in 1546, while the mighty castle of **Kanazawa-jō** took shape early in the seventeenth century. That was almost entirely destroyed by successive fires, however, most conclusively in 1881, so the area is now occupied by a **castle park** rather than an actual castle. Other than scattered ruins,

5

the sole relic of the original castle is a towering eighteenth-century gateway, the **Ishikawa-mon**, which can be reached via a road-spanning footbridge from the northernmost exit of Kenroku-en.

Since 2001, several buildings in the castle's inner enclosure have been rebuilt using traditional methods and plans from the Edo period. These include the **Hashizume** bridge and gate that leads into the enclosure; the three-storey, diamond-shaped **Hishi Yagura** and **Hashizume-mon Tsuzuki Yagura** watchtowers; and the 98m-long **Gojikken Nagaya** corridor that connects them. The sheer scale of these structures is impressive, especially considering they represent such a small proportion of the original complex. Inside they only hold scanty displays, but you can admire the intricate joinery and inspect the scale model that carpenters used to master their complex task.

21st Century Museum of Contemporary Art

金沢21世紀美術館, Kanazawa Nijū-ichi Seiki Bijutsukan • 1-2-1 Hirōsaka • Public spaces daily 9am–10pm, exhibits Tues–Thurs & Sun 10am–6pm, Fri & Sat 10am–8pm • ¥360, plus varying fees for special exhibits • ☎ 076 220 2800, ⓦ kanazawa21.jp

An enormous geometry puzzle, the hyper-modern **21st Century Museum of Contemporary Art** consists of a circle of glass that embraces several galleries along with a café, a library and a free crèche, and makes a dynamic hub for Kanazawa's forward-thinking arts scene. Exhibitions frequently change, but specially commissioned works on permanent display includes James Turrell's *Blue Planet Sky*, a great opportunity to relax and watch the clouds float by, and Leandro Elrich's trompe-l'oeil *Swimming Pool*, which encourages fun interaction between viewers upstairs around the edge, and those walking beneath. The twelve tuba-shaped pipes that sprout out of the lawns surrounding the gallery are by the German artist Florian Claar; if you speak into one, sound comes out of another.

Kanazawa Nō Museum

金沢能楽美術館, Kanazawa Nōgaku Bijutsukan • 1-2-25 Hirōsaka • Tues–Sun 10am–6pm • ¥300 • ☎ 076 220 2790, ⓦ kanazawa-noh-museum.gr.jp

The **Kanazawa Nō Museum** shines light on Japan's most refined dramatic art. On the virtual stage on the ground floor, you can try on a nō costume and get your picture taken. Upstairs displays include breathtakingly ornate costumes and eerie masks, as well as videos of performances.

Ishikawa Prefectural Museum of Art

石川県立美術館, Ishikawa Kenritsu Bijutsukan • 2-1 Dewa-machi • Daily 9.30am–6pm • permanent collection ¥360, up to ¥1000 for special exhibitions • ☎ 076 231 7580, ⓦ ishibi.pref.ishikawa.jp

The **Ishikawa Prefectural Museum of Art** displays beautiful examples of calligraphy, kimono, pottery, lacquerware and other relics of the Maeda clan, largely dating back to the seventeenth century, along with a more eclectic collection of contemporary local art. Regular special exhibitions showcase local and national art.

D.T. Suzuki Museum

鈴木大拙館, Suzuki Daisetsu Kan • 3-4-20 Honda-machi • Tues–Sun 9.30am–5pm • ¥300 • ☎ 076 221 8011, ⓦ kanazawa-museum.jp/daisetz

Kanazawa native son Daisetz Teitarō Suzuki (1870–1966), the philosopher and writer largely responsible for introducing Zen Buddhism to the Western world, is commemorated in the impressive **D.T. Suzuki Museum**. The highlight of the stylish contemporary building is its inner courtyard "contemplation zone", a wonderfully serene spot for peaceful reflection, built around a shallow pool and blending minimal architecture, simple materials, plants and natural light.

Nagamachi

長町

Scenic **Nagamachi**, west of Kōrinbō, is a compact neighbourhood of twisting cobbled streets, gurgling streams and old houses, protected by thick mustard-coloured earthen walls, topped with ceramic tiles. Samurai and rich merchants formerly lived here, and many of the traditional buildings remain private homes.

Nomura House

野村家, Nomura-ke • 1-3-32 Nagamachi • Daily: April–Nov 8.30am–5.30pm, Oct–March 8.30am–4.30pm • ¥550 • ☎ 076 221 3553, ⓦ nomurake.com

A former samurai home, **Nomura House** is noteworthy for its compact but beautiful garden, featuring a carp-filled stream, waterfall and stone lanterns. The rich, but unflashy, materials used to decorate the house reveal the wealth of the former patrons, while, in keeping with the culture of the era, a simple teahouse serves *matcha*, accompanied of course by sweets.

Higashi Chaya

東茶屋 • 15min walk northeast from Kenroku-en

Kanazawa is the only Japanese town apart from Kyoto where the old-style training of **geisha** still takes place. In the largest and most scenic of the three neighbourhoods where this is carried out – **Higashi Chaya**, northeast of Kenroku-en across the Asano-gawa – several old **teahouses** are open to visitors. **Ochaya Shima** (お茶屋志摩; 1-13-21 Higashiyama; daily 9am–6pm; ¥500; ☎076 252 5675, ⓦochaya-shima.com) is the most traditional, while **Kaikarō** opposite (懐華樓; 1-14-8 Higashiyama; daily 9am–5pm; ¥700; ☎076 253 0591, ⓦkenrokuen.jp/en/kaikaro) is decorated in a more modern style, and features an unusual Zen rock garden made of broken glass plus a tearoom with gilded tatami mats. Both offer tea (without geisha) for a small extra fee.

Tea is also part of the deal at the venerable **Shamisen-no-Fukushima** (三味線の福島; 1-1-18 Higashiyama; Mon–Sat 10am–4pm, closed second & fourth Sat of the month; ¥300; ☎076 252 3703), a shop-cum-teahouse where you can learn to pluck the Japanese stringed instrument, the *shamisen*.

Nishi Chaya

西茶屋 • 5min walk southwest of Sai-gawa Ōhashi bridge

Across from downtown Kazanawa, on the south side of the Sai-gawa, the pretty **Nishi Chaya** geisha district is less commercialized than Higashi Chaya. Wandering the streets is a pleasure, while to see inside the beautifully decorated teahouse **Hana-no-Yado** (華の宿; 2-24-3 Ichinomachi; daily 9am–5pm) you need only buy a coffee (¥300) or *matcha* (¥500).

Myōryū-ji

妙立寺 • 2-12 Nomachi • Daily: March–Nov 9am–4.30pm, Dec–Feb 9am–4pm • Visit by guided tour only, ¥800 • ☎ 076 241 0888 • 5min walk east of Nishi Chaya

The highlight of the temple-packed **Teramachi** (寺町) district, south of the Sai-gawa, is **Myōryū-ji**, also known as Ninja-dera. Completed in 1643 and belonging to the Nichiren sect of Buddhism, this specific temple has long been spuriously associated with Ninja assassins (see box, p.353) on account of its many secret passages, trick doors and concealed chambers, including a lookout tower that commanded a sweeping view of the surrounding mountains and coast. While you can walk freely through the precincts, you have to book a tour to see inside.

5

ARRIVAL AND DEPARTURE

By plane Komatsu Airport (☎076 121 9803, ⓦkomatsuairport.jp), 30km southwest of Kanazawa, is connected to Kanazawa Station by buses that stop first in the Katamachi district downtown (hourly, 50min; ¥1130; ⓦwww.hokutetsu.co.jp).

Destinations Fukuoka (4 daily; 1hr 20min); Naha (daily; 2hr 25min); Okayama (2 daily; 55min); Sapporo (daily; 1hr 30min); Sendai (2 daily; 1hr); Seoul (3 weekly; 1hr 55min); Shanghai (4 weekly; 2hr 20min); Tokyo Haneda (11 daily; 1hr); Tokyo Narita (daily; 1hr 15min).

By train Shinkansen trains from Tokyo, via Nagano, have been gliding into Kanazawa's magnificently upgraded train station, on the western edge of town, since 2015. The Hokoriku route is expected to extend to Fukui and Tsuruga by 2022, and will ultimately continue all the way to Kyoto and/or Osaka. For the moment, if you're coming from the Kansai area, take the Thunderbird express from Osaka, via Kyoto; there's also a direct express service from Kyoto and Nagoya.

Destinations Fukui (every 30min; 45min); Kyoto (every 30min; 2hr 5min); Nagano (hourly; 1hr 5min); Nagoya (4 daily; 3hr); Osaka (every 30min; 2hr 40min); Tokyo (hourly; 2hr 30min); Toyama (every 30min; 20min).

By bus The long-distance bus terminal is on the east side of the train station.

Destinations Nagoya (10 daily; 3hr); Niigata (2 daily; 4hr 40min); Osaka (2 daily; 3hr 40min); Sendai (daily; 8hr 30min); Shirakawa-gō (2 daily; 2hr); Takayama (4 daily; 3hr); Tokyo (8 daily; 7hr 30min); Toyama (8 daily; 1hr 15min); Wajima (4 daily; 2hr).

INFORMATION

Tourist information Kanazawa's excellent tourist information office, in the JR station (daily 9am–7pm; ☎076 232 6200, ⓦkanazawa-tourism.com), has English-speaking staff (daily 10am–6pm) who can arrange for a guide to show you around town for free, and will deliver your luggage to any hotel in the prefecture for ¥600. The *Eye on Kanazawa* website (ⓦeyeon.jp), run by a free English-language tourist paper, is another great resource for visitors.

International exchange foundations The Rifare Building, at 1-5-3 Hon-machi, a 5min walk southeast of the station, is home to both the Kanazawa International Exchange Foundation (KIEF; 金沢国際交流財団; 2F; Mon–Fri 9am–5.45pm; ☎076 220 2522, ⓦkief.jp), and the Ishikawa Foundation for International Exchange (国際交流石川財団; 3F; Mon–Fri 9am–6pm, Sat 9am–5pm; ☎076 262 5931, ⓦifie.or.jp). Both are good places to meet locals who want to practise English, while the latter also runs the Ishikawa International Lounge near Kenroku-en (石川国際交流ラウンジ; 1-8-10 Hirosaka; Mon–Fri 10am–5pm, Sat 10am–4pm; ☎076 221 9901), which offers free cultural and Japanese-language courses.

GETTING AROUND

By bus Frequent buses from stops #7, #8 and #9 at the train station head to both Kōrinbō and Katamachi (¥200). The useful Kanazawa Loop Bus (daily 8.30am–6pm; ¥200, one-day pass ¥500) runs clockwise around the city from the station, covering all the main sights.

By car Toyota Rent-a-Car (☎076 223 0100, ⓦrent.toyota .co.jp) has an office at Kanazawa Station.

By bike *Machinori* bikes can be rented from twenty docking stations around the city, including the station; simply swipe your credit card to get started (¥200 per day; additional fee for individual rides longer than 30min; see ⓦeyeon.jp/s/machinori.html).

On foot It takes a little over 10min to walk to Kanazawa's downtown neighbourhoods, Kōrinbō and Katamachi, from the east exit of Kanazawa Station, or you can catch a bus. Once there, the best way to explore the city is on foot.

ACCOMMODATION

A host of business hotels are concentrated near the train station, while the central **Kōrinbō** district offers easier walking access to Kenroku-en and other sights, and the **Higashi Chaya** neighbourhood to the east is also a pleasant place to spend a night. Local ryokan are listed on ⓦyadotime.jp/english.

★**Camellia Inn Yukitsubaki** カメリアイン雪椿 4-17 Kosho-machi ☎076 223 5725, ⓦwww.camellia.jp. Laura Ashley meets traditional Japan at this charming guesthouse that offers seven spacious, en-suite Western-style rooms and a lounge set in a *kura*. Rates include breakfast; add ¥4000 for a dinner of French cuisine served Mon & Wed only, on Kutani pottery. 🛜 **¥18,000**

Dormy Inn Kanazawa ドーミーイン金沢 2-25 Horai-kawa Shin-machi ☎076 263 9888, ⓦdormy-inn-kanazawa.hotel-rn.com. Stylish business hotel, opposite the slick Forus shopping mall a few metres to the left of the station's eastern exit, and offering full and half tatami rooms plus an indoor/outdoor rooftop spa with separate male and female sections, and a free laundry room. A large buffet breakfast (¥1000) is laid out in the pleasant lounge area. 🛜 **¥8700**

Ginmatsu 銀松 1-17-18 Higashi Chaya ☎076 252 3577, ✉ginmatsu@nifty.com. Pleasant, good-value and very welcoming minshuku, tucked away in the lovely Higashi Chaya district, where geisha are a familiar sight. The neat tatami rooms share a communal bathroom with shower, and they also provide free tickets for the local *sentō* bathhouse. **¥7000**

Good Neighbors Hostel グッドネイバーズホステル 4-19 Konohana-machi ☎806 890 0882, ⓦgoodneighbors.co. Small, basic but very friendly hostel, a couple of minutes' walk from the station's main, eastern exit, with one mixed and one female-only dorm, plus a double and a couple of family rooms, all sharing bathrooms. Helpful English-speaking staff, and rental bikes ¥500 per day. ☎ Dorms **¥2800**, doubles **¥6000**

Guesthouse Namaste ゲストハウスナマステ 6-14 Kasaichi-machi ☎076 255 1057, ⓦguesthouse-namaste .com. Conveniently located in a calm side street a 5min walk from the station, this well-priced option offers impeccably clean tatami male and female dorms, two Western-style twin rooms, and a tatami family suite, plus a communal bathroom, kitchen and lounge. The relaxed English-speaking owner will give you good tips on where to go and rents bikes for ¥500 a day. ☎ Dorm **¥2700**, double **¥5800**, suite **¥12,000**

Hotel MyStays Premier ホテルマイステイズプレミア金沢 2-13-5 Hirooka ☎076 290 5255, ⓦmystays.com. The comfortable Western-style rooms in this good-value business hotel are much larger than the Japanese norm, and even have full-sized baths, while there's a good café on the ground floor, and room service until midnight. It's also only a 5min walk from the station, albeit in the "wrong" direction, on its less frenetic western side. ☎ **¥10,500**

Murataya Ryokan 村田屋旅館 1-5-2 Katamachi ☎076 263 0455, ⓦmurataya-ryokan.com. Set in an old building, this central ryokan has some stylish touches and is run by a welcoming family well used to foreign guests. Internet access, laundry and a handy map of local restaurants are available. Western breakfast ¥550, Japanese ¥850. ☎ **¥9400**

Nikkō Kanazawa 日航金沢 2-15-1 Honmachi ☎076 234 1111, ⓦhnkanazawa.jp. Good views are guaranteed from rooms in this thirty-storey luxury hotel facing Kanazawa Station, where the sophisticated modern European design has been upgraded to a high standard. Rates include breakfast. ☎ **¥18,300**

★**Pongyi** ポンギー 2-22 Rokumai-machi ☎076 225 7369, ⓦpongyi.com. Convivial budget guesthouse, beside a gurgling stream a 5min walk south of the station, behind the old sake shop Ichimura Magotaro. The cosy dorms are in a converted *kura* warehouse, and a small but spruce tatami room sleeps up to four people. The hospitable English-speaking owner donates ¥100 of each night's accommodation charge to a charity that helps poor children in Asia. ☎ Dorms **¥3000**, doubles **¥9000**

EATING

Kanazawa's refined local cuisine, *kaga ryōri*, centres on **seafood** such as steamed bream, snow crab and prawns. Another local favourite is *jibuni*, boiled duck or chicken and vegetables in a viscous broth spiced up with a dab of *wasabi*. Sushi is also great – you'll find the freshest fish at the lively **Ōmichō Market**, where lots of stalls sell ready-to-eat raw and grilled snacks, small sushi bars and restaurants are scattered around the periphery, and several more formal restaurants upstairs stay open for dinner.

Café Dumbo カフェ ダンボ 2-11-6 Korinbo ☎076 255 6966. Bright, lively little coffee house run by a friendly young Japanese couple, which as well as good espresso drinks and cakes serves a simple lunch menu of omelettes and sandwiches, all costing under ¥1000. The upstairs room, with books and magazines, makes a great place to relax. Mon & Wed–Fri 8.30am–6pm, Sat & Sun 11.30am–6pm.

Fukuwauchi 福わ家 1-9-31 Hikoso-machi ☎076 264 8780. There's a warm welcome and equally warming udon, soba and *nabe* (stew) at this rustic complex of four restaurants in a 120-year-old building next to the Ko-bashi. Set lunch menus from ¥980, dinner from ¥2000. Mon, Tues, Thurs & Fri 11.30am–2.30pm & 5.30–8.30pm, Sat & Sun 11am–8.30pm.

Full of Beans フルオブビーンズ 41-1 Satomi-chō ☎076 222 3315, ⓦfullofbeans.jp. Cute café that's a real haven of peace, just metres from the busy Tatemachi shopping street. Settle into the upstairs dining room, which has the feel of a gallery, to enjoy the mixed Mediterranean/Japanese menu, with lunchtime pasta, risotto or curry sets starting at ¥950, and cheaper salad and vegetable dishes in the evening. ☎ Mon, Tues & Thurs–Sun 11.30am–11pm.

Ichinokura 市の蔵 88 Aokusa-machi ☎076 224 3371, ⓦichi-no-kura.jp. The pick of the half-dozen restaurants on the second floor above Ōmichō Market, this very lovely, formal Japanese place serves sashimi platters of ultra-fresh fish from ¥2000, but it's more fun to go à la carte and order specialities like steamed crab and meat dumplings for ¥734, or a duck-and-mushroom *kagajibuni* stew for ¥1026. Daily 11am–11pm.

Janome-sushi 蛇の目寿司 1-12 Katamachi ☎076 231 0093. Set in an attractive building that's reached across a gurgling stream, this venerable little sushi restaurant has reasonably priced set menus (5 pieces ¥2180, 8 pieces ¥3000) and also offers *kaga ryōri* dishes, and bowls of hot or cold udon noodles for under ¥1000. Sit at the counter to admire the chefs at work. Mon, Tues & Thurs–Sun 11am–2.30pm & 5–11.45pm.

Maimon Sushi 金沢まいもん寿司 Kanizawa Station ☎076 225 8988. For a quick high-quality meal at the station, you can't beat this tiny outlet of a successful local chain. Tucked in among the shops near the west exit, it only has a dozen seats, so you may have to wait outside before getting a chance to order a mixed sushi platter (lunch from

5

¥1280, dinner from ¥1800), or individual rolls from ¥150. Daily 11am–10pm.

Miyoshian 三芳庵 1-11 Kenroku-machi ☎076 221 0127, ⓦmiyoshian.net. Utterly irresistible century-old restaurant in Kenroku-en, alongside the waterfall just inside the garden's northern entrance, beyond the row of shops. Specializes in *kaga ryōri*; try the bentō boxed lunches (from ¥1620) or drop in for a cup of *matcha* tea and sweets (¥700). It only opens for dinner for groups of ten or more who reserve a week in advance. Mon–Wed & Fri–Sun 9am–2.30pm.

DRINKING, NIGHTLIFE AND ENTERTAINMENT

The epicentre of Kanazawa's **nightlife** is the buzzing **Katamachi Scramble**, the neon-lit drag that runs between the Sai-gawa to Kōrinbō, where the surrounding warren of streets is chock-full of **bars**. Check with the tourist office for upcoming **nō** plays (enthusiastically supported by Kanazawa's arty citizens), **classical music** performances, and free concerts by the city's **geisha**, who also perform at local festivals, especially during July and August.

Apre アプレズ 2-3-7 Katamachi ☎076 222 0002, ⓦaps-apre.com. Long-running *gaijin* bar, complete with pool table, up on the seventh floor of the Space Building, and run in conjunction with a Thai restaurant on the ninth. From July to Sept they also run a popular beach bar out at Uchinada, on the coast a few kilometres north. 🛜 Tues–Sun: bar 7pm–2am; restaurant 6–11pm.

Itaru Honten いたる本店 3-8 Kakinobatake ☎076 221 4194. Wildly popular with locals, Kanazawa's best *izakaya* is a great place to get acquainted with the excellent local sakes and enjoy some sashimi or grilled fish. Mon–Sat 5.30–11.30pm.

★**Machrihanish** マクリハニッシュ 2F Nishino Bldg, 2-4 Kigura-machi ☎076 233 0072. Haba-san used to work at the Royal St Andrew's Golf Club, and continues to communicate his passion for Scotch whisky and golf at this convivial bar stocking some 170 different single malts and blends; if spirits aren't your thing, you can always have a Guinness. Mon–Fri 6.30pm–2am, Sat 6.30pm–3am.

Mokkiriya もっきりや 3-6 Kakinokibatake ☎076 231 0096, ⓦspacelan.ne.jp/~mokkiriya. This snug little wood-panelled jazz bar is a local legend, serving a good range of well-priced coffee, drinks and snacks, and putting on live music on most nights (when there's a minimum spend). Advance booking is advisable for bigger acts. Daily noon–midnight.

Pole Pole ポレポレ 2-31-30 Katamachi ☎076 262 6510, ⓦpolepole-legian.com. Down by the river, and dedicated to the spirit of Bob Marley, Kanazawa's premier reggae bar is a laidback spot to while away an hour or two with friendly locals. Daily 7pm–5am.

RMX レミックス 2-30-2 Katamachi ☎076 262 0881. There's a friendly welcome at this relatively spacious gay bar, pronounced "remix". The cover charge is ¥1600 including one drink. Mon–Wed & Fri–Sun 8pm–2am.

Sturgis スタージス 4F Kirin Bldg, 1-7-15 Katamachi ☎076 262 9577. Like stumbling into a New Year's Eve party, circa 1975, this silver-streamer-festooned bar is the domain of rocker Nitta-san who, if things are quiet, takes to the stage to play a live set or two. There's a ¥1000 cover charge. Daily 8pm–6am.

SHOPPING

Kanazawa is a fantastic place to buy **souvenirs** and lovely objets d'art. Many shops sell the austerely rustic *Ōhi* and highly elaborate *Kutani* **pottery**; several good options line Hirozaka, the street leading up to Kenroku-en from Kōrinbō. For

---

TEMPLE OF ETERNAL PEACE

For a rewarding day-trip from Kanazawa, head south to the serene hillside temple of **Eihei-ji** (永平寺; daily 10am–5pm; ¥500; ☎077 663 3012, ⓦbit.ly/eiheiji). Consisting of more than seventy buildings that blend seamlessly into the cedar-covered hillside, the temple is one of the two headquarters of **Sōtō Zen Buddhism**. Established by the Zen master Dōgen Zenji in 1244, it's now home to two hundred shaven-headed monks.

Eihei-ji stands 15km east of Fukui (福井). Direct buses from JR Fukui Station, served by frequent trains from Kanazawa (45min; ¥1320), make it easy to reach the temple itself (¥760; 35min). As it's liable to be closed for special services, check before you set off, either with the temple, or with the tourist office in Fukui (daily 9am–6pm; ☎0776 21 6492, ⓦfuku-e.com). With an advance reservation, you can enjoy a vegetarian *shōjin-ryōri* meal as part of your visit.

Affiliates of Sōtō Zen Buddhist organizations can arrange to stay overnight here (¥8000) and participate in the monks' daily routine, including cleaning duties and pre-dawn prayers and meditation; serious devotees can join a four-day/three-night course (¥12,100). For details, see ⓦbit.ly/eiheijistay.

unusual modern design gifts, browse the shop in the 21st Century Museum of Contemporary Art (see p.392). Also check out the **Tatemachi shopping street** (タテマチストリート) for quirky design shops and individual independent retailers, while if you want to buy Japanese **snacks** to take home, look no further than the amazing shops in the station.

Hakuza 箔座 1-13-18 Higashiyama ✆ 076 251 8930, ⓦ hakuza.co.jp. Kanazawa produces 98 percent of Japan's gold leaf. Specialist shop in the heart of Higashi Chaya, selling all kinds of gold-leaf-decorated products, including chocolate cake. It's worth popping in just to take a look at their gilded *kura* (storehouse). Daily 9.30am–6pm.

Ishikawa-ken Kankō Bussankan 石川県観光物産館 2-20 Kenroku-machi ✆ 076 222 7788. Three-storey tourist shop with a good selection of everything from food products to *washi* paper and pottery. Craft classes take place in the second- and third-floor workshops. March–Nov daily 10am–6pm, Dec–Feb Mon, Tues & Thurs–Sun 10am–6pm.

Kaburaki Shōho 鏑木商舗 1-3-16 Nagamachi ✆ 076 221 6666, ⓦ kaburaki.jp. This *Kutani* pottery shop and restaurant-cum-bar in the heart of Nagamachi occupies an elegant old house surrounded by pleasant gardens. Their small museum displays some gorgeous pieces of pottery. Mon–Sat 9am–10pm, Sun 9am–6pm.

Kanazawa Crafts Hirosaka 金沢クラフト広坂 1-2-25 Hirosaka ✆ 076 265 3320, ⓦ crafts-hirosaka.jp. Gallery-like shop selling exquisite examples of Kanazawa's traditional crafts, as seen in the crafts museum (see p.391), and hosting special exhibitions upstairs. Tues–Sun 10am–6pm.

Sakuda さくだ 1-3-27 Higashiyama ✆ 076 251 6777, ⓦ goldleaf-sakuda.jp. A dazzling shop that specializes in gold-leaf products, from beautiful screens to gilded golf balls. You can watch gold leaf being made, and staff are happy to explain the process. Daily 9am–6pm.

DIRECTORY

Hospital Kanazawa Municipal Hospital, 3km south of Kenroku-en at 3-7-3 Heiwa-machi (✆ 076 245 2600).
Police The Police Help Line (✆ 076 225 0555) operates

Mon–Fri 9am–5pm.
Post office There are branches at Kōrinbō as well as the JR station.

Noto Hantō

能登半島

Jutting like a gnarled finger into the Sea of Japan, the **Noto Hantō** takes its name from an Ainu word, *nopo*, meaning "set apart". The peninsula's rural way of life, tied to agriculture and fishery, is certainly worlds away from fast-paced, urban Japan – there's little public transport, so it's best explored by car or bicycle. The rugged and windswept west coast holds the bulk of the Noto Hantō's low-key attractions, while the calmer, indented east coast harbours several sleepy fishing villages, with only the lapping of waves and the phut-phut of boat engines to break the silence.

Cosmo Isle Hakui

コスモアイル羽咋 • 25 Menda, Hakui • Mon & Wed–Sun 8.30am–5pm • ¥400 • ✆ 076 722 9888, ⓦ www.hakui.ne.jp/ufo

If you're travelling up the **west coast** of the Noto Hantō peninsula, drive past the wide, sandy beach **Chiri-hama** (千里浜), cluttered with day-trippers and their litter, and head briefly inland to the town of **HAKUI** (羽咋), 40km north of Kanazawa and a hotspot for UFO sightings. In a suitably saucerish hall 1km east of Hakui Station, you'll find **Cosmo Isle Hakui**, a fascinating museum devoted to space exploration which houses a great deal of authentic paraphernalia. The most impressive exhibit is the Vostok craft that launched Yuri Gagarin into space in 1961 – it looks like a giant cannonball. Space-related movies are shown in a large-screen theatre, and there's a quirky gift shop.

Keta-taisha

気多大社 • 1-1 Zyke-chō, Hakui • Daily 8.30am–4.30pm • Free • ✆ 076 722 0602, ⓦ keta.jp

Keta-taisha, Noto's most important shrine, stands in a wooded grove near the sea 4km north of Hakui Station. It's said to have been founded in the eighth century, but the

WAJIMA LACQUERWARE

Wajima is renowned for high-quality lacquerware (known locally as *wajima nuri*), sold in many shops around town. Three of the best places to see high-quality products and get involved in workshops are:

Ishikawa Wajima Urushi Art Museum (石川県輪島漆芸美術館; 11 Shijukari Mitomori-machi; daily 9am–5pm; ¥620; ☎076 822 9788, ⓦbit.ly/wajimamuseum). High-class lacquerware museum, 2km southwest of the centre, with a superb collection.

Nuritaro (塗太郎; 95-banchi (Asaichi-dōri); daily 8am–5pm; ☎076 822 6040, ⓦnuritaro.com). At this traditional workshop you can watch craftsmen and join lacquerware classes (from ¥1000).

Wajima Kōbō Nagaya (輪島工房長屋; 4-66-1 Kawai-machi; Mon, Tues & Thurs–Sun, May–Aug 9am–6pm, Sept–April 9am–5pm; free; ☎076 823 0011, ⓦbit.ly/wajimakobo). Complex of traditional-style wooden buildings near the sea, in the heart of town, displaying modern styles of lacquerware. Watch artists at work or, if you make an advance booking, engrave lacquerware yourself.

attractive complex seen today dates from the 1650s. Sadly, its charms are somewhat spoiled by commercialization, catering to young lovers who come to seek the blessing of the spirits.

Myōjō-ji

妙成寺 • 1 Takidani-machi • Daily: April–Oct 8am–5pm, Nov–March 8am–4.30pm • Temple free, pagoda ¥500 • ☎076 727 1226 • Catch bus headed for Togi from Hakui Station

A few kilometres further up the coast from Keta-taisha, **Myōjō-ji** is a seventeenth-century temple with an impressive five-storey pagoda. The surrounding area is pretty striking, too – millennia of poundings from the Sea of Japan have created fascinating rock formations and cliffs along this coastline.

Wajima

輪島

Straddling the mouth of the Kawarada-gawa, halfway up Noto's west coast, the appealing fishing port of **WAJIMA** is the peninsula's main tourist centre. Every morning, in the colourful if touristy **Asa Ichi** market (daily 8am–noon, closed second & fourth Wed of the month; ☎076 822 7653), around two hundred vendors set up stalls along the main street selling fish, vegetables and other local products. This is a good place to pick up lacquerware at reasonable prices, but to be sure of the best quality buy from the shops (see box above) rather than the stalls on the street.

Gō Nagai Wonderland Museum

永井豪記念館 • 123-banchi (Asaichi-dōri-zoi) • Daily 8.30am–5pm • ¥510 • ☎076 823 0715, ⓦwww.go-wonderland.jp

Anime and manga fans will enjoy the **Gō Nagai Wonderland Museum**, which celebrates the eponymous, locally born creator of series such as *Mazinger Z*, *Devilman* and *Cutie Honey*. In one section you can draw your own manga character on a computer and get a printout as a souvenir. No displays have English translations, however.

Kiriko-kaikan

キリコ会館 • 22-2 Tsukada-machi • Daily 8am–5pm • ¥620 • ☎076 822 7100, ⓦbit.ly/kiriko-kaikan

The **Kiriko-kaikan** exhibition hall, by the coast on the east side of Wajima, houses the enormous colourful paper lanterns that are paraded during the town's lively summer and autumn festivals. Videos of the highlights are shown.

Sosogi and around

曽々木

The scenic coastline northeast of Wajima towards the cape **Rokkō-zaki** (禄剛崎) is peppered with bizarre rock formations such as **Godzilla Rock** (ゴジラ岩). The **Shiroyone no Senmaida** rice paddies, near the village of **Sosogi**, make a stunning spectacle, while just south of the cape, a winding road leads down to the "secret onsen" inn of *Lamp-no-Yado* (see p.400).

Shiroyone no Senmaida

白米の千枚田 • Shiroyone-machi • LED light display mid-Oct to mid-March daily 6–8pm • ☎ 076 823 1146, ⓦ bit.ly/shiroyone • 20min by bus from Wajima

The dramatic coastal landscape at **Shiroyone no Senmaida**, 10km northeast of Wajima, is shaped by over two thousand rice paddies clinging in small, stepped terraces to the mountainside as it plunges towards the sea. The fields have to be tended by hand as the land is too steep to allow access by machine. Each night in winter, when no rice is grown, they host the world's largest display of solar-panelled LEDs – 21,000 lights line the paddies, making the hillside sparkle with colour.

The Tokikuni houses

Kami Tokikuni-ke 上時國家 • 13-4 Machinomachi • Daily: April–Nov 8.30am–6pm, Dec–March 8.30am–5pm • ¥500 • ☎ 076 832 0171 • **Shimo Tokikuni-ke** 下時國家 • 2-1 Machinomachi • Daily: April–Nov 8.30am–5pm, Dec–March 8.30am–4pm • ¥600 • ☎ 076 832 0075

A short way inland from the coast 10km northeast of Shiroyone no Senmaida, a total of 20km out of Wajima, two traditional thatch-roofed houses are open to visitors. The wealthy Tokikuni family, supposed descendants of the vanquished Taira clan (see box, p.603), were exiled here in the twelfth century. Their original homes have long vanished; the **Kami Tokikuni-ke**, towering 18m tall, was built in the nineteenth century, while the smaller **Shimo Tokikuni-ke**, a short walk away and boasting an attractive garden, dates from the sixteenth century.

ARRIVAL AND INFORMATION   NOTO HANTŌ

By plane Noto Airport (☎ 076 826 2000), 6km south of Wajima, is served by two flights daily from Tokyo's Haneda Airport.

By train Regular trains connect Kanazawa with Hakui (every 30min; 35min; ¥820), and terminate at the uninteresting east-coast resort town of Wakura Onsen

(和倉温泉).

By bus Buses cruise up the peninsula's central highway from Kanazawa to Wajima (4 daily; 2hr; ¥2400).

Tourist information Wajima Bus Station holds an information office (daily 8am–7pm; ☎ 076 822 1503, ⓦ wajimaonsen.com).

GETTING AROUND

By bus Infrequent local buses connect most places of interest.

By bike Rental bicycles are available from the information office in Wajima Bus Station (¥800/8hr).

ACCOMMODATION

Wajima holds the widest choice of places to stay on the peninsula. As eating options are limited in many parts of Noto, it's best to book accommodation with meals included.

Flatt's by the Sea 海のそばの元ふらっと 27-26-3 Otoritama Yanami, Hanami ☎ 076 862 1900, ⓦ flatt.jp. Cute seaside minshuku, restaurant and bakery, run by an Australian–Japanese couple, in Hanami (花見) at the northern tip of the Noto Hantō. The innovative restaurant, which prides itself on using local seafood and produce, is open to non-guests for lunch (¥4000) and dinner (¥6000), but closed Wed and Thurs. Rates include two meals. **¥28,000**

Fukasan ふかさん 4-4 Kawai-machi, Wajima ☎ 076 822 9933. There's a friendly welcome at this restored minshuku, which enjoys views over the Wajima coast. The four tatami-style rooms are simply furnished and share a large onsen bathtub. Rates include two meals, with plenty of delicious local seafood. **¥14,000**

Kagaya 加賀屋 80 Yobu, Wakura-machi, Wakura ☎ 076 762 1111, ⓦ kagaya.co.jp. An army of kimono-clad staff

5

greets guests outside this large hotel, regularly voted Japan's number one onsen resort, which combines Japanese elegance with Vegas-esque opulence. A host of restaurants, bars, karaoke, cabaret shows and souvenir shops are designed to keep you – and your wallet – occupied. Different onsen are ranged over three floors, with spectacular views over the bay – all in all, it's an experience to remember. Rates include two meals. **¥60,870**

★**Lamp-no-Yado** ランプの宿 10-11 Misakimachijike, Suzu ☎ 076 886 8000, ⓦ lampnoyado.co.jp. One of the peninsula's most famous ryokan, this centuries-old wooden complex is set in a spectacular cliffside location in Suzu (珠洲). Several of the thirteen rooms have their own rotemburo. **¥36,000**

Noto Isaribi Youth Hostel 能登漁火ユースホステル 51-6 Ogi-yo, Ogi ☎ 076 874 0150, ⓦ bit.ly/notohostel. Facing Tsukumo-wan in the sleepy village of Ogi (小木), this hostel has good-quality tatami dorms and is run by a friendly man who rustles up local seafood feasts. Taking breakfast and dinner costs ¥1800 extra. Buses from Kanazawa will drop you at Ogi-kō, an 8min walk away. Dorms **¥3900**

Wajima Minshuku 輪島民宿 2-5-1 Futatsuyamachi, Wajima ☎ 076 822 4243. Small minshuku, beside the river a 10min walk west of Wajima Bus Station, with good-sized and well-priced tatami rooms. Tasty, rustic meals feature home-grown rice and vegetables. **¥9500**

EATING

Kodawari こだわり 4-66-1 Kawai-machi, Wajima ☎ 076 823 1078. Caught by the owner himself, the fish in this little lunch place, close to the market, is superbly fresh. A seafood bowl costs ¥1000. Daily 11am–2pm.

Shoya No Yakata 庄屋の館 10-1 Maura-chō, Sosogi ☎ 076 832 0372. The best spot to enjoy local seafood in Sosogi, with lunch costing well under ¥1000. Daily 11am–2pm & 5.30–8pm.

Nagoya

名古屋

Completely rebuilt in the wake of devastating wartime air raids, **NAGOYA** is a modern metropolis of high-rise buildings, wide boulevards, multilane highways and flyovers, where business takes precedence over tourism. The local skill of *monozukuri* (making things) is epitomized by industrial powerhouse Toyota, which has its headquarters here, along with numerous other companies.

Japan's fourth-largest city, the capital of Aichi-ken is less overwhelming than Tokyo or Osaka. It provides an easily accessible introduction to urban Japan and all its contemporary delights, with its **food scene** as a particular highlight. The Tokugawa family celebrated taking control of Japan back in 1610 by constructing Nagoya's original **castle**, now partially restored, and their possessions are now proudly displayed in the grand **Tokugawa Art Museum**. In the city centre, the cutting-edge **Nagoya City Science Museum** boasts the largest planetarium in the world and a host of immersive displays to entertain kids of all ages, while the **Toyota Commemorative Museum of Industry and Technology** makes an appropriate tribute to Nagoya's industrial heritage. Off to the south, right by the sea, the remarkable **SCMaglev and Railway Park** celebrates Japan's cutting-edge railway technology.

Nagoya's sights are quite spread out, but walking from the main hub of train stations to Sakae and around, even down to Ozu, is quite feasible. Excellent transport links, including an international airport, also make Nagoya an ideal base for tours of the region. Day-trip possibilities include the castle towns of **Inuyama** (see p.410) and **Gifu** (see p.412), in both of which you can view the ancient skill of *ukai* – fishing with cormorants. The Shima Hantō lies within easy reach, too (see p.537).

Nagoya-jō

名古屋城 • 1-1 Honmaru • Daily 9am–4.30pm; free English tour Mon, Wed, Sat & Sun 1pm • ¥500, or ¥640 including Tokugawa-en • ☎ 052 231 1700, ⓦ www.nagoyajo.city.nagoya.jp • Shiyakusho subway, Meijō line

Nagoya's medieval castle, **Nagoya-jō**, stands on the northern edge of downtown, 2.5km from the stations and still partially surrounded by broad water-filled moats.

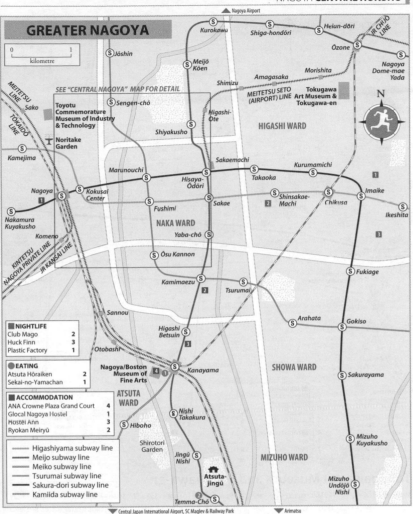

GREATER NAGOYA

0   1
kilometre

Nagoya Airport

Kurokawa
Jōshin
Shiga-hondōri
Heian-dōri
Ōzone
JR CHŪŌ LINE
Meijō Kōen
Morishita
Nagoya Dome-mae Yada
Amagasaka
Shimizu
MEITETSU SETO (AIRPORT) LINE
Tokugawa Art Museum & Tokugawa-en
SEE "CENTRAL NAGOYA" MAP FOR DETAIL
Sengen-chō
Higashi-Ōte
HIGASHI WARD
Toyotu Commemorature Museum of Industry & Technology
Shiyakusho
Noritake Garden
Sakaemachi
Kamejima
Marunouchi
Hisaya-Ōdōri
Takaoka
Kurumamichi
Nagoya
Kokusai Center
Imaike
Fushimi
Sakae
Shinsakae-Machi
Chikusa
Ikeshita
Nakamura Kuyakusho
NAKA WARD
Komeno
Yaba-chō
KINTETSU NAGOYA PRIVATE LINE
JR KANSAI LINE
Ōsu Kannon
Fukiage
Kamimaezu
Tsurumai
Sannou
Arahata
Gokiso
Higashi Betsuin
Otobashi
SHOWA WARD
NIGHTLIFE
Club Mago   2
Huck Finn   3
Plastic Factory   1
Nagoya/Boston Museum of Fine Arts
Kanayama
Sakurayama
EATING
Atsuta Hōraiken   2
Sekai-no-Yamachan 1
ATSUTA WARD
Nishi Takakura
ACCOMMODATION
ANA Crowne Plaza Grand Court 4
Glocal Nagoya Hostel   1
Hostel Ann   3
Ryokan Meiryū   2
Hiboho
Mizuho Kuyakusho
Shirotori Garden
Jingū Nishi
MIZUHO WARD
Mizuho Undōjō Nishi
----- Higashiyama subway line
----- Meijo subway line
----- Meiko subway line
----- Tsurumai subway line
----- Sakura-dori subway line
----- Kamiida subway line
Atsuta-jingū
Temma-Chō
Central Japan International Airport, SC Maglev & Railway Park
Arimatsu

Tokugawa Ieyasu, the founder of the Edo Shogunate, ordered the construction of this fortress in 1610, as the last of three mighty castles designed to demonstrate his new-found power.

The original structure was largely destroyed during World War II – only three turrets, three gates and some sequestered screen paintings survived – but a handsome concrete **replica** was completed in 1959. Steep stairs climb inside the central donjon, which holds interesting museum-like displays, including mock-ups of medieval streets and some fascinating archive photos, and is topped by huge gold-plated *shachi*, the mythical dolphins that are a symbol of Nagoya. The main attraction for visitors these days, though, is the gleaming **Honmaru Goten** (本丸御殿), the palace alongside, which has been meticulously reconstructed using traditional materials and techniques, and now displays sumptuous Edo-era painted screens including famous depictions of bamboo groves, leopards and tigers.

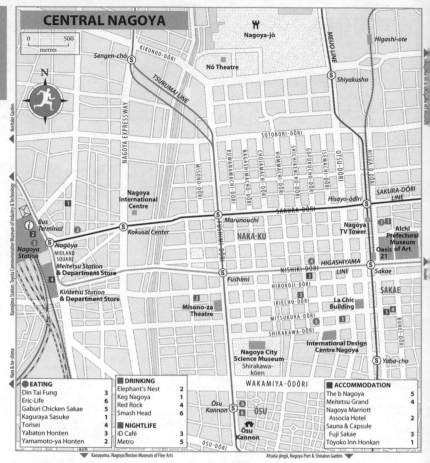

CENTRAL NAGOYA

EATING

Din Tai Fung	3
Eric-Life	6
Gaburi Chicken Sakae	5
Kaguraya Sasuke	1
Torisei	4
Yabaton Honten	3
Yamamoto-ya Honten	2

DRINKING

Elephant's Nest	2
Keg Nagoya	1
Red Rock	4
Smash Head	6

NIGHTLIFE

iD Café	3
Metro	5

ACCOMMODATION

The b Nagoya	5
Meitetsu Grand	4
Nagoya Marriott Associa Hotel	2
Sauna & Capsule Fuji Sakae	3
Tōyoko Inn Honkan	1

Tokugawa Art Museum and Tokugawa-en

Museum 徳川美術館 • 1017 Tokugawa-chō • Tues–Sun 10am–5pm • ¥1200, or ¥1350 with garden • **Tokugawa-en** 徳川園 • Daily
9.30am–5.30pm • ¥300 • ☎ 052 935 6262, ⓦ tokugawa-art-museum.jp • 15min walk north of Kurumamichi subway, Sakura-dōri line

In a hard-to-reach location northeast of downtown, the **Tokugawa Art Museum** is best
seen in conjunction with **Tokugawa-en**, the small but very lovely seventeenth-century
garden alongside. Focusing on heirlooms from the Owari branch of the Tokugawa
family who once ruled Nagoya, the museum offers a vivid sense of their rich and
cultured life. Displays include items inherited by the first Tokugawa shogun, Ieyasu,
reconstructions of the formal chambers of the *daimyō*'s residence, and a nō stage around
which magnificent traditional costumes are arranged. The single most treasured relic, a
twelfth-century painted scroll that's the earliest surviving version of *The Tale of Genji* (see
p.867), is so fragile that it's only displayed for a month each year, from November 10.

Nagoya City Science Museum

名古屋市科学館, Nagoya-shi Ragaku-Kan • 2-17-1 Sakae • Tues–Sun 9.30am–5pm, closed third Fri of month • ¥400, or ¥800 including
planetarium • ☎ 052 201 4486, ⓦ www.ncsm.city.nagoya.jp • 10min walk from Fushimi or Ōsu Kannon subway stations, Tsurumai line

An architectural *tour de force* at the southern end of Sakae, consisting of two towers

5

squeezing a colossal spherical planetarium between them – at 35m in diameter, reputedly the largest in the world – **Nagoya City Science Museum** is primarily targeted at kids, but makes a fun and enlightening experience for all ages. Hands-on exhibits inside range over four floors, covering everything from dinosaurs to hydraulics to natural phenomena, with highlights including a tornado machine and a deep-freeze lab. The main drawback is the shortage of information in English; if you don't understand Japanese, it's not worth paying for the fifty-minute planetarium shows.

Midland Square

ミッドランドスクエア・**Main building** Daily 11am–8pm (restaurants 11am–11pm)・Free・**Sky Promenade** Daily 11am–10pm・¥750・☎ 052 527 8877, ⓦ midland-square.com

Nagoya's trio of train stations forms the centre of a futuristic cityscape, with a vast network of tunnels, filled with shops and restaurants, radiating away underground, and a mini-Manhattan of tower blocks on all sides, including department stores topped by further hotels and restaurants.

Immediately across the street, the skyscraper known as **Midland Square** is the headquarters of the **Toyota** corporation. It too holds assorted shops and restaurants, plus a multiplex cinema. A partially open walkway, the **Sky Promenade** (スカイ・プロメナード), descends from the building's 46th to 44th floors to give panoramic views of the city. Every evening, at half-hourly intervals between 7pm and 9.30pm, coloured mist is sprayed into the hallways to enhance the effect.

Noritake Garden

ノリタケの森 トヨタ, Toyota Sangyō Gijutsu Kinen-kan, Noritake no Mori・3-1-36 Noritake Shinmachi・Tues–Sun 10am–6pm・Free; craft centre ¥500 (plate painting ¥1600), joint entry with Toyota Commemorative Museum ¥800・☎ 052 561 7114, ⓦ www.noritake.co.jp/mori・10min walk north of Nagoya Station

The grounds around a former china factory, run until 1975 by the still-extant Noritake company, have been transformed into a very pleasant park, **Noritake Garden**. Attractions on this spacious green site, a ten-minute walk north of the station, include a gallery of modern pottery and showrooms where you can buy Noritake products, plus a good café and a restaurant. If you pay to enter the garden's **craft centre** you can watch pottery being created, try your hand at painting a plate, and admire historic tableware in the museum section upstairs.

Toyota Commemorative Museum of Industry and Technology

産業技術記念館・1-35 Noritake Shinmachi・Tues–Sun 9.30am–5pm・¥500, or ¥800 with Noritake Garden・☎ 052 551 6115, ⓦ www.tcmit.org・10min walk northwest of Noritake Garden, near Sakō rail station on the Meitetsu Nagoya line

Housed in one of the car manufacturer's old red-brick factories, the **Toyota Commemorative Museum of Industry and Technology** traces the history of the corporation from its earliest days as a textile producer. At first, the rows of early twentieth-century

---

THE TOYOTA WAY

No business is more closely associated with Nagoya than **Toyota**, whose 47-floor headquarters are based in the Midland Square Tower (see above) opposite Nagoya Station. The automobile company was started in 1937 by Kiichiro Toyoda as a spin-off from Toyoda Automatic Loom Works, founded by his father Sakichi, who invented an improved **wooden handloom** in 1890 and subsequently moved on to power looms. As well as taking in the Toyota Commemorative Museum of Industry and Technology, you may like to visit one of Toyota's factories to see its famous production processes in action. The one-hour tours around the Kaikan factory are free, but you have to make a reservation online at ⓦ bit.ly/toyotanagoya, three months in advance.

5

looms make an incredible racket; in contrast, a computer-controlled air-jet loom at the end of that section purrs like a kitten. You then move on to the automobile area, encountering car-making robots that resemble giant menacing aliens, and to Technoland, where children can play with various toys intended to illustrate industrial processes.

Nagoya TV Tower

名古屋テレビ塔, Nagoya Terebi-tō · 3-6-15 Nishiki · Viewing deck daily 10am–10pm · ¥1000 · ☎ 052 971 8546, ⓦ nagoya-tv-tower.co.jp · Sakae subway, Higashiyama line

Hisaya Ōdōri-kōen, a swathe of parkland that runs north to south through **Sakae** (栄), Nagoya's central shopping and entertainment playground, is punctuated in the middle by the 180m **Nagoya TV Tower**. This handsome silver-painted structure, Japan's first TV signal transmission tower, built in 1954, has been designated a National Tangible Cultural Property. In summer, the ground-floor café and beer garden are good for a drink or snack in the sun.

The UFO-shaped complex opposite is **Oasis 21** (ⓦ sakaepark.co.jp). Its oval-shaped roof, covered with a pool of water, provides a great view of the surrounding cityscape; downstairs, as well as a cluster of restaurants, you'll find one of Nagoya's principal bus stations.

Aichi Prefectural Museum of Art

愛知県美術館, Aichi-ken Bijutsukan · 1-13-2 Higashisakura, behind Oasis 21 · Tues–Thurs, Sat & Sun 10am–6pm, Fri 10am–8pm · ¥500 · ☎ 052 971 5511, ⓦ www.aac.pref.aichi.jp · Sakae subway, Higashiyama line

The permanent collection at the excellent **Aichi Prefectural Museum of Art**, housed in the **Aichi Arts Centre** along with a major concert hall and theatre, provides a brisk romp through the superstars of twentieth-century art. Artists represented include Picasso, Klimt, Matisse and Modigliani, as well as Japanese painters such as Kishida Ryūsei and Takahashi Yuichi. The large galleries also host good temporary exhibitions, while the museum has since 2010 been the focus of the Aichi Triennale international arts festival (ⓦ aichitriennale.jp).

Ōsu

大須

Five minutes' walk southwest of Nadya Park, beside the Ōsu Kannon stop on the Tsurumai subway line, **Ōsu Kannon** (大須観音) is a vermilion-painted temple bustling with a steady stream of petitioners. A lively antiques and flea market is held in the temple's precincts on the 18th and 28th of each month; at other times it's still worth heading here to explore the bargain-hunters' district of **Ōsu**, where old-style arcades are lined with shops selling discount electronic goods, cheap clothes and used kimono. The area is popular with Nagoya's youth, and funky clothing and gift shops hereabouts include the mega-retailer *Komehyo* (ⓦ komehyo.co.jp), selling everything from electronics to used clothing priced by weight. Ōsu is also a good hunting ground for small, hip bars and restaurants.

Nagoya/Boston Museum of Fine Arts

名古屋ボストン美術館, Nagoya Bosutan Bijutsukan · 1-1-1 Kanayama-chō · Tues–Fri 10am–7pm, Sat & Sun 10am–5pm · ¥1300, after 5pm ¥1100 · ☎ 052 684 0101, ⓦ nagoya-boston.or.jp · Alongside Kanayama Station, on JR Tōkaidō line and Meijō subway line

A modern tower block next to the busy **Kanayama** (金山) Station holds a sister branch of one of the USA's most prestigious galleries. The **Nagoya/Boston Museum of Fine Arts** stages several high-quality temporary exhibitions each year; it's surprisingly small, though, so check what's on before paying the hefty admission fee. The plaza in front of the building is a favourite spot for buskers and impromptu dance performances.

5

WORLD COSPLAY SUMMIT

Cosplay is when fans dress up as their favourite characters, largely but not exclusively from anime, manga, video games or Japanese rock (J-rock) bands. Derived from "costume play", the word was coined by Japanese journalist Nobuyuki Takahashi in 1984, to describe US fans dressing up for a masquerade (a combination of a skit show and fashion parade for people in *cosplay* costumes) at a science fiction convention in Los Angeles. These days, every anime convention, anywhere in the world, incorporates a substantial *cosplay* element. At the ultimate level, the annual **World Cosplay Summit** (ⓦ worldcosplaysummit.jp) is staged in Nagoya in late July and early August, with participants from around twenty countries. The main events are a parade in the Ōsu district and the championship show itself, held in the public areas of Oasis 21 (see p.404).

Atsuta-jingū

熱田神宮 • 1-1-1 Atsuta-jingū • museum daily 9am–4.30pm, closed last Wed & Thurs of the month • free; museum ¥500 • ☏ 052 671 4151, ⓦ atsutajingu.or.jp/en •Jingū-Nishi subway, Meijō line

The Shintō shrine of **Atsuta-jingū**, said to be almost two thousand years old, but repeatedly remodelled since the nineteenth century, is 5km south of central Nagoya, amid extensive wooded grounds that give the feel of visiting a city park. The prized possession in the principal shrine, at the northern end, is the *kusanagi-no-tsurugi*, or "grass-cutting sword" – one of the three sacred treasures that symbolize the Imperial throne, along with jewels in Tokyo's Imperial Palace and the mirror at Ise-jingū (see p.537).

The precinct incorporates dozens of other structures, and at weekends especially tends to be thronged with proud parents and grandparents bringing month-old children for the traditional *miyamairi* blessing. Look out for a giant camphor tree, said to have been planted by the Buddhist saint Kōbō Daishi (see box, p.527) 1300 years ago.

A small **museum**, also known as the Treasure Hall, displays a changing selection of offerings donated to the shrine over the centuries, including robes, quivers of arrows, and many swords, among them a ferocious 2m-long blade in the entrance hall. As throughout Atsuta-jingū, nothing is translated into English.

SCMaglev and Railway Park

リニア, Rinia Tetsudō-kan • 鉄道館 • 3-2-2 Kinjofutu, Minato-ku • Mon & Wed–Sun 10am–5.30pm • ¥1000, plus ¥500 for Shinkansen Train driving simulator, ¥100 for Conventional Train driving simulator • ☏ 052 389 6100, ⓦ museum.jr-central.co.jp • 2min walk from Kinjofuto Station, on Aonomi line from Nagoya (20min; ¥350)

An enormous two-part hangar at the southernmost tip of Nagoya's docklands, 15km south of the city centre and overshadowed by an even more colossal bridge carrying the Isewangan Expressway, has been converted to hold the extraordinary **SCMaglev and Railway Park**. Pretty much irresistible for anyone exploring Japan by train – and absolute heaven, of course, for railway buffs – it traces the past, present and future of the Japanese rail network.

As well as climbing inside actual trains from all eras, you can admire a vast model railway that extends from Tokyo to Osaka, and learn all about the superconducting SCMaglev trains which it's currently hoped will connect those two cities by 2047, at speeds of up to 600kph. The biggest thrill, though, comes with the chance to enjoy a personal fifteen-minute **simulator** session, driving either a Shinkansen or conventional train. Admission tickets carry lottery tickets for both; drop them in the relevant boxes as soon as you enter, and pray that your number comes up.

Arimatsu

有松 • Direct trains from Meitetsu Nagoya Station (20min; ¥350)

Now a suburb 11km southeast of central Nagoya, **Arimatsu** dates back to 1608 and was once a town on the Tōkaidō highway. It's famous for its ongoing tradition of **shibori**, an intricate and time-consuming method of tie-dyeing cotton. Kimono made this way take up to six months to complete – hence the high prices they command. You can learn about tie-dyeing at the **Arimatsu-Narumi Shibori Kaikan** (有松鳴海絞会館; Mon, Tues & Thurs–Sun 9.30am–5pm; ¥300; ☏052 621 0111, ⓦshibori-kaikan.com), while shops selling examples line the picturesque street immediately south of Meitetsu Arimatsu Station, along with cafés and bakeries. Were it not for the utility poles and power lines, this could be a scene from a woodblock print: the old wooden houses with intricate tiled roofs provide the perfect backdrop to the parades of ornate floats that mark the spring and autumn **festivals** (third Sun in March & first Sun in Oct).

ARRIVAL AND DEPARTURE NAGOYA

BY PLANE

Centrair All international and some domestic flights arrive at Central Japan International Airport (☏056 938 1195, ⓦwww.centrair.jp). Also known as Chūbu Centrair, and commonly as simply Centrair, the airport stands on a man-made island in Isewan Bay, 45km south of Nagoya, and is a tourist attraction in its own right – locals visit just to sample its restaurants and bathe in its giant, runway-view onsen. Trains on the high-speed Meitetsu Airport line connect Centrair with Nagoya Station (28min; ¥1230), stopping previously at Kanayama (24min; ¥1170), while a taxi will cost around ¥16,000.

Destinations Akita (2 daily; 1hr 10min); Asahikawa (daily; 1hr 40min); Fukuoka (hourly; 1hr 15min); Hakodate (daily; 1hr 25min); Kagoshima (5 daily; 1hr 20min); Kumamoto (3 daily; 1hr 15min); Matsuyama (4 daily; 1hr 5min); Miyazaki (3 daily; 1hr 15imin); Nagasaki (2 daily; 1hr 20min); Niigata (2 daily; 55min); Okinawa (10 daily; 2hr 10min); Sapporo (15 daily; 1hr 35min); Sendai (6 daily; 1hr 5min); Tokyo Haneda (3 daily; 1hr); Tokyo Narita (4 daily; 1hr 10min).

Nagoya Airport (☏056 828 5633, ⓦwww.nagoya-airport -bldg.co.jp), 12km north of the city, this serves domestic destinations only, and is connected by bus with Midland Square, opposite the main train station (20min; ¥700).

Destinations Aomori (3 daily; 1hr 20min); Fukuoka (5 daily; 1hr 20min); Iwate-Hanamaki (3 daily; 1hr 20min); Izumo-Enmusube (2 daily; 1hr); Kita-kyūshū (2 daily; 1hr 15min); Kōchi (2 daily; 1hr); Kumamoto (3 daily; 1hr 20min); Niigata (1 daily; 1hr); Yamagata (2 daily; 1hr 5min).

BY TRAIN

Nagoya's main JR station, used by Shinkansen and regular JR

services, is the centrepiece of a giant complex on the west side of the city that also includes two other train stations, used by local lines, a subway station, and countless shops, restaurants and high-rise department stores. The Meitetsu line terminus, immediately south beneath the Meitetsu department store, serves Inuyama and Gifu, while the Kintetsu line terminus next door is used by services to Nara (see p.485) and the Shima Hantō region (see p.537).

Destinations Fukui (6 daily; 2hr 10min); Fukuoka (Hakata Station; every 30min; 3hr 25min); Gifu (very frequent; 20min); Hiroshima (every 30min; 2hr 20min); Inuyama (every 30min; 35min); Kanazawa (4 daily; 3hr); Kyoto (every 10min; 35min); Matsumoto (hourly; 2hr 10min); Nagano (hourly; 3hr); Okayama (every 30min; 1hr 40min); Osaka (every 10min; 1hr); Takayama (5 daily; 2hr 25min); Toba (8 daily; 2hr); Tokyo (every 10min; 1hr 40min); Toyama (5 daily; 3hr 45min).

BY BUS

Long-distance buses pull in at the terminal at the north end of the JR station as well as at the Oasis 21 terminal in Sakae.

Destinations Gujō Hachiman (2 daily; 2hr); Kanazawa (8 daily; 3hr); Kyoto (every 30min; 2hr 30min); Magome (daily; 2hr); Ogimachi (daily; 4hr); Osaka (14 daily; 3hr); Takayama (12 daily; 2hr 40min); Tokyo (hourly; 6hr).

BY FERRY

Ferries arrive at and depart from Nagoya-kō port, 10km south of the train stations (ⓦtaiheiyo-ferry.co.jp), and served by the Meitetsu bus (35min; ¥500).

Destinations Sendai (3–4 weekly; 21hr); Tomakomai (3–4 weekly; 38hr 45min).

INFORMATION

Tourist information Nagoya's very useful main tourist office is on the central concourse of the JR station (daily 9am–7pm; ☏052 541 4301, ⓦnagoya-info.jp); there's another office at Kanayama Station (daily 9am–7pm). The Nagoya International Centre, a 7min walk east of the JR

station (名古屋国際センター; 1-47-1 Nagono, Nakamura-ku; Tues–Sun 9am–7pm; ☏052 581 0100, ⓦnic-nagoya.or.jp), offers a library and the opportunity to meet English-speaking locals.

GETTING AROUND

By subway Nagoya's excellent subway is the easiest way to get around town. The four lines you're most likely to use

are Higashiyama (yellow on the subway map) and Sakura-dōri (red), both of which connect with the main train

5

stations, plus Meijō (purple) and Tsurumai (blue).

By bus The extensive local bus system includes the Me-guru route (メーグル; Tues–Sun, all-day ticket ¥500; ⓦncvb.or.jp /en/routebus), which loops around Nagoya's central sights.

Tickets Single journeys by subway or bus start at ¥200.

All-day tickets, valid on both the subway and buses, cost ¥850 on weekdays, or ¥600 at weekends, during national holidays and on the 8th of each month.

By car You can rent a car from Eki Rent-a-Car ⓣ052 581 0882 or Nissan Rent-a-Car ⓣ052 451 2300.

ACCOMMODATION

Nagoya has plenty of **accommodation**, with several options near the train stations. Thanks to the excellent public transport system, though, you can stay pretty much anywhere and get around quickly; choose **Sakae** or **Kanayama** if you're after lively nightlife. Be sure to book well in advance for weekends and public holidays.

ANA Crowne Plaza Grand Court クラウンプラザホテル 1-1-1 Kanayama-chō, Naka-ku ⓣ052 683 4111, ⓦanacrowneplaza-nagoya.jp; map p.401. This fine high-rise hotel, right by the subway station in groovy Kanayama, makes a handy base for southern Nagoya. There's a good array of restaurants, and even a choice of four different pillows for your bed. 🛜 **¥16,245**

The b Nagoya ビー 名古屋 4-15-23 Sakae, Naka-ku ⓣ052 241 1500, ⓦnagoya.theb-hotels.com; map p.402. Stylish enough to count as a boutique hotel as much as a business one, this modern block in the heart of the dynamic Sakae neighbourhood, a 3min walk from Sakae subway, offers comfortable contemporary rooms and free coffee in the lobby. 🛜 **¥10,200**

Glocal Nagoya Hostel グローカル名古屋ホステル 1-21-3 Noritake, Nakamura-ku ⓣ052 446 4694, ⓦfacebook.com/hostelnagoya; map p.401. Budget hostel, just over 5min walk west of the main station, with a welcoming ground-floor café and restaurant plus spacious dorms – one entire floor is women-only – and four-person private rooms. All the showers are on the same floor, so they can be a trek from your room. 🛜 Dorms **¥3200**, private rooms **¥12,500**

Hostel Ann 名古屋ゲストハウス Hostel Ann 2-4-2 Kanayama-chō, Naka-ku ⓣ052 253 7710, ⓦhostelann .com; map p.401. Relaxed hostel in a little old Japanese house a 10min walk northeast of Kanayama Station, with dorms and larger private rooms. They offer a kitchen, football table in the lounge, bike rental for ¥500 per day and no curfew. 🛜 Dorms **¥2900**, doubles **¥7000**

Meitetsu Grand 名鉄グランドホテル 1-2-4 Meieki, Nakamura-ku ⓣ052 582 2211, ⓦmeitetsu-gh.co.jp; map p.402. Long-established business hotel offering small

but perfectly adequate rooms in a great location in Nagoya's huge station complex. Turn right from the station's main east entrance, and it's on the upper floors of the Meitetsu shopping mall, reached by its own dedicated elevators. 🛜 **¥12,050**

Nagoya Marriott Associa Hotel 名古屋マリオットアソ シアホテル 1-1-4 Meieki, Nakamura-ku ⓣ052 584 1111, ⓦassocia.com/nma; map p.402. If money's no object, for convenience and luxury you can't beat staying here, high above the mammoth station and twin towers complex, in large comfortable rooms that enjoy a chintzy old European look and wonderful views. There's an excellent range of restaurants and a fitness club with a 20m pool. 🛜 **¥45,000**

Ryokan Meiryū 旅館名龍 2-4-21 Kamimaezu, Naka-ku ⓣ052 331 8686, ⓦwww.japan-net.ne.jp/~meiryu; map p.401. Friendly English-speaking owners run this simple ryokan, a couple of minutes' walk east of exit three at Kamimaezu subway station. The tatami rooms have a/c and TV, bathrooms are communal and a little café serves breakfast for ¥650 and dinner for ¥2300. 🛜 doubles **¥9000**

Sauna & Capsule Fuji Sakae サウナ＆カプセル フジ栄 3-22-31 Sakae, Naka-Ku ⓣ052 962 5711, ⓦfto.co.jp; map p.402. Nagoya's largest capsule hotel (men only) is a snazzy affair, with its own restaurant, comfortable lounge area, sauna and a huge communal bathing area. Non-guests can pay ¥1000 to use the sauna and bath for 1hr. Rates rise by ¥500 on Fri and Sat. 🛜 **¥3200**

Tōyōko Inn Honkan 東横 INN 本館 3-16-1 Meieki, Nakamura-ku ⓣ052 571 1045, ⓦtoyoko-inn.com; map p.402. The pick of the two branches of this reliable business chain hotel near the station, offering neat, good-value rooms 5min walk northeast. If you can't get in here, try the larger, older *Shinkan*, immediately west of the station. 🛜 **¥9500**

EATING

Nagoya's many **food specialities** include the flat, floury noodles *kishimen*, the succulent chicken dishes made from plump *Nagoya kochin* yardbirds, and assorted crab, pork and eel preparations. As for restaurants, the easiest area to look is in and around the **station**, but you'll get more of a night out if you head for bustling **Sakae**, which is packed with lively options, or, for a calmer and potentially more romantic alternative, **Ōsu**.

★**Atsuta Hōraiken** あつた蓬莱軒 503 Gōdo-chō, Atsuta-ku ⓣ052 671 8686, ⓦhouraiken.com; map p.401. This venerable mansion, a short walk from the

southern entrance of Atsuta-jingū, has been serving *hitsumabushi*, Nagoya's famous *unagi* (eel) dish, in its traditional tatami rooms ever since 1873. In summer, you'll probably have to queue before you tuck in; *hitsumabushi* set meals start at ¥3600, but you can also eat cheaper eel options à la carte. Mon, Tues & Thurs–Sun 11.30am–2pm & 4.30–8.30pm; closed second & fourth Thurs of month.

Din Tai Fung ディン タイ フォン 12F Takashimaya Dept Store, Nagoya Station ☎ 052 533 6030; map p.402. Hugely popular outlet of a prestigious Taiwanese dim sum chain, directly above the station on the twelfth floor of the Takashimaya department store. Most diners simply pick and choose from the long menu of *cha siu bao* buns and prawn or crab dumplings, but set meals start under ¥2000. Daily 11am–11pm.

Eric-Life エリック·ライフ 2-11-8 Ōsu, Naka-ku ☎ 052 222 1555; map p.402. There's a mid-century retro look to this hipsters' café behind Ōsu Kannon, where you can lounge on green velvet chairs enjoying *yoshoku* (Western-style) dishes such as *omu-raisu* (rice omelette) or ham bruschetta, or just nurse a cappuccino. Drinks from ¥400, main dishes from ¥800. Mon, Tues, Thurs, Fri & Sun noon–midnight, Sat 10am–midnight.

Gaburi Chicken Sakae がブリチキン 栄店 3-2-11 Sakae ☎ 052 262 8739; map p.402. Very lively little bar/restaurant on busy Mitsukura-dōri, in the heart of Sakae's nightlife zone, doling out platefuls of succulent fried chicken for under ¥1000, plus sweet-potato fries for ¥500 and cheap beers and whisky highballs. Daily 11.30am–11.30pm.

★ **Kaguraya Sasuke** 神楽家左助 1-10-6 Higashi Sakura, Higashi-ku ☎ 052 971 6203, ⓦ kaguraya-nagoya.com; map p.402. It feels incredible that this charming old building, overlooking lovely gardens, survives in the heart of modern Nagoya – even better is that they serve delicious, beautifully presented traditional food. Enjoy a set lunch from ¥3000 or dinner from ¥6000. Daily 11.30am–2pm & 5–10.30pm.

Sekai-no-Yamachan Kanayama Minami-ten 世界の山ちゃん金山南店 2-4-16 Kanayama-chō, Naka-ku; ☎ 052 684 2455, ⓦ www.yamachan.co.jp; map p.401. This fun *izakaya* serves addictively spicy chicken wings and other cheap, tasty dishes. Popularly known as *Yamachan*, it's a local phenomenon, with scores of branches across the city and more around Japan. Set meals start from ¥2400. Mon–Sat 5–11.30pm, Sun 5–10.30pm.

Torisei 鳥勢 3-19-24 Sakae, Naka-ku ☎ 052 951 7337, ⓦ torisei.jp; map p.402. You'll need to book ahead, especially at weekends, to enjoy the excellent *yakitori* and other chicken dishes at this restaurant, which has counter seating downstairs and tatami rooms upstairs. Lunch specials and *yakitori* meals are ¥900, dinner menus start at ¥3150. Mon–Sat 11.30am–1.30pm & 5–11pm.

Yabaton Honten 矢場とん 本店 9F Meitetsu Dept Store, Nagoya Station ☎ 052 241 5617, ⓦ english.yabaton.com; map p.402. High above the station, this quick-fire restaurant provides a convenient opportunity to sample *miso katsu*, breaded pork cutlets smothered in a sizzling miso sauce, which cost ¥1200 on their own, or ¥1600 as the centrepiece of a set meal. Check the website for this ever-expanding local chain's other outlets, or simply look out for their big fat pig signs. Mon–Fri 11am–3pm & 5–10pm, Sat & Sun 11am–10pm.

Yamamoto-ya Honten 山本屋本店 B1, Horiuchi Building, 3-25-9 Meieki ☎ 052 565 0278; map p.402. The chief outlet of this noodle café chain is on Sakura-dōri, a few minutes' walk from the JR station. The specialities are *miso nikomi* (thick udon noodles in a bean paste), locally reared *Nagoya kochin* (chicken) and Berkshire pork. Reckon on around ¥2000 per head. Daily 11am–10pm.

DRINKING

Drinking options are plentiful around Nagoya Station, south in Kanayama or in the eastern districts of Imaike and Ikeshita.

Elephant's Nest エレファントネスト 1-4-3 Sakae, Naka-ku ☎ 052 232 4360, ⓦ e-nest.jp; map p.402. For *gaijin* company, this British pub next to the *Hilton* is a good bet. There's free darts, English football on the telly, draught Guinness and staple British pub-grub dishes. During happy hour, 5.30–8pm, ¥100 is knocked off beers on weekdays, and any whisky costs ¥500 on Sun. Mon–Thurs & Sun 5.30pm–1am, Fri & Sat 5.30pm–2am.

Keg Nagoya ケグナゴヤ 1-10-13 Higashi Sakura, Higashi-ku ☎ 052 971 8211, ⓦ ameblo.jp/keg-nagoya; map p.402. Appealing real-ale bar that gives the chance to sample a great range of Japanese craft beers on tap. The food menu extends from curry rice to pizza. Mon–Fri 11.30am–1.30pm & 5–11pm, Sat 11am–1.30pm & 5–11pm, Sun 11am–1.30pm & 5–10pm.

Red Rock レッドロック 2F Aster Plaza Building, 4-14-6 Sakae, Naka-ku ☎ 052 262 7893, ⓦ theredrock.jp; map p.402. Spacious, centrally located bar with an Aussie theme, serving beers such as Coopers, VB and Cascade, as well as traditional pub grub like crocodile nuggets and kangaroo burgers (well, they're traditional in Australia). Mon–Thurs & Sun 5.30pm–1am, Fri & Sat 5.30pm–3am.

Smash Head スマッシュヘッド 2-21-90 Ōsu ☎ 052 201 2790, ⓦ smashhead.main.jp; map p.402. With "Zen and the Art of Motorcycle Maintenance" emblazoned above the entrance, this bar-cum-motorbike repair shop is one chilled spot, with exposed brick walls, retro furniture, and an extensive library of motorcycling, art and counterculture books. There's Guinness and Hoegaarden on tap and a good selection of spirits and bottled Belgian beers to choose from. Locals swear by the tasty handmade burgers, and daily lunch specials cost ¥950. Mon & Wed–Sun noon–midnight.

5

NIGHTLIFE

Sakae is the place to go for busy upbeat bars, clubs and karaoke boxes, while Ōsu offers quieter, hipper evenings out. Traditional **performing arts** are well supported, with a splendid nō theatre opposite the castle and the grand kabuki theatre, Misono-za, in the Fushimi area downtown. Nagoya also has an enthusiastically supported **live music** scene, and plenty of **cinemas**, including a modern multiplex in Midland Square. And you might like to try a game of **pachinko**, as Nagoya was where the noisy pinball pastime first took off, in the 1950s.

Club Mago マーゴ 2-1-9 Shin-Sakae, Naka-ku ☎052 243 1818, ⓦclub-mago.co.jp; map p.401. Big-name DJs front up at this high-energy mega-club, which has a welcoming vibe and hosts a recovery party every Sun from 5am. The same building contains the live venues *Diamond Hall* and *Apollo Base* (ⓦdiamond-apollo.sflag.co.jp). Opening hours vary; club nights generally 10pm–late.

Huck Finn ハックフィン 5-19-7 Imaike ☎052 733 8347, ⓦhuckfinn.co.jp; map p.401. Long-running punky club in the basement of the Ishii building, hosting regular live music nights of local and international bands. The entrance charge, typically ¥1500–2500, is cheaper if you buy in advance; drinks start around ¥500. Opening hours vary; typically Thurs–Sun 6pm–late.

iD Café iDカフェ 3-1-15 Sakae, Naka-ku ☎052 251 0382, ⓦidcafe.info; map p.402. Hip-hop, reggae and R&B can all be heard at this long-running bastion of the Nagoya club scene. The ¥2000 entrance fee includes four drinks. Daily 7pm–1am.

Metro メトロ Lover:z (club), 1-2-8 Shin-ei, Nakaku ☎090 4194 9722, ⓦthenagoyametroclub.com; map p.402. The fabulous Madame Matty hosts this long-running *gaijin*-friendly gay and lesbian club event, a guaranteed fun time for all, held monthly at *Lover:z club*, in the basement next to *Tōyōko Inn*. Entry is ¥2500 including two drinks. Second Sat of the month 10pm–6am.

Plastic Factory プラスチックファクトリー 32-13 Kanda-chō, Chikusa-ku ☎090 9894 9242, ⓦplasticfactory.jp; map p.401. Hosting an eclectic range of events in – guess what? – an old plastic factory, three blocks north of Imaike Station. Expect anything from progressive techno to live rock. Fri–Sun normally 8pm–2am.

DIRECTORY

Consulates Australia, 13F, Amnat Building, 1-3-3 Sakae, Naka-ku ☎052 211 0630; Canada, 6F, Nakatō Marunouchi Building, 3-17-6 Marunouchi ☎052 972 0450; UK, 15F, Nishiki Park Building, 2-4-3 Nishiki, Naka-ku ☎052 223 5031; USA, 6F, International Centre Building, 1-47-1 Nagono, Nakamura-ku ☎052 581 4501, ⓦnagoya.usconsulate.gov.

Emergencies The Prefectural Police Office is at 2-1-1 Sannomaru (☎052 951 1611). In an absolute emergency, contact the International Centre (☎052 581 0100). For other emergency numbers, see p.71.

Hospital The International Centre (☎052 581 0100) maintains a webpage of advice on local health and emergency facilities at ⓦbit.ly/nagoyahealth. The main hospital is the Nagoya Medical Centre, 4-1-1 Sannomaru, Naku-ku (☎052 951 1111).

Post office There are post offices in the main station, and a minute's walk north at 1-1-1 Meieki (Mon–Fri 9am–7pm, Sat 9am–5pm, Sun 9am–12.30pm).

Inuyama

犬山

The appealing castle town of **INUYAMA** lies beside the Kiso-gawa 25km north of Nagoya. Between May and October, the river is the stage for *ukai*, the centuries-old practice of fishing with cormorants (see box, p.412), to which the floodlit exterior of the privately owned castle, **Inuyama-jō**, provides a dramatic backdrop. The other major highlight in this picturesque area is the **Meiji Mura** architectural museum, which showcases buildings designed by Frank Lloyd Wright.

Inuyama-jō

犬山城 • 65-2 Kitakoken • Daily 9am–4.30pm • ¥500, joint ticket with Uraku-en ¥1200 • ☎056 861 1711, ⓦinuyamajohb.org

The riverside hill at the north end of Inuyama is crested by the only privately owned castle in Japan, **Inuyama-jō**. This toy-like fortress was built in 1537, making it the oldest in Japan (although parts have been extensively renovated), and it has belonged to the Naruse family since 1618. Inside, the donjon is ordinary, but there's a pretty view of the river and countryside from the top, where you can appreciate the castle's defensive strength.

Shirotomachi Museum

城とまちミュージアム · 8 Kitakoken · Daily 9am–5pm · ¥100 with Karakuri Museum, ¥600 with castle · ☎ 056 862 4802, ⓦ bit.ly/shirotomachi

The centrepiece of the attractive historic neighbourhood lining Inuyama's main street, immediately south of the castle and fifteen minutes' walk northwest of Inuyama Station, is the modern **Shirotomachi Museum**. Historical displays here include some fascinating maps and plans, and an impressive model of the town in its heyday. Across the street, the smaller **Karakuri Museum** celebrates the mechanical wooden puppets that adorn the towering, ornate floats (*yatai*) paraded around Inuyama during its major festival, on the first weekend of April. Operated from below rather than above, they're variously beautiful and grotesque, and can be seen in action on Fridays and Saturdays (10am–4pm).

Uraku-en

有楽苑 · 1 Gomonsaki · Daily: March to mid-July & Sept–Nov 9am–5pm, mid-July to Aug 9am–6pm, Dec–Feb 9am–4pm · ¥1000, combined garden & tea ¥1440, tea only ¥600; joint ticket with Inuyama-jō ¥1200 · ☎ 056 861 4608, ⓦ bit.ly/uraku-en

The grounds of the luxury *Meitetsu Inuyama Hotel* (名鉄犬山ホテル), a five-minute walk east of Inuyama-jō, hold the serene garden of **Uraku-en**. The mossy lawns and stone pathways act as a verdant frame for the subdued **Jo-an**, a traditional teahouse. Originally built in Kyoto during the sixteenth century, by Oda Uraku, the younger brother of the warlord Oda Nobunaga, the yellow-walled teahouse is so tiny that it has floor space for just over three tatami mats, and can only be viewed from the outside. Foaming green tea is served to visitors, in rather perfunctory style, in the larger modern Koan teahouse.

Meiji Mura

明治村 · 1 Uchiyama · March–July, Sept & Oct daily 9.30am–5pm; Aug daily 10am–5pm; Nov daily 9.30am–4pm; Dec–Feb Tues–Sun 4pm; check website for occasional closures · ¥1700, in-park trains & buses extra · ☎ 056 867 0314, ⓦ meijimura.com · Regular buses from Inuyama Station (20min; ¥410)

Ranging from churches and banks to a kabuki theatre, a lighthouse and a telephone exchange, the superb **Meiji Mura** open-air architectural museum consists of 67 structures spreading through a huge park 7km east of Inuyama. All date from the Meiji era, when Western influences were flooding into Japan and creating some unique hybrid architecture. The highlight is the facade of the original **Imperial Hotel**, designed by Frank Lloyd Wright.

Allow at least half a day to see Meiji Mura fully. An electric bus beetles from one end to the other, or you can travel part way on an old Kyoto tram and steam locomotive. There are several places to snack or eat lunch, including within the *Imperial Hotel* itself.

FRANK LLOYD WRIGHT IN JAPAN

Frank Lloyd Wright owes his fame in Japan largely to the fact that his grand **Imperial Hotel** in Tokyo survived the Great Kantō Earthquake, which hit the day after it opened in 1923. The US-born architect first visited Japan in 1905, and was so smitten that he pursued and eventually won the commission to build the hotel.

Wright lived in Tokyo between 1917 and 1923, working on the Imperial and thirteen other projects. Of the seven that were actually built, just five survive, in whole or in part: the front lobby of the *Imperial Hotel*, which now stands in **Meiji Mura**; the school **Jiyū Gakuen Myonichikan** (ⓦ jiyu.jp) and a portion of the **Aisaku Hayashi House**, both in Tokyo; JR Nikkō Station and Tazaemon Yamamura House (ⓦ www.yodoko.co.jp/geihinkan) in Ashiya, near Kōbe. For more information see ⓦ wrightinjapan.org.

5

By train Frequent trains on the Meitetsu railway take roughly 30min to reach Inuyama from either Nagoya to the south or Gifu to the west. The town has two stations; Inuyama-Yūen is a 10min walk east of the castle, Inuyama is a 20min walk southeast.

Tourist information Inuyama Station has an information booth (daily 9am–5pm; ☎ 056 861 6000, ⓦ ml.inuyama .gr.jp).

ACCOMMODATION AND EATING

Inuyama International Youth Hostel 犬山国際ユースホステル 162-1 Himuro, Tsugao ☎ 056 861 1111, ⓦ jyh.gr.jp/inuyama. Hotel-style modern hostel, 2km west of the castle, with both Western- and Japanese-style private rooms rather than dorms. It also has a good restaurant, serving breakfast for ¥750 and dinner from ¥1500. It's a 25min walk from the nearest station, Inuyama-

Yūen. ⓦ **¥6800**

Narita なり田 395 Higashikoken ☎ 056 865 2447, ⓦ f-narita.com. Set in a former kimono factory and mansion with lovely traditional gardens, a 5min walk north of Inuyama Station, this upmarket French restaurant offers a five-course set lunch for ¥3290. Mon & Wed–Fri 11am–2.30pm & 5–9pm, Sat & Sun 11am–2.30pm & 6–9pm.

Gifu

岐阜

The large city of **GIFU**, 35km northwest of Nagoya and 20km west of Inuyama, had to be entirely rebuilt after an earthquake in 1891 and blanket bombings during World War II. Like Inuyama, though, it's famed for offering traditional cormorant fishing – *ukai* – on a meandering river that's overlooked by a hilltop castle. *Ukai*-watching boat

---

WATCHING UKAI IN INUYAMA AND GIFU

Inuyama and Gifu are two of the main locations for **ukai**, or night-time fishing with **cormorants**, a skill developed back in the seventh century, and which draws appreciable crowds to watch the spectacle; other *ukai* spots include Kyoto, Iwakuni and Ōzu in Shikoku. The specially trained, slender-necked birds are used to catch *ayu*, a sweet freshwater fish, which is in season between May and September. Traditionally dressed fishermen handle up to twelve cormorants on long leashes, which are attached at the birds' throats with a ring to prevent them from swallowing the fish. The birds dive into the water, hunting the *ayu*, which are attracted to the light of the fire blazing in the metal braziers that hang from the bows of the narrow fishing boats.

The fast-moving show usually only lasts around thirty minutes, but an *ukai* jaunt is not just about fishing. Around two hours before fishing begins, the audience boards long, canopied boats, decorated with paper lanterns, which sail upriver and then moor to allow a pre-show picnic. Unless you pay extra you'll have to bring your own food and drink, but sometimes a boat will drift by selling beer, snacks and fireworks – another essential *ukai* component. Although you can watch the show for free from the riverbank, that way you won't experience the thrill of racing alongside the **fishing boats**, the birds splashing furiously in the reflected light of the pine wood burning in the brazier hanging from the boats' prows.

WATCHING UKAI IN INUYAMA

Boats sail from the dock beside the Inuyama-bashi bridge, five minutes' walk north of Inuyama Yūen Station. During the season, from June to mid-October, Kisogawa Ukai (☎ 056 861 2727, ⓦ kisogawa-ukai.jp) offer daily lunchtime trips (embark 11.30am, return 2pm; ¥4800 including obligatory lunch box), and much more exciting evening cruises, for which reservations are essential in summer (June–Aug 5.45–8.10pm, Sept to mid-Oct 5.15–7.40pm, ¥4800 with food or ¥2900 without, in which case you embark 1hr 45min later). There's no *ukai* on August 10 when Inuyama stages its riverside fireworks display.

WATCHING UKAI IN GIFU

Fishing takes place on the Nagara-gawa (長良川) between mid-May and mid-October (☎ 058 262 0104, ⓦ bit.ly/gifu-ukai; ¥3100–3400). Trips depart 6.15pm, 6.45pm or 7.15pm from the south side of the river bridge, which is just over 4km north of the town's JR and Meitetsu train stations.

trips start from the small but picturesque riverside neighbourhood of old wooden houses known as **Kawaramachi** (川原町), which also holds some good places to eat plus a handful of interesting galleries and craft shops.

Gifu is also renowned for its high-quality **paper crafts**, including umbrellas, lanterns, fans and the painted rice-paper fish you see flying off poles like flags.

Gifu-jō

岐阜城 • 18 Tenshukaku • **Castle** Daily: mid-March to mid-May 9.30am–5.30pm; mid-May to mid-Oct 8.30am–5.30pm; mid-Oct to mid-March 9.30am–4.30pm • ¥200 • **Ropeway** Daily: mid-March to mid-May 9am–6pm; mid-May to mid-Oct 8am–6pm; mid-Oct to mid-March 9am–5pm • ¥620 one-way, ¥1080 return • ☎ 058 265 3984, ⊛ bit.ly/gifu-jo

Seen from the city below, the castle of **Gifu-jō** is just a white speck, perched high above the densely forested, 329m Kinka-zan. Built originally in the thirteenth century, it fell into ruins after a major confrontation in the lead-up to the battle of Sekigahara in 1600, and was completely rebuilt in 1956. In itself it's nothing special, but it commands a panoramic view of Gifu. It takes around an hour to hike up there from the lovely city park, **Gifu-kōen** (岐阜公園), while a ropeway (cable-car) makes the climb in just three minutes.

Gifu City Museum of History

岐阜市歴史博物館, Gifu-shi Rekishi Hakubutsukan • 1-18-1 Omiya-chō • Tues–Sun 9am–5pm • ¥300 • ☎ 058 265 0010, ⊛ bit.ly/gifumuseum

Large dioramas in the excellent **Gifu City Museum of History**, in a concrete building in the Gifu-kōen, show how the city looked at the height of its military importance. Portuguese missionary Luís Fróis, who was here in 1569, compared Gifu to ancient Babylon. There's also a great re-creation of medieval streets, complete with soundtrack; in one "shop" visitors can try on kimono.

Shōhō-ji

正法寺 • 8 Daibutsu-chō • Daily 9am–5pm • ¥200 • ☎ 058 264 2760

The weatherworn **Shōhō-ji**, across the main road from Gifu-kōen, houses the Gifu Great Buddha (岐阜大仏), an imposing 13.7m-tall sculpture of Buddha that's one of the three biggest Buddhas in Japan. Made of lacquered bamboo and papier-mâché in the nineteenth century to remember the victims of earthquakes and epidemics, it took 38 years to complete.

Nagaragawa Ukai Museum

長良川うかいミュージアム • 51-2 Nagara • May to mid-Oct daily 9am–7pm; mid-Oct to April Mon & Wed–Sun 9am–5pm • ¥500 • ☎ 058 210 1555, ⊛ ukaimuseum.jp

Gifu celebrates its famous tradition of cormorant fishing in the high-tech **Nagaragawa Ukai Museum**, on the north bank of the river. For such a massive structure, though, it doesn't hold all that many exhibits, even if it does have a good café and beer garden. Apart from the entertaining introductory film, nothing is translated into English, so if it's at all possible you'd do better to see the real thing on a boat trip (see box opposite).

ARRIVAL AND INFORMATION   GIFU

By train Gifu's two train stations – JR and Meitetsu – stand 5min from one another at the south end of the city's commercial district, 4km south of the river. To reach Gifu-kōen or the Ukai Museum, catch any service except an express (快速) from stands 11 and 12 outside the JR station (¥210) or platform 4 at the Meitetsu station.

Destinations Inuyama (Meitetsu; hourly; 35min); Nagoya (JR or Meitetsu; very frequent; 20min–1hr).
Tourist information The tourist office is in the JR station (daily: March–Nov 9am–8pm, Dec–Feb 9am–6pm; ☎ 058 262 4415, ⊛ gifucvb.or.jp).

5

ACCOMMODATION

Jūhachirō 十八楼 10 Minato-machi ☎ 058 265 1551. This very pleasant large ryokan, overlooking the Nagara-gawa River, famously hosted the poet Bashō. The luxurious indoor and outdoor onsen have great panoramic views. Rates include two meals. **¥34,700**

Weekly Sho Gifu Daiichi Hotel ウィークリー翔岐卓第

一ホテル 2-5 Fukuzumi-chō ☎ 058 251 2111, ⓦ weekly -sho.jp. There's nothing remarkable about this basic business hotel, two blocks northwest of the JR station, but it is really good value. Most rooms are singles, but there are some twin rooms. Rates include breakfast. 📶 Singles **¥1900**, doubles **¥3800**

EATING AND DRINKING

Bunkaya 文化屋 35 Motohama-chō ☎ 058 212 0132. Facing the Nagara-gawa, this place is particularly alluring, with a traditional wooden interior, panoramic windows and innovative menu. Bookings are essential for its ¥2940 meal. Daily 11.30am–3pm & 5.30–10pm.

Kawaramachi Izumiya 泉屋 20 Motohama-chō ☎ 058 263 6788, ⓦ nagaragawa.com. Traditional restaurant by the river, serving the sweet river fish *ayu* in various styles, especially grilled with salt, on skewers. Main dishes around ¥1000. Mid-May to June & Sept to mid-Oct Mon, Tues & Thurs–Sun 11.30am–2pm & 5–8pm, July & Aug daily 11.30am–2pm & 5–8pm.

Kawaramachiya 川原町屋 28 Tamai-chō ☎ 058 266 5144, ⓦ kawaramachiya.com. This pleasant café/gallery, near the boat office and serving bowls of udon noodles for around ¥1000, is easily spotted by the old-fashioned red post box outside. 📶 Daily 9am–6.30pm.

Natural Café & Gallery ナチュラルカフェアンドギャラリー蔵 2-14 Hon-machi ☎ 058 269 5788, ⓦ natural -group.com. Bohemian café and gallery, in an old storehouse near the Hon-machi San-chōme bus stop, with meze-style sharing plates, a good selection of cocktails and wine, and live jazz some evenings. Mains cost around ¥800, sharing plates from ¥1200. 📶 Daily 11am–midnight, closed first & third Tues each month.

Gujō Hachiman

郡上八幡

It is a town of low, dark, wood-and-plaster buildings, paved lanes, and running water. The windows of the buildings are narrow and slatted. The lanes, too, are narrow, steeply walled, and end in dimly lanterned eating places or in small stone bridges that arch over splashing streams. It was like an Edo-era stage set.

Alan Booth, *Looking for the Lost*, 1995

Booth's romantic description captures **GUJŌ HACHIMAN**'s bygone-days atmosphere and mountain-bound location perfectly. It lies 55km north of Gifu, tucked in a valley on an old trade route that once led to the Sea of Japan. Two pristine rivers, the Yoshida and Nagara, add great appeal; the close link to water is honoured by the **Fountain of Youth** or Sōgi-sui (宗祇水), the town's natural spring.

The best time is in summer, when it hosts one of Japan's top three dance festivals, the **Gujō Odori**, and the sparkling rivers are tempting for swimmers. **Anglers** with long poles and tall straw hats can be seen along both rivers trying their luck for *ayu* (sweet fish) and trout.

Hakurankan

博覧館 • 50 Tonomachi • Daily 9am–5pm; during Gujō Odori 9am–6pm • ¥520, ¥650 with Gujō-Hachiman-jō • ☎ 057 565 3215, ⓦ gujohachiman.com

The high-quality **Hakurankan** museum, on the northern side of the Yoshida River, is a ten-minute stroll from the tourist office. Exhibits detail the town's history; arts and crafts; connection with water; folk dancing; and the Gujō Odori festival.

Gujō-Hachiman-jō

郡上八幡城 • Yanagimachi • Daily: March–May, Sept & Oct 9am–5pm; June–Aug 8am–6pm; Nov–Feb 9am–4.30pm • ¥310, ¥650 with Hakurankan • ☎ 057 567 1819, ⓦ gujohachiman.com/siro

A photogenic wooden reconstruction of the old castle, **Gujō-Hachiman-jō**, was erected

GUJŌ ODORI

While bon-odori festivals are common across Japan, nowhere is the dance so firmly rooted in the life of the community as at Gujō Hachiman, where the **Gujō Odori** has been celebrated since the 1590s. Nearly every night from mid-July to early September, between around 8pm and 10.30pm (the tourist information centre can tell you exactly when and where), locals don their *yukata* and *geta* and dance in the streets.

People dance in circles around a tall wood-and-bamboo structure, from which a singer, drummers, flute player and a chorus call the tune. The singer announces which of the ten kinds of **dance** is up next before each one commences. Watch the hand and feet movements of those in the inner circle, who will have learned these steps as children – and try to follow along.

During the **Obon holiday** in mid-August, dancing goes on all night, and thousands crowd into town. Don't worry if you can't find a bed, since there's always a place for revellers to rest during the festivities – check with the tourist office.

in 1934 on the stone foundations of the less elaborate original structure. From its ramparts you'll see that the town resembles a fish in shape, the elegant concrete span of the motorway accenting the tail.

ARRIVAL AND INFORMATION

GUJŌ HACHIMAN

By train From Gifu, take the JR line to Mino-Ōta then transfer to the private Nagaragawa line (2hr; ¥1850).
By bus Gujō Hachiman has direct bus connections with Nagoya (2hr) and Gifu (1hr 10min; ¥1580).

Tourist information The information office is in a handsome Western-style building, 1km north of the train station (daily 8.30am–5.15pm; ☎ 057 567 0002, ⓦ gujohachiman.com/kanko).

ACCOMMODATION

Gujō-Tōsen-ji Youth Hostel 郡上洞泉寺ユースホステル 417 Ozaki-machi ☎ 057 567 0290, ⓦ bit.ly /gujohostel. The best budget option, in the grounds of the Tōsen-ji temple along the river east of the station, with clean but basic rooms and amenities. Closed Wed. 🛜 Dorms **¥4000**

Nakashimaya 中嶋屋 940 Shinmachi ☎ 057 565 2191, ⓦ nakashimaya.net. Good traditional ryokan, on

the main shopping street where the all-night Obon dancing takes place. The rooms are meticulously maintained. Rates include breakfast. 🛜 **¥16,200**

Hotel Sekisuien ホテル積翠園 511-2 Hachiman ☎ 057 565 3101, ⓦ bit.ly/sekisuien. Halfway uphill to the castle, this modern hotel offers large, bright tatami rooms, excellent meals and a big public bath. Rates include two meals. 🛜 **¥24,600**

EATING

One curiosity about Gujō Hachiman is that around eighty percent of the plastic food samples displayed in restaurant windows in Japan are made here.

Hanamura 花むら Shinmachi ☎ 057 567 0056. Rustic, friendly place near the river, around the corner from *Nakashimaya*, where the set dinner of local dishes (*omikase*) is a great deal at ¥2500. Daily 11.30am–1.30pm & 5–10.30pm.

Soba-no-Hirajin そばの平甚 Honmachi ☎ 057 565 2004, ⓦ hirajin.com. Expect to wait for a table at this

popular noodle restaurant north of the river, close to the Fountain of Youth. A bowl of noodles costs around ¥700. Mon–Fri 11am–4pm, Sat & Sun 11am–5pm.

Uotora 魚寅 Shinmachi ☎ 057 565 3195, ⓦ uotora .co.jp. A great place to sample some tasty fish and *unagi* (eel) dishes, on the main shopping street; set meals cost around ¥2000. Mon & Wed–Sun 11am–2.30pm & 5–8pm.

Kyoto and Nara

KINKAKU-JI, KYOTO

Kyoto and Nara

The former imperial capitals of Kyoto and Nara are home to a sublime collection of temples, palaces, shrines and gardens. Both cities are deeply revered by the Japanese for their imperial history, their highly developed traditional arts and centuries-old festivals. Yet each has its own distinct personality. Kyoto is notoriously exclusive, whereas Nara has a relaxed dignity; as a result, the two cities complement each other well, with Nara displaying the foundations of traditional Japanese culture, which reached its zenith in Kyoto.

6

Until Emporer Meiji decamped for the bright lights of Tokyo in 1868, **Kyoto** was Japan's imperial capital, and despite modern trappings the city still represents a more traditional version of the country than the current capital. Kyoto maintains its reputation for cultural finesse – with its cuisine and traditional crafts – while fusing tradition with contemporary innovation. It's a delight to explore the exquisite **temples** and **gardens**, as well as designer shops and stylish cafés. It's also rewarding to spend at least a day in the surrounding districts; meander through rice fields in **Ohara** or tea fields in **Uji**, or view the city from atop **Hiei-zan**, where the temples of Enryaku-ji are nestled in a cedar forest.

Before Kyoto even existed, the monks of **Nara** were busily erecting their great Buddhist monuments under the patronage of an earlier group of princes and nobles. In 2010, this relaxed, appealing town celebrated the 1300th anniversary of **Heijō-kyō**, the site close to the centre of modern-day Nara city, where Japan's first permanent capital was founded in the early eighth century. A surprising number of buildings survive – notably the great **Tōdai-ji** with its colossal bronze Buddha – but Nara's real glory lies in its wealth of statues. Nowhere is this more evident than at the nearby temple complex of **Hōryū-ji**, a treasure-trove of early Japanese art. Kyoto and Nara house the bulk of Japan's sixteen Unesco World Heritage Sites – a truly impressive collection that makes a visit to both cities unmissable.

NISHIKI-KŌJI STREET MARKET

Highlights

❶ Kyoto International Manga Museum
Kyoto gets into "Cool Japan" with the first museum in the world devoted to Japanese comics. **See p.428**

❷ Nishiki-kōji street market Experience the city's food culture by touring "Kyoto's kitchen" – as Nishiki market is known. **See p.429**

❸ Kyoto's machiya Stay, shop or dine in one of Kyoto's narrow traditional wooden townhouses with inner gardens. **See p.439**

❹ Kinkaku-ji Kyoto's most elaborate Zen temple, the Golden Pavilion, was built as a

retirement home for a fourteenth-century shogun and is a beautiful sight in any season. **See p.444**

❺ Green tea Visit the tea fields of Uji and harvest your own green tea. Later enjoy the sophisticated *matcha* salons of Kyoto and a traditional tea ceremony. **See p.460**

❻ Ancient Nara In the historic capital city of Nara, see the monumental bronze Buddha at Tōdai-ji and wander the inner precincts of Kasuga Taisha, at the edge of a primeval forest. **See p.487**

❼ Asuka village Cycle around the picturesque village and explore ancient archeological sites where Japanese civilization began. **See p.499**

HIGHLIGHTS ARE MARKED ON THE MAP ON P.420

Kyoto

京都

The capital of Japan for more than a thousand years, **KYOTO** is endowed with an almost overwhelming legacy of ancient Buddhist temples, majestic palaces and gardens of every size and description, not to mention some of the country's most important works of art, its richest culture and most refined cuisine. For many people

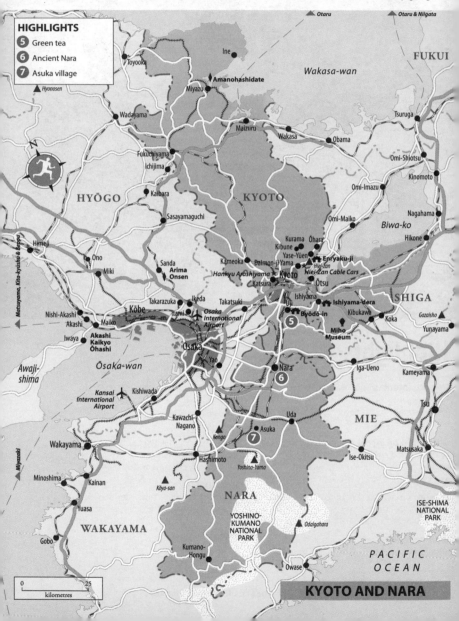

HIGHLIGHTS

5 Green tea
6 Ancient Nara
7 Asuka village

KYOTO AND NARA

0 — 25 kilometres

the very name Kyoto conjures up the classic image of Japan: streets of traditional wooden houses, the click-clack of *geta* (traditional wooden sandals) on the paving stones, geisha passing in a flourish of brightly coloured silks, and temple pagodas surrounded by cherry blossom trees.

While you can still find all these things, and much more, first impressions of Kyoto can be disappointing. Decades of haphazard urban development and a conspicuous industrial sector have affected the city, eroding the distinctive characteristics of the townscape. However, current regulations limiting the height of new buildings and banning rooftop advertising indicate that more serious thought is being given to preserving Kyoto's visual environment.

6

The vast amount of culture and history in Kyoto is mind-boggling, yet it's possible to get a good feel for the city within a couple of days. Top priority should go to the eastern, Higashiyama, district, where the walk north from famous **Kiyomizu-dera** to **Ginkaku-ji** takes in a whole raft of fascinating temples, gardens and museums. It's also worth heading for the northwestern hills to contemplate the superb Zen gardens of **Daitoku-ji** and **Ryōan-ji**, before taking in the wildly extravagant Golden Pavilion, **Kinkaku-ji**. The highlight of the central sights is **Nijō-jō**, a lavishly decorated seventeenth-century palace, while nearby **Nijō-jin'ya** is an intriguing place riddled with secret passages and hidey-holes. Also worth seeing are the imperial villas of **Shūgaku-in Rikyū** and **Katsura Rikyū**, and the sensuous moss gardens of **Saihō-ji**, in the outer districts. Take time to walk around the city's old merchant quarters, too; one of the best is found in the **central district**, behind the department stores and modern shopping arcades north of **Shijō-dōri**. Across the river in **Gion** you'll find the traditional **crafts shops** – selling everything from handmade bamboo blinds to geisha hair accessories – and the beautiful old **ryokan** for which the city is justifiably famous. The city is not all temples and tradition, however; the **Kyoto International Manga Museum**, alongside an increasing number of **designer shops** and **stylish cafés**, are examples of Kyoto's modern spirit, showing how the city manages to combine its heritage with contemporary culture.

Spring and autumn are undoubtedly the **best times to visit** Kyoto, though also extremely crowded; after a chilly winter, the cherry trees put on their finery in early April, while the hot, oppressive summer months (June–Aug) are followed in October by a delightful period of clear, dry weather when the maple trees erupt into fiery reds. While Kyoto has always been a major domestic tourism destination, in recent years the number of international visitors has surged dramatically. The city government is scrambling to increase accommodation facilities and provide more multilingual travel information. Local transportation services are strained, and it's not unusual to have to queue to enter popular sightseeing spots or restaurants.

KYOTO ORIENTATION

Kyoto is contained within a wide basin valley surrounded by hills on three sides and flanked by two rivers – the Katsura-gawa to the west and the smaller Kamo-gawa to the east. A grid street system makes this one of Japan's easier cities to find your way around. The **central district** of banks, shops and the main tourist facilities lies between the Imperial Palace in the north and **Kyoto Station** to the south; Nijō-jō and Horikawa-dōri define the district's western extent, while the Kamo-gawa provides a natural boundary to the east. Within this core, the **downtown** area is concentrated around Shijō-dōri and north along Kawaramachi-dōri to Oike-dōri. Shijō-dōri leads east over the Kamo-gawa into **Gion**, the city's major entertainment district, and to the eastern hills, **Higashiyama**, which shelter many of Kyoto's most famous temples. Much of this central area is best tackled on foot, but the city's other sights are widely scattered. To the northwest, **Kinkaku-ji** and **Ryōan-ji** provide the focus for a second group of temples, while tucked away in the southwestern suburbs are the superb gardens of **Saihō-ji** and the **Katsura Rikyū**.

6

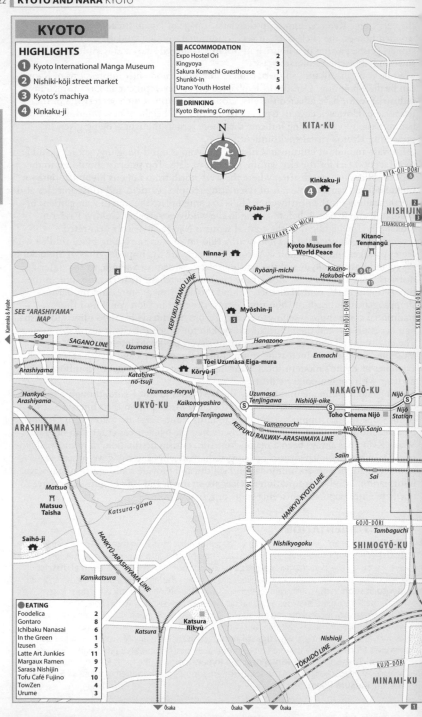

KYOTO

HIGHLIGHTS

1 Kyoto International Manga Museum

2 Nishiki-kōji street market

3 Kyoto's machiya

4 Kinkaku-ji

■ **ACCOMMODATION**

Expo Hostel Ori	2
Kingyoya	3
Sakura Komachi Guesthouse	1
Shunkō-in	5
Utano Youth Hostel	4

■ **DRINKING**

Kyoto Brewing Company	1

KITA-KU

Kinkaku-ji 4

KITA-ŌJI-DŌRI 6

1

Ryōan-ji

8

NISHIJIN 2

3

TERANOUCHI-DŌRI

KINUKAKE-NO-MICHI

Ninna-ji

Kyoto Museum for
World Peace

Kitano-
Tenmangū

Ryōanji-michi

Kitano-
Hakubai-chō

9 10

11

SEE "ARASHIYAMA"
MAP

4

KEIFUKU-KITANO LINE

Myōshin-ji

5

NISHIŌJI-DŌRI

SENBON-DŌRI

Saga

SAGANO LINE

Uzumasa

Hanazono

Arashiyama

Enmachi

Tōei Uzumasa Eiga-mura

Katabira-
no-tsuji

Kōryū-ji

Uzumasa-Koryuji

UKYŌ-KU

Kaikonoyashiro

Uzumasa
Tenjingawa

Nishiōji-oike

NAKAGYŌ-KU

Nijō

S

S

Toho Cinema Nijō

Nijō
Station

Hankyū-
Arashiyama

Randen-Tenjingawa

KEIFUKU RAILWAY–ARASHIMAYA LINE

Yamanouchi

Nishiōji-Sanjo

ARASHIYAMA

Saiin

ROUTE 162

Saiin

HANKYŪ-KYOTO LINE

Sai

Matsuo

Matsuo
Taisha

Katsura-gawa

GOJŌ-DŌRI

Tambaguchi

Saihō-ji

Nishikyogoku

SHIMOGYŌ-KU

HANKYŪ-ARASHIYAMA LINE

Kamikatsura

● **EATING**

Foodelica	2
Gontaro	8
Ichibaku Nanasai	6
In the Green	1
Izusen	5
Latte Art Junkies	11
Margaux Ramen	9
Sarasa Nishijin	7
Tofu Café Fujino	10
TowZen	4
Urume	3

Katsura
Rikyū

Katsura

Nishioji

Nishioji

TŌKAIDŌ LINE

KŪJŌ-DŌRI

MINAMI-KU

Kameoka & Ayabe

N

▼ Ōsaka   Ōsaka ▼   ▼ Ōsaka   ▼ 1

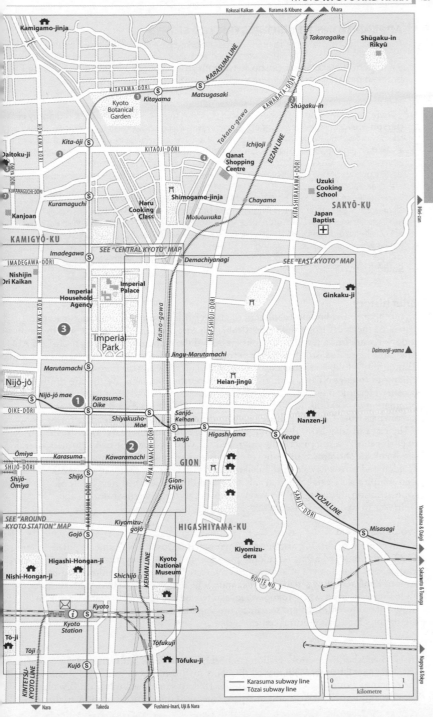

6

APPLICATIONS TO VISIT RESTRICTED SIGHTS

To visit some of Kyoto's most famous palaces and gardens it's necessary to apply in advance. Usually this is a fairly simple procedure if timed well, and is certainly worth the effort. Tours of the **Imperial Palace**, **Sentō Gosho**, **Katsura Rikyū** and **Shūgaku-in Rikyū** are all handled by the **Imperial Household Agency** office, 3 Kyōtogyoen, Kamigyō-ku (IHA; Mon–Fri 8.45am–noon & 1–4pm; ☎075 211 1215, ⓦ sankan.kunaicho.go.jp/english), on the west side of the Imperial Park, near Imadegawa subway station.

There are two ways to apply in advance: in person at the IHA office, or online. If you **apply in person** you must make a reservation seven days in advance; however, it is possible to apply the day before you intend to visit by 3.30pm if you have telephoned in advance and there are fewer than nine applications in your group. **Online applications** are accepted a month in advance and no later than four days prior to the date you intend to visit. Note that tour participants must be 18 years or older. Don't forget to take your passport with you to the office, and also for the tour itself.

For the Sentō Gosho, Katsura Rikyū and Shūgaku-in Rikyū, it is also now possible to take a chance and turn up at the attraction before 11am **on the day** to see if there are places available. Be aware that these entry tickets are distributed on a first-come first-served basis and are usually limited to around 20–30 visitors (check the website for capacity). However, due to the large volume of tourists wanting to visit these sights it is recommended to book in advance.

Other sights in Kyoto that require reservations in advance are **Nijō-jin'ya** (see p.428) and **Saihō-ji** (see p.448).

Brief history

Kyoto became the **imperial capital** in the late eighth century when Emperor Kammu relocated the court from Nara (see p.485). His first choice was Nagaoka, southwest of today's Kyoto, but a few inauspicious events led the emperor to move again in 794 AD. This time he settled on what was to become known as **Heian-kyō**, "Capital of Peace and Tranquillity". Like Nara, the city was modelled on the Chinese Tang-dynasty capital Chang'an (today's Xi'an), with a symmetrical north–south axis. By the late ninth century Heian-kyō was overflowing onto the eastern hills and soon had an estimated population of 500,000. In 894, imperial missions to China ceased and earlier borrowings from Chinese culture began to develop into distinct Japanese forms.

The city's history from this point is something of a roller-coaster ride. In the late twelfth century a fire practically destroyed the whole place, but two centuries later the **Ashikaga shoguns** built some of the city's finest monuments, among them the Golden and Silver Pavilions (Kinkaku-ji and Ginkaku-ji). Many of the great Zen temples were established at this time and the arts reached new levels of sophistication. Once again, however, almost everything was lost during the **Ōnin War** from 1467–77 (see p.823).

Kyoto's golden era

Kyoto's knight in shining armour was **Toyotomi Hideyoshi**, who came to power in 1582 and sponsored a vast rebuilding programme. The **Momoyama period**, as it's now known, was a golden era of artistic and architectural ostentation, epitomized by Kyoto's famous **Kanō school of artists**, who decorated the temples and palaces with sumptuous gilded screens. Even when **Tokugawa Ieyasu** moved the seat of government to Edo (now Tokyo) in 1603, Kyoto remained the imperial capital and stood its ground as the nation's foremost cultural centre.

Meiji modernization

In 1788 another huge conflagration swept through the city, but worse was to come; in 1869 the new **Emperor Meiji** moved the court to Tokyo. Kyoto went into shock, and the economy floundered for a while. In the 1890s a canal was built from Biwa-ko to the city, and Kyoto, like the rest of Japan, embarked on a process of industrialization.

Miraculously, the city narrowly escaped devastation at the end of **World War II**, when it was considered a potential target for the atom bomb. Kyoto was famously spared by American Defense Secretary Henry Stimson, who recognized the city's supreme architectural and historical importance.

Preserving Kyoto's heritage

After World War II, many of the city's old buildings were sold for their land value and replaced by ugly concrete structures or car parks. Despite continued modernization, however, a more enthusiastic approach to strengthening the city's traditional heritage is now being adopted by some of its residents, not least in efforts towards attracting foreign visitors. In particular, many people are becoming interested in not only preserving but also developing this historical legacy, evidenced by the growing number of businesses set in traditional townhouses, or *machiya* (see box, p.439).

Central Kyoto

The **Imperial Palace** is at the core of central Kyoto, just a short walk northeast of **Nijō-jō** – a lavish palace with magnificent screen paintings – and the intriguing **Nijō-jin'ya**. Nearby, Kyoto's **downtown** district is contained within the grid of streets bounded by Oike-dōri to the north, Shijō-dōri to the south, Karasuma-dōri to the west and the Kamo-gawa in the east. While there are few specific sights here, the backstreets still hide a number of traditional wooden buildings, including some of Kyoto's best ryokan. You'll also come across fine old craft shops (see p.465) among the boutiques and department stores, while the colourful shopping arcades of **Teramachi-dōri** and neighbouring **Shinkyōgoku** are worth a browse.

The Imperial Park and Palace

京都御苑, Kyōto Gyoen · 京都御所, Kyōto Gosho

Park open 24 hours a day · Palace tours (in Japanese, with free English-language audio guide) Tues–Sun 10am & 1.30pm; 1hr 15min · Free; guidebook ¥200 · Book tours in advance at the IHA office (see box opposite); bring your passport · Imadegawa subway, or bus to Karasuma Imadegawa

Earthen walls enclose the verdant **Imperial Park**, or Kyoto Gyoen, inside which wide expanses of gravel and clipped lawns have replaced most of the former palaces and subsidiary buildings. It's a popular spot for locals to picnic, exercise or walk the dog. Within the park, the **Imperial Palace** itself is by no means a high priority among Kyoto's wealth of sights, but it's a good idea to visit the **Imperial Household Agency** (IHA), in the park's northwest corner, early in your stay to make arrangements for visiting the city's more rewarding imperial villas and gardens (see box opposite).

The palace – the nation's physical and spiritual centre before the emperor moved to Tokyo in 1868 – originally stood about 2km further west, at Nijō-jō, but was relocated

---

KYOTO ADDRESSES

In general, Kyoto **addresses** follow the same pattern as for the rest of Japan (see box, p.43). There are, however, a few additional subtleties worth mastering. Unusually, most of the city's main roads are named and the location of a place is generally described by reference to the nearest major junction. Since the land slopes gently south, the most usual indicator is whether a place lies north (*agaru*, "above") or south (*sagaru*, "below") of a particular east–west road. For example, Kawaramachi Sanjō simply means the place is near the intersection of Kawaramachi-dōri and Sanjō-dōri; Kawaramachi Sanjō-agaru tells you it's north of Sanjō-dōri; Kawaramachi Sanjō-sagaru, that it's to the south. At a higher level of sophistication, the address might also indicate whether a place lies east (*higashi-iri*) or west (*nishi-iri*) of the north–south road.

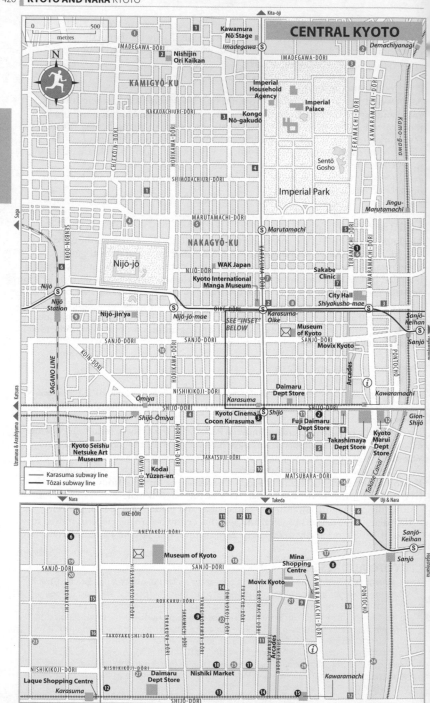

CENTRAL KYOTO

Kita-ōji

IMADEGAWA-DŌRI

Kawamura Nō Stage

Imadegawa

Nishijin Ori Kaikan

IMADEGAWA-DŌRI

Demachiyanagi

KAMIGYŌ-KU

NAKADACHIURI-DŌRI

Imperial Household Agency

Imperial Palace

HORIKAWA-DŌRI

CHEKON-DŌRI

Kongo Nō-gakudō

Sentō Gosho

SHIMODACHIURI-DŌRI

Imperial Park

Jingu-Marutamachi

MARUTAMACHI-DŌRI

Marutamachi

NAKAGYŌ-KU

TERAMACHI-DŌRI
KAWARAMACHI-DŌRI
KARASUMA-DŌRI

SENBON-DŌRI

Nijō-jō

NIJŌ-DŌRI

WAK Japan

Kyoto International Manga Museum

Sakabe Clinic

Nijō

Nijō Station

Nijō-jin'ya

Nijō-jō-mae

OIKE-DŌRI

City Hall
Shiyakusho-mae

Karasuma-Oike

Sanjō-Keihan

Museum of Kyoto

SANJŌ-DŌRI

SANJŌ-DŌRI

SEE "INSET" BELOW

Movix Kyoto

Sanjō

KŌIN-DŌRI

HORIKAWA-DŌRI

SAGANO LINE

Arcades

PONTOCHŌ

Ōmiya

NISHIKIKOJI-DŌRI

Daimaru Dept Store

Karasuma

Kawaramachi

SHIJŌ-DŌRI

Shijō-Ōmiya

Shijō

Kyoto Cinema Cocon Karasuma

Fuji Daimaru Dept Store

Gion-Shijō

Kyoto Seishu Netsuke Art Museum

Takashimaya Dept Store

Kyoto Marui Dept Store

OMIYA-DŌRI

Kodai Yūzen-en

HORIKAWA-DŌRI

TAKATSUJI-DŌRI

Takase Canal

TAKASHIMAYA

MATSUBARA-DŌRI

— Karasuma subway line
— Tōzai subway line

Nara

Takeda

Uji & Nara

OIKE-DŌRI

ANEYAKŌJI-DŌRI

Sanjō-Keihan

Museum of Kyoto

SANJŌ-DŌRI

Mina Shopping Centre

Sanjō

SANJŌ-DŌRI

Movix Kyoto

MUROMACHI-DŌRI

ROKKAKU-DŌRI

KAWARAMACHI-DŌRI

PONTOCHŌ

Higashiyama

TAKOYAKUSHI-DŌRI

Nishiki Market

NISHIKIKOJI-DŌRI

NISHIKIKOJI-DŌRI

Laque Shopping Centre

Daimaru Dept Store

Kawaramachi

Karasuma

SHIJŌ-DŌRI

■ ACCOMMODATION					
9h Nine Hours	8	Hale	25	Live Spot Rag	8
First Cabin	9	Honke Owariya	7	Miltons	7
Hiiragiya	12	Hotevila	10	Pub Karr	9
Itoya Hotel	10	Ippudo	27	Taku Taku	5
Kyoto Brighton Hotel	3	Iyemon Salon	20	Tato	11
Mitsui Garden Hotel Kyoto Sanjō	15	Kaboku Tearoom	6	UrBAN GUILD	10
Hotel Monterey	16	Kaji	5	World	12
Nishiyama Ryokan	7	Khanty	2		
Oil Street Guest House	1	Kiln	12	● SHOPPING	
Palace-Side Hotel	4	Kissa Master	18	Aritsugu	11
Petit Hotel Kyoto	2	Kushikura	8	Eirakuya/RAAK	6
Piece Hostel Sanjo	14	Menbakaichidai Ramen	4	Ippodo	1
The Screen	5	Nicora	1	Izutsu Yatsuhashi	14
Tawaraya	13	Ninja Kyoto	26	Kogetsu	12
Urban Hotel Kyoto Nijo Premium	6	Somushi Kochaya	19	Kyoto Design House	7
Yoshikawa Ryokan	11	Waka	13	Kyūkyo-dō	4
		Weekenders	22	Lisn	3
● EATING		Wontana	21	Maruzen	5
A Womb	23	Yoshikawa	16	Seisuke88	8
Anzukko	17			Sou Sou	15
Café Phalam	9	■ DRINKING AND NIGHTLIFE		Suzuki Shofudō	9
Fujino-ya	24	Ace Café	6	Takakuraya	10
Fukujuen	11	Before 9	2	Tanakaya	13
Giro Giro Hitoshina	14	Bungalow	4	Toraya	2
Grand Burger	3	Dublin Irish Pub	3		
Gyoza no Ohsho	15	Jittoku	1		

6

to its present site in the late twelfth century. However, nearly all of the buildings date from the mid-nineteenth century and the overwhelming impression is rather monotonous – wide spaces of pure white gravel, set against austere Meiji-period replicas of Heian-style (794–1185) architecture. The most important building is the ceremonial **Shishin-den** (紫宸殿), flanked by two cherry and citrus trees, where the Meiji, Taishō and Shōwa emperors were all enthroned. Further on, you can peer inside the **Seiryō-den** (清涼殿), which was once the emperor's private residence, while beyond there's a tantalizing glimpse of a pond-filled stroll-garden designed by the landscape gardener Kobori Enshū (1579–1647).

Sentō Gosho

仙洞御所 • In the southeast quadrant of the Imperial Park • Tours (in Japanese, with free English-language audio guide) Mon–Fri 11am & 1.30pm; 1hr • Free • Book tours in advance at the IHA office (see box, p.424); bring your passport

A fine example of Kobori Enshū's landscape design can be seen by taking a (compulsory) guided tour of the **Sentō Gosho** garden. Originally built as a retirement home for former emperors, the palace here burned down in 1854 and now only the peaceful garden remains. Apart from several graceful pavilions, its main features are a zigzag bridge – stunning when its wisteria trellis is in full bloom – and a cobbled "seashore", which lends the garden an extra grandeur.

Nijō-jō

二条城 • 541 Nijō-jō-chō, 1km southwest of the Imperial Park • 8.45am–4pm; closed Tues in Jan, July, Aug & Dec • ¥600, gallery ¥100, audio guide ¥500 • ☏ 075 841 0096, ⓦ www.city.kyoto.jp/bunshi/nijojo/english • The main entrance is the East Gate on Horikawa-dōri, near the Nijō-jō-mae subway station and bus stop

The swaggering opulence of **Nijō-jō** provides a complete contrast to imperial understatement. Built as the Kyoto residence of Shogun Tokugawa Ieyasu (1543–1616), the castle's double moats, massive walls and watchtowers demonstrate the supreme confidence of his new, Tokyo-based military government. Inside, the finest artists of the day filled the palace with sumptuous gilded screens and carvings, the epitome of Momoyama style (see p.840), leaving the increasingly impoverished emperor in no doubt as to where power really lay. The castle was built in 1603 and took 23 years to complete, paid for by local *daimyō*, but Nijō-jō was never used in defence and was rarely visited by a shogun after the mid-1600s.

After entering through the East Gate, head to the **Ninomaru Palace** (二の丸御殿), whose five buildings face onto a lake-garden and run in a staggered line connected by

6

THE KAMO-GAWA

Running through central Kyoto, the **Kamo-gawa** (鴨川) is a much-loved hangout for Kyoto's inhabitants, who flock to its banks for exercise and relaxation. The **Sanjō bridge** area is very popular with the city's youth, and buskers often perform here to large crowds. From late spring the river's western bank between **Shijō bridge** and **Ōike bridge** is covered with *yuka* (wooden platforms that extend out from the restaurants of Pontochō), which catch the cooling river breezes during humid summers. The river has an eventful history: **Kabuki** theatre began here in 1603, and in 1619 the "Martyrs of Kyoto", more than fifty **Christians** including women and children, were burned alive on the riverbank. The river was also used for hundreds of years to rinse out **kimono** fabric that had been dyed using the *kyō-yūzen* hand-dyeing technique. It's no surprise, then, that by the early 1990s it was very polluted. However, at the end of the decade the city government undertook a rejuvenation programme and now all 35km of the river and its surroundings support an abundance of bird and plant life.

---

covered corridors. Look out for the "nightingale floors" which squeak when trodden on and were specially designed to detect intruders. Each room is lavishly decorated with replicas of **screen paintings** by the brilliant Kanō school of artists, notably Kanō Tanyū and Naonobu. You can view the actual screens in a separate **gallery** to the north of the main gate.

Nijō-jin'ya

二条陣屋 • 137 Sanbō Ōmiya-chō • Tours in Japanese daily except Wed at 10am, 11am, 2pm & 3pm; non-Japanese-speakers will need an interpreter (volunteer information on website); 1hr • ¥1000 • ☎ 075 841 0972, ⓦ nijyojinya.net/English.html • Advance reservations only – book by phone (in Japanese) one day beforehand

The mysterious **Nijō-jin'ya** was built in the early seventeenth century as an inn for feudal lords who came to pay homage to the emperor. As these were days of intrigue and treachery, it is riddled with trap doors, false walls and ceilings, "nightingale floors", escape hatches, disguised staircases and confusing dead ends to trap intruders. It is owned by the Ogawa family and is a private residence, hence the strict rules for touring the house, and the rather frosty reception. The structure has been extensively restored in recent years, and is a fascinating example of traditional craftsmanship – it's worth organizing an interpreter for the tour (details on website) so that you can learn more about Nijō-jin'ya's clever safeguards against intruders.

Kyoto International Manga Museum

京都国際マンガミュージアム, Kyōto Jokusai Manga Myujiamu • Kanafuki-chō • 10am–5.30pm; closed Wed • ¥800 • ☎ 075 254 7414, ⓦ kyotomm.jp/english

The excellent **Kyoto International Manga Museum** recently celebrated its tenth anniversary as the world's first museum entirely devoted to **Japanese comics**. A joint project between Kyoto City and Seika University, it's housed in an old elementary school, which has been remodelled to accommodate the huge, all-encompassing collection of popular manga (see p.842), as well as provide plenty of space for art workshops (held at weekends) to teach the techniques of manga, and international conferences to discuss research. The great thing about the museum is that most of the manga can be taken outside and read on the lawn, and there is also an international section with some English-language manga.

Museum of Kyoto

京都文化博物館, Kyōto Bunka Hakubutsukan • 623-1 Higashikata-machi • Tues–Sun 10am–7pm; special exhibitions usually close at 5.30pm; check the website for screening times of Japanese classic movies • ¥500, film screenings ¥500 • ☎ 075 222 0888, ⓦ bunpaku.or.jp

In a trendy area of shops and cafés, the **Museum of Kyoto** incorporates a Meiji-era bank building and a replica Edo-period shopping street with craft shops and some reasonable restaurants. The museum's exhibits focus mainly on local history, culture and modern crafts, with some interesting historical dioramas, though there is little detailed explanation about the exhibits in Japanese or English. Check out the small section on Kyoto's film industry, which is enlivened by monthly screenings of classic movies (in Japanese).

Pontochō

先斗町

Running parallel to the west side of the Kamo-gawa between Sanjō and Shijō bridges, the geisha district of **Pontochō** is packed with teahouses, restaurants and bars – many of which are built in traditional wooden *machiya*. It's best visited at night, when lantern light fills the district's narrow lanes and you can often catch a glimpse of a geisha or trainee *maiko* on her way to an appointment. In July and August, Pontochō restaurants open wooden *yuka* terraces over the cooling Kamo-gawa, making Kyoto's sweltering summer nights a little more bearable.

Nishiki-kōji street market

錦小路通 · Parallel to Shijō-dori, one block north · Daily 9am–7pm, but varies from shop to shop · Ⓦ kyoto-nishiki.or.jp

Known as "Kyoto's kitchen", **Nishiki-kōji street market** has been one of the city's main fish and vegetable markets since the early seventeenth century. The tantalizing smells of fresh tofu, grilled fish and all kinds of pickled, fermented and dried Kyō-yasai (Kyoto vegetables) will greet you in this narrow covered alley. There are more than a hundred small shops here, many offering samples to taste, as well as plenty of restaurants. The Haru Cooking School offers a fun and informative one-hour **tour** of the market once a week (see p.452).

Kyoto Seishū Netsuke Art Museum

京都清宗根付館, Kyōto Seishū Netsuke-kan · 46-1 Mibukayōgosho-chō · Tues–Sun 10am–4.30pm · ¥1000 · ☎ 075 802 7000, Ⓦ netsukekan.jp · 10min walk southwest of Hankyu Ōmiya Station or Keifuku Shijō-Ōmiya Station

The fascinating **Kyoto Seishū Netsuke Art Museum** is home to a private collection of *netsuke* – hand-carved objects traditionally used for hanging pouches from *obi* sashes. These miniature pieces of art were originally made from ivory and mainly depict people and animals, as well as natural objects such as fruit and flowers. The antique and contemporary *netsuke* are displayed here over two floors of an old samurai mansion that has been beautifully restored.

Around Kyoto Station

Historically, the principal entrance to Kyoto lay through its great southern gate, so it's only fitting that this district, south of the city centre, should be home to the monumental **Kyoto Station**, the entry point for most visitors to the city. Opposite the station is the **Kyoto Tower**, which can clearly be seen throughout the city and makes a useful landmark when walking around. This area is also home to some of the city's more venerable temples – in their day, when their massive wooden halls were filled with shimmering gold, **Nishi-Hongan-ji** and **Higashi-Hongan-ji** were probably just as awe-inspiring as the modern train station. Across the tracks, **Tō-ji** boasts Japan's tallest original wooden pagoda and some of the city's oldest surviving buildings.

Kyoto Station

京都駅, Kyoto-eki · Karasuma Shichijō-sagaru

The city's main transport hub – where the JR, Kintetsu and Kyoto subway lines meet – **Kyoto Station** was rebuilt and enlarged in the 1990s by Tokyo architect Hara Hiroshi. The new building was initially the source of much local consternation, but over time many people have come to appreciate its shiny black bulk. Uncompromisingly modern, with its marble exterior and giant central archway, the station building also houses the Isetan department store, restaurants and underground shopping malls, plus a hotel and theatre.

Kyoto Tower

京都タワー • Karasuma Shichijō-sagaru • Observatory daily 9am–8.40pm • ¥770 • ☎ 075 361 3215, ⓦ keihanhotels-resorts.co.jp /kyoto-tower/en

The tallest structure in Kyoto, the 131m-high **Kyoto Tower** was built in the 1960s and caused controversy at the time for its modern design. Though still considered by many to be rather unsightly, the tower's observatory does provide fantastic panoramic views, which give you a good understanding of the city's geography – on a clear day you can even see parts of Osaka. The tower houses a hotel, restaurants, bars and even a public *sentō* bath.

Nishi-Hongan-ji

西本願寺 • Hanaya-chō sagaru • Daily: May–Aug 5.30am–6pm; Sept–April 5.30am–5.30pm • Free • ☎ 075 371 5181, ⓦ www.hongwanji.or.jp/english • 5min walk from Kyoto Station, on the west side of Horikawa-dōri

The vast temple complex of **Nishi-Hongan-ji** is the headquarters of the **Jōdo Shinshū** sect (see box opposite). Compared to other Kyoto temples, Nishi-Hongan-ji is relatively crowd-free and has a pleasant atmosphere. The gravel courtyard contains two huge halls, the oldest of which is the Founder's Hall, **Goeidō** (御影堂), built in 1636, and located on the left as you enter through the gate. The temple is dedicated to Shinran and was recently restored. The **Amida Hall** (阿弥陀堂) dates from 1760. Both are decked with

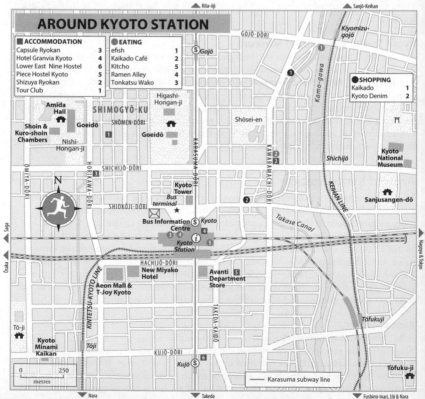

JŌDO SHINSHŪ

One of Japan's most popular and wealthy Buddhist sects, the **Jōdo Shinshū** (True Pure Land) was founded by the Kyoto-born priest **Shonin Shinran** (1173–1262). His simple creed, which at the time was regarded as heresy, asserts that merely chanting the *nembutsu*, "Praise to Amida Buddha", can lead to **salvation**. Not surprisingly, the sect grew rapidly, despite opposition from the established hierarchy, until eventually Toyotomi Hideyoshi granted them a plot of land in southern Kyoto in 1591 – today, this is the Nishi-Hongan-ji. By 1602, Shogun Tokugawa Ieyasu was sufficiently alarmed at the sect's power to sponsor a splinter group, Higashi-Hongan-ji, now based just a few hundred metres to the east of the Nishi-Hongan-ji. Even today, the two groups continue to differ over doctrinal affairs.

6

gold, including screens by Kanō artists in the Amida Hall. The temple's real highlights, the even more ornate **Shoin** (書院) and **Kuro-shoin Chambers** (黒書院), are only open to guided tours – ask in the green-roofed building, to the left of the Goeidō.

Higashi-Hongan-ji

東本願寺, Karasuma Shichijō sagaru • **Temple** Daily: March–Oct 5.50am–5.30pm; Nov–Feb 6.20am–4.30pm • Free • **Garden** Daily: March–Oct 9am–4.30pm; Nov–Feb 9am–3.30pm • ¥500 • ☏ 075 371 9181, ⊕ higashihonganji.or.jp/english • 5min walk from Kyoto Station, on the west side of Karasuma-dōri

Though **Higashi-Hongan-ji** was constructed in a similar style to its neighbour and rival, Nishi-Hongan-ji, it had to be completely rebuilt after a fire in 1864, and today only the two main halls are open to the public. The first hall, the **Goeidō** (御影堂), is one of Japan's largest wooden buildings – when it was built, ordinary ropes proved too weak to lift the massive roof beams, so female devotees from around the country sent in enough hair to plait 53 ropes. You can see an example of these black ropes preserved in the open corridor that connects the Goeidō to the **Amida Hall** (阿弥陀堂), with its image of Amida on an elaborate altar. Two blocks further east, the temple's shady garden, **Shōsei-en** (渉成園), provides a welcome respite from the surrounding city blocks, with teahouses, as well as stone and wooden bridges over a pond brimming with carp.

Tō-ji

東寺 • 1 Kujō-chō • **Temple grounds** Daily: mid-March to mid-Sept 8.30am–5.30pm; mid-Sept to mid-March 8.30am–4.30pm • **Gojū-no-tō** Daily 9am–4.30pm • ¥800 • **Kō-dō & Kon-dō** Daily 8.30am–4.30pm • ¥500 • **Miei-dō** Daily 8.30am–4.30pm • Statue can be seen on 21st of each month • Free • **Hōmotsu-kan** Approx mid-March to late May & mid-Sept to late Nov daily 9am–4.30pm, but check the temple's website for exact dates • ¥500 • ☏ 075 691 3325, ⊕ toji.or.jp • 10min walk southwest of Kyoto Station

Founded by Emperor Kammu in 794, the historic temple of **Tō-ji** contains some of Japan's finest esoteric Buddhist sculpture and its lovely **pagoda** is one of the symbols of Kyoto. The best time to visit is during the **monthly flea market**, held on the 21st of each month, when Tō-ji is thronged with pilgrims, hustlers and bargain hunters.

After the problems in Nara (see p.486), Emperor Kammu permitted only two Buddhist temples within the city walls: Tō-ji and Sai-ji, the East and West temples, which stood either side of Rashō-mon, the main entrance to eighth-century Heian-kyō. While Sai-ji eventually faded, Tō-ji prospered under **Kōbō Daishi**, the founder of Shingon Buddhism (see box, p.527), who was granted the stewardship of the temple in 823. Over the centuries, the temple gathered a treasure-trove of calligraphy, paintings and Buddhist statuary, the oldest of which were supposedly brought from China by the Daishi himself.

Tō-ji's most distinctive feature is the five-storey **Gojū-no-tō** (五重塔), Japan's tallest pagoda. Erected in 826 and last rebuilt in the mid-seventeenth century, it now stands in an enclosure alongside Tō-ji's greatest treasures, the **Kō-dō** (講堂) and more southerly **Kon-dō** (金堂). These buildings both date from the early seventeenth century, but it's the images inside, such as Heian-period Buddhist statues, that are the focus.

The **Miei-dō** (御影堂), or Founder's Hall, is said to be where Kōbō Daishi lived. The present building, erected in 1380, houses a thirteenth-century statue of him, which can be seen monthly, on the day that marks the entry of the Daishi into Nirvana, when hundreds of pilgrims queue up to pay their respects. Beyond the Miei-dō, the modern **Hōmotsu-kan** (宝物館) contains Tō-ji's remaining treasures, including priceless mandala, portraits of Kōbō Daishi and a 6m-tall Senju Kannon (thousand-armed Buddhist Goddess of Mercy), carved in 877. The museum opens for two seasons (spring and autumn), with different exhibitions each time.

East Kyoto

If you only have one day in Kyoto, it's best to concentrate on the wealth of temples and museums lining the eastern hills. Not only does this district include many of Kyoto's more rewarding sights, but it's also fairly compact and contains attractive lanes and traditional houses set against the wooded slopes behind. If you're pushed for time, head straight for **Kiyomizu-dera**, with its distinctive wooden terrace, and then follow cobbled **Sannen-zaka** north. **Gion**, the famous entertainment district traditionally associated with geisha and teahouses, has retained a surprising number of wooden facades and photogenic corners, though its seductive charms are best savoured after dark. Garden lovers should also arrange to visit **Shūgaku-in Rikyū** on the northeast edge of Kyoto, for its inspired use of borrowed scenery on a grand scale – you'll need to allow a half-day for this. The following account covers the sights of eastern Kyoto from south to north.

Fushimi-Inari Taisha

伏見稲荷大社 • 68 Yabunochi-chō • Daily 24 hours • Free • ☎ 075 641 7331, ⓦ inari.jp • From Kyoto Station take either the JR Nara line to Inari Station or the Keihan line to Fushimi-Inari Station; from eastern Kyoto, take a #202, #207 or #208 bus to Tōfuku-ji Station and get a train from there to JR Inari or Keihan Fushimi-Inari Station; it's a short walk east from either station to the shrine

The spectacularly photogenic **Fushimi-Inari Taisha**, about 2.5km southeast of Kyoto Station, is the head shrine of the Inari cult, dedicated to the god of rice and sake. In 711, the local Hata clan established a shrine on top of Inari-san, the mountain, although this was eventually moved in the ninth century to the site of the current sanctuary at the foot of the mountain. Don't linger here too long though – the real highlight is the 4km maze of **paths** that wind their way up through the forest to the summit of the mountain. More than 10,000 vermilion *torii* frame the paths, forming a mysterious tunnel that in some places cuts out most light, even on the brightest days. These painted wooden gates are replaced every ten years, each one an offering by local and national companies asking for success in business – the black lettering on each gate indicates the company that has donated it. Dozens of sub-shrines line the route, with hundreds of thousands of miniature wooden gates hanging from every available space, flanked by stone foxes, which are believed to be the messengers of the rice gods. It's quite a steep climb up to the top, but you'll be rewarded with great views of Kyoto, and along the way you can stop for tea and grab some *inari-zushi* – rice balls in pockets of fried tofu.

Tōfuku-ji

東福寺 • 778 Honmachi • Daily: April–Oct 9am–4pm; Nov–late Dec 8.30am–4pm; late Dec–March 9am–3.30pm • Garden ¥400, bridge ¥400 • ⓦ tofukuji.jp • Catch a #202, #207 or #208 bus from central or eastern Kyoto or a train from Kyoto Station on the JR Nara line to Tōfuku-ji Station; the temple is a short walk east from the station, across a busy road

Tōfuku-ji, a Zen temple, is most often visited during autumn, when the colours of the *momiji* (maple) leaves in the grounds provide a spectacular array of red and gold. The best place to view this classic scene is from the wooden **Tsūten-kyō** (Bridge to Heaven). The temple is part of the Rinzai sect of Zen Buddhism and was founded in 1236. This large, sprawling complex with 23 sub-temples is significant not only for its medieval

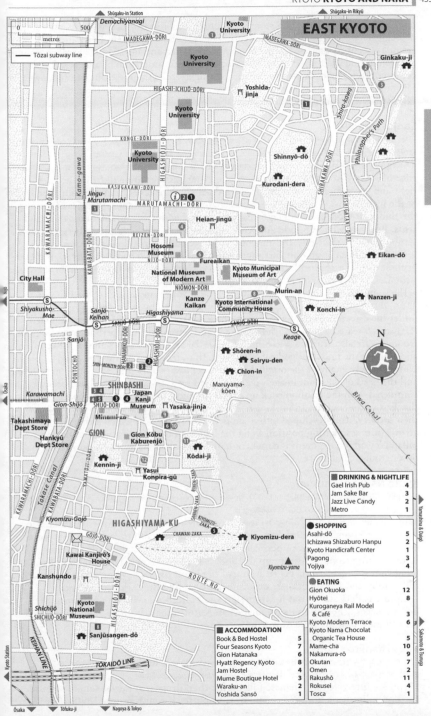

EAST KYOTO

Shūgaku-in Station
Shūgaku-in Rikyū
Demachiyanagi
Kyoto University
IMADEGAWA-DŌRI
IMADEGAWA-DŌRI
Ginkaku-ji
Kyoto University
Kyoto University
HIGASHI-ICHIJŌ-DŌRI
Yoshida-jinja
Kyoto University
KONOE-DŌRI
Kyoto University
Shinnyō-dō
Philosopher's Path
KASUGAKAMI-DŌRI
Kurodani-dera
Shira-kawa
Jingu-Marutamachi
MARUTAMACHI-DŌRI
Heian-jingū
REIZEN-DŌRI
Hosomi Museum
NIJŌ-DŌRI
Fureaikan
Eikan-dō
National Museum of Modern Art
Kyoto Municipal Museum of Art
NIŌMON-DŌRI
Murin-an
City Hall
Kanze Kaikan
Kyoto International Community House
Nanzen-ji
Konchi-in
Shiyakusho-Mae
Sanjō-Keihan
Higashiyama
SANJŌ-DŌRI
SANJŌ-DŌRI
Keage
Sanjō
Biwa Canal
Shōren-in
Seiryu-den
Chion-in
Higashiyama
Maruyama-kōen
Shinbashi
Japan Kanji Museum
Yasaka-jinja
Karawamachi
Gion-Shijō
SHIJŌ-DŌRI
Takashimaya Dept Store
Hankyū Dept Store
GION
Gion Kōbu Kaburenjō
Minami-za
Kōdai-ji
Kennin-ji
Yasui Konpira-gū
HIGASHIYAMA-KU
Kiyomizu-Gojō
GOJŌ-DŌRI
Kiyomizu-dera
Kawai Kanjirō's House
CHAWAN-ZAKA
Kiyomizu-yama
Kanshundo
ROUTE NO. 1
Shichijō
Kyoto National Museum
SHICHIJŌ-DŌRI
Sanjūsangen-dō
KEIHAN LINE
TŌKAIDŌ LINE
Kyoto Station
Ōsaka
Tōfuku-ji
Nagoya & Tokyo
Yamashina & Daigo
Sakamoto & Tsuruga

DRINKING & NIGHTLIFE
Gael Irish Pub	4
Jam Sake Bar	3
Jazz Live Candy	2
Metro	1

SHOPPING
Asahi-dō	5
Ichizawa Shizaburo Hanpu	2
Kyoto Handicraft Center	1
Pagong	3
Yojiya	4

EATING
Gion Okuoka	12
Hyōtei	8
Kuroganeya Rail Model & Café	3
Kyoto Modern Terrace	6
Kyoto Nama Chocolat Organic Tea House	5
Mame-cha	10
Nakamura-rō	9
Okutan	7
Omen	2
Rakushō	11
Rokusei	4
Tosca	1

ACCOMMODATION
Book & Bed Hostel	5
Four Seasons Kyoto	7
Gion Hatanaka	6
Hyatt Regency Kyoto	8
Jam Hostel	4
Mume Boutique Hotel	3
Waraku-an	2
Yoshida Sansō	1

0   500
metres

— Tōzai subway line

6

temple architecture – the two-storey San-mon gate, built in 1425, is the oldest example of Zen gate architecture still in existence – but also for its gardens. Revolutionary twentieth-century gardener Mirei Shigemori designed and installed the gardens around the **Hōjō** (main hall) in 1939, and his work here is considered to be a great example of **contemporary Japanese garden** design, creating abstract shapes with moss and gravel. His interpretation of the traditional Zen raked gravel garden is also interesting – lots of extra swirls and coned peaks.

Sanjūsangen-dō

三十三間堂 · 657 Sanjūsangendōmawari-chō, south of Shichijō-dōri · Daily: April–Oct 8am–4.30pm; Nov–March 9am–4pm · ¥600 · ☎ 075 525 0033, ⓦ sanjusangendo.jp · Take Raku bus #100, or city buses #206 and #208 from Kyoto Station

The ranks of 1001 gilded Buddhist statues inside **Sanjūsangen-dō**, on the southeastern edge of Kyoto, are a truly memorable sight. After passing through the turnstiles, turn right and leave your shoes in the porch; a short corridor takes you to the northern end of the hall. At first, the impassive, haloed figures appear as identical **images of Kannon**, the Buddhist Goddess of Mercy, usually portrayed with eleven heads and a thousand arms. But they all have subtle differences in their faces, clothes and jewellery, and in the symbols held in their tiny, outstretched hands. Rather than a thousand arms, the statues have been given only forty apiece (excluding the two hands in prayer), but each of these can save 25 worlds. In addition, every figure represents 33 incarnations, giving a total of 33,033 Kannon to help save mankind.

The statues were commissioned by the devout former emperor Go-Shirakawa in 1164, during the bloody Genpei Wars, and were carved by some seventy craftsmen under the direction of the renowned sculptor **Tankei** (c.1173–1256). He completed the central, seated Kannon at the age of 82, and several of the superb images along the front row are also attributed to him. Of these, 28 are disciples of Kannon, while Fujin and Kanjin, the muscular gods of Wind and Thunder, bring up the two ends. Unfortunately, many of the original statues were lost in a fire in 1249, but 156 Kannon and the head of the main image were saved, and by 1266 a replica hall had been completed with the Kannon back up to full strength. In the early seventeenth century, the west veranda of the 188m-long hall became a popular place for samurai to practise their **archery**. This developed into a competition, **Tōshiya**, in which archers had to fire arrows from a squatting position along the length of the building without hitting a pillar. Nowadays, the event is commemorated with an archery display outside the hall on or around January 15.

Kyoto National Museum

京都国立博物館, Kyōto Kokuritsu Hakubutsukan · 527 Chaya-machi · Tues–Sun 9am–4.30pm, Fri until 7.30pm · ¥500, plus extra during special exhibitions · ☎ 075 531 7509, ⓦ kyohaku.go.jp

Immediately across Shichijō-dōri from Sanjūsangen-dō is the southern entrance to the **Kyoto National Museum**, Kyoto's major art museum and the venue for important special exhibitions. The vast permanent collection, with 12,500 works covering Kyoto culture from prehistory up to 1868, is held in the new Heisei Chishinkan wing, and is organized by genre. Many of the items on display, including textiles, calligraphy and metalwork, are exquisite national treasures. The ground-floor sculpture gallery stands out for its design and collection of Heian and Kamakura period pieces. The museum's original Meiji Kotokan hall, built in 1895, was closed for restoration at the time of writing.

Kawai Kanjirō's House

河井寛次郎記念館, Kawai Kanjirō Kinen-kan · 569 Kanei-chō · Tues–Sun 10am–4.30pm; closed Aug 11–20 & Dec 24–Jan 7 · ¥900 · ☎ 075 561 3585, ⓦ kanjiro.jp · Turn west off Higashiōji-dori shortly before the Gojō-dōri flyover

If you are interested in Japanese folk crafts, then drop in at **Kawai Kanjirō's House**, the tastefully rustic home of the innovative potter Kawai Kanjirō (1890–1966), who helped revive *mingei* (folk crafts) in the 1930s. The house is as he left it, beautifully furnished with ceramics and sculptures from his long career, including the kilns where many of these pieces were made, as well as personal items, such as his opium pipe.

Kiyomizu-dera

清水寺 • 294-1 Kiyomizu • Daily 6am–6pm; Jishu-jinja daily 9am–5pm • ¥400 • ⓦ kiyomizudera.or.jp • The closest bus stops are Kiyomizu-michi or Gojō-zaka on Higashiōji-dōri, served by buses #100 (Raku bus), #202, #206 & #207

With its trademark wooden platform overhanging the valley, **Kiyomizu-dera** is one of Kyoto's defining sights. There's been a temple here since 778, when a visionary priest came across its fount of clear water (*kiyo-mizu*); however, nearly all the buildings you see today date from 1633. Just north of the Gojō-dōri flyover a right fork brings you to **Chawan-zaka** (茶わん坂), a quiet lane lined with shops selling local pottery. If you'd rather use the traditional approach, continue on to **Kiyomizu-zaka** (清水坂), where you'll find a colourful, crowded parade of souvenir shops and craft galleries.

Hon-dō

本堂

Beyond the three-storey pagoda, you can step for a moment into the monumental **Hon-dō** (Main Hall) to enjoy its surprisingly peaceful interior. There's little to actually see in here – its principal image, an eleven-headed Kannon, only goes on show every 33 years (next time will be 2033), so head for the wide terrace in front, originally a stage for sacred dances, to soak up the famous view over the wooded gorge and Kyoto beyond.

Jishu-jinja

地主神社主

On the hill behind the Hon-dō a jumble of shrine buildings competes for the attention of people looking for luck in love. **Jishu-jinja** is dedicated to several Shintō gods, of whom the most popular is Okuninushi-no-mikoto, an ancient deity in charge of love and good marriages; his messenger is a rabbit. To test your current love life, try walking in a straight line between the two "blind stones", set 18m apart, with your eyes closed and intoning your partner's name. If you arrive at the other stone without erring, all is well.

Otowa waterfall

音羽の瀧, Otowa-no-taki

At the base of the wooden terrace, the **Otowa-no-taki** waterfall is reputed to have magical powers if you drink its waters. There are three separate streams, each of which grants a different wish – success, health or beauty – though it's considered bad luck to sip from more than one. From the waterfall you can follow a short path up the opposite hillside from where you get the best views of Kiyomizu-dera.

SANNEN-ZAKA AND NINEN-ZAKA

Two charming cobbled lanes connect Kiyomizu-dera with Kōdai-ji. Known as **Sannen-zaka** (三年坂;"Three-Year Slope") and **Ninen-zaka** (二年坂;"Two-Year Slope"), these lanes preserve some of the last vestiges of the old Kyoto townscape (see box, p.439). There has been a path here since the ninth century, while the two-storey wooden **townhouses** date from the late 1800s. Many of these buildings still cater to passing pilgrims and souvenir hunters in time-honoured fashion, peddling Kiyomizu pottery, bamboo-ware, pickles and refreshments – look out for Hyōtan-ya, at the bottom of the steps at the Kiyomizu-dera end, which has been selling gourd flasks (*hyōtan*) for two hundred years. Be careful walking along these two lanes, though: according to popular belief, a fall here brings two or three years of bad luck.

6

Kōdai-ji

高台時 • 526 Shimokawara-chō • Daily 9am–5pm • ¥600 • Ⓦ kodaiji.com

At the north end of the cobbled lanes of Ninen-zaka (see box, p.435), walk straight ahead up the steps and through the car park to find the entrance to the peaceful gardens of **Kōdai-ji**. This temple was granted to Kita-no-Mandokoro, the wife of Toyotomi Hideyoshi, when she became a nun after his death in 1598. Kōdai-ji owes its finery, however, to the generosity of Hideyoshi's successor, Tokugawa Ieyasu, who donated buildings from his own castles and financed paintings by Kanō artists, before he wiped out the Toyotomi dynasty at Osaka in 1615. Nowadays, the temple buildings blend beautifully into their attractive hillside garden, its two ponds graced by a moon-viewing pavilion and the aptly named "**Reclining Dragon Corridor**", a covered walkway with a sloping roof. Between the ponds, check out the ceilings of the pretty **Kaisan-dō** hall, which are made from recycled panels from Ieyasu's ship and from the carriage of Kita-no-Mandokoro. But the temple's most important building lies at the top of the Reclining Dragon Corridor (though you have to walk round by a path), where statues of Hideyoshi and his widow are enshrined. The exquisite gold-inlay lacquer work is among the finest of its kind in Japan.

Chion-in

知恩院 • 400 Rinka-cho • Daily: March–Nov 9am–3.30pm; Dec–Feb 9am–4pm • Hall & gardens ¥500 • ☎ 075 531 2111, Ⓦ chion-in.or.jp

On the northern edge of Maruyama-kōen public park is the temple of **Chion-in**, a big, busy complex where everything is built on a monumental scale, starting with the huge **San-mon** (三門) gate. Founded in 1175 by the priest Hōnen, the temple is the headquarters of his popular Jōdo (Pure Land) sect of Buddhism. Behind the cavernous **Miei-dō** (御影堂) main hall – closed for restoration until 2018 – red arrows lead to the entrance of the **Ōhōjō** and **Kohōjō** halls and gardens representing Amida's paradise. The main feature of both halls is the Momoyama-period screens that fill them; since you can only peer in, they've placed replicas of the screens in a room behind the ticket desk – the most famous features a cat with uncannily lifelike eyes. The colossal **Daishō-rō** (大鐘楼) bell, the biggest in Japan, is located at the back of the complex; at New Year it takes seventeen priests to ring this 67-tonne monster.

Shōren-in

青蓮院 • 69-1 Sanjobo-cho • Daily 9am–4.30pm • ¥500 • ☎ 075 561 2345, Ⓦ shorenin.com

North of the bustling Chion-in, **Shōren-in** is a quiet little place surrounded by pleasant gardens and ancient camphor trees. The temple started life in the ninth century as lodgings for Tendai-sect priests from Enryaku-ji (see p.474) and later served as a residence for members of the imperial family. After seeing the collection of painted screens, the main reason to come here is to stroll along the paths that wind through the beautifully landscaped hillside garden. If you have the stamina, don't miss the steep climb up to **Seiryū-den** (青龍殿); perched on the top of the ridge behind Shōren-in, this small sub-temple has fine views of central and northern Kyoto from a wooden observation deck.

Yasaka-jinja

八坂神社 • 625 Gion-machi Kitagawa • Daily 24hr • Free • ☎ 075 561 6155, Ⓦ yasaka-jinja.or.jp

The main entrance to the lively shrine of **Yasaka-jinja** faces west onto the intersection of Higashiōji-dōri and Shijō-dōri. Instead of the usual *torii*, you enter through a brightly coloured Buddhist-style gate – a legacy of the days before 1868 when Buddhism and Shintō often cohabited. Located on the southern edge of Maruyama-kōen and the eastern edge of Gion, Yasaka-jinja is at the heart of many Kyoto cultural events – from cherry blossom viewing in spring, which brings thousands to the park, to the spectacular Gion Matsuri in July (see box opposite). Because of its role as the guardian shrine of Gion, many geisha-related ceremonies are conducted here too.

6

GION MATSURI

Each July, Yasaka-jinja hosts one of Kyoto's biggest spectacles, the **Gion Matsuri** (祇園祭; ⓦ gionfestival.com). This festival is one of the oldest in the world, and, except for wars and one case of interference from the shogunate, it has been held annually since 970. Lasting from July 1 to July 29, Gion Matsuri is more like a series of mini-festivals, with the highlight being the July 17 **Yamahoko Junkō** – a grand procession of 32 floats decorated with Silk Road treasures. The procession's traditional, ancient route, however, has had to be altered in the postwar era to avoid present-day obstacles such as power lines.

Japan Kanji Museum

漢字ミュージアム, Kanji Myūjiamu • 551 Gion-machi Minamigawa • Tues–Sun 9.30am–4.30pm • ¥800 • ☎ 075 757 8686, ⓦ kanjimuseum.kyoto

Kyoto's newest museum, the **Japan Kanji Museum** is devoted to the history and culture of **Kanji**, the Chinese characters that were introduced into the Japanese writing system in the fifth century. Disappointingly, apart from an interesting exhibit on the "*Kanji* of the Year" – showing the character that represents the annual situation of Japan – the museum currently has no English explanations, and the steep entrance fee will entice only the most dedicated *kanji* enthusiasts.

Kennin-ji

建仁寺 • 584 Komatsu-chō • Daily 10am–4pm • ¥500 • ☎ 075 561 6363, ⓦ kenninji.jp

Tucked away behind the bustling streets and teahouses of Gion is **Kennin-ji**, Kyoto's oldest Zen temple. Founded in 1202 by the priest Yōsai, who is also recognised as having introduced tea drinking to Japan, Kennin-ji belongs to the Rinzai sect. Of note are its two remarkably different gardens: the **Chō-ontei** (潮音庭), complete with moss and maple trees; and a modern-looking square **rock garden** based on the calligraphy of a circle, triangle and square. Don't miss the fantastic painting of two dragons on the ceiling of the **Hattō hall**, created in 2002 for the temple's 800th anniversary.

Gion entertainment district

祇園花街, Gion Hanamachi

The area around Shijō-dōri, east of the Kamo-gawa and west of Yasaka-jinja, is known as the **Gion entertainment district**. Its narrow lanes, which lead off to the north and south of Shijōdōri, contain dozens of traditional teahouses and geisha houses, as well as modern bars and nightclubs. Historically, the area grew into a vibrant **pleasure quarter** as the teahouses, kabuki theatres and geisha performers flourished. By the middle of the eighteenth century, Gion was Kyoto's largest "floating world" (as the urban, pleasure-seeking culture of the Edo period was referred to), and you can still get a flavour of this if you walk south along picturesque Hanamikōji-dōri, where many of the lovely wooden buildings function as exclusive teahouses with geisha holding court. It's best after dark when red lanterns hang outside each secretive doorway, allowing the occasional glimpse down a stone-flagged entranceway; early evening is also a good time to spot geisha and trainee *maiko* arriving at the teahouses for an appointment.

Gion Kōbu Kaburenjō

祇園甲部歌舞練場 • Near the south end of the Hanamikoji-dōri • Gion Corner performances daily at 6pm & 7pm (Dec–Feb Fri–Sun only) • ¥3150 • ☎ 075 561 1119, ⓦ kyoto-gioncorner.com

The **Gion Kōbu Kaburenjō** theatre is the nightly venue for a touristy sampler of traditional arts known as **Gion Corner** (ギオンコーナー), which includes *maiko* dancing. Though it's far better to spend a little extra to see the real thing, this is an easy opportunity to watch brief extracts of court dance, *bunraku* puppet theatre, slapstick *kyōgen*, demonstrations of ikebana (flower arranging) and a tea ceremony. English-language guided commentary is available to rent at the entrance. During

6

THE GEISHA OF KYOTO

Often mistakenly considered by foreigners to be high-class prostitutes, **geisha** (which means "practitioner of the arts") are in fact refined women who entertain affluent men with their various accomplishments, such as singing, dancing, conversation and playing a traditional instrument such as a *shamisen* (three-string banjo). In Kyoto, geisha are called **geiko**, which literally means "child of the arts". Foreign-language conversation skills are also becoming important, as a result of the increase in overseas visitors to the *hanamachi* ("flower towns"), where geisha live and work.

It takes five years for an apprentice geisha – known as **maiko** – to master her art, training with the same focus and dedication as an Olympic athlete in the various arts, and living according to a strict code of dress and deportment. From a pre-World War II peak of eighty thousand there are now reckoned to be no more than a few thousand geisha left, the majority concentrated in Kyoto, the centre of the tradition. Though few fifteen-year-olds are tempted to sign up as apprentices, the internet is beginning to change this – some geisha houses have established websites to recruit apprentices, with successful results.

It's also becoming more common to be able to meet and talk to geisha and *maiko* in person. Many hotels and ryokan now offer exclusive **dinner shows** (see p.462), where it is possible to experience a little of the elegant yet fun entertainment that has until recently been the exclusive playground of wealthy male customers. There are also **walking tours** (see p.452) that provide a chance to learn more about geisha culture. Don't be fooled by daylight groups of "geisha" in Kyoto tourist spots: they are likely to be visitors who have paid for the chance to wear the distinctive make-up, wig and costume for a couple of hours.

April's Miyako Odori (see box, p.463) the theatre also hosts local geisha giving performances of traditional dance.

Shinbashi

新橋

Gion north of Shijō-dōri consists mainly of high-rise blocks packed with clubs, bars and restaurants. But walk up Kiritoshi, one block west of Hanamikōji-dōri, and you eventually emerge into another area of teahouses, known as **Shinbashi**. Although it comprises just two short streets, the row of slatted facades reflected in the willow-lined Shirakawa Canal makes a delightful scene, day or night.

Minami-za

南座 • Shijō-Ōhashi Higashi-zume • Opening times depend on the performance schedule; tickets can be bought at the box office or on the website • ☎ 075 561 1155, ⦿ shochiku.co.jp/play/minamiza

One of the most distinctive buildings in Gion, on the corner overlooking the Kamo-gawa, is the **Minami-za**. This famous kabuki theatre, the oldest in Japan, was established in the early seventeenth century, though last rebuilt in 1929. Kabuki has been an integral part of Gion life since the late sixteenth century when a female troupe started performing religious dances on the riverbanks. Eventually this evolved into an equally popular, all-male theatre, patronized by an increasingly wealthy merchant class. In December Minami-za is the venue for a major kabuki festival featuring Japan's most celebrated actors (see box, p.463). At the time of research, the theatre was temporarily closed for building maintainence.

Heian-jingū

平安神宮 • Nishi Tenno-chō • **Shrine** Daily: March–Sept 6am–6pm; Oct 6am–5.30pm; Nov–Feb 6am–5pm • Free • **Gardens** Daily: March–Sept 8.30am–5.30pm; Oct 8.30am–5pm; Nov–Feb 8.30am–4.30pm • ¥600 • ☎ 075 761 0221, ⦿ heianjingu.or.jp • 10min walk north of Higashiyama subway station, or take one of the many buses that run along Higashiōji-dōri

In the late nineteenth century, after Emperor Meiji moved his imperial court to Tokyo, Kyoto authorities felt the need to reaffirm their city's illustrious past. The result was **Heian-jingū**, an impressive though rather garish shrine modelled on a scaled-down version of the original eighth-century emperor's Hall of State. Completed in 1895 to commemorate the 1100th anniversary of the founding of the city, it was dedicated to emperors Kammu and Komei (1846–67), Kyoto's first and last imperial residents. The present buildings are reconstructions from 1979, but this is still one of Kyoto's most famous and picturesque landmarks.

The shrine's bright orange and white halls have an unmistakably Chinese air. Two wings embrace a huge, gravelled courtyard, at the north end of which sits the main worship hall flanked by a couple of pretty two-storey towers representing the protective "Blue Dragon" and "White Tiger".

6

The gardens

More interesting than the actual shrine are the **gardens** behind, which were also designed in Heian style. They're divided into four sections, starting in the southwest corner and ending beside a large pond in the east. The south garden features a collection of plants mentioned in Heian literature, while the middle (third) garden is famous for a row of stepping stones made from the columns of two sixteenth-century bridges. The more spacious east garden boasts the shrine's most attractive buildings – the graceful Taihei-kaku pavilion and its covered bridge.

Fureaikan

ふれあい館 • 9-1 Seishoji-chō • Daily 9am–5pm • Free • ☎ 075 762 2670, ⓦ miyakomesse.jp/fureaika

Heian-jingū faces south towards a large vermilion *torii* across a park dotted with museums and other municipal buildings. The most rewarding of these is the **Fureaikan**, a museum of traditional crafts in the basement of the modern Miyako Messe exhibition building. Well designed and informative, the museum provides an excellent introduction to the whole range of Kyoto crafts, from roof tiles and metalwork to textiles, confectionery and ornamental hairpins. You can also watch the craftsmen and women at work here, or join a Yuzen dyeing class (Sundays only).

MACHIYA

Kyoto's traditional townhouses, **machiya**, were built in a unique architectural style and remain an enduring symbol of the city's **cultural heritage**. These long, wooden houses are made up of a succession of rooms, connected by a single corridor, sometimes stretching as far back as 100m from the front. Their design is a result of the taxes that were levied on buildings during the Edo period according to the size of their street frontage. *Machiya* were generally built by merchants, encompassing a front shop space, living quarters in the middle and a warehouse at the rear. A courtyard garden was also included to aid the flow of light and air through the centre. Their long, thin shape lead to their colloquial name, *unagi no nedoko*, or "bedroom of eels".

Machiya were built almost entirely out of wood, which means that because of fire and earthquakes few that remain today are more than a century old. Some of the best examples are protected by law, but this has not stopped others being demolished at an alarming rate (some figures estimate by more than ten percent a year) since the end of World War II, as land values increased and modern development was encouraged. However, you can still walk along **Sannen-zaka** (see box, p.435), **Shinbashi** (see p.438) or through the **Nishijin** weaving district (see p.444) in Western Kyoto and find some almost complete rows of these beautiful old houses, each dark facade showing subtle variations on the same overall design. Note the distinctive gutter-guards made of curved bamboo, and the narrow-slatted ground-floor windows, which keep out both the summer heat and prying eyes.

Encouragingly, though some continue to be demolished, many *machiya* now seem to be experiencing a period of revitalization, having been remodelled as restaurants, guesthouses, boutiques and galleries. You can find a selection of the best of these in the accommodation and restaurant listings (see pp.452–455 & pp.455–460).

Hosomi Museum

細見美術館, Hosomi Bijutsukan • 6-3 Saishōji-chō • Tues–Sun: museum 10am–6pm; café 10am–10.30pm; tearoom 11am–5pm • ¥1200 • ☎ 075 752 5555, ⓦ emuseum.or.jp

The cube-shaped **Hosomi Museum** is a private establishment whose inspiring collection includes Japanese painting, sculpture and decorative art from all major historical periods. It hosts seasonal exhibitions that are curated from the museum's collection. On the top floor is a traditional tearoom, while downstairs the *Café Cube* serves tasty Italian dishes. The museum's Artcube shop is also worth a visit for its excellent selection of contemporary crafts.

National Museum of Modern Art

京都国立近代美術館, Kyōto Kokuritsu Kindai Bijutsukan • Enshoji-chō • Tues–Sun 9.30am–4.30pm, until 7.30pm on Fri & Sat • ¥430, special exhibitions ¥1500 • ☎ 075 761 4111, ⓦ momak.go.jp

The **National Museum of Modern Art** focuses on local and international twentieth-century artists. On display in this smart modern building are paintings, sculptures, ceramics, crafts and photos. The museum also has an excellent collection of contemporary *nihonga* (Japanese-style painting) and *yōga* (Western-style painting). From the fourth floor, there are good views over the large red *torii* in front of the museum.

Kyoto Municipal Museum of Art

京都市美術館, Kyoto-shi Bijutsukan • Enshoji-chō • Tues–Sun 9am–4.30pm • Free, prices vary for special exhibitions • ☎ 075 771 4107, ⓦ www.city.kyoto.jp/bunshi/kmma/en

The brick-built **Kyoto Municipal Museum of Art**, inaugurated in 1933, hosts special exhibitions from its vast collection of post-1868 fine arts. On display are Japanese and foreign artists, and it's also possible to see visiting exhibitions of Baroque treasures or painters such as Van Gogh. Check the museum's website for the exhibition schedule.

Murin-an

無鄰庵 • Kusakawa-chō • Daily: April–June, Sept & Oct 8.30am–6pm; July & Aug 7.30am–7pm; Nov 7.30am–6pm; Dec–March 8.30am–5pm • ¥410 • ☎ 075 771 3909, ⓦ murin-an-jp.html • Walk east along the canal from the large *torii* between the Municipal Museum of Art and the Museum of Modern Art

At the same time that Heian-jingū was being built, Marshal Yamagata Aritomo, a leading member of the Meiji government, was creating his villa, **Murin-an**, a delightful haven beside the Biwa Canal. Even today, as you look east from the garden to the Higashiyama hills beyond, it's hard to believe that you're in the middle of a busy city. Designed by Yamagata himself, the unusually naturalistic garden incorporates a meandering stream, pond and lawns in a surprisingly small space. There are also three buildings: take a look upstairs in the two-storey brick house, where parquet floors and wood panelling blend beautifully with Kanō-school painted screens.

Nanzen-ji

南禅寺 • Fukuchi-chō • Daily: March–Nov 8.40am–5pm; Dec–Feb 8.40am–4.30pm • Temple complex free, Konchi-in ¥400, San-mon ¥500, Hōjō ¥400, Tenju-an ¥500 • ☎ 075 771 0365, ⓦ nanzenji.com • A 10min walk from Keage subway station, or #5 bus to Nanzenji/Eikandō-michi

Nestled in the eastern hills near the Biwa Canal is the stately **Nanzen-ji**. This large, active temple complex belongs to the Rinzai sect of Zen Buddhism and is one of the most important in Kyoto. Nanzen-ji is also famous for its **shōjin-ryōri** (Buddhist vegetarian cuisine) and **yūdōfu** (simmered tofu), which can be sampled in a number of its sub-temples.

Konchi-in

金地院

Before entering the main Nanzen-ji compound, it's worth exploring its quiet sub-temple, **Konchi-in**, on the right in front of the first gate. An arched gate leads straight into one of Kyoto's most beautiful dry gardens – one of the rare works by famed landscape gardener Kobori Enshū, with documents to prove it. Its centrepiece is a large rectangle of raked gravel with two groups of rocks set against a bank of clipped shrubs. The right-hand, vertical rock group represents a crane, in balance with the horizontal "tortoise"-shaped rock topped by a twisted pine, on the left; both these animals symbolize longevity.

San-mon
三門

Erected in 1628 to commemorate the soldiers killed during the siege of Osaka Castle (see box, p.509), the looming bulk of **San-mon**, the main gate to Nanzen-ji, seems excessively monumental after Konchi-in. Aside from the pleasant views from the gate, the main reason to pay the entry fee is to see the fabulous ceiling of birds and celestial beings painted by Tosa- and Kanō-school artists.

The Hōjō
方丈

Nanzen-ji's prize treasures can be found in the **Hōjō** (main hall), up to the right behind the San-mon. These include a series of beautiful screens painted by Kanō Tanyū that depict tigers in a bamboo grove, and the "Leaping Tiger" garden, also attributed to Enshū, though the space here is much more confined than that of Konchi-in.

Tenju-an
天授庵

Located on the south side of the San-mon gate, the sub-temple **Tenju-an** is often overlooked as visitors rush to the Hōjō of Nanzen-ji. However, the rock garden here is superb, and there's also a charming garden around the koi pond.

Oku-no-in
奥の院

Oku-no-in, a small Shintō shrine, is hidden away behind the main temple buildings – follow the path along the aqueduct into the forest until you come to a mossy grotto with a small waterfall. You may be lucky enough to see pilgrims praying and performing sacred rituals here, even in the winter months.

Eikan-dō
永観堂 • 48 Eikandō-chō • Daily 9am–4pm; maple-leaf viewing Nov daily 8.30am–5pm & 5.30–8.30pm • ¥600, or ¥1000 in Nov • ☎ 075 761 0007, ⊕ eikando.or.jp

Also known as Zenrin-ji due to its unusual Amida statue, the temple of **Eikan-dō** was founded in the ninth century by a disciple of Kōbō Daishi (see p.527), but later became the headquarters of a sub-sect of Jōdoshū (Pure Land Buddhism). In 1082 the then head

---

THE PHILOSOPHER'S PATH

One of the prettiest walks in Kyoto, especially during cherry blossom season, is the 2km-long **Philosopher's Path** (哲学の道), which starts just north of Nanzen-ji (see p.440) and leads to Ginkaku-ji (see p.442). Its name refers to a respected philosopher, **Nishida Kitarō** (1870–1945), who took his daily constitutional along the path through the wooded hillside on his way to Kyoto University. Every so often stone bridges link it to the tranquil residential lanes on either side, while the occasional souvenir shop or quaint teashop provides an additional distraction. You can reach the southern end of the path by exiting Eikan-dō (see p.441), and taking the first right turn; you'll emerge about thirty minutes later beside the Ginkaku-ji bridge and the road leading up to the temple. From here you can pick up bus routes #5, #203 and #204, and Raku buses #100 and #102, which stop nearby at Ginkaku-ji-michi.

6

priest, Eikan, was circling the altar and chanting the *nembutsu*, "Praise to Amida Buddha", when the Amida statue stepped down and started walking in front of him. When Eikan stopped in his tracks, Amida turned to encourage him. Soon after, the priest commissioned the statue you see today of Amida looking over his left shoulder. Eikan-dō is also an extremely popular location for **maple-leaf viewing** during November. Viewing the floodlit leaves in the evening is quite magical, if you don't mind sharing the experience with large crowds; weekends during this period are best avoided.

Ginkaku-ji

銀閣寺 • 2 Ginkakuji-chō • Daily: March–Nov 8.30am–5pm; Dec–Feb 9am–4.30pm • ¥500 • ☎ 075 771 5725, ⓦ shokoku-ji.jp

The Temple of the Silver Pavilion, **Ginkaku-ji**, is one of Kyoto's most celebrated sights. Though modelled on its ostentatious forebear, the golden Kinkaku-ji (see p.444), this simple building sits quietly in the wings while the garden takes centre stage, dominated by a truncated cone of white sand whose severity offsets the soft greens of the surrounding stroll-garden.

Ginkaku-ji originally formed part of a much larger villa built in the fifteenth century for Shogun **Ashikaga Yoshimasa** (1436–90), the grandson of Kinkaku's Ashikaga Yoshimitsu. Interrupted by the Ōnin War (1467–77) and plagued by lack of funds, the work continued for thirty years, until Yoshimasa's death in 1490. During that time, however, it became the focal point of Japanese cultural life. Yoshimasa may have been a weak and incompetent ruler, but under his patronage the arts reached new heights of aesthetic refinement; in this mountainside retreat, significantly turned away from the city, he indulged his love of the tea ceremony, poetry and moon-viewing parties while Kyoto succumbed to war. After 1490, the villa became a Rinzai Zen temple, **Jishō-ji**, and eventually fires razed all except two buildings, one of which was the famous pavilion.

The garden

The approach to Ginkaku-ji creates a wonderful sense of anticipation as you're funnelled between tall, thick hedges down an apparently dead-end lane. Inside, you're directed first to the **dry garden**, comprising a raised, rippled "Sea of Silver Sand" – designed to reflect moonlight – and a large "moon-facing" cone of sand. The jury's out on whether these enhance the garden or intrude, but it's almost certain that they weren't in the original design, and were probably added in the early seventeenth century. Behind the cone to the west, the small, dark two-storey building with the phoenix topknot is **Ginkaku-ji**, or "Silver Pavilion", despite its lack of silver plating.

Shūgaku-in Rikyū

修学院離宮 • Shūgaku-in • Tours (in Japanese, with free English-language audio guide) Tues–Sun 1.30pm & 3pm • Free • Book tours in advance at the IHA office (see box, p.424); bring your passport • City Bus #5 to the Shūgaku-in Rikyū-michi stop on Shirakawa-dōri, from where the villa is a signed 10min walk to the east; alternatively, take a train on the private Eizan line from Demachiyanagi Station (in northeast Kyoto) to Shūgaku-in Station (10min), located a couple of minutes west of Shirakawa-dōri

In the foothills of Hiei-zan (see p.473) in the far northeast of Kyoto, the imperial villa of **Shūgaku-in Rikyū** boasts one of Japan's finest examples of garden design using "borrowed scenery" – a technique which incorporates the existing landscape to give the impression of a much larger space. Emperor Go-mizuno'o, who reigned between 1611 and 1629, built Shūgaku-in Rikyū in the late 1650s as a pleasure garden rather than a residence. Just fifteen years old when he ascended the throne, the artistic and highly cultured Go-mizuno'o fiercely resented the new shogunate's constant meddling in imperial affairs – not least being forced to marry the shogun's daughter. After Go-mizuno'o abdicated in 1630, however, the shogun encouraged him to establish an imperial villa. He eventually settled on the site of a ruined temple, Shūgaku-in, and set about designing a series of gardens, which survived more than a century of neglect before the government rescued them in the 1820s. Though some of the original pavilions have been lost, Go-mizuno'o's overall design remains – a delightfully naturalistic garden that blends seamlessly into the wooded hills.

The gardens

Shūgaku-in Rikyū is made up of three separate **gardens**, each in their own enclosure among the terraced rice fields. Of these, the top lake-garden is the star attraction. Climbing up the path towards the upper villa, you pass between tall, clipped hedges before suddenly emerging at the compound's highest point. An airy pavilion, **Rin-un-Tei**, occupies the little promontory, with views over the lake, the forested, rolling hills in the middle distance and the mountains beyond. As you walk back down through the garden, the grand vistas continue with every twist and turn of the path, passing the intricate Chitose bridge, intimate tea-ceremony pavilions and rustic boathouses.

North Kyoto

Kyoto's **northern area** stretches from the confluence of the Kamo-gawa and Takano-gawa towards the Kitayama district. The sites described below can be visited together in a day, incorporating a leisurely stroll along the banks of the Kamo-gawa – spectacular during the cherry blossom season – with visits to the Unesco World Heritage-listed twin shrines of **Shimogamo** ("lower Kamo") and **Kamigamo** ("upper Kamo"). Both shrines predate the founding of Kyoto, and house the deities that protect the city. They jointly hold the annual Aoi Matsuri festival (see box, p.463), as well as many other cultural events.

Shimogamo-jinja

下鴨神社 • 59 Izumigawa-chō • Daily 6.30am–5pm • Free • ☎ 075 781 0010, ⓦ shimogamojinja.or.jp • City Bus #4, #205 or a 10min walk from Keihan Demachiyanagi Station

The approach to the vermilion shrine buildings of tranquil **Shimogamo-jinja**, nestled in the ancient Tadasu-no-mori ("Forest of truth"), is along a gravel path flanked by a gurgling narrow stream. There have been structures on the site since the eighth century, although the main hall, the **Honden** (本殿), was rebuilt in the mid-nineteenth century. The shrine's peaceful, shady setting offers a welcome respite from the heat of summer, and offers stunning foliage colours in autumn. Sadly, financial pressures have forced it to lease some of its land, and a condominium building project is currently under way on its southern edges.

Kamigamo-jinja

上賀茂神社 • 339 Motoyama • Daily 6am–5pm • Free • ☎ 075 781 0011, ⓦ kamigamojinja.jp • City Bus #4, #9, #46 or 20min walk from Kitayama subway station

At the northern edge of Kyoto's city limits, **Kamigamo-jinja** has the feeling of a park thanks to the large lawn at its entrance, which is used for various festivals and rituals including horseback archery, horseracing and children's sumo. After entering through two large *torii*, you'll come to the closely grouped shrine buildings. Look out for the **tatesuna** – two cones of sand topped with sprigs of pine – located in front of the **Hosodono** hall. They are said to represent the yin and yang principle.

Kyoto Botanical Gardens

京都府立植物園, Kyoto Furitsu Shokubutsuen • Shimogamo Hangi-chō • Daily 9am–4pm; Conservatory 10am–3.30pm • ¥200 • ☎ 075 701 0141, ⓦ pref.kyoto.jp/plant • City Bus #4 or a short walk from Kitayama subway station

Established in 1924, the **Kyoto Botanical Gardens** are the oldest in Japan, with an impressive collection of more than 12,000 native and foreign plants. A circuit takes you round the gardens: look out for the sunken garden (a fusion of Oriental and European styles), the conservatory of tropical plants, the bonsai garden and the cherry blossom garden with around 500 varieties.

West Kyoto

Compared to east Kyoto, sights in the city's **western districts** are more dispersed, but it is worth devoting a day to this area, particularly the northwest fringes, where the city meets the encircling hills. The extravagant **Kinkaku-ji** (the Golden Pavilion), the enigmatic Zen garden of **Ryōan-ji** and the dry gardens of **Daitoku-ji** should all not be missed, while the **Nishijin** weaving district is an interesting area to explore with its streets of *machiya* (see box, p.439) and the sounds of the silk-weaving looms.

Nishijin Ori Kaikan

西陣織会館 • Horikawa-dōri Imadegawa Minami-iri • Daily 9am–6pm; kimono shows hourly 10.30am–4pm • Free; kimono rental ¥4000–13,000 • ☎ 075 451 9231, ⓦ nishijin.or.jp • Raku Bus #101 & #102 or City Bus #9 & #12

Kyoto has long been famous for the high quality of its **weaving** of kimono and *obi* sashes, and the centre of the city's textile industry is the Nishijin district, to the west of the Imperial Palace. The number of weaving businesses has decreased rapidly in recent years, from more than twelve hundred in 1980 to fewer than six hundred now, due to the economic conditions and reduced local demand. However, as you walk through the area today you'll still hear the clatter of looms in dozens of family-run workshops, and you can watch demonstrations of Nishijin weaving at the **Nishijin Ori Kaikan**. Their display rooms have examples of exquisite silk kimono and *obi*, and you can also watch the **kimono shows**, which, although touristy, are a good basic introduction to the different types of kimono. It's also possible to **rent** different types of kimono and be professionally photographed (reservation required).

Daitoku-ji

大徳寺 • 53 Daitokuji-chō • Daily 24hr • Free • ☎ 075 491 0019, ⓦ zen.rinnou.net • Roughly 1500m west of Kita-ōji subway station (on the Karasuma line), or can be reached by City Bus #101, #102, #205 and #206 – get off at Daitoku-ji-mae

Lying halfway between the Kamo-gawa and the Kitayama hills, **Daitoku-ji** is one of Kyoto's largest Zen temple complexes, with over twenty sub-temples in its large, walled compound. Of these only four are open to the public, but within them you'll find a representative sampler of the dry gardens (*kare-sansui*) for which Japanese Zen Buddhism is renowned. Daitoku-ji is also an excellent place to sample top-quality **shōjin-ryōri**, Buddhist vegetarian cuisine.

Daisen-in

大仙院 • Daily: March–Nov 9am–5pm; Dec–Feb 9am–4.30pm • ¥400 • ☎ 075 491 8346, ⓦ b-model.net/daisen-in/index.htm

Entering Daitoku-ji from the east, head through the huge San-mon gate to the sub-temple of **Daisen-in** in the north of the compound: if you can, it pays to visit early in the day before the crowds arrive. Of the temple's two gardens, the most famous is on the right as you enter the main hall – it replicates a Chinese landscape painting and uses carefully selected rocks, pebbles and a few scaled-down plants to conjure up jagged mountains.

Ryōgen-in

龍源院 • Daily 9am–4.20pm • ¥350 • ☎ 075 491 7635

Founded in the early sixteenth century, **Ryōgen-in** is home to Japan's smallest Zen rock garden. The minuscule Tōtekiko garden, on your right-hand side as you continue along the corridor from the entrance, consists of waves of sand round a rock, symbolizing a Zen saying that the harder a stone is thrown, the bigger the ripples. This sub-temple also contains four other gardens, including the mossy Ryugin-tei, which claims to be the oldest garden in the compound.

Kinkaku-ji

金閣寺 • 1 Kinkakuji-chō • Daily 9am–5pm • ¥400 • ☎ 075 461 0013, ⓦ shokoku-ji.jp • City Bus #101, #102, #205 & #206

West of Daitoku-ji, the wooded hills of Kitayama are home to **Kinkaku-ji**, the famous Temple of the Golden Pavilion. The pavilion originally formed part of a larger retirement villa built by the former Shogun Ashikaga Yoshimitsu (1358–1408) on the site of an earlier aristocratic residence; it was converted into a Zen temple on his death. A noted scholar of Chinese culture, Yoshimitsu incorporated various Chinese motifs into the pavilion and its surrounding garden, the focus of which is a lake studded with rocks and pine-covered islets.

Even the crowds can't diminish the impact of seeing the temple for the first time – a hint of gold glimpsed though the trees, and then the whole, gleaming apparition floating above the aptly named **Kyōko-chi** (Mirror Pond). If you're lucky enough to see it against the autumn leaves, or on a sunny winter's day after a dusting of snow, the effect is doubly striking. Note the different architectural styles of the pavilion's three floors and the phoenix standing on the shingle roof. It's an appropriate symbol: having survived all these years, Kinkaku-ji was torched in 1950 by an unhappy monk. The replica was finished in just five years, and in 1987 the building was gilded again, at vast expense.

Ryōan-ji

龍安寺 • 13 Goryōnoshita-machi • Daily: March–Nov 8am–5pm; Dec–Feb 8.30am–4.30pm • ¥500 • ☎ 075 463 2216, ⓦ ryoanji.jp • Take bus #12 or #59 from Kinkaku-ji, or walk southwest along Kitsuji-dōri for about 20min

While Kinkaku-ji is all about displays of wealth and power, the dry garden of **Ryōan-ji** hides infinite truths within its riddle of rocks and sand. Thought to date back to the late fifteenth century, and said by some to be the work of Sōami, the most famous artist, landscape gardener and tea ceremony master of the time, it was largely unknown until the 1930s. Now it's probably Japan's most famous garden, which means you're unlikely to be able to appreciate the Zen experience thanks to intrusive loudspeaker announcements and almost constant crowds, though very early morning tends to be better.

The **garden** consists of a long, walled rectangle of off-white gravel, in which fifteen stones of various sizes are arranged in five groups, some rising up from the raked sand and others almost completely lost. In fact, the stones are placed so that wherever you stand one of them is always hidden from view. The only colour is provided by electric-green patches of moss around some stones, making this the simplest and most abstract of all Japan's Zen gardens. It's thought that the layout is a *kōan*, or riddle, set by Zen masters to test their students, and there's endless debate about its meaning. Popular theories range from tigers crossing a river to islands floating in a sea of infinity. Fortunately, it's possible to enjoy the garden's perfect harmony and in-built tension without worrying too much about the meaning. Walk round the veranda of the main hall and you'll find a stone water basin inscribed with a helpful thought from the Zen tradition: "I learn only to be contented".

Kitano Tenmangū

北野天満宮 • Bakuro-chō • Daily: April–Sept 5am–6pm; Oct–March 5.30am–5.30pm • Free • ☎ 075 461 0005, ⓦ kitanotenmangu .or.jp • City Bus #50, #101 or #203

Established in the mid-tenth century, the large, stately Shintō shrine complex of **Kitano Tenmangū** is dedicated to Heian scholar Sugawara Michizane (845–903), deified as Tenjin, the "god of education". Students of all ages flock here at exam time to make offerings and buy good-luck charms. The current shrine buildings, including the main **Honden** (本殿) hall, the outer Ro-mon and the inner Sanko-mon, were built by Toyotomo Hideyori in 1607. The shrine hosts the monthly **Tenjin-san flea market** (see box, p.466) and is also an excellent place to view *ume* (plum) blossoms in early spring and *momiji* (maple) leaves in autumn.

Myōshin-ji

妙心寺 • Myōshinji-chō • Daily 9am–5pm • ¥500 • ☎ 075 463 3121, ⓦ myoshinji.or.jp • For the North Gate take City Bus #10, for the South Gate take City Bus #91 or #93; alternatively, it's a 10min walk from JR Hanazono Station

Formerly a palace for Emperor Hanazono (1297–1348), the large **Myōshin-ji** complex houses the head temple of the Zen Rinzai school, Myōshin-ji, as well as 46 sub-temples. The complex is vast and its main thoroughfare is connected by two imposing wooden gates, in the north and south. Myōshin-ji's notable sights include a wonderful cloud dragon painting on the ceiling of the **Hattō** (法堂) main hall and a seventh-century Buddhist temple bell (still in use) that's believed to be the oldest in Japan. Most of the sub-temples can't be visited and are hidden from view behind high walls, but two, **Taizō-in** and **Shunkō-in**, are open to the public.

Taizō-in

退蔵院 • Daily 9am–5pm • ¥500 • ☎ 075 463 2855, ⓦ taizoin.com

Dating from the fifteenth century, **Taizō-in** has two splendid gardens: a *karesansui* (dry rock garden) by the Muromachi-period artist Kanō Motonobu; and a modern pond garden. The temple owns one of Japan's oldest and most famous ink **paintings** – *Hyonenzu* ("Catching catfish with a gourd") by the fifteenth-century artist Josetsu, and also contains some exceptional modern **fusuma-e** (screen door paintings) by artist Murabayashi Yuki, commissioned in 2013.

Shunkō-in

春光院 • Meditation classes daily 9am (no reservation required), 10.40am & 1.30pm (for large groups with reservation) • Meditation class & tour ¥2500 • ☎ 075 462 5488, ⓦ shunkoin.com

Established in 1590, the **Shunkō-in** temple holds several important artefacts related to Christianity in Japan, including the bell of Nanban-ji, Kyoto's first Christian church, which was destroyed in 1587. Shunkō-in offers *shukubō* temple lodging (see p.455) and **meditation classes** in English; tours of the temple are only offered as part of the classes.

Kōryū-ji

広隆寺 • 32 Hachioka-chō • Daily 9am–5pm • ¥700 • ☎ 075 861 1461 • The easiest way to get here is to take a train on the private Keifuku Arashiyama line from Shijō-Ōmiya Station in central Kyoto to Uzumasa Station; alternatively, it's a 10min walk from Uzumasa Tenjingawa subway station. Coming from central Kyoto, City Bus #11 and Kyoto Bus #71, #72, #73 and #74 all stop outside Kōryū-ji

In the Uzumasa district in western Kyoto, due south of Ryōan-ji, **Kōryū-ji** is said to have been founded in the early seventh century by Nara's Prince Shōtoku (see p.486), making it one of Japan's oldest temples.

The **Kōdō** (Lecture Hall) – straight ahead once you've entered the compound from the Heian-period gate – dates from 1165 and is one of the oldest buildings in Kyoto. The three Buddhas inside are imposing enough, but Kōryū-ji's main attractions are the statues kept in the modern **Reihōden** (霊宝殿) Treasure House at the back of the compound. The "newest" of these images is a thirteenth-century statue of Prince Shōtoku aged 16, his sweet face framed by bun-shaped pigtails. The oldest is the exquisite **Miroku Bosatsu** (弥勒菩薩), the Future Buddha rendered as a bodhisattva pondering how to save mankind. Originally, it was probably gilded and it is thought to have been a gift to Shōtoku from the Korean court in the early seventh century; its soft, delicate features are certainly unlike any other Japanese images from the time.

Tōei Uzumasa Eiga-mura

東映太秦映画村 • 10 Higashi Hachioka-chō • Daily: March–Nov 9am–5pm; Dec–Feb 9.30am–4.30pm • ¥2200, plus extra charges for some attractions; ¥1100 for children • ☎ 075 864 7716, ⓦ toei-eigamura.com • The easiest way to get here is to take a train on the private Keifuku Arashiyama line from Shijō-Ōmiya Station in central Kyoto to Uzumasa Station. Alternatively, it's a 10min walk from Uzumasa Tenjingawa subway station. Coming from central Kyoto, City Bus #11 and Kyoto Bus #71, #72, #73 and #74 all stop outside Kōryū-ji, from where it's a short walk to Eiga-mura

Run by one of Japan's major film companies, **Tōei Uzumasa Eiga-mura** (Tōei Kyoto Studio Park) is a functioning **film studio** that doubles as a theme park. Sets are open to the public, who can look round the location where directors such as **Kurosawa Akira** filmed their classics. One of the indoor studios is usually in action, nowadays mostly making historical TV dramas, while the outdoor sets – an Edo-period street, thatched

farmhouses, Meiji-era Western-style buildings and so on – are enlivened by roaming geisha and sword-fighting samurai. You can also rent a costume and stroll around as a geisha, samurai or ninja (from ¥8500 with professional photos).

Katsura Rikyū

桂離宮 • Katsura • Tours (in Japanese, with free English-language audio guide) Tues–Sun 1.30pm, 2.30pm & 3.30pm • Free • Book tours in advance at the IHA office (see box, p.424); bring your passport • 20min walk from Katsura Station, on the private Hankyū line from central Kyoto; alternatively, City Bus #33 will drop you at Katsura Rikyū-mae, the first stop after crossing the river, from where it's a 5min walk north to the gate – this bus stop lies just outside the bus-pass zones, so if you want to save a few yen, get off before the river and walk over

Located on the west bank of the Katsura-gawa, **Katsura Rikyū** is a former imperial villa that was built in the early seventeenth century as a residence for the imperial Prince Toshihito, and then expanded by his son, Toshitada, in the 1650s. Toshihito was a highly cultured man, who filled his villa and garden with references to *The Tale of Genji* and other literary classics, while also creating what is considered to be Japan's first **stroll-garden**. As the name suggests, these gardens were to be enjoyed on foot – rather than from a boat or from a fixed viewpoint – and although they were designed to look "natural", in fact they were planned in minute detail, so that scenes unfold in a particular order as the viewer progresses. Focused on a large, indented lake, the Katsura garden is famed for its variety of footpaths and stone pavings, and for its stone lanterns. Several tea pavilions occupy prime spots around the lake, the most attractive of which is **Shokin-tei** (松琴亭).

Saihō-ji

西芳寺 • 56 Jingatani-chō • Daily • ¥3000 • ☎ 075 391 3631 • Reserve at least two months in advance through ⓦ www.saihoji -kokedera-reservation.com • From Arashiyama or Kyoto Station, take City Bus #28 or Kyoto Bus #63 or #73 to Matsuo Taisha-mae (松尾大社前), just west of the river, and walk for 15min

In a narrow, tree-filled valley 3km northwest of Katsura Rikyū, you'll find the voluptuous and tranquil moss gardens of **Saihō-ji**, also known as Koke-dera (苔寺), or the "Moss Temple". A visit to Saihō-ji needs planning, but don't be put off by the application process (see above) or the distance from central Kyoto – this temple is well worth visiting and a memorable experience. All visitors are required to attend a short Zen service during which you'll chant a sutra, trace the sutra's characters in *sumi-e* ink and finally write your name, address and "wish" before placing the paper in front of the altar. After that, you're free to explore the garden at your leisure.

Like Kōryū-ji (see p.446), the temple started life in the seventh century as one of Prince Shōtoku's villas. Soon after, Jōdo Buddhists adopted the site for one of their "paradise gardens", after which the gifted Zen monk, **Musō Kokushi**, was invited to take over the temple in 1338. The present layout dates mostly from his time, though the lakeside pavilion – the inspiration for Kinkaku-ji (see p.444) – and nearly all Saihō-ji's other buildings burnt down during the Ōnin Wars (1467–77). In fact, given the temple's history of fire, flooding and periods of neglect, it seems unlikely that today's garden bears much resemblance to Musō's. Whatever their origin, the swathes of soft, dappled **moss** – some 120 varieties in all – are a magical sight, especially after the rains of May and June, when the greens take on an extra intensity.

ARRIVAL AND DEPARTURE
KYOTO

BY PLANE

The nearest airports to Kyoto are Kansai International Airport (KIX), which handles both international and domestic flights, and Osaka International Airport (also known as Itami Airport), which, despite the name, only handles domestic flights.

KANSAI AIRPORT

Kansai International Airport (KIX; 関西国際空港; ☎ 072 455 2500, ⓦ kansai-airport.or.jp) is on a man-made island in Osaka Bay, some 35km south of Osaka city centre, and approximately 100km from Kyoto. The international departure lounge is on the fourth floor and domestic

departures are on the second floor. Terminal 2 (KIX; 第2タ
ーミナル; ☎072 455 2911, ⓦkansai-airport.or.jp/t2) is
currently only used by Peach Aviation for Asian and some
domestic destinations. Shuttle buses connect Terminal 2
with the main building, Kansai International Airport
Terminal 1.

Destinations Fukuoka (6 daily; 1hr); Kagoshima (3 daily;
1hr 10min); Nagasaki (2 daily; 1hr 10min); Naha (11 daily;
1hr 15min); Sapporo (10 daily; 2hr); Sendai (3 daily; 1hr
10min); Tokyo Haneda (12 daily; 1hr); and Tokyo Narita (9
daily; 1hr 15min).

Trains to Kyoto If you're coming direct from Kansai
International Airport, the quickest and easiest option is a
JR Haruka Limited Express train, which whisks you direct
to Kyoto in just over an hour (¥3370 reserved, ¥2850
unreserved); JR passes are valid on this service for
unreserved seats. JR West sells a ICOCA+HARUKA prepaid
card for tourists, which includes a good discount on the
Haruka ticket (see ⓦwestjr.co.jp/global/en/ticket/icoca
-haruka for more details). For those not travelling with a
JR Pass, a cheaper option is to take an express train from
the airport to Osaka Station, changing there to an express
train on the JR Kyoto line; this takes a little under 2hr and
costs about ¥1800.

Buses to Kyoto Comfortable airport limousine buses do
the journey into Kyoto in under 2hr, traffic permitting, and
terminate on the south (Hachijō-guchi) side of Kyoto
Station (1–2 hourly, 6.20am–11.55pm; ¥2550 from
ticket vending machine). If you're heading from Kyoto
direct to Kansai Airport, it's a good idea to reserve your
transport in advance. Buses depart (1–2 hourly,
4.30am–9.40pm, 1hr 45min; ¥2550; ☎075 682 4400)
from outside the Avanti department store, just south of
Kyoto Station. Tickets are available from the ground floor
of the nearby *Hotel Keihan Kyoto*.

Taxi shuttles There are two "door-to-door" taxi shuttle
buses: the MK Skygate shuttle (¥3600; ☎075 778 5489,
ⓦmktaxi-japan.com), and the Yasaka Kansai Airport
Shuttle (¥3500; ☎075 803 4800, ⓦwww.yasaka.jp
/english/shuttle). The ride time varies, depending on the
traffic, but will be calculated to get you there on time for
check-in. Reservations for both services must be made at
least 2 days in advance.

OSAKA INTERNATIONAL AIRPORT

Osaka International Airport (ITM; 大阪国際空港;
☎06 6856 6781, ⓦosaka-airport.co.jp) is located in Itami,
10km north of Osaka city centre, and around 50km
southwest of Kyoto.

Destinations Akita (6 daily; 1hr 30min); Aomori (6 daily;
1hr 40min); Fukuoka (12 daily; 1hr); Kagoshima (13 daily;
1hr 10min); Kumamoto (11 daily; 1hr 5min); Miyazaki
(11 daily; 1hr 5min); Nagasaki (7 daily; 1hr 10min);
Naha (5 daily; 1hr 15min); Niigata (12 daily; 1hr 10min);

Ōita (8 daily; 1hr); Sapporo (10 daily; 2hr); Sendai (16 daily;
1hr 10min); Tokyo Haneda (30 daily; 1hr); Tokyo Narita
(4 daily; 1hr 15min); and Yamagata (3 daily; 1hr 20min).

Trains to Kyoto The easiest way to get to Kyoto by train
from Osaka International Airport is to ride the monorail to
Hankyū Hotarugaike Station, then take a train to Juso
Station where you can change to a Kyoto-bound express
train (72min; ¥650). JR Pass holders will need to take the
Hankyū line to its terminus in Umeda and then walk to JR
Osaka Station for a Kyoto-bound express train.

Buses to Kyoto Direct limousine buses run between the
airport and Kyoto Station (every 20min, 5.50am–6.55pm;
55min; ¥1310; ☎06 6844 1124).

Taxi shuttles The MK Skygate shuttle (☎075 778 5489,
ⓦmktaxi-japan.com; ¥3600) has services between Kyoto
and Osaka International Airport. Reservations must be
made more than 2 days in advance.

BY TRAIN

Kyoto Station Most visitors arrive in Kyoto at the JR
Station. The JR local lines all converge here, and Kyoto is
also linked by Shinkansen to Tokyo and Nagoya, in the east,
and Osaka, Hiroshima and Fukuoka, to the west. The
terminus for the Kintetsu Kyoto line – which links the city
to Nara, Kōya-san and Ise – is also located here, next to the
Shinkansen station.

Destinations Amanohashidate (7 daily; 2hr 30min);
Fukuoka (Hakata Station; 1–2 hourly; 2hr 50min); Hikone
(every hour; 50min); Himeji (1–3 hourly; 50min);
Hiroshima (1–2 hourly; 1hr 40min); Ise (hourly; 2hr);
Kanazawa (1–2 hourly; 2hr); Kansai International (every
30min; 1hr 15min); Kashikojima (hourly; 2hr 45min); Kobe
(& Shin-Kōbe) (1–3 hourly; 30min); Nagoya (every 15min;
40min); Nara (every 15–20min; 40min); Osaka (& Shin-
Osaka) (every 15min; 17min); Toba (hourly; 2hr 20min);
Tokyo (every 15min; 2hr 10min); Toyama (hourly; 2hr
40min); Uji (every 10–15min; 20min).

BY BUS

Long-distance buses arrive at and depart from terminals
either side of Kyoto Station.

JR Highway buses (ⓦnishinihonjrbus.co.jp) to
Hiroshima, Kanazawa, Kochi, Matsue, Nagano, Nagoya,
Takamatsu and Tokyo depart from a stand on the north side
of the station.

Keihan Bus (ⓦkeihanbus.jp) uses a terminal on the
south side of Kyoto Station, outside the *Hotel Keihan Kyoto*;
Keihan services cover Fukuoka, Iga, Kanazawa, Matsue,
Okayama, Tokushima, Tokyo and Tottori.

Willer Express (ⓦwillerexpress.com) runs services to
Fukuoka, Hiroshima, Matsuyama, Niigata, Takayama and
Tokyo from the Hachijō exit on the south side of the station.
Destinations Amanohashidate (2 daily; 2hr 40min);
Fukuoka (1 daily; 11hr); Hiroshima (4 daily; 6hr 45min); Iga

6

6

(2 daily; 1hr 30min); Kanazawa (5 daily; 4hr); Kochi (2 daily; 6hr); Kumamoto (1 daily; 11hr); Matsue (4 daily; 5hr); Matsuyama (1 daily; 9hr 35min); Nagasaki (1 daily; 11hr); Nagano (1 daily; 7hr); Nagoya (16 daily; 2hr 30min); Niigata (1 daily; 9hr); Okayama (3 daily; 4hr 30min); Takamatsu (7 daily; 3hr 30min); Takayama (4 daily; 4hr); Tokushima (7 daily; 3hr); Tokyo (6 daily; 8hr); Tottori (3 daily; 4hr); and Yokohama (1 daily; 7hr 30min).

GETTING AROUND

Walking is the best way to explore Kyoto so that you can avoid using the bus network, which is very congested throughout the year but especially during spring and autumn's peak visitor seasons. It's also easier to wander the narrow back lanes on foot. Public transport is useful for getting to further-flung sights.

BY SUBWAY

The lines Kyoto's two subway lines (5.29am–11.49pm; ¥210–350) are the quickest way to scoot around the city. The Karasuma line runs from southerly Takeda (where it connects with the Kintetsu line), via Kyoto Station and Kita-ōji, to Kokusai Kaikan in the north, while the Tōzai line starts at Uzumasa Tenjingawa in the west and cuts east through Sanjō-Keihan and Higashiyama to Rokujizō in the southeast suburbs; the two lines intersect at Karasuma-Oike Station.

Tickets As well as single tickets (minimum fare ¥210), you can buy various passes (see box below).

BY TRAIN

Hankyū railway Trains on Hankyū railway's Kyoto line for Osaka (Umeda) run beneath the city centre from Kawaramachi Station west along Shijō-dōri. A branch line heads northwest from Katsura Station in west Kyoto to Arashiyama, where it's a short walk across the Togetsu-kyō bridge to the main part of town.

JR The JR Sagano line runs west from Kyoto Station to Saga-Arashiyama Station. The JR Nara line runs south through the southern Kyoto suburbs and Uji, and the JR Biwa-ko line runs east through Yamashima, Otsu and Hikone.

Keifuku Railway Also known as Randen, the Keifuku Railway services Arashiyama from Shijō-Ōmiya Station, and Kitano-Hakubai-chō Station in northwest Kyoto.

Eizan line In northeast Kyoto, Demachiyanagi is the terminus for the Eizan line, which covers Shūgaku-in Rikyū and Yase-yūen, one of the routes up Hiei-zan (see p.473).

Keihan mainline services Keihan mainline services start from a separate station in Demachiyanagi and then head south via Sanjō-Keihan to Osaka (Yodoyabashi and Nakanoshima).

Kintetsu-Kyoto line Trains on the Kintetsu-Kyoto line depart from the south side of Kyoto Station, from where they link into the main Kintetsu network, with services to Nara, Kōya-san and Ise.

BY BUS

Kyoto's bus system is relatively easy to use. The buses are colour-coded, the majority show their route numbers on the front and the most important stops are announced in English, either on the electronic display or over the internal speakers. Within the city there's a flat fare of ¥230, which you pay on leaving the bus. You enter via the back door, where you may need to take a numbered ticket if the bus is going into the suburbs, though the flat fare still applies within the central zone. Most services stop running around 11pm, or earlier on less popular routes.

Bus companies Services are run by Kyoto City Bus and the far less comprehensive Kyoto Bus. You'll need to use Kyoto Bus services for Ōhara and Shūgaku-in, but otherwise you

---

KYOTO TRANSPORT PASSES

There are a number of transport passes that make travelling in Kyoto more convenient and economical, especially if you are switching between trains and buses.

Traffika Kyoto Card A stored-fare card (¥1000 or ¥3000) that can be used to buy subway tickets and tickets on City Bus services; available from the Kyoto Bus Information Center in front of Kyoto Station, as well as from train and subway stations.

Surutto Kansai Card Another stored-fare card that can be used on City Buses, the subway, and the Keihan and Hankyū train lines; it's available in ¥1000, ¥2000, ¥3000 and ¥5000 denominations from station vending machines and bus information centres.

Kyoto Sightseeing Pass Allows travel on City Buses, the subway and Kyoto Buses within an area marked on

the bus maps in white (one-day ¥1200; two-day ¥2000). Available from train and subway stations and the Kyoto Bus Information Center, and can also be purchased from bus drivers.

Kansai Thru Pass If you are planning day-trips from Kyoto to other parts of Kansai, this pass (two days ¥4000; three days ¥5200; ⓦ surutto.com/tickets /kansai_thru_english.html) is a good option for tourists, as it allows you to use almost any bus, subway or private railway in the region. It can be purchased from major tourist information centres and bus information centres by showing your passport.

can stick to City Bus for the central districts, including Arashiyama.

Maps Before leaping on board, get hold of the English-language Bus Navi route map from the Kyoto Tourist Information Centre, or the Bus Information Center in front of Kyoto Station. This map shows the central zone boundary and routes operated by both Kyoto City Bus and Kyoto Bus.

Terminals and routes The main bus terminal is outside Kyoto Station's Karasuma exit. Most routes loop around the city; the most useful is #206, with stops near the National Museum, Gion, Heian-jingū, Daitoku-ji and Nijō-jō. Buses running clockwise leave from boarding platform B, and anticlockwise from boarding platform A. The other major terminals are at Sanjō-Keihan, in east Kyoto, and Kita-ōji in the north. Many routes also converge centrally at Shijō Kawaramachi.

Raku tourist buses The Raku bus routes are tourist buses that stop at major sightseeing spots and have English-language commentary, and are ideal if you want to cover a lot of sights in a short amount of time. Buses #100 and #101 start from Kyoto Station, with Raku #100 travelling up the east side of Kyoto from Kiyomizu-dera to Ginkakuji, and Raku #101 heading towards Nijo and then Kinkakuji. Raku #102 starts from Ginkakuji and then heads across to Kinkakuji, where it terminates. The buses operate 8am–5pm, with route #100 buses running every 10min, but #101 and #102 only running every 15 or 30min. You can use any of the prepaid card systems (see box opposite) on the Raku buses, or it's ¥230 per ride.

Tickets The bus companies offer a range of discount tickets. The simplest, *kaisūken*, are booklets of five ¥220 tickets available for ¥1000 at the bus terminals, and valid on all buses. Next up are the one-day passes (*shi-basu ichi-nichi jyōshaken*, ¥500), which allow unlimited travel on City Bus services within the central zone; these are available at information centres, hotels, bus terminals and from the bus driver. To validate the pass, put it through the machine beside the driver when you get off the first bus – after that, just show it as you exit. Finally, there's the Kyoto Sightseeing Pass (see box opposite).

BY BIKE

Renting a bike is a viable option for exploring central Kyoto, though not much use along the eastern hills, where you're better off walking. The bike rental outlets listed below have terminals near Kyoto Station. Be aware that Kyoto City regularly impounds bicycles parked in prohibited zones, such as in front of train and subway stations, and it costs ¥2300, and a lot of effort, to recover them. Check ⓦ kyochari-navi .jp/churin/index.html for official bicycle parks.

Fuune Rental Cycles ⓣ 075 371 7800, ⓦ fuune.jp. Has a good range of electric (¥1800/day) and non-electric bicycles (¥1000/day), which can be returned by 10am the next day. Daily: April–Nov 8.30am–7pm; Dec–March 9am–6.30pm.

Kyoto Cycling Tour Project ⓣ 075 354 3636, ⓦ kctp .net. Rents various kinds of bikes from ¥1000/day, and also arranges tours (see p.452). Daily 9am–7pm.

Kyoto Eco Trip ⓣ 075 691 0794, ⓦ kyoto-option.com. The most basic bicycles cost ¥800/day, and electric bicycles are ¥2000/day. Daily 9am–6pm.

BY CAR

Car rental outlets with offices near Kyoto Station include Nippon Rent-a-Car (ⓣ 075 661 6680, ⓦ nipponrentacar .co.jp), Nissan Rent-a-Car (ⓣ 075 661 4123, ⓦ nissan-rentacar .com/english), Eki Rent-a-Car (ⓣ 075 681 3020, ⓦ www .ekiren.co.jp), and Europcar (ⓣ 075 681 7779, ⓦ europcar.jp).

BY TAXI

Taxis are useful for hopping short distances – the minimum fare is ¥580 for 2km. In 2016 Kyoto initiated a new "Foreigner Friendly" taxi service for visitors – with drivers speaking either English or Chinese – at Kyoto Station (9am–5pm); the stand is adjacent to the regular taxi stand on both sides of the station. Alternatively, MK Taxi (ⓣ 075 778 4141, ⓦ mktaxi-japan.com) and Yasaka Taxi (ⓣ 075 842 1212, ⓦ www.yasaka.jp) are both reliable services; since drivers won't always speak English, it's useful to have your destination written down in Japanese.

INFORMATION

Tourist information Kyoto's main source of information is the Kyoto Tourist Information Centre (daily 8.30am–7pm; ⓣ 075 343 0548), on the second floor of Kyoto Station next to the main entrance of Isetan department store. In the city centre, there's a small tourist information office on the west side of Kawaramachi, between Shijō and Sanjō. In eastern Kyoto, near Nanzen-ji, Kyoto International Community House (9am–9pm; closed Mon; ⓣ 075 752 3010, ⓦ kcif .or.jp/en) is aimed primarily at foreign students and longer-term residents, but will happily assist tourists where possible. Also in eastern Kyoto, the Kyoto Handicraft Center (10am–7pm; ⓣ 075 761 8001, ⓦ kyotohandicraftcenter .com) on Marutamachi has a tourist information office.

Maps Detailed bilingual maps of Kyoto are available free from the Kyoto Tourist Information Centre (see above).

Listings The free monthly tourist magazine, *Kyoto Visitor's Guide* (ⓦ kyotoguide.com), is the best source of information regarding what's on in Kyoto and also has useful maps for sightseeing. It includes details of festivals and cultural events; you can usually pick it up in tourist information offices, major hotels and other tourist haunts. The free monthly *Kansai Scene* (ⓦ kansaiscene.com) magazine also has a good listings section, with the latest on Kyoto events and exhibitions.

Websites Some useful online resources for general Kyoto travel and cultural information are Kyoto Travel Guide (ⓦ kyoto.travel) and Mago-no-Te (ⓦ kyoto-magonote.jp/en).

TOURS

BUS TOURS

Kyoto World Heritage Tour ☎ 075 672 2100, ⓦ kyoto -lab.jp/hirubus. Hop-on, hop-off service, which loops around Kyoto's major historical sites (¥2300/person; usually Sat, Sun & national holidays but daily during busy seasons, 8.40am–5.50pm). It runs approximately hourly, with audio commentary (¥500 extra) on the bus between sites.

Kyoto Night Cruise Bus Tour ☎ 075 662 7100, ⓦ kyoto-lab.jp/nc/rve.php. The same route as the above, but in the evening (¥2100/person; Thurs–Sat 7.50– 9.25pm), though it's not a hop-on, hop-off service.

CYCLING TOUR

Kyoto Cycling Tour Project ☎ 075 354 3636, ⓦ kctp .net. Daily guided English tours of Kyoto's backstreets and hidden alleyways (3hr; from ¥5500/person for groups of four), as well as tours of Unesco World Heritage Sites in east and west Kyoto (7hr; ¥8900/person for groups of four). The cost includes bicycle rental and any admission fees. Reservations must be made three days in advance.

FOOD TOUR

Haru Cooking School ☎ 090 4284 7176, ⓦ kyoto -cooking-class.com. This outfit guides small groups on a 90min tour through Nishiki-kōji street market (see p.429) in conjunction with their cooking classes (weekly from noon; ¥4000/person for groups of two to six people). As well as learning about the essential ingredients of Kyoto cuisine, you'll have plenty of chance to sample an array of pickles, dried fish and traditional sweets.

JINRIKISHA TOURS

Tours in traditional *Jinrikisha* – two-seater rickshaws (the name means "man-powered vehicle") – depart from *jinrikisha* stations in front of Heian-jingū near Nanzen-ji (☎ 075 533 0444, ⓦ ebisuya.com) and at Arashiyama (☎ 075 864 4444) on the northwest side of Togetsu-kyō bridge, and cover three routes: Kiyomizu-dera to Yasaka-jinja, Heian-jingū to Ginkaku-ji, and around Arashiyama. Tours (daily 9.30am–sunset) last from 12min (¥3000 for one person, ¥4000 for two) to 2hr (¥23,500 for one, ¥32,500 for two), depending on the route and whether you want to stop and take photos. Some of the *jinrikisha*-pullers speak English and will be able to give you a commentary on the sights.

WALKING TOURS

Cool Kyoto Walking Tour ☎ 077 377 5514, ⓦ cool -kyoto.net. A fun, theatrical-style exploration of Kyoto on foot, from Teramachi to the Imperial Park area, with "last samurai" Joe Okada (Sat 10am–3pm; ¥4000/person).

The Deepest Kyoto Tour ⓦ deepestkyototour.com. Small-group tours of *machiya* townhouse architecture and Kiyomizu pottery artisans (Wed 1–3pm; ¥3000/person). They also occasionally conduct more specialized artisan tours – check the website for details.

Geisha Culture Walking Lecture ⓦ kyotosightsand nights.com. Run by long-term resident Peter Macintosh, this 90min, small-group tour (¥3000/person) winds through the backstreets of Gion and Miyagawa-chō districts, and provides a chance to learn about where geisha live, study and entertain, accompanied by Macintosh's personal anecdotes.

Waraido ☎ 075 752 7070, ⓦ waraido.com/walking /index.html. Waraido's Daytime Walking Tour takes small groups on a slow amble through southern Kyoto from Higashi-Hongan-ji to the eastern hills (March–Nov Mon, Wed & Fri, except national holidays, 10am to mid-afternoon; ¥2000/person). They also run the Gion Night Walking Tour, from Shinbashi to Gion Corner, in collaboration with Kyoto City Tourism Association (Mon, Wed & Fri: March–Nov 6–7.40pm; Dec–Feb 5–6.40pm; ¥1000/person; reservations not required); this offers a basic introduction to Kyoto geisha culture and points of interest, though groups tend to be large and obtrusive.

ACCOMMODATION

Kyoto's accommodation options range from basic guesthouses, capsule hotels, youth hostels and temple lodgings (*shukubō*) to luxurious international **hotels** and top-class **ryokan**. One night in a full-blown Kyoto ryokan, enjoying some of the world's most meticulous service, is an experience not to be missed. Increasingly, old Kyoto houses (*machiya*) are being developed into **guesthouses**, offering visitors the chance to experience traditional Kyoto life. It's essential to make **reservations** at these places as far in advance as possible, but all accommodation in Kyoto gets very busy in spring and autumn, at holiday weekends and around the major festivals (see box, p.463); room rates may rise considerably during these times. In terms of **where to stay**, Central Kyoto is a popular choice, with its easy access to the main shops and nightlife as well as good transport links to sights around the city, while the area around the station may not be as pleasant as other parts of Kyoto but it's undoubtedly convenient, with an abundance of inexpensive accommodation. It's also worth considering east Kyoto, where many places are in quieter, more attractive surroundings but also within walking distance of Gion and the city centre. The range of accommodation in northwest Kyoto is increasing and the area is a good base for exploring the northern part of the city, as well as Arashiyama.

6

CENTRAL KYOTO

9h Nine Hours ナインアワーズ Teramachi-dōri Shijō-sagaru ☎075 353 7337, ⓦninehours.co.jp; map p.426. The design of this capsule hotel is minimalist bordering on sci-fi, and the capsules are actually quite spacious sleeping pods. After check-in, female and male guests take separate elevators to pods and shower rooms. Impeccably clean and comfortable and in a convenient central location. ¥4900

First Cabin ファーストキャビン 4F 331 Kamiyanagi-chō ☎075 361 1113, ⓦfirst-cabin.jp; map p.426. First-class air-travel-themed capsule hotel, for both men and women, close to Karasuma-Shijō, with good facilities and friendly staff. Cabins are bigger than the business capsules and all have their own TV and internet connections. Clean bathrooms and comfortable café/bar facilities. ¥3700

Hiiragiya 柊家旅館 Fuyachō Anekoji-agaru ☎075 221 1136, ⓦhiiragiya.co.jp/en; map p.426. One of the city's most famous ryokan, since the mid-nineteenth century it has hosted the rich and famous, including Elizabeth Taylor and Charlie Chaplin. You need to book well in advance, but it's worth it for a quintessential Kyoto experience. Choose between the charming traditional wing and the stylish modern wing. ¥69,120

★Itoya Hotel 糸屋ホテル Karasuma Matsubara-agaru ☎075 365 1221, ⓦitoyahotel.com/en; map p.426. Pleasant boutique hotel in a nice central location with friendly staff. The stylish rooms are compact but comfortable. 🛜 ¥27,000

Kyoto Brighton Hotel 京都ブライトンホテル Shinmachi Nakadachiuri-dōri ☎075 441 4411, ⓦkyotobrighton.com; map p.426. Top-end hotel in a quiet residential area just a stone's throw from the Imperial Palace, with particularly spacious and comfortable rooms. The service is efficient and friendly. The only downside is the rather pricey in-house restaurants. 🛜 ¥29,000

Mitsui Garden Hotel Kyoto Sanjō 三井ガーデンホテル京都三条 80 Mikura-chō, Sanjō Karasuma Nishi-iru, Nakagyō-ku ☎075 256 3331, ⓦwww.gardenhotels.co.jp/en/kyoto-sanjo; map p.426. Conveniently located very close to Karasuma-Sanjō shopping area, this reasonable mid-range hotel is surprisingly good value. There's an onsen bath that is open to guests in the morning and evening. 🛜 ¥19,000

Hotel Monterey ホテルモントレ京都 Karasuma Sanjō-sagaru ☎075 251 7111, ⓦhotelmonterey.co.jp/en/htl/kyoto; map p.426. With a stylish, classic European interior, Japanese and French restaurants, as well as a wedding chapel and a "British Library" themed café, this hotel is a reliable choice for location and convenience. 🛜 ¥18,000

Nishiyama Ryokan 西山旅館 433 Yamamoto-chō ☎075 222 1166, ⓦryokan-kyoto.com; map p.426. More a hotel than a ryokan, with Japanese and Western-style rooms, the *Nishiyama* is comfortable, good value and close to all the downtown shopping and sightseeing areas. There's an onsen bath in the basement and free monthly cultural events (tea ceremony, calligraphy) held in the lobby. 🛜 ¥40,000

★Palace-Side Hotel ザ・パレスサイドホテル Karasuma Shimodachiuri-agaru ☎075 415 8887, ⓦpalacesidehotel.co.jp; map p.426. Large hotel overlooking the Imperial Palace, with good views from the higher, more expensive rooms. Nothing fancy, and the rooms are small, but it's excellent value for the location, just 3min north of Marutamachi subway station. There are substantial discounts if you stay six days or more. ¥10,200

★Piece Hostel Sanjo ピースホステル三条 531 Asakura-chō ☎075 746 3688, ⓦpiecehostel.com; map p.426. Central Kyoto's best budget option, this stylish hostel is in an excellent location and is clean and well organized. The emphasis is on shared space for travellers to communicate with each other. Breakfast included. 🛜 Dorms ¥2800, doubles ¥9000

The Screen ザ・スクリーン Teramachi-dōri Marutamachi-sagaru ☎075 252 1113, ⓦscreen-hotel.jp/en; map p.426. Kyoto's first major boutique hotel is tastefully decorated with contemporary designs of traditional Kyoto crafts – from the lamps to the upholstery. Rooms are spacious and equipped with espresso machines. The in-house French restaurant uses local ingredients, and the champagne terrace has great views over the Imperial Park. 🛜 ¥30,000

★Tawaraya 俵屋旅館 Fuyachō Anekoji-agaru ☎075 211 5566, 🖷075 221 2201; map p.426. The epitome of Kyoto elegance and refinement, this exquisite and exclusive ryokan is so traditional that it doesn't even have a website. Impeccable service, and gorgeous interior gardens. ¥111,780

Urban Hotel Kyoto Nijo Premium アーバンホテル京都二条プレミアム 25-5 Mawari Minami-machi ☎075 813 1177, ⓦuh-urban.com/nijo; map p.426. Close to JR Nijō Station and the subway, this smart new hotel has comfortable rooms decorated with kimono fabric. On the top floor there's a shared bath for the use of guests only. The in-house restaurant, which can be entered from the street, is excellent. 🛜 ¥17,280

Yoshikawa Ryokan 吉川旅館 Tominokoji Oike-sagaru ☎075 221 5544, ⓦkyoto-yoshikawa.co.jp; map p.426. Intimate, traditional ryokan that's renowned for its tempura *kaiseki* cuisine (see p.456). Cypress-wood baths, an immaculate garden and all the understated luxury you could want in a traditional setting. 🛜 ¥97,200

AROUND KYOTO STATION

★Capsule Ryokan カプセル旅館京都 204 Tsuchihashi-chō ☎075 344 1510, ⓦcapsule-ryokan-kyoto.com; map p.430. Modern-style budget ryokan that boasts the world's first tatami capsules with futons (and mini-TVs) and en-suite

6

rooms for two. Security lockers and tea/coffee-making facilities. Managed by the same friendly and efficient team who run *Tour Club* (see below). 🛜 Capsules **¥3500**, doubles **¥7980**

Hotel Granvia Kyoto ホテルグランヴィア京都 657 Higashi-Shiokoji-chō ☎ 075 344 8888, �🌐 granviakyoto.com; map p.430. Deluxe hotel incorporated into the Kyoto Station building, with rooms on the upper floors overlooking southern Kyoto, and decorated with artworks by local artists. Facilities include a good range of restaurants and bars, an indoor swimming pool, boutiques and business suites. 🛜 **¥28,000**

★**Lower East Nine Hostel** ロワーイーストナインホステル 32 Minami Karasuma-chō ☎ 075 644 9990, �🌐 lowereastnine.com; map p.430. Stylish new hostel south of Kyoto Station with an in-house coffee counter (lattes ¥400). Dorms have wide bunk beds and shared bathrooms, while there's a choice of bunks or beds for the twin rooms. 🛜 Dorms **¥3800**, twins **¥10,000**

★**Piece Hostel Kyoto** ピースホステル京都 21-1 Higashi Kujō Higashisanno-chō ☎ 075 693 7077, �🌐 piecehostel.com; map p.430. Sleek modern backpacker hostel on the south side of Kyoto Station. Dorms and private rooms are functional, clean and well equipped. Shared spaces include a BBQ terrace and lounge with a library of art books. Breakfast included. 🛜 Dorms **¥2900**, doubles **¥7600**

★**Shizuya Ryokan** しづや旅館 460 Zaimoku-chō ☎ 075 351 2726, �🌐 shizuya-kyoto.com; map p.430. This formerly traditional ryokan has recently been renovated as a modern minimalist-style guesthouse. It has dormitories, twin rooms and even a *hanare* annexe, which is perfect for groups. There's also an adjacent coffee shop that serves curry and rice meals. Dorms **¥3300**, doubles **¥11,000**

Tour Club ツアークラブ 362 Momiji-chō ☎ 075 353 6968, ⌂ kyotojp.com; map p.430. Conveniently located, this popular backpacker hostel has a solid reputation and is a great source of sightseeing information. Facilities include a Japanese-style communal living room, internet access, coin laundry, showers, money-changing facilities, the chance to try on a kimono and very reasonable bicycle rentals. Rates get cheaper the longer you stay. Dorms **¥2450**, doubles **¥6980**

EAST KYOTO

Book & Bed Hostel ブック&ベッドホステル 200 Nakano-chō ☎ 075 201 3374, ⌂ bookandbedtokyo.com/en/kyoto; map p.433. If you love books then this newly opened hostel is a treat: you crawl into a capsule-like space between the bookshelves to sleep, though there's not a lot of privacy. There are also rooms, some of which have river views. 🛜 **¥5300**

★**Four Seasons Kyoto** フォーシーズンス京都 445-3 Myohin Maekawa-chō ☎ 075 541 8288, ⌂ fourseasons.com/kyoto; map p.433. This newly opened super-luxury

hotel is stunning in every way – location, architecture, interior design and food. Built on the grounds of a twelfth-century estate, the outlook from the common areas and rooms is exceptional. 🛜 **¥90,000**

Gion Hatanaka 祇園畑中 Yasaka-jinja Minamimon-mae ☎ 075 541 5315, ⌂ thehatanaka.co.jp; map p.433. Elegant ryokan in a fabulous location near Yasaka-jinja with quiet, spacious rooms. It effortlessly blends traditional service with modern style – don't miss their Kyoto cuisine and *maiko* evening (see p.463). 🛜 **¥66,960**

Hyatt Regency Kyoto ハイアットリージェンシー京都 644-2 Sanjūsangendo-mawari ☎ 075 541 1234, ⌂ kyoto.regency.hyatt.com; map p.433. Modern luxury hotel right next to Sanjūsangen-dō, with an emphasis on contemporary Japanese style – guest-room interiors are sleekly decorated with traditional Kyoto fabrics. There are three in-house restaurants to choose from, and the spa specializes in traditional Japanese therapies. **¥33,000**

Jam Hostel ジャムホステル 170 Tokiwa-chō ☎ 075 201 3374, ⌂ facebook.com/jamhostel/; map p.433. This modern hostel has a prime location in Gion overlooking the Kamo-gawa. Dorms and private rooms are clean and comfortable, with shared bathing facilities. There's also an in-house sake bar and café. 🛜 Dorms **¥2300**, doubles **¥5500**

★**Mume Boutique Hotel** ホテルムメ 261 Umemoto-chō ☎ 075 525 8787, ⌂ hotelmume.jp; map p.433. This charming boutique hotel is tucked away on a street of antique shops in Gion and overlooks the Shirakawa canal. The seven rooms are tastefully decorated with antique furniture. Staff are both discreet and attentive, and you also get complimentary cappuccinos and cocktails. **¥32,000**

Waraku-An 和楽庵 19-2 Sannō-cho ☎ 075 771 5575, ⌂ kyotoguesthouse.net; map p.433. Conveniently located *machiya* guesthouse, near the northwest of Heian-jingū. All the rooms are traditional in style and have shared bathing facilities. The deluxe room next to the garden is recommended for its pleasant outlook and can sleep up to four. 🛜 Dorms **¥2700**, doubles **¥6480**

Yoshida Sansō 吉田山荘 59-1 Shimo Ōji-chō ☎ 075 771 6125, ⌂ yoshidasanso.com; map p.433. Located on Mt Yoshida, this high-class ryokan is the former second residence of the current emperor's uncle. With such imperial associations, don't be surprised if your room has a historical connection, not to mention a lovely garden view. *Kaiseki* cuisine is served and there's also an in-house tea salon. **¥75,600**

NORTH AND NORTHWEST KYOTO

★**Expo Hostel Ori** エキスポホステル織 2-4 Fujinomori-chō ☎ 075 202 2282, ⌂ facebook.com/expohostel.ori2; map pp.422–423. Nicely renovated building with clean, modern interiors in the northern part of Nishijin, the weaving district. The Japanese-style rooms have tatami and comfortable futons, and there's also a shared kitchen. **¥9000**

Kingyoya 金魚家 243 Kanki-chō ☎075 411 1128, ⓦkingyoya-kyoto.com; map pp.422–423. Small and friendly guesthouse in a tastefully restored *machiya* located in the heart of Nishijin. Dorm rooms and private rooms have traditional interiors, and breakfast is also available for an extra ¥700. Dorms **¥2700**, doubles **¥7560**

Oil Street Guest House 87-2 Mizuochi-chō ☎075 432 8867, ⓦoilstreetkyoto.com; map p.426. This large *machiya* on a quiet street in Nishijin has been nicely renovated into a guesthouse and event space, and has a kitchen that guests can use. There are two rooms with en-suite bathrooms which can both sleep up to four guests on futons. Book well in advance. 🛜 **¥20,000**

Petit Hotel Kyoto プチホテル京都 281 Motosa-chō ☎075 431 5136, ⓦph-kyoto.co.jp; map p.426. Small, friendly hotel on busy Imadegawa-dōri in Nishijin that's convenient for exploring the north and west. The traditional Kyoto breakfast with fresh tofu is excellent (¥700). Bicycle rental available. **¥14,600**

Sakura Komachi Guesthouse ゲストハウス桜こまち

10-2 Kinugasa Gaino-chō ☎075 406 1930, ⓦkyoto-sakurakomachi.com; map pp.422–423. Friendly guesthouse close to Kinkaku-ji and Ryōan-ji with an in-house café. There's a shared dormitory as well as a choice of Western- and Japanese-style private rooms. Dorms **¥3000**, doubles **¥12,500**

Shunkō-in 春光院 42 Myōshinji-chō ☎075 462 5488, ⓦshunkoin.com; map pp.422–423. Welcoming and peaceful temple lodging in the historic Myōshinji temple complex, run by an American-educated Zen priest. All rooms are tatami-style with futons and private baths, and shared kitchen facilities are available. Zen meditation class daily at 9am (¥500). 🛜 **¥11,000**

Utano Youth Hostel 宇多野ユースホステル 9 Nakayama-chō Uzumasa ☎075 462 2288, ⓦyh-kyoto.or.jp/utano; map pp.422–423. Award-winning modern hostel with a good atmosphere and helpful, English-speaking staff. Set in its own grounds on Kyoto's western outskirts, it has an excellent range of facilities. The dorms are very clean and comfortable and there are also Japanese- and Western-style double rooms with private baths. Dorms **¥3300**, doubles **¥8000**

EATING

It's worth treating yourself to a meal in a traditional *Kyō-ryōri* (Kyoto cuisine) restaurant, such as **kaiseki** (a multi-course banquet of seasonal delicacies), **obanzai** (Kyoto home-style cooking), **shōjin-ryōri** (Buddhist vegetarian cuisine) or **yūdōfu** (simmered tofu). **Nishin soba**, a big bowl of soba noodles with a part-dried piece of herring on top, and **saba-zushi**, made with mackerel, are two of the more everyday Kyoto dishes. **Reservations** are nearly always essential at top-end *kaiseki* restaurants in the evening; elsewhere it's not a bad idea to book ahead at weekends and during peak holiday times. Kyoto also has some excellent coffee shops and teahouses.

CENTRAL KYOTO
RESTAURANTS

Anzukko 杏っ子 2F Le Shisemme Building Ebisu-chō ☎075 211 3801, ⓦanzukko.com; map p.426. This is the place to go for gourmet-style *gyōza* in Kyoto. Mouthwatering variations on fried, grilled and steamed dumplings. The pan-grilled 12 *gyōza* set (¥1020) and the boiled seafood dumplings dribbled with spicy oil (¥680) are highly recommended. Tues–Sun 6.30–11.30pm.

★**A Womb** アウーム 405 Nanba-chō ☎075 203 5277, ⓦawomb.com; map p.426. One of the most artistic meals in Kyoto, this restaurant serves *teori sushi*, "hand weaving sushi" – tiny morsels of *Kyō-ryōri* flavours beautifully presented on a slate (Standard ¥1680, Supreme ¥2970). You then add seasoning to taste and handroll each piece in seaweed. The flavours pair nicely with Kyoto-produced sake (¥900). At lunchtime arrive early or you'll have to queue; reservations are essential in the evening. Daily noon–2pm & 6–8pm.

Fujino-ya 藤の家 Pontochō Shijō-agaru ☎075 221 2446, ⓦkyoto-fujinoya.com; map p.426. One of Pontochō's more affordable restaurants, with the added attraction of a river view. The simple menu (in English)

offers either tempura or *kushi-katsu* (deep-fried pork skewers), with standard sets from around ¥2900. In the summer you can eat on the *yuka* (riverside terrace), but the price of dinner increases to ¥4300 for the minimum set. 5–10pm; closed Wed.

Giro Giro Hitoshina 枝魯枝魯ひとしな Nishi Kiyamachi Matsubara-sagaru ☎075 343 7070, ⓦguiloguilo.com; map p.426. Hip restaurant serving an innovative ten-course meal at the excellent price of ¥3800. Dishes are a superb fusion of traditional Japanese and European cuisine, making this a fun and unforgettable dining experience. Reservations are essential well in advance. Daily 5.30–11pm.

Grand Burger グランドバーガー Shinyodomae-chō ☎075 256 7317, ⓦgrandburger.com; map p.426. Small restaurant serving tasty burgers with handcut chips. The Grand Burger set (¥1480) with thickly sliced bacon and two types of cheese is recommended, as is the slightly healthier Avocado Burger set (¥1280). 11am–11pm; closed Tues & third Mon of the month.

Gyoza no Ohsho 餃子の王将 430 Tatsuike-chō ☎075 251 0177, ⓦohsho.co.jp; map p.426. A stylish branch of the well-known *Ohsho* chain, with superior decor and

6

menu. The speciality here is *gyōza*, with some unique flavour combinations such fried *gyōza* with cheese and chilli sauce (¥410) and boiled *gyōza* in sour cream and butter (¥595). Other Chinese-style dishes such as fried rice (¥435) are also available. Mon–Sat 11am–11.30pm, Sun & public hols 11am–9.30pm.

Hale 晴 Nishiki-koji Fuyachō Nishi-iru ☎ 075 231 2516; map p.426. Organic and vegan restaurant in a quaint *machiya* with a garden, down a narrow entrance off the bustling Nishiki food market. Healthy lunch sets are very reasonable at ¥1000, and six-course dinner sets (¥2200), with deliciously fresh tofu and steamed vegetables, can be shared between two. Tues–Sun 11.30am–2pm & 6–9pm.

Honke Owariya 本家尾張屋 Nishiki-koji Fuyachō Nishi-iru ☎ 075 231 2516; ⓦ honke-owariya.co.jp /english; map p.426. Lovely old soba restaurant in business since 1465, with a wide variety of hot and cold soba and udon noodle dishes on the menu. The local favourite Nishin soba is ¥1190, and the simple Seiro soba set (served cold in summer) is just ¥865. Daily 11am–6.30pm.

Hotevila ホテヴィラ 645 Kuma-chō ☎ 075 200 2885, ⓦ facebook.com/nonbq.hotevila; map p.426. Friendly restaurant serving tasty pasta, curry and daily special plates (¥1080). It's one of the few places in Kyoto still visibly concerned with environmental contamination caused by the March 2011 nuclear accident, and checks all of its ingredients for radioactivity levels. ⓦ Daily noon–8.30pm.

Ippudo 一風堂 653-1 Bantoya-chō ☎ 075 213 8800, ⓦ ippudo.com; map p.426. One of the most popular ramen places in Kyoto, so expect queues out the door at any time of day or night. It's worth the wait – their Hakata-style ramen soups are rich and flavoursome. The Akamaru Modern (¥1080) is highly recommended, and their *gyōza* (¥420) are also excellent. Daily 10.30am–2am.

Kaji かじ 112-19 Yokokaji-chō ☎ 075 231 3801, ⓦ kyoto-kaji.jp; map p.426. Reasonably priced, classic *kaiseki* is served in a traditional setting at this restaurant, which has a hushed and slightly frosty atmosphere. However, each of the ten courses is impeccably presented, with ingredients and even edible flowers to evoke the season. The cheapest Yuki course (¥3900) is a good first-time choice. Reservations essential. Noon–2pm & 5–9pm; closed Wed.

★Khanty カンティ 31-1 Omote-chō ☎ 075 741 7280, ⓦ khantykyoto.com; map p.426. A welcome addition to the Kyoto dining scene, this craft kitchen uses seasonal local ingredients to produce delightful dishes with Laotian and Italian flavours, such as home-made Laos sausage (¥1600) and mushroom *all'arrabbiata* (¥1400). The cocktails are inventive (from ¥750) and the wine list has some surprises too (bottles from ¥2900). 5pm–midnight, plus brunch Sat & Sun 11am–2pm; closed Wed.

Kiln キルン Kiyamachi Shijō-sagaru ☎ 075 353 3555, ⓦ kilnrestaurant.jp; map p.426. Stylish modern restaurant overlooking the Takase-gawa with shared table seating. The menu is fusion-style using local ingredients – confit of abalone and oyster mushrooms with preserved lemon (¥865) and Kawachi duck with red wine risotto (¥2160) are two excellent choices. The evening cover charge is ¥300. Noon–2pm & 5–11pm; closed Wed.

Kushikura 串くら Takakura-dōri Oike-agaru ☎ 075 213 2211, ⓦ kushikura.jp; map p.426. Premium *yakitori* and other skewer foods in a nicely restored old Kyoto house. Sit at the counter and watch the chefs grill your food over charcoal, or enjoy the privacy of the small dining rooms. Sets start at ¥2500, or you can order skewers separately (from ¥220). Daily 11.30am–2pm & 5–9.45pm.

★Menbakaichidai Ramen めん馬鹿一代 757-2 Iseya-chō ☎ 075 812 5818, ⓦ fireramen.com; map p.426. If you like your ramen served with maximum drama and a high level of danger, then a visit here is a must: your ramen (¥1250) will arrive on fire, and the friendly staff will even film it for you. Touristy but fun. Daily 11.30am–2.15pm & 5–11pm.

Ninja Kyoto 忍者京都 Shinkyōgoku Shijō-agaru ☎ 075 253 0150, ⓦ ninja-kyoto.com; map p.426. This ninja-theme restaurant, with its labyrinth of basement dining booths and costume-clad staff, is a lot of fun and the food's not too bad either. There's an à la carte menu, but given the level of theatrics it's better to go with a course menu (from ¥3000) and watch your food metamorphose with magic tricks performed by the staff. Daily 5–11pm.

★Waka 和香 397-9 Shinkai-chō ☎ 070 5657 0953, ⓦ oterahouse.com; map p.426. Friendly restaurant, dishing up delicious and healthy *shōjin-ryōri* (Buddhist vegetarian) lunch sets (¥850), with four seasonal vegetable dishes, rice and soup. Arrive early or call ahead to check availability as they sell out quickly. It's also a pleasant place to have an organic coffee (¥400). Wed–Sat 11am–3pm.

Wontana 魚棚 452 Matsugae-chō ☎ 075 221 2579, ⓦ wontana.com; map p.426. This *Kyō-ryōri* restaurant serves sophisticated lunch and dinner sets based on seasonal ingredients. Unlike the usual classic Kyoto-style dishes, *Wontana*'s are more colourful, and are served on beautiful ceramic and glass dishes. Lunch *kaiseki* courses start at ¥2215, while evening courses range from ¥3240 to ¥8640. Noon–3pm & 5–10pm; closed Wed.

★Yoshikawa 吉川 Tominokōji Ōike-sagaru ☎ 075 221 5544, ⓦ kyoto-yoshikawa.co.jp; map p.426. The best tempura restaurant in Kyoto is located inside this eponymous ryokan (see p.453). It's worth sitting at the counter to watch the chefs expertly deep-fry your meal. Lunch sets (¥3240) include hearty portions of seafood and

THE TEAHOUSES OF KYOTO

The world of **tea** tends to have a reputation for rigidity and rules, but fortunately there are now some innovative and modern ways in which to experience this quintessential Japanese drink. Whether you're looking for a tea ceremony or are just after a relaxing cuppa, both are easily accessible in these elegant Kyoto teahouses.

CENTRAL KYOTO

Fukujuen 福寿園 Shijō Tominokōji ☎075 221 6174, ⓦfukujuen-kyotohonten.com; map p.426. The flagship store of this tea company has five floors of tea-related activities – from the tea-making workshop in the basement (¥1620) to a 30min tea ceremony experience in the elegant fourth-floor tearoom (¥2700). There are also two tea-inspired restaurants and a ground-floor shop. Daily 10am–6.30pm.

Iyemon Salon 伊右衛門サロン Sanjō Karasuma Nishi-iri ☎075 222 1500, ⓦiyemonsalon.jp; map p.426. This large bustling teahouse, on Sanjō-dōri just west of Karasuma, is aiming to be Kyoto's trendiest teahouse – it has an internet café, bookshop, tea counter and a kitchen serving tea-inspired cuisine. *Matcha* from ¥750. Daily 8am–11pm.

Kaboku Tearoom 喫茶室嘉木 Teramachi Nijō-agaru ☎075 211 3421, ⓦippodo-tea.co.jp/en/index.html; map p.426. In the historic Ippodō teashop, this tearoom is a wonderful place to sample different types and grades of green tea (¥650–2050). It has a hushed atmosphere but the staff are friendly and happy to guide you through the extensive menu (in English). Daily 11am–5.30pm.

Somushi Kochaya 素夢古茶屋 Sanjō Karasuma Nishi-iri ☎075 253 1456, ⓦsomushi.com; map p.426. Just across from the *Iyemon Salon* is an artfully rustic Korean teahouse that's an incredibly calm space to try a variety of medicinal teas, such as ginseng and jujube (from ¥600), as well as healthy vegetarian Korean dishes. 11am–6.30pm; closed Wed.

EAST KYOTO

Kyoto Nama Chocolat Organic Tea House 76-15 Tenno-chō ☎075 751 2678, ⓦkyoto-namachocolat.com; map p.433. East of the Heian-jingū, this tranquil teahouse is set in an elegant old house with a rambling garden. They serve a variety of teas and coffee (¥550), as well as their own brand of delectable fresh soft chocolate, which is made on the premises (¥550 for 4 pieces). Noon–6pm; closed Tues.

Rakushō 洛匠 Kōdaiji Kitamonmae-dōri ☎075 561 6892, ⓦrakusyou.co.jp; map p.433. In eastern Kyoto, don't miss this charming old teahouse between Kōdai-ji and Yasaka-jinja. Enjoy a bowl of *matcha* and *warabi mochi* (jelly-like cakes rolled in sweet soybean flour) for ¥720 while gazing out over the pond of enormous carp. Daily 9am–5pm.

---

vegetables, while in the evenings, the tempura supper (¥8640) or tempura *kaiseki* course (¥12,960) are both recommended. Daily 11am–1.30pm & 5–8pm.

AROUND KYOTO STATION

RESTAURANTS

Kitcho 吉兆 3F Granvia Hotel, Kyoto Station ☎075 342 0808, ⓦkitcho.com/kyoto; map p.430. The Kyoto Station branch of this famous *kaiseki* restaurant (see box, p.50) serves bentō boxes (¥7130) and *kaiseki* courses (¥14,260) for lunch and dinner. It lacks the extravagance and sublime decor of its sister branch in Arashiyama (see p.471), but the food is excellent. Daily 11am–2pm & 5–8.30pm.

★**Ramen Alley** 京都拉麺小路 10F Isetan, Kyoto Station ☎075 361 4401; map p.430. Eight ramen noodle shops, serving Kyoto, Osaka, Hakata, Sapporo and other varieties, are tucked into this "alley" on the tenth floor of Kyoto Station's Isetan department store. Some of the shops display English menus outside. When you've

chosen, buy a ticket from the vending machine outside (from ¥500) and hand it to the staff when you are seated. Daily 10am–10pm.

Tonkatsu Wako とんかつ和幸 11F Eat Paradise, Isetan, Kyoto Station ☎075 342 0024; map p.430. The Kyoto Station branch of this well-known *tonkatsu* (fried pork cutlet) restaurant serves good-value lunch and dinner sets. All sets come with rice, cabbage salad and miso soup – try the Hirekatsu Gohan set (¥1190). Daily 11am–9.15pm.

CAFÉS

efish エフィッシュ 798-1 Nishi-Hashizumi-chō ☎075 361 3069, ⓦshinproducts.com/efish/cafe.php; map p.430. Riverside café east of the station near Gojo bridge, serving chunky bread sandwich sets (¥820–930), cheesecake (¥600) and coffee (¥480) in a very stylish interior, designed by the owner. A good place to gaze out at the river and eastern hills from a comfortable chair. Daily 10am–10pm.

6

Kaikado Cafe 開化堂カフェ 352 Sumiyoshi-chō ☎ 075 353 5668, ⓦ kaikadocafe.com; map p.430. Recently opened café in an atmospheric old fire station, run by a traditional tea-caddy maker. Drinks are stylishly presented but pricey (house-blend coffee ¥810, high-quality Gyokuro green tea ¥760), and the food menu consists of cheesecake (¥540) or toast (¥455). 10.30am–6.30pm; closed Thurs.

EAST KYOTO

If you want to treat yourself to traditional Kyoto cuisine, the city's eastern districts are a good place to head. One or two of the more affordable restaurants are recommended below, and these still offer a glimpse into the world of kimono-clad waitresses, elegant tatami rooms, carp ponds and tinkling bamboo waterspouts. There are also some pleasant cafés in this part of Kyoto serving healthy, organic food.

RESTAURANTS

★**Gion Okuoka** 祇園おくおか 44-66 Bishamon-chō Higashiōji-dōri ☎ 075 531 5155, ⓦ gion-okuoka .com; map p.433. At this friendly restaurant specializing in Kyoto cuisine you can make fresh *yuba* (tofu skin) at your table (¥2650). In the evening, they serve *kaiseki* courses from ¥6500 and a *yuba* pot course (¥3650). English menu available. 11.30am–2.30pm & 5–9.30pm; closed Thurs.

Hyōtei 瓢亭 35 Kusagawa-chō Nanzen-ji ☎ 075 771 4116, ⓦ hyotei.co.jp; map p.433. Next to Murin-an garden, this sublime thatch-roofed garden-restaurant started serving *kaiseki* cuisine in 1837. Their specialities are *asagayu*, a summer breakfast (served July & Aug

8am–10am; ¥6000), and *uzuragayu* (rice gruel with quail eggs) in winter (¥12,100). Prices are lower in the new annexe, but even here expect to pay ¥4500 for the cheapest meal. Reservations are essential. 11am–7pm; closed second & fourth Tues of the month.

★**Kyoto Modern Terrace** 京都モダンテラス 13 Okazaki Saishoji-chō ☎ 075 754 0234, ⓦ kyotomodernterrace .com; map p.433. Part of the newly renovated Rohn Theatre complex, this spacious, 1960s-styled restaurant, with an outdoor terrace, is both elegant and welcoming. The food menu is based on grilled vegetables, meat and seafood, with scrumptious sets for breakfast (¥1000), lunch (¥2800) and dinner (¥3800). Daily 8am–11pm.

★**Mame-cha** 豆ちゃ Yasaka-jinja Nanmon-sagaru Ishibekōji ☎ 075 532 2788, ⓦ commercial-art.net/wp /kansai/mamecha_kyoto; map p.433. Elegant *obanzai* restaurant in a modern-designed *machiya* up one of Kyoto's most scenic alleyways, just south of Yasaka-jinja. The eleven-course dinner (¥4500) has a wonderful combination of flavours and is beautifully presented. Counter seating or tatami rooms upstairs, plus English-speaking staff and menu. Reservations essential. Daily 5–11pm.

Nakamura-rō 中村楼 Gion-machi Minami-gawa ☎ 075 561 0016, ⓝ nakamurarou.com; map p.433. A wonderful four-hundred-year-old restaurant adjacent to the south gate of Yasaka-jinja serving exquisite Kyoto cuisine. It's surprisingly relaxed and informal, with tatami rooms overlooking a lush garden and a modern room with counter seating. However, even just a lunchtime bentō will set you back ¥5250. Full *kaiseki*

KYOTO COFFEE

Kyoto is famous for its **siphon coffee** technique, which was brought to Japan in the early twentieth century; the method often produces a bitter brew, which has traditionally been the local taste. In the last few years there's been a boom in speciality roasters, and Kyoto now boasts some fine **coffee shops** with world-class baristas.

CENTRAL KYOTO

Café Phalam カフェパラン 24 Hokusei-chō ☎ 075 496 4843, ⓦ phalam.jp; map p.426. Directly in front of JR Nijō Station, this speciality coffee shop is renowned for its smooth espresso (¥330) and delicious French press coffee (¥550). Mon–Fri 9am–7.30pm, Sat & Sun 9am–6.30pm.

Kissa Master 喫茶マスター 26 Nakano-chō ☎ 075 231 6828, ⓦ facebook.com/KissaMaster; map p.426. The baristas at this coffee shop, situated at the back of a men's fashion boutique, make excellent lattes

in large cups (¥500), made even more enjoyable by the wonderful view of a traditional Japanese garden. Daily 11.30am–7.30pm.

Weekenders ウィークエンダーズ 560 Honeyano-chō ⓦ weekenderscoffee.com; map p.426. The downtown coffee shop of this highly esteemed coffee roaster is in a newly built traditional house incongruously located at the back of an ugly car park. However, the cappuccinos (¥480) make up for the uninspiring setting. 7.30am–6pm; closed Wed.

NORTH AND NORTHWEST KYOTO

Latte Art Junkies ラテアートジャンキーズ 839-3 Kamiyagawa-chō ☎ 075 463 6677, ⓦ junkies-cafe .com; map pp.422–423. Newly opened coffee bar

near Kitano Tenmangu shrine. The owner is a latte art champion and serves up fabulous *caffe* lattes (¥450) as well as *matcha* lattes (¥550). Daily 10am–6pm.

dinners start at ¥13,000. Reservations essential. Daily 11.30am–2pm & 5–7pm.

Okutan 奥丹 Fukuchi-chō, Nanzen-ji ☎ 075 771 8709; map p.433. This small restaurant has been serving *yūdōfu* (simmered tofu) since the fourteenth century. It's half hidden in a bamboo grove on the east side of the Chōshō-in garden, just outside Nanzen-ji. The *yūdōfu* sets start at ¥3240. 11am–4.30pm; closed Thurs.

★**Omen** おめん Jōdo-ji Shibashi-chō ☎ 075 771 8994; ⊛ omen.co.jp; map p.433. Excellent udon restaurant near Ginkaku-ji, serving bowls of thick white noodles topped with the nutritious combination of fresh ginger, sesame seeds and pickled *daikon* radish (from ¥1150). The seasonal vegetable salad (¥850) is also delicious. Daily 11am–8.30pm.

★**Rokusei** 六盛 71 Okazaki Nishitenno-chō ☎ 075 751 6171, ⊛ rokusei.co.jp; map p.433. *Rokusei* has been serving *Kyō-ryōri* in this location for over a hundred years, and its retro interior is still stuck in the 1970s. The best meal to experience here is lunch, when you can sample the Teoke Bentō (¥4105), prepared under the supervision of a National Living Treasure and served in a handmade wooden pail. Tues–Sun 11.30am–3pm & 5–8pm.

CAFÉS

★**Foodelica** フーデリカ Kitayama-dōri Shirakawa ☎ 075 703 5208, ⊛ foodelica.com; map pp.422–423. Organic café serving home-made pasta and delicious crêpes. The fresh pasta lunch set (¥1350) includes coffee. If you are visiting Shūgaku-in Rikyū, this is a great place to stop for a meal or a snack: it's just a few steps east of the Eiden Station. 11.30am–2.30pm, Sat & Sun until 5pm; closed Tues & fourth Wed of the month.

Kuroganeya Rail Model & Cafe くろがねや 44-7 Hōnenin-chō ☎ 075 752 8450, ⊛ www4.plala.or.jp /kuroganeya-kyoto; map p.433. Cluttered and eccentric café with very helpful owners and a large collection of antique model trains, some of which are for sale. The only food on the menu is fried pork cutlet toast (¥1000) and cake (¥400), served with coffee or juice (¥500). 11am–6pm; closed Tues & Wed.

Tosca トスカ Kitashirakawa Oiwake-chō ☎ 075 721 7779, ⊛ tosca-kyoto.com; map p.433. Vegetarian café in a light, breezy space opposite Kyoto University. It's run by English-speaking Tomoka and Asuka (hence the name), and the menu is healthy and delicious. Lunch courses of soup, curry or burgers from ¥1250, and tasty dinner courses of seasonal vegetables from ¥1620. There's also an à la carte menu. 11.30am–2.30pm & 6–9pm; closed Tues.

NORTH AND NORTHWEST KYOTO
RESTAURANTS

Gontaro 権太呂 Kinukake-no-michi ☎ 075 463 1039, ⊛ gontaro.co.jp/english/kyoto/kinkakuji.html; map

pp.422–423. Suburban branch of the Shijō soba shop in an old house just a few minutes' walk west of Kinkaku-ji. Fresh, reasonably priced noodle dishes (tempura soba ¥1100) and a welcoming atmosphere. 11am–9pm; closed Wed.

Ichibaku Nanasai 一麦七菜 32-3 Shimowakakusa-chō ☎ 075 431 4970, ⊛ facebook.com/ichibakunanasai; map pp.422–423. This friendly udon restaurant serves delicious handmade noodles in exquisite ceramic bowls. In summer, the Reinanasai udon (¥890) with Kyoto vegetables in a cool soup is refreshing. At other times try the Yuba-kizami udon (¥750) with tofu skin and *kamaboko* fish cake. 🛜 11pm–3pm; closed Tues.

★**Izusen** 泉仙 Daitoku-ji ☎ 075 491 6665, ⊛ kyoto -izusen.com/html/store_daijin.html; map pp.422–423. Located in the gardens of Daiji-in, a sub-temple of Daitoku-ji, this is one of the nicest places to sample vegetarian *shōjin-ryōri* at an affordable price, though it's still around ¥3250 for the simplest lunch. Reservations recommended in spring and autumn. Daily 11am–4pm.

Margaux Ramen まあごラーメン 1015-3 Kamiyagawa-chō ☎ 075 464 3308; map pp.422–423. The owner of this ramen shop, a French wine lover, created the delicious Tomato Ramen (¥750) to be drunk with a glass of red – though sadly *Margaux* are only currently serving beer (¥480). There are some other unusual Western-inspired noodle soups on the menu too, such as Milk Ramen (¥750), pork and chicken stock in a milk sauce, with a slice of butter. 11.30am–3.30pm & 6–11pm; closed Tues.

★**Nicora** ニコラ 69-3 Itsuji-cho ☎ 075 431 7567, ⊛ sobaya-nicolas.com; map p.426. Michelin-starred soba restaurant in Nishijin with some excellent innovative buckwheat dishes. The best way to enjoy them is to order a tapas-style selection of three dishes (¥1180) with a side dish of soba noodles (from ¥980). Food photography is strictly forbidden here. 11.30am–2pm & 5.30–8.30pm; closed Wed & first and third Tues of the month.

TowZen 豆禅 13-4 Higashi Takagi-chō ☎ 075 703 5731, ⊛ mamezen.com; map pp.422–423. This ramen shop specializes in ramen made with soy milk soup, topped with tofu skin and mushrooms. Simply choose your bowl size: small (¥850), medium (¥950) or large (¥1050). The chef can cater for vegans – let him know so he can make the soup without fish stock. 11.30am–3pm & 6–9.30pm; closed irregularly.

Urume うるめ 51 Ōno-chō Kitaōji-dōri ☎ 075 495 9831; map pp.422–423. This pleasant soba restaurant in a lovely old *machiya* makes a good lunch stop: the menu includes dishes such as Zaru-soba (¥760) and tempura with soba (¥1510), and the private room at the back has a nice garden view. It's on the north side of Kitaōji-dōri between Shinmachi and Horikawa; there's no large sign in front so look for a *noren* curtain. 11am–5pm; closed Tues.

6

6

KYOTO FOOD AND TEA CULTURE CLASSES

It's possible to study Kyoto's culinary **arts and tea culture** at venues around the city. The main advantage of taking a class is to gain some insights into Kyoto's enduring food and tea traditions and special techniques, and to spend time with local people.

COOKING CLASSES

Haru Cooking Class Shimogamo Miyazaki-chō ☎ 090 4284 7176, ⓦ kyoto-cooking-class.com. Fun and friendly cooking class run by a charming young couple out of their home kitchen. They offer vegetarian and non-vegetarian (including Kōbe Beef) courses, and give useful explanations of essential ingredients and the fundamentals of Japanese cuisine such as dashi (stock) making (¥5900–10,900/person). Daily at 2pm.

Uzuki Cooking School Shirakawa-dōri Imadegawa-agaru ⓦ kyotouzuki.com. This cooking school in northeastern Kyoto holds classes for two to four people in seasonal Kyoto cuisine, mostly on weekday afternoons. The enthusiastic instructor brings you into her own kitchen and takes you through the steps of creating a delicious three- or four-course meal (¥4500–5500/person).

TEA CEREMONY

Kanjoan 緩徐庵 Nishijin ☎ 075 200 7653, ⓦ kanjoan .com. At this beautifully restored teahouse in the heart of Nishijin you can experience a 2hr introduction to the tea ceremony with a Swiss-born tea master (¥4000/person depending on programme and group size). As well as getting insider information on Kyoto tea culture, you will learn to make your own bowl of *matcha* and enjoy a traditional sweet. Day and time by appointment.

WAK Japan ワックジャパン Takakura Nijō-agaru ☎ 075 212 9993, ⓦ wakjapan.com. WAK Japan is a cultural organization which offers a 45min morning tea ceremony experience (¥3890/person for groups of two or more) in their traditional *machiya* townhouse classroom. Reservations must be made two days in advance. Daily 9.30am–3.30pm.

SWEET MAKING

Izutsu Yatsuhashi 井筒八つ橋 Teramachi Shijō-agaru ☎ 075 255 2121, ⓦ yatsuhashi.co.jp. Learn how to mix and bake Kyoto's famous cinnamon-flavoured biscuits in a 45min class (¥1080/person), and take home a special tin containing 32 biscuits. It's best to make a telephone reservation in advance. Daily 10am–8pm.

Kanshundo 甘春堂 Kawabata Shomen

Higashi-iru ☎ 075 561 1318, ⓦ kanshundo.co.jp. At this traditional Kyoto confectioner you can learn how to handcraft four different kinds of *kyō-gashi* (traditional Kyoto sweets made with pounded rice and bean paste) in a 1hr 15min class (¥2160/person, cash only). Reservations must be made on the website at least three days in advance. Classes daily at 9.15am, 11am, 1pm and 3pm.

CAFÉS

In the Green インザグリーン Shimogamo Hangi-chō ☎ 075 706 8740, ⓦ inthegreen.com; map pp.422–423. Located on the north side of the Kyoto Botanical Gardens, this is a large café with indoor and semi-outdoor seating, as well as a pizza oven. The lunch menu is mostly sets (daily, plate ¥950) but in the evening there is a variety of pizzas (from ¥850) as well as à la carte dishes such as shrimp and avocado green salad (¥930). Garden ticket holders can get a ¥200 discount here. Daily 11am–3pm & 5–10pm.

Sarasa Nishijin さらさ西陣 Kuramaguchi-dōri ☎ 075 432 5075, ⓦ cafe-sarasa.com/shop_nishijin; map pp.422–423. This café and bar in a converted *sentō* (public bathhouse) in the Nishijin weaving district still has its

lovely original tiled interior. The food is average (egg sandwiches ¥810), but it's a really nice place for a coffee (¥350) or a drink. Monthly live music performances. 🛜 Noon–11pm; closed Wed.

Tofu Café Fujino とうふカフェ藤野 Imadegawa-dōri ☎ 075 463 1028, ⓦ kyotofu.co.jp/shoplist/cafe; map pp.422–423. A little west of Kitano Tenmangū shrine, this modern café serves classic soy bean cuisine. There's only one item on the menu: the "Fujino Prix-Fixe Lunch" (¥1900), which includes five different types of tofu, as well as dessert and black bean coffee. For an extra ¥300 you can have seasonal *kamameshi* pot rice. The café gets extremely busy on the 25th of the month, when the shrine market is held (see box, p.466). Daily 11am–3pm.

DRINKING AND NIGHTLIFE

With boisterous *izakaya* and trendy wine **bars**, the epicentre of the city's nightlife can be found either side of the Kamo-gawa in downtown Kyoto, in the two traditional pleasure quarters of **Gion** and **Pontochō**. Most of the clubs are in the **Kiyamachi** area between Sanjō and Shijō, which heaves with buskers, fortune-tellers and bar touts at weekends. Like the rest of Japan, Kyoto hosts a growing number of **craft breweries** and an ever-increasing number of bars devoted to drinking them. In summer, look out for rooftop **beer gardens** on top of the big hotels and department stores. Be aware that even fairly innocuous-looking establishments can be astronomically expensive (many have a "seating" fee of over ¥1000), so check first to make sure you know exactly what you're letting yourself in for.

BARS

CENTRAL KYOTO AND PONTOCHŌ

Ace Café エースカフェ 10F Empire Biru Kiyamachi Sanjō-agaru Ⓦace-cafe.com; map p.426. Enjoy a cocktail (¥730) while sitting on a comfortable sofa with fabulous panoramic views over the Kamo-gawa and eastern hills from this popular tenth-floor bar and café. Also serves pasta and pizza (from ¥850). Daily 6pm–2am, Fri & Sat until 3am.

Before 9 ビフォアナイン 545 Nijoden-chō ☎075 741 6492, Ⓦsakahachi.jp; map p.426. Minimalist-style bar serving craft beer spread over two floors in a renovated *machiya* opposite the Manga Museum. Locally brewed Karasuma Pilsner or Brown (¥550/950) are popular choices. Order and pay at the front counter. Daily 10am–6.30pm.

Bungalow バンガロー 15 Kashiwaya-chō ☎075 256 8205, Ⓦbungalow.jp; map p.426. A large plastic curtain covers the front entrance to this cosy bar in an old *machiya*. There are ten local craft beers on tap (¥600–1200), and table service upstairs. Mon–Sat 3pm–2am, Sun noon–1am.

Dublin Irish Pub ダブリン Oike-dōri Kawaramachi higashi-iru ☎075 241 9155, Ⓦdublin.kyoto-pontocho .jp; map p.426. Right next to the *Kyoto Hotel Okura*, this popular Irish pub has Kilkenny and Guinness on tap (¥900 a pint), voluminous portions of hearty Irish food (Irish stew ¥1000, fish & chips ¥900), and an enjoyable atmosphere, especially on the live music nights. Happy hour 5–7pm. Mon–Sat 5pm–2am, Sun 4pm–1am.

Miltons ミルトン 2F Clarion Biru 246 Yamazaki-chō ☎080 5292 0606; map p.426. Charming bar next to the BAL building run by artist Milton Ogura, whose art adorns the walls. Milton's specially spiced gin (¥700) is recommended, and there's a good range of whisky too (from ¥500). Daily 3–10.30pm; closed 5th, 10th, 15th, 20th, 25th and 30th of the month.

Pub Karr パブカー 2F Anraku Biru 452 Matsugae-chō ☎075 212 4567, Ⓦfacebook.com/pub.karr; map p.426. Friendly bar serving craft beer just off Kawaramachi, with counter or table seating. A variety of local and international IPAs (¥600–1300) is on offer, plus their own home-cured ham (¥600). 📶 Daily 3pm–1am.

Tato タト 151 Takoya-chō ☎075 211 9090; map p.426. Popular Spanish bar with standing or seating area, and a multilingual soccer-mad owner who keeps everyone entertained. Large selection of Spanish and other European beers (from ¥750), as well as wine by the glass (¥500). The tapas menu is also extensive – the garlic prawns (¥900) are especially good. 5.30–11.30pm; closed irregularly.

GION AND EAST KYOTO

The Gael Irish Pub ゲールアイリッシュパブ 2F Ōto Bldg, Keihan Shijō Station ☎075 525 0680, Ⓦirishpubkyoto.com; map p.433. Popular expat hangout with a warm and friendly atmosphere, good-quality food (try the Gael Burger; ¥900) and a decent range of beers (from ¥650). Weekly live music and other events. Daily 5pm–1am.

Jam Sake Bar ジャムサケバー *Jam Hostel* 170 Tokiwa-chō ☎075 201 3374, Ⓦsakebar.jp; map p.433. At this casual sake bar in the *Jam Hostel* (see p.454), you can sample a selection of sake from all over Japan. The English-speaking bartender will help you make a selection. The tasting set (of three) is ¥1000, or you can have one shot for ¥400. Beers are ¥500. Daily 5pm–midnight.

SOUTH OF THE CENTRE

Kyoto Brewing Company 京都醸造株式会社 25-1 Nishikujō Takahata-chō ☎075 574 7820, Ⓦkyotobrewing.com; map pp.422–423. Inspired by American- and Belgian-style craft beers, this foreign-run craft brewery has successfully established itself in Kyoto, and now has a tasting room where you can sample beers for ¥600 each. Sat & Sun only 1–5.30pm.

CLUBS

Metro メトロ Keihan Marutamachi Station ☎075 752 4765, Ⓦmetro.ne.jp; map p.433. In the depths of the train station (take exit 2), this progressive club offers an eclectic selection of music, from local guitar bands and big-name foreign techno DJs to drag shows and hardcore dub reggae parties. It's small, loud and very popular. Entrance ¥1000–3000 (more for foreign DJs or bands), including one drink. Daily, but opening hours vary.

World ワールド京都 B1-B2 Imagium Building ☎075 213 4119, Ⓦworld-kyoto.com; map p.426. Cavernous basement club attracting big-name house, hip-hop and techno DJs from Japan and abroad. Weekday nights are quieter, but the place heaves at the weekend. Average entry is ¥1500–3000 (including one drink). Open most nights from around 9pm.

LIVE MUSIC

Jazz Live Candy ジャズライブキャンディ B1 Hanamikōji Shinmonzen-agaru ☎075 531 2148, Ⓦh3.dion .ne.jp/~candy-h; map p.433. Well-established jazz bar with top live acts (mostly local) every night, and a serious yet friendly atmosphere. Seating charge of ¥600, plus cover charge (¥1500–2500). Drinks from ¥700. Daily 7.30pm–1am.

6

Jittoku 拾得 Ōmiya Marutamachi-agaru ☎075 841 1691, ⓦwww2.odn.ne.jp/jittoku; map p.426. It's a little bit out of the way, north of Nijō-jō, but this wonderful old *kura* (storehouse) has good acoustics and hosts regular rock and blues band performances. Cover charge ¥1000–3000. Daily 5.30pm–midnight.

Live Spot Rag 京都ライブスポトラグ 5F Empire Biru Kiyamachi Sanjō-agaru ☎075 241 0446, ⓦwww.ragnet .co.jp; map p.426. Well-established musicians' hangout (they have rehearsal rooms and recording studios here as well) which hosts local and international bands, mainly playing jazz. Entry from ¥1500. Mon–Sat 7pm until late.

Taku Taku 磔磔 Tominokōji Bukkōji-sagaru ☎075 351 1321, ⓦgeisya.or.jp/~takutaku; map p.426. In the blocks southwest of Takashimaya department store, this converted *kura* makes a great live venue. The music's pretty varied but tends towards rock and blues, including the occasional international artist. Cover charge from ¥1000 (depending on performer), including one drink. Daily 7pm until late.

UrBAN GUILD アバンギルド 3F New Kyoto Biru, Kiyamachi Sanjō-sagaru ☎075 212 1125, ⓦurbanguild.net; map p.426. Avant-garde club with a good reputation for hosting interesting underground local and international acts playing psych-rock, acid folk and lo-fi electronica. Occasional butō dance performances. Entry ¥1800–3000. Daily 6.30pm–midnight.

ENTERTAINMENT AND THE ARTS

Kyoto is famous for its traditional **geisha dance** shows. Performances of **kabuki** and **nō** plays are more sporadic but worth attending if you happen to be in town when they are on. The **Kyoto Art Center** (☎075 213 1000, ⓦkac.or.jp/en) hosts a range of exhibitions and art performances as well as lectures, field trips and a well-regarded series of "Traditional Theatre Training" workshops (held every July) for those who want to learn more about nō and other Japanese performing arts.

GEISHA ODORI

Geisha (or *geiko*, as they are known locally) and *maiko* (trainee geisha) from each of the city's former pleasure quarters have been putting on *Odori* (dance performances) in spring and autumn since the late nineteenth century, though the music and choreography are much older. By turns demure and coquettish, they glide round the stage in the most gorgeous kimono, straight out of an Edo-period woodblock print of Japan's seductive "floating world". If you're in Kyoto during these seasonal dances, it's well worth going along, but note that the autumn dances are more like recitals, and not as extravagant as the spring dances. Performances take place several times a day, so it's usually possible to get hold of tickets; you can buy them from the theatre box offices and major hotels. At all of the *Odori*, you can also buy tickets that combine the show with a tea ceremony conducted by geisha and *maiko*, which is well worth the extra cost (¥3800–6000, depending on the district). Make sure you get there early enough to enjoy your bowl of *matcha* (powdered green tea).

Kitano Odori 北野をどり ☎075 461 0148, ⓦmaiko3 .com/index.html; tickets from ¥4000. Kyoto's northern geisha district holds their Odori in early spring (March 25–April 7) at the Kami-shichiken Kaburenjō, near Kitano Tenmangū shrine.

Miyako Odori 都をどり ☎075 541 3391, ⓦmiyako -odori.jp; tickets from ¥2000. The annual dance performances in the geisha districts kick off with the Miyako Odori (April 1–30) performed at Gion Kōbu Kaburenjō (see p.437) by the geisha and *maiko* of Gion. This is the most prestigious and well known of the *Odori*, mainly because it is the oldest, having started in 1872. The dances are based on a seasonal theme and have lavish sets and costumes. Live musicians playing *shamisen*, flutes and drums, as well as singers, perform in alcoves at each side of the stage.

Kyō Odori 京おどり ☎075 561 1151, ⓦmiyagawacho .jp; tickets from ¥2500 with tea. The smaller-scale Kyō Odori is held in the Miyagawa-chō district, south of Gion, from April 7–22. This is a more intimate production than Miyako Odori, though just as opulent.

Kamo-gawa Odori 鴨川をどり ☎075 221 2025, ⓦkamogawa-odori.com; tickets from ¥2000. The geisha and *maiko* of Pontochō stage their Kamo-gawa Odori once a year (May 1–24) in Pontochō Kaburenjō, at the north end of Pontochō-dōri.

Onshūkai 温習会 ☎075 541 3391, ⓦmiyako-odori.jp /onsyukai; tickets from ¥4000. The Onshūkai dances are held during the first week in Oct at the Gion Kōbu Kaburenjō.

Kotobukikai 寿会 ☎075 461 0148, ⓦmaiko3.com /event/ev-8.html; tickets from ¥4000. The Kotobukikai dances (around Oct 8–12) are held in northwest Kyoto's Kami-shichiken Kaburenjō, close to Kitano Tenmangū shrine.

Mizuekai みずえ会 ☎075 561 1151, ⓦmiyagawacho .jp/mizuekai; tickets from ¥4000. Miyagawa-chō's Mizuekai recital is usually held in mid-Oct at the Miyagawa-chō Kaburenjō.

Gion Odori 祇園をどり ☎075 561 0160, ⓦgionkaikan .jp; tickets from ¥3300. The Gion Odori, performed by the *maiko* and geisha of the smaller Gion Higashi district, wraps things up in early Nov (Nov 1–10) at the Gion Kaikan theatre near Yasaka-jinja.

MAJOR KYOTO FESTIVALS AND ANNUAL EVENTS

Thanks to its central role in Japanese history, Kyoto is home to a number of important **festivals**; the major celebrations are listed below. The **cherry-blossom** season hits Kyoto in early April – famous viewing spots include the Imperial Park, Yasaka-jinja and Arashiyama – while early November brings dramatic **autumn colours**. Many **temples** hold special **openings** in October and November to air their inner rooms during the fine, dry weather. This is a marvellous opportunity to see paintings, statues and other treasures not normally on public display; details are available in the free *Kyoto Visitors' Guide*. Kyoto gets pretty busy during major festivals and national holidays, especially Golden Week (April 29–May 5).

Febuary 2–4: Setsubun 節分 Annual bean-throwing festival celebrated at shrines throughout the city. At Yasaka-jinja, "ogres" scatter beans and pray for good harvests, while Heian-jingū hosts performances of traditional *kyōgen* theatre (see p.843) on Feb 3.

April 1–30: Miyako Odori 都をどり Performances of traditional geisha dances in Gion (see opposite).

April 7–22: Kyō Odori 京おどり Performances by the geisha and *maiko* of the Miyagawa-chō district (see opposite).

May 15: Aoi Matsuri 葵祭 The "Hollyhock Festival" dates back to the days when this plant was believed to ward off earthquakes and thunder. Now it's an occasion for a gorgeous, yet slow, procession of people dressed in Heian-period costume (794–1185). They accompany the imperial messenger and an ox cart decked in hollyhock leaves from the Imperial Palace to the Shimo-gamo and Kami-gamo shrines, in north Kyoto.

May 1–24: Kamo-gawa Odori 鴨川をどり Performances of traditional dances by geisha in Pontochō (see opposite).

June 1–2: Takigi No 薪能 Nō plays performed by torchlight at Heian-jingū.

July 1–31: Gion Matsuri 祇園祭 One of Kyoto's great festivals dates back to Heian times, when ceremonies were held to drive away epidemics of the plague. The festivities focus on Yasaka-jinja and culminate on July 17, with a grand parade through central Kyoto of tall, pointy *yama-boko* floats, richly decorated with local Nishijin silk. Night festivals are held three days prior to the parade, when the floats are lit with lanterns. Some can be viewed inside for a few hundred yen.

August 16: Daimonji Gozan Okuribi 大文字五山送り火 Five huge bonfires etch *kanji* characters on five hills around Kyoto; the most famous is the character for *dai* (big) on Daimonji-yama, northeast of the city. The practice originated from lighting fires after Obon (see p.57).

October 22: Jidai Matsuri 時代祭 This "Festival of the Ages" was introduced in 1895 to mark Kyoto's 1100th anniversary. More than two thousand people, wearing costumes representing all the intervening historical periods, parade from the Imperial Palace to Heian-jingū.

October 22: Kurama-no-Himatsuri 鞍馬の火祭 After the Jidai parade, hop on a train north to see Kurama's more boisterous Fire Festival (see box, p.479).

December 1–25: Kabuki Kaomise 顔見世 Grand kabuki festival.

December 31: Okera Mairi 白朮詣り The best place to see in the New Year is at Gion's Yasaka-jinja. Locals come here to light a flame from the sacred fire, with which to rekindle their hearths back home. As well as general good luck, this supposedly prevents illness in the coming year.

GEISHA SHOWS

If your visit doesn't coincide with any of the seasonal geisha performances there are several opportunities to see Kyoto's geisha and *maiko* dance.

Fureaikan ふれあい館 Every third Sun of the month you can see a free 15min dance performance by *maiko* at the Fureaikan museum (see p.439). Performances are at 2pm, 2.30pm and 3pm.

Gion Corner ギオンコーナー As part of Gion Corner's sampler of traditional performance arts, *maiko* perform *kyō-mai* (Kyoto-style) dances at the Gion Kōbu Kaburenjō (see p.437). Performances are at 6pm and 7pm (¥3150).

Gion Hatanaka 祇園畑中旅館 The *Gion Hatanaka* ryokan (see p.454) holds Kyoto Cuisine and Maiko Evening events (Mon, Wed, Fri & Sat at 6pm; ☎075 541 5315, ⓦ kyoto-maiko.jp; ¥19,000; reservations essential) which non-guests are welcome to attend. This is a great chance to see *maiko* performing at close range and to take photos.

KABUKI AND NŌ

Colourful and dramatic, kabuki (歌舞伎) theatre originated in Kyoto, though performances are, unfortunately, fairly sporadic these days. Nō theatre (能) is a far more stately affair; though it is often incomprehensible, even to the Japanese, it can also be incredibly powerful to watch.

Kanze Kaikan 観世会館 South of Heian-jingū ☎075 771 6114, ⓦ www.kyoto-kanze.jp. This is Kyoto's main venue for nō, with performances (including *kyōgen*) most

6

weekends (tickets from ¥3000, occasional free performances).

Kawamura Nō Stage 河村能舞台 On Karasuma-dōri near Dōshisha University ☎075 722 8716, ⓦwww .kid97.co.jp/kawamura. Lovely old nō theatre run by the Kawamura family, a long line of famous nō actors (tickets from ¥4000).

Kongo Nō-gakudō 金剛能楽堂 On Karasuma-dōri on the west side of the Imperial Park ☎075 441 7222, ⓦkongou-net.com. Large modern theatre holding regular performances of nō classics (tickets from ¥4500).

Minami-za 南座 Shijō-Ōhashi Higashi-zume ☎075 561 1155, ⓦshochiku.co.jp/play/minamiza. This theatre is the main venue to see a kabuki performance in Kyoto. Throughout December there's a major kabuki-fest here known as *kaomise*, or "face-showing" (Dec 1–25), when big-name actors perform snippets from their most successful roles.

CINEMA

Kyoto Cinema Karasuma Shijō-sagaru ☎075 353 4723, ⓦkyotocinema.jp. On the third floor of the Cocon

Karasuma shopping complex, this cinema has three screens and mainly shows local and foreign art-house films and documentaries. Daily 11am–7pm.

Minami Kaikan 79 Higashi Hieijō-chō ☎ 075 661 3993, ⓦkyoto-minamikaikan.jp. Small cinema near the junction of Ōmiya and Kujō, southeast of Kyoto Station, showing an interesting mix of alternative and mainstream films. Daily 10.30am–9.40pm.

Movix Kyoto 400 Sakurano-chō ☎075 254 3215, ⓦsmt-cinema.com/site/kyoto. Located at the top end of Shinkyōgoku, just south of Sanjō, this is Kyoto's largest cinema complex with an annexe. It screens the latest Japanese and Hollywood blockbusters. Daily 9.30am–11pm.

T-Joy Kyoto 1 Toriiguchi-machi ⓦt-joy.net/site/Kyoto. Cinema complex on the fifth floor of the Aeon Shopping Mall near Kyoto Station, showing Japanese and mainstream Hollywood movies. Daily 9am–midnight.

Toho Cinema Nijō 1-6 Togano-chō ☎075 813 2410, ⓦtohotheater.jp/theater/nijo. Large complex next to Nijō Station, showing all the mainstream Japanese and Hollywood blockbusters, including late-night screenings. Daily 9.30am–1.30am.

SHOPPING

Kyoto's main shopping district is focused around the junction of **Shijō-dōri** and **Kawaramachi-dōri**, and spreads north of Shijō along the **Teramachi** and **Shinkyōgoku** covered arcades. You'll find the big-name department stores, notably Takashimaya, Hankyū and Daimaru, all on Shijō. Souvenir shops, smart boutiques and even a few traditional craft shops are mostly situated on **Sanjō-dōri**, just west of the river. Beneath Oike-dori, between Teramachi and Kawaramachi, is the Zest underground shopping mall. The **Kyoto Station** area is home to the huge Isetan department store and an underground shopping mall, Porta, beneath the northern bus terminal. East Kyoto is best known for its wealth of shops around **Kiyomizu-dera** (see p.435), which sell the local pottery, while nearby **Sannen-zaka** (see box, p.435) hosts a lovely parade of traditional craft shops. Further north, Gion's **Shinmonzen-dōri** specializes in antiques – prices are predictably high, but it's a good area to browse.

BOOKS

Kyoto Handicraft Center 京都ハンディクラフトセンタ ー Marutamachi-dōri ☎075 761 8001, ⓦkyoto handicraftcenter.com; map p.433. On the ground floor of the east wing, there's a good range of cultural books on Japan, including photography books and guidebooks. Daily 10am–7pm.

Maruzen 丸善 Kawaramachi-dōri ☎075 253 1599, ⓦmaruzenjunkudo.co.jp; map p.426. This vast bookshop, taking up the two basement levels of the BAL building, is the best place in Kyoto to buy English books on Japan. There's also a large selection of novels, children's and academic books. Daily 11am–9pm.

FOOD

Kyoto is as famous for its beautiful foodstuffs as it is for crafts, all made with the same attention to detail and love of refinement. You can see this in even the most modest restaurant, but also in the confectionery shops, where the

window displays look more like art galleries. A popular local delicacy is pickled vegetables (*tsukemono*), which accompany most meals. If you take a walk down Nishiki-kōji market street (see p.429), you'll notice that pickles predominate among all the vegetables, tofu and dried fish. The shops listed below sell souvenir packaging of their famous products.

Ippodō 一保堂 Teramachi Nijō-agaru ☎075 211 3421, ⓦippodo-tea.co.jp; map p.426. This historic tea-seller has been in business since 1717. The shop sells all grades of Japanese green teas, locally grown in Uji – from top-quality *matcha* to the earthy roasted *hōjicha*. Daily 9am–6pm.

Izutsu Yatsuhashi 井筒八つ橋 Teramachi Shijō-agaru ☎075 255 2121, ⓦyatsuhashi.co.jp; map p.426. Yatsuhashi sweet cinnamon-flavoured biscuits and soft rice cakes are Kyoto favourites and make great souvenirs. At this Izutsu branch store you can also try your hand at baking the famous Yatsuhashi biscuits (see box, p.460). Daily 10am–8pm.

KYOTO SHOPPING COMPLEXES

The **Aeon Mall** near Kyoto Station is Kyoto's newest shopping complex, housing popular fashion stores and restaurant chains. There are two stylish shopping complexes on Karasuma-dōri: **Laque**, on the corner of Shijō, consists of six levels of boutiques, restaurants and a variety of goods shops; while **Cocon Karasuma**, south of Shijō, has designer furniture and contemporary Japanese craft shops, as well as restaurants and cafés. On Kawaramachi, the trendy **Mina** shopping complex houses fashion boutiques, cafés and the Loft department store. In northeastern Kyoto, the **Qanat** shopping complex at Takano has fashion boutiques, chain stores and a large basement supermarket and food hall.

6

Kogetsu 鼓月 681 Takanna-chō ☎ 075 221 1641, ⓦ kogetsu.com; map p.426. This elegant confectioner is famous for its *senju-semnbei* – a waffle biscuit filled with bean jam. The chrysanthemum-shaped Hana soft cakes with white bean fillings are also delicious. Daily 9am–7pm.

Takakuraya 高倉屋 Nishiki-kōji ☎ 075 231 0032, ⓦ takakuraya.jp; map p.426. Takakuraya is famous for its thinly sliced *daikon* (white radish) pickles, which are expertly prepared and have a fresh and flavoursome taste. Daily 10am–6.30pm.

Toraya とらや Gokomachi Nishi-iru Shijō-dōri ☎ 075 221 3027, ⓦ toraya-group.co.jp; map p.426. Toraya has been in business since the sixteenth century. It produces superbly artistic creations of seasonal sweets made from *mochi* (pounded rice) and sweet red or white beans. This store also has a second-floor tearoom. Daily 10am–7pm.

TEXTILES AND FASHION

Kyoto has long been famous for its high-quality kimono silk weaving and dyeing, with the Nishijin district (see p.444) the centre of the city's textile industry. Some of the wonderful traditional techniques have been revitalized by innovative Kyoto fashion designers in recent years.

Eirakuya/RAAK 永楽屋 Muromachi Sanjō-agaru ☎ 075 256 7811, ⓦ eirakuya.jp; map p.426. The main store of this traditional *tenugui* (cotton hand-cloth) manufacturer, which now reproduces stylish Taishō designs from the 1920s. The *tenugui* can be worn as a scarf or framed and hung on the wall, while modern styles are produced through the RAAK label. There are also smaller branches on Shijō, on both sides of the bridge. Daily 11am–7pm.

Kyoto Denim 京都デニム 79-3 Koinari-chō ☎ 075 352 1053, ⓦ kyoto-denim.jp; map p.430. Fashionable denim jeans and clothing incorporating local fabrics, such as cotton, silk and brocade, as well as hand-dyeing techniques. Custom orders are possible. Daily 9am–8pm.

Pagong パゴン 373 Kiyomoto-chō Gion ☎ 075 541 3155, ⓦ pagong.jp/en; map p.433. Traditional Yūzen dyer, now producing aloha shirts, camisoles, dresses, scarves and T-shirts with traditional patterns and designs. Look out for sister brand Sanjō by Pagong on Sanjō-dōri

between Fuyachō and Tominokōji. 11.30am–8pm; closed Wed.

Seisuke 88 セイスケ88 83 Nakajima-chō ☎ 075 211 7388, ⓦ seisuke88.com; map p.426. This shop has a colourful array of bags, purses and accessories made from fabric printed with designs originally used for kimono and *obi*. Tues–Fri 11am–8pm, Sat & Sun 10.30am–8pm.

Sou Sou ソウソウ 565-72 Nakano-chō ☎ 075 212 8005, ⓦ sousou.co.jp; map p.426. A winning combination of traditional footwear and modern style, this local label designs and produces *jikatabi*, split-toe workmen's shoes, in funky fabrics and styles. Also sells sportswear and kimono. Daily 11am–8pm.

TRADITIONAL ARTS AND CRAFTS SHOPS

Aritsugu 有次 Nishiki-kōji Goko-machi Nishi-iru ☎ 075 221 1091; map p.426. This top-end knife shop has been in business since the sixteenth century, when they specialized in sword production. Now they do a roaring trade in sashimi knives and other hand-crafted kitchen implements. Daily 9am–5.30pm.

Asahi-dō 朝日堂 1-280 Kiyomizu ☎ 075 531 2181, ⓦ asahido.co.jp; map p.433. The best and most famous of several pottery shops on the road up to Kiyomizu-dera, established in the Edo period and selling a wide variety of locally produced *Kiyomizu-yaki*. Daily 9am–6pm.

Ichizawa Shinzaburo Hanpu 一澤信三郎帆布 602 Takabatake-chō ☎ 075 541 0436, ⓦ ichizawa.co.jp; map p.433. Long-established canvas-bag manufacturer on Higashiōji-dōri, producing beautifully hand-stitched rucksacks, tote bags and purses in functional designs and a variety of colours. Prices start at around ¥6500. Mon–Sat 9am–6pm.

Kaikadō 開化堂 84-1 Umeminato-chō ☎ 075 351 5788, ⓦ kaikado.jp/english; map p.430. This traditional Kyoto tea caddy manufacturer has branched out into modern design and, using centuries-old techniques, is now producing stylish teapots, water pitchers, milk jugs, trays and boxes. Mon–Sat 9am–6pm.

Kyoto Design House 京都デザインハウス 105 Fukunaga-chō ☎ 075 221 0200, ⓦ kyoto-dh.com/en; map p.426. Premium selection of contemporary local

6

TEMPLE AND SHRINE FLEA MARKETS IN KYOTO

If you're in Kyoto towards the end of the month, don't miss its two big **flea markets**. On the 21st, Kōbō-san (in honour of the founder) is held at **Tō-ji** temple (see p.431), and on the 25th, Tenjin-san (in honour of the enshrined deity) is held at **Kitano Tenmangū** shrine (see p.445). Both kick off before 7am and it's worth getting there early if you're looking for special treasures. There's a fantastic carnival atmosphere at these markets, where stalls sell everything from used kimono to dried fruit and manga. Tō-ji has an antiques market on the first Sunday of every month.

A monthly market is also held at **Chion-ji** on the 15th of every month (16th if raining), which focuses more on crafts and other handmade goods. Chion-ji sits on the corner of Imadegawa-dōri and Higashiōji-dōri, close to Kyoto University.

---

designs – from sleek tableware to functional leather purses and wallets. The craftsmanship is excellent and this is a great place to buy sophisticated souvenirs. Daily 11am–8pm; closed last Wed of the month.

Kyoto Handicraft Center 京都ハンディクラフトセンタ – Marutamachi-dōri ☎075 761 8001, ⓦkyoto handicraftcenter.com; map p.433. A surprisingly decent range of traditional Kyoto crafts, souvenirs from all over Japan, and even antique *ukiyo-e* prints. It's also possible to join craft workshops such as fan painting or woodblock printing; check the website for reservation details. Located near the northwest corner of Heian-jingu. Daily 10am–6pm.

Kyūkyo-dō 鳩居堂玉堂 520 Teramachi ☎075 231 0510, ⓦkyukyodo.co.jp; map p.426. This wonderful old shop on Teramachi shopping arcade smells great thanks to all the incense on sale, but it's also a good place to purchase handmade cards and other stationery items, as well as *uchiwa* fans and calligraphy goods. Mon–Sat 10am–6pm.

Lisn リスン Karasuma-dōri Shijō-sagaru ☎075 353 6466, ⓦwww2.lisn.co.jp; map p.426. This stylish incense shop on the ground floor of Cocon Karasuma shopping complex has the decor of an exclusive nightclub. Choose from a wide range of modern seasonal blends. Daily 11am–8pm.

Suzuki Shofudō 鈴木松風堂 409 Izutsuya-chō ☎075 231 5003, ⓦshofudo-shop.jp; map p.426. Wonderful traditional paper shop selling a creative array of paper crafts such as boxes, trays and sugar pots with wooden spoons attached (¥1515). Daily 10am–7pm.

Tanakaya 田中彌 Shijō Yanaginobanba ☎075 221 1959; map p.426. This stately old shop on Shijō-dōri is one of the best places to shop for *Kyō-ningyō* – traditional Kyoto dolls – in all shapes and sizes. There's also a gallery upstairs with changing exhibitions of antique dolls. 10am–6pm; closed Wed.

Yojiya よーじや Shijō-dōri, Gion ⓦyojiya.co.jp/english; map p.433. Traditional Kyoto *aburatori-gami* (face oil blotting paper) manufacturer with branches all over the city. Powders, lipsticks and brushes, just like those used by geisha, as well as cute make-up pouches and hand-mirrors, are on sale. There is another central branch on Sanjō, which has an excellent in-house Italian café. Daily 10am–8pm.

DIRECTORY

Emergencies The main police station is at 85-3 Yabunouchi-chō, Shimodachiuri-dōri, Kamanza Higashi-iru, Kamigyō-ku (☎075 451 9111). In an absolute emergency, call ☎110 where you will be transferred to an English-speaker.

Hospitals and clinics The best Kyoto hospital with English-speaking doctors is the Japan Baptist Hospital, 47 Yamamoto-chō, Kitashirakawa, Sakyō-ku (☎075 781 5191, ⓦjbh.or.jp). Sakabe International Clinic, 435 Yamamoto-chō, Gokomachi Nijō-sagaru (closed Thurs & Sat afternoons and all day Sun; ☎075 231 1624, ⓦsakabeclinic.com), is run by English-speaking staff. For more information about medical facilities with English-speaking staff in Kyoto or throughout the region, call the AMDA International Medical Information Centre (☎06 4395 0555).

Immigration To renew your tourist or student visa, apply to the Immigration Bureau, 4F, 34-12 Higashi Marutamachi, Kawabata Higashi-iru, near Keihan Marutamachi Station (☎075 752 5997).

Mobile phone rental Kyoto-based company Rentafone Japan (☎075 752 5997, ⓦrentafonejapan.com) rents out mobile phones for ¥3900 a week and will deliver to your accommodation in Kyoto. Incoming calls are free and outgoing calls are charged at ¥35/minute.

Post offices The Central Post Office, 843-12 Higashi Shiokōji-chō, Shimogyō-ku, Kyoto-shi, is located in front of Kyoto Station. Downtown, the Nakagyō Ward Post Office, 30 Hishiya-chō, Nakagyo-ku, is near the Museum of Kyoto. Both have a 24hr window for stamps and express mail.

Around Kyoto

There's so much to see in Kyoto itself that most people don't explore the surrounding area. First priority should probably go to **Arashiyama**, to the west of Kyoto, which is famous for its gardens, temples and monkey park. **Uji**, to the south of Kyoto, is another quiet pocket of history, home to the magnificent **Byōdō-in**, whose graceful Phoenix Hall is a masterpiece of Japanese architecture, and to the tea fields which support Kyoto's cultural traditions. To the northeast of Kyoto is the sacred mountain of **Hiei-zan**, where age-old cedars shelter the venerable temple complex of **Enryaku-ji**. Below Hiei-zan, **Ōhara** contains a scattering of beguiling temples in a rustic valley, while the nearby villages of **Kurama** and **Kibune** make a fun day-trip taking in temples, a hot spring and a river lunch. Slightly further afield, but definitely worth the effort, are **Amanohashidate**, the "Bridge to Heaven", on the northern coast of Kyoto prefecture, and the picturesque fishing village of **Ine**. The attractive castle town of **Hikone** on Biwa-ko, Japan's largest lake, the leafy and secluded **Ishiyama-dera** and the architecturally stunning **Miho Museum**, nestled in the Shigaraki mountains, are also all worth visiting.

6

Arashiyama

嵐山

Western Kyoto ends in the pleasant, leafy suburb of **ARASHIYAMA**. Set beside the Hozu-gawa, Arashiyama, literally "storm mountain", was originally a place for imperial relaxation, away from the main court in central Kyoto, where aristocrats indulged in pursuits such as poetry-writing and hunting. The palaces were later converted into Buddhist temples and monasteries, the most famous of which is **Tenryū-ji**, noted for its garden, while the smaller, quieter temples have a more intimate appeal. In contrast with Tenryū-ji's somewhat introspective garden, that of **Ōkōchi Sansō** – the home of a 1920s movie actor – is by turns secretive and dramatic, with winding paths and sudden views over Kyoto.

The town's most interesting sights, as well as the majority of its shops, restaurants and transport facilities, lie north of the Hozu-gawa. Note that central Arashiyama can get unbearably crowded, particularly on spring and autumn weekends; however, if you head north along the hillside you'll soon begin to leave the crowds behind. A good way to explore the area is to rent a bike (see p.470) and spend a day pottering around the lanes and through magnificent bamboo forests; alternatively, it is possible to see some of the main sights by *jinrikisha* (rickshaw).

Togetsu-kyō

渡月橋 • A 3min walk south of Keifuku Arashiyama Station

Arashiyama is centred on the long **Togetsu-kyō** bridge, which spans the Hozu-gawa (known as the Katsura-gawa east of the bridge). This is a famous spot for viewing cherry blossoms in spring, maples in autumn, and *ukai* (cormorant fishing) in the summer.

Tenryū-ji

天龍寺 • 68 Susukinobaba-chō • Garden only ¥500, garden & temple ¥800 • ☎ 075 881 1235, ⓦ tenryuji.org

The first major sight in Arashiyama is the Zen temple of **Tenryū-ji**, which started life as the country retreat of Emperor Kameyama (1260–74), grandfather of the more famous **Emperor Go-Daigo** (1318–39). Go-Daigo overthrew the Kamakura shogunate (see p.823) and wrested power back to Kyoto in 1333 with the help of a defector from the enemy camp, **Ashikaga Takauji**. The ambitious Ashikaga soon grew exasperated by Go-Daigo's incompetence and staged a counter-coup. He placed a puppet emperor on the throne and declared himself shogun, thus also gaining the Arashiyama palace, while

6

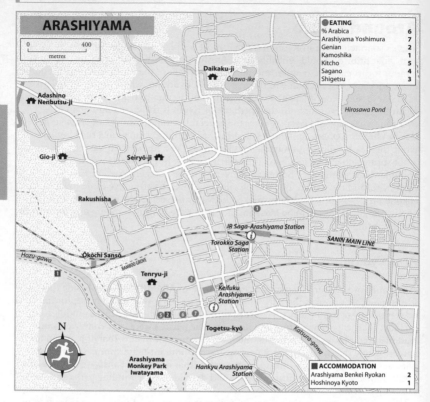

Go-Daigo fled south to set up a rival court in Yoshino, south of Nara. After Go-Daigo died in 1339, however, a series of bad omens convinced Ashikaga to convert the palace into a temple to appease Go-Daigo's restless soul.

The garden

The temple buildings are nearly all twentieth-century reproductions, but the **garden** behind dates back to the thirteenth century. It's best viewed from inside the temple, from where you get the full impact of the pond and its artfully placed rock groupings against the tree-covered hillside. The present layout of the garden is the work of **Musō Kokushi**, the fourteenth-century Zen monk also responsible for Saihō-ji (see p.448), who incorporated Zen and Chinese motifs into the existing garden. Look out for the garden's most admired feature, the dry Dragon Gate waterfall on the far side of the pond. Apparently inspired by Chinese Sung-dynasty landscape paintings, the waterfall's design is extremely unusual in Japanese garden design.

Bamboo grove

竹林, Takabayashi • Saga Ogura-yama Tabuchiyama-chō • Daily 24hr • Free • ⓦ hanatouro.jp/arashiyama • A 10min walk west of Keifuku Arashiyama Station

One of Arashiyama's most popular and photogenic sights, the beautifully maintained **bamboo grove** is spectacular in any season. The path through the grove begins to the north of Tenryū-ji, and runs west all the way to the entrance of Ōkōchi Sansō. It's usually best visited in daylight hours, but is lit up in the evening at certain times of the year; check the website for exact dates.

Ōkōchi Sansō

大河内山荘 · 8 Tabuchiyama-chō · Daily 9am–5pm · ¥1000, including green tea · ☎ 075 872 2233 · A 10min walk west of Keifuku Arashiyama Station

On the hillside at the edge of the bamboo grove you'll find the entrance to the very attractive **Ōkōchi Sansō**. Once the home of Ōkōchi Denjirō, a silent-film idol of the 1920s, this traditional Japanese villa has a spectacular location. The path through the villa's expansive grounds leads you all over the hillside, past tea-ceremony pavilions, a moss garden, a dry garden and stone benches, up to a ridge with views over Kyoto on one side and the Hozu gorge on the other. Finally, you drop down to a small museum devoted to the actor.

6

Giō-ji

祇王寺 · 32 Kozaka-chō · Daily 9am–5pm · ¥300 · ☎ 075 861 3574, ⓦ giouji.or.jp · A 20min walk northwest from JR Saga-Arashiyama Station

Named after one of its former inhabitants, **Giō-ji** is a pretty little Buddhist nunnery with a mossy, maple-shaded garden and bamboo groves. Princess Giō was a concubine of the notoriously ruthless Taira Kiyomori (1118–81), and retired to Arashiyama with her mother, sister and, later, another rejected concubine of Kiyomori. Their wooden statues are on display in a small pavilion alongside a Buddha image, and also a statue of Kiyomori.

Adashino Nenbutsu-ji

化野念仏寺 · 17 Adashino-chō · Daily 9am–4.30pm · ¥500, Sentō Kuyō ¥1000 · ☎ 075 861 2221, ⓦ nenbutsuji.or.jp · A 30min walk northwest from JR Saga-Arashiyama Station

On a hill at the northwestern edge of the Arashiyama district is the rather forlorn **Adashino Nenbutsu-ji**, notable for its ten thousand or so small Buddhist stone statues. It's a spectacular but sad landscape – centuries of unknown dead were buried here in paupers' graves. During the Obon season the **Sentō Kuyō evening ceremony** on August 23 and 24 sees thousands of lamps lit to commemorate the spirits of the dead.

Seiryō-ji

清凉寺 · 46 Fujinoki-chō · Daily 9am–4pm · ¥400 · ☎ 075 861 0343, ⓦ seiryoji.or.jp · A 15min walk north from JR Saga-Arashiyama Station

The main reason to visit the temple of **Seiryō-ji** is to see its wonderful statue of Shaka Nyorai (the Historical Buddha), though the compound itself is a pleasant place to wander around, too, and it's usually not crowded. The statue is currently on public display in April, May, October and November; at other times, a donation of ¥1000 will enable you to view it. The image was carved in China in 985 AD and is a copy of a much older Indian statue, which in turn is said to have been modelled on the Buddha while he was alive. When the statue was opened in 1953, several little silk bags in the shape of a heart, kidneys and liver were found; these "internal organs" are on display in the temple museum.

Daikaku-ji

大覚寺 · 4 Osawa-chō · Daily 9am–4.30pm · ¥500 · ☎ 075 871 0071, ⓦ daikakuji.or.jp · A 25min walk north from JR Saga-Arashiyama Station

The palatial-looking **Daikaku-ji** was founded in 876, when Emperor Saga ordered that his country villa be converted to a Shingon-sect temple. The main Shin-den hall was moved here from Kyoto's Imperial Palace in the late sixteenth century and still contains some fine screens painted by renowned artists of the Kanō school. Behind this building is the Shoshin-den, also noted for its panels of a hawk and an endearing group of rabbits. Afterwards you can wander along the banks of the picturesque Ōsawa-ike, Emperor Saga's boating lake and a popular spot for viewing the autumn Harvest Moon.

6

Rakushisha

落柿舎 • 20 Hinomyōjin-chō • Daily 9am–5pm • ¥250 • ☎ 075 881 1953, ⊛ rakushisha.jp • A 15min walk northwest from JR Saga-Arashiyama Station

A rustic seventeenth-century hermitage, **Rakushisha** belonged to Mukai Kyorai (1651–1704), one of the disciples of haiku master Bashō (see p.867), who composed his *Saga Nikki* (diary) here. Kyorai named Rakushisha (literally, "cottage of the fallen persimmons") after a storm stripped his persimmon trees of fruit. An English-language pamphlet has translations of the poem stones in the **garden**, which also contains special boxes in which you can leave your own haiku for the annual competition.

Arashiyama Monkey Park Iwatayama

嵐山モンキーパークくいわたやま • 8 Genryokuzan-chō • Daily: mid-March to mid-Nov 9am–5pm; mid-Nov to mid-March 9am–4pm • ¥550 • ☎ 075 872 0950, ⊛ kmpi.co.jp • Enter through the *torii* near the southern end of Togetsu-kyō

Located on the side of Mount Arashiyama, the **Arashiyama Monkey Park Iwatayama** is home to more than 120 Japanese macaque monkeys. The park is also a research centre, and is well worth a visit for a break away from the crowds. A steep path winds up Mount Arashiyama to the observation deck, where the monkeys are fed, and from here you can enjoy excellent views of Arashiyama, the Hozu-gawa and Kyoto city.

ARRIVAL AND DEPARTURE   ARASHIYAMA

By Keifuku train Three train lines connect Arashiyama with central Kyoto. The quickest and most pleasant way to get here is to take a train on the private Keifuku Electric Railway (nicknamed "Randen") from Kyoto's Shijō-Ōmiya Station (every 10min; 20min; ¥210) into the main Arashiyama Station in the centre of town. The "Randen All-Day Ticket" (¥500) allows unlimited travel on this Arashiyama line, as well as the Keifuku Kitano line, which connects with Kitano Hakubaichō Station in northwest Kyoto.

By JR train Alternatively, the JR Sagano line runs from Kyoto Station to Saga-Arashiyama Station (every 20min; 20min; ¥240), but it's roughly a 15min walk to central Arashiyama from here; make sure you get on a local JR train

from Kyoto and not the express, which shoots straight through.

By Hankyū train Finally, there's the less convenient Hankyū Electric Railway; from central Kyoto you have to change at Katsura Station, and you end up in the Hankyū Arashiyama Station on the south side of the river (every 20min; 30min; ¥220).

By bus Buses are slightly more expensive than trains and take longer, especially when the traffic's bad. However, Arashiyama is on the main Kyoto bus network and falls within the limits for the combined bus and subway pass (see box, p.450). City Bus routes #11, #28 and #93 all pass through central Arashiyama.

INFORMATION AND TOURS

Tourist information There's a tourist information booth (daily 9am–5pm) inside the Keifuku Arashiyama Station where you can pick up a free tourist map. There's also a small information office at the southern entrance to JR Saga-Arashiyama Station (daily 9am–4.30pm).

By bike If you plan to do more than just the central sights, it's worth considering bike rental. There are rental outlets at

each of the train stations (¥1000 per day).

Tours The Kyoto Sagano Walk (Tues & Thurs at 10am; 3hr; ¥2000; ⊛ kyotosaganowalk.main.jp) is a good way to discover some of Arashiyama's lesser-known sites on foot. Tours meet outside the ticket gate at JR Saga-Arashiyama Station. Reservations are not necessary.

ACCOMMODATION

Arashiyama Benkei Ryokan 嵐山辨慶旅館 34 Susukinobaba-chō ☎ 075 872 3355, ⊛ benkei.biz. This small high-class ryokan sits elegantly on the northern bank of the Hozu-gawa with Tenryū-ji at its rear. Located on the estate of a Heian court noble, the ryokan and its beautiful gardens have a special atmosphere. **¥130,200**

Hoshinoya Kyoto 星のや 11-2 Genryokuzan-chō ☎ 075 871 0001, ⊛ hoshinoyakyoto.jp. This luxury ryokan has become popular with celebrity visitors to Kyoto because of its secretive location on the southern bank of the Hozu-gawa. Guests are transported upriver by boat from a special jetty near Togetsu-kyō. ☎ **¥128,790**

EATING

Arashiyama is famous for its Buddhist vegetarian cuisine, *shōjin-ryōri*, and particularly for *yūdōfu* (simmered tofu), which is closely associated with the Zen tradition. Some of the top-end places are very pricey, but Arashiyama also has plenty of cheaper places to eat, mostly clustered around the main stations.

% Arabica アラビカ 3-47 Susukinobaba-chō ☎ 075 748 0057, ⊛ arabica.coffee. The Arashiyama branch of this hip coffee chain has probably the nicest view in Kyoto with which to enjoy your latte (¥550). It's situated in a kiosk with some outdoor seating, and also has a small indoor room with a perfect view of the river, available to rent by the half-hour (¥1000). Daily 8am–6pm.

★ Arashiyama Yoshimura 嵐山よしむら Togetsukyō Kitazume ☎ 075 863 5700, ⊛ arashiyama-yoshimura .com. This traditional soba restaurant near the Togetsu-kyō bridge has fantastic views of the Hozu-gawa and Mt Arashiyama from its second-floor dining area. Tasty soba set lunches start from ¥1600; the Tenzaru-zen (¥2180) includes a generous serving of assorted tempura. English menu available. Daily 10.30am–5pm.

Genian 玄以庵 Saga Tenryū-ji ☎ 075 881 9033, ⊛ oimatu.co.jp. The tranquil tearoom of renowned traditional sweet maker Oimatsu is a pleasant escape from the crowds. They serve beautifully crafted *kyo-qashi* served with *matcha* (¥1080), *sencha* (¥850) or *hoji-cha* (¥750). In summer, their citrus fruit jelly (¥650) is highly recommended. Daily 9.30am–4pm.

★ Kamoshika カモシカ 17-1 Wakamiya-chō ☎ 075 862 0106, ⊛ kamoshika.kyoto.jp. A delightful new addition to the Arashiyama dining scene, *Kamoshika* specializes in fermented foods, such as pickles, miso and fish. The delicious daily lunch set (¥1300) has eight different kinds of fermented dishes and is served with rice and soup. The simpler *donburi* set (¥900) – fermented soybeans on rice – comes with soup and pickles. It's best to reserve a table in advance, and allow plenty of time to eat. Tues–Sat 11am–3pm.

Kitcho 吉兆 58 Susukinobaba-chō ☎ 075 881 1101, ⊛ kitcho.com/kyoto. One of the most expensive restaurants in Japan, if not the world (science fiction writer Arthur C. Clarke described it as "frighteningly expensive"), *Kitcho* has a world-famous reputation for offering the best in culinary artistry, hospitality and decor. Each meal is uniquely designed to include the best produce of the season, with preparations beginning days in advance – infinite care is taken over everything, from the garnish to the antique ceramic plates on which the dishes are served. Set *kaiseki* lunches start at ¥43,200 and dinner courses are from ¥48,600. 11am–1pm & 5–7pm; closed Wed.

Sagano 嵯峨野 45 Susukinobaba-chō ☎ 075 871 6946, ⊛ kyoto-sagano.jp. In a graceful bamboo grove south of Tenryū-ji, *Sagano* is a tranquil place for lunch or an early dinner of tofu-based cuisine. The walls are lined with Imari chinaware, and their *yūdōfu* set meal is superb, accompanied by lots of dipping sauces and vegetarian side dishes (¥3800). Daily 11am–7pm.

★ Shigetsu 天龍寺篩月 68 Susukinobaba-chō ☎ 075 882 9725, ⊛ tenryuji.com/shigetsu. Located within Tenryū-ji, this is a truly authentic *shōjin-ryōri* experience in a lovely setting. There's a choice of three courses (the basic three-course set is ¥3000), and reservations are essential for the more expensive courses (from ¥5000). Note that if you're eating in the restaurant you will need to pay the ¥500 entry fee for the garden. Daily 11am–2pm.

Uji

宇治

The town of **UJI**, thirty minutes' train ride south of Kyoto, has a long and illustrious past and boasts one of Japan's most fabulous buildings, the **Byōdō-in** – for a preview, look at the reverse side of a ¥10 coin. Somehow this eleventh-century hall, with its glorious statue of Amida Buddha, survived war, fire and years of neglect, and today preserves a stunning display of Heian-period art at its most majestic. Uji is also famous for its **tea fields**; since the fourteenth century, this area's green tea leaves have been rated among the best in the country, and you'll find plenty of teashops where you can sample it on the way from the train station to Byōdō-in. Uji can easily be visited on a half-day excursion from Kyoto, and it's only a little bit further from Nara (see p.485).

Byōdō-in

平等院 • 116 Uji Renge • **Garden and treasure hall** Daily 8.30am–5.30pm • ¥600 • **Phoenix Hall** Daily 9.30am–4.10pm • ¥300 • Admission limited to 50 people every 20min • ☎ 0774 21 2861, ⊛ byodoin.or.jp • A 10min walk from JR or Keihan Uji Station

One of the nicest places to visit in western Japan, the elegant temple of **Byōdō-in** boasts a remarkable collection of Heian-period art, some impressive buildings and a

6

UJI TEA PLANTATION TOURS

The area around Uji is the second-biggest **tea-growing** region in Japan (the largest is Shizuoka in the east of the country) and the fields here have supplied Kyoto's tea culture since the fourteenth century, when seeds brought over from China were first planted. Uji tea is considered the finest in Japan and it is also the most expensive. The best times to visit Uji's tea fields and processing factories are in late spring, when the first leaves of the season, later drunk as *shin-cha* ("new tea"), are being picked, and in early autumn for the next harvest.

Obubu Tea Farm in Wazuka (ⓦobubutea.com), approximately 40 minutes south of Uji by train, holds **tea tours** on Tuesdays and Thursdays. The tour visits several tea fields, and includes tea tasting and a lunch of *cha-soba* (green tea noodles). Advance reservations are required up to one day in advance (ⓔinfo@obubutea.com). There are also three special **tea picking and rolling events** a year in spring, summer and autumn, where you can learn how to pick the best leaves, roast them and make your own Hōji-cha and *matcha*. The staff here (including foreign interns) are full of passion and energy for tea culture and warmly welcome foreign visitors, making it a memorable and worthwhile trip.

tranquil atmosphere. After the imperial capital moved to Kyoto in 794, Uji became a popular location for aristocratic country retreats. One such villa was taken over in the late tenth century by the emperor's chief adviser, **Fujiwara Michinaga**, when the Fujiwara clan was at its peak (see p.821). His son, Yorimichi, continued developing the gardens and pavilions until they were the envy of the court. Those pavilions have long gone, but you can still catch a flavour of this golden age through the great literary masterpiece, *The Tale of Genji* (see p.867), written in the early eleventh century. In 1052, some years after *The Tale of Genji* was completed, Yorimichi decided to convert the villa into a temple dedicated to Amida, the Buddha of the Western Paradise. By the following year, the great Amida Hall, popularly known as the Phoenix Hall, was completed. Miraculously, it's the only building from the original temple to have survived.

Phoenix Hall

鳳凰堂, Hōō-dō

The best place to view the **Phoenix Hall** is from the far side of the pond, where it sits on a small island; the exteriors have been recently restored and the reflection in the pond makes for an excellent photo. The hall itself is surprisingly small. Inside, the gilded statue of **Amida** dominates. It was created by a sculptor-priest called Jōchō, using a new method of slotting together carved blocks of wood, and is in remarkably fine condition. At one time the hall must have been a riot of colour, but now only a few traces of the **wall paintings** remain, most of which are reproductions. If you look very carefully, you can just make out faded images of Amida and a host of heavenly beings descending on billowing clouds to receive the faithful. Meanwhile, the white, upper walls are decorated with a unique collection of 52 carved bodhisattvas, which were also originally painted.

The original wall paintings, as well as the temple bell and two phoenixes, are now preserved in the excellent modern **treasure hall**, Hōmotsu-kan, partially submerged into a hill behind the Phoenix Hall. It's worth seeing them up close, especially as these are now the oldest examples of the *Yamato-e* style of painting (see p.839) still in existence.

The Tale of Genji Museum

源氏物語ミュージアム, Genji Monogatari Myūjiamu • 45-26 Higashiuchi • Tues–Sun 9am–4.30pm • ¥500 • ☎ 0774 39 9300, ⓦ uji-genji .jp/en • To get to the museum, cross Uji bridge, north of Byōdō-in, head towards Keihan Uji Station, and take a right turn up the hill

The small but engaging **The Tale of Genji Museum** is a delightful place to connect with Japan's literary history. *The Tale of Genji* (see p.867) was written in the early eleventh century by Murasaki Shikibu, the daughter of an official of the Imperial Court in Kyoto, and is regarded as the world's first novel. It is an epic saga of love affairs, court intrigues and political machinations, centring on Genji, the Shining Prince, the beautiful son of an emperor and his concubine. The book's finale is set in Uji, which Murasaki Shikibu would have known intimately – she was a distant relative of Fujiwara Michinaga and she served as lady-in-waiting to his daughter, Empress Akiko. At the museum, you can learn about the fictional world of Genji in 3-D format, which includes a reproduction of a Heian-period home and an animated film based on the heroine of the Uji chapters, Ukifune. Pick up an English-language pamphlet and free audio guide at the entrance which together provide useful information and commentary on the exhibits.

6

ARRIVAL AND DEPARTURE   UJI

By train Uji lies on the JR Nara line between Kyoto and Nara, with trains running roughly every 15min from Kyoto (15–30min; ¥240) and every 20min from Nara (30–50min;

¥500). The Keihan line, which runs between Kyoto and Osaka, stops at Chushojima, where you can change for the Keihan Uji line (¥320; 15min).

INFORMATION AND ACTIVITIES

Tourist information There's a tourist information office at JR Uji Station (daily 9am–5pm; ☎0774 24 8783) near the south exit. It's a good place to pick up a map in English before heading to the sights. The Uji City Tourist Information Centre (daily 9am–5pm; ☎0774 23 3334) is further along the riverbank from Byōdō-in.

Fishing demonstrations On summer evenings the river at Uji is used for demonstrations of *ukai* (cormorant fishing; see box, p.477) near Nakanoshima Park; it's best experienced from one of the fishing boats (mid-June to mid-Sept daily 7–8.30pm; ☎0774 21 2328; ¥2000).

EATING AND DRINKING

Magozaemon 孫左エ門 21 Uji Renge ☎0774 22 4068. Just opposite the entrance to Byōdō-in, this popular restaurant serves especially good and inexpensive handmade noodle dishes. The Uji green-tea udon sets, either hot or cold (¥1280), are delicious. 11am–3pm; closed Thurs.

Mitsuboshien Kanbayashi 三星園上林 27-2 Uji Renge ☎0774 21 2636, ⓦujicha-kanbayashi.co.jp. Long-established tea-seller with a tearoom and a reference library on the history and culture of Uji tea. You can join a class here and learn to make your own *matcha* (¥865 with a sweet). Reservations essential. Daily 9am–6pm.

Taihou-an 対鳳庵 2 Tokawa ☎0774 23 3334. This traditional teahouse is a lovely place to take a break and enjoy a fresh bowl of Uji's famous green tea with a seasonal sweet (¥500). Tickets to enter the teahouse and have tea

can be purchased at the Uji City Tourist Information Centre next door. Daily 10am–4pm; closed Dec 20–Jan 10.

★**Tatsumiya** 辰巳屋 3-7 Tokawa ☎0774 21 3131, ⓦuji-tatsumiya.co.jp. Overlooking the Uji-gawa, this *Kyō-ryōri* restaurant serves a wonderful lunch set. The Uji Maru Bentō (¥3240) is presented in a basket and consists of thirty artfully arranged bites of seafood, fish, tofu and vegetables served with rice balls and dessert. 11am–2.30pm & 4.30–8pm; closed Wed.

Tsūen-jaya 通園 1 Higashiuchi ☎0774 21 2243, ⓦtsuentea.com. Proudly claiming to be Japan's oldest teashop, *Tsūen-jaya* has been run by the same family for over 800 years. The current building, near to the Keihan Uji Station, dates back to the seventeenth century and is full of historical tea paraphernalia. Fresh *matcha* with a sweet is ¥680. Daily 9.30am–5.30pm.

Hiei-zan

比叡山

Protecting Kyoto's northeastern flank (traditionally considered the source of evil spirits threatening the capital), the sacred mountain of **Hiei-zan** is the home of Tendai Buddhism (see box, p.474). The sect's headquarters are housed in an atmospheric collection of buildings, **Enryaku-ji**, a pleasant place to meander along ancient paths through cedar forests. The route up to Enryaku-ji from Kyoto wriggles up the mountainside, then follows a ridge road north, and on a clear day you'll be rewarded with huge views west over **Biwa-ko**, Japan's largest lake and the second-oldest freshwater lake in the world after Lake Baikal in Siberia. Enryaku-ji lies about 800m above sea level and can get pretty chilly in winter; even in summer you'll find it noticeably cooler than Kyoto.

Enryaku-ji

延暦寺 • 4220 Honmachi • Daily 9am–4pm • Main compounds ¥700, English audio guide ¥500 • ☏ 077 578 0001, ⊚ hieizan.or.jp

The top of Hiei-zan consists of a narrow ridge, at the south end of which stand the central halls of **Enryaku-ji**. From this core area, known as the **Tō-tō** (Eastern Pagoda; 東塔), the ridge slopes gently northwest down to the **Sai-tō** (Western Pagoda; 西塔). A third compound, **Yokawa**, lies further north again, but this was a later addition and contains little of immediate interest.

Kokuhō-den and Daikō-dō

国宝殿 • 大講堂

Enryaku-ji's most important buildings are concentrated in the southerly **Tō-tō** compound. Immediately inside the entrance you'll find a modern treasure hall, the **Kokuhō-den**. Its most interesting exhibits are a fine array of statues, including a delicate, thirteenth-century Amida Buddha and a lovely Senjū Kannon (Thousand-Armed Kannon) of the ninth century. You can also see a scroll apparently recording Saichō's trip to China in 804 AD. Up the hill from the Kokuhō-den, the first building on your left is the **Daikō-dō**, the Great Lecture Hall, where monks attend lectures on the sutras and discuss doctrine. Keeping an eye on them are life-size statues of Nichiren, Eisai, Hōnen, Shinran and other great names from the past – a sort of Tendai Hall of Fame.

Konpon Chū-dō

根本中堂

Enryaku-ji's most sacred hall is the **Konpon Chū-dō**, located in the Tō-tō compound. This powerful, faded building marks the spot where Saichō built his first hut; his statue of Yakushi Nyorai is kept inside, though hidden from view. Despite the crowds, the atmosphere in the dark, cavernous hall is absolutely compelling. Unusually, the altars are in a sunken area below the worship floor, where they seem to float in a swirling haze of incense smoke lit by low-burning lamps. It's said that the three big lanterns in front of the main altar have been burning ever since Saichō himself lit them 1200 years ago. Monks tending the flames nowadays wear a mask in case they sneeze and accidentally blow the flame out.

ENRYAKU-JI AND THE TENDAI SECT

The mountain temple complex of **Enryaku-ji** was founded in 788 AD by a young Buddhist monk called Saichō (767–822), who was later sanctified as **Dengyō Daishi**. Saichō built himself a small hut on the mountain and a temple to house an image of Yakushi Nyorai (the Buddha of Healing), which he carved from a fallen tree. He then went to China for a year to study Buddhism; on his return to Hiei-zan in 805 AD he founded the Japanese **Tendai sect**. Based on the Lotus Sutra, Tendai doctrine holds that anyone can achieve enlightenment through studying the sacred texts and following extremely rigorous practices. Its followers went on to establish a whole host of splinter groups: Hōnen (who founded the Jōdo sect), Shinran (Jōdo Shinshū), Eisai (Rinzai Zen) and Nichiren all started out as Tendai priests.

In the early days, Enryaku-ji received generous imperial funding and court officials were sent up the mountain for a twelve-year education programme. As the sect expanded it became enormously rich and politically powerful, until there were three thousand buildings on the mountain. It owned vast areas of land and even maintained an army of several hundred well-trained **warrior monks** – many of whom were not really monks at all. They spent a good deal of time fighting other Buddhist sects, notably their great rivals at Nara's Kōfuku-ji (see p.487). In 1571, the warlord **Oda Nobunaga** (see p.874) put a stop to all this, leading 30,000 troops up Hiei-zan to lay waste to the complex, including the monks and their families. Nobunaga died eleven years later, and his successor, Toyotomi Hideyoshi, was more kindly disposed to the Tendai sect, encouraging the monks to rebuild.

FROM TOP TOGETSU-KYŌ BRIDGE (P.467); YOSHIKAWA RYOKAN, KYOTO (P.453) >

Kaidan-in and Amida-dō
戒壇院・阿弥陀堂

The pretty **Kaidan-in**, the Ordination Hall, and the reconstructed **Amida-dō** and its two-storey pagoda are surrounded by cherry blossoms in the spring, and maple trees in the autumn. Kaidan-in houses some important Buddhist images which are not on display to the public, while the bright-red Amida-dō is used for memorial services. Behind here, a path leads off through the woods to the Sai-tō compound.

6

Jōdo-in
浄土院

Located to the north of the Tō-tō compound, the peaceful **Sai-tō** compound is one of the highlights of a visit to Enryaku-ji. It houses some important buildings, including the **Jōdo-in**, a ten-minute walk along the path through the woods at the bottom of a lantern-lined staircase. Inside the temple's courtyard, behind the main hall, is **Saichō's mausoleum** (伝教大師御廟, Dengyō Daishi Gobyō), a red-lacquered building that stands in a carefully tended gravel enclosure and is one of Enryaku-ji's most sacred sites.

Ninai-dō
にない堂

Two identical square halls standing on a raised area in the Sai-tō compound are commonly known as **Ninai-dō**, which roughly translates as "shoulder-carrying hall"; this refers to the legendary strength of a certain Benkei, who's said to have hoisted the two buildings onto his shoulders like a yoke. Their official names are Jōgyō-dō (常行堂), the Hall of Perpetual Practice, and the Hokke-dō (法華堂), or Lotus Hall. They're used for different types of meditation practice: in the former, monks walk round the altar for days reciting the Buddha's name; in the latter, they alternate between walking and sitting meditation while studying the Lotus Sutra.

Shaka-dō
釈迦堂

The centre of the Sai-tō area is marked by the **Shaka-dō**, an imposing hall with a sunken centre and three lanterns. Though smaller and not as atmospheric as Konpon Chū-dō, this building is much older; originally erected in the thirteenth century on the shores of Biwa-ko, it was moved here in 1595 to replace the earlier hall destroyed by Nobunaga's armies. It's a lovely, quiet place to rest before you start heading back.

MARATHON MONKS

Followers of the Buddhist **Tendai sect** (see box, p.474) believe that the route to enlightenment lies through chanting, esoteric ritual and extreme physical endurance. The most rigorous of these practices is the "thousand-day ascetic mountain pilgrimage", in which **marathon monks**, as they're popularly known, are required to walk 40,000km through the mountains and streets of Kyoto in a thousand days – the equivalent of nearly a thousand marathons. The thousand days are split into hundred-day periods over seven years; during each period the monk has to go out every day in all weathers, regardless of his physical condition. He must adhere to a strict vegetarian diet and, at one point during the seven years, go on a week-long fast with no food, water or sleep, just for good measure.

Not surprisingly, many monks don't make it – in the old days they were expected to commit ritual suicide if they had to give up. Those who do finish (nowadays, about one person every five years) are rewarded with enlightenment and become "living Buddhas". Apparently, the advice of modern marathon monks is much sought-after by national baseball coaches and others involved in endurance training.

ARRIVAL AND DEPARTURE

HIEI-ZAN

By bus The quickest and simplest way of getting to Enryaku-ji is to take a direct bus (1hr; ¥800) from either Kyoto Station or Sanjō-Keihan Station in east Kyoto. The timetable varies according to the season, so check in Kyoto for the latest schedule and note that in winter the road is sometimes closed by snow. Buses loop around the rather tacky Garden Museum Hiei, an outdoor museum devoted to re-creating garden scenes from famous paintings by Monet and Renoir, and then stop at the Enryaku-ji Bus Centre, where you'll find the temple's main entrance.

Sakamoto Cable-car The most convenient of the mountain's two cable-cars is the eastern Sakamoto Cable (坂本ケーブル; every 30min; 11min; ¥860, or ¥1620 return), which has the added benefit of views over Biwa-ko. To reach the cable-car, take a JR Kosei line train from Kyoto

Station to Hiei-zan Sakamoto Station (比叡山坂本駅; every 15min; 20min; ¥320), then a bus (¥220). From the top station it's a 700m walk north to the central Tō-tō area along a quiet road.

Eizan Cable-car and Ropeway The western Eizan Cable and Ropeway (叡山ケーブル; every 30min; 20min; ¥850 one-way, or ¥1700 return) dumps you at the Sanchō Station (山頂駅), about 1.5km from the Tō-tō area: from the station you can catch a shuttle bus (see below), or walk along a footpath behind the Garden Museum Hiei. Eizan Cable leaves from near Yase-Hiei-zan-guchi Station (八瀬比叡山口駅) on the private Eizan line; to get there, either take a train from Kyoto's Demachiyanagi Station (every 12min; 14min; ¥260), or a Kyoto Bus headed for Ōhara from Kyoto Station (#17 and #18) or Sanjō-Keihan Station (#16 and #17).

GETTING AROUND

By bus Once you've arrived on the mountain, the best way to get around is on foot. If you're in a hurry, however, you can take the shuttle bus (late March to Nov; every 30min), which runs from Sanchō via the central Tō-tō car park to Sai-tō and Yokawa. The whole journey only takes about

20min and costs ¥740. It's best to get a one-day pass (*hiei-zan-nai ichi-nichi jyōshaken*; ¥800), which is available from the bus driver or at the Tō-tō bus terminal; this allows unlimited travel and also entitles you to a ¥100 discount on entrance to Enryaku-ji.

EATING

Minemichi 峰道レストラン 4220 Sakamoto Honmachi, 2km north of Sai-tō on the road to Yokawa ☎ 0775 78 3673. Large cafeteria serving standard fare with spectacular views of Biwa-ko. There's no English menu but

you can choose from the photo menu when you order at the counter – the Hieizan soba lunch set (¥1500) is a good choice. Daily 10am–5pm; closed mid-Dec to Feb.

Ōhara
大原

Though only a short trip north from Kyoto, the collection of temples that make up **ŌHARA** is almost in a different world. All are sub-temples of Enryaku-ji (see p.474), but the atmosphere here is quite different: instead of stately cedar forests, these little temples are surrounded by maples and flower-filled gardens that are fed by tumbling streams. The sights are divided into two sections: the easterly **Sanzen-in** and the melancholy **Jakkō-in** across the rice fields.

Sanzen-in

三千院・540 Raigōin-chō・Daily: March to Dec 7 8.30am–5pm; Dec 8 to Feb 9am–4.30pm・¥700・☎ 075 744 2531, ⌨ sanzenin.or.jp・A 10min walk up the hill from the bus terminal

A fortress-like wall contains Ōhara's most important temple, **Sanzen-in**. The temple is said to have been founded by Saichō, the founder of Tendai Buddhism (see box, p.479), but its main point of interest is the tenth-century **Ōjōgokuraku-in**, a small but splendid building standing on its own in a mossy garden. Inside is an astonishingly well-preserved tenth-century Amida Buddha flanked by smaller statues of Kannon (on the right as you face them) and Seishi, which were added later.

Shōrin-in

勝林院・187 Shōrinin-chō・Daily 9am–4.30pm・¥300・☎ 075 744 2537・A 10min walk from the bus terminal

With its thatched roof, the main hall of **Shōrin-in** is a very pretty sight in June when the surrounding hydrangea bushes are in bloom. Reconstructed in the 1770s and containing an image of Amida, the temple is used for studying *shōmyō*, the Buddhist incantations practised by followers of Tendai. *Shōmyō* were first introduced from China in the eighth century and have had a profound influence on music in Japan such as *gagaku* (court music); press the button in the booth on the left side of the altar and you can hear a short recital.

Hōsen-in

宝泉院 • 187 Shōrinin-chō • Daily 9am–5pm • ¥800, including green tea • ☎ 075 744 2409 • A 10min walk from the bus terminal

The main reason to visit the temple of **Hōsen-in** is for its intriguing garden, the highlight of which is a magnificent pine that is around seven hundred years old. The temple's ceiling is made from planks that were originally in Fushimi Castle in southern Kyoto, where more than three hundred samurai committed *seppuku* (ritual suicide) after losing a battle in 1600. If you look carefully, traces of blood are still visible.

Jakkō-in

寂光院 • 676 Kusao-chō • Daily 9am–5pm • ¥600 • ☎ 075 744 3341, ⊛ jakkoin.jp • A 15min walk west from Ōhara bus station across the river

Situated in a quiet garden which was landscaped in the late Edo period and is fringed by a row of tufted pines, the main hall of the **Jakkō-in** temple had to be rebuilt after it was destroyed in an arson attack in May 2000. This unfortunately damaged its Jizō Bodhisattva and also its one-thousand-year-old pine tree (mentioned in the *Tale of Heike*), which withered and died in 2004. The hall was completely rebuilt, and the temple and its surrounding area have lost much of their original allure. Photos of the devastating fire are on display in the Homotsuden.

ARRIVAL AND DEPARTURE ŌHARA

By bus To reach Ōhara from central Kyoto, take a cream-and-red Kyoto Bus either from Kyoto Station (#17 and #18), Sanjō-Keihan Station (#16 and #17) or Kita-ōji Station (#15). The journey takes 30–50min and costs a maximum of ¥580, or you can use the Kyoto-wide subway and bus pass (see p.450). The route takes you past Yase-yūen, the starting point of the Eizan cable-car up Hiei-zan (see p.473), making it possible to visit both places in one rather hectic day. Note that in autumn buses are very crowded and there are frequent traffic jams on the road to Ōhara. Visiting on a weekend during this time is best avoided.

ACCOMMODATION AND EATING

Ōhara Riverside Café Kirin 大原リバーサイドカフェ来隣 144 Raigōin-chō ☎ 075 744 2239, ⊛ ohara-kirin .com. Located behind the bus station, before the bridge over the river, this spacious café in a traditional building serves a variety of tasty dishes using local vegetables. Hungry travellers will find the daily Ōhara vegetable buffet (¥1500) an excellent (and filling) deal. Kirin's original blend drip coffee is ¥500 a cup. 11.30am–4.30pm; closed Tues.

Seryo 芹生 22 Shōrinin-chō ☎ 075 744 2301. If you want to enjoy Ōhara once the crowds have gone, consider a stay at this fine ryokan, which has a choice of comfortable tatami or Western-style rooms as well as open-air and indoor onsen baths. Even if you're not staying, *Seryo* is also one of the nicest places to eat in Ōhara, serving a beautifully presented bentō of seasonal vegetables (¥3500) as well as more expensive *kaiseki* meals (from ¥5500). In good weather you can eat outside on a riverside terrace. Daily 11am–4pm. ¥̲4̲4̲,̲0̲0̲0̲

Seryo Jaya 芹生茶屋 Sanzenin-mae ☎ 075 744 2301. At the top of the steps, just before the entrance to Sanzen-in, *Seryō Jaya* is a cheap option for lunch, with a variety of tasty soba lunch sets, served with rice and pickles, costing from ¥1000. Daily 9am–5pm.

Kurama and Kibune

鞍馬 • 貴船

Half an hour by train from Kyoto, the villages of **KURAMA** and **KIBUNE** make for a relaxing day-trip, especially during spring and autumn when the forest views are stunning. Picturesque Kibune is extremely popular in the summer, when many local restaurants erect special decks over the river. Other than the shrine of **Kifune-jinja**

KURAMA'S FIRE FESTIVAL

Kurama's boisterous **Kurama-no-Himatsuri** (fire festival; 鞍馬の火祭) is held every year on October 22. Villagers light bonfires outside their houses and local lads carry giant, flaming torches (the biggest weighing up to 100kg) to the shrine. Events climax around 8pm with a mad dash up the steps with a *mikoshi* (portable shrine), after which there's heavy-duty drinking, drumming and chanting till dawn. It's best to arrive at the festival early and leave around 10pm.

6

there's not a lot to see, so it's a good idea to combine a visit here with a trip to Kurama. Considered the spiritual home of the Japanese healing technique of reiki, Kurama's main draws are its **hot spring** and the mystical **Kurama-dera**.

Kurama Onsen

鞍馬温泉 • 520 Kurama Honmachi • Daily 10am–8pm • ¥2500, outdoor bath only ¥1000 • ☎ 075 741 2131, ⦿ jkurama-onsen.co.jp

Towards the northern end of Kurama village is **Kurama Onsen**, an attractive hot spring resort in a secluded setting surrounded by *sugi* (cedar) trees. The indoor "grand bath" has a sauna, but the spacious outdoor bath is recommended for its pleasant natural scenery.

Kurama-dera

鞍馬寺 • 1074 Kurama Honmachi • Daily 9am–4pm • ¥200, ropeway ¥200 one-way • ☎ 075 741 2003, ⦿ kuramadera.or.jp

Renowned for its spiritual atmosphere, **Kurama-dera** was founded in 770 by the monk, Gantei, of Tōshōdai-ji in Nara (see p.499), who is said to have been led to the spot by a white horse (the name Kurama literally means "horse's saddle"). Originally part of the Tendai Buddhist sect and a branch of Shoren-in (see p.436), Kurama-dera broke away in 1949 to form its own independent sect of nature worship, Kurama-Kokyo.

It's a steep thirty- to forty-minute climb up to the temple from Kurama village, or you can take the temple's own ropeway. The temple buildings have been repeatedly destroyed by fire, and most are modern constructions, including the main hall, the **Honden**, which contains replicas of several national treasures. It's worth spending a few minutes exploring the atmospheric basement, accessible via internal stairs at either side of the main hall, illuminated by hundreds of lanterns. There are wonderful views over the valley from the courtyard in front of the Honden.

Kifune-jinja

貴船神社 • 180 Kibune-chō • Daily 9am–4.30pm • Free • ☎ 075 741 2016, ⦿ kifunejinja.jp

The small shrine of **Kifune-jinja**, at the top of the valley, has existed since Heian times. The gods of water are enshrined here, hence its location adjacent to the river, and the stone boat and other water-related objects in the grounds. The shrine is one of the few places practising **water divination**: buy a *mikuji* from the booth (¥200), place it in the small stream nearby and your fortune (in Japanese) will become visible.

ARRIVAL AND GETTING AROUND **KURAMA AND KIBUNE**

By train Trains on the Eizan railway line from Demachiyanagi Station will take you directly to Kibune-guchi Station (every 15–20min; 30min; ¥420) and onto Kurama Station a few minutes later.

On foot It's possible to walk over the ridge on a 4.5km forest path linking Kurama-dera and Kifune-jinja.

EATING

KURAMA

Yoshūji 雍州路 1074-2 Kurama Honmachi ☎ 075 741 2848, ⦿ yoshuji.com. This *shōjin-ryōri* (Buddhist vegetarian) restaurant, in a traditional building, serves soba noodles (¥1080) and three different types of lunch sets. Try the Kurama Yama course (¥2700), which includes fresh *yuba* (tofu skin) sashimi, *tororo* (mountain yam) soba, rice and seasonal vegetables. 10am–6pm; closed Tues.

KIBUNE

Hirobun ひろ文 87 Kibune-chō ☎075 741 2147, ⓦhirobun.co.jp. In summer, you can enjoy cool breezes while slurping *somen* (thin white) noodles on a *kawaboko* (platform) jutting out over the river. The noodles (¥1300) are placed in bamboo water pipes, and patrons have to catch their noodles with chopsticks as they rush past, before dipping them into a sauce of vinegar and soy sauce. Off-season, try the Niyumen set consisting of hot *somen* noodles with *yuba* topping (¥1500). Daily 11am–7pm; closed late Dec–early Jan.

6 Amanohashidate

天橋立

At the northern tip of Kyoto-fu (Kyoto prefecture), the stubby peninsula of **Tango-Hantō** (丹後半島) leans protectively over Wakasa Bay, shielding the sand spit of **AMANOHASHIDATE**, the "Bridge to Heaven". As one of the trio of top scenic views in Japan (the other two are Matsushima and Miyajima), Amanohashidate has a lot to live up to. The "bridge" is actually a 3.6km-long ribbon of white sand and pine trees slinking its way between the villages of **Monju** (文珠) near the train station, and **Fuchū** (府中) across the bay.

Monju is the main tourist hub of Amanohashidate, and has an attractive wooden temple, **Chion-ji**, standing on the brink of the sand bar – a lovely area for a quiet stroll or cycle ride, or simply lazing on the beach. To reach the sand bar itself, cross the red bridge, Kaisenkyō, which swings around to allow boats through the narrow channel to the open sea. The sandy, crescent-shaped beaches on the east side of the pine-forested spit are at their busiest from July to August. Above Fuchū there are fantastic views over the bay and along the coast from the touristy sightseeing park of **Kasamatsu-kōen**, beyond which is the splendidly atmospheric **Nariai-ji**, on the upper slopes of Mount Nariai.

Chion-ji

智恩寺 • 466 Jimonju • Daily 8am–5pm • Free • ☎ 0772 22 2553, ⓦ monjudo-chionji.jp • A 5min walk north of Amanohashidate Station, at the end of a shopping street leading towards the sand spit

The attractive temple of **Chion-ji** is dedicated to the Buddhist saint of wisdom and intellect, Chie-no-Monju. Between the main gate and the hall (Monju-dō), which houses a revered image of the saint, stands the Tahoto, an unusual squat wooden pagoda dating from 1500. In the temple precincts, near the ferry jetty, you'll see the Chie-no-wa Torō, a granite ring monument symbolizing wisdom, which has been adopted as an emblem of the town. In front of the main gate is a row of traditional **teashops** all serving the same local speciality, *Chie-no-mochi* – small rice cakes topped with a sweet red bean paste; locals say eating them grants you wisdom.

Kasamatsu-kōen

傘松公園 • Fuchū • Funicular and chairlift daily 8am–5.30pm • ¥660 return

On the lower slopes of Mount Nariai is **Kasamatsu-kōen**, the principal lookout point over Amanohashidate. Signs demonstrate how best to do the "mata-nozoki": turn your back to Amanohashidate and bend over with your head between your legs, so that the view of the sand spit seems to float in midair like a bridge to heaven.

Nariai-ji

成相寺 • Fuchū • Daily 8am–4.30pm • ¥500 • ☎ 0772 27 0018, ⓦ nariaiji.jp • A 20min walk further up the mountain from Kasamatsu-kōen or catch a bus (¥700 return)

Founded in 704 AD and dedicated to Kannon, the Buddhist goddess of mercy, **Nariai-ji** is a charming rustic temple surrounded by lofty pines. It is one of the 33 temples on the Saigoku Kannon pilgrim route, and so attracts a steady stream of visitors, many of whom clutch elaborate hanging scrolls which are specially inscribed at each temple. Legend has it that if you pray at the temple and make a vow to Kannon, your prayer will be granted.

ARRIVAL AND INFORMATION — AMANOHASHIDATE

By train Trains to Amanohashidate Station (天橋立駅) in Monju run along the scenic Kita-kinki Tango Tetsudō line (北近畿丹後鉄道). When taking the express service from Osaka (hourly; 2hr; ¥5590) and Kyoto (hourly; 2hr; ¥4710), you may be required to switch in Fukuchiyama. There are a few direct JR trains from Amagasaki, Kyoto and Osaka, which take around 2hr 30min.

By bus Buses from both Kyoto Station (¥2800; 2 daily) and Shin-Osaka Station (¥2650; 3 daily) take around 2hr 40min.

Tourist information The staff at the tourist information office (daily 9am–6pm; ⊕0772 22 8030) inside Amanohashidate Station are helpful but don't speak much English, although they can provide English-language pamphlets on the area and help with accommodation bookings. There's also free wi-fi access here.

Services The post office ATM, opposite the station, takes international cards (Mon–Fri 9am–5.30pm).

GETTING AROUND

By bus Buses from Monju across the bay to Fuchū (15 daily; 20min; ¥400) and around the Tango-hantō peninsula leave from outside Amanohashidate Station until 7pm.

By ferry Ferries run between Monju and Fuchū (18 daily; 12min; ¥530; last ferry at 4.45pm) from the jetty beside Chion-ji, a 5min walk from the station, to the Fuchū-side jetty at Ichinomiya.

By bike Bicycles can be rented from various shops close to Amanohashidate Station and near the jetty (¥400–500 for 2hr).

On foot It takes about 50min to stroll the 2.4km across the sand bar from Monju to Fuchū.

ACCOMMODATION AND EATING

Monju has the widest range of **accommodation**. The tourist information desk at the station can help with accommodation but it's best to book in advance, especially if you arrive late in the day. Note that businesses in the area close early, especially in winter, so it's best to eat **meals** at your accommodation.

FUCHŪ

Amanohashidate Youth Hostel 天橋立ユースホステル Fuchū ⊕0772 27 0121, ⓦhashidate-yh.jp. This hostel is a 15min hike uphill to the right from the ferry and bus stop at Ichinomiya, but it's worth it for the pleasant location and wonderful views. It has bunk-bed dorms, a comfy lounge, helpful English-speaking staff and cheap bike rental (¥500/day). Dorms **¥3050**

MONJU

★**Café du Pin** カフェドパン 468 Jimonju ⊕0772 22 1313. One of the nicest places to take a break in Monju. It's near the bridge to the sand spit and serves curry and rice (¥1000), sandwiches (¥750), cake sets (¥800), good coffee and the award-winning local wine. Daily 9am–5.30pm.

Hashidatejaya はしだて茶屋 Monju ⊕0772 22 3363, ⓦhashidate-chaya.jp. Nestling amid the pines at the Monju end of the sand spit, this traditional restaurant serves good-value meals and snacks, including hearty bowls of *asari-don* (small shellfish and green vegetables on rice) for ¥1000. 9am–5pm; closed Thurs.

★**Monjusō Shōrotei** 文殊荘松露亭 Monju ⊕0772 22 2151, ⓦshourotei.com. Exquisite high-end ryokan behind Chion-ji temple, set amid private gardens at the tip of a mini-peninsula overlooking the sand bar. *Shōrotei*'s cuisine and hospitality are both excellent. Rates vary depending on the room and your choice of meals. **¥79,800**

★**Toriki** 鳥喜 Monju ⊕0772 22 0010, ⓦtoriki.jp. This *ryōri* ryokan (cuisine inn) doesn't look very fancy but it's well-known for serving top-class local cuisine. All the rooms are tatami-style, and there's also an onsen in the garden. The convenient location and friendly atmosphere make this an excellent choice. **¥32,400**

Ine

伊根

The charming fishing hamlet of **INE**, sheltering in a hook-like inlet towards the eastern end of the Tango-hantō pensinula, is a wonderful place to experience peaceful village life by the sea and eat deliciously fresh fish. The main tourist attraction is the picturesque rows of **funaya wooden boat houses**, some of which date from the Edo period. There are some 230 traditional houses built over the water, with space beneath for fishing boats to be stored – from a distance the houses appear to be floating on the water. Many films and television dramas have been filmed here, including the *Tora-san* series (see box, p.857).

ARRIVAL AND GETTING AROUND

By bus Buses for Ine depart from in front of Amanohashidate Station (15 daily; 50min; ¥400).
By bike You can borrow bikes for free 24hr a day (no deposit necessary) from the bus stop near the Ine Bay boat cruise jetty, with several drop-off/pick-up "ports" around the village.

INFORMATION AND TOURS

Tourist information The Ine tourist information office (daily 9am–5pm; ☎0772 32 0277, ⓦine-kankou.jp) is located in Fuya-no-Sato Park on the hill overlooking Ine. The staff speak a little English and can help with accommodation and sea taxi reservations.
Boat trips Sightseeing boats (伊根湾めぐり遊覧船, Ine-wan Meguri Yūransen; March–Dec daily 9am–4.30pm; every 30min; 30min tour ¥680; ☎0772 32 0009, ⓦtankai .jp) circle Ine Bay, providing a comprehensive but brief view of the unusual architecture of the *funaya*. A more satisfying experience is to rent a sea taxi (¥1000 per person for 30min; minimum two passengers) from one of the *funaya* and tour the bay at your leisure.

ACCOMMODATION AND EATING

★**Kagiya** 鍵屋 ☎0772 32 0356, ⓦine-kagiya.net. This comfortable modern *funaya* has a living and dining space on the first floor with sublime views of the bay. Upstairs there are two stylish bedrooms that can sleep up to eight guests. Rates include an excellent dinner and breakfast. Guests can also take *Kagiya's* private sea taxi tours of Ine Bay for ¥1000 per person. **¥43,200**
Kamome かもめ ☎0772 32 0025. This small restaurant and coffee shop is above a souvenir shop on the main road leading into Ine and has wonderful views of the bay. Tasty lunch sets with fresh local fish, miso soup and pickles are ¥1500. 9am–6pm; closed Thurs.

Shibatasō しばた荘 ☎0772 32 0254, ⓦshibata-sou .com. Located along the coast north of Ine, this large traditional-style minshuku serves excellent *kaiseki* cuisine as well as crab and yellowtail when in season. There are six tatami rooms which can sleep up to 20 guests. The owner can pick up guests by car from the boat cruise jetty. **¥21,390**
Yoshimura よしむら ☎0772 32 0062. This restaurant is a great spot for lunch, right in the centre of Ine. Multicourse lunch sets of various super-fresh fish dishes including sashimi are ¥2000. 11.30am–2pm; closed Wed.

Hikone

彦根

On the northeastern shore of Biwa-ko, Japan's largest lake, lies the stately castle town of **HIKONE**, an easy day-trip or a pleasant overnight stay from Kyoto. This attractive town not unreasonably claims that it has retained the look and feel of the Edo period more than any other place in the country. Its **castle** is one of the few in Japan to have remained intact since the early seventeenth century, and is well worth a visit. Hikone is also known for its *butsudan* (Buddhist altar) industry and the town has an abundance of shops with elaborate altars on display. Hikone's main attractions can all be seen on foot and, except during the cherry blossom season when the castle is engulfed by hordes of tourists, the town can be enjoyed at a leisurely and crowd-free pace.

Hikone-jō

彦根城 • 1-1 Konki-chō • Daily 8.30am–5pm • ¥600 combined ticket with Genkyū-en (see opposite), or ¥1000 combined ticket with Hikone-jō museum (see opposite) and Genkyū-en • ☎0749 22 2742

Very little has changed in the four hundred years and more that **Hikone-jō** has stood on the hill looking out onto the town and the lake. One of the most authentic castles remaining in Japan, it is also one of only four designated as a national treasure. There are spectacular views of Biwa-ko from the donjon on a clear day, and with very few modern buildings and little pollution to obscure the panorama it is possible to imagine something of what people in the Edo period may have seen.

Hikone-jō was built between 1602 and 1622 by the Ii family from the ruins of other castles in the area, including one on the original site. If you look at the stone walls as you climb up the hill, you can see that the style is inconsistent. The lower levels were constructed by untrained labourers while the upper levels have been assembled using the patchwork-like *gobo-zumi* masonry technique. Although the walls look rather precarious, they have successfully protected the castle from earthquake damage since their construction. The fortress is double-moated and also features many *yagura* or turrets: look out for the *tenbin-yagura*, in the unique shape of a *tenbin* (Japanese scales), and the *taikomon-yagura*, so-called because a *taiko* or Japanese drum was kept there to send warnings.

Hikone-jō Museum

彦根城博物館, Hikone-jō Hakubutsukan • Daily 9am–4.30pm • ¥500, or ¥1000 combined ticket with Hikone-jō (see opposite) and Genkyū-en (see below) • ☎ 0749 22 6100

Just inside the main gate of the castle, the **Hikone-jō Museum** was reconstructed in 1987 and is an exact copy of the Edo-period official quarter of the castle. Inside you can see how the Ii family lived: their nō stage, tearoom and living area have been re-created, and there are a large number of artefacts on display, including nō costumes, weaponry, calligraphy manuscripts and other artworks.

Genkyū-en

玄宮園 • Daily 8.30am–5pm • ¥200, or ¥600 combined ticket with Hikone-jō (see opposite), or ¥1000 combined ticket with Hikone-jō and Hikone-jō Museum (see above) • ☎ 0749 22 2742

On the northeast side of Hikone-jō is the **Genkyū-en**. Built in 1677, the garden is modelled on the ancient Chinese palace of Tang-dynasty emperor Genso and features a large pond full of carp. Genkyū-en has many imitation scenes of the region and the pond is Biwa-ko in miniature. The *Hoshō-dai* teahouse, where the Ii Lords entertained, is a good place to stop for a bowl of *matcha* and a sweet (¥500) while enjoying pleasant views of the garden and castle.

Yume-Kyōbashi Castle Road

夢京橋キャッスルロード • Ⓦ yumekyobashi.jp

The **Yume-Kyōbashi Castle Road**, south of Hikone-jō, is a charming imitation of a bustling Edo-period merchant area. The 350m-long stretch of road has modern reconstructions of traditional Japanese shops on both sides, housing a variety of cafés, restaurants, bars and souvenir shops. At the end of the road farthest from the castle, turn left into **Yonban-chō**, another reconstructed shopping and dining area. Here, dozens of small shops and restaurants have been built in a style reminiscent of the Taishō era of the 1920s.

Ryōtanji

龍潭寺 • 1104 Furusawa-chō • Daily 9am–4pm • ¥400 • ☎ 0749 22 2777 • A 10min taxi ride north of JR Hikone Station

The Zen temple **Ryōtanji**, located on the eastern edge of the town, was founded in 733 and was the family temple of the Ii Lords. The temple was once an important centre for Zen gardening and its gardens were designed by monks in training. The **Fudaraku stone garden**, dating from 1670, is considered to be a fine example of the genre, and is especially nice in autumn when it's framed by *momiji* maple leaves. Walking through the slightly dilapidated temple, with its odd assortment of displays, you reach the **dry waterfall garden**; here, naturally shaped stones and shrubs are evocatively arranged, seeming to tumble into a pond with an unusual tortoise-shaped rock.

Tennei-ji

天寧寺 • 232 Satone-chō • Daily 8am–4pm • ¥400 • ☎ 0749 22 5313 • A 30min walk from JR Hikone Station

East of Hikone-jō, at the well-kept Zen temple of **Tennei-ji**, 500 Buddhist disciples who reached Nirvana are enshrined as *Gohyaku Rakan* wooden statues. It is said that you should be able to find a face that resembles someone you know among the statues. From the temple's stone garden there is an excellent view of Hikone-jō. On the way out, don't forgot to rub the belly of Budai, the god of fortune, for good luck.

6

ARRIVAL AND INFORMATION
HIKONE

By train Express JR trains take 1hr 30min from Osaka (¥1940) and 50min from Kyoto (¥1140). On the Shinkansen Tokaido line, get off at Maibara Station (25min from Kyoto; ¥3300) and change for the JR Biwako line to Hikone Station (5min; ¥190). From here, it's about a 10min walk to the castle area.

Tourist information There's a helpful tourist office (daily 9am–5.30pm; ☎0749 22 2954) with English-speaking staff at JR Hikone Station, on your left-hand side as you exit: you can also pick up English pamphlets on Hikone here.

ACCOMMODATION

Hotel Estacion Hikone ホテルエスタシオンひこね 8-31 Asahimachi ☎0749 22 1500, ⓦestacion-hikone .com. This friendly and efficient business hotel is conveniently located near the JR station and shopping area. Rooms are on the small side but are clean and well appointed. Breakfast included. 🛜 **¥11,000**

Hikone Castle Resort & Spa 彦根キャッスルリゾート＆スパ 1-8 Sawa-chō ☎0749 21 2001, ⓦhch.jp. The best place to stay in Hikone, this hotel is situated right on the northeast corner of the castle moat, and has an in-house spa. Rooms are clean, spacious and most have clear views of the castle; superior rooms come with private semi-open air baths. The hotel restaurant serves local Omi beef lunch and dinner courses. 🛜 **¥17,500**

★**Honmachi Juku** 本町宿 3-55 Honmachi 3-chōme ☎0749 30 9932, ⓦhonmachi.hcdf.jp. This ryokan is in a beautifully restored traditional house close to Yume-Kyōbashi Castle Road. There's a choice of rooms, with either futon or bed, with shared facilities. The hearty breakfast made with local produce is particularly good. **¥10,800**

EATING AND DRINKING

Hokkoriya ほっこりや ☎0749 21 3567. This popular *izakaya* on the Yume Kyōbashi Castle Road is in an atmospheric traditional-style house serving a variety of local chicken dishes, such as *yakitori* (¥380 per stick) and chicken with rice *donburi* (¥1280). There's no English menu, but staff speak a little English and will also help with suggesting local Shiga sake (from ¥650 a glass) to pair with your food. 11.30am–2.30pm & 5.30–11pm; closed Wed.

Tachibana Shokudō たちばな食堂 ☎0749 24 3330. The speciality at this restaurant is *Hikone-aka-don* (¥870), a rice bowl dish topped with local Omi beef and red *konnyaku*

(yam cake). It's situated in the Taishō-style Yonban-chō (see p.483), where most restaurants and cafés are only open in the daytime. Daily 10am–5.30pm.

Yabuya やぶや ☎0749 20 4330. This Spanish bar is one of Hikone's most popular drinking spots and attracts a lively crowd on Friday and Saturday nights. Tapas plates are ¥380 each, or four for ¥1000. There's a standing bar area, but it's also a pleasant place to sit down for a main course of roast chicken (¥1200) or risotto (¥700). Cocktails and wine by the glass are ¥500. Mon–Thurs 5–11.30pm, Fri & Sat 5pm–1.30am.

Ishiyama-dera

石山寺 • 1-1-1 Ishiyama-dera, Ōtsu, Shiga-ken • Daily 10am–4pm • ¥600, special exhibitions ¥300–500 • ☎077 537 0013, ⓦishiyamadera.or.jp • From JR Kyoto Station, take a local train on the JR Biwa-ko line (for Nagahama or Maibara) two stops to JR Ishiyama Station (every 10–15min; 13min; ¥230), then change to the Keihan line for the short ride to Ishiyama-dera Station (¥160); the temple is a 10min walk from the station

At the southern edge of Biwa-ko, just 20km southeast of Kyoto city, is the quiet and secluded **Ishiyama-dera**. Founded in the eighth century, this Shingon-sect temple has an important literary connection: Murasaki Shikibu (see p.473) wrote **The Tale of Genji** here. The temple holds a vast collection of related manuscripts and art that are displayed at certain times of the year in the special exhibition hall (check the website for dates); in the temple itself there aren't any *Genji* relics on display except for a tacky mechanical robot of Murasaki Shikibu in a glass case. The pleasant gardens surrounding the temple can be explored by a network of meandering paths.

Miho Museum

ミホミュージアム • 300 Tashiro Momodani, Shigaraki, Shiga-ken • Tues–Fri & Sun 10am–5pm; only open for a few months every year – exact dates vary; check the website for details • ¥1100 • ☎0748 82 3411, ⓦmiho.jp/english

Around 50km south of Kyoto, the I.M. Pei-designed **Miho Museum** is one of the architectural highlights of the Kansai region, although it's only open at certain times of the year. Located in a rural, mountainous part of Shiga Prefecture, which is best known for its Shigaraki pottery, this stunning museum houses an incredible collection of artworks belonging to the late Koyama Mihoko and her daughter Hiroko. Koyama, after whom the museum is named, founded Shinji Shūmeikai, one of Japan's so-called "new religions", in 1970. There are an estimated 300,000 followers worldwide, hundreds of whom live and work here at the museum. The central tenet of Shinji Shūmeikai's philosophy is that spiritual fulfilment lies in art and nature, hence the setting.

From the entrance and restaurant, access to the museum proper is by an electric shuttle bus through a tunnel that opens onto a beautiful valley spanned by a 120m-high bridge; alternatively, you can walk – it takes about ten minutes on foot. Inside the museum, which is built into the mountainside, a continually shifting pattern of light and shadow is created by the innovative use of skylights, pyramid-shaped wall lights and ever-so-slightly uneven corridors which look out – through windows fitted with aluminium screens – onto bamboo gardens and tranquil green landscapes.

The collection

The museum has two wings. The **north wing** houses Japanese art, including priceless porcelain, scrolls, screens and Buddhist relics; the **south wing** has antiquities from the rest of the world, including jewellery, frescoes, textiles and statues produced by a range of civilizations, from ancient Egyptian to classical Chinese. Among the numerous treasures are a three-thousand-year-old silver-and-gold cult figure of a falcon-headed deity from Egypt's nineteenth dynasty, a fourth-century AD Roman floor mosaic and a statue dating from the second century AD of a Gandhara Buddha. Each artwork is labelled in English and Japanese and there are explanatory leaflets in some of the galleries, but the overall effect is one of art that is meant to be experienced for its intrinsic beauty rather than its historical or cultural import.

ARRIVAL AND DEPARTURE
MIHO MUSEUM

By train and bus There are tours available to the museum from Kyoto but it is better (and much cheaper) to make the journey there by yourself. From JR Kyoto Station, take a local train on the JR Biwa-ko line (for Nagahama or Maibara) two stops to JR Ishiyama Station (every 10–15min; 13min; ¥230). From here, buses run by the

Teisan Bus Company (ⓦteisan-konan-kotsu.co.jp) depart from outside the station's south exit (daily at 10min past the hour 9.10am–1.10pm, plus extra buses at 9.50am & 2.10pm on Sat, Sun & national holidays; 50min; ¥820). If you miss the last bus, you'll have to take a taxi, which is quite expensive (¥6000).

EATING

Peach Valley Miho Museum reception area ☏0748 82 3411. This excellent vegetarian organic restaurant is extremely popular with museum visitors. The lunch menu is seasonal and all dishes are made from locally grown

ingredients. The Onigiri-zen (rice ball set menu) is beautifully presented (¥1800), and the soba and udon lunch sets, served hot or cold (from ¥800), are also delicious. Arrive early to avoid disappointment. Daily 10am–3.30pm.

Nara

奈良

Before Kyoto became the capital of Japan in 794 AD, this honour was held by **NARA**, a town some 35km further south in an area that is regarded as the birthplace of Japanese civilization. During this period, particularly the seventh and eighth centuries, Buddhism became firmly established within Japan under the patronage of court nobles, who sponsored magnificent temples and works of art, many of which have survived to this day. Fortunately, history subsequently left Nara largely to its own devices and it remains today a relaxed, attractive place set against a backdrop of wooded hills.

Nara's grid-street system is well signposted in English, and the main sights, four of which are designated as Unesco World Heritage Sites, are all gathered on the city's eastern edge in the green expanse of **Nara-kōen**. Its greatest draws are undoubtedly the monumental bronze Buddha of **Tōdai-ji**, and Nara's holiest shrine, **Kasuga Taisha**, with its rows of lanterns and attractive new museum, while **Kōfuku-ji, Sangatsu-dō** and **Shin-Yakushi-ji** all boast outstanding collections of Buddhist statuary. The town also retains the well-preserved traditional merchant's quarter of **Nara-machi**, where some quaint old shophouses have been converted into museums and craft shops.

All Nara's sights are packed into a fairly compact space, and the central area is easily explored on foot. It can just about be covered in a day-trip from Kyoto, though if you want to visit the more distant temples (see p.495) you'll need to stay overnight – this gives you the added advantage of being able to enjoy a more peaceful atmosphere once the crowds have left. If at all possible, try to avoid Nara on Sundays and during holidays, when it can become exceptionally crowded.

Brief history

During the fifth and sixth centuries a sophisticated culture evolved in the plains east of Osaka, an area known as **Yamato**. Close contact between Japan, Korea and China saw the introduction of Chinese script, technology and the Buddhist religion, as well as Chinese ideas on law and administration. Under these influences, the regent **Prince**

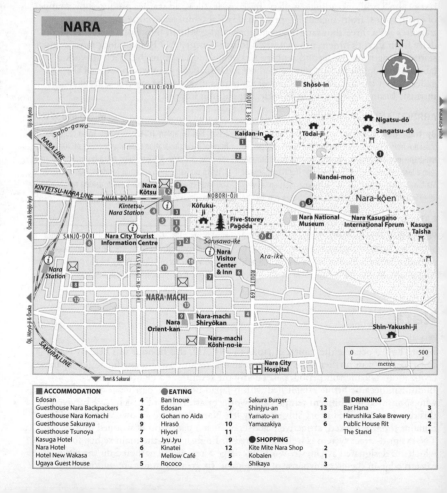

■ ACCOMMODATION		● EATING				■ DRINKING	
Edosan	4	Ban Inoue	3	Sakura Burger	2	Bar Hana	3
Guesthouse Nara Backpackers	2	Edosan	7	Shinjyu-an	13	Harushika Sake Brewery	4
Guesthouse Nara Komachi	8	Gohan no Aida	1	Yamato-an	8	Public House Rit	2
Guesthouse Sakuraya	9	Hirasō	10	Yamazakiya	6	The Stand	1
Guesthouse Tsunoya	7	Hiyori	11				
Kasuga Hotel	3	Jyu Jyu	9	● SHOPPING			
Nara Hotel	6	Kinatei	12	Kite Mite Nara Shop	2		
Hotel New Wakasa	1	Mellow Café	4	Kobaien	1		
Ugaya Guest House	5	Rococo	4	Shikaya	3		

Shōtoku (574–622) established a strictly hierarchical system of government. However, he's probably best remembered as a devout Buddhist who founded numerous temples, among them the great **Hōryū-ji** (see p.496). Though Shōtoku's successors continued the process of centralization, they were hampered by the practice of relocating the court after each emperor died, in line with purification rites. In 710 AD, therefore, it was decided to establish a permanent capital modelled on China's imperial city, Chang'an (today's Xi'an). The name chosen for this new city was **Heijō-kyō**, "Citadel of Peace", today known as **Nara**.

In fact, Heijō-kyō lasted little more than seventy years, but it was a glorious period in which Japanese culture began to take shape. A frenzy of building and artistic creativity culminated in the unveiling of the great bronze Buddha in **Tōdai-ji** temple by **Emperor Shōmu** in 752 AD. But beneath the surface things were starting to unravel. As the temples became increasingly powerful, so the monks began to dabble in politics, until one, Dōkyō, seduced a former empress and tried to seize the throne in 769. In an attempt to escape such shenanigans Emperor Kammu decided to move the court out of Nara in 784, and eventually founded Kyoto.

Nara-kōen
奈良公園

The ancient forested parklands on the eastern side of Nara are known as **Nara-kōen** and house many of the town's most important historical and religious sites. The park is also home to more than a thousand semi-wild **deer**, which were originally regarded as divine messengers of the Shintō gods – anyone who killed a deer was liable to be dispatched shortly afterwards. Vendors sell *shika sembei* (deer crackers) for feeding the deer throughout the park. The most pleasant route into Nara-kōen is along Sanjō-dōri, which cuts across the central district and brings you out near the pond of **Sarusawa-ike** (猿沢池).

Kōfuku-ji

興福寺 • 48 Noborioji-chō • Daily 9am–5pm • Tōkon-dō ¥300; Kokuhōkan ¥600 • ☏ 0742 22 4096, ⓦ kohfukuji.com

The picturesque **Five-Storey Pagoda** which rises from the trees on the northern edge of Sarusawa-ike belongs to **Kōfuku-ji**, which in the eighth century was one of Nara's great temples. Founded in 669 by a member of the Fujiwara clan, it was moved to its present location when Nara became the new capital in 710. The prime draw here is the fine collection of **Buddhist statues** contained in the **Tōkon-dō** and the **Kokuhōkan**. At the moment almost half of Kōfuku-ji is a building site as a new **Chukon-dō** (Central Hall) is being built in the temple grounds: completion is expected in 2018.

Tōkon-dō
東金堂

The **Tōkon-dō**, a fifteenth-century hall to the north of the Five-Storey Pagoda, is dominated by a large image of Yakushi Nyorai, the Buddha of Healing. He's flanked by three bodhisattvas, the Four Heavenly Kings and the Twelve Heavenly Generals, all beady-eyed guardians of the faith, some of which date from the eighth century. Perhaps the most interesting statue, though, is the seated figure of Yuima Koji to the left of Yakushi Nyorai; depicting an ordinary mortal rather than a celestial being, it's a touchingly realistic portrait.

Kokuhōkan
国宝館

The modern **Kokuhōkan** is a veritable treasure-trove of early Buddhist statues. The most famous image is the standing figure of **Ashura**, one of Buddha's eight protectors, instantly recognizable from his three red-tinted heads and six spindly arms. Look out, too, for his companion Karura (Garuda) with his beaked head. Though they're not all on display at the same time, these eight protectors are considered to be the finest dry-lacquer images of the Nara period. The large **bronze Buddha head**, with its fine, crisp features, comes from an even earlier period. Apart from a crumpled left ear, the head is in remarkably good condition considering that the original statue was stolen from another temple by Kōfuku-ji's warrior priests sometime during the Heian period (794–1185). After a fire destroyed its body, the head was buried beneath the replacement Buddha, only to be rediscovered in 1937 during renovation work.

Nara National Museum

奈良国立博物館, Nara Kokuritsu Hakubutkan • 50 Noboriōji-chō • Tues–Sun 9am–5pm; closed late Oct–early Nov for Shōsō-in Treasures exhibition • ¥520; ¥1100 for special exhibitions • ☎ 050 5542 8600, ⓦ narahaku.go.jp

The **Nara National Museum** holds a superb collection of centuries-old Buddhist art, of which only a small part is on display at any one time. The exhibits are arranged chronologically, so you can trace the development of the various styles, and there's plenty of English-language information available. The main Western-style building houses the sculpture collection, while the modern annexe is where the museum's **Shōsō-in Treasures exhibition** – a collection of treasures from Tōdai-ji – is shown once a year (see box below). In the lower-level passageway between the original building and the annexe you'll find an informative display that explains the forms, techniques and other characteristics of Buddhist art. It's an excellent primer before exploring Nara's temples.

Tōdai-ji

東大寺 • 406-1 Zoshi-chō • Daily: mid-March to mid-Sept 7.30am–5pm; mid-Sept to mid-March 8am–4pm • ¥500 • ☎ 0742 22 5511, ⓦ todaiji.or.jp

For many people Nara is synonymous with the great temple of **Tōdai-ji**, which was founded in 745 by **Emperor Shōmu**, ostensibly to ward off the terrible epidemics that regularly swept the nation, but also as a means of cementing imperial power. In doing so he nearly bankrupted his young nation, but the political message came across loud and clear; soon an extensive network of sub-temples spread throughout the provinces, where they played an important role in local administration. It took more than fifteen years to complete Tōdai-ji, which isn't surprising when you learn that the main hall is still the world's largest wooden building. Even so, the present structure (last rebuilt in 1709) is only two-thirds the size of the original. Avoid visiting Tōdai-ji at weekends, especially in spring and autumn, the two peak times for visiting Nara, when the temple is overrun with thousands of tourists and school groups.

Daibutsu-den

大仏殿

The main entrance to Tōdai-ji lies through the suitably impressive **Nandai-mon** (南大門), or Great Southern Gate. Rebuilt in the thirteenth century, it shelters two wonderfully expressive guardian gods (*Niō*), each standing over 7m tall. Beyond, you begin to see the horned, sweeping roof of the **Daibutsu-den**, the Great Buddha Hall, which houses Japan's largest bronze statue (see box opposite), a giant 15m-tall blackened

---

SHŌSŌ-IN TREASURES

Each autumn (late Oct to early Nov), the Nara National Museum is closed for two weeks while an exhibition of the **Shōsō-in Treasures** (正倉院) takes place in the annexe. This priceless collection was donated to Tōdai-ji in 756 by Empress Kōmyō, on the death of her husband Emperor Shōmu, and then added to with more treasures in 950. It contains unique examples of Buddhist art and ritual objects, musical instruments, household utensils, glassware and games, not only from eighth-century Japan but also from the countries of the Silk Road – China, Korea, India and Persia. The exhibition takes a different theme each year; check ⓦ narahaku.go.jp for details.

THE GREAT BUDDHA

Housed in the Daibutsu-den, the **great Buddha** (*Daibutsu*) depicts Rushana (later known as Dainichi Nyorai), the Cosmic Buddha who presides over all levels of the Buddhist universe. The statue was a phenomenal achievement for the time. Not surprisingly, several attempts at casting the Buddha failed, but finally in 752 the gilded statue was officially dedicated by symbolically "**opening**" its eyes. To achieve this, an Indian priest stood on a special platform and "painted" the eyes with a huge brush, from which coloured strings trailed down to the assembled dignitaries, enabling them to participate in the ceremony. Not only were there hundreds of local monks present, but also ambassadors from China, India and further afield, bearing an amazing array of gifts, many of which have been preserved in the Shōsō-in treasury – as has the original paintbrush.

The Buddha has had a rough time of it since then. As early as the ninth century an **earthquake** toppled his head, then it and his right hand were melted in a **fire** in 1180 and again in 1567. As a result, only tiny fragments of the original statue remain intact, the rest being made up of patchwork parts put together over the centuries. Nonetheless, the remodelled giant is definitely large, and it's hard not to be impressed by the technological triumph involved in re-creating it.

6

figure on a lotus throne, that seems to strain at the very walls of the building. As you walk round the hall, don't be surprised to see people trying to squeeze through a hole in one of the rear supporting pillars – success apparently reserves you a corner of paradise.

Nigatsu-dō

二月堂 • 406-1 Zoshi-chō • Daily 8am–4.30pm • Free

Built on the slopes of Wakakusa-yama, which forms Nara's eastern boundary, **Nigatsu-dō** is a sub-temple of Tōdai-ji. It's well worth a visit to enjoy the expansive views over the city from its second-floor wooden terrace, where dozens of lanterns hang and are lit every day at dusk – a rather beautiful sight. Next to the terrace, a rest area for pilgrims serves tea. Nigatsu-dō is the site of the O-Taimatsu and O-Mizutori ceremonies held in March every year (see box, p.494).

Sangatsu-dō

三月堂 • 406-1 Zoshi-chō • Daily 8am–5pm • ¥500

Another sub-temple of Tōdai-ji, the single-storey **Sangatsu-dō** was completed in 729, making it Nara's oldest building. Also known as Hokke-dō, it contains another rare collection of eighth-century dry-lacquer statues. The main image is a dimly lit, gilded figure of Kannon, bearing a silver Amida in its crown, while all around stand gods, guardians, bodhisattvas and other protectors of the faith.

Kasuga Taisha

春日大社 • 160 Kasugano-chō • **Shrine** Daily dawn–dusk • Free; inner shrine ¥500 • **Museum** Daily 9am–4.30pm • ¥500 • **Garden** Daily 9am–4.30pm • ¥500 • ☎ 0742 22 7788, ⓦ kasugataisha.or.jp

Some two thousand stone lanterns line the approach to **Kasuga Taisha** (Kasuga Grand Shrine), which is nestled in the hillside of Wakakusa-yama. It was founded in 768 AD as the tutelary shrine of the Fujiwara family and, for a while, held an important place in Shintō worship; indeed, the emperor still sends a messenger here to participate in shrine rituals. The four sanctuaries are just visible in the inner compound, while the thousand beautifully crafted bronze **lanterns** hanging round the outer eaves are easier to admire. Donated over the years by supplicants, they bear intricate designs of deer, wisteria blooms, leaves or geometric patterns. The best time to see them is when they are lit up twice a year for the Mantōrō ("Ten-thousand lantern") festivals: on February 3 marking *setsubun*, the beginning of spring; and during Obon, the festival of souls, in mid-August (Aug 14–15) for the Chūgen Mantōrō festival. Alternatively, try to visit in the early morning or dusk, when the stone lanterns are lit.

6

Kasuga Taisha museum

春日大社国宝殿, Kasuga Taisha Kokuhō Dono

Kasuga Taisha's small but beautifully laid out **museum**, on the east side of the main gate, recently reopened following major renovations under architect Yada Toshio, and contains the shrine's superb collection of designated national treasures. Kasuga Taisha's long connection with the samurai class between the Kamakura and Edo periods (1192–1867) accounts for the number of elaborately decorated swords and well-preserved armour. However, the highlights of the museum are the Dadaiko ("great drum") Hall, featuring drums used in the On-matsuri festival (see box, p.494), and the two stunning installations by artist Okayasu Izumi, intended to evoke the spirit of the forest as a place for communing with the gods.

Kasuga Taisha Shin-en garden

春日大社神苑

Near the entrance to Kasuga Taisha's inner shrine, the **Kasuga Taisha Shin-en** is especially charming in early May when the dozens of varieties of wisteria are in bloom. The garden is also a living museum of over nine hundred flowers, herbs and other plants mentioned in the verses of the *Manyōshū* ("Collection of Ten Thousand Leaves") poetry anthology, compiled in the Nara and early Heian periods.

Shin-Yakushi-ji

新薬師寺 • 1352 Takabatake-chō • Daily 9am–5pm • ¥600 • ☎ 0742 22 3737, ⓦ shinyakusiji.or.jp • From Kasuga Taisha, continue south through the woods, then cross over the main road into a quiet residential area; 5min further on you'll come to Shin-Yakushi-ji

The temple of **Shin-Yakushi-ji** was founded by Empress Kōmyō to pray for Emperor Shōmu's recovery from an eye infection; she apparently had some success, since he lived for another decade. Inside the temple's quiet precincts, a modest-looking hall houses a stunning collection of eighth-century Buddhist statues. The central image is a placid-looking, slightly cross-eyed Yakushi Nyorai (the Buddha of Healing), carved from one block of cinnamon wood. He's surrounded by a ring of clay statues of the Twelve Heavenly Generals; it's worth visiting just to see their wonderful manga-like expressions and poses.

Nara-machi

ならまち

The southern district of central Nara is known as **Nara-machi**. It's a quaint area of narrow streets, worth exploring for its traditional shops and lattice-front houses. The best approach is to start by the southwest corner of willow-fringed Sarusawa-ike, a good spot for views of the Five-Storey Pagoda, and then head south.

Nara-machi Shiryōkan

奈良町資料館 • 14-2 Nishonoshinya-chō • Daily 10am–4pm • Free • ☎ 0742 22 5509, ⓦ naramachi.co.jp

Strings of red-cloth monkeys (good-luck charms) hang outside the **Nara-machi Shiryōkan**, a small museum which occupies the former warehouse of a mosquito-net

---

NARA'S MASCOT

Many towns in Japan, as well as companies and even restaurants, have their own mascot – usually a cute manga-style character. As part of Nara's 1300th anniversary celebrations in 2010, a strange half-deer/half-boy monk called **Sento-kun** appeared as Nara's official mascot. Sento-kun received a lot of criticism from both the media and the public for being "creepy" and a waste of ¥5 million of taxpayers' money. Religious organizations were also not happy with his distinctive Buddhist appearance combined with deer antlers, and called the mascot "sacrilegious". However, Sento-kun has endured and can be found in different forms all over the city.

manufacturer. It houses a wonderful jumble of antique household utensils, shop signboards, Buddhist statues, pots and other folkloric objects from the local area. Of special note is the Zinemon Gara Ōzara, a large ceramic plate almost 2m in diameter, which was used to serve worshippers at festivals.

Nara-machi Kōshi-no-ie

ならまち格子の家 • 44 Gangōji-chō • Tues–Sun 9am–5pm • Free • ☎ 0742 23 4820

One of Nara-machi's best-preserved traditional houses, **Nara-machi Kōshi-no-ie** is an Edo-period merchant's dwelling with a long and narrow interior, including an inner courtyard garden. You can explore the house at will, but the staff will also happily demonstrate various features, such as the clever operating mechanism of the front door and kitchen skylights.

ARRIVAL AND DEPARTURE NARA

BY TRAIN

Nara has two competing train stations: the JR Nara Station, on the west side of the town centre, and the private Kintetsu-Nara Station, which is close to the main sights.

From Kyoto The quickest option is a Limited Express train on the private Kintetsu–Kyoto line (every 30min; 35min; ¥1130); the ordinary express takes a little longer and you have to change at Yamato-Saidaiji (1–2 hourly; 45min; ¥610). JR also has a choice of express trains (8 daily; 45min; ¥710) and regular trains (every 30min; 1hr 20min; ¥710) from Kyoto.

From Osaka Trains on the private Kintetsu–Nara line (from Osaka's Kintetsu-Namba Station) arrive at the Kintetsu-Nara Station (every 15min; 30–40min; ¥560). Alternatively, take a JR line train from Osaka Station (every 20min; 40min; ¥800) or from JR Namba Station (every 20min; 30–40min; ¥560) to JR Nara Station.

From Kansai International Airport You can go into central Osaka to pick up a train (see p.515) or hop on a limousine bus (hourly; 1hr 35min; ¥2050), which stops at both of Nara's train stations.

BY BUS

Long-distance buses Services from Tokyo (Shinjuku; 1 daily; 8hr), Yokohama (1 daily; 9hr) and Nagoya (5 daily; 2hr) stop outside both the Kintetsu and JR Nara train stations.

GETTING AROUND

By bus You'll need to use local buses for some of Nara's more far-flung sights – the main termini for these are outside the JR and Kintetsu-Nara train stations. The standard fare is ¥210 within the city centre, which you usually pay as you get on, though buses going out of central Nara employ a ticket system – take a numbered ticket as you board and pay the appropriate fare on exit. The one-day World Heritage Pass (¥500) covers buses in central Nara as well as Yakushi-ji and Tōshōdai-ji. For Hōryū-ji and other sites, use the one-day World Heritage Wide Pass (¥1000). Both passes are available from the JR and Kintetsu stations.

By car Rental outlets include Eki Rent-a-Car (☎ 0742 26 3929), next door to JR Nara Station. Toyota (☎ 0742 22 0100) and Nippon Rent-a-Car (☎ 0742 24 5701) have branches near the Kintetsu-Nara Station.

By bike Nara Rent-a-Cycle (daily: March–Nov 8.30am–5pm; Dec–Feb 9am–3pm; from ¥500/day; ☎ 0742 24 8111) is near exit 7 of the Kintetsu-Nara Station. It's possible to return your bicycle afterhours, or the following morning.

INFORMATION AND TOURS

Tourist information Nara is well provided with information offices, most impressive of which is the recently opened Nara Visitor Center & Inn (daily 8am–9pm; ☎ 0742 81 7461, ⓦ sarusawa.nara.jp), located to the south of Sarusawa-ike, with excellent facilities including temporary free baggage storage. On Sanjō-dōri the Nara City Tourist Centre (daily 9am–9pm; ☎ 0742 22 3900, ⓦ narashikanko.or.jp/en) has good information on special events and exhibitions. There's also an office next to the JR Station (daily 9am–9pm; ☎ 0742 27 2223), and one in Kintetsu Station (daily 9am–9pm; ☎ 0742 24 4858). All have English-speaking staff.

Listings magazines The free bilingual newspaper called *nara nara* (ⓦ naranara.jp) has features on local dining, shopping and sightseeing. It can be picked up at one of the tourist offices. The free monthly *Kansai Scene* also carries the latest information about what's on in Nara.

Services Nara's central hospital is the Nara City Hospital (市立奈良病院), 1-5-1 Higashi Kidera-chō (☎ 0742 24 1251), with a 24hr emergency department; it's located south of Nara-kōen on Route 169. The Central Post Office is on Ōmiya-dōri, a fair walk west of the centre. It has 24hr mail services, but for other purposes the sub-post offices opposite the JR station and in the centre of town are more convenient.

6

Tours There are a number of bus tours which take in some of the Unesco World Heritage Sites in and around Nara (ⓦ narakotsu.co.jp/teikan), but the best way is to walk and take public transport when needed. Alternatively, Nara Walk (ⓦ narawalk.com) offer a variety of guided walks starting at ¥2000, or there is the similarly priced Nara-machi Walking Tour (April–Nov Sat 10am–1pm; ¥2000; ⓦ eonet.ne.jp/~naramachiwalk), which departs from Kintetsu Nara Station. Reservations are not required.

ACCOMMODATION

★**Edosan** 江戸三 1167 Takabatake-chō ☎0742 26 2662, ⓦ edosan.jp. Located within Nara-kōen, this ryokan is the most exquisite place to spend the night in any season. All guests stay in their own private rustic cottage, from where deer can be seen wandering past as you dine on artistically presented top-class *kaiseki*. Despite *Edosan's* exclusivity, the service is warm and down-to-earth. The bathhouse is separate and can be used individually. **¥48,000**

Guesthouse Nara Backpackers 奈良バックパッカーズ 31 Yurugi-chō ☎0742 22 4557, ⓦ nara-backpackers .com. In a charming 100-year-old mansion just a 10min walk northeast of the Kintetsu-Nara Station, this budget guesthouse is a quiet and convenient place to stay. Retaining all the features of a traditional Japanese home, it has shared bathing and kitchen facilities, as well as a communal lounge overlooking the large internal garden. Private rooms, including a tea ceremony room, are very comfortable and there are also dorm rooms with bunk beds. 📶 Dorms **¥2400**, doubles **¥5800**

Guesthouse Nara Komachi ゲストハウス奈良小町 41-1 Surugamachi ☎0742 87 0556. Conveniently located close to the JR station, this clean modern guesthouse is a good deal. The dorms have bunk beds and there are also Japanese- and Western-style small private rooms, all with attached toilet and shower. 📶 Dorms **¥2500**, doubles **¥7600**

★**Guesthouse Sakuraya** ゲストハウス桜舎 1 Narukawa-chō ☎0742 24 1490, ⓦ guesthouse -sakuraya.com. This stylish guesthouse, located in historic Nara-machi, has been tastefully restored with three clean and comfortable tatami rooms and a lovely garden. The multilingual owner is very helpful and hospitable, and there are free tea- and coffee-making facilities. 📶 **¥10,400**

Guesthouse Tsunoya ゲストハウスつのや 5 Higashitera Bayashi-chō ☎0742 27 0055, ⓦ naratsunoya.com. A new addition to the Nara guesthouse scene, *Tsunoya* is at the southern end of Nara-machi in a smart, modern building. The shared dormitory is capsule-style, with futons on bunks separated by *shoji*

screens. The double rooms have comfortable futons or beds, as well as en-suite facilities. Staff are helpful and there's an in-house café (coffee ¥270). Dorms **¥3000**, doubles **¥8000**

Kasuga Hotel 春日ホテル 40 Noborioji-chō ☎0742 22 4031, ⓦ kasuga-hotel.co.jp. A short walk from Kintetsu-Nara Station, this luxurious ryokan-like hotel has both Japanese- and Western-style rooms, some of which have their own private outdoor baths. Locally sourced *kaiseki* cuisine is served in the evening (extra fee). The staff speak a little English and service is polite and efficient. **¥25,820**

★**Nara Hotel** 奈良ホテル 1096 Takabatake-chō ☎0742 26 3300, ⓦ narahotel.co.jp. Oozing with nostalgia, the *Nara Hotel* is one of Japan's most historic hotels. Its staff will gladly point out the hotel's unusual architectural features and tell stories of its famous guests, including Albert Einstein, Audrey Hepburn and the Dalai Lama. The rooms in the newer wing are smart and comfortable, but the Meiji-era ambience of the original rooms with their high ceilings and period furniture is recommended. The hotel is set in its own gardens on the edge of Nara-kōen and has two restaurants serving French and Japanese cuisine, as well as a bar and a tea lounge. 📶 **¥35,600**

Hotel New Wakasa ホテルニューわかさ 1 Kitahanda Higashi-machi ☎0742 23 5858, ⓦ n-wakasa.com. Conveniently located near Nara-kōen, this pleasant hotel has fantastic views from the rooftop terrace. Most of the tastefully decorated and fairly spacious rooms are Japanese-style. The hotel has a variety of hotspring baths, some of which can be used privately (¥2100/1hr). 📶 **¥30,100**

Ugaya Guest House 奈良ウガヤゲストハウス 4-1 Okukomori-chō ☎0742 95 7739, ⓦ ugaya.net. Formerly a pharmacy, this friendly guesthouse, located between the JR and Kintetsu stations, is a good place to make new friends and enjoy Nara's nightlife. It has women-only and mixed dorms with bunk beds, as well as private rooms – all with shared shower facilities. There's also an in-house library and an organic coffee shop. 📶 Dorms **¥2500**, doubles **¥5000**

EATING

Like Kyoto, Nara has its own brand of *kaiseki*, the elaborate meals that originally accompanied the tea ceremony, but local specialities also include some rather bland dishes. **Cha-ga-yu** may have evolved from the breakfast of poor people into a fairly expensive delicacy, but there's no escaping the fact that it's basically a thin rice gruel, boiled up with soya beans, sweet potatoes and green tea leaves. It's best as part of a set meal, when the accompaniments such as pickles add a bit of flavour. **Tororo** is pretty similar: thickened grated yam mixed with soy sauce, seaweed and barley, then poured over a bowl of rice – full of protein and rather sticky. Less of an acquired taste is **kakinoha-zushi**, sushi wrapped in persimmon leaves, and **Nara-zuke**, vegetables pickled in sake.

RESTAURANTS

★**Edosan** 江戸三 1167 Takabatake-chō ✆0742 26 2662, ⊛edosan.jp. If you can't stay at this ryokan, located within Nara-kōen, having a meal here is just as memorable. *Edosan* serves wonderful *kaiseki* meals to non-guests. The Mahoroba *kaiseki* lunch (¥5670) is a good example of their seasonal creations. Full *kaiseki* courses are priced from ¥8400. Reservations required. Daily 11.30am–2.30pm & 5–9pm.

Gohan no Aida ごはんの間 26 Hanashiba-chō ✆0742 24 1539. This popular restaurant is only open for lunch and serves mostly vegetarian dishes. Their speciality is tempura, and all set lunches (¥800) come with rice and miso soup. No English menu, but the staff will do their best to explain the dishes of the day. 11am–3pm; closed Wed.

Hirasō 平宗 30-1 Imanikadō-chō ✆0742 22 0866, ⊛kakinoha.co.jp/naramise. *Hirasō* specializes in *kakinoha-zushi*, though you'll also find all sorts of other tasty local delicacies on the menu. Sushi sets start at ¥1400, with multicourse meals including *kakinoha-zushi* and *cha-ga-yu* from around ¥3700. Tues–Sun 11am–8pm.

Hiyori ひより 26 Nakanoshinya-chō ✆0742 24 1470, ⊛narakko.com/hiyori. *Yamato-yasai*, the vegetable cuisine of Nara, is the speciality here, but it's not strictly vegetarian – there are also meat and fish dishes. Delicious and healthy *Yasai-biyori* lunch sets are ¥1650, and Hiyori's *kaiseki* dinner course, with seven vegetable dishes and one main dish, is just ¥3850. 11.30am–2pm & 5–9pm; closed Tues.

Jyu Jyu 樹樹 27 1 Mochiidono-chō ✆0742 27 6121, ⊛jyujyunara.com. Up a narrow alleyway off the arcade south of Sanjō-dōri, this friendly *izakaya* is in an old geisha house and serves Japanese home-style cooking. Try their avocado and anchovy pizza (¥780), tofu with miso sauce (¥470) or Korean *chijimi* pancake (¥730). Wine by the glass is ¥520 and draught beer is ¥630. Tues–Sun 5–11pm; closed first and third Tues of the month.

Kinatei 喜菜亭 25-1 Surugamachi ✆0742 20 6188, ⊛kinatei.com. This restaurant serves Japanese-style vegetarian lunch sets (¥1200), udon (from ¥700) and ramen (¥850) using fresh local ingredients. It's easy to miss – head south from the JR Station, and turn left at Toyota Rent-a-Car – it's 100m on the left. Tues–Sun 11.30am–2pm; closed irregularly.

Mellow Café メローカフェ Axe Unit, 1-8 Konishi-chō ✆0742 27 9099, ⊛mellowcafe.jp. This large, spacious Italian café-restaurant, specializing in oven-fired pizza, is up a lane off the Konishi Sakuradōri shopping street. The most adventurous topping on the menu is the Narazuke (pickles) and *sake lees* pizza (¥1300). The daily Mellow lunch plate is ¥900, and the dinner course with pasta, meat and fish dishes is ¥3600. Daily 11am–11pm.

★**Sakura Burger** さくらバーガー 6 Higashimuki Kita-chō ✆0742 31 3813, ⊛sakuraburger.com. One of the few places in Nara to get a healthy burger made with fresh ingredients. The patty is made from top-quality local beef, and comes with home-made bacon and French fries. For the super-hungry the Sakura Burger (¥1040) is a hearty lunch, but if you just want a snack the Momiji Burger (¥490) is very satisfying. 11am–4pm & 5–9pm; closed Wed.

★**Yamato-an** やまと庵 495-1 Sanjō-machi ✆0742 26 3585. Nara-produced beef, chicken and pork are the main ingredients in the scrumptious dishes served here. The Yamato chicken tempura (¥880) and the simmered Yamato pork are very popular (¥1080). Vegetarians are also catered for – the tofu dishes are excellent (from ¥640). Daily 11.30am–2.30pm & 5–11pm.

Yamazakiya 山崎屋 5 Higashimuki-chō ✆0742 27 3715, ⊛ajiyama.com. Located at the back of the eponymously named pickle shop, this traditional restaurant has a good range of set meals to choose from. The Hana-Gozen *chirashi-zushi* set is ¥900, the Tempura-Gozen set with Nara pickles is ¥2000, and *kaiseki* courses start at ¥3990. The staff are welcoming but don't speak English. It's easiest to check the window display first and then order from the English menu. Tues–Sun 11.15am–8.30pm.

CAFÉS

Ban INOUE 幡 INOUE 16 Kasugano-chō ✆0742 27 1010, ⊛asa-ban.com. Locally grown vegetables, as well as soy sauce and miso produced in Nara, are part of the macrobiotic-style meals served in this cheerful café and craft shop in the Yume-Kaze Plaza shopping complex. The Healthy Lunch Set (¥1245) includes three seasonal vegetable dishes, soup and rice. Daily 10am–6.30pm; closed irregularly.

Rococo ロココ 31 Nishimikado-chō ✆0742 23 4075, ⊛rococo-coffee.co.jp. Head here to sample Nara's best premium roasted beans and a good selection of speciality coffees, including original Nara coffee with local honey (¥700) and the Weekly Espresso Drinking Set (¥700), which includes an espresso and a cappuccino. Breakfast (¥650) and lunch (¥1100) sets with toast or sandwiches and coffee are also available. Daily 8am–8pm.

TEAHOUSE

Shinjyu-an 心樹庵 22 Nishishinya-chō ✆0742 27 3083, ⊛ryuuoukutu302.wixsite.com/shinjuan. High-quality Yamato-cha teas are served in this quaint teashop located in an 85-year-old *machiya* in Nara-machi. The daily tea set with sweets is ¥750, or you can just enjoy a cup (choose from 100 different kinds of tea) for ¥500. Tues–Sat 1–4.30pm; closed national holidays.

6

NARA FESTIVALS AND ANNUAL EVENTS

Several of Nara's **festivals** have been celebrated for well over a thousand years. Many of these are dignified court dances, though the fire rituals are more lively affairs. In spring and autumn the Nara Kasugano Internet Forum (☎0742 27 2630, ⓦpref.nara.jp/koukaido-e) in Nara-kōen stages a series of **nō dramas**, while the biggest cultural event of the year is undoubtedly the autumn exhibition of Shōsō-in's treasures.

January: Yama-yaki 若草山焼き On the fourth Saturday evening of January at 6pm, priests from Kōfuku-ji set fire to the grass on Wakakusa-yama – supervised by a few hundred firemen. The festival commemorates the settlement of a boundary dispute between Nara's warrior monks.

February 3: Mantōrō Lantern Festival 万燈籠 To mark *setsubun*, the beginning of spring, three thousand stone and bronze lanterns are lit at Kasuga Taisha (from 6pm).

March 1–14: O-Taimatsu and O-Mizutori お松明 and お水取り A 1200-year-old ceremony that commemorates a priest's dream about the goddess Kannon drawing water from a holy well. The climax is on the night of March 13 when, at around 6.30pm, priests on the second-floor veranda of Nigatsu-dō light huge torches and scatter sparks over the assembled crowds to protect them from evil spirits. At 2am the priests collect water from the well, after which they whirl more lit flares round in a frenzied dance.

Mid-May: Takigi Nō 薪御能 Outdoor performances of nō dramas by firelight at Kōfuku-ji and Kasuga Taisha: check at any of Nara's tourist offices (see p.491) or ⓦnarashikanko.or.jp/en for exact dates.

August 14–15: Chūgen Mantōrō 中元万燈籠 To celebrate Obon, the festival of souls, Kasuga Taisha's lanterns are spectacularly lit.

September: Uneme Matsuri 采女祭 On the night of the harvest moon, this festival takes place at the Sarusawa-ike pond as a dedication to Uneme, a court lady who drowned herself here after losing the favour of the emperor. At around 7pm two dragon-bowed boats bearing costumed participants and *gagaku* musicians commemorate the lady's death in multicoloured splendour. The festival lasts until 9.30pm.

Early to mid-October: Shika-no-Tsunokiri 鹿の角きり This is the season when the deer in Nara-kōen are wrestled to the ground and have their antlers sawn off by Shintō priests. It all takes place in the Roku-en deer pen, near Kasuga Taisha. Check at any of Nara's tourist offices (see p.491) or ⓦnarashikanko.or.jp/en for exact dates.

Late October–early November: Shōsō-in Treasures 正倉院 At the National Museum (see box, p.488).

December 15–18: On-matsuri おん祭 At around midday a grand costume parade sets off from the prefectural offices to Kasuga Wakamiya-jinja, stopping on the way for various ceremonies. It ends with outdoor performances of nō and courtly dances.

DRINKING

Bar Hana バー華 1 Hashimoto-chō ☎0742 22 3077. Small shot bar with a good range of local whiskies (from ¥900), as well as draught beer (¥600) and wine by the glass (¥700). There's an evening cover charge of ¥300 per person, but during happy hour (4–7pm) you can order two drinks for ¥1000. ☏ Mon–Fri 4pm–1am, Sat & Sun 1pm–1am.

Harushika Sake Brewery 春鹿醸造元 24-1 Fukuchi-in-chō ☎0742 2 2255, ⓦharushika.com. Producing high-quality sake since 1884, this sake brewery is a wonderfully atmospheric place to try rice wine produced in Nara. The front of the traditional premises has been remodelled into a comfortable tasting area where, for the very reasonable price of ¥500, you can sample five different kinds of sake and take

the glass home. Daily 8.15am–5.15pm.

Public House Ritz パブリックハウスリッツ 1-1 Hashimoto-chō ☎0742 31 6144. This bar is also Nara's only Tex-Mex restaurant, so you can enjoy tequila shots (¥500) or Corona beer (¥650) with nachos (¥480) or quesadilla (¥480). Daily 5–11pm.

The Stand ザ・スタンド 14 Higashimuki Minami-machi ☎050 5784 6458. Located on the busy Higashimuki shopping street north of Sanjō-dōri, this friendly standing bar serves large draught beers for ¥800, as well as *shōchū* (¥400), sake (¥400–600) and wine by the glass (¥600). The snack food menu changes daily, but small dishes start at ¥380. Daily 3–11.30pm.

SHOPPING

Kite Mite Nara Shop きてみてならショップ 1F Nara Commerce & Tourism Bldg ☎0742 26 8828, ⓦnara-shop.jp. Conveniently located just 2min east of Kintetsu-Nara Station, this shop sells a wide variety of tasteful Nara crafts, arts and food, and is a good place for last-minute

souvenir shopping. Tues–Sun 10am–6pm.

Kobaien Calligraphy Goods 古梅園 433-1 Zoshi-chō ☎0742 22 2646, ⓦkajisyouten.com. Nara is renowned for its high-quality *sumi-e* ink, calligraphy brushes (*fude*), tea whisks (*chasen*) and bleached hemp cloth (*sarashi*). At the foot of Wakakusa-yama, this traditional shop stocks the full range of top-quality calligraphy goods, plus various tea ceremony utensils. Calligraphy sets start from ¥5000. Daily 9am–5pm.

Shikaya 鹿屋 23 Kasugano-chō ☎ 0742 22 3181, ⓦ sikaya.co.jp. Catering to pop culture tastes, this eclectic

souvenir shop near the path that leads to Tōdai-ji stocks a large collection of cute character goods, such as Sento-kun (see box, p.490), as well as a range of ninja costumes and weapons, samurai swords and armour. They also sell kimono and the friendly staff will help you get kitted out. Daily 10am–5pm; closed irregularly.

6

Around Nara

Even before Nara was founded, the surrounding plains were sprinkled with burial mounds, palaces and temples. A few of these still survive, of which the most remarkable is the historic temple of **Hōryū-ji**, around 10km southwest of Nara, home to some impressive artworks and the world's oldest wooden building. Closer to Nara, the two temples of Nishinokyō district, **Yakushi-ji** and **Tōshōdai-ji**, contain yet more early masterpieces of Japanese art and architecture. These three temples are best visited together using local buses; the route described below starts at Hōryū-ji and then works back towards Nara. Also worth a visit nearby is the reconstructed palace of **Heijō Kyūseki** – the site of Japan's first real city.

Further south are two more enjoyable day-trip destinations. Burial mounds dot the landscape around the peaceful village of **Asuka**, where Japan's first Buddhist temple sits quietly next to rice fields. Nearby, **Yoshino-yama** attracts massive crowds of sightseers in spring when thousands of cherry blossoms bloom, and is also home to several magnificent temples and shrines.

Heijō-kyūseki

平城宮跡 • Daily 9am–4pm • Free, museum ¥500 • ☎ 0742 30 6753 • A 30min walk from the south exit of Kintetsu Yamato Saidaiji Station, one stop west of Nara on the Kintestu line (every 5–10min; 5min)

The site of Japan's first real city can be found at **Heijō Kyūseki**, some 2km northwest of Nara Station. The city was established by the Empress Genmei, who moved the capital from Asuka in 710, the third year of her reign. During the Nara Period (710–84) the site contained the emperor's palace, and at its height the city walls enclosed some 25 square kilometres, with a population thought to have numbered well over 100,000. In 784, when the capital moved to Heian-kyō – present-day Kyoto – the palace complex at Nara quickly fell into disrepair and the whole site was eventually swallowed up by rice paddies. Despite this, knowledge of its location and significance was not lost, and archeological work has been ongoing since 1959. As part of the 1300th anniversary of the founding of Nara City in 2010, the government embarked on a large-scale reconstruction of key parts of the site, based on evidence from archeological digs and the few surviving buildings from the period. Although the current structures on the site are modern reconstructions, Heijō-kyūseki is well worth a visit. There are detailed explanations in English of historical events and construction techniques, as well as some excellent illustrations of life in the Nara period.

Daigoku-den
第一次大極殿

The imposing **Daigoku-den** functioned as the main political centre of the palace for greeting dignitaries and ceremonial purposes. It was replaced by another audience hall later in the Nara period, the foundations of which can be found 100m to the east. Inside the hall you can see a replica of the **Takamikura**, the emperor's throne, which was used for state events and ceremonies.

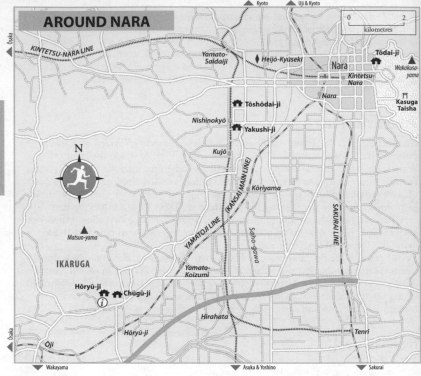

Heijō-kyo History Museum
平城京歴史館

The **Heijō-kyo History Museum**, located near the two-storey Suzaku-mon gate, was closed for a major expansion at the time of research. The upgraded museum is planning to focus on Japan's early relationship with China, and will have on display a reconstruction of a ship used by Japanese envoys to China, as well as a time tunnel and a virtual reality theatre.

Hōryū-ji

法隆寺 • Temple complex daily: mid-Feb to early Nov 8am–5pm; early Nov to mid-Feb 8am–4.30pm • ¥1500 • ⓦ www.horyuji.or.jp

As you walk round the Unesco World Heritage Site of **Hōryū-ji**, which was completed in 607 AD, it's worth bearing in mind that Buddhism had only really got going in Japan some fifty years earlier. The confident scale of Hōryū-ji and its superb array of Buddhist statues amply illustrate how quickly this imported faith took hold. One of its strongest proponents was Prince Shōtoku (574–622), the then-regent, who founded Hōryū-ji in accordance with the dying wish of his father, Emperor Yōmei. Though the complex burned down in 670, it was soon rebuilt, making this Japan's oldest-surviving Buddhist temple.

The main approach to Hōryū-ji is from the south, which takes you past the helpful information centre (see p.498). Walk north from here along a wide, tree-lined avenue to **Nandai-mon** (Great South Gate), which marks the outer enclosure. Inside lies a second, walled compound known as the **Sai-in Garan**, or Western Precinct. Within the Sai-in Garan's cloister-gallery, the **Five-Storey Pagoda** will inevitably catch your eye first. This is Japan's oldest five-tier pagoda, and inside you can see the early eighth-century clay images of Buddha entering Nirvana. However, it's actually the right-hand building, the **Kon-dō**, that is Hōryū-ji's star attraction.

Kon-dō
金堂

The **Kon-dō** (Golden Hall) is the world's **oldest wooden structure**, dating from the late seventh century, and although it's not very large, the building's multilayered roofs and sweeping eaves are extremely striking. Entering the east door, you're greeted by a bronze image of Shaka Nyorai (the Historical Buddha) flanked by two bodhisattvas still bearing a few touches of the original gold leaf that they were once covered in; this **Shaka triad** was cast in 623 AD in memory of Prince Shōtoku, who died the previous year. To its right stands **Yakushi Nyorai**, the Buddha of Healing, to which Hōryū-ji was dedicated, and to the left a twelfth-century **Amida Buddha** commemorating the Prince's mother.

Daihōzō-in
人宝蔵院

Exiting the Sai-in compound, walk east past two long, narrow halls, to the **Daihōzō-in** (Hall of Temple Treasures), which houses Hōryū-ji's priceless collection of more than 2300 national treasures in two halls. Look out for the bronze **Yume-chigae Kannon**. This "Dream-Changing" Kannon is credited with turning bad dreams into good, and has a soft, secretive smile.

Kudara Kannon-dō
百済観音堂

Connecting the two museum halls is the **Kudara Kannon-dō**, which houses the wooden **Kudara Kannon** (Kudara Goddess of Mercy) statue, thought to date from the seventh century. Not much is known about this unusually tall, willowy figure, but it has long been recognized as one of the finest Buddhist works of art in Japan. Kudara refers to an ancient province in Korea, and subsequently there has been some debate as to whether the statue came from there.

Chūgū-ji
中宮寺 • Daily: mid-March to Sept 9am–4.15pm; Oct to mid-March 9am–3.45pm • ¥600 • ☎ 0745 75 2106, ⊛ chuguji.jp

A gate in the northeast corner of the Tō-in Garan leads directly into **Chūgū-ji**. This intimate, peaceful nunnery was originally the residence of Prince Shōtoku's mother, which he converted into a temple on her death in 621. The main reason for coming here, however, sits inside a modern hall facing south over a pond. If you've already visited Kyoto's Kōryū-ji (see p.446), you'll recognize the central image of a pensive, boy-like **Miroku Bosatsu** (Future Buddha) absorbed in his task of trying to save mankind

---

THE HIDDEN BUDDHA OF HŌRYŪ-JI

Tō-in Garan is the eastern precinct of Hōryū-ji, which was added in 739. At its centrepiece is the octagonal **Yume-dono** (Hall of Dreams), with its magnificent statue, the **Kuze Kannon**. Until the late nineteenth century, this gilded wooden figure, said to be the same height as Prince Shōtoku (perhaps even modelled on him in the early seventh century), was a *hibutsu*, a hidden image, which no one had seen for centuries. Somewhat surprisingly, it was an American art historian, Ernest Fenellosa, who in the 1880s was given permission by the Meiji government, against the wishes of the temple, to unwrap the Kannon from the bundle of white cloth in which it had been kept. He revealed a dazzling statue in an almost perfect state of repair, carrying a sacred jewel and wearing an elaborate crown, with the famous enigmatic smile of the Kon-dō's Shaka Nyorai on its youthful lips. Unfortunately, the Kannon is still kept hidden for most of the year, except for brief spells in spring and autumn (usually April 11–May 15 & Oct 22–Nov 22).

from suffering. Here, the statue is of camphor wood, burnished black with age, and is thought to have been carved by a Korean craftsman in the early seventh century.

Chūgū-ji marks the eastern extent of the Hōryū-ji complex. If you exit from here it's a ten-minute walk south down to the main road and the Chūgū-ji-mae bus stop, one stop east of the Hōryū-ji-mae stop; alternatively, trek back and exit from the Nandai-mon, which will take you down to the Hōryū-ji bus depot.

ARRIVAL AND INFORMATION   HŌRYŪ-JI

By bus The simplest way of getting to Hōryū-ji from Nara is by #52 or #97 bus (hourly; 50min–1hr; ¥760) from Nara's JR or Kintetsu stations; get off at the Hōryū-ji-mae stop. The one-day World Heritage Wide Pass (¥1000) is the most economical way to visit this area from Nara by bus.

By train Osaka-bound trains from JR Nara stop at Hōryū-ji Station (every 10min; 15min; ¥220), from where it's a

20min walk to the temple on a fairly busy road, or you can catch a #72 bus (Mon–Fri 2–3 hourly, Sat & Sun every 10min; 10min; ¥180).

Tourist information The Information Centre (daily 8.30am–5pm ☏ 0745 74 6800, ⓦ www4.kcn.ne.jp/~ikaru-i) is across the road from the Hōryū-ji-mae bus stop.

Yakushi-ji

薬師寺 • Nishinokyō, 6km northwest of Hōryū-ji • Daily 8.30am–5pm • ¥1100 • ☏ 0742 33 6001, ⓦ nara-yakushiji.com

Emperor Tenmu first ordered the construction of **Yakushi-ji** sometime around 680 AD when his wife was seriously ill. Although she recovered, Tenmu himself died eight years later, leaving the empress to dedicate Yakushi-ji herself in 697. Over the centuries, fires have destroyed all but one of the original buildings, the **East Pagoda**, though Yakushi-ji's amazing collection of statues has fared better. **Major restoration work** is currently under way on the **East Pagoda** and is expected to continue until 2018. A special exhibition hall has been built to explain the restoration process and to display the pagoda's beautiful metal rooftop ornaments.

The inner compound

The only building of historical note in Yakushi-ji's inner compound is the three-storey **East Pagoda**, which was famously described as "frozen music" by Ernest Fenellosa (see box, p.497). He was referring to the rhythmical progression of the smaller double roofs that punctuate the pagoda's upward flow. It's the sole surviving remnant of the original temple and contrasts strongly with the spanking red lacquer of the new West Pagoda, the **Daikō-dō** (Great Lecture Hall) and the **Kon-dō** (Golden Hall), all of which have been rebuilt during the last thirty years. Inside the Kon-dō, the temple's original seventh-century bronze **Yakushi triad** sits unperturbed; past fires have removed most of the gold and given the statues a rich black sheen, but otherwise they are in remarkably fine condition.

The outer compound

Continuing through the outer compound, you come to a long, low wooden hall on your left, the **Tōin-dō**. Rebuilt around 1285, the hall houses a bronze image of **Shō-Kannon**, an incarnation of the goddess of mercy, which dates from the early Nara period. This graceful, erect statue, framed against a golden aureole, shows distinctly Indian influences in its diaphanous robes, double necklace and the strands of hair falling over its shoulders.

ARRIVAL AND DEPARTURE   YAKUSHI-JI

By train Kintetsu-line trains run from Nara to Nishinokyō Station (every 10min; 15min; ¥310) with a change at Saidai-ji; Yakushi-ji's north gate is a 3min walk east of the station.

By bus Buses #97 or #98 run from Hōryū-ji (35min; ¥560) or #52 bus from Nara (20min; ¥240) – get off at the Yakushi-ji Chūsha-jo stop, from where it's a short walk to

the temple's south gate. The World Heritage Pass (¥500) and World Heritage Wide Pass (¥1000) are the most economical way to visit this area from Nara by bus.

On foot From Yakushi-ji, after exiting the north gate, go straight ahead for 5min and you'll find the front entrance to Tōshōdai-ji.

Tōshōdai-ji

唐招提寺 • Nishinokyō • **Temple complex** Daily 8.30am–4.30pm • ¥600 • **Shin-Hōzō** March–May & Sept–Nov daily 8.30am–4pm • ¥100 • ☎ 0742 33 7900, ⓦ toshodaiji.jp

The weathered, wooden halls of **Tōshōdai-ji** in their pleasant shady compound are superb examples of late eighth-century architecture. The temple was founded in 759 by the eminent Chinese monk Ganjin when he was granted permission to move from the city to somewhere more peaceful.

The first thing you'll see on entering the south gate is the stately Chinese-style **Kon-dō** (Main Hall), which has been masterfully restored in recent years. Craftsmen who accompanied Ganjin from the mainland are responsible for the three superb dry-lacquer statues displayed here. The **Kō-dō** (Lecture Hall) behind the Kon-dō also dates from the late eighth century, and is more Japanese in styling. During the Nara period, this hall was a major centre of learning and religious training.

Just once a year – on June 6, the anniversary of Ganjin's death – the doors of the **Miei-dō** (Founder's Hall), in the northern section of the compound, are opened to reveal a lacquered image which was carved just before Ganjin died in 763 at the grand age of 76. He's buried next door, in the far northeast corner of the compound, in a simple grave within a clay-walled enclosure.

Shin-Hōzō

新宝蔵

On the compound's east side is the rather modern-looking concrete **Shin-Hōzō**, where, each spring and autumn, Tōshōdai-ji's stunning collection of treasures goes on display. These are mostly statues, of which the most celebrated is a headless wooden Buddha known as the "Venus of the Orient" – the voluptuousness of the statue contrasts with the more sculptural styles of the surrounding artworks. The exhibits are mostly labelled in English but staff also provide an explanation book in English.

ARRIVAL AND DEPARTURE   TŌSHŌDAI-JI

By train Kintetsu-line trains run from Nara to Nishinokyō Station (every 10min; 15min; ¥310) with a change at Saidai-ji; the main gate is a 1km walk northeast of the station.

By bus Buses #52 and #97 from Nara (every 30min; 20min; ¥240) drop you at the Tōshōdaiji Higashi-guchi bus stop on the main road, a 5min walk west of Tōshōdai-ji's main gate. The World Heritage Pass (¥500) and World Heritage Wide Pass (¥1000) are the most economical way to visit this area from Nara by bus.

On foot From Tōshōdai-ji's main gate it's a short walk south to Yakushi-ji.

Asuka

飛鳥

Located at the southern end of the Yamato plain, an hour south of Nara city by train, **ASUKA** is where the political and cultural foundations of the Japanese nation began, more than 1400 years ago. With its picturesque combination of traditional farmhouses, temples, rice terraces and verdant, low-lying hills, Asuka appears to be a quaint farming village. However, it is actually a major **archeological site**, dotted with **kofun** (tumuli) burial mounds that were probably constructed around the seventh century for burying the early emperors and empresses of Japan. Asuka is also the place where Buddhism first took root in Japan, and where many of the poems that make up the ancient anthology known as the *Man'yōshu* were composed. The main sights of Asuka are all less than 4km from the station and can be explored in a day-trip from Nara.

Takamatsuzuka Kofun

高松塚古墳 • 439 Hirata Asuka-mura, 1.2km from Asuka Station • Daily 9am–4.30pm • Museum ¥250 • ☎ 0774 54 3340, ⓦ asukabito.or.jp

You can't see inside the grassy mound that is the **Takamatsuzuka Kofun**, but the small **museum** next to it reveals all. Beautiful murals of dragons, tigers and turtle-snakes were discovered when the mound was first excavated in 1972, and removed for restoration in 2007. Photographic reproductions showing the delicate restoration process, as well as a full-sized replica of the internal crypt, are on display here.

Ishibutai Kofun

石舞台古墳 • Asuka-mura, 3.3km from Asuka Station • Daily 8.30am–5pm • ¥250 • ☎0774 54 4577

For centuries, **Ishibutai Kofun** was buried under vegetable fields, until its excavation in the 1930s. The *kofun* sits in an open park area and was constructed from massive boulders and slabs of stone to form a rectangular stone chamber. It's possible to enter the interior, which gives you a close-up view of the skilful ancient stonework.

Asuka-dera

飛鳥寺 • Asuka-mura, 3.5km from Asuka Station • Tues–Sun 10am–5pm • ¥350 • ☎0774 54 2126

Founded in 596, **Asuka-dera** is said to have been the first full-scale Buddhist temple in Japan. The current complex is much smaller than it was in its heyday but houses a rare treasure – the oldest known Buddhist statue in Japan, dating from the early seventh century. The 3m-high **Asuka Daibutsu** was crafted in a Chinese style from bronze, and is flanked by two exquisite fourteenth-century wooden sculptures.

Nara Prefecture Complex of Man'yō Culture

奈良県立万葉文化館, Nara Kenritsu Man'yō Bunkakan • Asuka-mura, 3.7km from Asuka Station • Tues–Sun 10am–5pm • ¥600 • ☎0774 54 1852, ⊛manyo.jp

The excellent **Nara Prefecture Complex of Man'yō Culture** brings to life the history and culture of the *Man'yōshu* – Japan's earliest collection of poetry. Many of the displays are interactive, re-creating daily life in the early centuries, and there's a film theatre too. Be sure not to miss the Sayakeshi Room, where you can relax to the natural sounds of Asuka with a soothing ceiling light display.

ARRIVAL AND INFORMATION   ASUKA

By train To get to Asuka Station, take a train from Kintetsu Yamato Saidai-ji Station (one stop west of Nara on the Kintetsu line), and change at Kashihara-jingūmae Station for the Yoshino line (1hr; ¥580).

Tourist information There's a small tourist information desk (daily 8.30am–5pm; ☎0774 54 3624) in the Asuka Bito-no-kan, on the left as you exit Asuka Station. Information in English is scant, but you can pick up a bilingual map of the area. English-language audio guides can also be rented from here (9am–5pm; ¥500).

GETTING AROUND

By bike There are a few bicycle rental shops in front of Asuka Station. Asuka Rent-a-Cycle (daily 9am–5pm; ☎0774 54 3919) has one-day bike rentals (Mon–Fri ¥900, Sat, Sun & public hols ¥1000).

By bus The Kame Loop Bus (¥180 per ride; 1-day pass ¥650) runs through Asuka village hourly, stopping at the major sights. It departs from in front of Asuka Station and terminates at the east exit of Kintetsu Kashihara-jingūmae.

EATING

Coccolo Cafe コッコロカフェ 137-1 Goen ☎0744 54 3039, ⊛bit.ly/2fQ34ON. Friendly café opposite the station with comfortable table or sofa seating. It's a great place to stop for breakfast (¥570), a healthy veggie lunch set (¥1030) or pumpkin cheesecake and coffee (¥570). 8am–7pm; closed Wed.

Yume-ichi-chaya 夢市茶屋 154-3 Shimasho ☎0744 54 9450. At the edge of the Ishibutai Kofun park, this spacious restaurant serves delicious lunch sets (¥1080) made with local vegetables, tofu and heirloom rice, and black rice curry (¥860). Order at the counter from the photo menu. Downstairs is a small shop selling fresh local produce and souvenirs. Daily 11am–4pm.

Yoshino
吉野

YOSHINO is the most famous and revered place in Japan to see **cherry blossoms**. More than 100,000 trees bloom on the sacred mountain of Yoshino-yama, usually from early April – attracting enormous crowds and traffic jams for a month. The small town at the top of Yoshino-yama, accessed via ropeway, is essentially one long street and is easily explored on foot. Home to several Unesco World Heritage Sites, it is also the headquarters of the Shugendō Buddhist sect of mountain aestheticism, and is renowned for its *kuzu* (arrowroot) sweets, making a visit at any time of the year worthwhile.

6

Kimpusen-ji
金峯山寺 • 2498 Yoshino-yama • Daily 8.30am–4pm • Main hall ¥500 • ☎ 0746 32 8371, ⓦ kimpusen.or.jp

Kimpusen-ji was established in the late seventh century by the En no Gyōja, a mountain ascetic monk and founder of Shugendō Buddhism. The impressive **Zaodo** main hall has burnt down five times, and the current structure dates from 1592. Inside are three important sixteenth-century wooden statues of Buddhist deities – Shakamuni, Kannon and Mitreya Bodhisattva – usually hidden behind curtains, and only displayed for one month a year. The morning worship service, accompanied by *horagai* (large conch shells used as trumpets) and *taiko* drums, is held here daily at 6.30am.

Yoshimizu-jinja
吉水神社 • 579 Yoshino-yama • Daily 9am–5pm • ¥400 • ☎ 0746 32 3024, ⓦ yoshimizu-shrine.com

The Shintō shrine **Yoshimizu-jinja** was founded in the seventh century as a Buddhist temple, and was converted in the mid-nineteenth century. During its lifetime it has sheltered various historical figures fleeing from strife, including Emperor Go-Daigo (see p.823), and it also hosted Toyotomi Hideyoshi's cherry blossom viewing party for 5000 guests in 1594. The shrine and gardens were under long-term restoration at the time of research, but it's worth visiting to see the interesting assortment of scruffy historical items on display inside.

ARRIVAL AND INFORMATION
YOSHINO

By train and ropeway The easiest way to get to Yoshino is on the Kintetsu line. From Yamato Saidai-ji Station (one stop west of Nara on the Kintetsu line), take a train to Kashihara-jingūmae Station and change there for the Yoshino line (1hr 30min; ¥850). Once you have arrived at Kintetsu Yoshino Station, it's a 10min walk to Senbonguchi Station, from where you take the ropeway to Yoshino-yama Station at the top of the mountain (daily 9.20am–5.40pm; ¥360 one-way, ¥510 return).

Tourist information The Yoshinoyama Visitor Information Centre (daily 9am–5pm in spring and summer only; ☎ 0746 32 1007, ⓦ yoshino-kankou.jp) is located next to Kimpusen-ji.

EATING

Nakai Shunpudo 中井春風堂 545 Yoshino-yama ☎ 0742 32 3043, ⓦ nakasyun.com. Friendly café devoted to serving fresh and delicious *kuzu*, or arrowroot – a traditional gelatinous sweet. You can watch the chef make your noodles (¥800) or *mochi* (jelly; ¥800), which can then be dipped in a choice of two flavours – *kinako* (crushed soybean powder) or *kuromitsu* (black sugar syruip). 🛜 10am–5pm; closed Wed & weekdays in winter.

Tofu Chaya Hayashi 豆腐茶屋林 551 Yoshino-yama ☎ 0746 32 5681, ⓦ yoshinoyama-tofu.jp. The tofu here is made from the spring water of Yoshino-yama and has a rich flavour. The tofu set meal (¥1405) and tofu ramen (¥865) are both excellent. If you have any room for dessert, try their tofu ice cream (¥325). 9am–4.30pm; closed Tues.

Kansai
関西

VIEW FROM FLOATING GARDEN
OBSERVATORY, OSAKA

Kansai

In a country so devoid of flat land, the great rice-growing plains of Kansai, the district around Osaka and Kyoto, are imbued with an almost mystical significance. This was where the nation first began to take root, in the region known as Yamato, and where a distinct Japanese civilization evolved from the strong cultural influences of China and Korea. Kansai people are tremendously proud of their pivotal role in Japanese history and tend to look down on Tokyo, which they regard as an uncivilized upstart. The former imperial capitals of Kyoto and Nara (see pp.418–501), with their enduring historical and cultural importance, are naturally a major part of the region's appeal. Today, Kansai's diverse legacy of temples, shrines and castles, combined with an increasing array of exciting modern architecture, makes it one of Japan's top tourist destinations.

7

After having been much maligned as an "ugly" city, **Osaka** is finally emerging as a popular destination for international visitors. In recent years, some dynamic urban design and infrastructure projects have improved parts of the city. One thing that has not changed is the city's commercial spirit – the source of its long-established wealth – and its enthusiasm for eating and drinking.

South of Osaka, the temples of **Kōya-san** provide a tranquil glimpse into contemporary religious practice in Japan. This mountain-top retreat – the headquarters of the Shingon school of Buddhism – has been an active centre of pilgrimage since the ninth century, and people of all faiths are welcome to stay in the quiet old temples and join in the morning prayer service.

Shintō, Japan's native religion, also has deep spiritual roots in Kansai. Not far from Kōya-san is the **Kumano Kodō**, an ancient pilgrimage route through the "Land of the Gods", where for centuries both emperors and peasants sought purification and healing at sacred sites and hot springs. Over on the far eastern side of the region is **Ise-jingū**, one of the country's most important Shintō shrines, dedicated to Amaterasu, the Sun Goddess, from whom all Japan's emperors are descended. **Ise** itself is the gateway to the attractive peninsula of **Shima Hantō**. Here, *ama* women divers still use traditional fishing methods to collect seafood. The unspoiled scenery of **Ago-wan**, the bay at the southern tip of the peninsula, is a rewarding destination for scenic boat rides which give a bird's-eye view of the cultured pearl industry.

The port of **Kōbe** is less than thirty minutes west of Osaka in a dramatic location on the edge of Osaka Bay. Kōbe's sights are less of a draw than its relaxed

Highlights

❶ Osaka nightlife Enjoy the neon-lit buzz of streets of Japan's third-largest city and sample some typical Osakan street food, such as *takoyaki* – grilled octopus dumplings – before hitting the city's bars and clubs. **See p.522**

❷ Kōya-san Spend an atmospheric night in temple lodgings atop a sacred mountain and participate in a dawn *gomataki* fire ritual. See p.526

❸ Kumano Kodō Wander the pilgrimage route through ancient forests, discover sacred mountain shrines and soak in the healing waters of isolated hot springs. **See p.533**

❹ Ninja Museum, Iga-Ueno Learn about the stealth arts of Japan's medieval spies and assassins, and see a live demonstration of ninja fighting techniques. **See p.537**

❺ Kōbe jazz Spend an evening in one of this cosmopolitan city's jazz clubs. **See p.550**

❻ Himeji-jō Japan's most impressive castle, dating from the seventeenth century and dominated by a towering six-storey donjon. See p.554

❼ Kinosaki Onsen Enjoy a luxury onsen experience in this picturesque hot-spring town. See p.556

HIGHLIGHTS ARE MARKED ON THE MAP ON P.506

cosmopolitan atmosphere, best experienced with a stroll around its harbourside and an evening in one its jazz clubs. Close by is the ancient hot-spring resort **Arima Onsen**, which has managed to retain some old-world hospitality in its elegant ryokan, while further to the north on the Sea of Japan coast there are more popular hot springs at **Kinosaki Onsen**.

Wherever you choose to stay in Kansai, don't miss **Himeji**, on the area's western edge, and **Himeji-jō**, Japan's most impressive castle. Himeji also has the lovely **Himeji Kōko-en**, nine connected gardens laid out according to traditional principles, and two intriguing museums in buildings designed by top contemporary architects.

HIGHLIGHTS

1. Osaka nightlife
2. Kōya-san
3. Kumano Kodō
4. Ninja Museum, Iga-Ueno
5. Kōbe jazz
6. Himeji-jō
7. Kinosaki Onsen

GETTING AROUND   **KANSAI**

BY TRAIN
The most convenient way of getting around the Kansai district is by train. The area is crisscrossed by competing JR and private rail lines, while the Tōkaidō Shinkansen provides a high-speed service between Osaka, Kyoto, Kōbe and Himeji.

Kansai Area Pass If you plan to travel intensively around the region, you might want to buy JR West's Kansai Area Pass. Valid for between one and four consecutive days (¥2200–6300), the pass allows unlimited travel on all local services operated by JR West, apart from the Shinkansen. It also offers discounts on admission to various cultural and tourist sights, including art museums and amusement parks along JR lines.

San'yō Area Pass For those travelling on to Fukuoka, the San'yō Area Pass covers JR services from Kansai Airport via Osaka, Kōbe and Himeji, including the Shinkansen (seven days; ¥19,000).

Kansai Thru Pass A convenient and economical way to access the region's private railway lines, subway networks and bus companies is with the Kansai Thru Pass (two days ¥4000, three days ¥5200), which enables travellers to ride on almost any bus, subway or private railway in the region. Even if you have a JR Pass, this pass is handy, as it saves the hassle of buying tickets each time you jump on a bus or ride the subway.

Kintetsu Rail Pass The Kintetsu Rail Pass (two days ¥2500, five days ¥3800) covers the whole of the extensive Kintetsu network, including three rides on limited express trains. The five-day pass includes a return trip from the airport and good discounts on entry to major sights.

7

Osaka

大阪

Japan's third-largest city after Tokyo and Yokohama, the vibrant metropolis of **OSAKA** is inhabited by famously easy-going citizens with a taste for the good things in life. It may lack the traditional townscapes found in nearby Kyoto, but having received a bad rap as a tourist destination for many years, Osaka has re-branded itself and improved its image over the last decade. Urban revitalization, ambitious architectural projects – such as the 300m-tall Abeno Harukas skyscraper – and schemes such as free wi-fi hotspots throughout the city have succeeded in making it a popular destination for tourists.

Osakans speak one of Japan's more earthy dialects, **Osaka-ben**, and are as friendly as Kyoto folk can be frosty. They may greet each other saying "Mō kari-makka?" ("Are you making any money?"), but Osakans also know how to enjoy themselves once work has stopped. There are large entertainment districts in the north and south of the city, and the Osaka live music scene showcases eclectic local talent as well as international acts. In a city that cultivated high **arts**, such as *bunraku* puppetry, the locals also have a gift for bawdy comedy; Takeshi "Beat" Kitano, the internationally famous film director, started his career as a comedian here. The city continues to produce successful comedy duos who dominate national TV variety shows, and Osakans are very proud that their dialect has now become popular as the language of comedians. Osaka is also one of Japan's great **food** cities, though the residents are not snobby about their cuisine – a typical local dish is *takoyaki*, grilled octopus dumplings, usually sold as a street snack.

OSAKA ORIENTATION

Like all big Japanese cities, Osaka is divided into wards (*ku*), but you'll often hear locals talking of Kita (north) and Minami (south), the split being along Chūō-dōri. **Kita** covers the areas of **Umeda**, where all the main railway companies have stations, and **Shin-Osaka**, north of the Yodo-gawa River and location of the Shinkansen station. On the east side of this area is **Osaka-jō**, the castle. The shopping and entertainment districts of Shinsaibashi, Dōtombori, Amerika-mura and Namba are all part of **Minami**.

Slightly further south is **Tennōji**, where you'll find Tennōji-kōen, the temple Shitennō-ji and Abeno Harukas, Japan's tallest skyscraper. Further south again is the ancient shrine of Sumiyoshi Taisha. West of these districts lies the patchwork of landfill islands edging Osaka Bay, home to Universal Studios Japan and the Osaka Aquarium Kaiyūkan at **Tempozan Harbour Village**.

Brief history

Osaka's history stretches back to the fifth century AD, when it was known as **Naniwa** and its port served as a gateway to the more advanced cultures of Korea and China. For a short period, from the middle of the seventh century, the thriving city served as Japan's capital, but in the turbulent centuries that followed it lost its status, changed its name to Osaka and developed as a temple town. It was on the site of the temple Ishiyama Hongan-ji that the warlord **Toyotomi Hideyoshi** decided to build his castle in 1583 (see box opposite), and it became a key bastion in his campaign to unite the country.

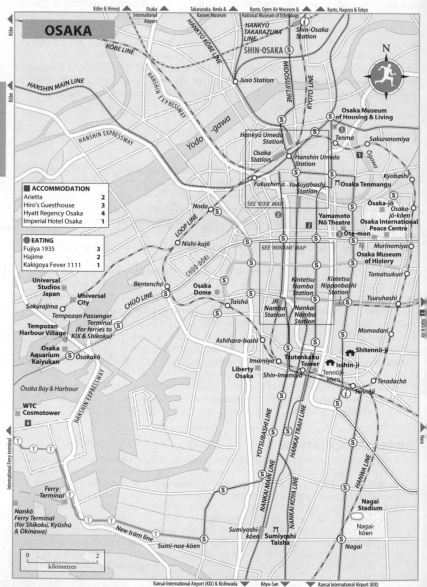

With Toyotomi's death in 1598, another period of political instability loomed in Osaka for his supporters, as rival **Tokugawa Ieyasu** shifted the capital to Edo. The shogun's troops besieged the castle in 1614 and destroyed it a year later. With Japan firmly under their control, the Tokugawa shoguns were happy to allow the castle to be rebuilt and for Osaka to continue developing as an economic and commercial centre. The wealth of what became known as the "kitchen of Japan" led to patronage of the arts, such as kabuki and *bunraku*, and a deep appreciation of gourmet pursuits (the origin of the famous Osaka expression "kuidaore", to eat oneself bankrupt) that still exists today.

Despite the city having a GDP comparable to that of New Zealand, the local government has been struggling financially for decades. In recent years, politicians have been arguing that Osaka should become the "back-up" capital in case Tokyo is affected by a disaster.

Osaka-jō

大阪城 • 1-1 Osaka-jō • Daily 9am–4.30pm • Park free; Osaka Castle ¥600 • ☎ 06 6941 3044, ⓦ osakacastle.net • Ōte-mon is a 2min walk northeast of the Tanimachi 4-chōme subway station; alternatively, take the JR loop line to Osaka-jō Kōen Station

Some cynics suggest that the only reason the castle **Osaka-jō** is the single most visited attraction in Japan – outdoing the country's best fortress Himeji-jō (see p.554) and even Mount Fuji – is because it's the only thing to see in the city. In fact, Osaka has plenty to see, but the castle is the main focus, and justly so.

There are several entrances to the park surrounding the castle, but the most impressive is through the **Ōte-mon** (Main Gate), dating from 1629, on the west side. If you enter though the southern Sakura-mon, keep an eye out for the 130-tonne **Tako-ishi** ("Octopus Stone") as you head up towards the donjon: with a surface area of sixty square metres, this is the largest rock used in the original construction of the castle walls.

Donjon

天守閣, Tenshukaku

It's long been a point of amusement that Osaka-jō's main tower, or **donjon**, has its own elevator inside, as well as one outside, so that the elderly and those in wheelchairs can

---

THE INDOMITABLE FORTRESS

Despite being largely a concrete reconstruction, **Osaka-jō** can be counted a great survivor, a tangible link with the city's illustrious past as Japan's one-time seat of power. The castle's roots go back to the early sixteenth century, when an influential Buddhist sect built its fortified temple headquarters **Ishiyama Hongan-ji** beside the confluence of the Ōgawa and Neya-gawa rivers. For a decade the monks held out against warlord Oda Nobunaga (see p.824), before handing their fortress over in 1580. Nobunaga's successor, **Toyotomi Hideyoshi**, decided to build the grandest castle in Japan on the temple site. For three years from 1583, tens of thousands of men laboured on the enormous castle, and craftsmen were drafted in from around Japan to give the eight-storey central donjon the finest gold-leaf decoration.

Hideyoshi died in 1598, and his son and heir Hideyori was immediately under threat from rival **Tokugawa Ieyasu**. In 1614, the would-be shogun laid siege to the castle, even though his favourite granddaughter Senhime, wife of Hideyori, was inside. A year later he breached the castle and reduced it to ruins. Hideyori and his mother committed suicide rather than surrender, but Senhime survived and went on to become mistress of Himeji-jō. When Ieyasu allowed the castle to be rebuilt in the 1620s, he made sure it was not on the same scale as his own residence in Edo. In 1665, the donjon was again burnt to the ground after being struck by lightning. It was not rebuilt until the 1840s and then only lasted another thirty years before the Tokugawa troops set fire to it during the civil war that briefly raged before the Meiji Restoration of 1868. Osaka's citizens, however, had grown fond of their castle, so the donjon was rebuilt once more in 1931 – this time from concrete – and it has remained standing despite the heavy bombing of the city during World War II.

avoid the steps to the entrance. Head up to the eighth floor for a panoramic view of the city and castle grounds; the orchards you can see between the moats on the castle's eastern flank are a riot of plum blossom in March. Working your way down the floors, you'll be guided through the life of Toyotomi Hideyoshi (see box, p.509) and the castle's colourful history. The displays include the highly detailed folding screen painting *Summer War of Osaka* and a full-scale re-creation of Toyotomi's famous golden tearoom. On the first floor, it's worth dropping by the mini-theatre to see the free history videos with English subtitles.

Osaka International Peace Centre

大阪国際平和センター, Ōsaka Kokusai Heiwa Senta • 2-1 Osaka-jō • Tues–Sun 9.30am–4.30pm • ¥250 • ☎ 06 6947 7208, Ⓦ peace-osaka.or.jp

The sobering **Osaka International Peace Centre** is located in the southern corner of the Osaka-jō-kōen. As at similar museums in Hiroshima and Nagasaki, the heavy-going displays attempt to explain Japan's experiences of World War II. Here, however, there is less emphasis on Japan's provocative actions before and during the war, and more prominence is given to the suffering of Osaka when it was heavily bombed. The displays detailing life during that time emphasize the misery of war, and visitors are asked to leave a message of peace.

Osaka Museum of History

大阪歴史博物館, Ōsaka Rekishi Hakubutsukan • 4-1-32 Otemae • 9.30am–4.30pm, Fri until 8pm; closed Tues • ¥600, audio guides ¥400 • ☎ 06 6946 5728, Ⓦ mus-his.city.osaka.jp

To the southwest of Osaka-jō, the stunning **Osaka Museum of History** is housed in a twelve-storey concrete and glass structure shaped like a giant ship's funnel – the "edge" pointing towards the castle is made of glass and offers excellent views. One of the city's premier attractions, the museum is built on the site of the Asuka-period Naniwa-no-Miya Palace, remains of which have been preserved in the museum's basement. Above that are four storeys of interesting displays featuring antique manuscripts and intricate scale models of street scenes and long-vanished buildings which once played important roles in Osaka's cultural and social life. English explanations are limited so it's worth renting an audio guide.

Umeda

梅田

In the north of Osaka, the meeting point of the JR, Hankyū and Hanshin railway lines, plus the Midosuji, Yotsubashi and Tanimachi subway lines, is the **Umeda** area, home to some interesting modern architecture. Even if you don't plan to take a train, the baroque entrance hall of the **Hankyū Umeda Station** (阪急梅田駅) is worth a look. JR Osaka Station houses two large department stores, as well as a shopping mall and cinema.

Hep Five

ヘップファイブ大阪 • 5-15 Kakuda-chō • **Shops** Daily 11am–9pm • **Restaurants** Daily 11am–10pm • **Ferris Wheel** Daily 11am–11pm • ¥700 • Ⓦ hepfive.jp

The eleven-storey **HEP Five** shopping and dining extravaganza is one of northern Osaka's landmark buildings. The huge red Ferris wheel on its roof offers excellent vistas of the city and, inside, you'll find more than 150 shops and restaurants. Outside the main entrance, Osaka's trendy urban youth congregate, making it a great place to observe the latest fashions.

Ohatsu Tenjin

お初天神 • 2-5-4 Sonezaki • Daily 6am–midnight • Free • ☎ 06 6311 0895, Ⓦ tuyutenjin.com/en • A 5min walk from JR Osaka or Hankyū Umeda stations

The atmospheric shrine of **Tsuyu no Tenjinsha**, founded more than 1300 years ago, is more popularly known as **Ohatsu Tenjin** because of the doomed romance of Ohatsu

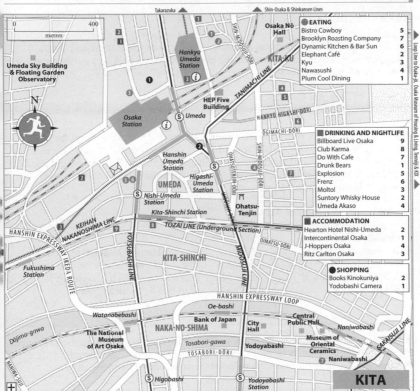

and her lover Tokubei, who committed suicide here in 1703. The shrine is a popular destination for young couples who want to pray for a strong relationship, and there is a variety of marriage charms for sale. A **flea market** is held here on the first and third Friday of each month.

Umeda Sky Building

梅田スカイビル • 1-1-88 Oyodonaka • Floating Garden Observatory daily 10am–10.30pm • ¥700 • ☎ 06 6440 3855, Ⓦ skybldg.co.jp

Immediately west of Hankyū Umeda Station, a tunnel leads beneath the railway sidings to the twin towers of the **Umeda Sky Building**, a striking skyscraper, where you can take a glass elevator up to the **Floating Garden Observatory**, 170m above the ground, and enjoy 360-degree views of north Osaka. The Shōwa-period **Takimi-koji** (滝見小路) restaurant street at the base of the building has a nice retro atmosphere and is a good place for a drink or a snack.

Osaka Museum of Housing and Living

大阪くらしの今昔館, Ōsaka Kusashi Konjyaku-Kan • 8F-10F 6-4-20 Tenjinbashi • 10am–4.30pm; closed Tues • ¥600 • Take Tanimachi subway line to Tenjinbashisuji 6-chome, and the museum is a 2min walk from exit 3 • ☎ 06 6242 1170, Ⓦ konjyakukan.com

The Osaka Museum of Housing and Living is a great place to get a sense of Naniwa, as the city was called in the Edo period. On one floor there's a complete replica of an 1830s neighbourhood with streets of shops, homes and other urban features of the time. Models and images showing how modern Osaka developed from the Meiji period to the post-World War II era take up the other floor of the museum.

Naka-no-shima
中之島

The thin island of **Naka-no-shima** is sandwiched between the Dōjima and Tosabori rivers, southeast of Umeda. As well as the pleasant riverside park and walkways, there are two excellent museums here.

Museum of Oriental Ceramics

東洋陶磁美術館, Tōyō Tōji Bijutsukan • 1-1-26 Naka-no-shima • Tues–Sun 9.30am–4.30pm • ¥500 • ☎ 06 6223 0055, ⓦ moco.or.jp

Housing an exemplary collection of ancient Chinese and Korean pottery, the impressive **Museum of Oriental Ceramics** has a hushed, reverential atmosphere that is a world away from the bustling city outside. The exhibits are well displayed and regular special exhibitions offer fascinating insights into the ancient flow of arts and crafts between China, Korea and Japan.

The National Museum of Art Osaka

国立国際美術館, Kokuritsu Kokusai Bijutsukan • 4-2-55 Naka-no-shima • Tues–Sun 10am–4.30pm, until 8pm on Friday • ¥420 • ☎ 06 4860 8600, ⓦ www.nmao.go.jp

At the western end of the island of Naka-no-shima, **The National Museum of Art Osaka** holds engaging exhibitions of contemporary Japanese and international art. The museum's entrance is above ground – look out for a large steel structure which is supposed to represent bamboo – while the galleries are housed in two floors underground.

Tennōji

South of the downtown area of Osaka, the **Tennōji** area, centred around the large green expanse of **Tennōji-kōen**, is home to one of Japan's earliest Buddhist temples, **Shitennō-ji**, as well as the country's tallest skyscraper, **Abeno Harukas**.

Tennōji-kōen

天王寺公園 • 1-108 Chausuyama-chō • Tues–Sun 9.30am–5pm; May–Sept Sat & Sun closes at 7.30pm • ¥150 • ☎ 06 6771 8401

Tennōji-kōen was opened as a botanical garden in 1909 on a historic site that includes an ancient tumulus (burial mound). The park is also home to **Keitakuen**, a pretty, traditional Japanese garden arranged around a central pond, which was donated to the city by Baron Sumitomo, whose family owned the trading company of the same name. As well as the modern **Great Conservatory**, a giant glasshouse brimming with plants from around the world, Tennōji-kōen also houses a rather depressing zoo.

Abeno Harukas

阿部野ハルカス • 1-1-43 Abeno-suji • Daily 9am–10pm • Observation deck ¥1500 • ☎ 06 6624 1111, ⓦ abenoharukas-300.jp/en • Directly above Kintetsu Osaka-Abeno Station, and next to JR and Tanimachi subway line Tennōji Station

Osaka's newest landmark is the 300m-tall **Abeno Harukas** skyscraper, designed by Argentinian-American Cesar Pelli. Completed in 2014, it's a massive commercial and office complex of sixty floors, with indoor and semi-outdoor **observatories**, a shop and a café on the top three floors. From here, there are spectacular panoramic views over Osaka city that are especially memorable at night.

Tsūtenkaku Tower

通天閣 • 1-18-6 Ebisu-higashi • Daily 9am–8.30pm • ¥700 • ☎ 06 6641 9555, ⓦ www.tsutenkaku.co.jp • A short walk east from Ebisuchō Station on the Hankai tramway line, or a 10min walk north from Shin-Imamiya Station on the JR loop line

On the western side of Tennōji-kōen is the retro 103m-high **Tsūtenkaku Tower**. Rebuilt in the 1950s after it was destroyed during World War II, the tower stands in the centre of the rather run-down area of **Shin-Sekai** ("New World"; 新世界), a raffish district of narrow shopping arcades, cheap bars, restaurants and pachinko parlours.

Shitennō-ji

四天王寺 • 1-11-18 Shitennō-ji • **Temple** Daily 8.30am–4.30pm • ¥300 • **Treasure house** Tues–Sun 8.30am–4pm • ¥200 • ☎ 06 6771 0066, ⓦ shitennoji.or.jp • The main entrance to the temple is a 5min walk south of Shitennō-ji-mae subway station and 15min north of the Tennōji overground station

One of the first Buddhist temples in Japan, **Shitennō-ji** lies on the northern edge of Tennōji-kōen. The temple has retained its classical layout but contains none of the buildings originally erected in 593 AD; the oldest feature of the windswept, concrete complex, with turtle ponds and a five-storey pagoda at its centre, is the late thirteenth-century *torii* at the main entrance gate. The **treasure house**, in the modern white building behind the central courtyard, contains gorgeous orange costumes and enormous mandalas, carved with fantastic birds and dragons, which are used for the ceremonial *bugaku* dances held at the temple three times a year (check the website for dates).

Liberty Osaka

リバティ大阪 • 3-6-36 Naniwaishi • Tues–Fri 10am–3.30pm, Sat 1–4.30pm • ¥500 • ☎ 06 6561 5891, ⓦ liberty.or.jp • An 8min walk south of Ashiharabashi Station on the JR Loop line

Popularly known as **Liberty Osaka**, the Osaka Museum of Human Rights contains remarkable exhibits that tackle Japan's most taboo subjects. There's an English-language leaflet and a portable audio guide that explains the displays, which include the untouchable caste (the Burakumin), Japan's ethnic minorities, the disabled, the sexist treatment of women, and the effects of pollution, most tragically seen in the exhibition about Minamata disease (see p.852). Unfortunately, at the time of writing the Osaka City government has cut funding to the museum and it is struggling to continue.

Sumiyoshi Taisha

住吉大社 • 2-9-89 Sumiyoshi • Dawn–dusk • ☎ 06 6672 0753, ⓦ sumiyoshitaisha.net • Take the Hankai tramway line from Tennōji to Sumiyoshi Tori-mae Station, or the Nankai line from Namba to Sumiyoshi Taisha Station

Built in 211 AD, Osaka's grandest shrine is **Sumiyoshi Taisha**, home of the Shintō gods of the sea. According to legend, the grateful Empress Jingō ordered its construction after returning safely from a voyage to Korea. With logs jutting out at angles from the thatched roofs, its buildings exemplify *sumiyoshi zukuri*, one of Japan's oldest styles of shrine architecture. Unlike similar complexes at Ise (see p.537) and Izumo Taisha (see p.624), Sumiyoshi Taisha is painted bright red, in sharp contrast with its wooded surroundings. The approach to the complex takes you over the elegant humpbacked **Sori-hashi** (arched bridge), donated to the shrine by Yodogimi, the warlord Toyotomi Hideyoshi's lover.

Osaka Bay

大阪湾, Ōsaka-wan • Take the Chūō line subway to Osaka-kō Station and walk north towards the Ferris wheel

The **Osaka Bay** area consists of man-made islands and reclaimed waterfront areas such as Saki-shima, home to the city's second-tallest building, the WTC Cosmotower, and Sakura-jima, where Universal Studios Japan is situated. The **Tempozan Harbour Village** (天保山ハーバービレッジ) district features a large Ferris wheel and an excellent aquarium.

Osaka Aquarium Kaiyūkan

大阪海遊館, Osaka Kaiyūkan • 1-1-10 Kaigan-dōri • Daily 10am–7pm • ¥2300 • ☎ 06 6576 5501, ⓦ kaiyukan.com

Inside an exotic butterfly-shaped building, decorated with a giant fish-tank mosaic, is the fabulous **Osaka Aquarium Kaiyūkan**. It's constructed so that you wind down, floor by floor between fourteen elongated tanks, each representing a different aquatic environment, from Antarctica to the Aleutian Islands. The beauty of the design means you can, for example, watch seals basking on the rocks at the top of the tank and see them swimming, torpedo-like, through the lower depths later. The huge central tank represents the Pacific Ocean and is home to a couple of whale sharks and several manta rays, among many other fish. The giant spider crabs, looking like alien invaders from *War of the Worlds*, provide a fitting climax to Japan's best aquarium.

Universal Studios Japan

ユニバーサル・スタジオ・ジャパン・2-1-33 Sakura-jima・Mon–Fri 10am–5pm, Sat & Sun 10am–6pm, longer hours during summer・Day pass ¥7600・☎ 06 6465 3000, ⓦ usj.co.jp/e・Direct express trains run from JR Osaka Station to Universal City Station on the JR Yumesaki line (every 10min; 14min). From other stations on the JR Loop line, change at Nishi-kujō Station

Covering some 140 acres on Osaka's western waterfront, **Universal Studios Japan** is one of the nation's leading theme parks and is hugely popular among young Japanese. Its attractions are based on Hollywood movies, such as the Harry Potter series, and there is a huge variety of rides, live shows and restaurants in the park.

North of the centre

A handful of museums to the north of central Osaka are worth a visit. If you don't have much time in rural Japan, then the **Open-Air Museum of Old Japanese Farmhouses** offers a glimpse of traditional *inaka* (countryside) living. Foodies will enjoy the interactive **Momofuku Andō Instant Ramen Museum**, where you can learn about the origins of one of the world's favourite fast foods.

Open-Air Museum of Old Japanese Farmhouses

日本民家集落博物館, Nihon Minka Shuraku Hakubutsukan・Tues–Sun 9.30am–4.30pm・¥500・Take the Midosuji subway line to Ryokuchi-koen; from here, it's a 30min walk from the west exit・☎ 06 6862 3137, ⓦ occh.or.jp/minka

The **Open-Air Museum of Old Japanese Farmhouses** in Ryokuchi-kōen is an outdoor architectural museum with a wonderful collection of eleven thatch-roofed *minka*, or traditional Japanese farmhouses. The original buildings have been transported here from all over Kansai, as well as from Kyūshū and Kantō, and immaculately reconstructed in the park. Many were built during the Edo period and were still in use up until the 1960s. The park is especially nice to visit during spring and autumn.

Momofuku Andō Instant Ramen Museum

インスタントラーメン発明記念館, Insutanto Rāmen Hatsumei Kinenkan・8-25 Masumi-chō・9.30am–3.30pm; closed Tues・Free・☎ 072 752 3484, ⓦ instantramen.museum.jp/en・Take the Hankyu Takarazuka line to Ikeda Station, from where it's a 5min walk

In 1958, Andō Momofuku, an immigrant from Taiwan, invented a new kind of fast-food culture in a small shed in Osaka; today, it's estimated that 100 billion servings of instant ramen are consumed annually. Everything you ever wanted to know about the origin and development of instant noodles is showcased in the well-designed **Momofuku Andō Instant Ramen Museum**. It's a great place for kids to interact with the exhibits before slurping a bowl of noodles.

National Museum of Ethnology

国立民族博物館, Kokuritsu Minzoku Hakubutsukan・10-1 Senri Expo Park・10am–5pm; closed Wed・¥420・☎ 06 6876 2151, ⓦ minpaku.ac.jp・Take the Midosuji subway line to Senri-Chūō Station, and then the Osaka Monorail to Banpaku-Kinen-Kōen Station

The fascinating **National Museum of Ethnology** has a massive collection of items relating to ethnology and cultural anthropology, as well as an excellent library of printed materials and films. The collection includes jewellery, costumes, musical instruments and even transportation from Japan and around the world. To make the most of a visit it's best to pick up a free audio guide at reception.

ARRIVAL AND DEPARTURE	OSAKA

Served by two airports, numerous ferries and buses, not to mention a slew of railway companies, Osaka is accessible from almost any point in Japan and, via Kansai International Airport, from many places overseas, too. There's also a weekly ferry service between Osaka and Shanghai in China.

BY PLANE

KANSAI INTERNATIONAL AIRPORT

On a man made island in Osaka Bay, some 35km south of the Osaka city centre, and approximately 100km from Kyoto, Kansai International Airport (KIX; 関西国際空港; ☎072 455 2500, ⓦ kansai-airport.or.jp) handles both international and domestic flights. The international departure lounge is on the fourth floor and domestic departures are on the second floor. KIX Terminal 2 (KIX第2ターミナル; ☎072 455 2911, ⓦ kansai-airport.or.jp/t2) services budget airlines, and is currently only used by Peach Aviation for Asian and some domestic destinations. Shuttle buses connect Terminal 2 with the main building, Kansai International Airport Terminal 1.

Destinations Fukuoka (6 daily; 1hr); Kagoshima (3 daily; 1hr 10min); Nagasaki (2 daily; 1hr 10min); Naha (11 daily; 1hr 15min); Sapporo (10 daily; 2hr); Sendai (3 daily; 1hr 10min); Tokyo Haneda (12 daily; 1hr); and Tokyo Narita (9 daily; 1hr 15min).

GETTING INTO TOWN FROM KANSAI

By train The fastest way into the city is by train, from the station connected to the second floor of the passenger terminal building. The regular Nankai Express, or *kyūkō* (急行; ¥920), takes 47min to reach Nankai Namba Station (南海難波駅), although it's hard to resist the chic Rapi:t, designed like a train from a sci-fi comic, which costs ¥1430 and does the journey in 38min. From Nankai Namba Station you can take a subway or taxi to other parts of the city. JR also runs trains directly to several stations in and around Osaka from KIX, and if you have a rail pass voucher you can exchange it at Kansai Airport Station. After that, you can either take a train with your pass to JR Namba Station (難波駅; 1hr; ¥1060), where it's easy to transfer to the subway, or take a taxi. Alternatively, JR Pass holders can also ride the Haruka limited express which stops at Tennōji Station (天王寺駅; 30min; ¥2230) and Shin-Osaka Station (新大阪駅; 45min; ¥2850), where you can catch the Shinkansen, before continuing on to Kyoto (15min; ¥3020). If you're in no hurry, the regular JR express trains to Tennōji Station (45min; ¥1060) and Osaka Station (70min; ¥1190), in the Umeda area of the city, are worth considering.

By limousine Limousine buses to various locations around Osaka, including several hotels, depart from international arrivals. All central city locations take 40min–1hr to reach, depending on the traffic, and cost ¥1550.

By taxi Taxis to central Osaka are expensive (from ¥15,000), and no faster than the buses.

ITAMI AIRPORT

Osaka International Aiport, also known as Itami Airport (大阪国際空港; ☎06 6856 6781, ⓦ osaka-airport.or.jp), is 10km north of the city centre and, despite the name, only handles domestic flights.

Destinations Akita (6 daily; 1hr 30min); Aomori (6 daily;

1hr 40min); Fukuoka (12 daily; 1hr); Kagoshima (13 daily; 1hr 10min); Kumamoto (11 daily; 1hr 5min); Miyazaki (11 daily; 1hr 5min); Nagasaki (7 daily; 1hr 10min); Naha (5 daily; 1hr 15min); Niigata (12 daily; 1hr 10min); Ōita (8 daily; 1hr); Sapporo (10 daily; 2hr); Sendai (16 daily; 1hr 10min); Tokyo Haneda (30 daily; 1hr); Tokyo Narita (4 daily; 1hr 15min); and Yamagata (3 daily; 1hr 20min).

GETTING INTO TOWN FROM ITAMI

By bus There are regular buses into the city (25–50min depending on destination; ¥640–930) and also to Shin-Osaka Station (25min; ¥500), where you can connect to the Shinkansen.

By limousine Direct limousine buses run to Osaka Station (30min; ¥1550) and on to Kyoto (1hr 55min; ¥2550) and Kōbe (45min; ¥1950).

By monorail A monorail (tickets from ¥200) links the airport with parts of north Osaka, connecting at various points to the city subway system and both the Hankyū and Keihan private railways.

By taxi A taxi to Umeda in central Osaka costs around ¥5000.

BY TRAIN

Shin-Osaka Station (新大阪駅) Shinkansen pull into Shin-Osaka Station, north of the city centre. You can transfer here to other JR services around the area or to the city's subway lines.

Destinations Fukuoka (Hakata Station; every 30min; 2hr 20min); Himeji (every 20min; 35min); Hiroshima (every 15min; 1hr 15min); Kansai International (every 30min; 45min); Kōbe (every 15min; 15min); Kyoto (every 15min; 20min); Nagoya (every 15min; 1hr 10min); Okayama (every 15min; 1hr 5min); and Tokyo (every 15min; 2hr 30min).

Osaka Station (大阪駅) JR services along the Tōkaidō line, connecting Nagoya, Kyoto and Kōbe with Osaka, arrive at the central Osaka Station in Umeda, where you'll also find the termini for the Hankyū and Hanshin lines (see below): these both provide cheaper connections to Kyoto and Kōbe than JR, if you don't have a rail pass.

Destinations Akita (daily; 12hr); Aomori (daily; 15hr); Kanazawa (24 daily; 2hr 30min); Kii-Tanabe (hourly; 2hr); Kōbe Sannomiya (every 15min; 22min); Kyoto (every 10min; 28–46min); Matsumoto (daily; 4hr); Nagano (daily; 4hr 50min); Nagoya (every 30min; 2hr 42min); Takarazuka (every 30min; 30min); and Toyama (14 daily; 3hr 5min).

Hankyu Umeda Station (阪急梅田駅) For Hankyū line services to Kyoto (every 15min; 50min), Kōbe Sannomiya (every 15min; 30min) and Takarazuka (every 30min; 30min).

Hanshin Umeda Station (阪神梅田) For Hanshin line services to Kōbe Sannomiya (every 15min; 30min).

Keihan Yodoyabashi Station (京阪淀屋橋駅) Just south of the island of Naka-no-shima. For Keihan line services to Kyoto Demachiyanagi (every 15min; 47min).

7

7

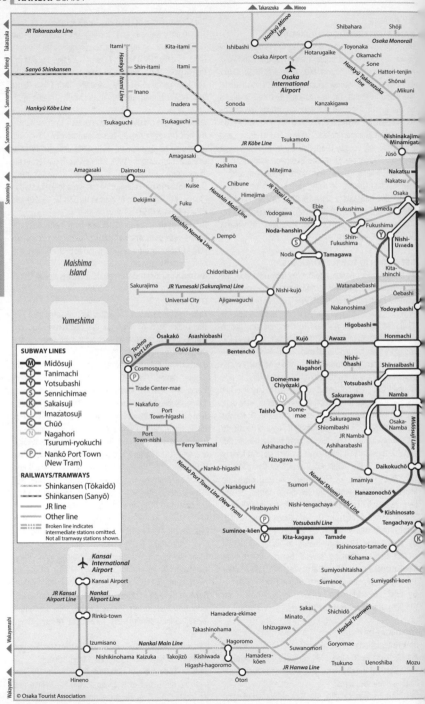

© Osaka Tourist Association

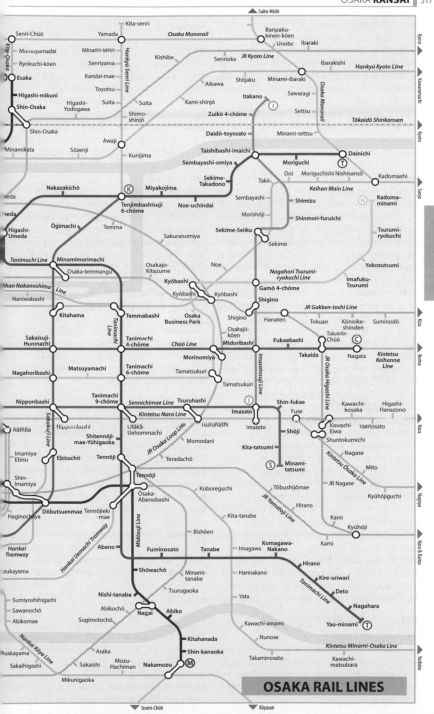

OSAKA RAIL LINES

7

Kintetsu Namba Station (近鉄難波駅) In the heart of the Minami district. For Kintetsu line services for Nara (every 15min; 30min) and outer Osaka.

Kintetsu Uehonmachi Station (近鉄上本町駅) For Kintetsu line services for Ise (every 15min; 1hr 45min), Kashikojima (1–2 hourly; 2hr 20min) and Toba (every 20–30min; 2hr) on the Shima Hantō.

Nankai Namba Station (南海難波駅) In the heart of the Minami district. For Nankai line services for Kansai International Airport (every 30min; 35min) and Kōya-san (every 20–30min; 1hr 15min).

BY BUS

Osaka has various long-distance bus stations with services mainly operated by Willer Express (ⓦ willerexpress.com) and JR Highway Buses (ⓦ nishinihonjrbus.co.jp). There are stations located beside the JR Osaka Station in Umeda; at the Namba Kaisoku Bus Terminal and Osaka City Air Terminal in Namba; at Kintetsu Uehonmachi, south of the castle; and at Abenobashi near Tennōji, 1km further south of the castle. All are beside or near subway and train stations for connections around the city. If you plan to depart from Osaka by bus, check first with one of the tourist information centres (see below) for timetables and which station to go to.

Destinations: Beppu (daily; 9hr); Fukuoka (daily; 9hr 30min); Hagi (daily; 12hr); Hiroshima (5 daily; 6hr); Kagoshima (daily; 12hr); Kumamoto (daily; 11hr); Miyazaki (daily; 12hr); Nagano (daily; 8hr); Nagasaki (1 daily; 10hr); Niigata (daily; 9hr); Tokyo (30 daily; 8hr 50min); Tottori (20 daily; 4hr); Wakayama (8 daily; 3hr); and Yonago (18 daily; 5hr).

BY FERRY

Osaka is a major port of call for many of the ferries plying routes around Japan, and sailing into Osaka Bay is a memorable way of approaching the city. The port is west of the city centre and has good transport links via the subway and train network.

Osaka Nankō Ferry Terminal (大阪南港フェリーター ミナル) Most domestic and international ferries use the Osaka Nankō Ferry Terminal, close to Ferry Terminal Station on the New Tram monorail, which connects to the city's subway network.

Tempozan East Wharf (天保山東岸壁) Ferries to and from Shikoku arrive and depart from the less busy Tempozan East Wharf; the nearest station to here is Osaka-kō (大阪港) on the Chūō subway line, a 10min walk away.

Ferry companies The main ferry operators are A Line Ferry (ⓦ aline-ferry.com), Ferry Sunflower (ⓦ ferry-sunflower .co.jp), and Hankyū Ferry (ⓦ han9f.co.jp). Services to Shanghai, China, are run by the Japan–China International Ferry Co (ⓦ shinganjin.com) and The Shanghai Ferry Company (ⓦ shanghai-ferry.co.jp), while Pan Star (ⓦ panstar.co.kr) runs ferries to Busan, in South Korea.

Destinations Beppu (daily; 11hr 30min); Busan, South Korea (weekly; 18hr 50min); Miyazaki (daily; 12hr 50min); Naha (weekly; 39hr); Shanghai, China (2 weekly; 48hr); Shibushi (daily; 14hr 40min); Shinmoji (daily; 12hr); Toyo (daily; 7hr 40min).

GETTING AROUND

By subway and train Like Tokyo, Osaka has an extensive subway and train system as well as a JR Loop line (see map, pp.516–517). The latter is handy if you're using a rail pass, but most of the time you'll find the subway more convenient and quicker for getting around the city. You can transfer between the nine subways and the New Tram line on the same ticket, but if you switch to any of the railway lines at a connecting station you'll need to either buy another ticket or a special transfer ticket when you start your journey. Most journeys across central Osaka cost ¥240.

Tickets and passes Because Osaka's attractions are widely scattered, investing in a one-day Osaka Visitors' Ticket (¥550) is worth considering if you're up for a hectic round of the sights. The pass is valid on all the subway lines and buses, and will be date-stamped when you first pass through the gate machines. You could also buy a one- or two-day Amazing Osaka Pass (¥2300–3000), valid for both trains and buses, and including free admission to 26 popular tourist sites. These can be bought at subway-ticket vending machines as well as station kiosks.

By bus There are plenty of buses, but you'll find the subways and trains with their English signs and maps much easier to use.

Car rental Several major car rental firms can be found at both Shin-Osaka and Osaka stations (both daily 8am–8pm) including Eki Rent-a-Car (Shin-Osaka ☎ 06 6303 0181, Osaka ☎ 06 6341 3388, ⓦ ekiren.co.jp) and Nippon Rent-a-Car (Osaka Reservation Center ☎ 06 6344 0919, ⓦ nipponrentacar.co.jp).

INFORMATION AND TOURS

TOURIST OFFICES

The Osaka Tourist Association (ⓦ osaka-info.jp/en) is very helpful, with information offices all over the city, as well as at Kansai International Airport. All the tourist offices have English-speaking staff and can help with accommodation and transport.

JR Osaka Station tourist information centre 1F north central gate, JR Osaka Station. The city's main tourist information centre, on the central concourse (daily 8am–5pm; ☎ 06 6345 2189).

Hankyu Station tourist office 1F Hankyu Umeda Station. For information about sights in the Hankyu area (daily 9am–8pm; w hankyu.co.jp/area_info/tourist).

JR Shin-Osaka Station tourist office 3F JR Shin-Osaka Station, next to the Shinkansen central ticket gates (daily 9am–6pm; ☎ 06 6305 3311).

JR Tennōji Station tourist office 1F JR Tennōji Station (daily 9am–6pm; ☎ 06 6774 3077).

Nankai Namba Station tourist information centre 1F Nankai Terminal Building, near the Nankai and Midosuji lines (daily 9am–8pm; ☎ 06 6631 9100).

Kansai International Airport 1F South Arrivals. The airport has a tourist information counter (daily 7am–10pm; ☎ 072 456 6025) along with a separate desk where you can make hotel reservations.

LISTINGS

Information on events is listed in the free monthly *Kansai Scene* (w kansaiscene.com), an English-language magazine that also has interesting features, and includes information on the Osaka club scene. It's available from tourist offices, as well as main bookshops and pubs.

TOURS

Cycle Osaka Full-day (5–6hr; ¥10,000) and half-day (3hr; ¥5000) tours of Osaka's main sights, in English, with bike and helmet rental included (☎ 080 6183 8765; w cycleosaka.com). They also run daily food tours by bicycle (3hr; ¥8000), which are a great introduction to Osaka's famous culinary culture.

ACCOMMODATION

7

Osaka's accommodation is predominantly Western-style hotels. The Umeda area in **Kita** hosts the bulk of the city's luxury hotels, while the shopping and nightlife districts of Shinsaibashi and Namba in **Minami** have a greater range of accommodation, catering to all budgets. Local transport is so efficient, however, that it's no great problem to be based outside the central area.

KITA

Hearton Hotel Nishi-Umeda ハートンホテル西梅田 3-3-55 Umeda ☎ 06 6342 1111, w www.heartonhotel .com/nis; map p.511. Popular business hotel just behind the main post office next to JR Osaka Station. It's not the newest hotel in Umeda but the rooms are smart, clean and functional, and come with cable TV and internet access. **¥18, 500**

Imperial Hotel Osaka 帝国ホテル大阪 1-8-50 Tenmabashi ☎ 06 6881 1111, w www.imperialhotel .co.jp/e/osaka; map p.508. This opulent hotel, overlooking the Ōkawa River, is just as luxurious as its famous Tokyo parent. Purified air, a golf driving range and a choice of elegant restaurants and bars are all part of the experience. 🛜 **¥24,900**

Intercontinental Osaka インターコンチネンタル大阪 3-60 Ofuka-chō ☎ 06 6374 5700, w icosaka .com; map p.511. Swish new luxury hotel with sweeping views over northern Osaka. The rooms are spacious and stylishly decorated, and also have Nespresso machines. There's a fitness centre with swimming pool, as well as a spa for relaxation treatments. **¥38,000**

J-Hoppers Osaka ジェイホッパーズ大阪 7-4-22 Fukushima ☎ 06 6453 6669, w osaka.j-hoppers.com; map p.511. This is Kita's best budget option, in a handy location for exploring Osaka. Rooms are clean, the staff are happy to help with travel information, and the breezy rooftop garden is very popular. Free PC usage. Bicycle rental (¥500/day) also available. 🛜 Dorms **¥2700**, doubles **¥6000**

Ritz Carlton Osaka リッツカールトン大阪 2-5-25 Umeda ☎ 06 6343 7000, w ritzcarlton.com; map p.511. Luxury hotel with the intimate feel of a European country house, liberally sprinkled with antiques and Japanese objets d'art. Rooms have fantastic views across the city, there's a great range of restaurants, plus live piano music and a pool and gym that are free to guests. **¥27,600**

MINAMI

Arietta アリエッタホテル 3-2-6 Azuchi-machi ☎ 06 6267 2787, w thehotel.co.jp/en/arietta_osaka; map p.508. Clean and smart business hotel conveniently located close to three subway lines with friendly English-speaking staff. There's a coin laundry, and breakfast and LAN internet access are free. **¥10,500**

Cross Hotel Osaka クロスホテル大阪 2-5-15 Shinsaibashi ☎ 06 6213 8281, w crosshotel.com/eng _osaka; map p.520. A stylish hotel with efficient service, just minutes away from the Minami shopping and nightlife scene. The decently sized rooms are tastefully decorated and include internet access. 🛜 **¥17,500**

First Cabin ファーストキャビン 4-2-1 Namba ☎ 06 6631 8090, w first-cabin.jp; map p.520. Smart capsule hotel for both men and women in the heart of Namba, with a first-class air travel theme. Cabins, for single occupancy, are bigger than the business capsules but all have their own TV and internet connection. Excellent bath, café/bar and communal lounge facilities. 🛜 **¥3500**

Fuku Hostel 福ホステル 3F 2-9-6 Sennichimae ☎ 06 6633 8029, w fukuhostel.jp; map p.520. Popular new hostel in a great location. There are shared kitchen and lounge areas, and the helpful staff are happy to give recommendations to help guests enjoy the surrounding Namba area. 🛜 Dorms **¥3300**, doubles **¥12,000**

Hotel Nikkō Osaka ホテル日航大阪 1-3-3 Nishi-Shinsaibashi ☎ 06 6244 1281, w hno.co.jp; map p.520. Deluxe hotel close to nightlife and shopping arcades, with spacious and comfortable rooms, attentive service and a good range of restaurants, including a coffee shop that serves an excellent buffet breakfast. 🛜 **¥15,500**

Rock Star Hotel ロックスターホテル 1-4-11 Awaza ☎ 06 6538 6909, w rockstar-hotel.jp; map p.520. Small

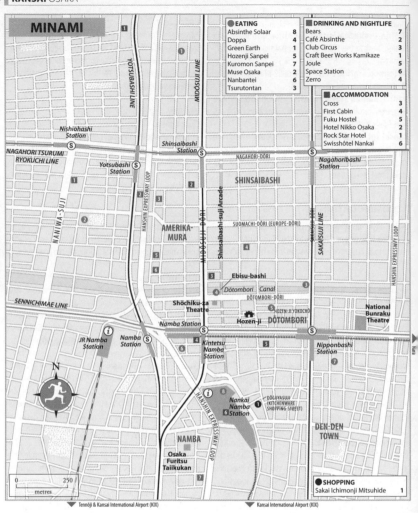

MINAMI

EATING	
Absinthe Solaar	8
Doppa	4
Green Earth	1
Hozenji Sanpei	5
Kuromon Sanpei	7
Muse Osaka	2
Nanbantei	6
Tsurutontan	3

DRINKING AND NIGHTLIFE	
Bears	7
Café Absinthe	2
Club Circus	3
Craft Beer Works Kamikaze	1
Joule	5
Space Station	6
Zerro	4

ACCOMMODATION	
Cross	3
First Cabin	4
Fuku Hostel	5
Hotel Nikko Osaka	2
Rock Star Hotel	1
Swissôtel Nankai	6

SHOPPING	
Sakai Ichimonji Mitsuhide	1

Tennōji & Kansai International Airport (KIX)

Kansai International Airport (KIX)

rock-music-themed boutique hotel close to Honmachi subway station. Rooms are compact but well equipped and decorated with artwork by cult Japanese photographer Moriyama Daidō.. In warmer months there's a rooftop lounge bar. 🛜 **¥14,700**

Swissôtel Nankai Osaka スイスホテル南海大阪 5-1-60 Namba ☎ 06 6646 1111, ⓦ swissotel-osaka.co.jp; map above. Large international hotel located above Nankai Namba Station which makes it ultra-convenient for direct airport access. Rooms are fresh and modern with comfortable beds, and the service is impeccable. 🛜 **¥22,500**

OTHER AREAS

Hiro's Guesthouse ヒロゲストハウス 4-9-7 Momodani ☎ 06 7897 6608, ⓦ hirosguesthouse.com; map p.508. Stylish and modern guesthouse in Korea Town in the Minami area, near Tsuruhashi Station on the JR loop line. Rooms are clean, with a/c. 🛜 Dorms **¥2500**, doubles **¥7000**

Hyatt Regency Osaka ハイアットリージェンシー大阪 1-13-11 Nankō-Kita ☎ 06 6612 1234, ⓦ hyattregency osaka.com; map p.508. Good luxury choice near the port area, offering well-equipped rooms with a minimalist design, elegant public areas and restaurants, and indoor and outdoor pools. 🛜 **¥23,800**

EATING

The best choice of **restaurants** and **cafés** is around the Kita areas of Umeda and Chayama, and the Minami areas of Shinsaibashi, Dōtombori and Namba. Strolling around the narrow streets dotted with stand-up noodle and *takoyaki* bars, and restaurants with flickering neon signs and crazy displays – especially along canal-side Dōtombori (道頓堀), with its redeveloped promenade – is an appetizing experience in itself. The major **hotels** and **department stores** are also worth checking out, especially at lunchtime, when many restaurants offer special deals.

KITA

Bistro Cowboy ビストロかうぼーい B2 Herbis Plaza, 2-5-25 Umeda ☎06 4799 1011, ⓦsteakcowboy.com /umeda; map p.511. Funky steakhouse serving Kuroge local beef that's been fattened with red wine. Select your steak size (150–600g) and choose from five different sauces. Prices start at ¥5900. Daily 11.30am–2.30pm & 5–10pm.

Brooklyn Roasting Company ブルックリンロースティン グ 2-1-16 Kitahama ☎06 6125 5740, ⓦbrooklynroasting .jp; map p.511. The best place in Osaka for a superbly brewed coffee – drip coffee is ¥390 and cappuccinos and lattes are ¥450. Sandwiches are also available at lunchtime (¥450). Mon–Fri 8am–7.30pm, Sat & Sun 10am–6.30pm.

Dynamic Kitchen & Bar Sun 燦 27F 4-5-10 Nishi-Tenma ☎06 6367 5512, ⓦdynac-japan.com/sun; map p.511. With stunning night views over the Kita area, this is a great place to enjoy modern Japanese cuisine. You can choose to sit at either *ozashiki* floor tables, or at the counter. Excellent-value dinner courses of Kōbe and Nara beef from ¥8000. Mon–Sat 11.30am–2pm & 5–10pm, Sun 11.30am–2pm & 5–9.30pm.

Elephant Café エレファントカフェ 2-28 Chaya-machi ☎06 6359 0136, ⓦug-gu.co.jp/restaurant/elephant /elephant.html; map p.511. International cuisine restaurant in the Chayama area with an exotically decorated interior of hanging lamps and fabrics, serving curries, noodles, pasta, dumplings, tapas and salads. The weekend set lunch (¥1200) is good value. Mon–Fri 5–11.30pm, Sat & Sun 11.30am–11.30pm.

★**Fujiya 1935** ふじや1935 2-4-14 Yariya-machi ☎06 6941 2483, ⓦfujiya1935.com; map p.508. Superb Michelin-starred European-Japanese fusion restaurant serving sophisticated dishes made with local ingredients. The seasonal fixed menu costs from ¥7200 for lunch, or from ¥15,000 for dinner. Reservations have to be made well in advance by a Japanese-speaker. Mon–Sat noon–1pm & 6–8pm; closed first Mon of the month.

Hajime ハジメ 1-9-11-1 Edobori ☎06 6447 6688, ⓦhajime-artistes.com; map p.508. Michelin-starred gourmet restaurant with a fabulous seasonal tasting menu (¥26,250) that fuses Japanese and French cuisine into a work of gastronomic art. There's also a shorter, and slightly less expensive, tasting menu (¥21,600). Reservations must be made in advance and there's a strict dress code and cancellation policy. Daily 11.30am–2pm & 5.30–8pm.

Kakigoya Fever 1111 かき小屋フィーバー1111 1-6 Ikeda-machi-chō ☎06 6352 3393, ⓦkakigoyafever.jp; map p.508. If you love oysters fresh, fried, or steamed, then this is the place to indulge. Prices are very reasonable – the all-you-can-eat course starts at ¥3480. Daily 3–11.30pm.

Kyu 大阪おでん久 7F Grand Front Osaka Bldg 4-20 Ōfuka-chō ☎06 6374 8999; map p.511. This small restaurant is a great place for a warming winter meal of *oden* (vegetables, tofu, fishcake and boiled eggs stewed in a *dashi* broth) and *yakiton* (pork pieces grilled on skewers). Lunch sets start at ¥1000 and dinner courses are ¥3000. Daily 11am–11pm.

Nawasushi 縄寿司 2-14-1 Sonezaki ☎06 6312 9891; map p.511. Generous servings of super-fresh sushi (from ¥400/plate) and sashimi platters (from ¥1050) in a no-frills traditional setting. Don't be shy about yelling out your order. Daily noon–1am; closed first and second Mon of the month.

Plum Cool Dining プラム 3F 4-6 Chaya-machi ☎06 6377 0701, ⓦplum.co.jp/chayamachi.html; map p.511. Everything on the menu here is intended to be paired with *umeshu* (sweet plum wine). Try the delicious tofu and avocado salad (¥780) or their "plum-style" rice (from ¥800); there's also an extensive *umeshu* list, from ¥400 a glass. Daily 5.30–11.30pm.

MINAMI

Absinthe Solaar アブサンソラー Namba Dining Maison 8F, 5-1-18 Namba ☎06 6633 1445, ⓦabsinthe-jp.com; map p.520. Rooftop restaurant with outdoor lounge area, great for enjoying the evening breeze

OSAKA: THE KITCHEN OF JAPAN

Osaka has a reputation as a **foodies' paradise**, and it boasts many excellent local specialities. You shouldn't leave town without going to an **okonomiyaki** restaurant, where you can eat the thick pancakes straight off the grill, or just grab some piping-hot **takoyaki** (octopus dumplings) from a street stall. Osaka's own style of **sushi** is *oshizushi*, layers of vinegared rice, seaweed and fish cut into bite-size chunks, and the city also has a particular way of cooking chunky udon noodles, simmering them in a veggie, seafood or meat broth.

7

during the hot summer months. The Mediterranean menu includes Greek salad (¥1000) and Moroccan-style lamb chops (¥2300). 11am–11.30pm; closed Wed.

Doppa ドッパ 2F 1-6-9 Dōtombori 06 6212 0530; map p.520. A friendly restaurant that's a good mix of Italian and Osakan – hearty portions served without fuss. There are thirty kinds of pasta dish on offer (from ¥980), as well as pizza (¥850). Daily noon–9pm.

Green Earth グリーンアース 4-2-2 Kitakyūhōji-machi 06 6251 1245, w osaka-vegetarian-ge.com/english; map p.520. This narrow café is one of the city's most popular vegetarian establishments. They serve jumbo sandwiches (from ¥500), good pasta (¥580) and filling veggie pizza (¥800). Mon–Sat 11.30am–4.30pm.

Hozenji Sanpei 法善寺三平 1-7-10 Dōtombori 06 6211 0399; map p.520. Long-running okonomiyaki restaurant with lots of retro atmosphere. Sanpei-style okonomiyaki is ¥950 and side dishes such as yakisoba start at ¥780. 5–10.30pm; closed Tues.

Kuromon Sanpei 黒門三平 1-22-25 Nipponbashi 06 6634 2611, w kuromon-sanpei.co.jp; map p.520. Fresh seafood shop with a dining area: choose what you'd like from the daily catch, and the chefs will prepare it in front of you. Their

seafood rice bowls (¥1600) are delicious. Daily 9am–6.30pm.

Muse Osaka ミュース大阪 1-21-7 Minamihorie 06 4391 3030, w muse-osaka.com; map p.520. Spacious café serving Italian and French-style course meals; pasta lunch sets are ¥1000, dinner courses ¥2900, and in winter they serve nabe (hotpot; from ¥2500). There's a hookah salon on the third floor. Daily 11.30am–4pm & 5–11.30pm.

Nanbantei 南蛮亭 4-5-7 Nanba 06 6631 6178; map p.520. In the alleyway behind the Shin Kabukiza Theatre, this popular yakitori-ya has a huge range of skewer food (from ¥120), an English menu and a friendly atmosphere. Because of its popularity, dining time is limited to 2hr. Daily 5pm–midnight.

★Tsurutontan つるとんたん 3-17 Soemon-chō 06 6211 0021, w tsurutontan.co.jp/shop/soemoncho-udon; map p.520. Fabulous udon restaurant that serves an amazing range of traditional and modern fusion dishes in extremely large bowls. The umeboshi (pickled plum) udon is unbeatable for its classic home-style cooking taste (¥880), while the carbonara udon (¥1800) really pushes the fusion boundaries by serving the thick white noodles with creamy seafood. Daily 11am–7.30pm.

DRINKING AND NIGHTLIFE

The epicentre of Osaka's frenetic nightlife is **Ebisu-bashi**, the bridge that crosses the Dōtombori canal just north of the Shōchiku-za Theatre, a 5min walk north of Namba Station; it's a dazzling area to wander around, if only to check out the wild youth fashions on view, and pose for a photo with locals in front of the landmark Glico Man sign. Don't miss out on strolling through the **Amerika-mura** area immediately west of **Shinsaibashi**, a street crowded with extremely cool shops and bars. In contrast, the **Hozen-ji Yokochō** area, around the paper-lantern-festooned temple Hozen-ji south of the Dōtombori canal, is old-time Osaka, a narrow alley of tiny watering holes. The **Kita** area also has its own fair share of bars and clubs, mostly close to Umeda's train stations; it's also where most of the city's LGBT scene (see opposite) is located.

BARS

★Café Absinthe カフェアブサン 1-2-27 Kita-Horie 06 6534 6635, w www.absinthe-jp.com; map p.520. Mediterranean-style bar with live music, DJs and photography exhibitions. Tabbouleh and hummus (¥800) are on the menu,

and they serve absinthe drinks (from ¥800). Mon–Thurs 11.30am–3am, Fri & Sat 11.30am–5am, Sun 2pm–3am.

Craft Beer Works Kamikaze カミカゼ 1-22-21 Kita-Horie 06 6539 7550, w cbw-kamikaze.com; map p.520. This craft beer specialist is a great place to get

YAMAZAKI WHISKY DISTILLERY

Whisky was introduced to Japan in the late nineteenth century, and in 1923 the **Yamazaki Whisky Distillery** – Japan's oldest distillery – was established by Suntory on a site halfway between Osaka and Kyoto. Suntory are today internationally recognized as the premium distillers of Japanese whisky, as well as being regular gold-medal winners at international competitions. The 2003 film Lost in Translation, with its iconic scene of actor Bill Murray flogging Suntory's tipple in a Japanese TV commercial, has also helped to cement the company's fame. In recent years, the distillery has become a popular destination for whisky lovers and there are now regular **tours** (¥2000; w suntory.com/factory/yamazaki). The tours (in Japanese, although free English audio guides are provided) give a good overview of the fermenting and ageing processes, but there's no denying that many participants are mostly interested in getting to the tasting room, where you can sample some top-grade drams at very reasonable prices. To get to the distillery from Osaka or Kyoto, take the JR line to Yamazaki Station, or the Hankyu line to Oyamazaki Station; from either station, it's a ten-minute walk.

acquainted with the local brews. They have 20 different Japanese craft beers on tap, plus a small selection of imported beers. Daily 5pm–12.30am.

Drunk Bears ドランクベアーズ B1 10-12 Chaya-machi ☎06 6372 7275; map p.511. Friendly tapas bar (from ¥480) in the NU Chayamachi shopping centre. Belgian beers on tap (from ¥850). Mon–Thurs 11am–11.30pm, Fri & Sat 11am–2am & Sun 11am–11.30pm.

Molto! モルト! 31F Hankyū Grand Building Umeda ☎06 6809 2641; map p.511. Popular craft beer restaurant with fantastic night views of Umeda. Half pints start at ¥600, and pints are ¥900–1200. Reservations are recommended. Daily 5–10.45pm.

Space Station スペースステーション 8F 2-3-2 Shinsaibashisuji ☎080 4151 6336; map p.520. Video game bar that has a serious, museum like atmosphere as patrons reconnect with older model Atari, Nintendo and Playstation machines. Drinks from ¥650. No seating charge. Daily 8pm–2am.

Suntory Whisky House サントリーウイスキーハウス 2F Grand Front Osaka Building, ☎06 6359 5177, ⓦsuntory .co.jp/whisky/whiskyhouse; map p.511. If you can't make it to the distillery itself (see box opposite), head to this vast whisky emporium, complete with gallery, bar and restaurant, and try a five-sample set of award-winning Suntory whisky (¥1200). They also sell furniture and accessories made from white-oak whisky barrels. Daily 11.30am–11pm.

Zerro ゼロ 2-3-2 Shinsaibashi ☎06 6211 0439; map p.520. Popular bar with foreign and Japanese staff that hosts DJ events on Sat nights. Drinks are rather pricey but there's no extra charge for enjoying the music and dance at weekends. Daily 8pm–late.

CLUBS AND LIVE MUSIC VENUES

Bears ライブハウスベアーズ B1 Shin-Nihon Namba Building, 3-14-5 Namba-naka ☎06 6649 5564, ⓦnamba-bears.main.jp; map p.520. The heart of the city's underground music scene, with a diverse range of local experimental and avant-garde acts playing every night. Daily 5.30–11.30pm.

Billboard Live Osaka ビルボードライブ大阪 B2 Herbis Plaza Ent Building, 2-2-2 Umeda ☎06 6342 7722, ⓦbillboard-live.com/club/o_index.html; map p.511. Top-class jazz, soul, R&B and folk performers regularly play at this small-scale supper club. It's pricey though, with tickets often in excess of ¥6000. Still, the sound system is excellent and the food's tasty and reasonably priced (from ¥1580). Mon–Fri 5.30pm–10pm, Sat & Sun 3.30–10pm.

Club Circus クラブサーカス 2F 1-8-16 Nishi-Shinsaibashi ☎06 6241 3822, ⓦcircus-osaka.com;

map p.520. One of Osaka's best clubs, with almost daily DJ events and theme parties. Door charge from ¥2000, depending on the event. Daily 5pm–late.

Club Karma カーマ B1 Zero Building, 1-5-18 Sonezaki-Shinchi ☎06 6344 6181, ⓦclub-karma.com; map p.511. Stark yet roomy bar and club that hosts a range of up-to-the-minute music and dance nights, with the added bonus of a good menu and a happy hour until 9pm. The all-night techno and house events are usually held on Fri and Sat, when there's a cover charge of ¥2500 (more if big-name foreign DJs are in town). Daily 5pm–2am.

Joule ジュール 2,3,4F Minami-sumiyamachi Building, 2-11-7 Nishi-Shinsaibashi ☎06 6214 1223, ⓦclub-joule .jp; map p.520. This very popular club in Amerika-mura has a fairly mainstream music policy and a laidback atmosphere. There's a third floor lounge for relaxing in when the dancefloor gets too full. Entrance ¥1500–3000. Daily 8pm–late.

★**Umeda Akaso** 梅田アカソ 16-3 Doyama-chō ☎06 7897 2450, ⓦwww.akaso.jp; map p.511. By local standards, this live-music venue is surprisingly large. *Akaso* regularly hosts well-known domestic and international acts – everything from folk to heavy metal. Depending on who's performing, entrance fees range from free to ¥8500 (including one drink). Daily 5pm–late.

LGBT BARS AND CLUBS

The city's gay scene is much smaller than that in Tokyo, and historically it's tended to be in the Doyama-chō area of Kita rather than Minami. Check the free magazine *Kansai Scene* for the latest info on clubs, bars and one-off dance events.

Do with Cafe B1 9-23 Asano-machi ☎06 6312 1778; map p.511. Dining bar with a nightly drag show, beginning at 9pm, and with an extra show at midnight on Fri and Sat nights. Mon–Thurs 6pm–3am, Fri & Sat 6pm–5am, Sun 6pm–midnight.

Explosion エクスプロージョン B1 Sanyo Kaikan, 8-23 Doyama-chō ⓦex-osaka.com; map p.511. This club hosts men-only, women-only and mixed nights, with drag shows and films. ¥2000 cover charge, with two drinks for Japanese and three drinks for non-Japanese customers. Daily 8pm–4am.

Frenz フレンズ 1F 8-14 Kamiyama-chō ☎06 6311 1386, ⓦfrenz-frenzy.jp; map p.511. The first gay bar in Japan to be run by a non-Japanese, *Frenz* has firmly established itself at the centre of the Kansai gay community. It's a relaxed and friendly place where you can drop by on your own or with friends, especially if you enjoy retro disco music. Sister bar *Frenzy*, which has hosted celebrities such as Lady Gaga, is in the same building but only open at weekends. Daily 8pm–2am.

7

ENTERTAINMENT AND THE ARTS

Traditional performing arts have flourished in Osaka since the Tokugawa shoguns in the seventeenth century. Full details of **performances** appear in the free monthly *Kansai Scene*, which you can pick up from tourist offices, pubs and large bookshops.

7

OSAKA FESTIVALS

Two spectacular festivals take place in Osaka during the summer season. **Tenjin Matsuri**, believed to be over 1000 years old, begins on July 24 with ceremonies at **Osaka Tenmangū** (ⓦtenjinsan.com) near Osaka-jō, where Heian scholar Sugawara Michizane is enshrined. The main event is the following day, when there's a parade of *mikoshi* (portable shrines), *taiko* drumming and a procession of boats, ending with a fabulous fireworks display.

In the far south of Osaka, one of Japan's most exciting festivals, **Kishiwada Danjiri Matsuri**, is held every September (usually mid-month but dates vary). Teams of men carry 35 heavy wooden "danjiri" floats at high speed through the streets of Kishiwada. It's a thrilling and dangerous spectacle, with each float ridden by a "daiku gata" whose job it is to encourage and pilot his team. Accidents resulting in fatalities are not unknown.

BUNRAKU

National Bunraku Theatre 国立文楽劇場 1-12-10 Nipponbashi ☎06 6212 2531, ⓦntj.jac.go.jp/english/.html. Weekly performances, at 11am and 4pm, in Jan, April, June–Aug and Nov. Tickets (price depends on performance) sell out quickly, but you can try at the theatre box office, a 3min walk from exit seven of Nipponbashi Station.

KABUKI

Osaka Shōchiku-za Theatre 大阪松竹座 1-9-19 Dōtonbori ☎06 6214 2211, ⓦshochiku.co.jp/play/shochikuza. Handsomely restored theatre, a 5min walk north of Namba Station. Tickets from ¥4000.

NŌ

Osaka Nō Hall 大阪能楽会館 3-17-2 Nakazakinishi ☎06 6373 1726, ⓦnougaku.wix.com/nougaku. You can sample nō plays at this theatre, a short walk east of Hankyū Umeda Station (or head to Nakazakichō Station on the Tanimachi line). Tickets cost from ¥5500; it also puts on occasional free performances at weekends and during national holidays.

Yamamoto Nō Gakudo 山本能楽堂 1-3-6 Tokui-chō ☎06 6942 5744, ⓦnoh-theater.com. A great place to see nō performances, a short walk from Tanimachi 4-chōme station. They also hold workshops and other traditional performing arts events.

SHOPPING

While Umeda, Shinsaibashi and Namba attract hordes of shoppers to their covered **malls**, there are other places in Osaka where window-shopping is just as interesting as picking up a bargain. In the Minami area, the **Den Den Town** (でんでんタウン) area, south of Nipponbashi Station, has long been the focus for electronic goods and, increasingly, has also become a handy place to pick up "character goods" for all your favourite manga and anime heroes. If you are keen on Japanese cuisine, **Dōguyasuji** (道具屋筋), just east of Nankai Namba Station, is the place to pick up an interesting souvenir – it's an entire street of kitchen and tableware shops, all stocked full with every kind of pot, pan, dish, knife and chopstick required for Japanese cooking.

Books Kinokuniya 紀伊国屋 1-1-3 Noda ☎06 6372 5821, ⓦkinokuniya.co.jp; map p.511. Located behind the main entrance to Hankyū Umeda Station, this branch of the nationwide chain has a good range of books and magazines in English. Daily 10am–10pm; closed third Wed of the month.

Sakai Ichimonji Mitsuhide 堺一文字光秀 Dōguyasuji ☎06 6633 9393, ⓦichimonji.co.jp; map p.520. This shop specializes in Sakai knives which are manufactured by veteran craftsmen in southern Osaka. It also stocks a huge range of blades for every type of culinary need. Daily 10am–7pm.

Yodobashi Camera ヨドバシカメラ 1 Ofuka-chō ☎06 4802 1010, ⓦyodobashi.com; map p.511. Directly across the street from the north exit of Osaka Station, this large electronics emporium has five floors of the latest camera, computer and other electronic equipment – there's an overwhelming range of choice and you can bargain here for a good deal. Daily 9.30am–9pm.

SPORTS

Baseball Osakans are mostly huge fans of the Hanshin Tigers baseball team and tend to get very excited when their team wins, often jumping into the Dōtombori canal to celebrate. The Hanshin Tigers play at the huge Osaka Dome during the professional baseball season, but the highlight of the city's sporting summer is the All-Japan High School Baseball Championship, held at Kōshien Stadium, a 5min walk from Kōshien Station on the Hanshin line. For ticket availability, check first with tourist information at JR Osaka Station (daily 9am–8pm; ☎06 6345 2189).

Sumo Osaka's fifteen-day sumo tournament is held mid-March at Osaka Furitsu Taiikukan (ⓦsumo.or.jp), a 10min walk from exit 5 of Namba Station. Seats for the bouts, which begin at 10am and run through to 6pm, sell out quickly, and you'll need to arrive early to snag one of the standing-room tickets (¥1500), which go on sale each day at 9am.

DIRECTORY

Consulates Australia, 29F, Twin 21 MID Tower, 2-1-61 Shiromi, Chuō-ku (☎06 6941 9448); China, 3-9-2 Utsubohon-machi, Nishi-ku (☎06 6445 9481); Russia, 1-2-2 Nishimidorigaoka, Toyonaka-shi (☎06 6848 3451); South Korea, 2-3-4 Nishi-Shinsaibashi, Chuō-ku (☎06 6213 1401); UK, 19F Epson Osaka Building, 3-5-1 Bakuro-machi, Chuō-ku (☎06 6120 5600); USA, 2-11-5 Nishitemma, Kita-ku (☎06 6315 5900).

Emergencies The main police station is at 3-1-16 Otemae, Chuō-ku (Mon–Fri 9.15am–5.30pm; ☎06 6943 1234). In an absolute emergency, contact the Foreign Advisory Service on ☎06 773 6533. For other emergency numbers, see p.71.

Hospitals and medical advice Yodogawa Christian Hospital, 2-9-26 Awaji, Higashi-Yodogawa-ku (☎06 6322 2250, ⓦych.or.jp/en), or the more central Sumitomo Hospital, 5-2-2 Naka-no-shima, Kita-ku (☎06 6443 1261, ⓦsumitomo-hp.or.jp). Otherwise contact one of the tourist information counters (see p.518).

Immigration Osaka's immigration bureau is at 1-29-53 Nankō Kita, Suminoe-ku (☎06 4703 2100).

Lost property The lost and found department for Osaka's buses and subways is at 1-17 Moto-machi (☎06 6633 9151).

Post office The Central Post Office (3-2-4 Umeda; ☎06 6347 8097) is immediately southwest of JR Osaka Station and open daily 7am–midnight.

7

Takarazuka

宝塚

When the Hankyū railway tycoon Kobayashi Ichizō laid a line out to the tiny spa town of **TAKARAZUKA**, 20km northwest of Osaka in Hyōgo Prefecture, in 1911, he had an entertainment vision that extended way beyond soothing onsen dips. By 1924 he'd built

---

THE WONDERFUL WORLD OF TAKARAZUKA

The all-female **Takarazuka Revue Company** (宝塚歌劇団) has been thrilling audiences with their Broadway-style shows since 1914. The company's founder, **Kobayashi Ichizō**, was impressed by cabaret shows he'd seen in Paris, and sensed that Japanese audiences were ripe for lively Western musical dramas, but he also wanted to preserve something of Japan's traditional theatre. So, as well as performing dance reviews and musicals, Takarazuka also act out **classical Japanese plays** and have developed **shows** from Western literature, including Gone with the Wind and War and Peace, and Hollywood movies. Even manga has been adapted, with The Rose of Versailles still one of Takarazuka's most successful and enduring productions. The dramatizations tend to be heavy on romance, allowing the otoko-yaku (male role) and musume-yaku (female role) stars to shine on stage as they sing, dance and act out epic love stories.

The Revue has **five troupes** – Hana (flower), Tsuki (moon), Hoshi (star), Yuki (snow) and Sora (cosmos) – with approximately 400 members in total. It is thought that the overwhelmingly female audiences come to see the Revue to escape the frustrations of their daily lives, and that they enjoy seeing the idealized gender performances of the otoko-yaku. Thousands of young girls apply annually to join the troupe at the age of 16, and devote themselves to a punishing routine of classes that will enable them to embody the "modesty, fairness and grace" (the company's motto) expected of a Takarasienne, as Takarazuka members are called.

Takarazuka Grand Theatre 宝塚大劇場 1-1-57 Sakae-machi ⓦkageki.hankyu.co.jp/english/index .html. Shows are also staged regularly in Tokyo (see p.158), but most fans prefer to see the troupe on their home ground, and perhaps glimpse one of the stars on her way to and from the theatre. There are daily performances (except Wed) at 11am and 3pm, and tickets cost ¥3500–12,000. Reservations should be made up to a month in advance via the ticket office (daily 10am–5pm except for four-day closures between shows; ☎0570 00 5100, ⓦkageki.hankyu.co.jp/ticket;

no English spoken, but tourist offices can often check availability on your behalf). Alternatively, tickets can be purchased from Ticket Pia outlets (ⓦt.pia.jp) or at Lawson convenience stores. The theatre is a 10min walk southeast of the train stations, along the Hana-no-michi, or Flower Road, an elevated platform along an avenue of cherry trees, which is supposed to be like a passage leading onto the stage. At the theatre, there's a vast complex of shops and cafés where you can easily pick up a bentō lunch or sandwiches.

the **Takarazuka Grand Theatre** (宝塚大劇場), which has been home ever since to the all-female musical drama troupe the **Takarazuka Revue** (see box, p.525). Almost two million people – mainly women – flock to the town each year to watch the theatre's lavish musical productions, while the Revue itself has become an enduring part of Japanese popular culture, Takarazuka is also the childhood home of the "God of Manga", **Tezuka Osamu**, and a **memorial museum** here celebrates his life and work. It's perfectly possible to see a performance and visit the museum in a day-trip from Osaka, Kōbe or Kyoto.

Tezuka Osamu Manga Museum

手塚治虫記念館, Tezuka Osamu Kinenkan • 7-65 Mukogawa-chō • 9.30am–4.30pm; closed Wed; check in advance for temporary closures • 40min animation workshops 10am–4pm • ¥700 • ☏ 0797 81 2970, ⓦ tezukaosamu.net/en/

The **Tezuka Osamu Manga Museum**, just beyond the Takarazuka Grand Theatre, celebrates the comic-book genius **Tezuka Osamu** (1928–89), creator of *Astro Boy* and *Kimba the White Lion* among many other famous manga and anime series. Tezuka was raised in Takarazuka, and as his mother was a big fan of the Revue, he saw dozens of its performances as a child. This apparently led him to create the romantic tale of the cross-dressing Princess Knight, and the Revue has subsequently adapted manga by Tezuka into its popular productions. This colourful museum charts his career, displays art from his books, comics and animated films, screens cartoons and gives you the chance to become an animator in the workshop.

ARRIVAL AND INFORMATION | TAKARAZUKA

By train The fastest train on the Hankyū Takarazuka line from Osaka's Umeda Station takes less than 30min to reach Takarazuka Station (¥280). There are also direct trains on the JR Fukuchiyama line, taking a few minutes more from JR Osaka Station to JR Takarazuka Station, next to the Hankyū terminus and department store. If you are coming from Kyoto, change at Jūsō for the Takarazuka line. From Kōbe, change at Nishinomiya-Kitaguchi for the Imazu line to Takarazuka Station.

Tourist information The town's tourist information office (daily 9am–5pm; ☏ 0797 81 5344) is in front of the second-floor Hankyū Station entrance; you can pick up a map here.

Kōya-san

高野山

Ever since the Buddhist monk Kōbō Daishi founded a temple here in the early ninth century, **KŌYA-SAN** has been one of Japan's holiest mountains. The town itself is in a high, cedar-filled valley near the top of the mountain, 800m above sea level, where more than one hundred monasteries cluster round the head temple of the Shingon school of Buddhism, **Kongōbu-ji**. This isolated community is protected by two concentric mountain chains of eight peaks, which are said to resemble an eight-petalled lotus blossom.

Whatever your religious persuasion, there's a highly charged, slightly surreal atmosphere about this group of temples suspended among the clouds. The journey alone, a dramatic ride by train and ropeway (cable-car), is spectacular, and Kōya-san is also a good place to step out of Japan's hectic city life for a day or two. One of its great delights is to stay in a *shukubō*, or **temple lodging**, and attend a dawn prayer service. Afterwards, head for the **Garan**, the mountain's spiritual centre, or wander among the thousands of ancient tombs and memorials which populate the **Okunoin cemetery**, where Kōbō Daishi's mausoleum is honoured with a blaze of ten thousand oil-fuelled brass lanterns.

Kōya-san may be remote but it is not unpopulated. Some six thousand people live in the valley and each year thousands of pilgrims visit the monasteries. In 2004 it became a UNESCO World Heritage Site, which has resulted in an increase in the number of overseas visitors. Life still moves at a fairly slow pace on Kōya-san: the town only has one convenience store, and by early evening the shops are shuttered and the streets almost deserted. Be aware that, while the mountain can be pleasantly cool in summer, winter temperatures often fall below freezing.

Brief history

The first monastery on Kōya-san was founded in the early ninth century by the monk Kūkai (774–835), known after his death as **Kōbō Daishi** (see box below). As a young monk, Kūkai travelled to China to study Esoteric Buddhism for two years. On his return in 806 he established a temple in Hakata (now Fukuoka) before moving to Takao-san near Kyoto, where his ardent prayers for the peace and prosperity of the nation won him powerful supporters. Kūkai was soon granted permission to found the **Shingon** school which, in a break from contemporary belief, held that enlightenment could be achieved in one lifetime. But city life was too disruptive for serious meditation, so Kūkai set off round Japan to find a suitable mountain retreat.

According to legend, when Kūkai left China he prayed for guidance on where to establish his monastery. At the same time he flung his three-pronged *vajra* (the ritual implement of Shingon monks) clear across the ocean. Later, as he drew near **Kōya-san**, he met a giant, red-faced hunter, who gave him a two-headed dog. The dog led Kūkai to the top of the mountain where, of course, he found his *vajra* hanging in a pine tree. In any event, the historical records show that Kūkai first came to Kōya-san in 816 and returned in 819 to consecrate the first temple. For a while after 823 he presided over Kyoto's Tō-ji (see p.431), but eventually returned to Kōya-san, where he died in 835. Even without his religious work it seems that Kūkai was a remarkable man. After his death, Kūkai's disciple **Shinzen** continued developing the monasteries, then collectively known as **Kongōbu-ji**, until there were more than 1500 monasteries and several thousand monks on the mountain top. The sect then had its ups and downs, of which the most serious was during the anti-Buddhist movement following the 1868 Meiji Restoration. Today there are 117 temples atop Kōya-san and it is once again a major centre of pilgrimage.

Kōya-san town

The secular centre of Kōya-san lies at the **Senjuin-bashi** junction, and the town's main sights are located either side of this crossroads: head west for Kōya-san's principal temple, **Kongōbu-ji**, and its religious centre, the **Garan**, or east for the mossy graves of **Okunoin cemetery**. Buses from the ropeway station also stop at the crossroads, and you'll find the tourist office, post office and police station all nearby, alongside restaurants and shops peddling souvenirs and pilgrims' accessories.

KŌBŌ DAISHI

Kōbō Daishi (known during his lifetime as Kūkai) was born in 774 AD in the town of Zentsūji, 30km from Takamatsu on the island of Shikoku. This pious man walked all over Shikoku as an itinerant priest and spent two years in Tang-dynasty China studying Esoteric Buddhism, before apparently gaining enlightenment at Muroto Misaki in Kōchi-ken and founding the **Shingon** ("True Word") school of Buddhism. Shingon was influenced by the Tibetan and Central Asian tantric Buddhist traditions and this is reflected in the Shikoku temples, with their exotic decor and atmosphere.

In addition to his significant efforts in the development of **Japanese Buddhism**, Kōbō Daishi is often referred to as the father of Japanese culture; in many ways, he was the Japanese Leonardo da Vinci. He is credited with a phenomenal number of cultural and technological **achievements**: devising the kana syllabary "(*katakana* and *hiragana*)", opening the first public school, inventing pond irrigation, discovering mercury, and compiling the first dictionary. In addition, he was also renowned as a master calligrapher, poet, sculptor and healer.

Kōbō Daishi died on April 22, 835, the exact day he predicted he would. For his achievements, he was posthumously awarded the title Daishi ("Great Saint") by the imperial court. Soon after his death, his disciples began a tour around the temples of Shikoku associated with the Daishi, thus establishing the **pilgrimage** as it is known today (see box, p.636).

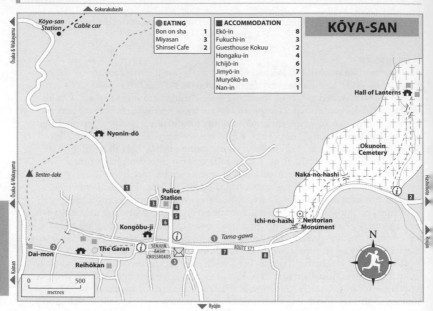

Nyonin-dō

女人堂 • Daily 8.30am–5pm • Free

The road into Kōya-san from the ropeway station winds through cool, dark cryptomeria forests for about 2km before passing a small temple called **Nyonin-dō**. This "Women's Hall" marks one of the original seven entrances to the sacred precincts, beyond which women weren't allowed to proceed; the practice continued until 1906 despite an imperial edict against it, issued in 1872. In the meantime, female pilgrims worshipped in special temples built beside each gate, of which Nyonin-dō is the last remaining.

Kongōbu-ji

金剛峯寺 • Daily: May–Oct 8.30am–5pm; Nov–April 8.30am–4.30pm • ¥500 • ☎ 0736 56 2011, ⊕ koyasan.or.jp

Though it originally applied to the whole mountain community, the name **Kongōbu-ji**, meaning "Temple of the Diamond Mountain", now refers specifically to the Shingon school's chief monastic and administrative offices. In fact, this temple was a late addition to the complex, founded in 1592 by the ruler Toyotomi Hideyoshi in honour of his mother. It only later became Shingon's headquarters.

Rebuilt in 1861 in the original style, the graceful building is famous largely for its late sixteenth-century **screen paintings** by Kyoto's Kanō school of artists. The best of these are the cranes and pine trees by Kanō Tanyū decorating the Great Hall, and Kanō Tansai's *Willows in Four Seasons* two rooms further along. Beside the temple's front entrance, the **Rokuji-no-kane** (六時の鐘) or "Six O'Clock Bell", cast in 1535, sits on a castle-like foundation; a monk comes out to ring it every even hour (6am–10pm).

The Garan

伽藍 • **Grounds** Daily 8.30am–5pm • Free • **Konpon Daitō** Daily 8.30am–5pm • ¥200 • **Kon-dō** Daily 8.30am–5pm • ¥200 •
☎ 0736 56 3215, ⊕ koyasan.or.jp

Kōya-san's most sacred precinct, the **Garan** is a large sandy compound, filled with cryptomeria trees, lanterns and wooden halls wreathed in incense. It is the spot where Kōbō Daishi's three-pronged *vajra* landed and where he founded his original monastery (see box, p.527).

The Garan's most important building is the monumental **Konpon Daitō** (根本大塔), the Fundamental Great Stupa, which is covered in strident, orange lacquer. The original stupa was established in 816, but the current building dates from the 1930s. A statue of the Dainichi Nyorai (Cosmic Buddha) and images of four Buddhist deities are enshrined inside. The more restrained **Kon-dō** (金堂), also rebuilt in the 1930s, marks the spot in the Garan where Kūkai gave his first lectures. Buddhist services are still held here today, and the Asuku Nyorai, or Buddha of Medicine, is enshrined here. Kūkai reputedly lived where the **Miei-dō** (御影堂) now stands, just to the west, which is regarded as one of the mountain's most holy places. Note the two sacred pines in front, which are said to be offspring of the tree in which Kūkai's *vajra* (ritual implements) landed.

Dai-mon
大門
The main road in front of the Garan eventually leads to the **Dai-mon**, or Great Gate, which was Kōya-san's main entrance until the ropeway was built in the 1930s. The huge, rust-red gate sits on the mountain's western edge, where on a clear day you can see right out to sea.

Reihōkan
霊宝館 • Daily 8.30am–4.30pm • ¥600 • ☎ 0736 56 2029, ⓦ reihokan.or.jp
Kōya-san's greatest treasures are in the **Reihōkan**, which contains a number of priceless works of esoteric Buddhist art, including Heian- and Kamakura-period wooden sculptures. Displays are changed every few months. If you're lucky you might get to see a triptych of Amida welcoming souls to the Western Paradise, painted in 965, or a Heian-era silk painting of Buddha entering nirvana; due to their fragile nature they are only on display every three years.

Okunoin
奥の院
About 1km east of Kōya-san's central crossroads, **Okunoin** is Kōya-san's vast forest **cemetery**. Stretching from Ichi-no-hashi to the cemetery's spiritual centre, Kōbō Daishi's mausoleum, a 2km-long forest path winds through more than 200,000 stone stupas of all shapes and sizes. A large number of historical characters are buried here, among them the great general Oda Nobunaga. You'll also find numerous *jizō* statues and the occasional war memorial. It's best to walk through Okunoin in the early morning or around dusk, when lamps light up the path; at these times the only other people you're likely to meet are the occasional white-garbed pilgrims with their tinkling bells.

Kōbō Daishi mausoleum
Once across the bridge over the Tama-gawa, the approach to the **mausoleum of Kōbō Daishi** begins. First comes the **Hall of Lanterns**, where ten thousand oil lamps donated by the faithful are kept constantly alight. Two of them are said to have been burning since the eleventh century, one donated by the former Emperor Shirakawa and another by an anonymous poor woman. After this blaze of light and colour, the **tomb** itself is surprisingly restrained. Indeed, it's only just visible within a gated enclosure behind the hall, sheltered by lofty cryptomeria trees and clouds of incense.

KŌYA-SAN FESTIVALS
Kōya-san's biggest **festival** takes place on March 21, when all the monks gather for a service at the **Miei-dō** in the Garan, which is fully opened to the public, and worshippers make flower and candle offerings. Everyone's out in force again for the **street parade** on Kōbō Daishi's birthday (June 15), while during Obon several thousand lanterns light the route through Okunoin cemetery as part of Japan's **festival for the dead** (Aug 13).

A VICTORIAN LADY ON KŌYA-SAN

Elizabeth Anna Gordon was a Victorian aristocrat and religious scholar who not only made an important contribution to the western study of Buddhism but is one of the few foreigners to be buried in Okunoin. Born in 1851, she was a lady-in-waiting to Queen Victoria and an Oxford University graduate with a strong interest in Japan. She was responsible for erecting a replica of the **Nestorian Monument**, a kind of Rosetta Stone of world religions discovered in China in around 1625, on Kōya-san in 1911. For Gordon, the monument was a symbol of the common roots of Buddhism and Christianity. Her activities on the mountain are remarkable for the time – women were banned until 1868, but only really began visiting in the early twentieth century. The monks welcomed this intrepid woman and the monument as a means of promoting Kōya-san around the world. Gordon died in a Kyoto hotel in 1925 and her grave is on the right side of the Nestorian Monument, close to the Ichi-no-hashi entrance to Okunoin.

7

According to Shingon tradition, the Great Master, Daishi, did not die in 835 but rather entered "eternal meditation". He's now waiting to return as Miroku, the Future Buddha, when he will help lead the faithful to salvation – which is one reason why so many Japanese wish to have their ashes buried on Kōya-san. Next to the Daishi's tomb you'll see the octagonal ossuary where ashes are collected.

The modern cemetery

Okunoin's modern cemetery lies south of the Tama-gawa bridge on a short cut back to the main road. It contrasts sharply with the atmospheric and ancient forested area leading up to Kōbō Daishi's mausoleum. Here, large companies maintain plots for past employees with some unusual memorials – the space rocket and coffee cup are two that stand out. Also note the "letter boxes" on some monuments for company employees to leave their *meishi* (business cards). The cemetery ends at Naka-no-hashi (中の橋), on the main road beside a clutch of restaurants and a bus park.

ARRIVAL AND DEPARTURE
KŌYA-SAN

By train Direct express and limited express trains from Osaka's Namba Station make the 50km journey south on the private Nankai line (every 20–30min; 1hr 15min–1hr 40min; ¥1230; ¥760 limited express train supplement), to Gokurakubashi Station, where they connect with the ropeway to Kōya-san (price included in the ticket); note that reservations are required on the limited express. From Nara and Kyoto you can either travel via Osaka or use the JR network as far as Shin-Imamiya (新今宮) or Hashimoto (橋本) and then change onto the Nankai line.

Destinations Hashimoto (every 20–30min; 45min); Nara (every 15–20min; 3hr); Osaka (every 20–30min; 1hr 15min–1hr 40min).

By ropeway Most visitors access Kōya-san's mountain-top hideaway via a ropeway (cable-car) which departs every 30min from Gokurakubashi Station (極楽橋駅), arriving at Kōya-san Station 5min later. Nankai trains usually arrive in time for ropeway departures, and the price is included in the train ticket.

By bus If you are travelling on from Kōya-san to Kumano Kodō (see p.533), there are buses to Tanabe (¥4430) at weekends and during peak seasons from April 1 to Nov 30; check the Tourism Bureau website (🌐 tb-kumano.jp/en /transport) for the latest information.

GETTING AROUND

By bus At the top ropeway station you'll find buses waiting for the 10min ride into town (every 20–30min; ¥280). If you plan on doing a lot of bus journeys, you can buy a one-day pass, or *ichi-nichi furii kippu* (¥800) at the ropeway station. All buses stop at the central Senjuin-bashi crossroads (千手院橋), where the routes then divide, with the majority of services running east to Okunoin and fewer heading past Kongōbu-ji to the western gate, Dia-mon.

On foot Kōya-san's major sights are within walking distance of each other, and it's most pleasant to explore on foot.

By bike You can rent bikes from the Kōya-san Tourist Association office (see p.532) for ¥400/1hr.

By taxi Taxis wait outside the ropeway station, or call Kōya-san Taxi (☎ 0736 56 2628).

INFORMATION AND TOURS

Tourist information The Kōya-san Tourist Association office (daily 8.30am–5pm; ☎0736 56 2616, ⓦshukubo.jp) is beside the Senjuin-bashi junction. You can book accommodation here, or in advance through their English website (ⓦeng.shukubo.net). The Kōya-san Visitor Information Center (10am–4pm, closed Tues & Thurs; ☎0736 56 2270, ⓦkoyasan-ccn.com) near Kongōbu-ji also has helpful staff and free internet access. They also offer a free interpreter service if you get stuck (☎090 1486 2588 or ☎090 3263 5184).

Tourist pass The Kōya-san World Heritage Ticket (¥3400) is valid for two days and covers a return trip from Namba to Kōya-san (limited express train), bus travel from the ropeway station and around the mountain top, and a twenty percent discount on admission to Kongōbu-ji, Kon-dō, Konpon Daitō and Reihōkan.

Tours The tourist office offers the Kōya-san Audio Guide (daily 8.30am–4.30pm; ¥500), which has a commentary in English of Kōya-san's places of interest, corresponding to numbered sites throughout the town. A better way to learn the stories and the secrets of this sacred site is with the Kōya-san Interpreter Guide Club (☎0736 56 2270, ⓔmail@koyasan-ccn.com), whose walking tours (from ¥1000/person depending on group size) include Okunoin, as well as Kongōbu-ji and the Garan; reservations must be made at least a day in advance. You can also do night tours of Okunoin with a local English-speaking monk as your guide, which is a great way to soak up the spiritual atmosphere (☎080 3108 4790, ⓦnight.koyasan-okunoin .com). The 1hr tour (¥1500) starts at the Eko-in shukubō (see below) at 7.15pm; call in the afternoon of the day you want to join the tour to check if it's running.

ACCOMMODATION

More than fifty monasteries on Kōya-san offer **accommodation** in *shukubō* – temple lodgings run by monks, and occasionally also by nuns (see box below). The rooms are all Japanese-style and usually look out over beautiful gardens or are decorated with painted screens or antique hanging scrolls; most have communal washing facilities. In recent years, some of the temples have upgraded rooms to include private bathing facilities, Western-style toilets, mini-refrigerators, TVs and internet connections. Note that accommodation is very hard to find during Kōya-san's festivals (see box, p.529), so if you plan to visit during any of these, book well in advance. Prices for temple accommodation quoted here are for one person and include dinner and breakfast.

Ekō-in 惠光院 ☎0736 56 2514, ⓦekoin.jp/en. This friendly temple has simple but comfortable rooms overlooking a garden. There's also a meditation hall for after-dinner sessions, as well as a *goma-taki* fire ceremony at dawn, which anyone can attend. Internet available. **¥12,000**

Fukuchi-in 福智院 ☎0736 56 2021, ⓦfukuchiin.com /en. This temple is famous for its modern dry landscape garden by Mirei Shigemori, who controversially used concrete and avant-garde shapes in the design. Even if you're not staying here, it's worth a visit to see the garden. The temple also has Kōya-san's only onsen hot-spring bath. **¥14,000**

★Guesthouse Kokuu ゲストハウスコクウ ☎0736 26 7216, ⓦkoyasanguesthouse.com. This popular guesthouse is in an impressively designed modern

building, and run by an English-speaking young couple. The space is compact (rather than dorms they have capsules) but light and airy. In winter there's a cosy wood stove. Capsules **¥3500**, doubles **¥9000**

★Hongaku-in 本覚院 ☎0736 56 2711, ⓦhongakuin .jp. One of the nicest temples to stay in Kōya-san, with a quiet atmosphere and some interesting Buddhist art; they also serve excellent *shojin-ryōri*. The prayer hall has recently been restored and the morning prayer service is welcoming and inclusive – listen out for your name. **¥17,280**

Ichijō-in 一乗院 ☎0736 56 2214, ⓦitijyoin.or.jp. Elegant and modern temple lodgings; all rooms have internet connection and TV and some have en-suite facilities. The *shojin-ryōri* meals here are especially good. **¥17,000**

STAYING IN A *SHUKUBŌ*

Shukubō are primarily **places of worship**, so you'll be asked to keep to fairly strict meal and bath times, and you shouldn't expect hotel-style service. Guests are usually welcome to attend the early-morning prayers (around 6am). At some temples this also includes a *goma-taki* **fire ceremony** – the burning of 108 pieces of wood which are said to represent the number of "defilements" that need to be overcome in order to gain enlightenment. All *shukubō* offer excellent **vegetarian meals** (*shōjin-ryōri*), which consist of seasonal vegetable and tofu-based dishes cooked without meat, fish, onion or garlic seasoning. Due to the number of foreign tourists making the journey to Kōya-san, there is usually someone at the temples who can speak English. It's a good idea to make **reservations** well in advance, either through the Kōya-san Tourist Association (see above) or by approaching the temples recommended above directly. **Prices** generally start at around ¥9500 per person per night, including two meals.

Jimyō-in 持明院 ☎ 0736 56 2222, ⓦ koyasan-jimyoin .com. This peaceful temple is surrounded by a large garden and some of the rooms have nice views. It's not as swish as some of the other temples but the monks are friendly and welcoming. The morning prayer service is at 6.30am. **¥10,800**

Muryōkō-in 無量光院 ☎ 0736 56 2104, ⓦ muryokoin .org. This large, rambling temple is known for its international atmosphere – a few of the monks and nuns are foreigners. The rooms are spacious and have the basic comforts. The morning service here, including a fire ceremony, is well worth rising at dawn for. **¥11,880**

★**Nan-in** 南院 ☎ 0736 56 2534, ⓦ sea.sannet.ne.jp /namikiri-nanin. This stately temple is adjacent to the Tokugawa Mausoleum, northwest of the Senjuin-bashi junction, and has a friendly atmosphere. The rooms are decorated with historic artworks and the bathing facilities are clean and modern. **¥9500**

EATING

★**Bon On Sha** 梵恩舎 ☎ 0736 56 5535. Welcoming café and art gallery run by a young Japanese and French couple, serving organic vegetarian lunch sets (¥1200), as well as delicious cake and coffee sets (¥550). It's east of the Senjuin-bashi intersection. Wed–Sun 9.30am–5.30pm.

Miyasan みやさん ☎ 0736 56 2827. Just south of Senjuin-bashi, this cheap and friendly *izakaya* serves up fried chicken (¥650), potato salad (¥380) and locally distilled plum wine (¥550). Mon–Sat 5–10pm.

Shinsei Café 心星カフェ ☎ 0736 56 5535. Friendly café with Kōya-san's first espresso machine, making cappuccino and lattes (¥380). They also serve breakfast sets of toast (¥450) and sandwiches (¥700). 7.30am–7pm; closed Wed.

7

Kumano Kodō

熊野古道

Set among the isolated mountain ranges of the **Kii Hantō** (紀伊半島) peninsula, in southern Wakayama prefecture, southeast of Osaka, is a network of ancient pilgrimage routes known as the **Kumano Kodō**. In 2004, Kumano Kodō, literally the "Kumano ancient road", became a UNESCO World Heritage Site. An area of stunning natural beauty – old-growth forests, charming mountain tea fields, magnificent waterfalls and healing hot springs – it is also the spiritual heartland of Japanese mythology and religion, and unique for its synthesis of Shintōism and Buddhism, in which indigenous Japanese deities were accepted as manifestations of Buddhist deities. This is where the mountain-worshipping Buddhist-Shintō practice of Shugendo evolved and is still active today. The Kumano Kodō is a special place to visit, both for its serene natural beauty and its ancient spiritual atmosphere. Despite its remoteness from modern, hi-tech Japan, it is an incredibly friendly place, with good transport and accommodation that caters well to international visitors.

Brief history

Though mentioned in the eighth-century *Kojiki* historical record as the "Land of the Dead", where the spirits of the gods reside, Kumano Kodō became popular from the tenth century mainly through Imperial pilgrimages by retired emperors and aristocrats, who made the trek from Kyoto to worship at the **Kumano Sanzan** (熊野三山), a set of three important Grand Shrines of **Kumano Hongū Taisha**, Kumano Hayatama Taisha and **Kumano Nachi Taisha**, and to perform rites of purification in the surrounding rivers and waterfalls. The working classes were also attracted to worshipping here, so, by the fourteenth century pilgrims from all over the country had forged routes here from other parts of the county. Unlike Kōya-san, some 70km away, female pilgrims have always been welcomed in Kumano from its earliest history.

Another reason for the historical popularity and significance of the Kumano Kodō is the number of excellent **hot springs**, many in remote villages, which since ancient times have been known for their healing and restorative powers. The area boasts Japan's only hot spring to be recognized as a UNESCO World Heritage Site – the 1800-year-old **Tsuboyu** at **Yunomine Onsen**.

> ### THE NAKAHECHI PILGRIMAGE ROUTE
>
> The Kumano Kodō is actually a rubric for the network of four pilgrimage routes; the **Imperial Nakahechi** route, the mountainous **Kohechi** route, the coastal **Ohechi** route and the eastern **Iseji** route. The Kohechi and Iseji routes link up Kumano with Kōya-san and Ise-jingū, respectively. Detailed information on all the routes, as well as suggested itineraries, are available in English (see opposite).
>
> The Nakahechi is the most popular route to the Grand Shrines. Beginning in **Tanabe**, it traverses the **mountains** eastwards towards Hongū, where it splits into a river route to Shingū and a mountain route to Nachi. The Nakahechi passes through some remote villages but has excellent accommodation facilities for **multi-day walks**. This route has many *oji*, small roadside shrines for worshipping various deities, hence many of the villages are named accordingly. Most pilgrims take a bus from Kii-Tanabe station to Takijiri-oji, a major trailhead, and walk to Chikatsuyu (6–7hr) on the first day, stopping at Takahara Kumano-jinja to see the wonderful vista of clouds and mountains. The second full-day walk leads to Hongū and its onsen. Many pilgrims continue on the trail for another few days, also taking in **Kumano Nachi Taisha** and its amazing waterfall, before arriving at the final destination in **Shingū**.
>
> It is also possible to use a combination of buses and selected trail walks to experience the Nakahechi route – either way, it takes in some of the most tranquil natural scenes in western Japan, and is a great way to visit the Kumano Sanzan Grand Shrines. Remember that this is a mountainous area and the weather can change quickly – be prepared for fluctuating temperatures.

Kumano Hongū Taisha

熊野本宮大社 • Hongū • Daily 8am–5pm • Free; Treasure Hall ¥300 • ☎ 0735 42 0009, ⓦ hongutaisha.jp • Bus from Tanabe (2hr; ¥2060)

The four pilgrimage routes converge at the stately **Kumano Hongū Taisha**, making it both the geographical and sacred centre of the Kumano Kodō. The most important of the three Grand Shrines of Kumano, it's similar in style to the architecture of Ise-jingū – note the thatched roofs and decorated gables. The shrine was moved to its current, and slightly more elevated, location after a massive flood in 1889 almost completely destroyed it at nearby Oyunohara, a sandbank on the Kumano-gawa, and where a gigantic *torii* now stands. Look out for the *yatagarasu* black crow symbol at the shrine – the sacred three-legged bird is believed to be both a heavenly messenger and a supernatural guide. Among the many pilgrims who visit the shrine are the Japanese national soccer team, who use the *yatagarasu* symbol as part of their official emblem.

Kumano Hongū Heritage Center

世界遺産熊野本宮館, Sekai Isan Kumano Hongū-kan • Hongū • Daily 9am–5pm • Free • ☎ 0735 42 0751, ⓦ city.tanabe.lg.jp /hongukan/en • Bus from Tanabe (2hr; ¥2060)

Just across the road from the entrance to the Kumano Hongū Taisha, the **Kumano Hongū Heritage Center** is a large modern building where you can learn more about the history, culture and religion of the area, and you can also see photos and models of the shrine before the 1889 flood.

Nachi-Katsuura

Nachi-Katsuura marks the confluence of the Nakahechi and Ohechi pilgrimage routes. The sacred mountain of **Nachisan**, with its Grand Shrine and ancient Buddhist temple, is just a few kilometres inland from the fishing port of **Katsuura**.

Kumano Nachi Taisha and Seiganto-ji

熊野那智大社 • 青岸渡寺 • Nachisan • **Kumano Nachi Taisha** Daily 8.30am–4.30pm • Free • ☎ 0735 55 0321, ⓦ www .kumanonachitaisha.or.jp • **Seiganto-ji** Daily 8.30am–4pm • Free • ☎ 0735 55 0401 • Bus from JR Kii-Katsuura Station (25min; ¥620)

Just outside the town of Katsuura is the Grand Shrine of **Kumano Nachi Taisha** and the adjacent Buddhist temple of **Seiganto-ji**. Perched on the side of Nachisan mountain,

KUMANO'S ONSEN

The Kumano region is blessed with some of western Japan's best **onsen** towns, which can be easily visited while walking the Kumano Kodō.

Kawayu Onsen 川湯温泉 In winter, the river at this onsen town near Hongū is transformed into a piping-hot giant outdoor bath called the Sennin-buro (仙人風呂), literally a bath for one thousand people (daily 6.30am–10pm; free). Given its very public, outdoor location, it's one of the few hot springs where swimwear is acceptable. It's also fine to dig your own spring in the river.

Ryūjin Onsen 龍神温泉 Slightly outside Hongū, in a remote mountain area, Ryūjin Onsen is worth considering for a visit if you are travelling from Kōya-san towards Hongū. Its waters are well known for their beautifying effects on the skin, and the views from the various onsen's outdoor baths in spring and autumn are sublime.

Wataze Onsen 渡瀬温泉 The main claim to fame of this onsen town near Hongū is having the largest rotemburo (outdoor bath) in western Japan (daily 6am–9.30pm; ¥700). It may not be as historic as the other two onsen in Hongū, but its garden setting is just as picturesque.

Yunomine Onsen 湯の峰温泉 In this 1800-year-old onsen town near Hongū, the main attraction is Tsuboyu (つぼ湯) – the only hot spring in Japan to be registered as a UNESCO World Heritage Site (daily 6am–9.30pm; ¥770). A small cloudy-coloured spring, built out of the narrow stream that runs through the town, Tsuboyu is covered by a wooden cabin that you can use privately for thirty minutes.

7

they are fine examples of the interconnectivity of Shintō and Buddhist faiths in the Kumano region, and attract large numbers of pilgrims.

Nachi-no-Ōtaki

那智の大滝 • Nachisan • Daily 7am–5pm • Free; viewing platform ¥300 • ☎ 0735 55 0321 • Bus from JR Kii-Katsuura Station (25min; ¥620)

An important place of nature worship for Shugendō followers, **Nachi-no-Ōtaki** is said to be the tallest waterfall in Japan. The water comes pounding out of a primeval forest and spectacularly drops 133m into the valley. If you don't have time to trek down to the waterfall, you can still enjoy the superb view from Seiganto-ji (see opposite).

Daimonzaka-chaya

大門坂茶屋 • Nachisan • Daily 9am–4pm; reservations necessary during high season • Kimono rental ¥2000/1hr, ¥3000/2hr • ☎ 0735 55 0244, ⓦ nachikan.jp • Bus from JR Kii-Katsuura Station (25min; ¥620)

If you've wondered what it felt like to walk the Kumano Kodō in Heian times, the **Daimonzaka-chaya costume rental** shop is a great place to find out. Here, you can dress up in a ninth-century-style kimono, *zori* shoes and veiled headwear, and wander a little way on Daimon-zaka – a cobblestone staircase set among towering ancient trees that's part of the pilgrimage route up to Kumano Nachi Taisha and Seiganto-ji. Female and male costumes are available, as well as children's.

ARRIVAL AND INFORMATION   KUMANO KODŌ

By train The main access point for the Kumano Kodō is the city of Tanabe (田辺); its JR station is Kii-Tanabe (紀伊田辺). Express train services run here from Kyoto (2–3 daily; 2hr 35min) and Shin-Osaka (15 daily; 2hr). From eastern Japan, trains from Nagoya (4 daily; 3hr) go to Shingū (新宮). Otherwise, you can get a train from Kōya-san, changing at Hashimoto for services towards Wakayama city and Tanabe (hourly; 1hr 20min).

By bus JR Nishi-Nihon and Meiko buses run from Osaka to Tanabe (10 daily; ¥2980) and from Kyoto to Tanabe (2 daily; ¥3910). From April 1 to Nov 30, buses run between Kōya-san and Tanabe (¥4430) at weekends and during peak seasons only; check the Tourism Bureau website

(ⓦ tb-kumano.jp/en/transport) for the latest information.

Tourist information The Tanabe Tourist Information Center (daily 9am–6pm; ☎ 0739 26 9025, ⓦ tb-kumano .jp/en) next to JR Kii-Tanabe Station is an excellent place to pick up English-language pamphlets and maps of the ancient routes. Their website is also the best source for up-to-date information on the Kumano Kodō, translated into English, including transport timetables and an accommodation reservation system (bookings must be made more than 7 days in advance and take 3 days to process). There are also visitor information centres at Takijiri-oji, the spiritual entrance to the sacred Kumano mountains, and at the Kumano Hongū Heritage Center, near Kumano Hongū Taisha (see opposite).

7

GETTING AROUND

By bus Pilgrims are usually intent on walking the Kumano Kodō, but there is also a good network of fairly regular bus services, depending on the season, which connect the main sights of the pilgrim routes and the surrounding areas; see the Tourism Bureau website (ⓦtb-kumano.jp/en/transport) for route details and timetables.

By bike Bike rental is available at Kii-Tanabe Station (daily 9am–6pm; ¥500/1 day) and also from the Kumano Hongū Heritage Center (daily 8.30am–5pm; ¥1500/day).

ACCOMMODATION

Along the Kumano Kodō there is a range of good-quality accommodation options for all budgets. Many ryokan or minshuku have their own onsen, or are close to one, and most places can provide dinner and breakfast, as well as a boxed lunch to take on the trail the next day. All the accommodation listed below can be booked through the Kumano Tourism Bureau reservation system (ⓦkumano-travel.com).

TANABE

Altier アルティエホテル Tanabe ☎0739 81 1111, ⓦaltierhotel.com. If you are starting your journey in Tanabe, this comfortable business hotel near the station, with free breakfast and internet, is a good choice. **¥13,000**

★**Konyamachiya Townhouse** 紺屋町家 Tanabe ☎0739 26 9025, ⓦkumano-travel.com. This nicely restored townhouse in Tanabe city sleeps up to six guests, and it's a lovely place to experience living in a traditional Japanese house. It's fully equipped for self-catering and also has a washing machine. Check-in is at the Kishifuan-En souvenir shop at Kii-Tanabe Station. **¥10,800**

THE NAKAHECHI ROUTE

Kiri no Sato Takahara 霧の郷たかはら Takahara ☎0739 64 1900, ⓦkirinosato-takahara.com. Friendly mountain lodge in Takahara village on the Nakahechi route. The comfortable Japanese- and Western-style rooms (with toilets) have stunning views looking directly out over the valley. Bathing facilities are shared and meals are included. **¥22,736**

Minshuku Chikatsuyu 民宿ちかつゆ Chikatsuyu ☎0739 65 0617. This minshuku on the Nakahechi route has comfortable private and shared tatami rooms, as well as its own onsen with water as smooth as silk. Rates include breakfast and dinner. **¥9405**

HONGŪ AND AROUND

Blue Sky Guesthouse 蒼空げすとはうす Hongū ☎0735 42 0800, ⓦkumano-guesthouse.com. A spacious modern building in a pleasant natural setting, this guesthouse has tatami rooms and excellent facilities. There's a friendly and international atmosphere, and breakfast is included in the price. **¥13,200**

Kamigoten Ryokan 上御殿 Ryūjin Onsen ☎0735 79 0005, ⓦkamigoten.jp. High-class ryokan at Ryūjin Onsen in an exquisite Edo-period building, serving multi-course dinners of hearty mountain cuisine. The onsen facilities are modern, with superb river valley views. **¥32,400**

Minshuku Ōmuraya 民宿大村屋 Kawayu Onsen ☎0735 42 1066, ⓦoomuraya.net. At Kawayu Onsen, near Hongū, this family-run inn is steps away from the Sennin-buro river bath, and offers a delicious evening meal, as well as a hearty breakfast and gourmet boxed lunch the next day. The clean and spacious tatami rooms all have their own WC. **¥9600**

Yoshinoya よしのや Yunomine ☎0735 42 0101, ⓦyunomine.com. This friendly inn, right on the narrow stream near the ancient Tsuboyu, has clean and comfortable tatami rooms, its own pleasant outdoor bath and meals featuring delicious local cuisine. **¥22,400**

EATING

TANABE

★**Kanteki** かんてき Tanabe ☎0739 26 1081. Friendly, and sometimes raucous, *izakaya* in the Ajikokoji area near the station with a fantastic menu of local fish and seafood dishes and *ume-shu* (plum wine). For around ¥3000 you can feast like a king. 5–11pm; closed Wed.

★**Shinbe** しんべ Tanabe ☎0739 24 8845, ⓦjpcenter .co.jp/shinbe. *Shinbe* serves delicious sashimi, sushi and fish dishes at very reasonable prices – top-quality sashimi platters are just ¥1800. The cheery chef will happily make recommendations from the menu for the best of the season. Mon–Sat 5–10.30pm.

THE NAKAHECHI ROUTE

Bocu 朴 Chikatsuyu ☎0739 65 0694, ⓦfacebook.com /cafebocu. Macrobiotic restaurant and bakery in a charming old farmhouse on the Nakahechi route. Delicious lunch sets, made with vegetables grown in the neighbouring field, are ¥1500. Wed–Sat 10am–4pm.

HONGŪ

Sangenjaya 三軒茶屋 Hongu ☎0735 42 1888, ⓦsangendyaya.com. At this small shop next to the Post Office, you can buy takeaway lunch packs of five fresh pieces of *mehari-zushi* for ¥700. 8am–5pm; closed Thurs & last Wed of the month.

IGA-UENO'S NINJA HERITAGE

During Japan's warring states period in the fifteenth century (see p.823), bands of mercenaries with advanced martial arts skills emerged, who were used by the ruling classes as spies and assassins. Excelling at espionage and possessing extraordinary abilities, the mercenaries – known as *shinobii* (though outside Japan they are mostly known as "**ninja**") – developed the art of **ninjutsu**, or stealth warfare. Two tribes of mercenaries dominated: the Koga of Shiga Prefecture, and the Iga of Mie Prefecture. Much of what is known about them today is based on myth and legends, but you can get a sense of their shadow world at Iga-Ueno's excellent **Ninja Museum** (伊賀流忍者博物館; Igaryū Ninja Hakubtsukan; 117-13-1 Ueno Marunouchi; daily 9am–5pm; ☏0595 23 0311, ⓦiganinja.jp). The exciting one-hour tour (¥756) here begins in a typical ninja house fitted with traps and hiding places, and includes demonstrations of the building's many tricks, including revolving doors and walls. After the tour, an interesting exhibition (with lots of ninja weaponry on display) details how the castle next door, Iga-Ueno-jō, was infiltrated using *ninjutsu* techniques. There's also a ninja show (¥400) which uses real weapons, as well as more fascinating displays in the gift shop.

It's possible to visit Iga-Ueno (伊賀上野) on the way from Osaka or Kyoto to Shima Hantō. See the local tourism association website for more information (ⓦiga-travel.jp).

7

NACHI-KATSUURA

★**Bodai** 母大 Nachi-Katsuura ☏0735 52 0039. Stylish restaurant directly opposite Kii-Katsuura Station serving super-fresh *maguro* tuna dishes. The *maguro chūtoro katsu* *teishoku* lunch set (¥1500), with tuna pieces delicately fried in breadcrumbs, is highly recommended. 11am–2pm & 5–11pm; closed Tues.

Shima Hantō

志摩半島

East of the Kii Hantō mountain ranges, on the far side of the Kii Peninsula, a small knuckle of land sticks out into the ocean. Known as **Shima Hantō**, this peninsula has been designated a national park, partly for its natural beauty but also because it contains Japan's spiritual heartland, **Ise-jingū**. Since the fourth century the Grand Shrine of Ise, on the edge of **Ise** town, has been venerated as the terrestrial home of the Sun Goddess Amaterasu, from whom it was once believed all Japanese emperors were descended. Beyond Ise it's **pearl** country. The world-famous Mikimoto company started up in **Toba** when an enterprising restaurant owner discovered the art of cultivating pearls, and now there's a whole island dedicated to his memory, **Mikimoto Pearl Island**. Today, most of the pearls are raised further east in **Ago-wan**, where hundreds of rafts are tethered in a beautiful, island-speckled bay. The **Ama women divers** of the peninsula have been diving for seafood, and pearls, for centuries, and it's possible to meet them at **Osatsu** and hear their stories of the sea.

Ise

伊勢

The town of **ISE** wears its sanctity lightly, and many visitors find the town a disappointingly ordinary place. However, the main reason to come here is to visit the two sanctuaries of Japan's most sacred Shintō shrine, **Ise-jingū**; even non-Japanese visitors will appreciate the spiritual atmosphere of these simple buildings, with their unusual architecture, deep in the cedar forests.

Ise-jingū

伊勢神宮・☏0596 24 1111, ⓦisejingu.or.jp

The two sacred sanctuaries of **Ise-jingū** are in separate locations in the town of Ise. The **Naikū**, or inner shrine, is some 6km to the southeast of town, while the southwestern quarter of Ise is taken up by a large expanse of woodland (which accounts for a full

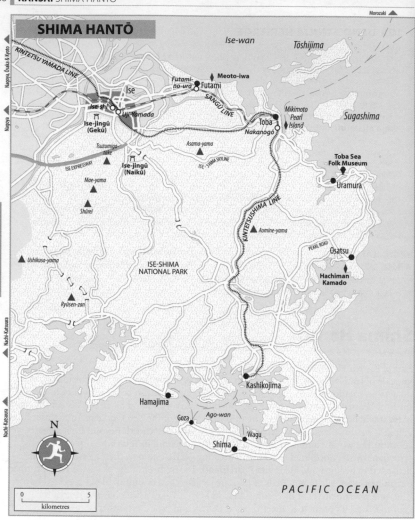

SHIMA HANTŌ

Nagoya, Ōsaka & Kyoto

KINTETSU TAMADA LINE

Ise-wan

Tōshijima

Nagoya

Futami-
no-ura

Meoto-iwa

Futami

Ise

SANGŪ LINE

Sugashima

Ise-shi

Uji-Yamada

Toba

Mikimoto
Pearl
Island

**Ise-jingū
(Gekū)**

Nakanogō

Tsuzumiga-
take

Asama-yama

Toba Sea
Folk Museum

ISE EXPRESSWAY

**Ise-jingū
(Naikū)**

ISE-SHIMA SKYLINE

Uramura

Mae-yama

KINTETSUSHIMA LINE

Shūrei

Aomine-yama

PEARL ROAD

Ōsatsu

Ushikusa-yama

ISE-SHIMA
NATIONAL PARK

**Hachiman
Kamado**

Ryūsen-zan

Nachi-Katsuura

Kashikojima

Nachi-Katsuura

Hamajima

Goza

Ago-wan

Wagu

Shima

N

PACIFIC OCEAN

0   5
kilometres

third of the town's area), in the midst of which lies the **Gekū**, or outer shrine. The two shrines follow roughly the same layout, so if you're pushed for time, head straight for the more interesting Naikū.

THE REBIRTH OF *NAIKŪ* AND *GEKŪ*

According to custom, both the **Naikū** (inner shrine) and **Gekū** (outer shrine) are rebuilt every twenty years in order to re-purify the ground. Each is an exact replica of its predecessor, following a unique style of architecture that has been passed down over the centuries and is free of any of the Chinese or Korean influences usually found in Buddhist architecture. Only plain *hinoki* (Japanese cypress) and grass thatch are used, plus a few gold embellishments. When the buildings are dismantled, the old timbers are passed on to other shrines around the country to be recycled. The next rebuilding will be in 2033.

ISE-JINGŪ EVENTS AND CEREMONIES

Ise-jingū is a top choice for the **first shrine visit** of the New Year (*hatsu-mōde*) on January 1. This is followed by more than 1500 annual **ceremonies** in honour of Ise's gods. The most important of these revolve around the agricultural cycle, culminating in offerings of sacred rice (Oct 15–17). In spring (April 5–6) and during the autumn equinox (Sept 22 or 23), ancient Shintō dances and a moon-viewing party take place at the inner shrine.

Naikū

内宮 • 1 Ujitachi-chō • Sunrise–sunset • Free • Take bus #51 or #55 from JR Ise-shi Station, Kintetsu Uji-Yamada Station, or from the stop outside the Gekū (every 10–15min; ¥410)

The **Naikū**, Ise-jingū's inner shrine, is Japan's most sacred shrine and was established sometime in the fourth century. Dedicated to **Amaterasu Ōmikami**, the ancestress of the imperial family, the shrine houses a **mirror** that Amaterasu gave her grandson Ninigi-no-Mikoto when she sent him to rule Japan. At first the mirror was stored in the Imperial Palace, along with the sacred sword and beads (these are now held in Nagoya's Atsuta-jingū and Tokyo's Imperial Palace), but the goddess gave instructions to move her mirror to somewhere more remote. Eventually they settled on a wooded spot beside Ise's Isuzu-gawa, which has been the mirror's home ever since.

After crossing the Uji-bashi, turn right and walk through a small, formal garden to reach the purification fountain just in front of the first sacred *torii*. A little further on, the path goes down to the river where, traditionally, pilgrims would purify themselves. The path loops round to approach the **inner sanctum** from the south. The main building is contained within four increasingly sacred enclosures, with the inner sanctum the furthest from view, making it difficult to see the details. Only members of the imperial family and head priests can enter the inner sanctuary where Amaterasu's **sacred mirror** is enshrined. It's wrapped in layers of cloth and, according to the records, no one has laid eyes on it for more than a thousand years.

Gekū

外宮 • Toyokawa-machi • Sunrise–sunset • Free • A 15–20min walk from from JR Ise-shi and Kintetsu Uji-Yamada stations, or buses #55 or #51 from the Naikū (every 10–15min; ¥410) will drop you at the bus stop on the main road opposite the Gekū's main entrance

The **Gekū**, or outer shrine, is located close to the southern edge of the modern business district of Ise city, and is much smaller, with fewer crowds, than Naikū. Its entrance lies over a small humped bridge and along a gravel path leading into the woods. It was constructed in the fifth century to honour the goddess **Toyouke-no-Ōmikami**, who was sent by Amaterasu to look after the all-important rice harvests. Another of her duties is to provide Amaterasu with sacred food, so twice a day priests make offerings to Toyouke in a small hall at the back of the compound. Having paid their respects to Toyouke by bowing deeply twice, clapping and bowing deeply a third time, most people hurry off to visit the Naikū.

Oharai-machi

おはらい町 • 48 Ujinakanokiri-chō • ☎ 0596 28 3705

Not far from the entrance to the Naikū, the pedestrianized shopping street of **Oharai-machi** sits on the exact site of the town's late Edo- and early Meiji-era merchants' quarter, and the buildings here are authentic reproductions of those that existed in that time. Despite being rather touristy, it's one of the nicest streetscapes in western Japan to stroll around, and there are also some decent places to eat local cuisine (see p.540).

Okageza History Museum

おかげ座 • 52 Ujinakanokiri-chō • Daily 10am–4.30pm • ¥300 • ☎ 0596 23 8844

Just off Oharai-machi, the Okage-Yokochō (おかげ横町) square is home to more replica Edo- and Meiji-era buildings, including the quaint **Okageza History Museum**. The museum re-creates the encounters between pilgrims and the people of Ise during the Edo period, using scale models and recordings of Edo-period stories and street sounds (in Japanese). On entering the museum, you'll be given a short introduction by the staff in Japanese, but after that you're free to wander unaccompanied, and an English-language pamphlet is provided that adequately explains the exhibits.

ARRIVAL AND GETTING AROUND

By train Regular trains run to Ise from Nagoya, Kyoto and Osaka: in all cases the private Kintetsu network offers the quickest and most convenient service. There are two stations in central Ise, with the more easterly, Uji-Yamada Station, being Kintetsu's main station. However, some Kintetsu trains also stop at Ise-shi Station, which is shared with JR. From Nagoya the fastest option is an express on the Kintetsu-Ise line to Uji-Yamada Station (hourly; 1hr 25min; ¥2770). If you've got a JR Pass, you can use JR's limited express trains direct from Nagoya to Ise-shi (hourly; 1hr 30min), though you have to pay a small supplement (¥470) for travelling on a section of Kintetsu track. Kintetsu also runs direct trains from Osaka's Namba and Tsuruhashi stations (every 15min; 1hr 45min; ¥3120) and from Kyoto (hourly; 2hr; ¥3620).

Destinations Futaminoura (1–3 hourly; 6min); Kashikojima (1–3 hourly; 50min–1hr); Kyoto (hourly; 2hr); Nagoya (every 20–30min; 1hr 25min–1hr 35min); Nara (every 15–20min; 2–3hr); Osaka (every 15min; 1hr 45min); Toba (every 20–30min; 15–20min).

By bus Each train station has its own bus terminal, with regular departures for the two shrines; buses #51 and #55 run via the Gekū to Naikū, after which the #51 route circles back round to the stations. There are also 7 buses daily to Toba (1hr).

By car Car rental is available through Kinki Nippon Rent-a-Car (📞 0596 28 0295), at Uji-Yamada Station, and Eki Rent-a-Car (📞 0596 25 5019), at Ise-shi Station.

By bike Bike rental is available at Ise-shi Station (daily 8.30am–5pm; ¥800 per day).

INFORMATION AND TOURS

Tourist information Ise's main tourist information office (daily 8.30am–5pm; 📞 0596 23 3323, 🌐 ise-kanko.jp /english) is located opposite the entrance to the Gekū, with a smaller office opposite the bus stop at the Naikū (daily 8.30am–4.30pm; 📞 0596 24 3501). At Uji-Yamada Station there is a helpful office with English-speaking staff (daily 9am–5.30pm; 📞 0596 23 9655), who can help arrange accommodation throughout the Shima Hantō area.

Tours Tours of both Ise-jingu sanctuaries with English-speaking guides can be arranged in advance through the local volunteer guide organization (📧 kk_sta@kanko-pro .co.jp).

ACCOMMODATION

Hoshidekan 星出館 2-15-2 Kawasaki 📞 0596 28 2377, 🌐 www.hoshidekan.jp. This eccentric, rambling old ryokan has tatami rooms centred around a garden, all with shared bath and toilet facilities. They serve macrobiotic food in their restaurant for breakfast. **¥12,500**

Ise City Hotel 伊勢シティホテル 1-11-31 Fukiage 📞 0596 28 2111, 🌐 greens.co.jp. Fairly bland business hotel with English-speaking staff, rather small rooms and an in-house steak restaurant. They have a slightly more expensive annexe just along the road towards the Kawasaki district. **¥11,400**

★ **Ise Guesthouse Kazami** 風見荘 1-6-36 Fukiage 📞 0596 64 8565, 🌐 ise-guesthouse.com. Ise's best backpacker hostel, in a former ryokan, has clean, comfortable rooms and shared bathing facilities. Run by a punk rocker, it's a friendly, vibrant place with occasional live music performances. There's also a shared kitchen and bike rental (¥500/day). Dorms **¥2600**, doubles **¥6000**

Town Hotel Ise タウンホテル伊勢 1-8-18 Fukiage 📞 0596 23 4621. Small and reasonably priced business hotel right next to the train tracks. The rooms are functional and, thankfully, double-glazed. There's no in-house restaurant or food available here so you'll need to eat out. **¥9670**

EATING

Ise's **speciality foods** include lobster (*Ise-ebi*) and the rather salty *Ise udon*, which consists of thick, handmade noodles served in a thin soy sauce. Matsuzaka beef, marbled and fatty like its Kōbe cousin, is another local favourite. **Oharai-machi** (see p.539), a pedestrianized shopping street, is a better, and more interesting, choice for lunch than the Gekū area.

Akafuku 赤福本店 26 Ujinakanokiri-chō 📞 0596 22 7000, 🌐 akafuku.co.jp. A 300-year-old sweet shop near the Shinbashi bridge on Oharai-machi that serves the local speciality – *akafuku mochi*, deliciously fresh pounded rice cakes covered with red bean paste (¥290 for three pieces including tea, or ¥550 with *matcha*). Daily 9am–5pm.

★ **Daiki** 大喜 2-1-48 Iwabuchi 📞 0596 28 0281, 🌐 ise .ne.jp/daiki. Touted as "Japan's most famous restaurant", *Daiki* has made its name catering to the imperial family. It's located in a traditional building near Uji-Yamada Station, and serves great bentō lunch sets (¥1000), as well as excellent-value *kaiseki* and *Ise-ebi* sets (both from ¥5000).

Daily 11am–9pm.

Kura de Pasta 蔵でパスタ 1-10-39 Miyajiri ☎ 0596 63 8555, ⓦ koujiya-ise.com/kura. Italian restaurant in a converted soy-sauce warehouse, with local specialities such as *Ise-ebi* (lobster) and Matsuzaka beef on the menu. Lunch sets (¥1000) include salad and a drink, and there is a variety of dinner courses (from ¥2250). Daily 11am–2pm & 5.30–9.30pm.

Okadaya 岡田屋 31 Ujimazaike-chō ☎ 0596 22 4554.

Very popular *Ise udon* restaurant in the main part of Oharai-machi. Their lunch sets (¥1350) are good value. Arrive early to avoid the long queues. 10.30am–5pm; closed Thurs.

Yamaguchi-ya 山口屋 1-1-18 Miyajiri ☎ 0596 28 3856, ⓦ iseudon.jp. Very friendly *Ise udon* restaurant down a shopping street across from the JR station, serving excellent, tasty udon noodles (¥500), as well as soba (¥550) and tempura (¥800). 10am–6.45pm; closed Thurs.

Toba and around

鳥羽

East of Ise, the ragged Shima Peninsula juts out into the Pacific Ocean. Most of this mountainous area belongs to the Ise-Shima National Park, whose largest settlement is the port of **TOBA**, home to the birthplace of cultured pearls, the famous **Mikimoto Pearl Island**. Although it's sited on an attractive bay, Toba's seafront is mostly a strip of car parks, ferry terminals and shopping arcades, behind which run the main road and train tracks. There is, however, a decent **aquarium** and an abundance of excellent seafood restaurants.

Mikimoto Pearl Island

ミキモト真珠島, Mikimoto Shinju-shima • Daily: Jan–Nov 8.30am–5pm; Dec 9am–4.30pm • ¥1500 • ☎ 0599 25 2028 • A 5min walk south of Toba's train and bus stations

In 1893, **Mikimoto Kokichi** (1858–1954), the son of a Toba noodle-maker, produced the world's first cultivated pearl using tools developed by a dentist friend. Just six years later he opened his first shop in Tokyo's fashionable Ginza shopping district, from where the Mikimoto empire spread worldwide. His life's work is commemorated – and minutely detailed – on **Mikimoto Pearl Island**, a complex of shops, restaurants and exhibition rooms, that is connected to the mainland by a short bridge. Devoted to the history and cultivation of pearls, the exhibitions are extremely well put together, with masses of information in English describing the whole process from seeding the oyster to grading and stringing the pearls. There's also a section devoted to Mikimoto's extraordinary pearl artworks and jewellery collection. The highlight of the visit is the **ama women divers** (see box, p.543), who stoically come out every hour in all weathers to demonstrate their diving skills.

Toba Aquarium

鳥羽水族館, Toba Suizokukan • 3-3-6 Toba • Daily: April–Oct 9am–5pm; Nov–March 9am–4.30pm • ¥2500 • ☎ 0599 25 2555, ⓦ aquarium.co.jp

Right on Toba seafront, next to Mikimoto Pearl Island, the **Toba Aquarium** is one of only two places in the world to house a captive dugong. This large aquarium is divided into twelve zones and has finless porpoises and sea otters on display, as well as sea lions and walruses.

Meoto-iwa

夫婦岩 • 575 Futami-chō • Daily dawn–dusk • ☎ 0596 43 2020 • 15min walk northeast of JR Futami-no-ura Station

Between Ise and Toba, the coastal town of Futami (二見) is famous for its "wedded rocks", **Meoto-iwa**. Joined by a hefty, sacred rope, this pair of "male" and "female" rocks lies just offshore from the Okitama shrine. They're revered as representations of Izanagi and Izanami, the two gods who created Japan, and it's the done thing to see the sun rise between them – the best season to do this is from May to August. On a clear day, you can also see Mount Fuji in the distance from above the rocks.

7

Toba Sea Folk Museum

海の博物館, Umi no Hakubutsukan • Uramura-chō • Daily: mid-March–Nov 9am–5pm; Dec to mid-March 9am–4.30pm • ¥800 •
☎ 0599 32 6006, ⓦ umihaku.com • The museum is on the Pearl Road driveway; take the Kamome bus for Ijika (石鏡) from the bus
terminal in front of Toba Station (hourly; 37min; ¥560), and get off at the Umi-hakubutsukan-mae (海博物館前) stop, from where it's
a 7min walk down the hill

The excellent **Toba Sea Folk Museum**, located 10km south of Toba in **Uramura**, is
housed in an award-winning wooden building overlooking the ocean. It houses some
informative 3-D exhibits on the historical relationship between the people of Toba and
the sea, as well as a short film and some comprehensive displays providing more
historical background on the *ama* women divers (see box opposite).

ARRIVAL AND DEPARTURE   TOBA

By train Kintetsu (¥300) and JR (¥240) trains both run
east from Ise to Toba. JR services are less frequent and
terminate at Toba, while the Kintetsu line continues south
to Kashikojima, for Ago-wan. Toba's JR and Kintetsu
stations and the bus terminal are all located next door to
each other in the centre of town.
Destinations Kashikojima (every 30min; 30–40min);
Kyoto (hourly; 2hr 20min); Nagoya (every 20–30min; 1hr
45min); Osaka (every 20–30min; 2hr).
By bus From Ise, the best option is the "Canbus" bus
service (Mon–Fri hourly, Sat & Sun every 30min), which

departs from Uji-Yamada Station and stops at all the major
sights and train stations between Ise and Toba, including
the inner and outer shrines, and Mikimoto Pearl Island.
One-day (¥1000) and two-day (¥1600) passes for the
"Canbus" can be bought at major train stations, the Gekū
tourist information office, Mikimoto Pearl Island and on the
bus; both passes come with a book of coupons offering
further discounts to attractions.
By ferry Isewan Ferry (☎ 0599 25 2880, ⓦ isewanferry
.co.jp) connects Toba with Irago, on the other side of Ise Bay
in Aichi prefecture (¥1550; 8 daily; 55min).

INFORMATION AND TOURS

Tourist information There's a very helpful tourist
information office with English-speaking staff (daily
9am–5pm; ☎ 0599 28 0001) in Kintetsu Station. The entire
station area is also a free wi-fi zone: tourist office staff can
give you the password.
Tours The Kaito Yumin Club (☎ 0599 28 0001, ⓦ oz-group.jp)

is run by a friendly all-female crew who lead eco-tours in
and around the Toba area. They offer lunch trips to fishing
villages by boat (¥7080), kayaking day-trips (¥7000) and
snorkelling tours (¥4800), as well as night-walking tours of
Toba (¥4500). Their office is next to the *Kaigetsu Inn*, a 3min
walk from Toba Station.

ACCOMMODATION

Kaigetsu Inn 海月 1-10-52 Toba ☎ 0596 26 2056,
ⓦ kaigetsu.co.jp. This friendly ryokan serves excellent
gourmet meals and is the best place to stay in Toba in terms
of convenience and value for money. The tatami rooms are
spacious and comfortable. Rates include breakfast. **¥12,000**
Road Inn Toba ロードイン鳥羽 1-63-11 Toba ☎ 0599
26 5678, ⓦ greens.co.jp/toba. This standard business
hotel is located on a hill behind the station, and has basic

but clean rooms, plus free internet. The sauna and
swimming pool next door can be used by guests. **¥9530**
Toba International Hotel 鳥羽国際ホテル 1-23-1
Toba ☎ 0599 25 3121, ⓦ tobahotel.co.jp. Pricey resort-
style hotel in a fine position on the headland overlooking
Toba Bay. Rooms are well appointed with marvellous views
and the in-house restaurant serves French cuisine. It takes
about 10min to walk from the station. **¥31,600**

EATING

Grand Blue グランブルー Ichibangai building,
opposite Toba Station ☎ 0599 26 3129. Café specializing
in "Tobarger" (Toba burgers), made with lobster, octopus
and other seafood patties (¥760). It's also a pleasant place
to sit and look out onto the harbour. Daily 10am–5pm.
Kippei 吉平 Ichibangai building, opposite Toba Station
☎ 0599 26 2085. This small noodle restaurant does a hearty
bowl of *asari* (shellfish) soba for ¥850, and also serves the
local speciality, *Ise udon* (¥700). Daily 10am–5pm.
Nagatokan 長門館 1-10-45 Toba ☎ 0599 25 2006,
ⓦ nagatokan.co.jp. Popular seafood restaurant with

hearty lunch and dinner set meals (from ¥1730/¥3240
respectively). They specialize in *awabi* (abalone) and *Ise-
ebi* lobster dishes. 11am–7pm; closed Tues.
Tenbinya Honten てんびん屋本店 1-4-61 Toba
☎ 0599 25 2223. Located in the streets just inland from
Mikimoto Pearl Island, *Tenbinya* makes a great choice for a
very reasonably priced seafood dinner. The speciality is
ama no kamameshi (¥1240) – seafood caught by the *ama*
women divers, served with rice. There's another branch in
the Ichibangai building opposite Toba Station. Tues–Sun
11.30am–2pm & 5–10.30pm.

Ōsatsu

鳥羽

The coastal village of **ŌSATSU** is home to one of Japan's largest communities of **ama women divers**, with more than 150 women still practising this 2000-year-old tradition (see box below). Ōsatsu is one of the few places that you can meet the women in their *amagoya* huts, where they grill freshly caught seafood and are happy to chat with visitors.

Ōsatsu Ama Bunka Shiryōkan

相差海女文化資料館 • 1238 Ōsatsu-chō • Daily 9am–5pm • Free • ☎ 0599 33 7453

The small museum of **Ōsatsu Ama Bunka Shiryōkan** details the history and culture of the *ama* women divers in the Shima-Hantō area. It's a good first stop to gain some insight into the history and traditions of the practice, and some of the exhibits have English explanations. There's also quite a bit of diving equipment on display, and seasonal exhibitions of *ama*-inspired artworks.

Ishigami Shrine

石神さん, Ishigami-san • 1385 Ōsatsu-chō • Dawn–dusk • Free

Located within Shinmei-jinja (神明神社), the small **Ishigami Shrine** is dedicated to Ishigami-san, the female deity who is the guardian of the *ama* divers. The shrine is also known for its mystical powers, and can apparently grant special wishes to women. Not only *ama*, but women from all over Japan, visit the shrine to pray for safety and happiness, and on May 5 each year, hundreds of *ama* gather here for a special festival. You can buy special protective amulets from the shrine for ¥800.

7

Hachiman Kamado

はちまんかまど • 1094 Ōsatsu-chō • Daily by appointment • From ¥3240 (including seafood snack) • ☎ 0599 33 6145, ⊕ amakoya.com

The highlight of a visit to Ōsatsu is meeting the *ama* divers, and the star of the show at **Hachiman Kamado** (divers' hut) is octogenarian Nomura Reiko, a veteran diver. Nomura-san and her *ama* friends are very welcoming, and, as they grill freshly caught seafood, they will tell you their stories of the sea and the *ama* lifestyle. Unless you speak Japanese, however, it's best to come with an interpreter to help you chat with the women.

ARRIVAL AND INFORMATION | ŌSATSU

By bus To get to Ōsatsu, take the Kamome bus from Toba Station (10 daily; 50min; ¥600).

Tourist information There's an information desk in the Ōsatsu Ama Bunka Shiryōkan, 1238 Ōsatsu-chō (daily 9am–5pm; ☎ 0599 33 7453), which can help with accommodation and transport information for the area.

Tours The Kaito Yumin Club (☎ 0599 28 0001, ⊕ oz-group .jp) runs "Land of Ama Divers" tours from Toba to Ōsatsu, including a visit to the Ishigami shrine and an *amagoya* hut (3hr; ¥7000–8500).

THE *AMA* WOMEN DIVERS

The female diving culture of Ise-shima dates back to the earliest annals of Japanese history. Known as *ama* (海女, literally "sea woman"), the women **free-dive** for shellfish, such as oysters and abalone, as well as harvesting seaweed. On average they'll spend three to four hours a day in the water, going down to a depth of 10–15m without any breathing apparatus; some are still diving past the age of 70. *Ama* usually dive year-round, either in small groups, or from boats skippered by their husbands. The reason for women-only divers is that they can hold their breath longer than men and have an extra layer of insulating fat, which protects them from the freezing waters.

Traditionally, *ama* harvested seafood in Ise Bay and transported it to Ise-jingū, where they presented their catch as an offering. The women played a major role in the development of the **cultured pearl industry** in the nineteenth century, helping to gather the *akoya* pearl oysters. Today, there are approximately 1300 *ama* in the Toba area; they still wear the customary white outfits, which apparently scare off sharks, and which are also marked with special protective star-shaped charms to ward off bad luck.

BOAT TRIPS FROM AGO-WAN BAY

A choice of **sightseeing boats and ferries** leaves from the tiny Kashikojima (賢島) harbour at the end of the Kintetsu train line. For ¥1600 you can cruise in the **Esperanza**, a very tacky mock-Spanish galleon (50min; every 30min; 9am–4.30pm) which stops off at a pearl farm. There are also **small boats** called *yūransen* (遊覧船), which take you further in among the islands (50min–1hr; from ¥1400). The cheapest option is one of the infrequent passenger **ferries** called *teikisen* (定期船). There are two ferry routes: across to **Goza** (御座), on the long arm forming the bay's southern edge, and back via **Hamajima** (浜島) to the west of Kashikojima (1hr 15min; ¥1800 for the round-trip); or via Masaki island (間崎) in the middle of the bay to **Wagu** (和具), a village east of Goza (25min; ¥600 one-way). You can get tickets and information about the ferries and Spanish cruise boat from an office beside the harbour – on the right as you walk down from the station – or buy *yūransen* tickets from one of the small booths opposite.

Ago-wan

あご湾

The Shima Hantō ends in a bay of islands known as **Ago-wan**. With myriad coves and deep inlets, this huge, sheltered bay is scattered with wooded islands between which float banks of oyster rafts. For centuries, divers have been collecting natural pearls from its warm, shallow waters, but things really took off when Mikimoto (see p.541) started producing his cultured pearls in Ago-wan early in the twentieth century. The main reason to visit Ago-wan is to take a **boat trip** round the scenic bay (see box above) and see the pearl industry at work, including a visit to a pearl farm.

ARRIVAL AND INFORMATION

AGO-WAN

By train The Kintetsu line from Ise runs through Toba and terminates at Kashikojima Station, a minute's walk north of the harbour. Trains from Toba cost ¥470.
Destinations Ise (1–3 hourly; 50min–1hr); Kyoto (hourly; 2hr 45min); Nagoya (hourly; 2hr 15min); Osaka (hourly; 2hr 20min); Toba (every 30min; 30–40min).

Tourist information For local maps and general information, head to the *Kashikojima Ryokan Annaijo* (賢島旅館案内所; Tues, Wed & Fri–Sun 9am–4.30pm; ☎0599 43 3061), on the right-hand side as you come down the escalator leading from the train station to the pier.

ACCOMMODATION

★**Prime Resort Kashikojima** プライムリゾート賢島 3618-33 Ago-chō ☎0599 43 7211, ⓦmiyakohotels .ne.jp. Spanish-style resort villa hotel in a lovely setting overlooking a cove. The rooms are spacious and have balconies, and the in-house French and Japanese restaurants are excellent. **¥17,460**

Ryokan Ishiyama-sō 旅館石山荘 Yokoyama-jima ☎0599 52 1527, ⓦlosmen.info. A great place to spend the night on the small island of Yokoyama-jima (横山島). The English-speaking owner will come and collect you in his boat from a jetty near Kashikojima pier for the 2min trip

to the island. After dining on a scrumptious feast of fresh seafood in their restaurant you can watch the sun go down over Ago-wan. The rooms are mostly tatami-style, but they also have a few Western-style ones. **¥18,000**

Shima Kankō Hotel 志摩観光ホテル 731 Ago-chō ☎0599 43 1211, ⓦwww.miyakohotels.ne.jp/shima. This classic luxury hotel was spruced up for the G7 Summit, held here in 2016, and is now more modern in style and better equipped, though the quaint, old-fashioned service remains. It's in a magnificent position overlooking the bay, and the spacious rooms have wonderful views. **¥25,240**

Kōbe

神戸

The historic port city of **KŌBE**, the capital of Hyōgo-ken, is nestled on a sliver of land between the sea and the steep slopes of Rokkō-san, and is renowned for its cosmopolitan atmosphere, eclectic food scene and jazz clubs. Although it's more than twenty years since the 1995 **earthquake**, Kōbe has far from forgotten this horrific event: the **Disaster Reduction and Human Renovation Institution** documents the quake and its aftermath, while the **Tetsujin** robot monument is a reminder of the spirit and effort of Kōbe citizens in rebuilding their city. The **Kōbe City Museum**, covering the port's earlier illustrious history, is also worth a look, as is the space-age-looking **Fashion Museum** on the man-made Rokkō Island, east of the city harbour. For the best view of the whole city and the Inland Sea, take the **Shin-Kōbe Ropeway** up Rokkō-san to the Nunobiki Herb Garden, where you might also be lucky enough to see one of the many wild boars that roam the city's mountainous northern districts.

Brief history

Kōbe's history is dominated by two important events; the opening of Japan's ports to foreign trade in 1868, and the Great Hanshin Earthquake of 1995. Although it had been a port as long ago as the eighth century, Kōbe's fortunes really took off when **foreign traders** set up shop in the city in the latter part of the nineteenth century, bringing their

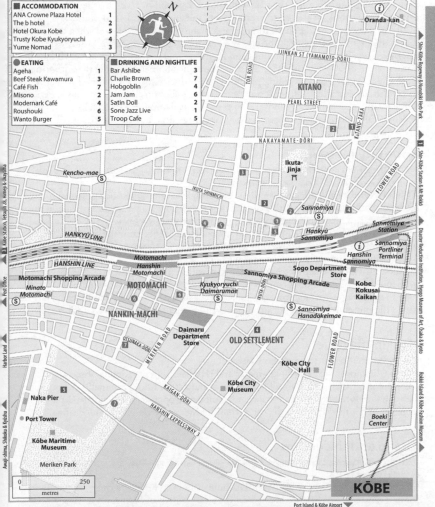

7

■ ACCOMMODATION	
ANA Crowne Plaza Hotel	1
The b hotel	2
Hotel Okura Kobe	5
Trusty Kobe Kyukyoryuchi	4
Yume Nomad	3

● EATING		■ DRINKING AND NIGHTLIFE	
Ageha	1	Bar Ashibe	3
Beef Steak Kawamura	3	Charlie Brown	7
Café Fish	7	Hobgoblin	4
Misono	2	Jam Jam	6
Modernark Café	4	Satin Doll	2
Roushouki	6	Sone Jazz Live	1
Wanto Burger	5	Troop Cafe	5

KITANO

IJINKAN ST (YAMAMOTO-DŌRI)

Oranda-kan

PEARL STREET

NAKAYAMATE-DŌRI

Kencho-mae

Ikuta-jinja

IKUTA SHINMICHI

Sannomiya

Hankyū Sannomiya

Sannomiya Station

Sannomiya Portliner Terminal

HANKYŪ LINE

HANSHIN LINE

Motomachi Hanshin

Hanshin Sannomiya

Motomachi Shopping Arcade

Minato Motomachi

Motomachi

Sannomiya Shopping Arcade

Sogo Department Store

Kobe Kokusai Kaikan

MOTOMACHI

Kyukyoryuchi Daimarumae

NANKIN-MACHI

Sannomiya Hanadokeimae

ŌTSUNAKA-DŌRI

Daimaru Department Store

OLD SETTLEMENT

Kōbe City Hall

KAIGAN-DŌRI

Kōbe City Museum

Naka Pier

Port Tower

HANSHIN EXPRESSWAY 3

Boeki Center

Kōbe Maritime Museum

Meriken Park

0   250
metres

KŌBE

> ### KŌBE ORIENTATION
>
> With its central area less than 3km wide, Kōbe is a great city for walking around. The city's sights are split into three main areas. South of the band of rail lines passing through Sannomiya Station is the commercial centre covering the **Old Settlement** area and, to the west, **Nankin-machi**, Kōbe's Chinatown. Immediately south of here are the **harbour** developments of Meriken Park, Kōbe Harbor Land, Port Island and Rokkō Island. North of Sannomiya Station lies Shin-Kōbe Station and **Kitano**, where the *ijinkan* (foreigners' houses) are clustered on the slopes of Maya-san.

new ways and styles of living with them. Japan got its first taste of beef and football in 1871 in Kōbe, the first cinema film was shown here in 1896, and the first golf course was laid down close to the city in 1903, designed by Arthur Gloom, a Brit. This trendsetting nature and booming trade made Kōbe very popular, and despite suffering heavy bombing during World War II, by the 1960s the city was bursting out of its narrow stretch of land between the mountains and the sea. A solution was found by levelling the hills and dumping the rubble in the sea to create Port Island and Rokkō Island in the bay.

All this came to a sudden halt, though, at 5.46am, January 17, 1995, when a devastating **earthquake** struck the city and surrounding area. As dawn broke, Kōbe resembled a war zone, with buildings and highways toppled, whole neighbourhoods in flames, some 6500 people dead and tens of thousands homeless. While the authorities were criticized for not responding promptly to the disaster, Kōbe recovered well and today the city bears little physical sign of the tragedy. Lessons learnt from this experience helped with relief efforts in Tōhoku after the 2011 tsunami (see box, p.225), and groups of Kōbe volunteers have also been active in assisting affected communities in Tōhoku.

Kōbe City Museum

神戸市博物館, Kōbe-shi Hakubutsukan • 24 Kyo-machi • Tues–Sun 10am–4.30pm • ¥200 • ☎ 078 391 0035, ⓦ city.kobe.lg.jp /museum/ • A 10min walk south of either Sannomiya or Motomachi stations

Around a century ago, the area south of Sannomiya Station was Kōbe's principal foreign settlement, although there's little evidence of it today. To get a better idea of what it once looked like, head for the **Kōbe City Museum**, which contains a finely detailed scale model of early twentieth-century Kōbe and many woodblock prints from the same era. The highlight of the museum, however, is its collection of *Namban* (southern barbarian) art. These paintings, prints and screens – some of extraordinary detail and beauty – by Japanese artists of the late sixteenth and seventeenth centuries, show how they were influenced by the art of the first Europeans, or "southern barbarians", to come to Japan. Due to their fragile nature, however, only a few of these artworks are on display at any one time. The museum will close for major renovation work from early 2018 until late 2019.

Nankin-machi

南京町 • South of JR Motomachi Station • ⓦ nankinmachi.or.jp

Kōbe's Chinatown is called **Nankin-machi** and is packed with restaurants, shops and colourful street stalls which are all fairly touristy but add to Kōbe's international atmosphere. The entrance is marked by the ornate Choan-mon gate opposite the Daimaru department store. It's better to visit during the day as most businesses are closed by mid-evening.

Kitano and the *ijinkan*

北野 • 1km north of Sannomiya Station • *Ijinkan* daily 9am–5pm • Oranda-kan ¥700; other *ijinkan* range in price from free up to ¥1050 • ⓦ kobeijinkan.com

Of primary interest to the hordes of Japanese visitors to Kōbe are the *ijinkan*, the foreign residences of **Kitano**, located on the slopes north of Sannomiya. After Kōbe opened as an international port in 1868, dozens of Western-style brick and clapboard houses were built on the hillside. Fewer than thirty now remain, as virtually all the *ijinkan* had to be rebuilt after the 1995 earthquake, and most are now fairly tacky reconstructions heavily focused on souvenir sales. The most popular *ijinkan* is the **Oranda-kan**, the former home of the Dutch consul-general. The area also has some fashionable cafés, restaurants and shops, and is a pleasant place to explore.

Shin-Kōbe Ropeway and Nunobiki Herb Garden

Ropeway 新神戸ロープウェー・Daily: mid-March to mid-July & Sept–Nov Mon–Fri 9.30am–4.45pm, Sat & Sun 9.30am–8.30pm; mid-July to Aug 9.30am–8.15pm; Dec to mid-March 10am–5pm・¥900 one-way, ¥1400 return (includes garden admission)・**Garden** 布引ハーブ園, Nunobiki Habu-en・Daily 10am–5pm・¥200・☎ 078 271 1160, ⓦ kobeherb.com

From the top of Kitano, it's a short walk across to the **Shin-Kōbe Ropeway** near Shin-Kōbe Station. The cable-car provides sweeping views of the bay on the way up to the restful **Nunobiki Herb Garden**, a flower garden with a field of lavender and glasshouses stocked with more exotic blooms. Hiking up the hill along the course, starting behind Shin-Kōbe Station, takes around thirty minutes. Once you make it to the top, it's only a fifteen-minute climb to the picturesque **Nunobiki Falls**, a 43m-tall waterfall.

Meriken Park

メリケンパーク・ⓦ kobe-meriken.or.jp

Kōbe's **port** lies directly south of Nankin-machi and is marked by the waterfront **Meriken Park**, which houses the Kōbe Port Tower, the Kōbe Maritime Museum (see below) and, partly submerged in the harbour, an unusual memorial to the victims of the Great Hanshin Earthquake.

Kōbe Maritime Museum

神戸海洋博物館, Kōbe Kaiyō Hakubutsukan・2-2 Hatoba-chō・Tues–Sun 10am–4.30pm・¥600・☎ 078 327 8983, ⓦ kobe-meriken .maritime-museum.com

The filigree roof of the **Kōbe Maritime Museum**, a swooping white framework symbolizing waves and sails, is the city's most striking architectural feature. The museum itself contains detailed models of a wide range of ships and intriguing audiovisual displays, and has good English explanations, although it lacks the impact of its exterior.

Kōbe Harbor Land

神戸ハーバーランド・ⓦ harborland.co.jp

Just west of Meriken Park, directly across the bay, is the **Kōbe Harbor Land** development, where spruced-up brick wharf buildings are joined by modern shopping malls, a cinema complex and a huge Ferris wheel.

GIGANTOR: THE KŌBE TETSUJIN PROJECT

In Wakamatsu Kōen, one of the areas of Kōbe that was hardest hit by the 1995 earthquake, stands an impressive 18m-tall, fifty-tonne replica of the famous manga and anime robot **Tetsujin 28** (鉄人28号; ⓦ kobe-tetsujin.com), known as Gigantor outside Japan. The citizens of Kōbe raised US$1.4 million to build the giant-sized statue of this fictional robot as a symbol of the city's revival after the earthquake. The manga artist who created Tetsujin 28, Mitsuteru Yokoyama, was a native of Kōbe. His Tetsujin, literally "iron man", was the first giant robot to appear in manga, in 1956. Later, the manga was adapted into an animated television series, which was first broadcast in 1963. The full-scale robot has now become a popular hub for manga and anime-related events in Kōbe. To get to Wakamatsu Kōen, take the JR line from Sannomiya to Shin-Nagata Station.

Kōbe Fashion Museum

神戸ファッション美術館, Kōbe Fasshon Bijutsukan • 2-9-1 Koyochonaka • Tues–Sun 10am–5.30pm • ¥500 • ☎ 078 858 0050, Ⓦ fashionmuseum.or.jp • Take the Rokkō Line monorail from JR Sumiyoshi or Hanshin Uozaki stations to Island Centre Station (¥250); the museum is a couple of minutes' walk from the southeast exit

East of the city centre, on the artificially built Rokkō Island (六甲アイランド), the main attraction is the **Kōbe Fashion Museum**. Housed inside what looks like a docked *Starship Enterprise*, this museum is a must for fashionistas, with regular special exhibitions that mainly focus on historical developments and classic couture collections. There's also an extensive multilingual library of fashion magazines.

Disaster Reduction and Human Renovation Institution

人と防災未来センター, Hito to Bōsai Mirai Senta • 1-5-2 Kaigan-dōri • Tues–Thurs & Sun 9.30am–4.30pm, Fri & Sat 9.30am–6pm • ¥600 for both museums • ☎ 078 262 5050, Ⓦ dri.ne.jp • About a 10min walk from Hanshin Iwaya or JR Nada stations' south exits

The **Disaster Reduction and Human Renovation Institution** consists of two conjoined museums dedicated to the **Great Hanshin-Awaji Earthquake**. The Disaster Reduction Museum is the more interesting of the two, and its high-tech multimedia facilities, interactive exhibits and film screenings devoted to the 1995 disaster make this one of Kōbe's highlights. Queue in the lobby and you'll be led up to the fourth floor, where you'll see two short films, and experience the sensation of a tremor, before proceeding to the incredibly detailed exhibits. Audio guides are available, and there are often English-speaking volunteers on hand, some of them quake survivors, who are happy to answer questions.

Hyōgo Prefectural Museum of Art

兵庫県立美術館, Hyōgo Kenritsu Bijutsukan • 1-1-1 Kaigan-dōri • Tues–Sun 10am–5.30pm • ¥510, special exhibitions ¥1400 • ☎ 078 262 0901, Ⓦ artm.pref.hyogo.jp • About a 10min walk from Hanshin Iwaya or JR Nada stations' south exits

The Andō Tadao-designed **Hyōgo Prefectural Museum of Art**, adjacent to the Disaster Reduction and Human Renovation Institution, is highly recommended. Exhibitions tend to focus on artists from the prefecture, but as this includes the postwar Gutai – a controversial group of loosely aligned 1950s artists who went very much against the local grain with their stunts and visceral visual art – the quality is extremely high.

SAKE BREWING

The Nada (灘) sake-brewing district, 5km east of the commercial centre, and just inland from Rokkō Island, is home to more than forty breweries. Take the Rokkō Liner train to Minami Uozaki Station and walk five minutes east to the Uozaki-Gō area (魚崎郷). Here you can visit three **sake breweries** and see the production of sake, as well as sample a few free thimblefuls.

Hakutsuru 白鶴 4-5-5 Sumiyoshi Minami-machi ☎ 078 822 8907, Ⓦ hakutsuru.co.jp. This large brewing company has turned one of its original brewing houses into a museum, with an emphasis on the tradition of sake brewing. There's a free tasting after you've toured the exhibits. Call in advance to make a reservation. Daily 9.30am–4pm.

Hamafukutsuru 浜副鶴 4-4-6 Uozaki Minami-machi ☎ 078 411 8339, Ⓦ hamafukutsuru.co.jp. You can observe the brewing process from decks overlooking the production area (with simple explanations in English) at this brewery. Samples of Hamafukutsuru's sake are available after the brewery tour. Tues–Sun 10am–5pm.

Sakuramasamune 櫻正宗 5-10-1 Uozaki Minami-machi ☎ 078 411 2101, Ⓦ sakuramasamune.co.jp. Check out the historical exhibits and the in-house restaurant, *Sakuraen*, where you can enjoy lunch (from ¥1500) and dinner (from ¥4000) with the house brews. There's also a counter bar, *Sanbaiya*, where you can sample different grades of sake by the cup (from ¥310). 10am–10pm; closed Tues.

ARRIVAL AND INFORMATION

KŌBE

By plane The nearest airports to Kōbe are Kōbe Airport on Port Island (神戸空港ターミナル; ☏078 304 7777, ⓦkairport.co.jp/eng), which only handles domestic flights, and Kansai International Airport (関西国際空港; ☏072 455 2500, ⓦkansai-airport.or.jp), 35km south of Osaka, where international flights arrive. To get from Kōbe Airport to Sannomiya, take the Port Liner monorail (18min; ¥330). The most convenient way of getting directly to Kōbe from Kansai International Airport is by limousine bus (1hr; ¥1950), which drops passengers at Sannomiya Station.

Destinations from Kōbe Airport Ibaraki (3 daily; 1hr 15min); Kagoshima (2 daily; 1hr 10min); Nagasaki (4 daily; 1hr 15min); Naha (5 daily; 2hr 15min); Sapporo (6 daily; 1hr 50min); and Tokyo Haneda (9 daily; 1hr 15min).

By train Shinkansen trains stop at Shin-Kōbe Station (新神戸) at the foot of Rokkō-san, around 1km north of Sannomiya Station in downtown Kōbe. JR services and trains on the Hankyū and Hanshin lines stop at Sannomiya Station (三宮駅); Hankyū and Hanshin services are the cheaper way of connecting with Osaka and Kyoto if you're not using a JR Pass.

Shin-Kōbe Station (Shinkansen) destinations Fukuoka (Hakata Station; every 15min; 2hr 10min); Himeji (every 30min; 20min); Hiroshima (every 30min; 1hr 10min); Kyoto (every 10min; 30min); Nagoya (every 10min; 1hr 10min); Okayama (every 30min; 35min); Shin Osaka (every 10min; 15min); Tokyo (every 10min; 2hr 50min).

By bus Long-distance buses operated by JR Highway Buses (ⓦnishinihonjrbus.co.jp) and Willer Bus (ⓦwillerexpress .com) depart from Sannomiya.

Destinations Fukuoka (daily; 10hr); Kagoshima (daily; 12hr); Kumamoto (daily; 9hr); Tokyo (30 daily; 8hr); Tottori (7 daily; 3hr 10min); Uwajima (2 daily; 7hr 30min); Yokohama (8 daily; 9hr); and Yonago (6 daily; 4hr).

By ferry Ferries (ⓦorange-ferry.co.jp and ⓦhan9f.co.jp) from Shikoku, Kyūshū and Awaji-shima arrive at the Rokkō Island Ferry Terminal, east of the city. From here you can take the Rokkō Liner monorail to JR Sumiyoshi or Hanshin Uozaki stations, from where it's 10min to either JR Sannomiya or Hanshin Sannomiya stations. The Japan–China International Ferry Co (☏06 6536 6541, ⓦshinganjin .com) heads to Shanghai from Kōbe on alternate weeks.

Destinations Imabari (daily; 6hr 40min); Matsuyama (2 daily; 8hr); Ōita (daily; 12hr); Shinmoji (daily; 12hr); Takamatsu (5 daily; 3hr 30min); Shanghai (twice a month; 48hr).

Tourist information The main tourist information office (daily 9am–7pm; ☏078 322 0220) is at the eastern side of the south exit of JR Sannomiya Station. There's also an information counter inside Shin-Kōbe Station near the main Shinkansen gate (daily 9am–6pm; ☏078 241 9550), and a small tourist information office at the top of the Kitano slope, near the *ijinkan* (daily 9am–5pm; ☏078 251 8360).

GETTING AROUND

By bus The city loop tourist bus (¥260 per ride, or ¥660 for a day pass) runs a regular circuit around Kōbe's main sights, and gives substantial discounts to many of the city's major attractions (Mon–Fri 9am–5pm, Sat & Sun 9am–6pm).

Car rental Nippon Rent-a-Car (☏078 231 0067) has branches at Kōbe Airport and near Sannomiya Station.

ACCOMMODATION

ANA Crowne Plaza Hotel Kōbe ANAクラウンプラザホテル神戸 1-7-14 Kitano-chō ☏078 291 1121, ⓦanacrowneplaza-kobe.jp. This upmarket hotel occupies a soaring skyscraper next to Shin-Kōbe Station, with fantastic views from all rooms, great service and a good range of restaurants both in the hotel and the connected shopping plaza. **¥16,400**

The b Kōbe ザ・ビー神戸 21-5 Shimoyamate-dōri ☏078 333 4480, ⓦkobe.theb-hotels.com/en. An excellent mid-range choice right in the middle of Sannomiya, close to the main nightlife area. The stylish rooms are comfortable, though on the small side, and are equipped with large-screen TVs and "tower showers". There's a coffee lounge in the lobby. **¥9700**

★**Hotel Okura Kōbe** ホテルオークラ神戸 2-1 Hatoba-chō ☏078 333 0111, ⓦkobe.hotelokura.co.jp. Elegant luxury hotel with smartly designed rooms, beside the Port Tower. Facilities include tennis courts, pools and a fitness

centre. The in-house restaurants serve a variety of Japanese cuisines, as well as French and Chinese, and the dimly lit Emerald bar has all the right atmosphere for a quiet drink. Free shuttle to and from Sannomiya Station. **¥14,000**

Trusty Kōbe Kyūkyoryūchi ホテルトラスティ神戸旧居留地 63 Naniwa-machi ☏078 330 9111, ⓦtrusty.jp /kobe. Located in the Motomachi district, not far from Chinatown, this stylish hotel is a good mid-range option, with clean, if somewhat pokey, rooms. On the second floor there's a pleasant outdoor terrace café serving a good breakfast buffet. **¥15,800**

★**Yume Nomad** ユメノマド 1-2-2 Shinkaichi ☏078 576 1818, ⓦyumenomad.com. Friendly backpacker hostel in a converted ryokan with a stylish café and bar, as well as an art gallery that doubles as an occasional cinema. All rooms, both shared and private, have an attached shower/toilet, and there's a well-equipped kitchen for self-catering. Dorms **¥2400**, doubles **¥6200**

EATING

Kōbe's long history of international exchange has given it a reputation for having the best Western-style and ethnic cuisine **restaurants**, all aimed at Japanese palates. Despite the density of restaurants catering to Chinese and Indian cuisine, it can be difficult to find authentic dim sum or curry. The most cosmopolitan dining area is between Sannomiya Station and Kitano-zaka, where you can also find the local delicacy, **Kōbe beef** – expensive slices of meat heavily marbled with fat.

Ageha あげは 2-4-8 Nakayamate-dōri ☎078 321 2780, ⓦcafe-ageha.jp. This bright and friendly café serves healthy meals made from locally grown organic vegetables. The most basic lunch set is ¥1080, and includes soup and salad. For dinner, there is a range of options, including curry (¥1300) and steamed vegetables with home-made dipping sauce (¥1515). Mon–Thurs 11am–8pm, Fri–Sun 11am–9pm.

Beef Steak Kawamura ビーフステーキカワムラ 6F 1-10-6 Kitanagasa-dōri ☎078 335 0708, ⓦbifteck.co.jp /en. *Kawamura* serves award-wining local beef in an opulent setting complete with Greco-Roman statues and chandeliers. The deluxe Kōbe beef lunch sets start at ¥10,000, while set dinner courses cost from ¥13,000. It's also possible to order à la carte. Daily 11.30am–3pm & 5–9.30pm.

Café Fish カフェフィッシュ 2-8 Hatoba-chō ☎078 334 1820, ⓦcafe-fish.com. Easily recognizable by the giant metal fish outside, this funky warehouse-style café in Meriken Park serves tasty fish and seafood burgers (¥1620) and is a relaxing place to while away a few hours gazing out on the harbour. Daily 11am–10pm.

★**Misono** みその 7F & 8F 1-1-2 Shimoyamate-dōri ☎078 331 2890, ⓦmisono.org. This restaurant proudly boasts that it is the originator of the *teppanyaki* grilling technique, but it also has a reputation for serving top-quality local beef. Locals flock here for the 100g fillet (¥12,960), grilled expertly on the counter hotplates. Daily 11.30am–1.30pm & 5–9pm.

Modernark Cafe モダナークカフェ 3-11-15 Kitanagasa-dōri ☎078 391 3060, ⓦmodernark-café .chronocle.co.jp. This vegetarian restaurant is spacious, light and bursting with indoor plants. The daily lunch plate (¥1350) has a delicious selection of veggie dishes, and the evening à la carte menu includes chilli bean burrito (¥1100). Also recommended are the organic fresh juices and scrumptious desserts. Daily 11.30am–9.30pm.

Roushouki 老祥記 2-1-14 Motomachi-dōri ☎078 331 7714, ⓦroushouki.com. Extremely popular *buta-man* (steamed pork bun) restaurant that's been in business since 1915, when it mainly catered to homesick Chinese sailors. Buns are just ¥90 each. Arrive early so as not to be disappointed, because there is usually a long queue. Daily 10am–6.30pm.

Wanto Burger ワントバーガー 3-10-6 Shimoyamate-dōri ☎078 392 5177, ⓦwantoburger.com. Hipster diner serving the latest in local cuisine – the Kōbe beef burger. *Wanto* has a number of variations, starting with a simple hamburger (¥1800) and culminating in the Super Wanto Burger (¥3800), a heart-attack-inducing stack of beef, bacon and fried egg. Tues–Sun noon–9.30pm.

DRINKING AND NIGHTLIFE

While Kōbe doesn't have as strong a club scene as neighbouring Osaka, it does have a good range of **bars**, most clustered around Sannomiya and Motomachi, and all within easy walking distance of each other. As Kōbe is the birthplace of Japanese jazz, it's worth spending an evening in one of the city's **jazz clubs**.

BARS

Bar Ashibe バーあしべ 2-12-21 Shimoyamate-dōri ☎078 391 2039. Dark and moody bar with lots of intimate seating space plus an extensive, but rather expensive (from ¥1000), cocktail menu. Popular with both locals and the expat crowd. Daily 6pm–3am.

Charlie Brown チャーリーブラウン 1-2-15 Kaigan-dōri ☎078 393 1514. Retro-rockabilly bar, established in 1969, and located down an extremely narrow alleyway. Once inside, order a drink (there's no menu but they have the basics, from ¥800) and marvel at the memorabilia adorning the walls. No seating charge. Mon–Sat 6pm–1am.

Hobgoblin ホブゴブリン 4-3-2 Kano-chō ☎078 325 0830, ⓦhobgoblin.jp. Bustling British pub with live music and sports broadcasts. There's a range of local and imported draught beers (from ¥900 a pint) as well as a large bar-food menu that includes fish & chips (¥1500) and chilli beef nachos (¥800). ⓦ Mon–Sat 5pm–late.

CLUBS

★**Jam Jam** ジャムジャム B1 1-7-2 Motomachi ☎078 331 0876, ⓦjamjam-jazz-kobe.com. Cavernous basement jazz club with two types of seating – listening only, and quiet conversation. No requests are allowed, but the playlist here is unforgettable. Noon–11pm; closed first and third Mon of the month.

Satin Doll サテンドール 2F 1-26-1 Nakayamate-dōri ☎078 242 0100, ⓦsatindollkobe.jp. Cosy, relaxing live jazz club serving French cuisine (from ¥3800). The acts are mostly local amateurs and there are usually only one or two performances a night. Cover charge ¥500. Tues–Sun 6–11pm.

★**Sone Jazz Live & Restaurant Kitano-zaka** ソネ

Kitano-zaka ☎078 221 2055, ⓦkobe-sone.com. The birthplace of Japanese jazz, attracting many top international artists as well as local talent. The first live set starts around 7pm and there are four performances a night; cover charge from ¥1200. Daily from 5pm.

Troop Cafe トループカフェ B1 2-11-5 Kitanagasa-dōri ☎078 321 3130, ⓦtroopcafe.jp. Popular club with regular weekend events of mainly house, techno and bass music. Cover charge, including one drink, from ¥1500. During the week it's a restaurant serving dinner courses (Kōbe beef and vegetables course ¥2500). Daily from 5.30pm.

DIRECTORY

Emergencies The main police station is at 5-4-1 Shinoyamate-dōri (☎078 341 7441). There's also a police box opposite the information centre at the Sannomiya Station south exit. In an emergency, contact the Foreign Advisory Service on ☎078 291 8441.

Hospital and medical advice Kōbe Adventist Hospital, at 8-4-1 Arinodai, Kita-ku (☎078 981 0161, ⓦkahns.org), has many English-speaking staff, but is a 30min drive north of the city. Kōbe Kaisei Hospital, at 3-11-15 Shinohara Kitamachi, Nada-ku (☎078 871 5201, ⓦkobe-kaisei.org), has an international division with many English-speaking staff, but, like the Adventist Hospital, is a little awkward to reach, being a 15min walk uphill from Hankyū Rokkō Station. Kōbe University Hospital, at 7-5-2 Kusunoki-chō (☎078 382 5111, ⓦhosp .kobe-u.ac.jp/e), is a 10min walk north of Kōbe Station.

Post office Kōbe Central Post Office is a 2min walk northeast of JR Kōbe Station. There's also a convenient branch in the Kōbe Kokusai Kaikan Building, directly south of Sannomiya Station, as well as a small postage-only branch beneath JR Sannomiya Station.

Arima Onsen

有馬温泉

On the northern slopes of Rokkō-san, northeast of Kōbe, is one of Japan's oldest hot-spring resorts, **ARIMA ONSEN**. Since the seventh century, Arima has been famous for attracting emperors, shoguns and, in more modern times, the literati, all of whom have come to bathe in its healing gold and silver waters. It's even mentioned in the ancient chronicle the *Nihonshoki*. Toyotomi Hideyoshi brought the tea master Sen no Rikyū here in the sixteenth century to perform a tea ceremony, an event commemorated annually in November with the Arima Great Tea Ceremony.

Arima has two kinds of **mineral-rich hot springs**, both recognized for their numerous health benefits, as well as some top-class ryokan, where you can soak yourself in luxury on an overnight trip. If you are only here for the day, you can either take a dip in the **public baths**, or (more expensively) visit the spas of some of Arima's ryokan and hotels: the tourist office can tell you which private spas accept non-residents.

Kin no Yu

金の湯 • 833 Arima-chō • Daily 8am–9.30pm; closed second and fourth Tues of the month • ¥650 • ☎078 904 0680 • A 5min walk uphill from the train station, close to the bus station and tourist office

At the large **Kin no Yu** public bath, you can soak in the sludgy brown *kinsen* (gold spring) waters, at their source, and get relief for a wide variety of common health complaints, including some forms of rheumatism and sensitive skin. Don't be put off by the colour – after bathing here your skin will feel wonderfully soft, and the *kinsen* waters also have a relaxing effect. Outside the bathhouse there is a free *ashi-yu* footbath, as well as a fountain of drinkable spa water.

Gin no Yu

銀の湯 • 1039-1 Arima-chō • Daily 9am–8.30pm; closed first and third Tues of the month • ¥550 • ☎078 904 0256 • Gin no Yu is at the top of Negai-zaka slope past Nembutsu-ji temple, a 15min walk from the train station

The **Gin no Yu** public bath is much quieter than Kin no Yu and has a high ceiling with skylights; the light streaming in through the steam is quite spectacular. The clear *ginsen* (silver spring) waters are believed to be effective for curbing high blood pressure and improving blood circulation, and drinking the water is reputedly good for your digestive system.

ARRIVAL AND INFORMATION

ARIMA ONSEN

By train To reach the resort by train from Kōbe, take the subway from Sannomiya to Tanigami, then transfer to the Kōbe Dentetsu line to Arima Guchi (有馬口), where you may have to change again (same platform) to reach the terminus at Arima Onsen. The journey takes around 40min and costs ¥930. If you're coming from Osaka, take a local JR train to Sanda (JR Fukuchiyama line), where you can change to the Kōbe Dentetsu line. The journey costs ¥1340 and takes 1hr 20min.

By cable-car and ropeway A more scenic route from Kōbe to Arima Onsen, though a little more time-consuming and expensive than the train, is to take a cable-car and ropeway via Rokkō-san. Take the Hankyū line to Rokkō Station and then transfer by bus (10min; ¥230) to the Rokkō cable-car (daily 8.15am–4.35pm, until 7.35pm in summer; w rokkosan.com/en/cablecar) for the 10min trip

(¥590) to the Rokkō Arima Ropeway Station. From here, it's another 10min by ropeway to Arima Onsen (daily 9.30am–5.10pm; ¥1010; w koberope.jp/en/rokko).

By bus There are direct buses from Sannomiya (50min; ¥700) via Shin-Kōbe Station to Arima, as well as JR West Japan highway buses from Shin-Kōbe Station (50min; ¥750) via Sannomiya. From Osaka, comfortable air-conditioned coaches from the Hankyū Bus Station beneath Hankyū Umeda Station cost ¥1370 and take just over an hour.

Tourist information The Arima Onsen Tourist Information Center (daily 9am–7pm; ☏ 078 904 0708, w arima-onsen.com) is located uphill from the train station. You can pick up a handy English map of the town here, and arrange accommodation, though it's best to book in advance.

ACCOMMODATION

★**Kami-ō-bō** 上大坊 1175 Arima-chō ☏ 078 904 0531, w kamiobo.com. Small and friendly inn just up the main street from Kin no Yu which serves delicious seasonal *kaiseki-ryōri* (two meals included in rates). The tatami rooms are compact but comfortable. Non-residents can bathe in the onsen here too (daily 3–6pm; ¥1000). **¥30,240**
Nakanobō Zui-en 中の坊瑞苑 808 Arima-chō ☏ 078 904 0787, w zuien.jp/en. A superb Arima resort, which has hosted the likes of Princess Grace of Monaco as well as other international celebrities. There is a variety of plush Japanese- and Western-style rooms to choose from, all looking out onto carefully manicured gardens, and superb *kaiseki-ryōri* meals are served in your room. You can soak in

both Kin and Gin waters here, and there's also a private family bath that can be reserved by guests (¥2160/hr). **¥78,060**
★**Tosen Goshobō** 陶渓御所坊 858 Arima-chō ☏ 078 904 0551, w goshoboh.com/en. This is the top place to stay in Arima: there have been lodgings in this exact location since the twelfth century, and its current incarnation – a fusion of Japanese and Western styles – is the height of onsen sophistication. Fortunately, they serve lunch to non-guests (daily 11am–2pm; from ¥2950), and accept day visitors to their stylish baths (daily 11am–2pm; ¥1650); both are great opportunities to experience the tasteful surroundings if you're not staying. **¥67,400**

Himeji

姫路

Of Japan's twelve surviving feudal-era fortresses, by far the most impressive is the one in **HIMEJI**, 55km west of Kōbe. The fortress, **Himeji-jō**, made the memorable backdrop to the Bond adventure *You Only Live Twice*, as well as countless feudal-era dramas and the Tom Cruise film, *The Last Samurai*, part of which was filmed here and around the city. The splendid gabled donjons of Himeji-jō – also known as Shirasagi-jō, or "white egret castle", since the complex is supposed to resemble the shape of the bird in flight – miraculously survived the World War II bombings that laid waste to much of the city, and in 1993 the castle was added to UNESCO's World Heritage list.

Himeji is a welcoming city, and although it can be visited as a day-trip it's a pleasant place to stay overnight. Other sights include the beautiful **Himeji Kōko-en**, nine linked traditional-style gardens, and a couple of **museums** with outstanding architecture around the fortress walls.

Himeji-jō

姫路城 • 68 Hon-machi • Daily: April 27–Aug 9am–5pm; Sept– April 26 9am–4pm • ¥1000, or ¥1040 combined ticket with Kōko-en (see opposite) • ☎ 079 285 1146, ⓦ himeji-castle.gr.jp • Tours (1hr 30min; included in price) are in English, and guides are usually waiting at the main castle gate, but it's best to ask about the start time of the next tour when buying your ticket; if you don't have a guide, finding your way around the castle is no problem, since the route is clearly marked and there are English explanations on plaques at many points of interest

Around 1km directly north of Himeji Station lies the main gateway to **Himeji-jō**. The present complex of moats, thick defensive walls, keeps and connecting corridors dates from the early seventeenth century, although there has been a fortress in the town since around 1346. By the time Tokugawa Ieyasu's son-in-law, Ikeda Terumasa, took control of the area in 1600, the country was at peace, and so when he set about rebuilding Himeji-jō, adding the central five-storey donjon and three smaller donjons, the aim was to create something visually impressive. Even so, the castle incorporates many cunning defensive features, which are explained in detail if you go on one of the **free guided tours** in English.

Nishi-no-maru

西の丸

To the west of the main gateway, the Hishi-no-mon, are the open grounds of the **Nishi-no-maru** (western citadel), where the *daimyō* and his family lived; the central donjon was only used in times of war. All that remains of the original palace are the outer corridor and "cosmetic tower", where Princess Sen adjusted her kimono and powdered her nose in the mid-seventeenth century. It was Sen's dowry that enabled the castle to be built in its present form.

Honmaru

本丸

From the Nishi-no-maru, a zigzag path leads up through more gates and past turrets and walls – from which defending soldiers could fire arrows, shoot muskets and drop stones and boiling liquids – to the **Honmaru** (inner citadel), which is dominated by the magnificent central donjon, **Tenshū** (天守). There are six levels within the dark and chilly keep, supported by a framework of huge wooden pillars, one of which is made from a 780-year-old cypress tree;

Map: HIMEJI

Hyogo Prefectural Museum of History

0   250
metres

HIMEJI-JŌ

Okiku-ido
Daitenshū & Honmaru
Harakiri-maru
Nishi-no maru
Hishi-no-mon

Himeji Kōko-en

Himeji City Museum of Literature, Senhime Tenman-gū & ❶

ACCOMMODATION

Guesthouse Engakudo	1
Himeji 588 Guesthouse	2
Hotel Nikko Himeji	4
Hotel Wing International	3

Otemae-kōen

ROUTE 2

EATING

Avanzar Sushi Bar	5
Kassui-ken	1
Menme	3
Wakajishi	2
Zen	4

DRINKING

Public House Hosanna	1

ŌTEMAE-DŌRI

Miyuki-dōri Shopping Arcade

EKI HIGASHI-DŌI

JUNISHOMAE

Sanyo Himeji Station

Shinki Bus Terminal

JR Himeji Station

N

Okayama & Hiroshima

Kōbe & Ōsaka

touch it and it's said you'll have long life. On the top level, where the lord and his family would have committed suicide if the castle were captured (which it never was), you can look out across the city and see as far as the Inland Sea on clear days.

Himeji-jō Kōko-en

姫路城好古園 • 68 Hon-machi • Daily: Jan–April & Sept–Dec 9am–4.30pm; May–Aug 9am–5.30pm • ¥300, or ¥1040 combined ticket with the castle (see opposite); tea ceremony ¥500 • ☎ 079 289 4120

On the west side of Himeji-jō's moat is the splendid **Himeji-jō Kōko-en**, a reconstruction of samurai quarters built in 1992 on the former site of the Nishi Oyashiki, the *daimyō*'s west residence for his samurai. The nine connected Edo-period-style gardens are separated by rustic mud walls topped with roof-tiles, like those which would have stood around each samurai villa. In the gardens are mini-forests, carp-filled pools, rockeries and an elegant teahouse where you can experience the tea ceremony. The *Kassui-ken* restaurant (see p.556) is located in a teahouse in the gardens.

Hyōgo Prefectural Museum of History

兵庫県立歴史博物館, Himeji Bungaku-Kan, Hyōgo Kenritsu Rekishi Hakubatsuken • 68 Hon-machi • Tues–Sun 10am–4.30pm • ¥210 • ☎ 079 288 9011, ⓦ hyogo-c.ed.jp/~rekihaku-bo/english/about.html

The informative **Hyōgo Prefectural Museum of History**, on the northeast side of Himeji-jō's moat, is in a striking building designed by the founding father of modern Japanese architecture, Tange Kenzō. Inside are scale models of the twelve castle donjons across Japan that survive in their original form, as well as a display of children's culture, beginning in the Edo period, and an interesting multimedia exhibition on Himeji's festivals. The museum also provides three opportunities a day to try on a Heian-style twelve-layered court kimono and samurai armour (at 10.30am, 1.30pm & 3.30pm): apply at reception on arrival, as spaces are limited to one visitor per session.

Museum of Literature

姫路文学館, Himeji Bungakukan • 84 Yamanoi-chō • Tues–Sun 10am–4.30pm • ¥300 • ☎ 079 293 8228, ⓦ www.himejibungakukan.jp

Tange Kenzō's contemporary rival, Andō Tadao, has made his mark on Himeji at the city's **Museum of Literature**, some 600m directly west of the Museum of History across the moat and just beyond the entrance to Princess Sen's shrine, **Senhime Tenman-gū** (千姫天満宮). The exhibits inside the museum are mostly in Japanese (the English-language leaflet only gives a summary), but the displays are imaginative; Japanese literature enthusiasts will find the novelist Shiba Ryōtarō's (see box, p.687) Memorial Hall of interest. If nothing else, come here to admire Andō's ultra-modern design – a disjointed arrangement of squares, circles and walkways made from rough concrete.

ARRIVAL AND INFORMATION
HIMEJI

By train Himeji is a stop on the Shinkansen line between Osaka and Okayama, and is also served by slower but cheaper *shinkaisoku* (Special Rapid Service) trains, which take 40min from Kōbe or 1hr from Osaka. The train station is around 1km south of the castle at the end of Ōtemae-dōri (大手前通り), the main boulevard.

Destinations Fukuoka (Hakata Station; hourly; 2hr 15min); Hiroshima (every 30min; 1hr); Kōbe (every 30min; 20min); Kyoto (every 30min; 1hr); Nagoya (30 daily; 1hr 50min); Okayama (every 30min; 20min); Osaka (every 30min; 30min); and Tokyo (hourly; 3hr 40min).

By bus Long-distance highway buses from Tokyo (Shinjuku; daily; 9hr) stop at the south side of the JR Himeji train station. Buses from Osaka and Kōbe also pull in here, though it's much easier and quicker to travel from these destinations by train.

Tourist information Pick up a map from the excellent Himeji Kanko Navi Port (daily 9am–7pm; ☎ 079 287 0003, ⓦ himeji-kanko.jp) on the west side of the central entrance to the station, which is staffed by English-speakers between 10am and 3.30pm. They can also make accommodation bookings here, and lend out free bikes (see p.556). There's a smaller tourist information office near the castle, but it only has maps and can't help with accommodation or other enquiries.

GETTING AROUND

Loop bus The city "loop bus" (ループバス; every 15–30min: March–Nov daily 9am–4.30pm; Dec–Feb Sat & Sun only 9am–5pm) starts from the Shinki Bus Terminal outside Himeji Station and stops at all the major tourist attractions. Rides cost ¥100, though the one-day pass (¥300) offers good value as it includes a twenty percent discount on entry to a number of the city's major sights, including the castle and some of the museums.

Bike rental Himeji has a convenient free bicycle loan service for tourists. Bikes can be picked up between 9am and 4pm, from outside the station, and must be returned by 5.30pm. Apply and register at Himeji Kankō Navi Port (see p.555).

ACCOMMODATION

Guesthouse Engakudou 縁楽堂 8-2 Yanagi-machi ☏079 260 7373, ⓦengakudou.com. Tucked away in a residential area, this guesthouse is in a rambling 100-year-old house with lots of character. The tatami rooms are clean and comfortable, and there's a shared kitchen and bathroom. Just across the road is a new annexe with more dorm beds and a library. Dorms ¥2500, doubles ¥6000

★**Himeji 588 Guesthouse** ガハハゲストハウス 68 Hon-machi ☏079 283 2588, ⓦhimeji588.com. This super-friendly guesthouse is conveniently located at the castle end of the shopping arcade that runs from the train station. Run with great care by the lovely Kyoko-san, it has been nicely renovated and has good facilities. It's a great place to get insider information on Himeji and meet fellow travellers. Dorms ¥2700, doubles ¥6000

Hotel Nikkō Himeji ホテル日航姫路 100 Minami-eki-mae ☏079 222 2231, ⓦhotelnikkohimeji.co.jp. Himeji's best upmarket option, conveniently located close to the station. The rooms are fairly spacious and some of the higher floors have good views of the castle. There are four in-house restaurants and a gym. ¥23,000

Hotel Wing International ホテルウィングインタナーショナル 132 Wata-machi ☏079 287 2111, ⓦhimeji .hotelwingjapan.com. Stylish budget hotel with castle views from some floors, and compact, comfortable rooms. Breakfast is optional (¥800). ¥10,500

EATING

The Miyuki-dōri covered shopping arcade (みゆき通り), one street east of Ōtemae-dōri, is a good place to stop for a snack or pick up a bentō to enjoy within the castle grounds. There are also several good lunch options closer to the castle.

★**Avanzar Sushi Bar** あばんさーる 227 Ekimae-chō ☏079 282 8866. Modern sushi restaurant run by the local fisheries co-op, and an excellent choice for lunch or dinner. Individual sushi pieces start at ¥120, and the chef's selection sushi plate is a very reasonable ¥1600. 11am–3pm & 5–10pm; closed Wed.

Kassui-ken 活水軒 68 Hon-machi ☏079 289 4131. Classic teahouse within Himeji Kōko-en serving the local speciality *anago* (grilled conger eel) cuisine. The *anago-don* set lunch, served with tempura, pickles and miso soup (¥1350), is the best deal here. Daily 10am–4.30pm.

Menme めんめ 68 Hon-machi ☏079 225 0118. A specialist udon shop, with noodles made on the premises throughout the day and a variety of healthy toppings such as tofu and vegetables to choose from. Bowls of noodles start at ¥550. 11.30am–7pm; closed Wed.

Wakajishi 若獅子 195-2 Soshahon-machi ☏079 282 5676. This family-run restaurant serves delicious home-style *teishoku* meal sets with generous portions from ¥600. The friendly English-speaking waitress will explain the day's specials. Daily 11am–1pm & 5–9pm.

Zen ぜん 96 Motoshio-machi ☏079 288 1039. Ramen noodle restaurant serving top-quality fusion Japanese and Asian fare at reasonable prices. The spring roll lunch set (¥800) is excellent value, while the evening à la carte menu offers some tasty stir-fries with seasonal ingredients (¥950). There's no English menu but the staff are helpful. 11am–2pm & 6–11pm; closed Wed.

DRINKING

Public House Hosanna パブリックハウスホサンナ 9 Tate-machi ☏079 288 3289, ⓦpub-hosanna.com. Cosy British-style pub-restaurant with ten local and imported draught beers on tap, and a wine bar. The food is a mishmash of typical *izakaya* fare, fish and chips (¥1420) and pizza (¥1360). Tues–Sun 5pm–midnight.

Kinosaki Onsen

城崎温泉

If you're after an indulgent onsen experience, the atmospheric town of **KINOSAKI ONSEN**, in the northern part of Hyōgo prefecture, is well worth the journey. Hot-spring aficionados flock here in droves – especially in the winter months – to soak in the therapeutic waters and feast on *kani* (crab) from the nearby Sea of Japan. There are seven hot-spring public **bathhouses** (known as *soto-yu*), but most of Kinosaki's ryokan also have their own private hot springs (*uchi-yu*). Because of its compact size, the town is easily explored on foot, and many visitors enjoy strolling along the ryokan-lined streets and willow-fringed canal in *yukata* (cotton kimono) and *geta* (wooden shoes); overnight stays usually include *yukata* rental and a pass to all of the public onsen.

Kō no Yu

鴻の湯 • 610 Yushima • 7am–11pm; closed Tues • ¥600 • ☎ 0796 32 2195 • A 20min walk from the train station

Kinosaki's oldest bathhouse is **Kō no Yu**, which according to legend was built on the spot where a stork was seen bathing its wounds over 1400 years ago. It is also the furthest away from the train station, and is therefore less hectic than Kinosaki's other bathhouses and perfect for a peaceful and relaxing soak.

Gosho no Yu

御所の湯 • 448 Yushima • Daily 7am–11pm; closed first and third Thurs of the month • ¥800 • ☎ 0796 32 2230 • A 15min walk from the train station

A dip in the waters at **Gosho no Yu** is believed to be not only beautifying but to make you lucky in love, too. The public bathhouse has both inside and outside baths (including a two-level rotemburo), and an entrance built in the opulent style of Kyoto's Imperial Palace. Other regal touches include painted screens and an abundance of *momiji* (maples) in the garden.

Sato no Yu

さとの湯 • 290-36 Imazu • Tues–Sun 1–9pm • ¥800 • ☎ 0796 32 0111

Located right next to the train station, **Sato no Yu** is Kinosaki's largest and most modern bathing complex, with Japanese- and Western-style baths that alternate between women and men on a daily basis. Facilities include jet baths, vapour baths and even an ice sauna. The rotemburo on the third floor has excellent views of the town.

ARRIVAL AND INFORMATION

KINOSAKI ONSEN

By train Kinosaki Onsen is on the JR San'in line, making it accessible from Tottori to the west, or from Kōbe, Kyoto or Osaka to the south. If you're approaching from Amanohashidate, take the Kyoto Tango Railway to Toyooka (hourly; 1hr 30min) and then change to the JR San'in line.
Destinations Kōbe (3 daily; 2hr 30min); Kyoto (6 daily; 2hr 30min); Osaka (7 daily; 2hr 40min); Tottori (hourly; 1hr 30min).

By bus There are direct buses from Osaka (Umeda; 2 daily; 3hr 20min) and Kōbe (Sannomiya; 1 daily; 3hr 10min).
Tourist information The Sozoro Kinosaki Onsen Tourist Information office (daily 9am–7pm; ☎ 0796 32 0013, ⓦ global.kinosaki-info.com) is run by a local bus company and located in front of the train station. They provide information in English and free wi-fi, and also rent out bikes and run local tours.

ACCOMMODATION

★ **Mikuniya** 三国屋 221 Yushima ☎ 0796 32 2414, ⓦ kinosaki3928.com. This friendly ryokan has Japanese-style rooms and serves delicious crab and Tajima beef cuisine. Three *uchi-yu* (hot springs) can be reserved for private use, and spa treatments such as massages (from ¥4000 for 40min) are available. **¥25,920**
Nishimuraya Honkan 西村屋本館 469 Yushima ☎ 0796 32 2211, ⓦ nishimuraya.ne.jp. This luxurious traditional ryokan is one of the best places to stay in Kinosaki. Some rooms have balconies with pleasant garden

views, while others have private gardens and baths. *Nishimuraya* also serves elaborate seasonal meals, such as *kaiseki* course dinners that include crab. **¥99,360**
Ryokan Yamamotoya 旅館山本屋 643 Yushima ☎ 0796 32 2114, ⓦ kinosaki.com. Proudly boasting that it is the oldest ryokan in Kinosaki, *Yamamotoya* has kept up with the times and has added a bar serving local brews that's very popular with guests. Most of the Japanese-style rooms have views over the canal, and *Yamamotoya*'s crab cuisine is excellent. **¥52,400**

Western Honshū

TOMONOURA PORT

Western Honshū

Long ago, western Honshū stood at the centre of the Japanese nation, sited between the country's earliest settlements in Kyūshū and the imperial city of Kyoto. Hence the region's official name, *Chūgoku*, which means "middle country" and is spelled with the same *kanji* that designates "China" in Japanese. It consists of two distinct geographical areas – the southern San'yō coast, which is blighted by heavy industry but borders the enchanting Inland Sea, and the rugged and sparsely populated northern San'in coast, which boasts some delightful small towns and a generally pristine landscape. While the southern coast is easy to travel around, with the east–west Shinkansen line supplemented by good local railway services and highways, it takes more planning to tour the northern coast by public transport, but the reward is to reach some properly remote destinations.

Despite the rich legacy of its past – both coasts hold burial mounds dating from the first century – western Honshū is best known as the site where the first atomic bomb was dropped, in 1945. Almost every visitor stops to pay respects at **Hiroshima**, the region's largest city, halfway along the San'yō coast. To the east, **Okayama** is home to one of Japan's most famous gardens, **Kōrakuen**, and makes a good base for visiting the beautifully preserved Edo-era town of **Kurashiki** and the island art project on **Inujima**. Closer to Hiroshima, two appealingly unspoiled coastal towns – the fishing village of **Tomonoura**, a five-minute ferry ride from the island of Sensui-jima, and the grittier port of **Onomichi**, stretching below a delightful array of hillside temples – enjoy views across the Inland Sea. Onomichi is also the jumping-off point for the Shimanami Kaidō, or Sea Road, which connects Honshū via a series of breathtaking bridges and islands to Imabari on Shikoku, taking in the laidback island of **Ikuchi-jima** en route.

Of the Inland Sea islands described in this chapter – several others, including Naoshima and the so-called "Art Islands", are covered in chapter 9 – make sure you don't miss **Miyajima**, the site of the ancient shrine **Itsukushima-jinja**, which is an easy day-trip from Hiroshima. On the southern coast of neighbouring Yamaguchi-ken, pause to admire the elegant Kintai-kyō bridge at **Iwakuni** and the spectacular view across the narrow Kanmon Straits to Kyūshū from **Shimonoseki**, at the tip of Honshū. Inland, the highlights of the prefecture's small capital, **Yamaguchi**, are an impressive pagoda and a classic Zen rock and moss garden.

Near the western end of the frequently deserted San'in coast, the old castle town of **Hagi** boasts a lovely cluster of samurai houses and atmospheric temples. Perhaps even more beautiful is **Tsuwano** to the east, another small castle settlement nestling in a tranquil valley inland. Shimane-ken prefecture is the heartland of Japan's eight million

PEACE MEMORIAL PARK, HIROSHIMA

Highlights

❶ Washū-zan Climb Washū-zan and watch the sun set over the Seto Ōhashi bridge and the islands of the Inland Sea. **See p.574**

❷ Onomichi A favourite with movie-makers from Ozu onwards, this time-forgotten little port offers dramatic hillside temples, memorable hotels and great cycling. **See p.580**

❸ Hiroshima Now a vibrant modern city, Hiroshima abounds in monuments to the devastation of the A-Bomb; the Peace Memorial Museum tells the full harrowing story. **See p.586**

❹ Miyajima Watch the summer fireworks explode over Itsukushima-jinja's magnificent *torii*, or swoon at the island's spectacular autumn foliage. **See p.594**

❺ Tsuwano Explore this picturesque old castle town by bicycle, then climb up to the Taikodani Inari-jinja through a tunnel of over a thousand red *torii*. **See p.614**

❻ Adachi Museum of Art Rural art museum renowned for its exquisite, look-but-don't-touch gardens. **See p.626**

HIGHLIGHTS ARE MARKED ON THE MAP ON P.562

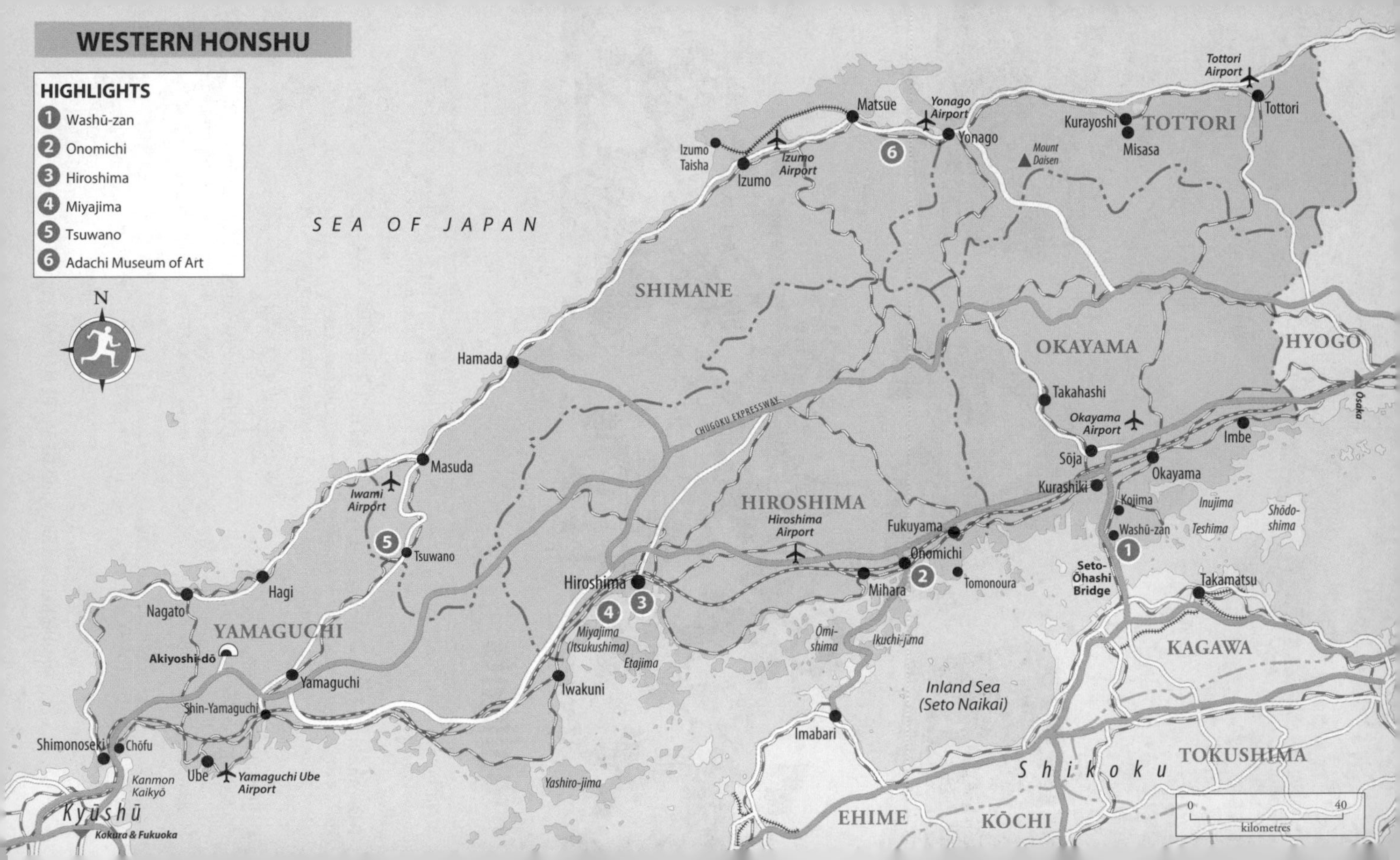

HIGHLIGHTS
1. Washū-zan
2. Onomichi
3. Hiroshima
4. Miyajima
5. Tsuwano
6. Adachi Museum of Art

SEA OF JAPAN

Inland Sea (Seto Naikai)

HYOGO
TOTTORI
OKAYAMA
SHIMANE
HIROSHIMA
YAMAGUCHI
KAGAWA
TOKUSHIMA
EHIME
KŌCHI
S h i k o k u
Kyūshū

Ōsaka
Tottori
Tottori Airport
Kurayoshi
Misasa
Mount Daisen
Yonago
Yonago Airport
Matsue
Izumo
Izumo Airport
Izumo Taisha
Hamada
Masuda
Iwami Airport
Tsuwano
Yamaguchi
Hagi
Nagato
Akiyoshi-dō
Shin-Yamaguchi
Ube
Yamaguchi Ube Airport
Chōfu
Kanmon Kaikyō
Shimonoseki
Kokura & Fukuoka

Imbe
Okayama
Okayama Airport
Takahashi
Sōja
Kurashiki
Washū-zan
Seto-Ōhashi Bridge
Kojima
Inujima
Teshima
Shōdo-shima
Takamatsu

Fukuyama
Onomichi
Mihara
Tomonoura
Ikuchi-jima
Ōmi-shima
Imabari
Yashiro-jima

Hiroshima
Hiroshima Airport
Miyajima (Itsukushima)
Etajima
Iwakuni

CHUGOKU EXPRESSWAY

N

0   40
kilometres

THE INLAND SEA

"They rise gracefully from this protected, stormless sea, as if they had just emerged, their beaches, piers, harbors all intact … Wherever one turns there is a wide and restful view, one island behind the other, each soft shape melting into the next until the last dim outline is lost in the distance."

Donald Richie, *The Inland Sea*

It would be hard to improve on Richie's sublime description of the **Inland Sea** (Seto Naikai), written in 1993. Despite his fears that it would all be ruined in Japan's rush to the twenty-first century, this priceless panorama has changed remarkably little. Boxed in by Honshū, Kyūshū and Shikoku, and dotted with more than three thousand other islands, the sea is one of Japan's scenic gems, often likened to the Aegean in its beauty.

Several islands are now connected by bridges and fast ferries to the mainland, reducing their isolation and much of their charm, but on many others you'll be struck by the more leisurely pace of life and the relative lack of modern-day blight. The best islands to head for are **Naoshima** (p.648), **Inujima** (p.654), **Ikuchi-jima** (p.583), **Ōmi-shima** (p.585), **Miyajima** (p.594) and **Shōdoshima** (p.656), all popular for their relaxed atmosphere and beautiful scenery.

If you don't have time to linger, consider a **boat trip** across the sea or heading to a vantage point such as Washū-zan (p.574) or Yashima (p.643) to look out over the islands. There are also several sightseeing cruises, though these are expensive for what they offer; you're better off putting together your own itinerary using individual ferry services.

Shintō deities, who gather each year in November at the ancient shrine Izumo Taisha. The attractive city of **Matsue**, nearby, holds the region's only original castle tower, as well as some old samurai houses and interesting museums. In neighbouring Tottori-ken, **Mount Daisen**, Chūgoku's highest peak, offers great hiking in summer and skiing in winter.

If you only have a few days, aim to take in Onomichi and Matsue, as well as Hiroshima and Miyajima. In a couple of weeks, you could make a circuit of both coasts, taking in most of the region's highlights.

GETTING AROUND

WESTERN HONSHŪ

By plane There are airports near Hiroshima; Okayama; Ube, near Shimonoseki and Yamaguchi; Iwami, east of Hagi; Izumo and Yonago, either side of Matsue; and Tottori.

By train Shinkansen trains cover the full length of the south coast only, heading east via Okayama to Shimonoseki and on to Kyūshū, but some delightful local routes thread through the inland valleys to reach and run along the north coast. A national JR Pass is the easiest way for most visitors to reach and explore the region, though if you're simply making a quick visit to western Honshū, various local passes, such as the seven-day JR West San'yō-San'in Pass,

are worth considering.

By bus While generally slower and more expensive than trains, buses are also an option. Long-distance bus services often travel overnight between the major cities.

By car Renting a car is a good idea, especially if you're planning to tour the quieter San'in coast, as you can make good use of the fast Chūgoku Expressway, which threads its way through the region's central mountainous spine, from where you can branch off to sights on either coast.

By ferry If time isn't an issue, schedule a leisurely ferry ride across the Inland Sea.

Okayama

岡山

The compelling reason to stop off in the capital of Okayama-ken, **OKAYAMA**, 730km west of Tokyo, is to stretch your legs on the lawns and footbridges of its famous **Kōrakuen** garden. Across the broad Ashi-gawa, though, you'll also find the majestic **Okayama-jō**, the castle around which the city developed during the Edo period. The sort of place that tends to grow on visitors, Okayama is all on a very manageable scale, with the main street, **Momotarō-dōri**, punctuated by a charming covered shopping arcade, **Omotechō-shōtengai**, as well as the pleasant, tree-lined **Nishigawa Greenway**

Canal. The ferry port to the south offers island excursions in the Inland Sea, while other attractions in the surrounding area make Okayama a potential base for a few days' sightseeing.

Kōrakuen

後楽園 • 1-5 Kōrakuen • Daily: late March to Sept 7.30am–6pm, Oct to late March 8am–5pm • ¥400, or ¥560 with Okayama-jō • ☎ 086 272 1148, ⓦ okayama-korakuen.jp

Okayama's star attraction, the magnificent **Kōrakuen**, occupies most of the comma-shaped Nakanoshima, cradled within a curve of the Ashi-gawa twenty minutes' walk east of the station. Acclaimed as one of the top three gardens in Japan – the others are Kenroku-en in Kanazawa and Ritsurin-kōen in Takamatsu – it was laid out in 1686 by Lord Ikeda Tsunamasa, and is notable for its broad, lush lawns, which are highly unusual in Japanese garden design. Otherwise, all the traditional elements, including artificial lakes, islands and hills, are present, while the black keep of Okayama-jō, across the river, has been nicely integrated into the scenery. It also holds a small **tea plantation** – relax over a bowl of delicious, foaming *matcha* in the Fukuda Teahouse alongside – and a flock of caged **red-crested cranes**.

Okayama-jō

岡山城 • 2-3-1 Marunouchi • Daily 9am–5pm • ¥300, or ¥560 with Kōrakuen • ☎ 086 225 2096, ⓦ okayama-kanko.net/ujo

Immediately south of Kōrakuen, across the river via the Tsukimi-bashi ("Moon-viewing Bridge"), the castle of **Okayama-jō** was built in 1597 by Lord Ukita Hideie, the adopted son of the great warlord Toyotomi Hideyoshi. Having fallen foul of both the Meiji restoration and World War II bombs, however, it was completely restored in 1966; the only original part of the compound is the **Tsukimi Yagura** ("Moon-Viewing Turret"), at its western corner. You can climb to the top of its donjon – the black wooden cladding of which gave rise to its nickname, U-jō ("Crow Castle") – for superb views over both garden and city. Historical displays within include a remarkable bearskin quiver, stuffed with arrows; few, though, are labelled in English. Visitors can however dress up in kimono or samurai armour for no extra charge.

Okayama Orient Museum

岡山市立オリエント美術館, Okayama Shiritsu Oriento Bijutsukan • 9-31 Tenjin-chō • Tues–Sun 9am–5pm • ¥300 • ☎ 086 232 3636, ⓦ www.orientmuseum.jp

In an award-winning modernist building, the atmospheric **Okayama Orient Museum** is devoted to the ancient Near East rather than what English-speakers would normally consider the Orient. The highlights of its unusual collection of ancient artworks and artefacts are the Assyrian reliefs, while other treasures include Syrian mosaics and recently acquired sculptures from central Asia.

Okayama Prefectural Museum of Art

岡山県立美術館, Okayama Kenritsu Bijutsukan • 8-48 Tenjin-chō • Tues–Sun 9am–5pm • ¥350, special exhibitions extra; ¥960 with Kōrakuen and Okayama-jō • ☎ 086 225 4800, ⓦ bit.ly/okayama-art

As the name suggests, the **Okayama Prefectural Museum of Art**, just north of the Okayama Orient Museum, holds art from the surrounding area. As well as dreamy ink paintings by the fifteenth-century artist and priest Sesshū Tōyō, it displays prime specimens of the local pottery style, *Bizen-yaki*, and also puts on temporary exhibitions.

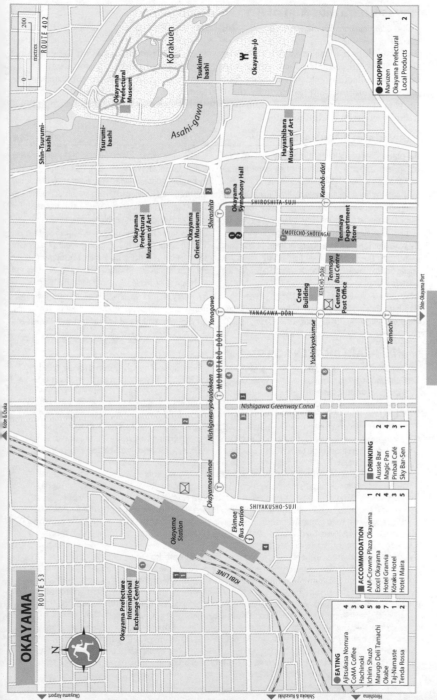

Hayashibara Museum of Art

林原美術館, Hayashibara Bijutsukan • 2-7-15 Marunouchi • Tues–Sun 10am–5pm • ¥500 • ☏ 086 223 1733,
🌐 hayashibara-museumofart.jp

The **Hayashibara Museum of Art**, just southwest of Okayama-jō, shows off the exquisite Asian art acquired by late local businessman Hayashibara Ichirō. Only some of its beautiful collection, which includes armour, paintings, ceramics, metalwork, delicate ink scroll paintings and ravishing nō theatre robes from the sixteenth century, is on show at any one time, so take a moment to leaf through the catalogue while sipping a free cup of green tea in the lounge.

ARRIVAL AND INFORMATION   OKAYAMA

By plane Okayama Airport, 15km northwest of town (🌐 okayama-airport.org), is connected by frequent buses with the train station (30min; ¥760).

Destinations Hong Kong (5 weekly; 4hr 20min); Okinawa (daily; 2hr); Sapporo (daily; 1hr 50min); Seoul (daily; 1hr 45min); Shanghai (daily; 2hr 15min); Taipei (3 weekly; 3hr 30min); Tokyo Haneda (10 daily; 1hr 5min).

By train Both Shinkansen and regular trains on local lines – including the JR Seto Ōhashi line, which crosses the Inland Sea to Shikoku – stop at Okayama Station, on the western edge of downtown.

Destinations Fukuyama (every 15min; 16min–1hr); Hiroshima (every 15min; 35min); Imbe (hourly; 40min); Matsue (hourly; 2hr 30min); Shin-Osaka (every 30min; 45min); Takamatsu (every 30min; 1hr); Tokyo (every 15min; 3hr 30min); Yonago (hourly; 2hr 10min).

By bus Long-distance buses arrive either at the Ekimae bus station on the east side of Okayama Station, or the Tenmaya Bus Centre, in the shopping district 1.4km southeast. For routes and schedules, visit 🌐 bit.ly/okayamabus.

Destinations Fukuoka (1 daily; 9hr); Kōbe (6–8 daily; 2hr 50min); Kōchi (9 daily; 2hr 30min); Kyoto (7 daily; 3hr 30min); Matsue (7 daily; 3hr 50min); Matsuyama (6 daily; 2hr 40min); Osaka (hourly; 4hr); Tokyo (3 daily, all overnight; 10hr 20min); Yonago (7 daily; 2hr 10min).

By ferry Ferries to Shōdoshima depart from Shin-Okayama, 10km south of town (hourly; 1hr 10min; 🌐 ryobi-ferry.com). Buses link the port with the bus and

---

KIBI PLAIN BICYCLE ROAD

Accessed from either Okayama or Kurashiki (see p.569), the 17km **Kibi Plain bicycle road** (吉備路サイクリングロード) provides an enjoyable opportunity to see a stunning expanse of countryside studded with ancient burial grounds, shrines and temples. The route takes about four hours to cycle – one-way rental bikes are available at the stations at either end, for around ¥1000 per day – or a full day to walk.

During the fourth century, this area, known as Kibi-no-kuni, was the cradle of early Japanese civilization. Lords were buried in giant keyhole-shaped mounds known as *kofun*, one of which can be visited along the cycle route. Starting from **Bizen-Ichinomiya Station** (備前一宮駅), three stops west of Okayama on the JR Kibi line, cross the tracks and follow the cycle path to **Kibitsuhiko-jinja** (吉備津彦神社; daily 5am–6pm; free), an ordinary shrine beside a pond notable only for its huge stone lantern, one of the largest in Japan. Around 300m further southwest, the much more impressive **Kibitsu-jinja** (吉備津神社; daily 5am–6pm; free), nestled at the foot of Mount Naka and dating from 1425, has a magnificently roofed outer sanctum, with twin gables. It's dedicated to Kibitsu-no-mikoto, the valiant prince who inspired the legend of **Momotarō**, the boy who popped out of the centre of a giant peach rescued from a river by a childless farmer's wife.

Several kilometres further west, the wooded **Tsukuriyama-kofun** (造山古墳) is a fifth-century burial mound, constructed in the characteristic keyhole-shape. Set amid rice fields and measuring 350m in length and 30m at its highest point, this is the fourth-largest *kofun* in Japan, but can only be fully appreciated from the air. A cluster of sights 1km east includes the foundation stones of Bitchū Kokubun-niji, an eighth-century convent; another burial mound; and the five-storey, seventeenth-century pagoda of **Bitchū Kokubun-ji** (備中国分寺; daily 10am–4pm; free).

It's another couple of kilometres to the train station at **Sōja** (総社), from where you can return to either Okayama or to Kurashiki. Before you leave, check out **Iyama Hōfuku-ji** (井山宝福寺; daily 5am–5pm; free), a pretty Zen Buddhist temple 1km north of the station along a footpath that follows the railway line. The celebrated artist and landscape gardener Sesshū Tōyō (1420–1506) trained here as a priest.

8

train stations in Okayama (hourly; 30min).

Tourist information The Momotarō Tourist Information Centre is in the underground mall outside the east exit of the train station (daily 9am–8pm; ☎086 222 2912, ⓦokayama-kanko.net), while there's a smaller information counter in the station itself (daily 9am–6pm).

GETTING AROUND

By tram Trams crisscross the city. The most useful route for visitors runs east from the station along the main road, Momotarō-dōri, to the Asahi-gawa, near Kōrakuen and the castle, which is otherwise a 20min walk.

By bus Buses head all over the city from the station; for Kōrakuen, catch #18 from platform 4.

By car Car rental is available at the station from Nippon Rent-a-Car (☎084 991 0919, ⓦwww.nrgroup-global .com) or Toyota Rent-a-Car ☎086 254 0100, ⓦrent.toyota .co.jp).

By bike Several outlets by the station rent out bicycles, from ¥300 a day.

ACCOMMODATION

ANA-Crowne Plaza Okayama ANAクラウンプラザホテ ル岡山 15-1 Ekimoto-chō ☎086 898 1111, ⓦanacp okayama.com. Plush business hotel, beside the train station and attached to the convention centre, with spacious elegant rooms, two restaurants and superb views from the twentieth-floor *Sky Bar-Sen* (see p.568). Ask for a corner room, for the especially large windows, or one that faces south, looking out over the station towards downtown. 🛜 **¥26,400**

Excel Okayama エクセル岡山 5-1 Ishiseki-chō ☎086 224 0505, ⓦwww.excel-okayama.com. Good-value mid-range hotel, smartly decorated and conveniently located close to the river, near to both Kōrakuen and the shopping arcades. 🛜 **¥12,600**

Hotel Granvia ホテルグランヴィア 1-5 Ekimoto-chō ☎086 234 7000, ⓦgranvia-oka.co.jp. A close second to *ANA-Crowne Plaza Okayama* in terms of luxury, this tall tower block in the station complex features large, tastefully furnished rooms with good bathrooms, plus several restaurants, bars and shops. 🛜 **¥28,512**

Kōraku Hotel 後楽ホテル 5-1 Heiwa-chō ☎086 221 7111, ⓦhotel.kooraku.co.jp. This hotel offers big, simple and stylish boutique rooms. They also have a Japanese restaurant on the second floor, and high-quality art in the public areas. 🛜 **¥13,400**

Hotel Maira ホテルマイラ 8-16 Nishiki-machi ☎086 233 1411. Small and charming hotel, attractively located beside a little canal a 10min walk southeast of the station. The rooms are large for the price, and the staff exceptionally friendly; rates include free non-alcoholic drinks and continental breakfasts. 🛜 **¥6500**

EATING

Okayama has a wide range of eating options, and is noted for its **izakaya**. The liveliest districts lie immediately east of the station, and along Omotechō-shōtengai, the covered shopping street closer to the river. Local specialities include *sōmen*, handmade noodles dried in the sun and often served cold in summer, and *Okayama barazushi* (festival sushi), a mound of vinegared rice covered with seafood and regional vegetables.

Ajitsukasa Nomura 味司野村 1-10 Heiwa-chō ☎086 222 2234. Pay at the vending machine outside – most dishes costs around ¥1000 – then step inside to enjoy either their signature breaded pork cutlet in thick brown gravy, or, for lighter appetites, perhaps a plate of raw fish. Daily 11am–11pm.

CoMA Coffee コマ コーヒー 1-1-5 Marunouchi ☎086 225 5530, ⓦcoma-coffee.com. Dainty little second-floor coffee joint, across from the Symphony Hall, with great views all the way down Momotarō-dōri. In addition to very good freshly brewed coffee (¥400), they sell sandwiches (peanut butter and jam, for example), plus coffee paraphernalia and bagged beans. Service can lag, but it's so calm and relaxing you may not notice. 🛜 Mon–Sat 9am–8pm, Sun 9am–7pm.

Hachinoki 鉢の木 5-20 Heiwa-chō ☎086 232 1088. There's no English spoken, let along an English menu, at this bustling little *izakaya*, but you won't go far wrong if you just point to the goodies on the open grill, ranging from fish and meat to delicious tofu. They also offer sashimi, with a plate of pretty much anything costing under ¥1000. Daily 6pm–2am.

Ichirin Shuzō 壱厘酒蔵 2-16 Hon-machi ☎086 231 0690, ⓦichirinshuzo.com. If you've a taste for adventure, there's plenty to tickle the palate at this popular *izakaya*, not far east of the station. How about *nattō* topped with raw squid and a raw quail's egg for ¥500, or boiled eel with scrambled egg for ¥800? Mon–Sat 5pm–midnight.

Marugo Deli Tamachi マルゴ デリ田町 1-1-11 Ta-machi ☎086 235 3532. Friendly, late-opening neighbourhood deli that's a lively local rendezvous thanks to its fine espresso coffee drinks and fresh-squeezed juices of all kinds. 🛜 Mon–Sat 11am–11pm, Sun 11am–9pm.

Okabe おかべ 1-10-1 Omote-chō ☎086 232 9167, ⓦtofudokoro-okabe.com. You'll encounter all forms of tofu in this small, no-nonsense lunch restaurant, just off the shopping arcade. Recommended dishes include the ¥820 *teishoku* and the ¥870 *yuba* (tofu skin) *donburi*, of

8

which they make only fifteen servings per day. Their adjoining shop sells take-away tofu until 7pm. Mon–Sat 11.30am–2pm.

Taj-Namaste タージナマステ Misawa building, 30-10 Ekimoto-machi ☎086 252 5006. Great little Nepali-run curry house, painted a just-bearable orange colour, and serving good-value lunch and dinner specials (from ¥900) that range from tandoori keema to fish biryani. Daily 11am–3pm & 5–10pm.

Tenda Rossa テンダロッサ 1-7-15 Nodaya-chō ☎086 227 9011, ⓦbit.ly/tenda-rossa. Plaid tablecloths and rustic decor complement the Japanese-style Italian menu at this large pink restaurant, where pasta, pizza and grilled meats and fish cost from ¥1400, and set menus start at ¥2700. 🛜 Tues–Sun 11.30am–2pm & 5.30–9.30pm.

DRINKING

Aussie Bar オーヅーバー 1-10-21 Ekimae-chō ☎902 290 8136. By the Nishigawa Greenway Canal, north of Momotarō-dōri – look for the yellow *Aussie* road sign outside – this smokey, divey spot is especially busy with foreigners at weekends. You won't find any Fosters here, though. 🛜 Daily 7pm–3am.

Magic Pan ハワイアンバー マジックパン Saiwai-chō 3-10 Hazlme Tomozawa Building ☎086 234 2121, ⓦmagicpan.net. Small Hawaiian-themed bar and restaurant doing a decent trade in colourful tropical cocktails, doled out by energetic bartenders who may have seen *Cocktail* one too many times – bottles of Blue Curaçao on fire and so on. Cover charge ¥300. Mon–Thurs 7pm–3am, Fri & Sat 7pm–5am, Sun 7pm–1am.

Pinball Café ピンボール カフ 4-18 Hon-machi ☎086 222 6966. Pinball is not actually on the menu in this casual, American-themed café, which turns bar in the evenings, but Guinness and live music are, and there's usually a foreign crowd clustered around the beer pumps. Take the escalators up from ground level. 🛜 Mon–Fri 11.30am–2.30pm & 7pm–2am, Sat & Sun 7pm–2am.

Sky Bar-Sen スカイバー「SEN」 ANA Hotel Okayama 15-1 Ekimoto-chō ☎086 898 2284, ⓦanacpokayama .com. Intimate bar on the twentieth floor of an upscale hotel, with white leather seating and stupendous views of the city and surrounding hills. Cocktails from ¥1200, with a happy hour from 5–7pm. 🛜 Mon–Fri 5pm–midnight, Sat & Sun 5–11pm.

SHOPPING

Maruzen 丸善 Okayama Symphony Hall, 1-5-1 Omote-chō ☎086 233 4640. Entered off the shopping arcade beside the Symphony Hall, the basement bookshop of this department store stocks a very extensive array of English books and magazines, stationery and Japanese language learning materials. Daily 10am–8pm.

Okayama Prefectural Local Products 岡山県観光プ ロダクトセンター 1-2-2 Omote-chō ☎086 234 2270. A good place for local foods and crafts, including *Bizen-yaki* pottery, masks and weaving, in the covered arcade opposite Okayama Symphony Hall. Daily 10am–8pm.

POTTERY IN IMBE

For dedicated lovers of ceramics, the otherwise dreary town of **IMBE** (伊部; often alternatively rendered in English spelling as "Inbe"), 30km east of Okayama on the local Aco railway, makes a worthwhile pilgrimage. This is the home of *Bizen-yaki*, Japan's oldest method of making pottery, which first developed over a thousand years ago and had its heyday during the sixteenth century. The distinctive earthy colour and texture of the ceramics are achieved without the use of glazes by firing in wood-fuelled kilns, whose brick chimneys you'll see dotted around town.

You can pick up an English leaflet about *Bizen-yaki* from the tourist office at Imbe Station (Tues–Sun 9am–6pm; ☎086 964 1100). Housed in the grey concrete block immediately north, the **Bizen Pottery Traditional and Contemporary Art Museum** (備前陶芸美術館, Bizen Dōgei Bijutsukan; 1659-6 Imbe; Tues–Sun 9.30am–5pm; ¥700; ☎086 964 1001, ⓦbit.ly /bizenmuseum) displays ceramic work both old and new, providing an overview of the pottery's style and development.

Simply strolling around Imbe, you'll see fine specimens of *Bizen-yaki* adorning temples and homes. Plenty of kilns have attached shops where you can browse for souvenirs, while some hold studios in which you can sculpt your own blob of clay for around ¥3000. This is then fired and shipped to your home (overseas deliveries cost extra). The most convenient such opportunity comes at the **Bizen-yaki Traditional Pottery Centre** (備前伝統産業会館, Bizen-yaki Dentō Sangyō Kaikan; ☎086 964 1001), on the third floor of Imbe Station, which holds workshops each weekend and on holidays.

Kurashiki

倉敷

The historic town of **KURASHIKI**, 18km southwest of Okayama, is a hugely popular day-trip destination, and arguably even more appealing as an overnight stop. Ten minutes' walk south of the station, its initially unpromising modern buildings and shops are replaced by a well-preserved enclave of picturesque, black-and-white walled merchants' homes (*machiya*), storehouses (*kura*) and canals. They date from Kurashiki's Edo-era heyday, when it became an important centre for trade in rice and rush reeds.

The compact **Bikan** (美観) district, cut through by a narrow, tree-fringed canal, is filled with museums and galleries, the best of which is the excellent **Ōhara Museum of Art**, containing four separate halls for Western art, contemporary Japanese art and local crafts. During the day, especially in summer, Bikan can all feel a bit too busy with tourists. Stay the night, and an early-morning or evening stroll can be quite magical.

Ōhashi House

大橋家住宅, Ōhashi-ke Jūtaku • 3-21-31 Achi • March, Oct & Nov daily 9am–5pm; April–Sept Mon–Fri & Sun 9am–5pm, Sat 9am–6pm; Dec–Feb Mon–Thurs, Sat & Sun 9am–5pm • ¥550 • ☎ 086 422 0007, ⊕ ohashi-ke.com

The **Ōhashi House**, a short detour west of the main road immediately before the Bikan district, was built for a rich merchant family in 1796. The Ōhashi had prospered

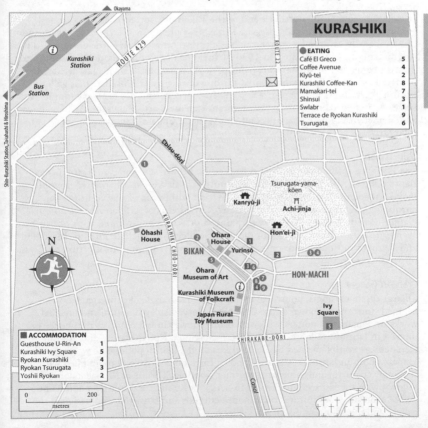

KURASHIKI

● **EATING**

Café El Greco	5
Coffee Avenue	4
Kiyū-tei	2
Kurashiki Coffee-Kan	8
Mamakari-tei	7
Shinsui	3
Swlabr	1
Terrace de Ryokan Kurashiki	9
Tsurugata	6

■ **ACCOMMODATION**

Guesthouse U-Rin-An	1
Kurashiki Ivy Square	5
Ryokan Kurashiki	4
Ryokan Tsurugata	3
Yoshii Ryokan	2

8

through salt production and land holdings, and designed their home to resemble those of the high-ranking samurai class, demonstrating how wealth was starting to break down previously rigid social barriers. After passing through a gatehouse and small courtyard, and listening to a recorded history of the house (in Japanese), you are free to wander through the spacious, unfurnished tatami rooms.

Bikan

美観

The approach to Kurashiki's showpiece **Bikan** district, 1km southeast of the station, is usually flagged by coaches unloading day-trippers. The pedestrianized avenues to either side of its willow-lined canal hold a succession of beautifully preserved merchant houses, granaries and warehouses, many of which now hold inn or restaurants, while out on the water swans drift, carp splash to the surface, and boatmen punt sightseers on short cruises. Notable buildings include the **Ōhara House** (大原家住宅), with its typical wooden lattice windows, and the Ōhara family's green-tiled guesthouse alongside, the **Yūrinsō** (有隣荘); neither is open to the public.

Ōhara Museum of Art

大原美術館, Ōhara Bijutsukan • 1-1-15 Chūō • late July to Aug daily 9am–5pm, Sept to late July Tues–Sun 9am–5pm • ¥1300 • ☎ 086 422 0005, ⓦ ohara.or.jp

Beside the canal at the northern end of the Bikan district, reached via a stone bridge adorned with carved dragons, Kurashiki's premier gallery, the **Ōhara Museum of Art**, is easily spotted by its creamy Neoclassical facade. This is the entrance to the original building, established in 1930 by local textile tycoon **Ōhara Magosaburō** to house a collection of **Western art** hand-picked on his behalf by his late friend, the painter Kojima Torajirō, who toured Europe during the 1920s. The first gallery to exhibit Western art in Japan, it was a roaring success, and has been expanding ever since. As well as contemporary Western and Japanese art, Magosaburō's heirs have added ancient Chinese artworks and an excellent range of top-class Japanese folkcrafts.

Main gallery

The entrance to the **main gallery** is flanked by bronze sculptures of St John the Baptist and the Burghers of Calais by Rodin – both were nearly melted down to make armaments during World War II. Artists within are displayed in roughly chronological order, with early appearances by El Greco, with an *Annunciation*; Gauguin, with *Te Nave Nave Fenua*, painted in Tahiti; and Monet, with one of his *Waterlilies* series. Big names from the twentieth century include Picasso, Matisse and Rothko; most are represented by relatively minor works, but it's still an impressive collection.

Craft Art Gallery

Ōhara's **ceramics rooms**, housed in an attractive quadrangle of converted wooden-beamed storehouses known as the **Craft Art Gallery**, display beautiful and unusual works by a quartet of potters who were prime movers in last century's resurgence of interest in Japanese folk arts (*mingei*). Hamada Shōji, Kawai Kanjirō and Tomimoto Kenkichi are complemented by Bernard Leach, the British potter who worked with Hamada both in Japan, at Mashiko, and in England at St Ives. A room filled with the strikingly colourful and sometimes abstract **woodblock prints** of Munakata Shikō follows, with the last section devoted to Serizawa Keisuke, a textile dyer and painter whose exquisite work features on kimono, curtains and fans, and who designed the gallery and the adjoining Asian Art Gallery.

Asian Art Gallery and Annex
The small collection in the **Asian Art Gallery**, on two levels, features displays of ancient East Asian art, including seventh-century Tang Dynasty ceramics and sculptures and serene Buddhas. The ground floor of the **Annex**, in a separate building behind the main gallery, displays unremarkable pastiches of Western-style art by Japanese artists, while downstairs is devoted to contemporary works.

Japan Rural Toy Museum

日本郷土玩具館, Nihon Kyōdo Gangu-kan • 1-4-16 Chūō • Daily 9am–5pm • ¥400 • ☎ 086 422 8058, ⓦ gangukan.jp

Room after room in the delightful **Japan Rural Toy Museum**, beside the canal, displays an entertaining assortment of wooden dolls, dioramas, puppets and animals, most of which are faded and tatty with age and use. The tumbledown hall at the end of the garden holds some fabulous kites and masks, as well as a large top in the corner that earned the museum's owner, **Ohga Hiroyuki**, a place in the Guinness World Records in 1983, after he spun it for 1 hour, 8 minutes and 57 seconds. The front of the museum is given over to an excellent gift shop, selling colourful modern versions of the traditional playthings on show further back.

Kurashiki Museum of Folkcraft

倉敷民芸館, Kurashiki Mingei-kan • 1-4-11 Chūō • March–July & Sept–Nov Tues–Sun 9am–5pm; Aug daily 9am–5pm, Dec–Feb Tues–Sun 9am–4.15pm • ¥700 • ☎ 086 422 1637, ⓦ kurashiki-mingeikan.com

A handsome restored granary at a curve in the canal is home to the **Kurashiki Museum of Folkcraft**. Pay the rather steep admission fee and you can explore dry-as-dust displays of local crafts such as *Bizen-yaki* pottery, baskets and traditional clothes, with no English translations to explain what you're seeing. It makes more sense to spend the money on buying the actual products instead, sold in the free-to-access shop beside the front desk – the small ceramics are particularly good value.

Hon-machi

本町

The seventeenth-century merchant houses in the **Hon-machi** district make a great destination for an afternoon amble. The streets just east of the canal hold cafés and artsy craft shops, while climbing up the hillside stairways into **Tsurugata-yama Park** (鶴形山公園) will bring you to the simple **Achi-jinja** (阿智神社; 24hr) shrine, and the **Hon'ei-ji** (本栄寺; 24hr) and **Kanryū-ji** (観龍寺; daily 6am–5pm) temples.

Further south in Hon-machi, the ivy-covered late nineteenth-century **Kurashiki Cotton Mill** has been redeveloped into a shopping, museum and hotel complex known as **Ivy Square**. This holds a good craft shop, as well as an atelier where you can try your hand at pottery (¥2100).

ARRIVAL AND INFORMATION

KURASHIKI

By train Trains on the JR San'yō line stop at Kurashiki Station, at the northwestern edge of town, which is 18km southwest of Okayama; 10km northeast of the nearest Shinkansen stop, Shin-Kurashiki; and 45km northeast of Fukuyama.

Destinations Fukuyama (frequent; 42min); Okayama (frequent; 15min); Onomichi (frequent; 1hr); Shin-Kurashiki (frequent; 10min).

By bus Regular buses from Okayama and Kojima

stop in front of Kurashiki Station.

Destinations Okayama Airport (10 daily, 35min; ¥1130); Osaka (2 daily; 3hr 50min); Tokyo (daily; 11hr).

Tourist information There are tourist offices at Kurashiki Station (daily: April–Sept 9am–7pm, Oct–March 9am–6pm; ☎ 086 424 1220, ⓦ www.kurashiki-tabi.jp), and in a stylish Meiji-era wooden building beside the canal in the Bikan district (1-4-8 Chūō; daily 9am–6pm; ☎ 086 422 0542).

ACCOMMODATION

Kurashiki offers great opportunities to experience a traditional ryokan or minshuku, the best of which are in the Bikan district. The town is also fairly well served with upmarket Western-style hotels.

★**Guesthouse U-Rin-An** 有鄰庵 2-15 Hon-machi ☎086 426 1180, ⓦu-rin.com. Charming and very welcoming Japanese-style hostel, in a venerable mansion in the Bikan district, with tasteful tatami dorms and a rather irresistible communal lounge/dining room, serving hot and cold drinks and simple meals. Rates drop for multi-night stays. ☎ Dorms **¥3780**, doubles **¥9500**

Kurashiki Ivy Square 倉敷アイビースクエアホテル 7-2 Hon-machi ☎086 422 0011, ⓦivysquare.co.jp. Part of a renovated factory complex at the southern corner of the Bikan district, this is a good mid-range stay with pleasantly decorated rooms, a couple of restaurants, a bar and shops. ☎ **¥13,200**

Ryokan Kurashiki 旅館倉敷 4-1 Hon-machi ☎086 422 0730, ⓦryokan-kurashiki.jp. Very swanky ryokan, housed in three converted rice and sugar storehouses in the heart of the Bikan district. Each suite has a Western-style bedroom and Japanese living room full of antiques, with ever-present women in blue kimono keeping everything meticulously correct. Rates include sumptuous *kaiseki-ryōri* meals, served in your room – extravagant, perhaps, but the genuine article. ☎ **¥64,000**

Ryokan Tsurugata 旅館鶴形 1-3-15 Chūō ☎086 424 1635, ⓦturugata.jp. Good-value ryokan, with atmospheric tatami rooms in a 250-year-old canalside merchant's house, overlooking a traditional rock garden. Rates include top-class *kaiseki-ryōri* dinners, also available to non-residents (see below). ☎ **¥17,820**

Yoshii Ryokan 吉井旅館 1-29 Hon-machi ☎086 422 0118, ⓦyoshii-ryokan.com. Set back from the canal, this peaceful little inn has eight large rooms, some peering out over beautifully manicured gardens, others over a courtyard. Rates include satisfying, seafood-rich *kaiseki-ryōri* dinners. ☎ **¥60,000**

EATING

Kurashiki holds a wide range of **restaurants**. The best lunchtime options line up in the Bikan district, but many close in the evening, and if you're not dining in your hotel you're probably best off heading for the station area. The town's signature dish is *mamakari-zushi*, a vinegared sardine-like fish on top of sushi rice. Kurashiki is better known for afternoon tea than late-night drinking. In summer, though, you can chill out at the beer garden in the inner courtyard of the red-brick, ivy-clad complex of Ivy Square (July & Aug daily 6–9.30pm).

Café El Greco カフェエルグレコ 1-1-11 Chūō ☎086 422 0297, ⓔelgreco.co.jp. Run by a delightful team of older ladies, this classic Bikan café, in an ivy-clad building facing the canal, is a popular pit stop for tea and cake. A coffee will set you back ¥500, green tea and cake ¥800, and blueberry cheesecake ¥450; seating is at shared tables. ☎ Tues–Sun 10am–5pm.

Coffee Avenue アベニュー 11-30 Hon-machi ☎086 424 8043. Friendly coffee shop, below the temple district on a street of old merchant houses; the grand piano and vinyl-packed DJ booth signal its nightly re-invention as the *Robert Brown Jazz Avenue* bar, featuring live jazz from 8pm (cover ¥500). ☎ Daily noon–11pm.

Kiyū-tei 亀遊亭 1-2-20 Chūō ☎086 422 5140, ⓦbit.ly /kiyutei. Attractive, rustic-looking steak restaurant at the head of the canal – there's a pretty garden, but you dine indoors – which serves a seasonal set lunch or dinner for ¥3240, or a simple curry rice for ¥1100. Tues–Sun 11am–3pm & 5–9pm.

Kurashiki Coffee-Kan 倉敷珈琲館 4-1 Hon-machi ☎086 424 5516, ⓦkurashiki-coffeekan.com. Buzzy coffee shop, tucked away beside the canal, where you can enjoy the best espresso in town – a genuine java jolt – overlooking a tranquil traditional garden. ☎ Daily 10am–5pm.

Mamakari-tei ままかり亭 3-12 Hon-machi ☎086 427 7112, ⓦhamayoshi-kurashiki.jp. This canalside restaurant is a great place to try the local delicacy *mamakari-zushi*; a set lunch including the sushi, alongside baked fish, tofu and soup, is ¥2500. Tues–Sun 11am–2pm & 5–10pm.

Shinsui 新粋 11-35 Hon-machi ☎086 422 5171, ⓦk-suiraitei.com/shinsui. Menu highlights in this delightful, romantically lit dinner-only restaurant include eggy *oden* (from ¥160), conger eel (¥1200), and creamy, crunchy croquettes (¥800). There's usually a jazz-piano soundtrack. ☎ Mon–Sat 5–10pm.

Swlabr スーラバー 2-18-2 Achi ☎086 434 3099. This funky little place, on the road into town from the station, may be a whole lot more shabby than it is chic, with its ramshackle wooden furniture and library of (Japanese) books, but it has a wonderfully laidback feel. During the day, it's a café, serving snacks such as BLTs and pasta from ¥800, plus smoothies, lassi and floats; then, after 8pm, it turns into a convivial bar. ☎ Daily 11.30am–3am.

★**Terrace de Ryokan Kurashiki** テラスデ旅館くらしき 4-1 Hon-machi ☎086 422 0730, ⓦryokan-kurashiki .jp. This elegant café opens out onto a beautiful traditional garden complete with moss-covered rocks, gnarled pines and stone lanterns. Indulge in tea and biscuits for ¥950. ☎ Daily 2–5pm.

Tsurugata 鶴形 1-3-15 Chūō ☎086 424 1635, ⓦturugata.jp. Even if you're not staying in the attached ryokan, this historic canalside house makes an appealing venue for a quick lunch – a set meal with tempura noodles costs ¥1100, with eel and eggs it's ¥1750 – or a more formal *kaiseki* dinner for around ¥6000. ☎ Tues–Sun 11am–2pm & 5.30–8pm.

Takahashi

高梁

The small and charming time-warped castle town of **TAKAHASHI** stands 45km northwest of Okayama, in the foothills of the mountains that divide western Honshū. Few visitors venture here, despite the fine old buildings and temples in the **Ishibiya-chō Furusato Mura** ("Hometown Village") area, a name evoking images of a long-lost Japan. Ranged attractively at differing levels along the hillside east of the train tracks, the temples extend north towards Furusato Mura. They're best viewed from above; the steep hike up to **Bitchū Matsuyama-jō**, Japan's highest castle, rewards visitors with excellent panoramas.

The castle aside, almost all Takahashi's sights lie within easy walking distance of Bitchū Takahashi Station and can be explored in half a day.

Raikyū-ji

頼久寺 • 18 Raikyūji-chō • Daily 9am–5pm • ¥300

Takahashi's most impressive temple, **Raikyū-ji**, is ten minutes' walk north of the station. Its exact date of construction is uncertain, but Kobori Enshū, governor of the province and expert gardener, is known to have lived here some centuries later, from 1604 onwards. The serenely beautiful raked-gravel **Zen garden** that he designed is maintained exactly as he left it, complete with islands of stones, plants and trimmed azalea hedges carefully placed to resemble a crane and a tortoise in the "well-wishing garden" style, and featuring the distant borrowed scenery of Mount Atago.

8

Bitchū Matsuyama-jō

備中松山城 • Yamashita • Donjon daily: April–Sept 9am–5.30pm, Oct–March 9am–4.30pm • ¥300 • ☎ 086 622 1487, ⓦ bit.ly/takahashicastle • Not served by local buses; the nearest road access (around ¥1300 by taxi from the station) leaves you with a steep 15min hike up to the castle

A strenuous hour-long hike north from the station, climbing a shaded track up through the hillside forest, will bring you to the castle, **Bitchū Matsuyama-jō**. Takahashi's fortunes prospered from the mid-thirteenth century, when warlord Akiba Saburo Shigenobu built the original fortress atop nearby Mount Gagyū. It's not really worth paying to go into the restored **donjon**, as there are few relics inside and poor views through its narrow windows. At 480m, this is the highest-altitude castle in Japan, and the vistas on the walk back downhill make the effort of hiking up worthwhile.

Ishibiya-chō Furusato Mura

石火矢町ふるさと村

It's well worth spending an hour or two exploring the **Ishibiya-chō Furusato Mura** area of old houses and buildings. Sandwiched between the rail tracks and the Takahashi-gawa, it's cut through by a stream that's spanned by stone bridges topped with miniature shrines.

Buke-yashiki-kan samurai houses

武家屋敷館 • Nishi 95 • Daily 9am–5pm • ¥400 for both • ☎ 079 552 6933

Several buildings in the Ishibiya-chō Furusato Mura have been turned into museums. At the most interesting, the two **Buké-yashiki-kan samurai houses**, you can explore the residence's various living spaces and wander around the gardens.

Takahashi Museum of History

高梁市郷土資料館, Takahashi-shi Kyoda Shiryōkan • 21 Muko-machi • Daily 9am–5pm • ¥300 • ☎ 086 622 1479

The clapboard Meiji-era Takahashi Elementary School, a small Western-style Meiji-era building 500m south of the station, now holds the **Takahashi Museum of History**.

Exhibits range from *mikoshi* (portable shrines) to a Morse-code machine, with some evocative black-and-white photos of Takahashi at the back of the ground floor. On the second floor, look out for the dancing doll models made from old cigarette packets – a nod to Japan Tobacco, which has a factory in town.

ARRIVAL AND INFORMATION   TAKAHASHI

By train Takahashi's train station, Bitchū-Takahashi (備中 高梁駅), is connected with Okayama and Kurashiki on the JR Hakubi line.
Destinations Kurashiki (frequent; 25–40min); Okayama

(frequent; 30–55min).
Tourist information There's a tiny information office at the bus terminal, beside the station (daily 9am–5pm; ☏ 086 622 8666, ⓦ takahasikanko.or.jp).

ACCOMMODATION AND EATING

Daichan 大ちゃん 895 Higashi-machi ☏ 086 622 5338. Thanks to its substantial portions of pancake-like *okonomiyaki*, a glorious fried concoction of everything under the sun which costs under ¥1000, this central restaurant is hugely popular with young locals. Daily 11am–11.30pm.

Takahashi Kokusai Hotel 高梁国際ホテル 2033 Masamune-chō ☏ 086 621 0080, ⓦ www.tkh.co.jp. The closest Takahashi comes to a reasonable business hotel, a 3min walk north of the station. Rooms are sizeable, as are the breakfasts, served in a decent on-site restaurant. Ask for a room on the opposite side to the station. ☏ **¥12,342**

Kojima and around

児島

The port of **KOJIMA**, 30km southwest of Okayama, has boomed since the 1988 opening of the nearby 12.3km-long **Seto Ōhashi** (Great Seto Bridge), a series of six bridges and four viaducts that hop across the Inland Sea from island to island all the way to Shikoku. The summit of **Washū-zan** on the prefecture's southern tip offers fantastic views, while outdoor lovers might want to explore fragments of the area's ancient history by taking the leisurely and relatively flat **Kibi Plain** bicycle route, which runs past fifth-century burial mounds and rustic temples and shrines. Kojima has also built up a reputation as the prime place to buy **jeans** in Japan; serious denim enthusiasts can shop to their hearts' content in downtown's **Kojima Jeans Street** (ⓦ jeans-street.com), 1km northwest of the station.

Seto Ōhashi

瀬戸大橋 • Boat tours 4–5 departures mid-March to Nov daily 9am–3pm, Dec to mid-March Sat & Sun 9am–3pm • 45min • ¥1550 • ☏ 086 473 6777

Boat tours from the sightseeing pier immediately east of Kojima Station offer a memorable opportunity to view the islands of the Inland Sea, and the series of bridges that make up the epic **Seto Ōhashi**.

If you'd rather view it all from dry land, head instead to **Washū-zan** (鷲羽山). The summit of this 134m-high promontory, which juts out to sea 4km south of Kojima, commands one of Japan's most glorious panoramas. Regular buses run to the official lookout spot from Kojima Station; stay on the bus beyond Shimotsui and the tacky Washū-zan Highland amusement park (鷲羽山ハイランド), then climb to the hilltop from the car park where it terminates.

Shimotsui

下津井

The "textile city" of Shimotsui, beneath Washū-zan and 4km south of Kojima, is home to the intriguing **Mukashi Shimotsui Kaisendonya** (むかし下津井回船問屋; Mon & Wed–Sun 9am–5pm; free; ☏ 086 472 1289), a "museum of port life" that covers local fishing traditions. It's also worth strolling around the old streets, taking in the castle ruins, the covered wells from which passing boats stocked up on fresh water, and the Gion shrine.

ARRIVAL AND INFORMATION KOJIMA

By train Kojima is on the Seto Ōhashi line from Okayama (frequent, 18–38min; ¥500). Look out for the jeans-shaped ticket barriers!

Tourist information For local information in English, visit the tourist office in Kojima Station (daily 9am–5.30pm; ☎ 086 472 1289, ⓦ kojima-cci.or.jp).

Fukuyama

福山

The old castle town of **FUKUYAMA**, 70km west of Okayama along the industrialized San'yō coast, has become the key industrial city of Hiroshima-ken's Bingo district. Best known for its summertime extravaganza of hundreds of thousands of rose blossoms, it's also the jumping-off point for trips to the lovely seaside town of **Tomonoura**.

Hiroshima Prefectural Museum of History

広島県立歴史博物館, Hiroshima Kenritsu Rekishi Hakubutsnkan • 2-4-1 Nishi-machi • Tues–Sun 9am–5pm • ¥290 • ☎ 084 931 2513, ⓦ bit.ly/fukuyama-museum

The memorable **Hiroshima Prefectural Museum of History** stands at the southwestern corner of the large **castle park** immediately north of the station, which as the name suggests also holds a restored version of the town's castle. Built around the excavated ruins of **Kusado Sengen** (草戸千軒), a medieval town that became buried in the riverbed of the nearby Ashida-gawa, the museum holds some imaginatively displayed artefacts. The highlight, though, is the reconstruction of an entire village street from the lost settlement, lit to re-create twilight in May.

Fukuyama Museum of Art

ふくやま美術館, Fukuyama Bijutsukan • 2-4-3 Nishi-machi • Tues–Sun 9.30am–5pm • ¥300 • ☎ 084 932 2345, ⓦ bit.ly/fukuyama-artmuseum

The **Fukuyama Museum of Art** is immediately north of the history museum in Fukuyama's castle park. Its permanent collection consists largely of Japanese art, with an emphasis on contemporary works by local artists. It does have some European works, especially from Italy, and there are some striking sculptures in the surrounding gardens.

ARRIVAL AND INFORMATION FUKUYAMA

By train Fukuyama Station is on both the Shinkansen and JR San'yō train lines.
Destinations Hiroshima (every 15min; 25min); Kurashiki (frequent; 42min); Kyoto (every 30min; 1hr 20min); Okayama (every 15min; 16min–1hr); Onomichi (every 15min; 20min).

By bus The bus terminus is outside the station's south exit, with services to Tomonoura (hourly; 30min).
Tourist information The information desk in the station has English maps and leaflets (daily 9am–5.30pm; ☎ 084 922 2869, ⓦ fukuyama-kanko.com).

ACCOMMODATION

Fukuyama Oriental Hotel 福山オリエンタルホテル 1-1-6 Shiromi-chō ☎ 084 927 0888, ⓦ fukuyama .oriental-web.co.jp. Mid-range business hotel, a block from the castle park 400m northeast of the train station, offering modern en-suite rooms – features include stylish desk chairs and futuristic phones – plus an indoor onsen bath. �🛜 **¥14,000**

Hotel AreaOne ホテルエリアワン福山 9-12 Sannomaru-chō ☎ 086 942 9999, ⓦ hotel-areaone .com/en/fukuyama. Good-value little high-rise hotel, 200m east of the station's south exit, with small but well-maintained rooms, friendly staff and free breakfasts. 🛜 **¥7500**

8

EATING

Forever Coffee Market フォーエバー コーヒー マーケット 4-16 Sannomaru-chō ☎084 931 8388. Busy espresso bar, handy for the station and offering lots of basement seating, serving inexpensive pizzas, sandwiches and all-day breakfasts. 🛜 Tues—Sun 10am–9.30pm.

Onomichi Ramen Icchō 尾道ラーメン 一丁 3-7 Sannomaru-chō ☎084 928 5280. A wildly popular ramen joint, just south of the station, where after-work locals flock to slurp its frankly fatty pork-bone broth. Mon—Wed & Fri—Sun 11am–11pm.

Tomonoura

鞆の浦

The historic port of **TOMONOURA** enjoys a spectacular location on the Inland Sea, 14km south of Fukuyama at the tip of the Numakuma Peninsula. With its narrow, twisting streets and temple-topped hills readily explorable on foot or by bicycle, it makes a great day-trip destination. Studio Ghibli maestro Hayao Miyazaki stayed here for several months while preparing his 2008 film *Ponyo*, in which various local landmarks make cameo appearances.

Fishing boats still unload their catch daily beside Tomonoura's horseshoe-shaped **harbour**, which can hardly have changed since the town's Edo-era heyday, when trading vessels would wait here for a shift in the tides or rest en route to mainland Asia. Today, you're just as likely to see locals dreaming the day away on the sea walls, rod in hand, waiting for the fish to bite (especially *sakura dai*, sea bream), or selling catches of prawns, squirming crabs and other seafood on the streets.

Get your bearings by climbing up to the ruins of **Taigashima-jō** on the southern headland, where you'll find a small monument to the celebrated haiku poet Bashō and great views from Empuku-ji. To the west, you can admire the gentle sweep of the harbour and the temple-studded slopes of Taishiden hill, while a five-minute ferry ride to the east lies the island of **Sensui-jima**.

Tomonoura Museum of History

鞆の浦歴史民俗資料館, Tomonoura Rekishi Minzoku Shiryokan • 536-1 Ushiroji • Tues—Sun 9am–5pm • ¥150 • ☎084 982 1121, ⓦ tomo-rekimin.org

From its hilltop vantage point in the heart of town, once the site of the local castle, the **Tomonoura Museum of History** enjoys splendid views across a patchwork of grey and blue tiled roofs that drop away to the harbour. Diverting exhibits within include a diorama of the sea bream-netting display that's staged in the harbour every day in May, when local fishermen use age-old methods to herd the fish into their nets.

Shichikyō-ochi Ruins

七卿落ち • 8-4-2 Tomo-chō • Mon & Wed—Sun 10am–5pm • ¥400 • ☎084 982 3553

Despite the name, the **Shichikyō-ochi Ruins** – "the ruins of the exile of the seven nobles" – is in fact a perfectly intact old sake brewery. Set amid eighteenth- and nineteenth-century wood-and-plaster warehouses that now hold gift- and coffee-shops, the building briefly sheltered a band of anti-shogun rebels during the turbulent lead-up to the Meiji Restoration.

Temples and shrines

Around a dozen **temples** are scattered in and around Tomonoura. The landmark **Iō-ji** (医王寺; 13-97 Ushiroji; 24hr; free), sitting pretty atop Taishiden hill 1km west of the centre, and reached via a steep hike up a narrow pedestrian alley, is said to have been founded in 826 AD by the revered Buddhist priest **Kōbō Daishi** (see box, p.527).

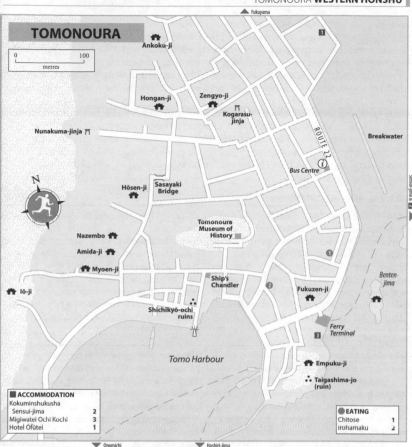

Set 400m northeast at the foot of a lesser hill, **Hōsen-ji** (法宣寺; 11-94-3 Ushiroji; 24hr; free) occupies a site where a 14.3m-wide Tengai pine tree once stood; only a stump now remains. A few minutes' walk northwest, the ancient shrine of **Nunakuma-jinja** (沼名前神社; 12-25 Ushiroji; 24hr; free) was recently rebuilt in concrete. The traditional wooden nō stage in the precinct used to be carried from battlefield to battlefield to entertain warlord Toyotomi Hideyoshi.

Fukuzen-ji

福禅寺 • 6-2-9 Tomo-chō • Daily 9.30am–5pm • Taichōrō ¥200 • ☎ 084 982 2705

The airy tatami space of the **Taichōrō** reception hall of the tenth-century **Fukuzen-ji**, immediately above the ferry terminal, features paper screens that open to reveal a striking panorama of the Inland Sea. That view has changed little since 1711, when a visiting Korean envoy hailed it "the most beautiful scenery in Japan".

Sensui-jima

仙酔島 • Frequent sailings from Tomonoura's ferry terminal • Daily, every 20min, 7.10am–9.30pm; 5min • ¥240 return

Clad in thick forest, the island of **Sensui-jima** looms out of the Inland Sea immediately east of Tomonoura. Regular year-round ferries make it simple to escape here for an hour or two, and it's also possible to stay overnight. En route, the ferry – a bizarre-looking vessel that's a scale model of an Edo-era steamship, the *Iroha Maru* – passes tiny, uninhabited **Benten-jima**. Little more than a solitary rock, the island is crowned by a temple dedicated to the Buddhist protector of fishermen.

From the dock near Sensui-jima's western tip, an obvious footpath crosses to the southern shore, where the *Kokuminshukusha* hotel surveys the main beach. An enjoyable **hiking trail** sets off from there up to the island's central hill, while if you continue along the paved coastal walkway, you'll soon reach a cliff face variously tinted black, red, blue, yellow and white. As what's said to be the only five-coloured rock in Japan, this is regarded as a spiritually auspicious spot. The shoreline path ends a few hundred metres later at a large beach, but a side trail climbs up to join the main round-island route, which will bring you back to the dock after a total circuit of roughly 6km, or two hours.

ARRIVAL AND INFORMATION TOMONOURA

By bus Buses leave platform 5 outside Fukuyama Station every 20min, and take around 30min to reach Tomonoura, where they stop at the Bus Centre at the north end of town (¥520) and beside the lighthouse in the port (¥550).

By ferry Ferries to Sensui-jima leave from the tiny terminal on Tomonoura's east-facing shoreline. In addition, an excursion boat plies back and forth between Tomonoura Harbour and Onomichi on summer weekends (May–Nov Sat & Sun 4 trips daily), and irregular services

also connect the harbour with the island of Hashiri-jima, 8km offshore.

Tourist information Pick up maps and brochures in Fukuyama, or in the local products shop alongside Tomonoura's Bus Centre (daily 9am–5.30pm; ☎084 982 3200, ⓦ bit.ly/tomonoura-tourism). You can also find useful local information at ⓦ tomomonogatari.com.

Services Bikes can be rented from the car park adjoining the ferry terminal (¥300/2hr, then ¥100/30min).

ACCOMMODATION

Kokuminshukusha Sensui-jima 国民宿舎仙酔島 3373-2 Tomochōshiroji, Sensui-jima ☎084 970 5050, ⓦ kokumin-shukusha.or.jp. Large resort hotel, facing the main beach on Sensui-jima island; some of its sizeable tatami and Western-style rooms have balconies. Be sure to reserve a sea-view room. A relaxing set of public baths includes an outdoor rooftop pool. Rates include two meals; there are no TVs, and wi-fi is only available in the lobby. In summer, they also offer camping, in tents fixed to platforms on the adjacent hillside. 🛜 Camping per person ¥4500, room ¥20,000

★**Migiwatei Ochi Kochi** 汀邸遠音近音 6-2-9 Tomochōtomo ☎084 982 1575, ⓦ ochikochi.co.jp.

Tomonoura's finest ryokan stands right at the edge of the sea, in an expanded 250-year-old building. Hugh Jackman stayed here when filming *The Wolverine*. Every room has its own black bamboo onsen, set on a large balcony looking out over the water, while the minimal interiors feature ultra-modern amenities. There's also a roof terrace. Rates include full *kaiseki* meals. 🛜 ¥56,800

Hotel Ōfūtei ホテル鴎風亭 136 Tomochōtomo ☎084 982 1123, ⓦ ofutei.com. Upscale (if, from the outside, strikingly ugly) hotel at the north end of town, with a large wooden waterfront deck for dining, spacious tatami and Western-style rooms, and a stylish array of rooftop baths. 🛜 ¥47,520

EATING

Chitose 千とせ 552-7 Tomo-chō ☎084 982 3165. A friendly place just behind the car park on the town's eastern waterfront, this spot is low on atmosphere but big on taste and value. A delicious set meal of many dishes, including the trademark catch of *tai* (sea bream), costs ¥2000, though more affordable is the tempura dinner (¥1100), which features an array of shrimp, octopus, squid and whitefish. Cash only. Mon & Wed–Sun 11.30am–2.30pm & 6–8.30pm.

★**Irohamaku** いろは 670 Tomochōtomo ☎084 982 1920, ⓦ bit.ly/tomonoura-iroha. Very traditional, very charming, lunch-only restaurant, set slightly back from the harbour, serving delicious seafood specialities in a relaxed atmosphere. Set meals start at ¥1400, with the star dish, sea bream served three ways – as sashimi, braised in hot tea, and as soup – costing ¥1750. The owners also operate a small separate inn. 🛜 Daily 11am–3pm.

RIGHT LIVING PICTURE SCROLLS VIEW, ADACHI MUSEUM OF ART (P.626) >

Onomichi

尾道

The rough-and-ready yet charming port of **ONOMICHI** lies 20km southwest of Fukuyama, its gritty waterfront facing the island of Mukai-shima across a narrow channel. Visitors come to stroll between the historic **temples** that cling to the steep forested slopes immediately inland, and explore the alleyways of the town itself, threaded through by a venerable roofed **arcade** that holds some intriguing shops and old cafés.

Onomichi has a big **movie** connection, its vertiginous byways being familiar to fans of local director Ōbayashi Nobuhiko, and of the 1950s classic *Tokyo Story*. It also serves as a gateway to the islands of the Inland Sea, with **Ikuchi-jima** and **Ōmi-shima** readily accessible by ferry, and active travellers use the town as a base for adventures on the island-hopping **Shimanami cycling road**.

The temple walk

古寺めぐり, Koji Meguri

A hugely enjoyable **temple walk**, clearly signposted from the station, undulates across the hillsides to connect most of Onomichi's 25 temples. Completing the entire course takes at least half a day, but there are several cafés and teahouses along the way, and the route dips back down to the town centre at several points. The twin highlights are **Senkō-ji**, atop the westernmost hill – which can also be accessed via cable-car, if you're looking to save time – and **Saikoku-ji**, up a separate slope further east.

Senkōji-kōen

千光寺公園 • **Temple** daily 8.30am–5pm • Free • ☎ 084 823 2310 • **Ropeway** daily 9am–5.15pm, extended hours in cherry-blossom season • ¥320 one-way, ¥500 return • **Museum of Art** Tues–Sun 9am–5pm • Admission depends on current exhibition • ☎ 084 823 2281

A large public park, **Senkōji-kōen** (千光寺公園), sprawls across the summit of Senkō-ji, the hill that looms over central Onomichi. You can reach it on the temple walk via a

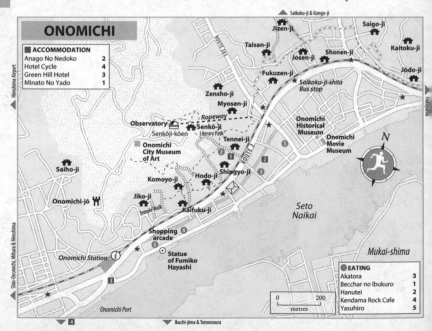

tangle of steep staircases, which twist up between the crags amid dense woods that are ablaze with cherry blossom and azaleas each spring. There's also a road up, from the west, while a **ropeway** (cable-car) climbs from Onomichi's central crossroads, 1km northeast of the station, dangling high over town and offering wonderful vistas.

You can enjoy even more spectacular views over the Inland Sea from the circular **Observatory** that crowns the very top of Senkō-ji, before perhaps pausing for tea or ice cream at its second-floor café. Just below, the **Onomichi City Museum of Art** stages changing exhibitions of predominantly local art.

The prime reason to come up here, however, is to visit the scarlet-painted **Senkō-ji** (千光寺) surrounded by *jizō* statues 100m below the summit. Said to have been founded in 806 AD, it long served as a landmark for passing ships, and boasts a hilltop belfry in which the huge bell tolls to celebrate New Year. The temple shop does a lively trade in devotional trinkets, particularly heart-shaped placards on which visitors scribble their prayers.

Literary path
文学のこみち, Bungaku no komichi
Along the "**literary path**", the section of the temple walk immediately below Senkō-ji, successive stone monuments hold inscribed quotations from famous writers, and assorted Japanese-only displays honour individual authors. Just east of the station, at the entrance to the shopping arcade, you'll encounter a bronze statue of female poet **Hayashi Fumiko**, who lived in Onomichi from 1917. She's depicted crouching pensively beside a wicker suitcase and umbrella.

Fukuzen-ji
福善寺 • Daily 9am–5pm • Free
Fukuzen-ji, 300m northeast of the ropeway base station on the lower slopes of Onomichi's eastern hills, dates from 1573. Its main gate is decorated with beautiful woodcarvings of cranes and dragons, while the vast spreading pine tree in its grounds is said to be shaped like an eagle. On the steps up to the temple, look out for **Tile-ko-michi** (Little Tile Street), a narrow hillside alleyway peppered with ceramic slabs inscribed by visitors.

Saikoku-ji
西国寺 • Daily 9am–5pm • Free • ☎ 084 837 0321, ⓦ saikokuji.jp
One of the largest temple complexes in western Japan, just east of Fukuzen-ji and reached via a broad staircase, **Saikoku-ji** is thought to have been built around 739. An enormous pair of straw sandals, each flanked in turn by a lesser pair, hang to either side of its imposing entrance gate. Pray here, in the hope you'll find the strength to continue your journey.

Jōdo-ji
浄土寺 • Daily 9am–5pm • Temple free, garden ¥500 • ☎ 084 837 2361
The squat two-storey pagoda of **Jōdo-ji**, usually engulfed by pigeons, rises 1km southeast of Saikoku-ji at the eastern end of the temple walk. There's an elegant Zen garden, with a tea-ceremony room transported from Kyoto's Fushimi castle, hidden behind the main hall of worship.

Onomichi Movie Museum
おのみち映画資料館, Onomichi Eigashi Shiryōkan • 1-14-10 Kubo • Mon & Wed–Sun 10am–6pm • ¥500 • ☎ 084 837 8141, ⓦ bit.ly/onomichi-cinema
Occupying a former rice warehouse near the waterfront, and filled with memorabilia ranging from stills and posters to vintage equipment, the **Onomichi Movie Museum**

8

makes for an enjoyable half-hour visit, even if almost nothing is translated into English. Much of Ozu Yazujirō's 1953 classic *Tokyo Story* – hailed in a recent poll of movie directors as the best film ever made – was set in Onomichi. Short films explore the connection, including one that shows shot for shot, then and now, where certain sequences were filmed. Tickets include admission to the neighbouring **Onomichi Historical Museum**, which is quite astonishingly small and devoid of interest.

ARRIVAL
ONOMICHI

By train Onomichi Station, just back from the waterfront at the southwest end of town, is on the JR San'yō line between Fukuyama and Hiroshima. The nearest Shinkansen station – Shin-Onomichi, 3km north – is a 15min bus ride away.
Destinations Fukuyama (every 15min; 20min); Hiroshima (every 15min; 20min); Okayama (hourly; 1hr 25min).
By bus Buses leave from outside Onomichi Station.
Destinations Hiroshima Airport (3 daily; 1hr; ¥1130);

Ikuchi-jima (10 daily; 1hr); Imabari, Shikoku (every 30min; 1hr 30min); Matsuyama, Shikoku (4 daily; 2hr 50min); Ōmishima (10 daily; 55min); Shin-Onomichi (frequent; 15min).
By ferry Ferries to Setoda on Ikuchi-jima leave from the jetty immediately in front of Onomichi Station (8 daily; 40min; ¥1050 one-way). On summer weekends, there are also direct boats along the coast to Tomonoura (May–Nov Sat & Sun 4 trips daily).

INFORMATION AND GETTING AROUND

Tourist information There's a helpful information counter, with lots of English-language leaflets and maps, in the station (daily 9am–6pm; ☎084 820 0005, ⓦononavi.com).
By bus On Saturday and Sunday, the Skip Line loops around central Onomichi from the station at half-hourly intervals

(all-day ticket ¥500). At weekdays, local buses reach all the same destinations; the closest stop to the foot of the ropeway, Nagaeguchi, is 5min east of the station (¥140).
By bike Rental cycles are available at the ferry terminal, opposite the station, and at several local hotels.

ACCOMMODATION

Anago No Nedoko あなごのねどこ 2-4-9 Tsuchidō ☎084 838 1005, ⓦanago.onomichisaisei.com. Part of a project to restore empty historic buildings, this budget hostel has taken over a long, thin wooden former store that snakes back from the shopping arcade – hence the name, *anago* meaning "eel". As well as simple dorm-style tatami accommodation, sharing toilets and showers (towels aren't provided, but can be rented), there's a café, lounge, cycle parking and bookstore. ☞ Dorms **¥2800**, rooms **¥6600**
Hotel Cycle ホテルサイクル 5-11 Nishigosho-chō ☎084 821 0550, ⓦonomichi-u2.com. Set 600m west of the station – follow the waterfront away from the town centre – this stylish modern hotel is the centrepiece of a converted warehouse complex dedicated to cyclists using the Shimanami Kaidō. The guest rooms are Western-style and sizeable by Japanese standards; all have twin beds and comfortable bathrooms with large baths, and there's also a restaurant, café, bakery on site, plus bike rental and servicing. ☞ **¥18,200**

Green Hill Hotel グリーンヒルホテル Onomichi 9-1 Higashigosho-chō ☎084 824 0100, ⓦshimanami-gho .co.jp. Western-style hotel, handily located on the waterfront just across from the train station, beside the Ikuchi-jima ferry terminal. From the outside it's a bit of an eyesore, but the rooms, done in beige and pale woods, are bright, decently sized and relatively cheap, and there's a good café with floor-to-ceiling sea-view windows. ☞ **¥13,500**
Minato No Yado 湊のやど 1-2-24 Kubo ☎084 838 1007, ⓦminatonoyado.jp. Built as a hillside residence in the 1930s, a hundred steps up the stairway from central Onomichi towards Senkō-ji, this opulent, elegant house combines Art Deco flourishes with Japanese traditions. It's now rented to visitors either in sections, sleeping 1–4 guests, or in its entirety, holding up to ten; shifting screens make the layout flexible. A glorious, spacious retreat, it holds a full kitchen, and modern bathroom with deep wooden bath. ☞ Half house **¥40,000**, whole house **¥80,000**

EATING

As a port, Onomichi is famous for its seafood, as sold in restaurants, sushi bars and *izakaya* throughout the old town. Look out too for *Onomichiyaki*, a local variation on the Hiroshima favourite *okonomiyaki* (see p.592) that features ingredients such as squid and chicken gizzards.

Akatora あかとら 2-4-43 Tsuchidō ☎084 822 2422. This friendly little restaurant just off the arcade in the heart of town, with counter seating as well as tatami rooms, is a great place to try local seafood specialities – though there's

no English menu. If in doubt, go for their signature *kaisen-don*, a ¥1650 bowl of raw fish with rice. Tues 5.30–10.30pm, Wed–Sun 11.30am–2pm & 5.30–10.30pm.
Becchar no Ibukuro ベッチャーの胃袋 5-9 Toyohi

CYCLING THE SHIMANAMI KAIDŌ

Onomichi is the northern gateway to the **Shimanami Kaidō**, the official name for the 60km driving route along the **Nishi-Seto Expressway** which hops from island to island across the Inland Sea to connect Honshū with Imabari on Shikoku. In total, it crosses six major islands via nine breathtaking bridges, including the **Tatara Ōhashi** between Ikuchi-jima and Ōmi-shima – which at 1480m was the world's longest cable-stayed suspension bridge when it was completed in 1999 – and culminating with the 4km **Kurushima-Kaikyō** from Ōshima to Imabari, the world's longest three-span suspension bridge.

All the bridges being open to both pedestrians and cyclists, the Shimanami Kaidō has become a hugely popular **cycling route**. While it's possible to ride all the way from Onomichi to Imabari in a single day, you'll probably enjoy it more if you take scenic detours to explore any islands that take your fancy, and spend a night or two in Ikuchi-jima (see below). **Rental bikes** (¥1000/day, plus ¥1000 deposit, refundable if you return your bike to the same place), along with route maps and left-luggage lockers, are available at the ferry terminal in Onomichi, and a dozen other locations along the way. Individual bridges charge cycle tolls ranging ¥50–200. For full details, visit ⓦbit.ly/shimanami-kaido.

Motomachi ☎084 837 3730. Lively central *izakaya* that's a welcoming spot where you can drink and eat well after most of Onomichi has shut down for the evening. Eel is the real speciality here, costing ¥1260 broiled or ¥1800 in a hot pot, but you can also get sashimi platters from ¥980 or full set meals from ¥3000. 📶 Mon & Wed–Sun 11.30am–2pm & 5pm–midnight.

Hanutei 帆雨亭 11-30 Higashitsuchidō-chō ☎084 823 2105. Delightful teahouse, tucked away in a historic home on the temple route, halfway up the stairs to Senkō-ji. Settle down in the peaceful tatami room, and enjoy green tea and cake as you savour the sweeping views. Daily 10am–5pm.

Kendama Rock Cafe ケンダマロックカフェ 1-17-13 Tsuchidō ☎084 824 8180, ⓦkendamarock.com. Very cute, very tiny coffee spot with rickety floorboards and half a dozen seats. Run by a gregarious professional kendama player, it's awash with the sport's paraphernalia, and serves good fresh Americano (¥500) plus a few snacks. 📶 Daily 11am–6pm.

Yasuhiro 保広 1-10-12 Tsuchidō ☎084 822 5639. Not surprisingly, after fifty years in the same seafront location this friendly, family-run sushi place has a devoted local following. The ¥1750 set lunch is the best value; full dinners cost from ¥5000. Tues–Sun 11.30am–2.30pm & 5.30–9pm.

Ikuchi-jima and Ōmi-shima

生口島・大三島

Of the various islands in the Geiyo archipelago, which peppers the Inland Sea between Honshū and Shikoku, IKUCHI-JIMA and ŌMI-SHIMA most merit a visit. Both are accessible by ferry or along the Shimanami Kaidō, but Ikuchi-jima is the better choice for an overnight stay and holds the dazzling **Kōsan-ji** complex and the exquisite **Hirayama Ikuo Museum of Art**.

Ikuchi-jima

生口島

Tourists flock in summer to the palm-fringed beaches of **IKUCHI-JIMA**, an island you may also see called **SETODA** (瀬戸田) after the quaint settlement at its northwest tip. Sun-kissed and covered with citrus groves, it can be comfortably toured by bicycle within a day, taking in Setoda itself, home to Kōsan-ji temple and the art museum; the separate islet of **Kōne-shima**, across a short bridge from Setoda; and the sweeping man-made **Sunset Beach**, further down the west coast towards the **Tatara Ōhashi bridge**. As you explore, look out for the seventeen outdoor sculptures, including a giant saxophone and a stack of yellow buckets, that comprise the "Island-Wide Museum".

Kōsan-ji

耕三寺 · 553-2 Setoda · Daily 9am–5pm · ¥1400 · ☎ 084 527 0800, ⓦ kousanji.or.jp

Ikuchi-jima owes its most famous attraction, the kaleidoscopic temple complex of **Kōsan-ji**, to steel-tube manufacturer **Kanemoto Kozo** (1891–1970), who made his fortune in the arms trade. In 1936, after his mother died, the bereft Kanemoto resigned from his company, grew his hair, and set about building a temple in her honour. He bought a priesthood from Nishi-Hongan-ji temple in Kyoto, took the name of the minor Kōsan-ji temple in Niigata, and became **Kōsanji Kozo**. His new Kōsan-ji incorporated replicas of Japan's most splendid temple buildings, including ten halls, three towers, four gates and an underground cave. Many of the re-creations are smaller than the originals, but Kanemoto cut no corners in terms of detail, even adding his own embellishments – most famously to his over-the-top version of the Yōmei-mon from Nikkō's Tōshō-gū, thereby earning Kōsan-ji its nickname **Nishi-Nikkō**, the "Nikkō of the west".

Senbutsudō and the Hill of Hope

千仏洞 · 未来心の丘, Mirai Kokoro no Oka

Reached from a gift-shop-lined street off the waterfront just west of Setoda's ferry landing, Kōsan-ji's gaudy entrance gate is modelled on one from the imperial palace in Kyoto. Head right from the main temple building, and an underground passage will lead you through the Valley of Hell, where miniature tableaux depict the horrors of damnation, and into the **Senbutsudō** or "Cave of a Thousand Buddhas", home to an enraptured heavenly host. You eventually emerge beneath the beatific gaze of a 15m-tall statue of Kannon (観音), the Buddhist goddess of mercy. The **Hill of Hope** beyond holds unusual modern marble sculptures with names like "Flame of the Future" and "Stage of the Noble Turtle", and offers wonderful views over Setoda.

Chōseikaku and the gallery

潮聲閣 · アートギャラリー · Daily 10am–4pm · Same ticket and contact details as Kōsan-ji

Kōsan-ji's five-storey **pagoda**, modelled on one at Murō-ji in Nara, is the last resting place of Kanemoto's beloved mother. Her holiday home, **Chōseikaku**, stands alongside. It's a fascinating combination of Western and traditional styles – two rooms have beautiful painted panels on their ceilings and a Buddha-like model of Mrs Kanemoto resting in an alcove. Kōsan-ji's plain-looking **art gallery** opposite holds sober displays of predominantly religious paintings and statues.

Hirayama Ikuo Museum of Art

平山郁夫美術館, Hirayama Ikuo Bijutsukan · 200-2 Sawa · Daily 9am–5pm · ¥900 · ☎ 084 527 3800, ⓦ hirayama-museum.or.jp

The **Hirayama Ikuo Museum of Art**, next door to Kōsan-ji's art gallery, is devoted to the Setoda-born painter **Hirayama Ikuo** (1930–2009). Hirayama was a junior-high-school student in Hiroshima when the bomb dropped; his *Holocaust at Hiroshima* can be seen in the city's Prefectural Museum of Art (see p.590). He subsequently travelled the world, becoming famous for his depictions of the Silk Road, while repeatedly returning to the Inland Sea for inspiration. Hirayama used a traditional Japanese technique for his giant canvases, working very quickly with a special fast-drying paint, *iwa-enogu*; the resultant brush strokes give the finished works a distinctively dreamy quality. This method requires the artist to create preparatory sketches for each picture, and many such full-sized blueprints, known as **oshitazu**, are displayed here alongside the completed paintings and watercolours.

Kōjō-ji

向上寺

One of Hirayama's most beautiful paintings was inspired by the view from the summit of the hill that looms immediately behind Setoda. A small park here overlooks the attractive three-storey pagoda of **Kōjō-ji**, emerging from the pine trees below, with the coloured tiled roofs of the village and the islands of the Inland Sea beyond.

ARRIVAL AND INFORMATION IKUCHI-JIMA

By bus Buses connect Setoda with both Onomichi on Honshū and Imabari on Shikoku.
Destinations Imabari (frequent; 30min); Onomichi (10 daily; 1hr).
By ferry Ferries connect Ikuchi-jima with both Onomichi (8 daily; 40min; ¥1050 one-way) and Mihara, further west along the coast, which is on both the San'yō and

Shinkansen rail lines (hourly; 25min; ¥820 one-way; ⓦ bit .ly/mihara-ferry).
Tourist information There's an information booth facing the art museum in Setoda (daily 9am–5pm; ☏ 084 527 0051).
Bike rental From the tourist information booth (¥1000/ day, plus ¥1000 deposit).

ACCOMMODATION

★**Ryokan Tsutsui** 旅館つつ井 216 Setoda-chō ☏ 084 527 2221, ⓦ www.tsutsui.yad.jp. Traditional establishment, right beside the ferry terminal, and run by a charming Japanese couple, with spacious, tastefully modernized tatami rooms and a deliciously invigorating lemon bath (many of Japan's lemons are grown on Ikuchi-jima). The lobby features comfy seating and an upright, well-tuned piano. Rates include two meals. 🛜 **¥23,760**

Setoda Private Hostel 瀬戸田ゲストハウス 58-1 Tarumi Setoda-chō ☏ 084 527 3137, ⓦ bit.ly/setoda -hostel. Also known as *Setoda Tarumi Onsen*, this no-frills hostel, south of Setoda near Sunset Beach, offers simple accommodation in tatami dorms, plus a rather amazing wood-panelled onsen set in rocks gathered from the seashore. Breakfast and dinner, rich in local seafood, cost ¥1800 extra per person. 🛜 Dorms **¥4500**

EATING

Chidori ちどり 530-2 Setoda-chō ☏ 084 527 0231, ⓦ chidori-onomichi.com. Octopus is the speciality at this smart seafood restaurant, at the main crossroads between the ferry and the temple, with a full set meal for ¥3000 and individual dishes from ¥1100. They also offer a ¥4000 lemon hot pot, containing oysters and sea bream as well, of course, as octopus. 🛜 Mon & Wed–Sun 11am–4pm & 6–11pm.
Keima 桂馬 251 Setoda-chō ☏ 084 527 1989. Highly

recommended little sushi spot, offering good food at down-to-earth prices. A sizeable set lunch goes for ¥1400. Mon–Wed & Fri–Sun 10am–9pm.
Mansaku Seto No Aji 万作 530-1 Setoda-chō ☏ 084 527 3028. Popular fish restaurant opposite Kōsan-ji, serving a wide range of tempura and hot-pot dishes as well as sushi and sashimi, with prices starting at ¥1300 and their signature broiled eel at ¥1800. Mon–Wed & Fri–Sun 11am–3pm.

Ōmi-shima

大三島

The Shimanami Kaidō only dips briefly into the eastern side of **ŌMI-SHIMA**, Ikuchi-jima's larger neighbour to the south, on its southward course towards Shikoku. The island is however home to one of Japan's oldest shrines, **Ōyamazumi-jinja**, in the undistinguished little port of **Miyaura** (宮浦) on its west coast. While Ōmi-shima's beaches are nothing special, it's still fun to spend a half-day circling the seashore by bike.

Ōyamazumi-jinja

大山祇神社 • Miyaura 3327 • Daily 8.30am–5pm • Free • ☏ 089 782 0032

The **Ōyamazumi-jinja**, which dates back to the end of the Kamakura era (1192–1333), is dedicated to Ōyamazumi, the elder brother of the Shintō deity Amaterasu. Between the twelfth and sixteenth centuries, it was a place of worship for pirates – its deities include one who protects sailors – who used Ōmi-shima as a base until the warlord Toyotomi Hideyoshi brought them to heel. The present structure, fifteen minutes' walk from the Miyaura waterfront, dates from the late fourteenth century and features a pleasant courtyard garden.

Ōyamazumi-jinja museum

大山祇神社宝物館, Ōyamazumi-jinja Homotsukan • 3327 Ōmishima-chō Miyaura • Daily 8.30am–5pm • ¥1000, with Kaiji Museum • ☎ 089 782 0032

The three modern buildings that comprise the **Ōyamazumi-jinja museum** stand to the right of the main shrine grounds. The Shiyōden hall and connected Kokuhō-kan claim to hold the largest collection of armour in Japan – over two-thirds of all national treasures in weaponry – but only samurai freaks are likely to find its dry displays interesting.

Kaiji Museum

絵画比肩, Kaiji Hiken • 3327 Ōmishima-chō Miyaura • ¥1000, with Ōyamazumi-jinja museum • Daily 8.30am–4.30pm • ☎ 089 782 0032

The intriguing **Kaiji Museum**, also known as the Ōmi-shima Maritime Museum, houses the *Hayama-maru*, a boat built in 1935 for Emperor Hirohito, who like his son Akihito was a keen student of marine biology. Some of the sea life in the museum's meticulously catalogued displays of fish, birds and rocks looks an awful lot like pickled aliens.

ARRIVAL AND DEPARTURE	**ŌMI-SHIMA**

By ferry Ferries connect Miyaura with Imabari (7 daily; 1hr–1hr 30min).

Hiroshima

広島

Since August 6, 1945, **HIROSHIMA**, western Honshū's largest city, has been a living monument to the devastating effects of the atomic bomb. Millions of visitors each year come to pay their respects at the Peace Memorial Park and museum, while the reconstructed city serves in its entirety as an eloquent testimony to the power of life over destruction. Where once there was nothing but ashes, there now stands a dynamic modern city which with its trundling trams and bustling alleyways retains an old-world feel.

Poised at the western end of the Inland Sea, Hiroshima is also the jumping-off point for several offshore islands, including **Miyajima**, home of the magnificent **Itsukushima-jinja** shrine.

Brief history

Hiroshima grew up on the delta of the Ōta-gawa; it remains very much a river city, threaded through by several waterways. During the twelfth century, the region where the city now stands was known as **Gokamura** ("Five Villages"). Its ruler, a scion of the Taira clan named Taira no Kiyomori, was for a while the power behind the throne in Kyoto, and commissioned the Ikutsushima shrine on Miyajima. Even after the Taira were vanquished by the Minamoto clan (or Genji), at the battle of Dannoura in 1185, Gokamura continued to grow, and it played a crucial part during warlord **Mōri Motonari**'s campaign to take control of Chūgoku during the latter half of the fifteenth century. When Motonari's grandson Terumoto built his castle, the city was renamed **Hiroshima** ("Wide Island") By the Meiji era the city had become an important base for the imperial army, a role that placed it firmly on the path to its terrible destiny.

A-bomb Dome

原爆ドーム, Genbaku Dōmu • 1-10 Ōte-machi

Hiroshima's most famous landmark, the **A-bomb Dome** or *Genbaku Dōmu*, is the twisted shell of what used to be the Industrial Promotion Hall, built in 1914. Almost at the hypocentre of the blast, the hall was one of the few structures in the surrounding 3km that remained standing, its skeletal dome open to the skies. It's been maintained ever since in its distressed state as a historical witness to Hiroshima's suffering, and

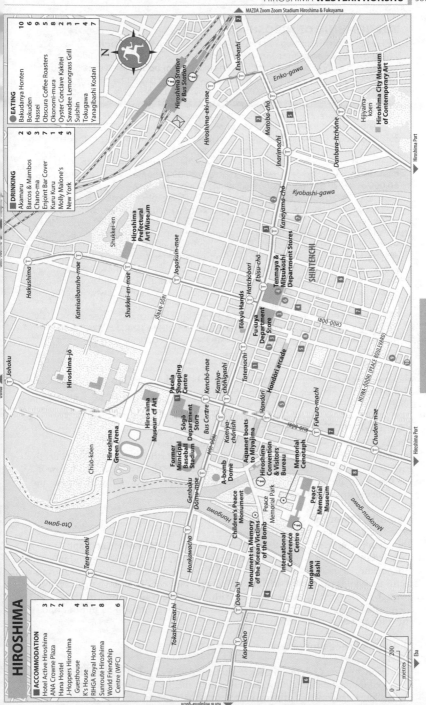

HIROSHIMA

■ ACCOMMODATION
Hotel Active Hiroshima	3
ANA Crowne Plaza	7
Hana Hostel	2
J-Hoppers Hiroshima Guesthouse	4
K's House	5
RIHGA Royal Hotel	1
Sunroute Hiroshima	8
World Friendship Centre (WFC)	6

● EATING
Bakudanya Honten	10
Bokuden	6
Hassei	9
Obscura Coffee Roasters	5
Okonomi-mura	8
Oyster Conclave Kakitei	2
Sawadee Lemongrass Grill	3
Suishin	1
Tokugawa	4
Yanagibashi Kodani	7

■ DRINKING
Akamaru	2
Barcos & Mambos	6
Chano-ma	3
Enjoint Bar Cover	7
Kuru Kuru	1
Molly Malone's	4
New York	5

MAZDA Zoom Zoom Stadium Hiroshima & Fukuyama

8

THE BOMBING OF HIROSHIMA

As a garrison town, Hiroshima was an obvious target during **World War II**. Until August 6, 1945, however, it had been spared Allied bombing. That may have been an intentional strategy by the US military, so that the effects of the **atom bomb**, when exploded, could be fully understood. Even so that, when the B29 bomber *Enola Gay* set off on its mission, Hiroshima was one of three possible targets, with the others being Nagasaki and Kokura. Its fate was sealed when reconnaissance planes reported clear skies over the city.

When "**Little Boy**", as the bomb was nicknamed, exploded at 8.15am, 580m above Hiroshima, it unleashed the equivalent destructive power of **15,000 tonnes of TNT**. Down below, some 350,000 people looked up to see what must have looked like the sun falling to the earth. Within less than a second, a kilometre-wide radioactive fireball consumed the city. The heat was so intense that all that remained of some victims were their outlines seared onto the rubble. Immediately, 70,000 buildings were destroyed and **80,000 people** killed. By the end of the year, **60,000** more had died from burns, wounds and radiation sickness; everyone within 2km of the explosion suffered severe internal organ damage. The final death toll is still unknown, the figure offered by the Hiroshima Peace Memorial Museum being "140,000 (plus or minus 10,000)". By way of context, almost 20,000 people died in Tokyo on a single night of bombing in 1945.

Many survivors despaired that anything would grow again in the city's poisoned earth, but their hopes were raised when fresh buds and blossom appeared on the trees less than a year after the blast. Since then, Hiroshima has been reconstructed to an astounding degree, and as a self-proclaimed "city of international peace and culture", it's now home to well over a million people. As of 2016, they include an estimated 60,000 **hibakusha**, literally "explosion-affected people", who survived the bombing. A total of around 170,000 survivors who were present in either Hiroshima or Nagasaki are still alive to bear witness.

On the anniversary of the blast, August 6, a **memorial service** takes place in front of the Cenotaph in the Peace Memorial Park. White doves are released, and ten thousand lanterns for the souls of the dead are set adrift on the Ōta-gawa.

packs a powerful punch as you emerge from the modern-day hustle and bustle of the Hondōri arcade. There's no entry to the dome itself.

Peace Memorial Park

平和記念公園, Heiwa Kinen-kōen • 1 Nakajima-chō • 24hr • Free • ☎ 082 504 2390

Immediately west of downtown Hiroshima, at the northern apex of what's effectively a narrow island, created when the Ōta-gawa divides for the last time 4km before it reaches the Inland Sea, the verdant **Peace Memorial Park** is dotted with statues and monuments to the victims of the A-bomb.

Memorial Cenotaph

原爆死没者慰霊碑, Genbaku Shibotsu-sha Irai Ijibumi

The main monument in the Peace Memorial Park, the **Memorial Cenotaph**, was designed by architect Kenzō Tange in the style of protective objects found in ancient Japanese burial mounds. A smooth arch of concrete and granite, it curves above a stone coffin that holds the names of all the direct and indirect A-bomb victims. Framed through it, along an axis that's aligned with the A-bomb Dome and the Peace Memorial Museum, the **Flame of Peace** was lit in 1964, and will be put out once the last nuclear weapon on earth has been destroyed.

Children's Peace Monument

原爆の子の像, Genbaku no Ko no Zō

The deeply moving **Children's Peace Monument** depicts a young girl standing atop an elongated dome, holding aloft a giant origami crane. Its base is always festooned in multicoloured garlands of origami cranes – a symbol of health and longevity – folded by schoolchildren not only from Japan but from all over the world. The tradition started when 12-year-old radiation victim Sasaki Sadako fell ill with leukaemia in 1955. She began to fold cranes on her sick bed in the hope that if she reached a thousand she'd be cured; she died despite reaching her goal, but her classmates continued after her death, and this monument was built using donations from children throughout Japan.

Monument in Memory of the Korean Victims of the Bomb

韓国人原爆犠牲者慰霊碑, Kankoku-jin Genbaku Giseisha Irei Ishibumi

The **Monument in Memory of the Korean Victims of the Bomb**, on the western side of the Peace Memorial Park, commemorates the estimated twenty thousand Koreans who died anonymously in the A-bomb blast. Korea was at the time occupied by the Japanese, and many Koreans had been brought over as forced labourers during the preceding decade. Only in 1970 were they officially memorialized, and even then this monolith, mounted on the back of a turtle and built in Korea, was erected outside the park; it finally moved into the park in 1999.

Peace Memorial Museum

平和記念資料館, Heiwa Kinen-Shiryōkan • Daily: March–July & Sept–Nov 8.30am–6pm; Aug 8.30am–7pm; Dec–Feb 8.30am–5pm • ¥200, audio commentary ¥100 extra • ☎ 082 241 4004, ⓦ www.pcf.city.hiroshima.jp

The **Peace Memorial Museum**, an essential port of call for every visitor, spreads through two large buildings at the southern end of the Peace Memorial Park. Hiroshima sees itself as the prime witness in the project to create a world without war, and the museum is the centrepiece of its endeavour. At the time of writing, it was being comprehensively renovated section by section, while remaining partially open throughout. When that overhaul is completed – in 2018, according to the latest schedule – the revamped museum is expected to retain many of its long-standing exhibits. Bear in mind, though, that certain details below may have changed.

Visitors enter the museum via the **east building**, where the ticket office is located and where the temporary exhibitions on the ground floor can be accessed without paying for admission. The upper floors are partly given over to displays on Hiroshima itself before and after the war – including a huge diorama of the moment of the blast, in which the bomb appears as a huge red ball suspended over the city – and partly to tracing the development and dangers of nuclear weapons.

The **west building** covers the events and aftermath of August 6, 1945, in shocking and gruesome detail. Cases display the pitiful possessions and torn clothing left by the dead; agonized mannequins stagger through a post-apocalyptic landscape, their skin melting away; stark photographs catalogue the effects of radiation; a stone step taken from a bank bears the silhouette of some nameless victim; and there are even pieces of bone, clumps of hair and a human tongue.

Eventually you come to a corridor looking down the full length of the park towards the resurrected city, which is used for press conferences by visiting dignitaries. President Obama was here in 2015, and expressed his hopes for a world free of nuclear weapons in a speech that's available in DVD form in the museum shop.

As the years go by, and fewer survivors of the bombing remain, the museum no longer schedules opportunities to meet actual *hibakusha*. Instead there's an English-language lecture at 2pm daily, by a designated "A-Bomb Legacy Successor".

Hiroshima-jō

広島城 • 21-1 Moto-machi • Daily: March–Nov 9am–6pm, Dec–Feb 9am–5pm • ¥370 • ☎ 082 221 7512, ⓦ www.rijo-castle.jp

Hiroshima's restored castle, **Hiroshima-jō**, stands twenty minutes' walk north of the Peace Park, at the northwest corner of a moated enclave that also holds the active **Gokoku-jinja** shrine. Originally erected in 1591, the castle became the city's military headquarters after the Meiji Restoration in the nineteenth century. After the war – remarkable photos show it reduced to a pile of timbers, but not actually incinerated, by the A-bomb – its five-floor donjon was swiftly reconstructed in concrete, and now doubles as a superb **historical museum**. Excellent displays, all with good English translations, tell the story of both castle and city, and include some stunning fifteenth-century armour.

Shukkei-en

縮景園 • 2-11 Kaminobori-chō • Daily: April–Sept 9am–6pm, Oct–March 9am–5pm • ¥260 • ☎ 082 221 3620, Ⓦ shukkeien.jp • Tram #9 from Hatchōbori to Shukkei-en-mae

Asano Nagaakira, who became *daimyō* of Hiroshima in 1619, laid out the **Shukkei-en** – literally, "shrunk scenery garden" – to present in miniature Xihu lake in Hangzhou, China. Fully restored after the war, bordered by the Kyōbashi River and centred on an artificial pond dotted with tiny islands, it's a ravishing place for a stroll, with several charming teahouses as potential breaks.

Hiroshima Prefectural Art Museum

広島県立美術館, Hiroshima Kenritsu Bijutsukan • 2-22 Kaminobori-chō • April to mid-Oct Tues–Thurs, Sat & Sun 9am–5pm, Fri 9am–8pm, mid-Oct to March Tues–Thurs, Sat & Sun 9am–5pm, Fri 9am–7pm • ¥510, temporary exhibitions extra • ☎ 082 221 6246, Ⓦ hpam.jp • Tram #9 from Hatchōbori to Shukkei-en-mae

As well as staging noteworthy temporary exhibitions, the impressive modern **Hiroshima Prefectural Art Museum**, alongside Shukkei-en, displays its permanent collection in three galleries. Two are devoted to Japanese artists, largely with connections to Hiroshima, while one ranges more widely over art from the 1920s and 1930s. The twin highlights are the fiery, awe-inspiring *Holocaust at Hiroshima* by Hirayama Ikuo (see p.584), who was in the city when the bomb dropped, and the floppy watches of Salvador Dalí's surreal *Dreams of Venus*.

Hiroshima Museum of Art

ひろしま美術館, Hiroshima Bijutsukan • 2-22 Kaminobori-chō • Tues–Sun 9am–5pm • ¥1000, temporary exhibitions extra • ☎ 082 223 2530, Ⓦ hiroshima-museum.jp

Less directly connected to Hiroshima itself than the city's other art museums, and pricier to boot, the **Hiroshima Museum of Art**, in Central Park just south of the castle, is arguably the one to skip if your time is limited. It does however hold a fine collection of European masterpieces, including Van Gogh's late *Daubigny's Garden* and Monet's *Morning on the Seine*, as well as Western-influenced works by twentieth-century Japanese artists.

Hiroshima City Museum of Contemporary Art

広島市現代美術館 • 1-1 Hijiyamakoen • Tues–Sun 10am–5pm • ¥370 • ☎ 082 264 1121, Ⓦ hiroshima-moca.jp • On Orange route of Sightseeing Loop Bus

Many of the thought-provoking works in the **Hiroshima City Museum of Contemporary Art**, atop the steep little Hiji-yama 1km south of the station, were inspired by the atomic bomb. Its permanent collection, though, also includes a triptych by Francis Bacon, while the surrounding leafy **Hijiyama-kōen** is dotted with sculptures, including some by Henry Moore, and provides splendid views across the city.

ARRIVAL AND DEPARTURE   **HIROSHIMA**

By plane Hiroshima Airport (Ⓦ www.hij.airport.jp) is 50km east of the city, and 35km west of Onomichi. Buses connect it with Hiroshima Station and the central Bus Centre (frequent; 50min; ¥1300), and also with the JR stations in Onomichi (3 daily; 1hr; ¥1130) and Fukuyama (3 daily; 1hr 5min; ¥1350). The smaller Hiroshima Nishi airport has been closed to aircraft since 2012.

Destinations Dalian (4 weekly; 1hr 55min); Hong Kong (3 weekly; 3hr 15min); Okinawa (1 daily; 1hr 55min); Sapporo (2 daily; 1hr 50min); Sendai (2 daily; 1hr 20min);

Seoul (5 weekly; 1hr 50min); Shanghai (daily; 2hr 15min); Taipei (daily; 2hr 50min); Tokyo Haneda (17 daily; 1hr 20min); Tokyo Narita (3 daily; 1hr 20min).

By train Shinkansen and local trains arrive at Hiroshima Station, on the east side of the centre.

Destinations Fukuoka, Hakata Station (every 15min; 1hr 10min); Fukuyama (every 15min; 25min); Kyoto (every 15min; 1hr 50min); Okayama (every 15min; 35min); Onomichi (every 15min; 20min); Shin-Osaka (every 15min; 1hr 30min); Tokyo (every 15min; 4hr).

By bus Long-distance buses arrive beside Hiroshima Station; some also use the Bus Centre (@h-buscenter.com), on the third floor of Sogō department store, at 6-27

Moto-machi in the city centre. Note that foreign visitors currently pay just ¥500 for the bus to Matsue (@bit.ly /matsue-bus).

Destinations Kyoto (3 daily; 6hr 15min); Matsue (hourly; 3hr); Okayama (5 daily; 2hr 30min); Osaka (5 daily; 5hr); Tokyo (daily; 12hr).

By ferry Hiroshima Port (☎082 253 1212, @setonaikaikisen.co.jp), 7km south of Hiroshima Station and served by regular trams (¥160), is linked by high-speed hydrofoils to Miyajima (see p.594), and also has ferry connections with Matsuyama on Shikoku.

Destinations Matsuyama (20 daily; ferry 2hr 40min, hydrofoil 1hr 15min); Miyajima (8 daily; 30min).

GETTING AROUND

Hiroshima has a good public transport system, including nine tramlines and an extensive bus network as well as the zippy Astram monorail line, which goes underground in the city centre, terminating beneath the Hondōri arcade. That said, traffic can make travelling by bus or tram frustratingly slow, and it's often quicker to get around on foot.

By tram Each journey within the city centre on the Hiroden tram network (@hiroden.co.jp) costs ¥160; a one-day pass is ¥640, or ¥840 including the Matsudai ferry to Myajima (*not* the JR ferry or the ferry from Hiroshima Port). From the station, trams #2 and #6 head west to the Peace Park and beyond.

By bus The Sightseeing Loop Bus, also known as Hiroshima Meipuru-pu, circles between the station and the Peace Park on two distinct routes – the Orange route takes in the Shukkei-en garden, the castle and all three art museums, while the Green route passes through the temple district north of the station (free for holders of JR rail passes, otherwise ¥200 per journey, one-day pass

¥400; ☎082 261 0622, @bit.ly/meipuru-pu).

By bike Under the Hiroshima City Rental Cycle scheme, you can use a credit card to rent a bicycle – or a Peacecle, as they're officially known – from any of 22 docking stations, including two at the station, one at the Peace Park, and one at the main Peacecle office (7-29 Koyobashi-chō, across the Enko-gawa from the station; one 30min trip ¥108, all-day pass ¥1080; ☎082 568 5760, @docomo-cycle.jp.hiroshima).

Car rental Companies based at the station include Eki Rent-a-Car (☎082 263 5933, @www.ekiren.co.jp) and Nippon Rent-a-Car (☎084 264 0919, @www.nrgroup -global.com).

8

INFORMATION

Tourist information Hiroshima Station holds two tourist offices, one on the Shinkansen concourse and a larger one in the underground tunnel outside the southern entrance (both daily 9am–5.30pm; ☎082 261 1877), while the Hiroshima Convention & Visitors Bureau has its main office

in the *Hiroshima Rest House*, beside the Motoyasu bridge in the Peace Park (daily: March–July & Sept–Nov 8.30am–6pm; Aug 8.30am–7pm; Dec–Feb 8.30am–5pm; ☎082 247 6738, @www.hiroshima-navi.or.jp or @visithiroshima.net).

ACCOMMODATION

Hotel Active Hiroshima ホテルアクティブ広島 15-3 Nobori-chō, Naka-ku ☎082 212 0001, @hotel-active .com/hiroshima. Smart, comfortable business hotel, 1km southwest of the station, across the second bridge on the tram route into the centre, and offering small but great-value Western-style hotel rooms. Rates include buffet breakfast. 🛜 **¥7980**

★ **ANA Crowne Plaza** ANAクラウンプラザホテル広島 7-20 Naka-machi, Naka-ku ☎082 241 1111, @anacrowneplaza-hiroshima.jp. Conveniently located in the heart of the city, just across the river from the memorial, the ANA is one of the city's largest and finest hotels, with top-notch service. Some of its 409 guest rooms are very small,

though; expect to pay around ¥5000 extra if you need more space. 🛜 **¥19,500**

Hana Hostel 広島花宿 1-15 Kojin-machi, Minami-ku ☎082 263 2980, @hiroshima.hanahostel.com. Handy little budget option, in what used to be a business hotel, facing a temple barely 5min southeast of the station's south exit; train noise may disturb light sleepers. As well as hostel-style four-bed tatami dorms, they offer twin and double private rooms with en-suite bathrooms, and rent bikes for ¥700/day. 🛜 Dorms **¥2500**, doubles **¥6000**

J-Hoppers Hiroshima Guesthouse ジェイホッパーズ 広島ゲストハウス 5-16 Dohashi-chō, Naka-ku ☎082 233 1360, @hiroshima.j-hoppers.com. This popular little hostel, in a former ryokan 3km west of the station beyond the Peace Park, has dorms and tatami rooms, a spacious lounge, a self-catering kitchen (with 24hr grocery nearby) and laundry facilities. 🛜 Dorms **¥2500**, doubles **¥6000**

★ **K's House** ケイズハウス広島 1-8-9 Matoba-chō, Minami-ku ☎082 568 7244, 🌐kshouse.jp/hiroshima. Welcoming, well-equipped backpackers hostel, just off the main road, 10min walk southwest from the station. As well as dorms (4–6 beds) – all mixed gender – they have simple tatami rooms and private doubles exactly resembling those of a standard business hotel, along with lounge, kitchen, laundry and lots of useful local advice. 🛜 Dorms **¥2600**, tatami rooms **¥7400**, en-suite doubles **¥7900**

RIHGA Royal Hotel リーガロイヤルホテル 6-78 Moto-machi, Naka-ku ☎082 502 1121, 🌐www.rihga.com /hiroshima. Soaring 33 floors, Hiroshima's grandest hotel was designed in the image of its neighbour, the reconstructed castle. It has spacious rooms, six restaurants,

two bars, a pool, a gym and a plush lobby, complete with a stunning painting of Itsukushima-jinja by Hirayama Ikuo. Breakfast is included. 🛜 **¥25,370**

Sunroute Hiroshima ホテルサンルート 3-3-1 Ōte-machi, Naka-ku ☎082 249 3600, 🌐bit.ly/sunroute -hiroshima. Upmarket branch of a well-established national chain of business hotels, very close to the Peace Park, with two good restaurants (the Italian *Viale* and the Japanese *Kissui*), rooms specially equipped for disabled guests, and decent prices. 🛜 **¥10,200**

World Friendship Centre (WFC) ワールドフレンドシップ センター 8-10 Higashi-Kannon-machi, Nishi-ku ☎082 503 3191, 🌐wfchiroshima.net. Run by a friendly American couple and devoted to peaceful commemoration of Hiroshima's tragic history, this small and homely non-smoking B&B offers accommodation in simple tatami rooms, sharing a bathroom. Rates include breakfast plus an optional talk by an A-bomb survivor and a tour of the Peace Park. 🛜 **¥7800**

EATING

Hiroshima has the finest selection of restaurants in western Honshū. As well as fresh **seafood** from the Inland Sea – especially oysters, which are cultivated on rafts in Hiroshima Bay – the major local speciality is *okonomiyaki*. The usual description of these amazing heaps of fried, concentrated goodness as being "pancakes" doesn't begin to do them justice; skilfully assembled by quick-fire chefs, they hold the diner's choice of noodles, cabbage, bean sprouts, meat, fish and all sorts of spices, powders and condiments. Unlike in Osaka, where all the ingredients are mixed up together, everything is painstakingly added level by level. Don't leave Hiroshima without sampling one.

Bakudanya Honten ばくだん屋本店 6-14 Fujimi-chō ☎082 245 5885, 🌐bakudanya.net. Simple noodle restaurant, a few blocks south of central downtown, whose recipe for *tsukemen* – a spicy local take on ramen, served cool with a separate dipping sauce, and costing well under ¥1000 – has been such a hit that they now have branches all over Hiroshima, and as far afield as Hong Kong. Daily 11.30am–midnight.

Bokuden ボクデン Takata Arei Biiru, 4-20 Horikawa-chō, Naka-ku ☎082 240 1000, 🌐bokuden.co.jp. Glossy, late-opening Korean restaurant, on the covered arcade behind downtown's Tenmaya department store, which centres on a large open kitchen. The menu holds something to suit most budgets, but it helps if you like your food spicy, whether it's fiery *chijimi* – a kind of omelette with leeks, meat and chilli – for ¥790, or a full crab *kimchi* dinner for ¥2500. 🛜 Daily 5pm–1am.

Hassei 八誠 4-17 Fujimi-chō, Naka-ku ☎082 242 8123. Bustling little place that lures in-the-know locals to the southern edge of downtown to watch a team of deft chefs whip up every imaginable variety of *okonomiyaki*; the seafood special costs ¥1300, but you can eat well for under ¥1000. Tues–Sat 11.30am–2pm & 5.30–11pm, Sun 5.30–11pm.

Obscura Coffee Roasters オブスキュラ 3-28 Fukuro-machi, Naka-ku ☎082 249 7453, 🌐www.obscura -coffee.com. This stylish modern café, a short walk east of the Peace Park, has a laidback, grown-up vibe – young

children are positively discouraged. As well as the best coffee in town, they also serve simple snacks. 🛜 Daily 9am–8pm.

★ **Okonomi-mura** お好み村 5-13 Shin-tenchi, Naka-ku ☎082 241 2210, 🌐okonomimura.jp. Budget food heaven: 25 separate little *okonomiyaki* counters are crammed into three upper floors of this narrow building, in the heart of the entertainment district with its own stop on the green route of the Sightseeing Loop Bus. Find a space at whichever one sets you salivating, and watch the expert chefs put their astonishing concoctions together. *Hasshō* on the second floor and *Itsukushima* on the elevator on the fourth floor are among the best in town. Expect to pay around ¥800 for a standard *okonomiyaki*, plus a few hundred more for special ingredients such as oysters. Daily 11am–2am.

Oyster Conclave Kakitei オイスターコンクラーベ牡蠣 亭 11 Hashimoto-chō, Naka-ku ☎082 221 8990, 🌐kakitei.jp. As the name suggests, the emphasis in this small pavilion, on the riverfront walkway beside the main bridge on the tram route, is firmly on oysters, with deep fried as the best of many different styles of preparation. Individual oysters cost around ¥200, with set lunches for ¥1600 and set dinners from ¥3300. In fine weather, you can sit outdoors by the river. Mon & Wed–Sun 11.30am–2.30pm & 5–10pm.

Sawadee Lemongrass Grill サワディー レモングラス グリル 4F Mozart House Building, Chūō-dōri, Naka-ku

☎082 241 0066. Casual Thai restaurant above the posh *Mozart* cake shop and café (take the elevator at the back). The most popular dishes, all at ¥1000–1500, are *tom yam kung* soup and the massaman and green curries. Portions can be small and the food isn't overly spicy, but this is the real deal. Daily 11am–2.30pm & 5–10.30pm.

Suishin 酔心 6-7 Tate-machi, Naka-ku ☎082 247 4411, ⓦsuishin.or.jp. The original location of a veteran local seafood restaurant – they now have branches all over town, including on the sixth floor of the station – serves sushi downstairs and *kamameshi* (rice casseroles) upstairs. Tasty crab, eel, oyster, shrimp and *chirimen* (boiled, dried local fish) *kamameshi* cost around ¥1000, while set menus start at ¥1350 for lunch, and ¥3000 for dinner. It can get very busy, though – in which case they stay open all afternoon – and seating is limited. Mon, Tues & Thurs

Sun 11.30am–2.30pm & 5–10pm.

Tokugawa 徳川 2F Tohgeki Building, Ebisu-chō, Naka-ku ☎082 241 7100, ⓦbit.ly/tokugawa -hiroshima. Large restaurant, halfway along the arcade behind the Tenmaya store, where you can cook your own *okonomiyaki* – Kansai-style, using wheat flour rather than Hiroshima's usual noodles – for around ¥800. Expect a bright, family-oriented atmosphere, but no English menu. Daily 11am–3am.

Yanagibashi Kodani 柳橋 こだに 1-1 Kanayama-chō, Naka-ku ☎082 246 7201, ⓦkodani.co.jp. The menu at Hiroshima's top eel specialist, near the Kyobashigawa, is really eely, ranging from an ¥880 grilled eel liver dish via the delicious ¥1730 eel-and-rice bowl to a large set meal for ¥4180; in winter, though, they also serve raw and baked oysters. 📶 Mon–Sat 11.30am–2pm & 5–9.30pm.

DRINKING

Come sundown, thousands of bars, crammed into the Nagarekawa and Shin-tenchi neighbourhoods just southeast of downtown, fling open their doors. In summer, several beer gardens sprout on city rooftops, including one at the *ANA Crowne Plaza* (see p.591).

Akamaru 赤まる 1-1-5 Matoba-chō, Minami-ku ☎082 264 2215. Hard-drinking salarymen heading home fill this classic, rough-and-ready *izakaya*, a few minutes' walk from the station, every evening. There's a ¥300 cover charge, but cocktails or beer cost under ¥500, and there's a great array of snacks, with seafood treats costing around ¥400, and beef or pork skewers ¥680. Seating is on upturned beer crates, in sections divided by flimsy rattan screens. Daily 5pm–midnight.

Barcos & Mambos バルコス & マンボス 2F, 3F, Sanwa Building 2, 7-9 Yagenbori ☎082 246 5800. The place to come if you want to mingle with an international crowd; head to *Mambos* (closed Sun) on the third floor for Latin vibes and salsa dancing. ¥1000 cover gets you one drink, and *Barcos* has a food menu too. 📶 Mon–Thurs & Sun 9pm–6am, Fri & Sat 8pm–6am.

Chano-ma チャノマ 2F, 2-19 Honden, Naka-ku ☎082 730 0035. This unusual and swish (but unpretentious) café-bar, above the *Cine Twin* cinema and extremely popular with teenage girls, is furnished with soft mattresses swathed in whites and off-whites. They serve a full menu of cocktails, plus tea and coffee and Asian-fusion food, including pasta dishes like an excellent avocado and tuna with spicy cod roe. Lunch set menus from ¥1000. 📶 Mon–Fri noon–2am, Sat & Sun 11.30am–2am.

Enjoint Bar Cover エンジョイントバーカバー 2F Hakubishi Daigo Building, 7-6 Nagarekawa, Naka-ku ☎082 249 3917. Considering the size of this friendly little

second-floor bar, its sound system packs a mighty punch, with DJs playing anything from reggae to house at the weekends and occasional other nights. 📶 Tues–Sun 8pm–late.

Kuru Kuru クルクル Hiroshima Kokusai Hotel, 3-13 Tate-machi, Naka-ku ☎082 240 7556, ⓦkokusai.gr.jp. The American-themed revolving restaurant on the top floor of the *Hiroshima Kokusai Hotel* is worth dropping by for a romantic evening cocktail (¥500). 📶 Daily 11.30am–11pm.

Molly Malone's モーリー・マロンズ 4F Teigeki Building, Chūō-dōri, Naka-ku ☎082 244 2554, ⓦmollymalones.jp. This popular Irish bar is a good place to meet local expats, and the chef rustles up generous-sized portions of tasty Irish food – try the Jameson chicken or Galway mussels (¥1150). Pints of Guinness go for ¥900. 📶 Tues–Thurs 5pm–1am, Fri 5pm–2am, Sat 11.30am–2am, Sun 11.30am–midnight.

New York New York ニューヨークカフェ 7-2 Fukuro-machi ☎082 541 7000. Industrial-style but with hints of traditional Japan, this all-day *izakaya* has dim lighting and comfortable seats, with a jazz soundtrack and Woody Allen films often playing. You can find just about anything on the expansive cocktail menu (all ¥500), while the food includes pastas, pizzas and snacks, from around ¥1000. 📶 Mon–Thurs & Sun 11.30am–midnight, Fri & Sat 11.30am–2am.

DIRECTORY

Bookshops There's a small selection of English-language books and magazines at Kinokuniya, on the 6th floor of Sogō

department store at 6-27 Moto-machi (daily 10am–8pm; ☎082 224 3232). The Book Nook Global Lounge, 2F Nakano

Building, 1-5-17 Kamiya-chō, has an excellent stock of secondhand English books (Mon–Thurs noon–9pm, Fri & Sat noon–11pm; ☎ 082 244 8145, ⓦ hiroshima-no1.com).
Emergencies The main police station is at 9-42 Moto-machi (☎ 082 224 0110).

Hospital Hiroshima City Hospital, 7-33 Moto-machi (☎ 082 221 2291).
Post office The Central Post Office is on Rijo-dōri, near the Shiyakusho-mae tram stop (Mon–Fri 9am–7pm, Sat 9am–5pm, Sun 9am–12.30pm).

Miyajima

宮島

Home to the ancient and venerated **Itsukushima-jinja** shrine, famous for the spectacle of its vermilion **Ō-torii** gate appearing to float above the tidal shallows, the island of **MIYAJIMA** is an unmissable excursion for anyone visiting Hiroshima. Even if you only have a few hours to spare, it's worth venturing out here; try if you can, though, to come for the full day, or, even better, to spend a night as well, in one of its classy ryokan.

Miyajima stretches parallel to the coast for 10km, just a few hundred metres offshore and 20km southwest of Hiroshima. All the island's major attractions, which as well as Itsukushima-jinja at sea level include the hillside **Daishō-in** temple plus several other temples and pagodas, are located in its principal **village**, beside the ferry dock near the northern tip. (Strictly speaking, Itsukushima is the island and Miyajima is the village,

but the entire island is usually referred to as "Miyajima".) The village itself is heavily commercialized but nonetheless appealing, packed with restaurants, cafés and gift shops. Among the souvenirs, the most distinctive is the **Miyajima dipper** (*kijakushi*), a wooden, lute-shaped spatula carved from local trees.

Given a bit more time, this hilly island holds much to explore. Atop its central peak, **Mount Misen**, reached via either a demanding hike or a mildly alarming cable-car ride, you'll find tremendous views as well as further sacred sites and a population of monkeys, while the shoreline is fringed with **beaches**. The most accessible is at the **Tsutsumigaura Recreation Park** (包ケ浦自然公園), a 3km walk from the ferry dock around the northern headland, where the long strand slopes gently into a sea that's ideal for paddling. Continue beyond that, and you'll come to beautiful empty beaches with crystal-clear water and fantastic views.

Ideally, you'd visit Miyajima either in **autumn**, when the myriad maple trees turn a glorious red and gold and perfectly complement Itsukushima-jinja, or for one of its many **festivals**. At such times especially, the island

MIYAJIMA

Tsutsumigaura Recreation Park & **1**

Ferry Terminal

Miyajima-guchi & Hiroshima

Ōmote-sandō Shopping Street

0 ——— 200
metres

N

Senjōkaku

Ō-Torii ⊙
Itsukushima-jinja

Mitarai-gawa

Misen-san & Momiji-dani-kōen

Kiyomori-jinja

Daigan-ji

Miyajima History & Folklore Museum

Aquarium

Daishō-in

● EATING

Fujitaya	4
Koumitei	1
Sarasvati	3
Yakigaki-no-Hayashi	2

■ ACCOMMODATION

Grand Hotel Arimoto	3
Guest House Kikugawa	2
Iwasō Ryokan	4
Miyajima Morinoyado	5
Tsutsumigaura Recreation Park and Campsite	1

8

can get very busy indeed, though no amount of crowding seems to deter its countless, theoretically wild **deer** from cadging and/or stealing visitors' snacks.

Itsukushima-jinja

厳島神社 • 1 Miyajima-chō • Daily: Jan, Feb & mid-Oct to Nov 6.30am–5.30pm; March to mid-Oct 6.30am–6pm; Dec 6.30am–5pm • ¥300, or ¥500 with Treasure Hall • ☎ 082 944 2020, ⓦ bit.ly/itsukushima-jinja

Propped on pillars and straddling the crescent bay that fronts Miyajima village, the **Itsukushima-jinja** shrine dates back to the sixth century. Its magnificent, bright-red, 16m-tall **Ō-Torii** (Grand Gate) is set 200m offshore, to denote that the entire island is a Shintō holy place. At low tide, both shrine and gate stand on exposed mudflats; when the sea rises, though, to lap beneath Itsukushima-jinja's low-slung halls and red-colonnaded, lantern-fringed corridors, you can see why it's called the "floating shrine", and why this is officially ranked as one of Japan's three most beautiful views.

Itsukushima-jinja took on its present splendid form in 1168, courtesy of the warlord Taira-no-Kiyomori, the central figure in the epic *Tale of Heike*. While it has been repeatedly reconstructed – the **Ō-Torii** no fewer than seventeen times – the classical beauty of its architecture, modelled after the *shinden*-style villas of the Heian period, endures. The whole ensemble is at its most enchanting come dusk, when the lights of the surrounding stone lanterns flicker on.

The shrine itself can only be entered from its northern side, a ten-minute walk south of the ferry dock. Visitors follow a route that leads past but not into various halls and subsidiary shrines, as well as the raised **Taka-Butai stage**, which is actually free-floating and is regularly used for performances of *bugaku* court dances. Across from the exit, on the south shore of the bay, the shrine's separate **Treasure Hall** holds priceless sutras, scrolls and sculptures.

Senjōkaku

千畳閣 • 1-1 Miyajima-chō • Daily 8.30am–4.30pm • ¥100 • ☎ 082 944 2020

Two remarkable structures stand atop the low hill that looms immediately north of Itsukushima-jinja. **Senjōkaku**, the "hall of a thousand tatami", was erected from 1587 onwards by Toyotomi Hideyoshi as part of Hokoku-jinja, a shrine that was left unfinished after the warlord's death. Originally a library for Buddhist sutras, this vast wooden hall, wide open to the elements and framing wonderful views, is decorated

---

MIYAJIMA FESTIVALS

As well as the regular celebrations, such as New Year, special **festivals** take place throughout the year on Miyajima at both Itsukushima-jinja shrine and the Daishō-in temple. See the island website for scheduled performances of *bugaku* (traditional court dancing) on the shrine's central stage.

Kaki Matsuri (second Sat in Feb): Free oysters, an island speciality, are served to sightseers.

Ceremony for Kitchen Knives (March 8): Thanksgiving service for old kitchen knives that are no longer fit for use, at Daishō-in.

Spring and Autumn festivals (April 15 & Nov 15): At Daishō-in, with firewalking by the resident monks.

Jin-Nō (April 16–18): As part of the spring peach-blossom festival, sacred nō plays, first performed for the *daimyō* Mōri Motonari in 1568, are re-enacted on the stage at Itsukushima-jinja.

Kangensai (June 16): Itsukushima-jinja's main annual festival includes an atmospheric night-boat parade, accompanied by traditional music.

Hanabi Matsuri (Aug 14): Western Japan's largest fireworks display explodes over Itsukushima-jinja.

Chinkasai (Dec 31): Groups of young men fight over huge pine torches, blazing in front of Itsukushima-jinja.

with intriguing votive plaques. Alongside it, the red-painted **five-storey pagoda** combines elements of both Chinese and Japanese design and dates from 1407; it's not open to visitors.

Daishō-in

大聖院 • 210 Miyajima-chō • Daily 8am–5pm • Free • ☎ 082 944 0111, ⓦ galilei.ne.jp/daisyoin

Miyajima's main temple, **Daishō-in**, spreads up the hillside towards Mount Misen, south of the village. Founded in the ninth century by **Kōbō Daishi**, who spent a hundred days in seclusion here, it belongs to the **Shingon** sect of Buddhism. Especially beautiful in autumn, it holds a wonderful array of halls and shrines, along with ornate wooden pavilions, hidden passageways, formal gardens, stone lanterns, and arched bridges spanning lily-dotted ponds. Look out for the little *jizō* images that line the stairways, and the "universally illuminating cave", hung with hundreds of lanterns and packed with mini-Buddhas laden with lucky talismans. The temple **teahouse**, accessible either side of its main gate, is a superb spot for a tranquil escape from the crowds.

Miyajima History and Folklore Museum

宮島歴史民俗資料館, Miyajima Rekishi Minzoku Shiryōkan • 57 Miyajima-chō • Tues–Sun 9am–5pm • ¥300 • ☎ 082 944 2019

In a former merchant's house on the south side of the village, complete with a lovely garden, the **Miyajima History and Folklore Museum** provides both a fascinating glimpse of nineteenth-century life on the island, and a detailed history of Itsukushima. Dioramas and displays tell the story of the 1555 **Battle of Miyajima**, fought in and around the shrine; as Shintō tradition forbids either birth or death near a shrine, the entire island had to be purified afterwards. Don't miss the excellent, subtitled short movie.

Misen-san

弥山 • Ropeway: daily, March–Oct 9am–5pm, Nov 8am–5pm, Dec–Feb 9am–4.30pm • One-way ¥1000, return ¥1800 • ☎ 082 944 0316, ⓦ miyajima-ropeway.info • Free shuttle buses run between Momiji-dani and the ropeway base station

Two distinct walking routes lead from Miyajima village to the top of the island's 530m sacred mountain, **Misen-san**; each takes a couple of hours, while combining the two makes for a half-day circuit. Most hikers go clockwise, and thus start by heading directly inland from Itsukushima-jinja via **Momiji-dani-kōen** (紅葉谷公園), a leafy hillside park. This route will also bring you in 800m to the base station for the **ropeway** (cable-car), which climbs 1.7km in two somewhat scary stages, with a transfer to larger gondolas for the final gorge-spanning stretch to the **Shishiwa station**, still well below the actual summit.

A lookout spot nearby commands stunning views across the Inland Sea. Up here, as well as the island's usual abundant deer you'll encounter a colony of wild **monkeys**. Cute as they look, keep your distance; the monkeys occasionally become aggressive.

The summit itself stands a good twenty minutes' walk further on. At first, the path drops, but it soon climbs once more, passing assorted small temples built in honour of Kōbō Daishi. Opposite the **Misen Hondō**, the main hall of worship on the mountain, the **Kiezu-no-Reikadō** holds a sacred fire. Originally kindled by the Daishi, it has burned for over 1200 years, and was used to light Hiroshima's Flame of Peace. Drink tea made from the boiling water in the suitably blackened iron pot that hangs over the fire, and it's said that all your ills will be cured. Five more minutes' climb will take you past mysterious giant boulders to the resthouse at the summit, which sells high-priced refreshments.

The main route down passes yet more small temples and provides tremendous views over Itsukushima-jinja, especially as you approach Daishō-in.

ARRIVAL AND DEPARTURE

By ferry from Miyajima-guchi The cheapest way to reach Miyajima is to take a ferry from Miyajima-guchi, the closest mainland town, 20km southwest of Hiroshima. Two separate ferries make frequent 10min crossings from neighbouring terminals: the JR Miyajima ferry (departures from Miyajima-guchi daily 6.25am–10.42pm, from Miyajima 5.45am–10.14pm; ☎ 082 956 2045, ⊚ jr -miyajimaferry.co.jp), and the Miyajima Matsudai ferry (departures from Miyajima-guchi 7.15am–8.35pm, from Miyajima 7am–8.15pm; ☎ 082 944 2171, ⊚ miyajima -matsudai.co.jp). Both charge ¥180 one-way, but you also have to factor in the cost of getting to Miyajima-guchi from Hiroshima. Trains on the JR San'yō line take 30min to reach Miyajima-guchi from Hiroshima Station, and cost ¥410. If you have a JR Rail Pass, though, both the train and the JR ferry are free. Alternatively, tram line 2 runs to Miyajima-guchi from central Hiroshima; travelling all the way from

Hiroshima Station to Miyajima-guchi takes around an hour and costs ¥260, while a one-day pass covering all tram journeys and the Matsudai ferry costs ¥840.

By ferry from central Hiroshima Aquanet run a high-speed ferry service to Miyajima from a dock immediately across the Ōta-gawa from Peace Memorial Park (15 daily, departures 8am–5.15pm; 45min; ¥2000 one-way, ¥3600 round trip; ☎ 082 295 2666, ⊚ mariho-miyajima.com).

By ferry from Hiroshima Port Setonai Kaikisen operate high-speed ferries to Miyajima from Hiroshima Port (6–8 daily, departures Mon–Fri 9.25am–4.25pm, Sat & Sun 8.25am–4.25pm; 30min; ¥1850 each way; ☎ 082 253 1212, ⊚ setonaikaikisen.co.jp). They also offer sightseeing cruises that include lunch (from ¥6000) or dinner (from ¥9000). The port is 7km south of Hiroshima Station, a 20min/¥160 ride on tram #5 from the station or tram #3 from the centre.

INFORMATION AND GETTING AROUND

Tourist information There's an information booth in the ferry terminal (daily 9am–6pm; ☎ 082 944 2011,

⊚ miyajima.or.jp).
Bike rental No cycles are available for rent on Miyajima.

ACCOMMODATION

8

While Miyajima does hold some relatively cheap accommodation options, this is a place where, if at all possible, it's worth splashing out on an upmarket ryokan. Note that rates tend to rise at weekends, as well as during peak holiday times.

★**Grand Hotel Arimoto** グランドホテル有もと 364 Minami-machi ☎ 082 944 2411, ⊚ miyajima-arimoto .co.jp. Rooms at this sprawling hotel complex, the closest to the shrine, come in tatami or Western style (or both); some have water views and/or private outdoor onsen. Several excellent dining options are on offer, and they also put on classical music concerts and storytelling evenings. Rates include breakfast and dinner. ☏ **¥18,360**

Guest House Kikugawa ゲストハウス菊川 796 Miyajima-chō ☎ 082 944 0039, ⊚ kikugawa.ne.jp. Set back in the village a couple of minutes from the ferry, this delightful pension is clean and comfortable, and holds both Western- and Japanese-style rooms. The owner, Kikugawa-san, is an excellent chef; dinner costs an extra ¥3900 per person, breakfast ¥1080, with an English-style cooked breakfast available. ☏ **¥11,880**

★**Iwasō Ryokan** 岩惣旅館 Momiji-dani ☎ 082 944 2233, ⊚ iwaso.com. The most famous ryokan on the island, and by far the most luxurious, with immaculate tatami rooms (not all en suite) and sumptuous meals. Rooms overlooking the gorge behind the building are

booked solid throughout autumn when the view transforms into a sea of red, yellow and orange. Rates include two meals. ☏ **¥42,000**

Miyajima Morinoyado 国民宿舎みやじま杜の宿 Omoto-Kōen, Miyajima-chō ☎ 082 944 0430, ⊚ morinoyado.jp. There's nothing very fancy about this minshuku, at the quiet southern end of the village, but it's hard to find a better deal on Miyajima; small wonder that the rooms, both Western and Japanese, tend to sell out well in advance. Rates include two meals. ☏ **¥24,440**

Tsutsumigaura Recreation Park and Campsite 宮島包ヶ浦自然公園キャンプ場 Miyajima-chō ☎ 082 944 2903. Miyajima's only real budget accommodation, around the island's northern tip 3km from the ferry. It takes a very hardy camper, though, and very good weather too, to appreciate its rather grim and basic tent space (tent rental available); the plush rental cabins are much better, with air conditioning, kitchen and bathroom. No wi-fi, reservations by phone only. Camping **¥400** per person, four-person cabins **¥15,000**

EATING

The bustling village holds lots of daytime restaurants and cafés, but almost everything shuts down in the evening, and most visitors dine at their hotels. The main local specialities are oysters, sold fried or grilled at the stalls lining the road south of the ferry terminal, and *anago*, a long eel-like fish, served broiled and sliced on top of rice (*anagoburi*).

Fujitaya ふじたや 125-2 Miyajima-chō ☏082 944 0151. This refined, busy restaurant, on the village street that leads up to Daishō-in, is the most famous place to sample *anago*. A large serving of *anagoburi*, accompanied by soup and pickles, costs ¥2300. Daily 11am–3.30pm.

Koumitei 好み亭 1162-1 Minato-machi ☏082 944 0177. Lively, dinner-only option on the seafront between the ferry and the shrine, where you can have your ¥810 *okonomiyaki* Hiroshima-style (layered and cooked for you) or Kansai-style (cook it yourself). There's a pretty ornamental garden at the back. Mon, Tues & Thurs–Sun 5–9pm.

Sarasvati サラスパティ 407 Miyajima-chō ☏082 944 2266, ⓦsarasvati.jp. Brimming with bags of coffee and grinders, set in a former granary with dark woods and brushed cobalt walls, this stylish café nails the industrial-rustic look. It's a great place to kick back over an excellent blended coffee (¥550; ¥250 to take away). They also serve sandwiches, scones and set lunches of oysters and pâté (¥1300). ☏ Daily 8.30am–8pm.

Yakigaki-no-Hayashi 焼がきのはやし 505-1 Miyajima-chō ☏082 944 0335, ⓦyakigaki-no-hayashi.co.jp. Hugely popular lunch spot on the main Omote-sandō shopping street, serving top-quality oysters, cultivated on their own beds and available all year, and fresh grilled eel. Both are available with noodles or rice, with set meals costing ¥1500–1700, and they also offer takeout bentō boxes too. ☏ Mon, Tues, Thurs, Fri & Sun 10.30am–5pm, Sat 10.30am–5.30pm.

Iwakuni

岩国

Heading south along the coast from Miyajima, you soon cross the border into western Honshū's last prefecture, Yamaguchi-ken. The first potential pause is the pleasant old castle town of **IWAKUNI**, 40km southwest of Hiroshima and home to a US marine base, as well as a remarkable bridge, a scattering of samurai houses and a mildly interesting museum. Also noteworthy as a good spot to watch the ancient practice of **cormorant fishing**, Iwakuni can be comfortably explored within a couple of hours.

Kintai-kyō

錦帯橋 • Open 24hr • ¥300 • ⓦbit.ly/kintai-kyo

Like a tossed pebble skipping across the water, one of Japan's top three **bridges**, the elegant five-arched **Kintai-kyō**, spans the rocky Nishiki-gawa 2km west of central Iwakuni. *Daimyō* Kikkawa Hiroyoshi ordered its construction in 1673, hoping to solve the problem of crossing the Nishiki-gawa during its frequent floods. His first bridge was promptly washed away during the rainy season of 1674, but the second attempt – a 210m-long structure built without a single nail and bound together with clamps and wires – survived until it was swept away by Typhoon Kijiya in 1950. What you see today is therefore an impressive reconstruction, from 1953. For once, the hordes of tourists, parading across the steep wooden arches like figures in an *ukiyo-e* print, add to the overall attraction. It looks even more wonderful at night, when it's glamorously floodlit.

Kikkō-kōen

吉香公園 • Park 24hr, Chōko-kan (徴古館) Tues–Sun 9am–5pm • Free

A grassy landscaped park, **Kikkō-kōen**, adjoins Kintai-kyō on the west bank of the Nishiki-gawa. Once the estate of the ruling Kikkawa clan, it still preserves some of its original layout and buildings. Immediately ahead of the bridge, on the right, stands the **Nagaya-mon** (長屋門), the wooden gate to the home of the Kagawa family, samurai to the Kikkawa *daimyō*. You can wander around several other samurai houses nearby, while the **Chōko-kan**, at the north end of the park, holds a mildly interesting collection of old maps and plans from feudal times, photos and prints featuring the bridge through the centuries, as well as craftwork from Iwakuni's past.

CORMORANT FISHING

If you stay overnight in Iwakuni between June and August, don't miss the **cormorant fishing** (*ukai*), which takes place on the Nishiki-gawa beside the bridge. This colourful and exciting method of fishing with birds (see box, p.412) can be watched from the pebbly riverbank for free, between 6.30pm and 9pm nightly.

Kikkawa Historical Museum

吉川史料館, Kikkawa Shiryōn • 9-3 Nichome • Mon, Tues & Thurs—Sun 9am—5pm • ¥500 • ☎ 082 741 1010, Ⓦ bit.ly/kikkawa-museum

The **Kikkawa Historical Museum**, alongside Kikkō-kōen park, holds artefacts from the family collection of the Kikkawa warlords. The weapons on show include a multitude of swords, and you can also peer at samurai armour, jewellery and hanging scrolls. However, all the explanations are in Japanese.

Shiro-yama

城山 • **Ropeway** daily 9am—5pm • ¥320 one-way, ¥550 return • **Castle** daily 9am—4.45pm • ¥260 • ☎ 082 741 1477, Ⓦ bit.ly/iwakuni-ropeway

Iwakuni's castle hill, **Shiro-yama**, looms above the northern edge of Kikkō-kōen park. You can get up there either on a forty-minute hike that starts beside the youth hostel, or via a **ropeway** (cable-car) from the park. The impressive view of the meandering river, town and Inland Sea from the summit makes the effort worthwhile. The **castle** itself though, which holds further displays of armour and swords, plus a miniature wooden model of the Kintai-kyō, isn't really worth entering.

8

ARRIVAL AND INFORMATION   IWAKUNI

By train Trains on the JR San'yō line stop at Iwakuni Station, 15min by bus east of the centre (¥240), while Shinkansen stop at Shin-Iwakuni Station, 10min by bus west of the centre (¥280).

Tourist information There's a tourist office immediately east of the bridge (daily 8.30am—5pm; ☎ 082 729 5116, Ⓦ kankou.iwakuni-city.net).

ACCOMMODATION AND EATING

Iwakuni Kokusai Kankō Hotel 岩国国際観光ホテル 1-1-7 Iwakuni ☎ 082 743 1111, Ⓦ iwakunikankohotel .co.jp. Large riverfront property, close to the bridge, that's popular with groups, and offers Japanese- and Western-style rooms as well as public indoor/outdoor onsen and a gift shop. Rates include two meals. 🛜 **¥39,100**
Shiratame Ryokan 白為旅館 1-5-16 Iwakuni ☎ 082 741 0074, Ⓦ siratame.justhpbs.jp. Iwakuni's best ryokan is a pretty spot, with rooms overlooking the bridge; even if

you can't afford to stay, try to go for lunch, where you can get great sushi as well as noodle soup with tofu and *kamaboko* (fish cake). Rates include two meals. 🛜 **¥31,200**
Yoshida よしだ本店 1-16-9 Iwakuni ☎ 082 741 0373. Just beyond some interesting antique shops as you approach the eastern side of the bridge, this is a good place to try such local fish dishes as *Iwakuni-zushi*, a block of vinegared rice topped with bits of cooked fish and vegetables, and costing from ¥600. Daily 9am—5pm.

Yamaguchi

山口

The coastal route west of Iwakuni is blighted by heavy industry, but head inland to the hills, a couple of stops off the Shinkansen line, and you'll come to sleepy **YAMAGUCHI**. Sometimes fancifully known as the "Kyoto of western Japan", Japan's smallest prefectural capital is a modern city, but with its waterways, green hills and unhurried pace, it has a certain old-world charm.

Yamaguchi's commercial heart is the point where Ekimae-dōri, the main street heading northwest towards the hills from the station, crosses the **Komeya-chō** shopping arcade. All the main highlights lie to the north, including the fifteenth-century temple garden of **Jōei-ji**, designed by the artist and priest Sesshū; the handsome five-storey pagoda at **Rurikō-ji**; and **St Francis Xavier Memorial Cathedral**, an ultra-contemporary church commemorating the first Christian missionary to Japan. Nearby attractions include the hot-spring resort neighbourhood **Yuda Onsen**, just one train stop west, and the intriguing caverns and rocky plateau of **Akiyoshi-dai** Quasi National Park, 20km northwest.

Brief history

Many of the temples around Yamaguchi, not to mention its artistic sensibilities, date from the late fifteenth century, when war raged around Kyoto, and the city became an alternative capital for fleeing noblemen and their retinues. The tolerant ruling family of **Ōuchi Hiroyo**, who settled in the area in 1360, allowed the missionary Francis Xavier to stay in Yamaguchi in 1549. By the Edo period, the **Mōri** clan had gained power over the whole of western Japan, and several Mōri lords now lie buried in Kōzan-kōen.

St Francis Xavier Memorial Church

サビエル記念聖堂, Zabieru Kinen Seidō · 4-1 Kameyama-chō · Mon, Tues & Thurs–Sun 9am–5pm · ¥300 · ☎ 083 920 1549, ⓦ xavier.jp

The 53m spires of the modern **St Francis Xavier Memorial Church** poke conspicuously from the trees atop the Kame-yama-kōen hill, north of central Yamaguchi. The church was named after the pioneering Basque missionary **Francis Xavier** who, having already had success in Goa and Malacca, landed in Japan on August 15, 1549, and in the following year was granted leave to preach in Yamaguchi. When he left, six months later, the city had a community of more than five hundred Christians, many of whom later died for their beliefs under the less tolerant Tokugawa government. A church was erected here in 1952 to commemorate the four-hundredth anniversary of Xavier's visit, but it burned down in 1991. It was replaced in 1998 by this striking contemporary structure, which incorporates a main building with a tent-like roof designed to resemble a tabernacle, as well as **twin square towers** topped by metallic sculptures, one hung with nine bells.

Rurikō-ji

瑠璃光寺 · Kōzan-kōen · **Temple** 24hr · Free · **Exhibition hall** Daily 9am–5pm · ¥300 · ☎ 083 924 9139

The charming **Rurikō-ji** temple complex stands in the foothills 1km north of Kame-yama-kōen, roughly half an hour's walk from Yamaguchi Station. Its beautifully preserved **five-storey pagoda**, designated one of the top three in the country, is made from Japanese cypress and picturesquely sited next to an ornamental pond. A small exhibition hall beside the temple holds a diverting collection of model pagodas, photographs of the other 53 pagodas scattered around Japan, and strange masks.

YAMAGUCHI

0 — 250 metres

N

Rurikō-ji

Kōzan-kōen & Cemetery

Five-storey Pagoda

Yamaguchi-kenchō (Prefectural office)

ROUTE 9

Yamaguchi Museum

Kame-yama-kōen

St Francis Xavier Memorial Church

Yamaguchi Prefectural Art Museum

Ichinosaka-gawa

ROUTE 204

Komeya-chō arcade

EKIMAE-DŌRI

Fushino-gawa

Yamaguchi Station

Yuda Onsen & Ogōri

Akiyoshi-dai

Tsuwano, Masuda & Kamiyamaguchi Station

EATING
Hondaya Kaikoan	4
Kaitenzushi Wasabi	3
Sakanaya Hidezo	2
Xavier Campana	1

ACCOMMODATION
Green Rich Hotel	2
Matsudaya Hotel	1
Sunroute Yamaguchi	3
Taiyō-dō	4

Kōzan-kōen

香山公園 · Kōzan chō · 24hr · Free

With its peaceful and atmospheric graveyard, the park of **Kōzan-kōen**, alongside Rurikō-ji, is a traditional Japanese place of worship. It's also the last resting place of the *daimyō* Mōri Takachika and his family. Takachika was a key figure in planning the overthrow of the Tokugawa government in 1867, and the park holds a couple of old wooden houses where he secretly met fellow plotters.

Sesshū-tei

雪舟庭 · 2001 Miyano-shimo · Garden and temple daily: April–Sept 8am–4.30pm, Oct–March 8am–4pm · ¥300 · ☎ 083 922 2272 · 10min walk north of Orimoto, the closest bus stop

The enchanting **Sesshū-tei** garden at the **Jōei-ji temple** (常榮寺) was created by the priest and master-painter Sesshū, who was born in Okayama-ken in 1420 and studied the arts in China. He settled in Yamaguchi towards the end of the fifteenth century, and was asked by the *daimyō* Ōuchi Masahiro to create a traditional garden for the grounds of his mother's summerhouse. Sesshū's Zen-inspired rock and moss design remains intact behind the temple, and, if you're fortunate enough not to coincide with a tour group, you'll be able to sit in quiet contemplation of the garden's simple beauty, looking for the volcano-shaped rock that symbolizes Mount Fuji. The surrounding forest and lily pond add brilliant splashes of colour, particularly in autumn, when the maple trees flame red and gold.

Yuda Onsen

湯田温泉

The spa resort of **Yuda Onsen**, one train stop or a short bus ride southwest of Yamaguchi, can be readily spotted by its cluster of large and not particularly attractive hotels. A cute legend about a white fox curing its injured leg in the natural spring water explains the origins of both the onsen and the town's mascot, immortalized by an 8m-tall cartoon-like fox statue beside the station.

The resort's main public bath, **Onsen no Mori** (温泉の森; 4-7-17 Yuda Onsen; daily 10am–midnight; ¥1000) – a modern spa complex that holds several jacuzzi baths plus saunas and a rotemburo – stands just north of the large central crossroads in its commercial district, a straightforward ten-minute walk northwest of the station. The *Kamefuku Hotel* (かめ福ホテル; 4-5 Yudaonsen-dōri; daily 11.30am–8pm; ¥2230; ⓦ kamefuku.com), roughly 300m east along the main street, also holds good spa facilities, with individual turtle-shaped baths outside.

ARRIVAL AND INFORMATION

By plane Yamaguchi Ube Airport (ⓦ www .yamaguchiube-airport.jp), 35km southwest near the coastal city of Ube, has bus connections to Shin-Yamaguchi Station (9 daily; 40min) and Yamaguchi Station (6 daily; 45min).
Destination Tokyo Haneda (10 daily; 1hr 25min).
By train Yamaguchi is on the JR Yamaguchi line, which connects the closest Shinkansen station, 13km southwest at Shin-Yamaguchi (新山口), with the coastal town of Masuda, 80km northeast.

YAMAGUCHI

Destinations Masuda (8 daily; 1hr 5min–2hr); Shin-Yamaguchi (every 20min; 22min); Tsuwano (8 daily; 50min–1hr 20min); Yuda Onsen (every 20min; 3min).
By bus All buses stop in front of Yamaguchi Station.
Destinations Akiyoshi-dai (19 daily; 55min); Hagi (12 daily; 1hr 20min); Shin-Yamaguchi (6 daily; 40min).
Tourist information The tourist office in Yamaguchi Station has English maps and leaflets (daily 9am–6pm; ☎ 083 933 0088, ⓦ yamaguchi-city.jp). There's also an information counter at Shin-Yamaguchi Station.

GETTING AROUND

By bike There are plenty of local buses, but the easiest way to get around is to rent a bicycle from the Fukutake

shop opposite the station (¥300/2hr, ¥700/day; ☎ 083 922 0915).

ACCOMMODATION

★**Green Rich Hotel** グリーンリッチホテル 4-7-11 Yuda Onsen ☎ 083 923 6000, ⓦ bit.ly/greenrich-yudaonsen. Modern hotel just north of the central crossroads in Yuda Onsen, offering spacious and comfortable rooms with good amenities, and copious Japanese breakfast for ¥550. There's also cut-price (¥450) admission to the Onsen no Mori next door, close enough that you can pad there in slippers and robe. 🛜 **¥9,300**

★**Matsudaya Hotel** 松田屋ホテル 3-6-7 Yudaonsen-dōri ☎ 083 922 0125, ⓦ matsudayahotel.co.jp. Cocooned by high walls, this historic 300-year-old ryokan, 1km north of Yuda Onsen Station on the main road through the resort, ranks among the very finest accommodation options in the west of Chūgoku. Ignore the modern high-rise extension, and opt for one of the elegant, sprawling tatami rooms, plus tasty meals and a peaceful, traditional garden. Rates include breakfast and dinner. 🛜 **¥34,500**

Sunroute International Yamaguchi サンルート国際 ホテル山口 1-1 Nakagawara-chō ☎ 083 923 3610, ⓦ bit.ly/sunroute-yamaguchi. Business-oriented chain hotel in a handy central location, a 15min walk north of Yamaguchi Station at the crossroads near Kame-yama-kōen. The spiffy rooms are smartly decorated and have decent amenities. 🛜 **¥10,660**

Taiyō-dō 太陽堂 2-3 Komeya-chō ☎ 083 922 0897. Surprisingly large, good-value ryokan, entered from the east side of the Komeya-chō shopping arcade. Tatami rooms with shared bathrooms, plus a small central garden. 🛜 **¥7000**

EATING

Most of the restaurants in Yamaguchi are clustered along Ekimae-dōri and the Komeya-chō arcade, while a few cafés dot the riverside beyond the arcade. Many shops sell the local speciality, *uirō*, a glutinous sweet made from pounded rice, said to have been a favourite of the ruling Ōuchi clan six centuries ago.

Hondaya Kaikoan 本多屋 懐古庵 1-4-5 Eki-dōri ☎ 083 925 1600, ⓦ kaikoan.com. Primarily a confectionery shop, this bright, roomy store, across the road from Yamaguchi Station, makes a lovely calm setting to unwind over fresh green tea and cakes, for under ¥1000. 🛜 Mon, Tues & Thurs–Sun 9am–6pm.

Kaitenzushi Wasabi 回転鮨和さび 1-3-2 Eki-dōri ☎ 083 921 5636. Cheap and cheerful conveyor-belt sushi stop near Yamaguchi Station, with decent cuts of fish starting at ¥280. Daily 11am–10pm.

Sakanaya Hidezo 魚屋ひでぞう 1-1-22 Aoi ☎ 083 920 0380. Friendly little restaurant at the main crossroads in Yuda Onsen, serving good-value sushi and sashimi plates, made with local seafood and costing around ¥1500, as well as succulent grilled chicken for under ¥1000. Daily 5.30–9.30pm.

Xavier Campana サビエル・カンパーナ 5-2 Kameyama-chō ☎ 083 923 6222. This mouthwatering bakery and restaurant serves a wide range of breads, cakes, salads and various European meals, including German-style dishes, fondue and pasta. The bakery, downstairs, also sells take-away snacks like udon cake (¥200). 🛜 Daily 7.30am–7pm.

Akiyoshi-dō

秋芳洞 • Daily 8.30am–4.30pm • ¥1200 • ☎ 083 762 0304, ⓦ karusuto.com

The vast caverns and rock-strewn tablelands of the **AKIYOSHI-DAI** (秋吉台) plateau occupy a remote area roughly 30km northwest of Yamaguchi and the same distance southwest of Hagi on the northern coast. The main attraction of this bleak landscape is the largest limestone cave in Japan, **Akiyoshi-dō**. In total it stretches around 10km underground, only a tenth or so of which is open to the public. Its main entrance is five minutes' walk from Akiyoshi-dō bus station, along a pedestrianized street packed with gift shops.

A raised walkway through a copse of lofty, moss-covered pine trees provides an atmospheric introduction to the gaping cavern mouth. Allow around an hour to follow the route inside, though you may find that the booming amplified voices of competing tour-group leaders, combined with unimaginative lighting, detract from the overall impact. It took more than 300,000 years of steady erosion and dripping to create the rock walls and formations, which have been given names like "Big Mushroom" and "Straw-Wrapped Persimmon".

From the bowels of the earth, an elevator whisks you up to the alternative cave entrance **Yano-ana**, a short walk from Akiyoshi-dai, Japan's largest karst plateau. A lookout point commands an impressive view of rolling hills, while various hiking trails enable you to explore the surrounding 130 square kilometres.

ARRIVAL AND INFORMATION

By bus Regular buses run from nearby towns. If you have a JR Rail Pass, the JR bus service from Yamaguchi will cost you nothing.

Destinations Higashi-Hagi (2 daily; 1hr 10min; ¥1800);

Shimonoseki (8 daily; 1hr 50min; ¥1730); Shin-Yamaguchi (7–9 daily; 43min; ¥1170); Yamaguchi (4–6 daily; 1hr; ¥1210).

Tourist information There's an information counter inside the bus centre (daily 9am–6pm; ☎083 762 1620).

Shimonoseki

The port of **SHIMONOSEKI** (下関) stands at the southern tip of Honshū, at the head of the narrow **Kanmon Channel**, which separates Honshū from Kyūshū, and is also known as the Straits of Shimonoseki. These waters played a major role in Japanese history, as the site of the twelfth-century battle of **Dannoura**, and over a thousand ships each day continue to sail through one of Asia's busiest maritime crossroads. Shimonoseki these days is thriving, thanks in part to its daily ferry link with Pusan in South Korea, and its waterfront now holds a state-of-the-art **aquarium** as well as the colourful ancient shrine of **Akama-jingū**.

Shimonoseki is also notorious as the home port of Japan's **whaling fleet**. By no coincidence, Japan's Prime Minister **Shinzō Abe**, a vocal supporter of whaling, represents the city in the House of Representatives. Despite the international ban on commercial whaling, in force since 1986, five vessels, including the world's only whaling factory ship, the 8145-tonne *Nisshin Maru*, sail from Shimonoseki to Antarctica each winter, returning with the carcasses of minke whales. Although the whales are supposedly slaughtered for research purposes only, **whale meat** is still sold at Shimonoseki's fish market, and served in many local restaurants.

8

Akama-jingū

赤間神宮 • 4-1 Amidaiji-chō • 24hr • Free; museum ¥100 suggested donation • ☎083 231 4138

Painted in a magnificent palette of vermilion, gold and pale-green, the hillside **Akama-jingū** shrine stands just above the coast road 2.5km east of Shimonoseki Station. Dedicated to the 8-year-old emperor Antoku, who drowned during the battle

---

SAMURAI CRABS OF SHIMONOSEKI

The naval battle of **Dannoura**, fought in the Straits of Shimonoseki in April 1185, was the decisive confrontation of the **Genpei War** between the **Taira** (also known as the Heike) and **Minamoto** (or Genji) clans. The war had broken out five years earlier, when Taira Kiyomori, the villain of the epic *Tale of Heike*, declared his infant grandson **Antoku** to be the 81st Emperor of Japan. Since then, the Minamoto, who felt they had a stronger claim to the imperial throne, had pushed the Taira ever further west.

Skilled sailors, the Taira made their desperate final stand in the waters off Shimonoseki. The tide, however, turned against them, and so too did some of their allies. Perceiving the battle to be lost, Antoku's grandmother clasped the 8-year-old emperor to her breast and leaped into the sea, with the immortal words "there is another capital beneath the waves". Many of the court followed suit, and certain imperial regalia was lost as well, including by some accounts the *kusanagi-no-tsurugi*, or "grass-cutting sword", though that's also said to be at the Atsuta shrine in Nagoya (see p.406). The leader of the victorious clan, Minamoto Yoritomo, celebrated by declaring himself **Shogun**, and thus established the shogunate, which ruled Japan for the next seven hundred years.

Local fishermen, meanwhile, believed the battle site was **haunted**, and claimed to see the faces of defeated Heike warriors staring from the shells of crabs caught off Shimonoseki. So-called **heikegani crabs** do indeed bear an eerie resemblance to angry samurai; prime specimens are displayed (and sold) at the Akama-jingū shrine. Scientist Carl Sagan, on the TV series *Cosmos*, famously cited the phenomenon as an example of human-aided evolution, arguing that centuries of throwing "samurai crabs" back into the sea had resulted in such crabs breeding in ever greater numbers.

of Dannoura, this was built as a Buddhist temple to appease the souls of the dead Taira warriors. It was originally known as Amida-ji, and was renamed Akama-jingū when it became a shrine in the Meiji period, after Shintō and Buddhism separated.

Look back through the Chinese-style arched gate at the temple entrance, and it frames a view of the straits where the battle was fought. Antoku's small mausoleum is near the foot of the stairs, while the main shrine, which encloses a small pool of limpid water, is directly ahead. Tucked away to the left, beyond a small **museum** of armour and scrolls, a **graveyard** holds fourteen ancient tombs of notable Taira warriors, along with a small statue of the blind and deaf priest, Hōichi Miminashi – the "earless Hōichi" immortalized in one of the Irish writer Lafcadio Hearn's most famous ghost stories (see box, p.620).

Karato

唐戸

The twenty-first century has seen a transformation of Shimonoseki's waterfront **Karato** district. While a handful of handsome brick and stone buildings still survive along the main road – among them is the former British Consulate, now a teahouse – the docks and warehouses nearer the sea have largely been swept away. An appealing **pedestrian promenade** now runs along the water's edge.

The busy **Karato Fish Market** (唐戸市場; daily 4am–noon; ✆083 231 0001) is still there, a cavernous place that starts each day supplying bulk orders to wholesalers, then turns its attentions to selling sashimi platters from 10am onwards. It's now complemented by the large **Kanmon Wharf**, a two-storey mall that's much more geared towards meeting the needs of visitors, with gift stores downstairs and some great restaurants on its upper level. Nearby, a double-decker London bus advertises an open-air amusement park equipped with a giant Ferris wheel. The centrepiece of this redevelopment project, though, is the enormous **Shimonoseki Marine Science Museum**, a huge hit with Japanese tourists.

Shimonoseki Marine Science Museum

市立しものせき水族館海響館, Shiritsu Shimonoseki Suizokukan Kaikyōkan • 6-1 Arukapōto • Daily 9.30am–5.30pm • ¥2000 • ✆083 228 1100, ⓦ kaikyokan.com

Despite the name, the enormous **Shimonoseki Marine Science Museum**

SENTEISAI MATSURI

The extraordinary **Senteisai Matsuri** festival is staged in the courtyard of Akama-jingū on May 3 and 4 each year. Preceded by a procession through the streets of Shimonoseki, it commemorates the legend that, from 1186 onwards, the surviving women of the Taira court would mark the anniversary of Emperor Antoku's death by making a ceremonial pilgrimage to his shrine. According to some accounts, they were forced to turn to prostitution after the defeat of their clan, and came here to purify themselves. The participants' costumes are breathtaking; in particular, it takes months of training to learn to walk in their utterly impractical clogs

---

is much more of an aquarium than it is a museum. Although it holds some remarkable displays, many visitors consider its **live dolphin and seal shows** sufficient reason to boycott the place altogether.

If you do choose to enter, highlights include an extraordinary tank designed to replicate the swirling waters of the Kanmon Channel outside, which you can walk right through via a glass-roofed tunnel; an indoor/outdoor penguin exhibit; some colossal fish from the Amazon River; and what's said to the world's largest collection of pufferfish. There's also a complete skeleton of a blue whale, donated by that other bastion of whaling, Norway.

Kaikyō-yume Tower

海峡ゆめタワー・3-3-1 Buzenda-chō・Daily 9.30am–9.30pm・¥600・☎ 083 231 5600, Ⓦ yumetower.jp

The **Kaikyō-yume Tower**, a 153m-high observation tower, made of glass and resembling a giant golf tee with a ball resting on top, soars ten minutes' walk east of Shimonoseki Station. The tower is at its most impressive at night, when the interior glows green and points of light dot its spherical **observation deck**, which as well as offering tremendous views holds a couple of restaurants.

Hino-yama

火の山・Ropeway (cable-car): late March to Nov daily 10am–5pm・one-way ¥300, round-trip ¥500・☎ 083 231 1838, Ⓦ bit.ly/hinoyama・Served by hourly buses from Shimonoseki Station

Starting alongside the Kanmon Bridge, a kilometre-long **pedestrian tunnel** makes it possible to walk under the straits to Moji, on Kyūshū (daily 6am–10pm; free). Alternatively, a number of trails lead uphill from the bridge to the 268m summit of **Hino-yama**. Especially dramatic as sunset approaches, the view from the top takes in the whole of the Kanmon Straits, as well as the islands to the west of Shimonoseki.

THE FERRY TO SOUTH KOREA

The Kampu Ferry service to Busan in South Korea (Ⓦ kampuferry.co.jp) leaves daily at 7.45pm from the **Shimonoseki Port International Terminal**, five minutes' walk from Shimonoseki Station. The ticket booking office is on the second floor of the terminal building (daily 9am–6pm; ☎ 083 224 3000); the cheapest one-way, second-class ticket costs ¥9000 for the tatami resting areas, or ¥12,500 for a bed in a cabin. There's a twenty percent discount for students and under-30s, and a ten percent discount on a return ticket, though it's still cheaper to buy another one-way ticket in Busan.

As one of the cheapest routes in and out of Japan, the ferry is often used by foreigners working illegally who need to renew their tourist visas. For this reason, the immigration officials at Shimonoseki have a reputation for being tough on new arrivals. Note that if you need a **visa** for South Korea, you must arrange it before arriving in Shimonoseki; the nearest consulate is in Hiroshima.

ARRIVAL AND DEPARTURE

BY TRAIN

Shimonoseki Station Beside the port at the west end of town and only served by local trains on the JR San'yō line.

Destinations Chōfu (every 20min; 14min); Shin-Shimonoseki (every 20min; 8min); Shin-Yamaguchi (every 20min; 1hr 10min).

Shin-Shimonoseki Station The nearest Shinkansen station, 9km north and two stops away on the San'yō line.

Destinations Fukuoka, Hakata Station (every 30min; 27min); Hiroshima (hourly; 1hr 15min); Shin-Yamaguchi (very frequent; 20min–1hr).

BY BUS

Long-distance buses stop in front of Shimonoseki Station.

Destinations Akiyoshi-dō (8 daily; 1hr 50min); Osaka (1 daily; 10hr); Tokyo (1 daily; 15hr 30min).

BY FERRY

By ferry to Kyūshū Although the fastest route to Kyūshū is by train or road across Kanmon suspension bridge, traditionalists can still make the 5min ferry hop between Karato Pier, 1.5km east of Shimonoseki Station, and Moji on Kyūshū's northwest tip (every 20min; ¥400; ☎ 083 222 1488, ⓦ kanmon-kisen.co.jp).

By international ferry Ferries to and from Pusan in Korea (daily; 11hr 15min) use the Shimonoseki Port International Terminal, just south of Shimonoseki Station (see above). Until recently, ferries also linked Shimonoseki with the Chinese ports of Qingdao and Shanghai, but both those services now carry cargo only, not passengers.

INFORMATION

Tourist information There are tourist offices at Shimonoseki Station (daily 9am–6pm; ☎ 083 232 8383, ⓦ bit.ly/shimonoseki-tourism), and beside the Shinkansen exit in Shin-Shimonoseki Station (daily 9am–6pm; ☎ 083 256 3422).

GETTING AROUND

By bus Shimonoseki stretches for several kilometres east along the waterfront from the station, so local buses can be useful. Buses from platforms 1 and 2 outside the station call at Akama-jingū and Hino-yama en route to Chōfu (¥390). A one-day bus pass costs ¥720.

By bike Rental bikes, costing around ¥500/day, are available at Shimonoseki Station, and at the youth hostel.

ACCOMMODATION

Kaikyō View Shimonoseki 海峡ビューしものせき 3-58 Mimosusogawa-chō ☎ 083 229 0117, ⓦ kv-shimonoseki.com. From its vantage point on Hino-yama, this low-rise concrete block enjoys fantastic views across the Kanmon Channel. There's a choice of spacious tatami rooms (not all en-suite) or Western-style suites. Rates include two meals. 🛜 **¥22,680**

Plaza Hotel Shimonoseki プラザホテル下関 11-10 Hanano-chō ☎ 083 223 3333, ⓦ plazahotel.co.jp. Hidden away off the road, in a convenient spot between the station and the waterfront, this veteran high-rise hotel has friendly staff and good-sized, well-equipped sea-view rooms. Rates include a good breakfast in its top-floor restaurant. 🛜 **¥10,400**

Shimonoseki Grand Hotel 下関グランドホテル 31-2 Nabe-chō ☎ 083 231 5000, ⓦ sgh.co.jp. A comfortable upmarket hotel, commanding a prime seafront location beside Karato Pier, with Western-style rooms and a couple of restaurants – one French, one Japanese. 🛜 **¥12,000**

FUGU

Shimonoseki is famous for its **fugu**, the potentially deadly **blowfish** or globefish, which provides inspiration for many local sculptures and souvenirs of spiky, balloon-shaped fish. It is known in Shimonoseki as *fuku*, homonymous with the character for fortune and wealth, in order to attract good luck and happiness. Around half Japan's entire national catch (3000 tonnes a year) passes through Haedomari, the main market for *fugu*, at the tip of the island of Hiko-shima, 3km west of Shimonoseki Station.

Chomping on the translucent slivers of the fish, which are practically tasteless, you may wonder what all the fuss is about. However, it's the presence of **tetrodotoxin** – a poison more lethal than potassium cyanide – in the *fugu's* ovaries, liver and a few other internal organs, that make this culinary adventure both dangerous and appealing. *Fugu* chefs train for up to seven years before they can obtain a government licence to prepare the fish. Even so, a small number of diners do die, the most famous fatality being kabuki actor **Bandō Mitsugorō** – a national treasure – who dropped dead after a globefish banquet in Kyoto in 1975.

★ **Shimonoseki Hino-yama Youth Hostel Kaikyō no Kaze** 下関火の山ユースホステル海峡の風 7-1 Mimosusogawa-chō ☎083 222 3753, ☎e-yh.net /shimonoseki. Fine hostel, overlooking the Kanmon Bridge almost 5km east of the station, a 2min walk downhill from the Hino-yama ropeway. Accommodation is in bunk-bed dorms or private twins, and the friendly English-speaking manager is a reasonable cook, preparing breakfast for ¥540, lunch for ¥650 and dinner for ¥1200. From Shimonoseki Station, catch a bus either to the ropeway, or to Mimosuso-gawa, a 10min walk away at the base of Hino-yama. Note there's a 9.30pm curfew. ☎ Dorms ¥3500, rooms ¥8000

Hotel Wing ホテルウィング下関 3-11-2 Takezaki-chō ☎083 235 2111, ☎hotelwing.co.jp/shimonoseki. Amenable, fairly classy Western-style rooms are on offer at this super central spot a 2min walk from the station. Rooms are kitted out with twee floral wallpaper, designer couches and comfy beds. ☎ ¥9200

EATING

The major emphasis in Shimonoseki is on seafood, with good restaurants in the **Sea Mall** near the station and the **Kanmon Wharf** mall by the port, and lots of **fugu** specialists in the old streets. To avoid inadvertently eating **whale meat**, look out for クジラ肉 (*kujira niku*) on menus. Thanks to the ferry link with Busan, there are also several **Korean** restaurants, especially *yakiniku* (barbecue) places, in and around the **Green Mall**, just north of the station.

★ **Sushi Yukan** すし遊館 Kanmon Wharf, Karato ☎083 228 1722, ☎bit.ly/sushi-yukan. This superb conveyor-belt sushi place, with sea views from the second floor of Kanmon Wharf, is much better than the equivalent operation on the second floor of the fish market nearby. Typical plates of squid or mackerel cost around ¥230, while pricier handmade rolls and mixed platters are prepared on request. ☎ Daily 11am–9.30pm.

Tsukasa つか佐 4-6 Akama-chō, Karato ☎083 231 4129, ☎tsukasa-shimonoseki.com. Excellent traditional fish restaurant, set back amid the tangle of old streets north of the port, where a team of motherly waitresses serves hearty set lunches at weekends for ¥1950. Otherwise *kaiseki* dinner menus start at ¥5400; be warned, though, that the "Three Major Special" option includes whale as well as *fugu*. Tsukasa is hard to find, incidentally; if you give up, settle for one of the many *izakaya* you'll pass en route. Mon, Tues, Thurs & Fri 5.30–10pm, Sat & Sun 11.30am–3pm & 5.30–10pm.

Yabure Kabure やぶれかぶれ 2-2-5 Buzenda-chō ☎083 234 3711, ☎yaburekabure.jp. The large plastic *fugu* hanging outside this place, on the shopping parade east of the station, tells you what to expect. All four of its ¥3240 set lunches focus on *fugu* – one comes with porridge – while dinner menus, featuring every imaginable variation on the theme, start at ¥5400. Daily 11am–10pm.

Yakiniku Yasumori 焼肉やすもり 2-1-13 Takezaki-chō ☎083 222 6542, ☎y-yasumori.com. One of Shimonoseki's finest *yakiniku* restaurants, just south of the Green Mall. Order plates of raw meat and vegetables to sizzle on a tabletop cooker (from ¥1250). Also try *pivinpa*, a traditional mix of rice and vegetables in a stone bowl. Mon–Wed & Fri–Sun 11am–midnight.

8

Chōfu

長府

It's well worth making the short excursion from Shimonoseki to neighbouring **CHŌFU**, an old castle town of the Mōri family. One of the joys of Chōfu is its relative lack of tourist development; as you wander round its authentic enclave of samurai houses and streets, sleepy temples and lovely garden, it's easy to feel that you have slipped back several centuries.

The elegant garden **Chōfu-teien** (長府庭園; 8-11 Kuromo; daily 9am–5pm; ¥200; ☎083 246 4120), at the south end of Chōfu just over 4km northeast of the Kanmon bridge, makes a civilized introduction to the town. Laid out during the Taishō era for the ruler of a Mori clan, it holds several teahouses dotted around an ornamental pond and babbling river.

Chōfu's original **castle district** begins a short walk north of the garden. Head inland at the next turning, and you'll come to a compact cluster of old **samurai houses**, shielded by wooden gates and crumbling earthen walls, topped with glazed tiles, with the roads bordered by narrow water channels. Further up the hill, in a leafy glade approached by a broad flight of stone steps, is the Mōri family temple, **Kōzan-ji** (功山寺; 1-2-3 Chōfukawabata; daily 9.30am–4.30pm; free; ☎083 245 0258). Dating from the fourteenth century, it's the oldest Zen temple in the country. Alongside, the small **Chōfu Museum** (長府博物館; 1-2-5 Chōfukawabata; Tues–Sun 9.30am–5pm; ¥200; ☎083 245 0555) holds beautiful scrolls decorated with calligraphy and intriguing old maps.

ARRIVAL AND DEPARTURE   CHŌFU

By train Frequent trains from Shimonoseki run to Chōfu's train station, at the north end of town 4km from the samurai district (every 20min; 14min).

By bus Buses to Chōfu (every 15min; 25min; ¥390) run from outside Shimonoseki Station. Buy a ¥720 one-day pass if you're making the return trip. For Chōfu-teien, get off at Shiritsu Bijutsukan-mae (市立美術館前); for the samurai district, head uphill from the Jōka-machi (城下町) stop.

EATING

★Chayashō 茶屋祥 2-1-6 Chōfukawabata ☎ 083 245 0080. Delightful café-cum-shop in a century-old kimono emporium, where the gracious hosts serve tea and coffee with cakes for ¥500. The delicious chocolate cake comes on indigo china plates and is decorated with a gold maple leaf. They also sell set lunches for around ¥1200, plus kimono, pottery and colourful knick-knacks. A large red-paper umbrella, just downhill from Kōzan-ji, marks the entrance. 🛜 Daily 9am–6pm.

Hagi

萩

The unspoiled historic town of **HAGI**, in a spectacular setting on Honshū's northern shores 85km northeast of Shimonoseki, dates back to 1604, when warlord Mōri Terumoto built his castle at the tip of an island between the Hashimoto and Matsumoto rivers. Follow the waterfront route here from Shimonoseki, along the sparsely populated **San'in** coast, and you'll encounter a marvellously bleak and rugged shoreline, where the savage Sea of Japan has eroded the rocks into jagged shapes.

Hagi is a delightful place to spend a little time, with a similarly relaxed, friendly atmosphere to other towns in Yamaguchi prefecture. Much of its charm lies in the potential for meandering strolls or bike rides along its attractive plaster-walled streets. Although the castle is long ruined, the atmospheric graveyards of the Mōri *daimyō*, the layouts of the **samurai** and merchants' quarters – **Horiuchi** (堀内) and **Jōka-machi** (城下町) – and the temple district of **Tera-machi** (*tera* means "temple") remain, with several significant buildings intact.

Hagi is also renowned for its pottery, **Hagi-yaki** – only surpassed, according to connoisseurs, by Kyoto's *raku-yaki*. You can barely move around town without coming across a shop selling the pastel-glazed wares.

The one drawback is that while Hagi has the feel of a small town, its attractions are very spread out. All three train stations lie across the rivers from the town centre, half an hour's walk from the samurai district or castle area. That said, with a rental bike, you

YOSHIDA SHŌIN

The charismatic **Yoshida Shōin** was born into a Hagi **samurai** family in 1830. When the industrialized world came knocking at Japan's door in 1853, in the insistent form of Commodore Perry (see p.826), Yoshida believed that the only appropriate response for his self-isolated, military-ruled country was to ditch the Tokugawa Shogunate, reinstate the emperor and move swiftly to emulate the ways of the West. To this end, he attempted, together with a fellow samurai, to leave Japan in 1854 on one of Perry's "black ships". However, he was handed over to the authorities, who imprisoned him in Edo (Tokyo) before banishing him back to Hagi.

Once at home, Yoshida didn't let up in his revolutionary campaign to "**revere the emperor, expel the barbarians**". From 1857, he was kept under house arrest in the Shōka Sonjuku (now within the shrine grounds of Shōin-jinja; see p.611), where he taught many young disciples, including the future Meiji-era prime minister Itō Hirobumi. Eventually, Yoshida became too big a thorn in the shogunate's side and he was executed in 1860, aged 29, for plotting to assassinate an official.

Five years later, samurai and peasants joined forces in Hagi to bring down the local Tokugawa government. This, and similar **revolts** in western Japan (see p.826), led to Yoshida's aim being achieved in 1868 – the restoration of the emperor to power.

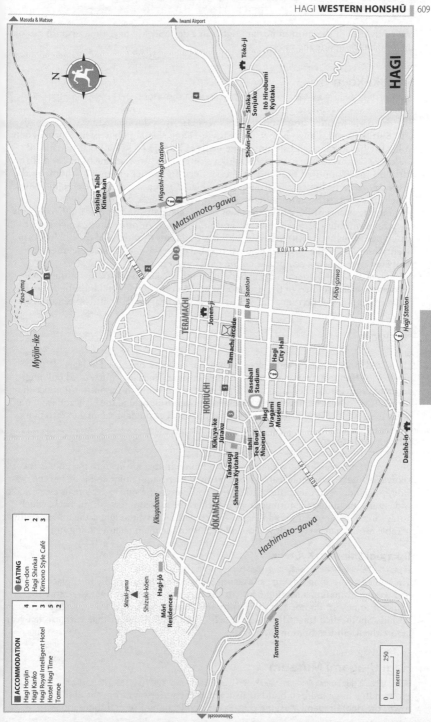

Masuda & Matsue

Iwami Airport

Shimonoseki

HAGI

Tokō-ji

Shōka Sonjuku

Itō Hirobumi Kyūtaku

Shōin-jinja

Yoshiga Taibi Kinen-kan

Higashi-Hagi Station

Matsumoto-gawa

ROUTE 262

Aiba-gawa

Kiso-yama

Myōjin-ike

TERAMACHI

Jōnen-ji

Bus Station

Tamachi arcade

Hagi City Hall

Hagi Station

8

HORIUCHI

Baseball Stadium

Hagi Uragami Museum

Kikuya-ke Jūtaku

Ishii Tea Bowl Museum

Takasugi Shinsaku Kyūtaku

JŌKAMACHI

Kikugahama

Daishō-in

ROUTE 191

Hashimoto-gawa

Shizuki-yama

Shizuki-kōen

Hagi-jō

Mōri Residences

Tamae Station

0   250
      metres

ACCOMMODATION	
Hagi Honjin	4
Hagi Kanko	1
Hagi Royal Intelligent Hotel	3
Hostel Hagi Time	5
Tomoe	2

● **EATING**	
Don-don	1
Hagi Shinkai	2
Kimono Style Café	3

can easily take in the most important sights in a day and still have time to crash out on the fine **beach** beside the castle.

Shizuki-kōen

指月公園 • Daily: March 8.30am–6pm; April–Oct 8am–6.30pm; Nov–Feb 8.30am–4.30pm • ¥210, including entry to Mōri soldiers' residence; tea at teahouse ¥500 • ☎ 083 825 1826

The dramatic wooded headland at Hagi's western tip is dominated by a 143m-high hill, **Shizuki-yama**. Down below, on its town-facing side, a public park, **Shizuki-kōen**, holds the broad moat and sloping stone walls of **Hagi-jō** (萩城), all that remains of the castle destroyed when Mōri Takachika shifted court to Yamaguchi in 1874. In addition to six hundred resplendent cherry trees, its former grounds are home to the rustic *Hananoe* teahouse, the atmospheric Shizuki-yama shrine, and the **Hagi-jō Kiln**, which sells exquisite ceramics (daily 8am–5pm; ☎ 083 822 5226).

Immediately east of the castle, the town beach, **Kikugahama** (菊ヶ浜), is officially only open for swimming between mid-July and mid-August. At other times, you'll have to watch out for jellyfish. Alternatively, a hiking trail leads to the top of the hill in around twenty minutes, while less energetic visitors may prefer to relax beside the quiet cove peppered with modern sculptures on the park's western side.

A long wood-and-plaster tenement building south of Shizuki-kōen contains the **Mōri residences**, where soldiers of the clan once lived. You can't literally go inside, but from the path outside you can peer into the various rooms and imagine daily life two centuries ago.

Horiuchi

堀内

High- and low-ranking samurai, along with rich merchants, once lived in Hagi's picturesque **Horiuchi** quarter, where the narrow lanes are lined by whitewashed buildings decorated with distinctive black-and-white lattice plasterwork. In season, you'll notice the *natsu mikan* (summer orange) trees heavily laden with fruit behind the high stone and mud walls; these were planted in 1876 as a way for the newly redundant samurai to earn money.

Kikuya-ke Jūtaku

菊屋家住宅 • 1-1 Gofuku • Daily 8.30am–5.15pm • ¥600 • ☎ 083 825 8282

The most interesting of the various houses in Horiuchi that are open to the public, the **Kikuya-ke Jūtaku**, was built in 1606 for a wealthy merchant family, and is one of the oldest such houses in the country. It's a large complex, so be sure to explore its every nook and cranny, including the former shops as well as the museum towards the back, which holds some intriguing scrolls and maps. The crowning glory, though, is the unexpectedly sizeable formal **garden**, which you can admire from the main tatami guest room.

Takasugi Shinsaku Kyūtaku

高杉晋作旧宅 • 2-9-3 Minami Furuhagi-machi • Daily 9am–5pm • ¥100 • ☎ 083 822 3078

The walled compound known as **Takasugi Shinsaku Kyūtaku** was the birthplace in 1839 of Takasugi Shinsaku, a leading figure in the nineteenth-century fight to restore the emperor to power. Photos and calligraphy tell the story of a man who, like his mentor, Yoshida Shōin, died tragically young, albeit of tuberculosis rather than execution, a year before the Meiji Restoration in 1867.

Hagi Uragami Museum

萩浦上記念館, Hagi Uragami Kinen-kan • 586-1 Hiyako • Tues–Sun 9am–5pm • ¥300 • ☎ 083 824 2400, ⓦ bit.ly/uragami

Housed in a huge modern building just across the waterways from the oldest parts of town, the **Hagi Uragami Museum** centres on a collection of several thousand *ukiyo-e* woodblock prints, including works by Hokusai and Hiroshige. These exhibits are complemented by displays covering the tools and processes employed in *ukiyo-e* printmaking, and galleries devoted to pottery from Korea and China as well as more contemporary local ceramics.

Shōin-jinja

松陰神社 • 1537 Chintō • **Temple** Daily 8am–5pm • Free • **Yoshida Shōin History Museum** (吉田松陰歴史館) Daily 9am–5pm • ¥500 • **Residence** Daily 9am–5pm • Free • ☎ 083 822 4643

Hagi's largest shrine – **Shōin-jinja**, dedicated to the nineteenth-century scholar and revolutionary figure Yoshida Shōin (see box, p.608) – stands 1km southeast of Higashi-Hagi Station, on the mountain side of the Matsumoto-gawa. Within its grounds are the **Shōka Sonjuku** (松下村塾), the small academy where Yoshida lived and taught during his final years; the **Yoshida Shōin History Museum**, illustrating various scenes from his life; and the **residence** where he was held under house arrest following his attempt to leave Japan in 1854.

Tōkō-ji

東光寺 • 1647 Chintō • Daily 8.30am–5pm • ¥300 • ☎ 083 826 1052, 🌐 toukouji.net

Following the riverside cycle path uphill from the Shōin-jinja shrine brings you to a family temple of the Mōri clan, **Tōkō-ji**, which was founded in 1691. There's a Chinese flavour to its many handsome buildings and gates. Look out for the giant wooden carp gong that hangs in the courtyard, as you walk behind the main hall towards its atmospheric graveyard, packed with neat rows of more than five hundred moss-covered stone lanterns. Here you'll find the **tombs** of five Mōri lords, all odd-numbered generations, save the first lord buried with the even-numbered generations in nearby Daishō-in. During the **Obon** (Aug 15), the lanterns are lit to send off the souls of the dead.

Continue uphill behind the temple and you'll come to **Tanjōchi** (誕生地), the birthplace of Yoshida Shōin, marked by a bronze statue of the samurai revolutionary and one of his followers. Take in the view of the town before heading back down, past the small thatched home of **Itō Hirobumi** (伊藤博文旧宅), another Yoshida disciple who later became prime minister and drafted the Meiji constitution.

Daishō-in

大照院 • 4132 Oazatsubaki Oumi • Daily 8am–5pm • ¥200 • ☎ 083 822 2124

Set at the foot of a wooded hill just above the south bank of the Hashimoto-gawa, 2km west of Hagi Station, the **Daishō-in** temple was built after the death of Mōri Hidenari, the first lord of the Hagi branch of the Mōri clan. A rickety gate at its entrance leads to a lantern-filled graveyard, similar to that at Tōkō-ji, where you'll find the corresponding tombs of all the even-numbered generations of Mōri lords. Hidenari himself also lies here, along with eight samurai who committed *seppuku* (ritual suicide) on his death.

Yoshiga Taibi Kinen-kan

吉賀大眉記念館 • 425-1 Chintō • Daily 9am–5pm • ¥500, pottery-making ¥2200, with advance reservation • ☎ 083 826 5180, 🌐 taibi-hagi.jp

Yoshiga Taibi Kinen-kan, 1.3km north of Higashi-Hagi Station along the coastal route Highway 191, ranks among Hagi's most respected pottery kilns. The attached museum displaying an outstanding collection of *Hagi-yaki*. If you book ahead you can make your own pottery, which will be fired and sent to you for an extra fee after a couple of months. Unlike some other kilns, they're happy to mail pottery abroad.

Kasa-yama

笠山

North of Hagi Station, the coast road passes through several succesive fishing villages, where squid hang drying on lines like wet underwear. The narrow promontory around 6km along was formed by a small **volcano**, now extinct and known as **Kasa-yama**. Down at sea level, beside a small shrine and set back from the **Myōjin-ike** (明神池), a saltwater pond teeming with fish, is an interesting natural phenomenon: the **Kazeana**, a shaded glade cooled by cold air rushing from cracks in the lava. Take the road that winds up to the summit, and you can enjoy panoramic views along the coast, and inspect the 30m crater, one of the tiniest in the world.

ARRIVAL AND DEPARTURE
HAGI

By plane Iwami Airport (☏ 085 624 0010, ⓦ hagiiwami.jp), 60km east along the coast outside Masuda, is served only by flights from Tokyo's Haneda airport (2 daily; 1hr 30min); a connecting bus (1hr 20min; ¥2070) runs to Hagi bus station.

By train Hagi has three train stations, spaced around its periphery, with services from all three stations, all of which are connected to Masuda (5 daily; 1hr 20min). Be careful: the most useful is not Hagi but Higashi-Hagi (東萩駅), immediately northeast of the centre. Tamae (玉江駅), two stops west of Higashi-Hagi, is more convenient if you're staying near Hagi-jō, or plan a quick visit to the castle area, while Hagi lies in between the two. All are on the San'in line. Note that if you're travelling to Hagi from Shimonoseki, the scenic route along the coast is much slower than the cross-country JR Mine line, which heads inland from Asa, 40km northeast of Shimonoseki on the JR San'yō and Shinkansen lines.

By bus Long-distance buses (ⓦ bochobus.co.jp) stop at the bus station in the town centre, near the Tamachi shopping arcade, a short walk east of Jōkamachi.

Destinations Akiyoshi-dai (2 daily; 1hr 10min); Kyoto (daily; 13hr); Osaka (daily; 12hr); Shin-Yamaguchi (12 daily; 1hr 10min); Tokyo (daily; 14hr 30min); Tsuwano (5 daily; 1hr 45min).

INFORMATION

Tourist information There are helpful tourist information booths at Higashi-Hagi (daily: March–Nov 9am–5.45pm, Dec–Feb 9am–5pm; ☏ 083 825 3145, ⓦ hagishi.com) and Hagi (same hours; ☏ 083 825 1750) stations.

GETTING AROUND

By bus Two buses – *nishi mawari* (西回り; west) and *higashi mawari* (東回り; east) – loop around the entire town and its attractions (every 30min, daily 7am–6pm; ¥100 per ride).

By bike Several shops at Higashi-Hagi Station offer bike rental from ¥200/hr, ¥1000/day.

ACCOMMODATION

★**Hagi Honjin** 萩本陣 385-8 Chintō ☏ 083 822 5252, ⓦ hagihonjin.co.jp. Though somewhat out of the way, perched on a low hill beyond Shōin-jinja 1.6km southeast of Higashi-Hagi Station, this features fabulous rotemburo baths, a monorail up to a viewpoint over the city, beautiful tatami rooms and exquisite meals. A great place to get away from it all. Prices include half-board. 🛜 **¥21,852**

★**Hagi Kanko** 萩観光ホテル 1189-541 Chintō ☏ 083 825 0211, ⓦ hagikan.com. Lovely ryokan, perched on the next headland north of Hagi, 1km below the summit of Kasayama. The spacious tatami rooms have tremendous views across to the town and towards misty islands scattered beyond, and the onsen has indoor and outdoor pools. You can book a room only, but there's nowhere else to eat nearby. Call ahead for the free shuttle service to and from Higashi-Hagi Station, 5km south. Rates include two meals. 🛜 **¥19,440**

Hagi Royal Intelligent Hotel 萩ロイヤルインテリジェントホテル 3000-5 Chintō ☏ 083 821 4589, ⓦ hrih.jp. This business hotel may be looking dated, but it's really pretty good, and has the huge advantage of being right next to Higashi-Hagi Station. As well as an onsen with rotemburo, it offers a large art gallery and fitness centre. Rates include breakfast. 🛜 **¥8100**

Hostel Hagi Time ホステルはぎタイム 20 Kawara-machi ☏ 083 821 7286, ⓦ hagitime-en.jimdo.com. Clean, modern and very welcoming hostel in an unexpected white clapboard house, on the edge of the historic Horiuchi district at the west end of the central shopping arcade. Rental bikes available for ¥500/day. 🛜 Dorms **¥2600**, rooms **¥6000**

★**Tomoe** 常茂恵 Hijiwara ☏ 083 822 0150, ⓦ tomoehagi.jp. Wonderful ryokan, a short walk from Higashi-Hagi Station, where guests enjoy Japanese hospitality and cuisine, presided over by Keiko, a charming local who speaks good English. The entire place exudes a cool Zen minimalism, with the 25 extremely well-equipped suites overlooking raked-gravel gardens. 🛜 **¥44,400**

8

EATING

Hagi is strangely short of restaurants, but you'll find a number of cheap noodle bars and fish restaurants around the central Tamachi shopping arcade and the main cross street, Route 262. The local speciality is *shirasu* (whitebait); in spring, you'll see fishermen on the Matsumoto-gawa sifting the water with giant nets hung from their narrow boats.

Don-don どんどん 177 Hijiwara 3-ku ☎083 822 7537. Bustling, inexpensive noodle joint near the Hagi-bashi across the Matsumoto-gawa. A bowl of udon noodles plus *taki-kome gohan* (vegetable rice) and pickles costs ¥750. Order at the counter. Daily 8am–8pm.

Hagi Shinkai 萩心海 370-71 Tsuchihara ☎083 826 1221, ⓦhagishinkai.com. You can't fail to spot this high-class seafood restaurant, topped by a lighthouse and standing just across the river from Higashi-Hagi Station. Expect to pay around ¥2500 for a meal of mixed sashimi or squid; if you're looking for a treat, they serve a special *fugu* (blowfish) set menu for ¥12,960 between October and

March, and switch to *harame* (flounder) in summer, costing ¥8640. 🛜 Daily 11am–2pm & 5–9pm.

Kimono Style Café キモノスタイルカフェ 2-39 Gofuku-machi, Jōka-machi ☎083 821 7000, ⓦkimono-raison -d-etre.com. Café, souvenir shop and kimono experience all in one, in a house near Kikuya-ke Jūtaku. You can simply admire the mini-garden and enjoy a ¥700 cake-and-coffee or mocha set, served by waitresses in kimono – simple snacks like soup or soba noodles are also available – or dress up in traditional style, with a "kimono rental experience" from ¥2990. 🛜 Mon–Wed & Fri–Sun 9am–6pm.

Tsuwano

津和野

The beautiful old castle town of **TSUWANO** stretches along the narrow valley of the Tsuwano-gawa, just over 50km east of Hagi and around 35km inland from the coast at Masuda. To either side, the soaring hills are thickly covered in trees that turn glorious colours when autumn sets in; the magnificent **Taikodani Inari-jinja** shrine pokes from the woods to the west, beneath the ruined castle of **Tsuwano-jō**, while the extinct, 908m-high **Aono-yama** volcano looms high above town to the east, surrounded at dawn by swirling mists.

Like many another small Japanese town, Tsuwano touts itself as a "Little Kyoto". For once, the nickname is entirely appropriate. Somehow, despite the many tourists, an air of courtly affluence still pervades its historic **Tono-machi** quarter, where the former samurai houses now hold shops, galleries, cafés and restaurants. What's more, in such a tiny place – home to fewer than ten thousand residents – a five-minute walk can take you out into open countryside, and, once the day-trippers have gone, Tsuwano lets out its breath and turns delightfully sleepy and peaceful.

Various annual **festivals** merit a special trip to Tsuwano. Between July 20 and July 27, the **Gion Matsuri** at the **Yasaka-jinja** (八坂神社; 625 Gionmachi) sees the ancient *Sagi-Mai* (**Heron Dance**) performed by men dressed as the white birds, complete with flapping wings and long-necked hats. It's also worth braving the crowds on the second Sunday in April, to watch the Yabusame Horseback Archery Competition at **Washibara Hachimangū** shrine (鷲原八幡宮; 6322 Washibara).

Tono-machi

殿町

Tsuwano's prosperity, born of peace and enlightened governance by local *daimyō*, is evident from the handsome buildings that fill the venerable **Tono-machi** neighbourhood, a few minutes' walk from the station. Cradled in a curve of the Tsuwano-gawa, this district was home to many **samurai** families, whose houses still retain their cross-hatched black-and-white plaster walls. As you stroll the semi-pedestrianized main street, look out for the three **sake breweries**, the perfectly preserved old **pharmacy**, and the many shops that sell traditional **sweets**, including *genji-maki*, a soft sponge filled with sweet red-bean paste. Most remarkable of all are the slender little **canals** that parallel the street on both sides – they're filled with live and very colourful **carp**, which were originally bred as emergency food supplies in case of famine.

Taikodani Inari-jinja

太鼓谷稲成神社 • 409 Ushiroda • 24hr • Free • ☎ 085 672 0219

From the west bank of the Tsuwano-gano River, an extraordinary and quite dazzling procession of over a thousand bright red *torii*, each crammed so close to the next that they form a "tunnel" through the trees, adorns a stairway that zigzags up the hillside to reach **Taikodani Inari-jinja** after a fifteen-minute climb.

This is one of the five largest **Inari** shrines in Japan, dedicated to a Shintō deity connected with fertility, agricultural bounty, and foxes – the vivid vermilion colour of the *torii* is closely associated with Inari, and so too are the matching male-and-female pairs of fox statues, *kitsune,* which you may see receiving loving caresses from devotees. All in all it's a magnificent spot, with its main eighteenth-century hall resplendent in gold and red, and presiding over a central patio where all the surrounding shrines repay further exploration.

Tsuwano-jō

津和野城 • Chairlift: daily: March–Nov 9am–5pm, Dec–Feb hours vary • ¥450 return

In a commanding hilltop location on the west side of the valley, the castle of **Tsuwano-jō** was built in 1295 by Lord Yoshimi Yoriyuki, as protection against potential Mongol invaders. The wooden parts of the structure were burned and dismantled at the start of the Meiji era, but its stone walls still stand surprisingly strong, guarding a grassy, levelled-off plateau above the thickly wooded slopes, from which the views are superb.

It takes around half an hour to **hike** up to the castle along a steep trail that starts a short way beyond the Taikodani Inari-jinja shrine. An old-fashioned and somewhat hair-raising hop-on hop-off **chairlift** also makes the climb to a point ten minutes' easy walking from the ruins. Make sure you get back in time for the last ride down; you really wouldn't want to be stuck up there after dark.

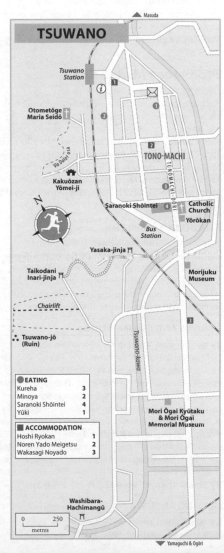

8

TSUWANO

Masuda

Tsuwano Station

Otometōge
Maria Seidō

Kakuōzan Yōmei-ji

TONO-MACHI

Saranoki Shōintei

Catholic Church
Yōrōkan

Bus Station

Yasaka-jinja

Taikodani Inari-jinja

Morijuku Museum

Chairlift

Tsuwano-jō (Ruin)

Tsuwano-kawa

● EATING
Kureha	3
Minoya	2
Saranoki Shōintei	4
Yūki	1

■ ACCOMMODATION
Hoshi Ryokan	1
Noren Yado Meigetsu	2
Wakasagi Noyado	3

Mori Ōgai Kyūtaku & Mori Ōgai Memorial Museum

Washibara-Hachimangū

0   250
metres

Yamaguchi & Ogōri

Morijuku Museum

杜塾美術館, Morijuku Bijutsukan · 542 Oazamori-mura · Daily 9am–5pm · ¥500 · ☎ 085 672 3200

Across the river just south of Tono-machi, in a restored farmhouse fronted by raked-gravel gardens, the **Morijuku Museum** is a smart modern gallery that exhibits works by local contemporary artists, as well as a small collection of etchings by Goya. Upstairs, the attendant will show you the pinhole camera in the *shōji* screen, capturing an image of the garden outside.

Mori Ōgai Memorial Museum

森鴎外記念館, Mori Ōgai Kinen-kan · 238 Machida · Tues–Sun 9am–5pm · ¥600 · ☎ 085 672 3210

The modern **Mori Ōgai Memorial Museum**, towards the southern end of Tsuwano, displays the personal effects of Mori Ōgai (1862–1922), a famed Meiji-era novelist, translator, poet and surgeon. His preserved wood-and-mustard-plaster home next door, **Mori Ōgai Kyūtaku** (森鴎外旧宅; daily 9am–5pm; ¥100), can be visited separately.

Otometōge Maria Seidō

乙女峠マリア聖堂 · 717-3 Ushiroda · 24hr · Free

A pleasant woodland hike leads through the hills immediately west of Tsuwano Station. Head southwest and cross the train tracks at the first opportunity, then double back and continue to the car park, from where a footpath leads up to the cosy chapel of **Otometōge Maria Seidō**, nestling in a leafy glade. In 1865, the Tokugawa shogunate transported some 150 Christians from Nagasaki to Tsuwano; 36 were eventually put to death for their beliefs before the new Meiji government bowed to international pressure, lifting the ban on the religion in 1874. This quaint wooden structure was built to commemorate the martyrs in 1951, and is the scene of the **Otometōge festival** on May 3.

Kakuōzan Yōmei-ji

覚皇山永明寺 · Daily 8.30am–5pm · ¥300 · ☎ 085 672 0137

Inside the charming temple of **Kakuōzan Yōmei-ji**, 200m south through the forest from the Maria Seidō chapel, stone steps lead up to an elegant collection of thatched wooden buildings, used by generations of Tsuwano lords since 1420. Inside, look out for the sumptuous screen paintings that decorate some of the tatami rooms, and take a moment to sit and admire the verdant traditional garden.

ARRIVAL AND INFORMATION   TSUWANO

By train Tsuwano Station, at the northwestern edge of the town centre, is on the scenic cross-country JR Yamaguchi line, which runs from the nearest Shinkansen stop, Shin-Yamaguchi on the south coast, via Yamaguchi (also served by more frequent, slower services), to Masuda on the north coast. To get to or from Hagi, you must change at Masuda; some trains from Tsuwano, however, continue east along the coast beyond Masuda to Matsue.

Destinations Masuda (7 daily; 40min); Matsue (2 daily; 2hr 40min); Shin-Yamaguchi (3 daily; 1hr); Yamaguchi (8 daily; 1hr 10min).

By steam train At weekends, JR run steam-train

day-trips to Tsuwano. The SL Yamaguchi-gō leaves Shin-Yamaguchi at 10.48am, and allows passengers a couple of hours in Tsuwano before setting off back to Shin-Yamaguchi at 3.45pm (late March to late Nov, Sat & Sun only; one-way ¥1660; ☎ 078 341 7903, ⌨ c571.jp).

By bus Direct services from Hagi arrive at the bus station, a few minutes' walk from Tono-machi (5 daily; 1hr 45min; ¥2190; ⌨ bochobus.co.jp).

Tourist information The tourist office is just outside the train station, off to the right in a separate building (daily 9am–5pm; ☎ 085 672 1771, ⌨ tsuwano-kanko.net).

GETTING AROUND

By bike Outlets offering rental bikes include Kamai Shoten, in the parade of shops opposite the station

(¥500/2hr, ¥800/day).

ACCOMMODATION

Tsuwano is a wonderful and relatively affordable place to spend a night in a traditional ryokan or minshuku.

Hoshi Ryokan 星旅館 53-6 Ushiroda ☎ 085 672 0136. Slightly ramshackle but charming and friendly ryokan, close to the station, which calls to mind the weathered home of an elderly aunt. Insulation is not the best, so if you're here in winter be sure the heater works. Add on ¥1250 per person per meal. ¥10,000

★**Noren Yado Meigetsu** のれん宿明月 665 Ushiroda ☎ 085 672 0685. This charming ryokan is great value, especially considering the sheer quality (and quantity!) of its food, with *kaiseki* dinners featuring local ingredients like seasonal mountain vegetables and carp. The spacious tatami rooms are arrayed around a small traditional garden, and there are plenty of polished wood fittings plus a small private onsen. Rates include two meals. 📶 ¥19,500

Wakasagi Noyado 若さぎの宿 93-6 Morimura ☎ 085 672 1146. This homely, somewhat kitsch minshuku has an English-speaking owner and offers good tatami rooms with TV and a/c. Rates include breakfast and dinner, but you can also pay ¥4500 per person without meals. ¥16,200

EATING

Although several *shokudō* and noodle shops are clustered near the station and around the Tono-machi area, very few restaurants in Tsuwano stay open in the evening, when most overnight visitors eat where they sleep. Don't miss *uzume-meshi*, the local dish of rice in a broth with shredded green mountain vegetables, pieces of tofu and mushrooms.

Kureha 紅葉 201 Ushiroda ☎ 085 672 1006. Cute little coffee house on the main street, with tatami and Western seating, English menu and English-speaking staff. You can pick up coffee and a cake (such as yummy cheesecake with tofu, or apricot tart) for ¥700, while breakfast toast is ¥480 and lunches such as beef curry cost ¥1000–1200. Try to avoid the noontime rush, please. 📶 Tues–Sun 9am–6pm.

Minoya みのや 75-11 Ushiroda ☎ 085 672 1531. Thatched-roof, teahouse-style dumpling restaurant, a short walk south of the station and festooned with a giant red paper lantern. A simple bowl of udon noodles with fried egg is ¥750; add meat and three dumplings and it's ¥1050; and a mixed set lunch costs ¥1300. Mon, Tues & Fri–Sun 9.30am–5.30pm.

Saranoki Shōintei 沙羅の木松韻亭 70 Ushiroda ☎ 085 672 1661, 🌐 saranoki.co.jp. Of several eating options within this large complex, the quickest and easiest is the cafeteria furthest from the street, where you pay at a vending machine for tasty soba (¥850) or udon (¥1000) noodles. There's also a more formal tatami dining room, overlooking a lovely traditional garden, and serving set meals from ¥2625 or ¥5250); an ice-cream counter; and a well-stocked gift shop alongside the main street. 📶 Daily 9am–6pm.

Yūki 遊亀 271-4 Ushiroda ☎ 085 672 0162. This renowned restaurant has a palpable sense of history, with tatami booths, pottery and porcelain on the walls and a carp-filled stream running right through the dining room – some of the fish end up on the plate, as sashimi or in the miso soup. Try the ¥2000 *Tsuwano teishoku*, a set meal of local dishes. Reservations recommended. 📶 Mon–Wed & Fri–Sun 11am–3pm.

Matsue

松江

The very charming prefectural capital of Shimane-ken, **MATSUE**, straddles a thin strip of land that separates the Shinji-ko and Nakaumi lagoons, around 16km inland from the San'in coast. Threaded through by canals and rivers, and centring on the intact 400-year-old castle of **Matsue-jō** – still encircled by a tranquil moat – Matsue has a soothing, faintly Venetian atmosphere. Its downtown core was left relatively unscathed by World War II, so walking through its main commercial districts you feel as though you could be in the 1930s. Going back a little further, it's still possible to catch glimpses of the old Japan that so enchanted author **Lafcadio Hearn** a century ago, such as fishermen casting their nets in Shinji-ko lake, or prodding its depths with poles, searching out shellfish.

Besides the castle, Matsue's finest attractions include the handsome samurai district of **Shiomi Nawate**, which holds Hearn's former home; the **Matsue Historical Museum**; and the lakefront **Shimane Art Museum**, south of the Ōhashi-gawa River which divides the city in two. While you could just about see them all in half a day, Matsue is quite spread out, and you'll probably enjoy it more if you take the time to amble from place to place, lingering beside the waterways and meandering around the various temples scattered near the river's south bank.

Matsue-jō

松江城 • 1-5 Tono-machi • **Castle grounds** daily: April–Sept 7am–7.30pm, Oct–March 8.30am–5pm • free • **Donjon** daily: April–Sept 8.30am–6.30pm, Oct–March 8.30am–5pm • ¥560, foreign visitors ¥280 • ☎ 085 221 4030 • English-speaking guides available at weekends, and on weekdays if booked through tourist information office (see p.622) • Bus from Matsue Station to Kenchō-mae; the castle grounds are straight ahead

Still very much the focal point of Matsue, just as it was when the *daimyō* Horio Yoshiharu ordered its construction in 1611, the five-storey donjon of **Matsue-jō** stands brooding atop the hill of Oshiro-yama. Even though, compared to the donjon of Himeji-jō (see p.554), it looks somewhat squashed, this is, in fact, the second largest of the twelve remaining original castle towers scattered around Japan. Extensively renovated during the 1950s, its sinister aspect is enhanced by the black-painted wood decorating the walls.

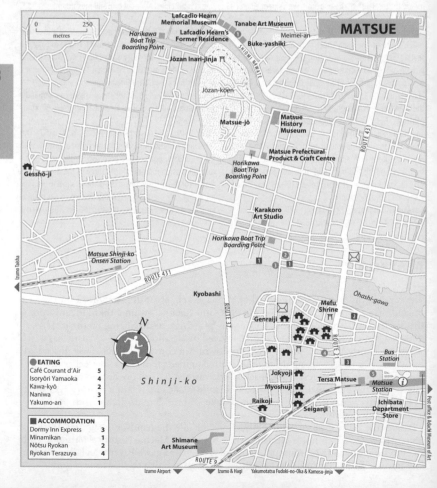

Leave your shoes at the entrance to the donjon, and climb the slippery wooden stairs in your socks to reach the fifth-floor *Tengu* ("Long-Nosed Goblin") room. Had there been any battles – which there weren't – the lords would have commanded their armies from this superb vantage point, with its views sweeping across the city towards the lake and sea. The lower floors hold some good historical exhibits, including the wooden *shachi* (mythical dolphins) that once topped the roof; huge ancient arrows; scale models of the city during different eras; and, best of all, fearsome samurai helmets, personalized with waves and antlers.

The grounds surrounding the castle, circumscribed by its wide inner moat, have been turned into a pleasant park, **Jōzan-kōen** (城山公園). Assorted footpaths undulate over and around the wooded slopes, making it a great spot for a picnic or a stroll, and there's also an Inari shrine at the northern end, **Jōzan Inari-jinja** (城山稲成神社).

Matsue History Museum

松江郷土館, Matsue Kyōdo-kan • Tono-machi 279 • Daily: April–Sept 8.30am–6.30pm, Oct–March 8.30am–5pm; closed third Thurs of month • ¥510, foreign visitors ¥250 • ☎ 085 232 1607, ⓦ matsu-reki.jp

A large, clearly signposted modern building, immediately across the moat east of the castle and designed to resemble a samurai home, holds the **Matsue History Museum**, which until recently was housed in the elegant whitewashed mansion outside the castle gate. Its extensively updated displays trace the story of Matsue from the building of the castle – which, as two talismans that were unearthed in 2012 confirm, was 1611 – via the city that Lafcadio Hearn knew, up to the present day. Contemporary Matsue is represented by a master **confectionery** maker, whom can you watch preparing sweets.

The same ticket also gives admission to the **Horan-enya Memorial Hall** next door, devoted to the city's huge **boat festival**, a Shintō ceremony celebrated every ten years (and next due in May 2019).

Shiomi Nawate

塩見縄手

The tranquil street that runs beside the moat along the northern flank of the castle park leads you to the **Shiomi Nawate** neighbourhood. Several former **samurai residences** here, still protected behind high walls capped with grey tiles, have been converted into museums and restaurants.

Lafcadio Hearn Memorial Museum

小泉八雲記念館, Koizumi Yakumo Kinen-kan • 322-4 Okudani-chō • Daily: April–Sept 8.30am–6.30pm, Oct–March 8.30am–5pm • ¥400, foreign visitors ¥200 • ☎ 085 221 2147, ⓦ www.hearn-museum-matsue.jp

Curated by Hearn's great-grandson, Bon Koizumi, the **Lafcadio Hearn Memorial Museum** provides an excellent introduction to the life and works of the revered writer. Exhibits spread across two floors, with plenty of English captions, and include Hearn's favourite writing desk and chair, specially designed to help him make the best use of his one good eye.

Lafcadio Hearn's Former Residence

小泉八雲旧居, Koizumi Yakumo Kyūkyo • 315 Kitahori-chō • Daily: April–Sept 8.30am–6.30pm, Oct–March 8.30am–5pm • ¥350, foreign visitors ¥150 • ☎ 085 223 0714

Alongside the writer's eponymous museum, **Lafcadio Hearn's Former Residence** is the small samurai house where he lived between May and November 1891. During that time, he started work on two of his best-known books, *Glimpses of Unfamiliar Japan* and the ghost story collection *Kwaidan*. As you sit in the calm of the tatami rooms, looking out over its exquisite little **garden** and reading the English leaflet that

LAFCADIO HEARN

"There is some charm unutterable in the morning air, cool with the coolness of Japanese spring and wind-waves from the snowy cone of Fuji …"

Lafcadio Hearn, My First Day in the Orient

The journalist **Lafcadio Hearn** was enchanted by Japan, and of all expat writers is by far the most respected by the Japanese. Celebrated by the people of Matsue as an adopted son, his books, including **Glimpses of Unfamiliar Japan** and **Kwaidan**, are considered classics.

The offspring of a passionate but doomed liaison between an Anglo-Irish army surgeon and a Greek girl, and named after the Greek island of Lefkada on which he was born on June 27, 1850, Hearn grew up in Dublin, a contemporary of Bram Stoker and Oscar Wilde. A schoolyard accident in 1866 left him permanently blind in his left eye, and in 1869, young and penniless, he decided to chance his fortune in the United States. Over the course of the next fourteen years, Hearn worked as a reporter and writer in Cincinnati, New Orleans and the West Indian island of Martinique (where he penned his first novel, *Chita),* with a brief marriage to an African-American girl along the way.

Commissioned by *Harper's Monthly* to write about Japan, Hearn arrived in Yokohama on April 4, 1890. By the end of the day, he had decided to stay, get a teaching job and write a book. The teaching post brought Hearn to Matsue, where he met and married Koizumi Setsu, the daughter of an impoverished samurai family.

Hearn would happily have stayed in Matsue, but the freezing winter weather made him ill, and in 1891 they moved south to Kumamoto, in Kyūshū, closer to Koizumi's relatives. The couple had four children, and in 1896 he adopted the name **Koizumi Yakumo** (Eight Clouds) and secured Japanese nationality. By the turn of the century, Hearn's novels and articles had become a great success; he had started teaching at Tokyo's prestigious Waseda University, and was invited to give a series of lectures at the University of London and in the United States. On September 30, 1904, however, at the age of 54, Hearn suffered a series of heart attacks and died. His gravestone in Zoshigaya cemetery, near Ikebukuro in Tokyo, proclaims him a "man of faith, similar to the undefiled flower blooming like eight rising clouds who dwells in the mansion of right enlightenment".

Hearn's **books** stand as paeans to the beauty and mystery of old Japan, something he believed worth recording, as it seemed to be fast disappearing in the nonstop modernization of the early Meiji years.

contains extracts from Hearn's essay "In a Japanese Garden", you can see how little has changed.

Tanabe Art Museum

田部美術館, Tanabe Bijutsukan • 310-5 Kitahori-chō • Tues–Sun 9am–5pm • ¥620 • ☎ 085 226 2211, ⓦ www.tanabe-museum.or.jp

A high wall shields the contemporary building of the **Tanabe Art Museum**, next door to Lafcadio Hearn's old house. Established in 1964 by the late prefectural governor Tanabe Chōemon XXIII, who was also a respected artist with a particular interest in the aesthetics of the tea ceremony, the museum contains the Tanabe family's refined collection, centred around pottery tea bowls and utensils. In the pleasant, breezy café that overlooks the garden, you can have *matcha* tea and cake for ¥410.

Buke-yashiki

武家屋敷 • 305 Kitahori-chō • Closed at press time, but normally daily: April–Sept 8.30am–6.30pm, Oct–March 8.30am–5pm • ¥300, foreign visitors ¥150 • ☎ 085 222 2243

Matsue's largest surviving samurai house, the **Buke-yashiki**, was built in 1730 as home to the Shiomi family, high-ranking retainers to the ruling Matsudaira clan. The attractive complex was closed for restoration as this book went to press, with a projected reopening date of April 2018. Assuming it has reopened by the time you read this, visits consist of wandering around the exterior, peering into tatami and wood rooms that offer an appealing glimpse of eighteenth-century samurai life.

Meimei-an teahouse

明々庵 · 278 Kitahori-chō · Daily: April–Sept 8.30am–6.30pm, Oct–March 8.30am–5pm · ¥410, foreign visitors ¥200; tea ceremony ¥410 · ☎ 085 221 9863, ⓦ www.meimeian.jp

Notable for the precise Zen beauty of the raked gravel and artfully positioned stones that surround it, the **Meimei-an teahouse** stands a short walk up the hill behind Shiomi Nawate. Originally designed by the *daimyō* Matsudaira Fumai to exact tea-ceremony principles, the tiny cottage has creamy beige plaster walls that hardly look capable of holding up its heavily thatched roof. In 1966, to celebrate its 150th anniversary, Meimei-an was restored and moved to this spot, beside an existing samurai mansion and enjoying a fine prospect of the castle. You can't enter the teahouse itself, but you can admire it – with tea and cake, for an additional fee – from the veranda of the adjoining mansion.

Karakoro Art Studio

カラコロ工房, Karakoro Kōbō · 43 Tono-machi · Daily: complex 9.30am–6.30pm, hours of individual businesses vary · Free · ☎ 085 220 7000, ⓦ www.karakoro-kobo.com

A stately former bank building across from the Kyobashi canal now holds the **Karakoro Art Studio**, a slightly misleading name for a complex that includes several cafés and restaurants as well as a small gallery exhibiting local glass art, kimono and fabric, and several **craft shops** selling jewellery, clothing and stained glass. Head upstairs to find the most interesting shops, while the central courtyard is a nice spot to relax over a green tea ice cream.

Shimane Art Museum

島根県立美術館, Shimane Kenritsu Bijutsukan · 1-5 Sodeshi-chō · Mon & Wed–Sun: March–Sept 10am until 30min after sunset, Oct–Feb 10am–6.30pm · free access to building and lake; museum ¥300, foreign visitors ¥150; with special exhibition ¥1150, foreign visitors ¥575 · ☎ 085 255 4700, ⓦ www.shimane-art-museum.jp

Strangely enough, the art itself is almost an afterthought at the **Shimane Art Museum**, which occupies a long, low contemporary structure a 1.2km walk southwest of Matsue Station. Instead it's the museum's dramatic location, facing the full sweep of the lake, that lures in the locals, who come to admire the sunset while strolling the broad **waterfront promenade** outside. The **permanent collection** on show inside, displayed in five upstairs galleries, ranges through some magnificent old painted scrolls and local crafts, and usually but not invariably includes some classic *ukiyo-e* prints, while changing temporary exhibitions cover Western as well as Japanese art.

Yakumotatsu Fudoki-no-Oka

八雲立つ風土記の丘 · 456 Oba-chō · **Park** 24hr · Free · **Museum** Mon & Wed–Sun 9am–5pm · ¥200 · ☎ 085 223 2485, ⓦ yakumotatu-fudokinooka.jp · Take #21 or #22 bus from Matsue Station towards Oba/Yakumo, and get off at Oba Shako

Amid the paddy fields on the southern fringes of Matsue, 6km out from the city centre, the site known as **Yakumotatsu Fudoki-no-Oka** preserves keyhole-shaped **burial mounds** (*kofun*) left by the region's earliest-known inhabitants. The **museum** displays a small assortment of archeological finds, including impressive pottery horses and some first- and second-century bronze daggers and bells.

As well as pleasant forest and nature walks, the surrounding **park** holds a couple of buildings promoting local culture, known as the **Izumo Kanbe-no-sato** (出雲かんべの里; ☎ 085 228 0040, ⓦ kanbenosato.com). For an additional ¥200, you can watch woodworkers, basket-makers, weavers, potters and a specialist in *temari*, the art of making colourful thread-decorated balls.

8

Kamosu-jinja

神魂神社 • 563 Oba-chō • 24hr • Free • ☎ 085 221 6379 • Take #21 or #22 bus from Matsue Station towards Oba/Yakumo and get off at Oba Shako, or take the bus for Kanbe-no-Sato and get off at the last stop

The handsome shrine of **Kamosu-jinja** stands 1km west of Yakumotatsu Fudoki-no-Oka, and 5.5km south of Matsue Station. Dedicated to the Shintō mother deity Izanami, it's set in a glade of soaring pines that's reached via stone steps lined with cherry trees. Raised on stilts, the main bare-wood structure dates from 1346 and is said to be the oldest remaining example of *Taisha-zukuri* or "Grand shrine style" left in Japan. The site itself, though, is even older, and preceded the more famous Izumo Taisha shrine to the west (see p.624), with which it remains associated.

ARRIVAL AND INFORMATION

By plane Connecting buses run from Izumo Airport (ⓦizumo-airport.co.jp), 25km west, to Matsue Station (30min; ¥1030). If you arrive at Yonago Airport (ⓦyonago -air.com), 25km east, you can either catch a shuttle bus to Matsue Station (45min; ¥990), or catch a train to Yonago Station, and change there for Matsue (1hr 10min/1hr 30min; ¥760/¥1830).

Izumo destinations Fukuoka (2 daily; 1hr 10min); Nagoya (daily; 1hr); Oki islands (daily; 35min); Osaka (5 daily; 55min); Seoul (3 weekly; 1hr 30min); Tokyo Haneda (5 daily; 1hr 15min).

Yonago destinations Seoul (3 weekly; 1hr 15min); Tokyo Haneda (6 daily; 1hr 10min).

By train JR trains arrive at Matsue Station, 450m south of the Ōhashi-gawa River and 2km southeast of the castle. The nearest Shinkansen stop, Okayama, is 180km away on the south coast and connected by cross-country local trains, while JR also run an overnight sleeper train from Tokyo. The private and totally separate Matsue Shinji-ko Onsen Station, across the river 1.2km southwest of the castle (and complete with public hot-spring footbath outside), is the terminus for Ichibata trains from Izumo Taisha (see p.624).

Destinations Izumo Taisha (hourly; 1hr); Okayama (hourly; 2hr 30min); Shin-Yamaguchi (2 daily; 3hr 45min); Tottori (5 daily; 1hr 30min); Tokyo (daily; 11hr 20min); Tsuwano (2 daily; 2hr 40min).

By bus Most long-distance buses arrive beside Matsue Station, while the rest go to Matsue Shinji-ko Onsen Station; for details, visit ⓦchugoku-jrbus.co.jp or ⓦichibata.co.jp. Foreign visitors currently pay just ¥500 for the trip to or from Hiroshima (ⓦbit.ly/matsue-bus).

Destinations Hiroshima (hourly; 3hr); Kyoto (4 daily; 5hr); Okayama (7 daily; 3hr); Nagoya (1 daily; 8hr); Osaka (8 daily; 4hr 30min); Tokyo (1 daily; 12hr).

GETTING AROUND

By bus Local bus routes radiate out from Matsue Station – check which bus stop you need at the tourist office alongside – and include frequent connections to Matsue Shinji-ko Onsen Station. The Lakeside Line, a red trolley bus, makes a complicated anticlockwise circuit around the city, taking in the castle, the samurai neighbourhood as well as both stations (every 20min; full circuit takes 50min; ¥200 per trip or ¥500 all-day pass; ⓦbit.ly/matsue-lakeside).

By bike Cycling is a good way to explore Matsue from top to bottom. Rental bikes are available at both stations, including from Eki Rent-a-Car at Matsue Station (daily 8am–7pm; ¥500/day; ☎085 223 8800).

INFORMATION AND TOURS

Tourist information Helpful staff at the tourist office outside the north exit of Matsue Station (daily 9am–6pm; ☎085 221 4034, ⓦvisit-matsue.com) can advise you on local sights and transport connections.

Boat tours An ideal way to appreciate Matsue's watery charms is to take a Horikawa Boat Trip, which takes 50min to complete a 3.7km circuit around the castle moat and canals. Passengers can get on and off at any of three points: across

---

KYŌDO RYŌRI IN MATSUE

Gourmets flock to Matsue for its **Kyōdo ryōri**, seven types of dishes using **fish and seafood** from Shinji-ko. Best sampled in winter when all the fish are available and tasting their freshest, these are: *amasagi*, smelt either cooked as tempura or marinated in teriyaki sauce; *koi*, carp baked in a rich, sweet sauce; *moroge-ebi*, steamed prawns; *shijimi*, small shellfish usually served in miso soup; *shirauo*, whitebait eaten raw as sashimi or cooked as tempura; *suzuki*, bass wrapped in paper and steam-baked over hot coals; and *unagi*, grilled freshwater eel. To sample the full seven courses, make an advance reservation with one of the top ryokan, such as *Minamikan* (see opposite), and be ready to part with at least ¥10,000.

from the Karakoro Art Studio; near the main castle entrance; and northwest of the castle near the Shiomi Nawate neighbourhood. An all-day pass costs ¥820 for foreigners (departures every 15–20min; daily: March–June & Sept to mid-Oct 9am–5pm; July & Aug 9am–6pm; mid-Oct to Feb 9am–4pm ☎ 085 227 0417, ⓦ matsue-horikawameguri.jp).

ACCOMMODATION

Matsue's accommodation options broadly divide between the usual cluster of business hotels around Matsue Station, and more upmarket options along the lakeshore south of Matsue Shinji-ko Onsen Station.

Dormy Inn Express ドーミーインEXPRESS松江 498-1 Asahi-machi ☎ 085 259 5489, ⓦ dormyinn-expressmatsue.hotel-rn.com. Chain hotel, just a 5min walk from Matsue Station, offering good rates for small but clean modern rooms, plus free laundry and free noodles in the lobby at night. ⓦ **¥11,000**

★ **Minamikan** 皆実館 14 Suetsugu-Hon-machi ☎ 085 221 5131, ⓦ www.minami-g.co.jp/minamikan. Matsue's top ryokan, facing the lake from the heart of the city, occupies a modern complex but has a distinctly traditional feel, from the courteous service to the neatly clipped pines in the gravel garden. Huge suites of tatami rooms in varying styles, plus the very finest local cuisine. Rates include two meals. ⓦ **¥45,200**

Nōtsu Ryokan 野津旅館 555 Isemiya-chō ☎ 085 221 1525. Smart, well turned out ryokan on the banks of the Ōhashi-gawa with rooms overlooking the river, a rooftop rotemburo and friendly service. The cheapest rates are for shared-bath tatami rooms with no meals, but the food is excellent, so it's worth looking for an all-in deal. ⓦ **¥9000**

★ **Ryokan Terazuya** 旅館寺津屋 60-3 Tenjin-machi ☎ 085 221 3480, ⓦ mable.ne.jp/~terazuya. In a quiet location above a sushi restaurant, a 10min walk southwest of Matsue Station, this quaint, excellent-value ryokan is run by a friendly couple who speak a bit of English, and has well-kept Japanese-style rooms with a/c. Rates include breakfast. ⓦ **¥9200**

EATING

Matsue doesn't have quite the range of restaurants you might expect, but there are some good places around, especially in the old streets between the Ōhashi-gawa and Kyobashi canal. The arcaded main street north of Matsue Station echoes to a vintage jazz soundtrack after dark, and feels as though it can have hardly changed in a hundred years, but the bars in the Isemiya district hereabouts tend to be seedy.

Café Courant d'Air カフェ クーラン デ エール 484-13 Asahi-machi ☎ 085 227 8577. This sophisticated café, right outside the station, has subdued lighting, classical music and classy decor, and offers thick slices of creamy sponge and strawberry shortcake (from ¥400) and espresso coffees (cappuccino ¥700). ⓦ Mon–Sat 11am–11pm.

Isoryōri Yamaoka 磯料理 やまおか 186 Tera-machi ☎ 085 225 9029. Friendly little local restaurant, 700m northwest of Matsue Station, just off the Tera-machi arcade, with counter seating downstairs and more formal private dining beyond. Sizeable set dinners, with meat as well as seafood, start at ¥3240. Mon–Sat 5–11pm.

★ **Kawa-kyō** 川京 65 Suetsugu-Hon-machi ☎ 085 222 1312. Everything is perfect at this tiny central *izakaya*, from the charming mother-and-daughter owners who prepare the consistently wonderful food to the sake-fuelled good cheer of your half-dozen fellow diners, crammed chopstick-to-chopstick along the counter. While serving all "Seven Delicacies from Lake Shiji", they're renowned for their broiled, basted eel, costing ¥1900 with rice and miso. Mixed

sashimi or a bowl of clams will cost around ¥1000, and be sure to try the paper-baked bass, too, or indeed whatever they happen to have on offer. Reserve ahead to be sure of squeezing in. Mon–Sat 6–10.30pm.

★ **Naniwa** なにわ 21 Suetsugu-Hon-machi ☎ 085 221 2835, ⓦ honten.naniwa-i.com. Popular, very classy lakefront restaurant, serving beautiful *kaiseki* meals and more modest "ladies" set dinners, with the cheapest option being an eel-and-rice set for ¥1940. It's also one of the best places to try *Kyōdo ryōri* (see opposite), with multi-course meals costing from ¥5400 to well over ¥10,000. ⓦ Daily 11am–9pm.

Yakumo-an 八雲庵 308 Kitabori-chō, Shiomi Nawate ☎ 085 222 2400, ⓦ yakumoan.jp. Popular, picturesque lunch-only restaurant in a former samurai residence across the castle moat, with a central garden, teahouse and carp-filled pond. The speciality here is good-value soba and udon noodles, including *warigo soba* (cold seaweed-seasoned buckwheat noodles, served in three-layer dishes, over which you pour stock), with nothing costing over ¥1400. Daily 10am–3.30pm.

8

Around Matsue

The region around Matsue, once known as **Izumo**, is among the longest settled areas in Japan, with a written history dating back to the seventh-century *Izumo-no-Kuni Fudoki*

(*The Topography of Izumo*). There's plenty to see, including the magnificent shrine of **Izumo Taisha** – holiday home of the Shintō pantheon of deities, and the reason Lafcadio Hearn dubbed Matsue the "chief city of the province of the gods" – and the stunning gardens of the **Adachi Museum of Art**.

Izumo Taisha

出雲大社 • 195 Kizuki-higashi • Daily 6am–6pm • Free • ☎ 085 353 3100, ⓦ www.izumooyashiro.or.jp

The sacred enclave of **Izumo Taisha**, a Shintō shrine second only in importance to the one at Ise (see p.537), spreads across a low eminence in the coastal foothills at the edge of the town of **Izumo**, 40km west of Matsue. At once grand and graceful, the shrine – which you may also see called by its official name, Izumo Ōyashiro – is said in legend to have been built by Amaterasu, the Sun Goddess. The current main building, which dates from 1744, stands 24m tall, which makes it Japan's tallest wooden structure, topping Nara's Tōdai-ji, home of the great statue of Buddha (see p.488). Three colossal pillars, unearthed in 2000, appear to confirm the belief that it was originally twice that size, raised 48m high and accessed by a vast, gently sloping staircase.

All eight million Shintō deities still visit Izumo Taisha each November, for their annual get-together (see box below). In this region, the tenth month of the lunar calendar is traditionally known as the "month with gods", while in all other parts of Japan it's known as the "month without gods". Since the shrine is dedicated to Okuninushi-no-mikoto, the God of Happy Marriage, many couples visit in the hope of living happily ever after; visitors to the shrine clap their hands four times, rather than the usual two, to summon the deity.

The shrine

At the top of the commercialized street that leads north from the little train station of Izumo Taisha-mae, a large concrete *torii* marks the southern limit of the park-like grounds. Set off along the path, and after 250m you'll come to a wooden *torii* at the start of the Seki-no-Baba, an avenue of gnarled pines that leads up to the shrine itself, at the foot of Yakumo-yama and entered via a final bronze *torii*. The branches of the trees on all sides, to which visitors tie *omikuji* (fortune-telling) papers for good luck, are so heavily laden they seem coated with snow.

Straight ahead stands the **Oracle Hall**, in front of which hangs a giant *shimenawa*, the traditional twist of straw rope. Legend has it that good fortune awaits those who can successfully toss a coin that lodges in the cut ends of the ropes. Inside the hall, Shintō ceremonies take place all day, with accompanying drumming and flute playing.

The inner shrine, or **Honden** (本殿), immediately beyond – recognizable by the projecting rafters that shoot from its roof – is closed to the general public. Instead, you'll have to stand outside its **Eight-Legged East Gate**, decorated with beautiful unpainted wooden carvings, and peer through to the inner courtyard. Even pilgrims are not allowed anywhere near the central Holy of Holies hall, buried deep within – only the head priest can enter.

Be sure to follow the footpath around the back of the enclosure, away from the crowds. Several little shed-like shrines nestle into the forest as it starts to climb up the

---

IZUMO TAISHA FESTIVALS

Apart from the usual Shintō festival days (see p.56), Izumo Taisha's most important festivals are:
Imperial Grand Festival (May 14–16): The welcome mat is rolled out for an envoy from the imperial family.
Kamiari-sai (A week between Oct and Nov): Celebration for the annual gathering of some eight million Shintō gods. During the festival, the gods are carried into the Honden, where they hold a conference to discuss, among other things, wedding matches between Japanese people.

hillside, and you're likely to encounter priests going about their duties – as well as lots of little rabbit statues.

The large modern hall near the west exit of Izumo Taisha hosts more daily ceremonies, and is also used for the sacred *kagura* dances on festival days. Here too visitors fling coins into the *shimenawa* that hangs in front, hoping they will stick and bring them luck.

Museum of Ancient Izumo

島根県立古代出雲歴史博物館, Shimanekenritsu Kodai Izumo Rekishi Hakubutsukan • 99-4 Kizuki-higashi • Daily: March–Oct 9am–6pm, Nov–Feb 9am–5pm; closed 3rd Tues of month • ¥610 • ☏ 085 353 8600, ⓦ www.izm.ed.jp

In a large modern building 500m southeast of the inner shrine, clearly signposted through the grounds, the superb **Museum of Ancient Izumo** tells the story of Izumo Taisha in compelling detail. Artefacts on display include 39 beautiful two-thousand-year-old brass bells, assorted clay figurines and woodblock prints, and all sorts of maps and scrolls depicting the growth of the shrine. There's also a nice little café, upstairs.

ARRIVAL AND INFORMATION   IZUMO TAISHA

By plane Two daily buses (35min; ¥850) connect the shrine with Izumo Airport (ⓦ izumo-airport.co.jp), 22km east.

By train The rather gorgeous little Art Deco station of Izumo Taisha-mae, a 5min walk south of the shrine, is served by trains on the Ichibata line from Matsue Shinji-ko Onsen Station, though you almost always have to change at Kawato, four stops east of Izumo Taisha (total 1hr; ¥810). JR trains between Masuda and Matsue stop at Izumo-shi Station, 9km southeast, from where you can either catch a direct bus to the shrine (25min; ¥520), or change trains

onto the Ichibata line, and then change once again at Kawato (22min; ¥490).

By bus The Izumo Taisha bus station, served by buses to and from Izumo-shi Station and Hinomisaki, is a minute's walk west of the shrine grounds.

By bike You can rent a bike at the station, but it's only worth it if you plan to visit Hinomisaki, 10km northwest, as well.

Tourist information There's a tourist office at Izumo-shi Station (daily 8.30am–7.30pm; ☏ 085 353 2298, ⓦ izumo -kankou.gr.jp), and you can also pick up English leaflets in Izumo Taisha-mae Station.

ACCOMMODATION AND EATING

With Matsue so close, there's no pressing reason to **stay** overnight in Izumo Taisha, though if need be you can grab a bite at any number of **restaurants** around the bus station near the shrine.

Arakiya 荒木屋 409-2 Kizuki-higashi ☏ 085 353 2352, ⓦ bit.ly/arakiya. Welcoming traditional restaurant, beyond the main throng of tourist canteens 400m west of the bus station, which makes a good place to try the local speciality, *warigo soba* (¥780), cold buckwheat noodles seasoned with seaweed flakes, served in three-layer dishes, over which you pour *dashi* (stock); a single layer of noodles, also served with a cup of hot soba-water soup,

costs just ¥260. Mon, Tues & Thurs–Sun 11am–5pm.

Hinode-kan 日の出館 776 Taisha-chō, Kizuki-nishi ☏ 085 353 3311, ⓦ bit.ly/hinode-kan. Set in pleasant gardens a couple of minutes' walk up from the train station towards the shrine, this simple Japanese-style inn offers air-conditioned rooms, not all en suite, plus a public bath. Rates include breakfast; dinner costs ¥2000 extra per person. 🛜 **¥16,000**

Hinomisaki-jinja

日御碕神社 • 455 Hinomisaki • **Shrine** Daily 8am–5pm • Free • **Lighthouse** Daily 9am–4.30pm • ¥150 • 20min by bus from Izumo Taisha bus station (¥540), or 30min on a rental bike

The scenic cape of **Hinomisaki** (日御碕), 9km northwest of Izumo Taisho, holds a quieter shrine complex, **Hinomisaki-jinja**. Built in 1644 under the shogun Tokugawa Ieyasu, it's been fully restored and painted bright orange. When the weather's good, you can climb the steep spiral staircase to the top of the 44m-tall white stone **lighthouse** in the complex, built in 1903, to get a splendid view out to the nearby islands. There are several bathing **beaches** around the cape, while the rocky cliffs close to the lighthouse are good for exploring.

Adachi Museum of Art

足立美術館, Adachi Bijutsukan • 320 Furukawa-chō, 20km southeast of Matsue and 9km southwest of the nearest village, Yasugi • Daily: April–Sept 9am–5.30pm, Oct–March 9am–5pm • ¥2300, foreign visitors ¥1150 • ☎ 085 428 7111, ⊕ adachi-museum.or.jp

Thanks to its extraordinary **garden**, consistently ranked as the finest in all Japan, the **Adachi Museum of Art** is something no visitor to western Honshū should miss. In truth, its collection of Japanese art is more forgettable, but it's still worth making the effort to reach this remote rural spot. Most people come as a day-trip from Matsue, but you can also simply stop off as you travel along the San'in coast.

The gardens

The founder of the museum, Adachi Zenkō, was an enthusiastic gardener, and his passion for the art form shows through in the six separate gardens that he created. All are meticulously crafted, with not a blossom, leaf or stone out of place, and no outsider could even dream of actually setting foot on the pristine raked gravel. Instead, you can only admire the perfection, at its most sublime in autumn, from a distance. Visitors proceed through the museum building along a set route, enjoying views of the Moss Garden, the Dry Landscape Garden, the Kikaku Waterfall, the Garden of Juryū-an, the Pond Garden and the White Gravel and Pine Garden from open-sided corridors or through spotless plate-glass walls. The experience culminates with a succession of so-called "living Japanese paintings", in which you sit in a tatami room and look out through a window that's precisely placed to frame a landscape and make it resemble a painted scroll.

Two traditional **teahouses** serve *matcha* and sweets from ¥1500. *Juryū-an* is a copy of a teahouse in Kyoto's former Imperial Palace, Katsura Rikyū, and looks over a peaceful moss-covered garden; in the smaller *Juraku-an*, bowls of green tea are made with water boiled in a kettle of pure gold, said to aid longevity. The two coffee shops in the museum are less atmospheric but cheaper, and the views just as fine.

The galleries

The museum's galleries, which also spread into a newer annexe, display Japanese artworks dating from 1870 to the present day. These include the largest collection of paintings by **Yokoyama Taikan**, whose delicate ink drawings and deep colour screens had a huge influence on modern Japanese art. There's also a section on kitsch art from children's books, and a ceramics hall holding works by Kawai Kanjirō – a local potter who participated actively in the *mingei* (folk art) movement begun by Yanagi Sōetsu – and Kitaōji Rosanjin, a potter and cook, whose pieces set out to complement and enhance the food served on them.

ARRIVAL AND DEPARTURE   ADACHI MUSEUM OF ART

By train The JR station at Yasugi (安来市) is on the San'in line, and holds luggage lockers plus a useful tourist information office (daily 9am–6pm; ☎ 085 922 6317). It's served by frequent trains between Matsue Station (18min; ¥410) and Yonago (8min; ¥200). Free shuttle buses, not timed to coincide with specific trains, make the 20min run between the station and the museum (17 daily). When you enter the museum, be sure to pick up a free ticket for the trip back to the station, as seats are limited; you have to choose an exact time, but you can swap for another one if necessary.

Mount Daisen

大山

East of Matsue, the coastal rail and road routes cross into the neighbouring prefecture of Tottori-ken, and pass through the uninteresting industrial city of **Yonago** (米子). The terminus for trains from Okayama on the JR Hakubi line, Yonago is also the gateway for **Mount Daisen**, which at 1711m is the highest mountain in the Chūgoku region, and home to beautiful beech forests and ancient temples. Daisen has the largest **ski slopes** in western Japan and sees heavy snowfall from November to April; it's also known for the **Daisen Ice and Snow Festival**, which takes place over three days at the end of January, with fireworks lighting up the night sky and an amazing display of ice sculptures. The main hub for accommodation is the village of **Daisen-ji** (大山寺), which offers access to the ski slopes in winter and to hiking trails in summer.

ARRIVAL AND INFORMATION — MOUNT DAISEN

By bus Buses depart from stop 4 outside Yonago Station for Daisen-ji (5 daily; 50min; ¥750).

Tourist information A couple of minutes' walk east of the bus stop, the tourist information booth (daily 8.30am–5pm; ⓣ 085 952 2502, ⓦ bit.ly/daisen-ji) stocks local maps and can help with accommodation.

Kurayoshi

倉吉

Set just inland from the coast, 60km east of Yonago and 50km east of Tottori, the small town of **KURAYOSHI** is the jumping-off point for the hot-spring resort of **Misasa** and the temple hike up to **Nageire-dō** on Mount Mitoku. In its own right, Kurayoshi holds some pleasant architecture and is a decent place to spend the night. It also attracts touring devotees of the hugely popular manga and anime series **Detective Conan**, known in English as *Case Closed*. The eponymous schoolboy detective comes from the coastal town of **Hokuei**, 10km northwest of Kurayoshi, and all sorts of tours, attractions and facilities in the prefecture now bear his name, including local trains, rail passes, and even Tottori's airport.

8

Akagawara

赤瓦

If you have an hour or two to spare in Kurayoshi, head for the picturesque **Akagawara** neighbourhood, 4km southwest of the station (follow signs for Shirokabe-dozō-gun, 白壁土蔵群). Several of the refurbished Edo- and Meiji-era black-and-white storehouses that stand next to the shallow Tama-gawa here now hold souvenir and craft shops. Look out for beautiful *Kurayoshi-gasuri* items, made from locally woven, indigo-dyed cloth.

ARRIVAL AND INFORMATION — KURAYOSHI

By train Kurayoshi Station is on the JR San'in line.

Destinations Matsue (hourly; 1hr); Tottori (every 30min; 30min).

Tourist information There's an information booth outside Kurayoshi Station, to the left beyond the bus stands (Mon–Fri 8.30am–5.30pm; ⓣ 085 824 5024, ⓦ bit.ly/kurayoshi), and another at 2568 Uo-machi in the Akagawara district (daily 8.30am–5pm; ⓣ 085 822 1200), which has three free bikes to lend visitors.

ACCOMMODATION AND EATING

★**Bokoro** 望湖楼 4-25 Hawai Onsen, Yurihama-chō ⓣ 085 835 2221, ⓦ bokoro.com. This wonderful ryokan, on the western shores of Lake Togo 6km northeast of Kurayoshi Station, holds large and very comfortable Japanese- and Western-style rooms, but the real reason to come Is for the fresh seafood dinners – crab is a local speciality – and the public baths, set out on a raised structure in the middle of the lake and offering 360-degree views. Rates include breakfast and dinner. **¥25,120**

Café Mela カフェ メーラ 2-2453 Shin-machi ⓣ 085 822 6445. Charming café on the second floor of the Sadar Chowk (サダルチョーク) crafts shop, opposite the storehouses in Akagawara, which serves up authentic curries for under ¥1000, plus lassi and chai in a large open room of exposed woods, with Indian clothing sold below. Mon–Wed & Fri–Sun 10am–7pm.

Misasa and around

The hot-spring resort of **MISASA** (三朝) stretches beside the Misasa-gawa, 10km southeast of Kurayoshi. Public onsen and hot-water footbaths punctuate its streets and alleyways, and there's even a free **rotemburo** (24hr) in the river itself. Bamboo screens partially surround the pools, but onlookers from the adjacent bridge have a bird's-eye view of proceedings, so this is one communal bathing experience that's not for the shrinking violet.

The narrow street that runs parallel to the river's south bank is dotted with interesting little craft shops and galleries, and there's an appealing shrine tucked away amid the trees a few blocks further back, not far west of the town's original hot springs.

Nageire-dō

投入堂 • 1010 Mitoku • April–Dec 8am–5pm • ¥400 • ☎ 085 843 2666, ⓦ mitokusan.jp • Bus from Misasa (15min; ¥390)

An 8km bus ride beyond Misasa will bring you to **Mount Mitoku** (三徳山), home to the legendary shrine of **Nageire-dō**, which belongs to the **Sanbutsu-ji** (山佛寺) temple. The rugged path up, which is equipped with chains in places to help you scramble over massive boulders, starts from the main temple complex, across the road from the bus stop. It takes an hour's climbing to reach Nageire-dō, during which you'll pass a belfry and several smaller temple buildings, including **Monju-dō** (文殊堂) and **Jizō-dō** (地蔵堂), similarly perched on a precipice and offering spectacular views.

Nageire-dō itself, nestling under an overhanging rock and balanced precariously on stilts that grip the cliff face below, is an incredible feat of engineering, No one knows quite how it was built; legend has it that it was thrown into place by an ascetic priest named Ennogyoja. Certainly Sanbutsu-ji has been a centre for Buddhism since the eighth century, and Nageire-dō is thought to date back to the eleventh or twelfth.

On your way down, try the local speciality of *sansai-ryōri*, mountain vegetables and tofu, at one of the **restaurants** at the foot of the main temple complex, near the bus stop.

ARRIVAL AND DEPARTURE — MISASA

By bus Buses to Misasa depart from platform 3 at Kurayoshi Station (19 daily; 24min; ¥470); get off at the Daigaku Byoin-mae stop.

ACCOMMODATION

Misasa is a picturesque place to spend the night, and you'll come across *yukata*-clad visitors wandering through the streets from inn to rotemburo or bar and back again.

★ **Kiya Ryokan** 木屋旅館 895 Miyasa ☎ 085 843 0521, ⓦ misasa.co.jp. This friendly old ryokan, on the river's south bank – you can spot its mint-green roofs from the bus stop – holds ravishing public spaces as well as spacious, en-suite tatami rooms and three onsen, two private and one communal. Rates include two excellent meals, served in private rooms, and shuttle service to and from Kurayoshi. 🛜 **¥31,320**

Tottori

鳥取

The provincial capital of **TOTTORI**, 120km east of Matsue, is famous in Japan for having the country's only substantial **sand dunes**, which belong to the **San'in Coast National Park**. The coastline around here is blessed with fetching beaches and headlands, bedecked with pretty flora and interesting geological formations.

Tottori sand dunes

鳥取砂丘, Tottori Sakyū • Chairlift daily 8.30am–5pm • ¥200 • ☎ 085 722 2111, ⓦ sakyu-daisen.jp/sakyu • Buses leave from bus platform 4 next to Tottori Station (¥380; 20min)

Designated a national monument, and the haunting setting for the existentially alarming 1960s novel and film *Woman in the Dunes*, the **Tottori sand dunes** are 7km north of the city centre, outside the satellite community of Hamasaka. Although they only cover a total area of around thirty square kilometres – and that's been dwindling for many years, despite attempts to shore them up by dumping sand into the sea nearby   once you're in the enclave they do feel quite magically exotic. The appeal is even augmented by the presence of **camels**, imported so visitors can unleash their inner Lawrence of Arabia.

Buses from the city centre can take you either to **Sakyū Kaikan**, right beside the dunes, or to the **Sakyū Centre** (砂丘センター), which overlooks them from a hill but is essentially just a souvenir and food stop for the many tour buses. A **chairlift** runs between the centre and the edge of the dunes, but you can just as easily walk between the two.

The Uradome coastline

浦富海岸, Uradome Kaigan

The **Uradome coastline** covers the 15km between the edge of the Tottori sand dunes and the eastern edge of the prefecture, which, together with the dunes, forms part of the **San'in Coast National Park**. Its shore is fringed with strangely shaped rocks and islands jutting out of the water, some topped with pine trees, and many sculpted with wave-carved tunnels, caves and openings. You get stunning **views** from the clifftop paths along much of the pine-covered coastline looking out over the blue-green Sea of Japan, and if you follow one of the steep paths down through the trees to the shore, you'll find numerous sandy **bays** and bathing **beaches**.

With a car, you can drive along the coast from the sand dunes on Route 178, stopping at the various parking places en route. If you're using public transport, take a bus bound for Iwai-onsen (岩井温泉) and get off at Uradome-kaigan-guchi (浦富海岸口). Otherwise, **sightseeing cruises** are a great way to enjoy the scenery (see below).

8

ARRIVAL AND INFORMATION
TOTTORI

By plane Tottori Airport (☏ 085 728 1150), 10km northwest of the city, is also known as Tottori Sand Dunes Conan Airport, in honour of the manga detective. It is linked by buses (20min; ¥460) timed to coincide with flights to and from Tokyo Haneda (5 daily; 1hr 15min).

By train Tottori Station is on the coastal San'in line, and is also served by direct JR trains to and from Himeji on the south coast, the nearest Shinkansen station. Destinations Himeji (8 daily; 1hr 30min); Matsue (5 daily;

1hr 30min); Osaka (5 daily; 2hr 30min); Yonago (8 daily; 1hr 40min).

By bus Long-distance buses stop next to the train station. Destinations Hiroshima (5 daily; 4hr 50min); Kyoto (3 daily; 4hr); Osaka (13 daily; 3hr 30min); Tokyo (daily; 10hr 30min).

Tourist information The local information booth is by the north exit of Tottori Station (daily 8.30am–5.30pm; ☏ 085 726 7218, ⓦ tottori-tour.jp).

TOURS

Sightseeing boats The Uradome Coast Excursion Boat operates 40min sightseeing tours from Iwami, 16km northeast of Tottori (daily, every 30min except in bad weather, March–Nov 9.10am–4.10pm; ¥1300; ☏ 085 773 1212,

ⓦ yourun1000.com). To reach the port, take a bus (40min; ¥620) bound for Iwai-onsen (岩井温泉) from platform 4 outside Tottori Station, and get off at Shimameguri Yuronsen-noriba (島巡り 湯論戦-のりば).

ACCOMMODATION AND EATING

There are plenty of good-value places to eat in the shopping arcades that run north of Tottori Station, and also a handful of restaurants out at the sand dunes.

Hotel New Ōtani Tottori ホテルニューオータニ鳥取 2-153 Ima-machi ☏ 085 723 1111, ⓦ newotani-tottori .jp. This upscale business chain next to the Daimaru department store has elegant standard and luxury contemporary rooms. Rates include breakfast. 🛜 **¥22,450**
Tottori Green Hotel Morris 鳥取グリーンホテルモーリス   1-107   Ima-machi   ☏ 085   722   2331,

ⓦ hotel-morris.co.jp/tottori. Set behind the Daimaru department store, across from the station, this good-value business hotel has a swanky lobby that leads to only slightly less swanky rooms, many of which look onto an alleyway. The economy doubles have slightly smaller beds but are otherwise the same as the pricier versions. A Western-style breakfast costs ¥550. 🛜 **¥11,500**

Shikoku

四国

NAMETOKO GORGE

9

Shikoku

With beautiful scenery, a laidback atmosphere, friendly people and several notable sights, it is perhaps surprising that Shikoku, Japan's fourth main island, is the least visited by international tourists. This tranquil place, nestling in the crook between Honshū and Kyūshū, offers elements of traditional Japan that are often hard to find elsewhere, making it an excellent destination for travellers wanting a more authentic experience. The remarkable 88-temple pilgrimage, historic castles and gardens, and unique arts and crafts are some of Shikoku's attractions – but equally appealing are the rural pace of life, little-visited villages and idyllic surrounding islands.

According to legend, Shikoku was the second island (after Awaji-shima) born to Izanagi and Izanami, the gods who are considered to be Japan's parents. Its ancient name was Iyo-no-futana, and it was divided into four main provinces: **Awa** (now Tokushima-ken), **Iyo** (Ehime-ken), **Sanuki** (Kagawa-ken) and **Tosa** (Kōchi-ken). These epithets are still used today when referring to the different prefectures' cuisines and traditional arts. Apart from being the scene of a decisive battle between the Taira and Minamoto clans in the twelfth century (see p.822), Shikoku has had a relatively peaceful history, due in part to its isolation from the rest of Japan. The physical separation ended with the opening of the **Seto Ōhashi** in 1988, a series of six bridges that leapfrog the islands of the Inland Sea, carrying both trains and cars. It has since been joined by the **Akashi Kaikyō Ōhashi suspension bridge**, connecting Shikoku to Honshū via Awaji-shima, the island to the east of Tokushima, and the **Nishi Seto Expressway** better known as the Shimanami Kaidō, running along ten bridges spanning nine islands on Shikoku's northern coast (see box, p.583).

Most of Shikoku's population of just over four million lives in one of the island's four prefectural capitals: **Takamatsu**, **Tokushima**, **Kōchi** and **Matsuyama**. The island is split by a vast mountain range that runs from Tsurugi-san in the east to Ishizuchi-san, Shikoku's tallest peak, in the west. The northern coast, facing the Inland Sea, is heavily developed, in contrast to the predominantly rural south, where the unimpeded *kuroshio* (black current) of the Pacific Ocean has carved a rugged coastline of sheer cliffs and oversized boulders. The climate across the island is generally mild, although the coasts can be lashed by typhoons, and the mountains see snow in the winter.

You should set aside at least a week to get around all of Shikoku's four prefectures. If you only have a day or two, head straight for Matsuyama's splendid castle and the hot springs at nearby Dōgo, or pay a visit to the landscaped gardens of Ritsurin-kōen in Takamatsu, before hopping on a ferry over to the idyllic, contemporary art-filled islands of the Seto-Naikai (Inland Sea). With more time, you could explore the lovely

RITSURIN-KŌEN

Highlights

❶ 88-temple pilgrimage Follow in the footsteps of Kōbō Daishi on the Shikoku pilgrimage, the longest and most famous in all of Japan, or opt for one of the shorter routes. **See p.636**

❷ Ritsurin-kōen Enjoy a peaceful bowl of *matcha* tea in the elegant teahouse of Takamatsu's beautifully landscaped garden, a century in the making. **See p.637**

❸ Art Islands of the Inland Sea Exciting contemporary art and architecture combine with friendly fishing villages on the islands of Naoshima, Teshima, Inujima and Shōdoshima in the Inland Sea. **See p.648**

❹ Awa Odori Over a million revellers let their hair down at Tokushima's annual summer dance festival, when the city's streets sway with dancers in colourful cotton kimono. **See p.659**

❺ Nametoko Gorge Explore the forest-fringed tracks of Nametoko for pristine waterfalls, wildlife spotting and outstanding natural beauty. **See p.681**

❻ Matsuyama This easy-going castle city boasts good nightlife, an important literary history, a famous hot-spring resort and a very unusual temple. **See p.686**

HIGHLIGHTS ARE MARKED ON THE MAP ON PP.634–635

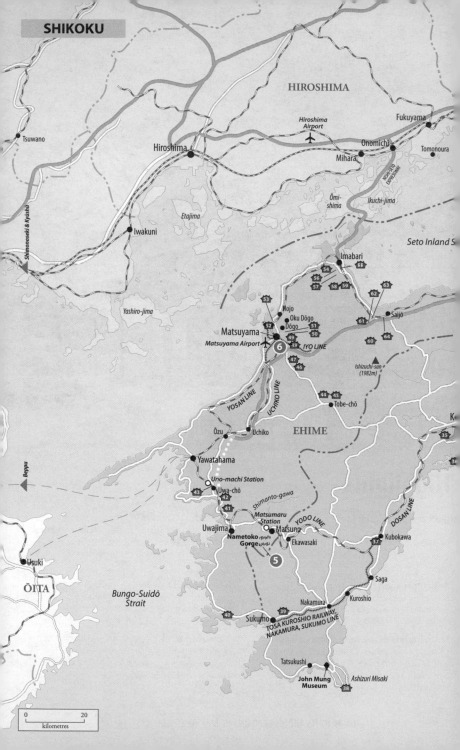

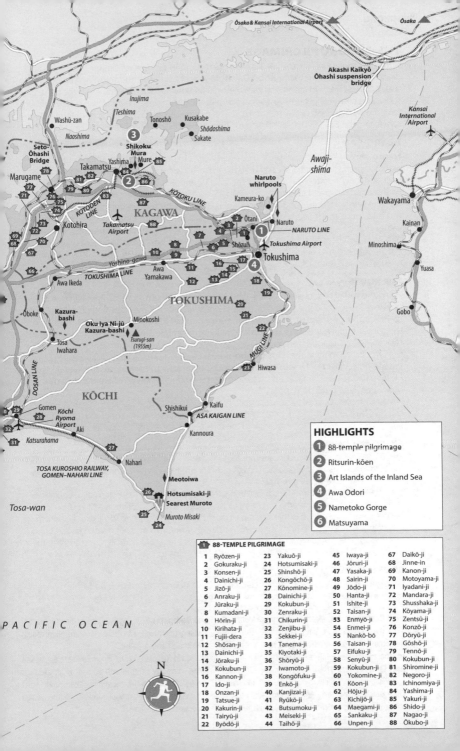

HIGHLIGHTS

1. 88-temple pilgrimage
2. Ritsurin-kōen
3. Art Islands of the Inland Sea
4. Awa Odori
5. Nametoko Gorge
6. Matsuyama

88-TEMPLE PILGRIMAGE

1	Ryōzen-ji	23	Yakuō-ji	45	Iwaya-ji	67	Daikō-ji
2	Gokuraku-ji	24	Hotsumisaki-ji	46	Jōruri-ji	68	Jinne-in
3	Konsen-ji	25	Shinshō-ji	47	Yasaka-ji	69	Kanon-ji
4	Dainichi-ji	26	Kongōchō-ji	48	Sairin-ji	70	Motoyama-ji
5	Jizō-ji	27	Kōnomine-ji	49	Jōdo-ji	71	Iyadani-ji
6	Anraku-ji	28	Dainichi-ji	50	Hanta-ji	72	Mandara-ji
7	Jūraku-ji	29	Kokubun-ji	51	Ishite-ji	73	Shusshaka-ji
8	Kumadani-ji	30	Zenraku-ji	52	Taisan-ji	74	Kōyama-ji
9	Hōrin-ji	31	Chikurin-ji	53	Enmyō-ji	75	Zentsū-ji
10	Kirihata-ji	32	Zenjibu-ji	54	Enmei-ji	76	Konzō-ji
11	Fujii-dera	33	Sekkei-ji	55	Nankō-bō	77	Dōryū-ji
12	Shōsan-ji	34	Tanema-ji	56	Taisan-ji	78	Gōshō-ji
13	Dainichi-ji	35	Kiyotaki-ji	57	Eifuku-ji	79	Tennō-ji
14	Jōraku-ji	36	Shōryū-ji	58	Senyū-ji	80	Kokubun-ji
15	Kokubun-ji	37	Iwamoto-ji	59	Kokubun-ji	81	Shiromine-ji
16	Kannon-ji	38	Kongōfuku-ji	60	Yokomine-ji	82	Negoro-ji
17	Ido-ji	39	Enkō-ji	61	Kōon-ji	83	Ichinomiya-ji
18	Onzan-ji	40	Kanjizai-ji	62	Hōju-ji	84	Yashima-ji
19	Tatsue-ji	41	Ryūkō-ji	63	Kichijō-ji	85	Yakuri-ji
20	Kakurin-ji	42	Butsumoku-ji	64	Maegami-ji	86	Shido-ji
21	Tairyū-ji	43	Meiseki-ji	65	Sankaku-ji	87	Nagao-ji
22	Byōdō-ji	44	Taihō-ji	66	Unpen-ji	88	Ōkubo-ji

9

THE SHIKOKU PILGRIMAGE

Wherever you are in Shikoku, you'll seldom be far from its famous pilgrimage, established by disciples of the Buddhist saint **Kōbō Daishi**, founder of Shingon Buddhism (see box, p.527). It usually takes over two months to walk the 1400km between the 88 temples on the prescribed route, and plenty of pilgrims, known as *henro-san*, still complete the journey this way – though far more now go by bicycle, motorbike, car, train or on bus tours. The number of temples represents the 88 evils that, according to Shingon Buddhism, bedevil human life.

HENRO-SAN

Henro-san are easy to spot, since they usually dress in traditional short, white cotton coats with coloured shoulder bands and broad-rimmed straw hats, and often clutch rosaries, brass bells and long wooden staffs. Many of the 150,000 annual pilgrims are past retirement age, but younger Japanese and even foreign visitors are increasingly experiencing this religious journey.

The expression "Daishi and I go together" is usually written on pilgrims' robes and hats, and this is thought to act as a symbolic link with the pilgrimage's founder and the Buddhist values that he represents. Many of the other accessories also have spiritual meaning and historical significance, such as the staff that's believed to be the embodiment of Kōbō Daishi. These items can be purchased at the first temple, **Ryōzen-ji**, and also at a number of shops in Tokushima.

THE ROUTE

The present-day headquarters of the Shingon sect is **Kōya-san**, in Wakayama-ken (see p.526) on the mainland, and it is traditional to visit here at the start of the pilgrimage before travelling to Shikoku. Once you're on the island, there are a number of ways to do the pilgrimage, but the conventional route starts at Ryōzen-ji, near Naruto in Tokushima-ken. From there, pilgrims typically follow a circular route that winds its way clockwise around the island, stopping at all the temples en route to the 88th, **Ōkubo-ji**, in Kagawa-ken. This approach, known as *jun-uchi*, has the practical advantage of making the route a bit easier to navigate, as the markers are set up for pilgrims travelling this way. It's also quite common to go in reverse order (called *gyaku-uchi*) and begin at Temple 88.

Many temples allow pilgrims to stay for around ¥4000 per person including meals. It's a lucrative business: you'll see lots of pilgrims dropping coins beside the thousands of Buddhas along the way, and they fork out again at the temples, where an official stamp costs around ¥300.

SHORTER COURSES

There's no obligation for you to attempt to do the entire 1400km pilgrimage; it's very common for both Japanese and overseas tourists to only complete sections of the journey, or try a few one-day walks to the major temples.

A popular one-day route is from Chikurin-ji (No. 31) to Sekkei-ji (No. 33), passing Godai-san and the beach at Katsurahama on the way; this 13.2km course is convenient if you're staying in Kōchi. An easier option is the 7.7km walk from Dainichi-ji (No. 13) to Ido-ji (No. 17), which can be done as a day-trip from Tokushima and takes you through quiet residential areas and rice fields. It's also possible to do a number of longer routes – check ⓦ bit.ly/2nzxZQ6 for these, as the website offers everything from detailed route maps to information on travel times.

BOOKS AND INFO

Check out ⓦ shikokuhenrotrail.com, created by the American *henro* David Turkington. Several books in English describe the 88-temple hike – here are a few of the best ones:

Paul Barach *Fighting Monks and Burning Mountains: Misadventures on a Buddhist Pilgrimage.* This is a humorous, honest and reflective account of Barach's unusual experiences while making the journey.
Amy Chavez *Running the Shikoku Pilgrimage: 900 Miles to Enlightenment.* A book by *Japan Times* columnist Chavez who ran the route (almost a marathon a day) and recounts the experience with humour and humility.

Lisa Dempster *Neon Pilgrim.* This first-hand account of a young, unemployed Australian woman's pilgrimage is both honest and inspiring.
Miyazaki Tateki *Shikoku Japan 88 Route Guide.* This guide, currently in its fourth edition, is an excellent choice. It has maps, accommodation and other information essential for a pilgrimage, whether you go on foot or use transport.

island of **Shōdoshima**, the whirlpools at **Naruto**, the coastal village of **Hiwasa** (where turtles come to lay their eggs each summer), or the surfing spots of **Kaifu** and **Shishikui**. Shikoku's southern coast and its dramatically rocky capes **Ashizuri** and **Muroto**, and the **Shimanto-gawa**, one of Japan's most beautiful rivers, also shouldn't be missed.

Despite Shikoku's laidback vibe, the popularity of the island's **88-temple pilgrimage** (see box opposite) means that, even in the countryside, you're unlikely to be stuck for somewhere to stay.

GETTING AROUND   SHIKOKU

By train Getting around by train is easy enough, but will require planning and coordination. JR Shikoku runs daily express trains, though the local train services are not as frequent as on the mainland. There are also five small, private railway companies. The All Shikoku Rail Pass (ⓦ shikoku-railwaytrip.com/railpass), which must be purchased outside Japan by tourist visa holders, allows travel on JR and the private lines for two days (¥7400), three

days (¥8500), four days (¥9400) or five days (¥10,000). Many Shikoku railway stations are now free wi-fi hotspots. **By car** Renting a car (see p.640) will give you more flexibility than public transport and really is the best option if you want to get to the villages of the Iya Valley or explore western Kōchi-ken and the Shimanto-gawa area. Major car rental companies such as Nippon Rent-A-Car (ⓦ nipponrentacar .co.jp) all have offices in Shikoku's main cities.

Takamatsu and around

Even before the Seto Ōhashi connected Shikoku's rail network with Honshū, the port of **TAKAMATSU** (高松), capital of **Kagawa-ken**, was a major gateway into the island. Warlord Chikamasa Ikoma built his castle here in 1588, but the city and surrounding area's history go back a long way before that. Most notably, the priest and mystic Kōbō Daishi (see box, p.527) was born in this prefecture, the banished Emperor Sutoku was murdered here in 1164 and, 21 years later, the Taira and Minamoto clans clashed at nearby **Yashima**. Chikamasa's castle was virtually destroyed in air raids during World War II, along with most of the city.

Today, Takamatsu is a sprawling yet attractive cosmopolitan city with close to 420,000 inhabitants, and is peppered with covered shopping arcades and chic boutiques. Next to Takamatsu Station, you can't miss the thirty-storey **Takamatsu Symbol Tower**, which is the city's tallest building and anchors the **Sunport** complex of offices, shops, convention halls and ferry piers. Northwest of here, the red-glass lighthouse at the end of the Tamamo breakwater is a good place to aim for if you're out for a seaside stroll or want to join local runners for a jog. Further east is the trendy **Kitahama Alley** (北浜アリー), a small area of brick warehouses and old buildings that have been converted into appealing cafés (see p.641) and boutiques. As twenty-first-century as all this is, the city's star attraction remains **Ritsurin-kōen**, one of Japan's most classical, spacious and beautifully designed gardens. They are easily accessible on a day-trip from Honshū, but it's well worth staying longer so you can also explore **Shikoku Mura** – the open-air museum of traditional houses at Yashima – or **Kotohira-gū** (see p.645), the ancient shrine an hour's train ride west of the city. Takamatsu is also a gateway to two of the most appealing islands in the Inland Sea: **Shōdoshima**, a mini-Shikoku with its own temple circuit and scenic attractions; and delightful **Naoshima**, a must for contemporary art and architecture fans with several outstanding galleries designed by Andō Tadao (see p.652).

Ritsurin-kōen

栗林公園 · Chūō-dōri · Daily, opening hours vary but usually summer 5.30am–7pm and winter 7am–5pm; check website for details · ¥410 · ☎ 087 833 7411, ⓦ my-kagawa.jp/ritsuringarden · The East Gate is the garden's main entrance, but JR trains stop at least every hour at Ritsurin-kōen Kita-guchi (栗林公園北口); at both entrances you can buy tickets and pick up a free English map

Takamatsu's one must-see sight, **Ritsurin-kōen**, is 2.5km south down Chūō-dōri from the JR station. The formal garden, Japan's largest at 750,000 square metres, lies at the foot of

9

TAKAMATSU

Teshima, Naoshima & Shōdoshima

0   250
metres

Sunport

Takamatsu
Symbol Tower
& Maritime Plaza

Bus Station
TIC

Kotoden
Takamatsu
Chikkō Station

MIZUKI-DŌRI

Takamatsu
Station

Takamatsu-jō

Tamamo-
kōen

Kagawa
Museum

SETO Ō-HASHI-DŌRI

Mitsukoshi
Department
Store

Hyogo-machi
arcade

Kotoden
Katahara-
machi
Station

N

Takamatsu City
Museum of Art

ROUTE 11

Matsugame-machi arcade

Lion-dori arcade

FERRY-DŌRI

Black Pumpkin
Sculpture

Kawaramachi
FLAG
Department
Store

I-PAL

ROUTE 11

Minami
Shin-machi
arcade

Tokiwa Shin-machi arcade

Kotoden
Kawaramachi
Station

Chūō-
kōen

Police

CHŪŌ-DŌRI

KIKUCHIKAN-DŌRI

Tamachi arcade

Tokiwa-gai
arcade

KANKO-DŌRI

NAGAO LINE

KANKO-DŌRI

Yashima

Ritsurin-kōen
Kita-guchi Station

JR KOTOKU LINE

North
Gate

Ritsurin
Station

Ritsurin-
kōen

Shiun-zan

Sanuki Folkcraft
Museum

East
Gate

KOTOHIRA LINE

Kotoden
Ritsurin-kōen
Station

Yashima & Tokushima

Takamatsu Airport

Kotohira

(left margin) Okayama, Kotohira-gū & Matsuyama

(right margin) Takamatsu-East Ferry Terminal & Kitahama Alley

■ ACCOMMODATION		
Guesthouse Chottoco-Ma	2	
JR Hotel Clement Takamatsu	1	
Hotel Kawaroku	5	
Takamatsu Terminal Hotel	3	
Takamatsu Tōkyū Rei Hotel	4	
● EATING		
Gowariyasu	6	
Merikenya	3	
Okageya	7	
Ramjhan	9	
Shigi China Kitchen	8	
Szechwan Restaurant Chin	1	
Tenkatsu	5	

Tokiwa Saryō	10	
Udon Ichiba	4	
Umie	2	
■ DRINKING AND NIGHTLIFE		
Amazon	2	
Bar & Flair Recommend	1	
King's Yawd	3	
Ruff House	4	
● SHOPPING		
Mingei Fukuda	2	
Miyawaki	3	
Shikoku Shop 88	1	

Shiun-zan. Its construction began in the early seventeenth century and took several feudal lords over a hundred years to complete. The gardens were designed to present magnificent vistas throughout the seasons, from an arched red bridge amid a snowy landscape in winter, to ponds full of purple and white irises in early summer.

From the East Gate main entrance you can either follow a route through the **Nantei**, South Garden, to the left or **Hokutei**, North Garden, to the right. It's possible to enter or exit the garden at the North Gate, but the route from the East Gate makes for a more pleasant meander.

Nantei

南庭 • **Kikugetsu-tei teahouse** (掬月亭) Daily 9am–4.30pm • Free; *sencha* or *matcha* ¥500/¥700 • **Higurashi-tei teahouse** (日暮亭) Sat & Sun 9am–4.30pm • Free; *matcha* ¥500

The more stylized of the two gardens, **Nantei** has paths around three lakes, dotted with islands with carefully pruned pine trees. The highlight here is a visit to the delightful *Kikugetsu-tei* (or "Scooping the Moon") teahouse overlooking the South Lake; the experience is all the better if you stop in for a cup of *sencha* or *matcha*. Dating from around 1640 and named after a Tang-dynasty Chinese poem, the teahouse exudes tranquillity, with its screens pulled back to reveal perfect garden vistas. Viewed from across the lake, it's just as impressive, swaddled in trees that cast a shimmering reflection over the water. The Nantei also has the less elaborate but more secluded *Higurashi-tei* teahouse, set in a shady grove, where you can also enjoy a cup of *matcha*.

Hokutei

北庭

Hokutei has a more natural appearance than the South Garden and is based around two ponds –

Fuyosho-ike, dotted with lotus flowers, and Gunochi-ike, where feudal lords once hunted ducks and which now blooms with irises in June. Keep an eye out for Tsuru Kame no Matsu, just to the left of the main park building, a black pine tree shaped like a crane spreading its wings and considered to be the most beautiful of the 29,190 trees in the gardens. Behind this is a line of pines called the Byōbu-matsu, after the folding-screen painting (*byōbu*) they are supposed to resemble.

Sanuki Folkcraft Museum

讃岐民芸館 • Sanuki Mingeikan • Wed–Sun 8.30am–5pm • Free

After you've viewed the gardens, head towards the East Gate, where you'll find the **Sanuki Folkcraft Museum** displaying beautiful examples of local basketwork, ceramics, furniture and huge, brightly painted banners and kites. Though some of the pieces are over a hundred years old, the designs are surprisingly modern. Also of interest are some pieces by twentieth-century Japanese-American architect and furniture designer George Nakashima.

Takamatsu-jō

高松城 • Ferry-dōri • Daily, opening hours vary but usually summer 5.30am–7pm and winter 7am–5pm; check website for details • ¥200 • ☏ 087 851 1521, ⓦ takamatsujyo.com

A couple of minutes' walk east of the JR station is **Tamamo-kōen** (玉藻公園), a small but pleasant park that contains the ruins of the city's castle, **Takamatsu-jō**. Four hundred years ago, the stronghold was one of the three major Japanese fortresses protected by sea, with three rings of moats surrounding the central keep. Like many of Japan's castles, Takamatsu-jō was decommissioned in 1869 following the Meiji Restoration (see p.827); all that remains today are a couple of turrets, parts of the moat, and grounds that are only a ninth of their original size. Still, the castle grounds host a fantastic display of blossom on the cherry trees in spring, and there are great views out across the Inland Sea. At the park's east end, you can also look around the very traditional **Hiunkaku**, a sprawling wooden mansion surrounded by stunted pines. Rebuilt in 1917, it's now used as a public event space.

Kagawa Museum

香川県立ミュージアム, Kagawa Kenritsu Myūjimu • Ferry-dōri • Tues–Sun 9am–4.30pm • ¥410 • ☏ 087 822 0002, ⓦ www.pref .kagawa.jp/kmuseum/foreign

Immediately east of Tamamo-kōen is the **Kagawa Museum**, built on part of the old castle grounds. This museum is housed in a modern building and combines displays of historical information and fine art. Head to the third floor to see the main exhibition, which has lots of high-tech displays as well as some impressive relics and life-sized replicas of local landmarks, such as the 7m-tall copper lantern from Marogame. There is also a special section relating to Kōbō Daishi (see box, p.527), with some amazing giant mandala paintings and ancient statues. On the ground floor, you can try on a multilayered kimono or a samurai warrior's armour and have your photo taken.

Takamatsu City Museum of Art

高松市美術館, Takamatsu-shi Bijutsukan • Bijutsukan-dōri • Tues–Sun 9.30am–5pm • ¥200 • ☏ 087 823 1711, ⓦ www.city .takamatsu.kagawa.jp/museum/takamatsu

Just off Chūō-dōri is the modern **Takamatsu City Museum of Art**. The small but impressive permanent collection includes a large variety of Sanuki lacquerware, as well as a superb display of Western and Japanese contemporary art. The Western art collection is almost entirely made up of works by major artists such as Pablo Picasso, Jasper Johns, Andy Warhol, David Hockney and Henri Matisse, making the entrance ticket a real

9

bargain. There's also a library where you are free to browse art books and videos – some in English – and the spacious entrance hall is used for dance and music performances.

Shōtengai

East of Chūō-dōri are Takamatsu's main commercial and entertainment districts, which are connected by covered **shōtengai** (shopping arcades). This is a lively area to wander around, both day and night, with a seemingly endless array of shops and restaurants. The longest *shōtengai* – comprised of the **Marugame-machi**, **Minami Shin-machi** and **Tamachi** arcades – stretches for 2.7km and is said to be the longest in Japan. Running parallel is **Lion-dōri**, which leads from Katahara-machi arcade into the Tokiwa Shin-machi and then Tokiwa-gai arcades. The southern end of the Marugame-machi arcade has been updated and boasts one of Yayoi Kusama's pumpkin sculptures, the *Black Pumpkin*.

ARRIVAL AND DEPARTURE
TAKAMATSU

By plane Takamatsu Airport (☎087 814 3355, ⓦtakamatsu-airport.com) lies 16km south of the city, 35min away by bus (¥760) or taxi (¥4700).
Destinations Hong Kong (4 weekly; 3hr 25min); Naha (daily; 1hr 55min); Seoul (5 weekly; 1hr 50min); Shanghai (5 weekly; 1hr 30min); Taipei (4 weekly; 2hr 35min); Tokyo Haneda (13 daily; 1hr 15min); Tokyo Narita (1–2 daily; 1hr 45min).

By train Takamatsu Station is at the northern, seaside, end of the central thoroughfare, Chūō-dōri, and a 10min walk from the heart of the city.
Destinations Kōchi (16 daily; 2hr 5min); Kotohira (24 daily; 55min); Matsuyama (hourly; 2hr 30min); Okayama (every 30min; 1hr); Tokushima (17 daily; 1hr 5min); Uwajima (15 daily; 4hr).

By bus Long-distance and most local buses pull in nearby to the JR train station, at the northern end of Chūō-dōri.
Destinations Kōbe (20 daily; 2hr 35min); Kōchi (13 daily; 2hr 10min); Matsuyama (15 daily; 2hr 40min); Osaka (32 daily; 3hr 25min); Tokyo (daily; 11hr); Yokohama (daily; 10hr 30min).

By ferry Ferries from Kōbe (¥1990 one-way, ¥3480 return; ⓦferry.co.jp) dock a 10min bus ride from the city centre at Takamatsu-East; a free shuttle bus transports passengers to JR Takamatsu Station. Ferry connections with Shōdoshima, Naoshima and Uno are at the Sunport ferry terminal, a short walk east of the train station.
Destinations Kōbe (4 daily; 3hr 40min); Naoshima (8 daily; 1hr); Shōdoshima (hydrofoil: 21 daily; 35min; & ferry: 28 daily; 1hr); Uno (22 daily; 1hr).

GETTING AROUND

Laid out on a grid, Takamatsu is an easy city to walk or cycle around. Otherwise, you'll find that trains and buses are perfectly user-friendly, and good for getting to sights outside the city.

By train As well as JR, Takamatsu has the Kotoden network whose trains run to Yashima or Kotohira. Kawaramachi Station (瓦町), where the Kotoden's three main lines intersect, is beside the Kawaramachi FLAG department store at the end of the Tokiwa arcade, while Kotoden Takamatsu Chikkō Station (高松築港) is next to Tamamo-kōen, a few minutes' walk from JR Takamatsu Station. If you're heading from Takamatsu Chikkō Station to Yashima, you'll need to change at Kawaramachi.
By bus Buses for Ritsurin-kōen and Yashima run from the stops outside Chikkō Station at the top of Chūō-dōri.

By bike You can rent bikes from the cavernous rent-a-cycle offices and parking lot beneath JR Takamatsu Station. At ¥100 for six hours or ¥200 for a full day, this is an absolute steal and the best way to see the city. You need to register first, but it's a very quick and simple process; the paperwork can be done in English. Make sure to park your bicycle in designated areas otherwise it could be impounded and incur a ¥1500 retrieval fee.
By car Eki Rent-a-Car (☎087 821 1341) and Toyota Rent-a-Car (☎087 851 0100) both have offices at Takamatsu JR Station.

INFORMATION

Tourist information There's a helpful tourist office (daily 9am–8pm; ☎087 826 0170) with friendly English-speaking staff on the first floor of the train station.
I-PAL The Kagawa International Exchange Centre, better known as I-PAL (Tues–Sun 9am–6pm; ☎087 837 5908, ⓦi-pal.or.jp), is a convenient facility with a library of

foreign-language books, magazines and newspapers and free computer terminals with internet access (30min). Here you can pick up the free information sheet *Takamatsu Information Board* (*TIA*), which carries details of what's on in town. I-PAL is at the northwest corner of Chūō-kōen, 750m south of Takamatsu Station.

ACCOMMODATION

Takamatsu has many business hotels, with plenty near the station – the better ones are listed below. More upmarket options can be found around Chūō-dōri.

Guesthouse Chottoco-Ma ちょっとこま 3-7-5 Ogimachi ☎090 6548 8735, ⊛chottoco-ma.com. A small, recently opened guesthouse with friendly and helpful owners, this is one of the very few budget options in Takamatsu. It's just one stop by train from JR Takamatsu Station. All facilities are shared. ☏ Dorms **¥2500**, doubles **¥6000**

★JR Hotel Clement Takamatsu JRホテルクレメント 高松 1-1 Hamanochō ☎087 811 1111, ⊛jrclement .co.jp. With great Inland Sea views, stylish, spacious rooms and plenty of top-notch facilities including six bars and restaurants, this remains the city's swankiest hotel, right next to JR Takamatsu Station. From May to Aug they also open the beer garden on the fifth floor. ☏ **¥24,948**

Hotel Kawaroku ホテル川六エルステージ 1-2 Hyakken-machi ☎087 821 5666, ⊛kawaroku.co.jp /english. Centrally located business hotel that has been designed to appeal to female visitors, with on-site spa facilities and a women-only floor. The excellent tatami rooms are the same price as the standard Western-style ones, and all are clean and functional. Breakfast and laptop computer rentals are available for an additional charge, and there is also a large public bath. ☏ **¥11,750**

Takamatsu Terminal Hotel 高松ターミナルホテル 10-17 Nishinomaru-chō ☎087 822 3731, ⊛www .webterminal.co.jp. There are both Western- and Japanese-style rooms at this welcoming business hotel, just a short walk from the JR station. The rooms are clean, though rather pokey, and some double rooms have a sofa that can be turned into a bed if you want to share a room between three and bring the cost down. ☏ **¥10,800**

Takamatsu Tōkyū Rei Hotel 高松東急REIホテル 9-9 Hyogo-machi ☎087 821 0109, ⊛tokyuhotelsjapan .com. Nothing fancy, but the rooms at this well-placed chain hotel are modern, very reasonably priced and have a good range of facilities. There are non-smoking floors. ☏ **¥10,000**

EATING

Takamatsu has a wide range of **restaurants** and **cafés**, many conveniently concentrated around the central arcade district, just off Chūō-dōri. Like Shikoku's other seaside cities, this is a great place to sample fresh and delicious **seafood**. The other local speciality is **sanuki udon**, thick white noodles usually served with a separate flask of stock and a variety of condiments.

Gowariyasu 吾割安 6-3 Fukudamachi ☎087 851 5030. This atmospheric *izakaya*, decorated with old film posters, record covers and other memorabilia, offers a wide range of tasty, inexpensive dishes such as *yakitori* (from ¥120), ramen noodle soup (¥600) and *gyōza* dumplings (¥400). Mon–Sat 6pm–1am, Sun 6pm–midnight.

Merikenya めりけんや 6-20 Nishinomaru-chō ☎087 811 6358, ⊛merikenya.com. Located just opposite the plaza in front of the JR station, this branch of the *Merikenya* chain has high-quality udon noodles, hence the long queues at lunchtime. Meat-topped *niku-bukkake* noodles and mountain vegetable *yama-bukkake* noodles start at ¥380 for the smallest size. Daily 7am–8pm.

★Okageya おかげや Tamura Building, 1-12-1 Kawara-chō ☎087 862 6004. This place, specializing in fish and country-style cuisine, serves gourmet standard dishes at very reasonable prices. A beautifully presented sashimi platter for four is ¥2400, and there are many tasty side dishes to choose from, such as mountain potato tempura (¥430), grilled ika (¥570) and tofu salad (¥520). You can opt for counter or private tatami room seating. Mon, Fri & Sat 5–11.30pm, Tues–Thurs 11.30am–1pm & 5–11.30pm.

Ramjham ラムジャム Minami Building, 2-3 Tamachi ☎087 834 8505. Friendly, Indian-run place serving thirty different kinds of Indian and Nepali curries, tandoori-cooked meats (from ¥650) and six types of naan (from ¥300). Dinner shouldn't cost more than ¥2000, and if you really want to indulge there's an all-you-can-eat-and-drink deal for ¥4000. Lunch sets are available from ¥600. Daily 11am–3pm & 5–10pm.

★Shigi China Kitchen シギチャイナキッチン 2-1-28 Kawaramachi ☎087 802 5788. It's easy to spot this dining bar with its distinctive orange sign. Shigi, the friendly chef, cooks a wide variety of Chinese-style dishes using local seasonal ingredients. The *mabo-dōfu* (tofu in spicy sauce; ¥700), and fish and vegetable *itame* stir-fries (from ¥600) are highly recommended. Tues–Sun 6pm–1am.

Szechwan Restaurant Chin スーツアンレストラン陳 29F Maritime Plaza, 2-1 Sunport ☎087 811 0477, ⊛sisen.jp/takamatsu. This is the most appealing and certainly the most welcoming of Sunport's top-of-the-tower trio of upmarket restaurants. The Chinese cuisine is authentically spicy, the decor is chic and the views are spectacular. The menu is mostly seasonal courses, but you can also order dishes such as swallow nest soup (¥3000)

9

and sauteed lobster with chilli sauce (¥3500). Expect to pay around ¥5000 for dinner and from ¥1500 for lunch. Daily 11.30am–2pm & 5–9pm.

Tenkatsu 天勝 7-8 Hyogo-machi ☎087 821 5380. The interior of this reputable fish restaurant is dominated by a central sunken tank, around which you can sit, either at the jet-black counter bar or in tatami booths. Kimono-clad waitresses will bring you your pick of the fish served raw, as part of a sushi platter (from ¥1080 per person) or cooked in a *nabe* stew (from ¥3240 per person). Set lunches start from as little as ¥1080. Mon–Fri 11am–2pm & 5–9.40pm, Sat & Sun 11am–9pm.

Tokiwa Saryō ときわ茶寮 1-8-2 Tokiwa-chō ☎087 861 5577, ⌨trs1515.com. Much of the lovely interior decoration of this old ryokan has remained intact in its transformation into a restaurant. Set courses of local delicacies (mainly seafood and vegetables) start at as little as ¥2000 for lunch and ¥4200 for dinner. It can be difficult to find, so look out for the giant white lantern hanging outside. Daily 11am–2.30pm & 5–9.30pm.

Udon Ichiba うどん市場 2-8 Hyogo-machi ☎087 823 0388, ⌨udon-ichiba.jp. This popular sanuki udon restaurant is a great place to fill up if you're on a budget – it's just ¥270 for a large bowl of the simplified kake-udon, which comes without toppings. If you're really famished, there is also a set menu for lunch (¥500) and dinner (¥580). *Honetsuki-dori* (chicken on the bone) served with a spicy dipping sauce is popular as a side dish (¥850). Mon–Sat 10am–9pm, Sun 10am–7pm.

★**Umie** ウミエ Kitahama Alley, 3-2 Kitahama-chō ☎087 811 7455, ⌨umie.info. Relax over great coffee (¥600) or tasty meals like hearty beef stew (¥1200), bagels (¥600) and pizza (¥1000) at this trendy joint, decorated with retro furniture and stacks of art books, magazines and LP records. Sometimes there are live music events here, and within the same complex are a gift and stationery shop, gallery and secondhand furniture store. Mon, Tues, Thurs, Fri 11am–11.30pm, Sat 10am–11.30pm, Sun 10am–9pm.

DRINKING AND NIGHTLIFE

Takamatsu has a large nightlife scene for a provincial city. There is a surprisingly good range of bars to explore in the lanes off the central *shōtengai* (shopping arcades).

Amazon アマゾン 3F One Foot Building, 4-21 Kajiyamachi ☎087 851 4560. Lively international bar playing 80s and 90s pop and rock, with dancing and retro video games. Shin-san, the owner, speaks fluent English and will mix any cocktail you desire from ¥500–700. Shots are ¥300 each, and there's a variety of bar snacks such as pizza (¥700) and hot dogs (¥600) to nibble on. Closed first Mon of the month. Daily 8pm–5am.

★**Bar & Flair Recommend** レコメンド 2F Shincho Building, 8-52 Furubaba-chō ☎087 823 3757. Takamatsu seems an unlikely place to find an Asia-Pacific Flair champion bartender, but Komoda-san's nightly performances are not to be missed. This bar has low lighting, plush sofas and smart counter seating, attracting a smartly dressed local crowd. Prices range from ¥800 for a standard mix, and from ¥1000 for a tropical cocktail. Mon–Sat 8pm–5am.

King's Yawd キングスヤード 1-2-2 Tokiwa-chō ☎087 837 2660, ⌨blog.livedoor.jp/kingsyawd. This laidback Jamaican bar has a friendly atmosphere and is presided over by the dreadlocked Satoko-san, who knows how to whip up a tasty plate of ackee and saltfish (¥1200) or a rum dessert (¥400). Drinks are reasonably priced (beer ¥500) and cocktails (¥600) are poured generously. There are regular DJ, hip-hop and reggae events. Mon–Sat 6pm–2am.

Ruff House ラフハウス B1F Oka Building, 2-3 Tamachi ☎087 835 9550, ⌨barruffhouse.com. A relaxed basement bar with nightly musical performances by young and upcoming local musicians. The schedule is eclectic – anything from Okinawan *shamisen* banjo to punk acoustic guitar – and the audience is enthusiastic. Beer from ¥600 and cocktails from ¥700. Arrive early to get a seat. Daily 7pm–midnight.

SHOPPING

Sanuki lacquerware and papier-mâché dolls are the main local crafts in Takamatsu. The **gift shops** in Ritsurin-kōen (see p.637) and the Kagawa Museum (see p.639), as well as the **shops** in the *shōtengai*, are good places to hunt for souvenirs.

Mingei Fukuda 民芸福田 9-7 Hyakken-machi ☎087 821 3237, ⌨mingei-fukuda.com. A fine emporium of locally produced folk crafts, pottery, glassware and paper goods. Look out for their beautiful hand-painted, traditional paper kites (¥8000). Tues–Sun 10am–6pm.

Miyawaki 宮脇書店 4-8 Marugame-chō ☎087 851 3733, ⌨www.miyawakishoten.com. Has a small selection of English-language, mass-market paperbacks

and books about Japan on the sixth floor. Daily 9am–10pm.

Shikoku Shop 88 四国ショップ88 Maritime Plaza ☎087 822 0459, ⌨shikokushop88.com. This shop sells different types of well-known food and crafts produced in all of Shikoku's prefectures. It's a great place to pick up packaged *sanuki udon* noodles (from ¥300) or *senbei* rice crackers (¥580). Daily 10am–9pm.

DIRECTORY

Hospital Kagawa Kenritsu Chūō Byōin (Kagawa Prefectural Central Hospital) is at 1-2-1 Asahimachi (☎ 087/ 811 3333).
Internet There are free terminals at I-PAL (see p.640) and free wi-fi spots at Kagawa Plaza (3F Symbol Tower, daily 10am–6pm), Ritsurin-kōen and the Kagawa Museum. Right next door to the entrance of the *Tōkyū Rei Hotel* (see p.641) there is also Hyokotto Comic & Internet Café (24hr),

where access starts at ¥270/30min.
Police The main police station is at 4-1-10 Banchō (☎ 087 833 0110). Emergency numbers are listed on p.71.
Post office The main post office (Mon–Fri 9am–7pm, Sat 9am–5pm, Sun 9am–12.30pm) is at the north end of the Marugame arcade, opposite the Mitsukoshi department store.

Yashima

屋島

Literally meaning "rooftop island" (which thousands of years ago it was), the **YASHIMA** plateau lies 6km east of Takamatsu's city centre. It was at Yashima that, in 1185, the Taira and Minamoto clans famously battled to determine who ruled Japan (see p.822). A small detachment of Minamoto forces surprised the Taira by attacking from the land side of the peninsula – the Taira had expected the attack to come from the sea. Within a month, the Taira were defeated at the Battle of Dannoura and forced to flee to the mountainous hinterland of Shikoku.

Buses run to the top of the 293m-high volcanic lava plateau (see p.644), or you can spend an hour hiking up a steep, winding path starting to the west of the decommissioned cable-car. Once at the top, you might be a little disappointed, as on the southern ridge of the plateau is a car park. However, the expansive views out over the Inland Sea and the stone workshops of Mure make the trek worthwhile.

Yashima-ji

屋島寺 • **Temple** Daily, dawn to dusk • Free • **Treasure House** Daily 9am–5pm • ¥500 • ☎ 087 841 9418

Supposedly founded in 754 by the Chinese monk Ganjin (see p.499), **Yashima-ji** temple is number 84 on the Shikoku pilgrimage. Look out for the racy granite carvings of tanuki, a type of Japanese racoon dog, next to the temple's main hall, and elephants carved into the eaves of the smaller halls near the front gate. Yashima-ji's **Treasure House** is worth popping into for its collection of screens, pottery and a mixed bag of relics from the battle between the Taira and Minamoto. There's also a traditional garden near the front gate, with the distinctly unbloody "Pond of Blood", believed to be the spot where the Minamoto soldiers cleansed their swords after the Battle of Yashima.

Shikoku Mura

四国村 • 91 Yashima Nakamachi • Daily: April–October 8.30am–5pm; Nov–March 8.30am–4.30pm • ¥1000 including Shikoku Mura Gallery • ☎ 087 843 3111, ⓦ www.shikokumura.or.jp • A 5min walk north of Kotoden Yashima Station

At the base of the Yashima plateau is the outdoor museum of **Shikoku Mura**. More than thirty traditional buildings from across the island and Inland Sea were relocated here in an imaginatively landscaped park. The route around the grounds, which takes about an hour, starts with a small replica of the Iya Valley's Kazura-bashi (see p.667), a bridge made of vines and bamboo that crosses a pond to an impressive thatched-roof kabuki theatre from Shōdoshima. Plays are occasionally performed here – check with the tourist information office in Takamatsu (see p.640). Look out also for the circular Sato Shime Goya (Sugarcane Press Hut) with a conical roof. Each of the houses has an excellent English explanation of its history.

Shikoku Mura Gallery

四国村ギャラリー • 91 Yashima Nakamachi • Daily: April–Oct 8.30am–5pm; Nov–March 8.30am–4.30pm • ¥1000 including Shikoku Mura • ☎ 087 843 3111, ⓦ www.shikokumura.or.jp

Near the top of Shikoku Mura is the Andō Tadao-designed **Shikoku Mura Gallery**. Inside the polished concrete building is a single long gallery featuring original paintings

9

by the likes of Marc Chagall and Pablo Picasso, and sculptures by Auguste Rodin, as well as regularly changing themed exhibitions of contemporary art.

ARRIVAL AND DEPARTURE   YASHIMA

By train From Takamatsu JR, trains run at least every hour to Yashima Station (15min; ¥220), from where it's a 15min walk north to the base of the plateau. More convenient is the Kotoden line (every 20min; 20min; ¥320 from Kotoden Takamatsu Chikkō Station), as Kotoden Yashima Station is only a 5min walk from Shikoku Mura.

By bus Between 9am and 5pm there's a shuttle bus every hour from outside both the JR and Kotoden stations running to the top of the plateau (10min; ¥100).

EATING

Ikkaku 一鶴 220-1 Yashima Nakamachi ☎ 087 844 3711. A short walk east of Kotoden Station, this cavernous beer hall-style restaurant specializes in *honetsukidori*, local chicken cuisine. Dishes start at ¥360. Mon–Fri 11am–2pm & 4–10pm, Sat & Sun 11am–10pm.

Waraya わら家 Shikoku Mura 91 Yashima Nakamachi ☎ 087 843 3115. This branch of a famous udon chain is beside the entrance to Shikoku Mura, in a building with a thatched roof and water wheel. You can sit and slurp a variety of delicious udon dishes (from ¥460); they also serve plates of assorted tempura (from ¥600). Admission to Shikoku Mura gives you a ¥100 discount coupon here. Daily 10am–6.30pm.

Mure

A few kilometres east of Yashima in **Mure**, the streets resound to the clack of hammers on granite and are lined with fantastic stone sculptures and designs – everything from traditional lanterns to pot-bellied Buddhas and long-necked giraffes. It was in this long-established stonemasons' town that the celebrated American-Japanese sculptor **Isamu Noguchi** (see box below) created a traditional-style home and sculpture studio during the latter part of his life.

Isamu Noguchi Garden Museum Japan

イサムノグチ庭園美術館, Isamu Noguchi Teien Bijutsukan • 3519 Mure-chō • Tues, Thurs & Sat 10am, 1pm & 3pm • ¥2160; it's best to book two weeks in advance by email • ☎ 087 870 1500, ⓦ isamunoguchi.or.jp • Take the Kotoden train either in Takamatsu or at Kotoden Yashima Station, alight at Yakuri Station (八栗駅), and then walk 20min northeast

Although you must make an appointment and the entrance fee is more expensive than most museums, a visit to the **Isamu Noguchi Garden Museum Japan** is highly recommended. The lovely traditional house Noguchi lived in, filled with his signature paper lanterns, the inspiring stone sculpture gardens and his large studio (where you can still see all his tools) have been left exactly as they were when he died. You can see more than 150 of Noguchi's sculptures, some only partly finished,

---

ISAMU NOGUCHI

Born in Los Angeles in 1904 to an Irish-American mother and a Japanese father, renowned artist and architect **Isamu Noguchi** spent part of his childhood in Japan before returning to the States, aged 13. In his late 20s he settled in New York, where his main studio (also a museum) can be found. It was here that he began to establish his reputation through his **iconic designs** for paper lanterns and furniture, as well as high-profile commissions for sculptures and landscape works around the world. Noguchi travelled widely prior to World War II, studying art in Paris, Kyoto and Beijing. He returned to Japan after the war, creating numerous site-specific pieces such as the two bridges in the Hiroshima Peace Park (1952) and the lobby of the Sōgetsu Kaikan in Tokyo (1977). Noguchi had many love affairs with famous twentieth-century women such as French writer Anaïs Nin and Mexican artist Frida Kahlo, and he was married to Chinese-born Japanese actress Ōtaka Yoshiko for five years. In 1988, the year of his death, he completed his design for Moerenuma Park in Sapporo (see p.300). Apart from the work at his studio in Mure, near Takamatsu, another of Noguchi's sculptures, *Time and Space*, stands at Takamatsu Airport.

including the signature pieces *Energy Void,* a 3.6m-tall work that looks more like a giant rubber tube than solid black granite, and the two-coloured stone ring *Sun at Midnight*. Exactly an hour is granted to wander the studio and grounds, soaking up the singular atmosphere. No photography is allowed, but there are some excellent books in English for sale at the reception area.

Kotohira

琴平

Approximately 30km southwest of Takamatsu, **KOTOHIRA** is home to the ancient shrine Kotohira-gū, popularly called **Kompira-san**. Along with the Grand Shrines of Ise and Izumo Taisha, Kotohira is one of the major Shintō pilgrimage sites, attracting some four million visitors a year. Despite the crowds, it is still one of Shikoku's highlights. The town itself is pleasantly located, straddling the Kanakura-gawa at the foot of the mountain Zozu-san, so-called because it is said to resemble an elephant's head (*zozu*). Kotohira can easily be visited on a day-trip from Takamatsu, one hour away by train, or en route to Kōchi or the mountainous interior. However, it has a number of enjoyable attractions as well as a traditional atmosphere, making it a worthwhile overnight stay.

Kotohira-gū

金刀比羅宮 • 892-1 Kotohira-chō • Daily: April–Sept 6am–6pm; Oct–March 6am–5pm • Free • ☎ 087 775 2121, ⓦ www.konpira.or.jp

Kotohira's star attraction, **Kotohira-gū**, is also known as **Kompira-san**. It's a venerable shrine, dating back to at least the tenth century, and the mainly wooden hillside complex can only be accessed via a long staircase ascent. It's a total of 1368 steps to reach the Oku-sha inner shrine at the top. You'll see many people huffing and puffing on the slopes, and some even hire traditional *kago* (palanquins) to carry them to the top. Depending on weather and crowd conditions, it will take about an hour to make your climb at a leisurely pace.

Kompira-san is one of only two places in Japan where you can see the ancient sport of *kemari* performed. Deemed an Intangible Cultural Property, this ninth-century forerunner of soccer is played by the shrine's monks on May 5, July 7 and in late December.

9

The museums

Daily 8.30am–4.30pm • ¥800 each

The Kompira-san shrine grounds begin at the Ō-mon (大門), a stone gateway just beyond which you'll pass the Gonin Byakushō (五人百姓) – five red-painted stalls shaded by large white umbrellas. The souvenir sellers here stand in for the five farmers who were once allowed to hawk their wares in the shrine precincts. Further along to the right of the main walkway, lined with stone lanterns, are three small museums housing different collections of the shrine's artistic treasures: the **Hōmotsukan** (宝物館), the **Gakugei Sankō-kan** (学芸参考館) and the **Takahashi Yuichi-kan** (高橋由一館). Only the latter, displaying the striking paintings of the nineteenth-century artist Takahashi Yuichi, is really worth the entrance fee.

Omote Shoin

表書院 • Daily 8.30am–4.30pm • ¥800

Before climbing to the shrine's next stage, look left of the steps to see a giant gold ship's propeller, a gift from a local shipbuilder. To the right is the entrance to the serene reception hall **Omote Shoin**, built in 1659. Delicate screen paintings and decorated door panels by the celebrated artist Maruyama Okyo (1733–95) are classified as Important Cultural Assets; they're so precious you have to peer through glass into the dim interiors to see them.

Asahi-no-Yashiro and the Hon-gū

朝日の社 • 本宮

Returning to the main ascent, the next major building you reach after the Omote Shoin is the grand **Asahi-no-Yashiro**, the Rising Sun Shrine. Dedicated to the sun goddess Amaterasu, it is decorated with intricate woodcarvings of flora and fauna, and topped with a green copper roof. Two flights of steep steps lead from here to the thatch-roofed **Hon-gū**, the main shrine, built in 1879 and the centre of Kompira-san's daily activities. Priests and their acolytes in traditional robes rustle by along a raised wooden corridor linking the shrine buildings.

Oku-sha

奥社

Many visitors stop at **Hon-gū**, but the hardy, and truly faithful, trudge on up the last 583 steps to the **Oku-sha**, following a path to the left of the main shrine. When you reach this inner shrine, located almost at the top of Zozu-san, look up at the rocks on the left to see two rather cartoonish stone carvings of the demon Tengu.

KOMPIRA'S BUDDHIST CONNECTION

Kompira-san, the unofficial but more commonly used name for Kotohira-gū, comes from the nickname for Omono-nushi-no-Mikoto, the spiritual **guardian of seafarers**. Kompira was originally Kumbhira, the Hindu crocodile god of the River Ganges, and was imported as a deity from India well before the ninth century, when Kōbō Daishi chose the shrine as the spot for one of his Buddhist temples. For a thousand years Kompira-san served as both a **Buddhist** and **Shintō** holy place and was so popular that those who could not afford to make the pilgrimage themselves either dispatched their pet dogs, with pouches of coins as a gift to the gods, or tossed barrels of rice and money into the sea, in the hope that they might be picked up by sailors who would take the offering to Kompira-san on their behalf.

When the **Meiji Restoration** began, Shintō took precedence, and the Buddhas were removed from the shrine, along with Kompira, who was seen as too closely associated with the rival religion. While there are no representations of Kompira at the shrine today, an open-air gallery decorated with pictures and models of ships (see opposite) serves as a reminder of the shrine's original purpose, and the Chinese architectural style of some of the buildings hints at the former Buddhist connection.

Ema-dō Gallery
絵馬堂

From the main shrine area, head to the wooden platforms for magnificent views of the surrounding countryside – on a clear day you can see as far as the Inland Sea. To the left of the main shrine is the open-air **Ema-dō gallery**, which displays votive plaques, paintings and models of ships. These are from sailors who hope to be granted good favour on the seas. The offerings extend to one from Japan's first cosmonaut, a TV journalist who was a paying passenger on a Russian Soyuz launch in 1990.

Kinryō Sake Museum

金陵の郷, Kinryō no Sato • 623 Kotohira-chō • Mon–Fri 9am–3.30pm, Sat, Sun & public holidays 9am–5.30pm • Free • ☎ 087 773 4133, ⓦ nishino-kinryo.co.jp

The **Kinryō Sake Museum**, at the start of the main approach to Kompira-san, is also well worth a visit. There has been a sake brewery on this spot since 1616, and the buildings arranged around a large courtyard have changed little over the centuries. Inside, the well-presented exhibition runs step by step through the sake-making process, using life-size displays and recordings of traditional brewers' songs. At the end of the displays there is an informative video in English that you can enjoy while sampling Kinryō's high-quality sake.

Kanamaru-za

金丸座 • 817-10 Enoi Kotohira-chō • Daily 9am–5pm; plays April only • ¥500 • ☎ 087 773 3846, ⓦ konpirakabuki.jp

On the hill to the left of the lower shrine steps of Kompira-san is **Kanamaru-za**. This performance hall, built in 1835, is said to be the oldest-surviving kabuki theatre in Japan and was fully restored when it was moved to this location from the centre of Kotohira in 1975. Plays are only performed here one month of the year, but the theatre itself merits a visit, especially for its impressive wooden-beamed and lantern-lit auditorium, and intriguing trapdoors and tunnels.

Nakano Udon School

中野うどん学校, Nakano Udon Gakkō • 720 Kotohira-chō • Daily 9am–3pm; classes 40min–1hr • ¥1620; reservations are required in advance • ☎ 087 775 0001, ⓦ nakanoya.net

Kagawa Prefecture is full of udon noodle restaurants, but there aren't so many places where you can actually learn how to make them. On the second floor of a hundred-year-old udon noodle shop, on the left side of the shrine approach, is the **Nakano Udon School**, which will teach you these special skills. The class is a fun experience, and though the teachers don't speak much English, they are welcoming and the demonstrations are easy to follow. You can eat your noodles on site, or take them home.

ARRIVAL AND INFORMATION
KOTOHIRA

By train JR Kotohira Station is a 10min walk northeast of the town centre. Left of the exit are coin lockers (24hr; ¥300–700). If you've travelled by Kotoden train from Takamatsu, you'll arrive at the smaller Kotoden Kotohira Station closer to the town centre on the banks of the Kanekura-gawa.

Tourist information The new tourist information office (daily 10am–6pm; ☎ 087 775 3500) is in the shopping arcade near Nakano Udon School, next to the shop Shoyu Mame, which specializes in the regional speciality, soy-flavoured beans.

ACCOMMODATION

Places to stay in Kotohira are always in high demand, and prices can rise substantially at weekends and during public holidays. The town is famed for its top-notch **ryokan**; unless mentioned, rates include breakfast and dinner, usually of high quality.

Kōbaitei 紅梅亭 556-1 Kotohira-chō ☎ 087 775 1111, ⓦ koubaitei.jp. Charming ryokan with lovely public areas including a tea lounge, traditional garden, small swimming pool and public onsen bath. There's a choice of tatami and

9

Western-style rooms. 🛜 **¥21,168**

★**Kotobuki Ryokan** ことぶき旅館　Kotohira-chō ☎ 087 773 3872, 📧 kotobukiryokan@hotmail.co.jp. The best deal in Kotohira, this small and attractive ryokan is run by a friendly couple and has a quaint traditional interior. Rooms and bathing facilities are spotless, and it's conveniently located by the river and shopping arcade. 🛜 **¥7,750**

Kotohira Riverside Hotel 琴平リバーサイドホテル 246-1 Kotohira-chō ☎ 087 775 1880, 🌐 hananoyu .co.jp/river. This small, Western-style hotel, located on the west bank of the Kanekura-gawa, is a good mid-range option, where the modern rooms are clean and fairly spacious. 🛜 **¥14,256**

Mi Casa Su Casa Guesthouse ゲストハウス ミカサス カサ　1230-1　Konzoji-chō ☎ 087 763 1353, 🌐 micasasucasa.jp. This small, budget guesthouse is two stops east on JR from Kotohira Station and right next to Konzoji Station. Rooms are simple but very clean, and there's also a shared kitchen area. The friendly English-speaking owner is on hand to give travel advice. 🛜 Dorms **¥2800**, doubles **¥7000**

Sakura-no-Shō 桜の抄 977-1 Kotohira-chō ☎ 087 775 3218, 🌐 sakuranosho.jp. At the foot of the steps leading up to Kompira-san, this large modern ryokan has comfortable Japanese- and Western-style rooms as well as some nice public baths. If you fancy a splurge, it's also worth visiting for the beautifully presented mix of traditional and contemporary Japanese dishes at its main restaurant, *Ikiri* (いきり), a large, sleek affair with an open kitchen at its centre and romantic views out over the illuminated Ō-mon at night. 🛜 **¥15,560**

EATING

Henkotsu-ya へんこつ屋 240 Shin-machi Kotohira-chō ☎ 0877 75 2343. This traditional shop is worth stopping at for a refreshing cup of *matcha* and some *manju* (baked rice flour cakes with sweet bean filling; set ¥650) after climbing Kompira-san. The unusual tearoom, decorated with calligraphy, is at the end of a narrow hallway stacked with samurai armour and other antiques. You'll find it on the same street as the *Kotobuki Ryokan* (see above). Daily 8.30am–6.30pm.

Kamitsubaki 神椿 892-1 Kotohira-chō ☎ 087 773 0202, 🌐 kamitsubaki.com. Located in the Kompira-san grounds, this elegant restaurant and café has a tranquil atmosphere and pleasant views. The restaurant serves pricey Western-style courses – expect to pay more than ¥2500 for lunch and from ¥5000 for dinner. The café, with a beautifully tiled feature wall, serves food such as sandwiches (¥600) and curry (¥1550), as well as tea (¥400) and coffee (¥450). Restaurant Tues–Sun 11.30am–2.30pm & 5–9pm; café daily 9am–5pm.

★**Kompira Udon** 金比羅うどん 810-3 Kotohira-chō ☎ 087 773 5785, 🌐 konpira.co.jp. Large, bustling restaurant close to the Kompira-san steps, serving all types of delicious *sanuki udon*. A bowl topped with tempura is ¥670, while sets with noodles, tempura, rice and a tofu side dish are good value at ¥870. Daily 8am–5pm.

New Green ニューグリーン 722-1 Kotohira-chō ☎ 087 773 3451, 🌐 new-green.sakura.ne.jp. If you're looking for somewhere to eat after 5pm, this friendly café at the shrine end of the shopping arcade is a cheap and cheerful choice. It serves Japanese and Western food including hearty set meals (from ¥850), pasta (¥700) and curry (¥750). English menu available. Mon–Wed & Fri–Sun 8am–8.30pm.

Naoshima and the Art Islands of the Inland Sea

The islands of the **Seto Inland Sea**, between Shikoku and the main island of Honshū, are some of the most scenic and friendly places in Japan. For centuries, they were at the crossroads of maritime transportation, including piracy, and developed their own unique culture and ecological lifestyle. In Japan's rapid economic growth period, despite the islands collectively becoming Japan's first **national park**, natural resources were exploited and illegal industrial waste dumping was rampant, destroying forests and polluting the waters. After the collapse of the "bubble" economy in the late 1980s, the islands suffered from depopulation and neglect.

Since then, the cultural foundation of publishing company Benesse has been a major force for revitalizing these island communities through ambitious **art and architectural projects** and **sustainable tourism**. The main focus was originally **Naoshima**, but there are currently eleven other Inland Sea islands being developed as art sites and attracting thousands of visitors for the **Setouchi Triennale**, an international art festival featuring exciting contemporary artworks (see box, p.650).

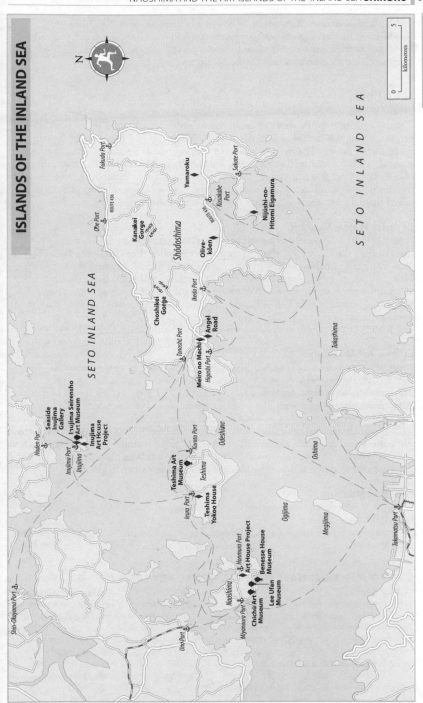

ISLANDS OF THE INLAND SEA

9

The islands described here can be visited in a loop from either Naoshima or Shōdoshima on day-trips, as both are easily accessed from Takamatsu or Okayama. Note that nearly all the museums and art sites on the islands are closed on Mondays, or Tuesdays if a public holiday falls on the Monday.

Naoshima
直島

The dynamic hub for Benesse's ongoing "community revitalization through art" project, idyllic **NAOSHIMA**, 13km north of Takamatsu, is now home to six stunning Andō Tadao-designed galleries as well as several large-scale installations and outdoor sculptures from major international and Japanese talent. In **Miyanoura** (宮浦), the island's ferry port and main town, there is an amazing public bathhouse, while around the southern Gotanji area there are sheltered beaches with glorious Inland Sea views – all of these things combine to make Naoshima a blissful escape.

Benesse House Museum

ベネッセハウスミュジアム • Gotanji • Daily 8am–9pm, last entry 8pm • ¥1030 • ☎ 087 892 3233, ⓦ benesse-artsite.jp

Overlooking the Inland Sea, the contemporary art gallery **Benesse House Museum**, 2km southeast of Miyanoura, is home to some stunning art including works by Bruce Nauman, Jasper Johns, Andy Warhol, David Hockney and Frank Stella. Scattered around the museum are seventeen outdoor sculptural works ranging from Yayoi Kusama's *Pumpkin* to Cai Guo-Qiang's witty and practical *Cultural Melting Bath*, an open-air jacuzzi surrounded by jagged limestone rocks. Guests of *Benesse House* (see p.653) can use the jacuzzi (Wed, Fri & Sun 4–5pm, closed Dec–Feb; ¥1030).

Chichū Art Museum

地中美術館, Chichū Bijutsukan • 3449-1 Naoshima • Tues–Sun: March–Sept 10am–6pm; Oct–Feb 10am–5pm • ¥2060 • ☎ 087 892 3755, ⓦ benesse-artsite.jp

The serene hilltop **Chichū Art Museum** is a naturally lit gallery, housing five of Monet's *Water Lilies* series of paintings. The artworks are the climax of a wonderful winding tour through towering corridors of polished concrete spaces dedicated to a dazzling installation by Walter de Maria and three signature "playing with light" pieces by James Turrell. The museum's lovely café offers a spectacular panorama of the Inland Sea. On the approach to the museum, the picturesque (and free) **Chichū Garden** has been planted with flowers and plants similar to those cultivated by Monet in his famous garden in Giverny.

Lee Ufan Museum

李禹煥美術館, Li Ūfan Bijutsukan • 1390 Azakuraura • Tues–Sun: March–Sept 10am–6pm; Oct–Feb 10am–5pm • ¥1030 • ☎ 087 892 3754, ⓦ benesse-artsite.jp

Situated between the Benesse House Museum and the Chichū Art Museum is the **Lee Ufan Museum**. This minimalist, three-room gallery and courtyard garden, also designed

---

SETOUCHI TRIENNALE INTERNATIONAL ART FESTIVAL

The attractive islands of the Inland Sea are the exhibition spaces for the **Setouchi Triennale** (瀬戸内国 際芸術祭, Setouchi Kokusai Geijutsusa; ⓦ setouchi-artfest.jp), a **contemporary art festival** held every three years. Japanese and international artists are invited to exhibit their works on the eleven participating islands, and many collaborate with the local community to produce fantastic sculptures, installations and audiovisual works. Local people are enthusiastic about the festival, and there are pop-up restaurants and cafés near the art sites. First held in 2010, the 2013 festival exhibited more than 150 pieces. Visiting the islands to see the festival sites is relatively easy thanks to the well-organized ferry services, and detailed information is available in English at many festival locations. The next Triennale is expected in 2019.

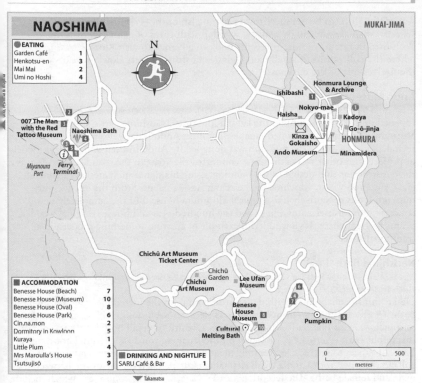

by Andō Tadao, showcases the work of renowned Korean artist **Lee Ufan**, a major force in the contemporary Japanese art movement of the 1970s. At the entrance to the gallery is a pole sculpture by Lee, and as you go through the angular corridors of the museum you'll pass several of his works, culminating in the hushed atmosphere of the final room where you must take your shoes off before entering.

Art House Project

家プロジェクト, le Purojekuto • Honmura • Tues–Sun 10am–4.30pm • Multi-entry ticket ¥1030 (six sites, not including Kinza) or ¥410 per site (Kinza ¥510; advance booking essential); tickets and information are available from Honmura Lounge and Archive (same hours), around the corner from the Nokyo-mae bus stop • ☎ 087 892 3233, ⓦ benesse-artsite.jp

The charming fishing village of **Honmura** (本村), located midway down Naoshima's east coast, is the base for the **Art House Project**, in which five old wooden houses, a temple and a shrine have been transformed into artworks.

Kadoya (角屋), an art house close to two hundred years old, is the forum for a trio of works by Miyajima Tatsuo, including the beguiling light-and-water installation *Sea of Time '98*. On the small hill to the east stands the Edo-era shrine **Go-ō-jinja** (護王神社), which was renovated to include a stone chamber and a glass staircase. **Minamidera** (南寺) is a collaboration between Andō Tadao and American artist James Turrell: Andō designed the stark building that stands on the site of a long-since-demolished temple, and incorporates the charred wooden walls that are typical of the village. As you enter, you'll be plunged into darkness (staff are on hand to assist) and Turrell's artwork will be revealed after some fumbling around.

A former dental clinic now houses the scrapbook-style **Haisha** (はいしゃ) by Ōtake Shinrō, which includes a partial life-sized copy of the Statue of Liberty. Beautiful

9

waterfall paintings by Senju Hiroshi decorate **Ishibashi** (石橋), while **Gokaisho** (碁会所) displays amazingly realistic wooden sculptures of camellias by Suda Yoshihiro in tatami rooms. You must book in advance to visit **Kinza** (きんざ), where the collections of small wood, glass and stone objects slowly reveal themselves out of the darkness.

Andō Museum

安藤ミュージアム • 736-2 Naoshima • Tues–Sun 10am–4.30pm • ¥510 • ☎ 087 892 3754, ⓦ benesse-artsite.jp

Opened in 2013 in Honmura, the latest addition to Naoshima's art sites is the **Andō Museum**, a tribute to renowned Japanese architect **Andō Tadao** who was key in revitalizing the island. The museum was designed by Andō himself and displays models of projects and other works that have connected the artist to the island. However, it is the construction and design of the building, using his signature materials of concrete, glass, steel and wood, which really showcases Andō's talent. From the outside, the museum looks deceptively like a typical Honmura house, but the completely new concrete interior uses natural light and the hundred-year-old house's original wooden beams to great effect. It's a wonderful example of creating something modern in a traditional space.

Naoshima Bath "I ♥ 湯"

直島銭湯「I 湯」, Naoshima Sentō "I yu" • 2252-2 Naoshima • Tues–Fri 2–9pm, Sat, Sun & public holidays 10am–9pm • ¥510; *ofuro* sets ¥1000 • ☎ 087 892 2626, ⓦ benesse-artsite.jp

Ōtake Shinrō collaborated with design studio Graf on the incredible *sentō* **Naoshima Bath "I ♥ 湯"**, 150m or so from Miyanoura's sleek SANAA-designed Naoshima ferry terminal. As with Haisha (see p.651), there's a wealth of detail both inside and out of this public bath (even "I ♥ 湯" is a pun on the Japanese word *yu*, meaning hot water). You can expect to see recycled ceramic tile mosaics, pop art paintings and photo collages, videos, erotica and a small elephant statue perched on the divide between the male and female baths. The reception area sells special "I ♥ 湯" *ofuro* sets, which include towels, soap and shampoo.

007 The Man with the Red Tattoo Museum

007赤い刺青の男記念館, 007 Akai Seisei no Otoko Kinenkan • Miyanoura • Daily 9am–5pm • Free • ☎ 087 892 2299

James Bond fans will want to drop by Miyanoura's tiny **007 The Man with the Red Tattoo Museum**. Plastered with posters, photos and other memorabilia, it feels a bit like a shrine created by an obsessive teenage fan and is part of the island's campaign to feature as a location in a future Bond film – not too big a stretch, since Raymond Benson set his 007 novel *The Man With The Red Tattoo* on Naoshima. Don't miss watching the locally produced video that introduces the island – James Bond style.

ARRIVAL AND INFORMATION   NAOSHIMA

By ferry Regular ferries sail to Miyanoura from Takamatsu (1hr; ¥520) and from Uno on Honshū (20min; ¥290), which is 1hr by train from Okayama (see p.563). Timetables are regularly updated on the Benesse website (ⓦ benesse -artsite.jp/en/access). There are irregular summertime or Triennale-time only ferries from Honmura. However, it's much easier and more convenient to depart from Miyanoura.

Tourist information The information desk in the ferry terminal (daily 8.30am–6pm; ☎ 087 892 2299) has an excellent English map and guide to the island.

GETTING AROUND

By bus There's a regular minibus (¥100) that runs between Miyanoura and the Chichū Art Museum via Honmura and *Benesse House*. The bus timetable is available from the tourist information desk in the ferry terminal. *Benesse House* also have their own shuttle service on the same route, which is free for guests.

By bike Cycle rental is available from *Café Ogiya* in the ferry terminal and from the TVC bike shop opposite the terminal (both ¥500/day). TVC also have electric-powered bicycles for ¥1500/day. Some of the guesthouses (see opposite) also rent out bicycles.

ACCOMMODATION

During Japanese holidays and the Setouchi Triennale, **accommodation** is almost impossible to find on Naoshima. Even outside of these periods, the island is a very popular destination. Book well in advance if you can – note that some places will charge higher rates on arrival if you don't.

★**Benesse House** ベネッセハウス Gotanji ☎087 892 3223, ⓦbenesse-artsite.jp/en/stay/benessehouse. This is a fine hotel offering comfortable, spacious rooms in four separate blocks: one in the museum (see p.650), one in the adjoining Oval and two within the hotel's newer complex, *Benesse House Park and Beach*. The latter is closer to the water and has a Scandinavian feel, as well as a spa, library and guest lounge. Although this hotel is on the pricey side, you'll get the opportunity to see artworks created by world-famous artists that aren't on display to the general public. 🛜 **¥37,000**

Cin.na.mon シナモン Miyanoura ☎087 840 8133, ⓦwww.cin-na-mon.jp. This stylishly renovated wooden house has three basic tatami bedrooms that all share a bathroom, as well as a trendy café-bar (Tues–Sun 11am–3pm & 5–9.30pm) that's decorated with a collection of colourful plastic models of characters from *Star Wars*, *Dragon Ball* and the like. They offer a selection of curry dishes (from ¥700) and have a 1hr 30min all-you-can-drink deal for ¥2000. Rates include breakfast, and bicycle rental is also available. 🛜 **¥8000**

Dormitory in Kowloon ドミトリーin九龍 Miyanoura ☎090 7974 2424, ⓦdomi-kowloon.com. This friendly, simple hostel is one of the cheapest places to stay on Naoshima and is a solid choice. It's just steps from the ferry terminal, with clean and comfortable rooms, self-catering facilities and a communal lounge area. 🛜 Dorms **¥3240**

★**Kuraya** くらや Honmura ☎087 892 2253, ⓦkuraya -naoshima.net. Set in a traditional but somewhat

unkempt Naoshima house with a central courtyard, this unconventional B&B is run by an English-speaking artist who keeps a large number of cats on the premises. *Kuraya* is also a gallery, and it's possible to stay in the exhibition space. Vegetarian breakfasts are available for an additional ¥500. **¥8000**

Little Plum リトルプラム Miyanoura ☎087 892 3751, ⓦlittleplum.net. Behind the bathhouse (see opposite) is this cute hostel and café-bar (Tues 5–10pm, Wed–Sun 11am–10pm) made out of shipping containers. *Little Plum* offers four comfortable bunk beds in each of the crates and a shared bathroom between them all. Bicycle rental is also available. 🛜 Dorms **¥3000**

★**Mrs. Maroulla's House** マローラおばさんの家 Miyanoura ☎090 7979 3025, ⓦyado-sevenbeach.com. This gaudy, self-catering cottage is a riot of colour both inside and out – no other house on Naoshima is painted hot pink. It's comfortably furnished, the kitchen area and shower room have all the mod cons, and the place can sleep up to five guests. **¥15,500**

Tsutsujisō つつじ荘 Gotanji ☎087 892 2838, ⓦtsutsujiso.com. You can choose between chalets with tatami floors, caravans or "*pao*" (spacious Mongolian circular tents with four beds, table and chairs) at this great seaside-facing camp. There's a small café (daily 11am–2.30pm; open Sat, Sun & public holidays in winter) selling drinks and snacks, and the BBQ cooking area and shower rooms have recently been upgraded. Prices are per person. **¥4320**

EATING

Garden Café ガーデンカフェ Honmura ☎087 892 3301. Look out over Honmura port at this popular restaurant, which is based in a historic house and offers bike rental. The seafood curry (¥800) is delicious and served with a side salad, while the fresh orange juice (¥500) and apple cake (¥350) are also particularly good. Tues–Sun 11.30am–5pm.

Henkotsu-en へんこつ苑 Miyanoura ☎087 840 8266, ⓦhenkotsuen.com. Just a minute from the port on foot, this stylish seafood and barbecue restaurant offers excellent *kaiseki*-style bentō lunch sets for ¥1500. There is also a counter bar where you can enjoy a glass of wine or a cocktail (from ¥500) while watching the ocean. Tues–Sun 11.30am–2pm & 5–10pm.

Mai Mai マイマイ Honmura ☎090 8286 7039, ⓦmaimaipj.exblog.jp. Operating out of a garage with courtyard seating, this burger café sells the popular Naoshima Burger (¥640) and the Hawaiian-style RocoMoco burger plate (¥680), which you can wash down with a fresh juice (¥400) or draught beer (¥300). Daily 10am–5pm.

★**Umi no Hoshi** 海の星 Benesse Park, Gotanji ☎087 892 3223, ⓦbenesse-artsite.jp. Offering wonderful Inland Sea views, the *Umi no Hoshi* restaurant serves superb Mediterranean-style cuisine featuring fresh local produce. The breakfast buffet is ¥2613, while the elegant dinner courses range from ¥9500–13,000. Daily 7.30–9.30am & 6–9pm.

DRINKING AND NIGHTLIFE

SARU Café & Bar カフェ&バーSARU Miyanoura ☎090 6414 6694. From the outside *SARU* looks a bit like a shed, but inside it's been renovated into an arty drinking spot. It's probably the only real watering hole on the entire

island, and you shouldn't miss sampling one of the series of original Naoshima craft beers, named "The Tale of Naoshima" (¥700). It's quite a cosy place, so it can get lively at times.

9

Inujima
犬島

The tiny island of **INUJIMA** is home to the dramatic Inujima Seirensho Art Museum and the ongoing Inujima Art House Project. These two sites are another excellent example of how the history, traditional architecture and natural environment of the Inland Sea have been skilfully combined with contemporary art. Currently, the island has a population of around fifty, and it's likely you'll meet at least half the residents as you wander around the sites. In total, it's probably worth setting aside two or three hours to visit the island.

Inujima Seirensho Art Museum
犬島精錬所美術館, Inujima Seirensho Bijutsukan • 327-4 Inujima • **Museum** March–Nov Mon & Wed–Sun 10am–4.30pm; Dec–Feb Mon & Fri–Sun 10am–4.30pm • ¥2060 (combined ticket with Inujima Art House Project and Seaside Inujima Gallery) • **Café** Daily 10.30am–4pm • ☎ 086 947 1112, ⓦ benesse-artsite.jp

The industrial-looking **Inujima Seirensho Art Museum** has been built into the ruins of a copper refinery constructed in 1909. Using local granite and waste products from the smelting process, architect **Sambuichi Hiroshi** has transformed the previously abandoned structures and smokestacks into a fantastic eco-building and art space, with solar power and geothermal cooling creating a naturally air-conditioned environment. The museum displays the work of **Yanagi Yukinori**, who has used parts of the dismantled home of controversial writer **Mishima Yukio** to explore the contradictions of Japanese modernization. The museum's café serves delicious lunches made from locally sourced ingredients, such as tako-meshi (octopus rice bowl; ¥1230).

Inujima Art House Project
犬島家プロジェクト, Inujima Ie Purojekuto • Inujima • March–Nov Mon & Wed–Sun 10am–4.30pm; Dec–Feb Mon & Fri–Sun 10am–4.30pm • ¥2060 (combined ticket with Seirensho Art Museum and Seaside Inujima Gallery) • ☎ 086 947 1112, ⓦ benesse-artsite.jp

The vibrant **Inujima Art House Project** opened in 2010. Given that Inujima is quite small, the project has taken over the entire village and local residents live among the five Art House galleries and other installation spaces. Of note is Kojin Haruka's *Contact Lens* – which shows distortions of the surrounding environment through different lenses – and Asai Yusuke's *Listen to the Voices of Yesterday Like the Voices of Ancient Times*, an installation built on the site of a former stonecutter's house with stone pillars and painted tribal motifs.

Seaside Inujima Gallery
シーサイド犬島ギャラリー, Shīsaido Inujima Gyararī • Inujima • March–Nov Mon & Wed–Sun 10am–4.30pm; Dec–Feb Mon & Fri–Sun 10am–4.30pm • ¥2060 (combined ticket with Seirensho Art Museum and Inujima Art House Project) • ☎ 086 947 1112, ⓦ benesse-artsite.jp

The most recent of the three Benesse-run sites on the island, the small **Seaside Inujima Gallery** is located inside the Inujima Ticket Center near the port, where an old inn and the gallery's namesake, the *Seaside Inujima*, was once located. It centres on a video installation by visual artist Takahashi Keisuke, where images are projected onto an island of black slag – a nod to the island's copper smelting past.

ARRIVAL AND GETTING AROUND

INUJIMA

By ferry Ferries sail to Inujima port from Miyanoura (¥1850; 45min) and Teshima (¥1200; 25min). There's also a ferry to Inujima from Hoden port in Okayama (¥300; 10min). Timetables are regularly updated on the Benesse website (ⓦ benesse-artsite.jp/en/access).

On foot There's no public transport once you're on the island, so you'll need to walk between the sights.

INFORMATION

Tourist information The Inujima Ticket Center (10am–4pm: March–Nov Mon & Wed–Sun; Dec–Feb Mon, Fri–Sun & public hols; ☎ 086 947 1112, ⓦ benesse-artsite.jp) is on your left as you exit the port. You can buy museum and ferry tickets here, as well as pick up a map to the sites. There's also a small café (daily 10am–4.30pm) and coin lockers.

9

Teshima

豊島

The lush island of **TESHIMA** is home to prosperous fishing and dairy-farming industries. Amid this verdant environment are numerous enchanting art sites – all of which you can see in a single day-trip – located between the island's two ports, Ieura and Karato. Out of all of them, make sure you don't pass up seeing **Teshima Art Museum** and **Teshima Yokoo House**.

Teshima Art Museum

豊島美術館, Teshima Bijutsukan • 607 Karato • March–Sept Mon & Wed–Sun 10am–5pm; Oct & Nov Mon & Wed–Sun 10am–4pm; Dec–Feb Mon & Fri–Sun 10am–4pm • ¥1540 • ☎ 087 968 3555, ⓦ benesse-artsite.jp

The splendid **Teshima Art Museum**, a collaboration between architect **Nishizawa Ryūe** and artist **Naito Rei**, is a concrete shell open to the elements on the edge of a rice terrace. From the outside, the museum looks something like a UFO, and once inside you'll feel even more like you've entered another world. You must take your shoes off to enter the hushed interior space, where small springs of water spontaneously erupt from the floor and then travel around, fascinating visitors who lie all over to observe them. It's recommended that you spend at least thirty minutes sitting here, observing the mobile puddles of water and listening to the wind whistling through the roof openings. The museum's café (same as museum hours) is a smaller version of the museum, with a white-carpeted lounge and glass roof.

Teshima Yokoo House

豊島横尾館 • 2359 Ieura Teshima Yokookan • March–Sept Mon & Wed–Sun 10am–5pm; Oct & Nov Mon & Wed–Sun 10am–4pm; Dec–Feb Mon & Fri–Sun 10am–4pm • ¥510 • ☎ 087 968 3555, ⓦ benesse-artsite.jp

Compared to the serenity of the Teshima Art Museum, the **Teshima Yokoo House** is an abrupt shock of pop culture collage. Exploring the themes of life and death, the house is a collaboration between architect **Nagayama Yuko** and artist **Yokoo Tadanori**, whose works are exhibited throughout. Yokoo's style is eccentric and provocative: a carp pond flows under the perspex floors of the main house; nine-hundred postcards of waterfalls are displayed on the walls of a 14m-high tower; and the amazing "outhouse" installations are definitely worth a look, whether nature calls or not.

ARRIVAL AND INFORMATION
TESHIMA

By ferry Ferries sail to Ieura port from Miyanoura (¥620; 55min), Inujima (¥1230; 25min), Uno (¥770; 25min) and Tonosho (¥770; 35min), as well as to Karato port from Uno (¥1030; 40min) and Tonosho (¥770; 35min). Timetables are regularly updated on the Benesse website (ⓦ benesse-artsite.jp/en/access).

Tourist information The desk in the ferry terminal (Mon & Wed–Sun 9am–5pm; ☎ 087 968 3135) has an English map and guide to the island.

GETTING AROUND

By bus A regular bus (¥200) runs between Ieura's port and Karato, stopping at some art sites and the Teshima Art Museum along the way.

By bike The best way to get around is by bicycle, and you can rent bikes from both Ieura and Karato ports (¥100/1hr). The island is quite hilly, so it's advisable to rent an electric-powered bicycle if possible (¥1000/4hr). The rental shops will also mind your luggage for a small fee (¥300).

Shōdoshima

小豆島

It may not have quite the same idyllic appeal as its smaller Inland Sea neighbours like Naoshima (see p.650) and Teshima (see above), but thanks to its splendid natural scenery and a collection of worthwhile sights, **Shōdoshima** should still be high on any list of places to visit in Shikoku. The mountainous, forested island styles itself as a Mediterranean retreat, and has a whitewashed windmill and mock-Grecian ruins strategically placed amid its terraced olive groves. But local culture also gets a look-in, since Shōdoshima – which translates as "island of small beans" – promotes its own version of Shikoku's 88-temple pilgrimage and its connection with the classic Japanese book and film *Nijūshi-no-Hitomi* (*Twenty-Four Eyes*). This tear-jerking tale of a teacher and her twelve young charges, set on Shōdoshima between the 1920s and 1950s, was written by local author **Tsuboi Sakae**. In recent years, Shōdoshima has become part of the Setouchi Triennale International Art Festival (see box, p.650), and there are now several interesting art installations on the island.

Though most of the main sights can be covered in a day, it's a bit of a rush if you don't have your own transport – in this case, it's better to spend at least one night on the island.

Meiro no Machi
迷路のまち

The town of Tonoshō was originally built during the Edo period in a complicated **maze** (*meiro*) pattern to protect the inhabitants from pirate attack; it was believed that pirates wouldn't enter if they couldn't retreat quickly. The labyrinth of narrow streets, some less than 2m wide, is known as **Meiro no Machi**. Having survived the centuries, the area has an intriguing atmosphere and is worth a wander. There are a considerable number of Taishō and Shōwa-era houses in the streets, some of which have started to be used for the Setouchi Triennale International Art Festival (see box, p.650). Check the festival information office for details of the latest exhibitions.

Olive-kōen
オリーブ公園 • Park & museum daily 8.30am–5pm • Free; onsen ¥700 • ☎ 087 982 2200, ⓦ olive-pk.jp

Along the main Highway 436 heading east from Tonoshō and around the south of Shōdoshima lies **Olive-kōen**, a pleasant but touristy hillside park of olive groves and fake Grecian ruins where, among other things, you can buy green-olive chocolate or take an onsen bath followed by a moisturizing session with olive-oil creams. There's also an interesting small **museum** in the park that explains the history of olive growing on the island.

Nijūshi no Hitomi Eigamura
二十四の瞳映画村 • Tanoura • Daily 9am–5pm • ¥830 (including entry to the old school in Tanoura) • ☎ 087 982 2455, ⓦ 24hitomi.or.jp

Just a little further along the southern coast of Shōdoshima than Olive-kōen is **Nijūshi no Hitomi Eigamura**, a mini-theme park dedicated to the 1954 film *Twenty-Four Eyes*. This fake village, which was used in the 1980s remake, has some charming old buildings. If you're not familiar with the film, you can watch it on site. Also in the park you'll find a museum dedicated to the prolific author Tsuboi Sakae, best known for the novel on which the film was based, and the very stylish *Café Shinema Kurabu*, which is a good place for lunch and part of a display devoted to classic Japanese films of the 1950s and 1960s. Just before reaching Eigamura, as you come along the road from Sakate, is the rustic fishing village of **Tanoura** (田の浦), where the original schoolhouse that served as an inspiration for the book is also open to visitors (daily 9am–5pm; ¥220).

Yamaroku
ヤマロク醤油, Yamaroku shōyu • 1607 Yasuda-ko • Daily 9am–5pm • Free • ☎ 087 982 0666, ⓦ yama-roku.net

Scattered around the southeastern part of Shōdoshima, between Eigamura and the youth hostel, you'll find several **soy sauce** factories, the most worthwhile of which is **Yamaroku**. Here, each batch of the local sauce is fermented for two years in hundred-year-old, 2m-high wooden barrels, and carefully watched over by a fifth-generation soy master. The staff don't speak much English, but are happy to show you around and let you climb up and peer into the pungent, bacteria-coated barrels. They also have a small souvenir shop where you can sample their different sauces.

9

By boat and ferry Shōdoshima is best reached with ferries from Takamatsu (1hr 15min; ¥690) or with the high-speed boats (30min; ¥1140) that depart daily for several ports on the island. If you're coming from Honshū, there are also ferries from Himeji (1hr 40min; ¥1520), Hinase (1hr; ¥1030), Okayama (1hr 10min; ¥1050) and Uno (1hr 30min; ¥1230). The island's main port of Tonoshō, on the west coast, is served by the most services. If you intend to stay at the youth hostel (see below), take a ferry from Takamatsu to Kusakabe (1hr; ¥690).

Tourist information There's a helpful tourist information desk (daily 9am–5pm; ☏ 087 962 0649) inside Tonoshō's ferry terminal, but if you're coming from Takamatsu, you can easily pick up information on the island from the tourist information centre there (see p.640).

GETTING AROUND

By bus Buses for main sights around the island depart from the terminal next to the Tonoshō port building. Here you can buy a one-day ticket for ¥1000 or a two-day ticket for ¥1500 – only worthwhile if you intend to do a lot of sightseeing by bus. Note that the frequency of the bus services changes seasonally, and some routes around the island don't operate in Jan, Feb or June; check with the tourist information desk before setting off.

By bike Rental bicycles are available at both Tonoshō port, where the high-speed passenger boats arrive (from ¥500; daily 10am–5.30pm; ☏ 087 962 0162), and also the youth hostel (¥200/day). For scooters, try Ishii Rent-a-Bike on Olive-dōri (☏ 087 962 1866).

By car Based at the port, Orix Rent-A-Car (☏ 087 962 4669) is worth checking out if you'd like to rent a car.

ACCOMMODATION AND EATING

Tonoshō offers plenty of business and tourist hotels that charge around ¥8000 per person, including two meals. Shōdoshima doesn't have many good places to eat, so it's best to plan on having dinner and breakfast at your hotel.

Business Minshuku Maruse ビジネス民宿マルセ Tonoshōchō-kō ☏ 087 962 2385, ⓦ new-port.biz. This is a small, clean minshuku with Japanese- and Western-style rooms and a coin laundry for guests. A Japanese-style breakfast is an extra ¥600, and dinner can be arranged in advance for ¥930–1980. **¥7780**

Celeste Shodōshima チェレステ小豆島 1462 Kashima-kō ☏ 087 962 5015, ⓦ celesteshodoshima .com. This is a smart hotel with spacious, well-appointed Japanese-style rooms with excellent views of the bay and "Angel Road", a slinky sandbar linking three tiny islands. Rates include meals in the hotel's Italian restaurant, and there's also an in-house art gallery and rooftop jacuzzi. ⬚ **¥36,000**

New Port ニューポート Tonoshōchō-kō ☏ 087 962 4620, ⓦ new-port.biz. This is a friendly business hotel run by the same management as *Business Minshuku Maruse*. You'll find Japanese- and Western-style rooms with private bathrooms and TVs. Japanese-style breakfasts cost an additional ¥600, and dinner can also be arranged in advance. ⬚ **¥7960**

Shōdoshima International Hotel 小豆島国際ホテル 24-67 Tonoshōchō-kō ☏ 087 962 2111, ⓦ shodoshima -kh.jp. This is a big, resort-style hotel in a beautiful location on the south side of Tonoshō, next to "Angel Road". Rooms are quite luxurious, and if you aren't lucky enough to get your own outdoor onsen bath, you can always use the hotel's own spa. ⬚ **¥32,400**

Shōdoshima Olive Youth Hostel 小豆島オーリブユー スホステル 1072 Nishimura ☏ 087 982 6161, ⓦ shodoshima-oliveyh-en.tumblr.com. Just a 10min walk west of Kusakabe port, this hostel has clean dorms and private tatami rooms for two. The friendly, English-speaking manager whips up a good *teishoku* dinner (set meal including a main dish, rice, miso soup and pickles ¥1080), and a filling breakfast for ¥648. ⬚ Dorms **¥3948**

Tokushima

徳島

Built on the delta of the Yoshino-gawa – Shikoku's longest river – and bisected by the Shinmachi-gawa, **TOKUSHIMA**, the capital of Tokushima-ken, is known across Japan for its fantastic summer dance festival, the Awa Odori, which is attended every year by over a million people (see box opposite). If you're not among them, then don't worry, as Tokushima does its best to provide a flavour of the Awa Odori experience year-round at the Awa Odori Kaikan, at the foot of Mount Bizan, a parkland area providing sweeping views of the city.

THE DANCING FOOLS

Every year in mid-August, many Japanese return to their family homes for **Obon** (Festival of the Dead), which is as much a celebration as a remembrance of the deceased. Towns all over the country hold *bon* dances, but none can compare to Tokushima's **Awa Odori** – the "Great Dance of Awa" – a four-day festival that runs every year from August 12 to 15. Over a million spectators come to watch the eighty-thousand participants, dressed in colourful *yukata* (summer kimono) and half-moon-shaped straw hats, who parade through the city, waving their hands and tapping their feet to an incessant two-beat rhythm, played on *taiko* drums, flutes and *shamisen* (traditional stringed instruments). With plenty of **street parties** and sideshows, this is as close as Japan gets to Rio's Carnival, and there's plenty of fun to be had mingling with the dancers, who famously chant, "The dancing fool and the watching fool are equally foolish. So why not dance?"

If you plan to attend the festival, book **accommodation** well in advance or arrange to stay in one of the nearby towns and travel in for the dances, which start at 6pm and finish at 10.30pm (though street parties continue well into the night). To take part as a dancer, contact the Tokushima International Association or Tokushima Prefecture International Exchange Association (see p.661), who organize dance groups on one of the festival nights.

Home to the first temple of the Shikoku pilgrimage (see box, p.636), Tokushima has a long history of welcoming visitors, and you'll find it a noticeably friendly and relaxed place, as well as a good base from which to explore the rest of the prefecture. The city's sights are all within easy walking distance of Clement Plaza mall.

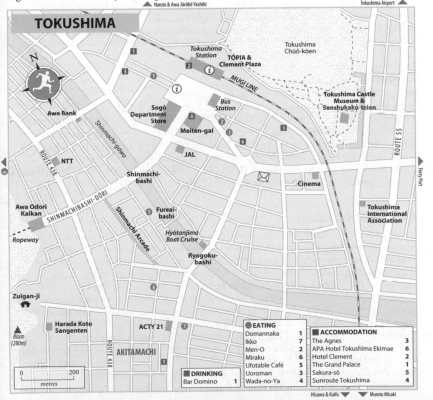

9

Bizan

眉山 • **Ropeway** Daily: April–Oct 9am–9pm; Nov–March 9am–5.30pm • One-way ¥610, return ¥1020 • If you take the ropeway, the entrance to the station is on the fifth floor of the Awa Odori Kaikan (see below)

On a clear day, it's worth ascending the 280m-high **Bizan** for the panoramic views, and it's not too difficult a hike if you want to save on the ropeway fee or fancy the exercise; a route starts from the temple to the left of the *kaikan* (hall) at the end of Shinmachibashi-dōri. At the summit, there's an observatory with telescopes and an outdoor observation deck, a park with a stupa, called **Tokushima Pagoda** in memory of the Japanese soldiers who served in Myanmar (Burma) during World War II, and **Kenzan-jinja**, a small and unremarkable shrine dedicated to the *kami* (gods) of the mountain. Of more interest is **Mayuhana-kyo** ("eyebrow mirror"), a 6m-high kaleidoscopic monument of light and colour made up of 4100 LED lights which can be viewed daily from sunset to 10.30pm.

Awa Odori Kaikan

阿波踊り会館 • 2-20 Shinmachi-bashi, Higashi Yamate • **Complex** Daily 9am–9pm Free • **Museum** Daily 9am–5pm • ¥300 **Awa Odori Hall Performances** Mon–Fri 2pm, 3pm, 4pm & 8pm, Sat & Sun also 11am • Day dance performance ¥600; evening dance performance ¥800; combined ticket for day dance performance, museum and ropeway ¥1620; combined ticket for just museum and day dance performance ¥800 ☎ 088 611 1611, ⓦ awaodori-kaikan.jp

Five minutes' walk south of the river, at the base of Bizan, is the **Awa Odori Kaikan**. The complex is dedicated to the city's famous dance (see box, p.659) and houses a good souvenir shop on the ground floor, a **ropeway** on the fifth floor that goes to the top of Bizan (see above), a museum dedicated to the history of the dance on the third floor, and the **Awa Odori Hall**, where there are at least four live dance performances daily. The daytime performances are explanatory and highly interactive – don't be surprised if you end up on stage – and the evening performances showcase Tokushima's most distinguished dance troupes.

Zuigan-ji

瑞巌寺 • 3-18 Higashi Yamate-chō • Daily 8am–5pm • Free • ☎ 088 652 5968

Walk east around the base of Bizan and you'll come to the delightful Buddhist temple **Zuigan-ji**. Built in the Momoyama style, Zuigan-ji dates from 1614 and has an elegant traditional garden with carp-filled pools, a waterfall and rock paths across mossy lawns leading up to a picturesque red pagoda. Look out for one of the lamps in the garden – it had the image of the Virgin Mary engraved on it during the Edo period, when Christianity was forbidden in Japan. While here, drop by the small music shop, Harada Koto Sangenten (daily 10am–6pm; ☎ 088 652 5625).

Awa Jūrōbē Yashiki

阿波十郎兵衛屋敷 • 184 Miyajima Motoura, Kawauchi-chō (4km north of Tokushima Station) • Daily 9.30am–5pm; check website for performance times • ¥410 • ☎ 088 665 2202, ⓦ joruri.info/jurobe • A 25min bus journey from stop number 7 at the bus terminal

Traditional Japanese puppetry, *bunraku*, is a highly skilled performance art which takes years of training to master, and it's one of Tokushima's enduring traditions. At the historic premises of the Jūrōbē family, **Awa Jūrōbē Yashiki**, you can immerse yourself in the world of *ningyō jōruri*, as it's called locally. This former samurai residence, with an enclosed garden and display room of beautifully made antique puppets, was once the home of the tragic figure Jūrōbē, who was immortalized in *Keisei Awa no Naruto*, the epic eighteenth-century play by Chikamatsu. The theatre has recently been completely rebuilt in the traditional manner, and you can see part of the play performed here, usually the classic scene where Jūrōbē's wife, Oyumi, turns away their daughter Otsuru as a stranger. Live performances are held regularly, and a video of the play is also shown inside a large tatami hall. The theatre staff are welcoming and there's a helpful English pamphlet.

HYŌTANJIMA BOAT CRUISE

Central Tokushima city is encircled by two rivers, the Shinmachi-gawa and the Suketo-gawa, in the shape of a hyōtan, or gourd. A relaxing thirty-minute **Hyōtanjima Boat Cruise** (ひょうたん島クルーズ; July & Aug daily 11am–3.40am & 5–7.40pm, Sept–June daily 11am–3.40pm; every 40min (or every 15min from 9am–10pm during Awa Odori festival); ¥200; ☎088 621 5232) takes in all **fifteen bridges** that connect this urban island, called Hyōtanjima, to the rest of the city, and some of them are decorated with sculptures and art related to Awa Odori. The cruises leave from the boathouse in front of the Shinmachi-gawa Riverside Park (新町川公園), at the northern end of the Ryōgoku-bashi (両国橋).

Tokushima Chūō-kōen

徳島中央公園 • **Senshūkaku-teien** 千秋閣庭園 Tues–Sun 9am–5pm • ¥50 • **Tokushima Castle Museum** 徳島城博物館
Tues–Sun 9am–5pm • ¥300 • ☎088 656 2525 • A 5min walk east of the JR station

The attractive park of **Tokushima Chūō-kōen** lies on the site of *daimyō* Hachisuka Iemasa's fortress. From 1586, Hachisuka's clan lived in the castle for 280 years, creating the town that is now Tokushima. All that remains of the castle, which was destroyed in 1896, are a few stone walls, part of the moat and the **Senshūkaku-teien**, a beautiful formal garden. Beside the garden is the small **Tokushima Castle Museum**, with informative, modern displays explaining the history of the Hachisuka clan and a large model that gives a good idea of what the fortress and its surrounding compound once looked like.

ARRIVAL AND DEPARTURE   TOKUSHIMA

By plane Tokushima's domestic airport (☎088 699 2831, ⓦtokushima-airport.co.jp) lies 12km north of the city centre; there are buses from here to Clement Plaza (30min; ¥440).
Destinations Fukuoka (daily; 1hr 15min); Tokyo (11 daily; 1hr 15min).

By train Trains pull in at JR Tokushima Station, next to the Clement Plaza shopping centre, at the head of Shinmachibashi-dori, the main thoroughfare.
Destinations Awa Ikeda (6 daily; 1hr 20min); Kaifu (3 daily; 1hr 40min); Naruto (14 daily; 40min); Takamatsu (17 daily; 1hr).

By bus Long-distance buses come and go from the bus station in front of the JR train station.
Destinations Awaji-shima (4 daily; 45min); Matsuyama (7 daily; 3hr 10min); Osaka (every 30min; 2hr 40min); Takamatsu (12 daily; 1hr 35min); Tokyo (3 daily; 10hr 40min).

By ferry Ferries arrive at Tokushima port, 3km east of the centre.
Destinations Kita-Kyūshū/Kokura (daily; 17hr); Tokyo (daily; 17hr 30min); Wakayama (8 daily; hydrofoil 1hr, ferry 2hr).

By car Eki Rent-a-Car (☎088 622 1014) is situated in front of Tokushima Station, while Nippon Rent-a-Car (☎088 699 6170) is at the airport.

INFORMATION

Tourist information Although there is a tourist information booth outside Clement Plaza, it's better to go to Tokushima Prefecture International Exchange Association (TOPIA) on the plaza's sixth floor (daily 10am–6pm; ☎088 656 3303, ⓦtopia.ne.jp), as the English-speaking staff are more helpful. There's also a small library of English books and

magazines there, as well as free wi-fi and computer terminals with internet access. The Tokushima International Association (Mon–Fri 10am–5.30pm; ☎088 622 6066, ⓦtia81.com), one block beyond the city hall to the east of the JR station, offers similar services. For longer-term visitors, both facilities offer Japanese classes.

ACCOMMODATION

Tokushima has a decent range of **accommodation**, most of it of a high standard and conveniently located around the JR station. Book well in advance if you plan to visit during the Awa Odori in August. If you're having problems finding somewhere to stay, pop into TOPIA (see above), as the staff can make enquiries for you.

★**The Agnes** アグネスホテル徳島 1-28 Terashima Honchō Nishi ☎088 626 2222, ⓦagneshotel.jp. West of the JR station, this hip, monochrome hotel has decent-sized, well-equipped rooms and a trendy patisserie on the

ground floor. The in-house café is open from breakfast until late evening serving sandwiches, pasta and other Western-style food. There's also a coin laundry. ⬚ **¥19,444**
APA Hotel Tokushima Ekimae アパホテル徳島駅前

9

2-21 Ichibanchō ☎088 655 5005, ⓦapahotel.com. You'll find tiny but clean rooms at this convenient and modern business hotel. Rates are lower for online bookings and eco-plans (room cleaning every second day). Breakfast is extra (continental ¥380, Japanese ¥680), but there are non-smoking rooms. 🛜 **¥6667**

Hotel Clement ホテルクルメント徳島 1-61 Terashima Honchō Nishi ☎088 656 3111, ⓦhotelclement.co.jp. Upmarket hotel next to the station with spacious, tastefully furnished rooms and polite, friendly staff. There's an eighteenth-floor bar and Japanese restaurant with a fabulous view of Bizan, as well as an in-house spa. 🛜 **¥15,444**

The Grand Palace ザ・グランドパレス 1-60-1 Terashima Honchō Nishi ☎088 626 1111, ⓦgphotel.jp. Going for the shiny and sleek black look in a big way, this boutiquish hotel offers larger than average rooms, with very comfortable beds, as well as an excellent breakfast buffet.

The staff don't speak much English, but they do make an effort to ensure your stay is enjoyable. 🛜 **¥7350**

Sakura-sō さくら荘 1-25-1 Terashima Honchō Higashi ☎088 652 9575. Don't be put off by the drab exterior – this minshuku is the best budget choice in Tokushima and is conveniently located a few blocks east of the station. It has simple but clean and spacious tatami rooms, with shared bathing facilities. The friendly owner speaks a little English and is very welcoming. **¥6600**

★Sunroute Tokushima サンルート徳島 1-5-1 Motomachi ☎088 653 8111, ⓦsunroute-tokushima.com. The reception for this slick, modern hotel is on the third floor of the Meiten-gai block, directly opposite Tokushima Station. The comfortable rooms are decorated in monochrome hues and each comes equipped with its own computer. There's also free access to the rooftop onsen bath, jacuzzi and sauna (¥520/¥720 for non-guests). 🛜 **¥11,000**

EATING

★Domannaka どまん中 1-47 Honmachi Nishi ☎088 623 3293, ⓦwa-domannaka.jp. This stylish *izakaya* serves delicious local fish, chicken and vegetarian cuisine (English menu available). There are grilled dishes such as *yakitori* (from ¥160) and *robata-yaki* (from ¥430), as well as sashimi platters (from ¥1580) and *nabe* hotpots. The hearty chicken and dumpling *nabe* for two (¥1050) is especially tasty. Mon–Thurs 11.30am–2pm & 5–10pm, Fri & Sat 5–10pm.

★Ikko 一鴻 2F Acty Annex ☎088 623 2311, ⓦi-kko .com. *Ikko* is the place to go to fully sample all the different ways Tokushima's famous Awa-Odori brand of chicken can be cooked. Specializing in *honetsuki-dori* (chicken on the bone) cuisine, you can enjoy superbly grilled chicken breasts (¥1280) or chicken sashimi (¥790) with a fresh salad of locally grown vegetables (¥580). Wash it all down with a draught beer (¥520) or locally brewed *sudachi-shu*, which is a kind of citrus vodka (¥580). Daily 5–11.30pm.

Men-O 麺王 240-1 Kawauchi-chō ☎088 623 4116, ⓦ7-men.com. Arrive here early to sample Tokushima ramen, because the queues are often out the door and along the street. This local ramen style is distinguished by noodles in a salty-sweet pork belly soup and topped with roast pork and a raw egg. Regular bowls are ¥480 – you can buy a ticket from the vending machine at the entrance. Daily 11am–midnight.

Miraku 味楽 1-20 Tomita-chō ☎088 655 1530, ⓦmiraku.jp. At this up-market barbecue restaurant grills a range of meat dishes at the table using charcoal,

including the local Awa pork that's known for being sweet and juicy. *Nabe* dishes are also on the menu, and the pork *shabu-shabu* (¥2700) comes highly recommended. Draught beer is ¥500 and glasses of *shōchū* start at ¥450. Daily 5–10pm.

Ufotable Café ユーフォーテーブルカフェ 1-13 Higashi Senba-chō ☎088 655 8805. Produced by animation studio Ufotable, this theme café is a popular hangout among Tokushima's anime fans, and there are original drawings from the studio's artists on the walls. There's a regular menu that includes dishes such as Thai curry and pork *donburi* (¥850), though there are also special menus made up for regular events inspired by anime titles and characters. Tues–Sun 11.30am–11pm.

★Uoroman 魚貝のビストロUOROMAN 2-15 Ichiban-chō ☎088 623 3917, ⓦtokushimaekimae -uoroman.owst.jp. Just a stone's throw from the station, this spacious, two-storey Italian seafood restaurant brings in the crowds. It has a very extensive range of wines that are listed by country (¥2600 per bottle), and the signature dish, a plate of raw *uni* (sea urchin) wrapped in succulent strips of *hon-maguro*, is very reasonably priced at ¥1200. Daily 5pm–12.30am.

Wada-no-Ya 和田の屋 5-3 Otakiyama ☎088 652 8414, ⓦwadanoya.com. This is a delightful teahouse at the foot of Bizan with a view onto a rock garden. *Matcha* and Tokushima's signature *yaki-mochi* (small, lightly toasted patties of pounded rice and red beans) cost ¥650. There's also a small branch in the Awa Odori Kaikan. Mon–Wed & Fri–Sun 10am–5pm.

DRINKING

Tokushima has no shortage of **bars**, with the densest concentration in Akitamachi, Tokushima's lively entertainment area. Rooftop beer gardens open during the summer at several hotels, including the *Hotel Clement* (see above).

Bar Domino どみの 1-33 Akitamachi ☎088 655 6556. This sophisticated and intimate mood-lit cocktail and whisky bar is located in a 50-year-old traditional house with a modern interior. Cocktails are priced from ¥800, whisky shots from ¥1000, and the snack menu includes pizza (¥900) and fried octopus (¥700). You can opt for counter or table seating. Daily 7pm–4am.

DIRECTORY

Hospital Tokushima Prefectural Central Hospital (Kenritsu Chūō Byōin), 1-10-3 Kuramoto-chō ☎088 631 7151.
Laundry There's a Laundry Queen at 1-19-1 Ryogoku Honmachi, open 24 hours.
Police The main police station is close to Kachidoki-bashi

☎088 622 3101. Emergency numbers are listed on p.71.
Post office The Central Post Office is just south of the JR station at 1-2 Yaoya-chō (Mon–Fri 9am–7pm, Sat 9am–5pm & Sun 9am–12.30pm).

Around Tokushima

North of Tokushima are the whirlpools of **Naruto**, and to the south there are popular surf beaches, the pretty coastal village of **Hiwasa** (where turtles lay their eggs on the beach each summer) and the jagged cape at **Muroto**, across the border in Kōchi-ken. Inland, the best place to head is the spectacular **Iya Valley**, where you'll find the river gorge at **Ōboke**.

Naruto Whirlpools

鳴門・**Cruise boats** Daily 9am–4.20pm; around 30min・¥1800 (¥2800 for first-class cabin)・☎088 687 0101, ⓦuzusio.com・
Uzu-no-Michi walkway 渦の道・Daily: March–Sept 9am–6pm (last admission 5.30pm); Oct–Feb 9am–5pm (last admission 4.30pm); Golden Week & summer holidays 8am–6.30pm・¥510・ⓦuzunomichi.jp・Take the regular direct bus from Clement Plaza (around 1hr 20min; ¥690)

The 88-temple pilgrimage (see box, p.636) begins in Shikoku at **NARUTO**, around 13km north of Tokushima. However, the town is most famous for the **whirlpools** that form nearby as the tides change and water is forced through the narrow straits between Shikoku and Awajishima. This is one of Tokushima's most heavily hyped attractions, but it's not a reliable phenomenon. The whirlpools are at their most dramatic on days of the full and new moon; to avoid a wasted journey, check first on the tidal schedule with tourist information in Tokushima (see p.661) or the timetables on the Uzusio website (ⓦuzusio.com/en/siomi).

One way to see the whirlpools up close is to hop on a tourist cruise boat from Kameura-ko. There are two options for viewing the whirlpools on foot: you can traverse the **Uzu-no-Michi**, a walkway under Naruto's bridge that puts you 45m directly above the maelstrom, or go for the cheaper alternative – a bird's-eye view from Naruto-kōen, the park on Oge Island just to the north of Naruto town.

Hiwasa

日和佐
Picturesque **HIWASA**, 55km south of Tokushima, is worth a visit for its intriguing temple, castle, quaint harbour and pretty beach. Facing the Pacific Ocean, the coast around it offers some of the best surfing spots in Japan, and attracts wave-seekers all year round. From November to February, it's also a well-known spot for viewing the sunrise as it emerges from across the ocean.

Yakuō-ji

薬王寺・285-1 Okugawauchi Teramae・Pagoda basement ¥100・☎088 477 0023, ⓦyakuouji.net
Yakuō-ji, the 23rd temple on the Shikoku pilgrimage, is on the hillside as you pull into Hiwasa train station. It's particularly popular as a temple, as it's claimed to have

SURFING AROUND HIWASA

Big waves and warm currents from the Pacific make the southern part of Tokushima prefecture one of the best places for surfing in western Japan. The popular surfing spot of **Kaifu** (海部), 26km south of Hiwasa, is where the JR train line ends and is replaced with the private Asa Kaigan railway. To continue south, you'll nearly always have to change trains here – simply cross over to the opposite platform. There's a ¥270 extra charge to travel the remaining two stops – the first is **Shishikui** (宍喰), Tokushima's top surf beach, where there's a good range of accommodation and surf shops that rent out boards (from ¥2000 per day). The end of the line is **Kannoura** (甲浦), a sleepy village with another popular surfing beach, **Ikumi** (生見), located just over the border in Kōchi prefecture. If you're travelling from further afield, an express bus also departs from Osaka (Nankai Namba Station) directly for Shishikui (4–5hr ¥5200 one-way, ¥9100 return), which can be boarded at Tokushima and other locations along the route.

powers to ward off bad luck. Climbing the steps to the main temple, you won't fail to notice lots of ¥1 coins on the ground: some pilgrims place a coin on each step for luck as they head up. At the top of the steps is the main temple area, where the buildings date from 815 and there's a striking statue of a goddess carrying a basket of fish and flanked by lotus blooms. Off to the right is a more recently built single-storey **pagoda**. There's a good view of Hiwasa's harbour from the platform, but the highlight here is the descent into the pagoda's darkened basement, where you can fumble your way around a pitch-black circular corridor to a central gallery containing Brueghel-like painted depictions of all the tortures of hell. In a second gallery is a creepy scroll showing the steady decay of a beautiful, but dead, young woman.

Hiwasa-jō

日和佐城 • 445-1 Hiwasaura • Daily 10am–4pm • ☎ 088 477 1166

About 1km south of Hiwasa harbour, the reconstructed castle **Hiwasa-jō** sits atop Shiroyama and has impressive views of the town and coastline. Aside from that, there's not a lot to see on display, but the grounds are very pleasant during March and April when the cherry blossoms bloom.

Sea Turtle Museum

うみがめ博物館カレッタ, Umigame Hakubutsukan Karetta • 374-4 Hiwasaura • Tues–Sun 9am–5pm • ¥600 • ☎ 088 477 1110

Turtles lay their eggs between May and August at **Ōhama beach** (大浜), north of the harbour. During this time, the beach is roped off and spectators must watch the action from a distance. For a closer look, make your way to the **Sea Turtle Museum** beside the beach. The displays here are mainly in Japanese, but they depict step-by-step photos of turtles laying their eggs. You can also see some turtles swimming in indoor and outdoor pools. In mid-July, there's a turtle festival involving ceremonies on Ōhama beach, as well as some events at the museum.

ARRIVAL AND INFORMATION   HIWASA

By train Limited express (56min; ¥2590) and local trains (1hr 36min; ¥1090) link Hiwasa to Tokushima daily.

Tourist information There's a left-luggage service (¥200 per bag) at the small tourist information office at the Hiwasa station (daily 10am–3pm; ☎ 088 477 0768), where

you can also pick up an English map of the town. There is also a tourist information desk (Mon–Fri 9am–6pm, Sat & Sun 9am–7pm; ☎ 088 477 2121) in the Michi-no-eki rest stop on the other side of the station, which also has a free wi-fi spot.

GETTING AROUND

By bike Renting a bicycle for the day is a good idea, as the town's sights are quite spread out. The tourist information

desk at the Michi-no-eki rest stop (see above) rents bicycles for ¥500 per day, though they have to be returned by 5pm.

ACCOMMODATION

Business Hotel Cairns ビジネスホテルケアンズ 75-16 Okugawauchi Benzaiten ☎088 477 1211, ⚓hotel-cairns.net. This no-frills business hotel is conveniently located right across from the station – particularly useful if you arrive in Hiwasa late in the day. It's clean and friendly, but facilities are minimal. All rooms have futons on tatami platforms. **¥8500**

Umigamesō うみがめ荘 370 Hiwasaura ☎088 477 1166, ⚓umigamesou.com. This large minshuku is close to the Sea Turtle Museum and beach, with tatami-style rooms. Guests use the public bath, which has stunning sea views. If you want to eat dinner or breakfast here (which is not included in the room price) you must reserve in advance. 📶 **¥8000**

White Lighthouse ホテル白い燈台 455 Hiwasaura ☎088 477 1170, ⚓shiroitodai.jp. Situated on the edge of a rocky cliff, this is the most scenic place to stay in Hiwasa. Choose from Western- or Japanese-style rooms, all with gorgeous ocean views. Rates include two meals, such as the beautifully presented seafood dinner. **¥12,960**

EATING

Hiwasaya ひわさ屋 122 Okugawauchi Teramae ☎088 477 3528. This popular restaurant is a good lunch spot and serves a variety of chicken dishes. The tasty *oyakodon* ("parent-and-child bowl"), a serving of rice topped with soy-sauce-flavoured chicken and egg (¥1000), is highly recommended. Mon, Tues & Thurs–Sun 11.30am–1.30pm & 5.30–9pm.

Murakami むらかみ 68-1 Okugawauchi Benzaiten ☎088 477 0083. *Murakami* serves locally fished *aori-ika* (reef squid). The super-fresh sashimi on rice *aori-ika-don* sets, served with soup and pickles, are great value at ¥1500. Mon & Wed–Sun 11.30am–2.30pm & 5–9pm.

Muroto Misaki

室戸岬

From Kannoura, buses continue south to the black-sand beaches and rugged cape of **MUROTO MISAKI**, an important stop on the pilgrimage route. On the way, look out for **Meotoiwa** (夫婦岩) – two huge rocky outcrops between which a ceremonial rope has been strung, creating a natural shrine. Virtually at the cape, a towering white **statue of Kōbō Daishi** commemorates the spot where the priest gained enlightenment when he had a vision of the Buddhist deity Kokūzō in a nearby cavern.

Apart from bathing in deep-sea water at **Searest Muroto**, there's not much else to do at Muroto Misaki other than take in the spectacular views and follow a series of paths along the shore and up the mountainside to the rustic temple.

Searest Muroto

シレストむろと • 3795-1 Muroto Misaki-chō • Daily except every second Wed 10am–9pm • ¥1300 • ☎ 088 22 6610, ⚓searest.co.jp

In recent years, Muroto Misaki has attracted pilgrims of a different ilk to those hiking the *henro* trail. Here, unusual currents off the cape push mineral-rich seawater from as deep as 1000m closer to the surface. Near the Kōbō Daishi statue, this deep-sea water is pumped into **Searest Muroto**, a state-of-the-art bathing complex where you can choose to be pummelled by high-pressure water jets, relax in a spa bath or follow a workout video on a pool-side touch-controlled screen.

Hotsumisaki-ji

最御崎寺 • 4058-1 Muroto Misaki-chō • 24hr • Free

Pilgrims pay their respects at the Kōbō Daishi statue before tackling the steep climb up to the glade of lush vegetation swaddling **Hotsumisaki-ji**. The appealingly shabby Buddhist temple, known locally as **Higashi-dera** (East Temple), is the 24th on the pilgrimage circuit.

ARRIVAL AND INFORMATION   MUROTO MISAKI

By train and bus Most trains run to Nahari all the way from Kōchi, though the Kōchi-to-Gomen stretch is on the JR lines. From Nahari, you can take a local bus, which runs hourly, to get to the cape (1hr; ¥1200). With an early start from Tokushima, it's also possible to visit the cape and make it all the way to Kōchi in a day (and vice versa), but you should allow two days if you plan to linger at any point along the route. If you are coming from Tokushima, you'll have to take a bus (¥1470) from Kannoura Station, where the Asa Kaigan line ends.

Tourist information The Muroto Geopark Information Centre (daily 8.30am–5pm; ☎ 088 722 5161, ⓦ muroto -geo.jp) has maps in English and will be able to assist if you're stuck for somewhere to stay.

ACCOMMODATION

Hoshino Resort Utoco Auberge & Spa 星野リゾートウトコオーベルジュ＆スパ 6969-1 Muroto Misaki-chō ☎ 057 007 3022, ⓦ utocods.co.jp. This hotel and spa resort, next door to Searest Muroto, is housed in a series of striking circular buildings. English-speaking staff glide around in white coats, administering high-end beauty treatments designed by the renowned Japanese cosmetics artist Shu Uemura (packages from ¥14,000). The attached hotel has seventeen chic rooms, all with unimpeded views of the Pacific. You can dine on local seafood at the hotel's classy Italian *Auberge* restaurant, where a set lunch starts at ¥1500. 🛜 **¥46,000**

Hotsumisaki-ji Youth Hostel 最御崎寺ユースホステル 4058-1 Muroto Misaka-chō ☎ 088 23 0024. Just behind Hotsumisaki-ji, this friendly temple-lodging facility offers spacious, clean tatami and Western rooms with separate bathrooms. The food here is excellent and guests are served a hearty breakfast and dinner, but you must order your meals when you book. **¥7000**

Ōboke Gorge and Iya Valley

大歩危・祖谷

Inland from Tokushima, Highway 192 shadows the JR Tokushima line for around 70km to the railway junction at **Awa Ikeda** (阿波池田), which is also easily reached from Kotohira (see p.645). From Awa Ikeda, the road and railway enter the spectacular **Ōboke Gorge**, created by the sparkling Yoshino-gawa. The vertiginous mountains here and around the adjacent **Iya Valley** can be coated in snow during the winter – a stark contrast, considering the palms of Kōchi sway in the sunshine around an hour's drive south.

It was this sense of remoteness from the rest of the island that made the gorge an ideal bolt hole for the Taira clan in 1185, following their defeat at Yashima. Here, the warriors traded their swords for farm implements and built distinctive thatch-roofed cottages on the steep mountainsides. Decades of ugly construction projects and depopulation have since disrupted this traditional lifestyle, but there is a growing awareness of the importance of conserving Iya's cultural heritage. Deep in the mountainous heart of Shikoku, the valley continues to retain a special atmosphere, and is often referred to as the Tibet of Japan.

Chiiori

篪庵・209 Tsurui Higashi Iya・Day visit by appointment only・¥500・☎ 088 388 5290, ⓦ chiiori.org

High up in the Iya Valley, in the village of **Tsurui** (釣井), is a beautifully restored 300-year-old thatched cottage called **Chiiori**, meaning the "house of the flute". The story of how American writer **Alex Kerr** saved Chiiori from the elements and spent decades restoring it is an unforgettable part of his award-winning book, *Lost Japan* (see p.863). The cottage retains the traditional features seen in Iya architecture, such as wooden floors and an *irori* sunken hearth, and has been decorated using traditional Japanese crafts and design. A modern kitchen and bathroom have also been recently installed, and the overall result is exceptional.

As part of Kerr's vision to revive rural areas through sustainable tourism based on **cultural heritage**, it's possible to stay at Chiiori (see p.668). Getting away from the noise, clutter and pollution of contemporary urban life in such an idyllic retreat, where you can enjoy broad views out across the misty valleys, is a memorable experience. The Chiiori Trust is also helping to restore other **thatched cottages** in the area, and eight of these are now available to visitors for short-term stays – see ⓦ tougenkyo-iya.jp for more details.

Roadside Station Lapis Ōboke Stone Museum

道の駅大歩危石の博物館, Michi no Eki Ōbake Ishi no Hakubutsukan・1553-1 Kamimyo Yamashiro-chō・March–Nov daily 9am–5pm; Dec–Feb Tues–Sun 9am–5pm・¥500・☎ 088 384 489, ⓦ yamashiro-info.jp/lapis

To learn more about the area's geology, pop into the **Roadside Station Lapis Ōboke Stone Museum** across the river and about 1km north from Ōboke Station. Inside, there's a model of the gorge and all manner of stones, including a meteorite from Mars and various glittering gems. It also doubles as a **tourist information centre**, and you can pick up pamphlets in English. The museum also recently added a colourful *yōkai* ("ghost") exhibition, featuring all the goblins that are said to exist in the area.

Iya Onsen

祖谷温泉 • Old Route 32, between the Iya-guchi and Nishi Iya junctions • Daily 7.30am–5pm • ¥1700; free if you're staying at the *Iya Onsen* hotel • ☎ 088 375 2311, ⊛ iyaonsen.co.jp

If you've been cycling up and down Iya's valleys or whitewater rafting (see box, p.668), then you'll want to relax your tired muscles in the soothing waters of **Iya Onsen**. Guests take a short funicular train ride down a ravine to the hot spring right beside the river, which offers panoramic views across the valley. Don't be put off if the water is murky white – it's just proof that it's loaded with minerals.

Iya no Kazura-bashi

祖谷のかずら橋 • 162-2 Zentoku Nishi Iya • Daily 7am–9pm • ¥550 • ☎ 0120 404 344, ⊛ miyoshinavi.jp

At **Nishi Iya** (西祖谷), Iya no Kazura-bashi is one of only three bridges left in the area dating from Taira times, when bridges were made out of *shirakuchi* (mountain vines) and bamboo so they could easily be cut down to block an enemy. The Taira would have a tougher time chopping down the Kazura-bashi today, since it's been strengthened with carefully concealed steel cables.

Just like other attractive tourist spots in Japan, the developments surrounding this vine bridge – such as the large concrete car park lurching over the ravine and the rows of tourist shops – detract a little from the natural beauty of the area, and there are often hordes of tourists lining up to cross. It's also now possible to visit at night, thanks to the recent addition of coloured lights. If you're looking for a less touristy alternative, visit Oku Iya Ni-jū Kazura-bashi (see below).

Oku Iya Ni-jū Kazura-bashi

奥祖谷二重かずら橋 • 620 Yamason Higashi Iya • April–Nov daily 7am–5pm; closed Dec–March • ¥550 • ☎ 0120 404 344

Some 30km further into the Iya Valley from Nishi Iya is the picturesque **Oku Iya Ni-jū Kazura-bashi**, a pair of vine bridges also known as the "Fufu-bashi" ("husband and wife bridges"). The bridges tend to sway as you cross them, so it can be a little unnerving if

---

Map:

Kotohira & Takamatsu

Tokushima

Awa Ikeda

TOKUSHIMA EXPRESSWAY

Minawa

ROUTE 32

Yoshino-gawa

Iya-guchi

Awa-Kawaguchi

OLD ROUTE 32

Yoshino-gawa

Iya-gawa

Iya-ke Camp Village

Koboke Gorge

TOKUSHIMA-KEN

Koboke

Iya Onsen

MOUNT TSURUGI QUASI NATIONAL PARK

Ōboke Gorge

Nishi Iya

Ōboke

Iya no Kazura-bashi

Roadside Station Lapis Ōboke Stone Museum

Mont-bell Outdoor Challenge

Tosa Iwahara
Happy Raft

ROUTE 439

Kōchi

JR DOSAN LINE

Toyonaga

Jōfuku-ji

KŌCHI-KEN

ŌBOKE GORGE AND IYA VALLEY

0   3
kilometres

N

Chiiori, Oku Iya Kazura-bashi & Mt Tsurugi-san

● EATING	
Iya Bijin	2
Nishiri Ramen & Riverside Cafe	1

■ ACCOMMODATION	
Awa Ikeda Youth Hostel	1
Chiiori	5
Iya Bijin	3
Iya Onsen	2
Kazuraya	4
Ku Nel Asob	6

9

RIDING ŌBOKE'S RAPIDS

With thrilling rapids and spectacular rocky scenery, a **boat trip** (daily 9am–5pm; 30min; ¥1080) down the Yoshino-gawa is the best way to view the Ōboke Gorge. Boats leave from the *Mannaka* restaurant (☏ 088 384 1211), a five-minute walk past the Lapis Ōboke Stone Museum.

More exciting **rafting and canyoning trips** on the Yoshino-gawa are offered between March and October by the Australian-run *Happy Raft* (☏ 088 775 0500, ☻ en.happyraft.com) further upriver near Tosa Iwahara Station; half-day trips start at ¥5000, while full-day ones start at ¥9000. MontBell Outdoor Challenge (☏ 088 775 0898) also offers whitewater-rafting trips (April–Nov from ¥5000).

there are many others crossing at the same time. There's also a man-powered three-seater wooden cable cart, which is another traditional form of transportation in the area and an entertaining way to cross the river.

Tsurugi-san

剣山 • Ropeway May–Oct daily 9am–4.45pm; closed Nov–April • ¥1030 one-way, ¥1860 return • ☏ 088 362 2772

At 1955m, **Tsurugi-san** is Shikoku's second-highest mountain and is worth visiting for its enchanting forest paths and pure mountain springs. As it's a sacred site, it was off-limits to women up until the early twentieth century. You can time your visit to coincide with the first day of August, when a festival is held at the summit, but visitors more often come to Tsurugi-san on a day hike. It's a four-hour round trip starting at **Minokoshi** (見ノ越), from where there's a ropeway that'll lead you most of the way up.

ARRIVAL AND DEPARTURE   ŌBOKE GORGE AND IYA VALLEY

By train Regular express trains from Okayama and Kōchi stop at Awa Ikeda, though most also stop at Ōboke. Several local trains also ply the route through the Iya Valley between Awa Ikeda and Ōboke daily, but they are infrequent, as are buses. The Miyoshi City Tourist Information Centre (daily 9am–6pm; ☏ 088 376 0877) beside Awa Ikeda Station has

details, and they're also available from Ōboke Station and at Lapis Ōboke 9 (☏ 088 384 1489, ☻ yamashiro-info.jp/lapis), which doubles as a tourist information centre for the area.
By car It's possible to rent a car for as little as ¥5000 for three hours from the *Mannaka* restaurant (☏ 088 384 1211, ☻ mannaka.co.jp).

GETTING AROUND

By car and bike To get to Chiiori and many of the area's other attractions, you're best off using either a car or bicycle – but keep in mind that pedalling up and down the valleys is tough work, if you opt for the latter. With your own transport, you'll have the choice of taking the quieter Route 32 through the Iya Valley.
By taxi Without your own transport, your best bet is

getting around by taxi (Ōboke Taxi; ☏ 088 387 2017).
By bus The Shikoku Transit Information Bureau (☏ 088 372 1231) runs "Bonnet Bus" tours from March to the end of November, starting and finishing in Awa Ikeda and taking in most of the area's sights for ¥7500 (includes lunch and site admission).

ACCOMMODATION

With its rustic onsen and river-rafting possibilities, the Iya Valley is a popular tourist spot that offers a good range of accommodation in beautiful natural settings.

Awa Ikeda Youth Hostel 阿波池田ユースホステル 3798 Nishiyamasako, Ikeda-chō ☏ 088 372 5277, ☻ awaikeda-yh.com. Part of a temple, this hostel is in a spectacular location on the side of the mountain overlooking the town. The manager will pick you up at the station if you call ahead. Accommodation is in high-standard tatami rooms, which share a bathroom between them. There's also

a cosy communal lounge with a TV, and meals (breakfast ¥540, dinner ¥1080) are excellent. Dorms <u>¥3888</u>
Chiiori 篪庵 209 Tsuirui Higashi Iya ☏ 088 388 5290, ☻ chiiori.org. The *Chiiori* traditional mountain lodge (see p.666) can sleep up to ten guests on futons; price per head increases for smaller groups. The Chiiori Trust can help organize some meals, but you'll mostly have to self-cater. If

you don't have your own transportation to get to *Chiiori*, you will need to organize a taxi from Ōboke Station (Ōboke Taxi; ☎088 387 2017), as there is no shuttle service for guests. **¥22,000**

★**Iya Bijin** 祖谷美人 9-3 Zentoku Nishi Iya ☎088 387 2009, ⊚iyabijin.jp. Housed in a modern building with traditional style, this ryokan and restaurant (see below) is in a lovely setting overlooking the river gorge. The luxurious tatami rooms are spacious and elegantly decorated, and the more expensive rooms have their own onsen baths. 🛜 **¥18,500**

Iya Onsen ホテル祖谷温泉 Old Route 32, between the Iya-guchi and Nishi Iya junctions ☎088 375 2311, ⊚iyaonsen.co.jp. One of the most stylish ryokan in Shikoku, *Iya Onsen* is based up in the mountains and offers spectacular panoramic views of the gorge. It's highly recommended for its excellent food and luxurious, traditional rooms, which

feature beautiful riverside vistas. 🛜 **¥19,590**

Kazuraya かずらや 78 Kanjo Nishi Iya ☎088 387 2831, ⊚www.ctm.ne.jp/~kazuraya. This smart ryokan-style hotel is close to the Iya no Kazura-bashi vine bridge. Rooms are tatami-style and have wonderful valley views, and the hotel's indoor and outdoor onsen bathing areas are nicely situated and very clean. Rates include delicious country-style meals. **¥12,000**

Ku Nel Asob 空音遊 442 Enoki Nishi Iya ☎080 6282 3612, ⊚k-n-a.com. Three kilometres' walk south of JR Ōboke Station (call and someone will come and pick you up), this eco-friendly guesthouse, also known as *K & A*, offers large tatami dorms in a ninety-year-old house by the river. There's no shower, but the friendly owners will take you to the local onsen, free of charge. Macrobiotic, vegetarian or vegan meals are available and guests eat communally, like a big family. **¥10,800**

EATING

Several tourist restaurants around the Iya no Kazura-bashi serve *yakisakana* – fish roasted on sticks over hot coals. Set meals start at around ¥1000.

Iya Bijin 祖谷美人 9-3 Zentoku Nishi Iya ☎088 387 2009, ⊚iyabijin.jp. This restaurant serves *Iya soba* noodles and has both indoor and outdoor seating with stunning views of the river below. The noodles are made using locally grown buckwheat and mountain spring water, which gives them a rich flavour. Make sure you order a bowl of the *Genpei* soba with beef and egg (¥1300), or the *Sansei* (mountain vegetable) soba (¥900). Daily 8am–5pm.

Nishiri Ramen & Riverside Café にし利ラーメン 1468-1 Nishi Yamashiro-chō ☎088 384 1117, ⊚west -west.com/shops/nishiri. Located in the River Station West-West complex, this friendly ramen restaurant and café is a great place to stop for a snack. Bowls of Tokushima ramen start at around ¥700, while tasty *gyōza* dumplings are just ¥310 per plate. They also serve a small range of fresh juices, including *sudachi* citrus juice (¥420). Daily 11am–5pm.

Kōchi and around

高知

Sun-kissed **KŌCHI** lies dead in the centre of the arch-shaped southern prefecture of Shikoku. With its palm-lined avenues, network of rivers, enjoyable shopping arcades and gently trundling trams, it's a pleasant town to explore. The area's old name of **Tosa** is still used today, particularly when referring to the local cuisine. It wasn't until 1603, when ruling *daimyō* Yamauchi Kazutoyo named his castle Kōchiyama (now Kōchi-jō), that the city adopted its present name.

The magnificent **castle** remains Kōchi's highlight; to see the other places of interest, you'll generally need to journey away from the city centre. The most immediately rewarding trip is to **Godai-san-kōen**, a beautiful mountain-top park overlooking the city, and the nearby **Chikurin-ji**, which is the 31st temple on Shikoku's famous pilgrimage circuit. South of the city lies **Katsurahama**, with its idyllic but slightly over-hyped beach, and the **Sakamoto Ryōma Memorial Museum** that's dedicated to a local hero of the Meiji Restoration (see box, p.671). In the right season, Kōchi can also be a good base from which to take a whale-watching tour (see box, p.676). The weekly **Sunday Market** (5am–6pm) on Kōchi's Otesuji-dōri is worth attending, as it sees farmers from all over the prefecture bringing their produce to town, while the colourful **Yosakoi Matsuri** (around Aug 9–12 each year) welcomes fourteen thousand dancers for a vibrant parade along the city's streets.

9

Kōchi Prefectural Museum of Art ▲   ▲ Godai-san-kōen, Chikurin-ji & Makino Botanical Garden

KŌCHI

■ ACCOMMODATION	
Jyoseikan	5
Katsuo Guest House	1
Katsurahama-so	1
Kokuminshukusha	7
Kōchi Youth Hostel	2
Los Inn Kōchi	3
Sansuien	6
Tosa Bekkan	4

● EATING	
5019 Premium Factory	3
Café de Libre	7
Habotan	5
Hirome Ichiba	4
Issyun	2
Tokugetsuro	6
Tosa Ichiba Sushi	1

■ DRINKING AND NIGHTLIFE	
Irish Pub Amontillado	2
Love Jamaican	1
Verite	3

● SHOPPING	
Papier	1
Tencosu	2

Kōchi Station
Kōchi-eki
Bus Station
Police Station
Bowl Jumbo Centre
Yatai stalls
Enokuchi-gawa
Hasuike-machi
Kōchi-bashi
Yosakoi Information Exchange Center
Harimaya-bashi
Dentetsu Teminal-mae
Umenotsuji
Yokoyama Ryuichi Memorial Manga Museum
Kōchi Cultural Plaza
Saenba-chō
HARIMAYA-BASHI-DŌRI
OTESUJI-DŌRI
Ok Parking (Bicycle Rental)
Yanagi-machi
Daimaru Department Store
Chūō-kōen
Harimaya-bashi
Horizume
Kagami-gawa
Obiya-machi arcade
OBISAN-DŌRI
Sunday Market
Hirome Ichiba
Ōte-mon
Ōhashi-dōri
Kōchijō-mae
NTT
Kyu-Yamanouchi-ke Shimoyashiki Nagaya
Kōchi International Association
Itagaki Taisuke Statue
Kōchi-jō
Donjon
Josei-koen
Kencho-mae
KENCHO-MAE DŌRI
Gurando-dori
Masugata
Kamimachi 1-chōme
Iriake Station

N

0   250   metres

Ryūga-dō, Awa Ikeda & Takamatsu
Nakamura, Uwajima & S

Kōchi-jō

高知城 • 1-2-1 Marunouchi • Daily 9am–4.30pm • ¥420 to enter the donjon • ☎ 088 824 5701, ⓦ kochipark.jp/kochijyo

Follow the covered Obiya-machi shopping arcade west of Harimaya-bashi to reach the hilltop **Kōchi-jō**. The feudal lord Yamauchi Kazutoyo began construction in 1601, but what you see today dates mainly from 1748, when reconstruction of the donjon turrets and gates was completed following a major fire just over twenty years earlier.

The main approach is through the **Ōte-mon**, an impressive gateway flanked by high stone walls at the end of Otesuji-dōri. In the anti-feudal fervour that heralded the beginning of the Meiji era, almost all the castle's buildings were demolished, leaving the steeply sloping walls surrounding empty courtyards. The exception was the three-storey donjon, within the inner citadel (*honmaru*). To the left of the entrance, there's an exhibition of old samurai armour and a scroll from 1852 showing the English alphabet, written by John Mung (see box, p.678). In the main building, look out for a beautifully painted palanquin before you ascend to take in the superb view from the top storey.

To the west of the castle is adjacent Josei-kōen, which is popular with local families and has an attractive, well-manicured pond area with a couple of interesting metal sculptures. The park is bordered by the Enokuchi-gawa on its western side and is a popular spot for riverside cherry blossom-viewing parties in spring.

Kōchi Prefectural Museum of Art

高知県立美術館, Kōchi Kenritsu Bijutsukan • 353-2 Takasu • Tues–Sun 9am–4.30pm • ¥360 • ☎ 088 866 8000, ⓦ kochi-bunkazaidan.or.jp • 15min tram journey east of Harimaya-bashi – ask to get off at Kenritsu Bijutsukan-dōri

The **Kōchi Prefectural Museum of Art** is a stylish building set in landscaped grounds, and it's home to an impressive collection of modern art including a gallery of lithographs, paintings by Marc Chagall and Paul Klee, and a theatre with a specially designed stage for nō plays. Films and other performances are occasionally held here too.

Yokoyama Ryūichi Memorial Manga Museum

横山隆一記念まんが館, Yokoyama Ryūichi Kinen Manga-Kan • 2-1 Kutanda • Tues–Sun 9am–6pm • ¥400 • ☎ 088 883 5029, ⓦ bunkaplaza.or.jp/mangakan

The Kōchi Cultural Plaza is home to the **Yokoyama Ryūichi Memorial Manga Museum**. Though Tezuka Osamu is credited with revolutionizing the world of manga after World War II, it was Yokoyama (1909–2001), a native of Kōchi, who paved the way for Tezuka's success by founding the *Shinmanga-ha Shudan* manga group in Tokyo in 1932. It was the members of this group who brought a freshness and vitality to the previously staid world of Japanese animation. The museum is full of examples of Yokoyama's work, including his signature creation "Eternal Boy" Fuku-chan, a comic strip that clocked up a record 5534 serializations before bowing out in 1971. There's also an exact replica of one of his ateliers, as well as a mock-up of the quirky bar he used to have in his house.

SAKAMOTO RYŌMA

You'd have to be blind to miss the scowling features of Kōchi's favourite son, **Sakamoto Ryōma**, on posters and other memorabilia around the area. Born in 1835 to a mixed samurai and farming family, Sakamoto directly challenged the rigid class structure of the Shogunate years by leaving the city to start a trading company in Nagasaki (samurai never normally dirtied their hands in business). In his travels around Japan, he gathered support for his pro-Imperial views, eventually forcing the shogun, Tokugawa Yoshinobu, to agree to give supreme power back to the emperor. But one month later, on December 10, 1867, Sakamoto was **assassinated** in Kyoto. Although he was just 33 at the time, his writings included an enlightened plan for a new political system for Japan, aspects of which were later embraced by the Meiji government

9

Yosakoi Information Exchange Center

よさこい情報交流館, Yosakoi Jōhō Kōryūkan • 1-10-1 Harimaya-machi • Mon, Tues & Thurs–Sun 10am–6pm • Free • ☎ 088 880 4351, ⓦ honke-yosakoi.jp

Kōchi's famous dance festival Yosakoi Matsuri, held in early August, might not be as historical as Tokushima's Awa Odori (see box, p.659), but it's just as colourful. Yosakoi, a highly energetic and fast-paced dance form, developed in Kōchi during the postwar era, combining traditional dance moves with modern music, and the first festival was held in the city in 1954. At the **Yosakoi Information Exchange Center** you can learn more about the history of Yosakoi through the colourful displays of costumes and the use of *naruko*, the small wooden clappers held by each dancer. There's also a theatre where you can watch dance teams from previous festivals and a dance studio where you can learn the steps from an instructional video.

Godai-san-kōen

五台山公園 • The MY-Yu tourist bus stops at Godaisan Observatory from Kōchi Station (see opposite); local buses also run daily from Harimaya-bashi to Aoyogi-bashi Higashi-zume (around 20min), from where it's a 30min walk uphill

Perched 2km south of the city centre on the mountaintop overlooking Kōchi's harbour is **Godai-san-kōen**, famous for its beautiful cherry blossoms and azaleas. It's a pleasant place to stroll around or take a picnic lunch, and there's an observatory with a rooftop deck where you'll find excellent views across the city.

Chikurin-ji

竹林寺 • 3577 Godaisan • **Temple** Daily 8.30am–5pm • Free • **Treasure House** Daily 8.30am–4.30pm • ¥400 • ☎ 088 882 3085, ⓦ chikurinji.com

Alongside Godai-san-kōen lie the equally pleasant grounds of the **Chikurin-ji**. This temple (the 31st on the pilgrimage circuit) was founded in 724, so it's among the oldest temples in the prefecture – its atmospheric main building, decorated with intricate carvings of animals, dates from the Muromachi period. The pagoda, built in the 1970s, is said to contain a bone of the Buddha from Bodh Gaya in India, but there's no way of seeing this for yourself since the tower is closed to the public. The **Treasure House**, to the right of the temple's main entrance gate, is worth a visit for its traditional gardens, overlooked by an Edo-era villa, and small collection of Tantric statues and Buddhas.

Makino Botanical Garden

牧野植物園, Makino Shokubutsuen • 4200-6 Godaisan • Daily 9am–5pm • ¥720 • ☎ 088 882 2601, ⓦ makino.or.jp

Opposite Chikurin-ji sits the large **Makino Botanical Garden**, a pleasant parkland which has lovely views out to the coast. It was dedicated to celebrated local botanist Dr Makino Tomitarō, who died in 1957 aged 95. The large greenhouse and fossil gallery, easily spotted since it has a giant model of a *Tyrannosaurus* rex outside, are blots on an otherwise peaceful landscape. The rather more tasteful **Makino Museum of Plants and People** is designed to harmonize with the environment.

Katsurahama

桂浜 • 13km south of Kōchi • Frequent buses head to Katsurahama from Kōchi's Harimaya-bashi (¥610; 40min); the My-Yu bus runs directly from Kōchi Station

Katsurahama is famous for two things: its beach and the Tosa fighting dogs that compete in mock sumo tournaments. The crescent-shaped beach, though capped off at one end with a picturesque clifftop shrine, is rather pebbly, and swimming isn't allowed because of strong currents. You should give the vicious canine bouts a wide berth, too. The main reason to come here is to learn more about Kōchi's hero, Sakamoto Ryōma.

Sakamoto Ryōma Memorial Museum

高知県立坂本龍馬記念館, Kōchi Kenritsu Sakamoto Ryōma Kinenkan • 830 Urado-shiroyama • Daily 9am–5pm • ¥500 •
☎ 088 841 0001, ⓦ ryoma-kinenkan.jp

The architecturally stunning building that houses the **Sakamoto Ryōma Memorial Museum** is on the headland above Katsurahama beach. Dedicated to local hero Sakamoto (see box, p.671), the building uses bold colours and a radical freestanding design for the main exhibition halls. There's a good English pamphlet which helps guide you through the exhibition spaces. Inside, there are state-of-the-art displays using touchscreens, as well as artefacts like the blood-spotted screen from the room in which Sakamoto was assassinated in Kyoto. If the weather is good, you can walk out onto the top of the building for spectacular views of the Pacific. Down on the beach, there's a large statue of Sakamoto gazing out over the ocean.

ARRIVAL AND INFORMATION
KŌCHI

By plane Kōchi Ryoma Airport (☎ 088 863 2906, ⓦ kochiap.co.jp) is a 40min drive east of the city; a bus (¥720) runs at least hourly from the airport to Kōchi Station, while a taxi into the city will cost around ¥4500.
Destinations Fukuoka (3 daily; 1hr 10min); Nagoya (2 daily; 1hr); Osaka Itami (8 daily; 45min); Tokyo Haneda (8 daily; 1hr 25min).

By train All trains arrive at Kōchi Station, at the top of Harimaya-bashi-dōri around 500m north of the city centre.
Destinations Awa Ikeda (14 daily; 1hr 5min); Kotohira (16 daily; 1hr 30min); Nakamura (9 daily; 1hr 50min); Okayama (hourly; 2hr 25min); Takamatsu (5 daily; 2hr 15min).

By bus Most buses arrive at and depart from just outside Kōchi Station.

Destinations Okayama (9 daily; 2hr 20min); Osaka (21 daily; 5hr 35min); Takamatsu (13 daily; 2hr 10min); Tokyo (daily; 11hr 40min).

Tourist information Just outside the south exit of Kōchi Station, in a swanky wooden building called the Tosa Terrace, you'll find Kōchi's excellent tourist information centre (daily 8.30am–6pm; hotel information window open till 7.30pm; ☎ 088 826 3337). Also helpful is the Kōchi International Association (KIA), close to the castle on the second floor of the Marunouchi Biru (4-1-37 Honmachi; Mon–Sat 8.30am–5.15pm; ☎ 088 875 0022, ⓦ kochi-kia .or.jp), which also has a small library of English books and magazines.

GETTING AROUND

While central Kōchi is easily negotiated on foot, the distances between the major sights make catching a tram or bus a sensible option.

By tram The tram terminus is immediately outside the south exit of Kōchi Station. The system consists of two lines, with one running north to south from the station to the port, crossing the east to west tracks at Harimaya-bashi. To travel within the city it costs a flat ¥200, paid to the driver upon leaving the tram; you'll need to ask for a transfer ticket (*norikae-ken*) when you switch lines at Harimaya-bashi. A one-day ticket covering the central city area costs ¥500; an ¥800 ticket gives you access to everywhere on both lines.

By bus The My-Yu tourist bus leaves from Kōchi Station

and takes a circular route to Katsurahama and Godai-san. A one-day pass costs ¥1000, a two-day pass is ¥1,600, and a Godai-san one-day pass is ¥600. These can be purchased from the tourist information office at Tosa Terrace and are half-price for overseas tourists (you'll have to show your passport).

By bike Bicycles are available for ¥500/day from OK Parking (OKパーキング; ☎ 088 871 4689), 100m east of the Sunday Market site along Otesuji-dōri.

By car Try Times Car Rental (☎ 088 872 4591); Toyota Rent-a-Car (☎ 088 823 0100); or Nissan (☎ 088 883 4485).

ACCOMMODATION

You'll find the usual cluster of business **hotels** close to the train station. More convenient for the shopping and entertainment districts are the hotels between Dencha-dōri and the city's principal river, Kagami-gawa.

Jyoseikan 城西館 2-5-34 Kamimachi ☎ 088 875 0111, ⓦ jyoseikan.co.jp. This elegant ryokan may be housed in a modern building, but it has a long history and offers top-grade, spacious tatami rooms with service fit for an emperor – which is probably why he stays here when he

visits town. Its public bath is open to non-guests (noon–4pm; ¥1000). They also run night "*ozashiki-asobi*" tours, introducing traditional entertainment and popular night food stands. ☞ **¥14,900**

★**Katsuo Guest House** かつおゲストハウス 4-7-28

9

Kitajima ☎ 070 5352 1167, ⓦ katuo-gh.com. Run by an energetic mother-and-daughter team, this friendly guesthouse has comfortable rooms (with futons) decorated creatively with different themes – the "Katsuo Room" is dedicated to the local bonito fish. There's a shared kitchen and lounge area for guests. ⓦ Dorms **¥2800**, doubles **¥7600**

Katsurahama-so Kokuminshukusha 桂浜荘国民宿舎 830-25 Urato Shiroyama ☎ 088 841 2201. Located 13km south of central Kōchi, this modern hotel has spectacular views across the beach from its clifftop location and good-value, high-standard tatami rooms. ⓦ **¥19,440**

Kōchi Youth Hostel 高知ユースホステル 4-5 Fukui Higashi-machi ☎ 088 823 0858, ⓦ kyh-sakenokuni .com. This is one of Shikoku's best youth hostels, based in a rustic building with lots of character. The friendly English-speaking manager used to work in a sake brewery, and offers sake-tasting courses after dinner each evening (¥500). You can stay in single rooms or dorms, and the nearest train station is Engyōji, two stops west of Kōchi Station, then a 5min walk. Dorms **¥2500**, singles **¥3000**

Los Inn Kōchi ロスイン高知 2-4-8 Kitahonmachi ☎ 088 884 1110, ⓦ losinn.co.jp. Close to the station, this friendly place has kitsch decor (a mixture of reproduction antiques, heavy leather sofas and 1970s-style chandeliers), an English-speaking manager and comfortable Western- and Japanese-style rooms. Guests may use bicycles for free. ⓦ **¥7600**

Sansuien 三翠園 1-3-35 Takajō-machi ☎ 088 822 0131, ⓦ sansuien.co.jp. Don't judge this ryokan by its modern exterior; it has a refined interior, and the attached traditional gardens and buildings beside the Kagami-gawa are reminiscent of old Japan. Some slightly cheaper Western-style rooms are also available. The onsen bath complex is also open to non-residents (Daily 10am–4pm; ¥900). **¥7350**

Tosa Bekkan とさ別館 1-11-34 Sakurai-chō ☎ 088 883 5685. This is a friendly and relaxed minshuku-style hotel. The clean tatami rooms have TVs, air conditioning and toilets, though bathrooms are communal. Meals are available, and there's a coin-operated laundry facility outside. **¥7600**

EATING

The best area for **eating** in Kōchi is around the Obiya-machi arcade, although on Wednesdays you might find several places are closed. The warm weather and convivial atmosphere mean locals tend to favour the many cheap **yatai** (street stalls) around town, serving *oden*, ramen, *gyōza* and beer – check out the area beside the Enokuchi-gawa, near the Bowl Jumbo Centre. If you want to splash out, try *sawachi-ryōri*, Kōchi's most refined style of cuisine, which features lots of fresh seafood like the famous local tuna, *katsuo*.

5019 Premium Factory 1-10-21 Obiya-machi ☎ 088 872 5019, ⓦ 5019.co.jp/premium. This laidback café and wine bar is a great spot to grab a midnight snack. Try the Ryōma Burgers – grilled *katsuo* patties with Kōchi vegetable salad (¥790). Glasses of wine start at ¥500. Mon–Thurs 11am–2am, Fri & Sat 11am–3am, Sun 11am–1am.

Café de Libre 3F Kōchi Cultural Plaza, 2-1 Kutanda ☎ 088 882 7750. In the same building as the Yokoyama Ryūichi Memorial Manga Museum (see p.671), this stylish and spacious café serves a good range of light meals, such as pasta and quiche, for around ¥1000, as well as some very tasty desserts and cakes. Tues–Sun 11am–5pm.

Habotan 葉牡丹 2-21 Sakaia-machi ☎ 088 823 8686, ⓦ habotan.jp. This is a cheerful *izakaya* serving good local food, such as *tataki-moriawase* platters (¥1080) and "stamina" tofu (¥280). This is probably the only *izakaya* in Shikoku that opens for lunch – tuna rice bowls are ¥630 and grilled chicken lunch sets go for ¥698. Daily 11am–11pm.

★**Hirome Ichiba** ひろめ市場 2-3-1 Obiya-machi ☎ 088 822 5287. At the end of the Obiya-machi arcade, this lively indoor market has over sixty stalls selling a range of Japanese food, as well as Indian and Chinese specialities and even toasted sandwiches. You'll eat well for under

¥1000, and the cheap beer and lively atmosphere mean you may even make a lot of new friends. Local food items and other sundries can also be purchased as souvenirs here. ⓦ Mon–Sat 8am–11pm, Sun 7am–11pm.

Issyun 一旬 2-1-3 Harimaya-chō ☎ 088 824 2030, ⓦ issyun.jp. Appealing contemporary *izakaya* with a long counter bar and discreet nooks. It specializes in sake from around Shikoku as well as local beers and nicely presented seasonal food. *Katsuo* tuna dishes start at ¥1000, and lunchtime set meals are good value, from ¥840. Mon–Fri 11.30am–11pm, Sat & Sun 11.30am–midnight.

Tokugetsuro 得月楼 1-17-3 Minami Harimaya-chō ☎ 088 882 0101, ⓦ tokugetsu.co.jp. This traditional restaurant with kimono-clad waitresses and tatami rooms is the place to sample a *sawachi-ryōri* meal (lunch from ¥6300, dinner ¥8400). The lunch bentō (from ¥2635) are a more affordable option. Bookings essential. Daily 11am–2pm & 5–10pm.

Tosa Ichiba Sushi 土佐市場寿し 5-1 Nijudai-machi ☎ 088 823 01130. This sushi restaurant is an excellent place to sample the local favourite, *katsuo no tataki* – seared bonito tuna (¥1200). It's served with salt or ponzu vinegar dipping sauce. Outside the front of the restaurant is a barbecue, and you can choose any type of seafood you'd like grilled. Mon–Sat 5pm–2am.

DRINKING AND NIGHTLIFE

As the largest city on Shikoku's southern coast, Kōchi attracts many people looking for a night on the town, so it's not short of **bars** and has a lively atmosphere, especially at weekends. The city's famous drinking street is **Yanagi-machi**, which runs parallel to the Obiya-machi arcade. During the summer Kōchi's many *yatai* and rooftop beer gardens are the ideal places to relax with a cold brew.

Irish Pub Amontillado 1-1-17 Obiya-machi ☎ 088 875 0599, ✆ facebook.com/IrishpubAmo. Owner Shimai-san's fascinating tale of how this Irish bar ended up with a Spanish name trundles on for at least a couple of pints of Guinness or Kilkenny (¥900 a pint). There's also decent fish 'n' chips and Irish stew (both ¥800), as well as occasional live music. Happy Hour runs from 5–8pm. Daily 5pm–1am.

Love Jamaican B1 1-9-1 Obiya-machi ☎ 090 8973 4736.

If you feel like dancing, this hip-hop and reggae bar is the place to mix it up with the locals. The door charge is usually ¥1000. Daily 9pm–late.

Verite 2F 1-7-19 Obiyamachi ☎ 088 873 5560. This cosy cocktail bar offers both standard and original drinks from ¥600, as well as a large range of Belgian beers from ¥800. The tasty bar snacks start from ¥300. Mon, Tues & Thurs–Sun 6pm–2am.

SHOPPING

Kōchi is well known as a centre for handmade paper products, and the local variety is known as *tosa washi*.

Papier パピエ 2-8-11 Harimaya-chō ☎ 088 880 9185. Papier has a lovely selection of wrapping papers, cards and small paper goods. You can also buy metres of plain or dyed paper. Mon & Wed–Sun 10am–6pm.

Tencosu てんこす 1-11-40 Obiya-machi ☎ 088 855 5411.

This huge vendor of Kōchi crafts is a great place to pick up souvenirs. Prices are reasonable, and there's a good range of cute *tenugui* hand towels and rustic local pottery. Daily 9am–9pm.

DIRECTORY

Hospital The Red Cross Hospital (☎ 088 822 1201) is behind Kōchi Station.

Internet There are free computer terminals with internet access at the Kōchi International Association and the Kōchi Tourist Information Center in Tosa Terrace (see p.673), which is also a wi-fi hotspot. Most of the Obiyamachi and Harimaya-bashi shopping street area is also a free wi-fi zone, but a limit of up to four fifteen minute sessions

applies per day.

Laundry There are coin-operated machines outside the *Tosa Bekkan* (see opposite).

Police The main police station is opposite Kōchi Station. Emergency numbers are listed on p.71.

Post office The post office is just to the west of Kōchi Station (Mon–Fri 9am–7pm, Sat 9am–5pm, Sun 9am–12.30pm).

Western Kōchi-ken

Some of Shikoku's best scenery is in western Kōchi-ken. Inland, you can raft or kayak down the beautiful **Shimanto-gawa**, while along the indented coast, carved by the savage Pacific Ocean, there are several fishing communities, including **Kuroshio** (黒潮), from where you can take **whale-watching tours** (see box, p.676). The rocky cape at **Ashizuri Misaki**, 180km southwest of Kōchi with its twisting scenic roads, temple and lush foliage, is well worth the journey.

Shimanto-gawa and around

四万十川

Often claimed to be the last free-flowing river in Japan, the **Shimanto-gawa** actually has one small dam along its 196km length, though this doesn't detract from its beauty, winding as it does through green countryside past pine-clad slopes and terraced rice fields. This is the place to head for tranquil boating, cycling, fishing and canoeing (see box, p.676). The river can be accessed from either Ekawasaki (江川崎) at the top end or Nakamura (中村) to the south.

9

WHALE-WATCHING TOURS

It's said that the **whaling industry** in Kōchi dates from 1591, when the local *daimyō* Chōsokabe Motochika gifted the warlord Toyotomi Hideyoshi in Osaka a whale and in return received eight hundred bags of rice. Japan and whales have, in recent times, become a **controversial** combination, but along Kōchi-ken's coast few are complaining, as whale-watching tours are replacing the old way of making a living. The best time to see whales is May and August, though the season runs from spring through to autumn. Nothing's guaranteed, but with a good skipper you can expect to see **Bryde's whales** and **false killer whales**, as well as schools of white-sided and Risso's **dolphins**.

TOURS

Ōgata Whale Watching 3573-5 Ukibuchi Kuroshio-chō ☏ 088 043 1058, ⓦ nitarikujira.com.

Tours typically last 4hr and cost around ¥6000 per person in small boats holding eight to ten people.

Nakamura
中村

Nakamura, formally called Shimanto-shi, is larger than Ekawasaki and is the better-positioned option for those planning to travel south to Cape Ashizuri after spending time on the river. In addition to all the usual river-related leisure activities, the small town also has a few historical sites worth seeing, such as the Shimanoto City Historical Museum that was built on the ruins of Nakamura's castle, and a number of shrines and ancient graves.

ARRIVAL AND INFORMATION   SHIMANTO-GAWA

By train The nearest train station to Matsuyama and Uwajima is Ekawasaki on JR's plodding Yodo Line (ⓦ jr-shikoku.co.jp/yodo3bros), which runs from Kubokawa (窪川) on the bay side of Kōchi-ken to Uwajima. The trains that traverse the scenic route are tourist attractions in their own right (see box opposite). Nakamura Station is on the Tosa Kuroshio Line, which runs southwest from Kubokawa and terminates in Sukumo.
By bus There are a few buses (Mon–Sat) from Nakamura to Kuchiyanai, a stop-off point on the river roughly halfway to Ekawasaki.

By bike Cycling is also a good way to see the Shimanto-gawa, and numerous cycling tracks follow the river's banks. Bikes are available to rent from various outlets in both Ekawasaki and Nakamura.
Tourist information The Shimanto City Tourist Information Centre is a 5min walk south of the JR station (daily 8.30am–5.30pm; ☏ 088 035 4171). The English-speaking staff are very helpful, and there's free wi-fi and a good selection of maps and pamphlets in English. Bicycle rental is also available here (¥600 for 5hr; ¥1000 for 24hr).

ACCOMMODATION

Hotel Seira Shimanto ホテル星羅四万十 1100 Nishi-Tosamochii, Shimanto-shi ☏ 088 052 2225, ⓦ seirashimanto.com. The views from this modern, elegant hotel, located on a hill in Ekawasaki overlooking the Shimanto-gawa, are superb. The hotel's relaxing hot-spring spa also has great views, and the Japanese- and

Western-style rooms are tastefully decorated. The in-house restaurant serves sweetfish and shrimp from the river, and breakfast and dinner are included. 🛜 **¥23,400**
Nakamura Daiichi Hotel 中村第一ホテル 5-15 Ekimae-chō, Shimanto-shi ☏ 088 034 7211, ⓦ park18.wakwak .com. Conveniently located right in front of Nakamura

SHIMANTO-GAWA CANOE TOURS

The best way to enjoy the beautiful **Shimanto-gawa** is to paddle along its gentle waters. There are a number of **boat cruises**, including in the traditional white-sailed Senba boats, which take large groups up and down the river. However, joining a **canoe tour** is both fun and relaxing, and the young Japanese guides are very enthusiastic and helpful for beginners. Depending on weather conditions, tours usually run from April until November. Both full-day and half-day canoeing courses are available, and all equipment is provided. For more details, see Soramil (ⓦ soramil.co.jp), Canoe House (ⓦ canoekan.com) and Kawarakko (ⓦ kawarakko.com).

THE YODO LINE BROTHERS

The three trains traversing the Yodo Line, namely the Shiman Torocco, Kaiyodo Hobby Train and Tetsudo Hobby Train, are affectionately known to railway enthusiasts as the Yodo Line Brothers (Ⓦ jr-shikoku.co.jp/yodo3bros). The **Shiman Torocco**, which was the brainchild of noted industrial designer Mitooka Eiji, is of particular interest, as you can ride part of the line in an open-air carriage (*torokko ressha*) during August and on most weekends from March to November – a rarity in Japan, and an opportunity to better view and photograph the natural scenery en route. The **Kaiyodo** and **Tetsudo** hobby trains, which operate year-round, both have novel themes: the former was inspired by the animal figurines of its namesake Kaiyodo Co., and the latter is modelled on the first generation of Shinkansen (bullet trains).

Station, this no-frills business hotel has clean and functional Western-style rooms. There's an attractive Japanese restaurant on the second floor that serves decent meals, and the hotel staff are polite and helpful. ☞ **¥10,500**

Ashizuri Misaki
足摺岬

The tourist trail has beaten a steady path to **ASHIZURI MISAKI**, a small, friendly village spread thinly around the cape that makes up Shikoku's most southerly point. Pilgrims have long been coming here to pay their respects at picturesque **Kongōfuku-ji** (金剛福寺), the 38th temple on the sacred circuit. Dedicated to the Buddhist deity Kannon, who symbolizes infinite compassion, the temple has a two-storey pagoda and is situated amid a palm grove at the eastern end of the village. Ashizuri's white-painted lighthouse stands atop 80m-high cliffs, while at shore level there's a natural rock arch, crowned by a small shrine. Also look out for the stern-looking bronze statue of **John Mung** (see box, p.678) at the cape, which is a popular photo spot with local tourists. All these sights are within easy walking distance of each other, along clifftop pathways that burst with crimson camellia blossoms each February.

John Mung Museum

ジョン万次郎資料館, John Manjirō Shiryōkan • Umi no Eki Ashizuri, Tosa Shimizu (18km from Ashizuri) • Daily 8.30am–5pm • ¥400 • ☎ 088 082 3155, Ⓦ johnmung.info • Buses bound for Nakamura or Ashizuri stop at Tosa Shimizu

Nakahama Manjirō, also known as John Mung (see box, p.678), was a local lad who travelled the world and pioneered relations between Japan and the USA in the early years of the Meiji Restoration. The interesting **John Mung Museum**, relocated from Ashizuri Misaki to the nearby town of Tosa Shimizu, includes some of Mung's personal possessions, including a re-creation of his study and some fascinating displays on the whaling industry he was once part of.

ARRIVAL AND INFORMATION

ASHIZURI MISAKI

By train and bus To reach the cape by public transport, take a train to Nakamura (中村), then transfer to a bus (7 daily; 1hr 45min; ¥1900) directly outside the station. The bus journey becomes progressively more spectacular the closer to the cape you get, as the driver whips the bus around the narrow, cliff-hugging road. The buses all go to Kongōfuku-ji, but most accommodation is closer to Ashizuri's tiny bus station.

By car In your own car, you can opt for the less hair-raising but equally scenic Skyline Rd which runs down the middle of the peninsula to the cape.

Tourist information There's a tourist information centre near the John Mung statue, which can provide general advice and help you with finding accommodation.

Services The Ashizuri Misaki post office has an ATM (Mon–Fri 9am–5.30pm, Sat 9am–12.30pm).

ACCOMMODATION AND EATING

Above the souvenir shops opposite Kongōfuku-ji, there are a few *shokudō* (cafeterias) serving **lunch** as well as hot drinks. In the evening, it's advisable to arrange **dinner** with your accommodation, as night-time dining options in the area are very limited.

9

JOHN MUNG

In the normal course of life, **Nakahama Manjirō**, born in 1827 into a poor family living near Ashizuri Misaki, would have lived and died a fisherman. However, his fortunes changed when he was marooned on an uninhabited volcanic island some 580km south of Tokyo, along with four shipmates. After nearly five months, they were saved by a landing party from a passing US whaling ship, who had come to the island in search of fresh water.

John Mung, as he was nicknamed, ended up serving with the American crew for four years, before returning with the captain, **William Whitfield**, to his home in Bedford, Massachusetts. This was the first known case of a Japanese person ever visiting the continental United States, as it was during Japan's *sakoku* period when it was a capital offence to leave the country – or return from abroad. A bright student, Mung mastered English, mathematics, surveying and navigation, and undertook journeys to Africa, Australia and around Southeast Asia. After profiting from the California Gold Rush of 1849, Mung returned to Japan in 1851, where he soon found himself serving as an advisor to the feudal lord of Tosa. Two years later, Mung was summoned to Tokyo to assist with the drawing up of international trade treaties, and in 1860 he returned to the US as part of a national delegation.

Before his death in 1898 he taught at the **Kaisei School for Western Learning** in Tokyo (later to become part of the prestigious Tokyo University), sharing the knowledge he had accumulated during a period when Japan was still living in self-imposed isolation from the rest of the world.

Ashizuri Kokusai Hotel 足摺国際ホテル 662 Ashizuri Misaki ☎088 088 0201, ⓦashizuri.co.jp. This fairly standard-looking hotel has fabulous ocean views and plenty of facilities, such as a spa, karaoke room and coin laundry, and the Japanese-style rooms are clean and spacious. The food is excellent, as it focuses on local Ashizuri seafood, and you can enjoy a soak in the *rotenburo* (outdoor bath) after dinner while gazing out to sea. 📶 **¥32,400**

Ashizuri Thermae 足摺テルメ 1433-3 Higashihata Ashizuri Misaki ☎088 088 0301, ⓦterume.com. This large hotel and spa resort complex offers Western- and Japanese-style rooms of a good standard, and also has a stylish French restaurant. The hotel has a number of terraces and observation decks designed to help you enjoy the panoramic views of the Pacific. 📶 **¥14,185**

Ashizuri Youth Hostel あしずりユースホステル 1351-3 Ashizuri Misaki ☎088 088 0324. This basic but friendly and relaxed hostel is next to a small shrine, and it's the best budget option for the area. Accommodation is in small, clean tatami dorms, and meals are available if you reserve in advance. 📶 Dorms **¥4100**

Uwajima and around

宇和島

From Sukumo, Route 56 continues through countryside before emerging on the coast. The cliff-side road, passing though small fishing communities, provides unforgettable views of the deep-blue sea, carpeted with nets held up by a crisscross network of buoys. Pearls are cultivated here, and at the port of **UWAJIMA**, 67km north of Sukumo, there are plenty of shops selling them. The town's main sights – which include a **castle** and a **fertility shrine** – can be seen easily in half a day, though it's worth staying a night and using Uwajima as a base from which to explore the small country town of Uwa-chō (see p.682) to the north.

WAREI TAISAI

The major festival of **Warei Taisai**, held at **Warei-jinja** from the evening of July 22 to July 24, involves huge models of devilish bulls (*ushi-oni*) and ornate portable shrines being paraded in the streets – the aim being to dispel evil. The bulls, like giant pantomime horses, eventually do battle in the river, while at the shrine there's much banging of *taiko*, lots of bonfires and a fireworks finale.

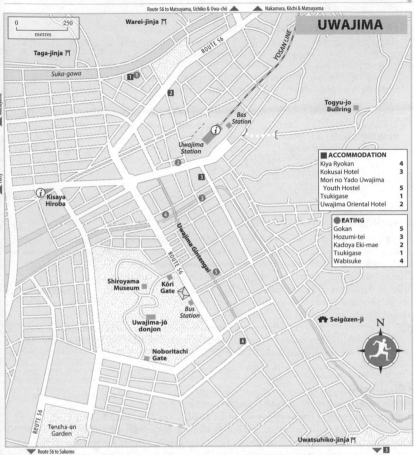

Route 56 to Matsuyama, Uchiko & Uwa-chō ▲   ▲ Nakamura, Kōchi & Matsuyama

UWAJIMA

Warei-jinja 鳥

Taga-jinja 鳥

Suka-gawa

ROUTE 56

YOSAN LINE

Togyu-jo
Bullring

Bus
Station

Uwajima
Station

Kisaya
Hiroba

■ ACCOMMODATION
Kiya Ryokan	4
Kokusai Hotel	3
Mori no Yado Uwajima Youth Hostel	5
Tsukigase	1
Uwajima Oriental Hotel	2

Uwajima Gintengai

ROUTE 56

● EATING
Gokan	5
Hozumi-tei	3
Kadoya Eki-mae	2
Tsukigase	1
Wabisuke	4

Shiroyama
Museum

Kōri
Gate

Bus
Station

Uwajima-jō
donjon

Seigōzen-ji

Noboritachi
Gate

N

ROUTE 56

Tensha-on
Garden

Uwatsuhiko-jinja 鳥

▼ Route 56 to Sukomo

▼ 5

Taga-jinja

多賀神社 • 1340 Fujie • Sex museum daily 8am–5pm • ¥800 • ☎ 089 522 3444, ⓦ www.geocities.jp/taga_shrine • A 10min walk north of the JR station, across the Suka-gawa

Uwajima's most provocative attraction, the fertility shrine **Taga-jinja**, is set back from the Suka-gawa in a small compound packed with various statues, most of which are stone or log phalluses. The attached **sex museum**, spread over three floors of a bland modern building, contains wall-to-wall erotica, with display cases packed to bursting point with all manner of sexual objects, literature and art.

On the ground floor is a collection of Japanese fertility symbols and figurines dating back centuries, including an ivory *netsuke* collection. The first floor holds similar objects from around the world, including displays devoted to Tibet, India, Europe and elsewhere; some of these exhibits are claimed to be the best part of two thousand years old. On the top floor is a large selection of Japanese erotic books and prints (*shunga*) dating all the way back to the Edo and Meiji periods. The larger shrine to the east of Taga-jinja is **Warei-jinja** (和霊神社; daily, 24 hours; ☎089 522 0197), the focal point of the spectacular Warei Taisai, one of Shikoku's numerous major festivals (see box opposite).

9

JAPANESE-STYLE BULLFIGHTING

The best time to visit Uwajima is for one of its bloodless **bullfights**, or *tōgyū*, the bovine equivalent of sumo wrestling. Some accounts date the sport back four hundred years, while others pinpoint the origins to an event in the nineteenth century, when a Dutch captain made a gift of bulls to the town after local fishermen came to his ship's aid during a typhoon. The bulls, weighing in at up to a tonne and treated like pampered pets by their owners, lock horns and struggle either to push each other to the floor or out of the tournament ring. The fights are held five afternoons per year (Jan 2, the first Sunday in April, July 24, Aug 14 and the fourth Sun in Oct; details at ⓦ www.tougyu.com) at the **Tōgyū-jō Bullring**, a white-walled arena in the hills a twenty-minute walk east of the JR train station, above the city. Get there an hour early to soak up the atmosphere and watch the bulls being paraded around the ring. The bouts are very good-natured and the enthusiastic crowd is welcoming and friendly. Tickets cost ¥3000 (¥2500 if purchased in advance) and can be bought on the day at the arena.

Uwajima-jō

宇和島城 • 1 Marunouchi • Daily: April–Sept 9am–5pm; Oct–March 9am–4pm • ¥200 • ☏ 089 522 2832 • A 15min walk south of the JR station; there are two routes up to the donjon, either from the north through the gate of the Kōri samurai family, tucked back from the main road behind the post office, or from the Noboritachi-mon on the south side of the castle hill

One of just twelve remaining original castles in Japan, **Uwajima-jō** sits atop the hillside park that rises west of Route 56. The steep and somewhat gruelling walk up Shiro-yama to reach the castle is worth the trouble, as you'll climb beautiful moss-covered steps amid the surrounding forest. The compact, three-storey donjon may be authentic, and certainly gives a fine view of the surrounding city and port, but there's little other reason to pay the entrance charge because there's hardly anything to see on display inside.

Tensha-en

天赦園 • 1 Tensha-kōen • Daily: April–June 8.30am–5pm; July–March 8.30am–4.30pm • ¥300 • ☏ 089 522 0056

A short walk south of the castle park is the small formal garden of **Tensha-en**. Dating from 1866, the pretty garden is laid out in circular style with a feature made of a wisteria trellis over a pond. Nearby, you can also explore the narrow residential streets immediately southeast of the centre. Here shrines, temples and graveyards are huddled on the slopes leading up to the *Mori no Yado Uwajima Youth Hostel* (see opposite). Even if you're not staying at the hostel, the hill is worth climbing for the sweeping views of the town.

ARRIVAL AND INFORMATION   UWAJIMA

By train Uwajima Station is the terminus for both the JR Yodo line running from Kubokawa and the JR Yosan line from Matsuyama.
Destinations Kubokawa (6 daily; 2hr 20min); Matsuyama (14 daily; 1hr 25min).
By bus Buses to and from Sukumo stop in front of Uwajima Station as well as at the main bus centre at the foot of the castle hill on Route 56.
Destinations Matsuyama (15 daily; 2hr 20min); Sukumo (11 daily; 2hr).

Tourist information Inside the JR station is a small tourist information booth (daily 9am–6pm). The Uwajima Sightseeing Information Centre at Kisaya Hiroba, near the port, is staffed with English-speakers and has English maps and pamphlets for the area (daily 9am–6pm; ☏ 089 522 3934).
Services You can change money at Iyo Bank just off the Gintengai, and there's an ATM at the main post office near the Kōri Gate to the castle. Out of hours, the convenience store next to the *Uwajima Oriental Hotel* has a 24-hour ATM.

GETTING AROUND

By bike Renting a bike to get around is a good idea; the information booth at the station (see above) can provide assistance with arranging bicycle rental (¥100/hr).

ACCOMMODATION

★**Kiya Ryokan** 木屋旅館 2-8-2 Oute-Honmachi ☎089 522 0101, ⓦkiyaryokan.com. The chance to spend the night in the stylishly restored Meiji-era *Kiya Ryokan* is a good reason to stay in Uwajima. More of a boutique hotel than a traditional ryokan, you'll have the place to yourself, and the staff only appear at breakfast time. There are three gorgeous guest rooms, sleeping up to eight in total between them, as well as a library and living room. 🛜 **¥32,400**

Kokusai Hotel 国際ホテル 4-1 Nishiki-machi ☎089 525 0111, ⓦuwajima-kokusaihotel.jp. Close to the station, this friendly and traditional hotel offers large, well-appointed Japanese rooms, as well as some Western-style rooms with outlandish 1970s decor. 🛜 **¥10,186**

Mori no Yado Uwajima Youth Hostel 森の宿宇和島ユースホステル Atago-kōen ☎089 522 7177, ⓦuwajimayh.iku4.com. The building's a bit dreary, but the views on the way up the hill and the friendly reception from the young, English-speaking couple who run the place make this a worthwhile place to stay. There's a pool table, a treehouse and free bike rental. The hostel is at the top of a steep hill, a 20min walk south of the JR station. If you're carrying heavy luggage, it's best to take a taxi there (around ¥1000) or ask the manager to pick you up. Dorms **¥3600**, doubles **¥7000**

Tsukigase 月ヶ瀬 1-5-6 Miyukimachi ☎089 522 4788, ⓦsanyukai.sakura.ne.jp/tukigase.html. This old-fashioned ryokan is a little quirky, but the rooms are spacious and well kept, and there's a fine attached restaurant, *Tsukigase* (see below), and a rooftop communal bath. Rates are substantially cheaper on weekdays and include two meals. **¥16,700**

Uwajima Oriental Hotel 宇和島オリエンタルホテル 6-10 Tsurushima-chō ☎089 523 2828, ⓦoriental-web .co.jp/uwajima. This stylish business hotel, a few minutes' walk from the station, has comfortable rooms and budget rates. At check-in, you'll be offered the luxury of a pillow menu. There's a decent restaurant, and they also offer free use of a bicycle for three hours. 🛜 **¥8000**

EATING

Not surprisingly for a port, Uwajima offers ample opportunity to eat **fresh fish** – two popular dishes are *tai-meshi* (sea bream sashimi on top of hot rice) and *iyo satsuma* (strips of fish mixed with a white miso sauce and eaten with rice). For cheaper lunch options and cafés, try Uwajima Gintengai shopping arcade.

Gokan カフェ五感 2-4-6 Chūō-chō ☎089 5287 459. Located just off the town's main shopping arcade, this trendy *izakaya* is very popular with the locals. It has an eclectic menu of Italian-influenced food, but with some unusual Japanese touches. The *nama-hamu* (raw ham) pizza (¥1050) is very tasty, and their original tomato *nabe* (¥850), which uses tomato soup stock and herb sausages, is a unique take on the classic Japanese dish. Mon–Wed, Fri & Sat 5.30pm–1am, Sun 4–10pm.

Hozumi-tei ほづみ亭 2-3-8 Shin-machi ☎089 522 0041, ⓦuwajima-hozumitei.com. An appealingly rustic fish restaurant with tables and tatami seating areas overlooking a stream. An evening meal will cost around ¥2000. Mon–Sat 11am–1.30pm & 5–9.40pm.

★**Kadoya Eki-mae** かどや駅前 8-1 Nishiki-machi ☎089 522 1543, ⓦkadoya-taimeshi.com. With reasonable prices and friendly service, this is one of the best places in town offering seafood dishes, including *taimeshi*, with various set menus from around ¥1500. There's also a useful picture menu. Mon–Wed & Fri–Sun 11am–2.30pm & 5–9pm, Thurs 5–9pm.

Tsukigase 月ヶ瀬 1-5-6 Miyuki-machi ☎089 522 4788. Bamboo grows in the centre of this restaurant specializing in *fugu* (in winter) and tempura. Set lunches start from as low as ¥790, while their *satsuma-jiru* meal is ¥1500. Daily 11am–10.30pm.

Wabisuke 和日輔 1-2-6 Ebisu-chō ☎089 524 0028. This large restaurant near the castle combines traditional decor with a friendly welcome, and has a range of set meals including sashimi sets, soba, udon and *kamameshi* (a kind of pilaf). Lunches are available from ¥840. Mon–Sat 11am–2pm & 5–10pm, Sun 11am–3pm & 5–9.30pm.

Nametoko Gorge

滑床渓谷, Nametoko Keikoku

Unlike the better-known and well-trodden Iya Valley in Tokushima, **Nametoko Gorge** really is Shikoku's secret mountain paradise. Driving from Matsumaru Station (the jumping-off point for the gorge), the road becomes increasingly narrow and winding as you head deeper into the valley, and the surroundings begin to take on the otherworldly quality characteristic of Nametoko. Pressing on along the forest-fringed tracks, you'll eventually come across the Shimanto-gawa below, with its gigantic boulders and crystal-clear water. Look out for the vast carpets of moss covering every surface – which even stretch onto the road in places.

9

Wildlife is plentiful in the area, so it's not uncommon to see wild deer, boar and monkeys. There are also numerous walking tracks and paths on both sides of the river, so it's relatively easy to explore the area on foot and discover a number of excellent sights, such as the Yukiwa no Taki. The thirty-minute walk to this waterfall from Mannen-bashi is well worth it, as the pristine water cascading down the 80m-high slab of granite makes for an impressive sight – it's considered one of the best waterfalls in Japan. The gorge is also a popular spot for canyoning in the warmer months, and in autumn it's one of the top *kōyō* (autumn leaf-viewing) spots in Shikoku.

ARRIVAL AND INFORMATION

NAMETOKO GORGE

By train The closest station to Nametoko Gorge is Matsumaru on the JR Yodo line, though it's too far to walk from there and onward transport should be arranged.

By taxi There are no local buses to Nametoko, so you will need to take a taxi from Matsumaru Station (30min; ¥4000) if you don't have your own transport. However, the

Mori no Kuni Hotel (see below) will pick you up from the station for free if you call ahead.

Tourist information The Popo Onsen next to Matsumaru Station also doubles as a visitor centre and has wi-fi. Closer to the gorge, the Nametoko Outdoor Centre near the Mannen-bashi is a good spot to stop for a rest.

ACCOMMODATION

There is only one option in the actual valley, but it would be possible to stay in nearby Matsuno and take a day-trip to the gorge. There is also an attractive riverside campsite located near the main road on the approach to the hotel, but facilities there are very limited.

★**Mori no Kuni Hotel** 森の国ホテル Meguro, Matsuno-chō ☎089 5430 331, ⓦmorinokunihotel .com. Perfectly located in the heart of the Nametoko Valley, surrounded by all the natural beauty one could want, this luxury hotel is reminiscent of a Swiss mountain chalet with its cute white facade and triangular red roof.

The rooms are very spacious and comfortable, and there is a communal lounge/bar with a hearth and open fire. The hotel grounds are extensive, with a bridge and numerous paths leading into the surrounding forest or down to the river. Breakfast and dinner are included. 📶 **¥29,000**

North of Uwajima

Between Uwajima and Matsuyama are three appealing small towns – **Uwa-chō**, **Ōzu** and **Uchiko**. They are interesting places to explore, mainly for their preserved streetscapes that evoke Japan's Edo and Meiji periods. All three can easily be visited in a day via train.

Uwa-chō

宇和町

Less than 20km north of Uwajima, the small country town of **UWA-CHŌ**, with its lovely traditional townscape and excellent museum, makes a very pleasant half-day trip from Uwajima. Large tour groups don't stop here, so there are few crowds.

Museum of Ehime History and Culture

愛媛県歴史文化博物館, Ehime-ken Rekishi Bunka Hakubutsukan • 4-11-2 Uno-machi • Tues–Sun 9am–5.30pm • ¥510, English audio guide ¥200 • ☎089 462 6222, ⓦi-rekihaku.jp • The museum can be reached by an infrequent bus (¥150) from the stop about a 5min walk south of the JR Uno-machi Station, along Route 56; the walk up the hill to the museum takes around 20min

Uwa-chō's highlight is the outstanding **Museum of Ehime History and Culture**. Inside this ultra-modern building there are spectacular and informative displays, which include full-sized **replicas of buildings**, including a Yayoi-era (330 BC to 300 AD) hut, a street of Meiji-era shops and a small wooden temple. In the centre of the museum is a **folklore exhibit**, which includes examples of the fabulous portable shrines, costumes and other decorations used in local festivals, such as Uwajima's

9

Warei Taisai (see box, p.678). There's also an interesting display on the Shikoku Pilgrimage. The audio guide in English is essential, as all displays are in Japanese. The museum's café is a good place to have lunch.

Kaimei School

開明学校, Kaimei Gakkō · 3-109 Uno-machi · Tues–Sun 9am–4.30pm · ¥500 (also includes entry to the Uwa Folkcraft Museum, Rice Museum and Memorial Museum of Great Predecessors) · ☎ 089 462 4292

Uwa-chō's street of well-preserved, white-walled houses is known as **Naka-chō**, which is also the name given to this part of town. Some of the buildings date from the Edo period, and most have been very well maintained. Along here is the **Kaimei School**, which is a lovely example of a Meiji-period school and one of the oldest remaining examples in western Japan. Founded in 1882, the architectural style is considered to be Western-influenced. Inside, there's a fascinating collection of antique textbooks and educational posters.

Uwa Folkcraft Museum

宇和町民具館, Uwa-chō Mingu-kan · Tues–Sun 9am–4.30pm · ¥200 (or ¥500 combined ticket with Kaimei School, Rice Museum and Memorial Museum of Great Predecessors) · ☎ 089 362 1334

Opposite the old schoolhouse is the **Uwa Folkcraft Museum**, which has a well-organized exhibition containing a wide range of interesting items that were once in daily use in the town. You can expect to see bamboo swords and deer costumes used in local festivals, as well as old record players and dioramas depicting life during the Edo period.

ARRIVAL AND INFORMATION UWA-CHŌ

By train The JR train station for Uwa-chō is Uno-machi (卯之町), less than 20min from Uwajima by the hourly limited express.

Tourist information You can pick up a simple map and guide to the town's sites in English from the Uwa Folkcraft Museum (see above).

Ōzu

大洲

Further north along the Yosan line from Uwa-chō, the train hits the coast at **Yawatahama** (八幡浜) before turning inland to reach **ŌZU** on the banks of the Hiji-kawa. Although the town's billing as a mini-Kyoto is certainly exaggerated, Ōzu is still a charming and attractive place, with paved streets and well-preserved Edo- and Meiji-era houses. From June 1 to September 20, the river is the location for **ukai**, a unique summer activity involving fishing with cormorants, which you can watch for a fee (¥3000; see box, p.412). For bookings call Ōzu tourist office (see opposite).

Ōzu-jō

大洲城 · 903 Ōzu · Daily 9am–4.30pm · ¥500, or ¥800 with entry to Garyū Sansō · ☎ 089 324 1146

The picturesque **Ōzu-jō** is in a commanding position overlooking the town and river. Destroyed in 1888, the four-storey donjon of this fortress was rebuilt in 2004 to its original sixteenth-century specifications. The grounds are a riot of pink in cherry-blossom season, and locals flock here for picnics, day and night.

Garyū Sansō

臥龍山荘 · 411-2 Ōzu · Daily 9am–4.30pm · ¥500 or ¥800 with entry to Ōzu-jō · ☎ 089 324 3759

Along the river from Ōzu-jō, on the other side of the town, is the **Garyū Sansō**, a beautiful example of a traditional villa built in the *sukiya kenchiku* architectural style with a triangular, thatched roof. Exquisitely detailed woodcarvings and fixtures inside are matched by a lovely moss-and-stone garden outside, leading to a teahouse and a separate moon-viewing platform overlooking the river.

Ōzu Aka-renga-kan

おおず赤煉瓦館・60 Ōzu・Daily 9am–5pm・Free・☎ 089 324 1281

Worth a look before leaving the town is the gallery, gift shop and café in the **Ōzu Aka-renga-kan**, a handsome red-brick complex dating from 1901 and once used as a bank. The architectural style is significant because it combines Western-style brickwork with a Japanese-style tiled roof. Inside, the high ceilings and large windows contrast markedly with the traditional Japanese interiors.

ARRIVAL AND INFORMATION   ŌZU

By train Ōzu is 40min by express train from either Uwajima or Mastuyama. The town's train station, Iyo Ōzu (伊予大洲), is around 2km north of the Hiji-kawa and the castle.

By ferry At Yawatahama (八幡浜) there are ferries to Beppu (6 daily; 2hr 50min) and Usuki in Kyūshū (7 daily; 2hr 25min).

Tourist information The tourist information centre (daily 8.30am–5pm; ☎ 089 324 2664) is in the Michi no Eki Asamoya complex on the south side of Ōzu. You can pick up an excellent local guide and map in English from here, as well as rent bicycles between 9am and 5pm (¥400/2hr). You can also buy a bentō lunchbox and other snacks.

Uchiko

内子

A trip to Ōzu can easily be combined with a visit to the appealing small town of **UCHIKO**, about 15km northeast. Uchiko was once an important centre for the production of Japanese **wax** (*moku-rō*), made from the crushed berries of the sumac tree. The wax is still used in candles, polishes, crayons, cosmetics, food and even computer disks. The wealth generated by the industry has left Uchiko with many fine houses preserved in the picturesque **Yōkaichi** (八日市) district of the town, where craftsmen can still be seen making candles by hand. Recently, Uchiko has become a popular destination for both domestic and international visitors, mainly due to its handsome streetscapes that are reminiscent of old Japan.

Uchiko-za

内子座・2102 Uchiko・Daily 9am–4.30pm・¥400 (or ¥900 combined ticket for all museums in town)・☎ 089 344 2840

The best place to start your tour of Uchiko – which is easily explored on foot – is at the handsomely restored kabuki theatre **Uchiko-za**, which lies around 500m northeast of the train station. Performances are held once or twice a week at the theatre, which was built in 1916 to celebrate the accession of the Emperor Taishō; during the day, you can wander around the auditorium and stage.

Museum of Commercial and Domestic Life

商いと暮らし博物館, Akinai-to-Kurashi Hakubutsukan・Daily 9am–4.30pm・¥200 (or ¥900 combined ticket for all museums in town)・☎ 089 344 5220

The **Museum of Commercial and Domestic Life** is set in a charming converted merchant's house, and has mechanical wax dummies that help show the daily life of a shopkeeper during the Taishō era (1912–26). The mannequins, electronically activated to start speaking (in Japanese), include a moaning pharmacist in the upstairs storeroom. Make sure to pick up an English pamphlet at the door.

Takahashi Residence

高橋邸, Takahashi-bei・2403 Uchiko・Mon & Wed–Sun 9am–4.30pm・Free・☎ 089 344 2354

If you're planning on heading northwest uphill into the **Yōkaichi** district, take a detour towards the Oda-gawa to admire the venerable **Takahashi Residence**, the birthplace of Takahashi Ryūtarō, a politician and founder of the Asahi Beer company. The elegant, two-storey building has castle-like stone walls as well as a lovely garden, which you can admire from the café inside.

9

Ōmura and Hon-Haga Residences

大村家, Ōmura-ke • 本芳我家, Hon-Haga-ke • South end of Yōkaichi historical district • Free • Both residences can only be viewed from outside, but part of the garden of the Hon-Haga Residence can be entered

The two most picturesque buildings in the town are the **Ōmura Residence**, the Edo-era home of a dye-house merchant, and the neighbouring **Hon-Haga Residence**, home of the primary family behind Uchiko's wax industry. The Hon-Haga Residence is more elaborate than the other houses in the district, with ornate gables, a facade decorated with intricate plaster sculptures, and a small, attractive garden.

ARRIVAL AND INFORMATION
UCHIKO

By train Uchiko is 10min by express train north along the Yosan line from Ōzu. The fastest train to Uchiko from Uwajima takes 1hr and from Matsuyama takes 25min. JR offers a handy ¥2700 day-pass ticket covering Matsuyama, Uchiko and Ōzu.

By bus Several buses run daily from Matsuyama (1hr), Ōzu (20min) and Uwajima (50min), stopping a couple of hundred metres to the east of Yōkaichi.

Tourist information There's a tourist information centre next to the train station (☎ 089 343 1450) with English maps and pamphlets. The Uchiko Visitor Centre (Mon–Wed & Fri–Sun: April–Sept 9am–5.30pm, Oct–March 9am–4.30pm; ☎ 089 344 3790, ⓦ we-love-uchiko.jp) is staffed by English-speakers and has more detailed information on the town. If you plan to enter all the buildings and museums around town, a small saving can be made by purchasing the ¥900 combination ticket from Uchiko-za, the Japanese Wax Museum and Kamihaga Residence (north end of Yōkaichi; ☎ 089 344 2771) or the Museum of Commercial and Domestic Life.

GETTING AROUND

By bike Bicycle rental is available at the tourist centre next to the train station (daily 9.30am–5pm; ¥350 for first 2hrs, additional time ¥200/hr).

By bus The Chagamaru Retro Bus shuttles back and forth from the station to the north end of Yōkaichi, passing all the sights on the way (Fri–Sun; ¥360 per trip).

Matsuyama and around

松山

Historic **MATSUYAMA** is Shikoku's largest city – with a population of over 500,000 – and it has a fascinating cultural heritage. Despite its size, Matsuyama is a convivial, friendly place that's easy to get around, thanks to a tram network that bestows an old-fashioned grace to a city that also proudly promotes its literary connections (see box opposite). Most points of interest are centred on the impressive castle, **Matsuyama-jō**, and the popular hot-spring suburb of **Dōgo**, 2km east of the centre, which is home to one of Japan's most magnificent bathhouses.

Local warlords from the **Kono clan** built a fortress in Dōgo in the fourteenth century, while Matsuyama was created in 1602 by *daimyō* Katō Yoshiaki when he built his castle on Katsu-yama. In 1635, the **Matsudaira clan** took charge of the castle and ruled the area until the **Meiji Restoration** in 1868. Rebuilt following the drubbing it received during **World War II**, this largely modern city is now the capital of Ehime-ken and has expanded to encompass the once separately administered Dōgo.

You can see Matsuyama's main sights in a day, but it's better to give yourself an extra day or two to savour the relaxed mood induced by Dōgo's onsen. The city is also a good base for day-trips to Uchiko, Ōzu and Uwajima.

Matsuyama-jō

松山城 • 1 Marunochi • Daily: March–July & Sept–Nov 9am–5pm; Aug 9am–5.30pm; Dec–Jan 9am–4.30pm • ¥510; ropeway and chairlift ¥270 each way, ¥510 return • ☎ 089 921 4873, ⓦ matsuyamajo.jp

The 132m-high Katsu-yama dominates the centre of Matsuyama, and on its summit stands the city's prime attraction, **Matsuyama-jō**. Warlord Katō Yoshiaki began building his fortress in 1602, but by the time it was finished, 26 years later, he had

MASAOKA SHIKI

Matsuyama heavily promotes its Japanese literary connections, and one of the most prominent is with the poet **Masaoka Shiki**, a rather tragic figure who died at 35 from tuberculosis. He took his pen name, Shiki, from that of a bird, which – according to legend – coughs blood as it sings. His life story can be traced at the **Shiki Kinen Museum** in Dōgo (see p.691) and there are two houses connected with the poet preserved as tourist attractions in Matsuyama, including the villa he shared for a short period with **Sōseki Natsume**, one of Japan's most famous authors, whose novel *Botchan* draws on his experiences as a young teacher working in Matsuyama in 1895.

Masaoka made his reputation by encouraging reforms to the then hidebound traditional poetic form **haiku**, which comprises just three lines of five, seven and five syllables and has a subject matter traditionally connected with the seasons. Famously criticizing the master of the genre, Bashō, Masaoka advocated that poets be allowed to use whatever words they wanted for haiku, on any subject matter, while striving to be more reflective of real life. Encapsulating his approach is one of his most famous poems: *"Kaki kueba kane-ga narunari Hōryū-ji"* ("I was eating a persimmon. Then, the bell of Hōryū-ji temple echoed far and wide").

Masaoka is also one of the principal characters in *Saka no Ue no Kumo* (*Clouds Over the Hill*) by Shiba Ryōtarō, a bestseller about Japan's destruction of the Baltic fleet during the Russo-Japanese War, and Japan's modernization. *Saka no Ue no Kumo* was recently filmed as an NHK TV drama series, and has been translated into English. The novel and its heroes are celebrated at the modern **Saka no Ue no Kumo Museum** (see p.689).

moved to Aizu in Tōhoku. As with many of the Japanese castles that are hailed as "original", this one has gone through several incarnations throughout its lengthy lifetime. The main five storey donjon was destroyed by lightning on New Year's Day in 1784 and rebuilt two storeys shorter in 1820 – the three lesser donjons are all modern-day reconstructions. Despite this, the castle is one of Japan's more impressive fortresses, and its location certainly provides commanding views right across the city and shimmering Inland Sea.

You can get up to the castle using the ropeway or rickety chairlift on the eastern flank of the hill. There are also several steep walking routes – the main one starts just beside the ropeway, at the steps up to **Shinonome-jinja** (東雲神社), also on Katsuyama's east side. This picturesque shrine is famous for its Takigi festival, held every April, when nō plays are performed by the light of flaming torches. Other routes run up the west side of the hill, and can be combined with a visit to the Ninomaru Shiseki Teien (see below).

Whichever route you take, you'll end up at the Tonashi-mon gateway to the castle, through which you emerge onto a long plateau surrounded by walls and turrets and planted with blossom trees. Inside the main donjon, climb up to the **top floor** for the view and, on the way down, pass through the **museum** which has displays of calligraphy, old maps, samurai armour and some gorgeously painted screens.

Ninomaru Shiseki Teien

二之丸史跡庭園 • 5 Marunouchi • Daily: Feb–July & Sept–Nov 9am–5pm; Aug 9am–5.30pm; Dec–Jan 9am–4.30pm • ¥200 • ☎ 089 921 2000

On the western side of the castle slope of Matsuyama-jō are the tranquil gardens of the **Ninomaru Shiseki Teien**. The gardens, which look a bit like a giant geometry puzzle, are built on the site of the Ninomaru, the outer citadel of the castle. The pools and pathways at the front of the gardens represent the floor plan of the former structure, which succumbed to fire in 1872. To the rear, as the grounds climb Katsu-yama, the design becomes more fluid, and there are rockeries, a waterfall and two teahouses, one of which serves tea and *wagashi* (a sweet cake) for ¥300.

9

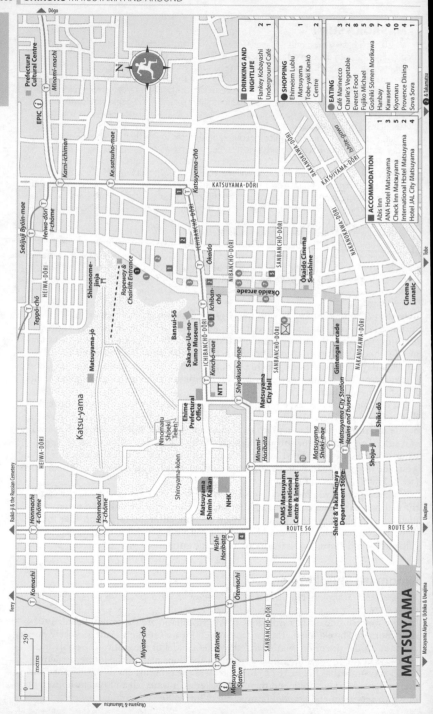

▲ Dōgo

Prefectural
Cultural Centre

EPIC ⓘ

Minami-machi

N

KATSUYAMA-DŌRI

Katsuyama-chō

Kami-ichiman

Ke satsuho-mae

ICHIBANCHŌ-DŌRI

NAKANOKAWA-DŌRI

Sekijūji Byōin-mae

Heiwa-dōri 1-chōme

Okaido

Ōkaido Cinema Sunshine

Teppō-chō

HEIWA-DŌRI

Shinonome-jinja

Ropeway & Chairlift Entrance

NIBANCHŌ-DŌRI

SANBANCHŌ-DŌRI

Ōkaidō arcade

Bansui-Sō

Saka-no-Ue-no-Kumo Museum

Ichiban-chō

ICHIBANCHŌ-DŌRI

Kenchō-mae

Matsuyama-jō

Katsu-yama

Ninomatu Shiseki Telen

Ehime Prefectural Office

Shiyakusho-mae

Matsuyama City Hall

SANBANCHŌ-DŌRI

Gintengai arcade

Cinema Lunatic

Matsuyama City Station (trains and buses)

NTT

Shiroyama-kōen

Minami-Horibata

Matsuyama Shieki-mae

Shoju-ji

Shiki-dō

 Railo-ji & the Russian Cemetery

Honmachi 4-chōme

Honmachi 3-chōme

HEIWA-DŌRI

Matsuyama Shimin Kaikan

NHK

COMS Matsuyama International Centre & Internet

ROUTE 56

Shieki & Takashimaya Department Store

ROUTE 56

Tobe ►

Uwajima ►

Ferry ◄

Komachi

Otemachi

Nishi-Horibata

SANBANCHŌ-DŌRI

Miyata-chō

JR Ekimae

Matsuyama Station

ⓘ

Okayama & Takamatsu ▼

Matsuyama Airport, Uchiko & Uwajima ▼

250
metres
0

MATSUYAMA

► to Takamatsu

Saka no Ue no Kumo Museum

坂の上の雲ミュージアム・3-20 Ichiban-chō・Tues–Sun 9am–6pm (open Mon if public holiday)・¥400; English audio guide ¥100・
☎ 089 915 2600, ⓦ www.sakanouenokumomuseum.jp

At the base of the south side of the castle hill is the modern **Saka no Ue no Kumo Museum**, devoted to the famous novel by Shiba Ryōtarō (see box, p.867). The museum is housed in a highly contemporary polished concrete-and-glass building designed by Andō Tadao. The displays, which focus on many fascinating aspects of the Meiji period and Shiba's novel, are all in Japanese. Thankfully, there is a superb **audio guide** in English, which takes you through the museum's exhibition rooms, making this well worth a visit.

Bansui-sō

萬翠荘・3-3-7 Ichiban-chō・Tues–Sun 9am–6pm・¥300・☎ 089 921 3711

The Saka no Ue no Kumo Museum contrasts nicely with the striking French-style villa, **Bansui-sō**, a little further up the hill. Built in 1922 for Count Sadakoto Hisamatsu, a descendant of the lord of the Iyo-Matsuyama Domain, the villa now houses the **Annexe of the Prefectural Art Museum**. It's no longer possible to go inside, but it's the exterior of the building that's most impressive, particularly the juxtaposition of trees pruned like poodles and the wild palms in the forecourt.

Shiki-dō

子規堂・16-3 Suehiro-machi・Daily 8.30am–5pm・¥50・☎ 089 945 0400

South of the Iyo Tetsudō rail line is the **Shiki-dō**, an evocative re-creation of the poet Masaoka Shiki's (see box, p.687) **childhood home** sandwiched between his family's local temple, Shoju-ji, and the cemetery, where there's a memorial to the poet. Inside the tiny one-storey house are some of his personal effects, his writing desk and examples of his calligraphy. It's rather dusty in places but, thanks to the photographs and other memorabilia, it's easy to imagine something of the life of the nineteenth-century poet.

Raikō-ji

来迎寺・1-525 Miyuki・Daily dawn till dusk・Free・Raiko-ji is a 15min walk northeast of the Takasago-chō tram stop

In the Yamagoe district are a number of temples whose purpose it was to defend the area immediately to the north of the castle. The most worthy of a visit is **Raikō-ji**, originally located in Dōgo but reconstructed in its present location in the eighteenth century.

Russian Cemetery

ロシア人の墓地, Roshia-jin no Bochi・1 Goko・Daily dawn till dusk

Beside Raikō-ji, up a steep incline, is the **Russian Cemetery**. Some six thousand Russian prisoners were interned at the POW camp here during the Russo-Japanese War of 1904–5. The prisoners – being something of a novelty and having little chance of escaping back to Russia – were allowed a fair amount of freedom. Ninety-eight prisoners died from natural causes during their imprisonment, and their graves are still kept immaculate, with fresh flowers regularly placed in front of each of the crosses. An impressive commemorative bust of a fierce-looking, bearded Russian officer stands watch at the entrance to the cemetery.

Dōgo

道後・15min by tram from JR Matsuyama Station

Like many other places in Matsuyama, **DŌGO** onsen has a literary history and a reputation for high-quality hot-spring water. Like many other onsen towns in Japan, it

9

has a seedy side, as well as an abundance of somewhat tacky souvenir shops. However, Dōgo's bathtime delights more than make up for this. Once you've sampled the **onsen**, there are also a couple of interesting museums to explore, along with the appealing **Isaniwa-jinja** and over-the-top **Ishite-ji**.

Dōgo Onsen Honkan

道後温泉本館 • 5-6 Dōgo Yuno-machi • **Kami-no-yu bath** (神の湯) Daily 6am–10.30pm (9pm for lounge) • ¥410 (bath only); ¥840 (bath & 2nd-floor lounge) • **Tama-no-yu bath** (霊の湯) Daily 6am–9.30pm • ¥1250 (bath & 2nd-floor lounge) • **Private room** Daily 6am–8.40pm • ¥1550 (Tama-no-yu bath & 3rd-floor tatami room) • **Yushinden** (又新殿) Daily 6am–9pm • ¥260; the extra fee is waived if you've opted for one of the Tama-no-yu bath courses • ☏ 089 943 8342

The cheapest way to soak at **Dōgo Onsen Honkan** is to use the rather raucous **Kami-no-yu**, or "Hot Water of the Gods", a section with two identical baths, decorated with mosaics of the heron, on each side of the changing rooms. For an extra fee you can relax afterwards in the second-floor public room, where you'll be served green tea and rice crackers, and you also get to borrow a cotton *yukata* robe. The next level up is the **Tama-no-yu** or "Hot Water of the Spirits", a more exclusive bath at the back of the complex. There's a view of a small garden from the changing room, and you relax afterwards in a separate section on the second floor. The first-class experience recommended by the title character of *Botchan* entitles you to a **private room** on the third floor, where you'll be offered green tea and three-coloured *dango* (sweet rice-dough balls on a stick) after your dip.

Even if you opt for the no-frills bath, the staff will allow you to explore the rest of the building. On the second floor, look out for a display of tea-ceremony items and old calligraphy scrolls to the side of the large tatami resting-room with carved wooden verandas. On the third floor, the corner room has a small exhibition (all in Japanese) of items related to *Botchan* and his creator **Sōseki Natsume**.

You'll need to return to the second floor to gain entrance to the **Yushinden**, which has been empty since 1950 (it was only ever used ten times), but the imperial apartments, with their silver- and gilt-coated screens and ornamental gardens, have been preserved.

DŌGO

0 ── 100 metres

Giyaman Glass Museum

Dōgo Kan

Tsubaki-no-yu

Dōgo Onsen Honkan

Isaniwa-jinja

Bus Stop ★

Dogo Onsen

Ehime Bank

Shiki Kinen Museum

Dōgo-kōen

■ **DRINKING AND NIGHTLIFE**
Wani to Sai Circus Bar 1

● **EATING**
Cha-Raku 1
Daikokuya 2
Dōgo no Machiya 3
Nikitatsu-an 4

■ **ACCOMMODATION**
Hotel Dōgo Yaya 2
Dōgo Yumekura 4
Sen Guesthouse 1
Yamatoya Honten 3

▼ City centre

Ishite-ji & Oku Dōgo ▶

DŌGO ONSEN'S CULTURAL HERITAGE

"If you went first class, for only 8 sen they lent you a bathrobe, an attendant washed you, and a girl served you tea in one of those elegant, shallow cups that they use in the tea ceremony. I always went first class".

Botchan by Sōseki Natsume, 1906

It may no longer be so cheap, nor do the attendants scrub your back, but a bath at the grand **Dōgo Onsen Honkan** is still a treat, as Sōseki lovingly described in his classic novel, set in Matsuyama in the early twentieth century. This is purportedly the oldest **hot-spring** resort in Japan, and is mentioned in the 1300-year-old history book the *Nihon Shoki*. According to legend, a white **heron** dipped its injured leg into the hot water gushing out of the rocks and found that it had healing properties. By the sixth century, the onsen's fame reached the ears of Prince Shotoku, and his royal patronage cemented its reputation. By the seventeenth century, the local *daimyō* Matsudaira Sadayuki had **segregated** the baths into those for monks and samurai, and those for lower-class merchants and craftsmen. He also introduced women-only baths and created facilities for animals to soak away their ills (the animal baths were only closed in 1966).

The present architectural extravaganza was built in 1894, and the heron, which has become the symbol of the baths, is commemorated in a statue atop the three-storey building's ornate roof. Inside, there are two types of bath, plus the Yushinden, a special bath built in 1899 for the Imperial family, but now drained of water.

You'll be guided around by one of the no-nonsense female attendants who'll explain, in Japanese, how the rooms were specially constructed to foil any would-be assassins.

Tsubaki-no-yu

椿の湯 • 19-22 Dōgo Yuno-machi • Daily 6am–10.30pm • ¥400 • ☎ 089 935 6586

A minute's walk along the arcade from the Dōgo Onsen Honkan is the separate modern bathhouse **Tsubaki-no-yu**, meaning "Hot Water of Camellia". The granite bath here is much larger than those at the Honkan and uses water from the same hot-spring source. You won't find so many tourists here – rather, elderly locals who take their bathing seriously.

Shiki Kinen Museum

子規記念博物館, Shiki Kinen Hakubutsukan • Tues–Sun 9am–4.30pm • ¥400 • ☎ 089 931 5566, ⓦ sikihaku.lesp.co.jp • Contact in advance to organize English-language tour

In the eastern corner of Dōgo-kōen is the **Shiki Kinen Museum**, which houses some rather dry displays telling the life story of Masaoka Shiki (see box, p.687) and setting his literature in its cultural context. The displays have English translations, and it's also possible to book an English-language tour that provides more insight into the displays and Shiki's life. The park itself is also worth visiting for its attractive river vista lined with cherry trees, as well as its historical significance – it is the former site of Yuzuki-jō and contains a number of historical monuments.

Giyaman Glass Museum

瓶泥舎びいどろぎやまんガラス美術館, Bindeisha Biidoro Giyaman Garasu Bijutsukan • 7-21 Dōgo Midoridai • Mon & Thurs–Sun 10am–5pm • ¥1000 • ☎ 089 922 3771, ⓦ bindeisha.co.jp

Near the *Sen Guesthouse* (see p.693) and housed in a private home away from the bustle of downtown Dōgo is the charming **Giyaman Glass Museum**. There are exquisite Edo-, Meiji- and Taishō-period pieces of glass from the owner's private collection, and the designs and colours are surprisingly modern. It's remarkable that so many fragile objects, such as a set of small glass plates made in 1788, have survived more than two hundred years of earthquakes and war. Don't be put off by the museum manager escorting you through the exhibition rooms – it's because of the fragile nature of the objects on display.

9

Ishite-ji

石手寺 • 2-29-21 Ishite • **Temple** Daily • Free • **Museum** Daily 8am–5pm • ¥200 • Walk for 15min east of the Dōgo tram terminus along the main road or hop on the #8 or #52 bus (¥150) to Oku Dōgo, which will drop you outside the temple gate • ☎ 089 977 0870

Eight of the 88 temples on Shikoku's sacred circuit are in Matsuyama, but the most famous – and without a doubt the most unusual – is the 51st, **Ishite-ji**. Unlike the pilgrimage's other 87 temples, Ishite-ji has used its accumulated wealth to branch out into **surreal forms** of religious expression. Tucked away behind the main temple buildings are dimly lit tunnels lined with hundreds of Buddhas and other icons. Condensation drips heavily from the tunnel ceiling if it's been raining, adding to the slightly foreboding atmosphere. Further on, in the tunnel which heads upwards, flashing fairy and strobe lights (activated as you approach) and the piped sound of a priest wailing mantras create the impression that you've stumbled into an esoteric rave.

The main tunnel emerges from behind a rock on the hill above the temple, close to the crumbling entrance to a **park** containing more bizarre statues, at the centre of which is a squat, golden-domed 3D **mandala**. Enter this dimly lit, circular hall and you'll be confronted by a two-hundred-strong congregation of wooden *jizō*, between 1m and 3m high, carved with Buddhist sexual symbols and arranged in tiered circles. Oddly, while the main temple is usually heaving with pilgrims, very few bother to head up to the park, making it a nice place to relax for a few minutes and take in your unusual surroundings. Climbing up the slope from the mandala will lead to a large graveyard and, on the summit of the adjoining hill, the looming statue of Buddhist saint Kōbō Daishi, founder of Shikoku's pilgrim trail (see p.636).

ARRIVAL AND DEPARTURE

By plane Matsuyama's airport (☎089 972 5600, ⓦ matsuyama-airport.co.jp) lies 6km west of the centre; bus #52 from here takes about 15min to reach the JR station (¥310) and continues on to Dōgo, and there's also a more comfortable, though less frequent, limousine bus (¥410). A taxi from the airport to the centre of town costs around ¥2500.
Destinations Fukuoka (4 daily; 45min); Kagoshima (daily; 1hr); Nagoya (4 daily; 1hr 10min); Naha (daily; 1hr 40min); Osaka Itami (11 daily; 50min); Osaka Kansai (daily; 1hr); Shanghai (2 weekly; 1hr 50min); Tokyo Haneda (12 daily; 1hr 35min); Tokyo Narita (2 daily; 1hr 55min).
By train Trains pull in at the JR Matsuyama Station, just west of the city centre – from here it's roughly a 10min walk to the castle.
Destinations Okayama (hourly; 2hr 45min); Takamatsu (hourly; 2hr 30min); Uwajima (hourly; 1hr 25min).
By bus Buses pull in beside the train station.

Destinations Kōbe (9 daily; 4hr 30min); Kōchi (11 daily; 2hr 30min); Kyoto (2 daily; 5hr 30min); Nagoya (daily; 10hr 20min); Okayama (6 daily; 2hr 50min); Onomichi (2 daily; 2hr 10min); Osaka (15 daily; 5hr 30min); Takamatsu (15 daily; 2hr 40min); Tokyo (daily; 11hr); Tokushima (7 daily; 3hr 10min).
By ferry and hydrofoil Ferries from several ports in western Honshū and Kyūshū dock at Takahama and Matsuyama Kankō ports – both around 10km north of Matsuyama. The terminus of the Iyo Tetsudō train line (Takahama Station) is within walking distance of both ports, from where it's a 25min journey (¥410) into Shi-eki just south of the castle. The fastest connection with Honshū is the hydrofoil from Hiroshima (1hr 8min; ¥6900).
Destinations Beppu (daily; 3hr 30min); Hiroshima (hydrofoil: 14 daily; 1hr 8min; ferry: 10 daily; 2hr 40min); Kita-kyushu (daily; 7hr); Oita (daily; 3hr 45min); Osaka (daily; 9hr 20min); Yanai (4 daily; 2hr 20min).

GETTING AROUND

By tram Matsuyama's city centre is easily covered on foot, but to travel between here and Dōgo you'll most likely need to use the tram network. There are four main tram routes: one loop line and three other routes all running through the city centre at Ichiban-chō, past the castle and ending at the delightfully old-fashioned Dōgo terminal. Fares are a flat ¥160 and must be paid to the driver on leaving the tram. A one-day ticket, offering unlimited travel on the trams, is a bargain at ¥500, and can be bought onboard. A couple of special tram services are pulled by the Botchan Ressha, designed like the steam trains that ran through the city during the Meiji era; a single trip on these costs ¥800, or an extra ¥300 for one-day ticket holders.
By bus The regular buses from the station are most useful for reaching further-flung areas of the city, such as the airport and Oku Dōgo.
By car Budget Rent-a-Car has a branch at the airport (☎0120 054 317).
By bike Apart from the castle hill, Matsuyama is reasonably flat so it's a good city to cycle around. Bicycles can be rented from the cycle port in front of the station, the castle or Dōgo Station for ¥300 per day.

INFORMATION

Tourist information is available all over Matsuyama, starting with booths at the train station and the airport. For more detailed help, head for EPIC – Ehime Prefecture International Centre (Mon–Sat 8.30am–5pm; ☏089 917 5678, ⍵epic .or.jp) – a couple of minutes' walk from the Minami-machi tram stop. As well as a small library of English-language books, free wi-fi and bicycle rental (for up to two weeks), EPIC can arrange goodwill guides to show you around the city and also hosts classes on Japanese traditional arts. Another option for free volunteer guides is the Matsuyama International Centre (Tues–Sun 9am–5.30pm; ☏089 943 2025), on the ground floor of COMS, 6-4-20 Sanbanchō. The Dōgo tourist information office (daily April–Sept 8am–9pm, Oct–March 8am–8pm; ☏089 921 3708), across the road from the Dōgo tram terminus, can provide English maps and leaflets, as well as bicycle rental (¥300/day).

ACCOMMODATION

With its baths and great range of accommodation, the most pleasant **place to stay** in Matsuyama is Dōgo. If you want to be based more centrally, you'll find plenty of cheap business hotels around the JR station as well as in the city centre – expect to pay around ¥5000 for a single room or ¥8000 for a double or twin.

MATSUYAMA

Abis Inn アビスイン 2-3-3 Katsuyamachō ☏089 998 6000, ⍵abis.ne.jp/dogo/index.html; map p.688. This standard business hotel is well positioned at the end of Ichiban-chō. Rooms are well maintained, and singles are good value. Rates include a light breakfast. ☈ **¥7980**

ANA Hotel Matsuyama 松山全日空ホテル 3-2-1 Ichiban-chō ☏089 933 5511, ⍵anahotelmatsuyama .com; map p.688. This smart hotel in the city centre has a range of stylish rooms, several restaurants and a shopping arcade. Rates for the less flash rooms in the annexe are substantially cheaper, especially the singles (¥7500). ☈ **¥30,000**

Check Inn Matsuyama チェックイン松山 2-7-3 Sanbanchō ☏089 998 7000, ⍵checkin.co.jp /matsuyama; map p.688. Emerald-green leather sofas, a Rococo-style grandfather clock and chandeliers in the lobby, plus even more chandeliers in the rooms, give this comfortable, well-priced business hotel in the centre of the city more than a touch of elegance. The rooftop onsen baths are also a plus. ☈ **¥7510**

International Hotel Matsuyama 国際ホテル松山 1-13 Ichiban-chō ☏089 932 5111, ⍵kokusai-h.jp; map p.688. Good-value mid-range hotel near the castle and shopping district, with comfortably furnished rooms and some striking interior design in its public areas and restaurants. The retro-to-the-max top-floor Chinese restaurant has to be seen to be believed. **¥12,400**

Hotel JAL City Matsuyama ホテルJALシティ松山 1-10-10 Ōtemachi ☏089 913 2580, ⍵matsuyama .jalcity.co.jp; map p.688. This hotel is surprisingly good value for the price and location. Rooms are super-clean, comfortable and well appointed, and some have castle views. Staff are helpful and attentive, and there's both an Italian and Japanese restaurant in house. ☈ **¥18,480**

DŌGO

Hotel Dōgo Yaya 道後ややホテル 6-1 Dōgo Tako-chō ☏089 907 1181, ⍵yayahotel.jp; map p.690. Elegant, new hotel decorated in a modern style with tatami and wood. Rooms are chic and comfortable. The in-house buffet restaurant serves up healthy vegetable and seafood dishes. **¥26,000**

Dōgo Yumekura 道後夢蔵 4-5 Yugetsu-chō ☏089 931 1180, ⍵yume-kura.jp; map p.690. This fancy ryokan is just behind the Honkan. The rooms are modern and luxurious with their own wooden bathtubs and deluxe amenities. The food is beautifully presented *kaiseki-ryori*, served in your room. ☈ **¥31,629**

★ Sen Guesthouse 鷺ゲストハウス Dōgo Tako-chō ☏089 961 1513, ⍵senguesthouse-matsuyama.com; map p.690. This friendly, well-run guesthouse is the best budget option in Matsuyama, and it's also an excellent place to pick up information about further travels in Shikoku. The facility is spacious, with pleasant communal areas and a roof terrace. Rooms are stylish and well equipped with comfortable mattresses and lockers. ☈ Dorms **¥2700**, doubles **¥7000**

Yamatoya Honten 大和屋本店 20-8 Dōgo Yunomachi ☏089 935 8880, ⍵yamatoyahonten.com; map p.690. Hotels with their own nō stage are few and far between, but not only does the *Yamatoya Honten* have one, it also stages two short nightly performances (30min and 10min). The tatami rooms are well up to deluxe standard, but there are also more modest, slightly dated Western-style single rooms and a rotemburo in the basement. ☈ **¥25,920**

EATING

As befits a big city, Matsuyama has a wide range of **restaurants** and **cafés**. Local specialities include the sponge roly-poly cake called *taruto* (タルト), inspired by a Portuguese confection introduced to Japan 350 years ago through the port of Nagasaki; the three-coloured rice dumplings on sticks called *Botchan dango*, after the character's favourite sweet; and *goshiki sōmen*, thin noodles made in five colours.

9

MATSUYAMA

Café Marinecco カフェマリネコ 3-1-3 Ōkaidō ⓣ089 935 5896; map p.688. This is a convivial café-cum-wine bar with stylish wooden interiors and menus handwritten on chalkboards. It has a good selection of lunch dishes such as pasta (from ¥680), while the outdoor tables are the perfect place for watching the world go by with a pint of Guinness or Kilkenny (¥800) and a pizza (¥980). Daily 11.30am–3pm & 5pm–2am.

★**Charlie's Vegetable** チャーリーズ・ベジタブル 2-3-16 Ōkaidō ⓣ089 915 6110, ⓦcharlies-vegetable.com; map p.688. This stylish restaurant is entirely devoted to vegetarian cuisine. The first floor is the buffet area, where you can choose from a huge array of fresh salads, soups, curries and even vegetable desserts. Table seating is upstairs. Lunch from ¥1280 and dinner from ¥1750. Mon & Wed–Sun 11am–3pm & 6pm–midnight.

Everest Food エベレスト・フード 2-2-7 Ōkaidō ⓣ089 945 7577; map p.688. This is a popular Indian and Nepali restaurant serving twenty different types of curry (from ¥590), tandoori mixed grills (¥1590), momos (¥600), samosas (¥490) and naans (¥300). Indian and Nepali beers are also available (from ¥390). Daily 11am–10.30pm.

★**Fujiko Michael** 不二子マイケル 2-4-9 Niban-chō ⓣ089 943 0600; map p.688. Wildly popular *izakaya* with counter seating and small tatami booths. The menu is mostly fish and seafood dishes. The *kamameshi no dashi kake* (¥450), a rice and fish stew cooked in an iron pot, is highly recommended. Mon–Thurs & Sun 5pm–1am, Fri & Sat 5pm–3am.

Goshiki Sōmen Morikawa 五色そうめん森川 3-5-4 Sanban-chō ⓣ089 933 3838; map p.688. This is the most famous place in town to sample *somen*, the five-coloured noodles. In front of the restaurant is a shop where you can buy the noodles, packed as souvenir sets, for around ¥300. Lunchtime set menus start at ¥880; noodles on their own are cheaper. Daily 11am–10.30pm.

Hanbay 薄利多賣半兵ヱ 1-6-2 Ōkaidō ⓣ089 931 3131, ⓦhanbey.com; map p. 688. This retro *izakaya* in the heart of Ōkaidō is decked out with kitch decor and curios from the Shōwa Era. The food is also old-school drinkers' fare and very, very cheap. Virtually everything on the menu seems to come on a skewer, with classics such as *yakitori* (from ¥50), *kushi-age* (from ¥80) and *yaki-soba* (¥280). Mon–Thurs 5pm–midnight, Fri & Sat 5pm–1am.

Kawasemi 川瀬見 2-5-6 Niban-chō ⓣ089 933 9697, ⓦkawasemi.ecnet.jp; map p.688. The portions in this stylish *kaiseki* (Japanese haute cuisine) restaurant are small, but your taste buds will be subtly challenged. Look for the word "club" in English on the mauve sign and go up to the second floor. You can get a *kaiseki*-style lunch/dinner from ¥2100/7000. Daily noon–2pm & 5–10pm.

Kiyomaru 清まる 4-6 Hanazonomachi ⓣ089 948 9588, ⓦtonkatsupafe.jp; map p.688. *Tonkatsu* (pork cutlet) restaurants are a dime a dozen in Japan, but *Kiyomaru* has reinvented the old classic by creating a range of *tonkatsu* desserts. The restaurant's "abnormal menu" lists bizarre hybrids, such as sweet chocolate katsu with spicy mayonnaise and custard cheese katsu (¥650 small; ¥1050 large), but its signature dish is the *tonkatsu parfait* (¥800) where pork cutlets are served with green tea ice cream and fresh fruit. Oh, and they have regular *tonkatsu-teishoku* sets (from ¥850) for those who just want to eat something normal. Daily 11am–9pm.

Provence Dining プロヴァンス ANA Hotel Matsuyama, 3-2-1 Ichiban-chō ⓣ089 933 5511, ⓦanahotel matsuyama.com; map p.688. The best thing about the *ANA*'s top-floor restaurant is its grandstand view of Katsuyama Hill and the Bansui-sō villa, which is especially romantic when the buildings are lit up at night. The lunch buffet (¥1950) offers a selection of Mediterranean dishes. Dinner courses start at ¥2800. Daily 6.30am–9pm.

Sova Sova ソバソバ 3-2-35 Ōkaidō ⓣ089 945 5252; map p.688. Chic, laidback café-bar serving a range of simple dishes such as cold soba and rice bowls for under ¥1000. It's also a pleasantly quiet place for a drink in the evening. Closes irregularly. Mon, Tues & Thurs–Sun 11am–9pm.

DŌGO

Cha-Raku 茶楽 5-13 Yugetsu-chō ⓣ089 921 5388, ⓦyamadayamanju.jp/charaku; map p.690. This elegant, modern tearoom serves a variety of traditional teas and their signature *manju* (baked rice flour cakes with sweet bean filling). A *matcha* and *manju* set is ¥864. Daily 10am–7pm.

Daikokuya 大黒屋 8-21 Dōgo Tako-chō ⓣ089 925 5005, ⓦdaikokuya-udon.co.jp; map p.690. An udon and *kamameshi* (rice dishes cooked in a traditional iron pot) restaurant serving reasonably priced set meals, from ¥1870. There's also a 100min all-you-can-drink deal for ¥1600. Closed every third Wed of the month. Daily 11am–10pm.

Dōgo no Machiya 道後の町家カフェ 14-26 Yunomachi ⓣ089 986 8886, ⓦdogonomachiya.com; map p.690. Burger (¥670) and sandwich (¥460) café in a traditional house with a lovely garden at the rear. The space is split into smoking and non-smoking areas. Hearty breakfast sets go for ¥630. Closed third Wed of each month. Mon & Wed–Sun 10am–10pm.

Nikitatsu-an にきたつ庵 3-18 Dōgo Kitamachi ⓣ089 924 6617; map p.690. This sake brewery and restaurant serves imaginative modern Japanese cooking alongside superbly brewed sake and beers. Lunches start at ¥1470, dinners from ¥3150 and drinks from ¥450. There's also an outdoor deck for balmy nights. Tues–Sun 11am–9.30pm.

DRINKING AND NIGHTLIFE

The tight grid of streets between Niban-chō and Sanban-chō in Matsuyama heaves with **bars** and, in the summer, **beer gardens** appear on the roofs of several hotels including the *ANA Hotel Matsuyama* (see p.693).

MATSUYAMA

★**Flankey Kobayashi** フランキー小林 2-3 Ichiban-chō; map p.688. Drinks are a bargain at this lively standing bar popular with an international crowd, with beers and sake starting at ¥300. There's also dirt-cheap but fairly decent food available, such as pasta and curry (from ¥300). Mon–Sat 5pm–3am, Sun 5pm–midnight.

Underground Café アンダーグラウンド・カフェ 3-3-6 Ōkaidō ☏ 089 998 7710; map p.688. Down a side street on the way to the castle chairlift, this retro-chic café-bar has a very laidback vibe. Look out for the large Union Jack

flag hanging outside. The food is reasonable and there are occasional club events. Closed second and fourth Wed of every month. Daily noon–4am.

DŌGO

Wani to Sai Circus Bar ワニとサイ 1-39 Yunomachi ☏ 080 3319 2765; ⓦ facebook.com/wanitosai; map p.690. Quirky "artspace" bar and café run by a musician and puppeteer, serving Ehime sake (¥600) and noodles (¥800). It's located up near the steps to Isaniwa-jinja. Closes irregularly. Daily 8pm–late.

ENTERTAINMENT

Cinema Lunatic シネマルナティック 2F Matsuaeki Building ☏ 089 933 9240, ⓦ bit.ly/CinemaLunatic. This cinema shows independent foreign films. Closed Tues.

Matsuyama Shimin Kaikan 松山市民会館 Horinouchi ☏ 089 931 8181, ⓦ cul-spo.or.jp/mcph. Theatre, dance and orchestral performances are held at this venue, located in the southwest corner of Shiroyama-kōen near the castle.

Ōkaido Cinema Sunshine シネマサンシャイン大街道 1-5-10 Ōkaidō ☏ 089 986 6633, ⓦ cinemasunshine .co.jp/theater/okaido. Shows mainstream Hollywood and Japanese films. Daily.

Prefectural Cultural Centre 県民文化会館 2-5-1 Dōgo-machi ☏ 089 923 5111, ⓦ ecf.or.jp/himegin _hall. Orchestral and other music performances are held at this venue.

SHOPPING

Local products that make good **souvenirs** include *iyo-kasuri*, an indigo-dyed cloth; *hime temari*, colourful thread-covered balls that bring good luck; and *Tobe-yaki*, distinctive blue-patterned pottery. Check out Ōkaidō and Gintengai **arcades** for souvenir shops. Tobe-yaki pottery is distinguished by its robust feel and simple blue-and-white glaze.

Ehimeism Lublu Matsuyama エヒメイズムルブリュ松山 3-2-45 Ōkaidō ☏ 089 993 7557; map p.688. This is one of Matsuyama's most elegant souvenir shops. All the locally produced art and craft objects for sale here are stylish, functional and well designed. They also sell citrus essential oils (¥1500), room fragrances and other aromatherapy goods manufactured in Ehime Prefecture. Daily 9am–7pm.

Tobe-yaki Kankō Centre 砥部町芸創作館 82 Gohonmatsu, Tobe ☏ 089 962 6145, ⓦ www.town .tobe.ehime.jp/site/sousakukan; map p.688. The centre of the local pottery industry is Tobe, 13km from Matsuyama. Take a #18 or #19 bus here from Shi-eki (45min; ¥600) to visit the Tobe-yaki Kankō Centre, where you can watch pottery being made and make or decorate some pieces yourself. Mon–Wed & Fri–Sun 9am–5pm.

DIRECTORY

Bookshop Junkudo (5-7-1 Chifune-machi; ☏ 089 915 0075) has English books and magazines on the fourth floor (daily 10am–9pm).

Hospital The central prefectural hospital, Ehime Kenritsu Chūō Byōin (☏ 089 947 1111), is in Kasuga-machi, south of Shi-eki.

Laundry Okaya Coin Laundry, 43 Minami-Mochida (daily 6am–10.30pm).

Police The main police station is at 2 Minami Horibata (☏ 089 941 0111). Emergency numbers are listed on p.71.

Post office Matsuyama's main post office is at 3 Sanban-chō (Mon–Fri 9am–7pm, Sat 9am–5pm & Sun 9am–12.30pm). There's also a branch in Dōgo (Mon–Fri 9am–5pm), to the west of the shopping arcade. Both have ATMs that accept credit cards.

Kyūshū

九州

VOLCANIC POOL AT BEPPU

10

Kyūshū

The spectacular array of natural attractions on Kyūshū makes this, Japan's third-largest island, a feasible holiday destination on its own, providing a thrilling alternative to the regular Kantō and Kansai circuits. Here visitors can find themselves hiking the rim of the world's largest caldera, taking a lonesome onsen dip in the forest, surfing Japan's gnarliest waves, tracking down moss-coated cedar trees that predate Christianity or being showered with ash from a live volcano. It's perfectly possible to just scoot round the main cities in a week, but you'll need more like two to do the region justice, allowing time for the splendid mountainous interior and a boat trip out to Yakushima.

Closer to Korea than Tokyo, Kyūshū has long had close links with the Asian mainland, and its chief city, **Fukuoka**, is an important regional hub. An energetic city on the island's heavily developed north coast, Fukuoka is worth a stop for its museums, modern architecture and vibrant nightlife. If you've only got a couple of days on Kyūshū, however, **Nagasaki** represents the best all-round destination. Though its prime draw is the A-Bomb museum and related sights, the city also has a picturesque harbour setting, a laidback, cosmopolitan air and a smattering of temples and historical museums. From here it's a short hop east to **Kumamoto**, famous for its castle and landscaped garden, and the spluttering, smouldering cone of **Aso-san**. This is great hiking country, while hot-spring enthusiasts will also be in their element – from **Kurokawa Onsen**'s delightful rotemburo to the bawdy pleasures of **Beppu** on the east coast. The mountain village of **Takachiho** requires a fair detour, but it's worth it to see traditional dance performances depicting the antics of Japan's ancient gods. The island's southern districts contain more on the same theme – volcanoes, onsen and magnificent scenery. Highlights include **Sakurajima**, one of the world's most active volcanoes, which looms over the city of **Kagoshima**, while the lush island of **Yakushima**, 60km off the southern tip of Kyūshū, sports towering, thousand-year-old cedar trees.

Brief history

The ancient chronicles state that **Emperor Jimmu**, Japan's legendary first emperor, set out from southern Kyūshū to found the Japanese nation in 660 BC. Though the records are open to dispute, there's evidence of human habitation on Kyūshū from before the tenth

GOKASE-GAWA, TAKACHIHO

Highlights

❶ Fukuoka Slurp a bowl of ramen noodles at one of the open-air *yatai* stalls along the Tenjin River. **See p.702**

❷ Arita Admire and shop for gorgeous porcelain, amazing feats of clay with a 400-year history. **See p.714**

❸ Aso-san The peaks of this active volcano offer superb views across the largest caldera in the world. **See p.739**

❹ Takachiho Go boating through a gorge on the emerald-green Gokase-gawa, then watch the gods cavort at a *kagura* performance in this beguiling mountain village. **See p.743**

❺ Beppu Relaxing hot-spring resort where you can take a sand-bath or hike up to a couple of hidden onsen in the western hills. **See p.746**

❻ Usuki Contemplate Japan's finest stone-carved Buddhas, sitting serenely in their wooded valley for more than seven hundred years. **See p.752**

❼ Yakushima Go hiking in the rainiest place in Japan, through lush green forests up to the ancient Yaku-sugi cedars, some of the oldest trees in the world. **See p.773**

HIGHLIGHTS ARE MARKED ON THE MAP ON P.700

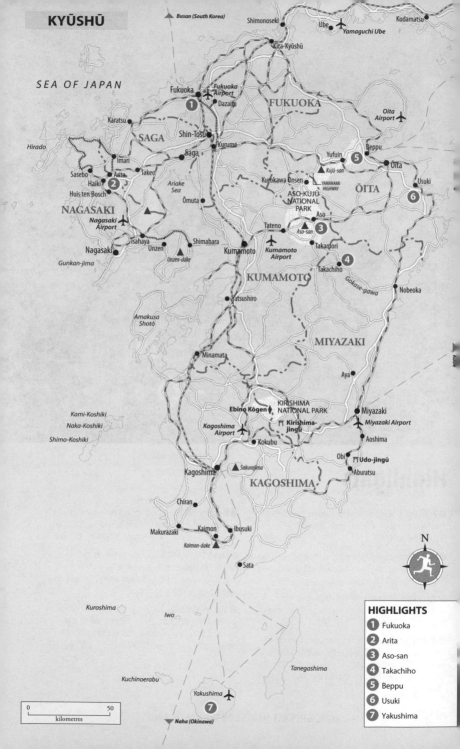

century BC, and by the beginning of the Yayoi period (300 BC–300 AD) the small kingdom of **Na** (as it was then known) was trading with China and Korea. Local merchants brought rice-farming and bronze-making techniques back to Japan, while in the twelfth century monks introduced Zen Buddhism to northern Kyūshū. Less welcome visitors arrived in 1274 and 1281 during the **Mongol invasions** under Kublai Khan. The first ended in a narrow escape when the Mongols withdrew, and the shogun ordered a protective wall to be built around Hakata Bay. By 1281 the Japanese were far better prepared, but their real saviour was a typhoon, subsequently dubbed *kami kaze*, or "wind of the gods", which whipped up out of nowhere and scattered the Mongol fleet on the eve of their massed assault.

Three hundred years later, in 1543, the first **Europeans** to reach Japan pitched up on the island of Tanegashima, off southern Kyūshū. Finding an eager market for their guns among the local *daimyō*, the Portuguese sailors returned a few years later, bringing with them **missionaries**, among them the Jesuit priest Francis Xavier. Within fifty years the Catholic Church, now also represented by Spanish Franciscans and Dominicans, was claiming some 600,000 Christian converts. The centre of activity was **Nagasaki**, where Chinese, Dutch and British merchants swelled the throng. In the early 1600s, however, the government grew increasingly wary of the Europeans in general and Christians in particular. By fits and starts successive shoguns stamped down on the religion and restricted the movement of all foreigners, until eventually only two small communities of Dutch and Chinese merchants were left in Nagasaki.

This period of isolation lasted until the mid-1850s, when Nagasaki and Kagoshima in particular found themselves at the forefront of the modernizing revolution that swept Japan

10

KYŪSHŪ'S TRAINS

Everyone knows that Japanese trains are among the best in the world – in Kyūshū, they go that little bit further. JR Kyūshū, the local division of Japan Rail, has won several international awards for the design of its trains, and some of them count as tourist sights in themselves. The bad news is that you'll have to pay extra for a ticket on the more interesting services; the good news is that they're all (bar the very fastest of the Shinkansen) included on the island- and nation-wide rail passes (see p.36). Such refinement has also come at a price: you may notice, on your way around the island, that some of the tracks are a little bumpy, the result of investment being directed to the trains themselves.

Kyūshū Shinkansen Completed in 2011, the Fukuoka–Kagoshima route is one of Japan's newest high-speed lines. Though slower than many mainland trains, with a top speed of 260km/hr, they have had much attention lavished on their carriages – check out the stylish seat design, and the rope curtains on the way to the bathrooms.

Yufuin-no-mori A green beast reflecting the colour of the mountains it passes through on its Fukuoka-to-Yufuin route (continuing to Beppu once a day), this features cabin-like relaxation rooms whose large windows allow you to enjoy superb views over a coffee (seat reservations required).

Kamome and **Sonic** Heading from Fukuoka to Nagasaki and Ōita respectively, these passenger trains come with wonderfully comfy seating. If riding the Kamome, check out the backlit ink-brush paintings in between carriages – the only time you'll ever want to take a picture of a train's toilet area.

Huis ten Bosch Linking the eponymous sight to Fukuoka, this train's carriages have been designed to an appropriately European template.

Aso Boy! Rather like a rolling amusement park, this train features a toy box and wooden ball pool, space-age white seating in the family car and a cartoon-meets-hotel-lobby lounge car. The Kumamoto–Aso tracks are currently under long-term repair, so Aso Boy pops up on various other lines around the island (seat reservations required).

Ibusuki-no-tamatebako If you're heading from Kagoshima to Ibusuki, adjust your schedule to ride this train, which features ocean-facing seats and a pine-lined interior (seat reservations required).

after the **Meiji Restoration**. Indeed, it was the armies of the Satsuma and Chōshū clans, both from Kyūshū, which helped restore the emperor to the throne, and many members of the new government hailed from the island. In 1877, however, Kagoshima's **Saigō Takamori** led a revolt against the Meiji government in what became known as the **Satsuma Rebellion**. Saigō's army was routed, but he's still something of a local hero in Kyūshū.

GETTING AROUND   KYŪSHŪ

By train Fukuoka's Hakata Station handles Shinkansen through-trains from Osaka to Kumamoto and Kagoshima, as well as firing its own trains out on the line south. From Hakata, other JR Kyūshū trains fan out to all the major towns; the vehicles are a cut above Japan's already sky-high standards (see box, p.701). Frustratingly, the company's English-language website (⊛ jrkyushu.co.jp/english) gives timetables only for the major lines, and even then only for the main stations; to plug the gaps, head to ⊛ hyperdia .com. JR Kyūshū offers its own three- and five-day rail passes (¥15,000 and ¥18,000) for travelling round the whole island, or just the north (including Nagasaki, Kumamoto, Aso, Yufuin and Beppu; ¥8500 and ¥10,000). There are more details on JR passes and discount tickets in Basics (see p.36). None of these passes are valid on the very

fastest of JR Kyūshū's Shinkansen services, the Mizuho.
By bus In the central uplands and southern Kyūshū, you'll need to supplement the trains with local buses. If you're on a whistle-stop tour, you might want to consider one of the SunQ bus passes (⊛ sunqpass.jp/english), which offer unlimited travel on most highway buses and local services throughout Kyūshū (¥10,000 for 3 consecutive days, ¥14,000 for 4) or just the five northern prefectures (¥8000 for 3 consecutive days). Not all bus companies are covered, however, nor are some of the fastest express services between cities. For English-language timetables on the main lines, go to ⊛ atbus-de.com.
By car For exploring the more remote areas, car rental is an excellent option; there are outlets in almost every town and in all the main tourist areas.

Fukuoka

福岡

The country's sixth-largest city, **FUKUOKA** ("Happy Hills") is one of the most likeable places in Japan – indeed, despite the fact that it's not exactly a household name abroad, it regularly pops up on global best-places-to-live lists. While it boasts few actual sights, there's a certain Kyūshū-style *joie de vivre* here, best exemplified at the umpteen rustic street-side *yatai*, where locals slurp happily away on their ramen while knocking back beer, sake or whatever takes their fancy. Until recently, the city was an industrial nonentity, notable only for its transport connections to Korea and the rest of the island, but its renaissance has been remarkable. Visit today and you'll find a squeaky-clean metropolis that makes for a great introduction to Kyūshū, or indeed Japan as a whole; as such, it deserves a day or two of any traveller's time.

Highlights include a couple of excellent museums and ranks of eye-catching modern architecture, notably the shopping and leisure complex of **Canal City**. As with any self-respecting Japanese city of this size, Fukuoka maintains a lively entertainment district, in this case crammed onto the tiny river island of **Nakasu**, though it's safer on the wallet to head for the less glitzy bars and restaurants of **Tenjin**, the city's main downtown area. Further west is **Ōhori-kōen**, where you'll find the ruins of Fukuoka castle, as well as an art museum with an important collection of twentieth-century works; and **Momochi**, home to the iconic Fukuoka Tower.

An excellent, easy day-trip can be made south of Fukuoka to the ancient town of **Dazaifu** (see p.760), once the seat of government for all of southern Japan, but now a pleasant backwater with a fine collection of temples and shrines and a fascinating museum.

Hakata

博多

Even today the old cultural and economic divide between the original castle town, Fukuoka, on the west bank of the river and the former merchants' quarter of **Hakata** on

FUKUOKA

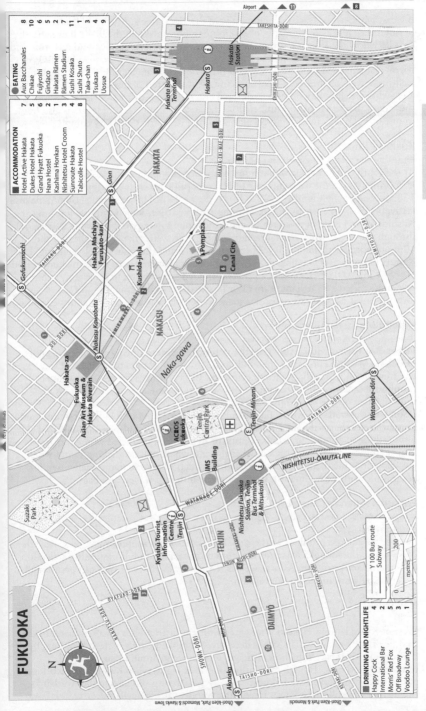

10

■ ACCOMMODATION
Hotel Active Hakata   7
Dukes Hotel Hakata   5
Grand Hyatt Fukuoka   6
Hana Hostel   2
Kashima Honkan   1
Nishitetsu Hotel Croom   3
Sunroute Hakata   4
Tabicolle Hostel   8

● EATING
Aux Bacchanales   8
Chikae   10
Fujiyoshi   6
Gindaco   5
Hakata Ramen   2
Ramen Stadium   7
Sushi Kosaka   11
Sushi Shuto   4
Taka-chan   1
Tsukasa   3
Uosue   9

■ DRINKING AND NIGHTLIFE
Happy Cock   4
International Bar   2
Morris' Red Fox   5
Off Broadway   3
Voodoo Lounge   1

Y100 Bus route
Subway

0   200
metres

10

the east bank can be traced, albeit faintly, in the city's streets. Much of Hakata consists of dull office blocks, with plenty of shopping opportunities in the malls above and the arcades below the JR station, but the district is also home to the city's oldest shrine and its most rumbustious festival. You'll also still find the occasional wooden building, narrow lane or aged wall, while some of the unique Hakata culture is showcased in its well-presented folk museum. Not surprisingly, many **craft** industries originated in this area, while geisha still work the traditional entertainment district of **Nakasu** (though these days they're vastly outnumbered by the area's working girls). Hakata is also home to one of Fukuoka's most famous landmarks, the futuristic **Canal City** complex.

Kushida-jinja

櫛田神社 • 1-41 Kamikawabata-machi • Museum daily 10am–5pm • ¥300

At the south end of **Kamikawabata-dōri**, a covered shopping arcade, a left turn under a *torii* brings you to the back entrance of Hakata's principal shrine, **Kushida-jinja**, built in 1587 but originally founded in 757. This is the home of Hakata's annual **Gion Yamakasa festival** (July 1–15), which climaxes on the 15th in a 5km-long dawn race finishing at Kushida-jinja, in which seven teams manhandle one-tonne portable shrines (*yamakasa*) through the streets while spectators douse them with water; they use replicas of the 10m-tall portable shrine you'll see between the *torii* and the main temple building. Like Kyoto's Gion festival (see box, p.437), the Yamakasa harks back to the Kamakura period (1185–1333 AD) when Buddhist priests sprinkled sacred water to drive away summer epidemics. There's a small **museum** of shrine treasures in the grounds – it's not of great interest, but it does stock English-language leaflets about Kushida-jinja and the festival.

Hakata Machiya Furusato-kan

博多町家ふるさと館 • 6-10 Reisen-machi • Daily 10am–6pm • ¥200 • ⓦ 092 281 7761, ⓦ hakatamachiya.com

Just east of Kushida-jinja, you'll see the traditional whitewashed walls and grey roofs of **Hakata Machiya Furusato-kan**, a folk museum which evokes the Hakata of the late nineteenth and early twentieth centuries. Its centrepiece is a restored wooden shophouse (*machiya*) from the mid-Meiji era, but be sure also to catch the twenty-minute video on the Gion Yamakasa festival.

Some of the **crafts** for which Fukuoka is renowned can be seen in the museum (and bought in the shop): the most famous are Hakata *ningyō*, hand-painted, unglazed clay dolls fashioned as samurai, kabuki actors, or demure, kimono-clad women; *champon*, long-stemmed, glass toys with a bowl at the end which make a clicking sound when you blow into them; and Hakata *ori*, slightly rough silk fabric traditionally used for *obi* (sashes worn with kimono), but now made into ties, wallets and bags.

Fukuoka Asian Art Museum

福岡アジア美術館, Fukuoka Ajia Bijutsukan • 7F 3-1 Shimokawabata-machi • 10am–8pm; closed Wed • ¥200 • ⓣ 092 263 1100, ⓦ faam.city.fukuoka.lg.jp

Located on the seventh floor of the ritzy Hakata Riverain shopping complex, near the Naka-gawa, the **Fukuoka Asian Art Museum** boasts a modest but interesting collection of contemporary art from Asia, as well as temporary exhibitions. You can occasionally see artists at work in the upstairs studio.

Nakasu

中洲

West of Kushida-jinja, **Nakasu** is an entertainment district built on a sandbank in the middle of the Naka-gawa. Its size is deceptive – despite being a mere 1.5km long by 250m wide, this space somehow manages to squeeze in around two thousand restaurants and bars. Though most atmospheric at night, when hundreds of working girls clamour for custom and almost as many *yatai* set up shop along the riverbanks, the district can still make for an interesting wander during daylight.

Canal City

1-2 Sumiyoshi • Ⓦ canalcity.co.jp

The weird and wonderful multicoloured blocks of **Canal City**, a showpiece urban renewal project inaugurated in 1996, lie near Nakasu's southernmost point on the east bank of the river. Apart from two large hotels, a major theatre and a thirteen-screen cinema with seating for nearly 2600, the complex also houses shopping arcades and a host of bars and restaurants. The liveliest part, however, is the interior court, where the salmon-pink and turquoise buildings wrap round the "canal", which erupts every half-hour during the day with five-storey-high jets of water, augmented by special light and animation shows on the hour in the evening.

Tenjin

天神

West of the Naka-gawa, the city's downtown area, **Tenjin**, has upmarket boutiques, galleries, department stores and "fashion buildings", as well as plenty of bars, restaurants and *yatai*, but little in the way of sights.

ACROS Fukuoka

1-1 Tenjin • **Step garden** Daily: March, April, Sept & Oct 9am–6pm; May–Aug 9am–6.30pm; Nov–Feb 9am–5pm • Free • **Rooftop observation deck** Sat & Sun 10am–4pm • Free • **Crafts gallery** Daily 10am–6pm • Free

The unusual **ACROS Fukuoka** building, meaning "Asian CrossRoads Over the Sea", was completed in 1995 as a cultural centre. Its terraced south side forms a "step garden", facing Tenjin Central Park and leading up to a rooftop observation deck, while inside there is a symphony hall, an information centre (see p.707), an interesting prefectural crafts exhibition space, shops and restaurants.

Ōhori-kōen

大濠公園

In 1601, the Kuroda lords built their castle on a low hill sitting among coastal marshes to the west of the Naka-gawa. Today, just a few old stone walls and ruined watchtowers remain, but the castle grounds have been landscaped to form **Ōhori-kōen**, a large public park. It's most easily accessible from the subway; exit 3 of Ōhori-kōen Station brings you up beside a large lake spanned by a pleasing necklace of islets and bridges.

Fukuoka Art Museum

福岡市美術館, Fukuoka-shi Bijutsukan • 1-6 Ōhorikōen • Closed for renovation until March 2019 • ☎ 092 714 6051, Ⓦ fukuoka-art-museum.jp

Ōhori-kōen's foremost attraction is the **Fukuoka Art Museum**, situated in its southeast corner. Its three ground-floor rooms contain a hotchpotch of early Japanese and Asian art, including the Kuroda family treasures and several eye-catching statues of Buddhism's twelve guardian generals (Jūni Jinshō), each crowned with his associated zodiacal beast. Upstairs you leap a few centuries to the likes of Dalí, Miró and Chagall in a great retrospective of twentieth-century Western art, displayed alongside contemporary Japanese works.

Momochi

モモチ

To the west of central Fukuoka, the **Momochi** district has only recently been reclaimed from the sea, and handed over to ambitious city planners. A fair proportion of international visitors to the area are English teachers on visa runs from Korea, while locals swing by for baseball games at the Fukuoka Dome and retail therapy at the district's several outlet malls. However, it's worth heading this way for a zip up the **Fukuoka Tower** or a visit to the excellent **Fukuoka City Museum**.

Fukuoka Tower

福岡タワー • 2-3-26 Momochihama • Observation deck daily 9.30am–10pm • ¥800 • ⓦ fukuokatower.co.jp • 15min walk from Nishijin subway station, or bus #306 from Hakata or #302 from Tenjin (bus stop on Watanabe-dōri, south of Nanotsu-dōri)

Momochi's most striking building by far is the 234m-high, pencil-thin **Fukuoka Tower**, which has become one of the city's most famous icons. Primarily a communications tower, its first section is an empty shell coated with 8000 sheets of mirror glass, while the top third bristles with radio transmitters. In between, at 123m, the architects slipped in an observation deck to capitalize on the spectacular views of Fukuoka and Hakata Bay.

Fukuoka City Museum

福岡市博物館, Fukuoka-shi Hakubatsukan • 3-1-1 Momochihama • Tues–Sun 9.30am–5.30pm • ¥200 • ☏ 092 845 5011, ⓦ museum.city.fukuoka.jp

Five minutes' walk south of the Fukuoka Tower is the excellent **Fukuoka City Museum** which occupies an imposing, late-1980s structure of mirrored glass and grey stone. The museum's most famous exhibit is the two-centimetre-square **Kin-in gold seal**, ornamented with a dumpy, coiled snake. According to its inscription, the seal was presented by China's Han emperor to the King of Na (see p.701) in 57 AD – it was only rediscovered in 1784 in a grave on an island in Hakata Bay.

ARRIVAL AND DEPARTURE   FUKUOKA

By plane So close to the city centre that you could walk into town in half an hour, Fukuoka Airport (domestic terminal ☏ 092 621 6059, international ☏ 092 483 7007, ⓦ fuk-ab.co.jp) is handily located only two subway stops east of Hakata and five from Tenjin; the subway station is located in the domestic terminal, which is linked to the international terminal by shuttle bus (10–15min; free). There are also Nishitetsu buses every 20min direct to Hakata Station (15min; ¥260) and Tenjin's Nishitetsu-Fukuoka Station (30min; ¥310) from the international terminal. International flights arrive from all over East and Southeast Asia, as well as from Helsinki (with Finnair). And yes, the airport's code really is "FUK".

Destinations Kagoshima (1 daily; 55min); Kansai International (6 daily; 1hr); Miyazaki (13 daily; 40min); Nagoya (1–2 hourly; 1hr 10min); Naha (1–2 hourly; 1hr 40min); Niigata (3 daily; 1hr 30min); Osaka (Itami; 10 daily; 1hr 10min); Sapporo (5 daily; 2hr 10min); Sendai (6 daily; 1hr 40min); Tokyo (2–4 hourly; 1hr 30min); Yakushima (1 daily; 1hr).

By train Don't go looking for a Fukuoka Station; the vast majority of trains to the city arrive at Hakata, a station to the east of the centre, its somewhat confusing name dating from before the two neighbouring towns of Fukuoka and Hakata merged. Hakata Station is where the Tōkaidō and Kyūshū Shinkansen meet, and is also the focal point of Kyūshū's local JR services. Further west, across the Naka-gawa in Tenjin, Nishitetsu-Fukuoka Station serves Dazaifu.

Hakata Station destinations Arita (1–2 hourly; 1hr 25min); Beppu (1–3 hourly; 2hr–3hr 20min); Hiroshima (every 15min; 1hr 10min–1hr 50min); Huis ten Bosch (hourly; 1hr 45min); Kagoshima (every 30min; 1hr 20min–2hr 30min); Kumamoto (every 30min; 40min–1hr 20min); Kyoto (every 30min; 2hr 50min); Miyazaki (hourly, usually with a change in Ōita; 5hr 45min); Nagasaki (every 30min–1hr; 2hr); Osaka (every 15–20min; 2hr 35min); Takeo (hourly; 1hr 10min); and Tokyo (every 30min; 5hr–5hr 20min).

Nishitetsu-Fukuoka Station destinations Dazaifu (3–4 hourly, with a change at Nishitetsu-Futsukaichi; 30min).

By bus Most long-distance buses call at the Tenjin Bus Terminal in the Nishitetsu-Fukuoka Station, before terminating at the Hakata Bus Terminal (aka Fukuoka Kōtsu Centre), immediately northwest of Hakata Station.

Destinations Beppu (roughly hourly; 2hr 30min); Dazaifu (2–4 hourly; 45min); Kagoshima (every 30min–1hr; 4hr 30min); Kumamoto (every 10–20min; 2hr 20min); Kyoto (1 daily; 10hr 30min); Miyazaki (every 20min–1hr; 4hr 30min); Nagasaki (every 20–30min; 2hr 30min); Osaka (2 daily; 9hr 20min–10hr 40min).

By ferry Fukuoka is connected by ferry and hydrofoil to Busan, Korea's second-largest city. Most travel on one of Beetle's hydrofoils (2 daily; 3hr; ☏ 092 281 2315, ⓦ jrbeetle.co.jp), which cost ¥13,000 one-way (¥8900 if booked in advance); round-trips can be as low as ¥9800 if booked ahead. Some find the journey uncomfortable – it's a little like sitting on a washing machine for a few hours – but a more leisurely trip can be enjoyed on the daily Camellia Line ferry (☏ 092 262 2323, ⓦ camellia-line .co.jp), which costs from ¥9000 one-way. The ferry heads to Busan by day in under 6hr, then back to Fukuoka overnight. From the ferry terminals, take a Nishitetsu city bus for the 10min ride to either Tenjin (¥190) or Hakata Station (¥230).

GETTING AROUND

By subway The easiest way of getting around Fukuoka is on its fast and efficient subway system; most places of interest fall within walking distance of a station. Trains run from 5.30am to midnight, and the minimum fare is ¥200. If you expect to make several journeys, it's worth buying a one-day subway card (¥620), which also gets you small discounts at several museums.

By bus For those places not within immediate striking distance of the subway, such as the Hawks Town area, you'll need to use Nishitetsu city buses, most of which funnel through the Hakata Station–Tenjin corridor. The "Tourist City Pass" (¥820) is a one-day card that covers both city buses and the subway. Look out for the handy "100-yen bus" – where you pay a flat fare of ¥100 – which loops round from Hakata Station in both clockwise and anti-clockwise directions, via Nishitetsu-Fukuoka Station, Nakasu and Canal City.

Car rental Eki Rent-a-Car has offices in Hakata Station (☎092 431 5152) and at the airport's international terminal (☎092 281 2374).

INFORMATION

Information offices Fukuoka has a good sprinkling of information offices with English-speaking staff. There are desks in both airport terminals, but the main tourist office (daily 8am–9pm; ☎092 431 3003) is located on Hakata Station's central concourse. In Tenjin, there's an office on the ground floor of the Mitsukoshi store (daily 10am–6.30pm; ☎092 751 6904), in the same complex as the Nishitetsu-Fukuoka Station. Just north of here on Meiji-dōri, the attractive, new Kyūshū Tourist Information Centre (daily 9am–7pm; ☎092 731 7711, ⊛welcomekyushu .com) covers the whole island and offers a plethora of helpful services, including a currency exchange machine, wi-fi and PCs, and luggage storage and delivery. There's also a cultural and tourist information centre at ACROS Fukuoka (daily 10am–6pm, volunteer interpreters available 11am–5pm; ☎092 725 9100; see p.705).

Listings and map The free monthly magazine, *Fukuoka Now*, and its website ⊛fukuoka-now.com are worth a look for local events; it also produces a useful, free city map. Both magazine and map are available at tourist information offices and at various hotels, shops and restaurants.

ACCOMMODATION

Fukuoka has several modern, world-class **hotels** and a good selection of business hotels scattered around the city centre. The standard of budget accommodation has also improved recently; it's mostly located around Hakata Station.

Hotel Active! Hakata ホテルアクティブ！博多 3-20-16 Hakata-eki-mae ☎092 452 0001, ⊛hotel-active.com. Good-value option between Nakasu and the train station. They've got the basics right and a lot more besides – witness the hot-drink vending machines by the lift on every floor, stylishly decorated corridors, coin laundry with free detergent, and the excellent buffet breakfasts. Rooms are small, but that's a given at this price level. 🛜 **¥10,800**

★**Dukes Hotel Hakata** デュークスホテル博多 2-3-9 Hakata-eki-mae ☎092 472 1800, ⊛dukes -hotel.com. A lobby heavy with the scent of flowers sets a suitable tone for this elegant, British-styled business hotel, whose lovingly decorated rooms are excellent value for the price and location. 🛜 **¥9500**

Grand Hyatt Fukuoka グランドハイアット福岡 Canal City ☎092 282 1234, ⊛fukuoka.grand.hyatt.com. Landmark luxury hotel, offering a lively piano bar in the plunging atrium and large, beautifully designed rooms in a modern Japanese style, with elegant lighting, contemporary artworks and acres of light wood. Consider upgrading to a Club room (about ¥10,000/night extra) to score breakfast, afternoon tea and evening cocktails in the Grand Club lounge, which is set in a tranquil rooftop garden, as well as free access to the lap pool, gym and onsen (otherwise ¥2000/person/day for standard guests). 🛜 **¥22,000**

★**Hana Hostel** 福岡花宿 4-213 Kamikawabata-machi ☎092 282 5353, ⊛fukuoka.hanahostel.com. One of the best hostels on the island, with cheery staff and a fantastically central location, just off Kamikawabata shopping arcade. The curtained-off dorm beds are surprisingly large, and the many private rooms (with bunks or futons) are well appointed. There's also a roof terrace, kitchen, coin laundry, free luggage storage, communal PCs and rental bicycles. On Sat nights it costs ¥300/person extra. 🛜 Dorms **¥2800**, doubles **¥7200**

Kashima Honkan 鹿島本館 3-11 Reisen-machi ☎092 291 0746, ✉kashima-co@mx7.tiki.ne.jp. The first building in Fukuoka to be designated an important cultural property, this homely, hundred-year-old ryokan is located on a pleasant backstreet, just round the corner from Gion subway station. The 27 tatami rooms are elegant, with antique screens and wall hangings, though none is en suite. English is spoken. Breakfast is available for an extra fee. 🛜 **¥9000**

Nishitetsu Hotel Croom 西鉄ホテルクルーム 1-17-6 Hakata-eki-mae ☎092 413 5454, ⊛croomhakata.com. At this convenient, newly renovated business hotel, the compact, sound-proofed rooms offer a good dose of contemporary style. There's an indoor onsen and coin laundry. 🛜 **¥19,000**

Sunroute Hakata 4-10 Hakata-eki-chūōgai ☎092 434 1311, ⊛sunroute.jp. Just a 2min walk from Hakata

Station, this good-value, twelve-storey business hotel offers small but comfortable and well-designed bedrooms and helpful staff; it occupies a narrow plot, so most rooms are set back from the main road. ☎ **¥8880**

Tabicolle Hostel タビコレホステル 3-7-14-2F Hakata-eki-minami ☎ 092 473 6767, ⓦ tabicolle.com. Just a short walk southeast of Hakata Station, this is a laidback place with a stylish common area that's the ideal place to meet some travel buddies. Dorms are more than adequate, while the rooftop is a lovely place for a relaxing coffee by day, or something stronger by night. Also offers a coin laundry, a communal PC and rental bicycles. ☎ Dorms **¥3000**

EATING

Not surprisingly for such a cosmopolitan city, Fukuoka boasts a range of international cuisines. For a cheap meal, however, try some of the city's characteristic **yatai kitchens** (see box below), many of which serve the pork-based ramen that the city is known for. **Tenjin** is a good bet for traditional restaurants, particularly the **Daimyō** district, immediately west of Tenjin Nishi-dōri, which is packed with little bars and funky designer boutiques. Fukuoka's most notorious **speciality food** is *fugu*, the poisonous blowfish eaten only in winter (Nov–March); though you'll find *fugu* throughout Japan, the best is said to come from the waters off northern Kyūshū.

Aux Bacchanales オーバカナル 1-4-1 Chūō ☎092 762 7373. A French-style bar-café-brasserie with red leather booths, brass rails and windows looking out onto a covered arcade to the east of Nishitetsu Fukuoka Station. Despite the charming decor and the dickie-bow-wearing waiters, prices aren't all that high – coffees cost from ¥300, while *petits plats* such as *saucisse frites* start at around ¥650. Cheese and scrumptious cakes are also on the menu. Daily 10am–9.30pm.

Chikae 稚加榮 2-2-17 Daimyō ☎092 721 4624. Famous, fifty-year-old fish restaurant where you sit at a counter overlooking the open fish tanks, or at tables to the side. Kimono-clad staff bustle about bearing platters laden with ultra-fresh sashimi and sushi, adding to the spectacle. It's a good place to try the local speciality *karashi mentaiko* (marinated spicy fish eggs), as well as *fugu*. Sashimi platters start at ¥2500, sushi at ¥2800, while lunch sets are a bargain ¥1500. Daily 11am–10pm.

★**Fujiyoshi** 藤よし 9-6 Nishi-nakasu ☎092 761 5692. Businessmen, designers and families with young kids all crowd into this warm, lively *izakaya* in a distinctive half-timbered building. *Yakitori*'s the thing here, with chicken skewers for ¥130, accompanied by asparagus in summer or ginkgo nuts in winter, but the big plates of deep-fried chicken (*kara-age*) are excellent, too. Mon–Sat 4–10.30pm.

Gindaco 銀だこ B1 Canal City ☎092 263 2700. Great little *takoyaki* joint which serves octopus balls in an intriguing range of flavours – Kansai folk may sneer at the cod-roe-mayonnaise-and-cheese variety (¥650 for eight), but they're pretty darn tasty. It's right next to the Canal City fountains – grab your meal to take away and munch it while watching the show. Daily 10am–9pm.

Hakata Rāmen 博多ラーメン Kamikawabata-dōri. This round-the-clock operation is one of the cheapest noodle bars in town, with bowls going from just ¥290; surprisingly, they're not bad at all, and the same can be said for the ¥160 *gyōza*. Daily 24hr.

Rāmen Stadium ラーメンスタヂアム 5F Canal City ☎092 282 2525. A funny little place on the top floor of the

YATAI

Forget the sights – *this* is Fukuoka. Come evening, steam billows out from more than one hundred **mobile street-kitchens**, each cocooning a fascinating little world of its own. Customers push their way through a thin drape of plastic sheets to find a garrulous clutch of locals, crammed onto narrow benches and filling up on scrumptious food – pork-based **tonkotsu ramen** is the meal of choice (¥600 or so), usually accompanied by flasks of sake and a few new friends. Mobile in nature, none of these **yatai** has a fixed location, but this being Japan they rarely venture too far from their original mark, and you'll usually find them open from around 7pm to 3am, often closing on Sunday. The greatest concentrations of *yatai* are around the intersection of Tenjin Nishi-dōri and Shōwa-dōri, and at the south end of Nakasu along the southwest bank, but you'll bump into them on pavements all over the centre; *Fukuoka Now*'s free map (see p.707) marks locations. These are some of the most enjoyable places to eat in all Japan, and the focus on merry-making means that any noisy *yatai* is worth a go, but a couple certainly stand out from the crowd.

Taka-chan たかちゃん. *Kokin-chan* is a local institution, having dished out ramen for over four decades, and at the south end of Nakasu along the southwest bank, but here's the secret – the place next door is just as good, and you won't have to queue for an hour to get in.

★**Tsukasa** 司 ⓦ yatai-tsukasa.com. The best of a clutch on the riverside (it even has a website), this shack specializes in *mentaiko* tempura – spicy cod roe fried in batter (¥900). A plate of assorted *yakitori* skewers goes for the same price. Mmm . . . *oishii*.

Canal City complex, which proves Fukuoka's love affair with ramen beyond doubt. No fewer than eight ramen restaurants from Fukuoka and all over Japan set up shop here on a regularly changing basis. Bowls go from ¥700; take your pick from various picture menus. Daily 11am–11pm.

Sushi Kosaka 鮨香坂 3-9-3 Hakata-eki-higashi ☎092 481 2887. Superb sushi bar that's well worth seeking out, 5min walk southeast of Hakata Station. Design is minimalist, all blonde wood and polished concrete, and there are just seven counter seats. Evening prices are stratospheric, but ¥3240 for a lunchtime set of ten nigiri sushi pieces, including excellent fatty tuna, pickled mackerel and gari (pickled ginger), represents very good value. Tues–Sun noon–2pm & 5–10pm.

Sushi Shuto 鮨しゅ藤 5–9 Tsunabamachi ☎092 272 1324. An excellent sushi bar that makes itself affordable at lunchtime: a bargain ¥1890 for an eight-piece set that might include such delights as tuna, fatty tuna and anago (sea eel), followed by toothsome miso soup. Come the evening and you're looking at over ¥8000 for a set. Reservations recommended. Mon–Sat 11.30am–1.30pm & 5.30–9.30pm.

★**Uosue** 魚末 2-1-30 Daimyō ☎092 713 7931. Old-fashioned, few-frills sashimi restaurant with a great atmosphere. It's famous for having the freshest fish in town, while all kinds of tempting vegetables for grilling are piled on the counter. Generous, melt-in-the-mouth plates of mixed sashimi start at ¥1980. Daily 6pm–1am; closed first, third & fifth Mon of the month.

DRINKING AND NIGHTLIFE

Fukuoka's famous **Nakasu** nightlife district is crammed full of clubs, restaurants and bars, as well as a whole clutch of seedier establishments aimed at Japanese businessmen. It's a great area to wander round, but most places are extortionately expensive and only take customers by recommendation, if they accept foreigners at all. A happier hunting ground lies around Tenjin's main crossroads, particularly **Oyafukō-dōri** and the streets immediately to the east, which are packed with bars and clubs; roughly translated, Oyafukō-dōri means "street of disobedient children", originally referring to a local school but nowadays more applicable to groups of drunken college kids who gather here at weekends under the blind eye of the *kōban* (neighbourhood police) on the corner. Lastly, any *yatai* worth its salt serves booze, and they're certainly the city's most characterful and atmospheric drinking spots (see box opposite).

Happy Cock 9F, 2-1-51 Daimyō ☎092 734 2686. It's elbow room only at weekends in this large, laidback bar just off Tenjin Nishi-dōri. DJs, party nights and *nomihōdai* (all-you-can-drink deals, typically ¥3000 for men, ¥2000 for women) pull a younger crowd. Wed, Thurs & Sun 10pm–5am, Fri & Sat 9pm–5am.

International Bar 4F, 3-1-13 Tenjin ☎092 714 2179, ⊛internationalbar.jp. This ordinary little bar, with no cover charge and inexpensive bar food, is a good place to meet local *gaijin*. Look out for the English sign on the main street opposite the Matsuya Ladies store, north of the main Tenjin crossroads. 🛜 Mon–Sat from 7pm.

Morris' Red Fox モーリスレッドフォックス 7F, 2-1-4 Daimyō ☎092 771 4774. The first of a chain of Morris bars across the city, this British-style pub has red leather banquettes and big-screen sports, but the real draw, at least on summer

evenings, is the large, south-facing balcony. Well-kept beers on tap (from ¥750/pint) include Guinness, Hoegaarden and a couple of guest Japanese craft brews, to wash down fish'n'chips, shepherd's pie and the like. 🛜 Mon–Thurs 5pm–1am, Fri & Sat 5pm–3am, Sun 5pm–midnight.

Off Broadway 2F, 1-8-40 Maizuru ☎092 724 5383. Imagine a processed chunk of New York – fries, burgers and buffalo wings on the menu, and a sophisticated, multinational clientele, who find themselves serenaded by live jazz and Latin music on Fri and DJs every night. Mon–Thurs & Sun 7pm–3am, Fri & Sat 7.30pm–5am.

Voodoo Lounge 4F, 1-8-38 Tenjin ☎092 732 4662, ⊛voodoolounge.jp. Boogie the night away or chill out in this lively bar that's recently moved to Oyafukō-dōri. Stages an eclectic programme of DJs, live bands and other events. Entry charges and opening times vary.

ENTERTAINMENT

To find out what's on, consult *Fukuoka Now* (see p.707) or ask at any of the tourist offices; tickets are available through the Kyūshū Tourist Information Centre (see p.707).

Hakata-za 博多座/ 2-1 Shimokawabata-machi ☎092 263 5555, ⊛hakataza.co.jp. As well as musicals such as *Les Misérables*, this large theatre next to Hakata Riverain Mall stages regular kabuki performances, especially in June and Nov; it's best to book in advance and, when you arrive, ask for an English-language leaflet to guide you through proceedings.

United Cinemas 4F Canal City ☎092 291 0730, ⊛unitedcinemas.jp. Film fans should check the current week's showings at United Cinema's thirteen-screen multiplex, where English-language films are shown with Japanese subtitles (¥1800 all day Sat and before 8pm Sun–Fri, ¥1200 after 8pm Sun–Fri). Also houses an IMAX cinema and a restaurant-cinema.

10

10

FUKUOKA FESTIVALS AND EVENTS

Hakata celebrates a whole host of **festivals**, of which the biggest are the **Gion Yamakasa** (see p.704) and the **Hakata Dontaku**, now held during Golden Week (May 3 & 4). In feudal times, Hakata townspeople were permitted across the river once a year to convey New Year greetings to their lord. Today's festival centres on a parade along Meiji-dōri to the old castle.

On a similarly traditional theme, the **sumo** circus comes to town each November for Japan's last *basho* of the season, held over fifteen days at the Fukuoka Kokusai Centre (15min walk northwest of Gofuku-machi or Nakasu Kawabata subway stations). The Kokusai Centre is smaller than the main Tokyo sumo stadium, which means that the cheap seats are a bit closer to the action and the atmosphere is livelier, especially when local favourites are wrestling. Book tickets in advance on Ⓦ sumo.pia.jp/en or buy the cheapest unreserved seats on the door on the day of competition (from 8am) and save some money for seasonal roast chestnuts, the snack of choice at the Fukuoka *basho*.

A much newer festival is the **Isla de Salsa** (Ⓦ tiempo.jp), a celebration of Latin music held mid-August on Nokono-shima, a ten-minute ferry ride from Fukuoka.

DIRECTORY

Consulates Australia, 7F, 1-6-8 Tenjin ☎ 092 734 5055, Ⓦ japan.embassy.gov.au/tkyo/location_fukuoka.html; China, 1-3-3 Jigyohama ☎ 092 713 1121; South Korea, 1-1-3 Jigyohama ☎ 092 771 0461; US, 2-5-26 Ōhori ☎ 092 751 9331, Ⓦ fukuoka.usconsulate.gov.
Emergencies The main police station is at 7-7 Higashikoen, Hakata-ku (☎ 092 641 4141). Emergency numbers are listed in Basics (see p.71).
Hospitals and clinics The largest general hospital with English-speaking staff is Kyūshū Medical Centre, 1-8-1 Jigyohama (☎ 092 852 0700), near Hawks Town. Also on the west side of town, there's the International Clinic

Tojin-machi, two blocks east of Tojin-machi subway station on Meiji-dōri (☎ 092 717 1000, Ⓦ internationalclinic.org), run by a Dutch general practitioner.
Immigration For visa renewals, contact Fukuoka Regional Immigration Bureau, in the airport's domestic terminal (☎ 092 626 5151, Ⓦ immi-moj.go.jp/english /soshiki/kikou/fukuoka.html).
Post offices Fukuoka Central Post Office (4-3-1 Tenjin), just north of Tenjin subway station, offers foreign exchange and a 24hr mail service. There's another big branch beside the west exit of Hakata Station.

Dazaifu

太宰府

Only 15km southeast of Fukuoka, **DAZAIFU** only just breaks free of the urban sprawl, but manages to retain a definite country air. The town is very much on Kyūshū's tourist map, thanks to the important **Kyūshū National Museum**. The crowd of art lovers and historians gets a boost in late February and March, when plum blossoms signal both the start of spring and the onset of the exam season, and anxious students descend on **Tenman-gū**, Japan's foremost shrine dedicated to the god of learning. Thankfully, the nearby **temples** and other historical relics remain surprisingly peaceful. Everything is within easy walking distance of the station, making it possible to cover the main sights in a day.

Brief history

Dazaifu rose to prominence in the late seventh century, when the emperor established a regional seat of government and military headquarters (known as the Dazaifu) here, responsible for defence, trade and diplomatic ties, particularly with China and Korea. For more than five hundred years successive governor generals ruled Kyūshū from Dazaifu, protected by a series of ditches, embankments and hilltop fortresses, until political circumstances changed in the twelfth century and the town gradually fell into decline.

CLOCKWISE FROM TOP YATAI STREET STALL, FUKUOKA (BOX, P.708); STONE BUDDHA, USUKI (P.752); KAGURA PERFORMANCE, TAKACHIHO (BOX, P.744); >

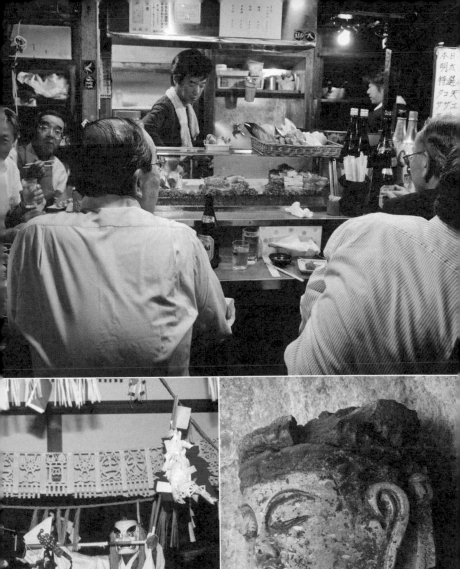

Tenman-gū

天満宮 • 4-7-1 Saifu • **Shrine** Daily 6/6.30am–6.30/7.30pm • Free • **Kanko Historical Museum** Mon & Thurs–Sun 9am–4.30pm • ¥200 • **Treasure house** Tues–Sun 9am–4.30pm • ¥400 • ⓦ dazaifutenmangu.or.jp

From the train station, it's a short walk east up pedestrianized Tenjin-sama-dōri, which is lined with *torii*, to Dazaifu's main historical sight, **Tenman-gū**. This tenth-century shrine was built over the grave of Tenjin, the guardian deity of scholars, also known as Sugawara-no-Michizane, and is dedicated to him (see box below).

The approach to Tenman-gū lies over an allegorical stone bridge, **Taiko-bashi**; its first, steep arch represents the past, the present is flat, while the final, gentler hump indicates difficulties yet to come. While negotiating the bridge, take a close look at the second of the two little shrines on the right, which was constructed in 1458 for the three gods of the sea – its intricate, Chinese-style roof shelters some particularly fine carving. Beyond, a two-storey gate leads into a courtyard dominated by the main **worship hall**, built in 1591 but resplendent in red and gold lacquer under its manicured thatch. A twisted plum tree stands immediately to the right (east) of the hall. Known as the "flying plum tree", it's said to be over a thousand years old and, according to legend, originally grew in Michizane's Kyoto garden. On the eve of his departure he wrote a farewell poem to the tree, but that night it upped roots and "flew" ahead of him to Dazaifu.

To the left and behind the worship hall, a modern building houses the small **Kanko Historical Museum** detailing the life of Michizane through a series of tableaux. You can see a few older portraits, alongside a poem supposedly written by Michizane and other historical items, in the **treasure house** (aka the Dazaifu Tenmangu Museum), set back to your left as you leave the main cloisters.

Kyūshū National Museum

九州国立博物館, Kyūshū Kokuritsu Hakubutsukan • 4-7-2 Ishizaka • 9.30am–5pm; closed Mon • ¥430 • ⓦ kyuhaku.com

A path beside the Tenman-gū treasure house leads to an escalator that tunnels through the rock to emerge beside a magnificent, wave-shaped building housing the **Kyūshū National Museum**. Japan's fourth national museum after Tokyo, Kyoto and Nara, it focuses on the history of Japan's trade with other Asian countries and illustrates the profound impact these interactions had on local art and culture. It's fascinating to see Chinese, Korean, Japanese and Egyptian ceramics side by side, and to compare Japanese Buddhist statues, musical instruments and lacquerware with those from neighbouring countries.

The permanent **exhibition hall**, on the fourth floor, is beautifully laid out, loosely divided by era into five spaces, covering prehistoric times to the Edo period. Look out here for the graceful folds of the golden robe of a tenth-century Buddha from nearby Kanzeon-ji; hand grenades from a Mongol ship wrecked at the Battle of Takashima in 1281; and a nineteenth-century textile swatch book that allowed the merchants of Nagasaki to choose which fabrics they wanted the Dutch to import

---

THE STORY OF TENJIN

Tenjin is the divine name of **Sugawara-no-Michizane**, a brilliant scholar of the Heian period, who died in Dazaifu in 903 AD. By all accounts, Michizane was a precocious youngster – composing *waka* poems at five years old and Chinese poetry by the age of eleven – and went on to become a popular governor of Shikoku before rising to the second-highest position at court as "Minister of the Right". Not surprisingly, he found no favour with his powerful superior, Fujiwara Tokihira, who persuaded the emperor to banish Michizane. So, in 901 Michizane, accompanied by his son, daughter and a retainer, travelled south to take up a "post" as deputy governor of Dazaifu. He was kept under armed guard until he died in despair – though still loyal to the emperor – two years later. Soon after, a succession of national disasters was attributed to Michizane's restless spirit, so in 905 Tenman-gū was founded to pray for his repose. This was the first of an estimated 12,000 shrines dedicated to Tenjin in Japan.

from India for them. Running off the main hall, small **auxiliary galleries** pursue fascinating cross-cultural themes, such as "the ideal image of Asian people", which features Greco-Roman-style Buddha images from Gandhara in Pakistan. There's plenty of English labelling throughout, but it's still worthwhile picking up a free audio guide at the desk before going in.

Kōmyōzen-ji

光明禅寺 • 2-16-1 Saifu • Hours irregular • ¥200 donation

From Tenman-gū, it's about a 100m walk south to the small, serene Zen temple of **Kōmyōzen-ji**, which was dedicated in the mid-thirteenth century to Tenjin – Michizane's deified spirit is said to have flown to China to study Zen Buddhism. Popular for its rhododendrons in early summer and its autumn foliage, the temple is an appealing collection of simple, wooden buildings whose tatami rooms contain Buddha figures or works of art. There's usually no one around, but you're welcome to explore – take your shoes off and follow the polished wooden corridors round to the rear, where there's a contemplative garden made up of a gravel sea swirling round moss-covered headlands and jutting rocks, caught against a wooded hillside. The stones in the garden at the front of the temple are arranged in the character for "light", referring to the halo of the Buddha.

10

Kanzeon-ji

観世音寺 • 1-1 Kanzeonji

Dazaifu's other major sights lie about twenty minutes' walk – or a short bicycle ride – west of the station; to avoid the main road, head west from the station to pick up a riverside path and then follow signs pointing you along a quiet lane (maps from the tourist office show the route). Take a left down a footpath just before a set of old foundation stones lying in the grass and the route brings you to the back of **Kanzeon-ji**. Founded in 746 AD by Emperor Tenji in honour of his mother, Empress Saimei, at one time Kanzeon-ji was the largest temple in all Kyūshū and even rated a mention in the great eleventh-century novel *The Tale of Genji* (see p.867). Only some Buddhist statues and the bronze **bell**, the oldest in Japan, remain from the original temple, while the present buildings – unadorned and nicely faded – date from the seventeenth century.

Treasure house

Daily 9am–5pm • ¥500

Kanzeon-ji's main hall holds a graceful standing Buddha, but you'll find its most magnificent statues in the modern **treasure house**, to the right as you face the hall. The immediate impression is of the sheer power of the huge wooden figures, of which even the newest is at least 750 years old. The oldest is Tobatsu-Bishamonten (fittingly the god of treasure, with a flaming halo), standing second in line, which was sculpted from a single block of camphor wood in the eighth century. An informative English brochure provides further details, starting with the **jizō** figure facing you as you come up the stairs and working clockwise from there.

Kaidan-in

戒壇院 • 5-7-10 Kanzeonji

A short walk west of the Kanzeon-ji treasure house (see above) is the two-tiered roof of **Kaidan-in**, built in the late eighth century for the ordination of Buddhist priests and originally part of Kanzeon-ji. This is one of only three such ordination halls in Japan – the other two being at Tōdai-ji in Nara (see p.488) and Yakushi-ji in Tochigi Prefecture – and again the statuary is of interest, in this case an eleven-headed Kannon from the Heian period, dressed in fading gold.

ARRIVAL AND INFORMATION DAZAIFU

By train The easiest way of getting to Dazaifu is by private train from Fukuoka's Nishitetsu Station in Tenjin (3–4 hourly; 30min; ¥400), with a brief change at Nishitetsu-Futsukaichi Station (not to be confused with JR Futsukaichi Station, which is a 10–15min walk away).

By bus There are now also buses from Hakata Bus Terminal to Dazaifu (2–4 hourly; 45min; ¥600), via the international terminal of Fukuoka Airport.

Tourist information There's a helpful tourist office outside Dazaifu Station (daily 9am–5pm; ☎ 092 925 1880, ⓦ dazaifu.org), with local maps and brochures in English.

Bike rental At the train station you can rent a bicycle (¥500/day) or electric bike (¥800/day) to visit the western sights.

EATING

Dazaifu's most famous foodstuff, sold at over thirty shops along Tenjin-sama-dōri, is *umegaemochi*, a delicious pounded rice cake filled with sweet bean paste and decorated with a plum-flower motif, in honour of Tenjin (see box, p.712).

Ume-no-hana 梅の花 4-4-41 Saifu ☎ 092 928 7787, ⓦ umenohana.co.jp. This restaurant in the lanes east of Kōmyōzen-ji is by far the best in Dazaifu, famed for its melt-in-the-mouth tofu creations, such as steamed dumplings and sweet almond puddings. Served in tatami rooms overlooking a pretty garden, set meals will set you back around ¥4000; arrive before noon if you haven't got a reservation. Daily 11am–3.30pm & 4.30–9pm.

Yasutake やす武 Tenjin-sama-dōri ☎ 092 922 5079. This little place is popular for its inexpensive handmade soba dishes (from ¥800), as well as its *umegaemochi*; it's on the right-hand side of Tenjin-sama-dōri, just beyond the first *torii*. Daily: café 10am–6pm; take-away mochi 9am–7pm.

Arita

有田

One of Japan's leading pottery towns, **ARITA** has been producing typically sparse, elegant **porcelain** for four centuries. The excellent **Kyūshū Ceramic Museum** is the place to start your explorations, but the main historic kilns each have their own museum and store. Dozens of other galleries and workshops dot the town, so there's plenty of opportunity to shop and, in some places, watch the potters at work. In early May and late November, the town holds big **fairs** to sell ceramics at discount prices.

Bicycles are a good way of getting around Arita, which spreads east–west along a narrow valley for several kilometres. The western half is Arita proper, with the main JR station, while to the east, the more historic **Kami-Arita** (Upper Arita, aka Uchiyama, "Inner Mountain") has its own station for local trains. The town supports several nice guesthouses, but if you're after a full-service ryokan, you could happily base yourself in Takeo (see p.717), fifteen minutes away by train.

Kyūshū Ceramic Museum

九州陶磁文化館, Kyūshū Tōji Bunkakan • South side of Highway 35, the main east–west through road, about 1km south of Arita Station • Tues– Sun 9am–5pm • Free • ☎ 0955 43 3681, ⓦ saga-museum.jp/ceramic

The lovely, modern **Kyūshū Ceramic Museum**, with plenty of English labelling, covers not only Arita ware (*arita-yaki*), but other Kyūshū styles such as Karatsu ware, a simple pottery that's popular for tea ceremonies, as well as contemporary ceramics. Downstairs, don't miss the **Shibata Collection**, which chronologically traces the development of Arita ware in the Edo period through both objets d'art and functional pieces.

Kakiemon

柿右衛門 • South off Highway 35, about 2km southwest of Arita Station • Daily 9am–5pm • Free • ☎ 0955 43 2267, ⓦ kakiemon.co.jp

One of Arita's two most important kilns, **Kakiemon** is set in a lovely complex of thatched houses with a museum and a shop (best considered as a gallery, considering the stratospheric prices). The current master potter and head of the family, designated

"WHITE GOLD" – THE PORCELAIN OF ARITA

In 1616, according to tradition, high quality **kaolin** (soft white clay) was discovered at Izumiyama, in the hills north of Arita, by a potter who'd been captured by Toyotomi Hideyoshi during his ill-fated campaigns against Korea in the 1590s. For the first time in Japan, it became possible to make white, strong, semi-translucent **porcelain**, rather than earthenware. Initially, only underglaze blue on a white background was produced, but further enhancements fusing Chinese techniques with Japanese aesthetics were made over the following decades.

In the 1640s and 1650s, **Kakiemon** – still one of Arita's leading kilns – successfully fired porcelain with multicoloured overglaze painting for the first time, and developed its own distinctive underglaze, *nigoshide*: thin, matt and milky-white, it gives a warm tone to backgrounds, but is very difficult to fire, with only a forty percent success rate. Out of these innovations, Kakiemon established an emblematic style: naturalistic, painterly plant and animal designs in bold, asymmetric compositions, using translucent blue, green and – notably – orange-red (made from oxidized iron, to a recipe that's still secret), set against large, undecorated areas of white.

EXPANSION AND DECLINE

During the upheavals in China that followed the collapse of the Ming dynasty in 1644, Arita was able to corner the **export market**. Porcelain was shipped from the local port, **Imari** (hence it's sometimes known as "Imari ware"), to the Dutch enclave at Nagasaki (see p.723), and then to Europe and the Middle East, reaching a peak in the 1660s when the **Dutch East India Company** exported over 25,000 pieces. Pottery was so valuable around this time that a method of repairing damaged pieces using gold – **kintsugi** – was developed. In the 1690s, Kakiemon ware found its way to William and Mary's palace at Hampton Court, outside London, where it's still on display.

As China recovered, however, its kilns were able to churn out "Chinese Imari" for a third of the price of the real thing, and in the eighteenth century further competition came from imitators in Europe such as Meissen and Chelsea. Kakiemon and many other kilns in Arita joined the race downmarket, turning out cheap and cheerful pottery to try to compete with the Chinese, but in 1757 the Dutch placed their last order with Arita, for just three hundred pieces.

In the mid-twentieth century, Western academic interest brought about a revival. In Kakiemon's case, luck played a large part: family secrets were usually passed on by word of mouth, but around 1700, the head of the family, knowing that he was dying, had written a confidential handbook for his one-year-old son. This was dug out and used to reinvent the original techniques such as *nigoshide* that had been discontinued.

OKAWACHIYAMA AND THE NABESHIMA CLAN

Meanwhile, the major part of Arita's **domestic production** in the Edo period was reserved for tribute payments: every year, the local **Nabeshima** lords had to give extravagant quantities of the highest-quality artworks to the shogun. To safeguard production, the Nabeshimas forcibly relocated thirty of Arita's best potters to **Okawachiyama**, a remote village on the other side of Mt Kurokami, with only one road in and out. The potters were elevated to the rank of samurai, given swords even, but they were not allowed to leave. With no commercial pressures, Okawachiyama could develop the most sophisticated techniques to produce exquisite and varied works. After the Meiji Restoration of 1867, however, the Nabeshima clan kiln was closed down, though small-scale porcelain-making continues at Okawachiyama to this day.

Kakiemon XV, was mentored by Kakiemon XIII – to better preserve the family secrets, knowledge is passed from grandfather to grandson. He's introduced a freer, more dynamic style than his father, the technically brilliant Kakiemon XIV, who was made a National Living Treasure. Examples of both men's work can be seen in the small but well-chosen **museum**, alongside very early polychromatic pieces by Kakiemon I.

Gen-emon

源石衛門 • About 2km northwest of Arita Station • Daily 8am–5pm (workshops closed Sat & Sun) • Free • ☎ 0955 42 4164, ⦾ gen-emon.co.jp

Set in venerable buildings around a lovely garden, **Gen-emon** is a relative newcomer to the Arita porcelain scene, having started in 1753. Perhaps less burdened by the weight

10

of history, the kiln now collaborates with outside designers and specializes in bright contemporary porcelain, at accessible prices. Visitors are allowed to walk around the atmospheric wooden **workshops** and kiln at the back of the compound, to watch men and women forming the clay, painting and underglazing (though the overglaze painting is off-limits). Traditionally, men would paint with the smaller brushes, made of weasel hair, while women wielded the big brushes, which are now made with hair from virgin female deer, though in times past the hair of well-nourished Kyoto ladies was used. Ask in the shop to visit the **museum** of Edo-period porcelain, which contains some fascinating early nineteenth-century blue and white plates: downstairs, one shows Dejima (see p.723) and a Dutch ship on fire; upstairs, several are decorated with primitive maps of Japan.

Imaemon

今石衛門 • Kami-Arita main street • **Museum** 9.30am–4.30pm; closed Mon • ¥300, or ¥500 if they put the best china out for special occasions • **Shop** Daily 8am–5pm; closed first Sun of the month • ☎ 0955 42 3101, ⓦ imaemon.co.jp

Kakiemon's big rival, **Imaemon** started out in the seventeenth century as the Nabeshima lord's favourite painter of multicoloured overglaze, but took on the whole production process after the Meiji Restoration. The kiln maintains the highest technical capabilities, turning out intricate shapes and designs, sometimes using several different glazing techniques on the same piece, for customers that include the imperial household. The current master, **Imaemon XIV**, who favours geometrical snowflake patterns, is a National Living Treasure, as was his father, the innovative Imaemon XIII, who invented a method of blowing blue and grey underglaze paint through a straw to give a softer texture. The two-storey **museum** contains some gorgeous pieces dating back to the seventeenth century, with the newer work upstairs. It's also well worth having a gander at their **shop** two doors away, where you're as likely to be stunned by the prices as the designs. Occupying the early nineteenth-century painting workshop, it's the oldest building in town, crowned by a gruesome devil to ward off evil.

ARRIVAL AND INFORMATION

ARITA

By train Arita is on the JR line from Fukuoka's Hakata Station (1–2 hourly; 1hr 25min), via Takeo, to Sasebo and Huis ten Bosch. There are no direct trains to Isahaya and Nagasaki, but it's an easy change at Haiki.

Information The tourist office is just in front of the station on the right (daily 9am–5pm; ☎ 0955 43 2121, ⓦ arita.jp). Saga Prefecture has a useful English-language call centre for tourists (☎ 0952 20 1601).

Guide To get to grips with the intricacies of porcelain making, you might want to hire a guide in Arita. Engaging and entertaining, Miyuri Tsuru (☎ 090 4274 9744, ⓔ miyuritsuru@msn.com) knows porcelain inside and out, and speaks excellent English.

GETTING AROUND

By bicycle You can rent bikes (¥500/day) and electric bikes (¥1000/day) at Arita Station.

By bus Ask at the tourist office about Arita's complicated community bus routes (all passing the station), which take in most of the sights several times a day; a single journey costs ¥200, a day pass ¥500.

ACCOMMODATION AND EATING

★**Iori Hisashi** 庵久 5min walk from Kami-Arita Station ☎ 0955 43 2764 or ☎ 090 4274 9744, ⓦ hisasih .com. Elegant homestay in a hundred-year-old *machiya* (merchant's house), where you'll stay in a lovely tatami room with a cedar vaulted ceiling, antique porcelain and a seating area overlooking the small formal garden (private toilet, shared bathroom). The owner's a master potter and offers all kinds of pottery and antiques appraisal courses (with interpreter). Excellent lunches and dinners provided on request; breakfast included. ☎ **¥17,000**

Keramiek ケラミック Kami-Arita main street, near Imaemon ☎ 080 3998 0477, ⓦ keramiekarita.wixsite .com/keramiek. Friendly, Dutch-owned guesthouse with very comfortable Western- and Japanese-style rooms and shared bathrooms. No meals available. ☎ **¥8000**

Sō Gallery Ōta 創ギャラリーおおた About 2km west of Arita Station on Highway 35 ☎ 0995 42 4275; also a branch at Arita Sato Plaza (see opposite). Arita's nationally famous dish is the bentō sold at the station, hearty beef curry and rice with cheese, served in a handmade porcelain bowl that you get to keep. Here you can enjoy the curry (from ¥1750) in a charming café and porcelain gallery that's handy for Kakiemon. It also serves home-made bread, delicious desserts and good coffee. Daily 11am–5pm, sometimes closed Wed; Arita Sato Plaza branch Wed–Sun noon–4pm.

★**Yasuna** 保名 On Arita's main street about 10min walk west of the station ☎0955 42 2783, ⓦyasuna.net. Gorgeous restaurant decorated with antique porcelain and furniture, serving very good *kaiseki* dinners (from ¥3000) that use plenty of seafood and local, seasonal produce such as wild mushrooms in autumn. Daily 11.30am–2pm & 5–9pm.

SHOPPING

Arita Sato Plaza 有田陶磁の里プラザ About 1.5km northwest of Arita Station ⓦarita.gr.jp. Sometimes labelled the Wholesale Ceramics Plaza, this is the best place to buy local porcelain. About twenty shops sell everything from tableware and gifts to top-dollar art pieces, at wholesale prices. Most shops daily 9am–5pm.

10

Takeo

武雄

Squeezed into a narrow valley, **TAKEO** is a pleasant onsen resort with several appealing ryokan and makes a good base for visiting Arita, just fifteen minutes away by train. The **public bathing** facilities are a ten-minute walk northwest of the station, behind a red-lacquered two-storey *rōmon* tower gate. First on the left through the gate is **Moto-yu** (元湯; daily 6.30am–midnight; ¥400), built in 1876 and the most traditional of the baths.

ARRIVAL AND DEPARTURE

By train There are direct trains to Takeo from Fukuoka's Hakata Station (hourly; 1hr 10min; ¥1650). Connections to Arita a little further down the line are even more frequent (1–2 hourly; 15min; ¥280).

ACCOMMODATION

★**Mifuneyama Kankō** 御船山観光 4100 Takeo-chō ☎0954 23 3131, ⓦmifuneyama.co.jp. Probably the best value in the area is to be had at this delightful place, 5min by car from the station (pick-ups offered) and set in lovely parkland at the foot of Mt Mifune. The tatami rooms have been designed with the attention to detail you'd expect at a

---

HUIS TEN BOSCH: A DUTCH HOUSE IN THE JAPANESE WOODS

Opened in 1992 at a cost of ¥250 billion, the resort town of **HUIS TEN BOSCH** ("House in the Woods"; ハウステンボス; ⓦenglish.huistenbosch.co.jp) is a meticulously engineered replica of an old Dutch port, featuring a faithful re-creation of the royal palace in The Hague after which the town is named. Part theme park, part serious experiment in urban living, it owes its existence to the drive and vision of **Kamichika Yoshikuni**, a local entrepreneur who was so impressed with Dutch land reclamation and environmental management that he persuaded his financiers it could work in Japan as a commercial venture. While the result may seem quaintly old world, it's equipped with the latest technology to manage its sophisticated heating systems, wave control, desalination, water recycling and security. All the pipes, cables and wires are hidden underground, and it's designed to be as environmentally benign as possible. Unfortunately, Huis ten Bosch went bankrupt in 2003 with debts of ¥220 billion, but was rescued in 2010 by the HIS travel agency.

The town is divided into an exclusive residential district, Wassenaar, and public areas where you'll find a raft of **museums and attractions** (daily 9am–10pm, though hours may change for special events; 1-day passport ¥6700), plus dozens of souvenir shops, numerous restaurants and hotels, including the world's first robot hotel. There's a wealth of themed rides and shows on site, including **Horizon Adventure Plus**, which re-creates a real-life Dutch flood with 800 tonnes of water cascading into the theatre. In the harbour zone lies a full-size replica of the first Dutch ship to reach Japan, *De Liefde*, which landed on the east coast of Kyūshū near Usuki in 1600.

The easiest way to get to the resort is on JR's special **Huis ten Bosch Express** direct from Fukuoka's Hakata Station (hourly; 1hr 45min; ¥2130), via Takeo and Arita, or on the **Seaside Liner** from Nagasaki (hourly; 1hr 30min; ¥1470). For those in a hurry, **high-speed boats** zip across Ōmura Bay direct to Huis ten Bosch from Nagasaki Airport (5 daily; 50min; ¥1960).

higher-class venue, and there are several gorgeous onsen to choose from, among which the hillside-backed outdoor ones are best. As well as the half-board price quoted here, room-only and B&B deals are available. 📶 **¥19,000**

Toyokan 東洋館 7408 Takeo-chō ☎0954 22 2191, 🌐takeo-toyokan.jp. Large ryokan in front of the *rōmon*,

with several onsen and elegant Japanese-style rooms; those on the second floor enjoy views of the gate and the mountains, while the Sasana annexe room has its own lovely tea room and a cypress-wood bath. Seasonal kaiseki dinners are served on handmade pottery; B&B rates are also available. **¥28,080**

10

Nagasaki

長崎

Gathered in the tucks and crevices of steep hills rising from a long, narrow harbour, and spreading its tentacles along several tributary valleys, **NAGASAKI** is one of Japan's more picturesque cities, and one of the most popular with international visitors. This appeal is furthered by an easy-going attitude and an unusually cosmopolitan culture, resulting from over two centuries of contact with foreigners when the rest of Japan was all but closed to the world.

However, it does have to be said that "dark tourism" is Nagasaki's biggest draw. The city would probably have remained little more than a bustling harbour town had a chance break in the clouds on August 9, 1945, not seared it into the world's consciousness – within minutes, it became the target of the world's second **atomic bomb**. It's the A-Bomb hypocentre and nearby museum, as harrowing as that in Hiroshima, that brings most people to Nagasaki, yet the city has much else to offer. Communities of Chinese, Dutch, Portuguese and British have all left their mark here, building colourful **Chinese temples**, Catholic **churches** and an array of European-style houses gathered in **Glover Garden**, as well as influencing the local cuisine and festivals. The tightly controlled Dutch enclave of **Dejima**, which was Japan's only link with Europe for two hundred years, has been impressively reconstructed, while the **Museum of History and Culture** further fleshes out Nagasaki's multicultural past and the stylish **Art Museum** evinces the city's long-standing connections with Spain. Despite efforts to stamp out another European import, the Catholic faith, Nagasaki remains Japan's centre of **Christianity**, claiming one-sixth of the country's believers.

It's possible to cover the city's three main areas – the hypocentre in the northern suburb of Urakami; Dejima and the nearby Art Museum; and the area around Glover Garden – in a long day, capped off by a twilight ropeway ride up to the top of **Inasa-yama**, on the northwest side of the harbour. However, Nagasaki deserves at least one extra night's stopover to explore its backstreets, soak up some atmosphere and sample a few of the city's culinary treats.

Brief history

Portuguese traders first sailed into Nagasaki in 1570, establishing a trading post and **Jesuit mission** in what was then a small fishing village of just 1500 inhabitants. For a brief period, Christianity was a major influence here: several local *daimyō* were converted and the town earned the nickname "Little Rome". However, in the late sixteenth century Toyotomi Hideyoshi, fearing the missionaries would be followed by military intervention, started to move against the Church. Though the persecutions – which provided the subject for Martin Scorsese's 2016 film *Silence*, adapted from Endō Shūsaku 1966 novel – came in fits and starts, one of the more dramatic events occurred in Nagasaki in 1597 when Hideyoshi ordered the crucifixion of 26 Christians.

After 1616 the new shogun, Tokugawa Hidetada, gradually took control of all dealings with foreigners, and by the late 1630s only Chinese and Portuguese merchants continued to trade out of Nagasaki. The latter, however, were expelled in 1639 following a Christian-led rebellion in nearby Shimabara (see box, p.732). Two years later, their place was filled by **Dutch merchants** who had endeared themselves to the

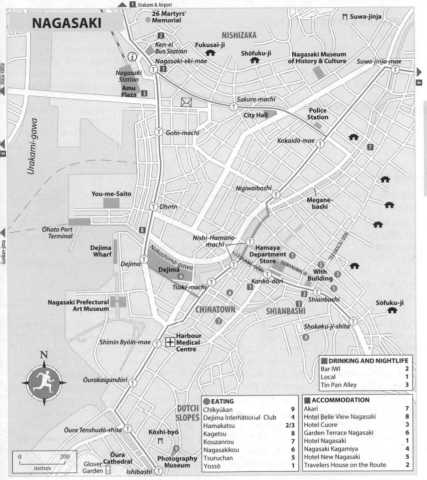

NAGASAKI

10

1 Urakami & Airport

26 Martyrs' Memorial

Suwa-jinja

Ken-ei Bus Station
Fukusai-ji
NISHIZAKA
Shōfuku-ji
Nagasaki Museum of History & Culture
Suwa-jinja-mae

Nagasaki-eki-mae

Nagasaki Station
Amu Plaza

Sakura-machi

City Hall
Police Station

Goto-machi
Kokaidō-mae

You-me-Saito
Nigiwaibashi
Megane-bashi

Ōhato
Ōhato Port Terminal

Dejima Wharf
Nishi-Hamano-machi
Hamaya Department Store
Dejima
Nakashima-gawa
Dejima
HAMANOMACHI
With Building

Tsuki-machi
Kankō-dōri
Shianbashi

Nagasaki Prefectural Art Museum
CHINATOWN
SHIANBASHI
Sōfuku-ji

Shimin Byōin-mae
Harbour Medical Centre
Shokaku-ji-shita

N

Ōurakaigandōri

DRINKING AND NIGHTLIFE
Bar IWI	2
Local	1
Tin Pan Alley	3

DUTCH SLOPES

Ōura Tenshudō-shita
Kōshi-byō

EATING
Chikyūkan	9
Dejima International Club	4
Hamakatsu	2/3
Kagetsu	8
Kouzanrou	7
Nagasakikou	6
Tsuruchan	5
Yossō	1

ACCOMMODATION
Akari	7
Hotel Belle View Nagasaki	8
Hotel Cuore	3
Garden Terrace Nagasaki	6
Hotel Nagasaki	1
Nagasaki Kagamiya	4
Hotel New Nagasaki	5
Travelers House on the Route	2

Ōura Cathedral
Photography Museum
Glover Garden
Ishibashi

0   200
metres

shogun by sending a warship against the rebels. For the next two hundred years this tiny Dutch group, who were confined to the artificial island of **Dejima**, and the much larger Chinese community in the city provided Japan's main access to the outside world (there were also trading links with Korea, through the large offshore island of Tsushima). Dutch imports such as coffee, chocolate, billiards and badminton were introduced to Japan via Dejima.

Eventually, the restrictions began to ease, especially after the early eighteenth century, when technical books were allowed into Nagasaki, making the city once again Japan's main conduit for **Western learning**, known as *rangaku* (from *oranda gaku*, "Dutch knowledge"). Nevertheless, it wasn't until 1858 that five ports, including Nagasaki, opened for general trade. America, Britain and other nations established diplomatic missions as Nagasaki's foreign community mushroomed and its economy boomed. New inventions flooded in: the printing press, brick-making and modern shipbuilding techniques all made their Japanese debut in Nagasaki. Then came high-scale industrial development and, of course, the events of 1945 (see box, p.720).

10

NAGASAKI ORIENTATION

Nagasaki's principal sights are widely spread, starting in the north in the district of **Urakami**, home of the Peace Park and the gruelling but informative **Atomic Bomb Museum**. Today, the district's prosperous residential streets make it hard to imagine the scenes of utter devastation left by the atomic explosion on August 9, 1945. From Urakami, it's a tram ride down to Nagasaki Station and a gentle stroll along the slopes of **Nishizaka** from the **26 Martyrs' Memorial**, via Nagasaki's informative history museum, to its most imposing shrine, Suwa-jinja. The focus of interest in the **central district** is a row of quiet **temples**, the former Dutch enclave of **Dejima** and, by night, the bars and clubs of **Shianbashi**. Down in the far south, several European houses have been preserved on the former hilltop concession, now known as **Glover Garden**, overlooking Nagasaki's magnificent harbour and a colourful Confucian shrine.

Atomic Bomb Museum

長崎原爆資料館, Nagasaki Genbaku Shiryōkan • 7-8 Hirano-machi • **Museum** Daily: May–Aug 8.30am–6.30pm; Sept–April 8.30am–5.30pm • ¥200 • **Peace Memorial Hall** Same hours • Free • ☎ 095 844 1231, ⓦ city.nagasaki.lg.jp

Located in the northerly suburb of Urakami, Nagasaki's much-vaunted **Atomic Bomb Museum** is entered via a symbolic, spiralling descent. Views of prewar Nagasaki then lead abruptly into a darkened room full of twisted iron girders, blackened masonry and videos constantly scrolling through horrific photos of the dead and dying. It's strong stuff, occasionally too much for some, but the most moving exhibits are always those single fragments of an individual life – a charred lunchbox, a twisted pair of glasses or the chilling shadow of a man etched on wooden planks.

The purpose of the museum isn't merely to shock, and the displays are packed with information, much of it in English, tracing the history of atomic weapons, the effects of the bomb and the heroic efforts of ill-equipped emergency teams who had little idea what they were facing. There's a fascinating video library of interviews with survivors, including some of the foreigners present in Nagasaki at the time; figures vary, but probably more than 12,000 non-nationals were killed in the blast, mostly Korean forced labour working in the Mitsubishi shipyards, as well as Dutch, Australian and British prisoners of war. The museum then broadens out to examine the whole issue of nuclear weapons and ends with a depressing video about the arms race and test ban treaties.

Just outside the museum, in **Hypocentre Park**, an austere black pillar marks the precise spot where the bomb exploded 500m above the ground, while the **Peace Memorial Hall**, right by the museum, is another place for quiet reflection: its centrepiece is a remembrance hall where the names of victims are recorded in 141 volumes.

AUGUST 9, 1945

In the early twentieth century, Nagasaki became an important naval base with huge munitions factories that supplied Japan's wars in China and the rest of Asia, making it an obvious target for America's second **atomic bomb** in 1945. Even so, it was only poor visibility at Kokura, near Kita-Kyūshū (see map, p.700), that forced the bomber, critically short of fuel, south to Nagasaki. The weather was bad there too, but as the B-29 bomber **Bock's Car** flew down the Urakami-gawa at 11am on August 9, a crack in the cloud revealed a sports stadium just north of the factories and shipyards. A few moments later "Fat Boy" exploded. It's estimated that over 70,000 people died in the first few seconds; 75,000 were injured and nearly forty percent of the city's houses were destroyed by the blast and its raging fires. By 1950, radiation exposure and other after-effects had increased the death toll to 140,000. Horrific though these figures are, they would have been higher had the valley walls not contained much of the blast; a spur of hills shielded southern Nagasaki from the worst of the damage. An American naval officer visiting the city a few weeks later described his awe at the "deadness, the absolute essence of death in the sense of finality without resurrection. It's everywhere and nothing has escaped its touch." But the city, at least, did rise again; like fellow bomb-victim Hiroshima, it's now a centre for anti-nuclear protest, and hosts many ardent campaigns for world peace.

The Peace Park

平和公園, Heiwa Kōen

A few hundred metres north of the Atomic Bomb Museum, a long flight of steps leads up into the **Peace Park**, as popular with young kids skateboarding among the donated plaques and memorials as it is with anti-nuclear lobbyists trawling for signatures. The park is watched over by sculptor Kitamura Seibō's muscular **Peace Statue**, unveiled in 1955: the figure's right hand points skyward at the threat of nuclear destruction, while its left hand is extended to hold back the forces of evil. As Kazuo Ishiguro remarked in *A Pale View of Hills*, from a distance the figure resembles a "policeman conducting traffic", but when an elderly person pauses on the way past, head bowed, it's not easy to remain cynical.

10

Urakami Cathedral

浦上天主堂, Urakami Tenshudō • 1-79 Moto-machi • Tues–Sun 9am–5pm • Free

From the Peace Park you can see the twin red-brick towers of **Urakami Cathedral**, dominating a small rise 400m to the east. The present building is a postwar replica of the original, which was completed in 1925 and destroyed when the atomic bomb exploded only 500m away. The blast left scorch marks on the statues now preserved at the top of the steps, and tore off huge chunks of masonry, including a section of the bell tower which still rests on the bank under the north wall. Inside the south door, a chapel is dedicated to the "Bombed Mary", from whose charred face stare sightless eyes.

26 Martyrs' Memorial

日本二十六聖人記念館, Nihon Nijūroku Seijin Kinenkan • 7-8 Nishizaka-machi • Museum daily 9am–5pm • ¥500 • ⓦ 26martyrs.com

In 1597, six foreign missionaries and twenty Japanese converts were the unlucky victims of the shogunate's growing unease at the power of the Church. They were marched from Kyoto and Osaka to Nagasaki, where they were crucified on February 2 as a warning to others. The group was canonized in 1862, and a century later the **26 Martyrs' Memorial** was erected on the site to commemorate Japan's first Christian martyrs, comprising a bizarre, mosaic-clad church, an outdoor memorial shrine and a small **museum** telling the history of the martyrs and of Christianity in Japan. A surprising amount survives, including tissue-thin prayer books hidden in bamboo and statues of the Virgin Mary disguised as the goddess Kannon. One document records the bounties offered to informers: 500 silver pieces per priest, down to 100 for a lowly catechist.

Fukusai-ji

福済寺 • 2-56 Chikugo-machi • Daily 7am–5pm • Free

The original Zen temple, **Fukusai-ji**, was founded in 1628, destroyed in 1945 by the bomb, then replaced with a quirky, turtle-shaped building, topped by an 18m-tall, aluminium-alloy statue of the goddess Kannon and a circle of supplicating infants. Inside the temple, a 25m-long Foucault's pendulum represents a perpetual prayer for peace, oscillating over the remains of 16,500 Japanese war dead buried underneath. For the best views of the goddess, head up the hill to the graveyard behind the temple;

with high-rise buildings stretching towards the ocean, it brings to mind Rio's Christ the Redeemer, and makes for a particularly beautiful view at sunset.

Shōfuku-ji

聖福寺 • 3-77 Tamazono-machi • Daily 24hr • Free

Showing its age somewhat, the Zen temple **Shōfuku-ji**, which originally dates from the early seventeenth century, was rebuilt in 1715 and survived the bomb. Inside the imposing gateway you'll find an attractive collection of aged wooden buildings surrounded by rustling bamboo stands and shady trees. Its main attributes are some detailed carving on the gates and unusual decorative features such as the red balustrade around the worship hall.

Nagasaki Museum of History and Culture

長崎歴史文化博物館, Nagasaki Rekishi Bunka Hakubutsukan • 1-1-1 Tateyama • Daily 8.30am–7pm • ¥600 • ☎ 095 818 8366, Ⓦ nmhc.jp

The engaging **Nagasaki Museum of History and Culture** focuses on the city's role as a conduit for cultural exchange. It's set in a pretty building in a large, grassy compound that's worth visiting even if you don't fancy seeing the exhibits. Inside, there are plenty of original materials, including an exquisite seventeenth-century folding screen depicting British and Dutch ships in Nagasaki harbour, and the first Japanese–English dictionary compiled by Dutch interpreters in 1814. Alongside scale models and videos, there's a room devoted to local crafts, some showing distinctly foreign influences, and you exit through a reconstruction of the Nagasaki Magistrate's office.

Suwa-jinja

諏訪神社 • 18-15 Kaminishiyama-machi • 24hr • Free

Accessed via a challenging flight of steep steps, **Suwa-jinja** is Nagasaki's major shrine. It was founded in 1625 when the shogunate was promoting Shintoism in opposition to the Christian Church. Its main hall, rebuilt in 1869, is fresh and simple, but for most foreigners its greatest attraction is the English-language fortune papers on sale beside the collecting box (¥200). The grounds are scattered with unusual subsidiary shrines, notably two *koma-inu* (guardian lions) known as the **stop lions**, where people vowing to give up unwanted habits fasten paper strings around the front legs, like plaster casts; you'll find them just around the corner from the main hall.

Megane-bashi

眼鏡橋

Below Suwa-jinja, the **Nakashima-gawa** flows west through central Nagasaki under a succession of stone bridges linked by a pleasant riverside walk. The most noteworthy of these is the double-arched **Megane-bashi**, aptly named "Spectacles Bridge", which is

---

KUNCHI MATSURI

Each autumn, Suwa-jinja hosts the famous **Kunchi Matsuri** (Oct 7–9). This festival is believed to have originated in 1633 when two geisha performing a nō dance attracted huge crowds during celebrations to mark the ninth day of the ninth lunar month. Gradually, European and Chinese elements were incorporated – this was one of the few occasions when Dutch merchants were allowed to leave Dejima – and the jollities now consist of dragon dances and heavy floats, some fashioned as Chinese and Dutch ships, being spun round outside the shrine.

Japan's oldest stone bridge, dating from 1634. Across Megane-bashi, **Teramachi-dōri** (Temple-town Street) parallels the river; in between this street and the river lies a lattice of quiet alleys that constitutes one of Nagasaki's most charming areas.

Chinatown

新地中華街, Shinchi Chūka-gai

From the seventeenth to the nineteenth centuries, Nagasaki's Chinese community, like the Dutch on nearby Dejima, was restricted to a designated area, which roughly corresponds with today's **Chinatown**. The area was surrounded by high walls and only men were permitted to live there, but at certain times its population rose above a thousand, including Vietnamese-Chinese and Thai-Chinese traders. Today, four elaborate gates signpost Chinatown's colourful grid of six blocks packed with shops and restaurants, while a bare earth park over on the south side houses an older wooden gate and a Chinese pavilion where old men sit and gossip over chess pieces.

Dejima

出島 • Daily: mid-July to early Oct 8am–7pm; early Oct to mid-July 8am–6pm • ¥510 • ⓦ nagasakidejima.jp • Dejima tram stop for west entrance, Tsuki-machi tram stop for east entrance

Immediately northwest of Chinatown, the old Dutch enclave of **Dejima**, which provided Japan's only access to the Western world for over two hundred years (see p.825), has been ambitiously re-created, to outstanding effect. Built in 1636 as a tiny artificial island, Dejima was intended to house Portuguese traders, but in 1639, a year after the end of the Shimabara Rebellion (see box, p.732), they were expelled from Japan for evangelizing and smuggling. In stepped the enterprising Dutch, who were prepared to transfer their trading post from nearby Hirado to this virtual prison in 1641 and to pay the equivalent, in today's terms, of ¥100 million rent each year for the privilege. As vividly evoked in David Mitchell's novel *The Thousand Autumns of Jacob de Zoet* (see p.868), only about a dozen men employed by the Dutch East India Company (the VOC) were permitted to live on Dejima under strict rules, visited from the mainland only by civil servants and prostitutes.

The site

The island was swallowed up in later land reclamations, but the buildings have now been lovingly replicated exactly as they were in the 1820s, and in the exact positions suggested by excavations. (The 1820s were chosen partly because at that time the Dutch made a highly accurate scale model – now in the possession of the University of Leiden – of this most peculiar outpost, right down to the wallpaper, to satisfy the curiosity of people back home in the Netherlands.) It's best to start at the west gate, where the **Chief Factor's Residence** is the ghetto's grandest edifice, a strange fusion of Dutch style and Japanese craftsmanship, covered in green ship's paint on the outside and chrysanthemum wallpaper inside – for which local artisans were obliged to use small sheets of *fusuma* paper printed with woodblocks. The tatami-matted dining room is laid out for a lavish meal to celebrate the winter solstice (like all other displays of Christianity, Christmas was banned). The fascinating exhibition, most of which is translated into English, continues in the nearby, hi-tech **Clerk's Quarters**, where you'll learn that striped fabric – so commonly used for kimono today – was introduced to Japan by the VOC from India. Every day, Japanese officials used to cross the only, heavily guarded bridge from the mainland (currently under reconstruction) to keep an eye on the Dutch from the **Town Elder's Room**, a purely Japanese building right opposite the main gate.

It's well worth timing your visit to Dejima to coincide with lunch at the on-site **restaurant**, the *Dejima International Club* (see p.728).

10

MADAME BUTTERFLY

Puccini's opera, written in the early twentieth century, tells the story of an American lieutenant stationed in Nagasaki who marries a Japanese woman known as **Madame Butterfly**. Whereas she has given up her religion and earned the wrath of her family to enter the marriage, Lt. Pinkerton treats the marriage far less seriously, and is soon posted back to the US. Unknown to Pinkerton, Butterfly has given birth to their son and is waiting faithfully for his return when he arrives back in Nagasaki three years later. Butterfly pretties up her house and prepares to present her child to the proud father. Pinkerton, meanwhile, has remarried in America and brings his new wife to meet the unsuspecting Butterfly. When he offers to adopt the child, poor Butterfly agrees and tells him to come back later. She then embraces her son and falls on her father's sword.

The opera was adapted from a play by David Belasco, though some attribute it to a book by Frenchman Pierre Loti who wrote *Madame Chrysanthème* after spending a month in Nagasaki in 1885 with a young Japanese woman called Kane. Whatever its origin, the opera was not well received at its debut and Puccini was forced to rewrite Pinkerton and his American wife in a more sympathetic light. Efforts to trace the real Pinkerton have led to a William B. Franklin, but there are many contenders; it was common practice in the late nineteenth century for Western males stationed in Japan to "marry" a geisha in order to secure their companion's faithfulness and reduce the spread of venereal disease. In return, they provided accommodation plus some remuneration. As soon as the posting ended, however, the agreement was considered null and void on both sides.

Nagasaki Prefectural Art Museum

長崎県美術館, Nagasaki-ken Bijutsukan • 2-1 Dejima-machi • Daily 10am–8pm; closed second & fourth Mon of month • ¥400 • ☎ 095 833 2110, Ⓦ nagasaki-museum.jp

A couple of minutes' walk southwest of Dejima, the modern **Nagasaki Prefectural Art Museum** occupies a splendidly airy building on the waterfront. Designed by Kengo Kuma, it has great views of the port from its roof terrace and a lovely café. The museum is particularly strong on Spanish art, including works by Picasso, Dalí and Miró, and Meiji-era art from Nagasaki, though only part of the collection is on show at any one time.

Sōfuku-ji

崇福寺 • 7-5 Kajiya-machi • Daily 8am–5pm • ¥300

Near the southern end of Teramachi-dōri, which is lined with temples on one side and neighbourhood shops on the other, you'll see signs pointing left to **Sōfuku-ji**. This is Nagasaki's most important Chinese Zen temple, founded in 1629 by Fujian immigrants and containing a monumental red gate among other rare examples of Ming-period Chinese architecture.

Ōura Cathedral

大浦天主堂, Ōura Tenshudō • 5-3 Minamiyamate-machi • Daily 8am–6pm • ¥600

In the south of the city, a parade of souvenir shops lines the road up to **Ōura Cathedral**, Japan's oldest extant Christian place of worship. A pretty little white structure housing exhibits in English on the history of Christianity in Japan, it was built by French missionaries in 1864 to serve Nagasaki's growing foreign community. A few months later Father Petitjean was astonished to find outside his door a few brave members of Nagasaki's "hidden Christians" who had secretly kept the faith for more than two centuries.

Glover Garden

グラバー園, Gurabā-en • 8-1 Minamiyamate-machi • Daily: mid-July to early Oct & around Golden Week (late April/early May) 8am–9.30pm; rest of year 8am–6pm, till 8/9pm on certain days in Oct, Nov & Dec • ¥610 • ☎ 095 822 8223, Ⓦ glover-garden.jp • From Ishibashi tram stop, take the elevator-like structure (the "Sky Road") which whisks you diagonally to an upper vantage point, from where a more regular lift will take you up to the garden's upper entrance

THOMAS GLOVER

Scotsman **Thomas Glover** arrived in Nagasaki from Shanghai in 1859, aged just 21, and became involved in various enterprises, including arms dealing. In the mid-1860s, rebels seeking to overthrow the shogun approached Glover for his assistance. Not only did he supply them with weapons, he also furthered their revolutionary cause by smuggling some of them abroad to study, including Ito Hirobumi, who eventually served as prime minister in the new Meiji government. For this, and his subsequent work in modernizing Japanese industry, Glover was awarded the Second Class Order of the Rising Sun – a rare honour – shortly before his death in Tokyo, aged 73.

Glover built the bungalow now known as **Glover House** in 1863, where he lived with his wife Tsuru, a former geisha, and his son from an earlier liaison, Tomisaburō. After his father's death, Tomisaburō was a valued member of both the Japanese and foreign business communities, but as Japan slid towards war in the mid-1930s his companies were closed and he came under suspicion as a potential spy. Forced to move out of Glover House, with its bird's-eye view of the harbour, and kept under virtual house arrest, he committed suicide two weeks after the atomic bomb flashed above Nagasaki.

10

Despite the crowds, and day-round piped music, pretty **Glover Garden** is well worth a visit. As well as offering some of Nagasaki's best views, it features seven late nineteenth-century, European-style buildings, each typically colonial with wide verandas, louvred shutters and high-ceilinged, spacious rooms. The houses also contain odds and ends of furniture and evocative photos of the pioneering inhabitants they once housed.

The best approach is to take the "Sky Road" up to the garden's upper entrance and work down. From here, the first building you'll come across is **Walker House**, a modest bungalow built in the 1870s for the British born captain of a Japanese passenger ship after he helped provide transport for government troops in the Satsuma Rebellion (see p.763). On retiring from the sea in 1898 he joined Thomas Glover, the bluff's most colourful and illustrious resident (see box above), in setting up Japan's first soft drinks company, which produced a popular line in "Banzai Lemonade" and "Banzai Cider" and eventually became Kirin Brewery. Glover's house, the oldest Western-style building in Japan, is worth a look around, as are those formerly belonging to Frederick Ringer, founder of the Nagasaki Press, and tea merchant William Alt.

The exit from Glover Garden takes you through the **Museum of Traditional Performing Arts** (same ticket), which displays the beautifully fashioned floats and other paraphernalia used during the Kunchi festivities (see box, p.722).

The Dutch Slopes

オランダ坂, Oranda-Saka

On the opposite bluff to Glover Garden, and divided from it by a small stream, is a prettified hillside district known as the **Dutch Slopes**. Though it's only a short walk from Glover Garden and the cathedral, few visitors bother to venture into this area, which is centred on the **Higashi-yamate** (東山手) clutch of blue, wooden Western-style buildings that have been preserved on roads still paved with their original flagstones. The first group of period wooden houses on the left consists of two neat rows: the lower row houses a **photography museum** (Tues–Sun 9am–5pm; ¥100) displaying fascinating early photos of Nagasaki.

Kōshi-byō

孔子廟 • 10-36 Oura-machi • Daily 8.30am–5.30pm • ¥600

Walking along the Dutch slopes you can't miss the bright yellow roofs of **Kōshi-byō**, nestling at the foot of the hill within its stout, red-brick wall. Interestingly, the land beneath this **Confucian shrine**, completed in 1893, belongs to China and is administered

10

by the embassy in Tokyo. Its present pristine state is due to an extensive 1980s rebuild using materials imported from China, from the glazed roof tiles to the glittering white marble flagstones and the statues of Confucius's 72 disciples that fill the courtyard.

Inasa-yama

稲佐山 • **Ropeway** Daily 9am–10pm; closed first 10 days of Dec • Every 20min • ¥720 one-way, ¥1230 return • Take Nagasaki Bus #3 or #4 from outside Nagasaki train station and get off across the river at Ropeway-mae bus stop, from where the entrance is up the steps in the grounds of a shrine; in the evening, there's a free shuttle bus from five hotels, including the Belle View and the Hotel Nagasaki • ☎ 095 861 3640, ⓦ nagasaki-ropeway.jp

Nagasaki is not short of good viewpoints, but none can compare with the spectacular night-time panorama from **Inasa-yama**, a 333m-high hill to the west of the city. A **ropeway**, or cable-car, whisks you up there in just five minutes. From the top, you get stunning views of the contorted local coastline, as well as the confetti of nearby islands and islets.

ARRIVAL AND INFORMATION   NAGASAKI

By plane Nagasaki Airport (☎ 095 752 5555, ⓦ nagasaki -airport.jp) occupies an artificial island in Ōmura Bay, 40km from town. It is served by three bus routes to the city, all of which pass Nagasaki Station (45min–1hr 10min; ¥900), as well as by buses to Shimabara ferry terminal (1hr 50min; ¥1800) via Isahaya Station. It receives a few international flights from neighbouring Asian countries, including

regular services from Seoul and Shanghai.
Destinations Kōbe (2–4 daily; 1hr); Nagoya (2–3 daily; 1hr 10min); Osaka (Itami & Kansai; 8 daily; 1hr 5min); and Tokyo (Haneda; 1–2 hourly; 1hr 30min).
By train The train station is roughly 1km north of the main downtown area.
Destinations Fukuoka's Hakata Station (1–2 hourly; 2hr);

BATTLESHIP ISLAND

Jutting out of the sea about 20km southwest off Nagasaki lies the city's most fascinating attraction, and one that may well be familiar as it was re-created for a menacing scene in the 2012 James Bond film *Skyfall*. Properly known as Hashima, it's more commonly referred to as **Gunkan-jima**, or "Battleship Island"; this may sound like a board game or pirate film, but the reality is far more interesting.

Gunkan-jima was once one of Japan's most important sources of coal, and from 1890 to 1974 it was inhabited by hundreds of miners and their families, with a population of over 5000 at its high point around 1960; slag from the mine was used to enlarge the island from a small, steep-sided rock. This dense concentration of people gave Japan a sneak preview of what it has become today – Gunkan-jima boasted the country's first ever high-rise concrete buildings (complete with rooftop farms), which together with the island's high sea walls make it appear from a distance like some huge and rather monstrous ship, hence the name. For a time it functioned quite well, with just enough schools, shops and housing – plus a cinema and pachinko hall – to keep its tiny population satisfied. However, development in mainland Japan soon raced ahead, giving this brave attempt at urban utopia a relatively improverished appearance. Its fate was sealed when the domestic coal industry collapsed in the mid-1970s; the island was abandoned and left to decay.

Gunkan-jima only opened to tourists in 2009, and it is now possible to visit on short trips. Interest has ballooned since the place inspired the scene from *Skyfall* – if you look anything like Daniel Craig or Javier Bardem (in other words, male and white), you may well become photo-fodder for local tourists. Once on the island, you'll be taking plenty of pictures yourself, as it's unique, and quite spectacular – with a little imagination, you'll discern echoes of Cappadocian caves, Pompeii or (suitably, given its proximity to Nagasaki) a nuclear disaster.

Five companies run **tours**, including Gunkanjima Cruise, who offer an English audio guide for the whole trip, as well as online booking (ⓦ gunkanjima-cruise.jp); otherwise, your accommodation or the tourist office should be able to book you a place. It's wise to book at least a couple of days ahead (the most popular dates sometimes sell out two months in advance), and note that in bad weather it may not be possible to land on the island or trips can be cancelled altogether. Tours cost from ¥3600 (plus ¥300 entrance fee to the island) and last around 3hr, including a short guided tour on the island itself, where you're restricted to a 200m-long walkway (there's no access to the buildings, which have been left to the elements for over forty years).

Huis ten Bosch (hourly; 1hr 30min); Isahaya (1–2 hourly; 25min).

By bus Most long-distance buses either stop outside the train station, or pull into Ken-ei bus station on the opposite side of the road.

Destinations Beppu (5 daily; 3hr 30min); Fukuoka (every 20–30min; 2hr 30min); Kumamoto (8 daily; 3hr 20min); Unzen (3–4 daily; 1hr 45min).

Tourist information You can pick up city maps and a few English pamphlets at Nagasaki City Tourist Information (daily 8am–8pm; ⓦ travel.at-nagasaki.Jp), Inside the train station by the ticket barrier. There's also an English-language call centre for the city (☏ 095 825 5175; daily 8am–8pm). Nagasaki Prefecture no longer operate a tourist information centre but they do have a good website (ⓦ visit-nagasaki.com).

GETTING AROUND

By tram Given its elongated shape, Nagasaki's sights are all fairly spread out. However, it's one of the easier cities for getting around, thanks mainly to its cheap and easy tram system. There are five numbered lines, each identified and colour-coded on the front. Transfers on the same fare are allowed only at Tsuki-machi stop (ask for a transfer ticket, *norikae-kippu*). There's a flat fare of ¥120 which you feed into the driver's box on exit, or you can buy a one-day pass (¥500) at the tourist information centre and hotels. While

you're clanking along, take a look around: some of these trolley cars are museum pieces – the oldest dates from 1911 – which were snapped up when other Japanese cities were merrily ripping up their tramlines.

By bus City buses are more complicated than trams, but the only time you're likely to need them is to get to the Inasa-yama Ropeway (see opposite).

Car rental Nissan Rent-a-Car has an office near the station (☏ 095 825 1988) and at the airport (☏ 095 754 1688).

ACCOMMODATION

Nagasaki offers a broad range of rooms, widely dispersed around the city. Forty or so hotels and hostels, including most of those listed below, can give guests a card that earns considerable **discounts** at many of Nagasaki's sights, including the Atomic Bomb Museum, the Museum of History and Culture, Dejima, Glover Garden and the Ropeway (ⓦ travel.at-nagasaki.jp/en).

★**Hostel Akari** ホステルあかり 2-2 Kojiya-machi ☏ 095 801 7900, ⓦ nagasaki-hostel.com. Home to pretty much every backpacker who swings through, and rightly so – dorms and en-suite private rooms alike are cosy places to bunk down, there's a cool common room to relax in, and the riverside location is very pleasant. In addition, the knowledgeable, super-friendly staff are able – and, more importantly, willing – to advise on all things Nagasaki. 🛜 Dorms **¥2700**, doubles **¥6800**

Hotel Belle View Nagasaki ベルビュー長崎出島 1-20 Edo-machi ☏ 095 826 5030, ⓦ hotel-belleview.com. Non-smoking, eco-friendly business hotel in a central location, with helpful and efficient service plus a restaurant and coin laundry. Computer available for guests. 🛜 **¥10,280**

Hotel Cuore クオーレ長崎駅前 7-3 Daikoku-machi ☏ 095 818 9000, ⓦ hotel-cuore.com. Spruce, eco-friendly, sound-proofed business hotel opposite the station, where the top floor is women-only. Everything you could possibly need, including trouser press and tea-making equipment, is squeezed into the smallest space imaginable in the single rooms (from ¥5900); double and twins are slightly more spacious. Coin laundry and computer available for guests. 🛜 **¥7400**

★**Garden Terrace Nagasaki** ガーデンテラス長崎 1-20 Akizuki-machi ☏ 095 864 7777, ⓦ gt-nagasaki.jp. Imagine a giant Rubik's Cube made of pine, and you're halfway to visualizing award-winning architect Kengo Kuma's stunning modern hotel. Sitting halfway up a mountain on the other side of the bay, its various suites are

decked out with angular furniture, and each provides a wonderful city view – in some cases, even from the bathtub. The infinity-edge summertime pool shares the view, and there's a private onsen. Breakfast included. 🛜 **¥44,000**

Hotel Nagasaki ホテル長崎 2-26 Takara-machi ☏ 095 821 1111, ⓦ landowner.jp/english/nagasaki; Takara-machi tram stop. Two tram stops or a 10min walk north of the station, this welcoming luxury hotel (formerly the *Best Western Premier*) overlooks the train lines and the harbour. Above its opulent lobby, there's a huge variety of spacious, sound-proofed accommodation, including Japanese-style rooms and a women-only floor. Discounts for advance bookings. 🛜 **¥16,200**

Nagasaki Kagamiya 長崎かがみや 1-12-9 Hongouchi ☏ 095 895 8250, ⓦ n-kagamiya.com; 5min walk from Hotarujaya tram stop, 6 stops east of the station on tram #3. Charming hostel offering dorms with bunk beds (female) or futons (male) and Japanese-style private rooms, as well as a computer and fridge in the cosy common area (no kitchen). The friendly, clued-up owners are experts on kimono and rent out beautiful antique kimono by the day. Free toast and coffee for breakfast. 🛜 Dorms **¥2500**, twins **¥6000**

Hotel New Nagasaki 14-5 Daikoku-machi ☏ 095 826 8000, ⓦ newnaga.com. Central Nagasaki's top hotel, conveniently placed just outside the station, has all the trimmings: grand marble lobby, shopping arcade, several restaurants (Japanese, Chinese and Western), "cake boutique" and bar. The rooms are mostly Western-style, some boasting harbour views. Discounts for advance bookings. 📶 **¥27,300**

Travelers House on the Route 5-14 Nishizaki-machi 📞 095 895 8965, 🌐 nagasaki-route.com. New branch of *Hostel Akari* near the station, overlooking the 26 Martyrs'

Memorial church, offering smart, individual cabin-like capsules, each with a small locker, light and power socket. The accommodation and a small kitchen are on the second floor, above a cool café and a bike rental outlet. Computer for guest use. 📶 Dorms **¥3900**

EATING

★ **Chikyūkan** 地球館 6-25 Higashi-yamate 📞 095 822 7966. A fun little place in the delightful, late nineteenth-century wooden buildings on the Dutch Slopes, set up to promote international exchange. On normal days it's a simple café serving English apple cake (¥300) and the like; at weekend lunchtimes, they dole out meals from a different country each week – over 70 nationalities so far – usually cooked by international students from the city universities. 10am–5pm; closed Tues & Wed.

Dejima International Club 内外倶楽部出島 Dejima 📞 095 893 8015. Dejima's former international club, built in 1903, is now a restaurant. As well as Toruko rice and Castella cake, dickie-bowed waiters serve up excellent versions of the fusion dishes that normally form part of a *shippoku*, including braised Chinese pork belly and a very tasty *pasti* (¥1500), a Dutch-style lattice pie filled with meat, ginkgo nuts, local mountain yam and beansprouts and served with a cup of *hikado* (Portuguese chicken and vegetable soup). Daily 10.30am–2.45pm.

★ **Hamakatsu** 浜勝 1-14 Kajiya-chō. Popular restaurant on Teramachi-dōri specializing in juicy *tonkatsu* (pork cutlets). Though it looks smart, with its gold signboard and iron lantern, prices are reasonable (¥1100–1700), with lunch sets starting as low as ¥700. Daily 11am–10.30pm.

Hamakatsu 浜勝 6-50 Kajiya-chō 📞 095 826 8321, 🌐 sippoku.jp. This even smarter *Hamakatsu* offers good-value *shippoku* meals. You can try a mini-*shippoku* for ¥3900 or the real thing from ¥5900 up to over ¥12,000/person; it's best to reserve, and for a full *shippoku* they

require a minimum of two people. Daily 11am–10pm (last orders 8.30pm).

Kagetsu 花月 2-1 Maruyama-machi 📞 095 822 0191, 🌐 ryoutei-kagetsu.co.jp. Set in a lovely, 375-year-old wooden building, a former geisha house that blends elements of Japanese, Chinese and Western design, with an exquisite traditional garden, this is the best spot in town for *shippoku*. Lunchtime prices start at ¥5400 for a *shippoku* bentō (Mon–Fri only) or ¥10,240 for the full meal; in the evening you'll pay upwards of ¥14,000. Booking is essential and you need at least two people to order the full *shippoku*. Noon–3pm (last orders 2pm) & 6–10pm (last orders 8pm); closed one day a week, usually Tues.

Kouzanrou 江山楼 12-2 Shinchi-machi 📞 095 824 5000. Chinatown is packed with tempting restaurants, but this Fukien establishment is recommended for its reasonably priced *champon* and *sara udon* (both ¥860), as well as more mainstream Chinese dishes. Try to nab a table by the window. It often closes 3–5pm for staff lunches, in which case just head across the road to its newer, swankier branch. Daily 11am–8.30pm.

Nagasakikou 長崎港 3-15 Doza-machi 📞 095 895 9179, 🌐 nagasakikou.com. On the north side of Chinatown, this lively, well-run, no-frills restaurant is justifiably popular for its generous portions of super-fresh seafood on rice (*donburi*; ¥1830); look out for a big blue fish and fairy lights on the façade. 📶 Daily 11am–9.30pm.

Tsuruchan ツル茶ん 2-4-7 Aburaya-machi 📞 095 824 2679. This claims to be the restaurant where Toruko rice,

NAGASAKI'S MULTINATIONAL CUISINE

Nagasaki's most famous culinary **speciality** is **shippoku**, its own multicultural version of *kaiseki-ryōri*, in which various European, Chinese and Japanese dishes are served simultaneously in the Chinese style at a lacquered round table, to be shared between diners. It's not cheap, starting at around ¥4000 per head; for the best *shippoku* you need to reserve the day before, although most of the big hotels also offer a less formal version.

Nagasaki's other home-grown dishes include the cheap and cheerful **champon**, in which morsels of seafood, meat and vegetables are served with a dollop of thick noodles in a salty, milky soup; fusing Japanese ingredients and Chinese cooking techniques, it was invented in 1899 to comfort homesick Chinese students. **Sara udon**, an import from Hong Kong and southern China, blends similar ingredients into a thicker sauce on a pile of crispy noodle strands. One bizarre local dish is **Toruko rice**, an unwieldy fusion of spaghetti, rice, salad, breaded pork cutlet and curry sauce, all co-existing on the same plate; the first component of its name means "Turkish", possibly due an old, erroneous presumption that Turkish folk, being exotic, eat curry.

If you've still got room for dessert, pick up some **Castella** (*kasutera*), a brick-like sponge cake which arrived with the Portuguese in the sixteenth century and is now sold all over town.

NAGASAKI FESTIVALS

Chinese New Year is celebrated in Chinatown with a Lantern Festival, dragon dances and acrobatic displays (late Jan to mid-Feb). **Dragon-boat races**, here called *Peiron*, were introduced by the Chinese in 1655 and still take place in Nagasaki harbour every summer (June–July). The last evening of **Obon** (Aug 15) is celebrated with a "spirit-boat" procession, when recently bereaved families lead lantern-lit floats down to the harbour. The biggest bash of the year occurs at the **Kunchi Matsuri** held in early Oct at Suwa-jinja (see box, p.722).

10

Nagasaki's prime culinary oddity (see box opposite), was invented in 1925: whether this should invoke pride or shame is anyone's guess. The "regular" variety of this irregular dish goes for ¥1180, and the place doubles as a decent, atmospheric little café. Daily 9am–10pm.

Yossō 吉宗 8-9 Hamano-machi ☎095 821 0001,

🌐 yossou.co.jp. Famous 150-year-old restaurant specializing in *chawan-mushi*, a steamed egg custard laced with shrimp, shiitake mushroom, bamboo shoots and other goodies. You'll pay around ¥750 for a basic bowl, or ¥1350 with rice and pickles, while a *teishoku* will set you back ¥1940. Tinkling *shamisen* music sets the tone. Daily 11am–8pm.

DRINKING AND NIGHTLIFE

Nagasaki's entertainment area, **Shianbashi** (思案橋), has its own tram stop to the south of the Hamano-machi arcades. The name translates as "bridge of contemplation", referring to men loitering on the bridge, deliberating whether or not to cross over into this former geisha district. The area is now packed with bars, clubs, pachinko parlours, *izakaya* and "soaplands" (seedy massage parlours), where nothing really gets going until 10pm and ends at dawn.

Bar IWI バーイウィ 1-9 Motoshikkui-machi. Run by a Kiwi and fittingly painted all black, this small, lively bar keeps its prices low (most drinks ¥500, apart from a few craft beers) to pull in the punters, who spill out onto the pavements of Harusame-dōri. Mon–Sat 8pm–3am.

Local ローカル 7-8 Dōza-machi ☎095 823 0022. This bright, friendly bar on a prominent corner just south of Kankō-dōri tram stop is standing only downstairs, but has a few picnic

tables on the floor above. The imported beers on draught are good – try a four-brew sampler (¥900) – and there are plenty of mostly American craft beers in bottles. Daily 5pm–2am.

Tin Pan Alley 4F, 5-10 Motoshikkui-machi ☎095 818 8277, 🌐 tin-pan-alley.jp. The house band struts its stuff nightly here, with a playlist ranging from mellow groove to rock and pop classics. Entry charge ¥1800 for men, ¥1300 for women. Tues–Sun 7pm–3am.

DIRECTORY

Hospital Harbour Medical Centre, 6-39 Shinchi-machi (☎095 822 3251), is an emergency hospital on the western edge of Chinatown.

Police 6-13 Okeya-machi (☎095 822 0110). Emergency numbers are listed in Basics on p.71.

Post office Nagasaki Central Post Office is 300m east of

the station at 1-1 Ebisu-machi.

Travel agents For domestic travel, head for the JR Travel Agency in the station (☎095 822 4813). International tickets can be bought at H.I.S., on the north side of the Hamano-machi arcade (☎095 820 6839, 🌐 his-j.com).

Shimabara Hantō

East of Nagasaki, the **Shimabara Hantō** bulges out into the Ariake Sea, tethered to mainland Kyūshū by a neck of land just 5km wide. The peninsula owes its existence to the past volcanic fury of **Unzen-dake**, which still grumbles away, pumping out sulphurous steam, and occasionally spewing lava down its eastern flanks. Buddhist monks first came to the mountain in the eighth century, followed more than a millennium later by Europeans from nearby Nagasaki, attracted by the cool, upland summers. Even today, **Unzen**, a small onsen resort surrounded by pine trees and billowing clouds of steam, draws holiday-makers to its hot springs, malodorous "hells" and scenic hiking trails. One of the most popular outings is to the lava dome of **Fugen-dake**, which roared back into life in 1990 after two centuries of inactivity, and now smoulders menacingly above the old castle town of **Shimabara** – this was protected from the worst of the eruption by an older lava block, but still suffered considerable damage to its southern suburbs.

Previously, Shimabara was famous largely for its association with a Christian-led rebellion in the seventeenth century when 37,000 peasants and their families were massacred. Both towns can be covered on a long day's journey between Nagasaki and Kumamoto, but if time allows, Unzen makes a relaxing overnight stop.

GETTING AROUND   **SHIMABARA HANTŌ**

Travel passes Shimatetsu one-day passes for transport on the peninsula (¥1200, or ¥1000 on the second and fourth Sun of the month) cover the private train between Isahaya and Shimabara and buses from Isahaya and Shimabara to Unzen, as well as local buses in Shimabara.

Unzen
雲仙

Little more than a village, the lofty resort of **UNZEN** sits contentedly on a plateau of the same name. Its name means "fairyland among the clouds", perhaps inspired by the pure mountain air and colourful flourishes of vegetation – azaleas in late spring, fiery-red leaves in the autumn and rime ice on the trees in winter. Competing for attention against this sumptuous backdrop are the town's **onsen**, renowned for their silky-smooth, sulphur-rich water that's good for the skin, and the spitting, scalding **jigoku** (地獄), whose name translates as "hells". Unzen consists largely of resort hotels and souvenir shops strung out along the main road, but fortunately there's plenty of space around and a variety of **walking trails** leads off into the surrounding national park. The best hikes explore the peaks of Unzen-dake; from the top of **Fugen-dake** you're rewarded with splendid views of the Ariake Sea and, if you're lucky, Aso-san's steaming cauldron.

Brief history

A Shingon Buddhist priest is credited with "founding" Unzen when he built a temple here in 701 AD; the area developed into a popular retreat where up to a thousand monks could contemplate the 84,000 tortures awaiting wrongdoers in the afterlife as they gazed at Unzen's bubbling mud pools. The first commercial onsen bath was opened in 1653, and two hundred years later Europeans arriving from Nagasaki, Hong Kong, Shanghai and east Russia prompted the development of a full-blown resort, complete with mock-Tudor hotels, dance halls and Japan's first public golf course, laid out in 1913. The volcanic vents are less active nowadays but still emit evil, sulphurous streams and waft steam over a landscape of bilious-coloured clay. Only the hardiest of acid-tolerant plants can survive, and local hoteliers have added to the satanic scene by laying a mess of rusting, hissing pipes to feed water to their onsen baths.

The jigoku

The *jigoku* provide an interesting hour's diversion, particularly the more active eastern area. The paths are well signposted, with lots of maps and information along the way, and there's also a descriptive English-language brochure available free at the information centre (see opposite). **Daikyōkan Jigoku**, the highest and most active "hell", takes its name ("great shout") from the shrill noise produced as it emits hydrogen sulphide steam at 120°C. The noise is likened to the cries of souls descending to hell, but could well be

---

UNZEN'S ONSEN

The nicest of Unzen's **public baths** is the old-style **Kojigoku Onsen** (小地獄温泉; daily 9am–9pm; ¥420; ⓦ seiunso.jp/kojigoku.html), which occupies two octagonal wooden buildings roughly ten minutes' walk south of town; take the left turn just past the *Fukuda-ya* hotel. More central is **Shin-yu** (新湯; 9am–11pm, closed Wed; ¥100), a small but traditional bathhouse founded in 1878, overlooking a car park at the southern entrance to the *jigoku*. In addition, most hotels also open their baths to non-residents during the day, for a fee.

the howls of the 33 Christian martyrs commemorated on a nearby monument, who were scalded to death here around 1630 by the Shimabara lords (see p.732). Another unhappy end is remembered at **Oito Jigoku**, which, according to legend, broke out the day a local adulteress, Oito, was executed for murdering her husband. The tiny, bursting bubbles of **Suzume Jigoku**, on the other hand, supposedly resemble the twittering of sparrows. Over in the western section, the main point of interest is **Manmyō-ji** temple, beside the Shimatetsu bus station. Founded nearly 1300 years ago, the temple is now home to a large gilded Shaka Buddha sporting a natty blue hairdo.

10

Fugen-dake

普賢岳 • Ropeway daily 8.30am–5.10/5.20pm • ¥630 one-way • 3 shared taxis daily run from Mt Unzen Visitor Centre in Unzen (see below) to Nita Pass (20min; ¥860 return), the departure point for the Ropeway, and back, waiting for their passengers for 1hr at the pass (enough time to take the Ropeway up and back but no more); you have to return to Unzen in the same taxi you go up in. It's possible to buy a one-way taxi ticket up to the pass for ¥430, then explore the mountain in your own time and walk back down to Unzen

While Unzen-dake is the name of the whole volcanic mass, **Fugen-dake** (1359m) refers to its central peak. Fugen-dake erupted for the first time in two hundred years in November 1990, reaching a crescendo in June 1991 when the dome collapsed, creating a newer cone, Heisei Shinzan (1483m), on its east side and sending an avalanche of mud and rocks through Shimabara town. Forty-three people were killed and nearly two thousand homes destroyed. There have been some minor rumbles since, but the eruption officially ended in 1996 and for now Fugen-dake just steams away gently.

A **ropeway** takes visitors up from Nita Pass to an observation platform to the southwest of Fugen-dake; cars run every twenty minutes, though not in bad weather or if the volcano is misbehaving. From the top station, you can walk up Fugen-dake in about an hour, or you could add on ninety minutes to two hours for a new loop trail that skirts within 400m of the top of Heisei Shinzan, for closer views of the new peak. For a satisfying day walk (5–6hr round trip from Unzen), you could climb the trails up to Nita Pass then take a much bigger loop that includes Fugen-dake and the slopes of Heisei Shinzan, before descending from Nita Pass the same way that you came up.

ARRIVAL AND INFORMATION   UNZEN

By bus Direct buses leave from Nagasaki's Ken-ei bus station (3–4 daily; 1hr 45min; ¥1800), or JR Pass holders can take the train to Isahaya Station (諫早; 1–2 hourly; 25min) and transfer to a Shimatetsu bus to Unzen (13 daily; 1hr 20min; ¥1350). Both of these services, as well as the Shimatetsu buses for the onward journey to Shimabara (12 daily; 45min; ¥750), stop at the station on the main road in the centre of Unzen.

Tourist information The Mt Unzen Visitor Centre at the south end of the main street (9am–5pm, closed Thurs, ☎0957 73 3636, ⊛unzenvc.com) provides maps and information about walks in the area, as well as exhibitions about the national park's birds and plants. For general information about accommodation and transport, head next door to the Unzen Tourism Association Information Centre (daily 9am–5pm; ☎0957 73 3434, ⊛unzen.org).

ACCOMMODATION AND EATING

Fukuda-ya 福田屋 South end of town, near the start of the Nagasaki road ☎0957 73 2151, ⊛fukudaya .co.jp. A modern hotel with good-sized rooms and a choice of rotemburo (open to non-residents noon–9pm; ¥1000). Even if you're not staying, try the hotel restaurant's Hayashi rice, a tasty dish of beef hash with rice that was invented in the nineteenth century for Western visitors from China. Restaurant daily 11am–2.30pm. 📶 Half-board **¥23,600**
★**Tsudoi** 集 On the main square next to the bus station ☎0957 60 4225, ⊛unzen-tsudoi.jp. Friendly, helpful new hostel above a stylish café-bar, where there's a small kitchen area for guests. The two attractive dorms (mixed and women-only) feature capsule-like bunk beds

and smart, well-equipped bathrooms. Guests get free tickets to the Yunosato Onsen, a nearby public bathhouse. 📶 Dorms **¥3564**
★**Unzen Miyazaki Ryokan** 雲仙宮崎旅館 Just off the south end of the main street ☎0957 73 3331, ⊛miyazaki -ryokan.co.jp. Excellent traditional ryokan with immaculate standards of service and three lovely rotemburo (for men, women and families). Superb *kaiseki* dinners – seasonal and featuring plenty of local seafood – are served in the guest rooms, which overlook the eastern *jigoku* and the wooded hills behind; indeed, the hotel has its own *jigoku* in its pretty, formal garden. Free daily shuttle bus from Nagasaki and Isahaya stations. 📶 **¥40,000**

10

Shimabara

島原

With its superb castle and the brooding, volcanic backdrop of Fugen-dake, the small port town of **SHIMABARA** makes for a pleasingly relaxed stay, or a day-trip from Nagasaki, Kumamoto or Unzen. Its quiet streets, which are lined with spring-fed streams, run parallel to the coast for more than 2km from the southerly Shimabara-kō ferry terminal to the main centre, Ōte, just below the castle. Following the ructions of the **Shimabara Rebellion** (see box below), the place was decimated when Unzen-dake erupted in 1792. An estimated 15,000 people died in the disaster, mostly from huge tsunamis that swept the Ariake Sea. The volcano then lay dormant until Fugen-dake burst into life again in 1990 and cut a swathe through the town's southern reaches. To the outsider, there's little visible evidence of the devastation wreaked by the mud flows, beyond some heavy-duty retaining walls aimed at channelling any future flows directly down to the sea.

Shimabara-jō

島原城 • Daily 9am–5.30pm • Grounds free; museum ¥540 • ☎ 0957 62 4766, ⓦ shimabarajou.com

Completed in 1625, **Shimabara-jō** castle took seven years to build – it was partly the taxes and hard labour demanded for its construction that provoked the Shimabara Rebellion. The reconstructed turrets contain a **museum**, spread among three buildings – most interesting is the main keep, which features local history exhibits, including relics of clandestine Christian worship, and an awesome observation deck on the fifth floor. The modern building on the west side shows a short film about Fugen-dake, while fans of Nagasaki's Peace Statue (see p.721) will be interested in the Kitamura Seibō Memorial Museum located in the southeast turret. Kitamura, a local sculptor who died in 1987, specialized in powerful bronzes, the best of them gripped by a restless, pent-up energy.

Bukeyashiki

武家屋敷 • Houses daily 9am–5.30pm • Free • ☎ 0957 63 1087

A few remnants of the old castle-town still exist. Five minutes' walk northwest of the castle, **Bukeyashiki** is a pretty little unpaved street of samurai houses, which runs north–south for 400m around a stream, flanked by trees and the original Cyclopean stone walls. You can wander round the gardens and peek inside three of the grander, thatched houses towards the street's northern end.

Shimabara Yūsuikan

しまばら湧水館 • 800m southeast of the castle entrance, just south of the central tourist office on the opposite side of the road • Daily 8.30am–6pm; *kanzarashi* making 10am, 11am, 1pm, 2pm, 3pm & 4pm • *Kanzarashi* making ¥300 • ☎ 0957 63 1111

The welcoming **Shimabara Yūsuikan**, a hundred-year-old summer house, is decorated with lovely carved screens of red hemlock wood and set in a pretty garden. You can have a go at making the local speciality *kanzarashi*, riceflour dumplings soaked in a light syrup with spring water.

THE SHIMABARA REBELLION

In 1637, exorbitant taxes and the oppressive cruelty of two local *daimyō* sparked off a large-scale **peasant revolt** in the Shimabara area, though the underlying motive was anger at the **Christian persecutions** taking place at the time. Many of the rebels were Christian, including their leader, a 16-year-old boy known as Amakusa Shirō, who was supposedly able to perform miracles. His motley army of 37,000, which included women and children, eventually sought refuge in abandoned Hara castle, roughly 30km south of Shimabara town. For three months they held off far-superior government forces, but even Shirō couldn't save them when Hara was stormed in April 1638 and, so it's said, all 37,000 were massacred. Rightly or wrongly, Portuguese missionaries were implicated in the rebellion, and soon afterwards all foreigners were banished from Japan as the country closed its doors.

Shimeisō

四明荘 • Just south of Shimabara Yusuikan on the same side of the road • Daily 9am–6pm • Free • ☎ 0957 63 1121

Shimeisō is a restored "water villa", open-sided and set on stilts above a spring-water pond filled with carp. Relax over a free cup of green tea, enjoying the lovely garden of miniature trees, rocks and moss.

Mount Unzen Disaster Memorial Hall

雲仙岳災害記念館, Unzen-dake Saigai Kinenkan • Highway 251, 5km south of central Shimabara • Daily 9am–6pm, last entry 5pm • ¥1000 (or ¥800 if you pick up a discount coupon from the tourist office) • ☎ 0957 65 5555, ⓦ udmh.or.jp • Take Shimatetsu bus (covered by the one-day pass – see p.730) south from Ōte via Shimabara-kō ferry terminal, and get off at Arena-iriguchi stop (1–3 hourly; 15min)

At the foot of the 1991 lava flow, the **Mount Unzen Disaster Memorial Hall** (aka Gamadasu Dome) contains a moderately interesting museum commemorating the eruption. There's an English audio guide to the exhibits, of which the most accessible are videos of the disaster and a technologically impressive but ultimately rather tacky Great Eruption Theatre which places you in the middle of the pyroclastic flows.

Suffer House Preservation Park

土石流被災家屋保存公園, Dosekiryū Hisai Kaoku Hozon Kōen • Daily 9am–5pm • Free • ☎ 0957 72 7222, ⓦ mizunashi-honjin .co.jp • Take Shimatetsu bus (covered by the one-day pass – see p.730) south from Ōte via Shimabara-kō ferry terminal, and get off at Arena-iriguchi stop (1–3 hourly; 15min)

A solemn memorial to the dead from 1991, the **Suffer House Preservation Park** is a small area of **half-buried houses**. The houses are preserved beneath two plastic domes, about ten minutes' walk across the river from the Memorial Hall (see above); don't go expecting Pompeii, but the area is certainly worth the effort to get to.

ARRIVAL AND INFORMATION

SHIMABARA

By train From Isahaya Station (諫早), which is connected to Nagasaki by JR services (1–2 hourly; 25min), trains on the private Shimatetsu line run east to Shimabara (1–2 hourly; 1hr–1hr 15min; ¥1510). They stop at the main Shimabara Station, a couple of minutes' walk east of Ōte, and then continue three more stops to Shimabara-Gaikō Station, just inland of the ferry point.

By bus Buses from Unzen (12 daily; 45min; ¥750) call at Shimabara-kō before proceeding into town, where they either terminate at the Shimatetsu bus station or stop a little further on in Ōte.

By ferry High-speed and regular ferries sail from Kumamoto-kō (熊本港; see p.737): Kumamoto Ferry (☎ 096 311 4100, ⓦ kumamotoferry.co.jp) runs the high-speed ferries (6–7 daily; 30min; ¥1000), while Kyūsho Ferry (☎ 096 329 6111, ⓦ kyusho-ferry.co.jp) operates the regular service (10 daily; 1hr; ¥780). From Shimabara-kō, buses run to the central Shimabara Station (2–4 hourly; 10min; ¥170).

Tourist information The main tourist office (daily 8.30am–5.30pm; ☎ 0957 62 3986, ⓦ shimabaraonsen .com) is inside the Shimabara-kō port building. It provides good English-language maps and brochures, and rents out bikes for ¥150/hr and electric bicycles for ¥300/hr (also available at Shimabara Station). There's also a new tourist office in the centre near Shimabara Yūsuikan, on the opposite side of the street a little to the north (daily 9am–6pm; ☎ 0957 64 2450).

ACCOMMODATION

Hotel Nampuro ホテル南風楼 On the seashore near Shimatetsu Honsha-mae, the next station down from Shimabara Station ☎ 0957 62 5111, ⓦ nampuro.com. This sprawling, welcoming new hotel offers great views of the Ariake Sea, notably from its outdoor and indoor rooftop onsen. Smart rooms come in all shapes and sizes, both Western- and Japanese-style, some with their own outdoor or semi-outdoor onsen. Free bicycles for guests. Very good rates for singles (¥7500). ☞ **¥14,000**

Shimabara Youth Hostel 島原ユースホステル 7938-4 Shimokawashiri-machi ☎ 0957 62 4451, ⓦ jyh.or.jp. There's something delightful about a youth hostel with an onsen – just what's on offer at this chalet-like building behind Shimabara-Gaikō Station. Dorms **¥3550**

EATING

Aoi Rihatsu-kan 青い理髪館 888-2 Ueno-machi ☎ 0957 64 6057. Eighty-year-old café immediately east of the castle (look out for the blue clapboard building) in an old barber shop. They serve a limited range of set lunches

10

on weekdays and delightful home-baked cakes and cookies. Mon 10.30am–5pm, Tues–Sun 10.30am–6pm; closed one day a week (day varies).

Himematsu-ya 姫松屋 1-1208-3 Jonai, opposite the entrance to Shimabara-jō. Popular restaurant that serves Shimabara's speciality food, *guzōni* – a delicious clam broth packed with rice cakes, fish, pork, lotus root, tofu and egg – at ¥980 for a regular portion or ¥1180 for large. It also offers a choice of well-priced sets and mainstream Japanese dishes. Daily 11am–7pm.

★ **Inohara** 猪原金物店 9-12 Ueno-machi ☎ 0957 62 3117, ⓦ inohara.jp. At the back of this traditional,

140-year-old ironmonger's, there's a delightful patio by a small pond, where you can tuck into handmade *somen* (thin wheatflour noodles; from ¥550), delicious *tonkatsu* curry sets, cakes, desserts (including *kanzarashi* – see p.732) and excellent espresso coffees. Also hosts theatre, storytelling and art events. 11am–6pm; closed Wed.

Shimabara Mizuyashiki しまばら水屋敷 513 Yorozu-machi, in the shopping arcade southeast of the castle ☎ 0957 62 8555. One of several Meiji-era houses in the area, this place serves drinks and snacks – and *somen* noodles in summer – above a delightful garden and spring-fed pond. Daily 11am–5pm.

Kumamoto

熊本

A fair proportion of travellers to Kyūshū find themselves in **KUMAMOTO** at some point. Not only is the city handily located between Fukuoka in the north and Kagoshima down south, but it also lies within striking distance of Aso to the east and Shimabara and Unzen to the west; it's possible to pop by and tick off the main sights on a day-trip from any of these places, but the city itself is attractive and rewards an overnight stay. Chief among its sights is the fearsome, fairy-tale **castle** dominating the town centre, though at the moment it's only possible to admire this at a distance: in April 2016, Kumamoto suffered a magnitude 7 earthquake, which killed around fifty people, injured three thousand and severely damaged the fortress. There's now little evidence elsewhere in the city of the quake's effects, and it's still possible to visit the excellent **Prefectural Traditional Crafts Centre** and **Suizenji-jōjuen**, one of Japan's most highly rated gardens, in the eastern suburbs. Wars and development have meant that little else of particular note survives, though you've got to admire a city which invented the endearingly offbeat "Kobori-style" swimming which "involves the art of swimming in a standing posture attired in armour and helmet".

Brief history

Kumamoto owes its existence to the Katō clan, who were given the fiefdom in the late sixteenth century in return for supporting Tokugawa Ieyasu during his rise to power. **Katō Kiyomasa**, first of the feudal lords, not only built a magnificent fortress but is also remembered for his public works, such as flood control and land reclamation. However, political intrigue resulted in the Katō being ousted in 1632 in favour of the **Hosokawa** clan, who had previously held Kokura. Thirteen generations of Hosokawa lords ruled Kumamoto for more than two centuries, during which time the city thrived as Kyūshū's major government stronghold, until feudal holdings were abolished in 1871. Six years later, the final drama of the Meiji Restoration was played out here when Saigō Takamori's rebel army was defeated by government troops, but not before destroying much of Kumamoto's previously impregnable castle.

Kumamoto-jō

熊本城 • Closed after 2016 earthquake damage – check with the tourist office (see p.737) if it's reopened

Completed in 1607 after only seven years' work, **Kumamoto-jō** is Japan's third-largest castle (after Osaka and Nagoya) and one of its most formidable. It was, however, powerless to resist the April 2016 earthquake, which brought down roofs, outbuildings and even parts of the outer wall. Complete reconstruction will take decades, but it's hoped to re-establish public access to the main keep some time around 2019. For the moment, it's still worth walking up through the park on the castle's west flank to appreciate its architecture as well as the power of the earthquake.

Kumamoto-jō was designed by lord **Katō Kiyomasa**, a brilliant military architect who combined superb fortifications with exquisitely graceful flourishes – as Alan Booth observed in *The Roads to Sata* (see p.866), the main keep seems like "a fragile bird poised for flight". At its peak, the castle had an outer perimeter of 13km and over 5km of inner wall built in what's called *musha-gaeshi* style, meaning that no invading warrior could scale their smooth, gently concave surfaces. In case of prolonged attack, 120 wells were sunk, while camphor and ginkgo trees provided firewood and edible nuts. These defences were severely tested during the 1877 **Satsuma Rebellion** (see box, p.763), when Saigō Takamori's army besieged Kumamoto-jō for fifty days. Government reinforcements eventually relieved the garrison, soon after trouncing the rebels. Though the castle held, most of its surrounding buildings were burnt to the ground and left in ruins until 1960, when the complex was magnificently restored.

The best approach to the castle, once it reopens, is from its south side, which brings you up into the grassy expanse of **Ninomaru** and the main, west, gate into the **inner citadel**. Inside to the left, **Uto Yagura** was the only turret to survive the 1877 battle,

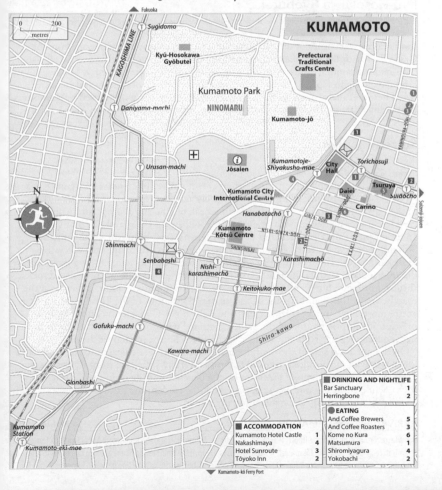

■ DRINKING AND NIGHTLIFE	
Bar Sanctuary	1
Herringbone	2

● EATING	
And Coffee Brewers	5
And Coffee Roasters	3
Kome no Kura	6
Matsumura	1
Shiromiyagura	4
Yokobachi	2

■ ACCOMMODATION	
Kumamoto Hotel Castle	1
Nakashimaya	4
Hotel Sunroute	3
Tōyoko Inn	2

10

while straight on, a high-sided defile leads to the imposing central keep, which hosts an excellent historical **museum** about the castle and the Hosokawa lords. Immediately south of the keep stands the resplendent **Go-ten Ōhiroma**, the main reception hall.

Prefectural Traditional Crafts Centre

熊本県伝統工芸館, Kumamoto-ken Dentō Kōgeikan • 3-35 Chibajo-machi • 9am–5pm; closed Mon • Kumamoto craft display ¥210 • ☎ 096 324 4930

Opposite the castle's northeastern gate (Akazu-no-mon), the **Prefectural Traditional Crafts Centre** hosts free exhibitions promoting local artists and an excellent display of Kumamoto crafts on the second floor, many of which are for sale in the ground-floor shop. The most famous traditional craft is *Higo zogan*, a painstaking method of inlaying gold and silver in a metal base. Developed in the seventeenth century for ornamenting sword hilts, it's now used for jewellery, decorative boxes and the like. Look out among the toys for a little red-faced fellow with a black hat, the ghost Obake-no-kinta – try pulling the string.

Kyū-Hosokawa Gyōbutei

旧細川刑部邸 • 3-1 Furukyō-machi • Closed after 2016 earthquake damage – check with the tourist office (see opposite) if it's reopened • Sugidomo tram stop

In the northwest corner of the castle grounds, roughly fifteen minutes' walk from the Crafts Centre, is **Kyū-Hosokawa Gyōbutei**, an immaculately restored and unusually large high-ranking samurai residence set in traditional gardens – one of the few buildings of its kind remaining in Japan. There are some gorgeous examples of pottery and lacquered wood here and there, many featuring the distinctive nine-circle motif used by the house's former inhabitants. There's also a lovely tearoom on the northern side of the complex.

Suizenji-jōjuen

水前寺成趣園 • 8-1 Suizenji-kōen • Daily: March–Oct 7.30am–6pm; Nov–Feb 8.30am–5pm • ¥400; tea ¥550 outside, ¥650 in ceremony room • ☎ 096 383 0074, ⓦ suizenji.or.jp • Suizenji-kōen tram stop, then 200m walk north

It pays to visit **Suizenji-jōjuen** early, before crowds arrive. In any case, the garden is at its best with an early-morning mist over the crystal-clear, spring-fed lake, its surface broken by jumping minnows or the darting beak of a heron. Plump, multicoloured carp laze under willow-pattern bridges, while staff sweep the gravel paths or snip back an errant pine tuft. Considered to be one of Japan's most beautiful stroll-gardens, Suizenji-jōjuen was created over eighty years, starting in 1632, by three successive Hosokawa lords. The temple from which the garden took its name is long gone, but the immaculate, undulating landscape has survived, dotted with artfully placed rocks, shrubs, miniature pines and plum trees. The design supposedly mimics scenes on the road between Tokyo and Kyoto, known as the "53 stations of the Tōkaidō" – the ones you're most likely to recognize are Fuji and Lake Biwa. Considering Suizenji-jōjuen's prestige, it's surprising to find the garden cluttered with souvenir stalls; many of the items on sale feature Kumamon, the cartoon black bear seen all over the city.

On the northern side of the complex is the Izumi shrine, dedicated to the Hosokawa lords, while a four-hundred-year-old **teahouse** overlooks the lake from its west bank. Here you can drink a cup of green tea on the benches outside or in the tea ceremony room, while admiring one of the best views of the garden; the price includes an *izayoi*, a white, moon-shaped cake made using egg white.

ARRIVAL AND INFORMATION   **KUMAMOTO**

By plane From Kumamoto Airport (☎ 096 232 2810, ⓦ kmj-ab.co.jp/eng), roughly 15km east, limousine buses shuttle into town (approx 1hr; ¥700–800), stopping at Shimo-dōri and the Kumamoto Kōtsū Centre before ending up at the train station. There are also free buses to Higo-Ozu Station on the railway line between Kumamoto and Aso.

Destinations Nagoya (6 daily; 1hr 15min); Naha (1 daily; 1hr 30min); Osaka (Itami; 10 daily; 1hr 5min); Tokyo (1–2 hourly; 1hr 35min).

By train The main train station lies some 2km south of the city centre.

Destinations Fukuoka (every 30min; 40min–1hr 20min); Kagoshima (every 30min; 40min–1hr 15min); Osaka (1–2 hourly; 3hr–3hr 45min).

By bus Kumamoto Kōtsū Centre (熊本交通センター) is the city's central bus station, and most long-distance buses terminate here, though a few continue through to the train station; in addition, most buses from the ferry port, Kumamoto-kō, stop at the train station first.

Destinations Aso (9 daily; 1hr 45min–2hr); Beppu (1 daily; 4hr 40min); Fukuoka (every 10–20min; 2hr 20min); Kagoshima (4 daily; 3hr 20min); Miyazaki (1 hourly; 3hr); Nagasaki (8 daily; 3hr 20min); and Takachiho (2 daily; 3hr 30min).

By ferry Kumamoto Ferry (☎ 096 311 4100, ⓦ kumamotoferry.co.jp) operates high-speed ferries from Kumamoto-kō (熊本港) to Shimabara (6–7 daily; 30min; ¥1000), while Kyūshō Ferry (☎ 096 329 6111, ⓦ kyusho-ferry.co.jp) runs a regular service to Shimabara (10 daily; 1hr; ¥780). To get to the port, take a bus from the Kumamoto Kōtsū Centre via Kumamoto Station (9 daily; 35min; ¥550).

10

GETTING AROUND

By tram Getting around central Kumamoto is fairly straightforward thanks to the tram system, which covers most sights. Trams run every 5–10min from 6.30am–11pm, with a flat fare of ¥170. There are just two lines (A and B), both of which run from the eastern suburbs through the city centre before splitting near the Kumamoto Kōtsū Centre. Line A then heads off south to Kumamoto Station, while Line B loops north round the castle. You can change from one line to another at Karashima-chō, where the lines split; ask for a

transfer ticket (*norikae-kippu*) to avoid paying twice.

Transport passes If you're moving about a lot, you can buy a one-day pass (*ichi-nichi jōshaken*; ¥500 for trams, or ¥900 for trams and buses, including the bus to the port), which also entitles you to discounted tickets to various sights.

Car rental Toyota Rent-a-Car has branches near Kumamoto Station (☎ 096 311 0100) and at the airport (☎ 096 232 0100).

INFORMATION

Tourist information Kumamoto's helpful tourist information service (daily 9am–5.30pm; ☎ 096 322 5060, ⓦ manyou-kumamoto.jp for the city, ⓦ kumanago.jp for the prefecture) can be found at Jōsaien, a visitor complex of crafts shops and restaurants on the southwest side of the castle. There are also two branches at the station (daily

8/8.30am–7pm) and one at the airport (daily 6.30am–9.30pm).

Services Kumamoto National Hospital (☎ 096 353 6501) is immediately south of Ninomaru Park. The Kumamoto Prefectural Police Headquarters is at 6-18-1 Suizenji (☎ 096 381 0110).

ACCOMMODATION

★**Kumamoto Hotel Castle** 熊本ホテルキャッスル 4-2 Jyōtō-machi ☎ 096 326 3311, ⓦ hotel-castle.co.jp. One of the few places in Kumamoto boasting views of the city's most famous sight – despite this, and the high quality of the rooms and service, it's not that expensive. Repair to the top-floor restaurant bar for evening drinks and wonderful castle vistas. 🛜 **¥15,000**

Nakashimaya 中島屋 2-11-6 Shin-machi ☎ 096 202 2020, ⓦ nakashimaya.ikidane.com. A wonderful women-only hostel: friendly, decorated with traditional flourishes, comfy futons on tatami mats, free computer access, rooftop deck, coin laundry ... and you can try your hand at dyeing your own shoes or T-shirts. 🛜 Dorms **¥2800**, singles **¥3300**, twins **¥5900**

★**Hotel Sunroute** ホテルサンルート熊本 1-7-18

Shimotori ☎ 096 322 2211, ⓦ sunroute-kumamoto.jp. Stylish, welcoming and very central hotel with a free espresso machine in the lobby and a wide choice of rooms: especially recommended are the spacious Japanese-style twins (¥16,000), with a retro feel, stylish modern *shōji* and enough room for two extra people to sleep on the tatami mats (¥3000 each). Very good rates for singles, too (¥7000). 🛜 **¥12,000**

Tōyoko Inn 東横INN 1-1 Suidō-chō ☎ 096 325 1045, ⓦ toyoko-inn.com. Typically good-value option from the business hotel chain, handily located on Kumamoto's main shopping street, right beside the Suido-cho tram stop. There's another branch next to the train station. Japanese breakfast included. 🛜 **¥7020**

EATING

Local **speciality foods** include horsemeat sashimi (*basashi*) eaten with lots of garlic, and *karashi renkon*, which consists of lotus-root slices stuffed with a mustard and bean paste, dipped in batter and deep-fried. In addition to the restaurants listed below, you'll find a good variety on the seventh floor of Tsuruya department store's main building.

KUMAMOTO FESTIVALS

Kumamoto's main events are the **Hinokuni Festival** (mid-Aug), celebrated with folk dances, a city-centre parade and fireworks; and the **Fujisaki Hachiman-gū autumn festival** (5 days in mid-Sept), on the final morning of which around sixty colourfully decorated horses and twenty thousand people in historical garb parade through the streets.

And Coffee Roasters Kaminoura-dōri ☎096 273 6178, ⍟andcoffeeroasters.com. Earnest, pared-down, third-generation coffee house that stretches to a few tables upstairs and a few cakes. The espresso (¥300), filtered and cold-brew coffees are excellent, of course. Also has a more central branch, *And Coffee Brewers* (daily 10am–8pm), on Floor 2 of Tsuruya department store. 🛜 Daily 8am–8pm.

Kome no Kura 米の蔵 2F, 1-6-27 Shimo-dōri ☎096 212 5551. Hugely stylish *izakaya* at the top of a grand staircase, where a garden path set under the glass floor leads you to the tables, each partitioned with dark-wood sliding doors and carved screens. It lives up to the name on its sign, "Dynamic Kitchen": try the delicious fishcakes stuffed with potato salad and deep-fried (¥470), and leave room for *zenzai* (winter only), a tasty sweet soup with riceflour dumplings. 🛜 Daily 5–11.15pm.

Matsumura まつむら 1F Kaminoura-dōri ☎096 356 6825. White *noren* (split curtains) give onto a refined interior, decorated with cream paint and bamboo, at this excellent oden restaurant. You can order small dishes individually, such as superb minced chicken balls with radish (¥470) and oysters with edible chrysanthemum leaves, or plump for a set menu, which might cost you ¥4200 for sashimi, a fried dish, a grilled dish and six stewed (oden) dishes. Mon–Sat 5.30–10pm.

★**Shiromiyagura** 城見櫓 1-10 Hanabata-chō ☎096 356 1146. One of the few Kumamoto restaurants with castle views, which are especially good from the uppermost of its four levels. *Kaiseki* dinners that include local specialities such as *karashi renkon*, horsemeat and free-range chicken start from ¥5000, though it's a lot cheaper at lunchtime when you can get a *kaiseki* for ¥2200. The entrance is a little hard to spot, but the building stands out: it's by the river, topped with a tiled gable roof that's designed to imitate the castle opposite. Daily 11.30am–1.30pm & 5.30–9pm.

Yokobachi ヨコバチ 11-40 Kamitorōri-chō ☎096 351 4581. Enjoy *karashi renkon* or Higo beef, the local *wagyu*, at this bustling *izakaya* on Kaminoura-dōri, where the tatami-mat rooms overlook a pretty Japanese garden. Set meals start at ¥2500, and you can add on ¥1500 for all-you-can-drink in 90min. Mon–Sat 5–11.30pm, Sun 5–11pm.

DRINKING AND NIGHTLIFE

Bar Sanctuary 4-16 Tetori-hon-machi. Kumamoto's one-stop party venue, with a dance club that attracts top local and national DJs, a bar, a darts room and karaoke. Entry charge depends on what's on, starting from ¥500 including one drink. Mon–Thurs & Sun 8pm–4am, Fri & Sat 8pm–5am.

Herringbone 3F, T Zone Building, Sakae-dōri, just south of Nishi-ginza-dōri ☎096 356 4747, ⍟herringbone0601.blog.fc2.com. Small, sparse but friendly bar for serious beer-spotters: five Japanese craft beers, mostly British-, Belgian- or American-style, are always on draught (from ¥1300/pint) and are changed weekly. 🛜 Daily 6/7pm–5am.

Aso and the central highlands

Central Kyūshū is dominated by sparsely populated, grassy highlands, in places rising to substantial peaks, which offer some of the island's most magnificent scenery and best walking country. These mountains are relics of ancient volcanic upheavals and explosions of such incredible force that they collapsed one gigantic volcano to create the **Aso caldera**, the world's largest crater. Today the floor of the caldera is a patchwork of fields like many tatami mats, and the surrounding uplands form a popular summer playground, but the steaming crater of Aso-san at its centre provides a potent reminder that the volcano is still very much alive.

All this subterranean activity naturally means a wealth of hot springs to wallow in, mostly within the caldera itself, although there are a few gems hidden deep in the highlands. One is the picturesque village of **Kurokawa Onsen**, squeezed in a narrow gorge on the Senomoto plateau, which makes a great overnight stop on the road to Beppu. The village lies a few kilometres off the **Yamanami Highway**, the main route between Aso and Beppu, providing a spectacular mountain ride through the **Aso-Kujū**

National Park. In the opposite direction, another dramatic road climbs over the crater wall and heads southeast to **Takachiho**. Perched above an attractive gorge of angular basalt columns, this is where the mythical Sun Goddess Amaterasu hid, according to legends about the birth of the Japanese nation. A riverside cave and its neighbouring shrine make an easy excursion, but a more compelling reason to stop here is to catch a night-time performance of the story told through traditional folk dances.

The Aso Caldera

The ancient crater of **Aso Caldera**, measuring 18km from east to west, 24km north to south and over 120km in circumference, was formed about 100,000 years ago when a vast volcano collapsed. As the rock cooled, a lake formed, but the eruptions continued, pushing up five smaller cones, today known collectively as **Aso-san**. Eventually the lake drained and the area became inhabited; local people attribute their fortune to the god Takeiwatatsu-no-mikoto, grandson of Emperor Jimmu, who kicked a gap in the western wall – the same gap the train uses – to give them rice land. Now some 70,000 people live within the crater, working the rich volcanic soils, while cattle and horses graze the higher meadows in summer. **ASO TOWN** (阿蘇市) is a grandiose name for a scattered group of villages located within the massive caldera on the north side of Aso-san, including a tourist area around Aso Station, which represents the centre of local life.

Aso-san

阿蘇山 • 2 daily buses from Aso Station to Aso Volcano Museum (30min; ¥570)

The five peaks of **Aso-san** line up across the caldera. At the eastern end of the chain lies the distinctively craggy Neko-dake (1433m), while the next peak west is Taka-dake

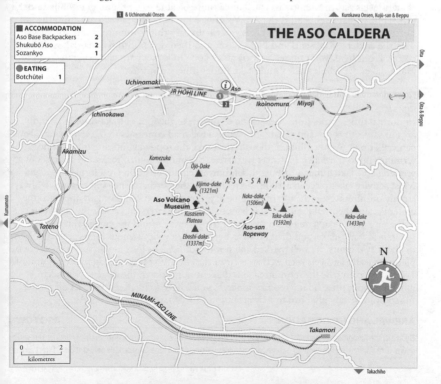

(1592m), the highest of the five summits, and its volcanic offshoot Naka-dake (1506m). West of here lie Eboshi-dake (1337m) and Kijima-dake (1321m).

Naka-dake has become active again since 2014, including a forceful eruption in October 2016, and at the time of writing, there's **limited access** to Aso-san. Kijima-dake, Naka-dake, the ropeway, Taka-dake and all the walks described below are currently **off-limits**. (Aso-san's bad luck continued in April 2016, when the Kumamoto Earthquake damaged several roads here: the only road up the mountain that's currently passable is the one due south from Aso Town.) It's still possible to drive or take the bus up as far as the Aso Volcano Museum. The museum itself is missable, but you'll be rewarded with great views, especially from the two **lookout points** above the museum: smoke rising to the east from the unearthly grey crater of Naka-dake; to the west, Kumamoto and Unzen-dake, beyond the gap in the caldera wall at Tateno; and to the north, the awesome expanse of the caldera's rim, with the perfect cone of **Komezuka**, the "hill of rice", below in the foreground – its dimpled top is said to have been created when Takeiwatatsu-no-mikoto scooped up a handful of rice to feed his starving people.

You're also free to walk on the hyperbolically named **Kusasenri** ("Thousand-Mile Meadow"), a grassy bowl on the south side of the Aso Volcano Museum speckled with shallow crater lakes, though the satisfying ninety-minute circuit of Kusasenri that takes in the crumpled peak of Eboshi-dake is off-limits at the moment.

Aso tourist office can give advice about the **current volcano alert level** and how it affects access, though it's tricky to get good information in English online – try ⓦaso.ne.jp/~volcano or the ropeway website, ⓦkyusanko.co.jp/aso/lang_en.

Kijima-dake
杵島岳

If alert levels return to normal, you'll once more be able to climb up grassy **Kijima-dake** (1321m), which rises behind the Aso Volcano Museum. The paved path from the far northeast corner of the car park takes you on an easy thirty-minute climb, for views over the caldera, Kusasenri and Naka-dake, and then down into Kijima-dake's extinct crater. From here, you can descend via a ski slope to join a path alongside the road to Naka-dake; the whole walk should take under ninety minutes.

Naka-dake and Taka-dake
中岳・高岳

In normal times, buses from Aso Station terminate at the foot of **Naka-dake** in a scruffy area of souvenir shops and restaurants, while a toll road continues to the top for cars. You can walk up in twenty minutes, though most take the **ropeway** running from the bus terminus up to the crater. However you arrive, the multicoloured rocks and glimpses of a seething grey lake through turbulent, sulphurous clouds of steam are a forbidding sight. Most activity takes place in a 100m-deep crater at the northern end, and this area is always strictly off-limits. Near the top of the ropeway, however, you can normally approach the crater lip and then walk south beside barren, dormant craters and across the lava fields.

There's a great **hiking trail** from the top of the ropeway round the crater's rim to the summit of Naka-dake, and then down to **Sensuikyō**, a valley famous for its azaleas in May, in about two hours. It's well marked and not too difficult as long as you've got good boots, plenty of water and you keep well away from the edge. If you detour up to the summit of **Taka-dake**, then take the more strenuous descent north down the ridge to Sensuikyō, it will take about three hours. From Sensuikyō, you'll have to hitch a ride or set off on the ninety-minute downhill trot to Miyaji Station (宮地駅), two stops east of Aso.

ARRIVAL AND INFORMATION
ASO TOWN

By train The Kumamoto Earthquake of April 2016 brought down a major rail bridge west of Tateno, and services between Kumamoto and Aso (normally hourly; 1hr) will be suspended for a considerable period of time. Direct services

to Aso from Beppu (3 daily; 2hr) are still running.

By bus Aso bus station is to the right as you exit the train station.

Destinations Beppu (1 daily; 3hr); Kumamoto (usually via Kumamoto Airport; 9 daily; 1hr 45min–2hr); Kurokawa Onsen (2 daily; 1hr); Yufuin (2 daily; 2hr 15min).

By car Toyota have a car rental office just east of the train station (☎ 096 735 5511).

Tourist information On the east side of the train station,

the Michi-no-eki visitor centre contains a well-organized tourist office (daily 9am–6pm; ☎ 096 735 5077, ☯ asocity-kanko.jp), where you'll find helpful, English-speaking staff and a wealth of information on local transport and accommodation, including a useful sketch map of Aso Town's restaurants and other facilities. The visitor centre also sells bentō boxes, which can be eaten at outdoor tables, and local products.

ACCOMMODATION AND EATING

★**Aso Base Backpackers** 阿蘇ベースバックパッカーズ 1498 Kurokawa ☎ 0967 34 0408, ☯ aso-backpackers.com. A short walk south of the train station, this sociable, squeaky-clean, pine-lined venue is a great place, its comfy beds augmented by a pleasing, lodge-style atmosphere. Closed in winter (months vary). ☞ Dorms ¥2800, twins ¥6000

Botchūtei 坊中亭 Aso train station. Surprisingly good restaurant inside the train station. The fantastically warming *dango-jiru* stew (see box, p.751) costs ¥1350 for a set, or try the huge *tonkatsu* curry rice (¥1000). Generally daily 9.30am–4pm.

Shukubō Aso 宿坊あそ 1076 Kurokawa ☎ 0967 34 0194. By far the fanciest place to stay in Aso Town itself, this minshuku in a wonderful old cedarwood farmhouse has beautiful, traditional rooms with toilets and washbasins, and shared lava-stone onsen. Good dinners feature vegetables and rice from their own organic farm, and the English-speaking owner will collect you from the station. ☞ ¥22,222

★**Sozankyo** 蘇山郷 Opposite the post office in Uchinomaki Onsen, 6km northwest of Aso Station ☎ 0967 32 0515, ☯ sozankyo.jp. Outstanding hospitality is offered at this ryokan which has 22 spacious, graceful rooms; most have futons, toilets and washbasins, leaving guests to bathe in the indoor onsen or two private, semi-outdoor baths, one of which is an old sake barrel. The price quoted below includes very fine breakfasts and excellent, creative dinners, which might include local beef, duck and rice from the volcanic fields; B&B rates also available. Free bicycles. ¥26,000

Kurokawa Onsen
黒川温泉

One of the most popular upmarket hot-spring resorts in Japan, **KUROKAWA ONSEN** is made up of twenty-odd ryokan, which lie higgledy-piggledy at the bottom of a steep-sided, tree-filled valley scoured into the **Senomoto Kōgen** plateau (瀬の本高原) by the gushing Tanoharu River, some 6km west of the Yamanami Highway. The village is completely devoted to hot-spring bathing and most of its buildings are at least traditional in design, if not genuinely old, while *yukata*-clad figures wandering between the boutiques and cafés on the narrow alleys add to its slightly quaint atmosphere. Kurokawa is

---

THE YAMANAMI HIGHWAY

From Aso, the **Yamanami Highway** (Highway 11) heads north over the Kujū mountains to Beppu. The road breaches the caldera wall at Ichinomiya, from where the classic profile of Aso-san's five peaks supposedly conjures up a sleeping Buddha with head to the east and Naka-dake's steaming vent at his navel, although it's a little more convincing from Daikambō lookout further west. North of here, and a little west of the highway, **Kurokawa Onsen** (see above) offers a choice of rotemburo along a picturesque valley. The highway then climbs again through the **Kujū range**, which for some reason receives far less attention than Aso-san or Ebino Kōgen (see p.759), although it offers good hiking and the Kyūshū mainland's highest peaks. The tallest, Kujū-san (1787m), is no longer active, but even here wisps of steam mark vents high on the north slopes. More spa towns lie strung along the route from here, and then start again at **Yufuin** (see p.751) before the road makes its final descent into Beppu.

While the Yamanami Highway is best avoided during peak holiday periods, for the most part it's fairly traffic free. A daily **bus** plies the whole route between Kumamoto and Beppu, stopping at Aso, Kurokawa Onsen, Yufuin and a few other places en route.

KUROKAWA'S BATHS

All the baths in town are attached to ryokan and you can buy **tickets** at the reception of each individual ryokan (from ¥500). Alternatively, get a **pass** allowing entry to any three ryokan (¥1300, valid for 6 months) from the ryokan or the tourist office (see below). The tourist office can also provide a good English map showing the location of all the public rotemburo, with a key indicating whether they're mixed or segregated.

If you only have time for one, try the central *Okyaku-ya Ryokan* (see below) for all-round atmosphere, or *Yamabiko Ryokan* (see below) for its unusually large rotemburo set among the trees; the latter also offers lunch/dinner plus onsen packages from ¥5000/person. Alternatively, *Yumotosō* (湯本荘) has a gorgeous little rotemburo, with a bath made from a sake barrel. A few kilometres out of central Kurokawa, the riverside baths at *Yamamizuki* (山みず木) or *Hozantei* (帆山亭), set in wooded hills away from the crowds, are also worth a visit; *Yamamizuki* offers a regular shuttle bus from town.

10

particularly famous for its rotemburo: there are 24 different locations in total, offering rocky pools of all shapes and sizes. Out of the main tourist season, when the crowds have gone, it's well worth making the effort to get here, and Kurokawa makes an excellent overnight stop, if you don't mind paying a little extra for accommodation.

ARRIVAL AND INFORMATION

KUROKAWA ONSEN

By bus Buses stop on Route 442, just south across the river from the centre of town.
Destinations Aso (2 daily; 1hr); Beppu (1 daily; 2hr 25min); Fukuoka (via Fukuoka Airport; 4 daily; 3hr); Kumamoto (2 daily; 2hr 30min); Yufuin (2 daily; 1hr 30min).

Tourist information The tourist office (daily 9am–6pm; ☎ 0967 44 0076, ⊛ kurokawaonsen.or.jp) is beside a car park in the centre of town, on the north side of the river, and produces a map of local walking trails. Electric bicycles can be rented from the adjacent building (¥500 for 2hr).

ACCOMMODATION AND EATING

Aso Kujū-kōgen Youth Hostel 阿蘇くじゅう高原ユー スホステル 6332 Senomoto ☎ 0967 44 0157, ⊛ asokujuuyh.sakura.ne.jp. The closest acceptable budget accommodation lies 5km east, near the Yamanami Highway; buses bound for Kurokawa stop at the end of the drive. Meals are available and staff can provide good hiking information. Dorms **¥2600**, doubles **¥6480**
Okyaku-ya Ryokan 御客屋旅館 6546 Manganji ☎ 0967 44 0454. Founded in 1722, this ryokan occupies a lovely wooden building right in the centre of things, and (trinket shop aside) maintains a pleasant Edo-era atmosphere. All rooms have river views and the on-site baths are nothing short of spectacular. **¥26,000**

Warokuya わろく屋 6600-1 Manganji ☎ 0967 44 0283. Amiable, cosy restaurant just down the bank from the tourist office by a river bridge. The emphasis is on quirky curry dishes (¥1300 for a medley of three curries): spicy horsemeat curry is the "no.1 favourite" but the *yakikare* (baked with mozzarella) is more likely to be palatable. The chocolate cakes are rather tempting, too. 10am–6pm, though it's sometimes closed by 4pm; closed Thurs.
★**Yamabiko Ryokan** やまびこ旅館 6704 Manganji ☎ 0967 44 0311, ⊛ yamabiko-ryokan.com. The place for a splurge, this grand riverside ryokan with outdoor rotemburo is set in spacious grounds on the west side of the centre. The meals are simply delectable. **¥34,000**

Takachiho
高千穂

The small town of **TAKACHIHO** lies on the border between Kumamoto and Miyazaki prefectures, where the Gokase-gawa has sliced a narrow channel through layers of ancient lava. In winter, when night temperatures fall below freezing, local villagers perform time-honoured **Yokagura dances** in the old farmhouses, bringing back to life the gods and goddesses who once inhabited these mountains (see box, p.744). The main reason for visiting Takachiho is to see a few excerpts from this dance-cycle, but combine that with **Takachiho gorge**, a pretty spot whose strange rock formations are woven into local myths, plus a dramatic journey from whichever direction you arrive, and Takachiho becomes somewhere to include on any Kyūshū tour.

Takachiho sits on the north bank of the **Gokase-gawa**, grouped around the central Hon-machi crossroads. Both the gorge and Takachiho-jinja, where nightly Yokagura dances are held, are on the southwest edge of town, within easy walking distance, while its other main sight, a mildly interesting riverside cave, lies a short drive or bus ride to the east. It's possible to cover both areas in a day, see a Yokagura performance in the evening and travel on the next morning.

Takachiho's shops are full of sweet-potato *shōchū* and other local produce, alongside *kagura* dolls and masks, which are carved from camphor-wood, making unusual **souvenirs**.

10

Takachiho-jinja
高千穂神社 • Yokagura dances at 8pm • ¥700

The road southwest to the gorge first passes **Takachiho-jinja** – founded in the second century AD – at the top of mossy steps roughly 800m from the Hon-machi crossing. It's a simple wooden building, engulfed in ancient cryptomeria trees and mainly of interest for a high-relief carving of the guardian deity dispatching a demon; to find the carving, facing the shrine, walk round to the right of the building. The wooden **Kagura-den** next door is where the nightly **Yokagura** dances are held (see box below).

Takachiho gorge
高千穂峡, Takachiho-kyō • Rowing boat rental daily 8.30am–4.30pm • ¥2000 for 30min; 3 people per boat

Beyond Takachiho-jinja, turn left after the *Takachiho Hotel*, then corkscrew down for about 1km on a series of hairpin bends, and you'll emerge at Mihashi Bridge at the south end of **Takachiho gorge**. At its narrowest point the gorge is just 3m wide and plunges 100m between cliffs of basalt columns, which in one place fan out like a giant cockleshell. If you want to see what the gorge looks like from below you can rent rowing boats at Mihashi Bridge – it's particularly impressive when viewed from the emerald-green river. Otherwise, follow the path along the east bank, which takes you along the gorge's most scenic stretch, passing lovely Manai Waterfall. Six hundred metres later you come out at the old stone Shinbashi Bridge. Before tackling the climb back into Takachiho, you might want to stop off at *Araragi-no-chaya* restaurant (see opposite).

MYTHS AND DANCE IN TAKACHIHO

Takachiho's famous **traditional dances** have their roots in local legend. The story goes that the Storm God, Susano-ō, once destroyed the rice fields of his sister, the Sun Goddess **Amaterasu**, and desecrated her sacred palace. Understandably offended by these actions, Amaterasu hid in a cave and plunged the world into darkness. The other gods tried to entice her out with prayers and chants, but nothing worked until, finally, a goddess named Ama-no-uzume broke into a provocative dance. The general merriment was too much for Amaterasu, who peeped out to see the fun, at which point the god of power, Tajikarao, hauled away the rock blocking the cave entrance – one of the climactic scenes of the dance-drama – and brought light back to the world. Takachiho locals also claim that nearby mountain Takachiho-no-mine – not the mountain of Ebino Kōgen (see p.759) – is where Amaterasu's grandson, Ninigi-no-mikoto, descended to earth with his mirror, sword and jewel to become Japan's first emperor.

A visit to Takachiho is not complete without viewing a sample of this rustic, masked dance-drama, accompanied by flute and drum, at the Kagura-den (see above). In one hour you see three or four extracts from the full cycle, typically including the story of Amaterasu and her cave, and ending with an explicit rendition of the birth of the Japanese nation in which the two "gods" leave the stage to cavort with members of the audience – to the great delight of all concerned. The performers are drawn from a pool of around 550 local residents, aged from 5 to 80 years, who also dance in the annual **Yokagura festival** (mid-Nov to mid-Feb, usually weekends). In a combination of harvest thanksgiving and spring festival, 24 troupes perform all 33 dances in sequence in private homes and village halls, lasting through the night and into the next day. You can sign up for one of these all-nighters at the tourist office; food is provided but you're expected to bring a donation of two large bottles of sake.

Amano Iwato-jinja

天岩戸神社 • Buses leave Takachiho's central station every 90min or so (fewer on Sat & Sun; 15min; ¥300)

Head east of Takachiho along the Iwato-gawa and after 8km you'll reach **Amano Iwato-jinja**, in an attractive setting among venerable cedars. The shrine buildings are closed to the public, but from behind the shrine it's just possible to make out Amaterasu's cave (see box opposite) on the river's far bank. Unfortunately, you can't reach it, but a second cave, **Amano Yasugawara**, on the same side of the river as the shrine, is more accessible: it was into this cave that Amaterasu's fellow gods crammed – all eight million of them – while they were deciding their strategy. The cave, with its diminutive shrine beneath a sacred rope, is about a fifteen-minute walk east, down some steps and beside the river.

10

ARRIVAL AND INFORMATION

TAKACHIHO

By bus from Aso Town and Kumamoto Takachiho bus station lies about 100m south of the central Hon-machi crossroads. To get here from Aso Town, you would normally take a private Minami-Aso line train from Tateno (立野), three stops west of Aso on the JR line, round the caldera's south side as far as Takamori (高森), then a thrice-daily bus to Takachiho. However, both the JR and Minami-Aso lines will be partially suspended for a considerable period of time following the 2016 Kumamoto Earthquake (see p.734); in the meantime, you'll need to catch a bus from Aso to Kumamoto Airport (7 daily; 1hr), then hook up with

one of the twice-daily services from Kumamoto to Takachiho (3hr 30min; 2hr 40min from the airport).
By bus from Nobeoka and Miyazaki In the opposite direction, Miyazaki Kōtsū buses track the Gokase valley up from Nobeoka on the east coast (延岡; roughly hourly; 1hr 20min). Nobeoka lies on the JR train line between Beppu and Miyazaki and receives regular buses from Miyazaki (every 30min; 1hr 10min–1hr 30min); at weekends, there's a daily bus all the way from Miyazaki to Takachiho in 3hr. The latter journey costs ¥2500, but tourists can buy a one-day bus pass for Miyazaki Prefecture (including Takachiho) for ¥1000.

INFORMATION

Tourist information The tourist office is opposite the bus station (daily 8.30am–5.30pm; ☎ 0982 72 3031, ⓦ takachiho-kanko.info; English-speaking helpline on ☎ 090 4723 0471 or ☎ 090 5208 5622). It rents out electric

bicycles (¥300/hr, ¥1500/day).
ATM There's an international ATM at the post office, buried in the backstreets to the northeast of the Hon-machi crossing.

ACCOMMODATION

Hotel Takachiho ホテル高千穂 1037-4 Mitai ☎ 0982 72 3255. On a promontory overlooking the gorge, just beyond Takachiho-jinja, this grand hotel is a good option if you want to sleep in a bed. It has spick-and-span Western-style en-suite rooms (Japanese-style rooms also available), with views of the gorge from the west side of the hotel. If you phone ahead they'll collect you from the bus station. The price includes meals. 🛜 **¥23,030**
Takachiho Youth Hostel 高千穂ユースホステル 5899-2 Mitai ☎ 0982 72 3021. In the countryside about 3km east of town, this spick-and-span hostel with

Japanese-style dorms is run by a wonderfully friendly woman, who will happily pick you up and take you back out for the Yokagura dances. 🛜 Dorms **¥3400**
Yamatoya 大和屋 About 100m southwest of the Hon-machi crossroads on the main street, on the left ☎ 0982 72 2243, ⓦ yado-sagashi.com/yamatoya. Basic but comfortable ryokan in a modern building in the centre, serving hearty, rustic meals. Most rooms have toilets and small showers, and there's a large shared bath upstairs. Room-only and B&B plans also available. **¥20,600**

EATING

Araragi-no-chaya あららぎ乃茶屋 1245 Oshikata. Friendly restaurant-cum-souvenir shop beside Shinbashi Bridge, with outdoor tables overlooking Takachiho gorge; stop here for a light meal or a taste of the local speciality, *kappo sake* – sake heated in a pipe of fresh green bamboo. Daily 8.30am–5pm.
Nagomi 和 Gamadase Ichiba, 5min walk southwest down the main street from Hon-machi crossroads, on the left ☎ 0982 73 1109, ⓦ takachiho.ja-miyazaki.jp. Part of an agricultural co-operative market, this restaurant

is stylishly lit to show off the local black-cow beef at its best. A Takachiho steak set dinner costs ¥2600; portions are smaller but cheaper at lunchtime. Look out for the statues of two prize-winning, now-deceased cattle outside. Daily 11am–2pm & 5–8.30pm.
★Ten-an 天庵 1180-25 Mitai ☎ 0982 72 3023. Charming noodle joint done out in lovely wood from floor to ceiling, serving excellent home-made soba made with stoneground buckwheat flour (from ¥870). To find it, walk southwest from the Hon-machi junction, straight over the

next set of lights (the Shiroyama crossing), take the first right and it's on the right. Daily 11am–3pm.

Tentsukuten てんつくてん 805 Mitai ☎ 0982 72 3858. This popular, cosy *izakaya* is hidden behind a plain wooden facade festooned with paper lanterns and fairy lights, just south round the corner from the bus station. You can sample some of Takachiho's well-rated *shōchū*, and eat well. 5.30pm–midnight; closed Sun.

Beppu

別府

10

Walking around the relaxed, coastal city of **BEPPU**, it is at times tempting to think that the place was built atop the den of some giant dragon – spirals of steam billow skywards from a thousand holes, lending certain streets a magical, otherworldly air. However, this is no myth or fairy tale, simply one of the world's most geothermically active regions. Over one hundred million litres of near-boiling water gush out of more than three thousand springs each day, harnessed for use by local homes and swimming pools, for heating and medicinal purposes, or to fill the dozens of public and private baths that make this one of Japan's most popular **onsen** resorts. The place is unashamedly commercial in nature, yet despite receiving over ten million visitors per year, it manages to feel like a town in decline – largely built during the domestic tourism boom of the 1970s, it seems half-forgotten by modern Japan. Still, the humble, throwback air that this creates enhances the city's pleasure, and it's easy to escape from the crowds.

There's not a lot more to do in Beppu than soak in a tub. The next most popular activity is to go to look at the **jigoku**, which spew out steaming, sulphurous mud and form simmering lakes in lurid hues; they're named after the Japanese word for the Buddhist notion of hell. Beppu's *jigoku* are located in two main clusters: seven in the northern district of **Kannawa** – these are of the most interest – and two in Shibaseki Onsen, 3km further north. If you're feeling adventurous, however, you'd do better to head for a clutch of **secret onsen** hiding away in the western hills (see box, p.749). Beppu is also one of only two places in Japan where you can take a real, ocean-side **sand bath**, or *suna-yu*. Alternatively, you can visit the lovely **Traditional Bamboo Crafts Centre** or ride the ropeway to the top of **Tsurumi-dake** for superb views over Beppu Bay and inland to the Kujū mountains.

The Beppu region is famed for its bamboo **handicrafts**, which you'll find in the station malls and department stores on Ekimae-dōri. Another popular souvenir, which is on sale all over town, is *yu-no-hana*, natural bath salts to create that instant hot-spring feel back home.

BEPPU

Ōita Airport

Beppu Medical Center ✚

Kamegawa Station

0   500
metres

N

SHIBASEKI ONSEN

KANNAWA ONSEN

Beppu Daigaku Station

SEE MAP "KANNAWA & THE JIGOKU" FOR DETAILS

Beppu Beach Sand Bath

Shoningahama Beach

Ferry Sunflower

Uwajima Unyu Ferry

Traditional Bamboo Crafts Centre

SEE MAP "CENTRAL BEPPU" FOR DETAILS

Tsurumi-dake & Yufuin ◀

Global Tower and B-Con Plaza

Beppu Park

Police Station

Beppu Station

Takegawara Onsen

● EATING
Sabou-Shinanoya   1

Ōita & Usuki ▼

Takegawara Onsen

竹瓦温泉 • 16-23 Moto-machi • **Bath** Daily 6.30am– 10.30pm • ¥100 • **Sand bath** Daily 8am–10.30pm • ¥1030 • ☎ 0977 23 1585

Takegawara Onsen is a grand old Meiji-era edifice in the backstreets south

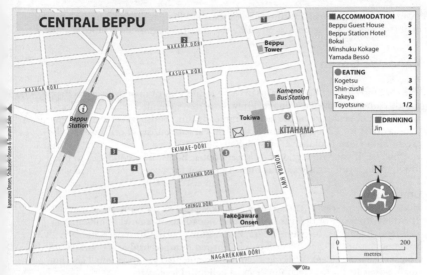

of Ekimae-dōri. Its ordinary bath is hot and nicely traditional, but try the **sand bath** first. After rinsing in hot water, you lie face up on a bed of coarse, black sand while an attendant gently piles sand on to you – a heavy, warm cocoon (around 42°C) that comes up to your neck. Then just relax as the heat soaks in for the recommended ten minutes, before another rinse and then a soak in the hot tub.

Beppu Beach Sand Bath

別府海浜砂湯, Beppu Kaihei Sunaba • On Shoningahama beach, near Beppu Daigaku Station • Daily: March–Oct 8.30am–6pm; Nov–Feb 9am–5pm • ¥1030 • From central Beppu, take bus #20 to Betsudai-mae stop or #26 to Rokushoen stop (20min; ¥240) • ☎ 0977 66 5737

On a fine day, the seaside location of **Beppu Beach Sand Bath** may seem preferable to Takegawara, but it's slightly marred by the busy main road behind and a concrete breakwater that dominates the view. The end result after a bath here, however, is still an overall sense of wellbeing. You'll need a swimsuit, but they provide *yukata* to wear in the "bath".

Global Tower

Fujimi-dōri • Daily: March–Nov 9am–9pm; Dec–Feb 9am–7pm • ¥300 • ☎ 0977 26 7111

About twenty minutes' walk northwest of the station, just beyond Beppu Park, stands the pencil-thin **Global Tower**, which serves as both viewing platform and a landmark for **B-Con Plaza**, Beppu's lavish convention centre and concert hall. The 100m-high, open observation deck provides giddying views, but if you've got time you'll get a better all-round panorama from the western hills.

Traditional Bamboo Crafts Centre

竹細工伝統産業会館, Takezaiku Dentō Sangyō Kaikan • 8-3 Higashisōen, 3km northwest of Beppu Station • Tues–Sun 8.30am–5pm • ¥300 • ☎ 0977 23 1072 • Bus #25 from the station's east exit to Takezaiku Densankan-mae

The art of weaving bamboo flourished in the Edo period in Beppu – where bamboo can grow up to 20m tall – to make souvenirs for tourists, who came to take the waters here. The **Traditional Bamboo Crafts Centre**, a neat little museum with a few choice pieces for sale, showcases a varied collection, from hats and kitchen utensils to jars and bags, some of

10

them by Living National Treasures. There's some labelling in English, but the beautiful craftworks speak for themselves, especially the modernist lights and geometric objets d'art.

Kannawa Onsen

鉄輪温泉

The charming area of **Kannawa Onsen** is the focal point of many visitors to Beppu, who mostly come here to see the *jigoku*. Only those recommended below are really worth it – any more and you'll tire of the tacky commercialism, loudspeakers and tour groups. A two-day **pass** for ¥2000 (discounted to ¥1800 at the tourist office) covers all the *jigoku* except Hon-Bōzu Jigoku and Yama Jigoku, but you'd have to visit several to make it worthwhile. If you visit any of the district's **public baths**, it's a good idea to bring a towel, though you can always buy one on the spot for a couple of hundred yen.

Umi Jigoku

海地獄 • Daily 8am–5pm • ¥400 • Bus #5, #24 or #41 from Beppu Station to Umijigoku-mae stop (18–24min; ¥330–370)

The most attractive of Beppu's *jigoku* is **Umi Jigoku**, set in a bowl of hills among well-tended gardens. Its main feature is a sea-blue pool – 120m deep and, at 90°C, hot enough to cook eggs – set off by a bright-red humped bridge and *torii* swathed in clouds of roaring steam. Walking around the manicured grounds, you'll also find a small, onsen steam-fed greenhouse, and a delightful footbath.

Oniishi-Bōzu Jigoku

鬼石坊主地獄 • Daily 8am–5pm • ¥400 • Bus #5, #24 or #41 from Beppu Station to Umijigoku-mae stop (18–24min; ¥330–370)

An easy walk from Umi Jigoku, the speciality of **Oniishi-Bōzu Jigoku** is mud – boiling, smelly, steaming, hiccuping pools of it. Indeed, the place takes its name from the belief that the largest mud bubbles look like the bald pate of a Buddhist monk, a *bōzu* – and, in fact, the resemblance is quite uncanny.

Hyōtan Onsen

ひょうたん温泉 • Daily 9am–1am; sand bath closes midnight • ¥750, ¥550 after 6pm; ¥330 extra for the sand bath • ☎ 0977 66 0527, ⓦ hyotan-onsen.com • Bus #5, #24 or #41 to Kannawa Bus Terminal (16–22min; ¥340)

Hyōtan Onsen is a modern bath complex at the bottom of the hill, offering a rotemburo, sauna, a range of indoor pools and a sand bath. Should you feel peckish, you can even buy *jigoku mushi* (see box, p.751) to snack on.

Shibaseki Onsen

柴石温泉 • Both jigoku daily 8am–5pm • ¥400 • Bus #16 from Kannawa Bus Terminal (6min; ¥190); bus #26 from Beppu Station (30min; ¥390) via Beppu Beach Sand Bath

There are two *jigoku* in **Shibaseki Onsen**, a five-minute bus ride north of Kannawa. **Chi-no-ike Jigoku** (血の池地 獄), "Blood Pond", is the better of the two, a huge bubbling pool whose vermilion fringes result from a high iron-oxide content. Fifty metres down the road, **Tatsumaki Jigoku** (龍巻地獄) consists of an unimpressive geyser that spouts around 5m into the air roughly every half-hour; it used to reach 50m until a stone block was placed over it for safety.

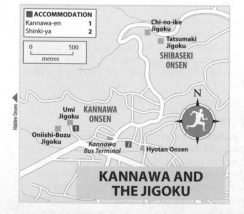

■ ACCOMMODATION
Kannawa-en — 1
Shinki-ya — 2

0 ——— 500
metres

Chi-no-ike Jigoku
Tatsumaki Jigoku
SHIBASEKI ONSEN

N

Umi Jigoku — KANNAWA ONSEN
Oniishi-Bozu Jigoku
Kannawa Bus Terminal
Hyotan Onsen

Hidden Onsen

KANNAWA AND THE JIGOKU

BEPPU'S HIDDEN ONSEN

If you're looking for something less commercial than the Beppu onsen, a few "hidden" baths can be found in the tranquil forests of the western hills – they are not exactly holes in the ground, but close enough. However, they are pretty isolated, and women in particular should think twice about going alone. Nabeyama-no-yu has officially been off-limits since a grisly murder took place there in 2010.

If you want to make the journey, the first step is to get to Myoban (明礬), an onsen area accessible from Beppu Station on buses #5, #24 and #41 (25–30min; ¥360–430), all of which pass Kannawa Bus Terminal and Umijigoku-mae. From here directions are a little tough; it's best to arm yourself with a rough map from the tourist office. A twenty-minute walk on a road heading up and left from Myoban bus stop will bring you to a fork. Take a left, and follow the road around for twenty minutes to **Hebin-yu** (へびん湯), a valley-based cascade of pools attended by a ramshackle hut. Turning right instead at the aforementioned fork, then scrambling up a rock path at the second gate, will bring you to **Nabeyama-no-yu** (鍋山の湯), a pair of onsen sitting in a forest-like setting. The first is a black-water pool, the second filled with clay that you can use for a free mud bath. Beppu is visible below, yet all one can hear are the sounds of nature – there isn't even a place to put your clothes. To hit the third spring, **Tsuru-no yu** (鶴の湯), you'll have to get off the bus just before it passes under the highway, and head up the dirt track alongside a graveyard for thirty to forty minutes. Not easy – but it's Beppu at its purest.

10

Tsurumi-dake

鶴見岳 • 6km west of Beppu Station • Ropeway daily 9am–5pm, closes 4.30pm mid-Nov to mid-March • ¥1000 one-way, ¥1600 return • ⓦ beppu-ropeway.co.jp • Buses #34, #36 or #37 from Beppu Station drop you at the ropeway's lower terminus (1–2 hourly; 30min; ¥420)

There are spectacular views from the summit of **Tsurumi-dake** (1375m) – it's even possible to see Shikoku in the distance on a clear day. Though it's perfectly climbable, the majority of visitors use the **ropeway** instead to get to the top. Buses here from Beppu continue to Yufuin (see p.751), meaning that you could combine the two into a long day-trip.

ARRIVAL AND INFORMATION   BEPPU

By plane Beppu is served by Ōita airport (ⓣ 0978 67 1174, ⓦ oita-airport.jp), 40km away on the north side of the bay; frequent airport buses run south to Ōita city, stopping at Kitahama, Beppu's central seafront district, on the way (40min; ¥1500), and a few terminate at Beppu Station.
Destinations Nagoya (2 daily; 1hr); Osaka (Itami; 7 daily; 55min); Tokyo (17 daily; 1hr 30min).

By train Beppu's main station is conveniently located right in the centre of town. Among the Fukuoka services listed below, three trains a day take the slower, more scenic route over the mountains via Yufuin and Ōita. The service from Kumamoto is currently suspended, following the 2016 Kumamoto Earthquake (see p.734).
Destinations Aso (3 daily; 2hr); Fukuoka (1–3 hourly; 2hr–3hr 20min); Miyazaki (usually with a change at Ōita; roughly hourly; 3hr 50min); Usuki (usually with a change at

Ōita; 1–3 hourly; 30min–1hr 15min); Yufuin (3 daily; 1hr).
By bus Long-distance buses mostly stop at the Kamenoi bus station, in Kitahama, although some services terminate at Beppu train station.
Destinations Aso (1 daily; 3hr); Fukuoka (roughly hourly; 2hr 30min); Hiroshima (1 daily; 6hr); Kumamoto (1 daily; 4hr 40min); Nagasaki (5 daily; 3hr 40min); Yufuin (1–2 hourly; 1hr).
By ferry Ferries from Honshū and Shikoku dock a couple of kilometres north of the centre at the International Tourist Port. To reach the port from Beppu train station, take bus #20 or #26 and get off at Kansai Kisen-mae.
Destinations Osaka (1 daily; 12hr; from ¥10,600) with Ferry Sunflower (ⓣ 0977 22 2181, ⓦ ferry-sunflower .co.jp); Yawatahama on Shikoku (6 daily; 2hr 50min; ¥3100) with Uwajima Unyu Ferry (ⓣ 0977 21 2364).

GETTING AROUND

By bus Local buses are the best way of getting around Beppu. Fortunately, they're not too complicated and there's a fair amount of information in English for the major routes. Most routes start at Beppu Station, but could leave from either the west or east sides – ask to make sure you're waiting in the right place.

Bus passes It may be worth buying a one-day "Mini Free Pass" (¥900) or "Wide Free Pass" (¥1600), available at the station information desk or the Kamenoi bus station in Kitahama. Both passes include all buses within the city centre, which covers the *jigoku*, sand baths and even the ropeway, while the "Wide" pass covers buses to Yufuin too

10

(otherwise ¥900 each way). They also entitle you to a ten percent discount on entry to the main sights, including the *jigoku* pass (see p.748).

Car rental Eki Rent-a-Car (☎0977 24 4428) and many others have offices near Beppu Station.

INFORMATION

Tourist information The town's main tourist office (daily 8.30am–5pm; ☎0977 21 6220) lies just inside the central east exit of Beppu Station and has maps, brochures and information on local bus routes. The English-speaking staff can also assist with hotel reservations.

Services Beppu Medical Centre (☎0977 67 1111) is in north Beppu's Kamegawa district, inland from Kamegawa Station. The main police station (☎0977 21 2131) is a 5min walk west of the station (left at the second traffic lights).

ACCOMMODATION

The most convenient place to look for **accommodation** is around Beppu Station, where you'll find a clutch of business hotels, a couple of appealing ryokan and some good-value budget options. Though less central, the **Kannawa** area offers a few atmospheric alternatives buried among its old streets. Prices tend to go up at weekends, when it can be hard to find a room anywhere in Beppu – make sure you book ahead.

AROUND THE STATION

Beppu Guest House 1-12 Ekimae-chō ☎080 4642 9044, ⓦ beppu-e.cloud-line.com. Comfortable hostel just a stone's throw from the station, with Western- and Japanese-style dorms and spacious common areas, including a well-equipped kitchen, computers and washing machine. Bicycles for rent. 🛜 Dorms **¥2000**, doubles **¥6000**

Beppu Station Hotel 別府ステーションホテル 12-8 Ekimae-chō ☎0977 24 5252, ⓦ station-hotels.com. Rooms here are pretty sharp for a business hotel, and as the name suggests, it's right next to the station. The cheapest singles (¥4000) are a little tight, but regular singles, twins and triples are a decent size. There's also an onsen bath. 🛜 **¥7400**

Bokai 望海 3-8-7 Kitahama ☎0977 22 1241, ⓦ bokai .jp. Excellent ryokan facing the beach. Bedrooms are all en suite and extremely comfortable (there's a choice of tatami or Western styles), with views of Beppu Bay, which are shared by the lovely indoor and outdoor onsen on the rooftop. Exquisite dinners are served in your room. 🛜 **¥26,000**

Minshuku Kokage 国際民宿こかげ 8-9 Ekimae-chō ☎0977 23 1753, ⓦ ww6.tiki.ne.jp/~kokage. Popular, seventy-year-old cheapie with a choice of tatami or Western rooms, mostly en suite using hot-spring water, and a stone onsen downstairs. Free breakfast of coffee and toast included. 🛜 **¥7650**

★**Yamada Bessō** 山田別荘 3-2-18 Kitahama ☎0977 24 2121, ⓦ yamadabessou.jp. Welcoming, family-run

ryokan occupying a nicely faded eighty-year-old wooden building, set in gardens a couple of blocks north of Ekimae-dōri. Cheaper rooms have no en-suite facilities, but the onsen and gorgeous outdoor rotemburo more than compensate; non-guests can use these facilities for just ¥500 (daily 11am–3pm). Meals are available on request, though prices almost double if you go for the full dinner-and-breakfast deal. 🛜 Room only **¥13,000**

KANNAWA

Kannawa-en 神和苑 6-kumi Miyuki ☎0977 66 2111, ⓦ kannawaen.jp. This beautiful old ryokan boasts lovely tatami rooms (some in individual buildings, all with their own wooden hot-spring bath), picturesque rotemburo and a classic, hillside garden featuring waterfall-fed ponds, a nō theatre and a thatched teahouse. Rates include Japanese or Western breakfast and seasonal *kaiseki* or *teppanyaki* dinner. 🛜 **¥36,720**

★**Shinki-ya** しんき屋 2-kumi Furimoto ☎0977 66 0962, ⓦ shinkiya.com. Five minutes' walk downhill from the bus terminal, tucked up a small lane on the right, this little ryokan has been beautifully renovated with seven gleaming tatami rooms (most with washbasin and toilet), a kitchen and washing machines for guests' use; bathe in the *hinoki* onsen baths or rotemburo. Meals are offered on request (for much higher rates), including home-steamed *jigoku mushi* (see box opposite). 🛜 Room-only **¥8900**

EATING

Beppu has a pleasing range of **speciality foods** to look out for (see box opposite). When it comes to finding a **restaurant**, you're best off in the downtown area, while ramen joints are everywhere you look.

Kogetsu 湖月 In a narrow alley east of the covered arcade, just off Ekimae-dōri ☎0977 21 8062. Homely mom-and-pop shop with just seven counter seats that's nationally famous for its *gyōza* (¥650 for a big plate), washed

down with Kirin beer. Look out for the window display of lucky cat figurines – and the queue. 2–9pm; closed Tues.

★**Sabou-Shinanoya** 尾信濃屋 6-32 Nishinoguchi ☎0977 25 8728. Set in a delightful old Shōwa-era holiday

BEPPU'S CULINARY SPECIALITIES

Beppu's **speciality foods** include the local *wagyu*, Bungo beef, as well as *fugu* (blowfish) and *karei* (flounder), which are traditionally winter dishes, though they're often available year-round. Far cheaper are the piping-hot *dango-jiru*, a cheap, filling soup which comes with thick white noodles, assorted vegetables and chunks of either chicken or pork; *toriten*, a local chicken tempura; and *reimen*, buckwheat noodles in a cold soup. You might also like to try *jigoku mushi*, a name given to a whole assortment of comestibles (vegetables and eggs are most prominent) slow-cooked in steam from Beppu's hells; you'll find it on sale at stalls and supermarkets in the Kannawa area, where it also often features in ryokan meals.

home with a manicured garden, this elegant *kissaten* is the place to head for *dango-jiru*, Beppu's tasty local noodle soup. Take the main road west from the station, turn right at the second traffic lights and it's 100m on the left (5min walk). 9am–9pm; closes 6pm Tues & Wed.

Shin-zushi 新鮨し 8-15 Ekimae-chō T 0977 25 0005. Sushi fans should head to this pristine restaurant, where nigiri sushi starts at ¥400 for two pieces, and there's a good choice of sushi, sashimi and tempura set dishes from ¥2400. Daily 5.30pm–1.30am.

Takeya 竹屋 15-7 Gen-chō T 0977 23 1006. Sweet little café with a bamboo theme (hence the name) and good coffee, opposite Takegawara Onsen. Also does tasty *dango-jiru* sets (¥850). Generally daily 11am–6pm.

Toyotsune とよ常 3-7 Ekimae-chō T 0977 23 7487, W toyotsune.com. Unpretentious restaurant opposite Beppu Station specializing in *fugu* (Oct–March; sashimi ¥2700). Bungo beef and *toriten* are also on the menu, as well as less exotic dishes including well-priced tempura or sashimi sets (from ¥750); there's a good range of local *shōchū*, too. Also has a branch in *Hotel Yuuhi* near the seafront (closed Wed). 11am–2pm & 5–10pm; closed Thurs.

DRINKING

Jin 仁 1-15-7 Kitahama T 0977 21 1768. Lively *robatayaki* and pub at the east end of Ekimae-dōri, with plenty of cheap local *shōchū* and an English menu listing a good range of fish, vegetable and tofu dishes, as well as *yakitori* skewers (¥330 for three). Daily 5pm–midnight.

Yufuin

湯布院

The small resort town of **YUFUIN** sits in a mountain-surrounded hollow just 25km inland from Beppu. It's perfect day-trip distance so hordes of tourists converge here at weekends and holiday times. However, Yufuin has made great efforts to protect its original character, and if you stay overnight, you'll better appreciate its charming, thatched-roof-lined alleyways.

Head roughly northeast from the station towards the biggest mountain, Yufu-dake (pick up a map from the tourist office), and after twenty or so minutes' walking you'll be by a beautiful little lake, **Kinrin-ko** (金鱗湖), surrounded by trees, cafés and boutiques. On the north bank of the lake, you'll find the tiny **Shitan-yu** (下ん湯), a mixed-gender onsen with rustic thatched roofing.

There are few other sights as such, though Yufuin boasts a number of picturesque temples, as well as the opportunity to climb **Yufu-dake**, the double-headed volcano that rears up above town. Yufuin–Beppu buses stop after about 6km at a car park by the trailhead, leaving a steep but straightforward walk to the 1584m-high summit; allow about four hours return.

Yufuogō Saigakukan Onsen

柚富の郷彩岳館 • About 1.5km southeast of the station on Route 11 • Daily 11am–4pm, last admission 3pm • Public baths ¥620/person; private bath ¥2100 for 50min • T 0977 44 5000, W saigakukan.co.jp

Yufuin's appeal for many visitors centres around tripping from one **onsen** to the next, though they are frustratingly rather spread out. Less than 2km from the station, the delightful onsen at the **Yufuogō Saigakukan** ryokan (see below) is definitely worth the effort. Men's and women's rock-lined rotemburo, as well as the outdoor sections of the two private baths, all enjoy the best views of Yufu-dake in town, and there's a gorgeous relaxation lounge set around a traditional sunken fireplace, looking out onto a small, elegant garden. Good-value lunches at their fine restaurant are also available, as well as lunch-and-onsen packages (from ¥2700 for a dip and *wagyu* steak on rice).

ARRIVAL AND INFORMATION   YUFUIN

By train Most visitors arrive by train on the special Yufuin-no-mori service that comes over the mountains from Fukuoka's Hakata Station three times a day (see box, p.701). There are three direct trains a day from Beppu, or you can change at Ōita.
Destinations Beppu (3 daily; 1hr); Fukuoka (6 daily; 2hr 15min).

By bus The bus station is a stone's throw away from the train station, along the main street on the left.

Destinations Aso (2 daily; 2hr 15min); Beppu (1–2 hourly; 1hr); Fukuoka (via Fukuoka Airport; roughly hourly; 2hr 20min); Kumamoto (2 daily; 4hr 15min); Kurokawa Onsen (2 daily; 1hr 15min).

Tourist information There's a very helpful booth in the station (daily 9am–5pm; ☎ 0977 84 2446); the booth opposite rents out bikes (¥250/hr) and electric bikes (¥500 for 2hr).

ACCOMMODATION

Country Road Youth Hostel カントリーロードユースホステル 2.5km northeast of the station ☎ 0977 84 3734, ⓦ countryroadyh.com. The town's budget choice, a superb place with its own onsen and a rarefied location on a hillside overlooking town – try to arrange pick-up in advance. Dinner and breakfast available. ☎ Dorms **¥3800**, doubles **¥8600**

Makiba-no-ie 牧場の家 About 500m southeast of the station ☎ 0977 84 2138, ⓦ ryosoumakibanoie.com. This ryokan is the most atmospheric option in town, with Japanese-style thatched-roof cottages set around a charming rotemburo. Their meals are fantastic. ☎ **¥39,180**

★**Yufuogō Saigakukan** 柚富の郷彩岳館 About 1.5km southeast of the station on Route 11 ☎ 0977 44 5000, ⓦ saigakukan.co.jp. Traditional but well used to catering to foreigners, this delightful rural ryokan is decorated throughout with hundreds of watercolour and oil landscapes. The lovely onsen (see above; public and private baths free to guests) shares fine views of Yufu-dake's twin peaks with the restaurant, where excellent *kaiseki* cuisine, including local ingredients such as sweet chestnuts and Bungo *wagyu* beef, is served. Free pick-ups from the station, and bicycles available for rent. ☎ **¥29,580**

EATING

Cafe la Ruche カフェラロシュ Kinrin Lake ☎ 0977 28 8500. It's hard to beat the stunning setting at this gallery café, with outdoor tables right next to the north bank of Kinrin Lake. Very good espresso coffees start at ¥486, and they serve a range of snacks and small meals. ☎ Mon–Sat 9am–5pm, Sun 7.30am–5pm.

Hidamari 陽だまり On the south side of a five-way junction with a stone torii, about 100m east of the station ☎ 0977 84 2270. At this agricultural co-operative, the cheap, functional but friendly café serves very tasty

dango-jiru (¥540), tempura and beef and burdock croquettes, while the shop does good-value bentō to take away. Daily: café 11am–3pm; shop 8.30am–5pm.

Izumi 泉 Kinrin Lake ☎ 0977 85 2283. Just west of *Cafe la Ruche* and also overlooking the lake, this beautiful venue is the best place in the area for a meal. It sells tasty handmade soba, including cold *seiro soba* (¥1296) – you can even watch the noodles being pounded and whacked out in an open area at the front of the restaurant. Daily 11am–5pm.

Usuki

臼杵

The small and attractive castle town of **USUKI**, some 40km to the south of Beppu, offers a reminder of the spiritual side of life, and makes a pleasant stop on the coastal route to or from Miyazaki. Between the twelfth and fourteenth centuries, in a little valley around 5km southwest of town, skilled craftsmen sculpted some sixty **Buddha statues** in the soft lava tuff. The weather has taken its toll since then, but restoration work has saved several of these serene statues, which continue their vigil unperturbed.

Seki Butsu

石仏 • Daily: April–Sept 6am–7pm; Oct–March 6am–6pm • ¥530 • Bus from Usuki Station (7 daily; 20min; ¥310); 30min by bicycle (available from station, free); or about ¥2000 by taxi

The stone Buddhas, or **Seki Butsu**, are grouped around the sides of a narrow north–south valley and divided into four clusters, of which the first and last are the most interesting. Following the path anticlockwise, you'll reach the Hoki Second Cluster first of all; it's dominated by a 3m-tall figure of **Amitabha Buddha** and his two attendants, each individually expressed. The path then takes you round via the Hoki First Cluster – comprising over twenty statues – and the rather worn Sannōsan trinity of Buddhas, to the Furuzono Cluster. Here, the central **Dainichi Nyorai** is considered one of Japan's finest stone-carved Buddhas. While the lower body has partly rotted away, the Buddha's face, picked out with faded pigment, is still sublime.

10

The old town

After you've walked round the stone Buddhas, which won't take much over thirty minutes, it's worth taking a quick stroll through the **old centre** of Usuki on the way back to the station; if you're travelling by bus, ask to get off at the *Hirasōzu* stop on the west side of town. From here, a stone-paved street leads northeast between high mossy walls and past temples and samurai houses. You'll eventually come out on a traditional shopping street, where the local speciality, *fugu*, is much in evidence, either for sale dried in shops or on restaurant menus. Where you come to the big red *torii* on the far east side of town, turn right and you'll be back at the station.

ARRIVAL AND INFORMATION USUKI

By train You'll usually need to make a quick change at Ōita if you're coming from Beppu.

Destinations Beppu (1–3 hourly; 30min–1hr 15min); Miyazaki (hourly; 3hr); Nobeoka (hourly; 1hr 30min).

Tourist information Staff at the station hand out basic sketch maps, but for anything more complicated, you'll need to walk into the centre of town (around 10min) to the tourist office (daily 9am–6pm; ☎ 0972 63 1715) on the main shopping street.

Miyazaki

宮崎

There's a relaxed, summery feel to the breezy city of **MIYAZAKI**, with its palm trees, flower-lined streets and the longest sunshine hours in Japan. It's best used as a base for exploring the **Nichinan coast** to the south, which is particularly appealing to the **surfers** who head here in droves in warmer months (see box, p.757). Sights in the city itself, however, won't appear on anyone's bucket list, though they're sufficiently interesting to fill a half-day. **Heiwadai-kōen** is a hilltop park with a delightful collection of clay *haniwa* figurines – replicas of statues found in ancient burial mounds – while the grounds of nearby **Miyazaki-jingū**, the city's foremost shrine, contain a good municipal museum.

Heiwadai-kōen

平和台公園 • Bus #8 from Miyazaki Station, east exit (30min; ¥320)

Low hills rise to the north of Miyazaki, where the rather Stalinist "Tower of Peace" dominates a large public park, **Heiwadai-kōen**. Behind the tower you'll find the **Haniwa Garden**, where dozens of clay statues of houses, animals and people populate a mossy wood. Look out for the charming warriors with elaborate uniforms and the pop-eyed, open-mouthed dancers. These are copies of the *haniwa* figures discovered in fourth-century burial mounds at nearby Saitobaru; it's believed the statues were used to "protect" aristocratic tombs.

10

Miyazaki Prefectural Museum of Nature and History

宮崎県総合博物館, Miyazaki-ken Sōgō Hakubutsukan · 2-4-4 Jingū · 9am–5pm; closed Tues · Free · ☎ 0985 24 2071

Around 1km southeast of Heiwadai-kōen, and close to Miyazaki-jingū Station, the **Miyazaki Prefectural Museum of Nature and History** is worth visiting for its displays of local folklore. The same complex includes an archeological centre, where you can watch people patiently glueing together pottery shards, and the **Minka-en**, a collection of four thatched farmhouses from around the area. Don't miss the two traditional stone baths; the water was heated by lighting a fire underneath, like giant cauldrons.

Miyazaki-jingū

宮崎神宮 · 2 Jingū · 24hr · Free

Just south across the park from the nature and history museum lies **Miyazaki-jingū**, dedicated to Japan's first emperor, Jimmu Tennō. An unusually large shrine at the end of an imposing avenue, the sanctuary itself is typically understated, though if you're lucky you'll catch a festive ceremony, or at least spot some of the colourful, semi-wild chickens scurrying round the raked-gravel compound.

Prefectural Art Museum

宮崎県立美術館, Miyazaki Kenritsu Bijutsukan · Tues–Sun 10am–6pm · Free · ☎ 0985 20 3792

Five minutes' walk west of Miyazaki-jingū is the aptly named Culture Park, a complex of public buildings, including a theatre, a library and a concert hall that contains Japan's largest pipe organ. It is also home to the monumental **Prefectural Art Museum**, which has a collection of twentieth-century Japanese and Western painting that includes works by Picasso, Klee and Magritte.

DRINKING	
The Bar	1

● EATING	
Gunkei	1/3
Hidaka Honten	4
Ogura	2
Suginoko	5

■ ACCOMMODATION	
APA Hotel	2
Green Rich Hotel	4
Guesthouse Heiwa	1
Sheraton Grande	3

ARRIVAL AND INFORMATION

By plane The airport (☎0985 51 5114, ⓦmiyazaki-airport.co.jp) is 5km south of the city centre and connected to Miyazaki Station by both train (1–3 hourly; 10min; ¥350) and bus (2–5 hourly; 30min; ¥440).

Destinations Fukuoka (14 daily; 45min); Nagoya (3 daily; 1hr 10min); Naha (1 daily; 1hr 25min); Osaka (12 daily; 1hr); Tokyo (1–2 hourly; 1hr 30min).

By train If you're coming to Miyazaki from Beppu or Fukuoka, you'll usually have to make a quick change at Ōita.

Destinations Aoshima (roughly hourly; 30min); Beppu (roughly hourly; 3hr 50min); Fukuoka (hourly; 5hr 45min); Kagoshima (10 daily; 2hr–2hr 10min); Nobeoka (roughly hourly; 1hr); Obi (roughly hourly; 1hr 10min); Usuki (hourly; 3hr).

By bus Long-distance buses stop outside Miyazaki Station's west exit. Tourists can buy a one-day bus pass (¥1000) at the train station tourist office, which covers all Miyazaki Kōtsū services within the prefecture, as far afield as Obi and Takachiho.

Destinations Aoshima (1–3 hourly; 45min); Fukuoka (1–2 hourly; 4hr); Kagoshima (7 daily; 2hr 40min); Kumamoto (1 hourly; 3hr); Obi (10 daily; 2hr); Udo-jingū (8 daily; 1hr 30min).

By ferry Ferries from Kōbe (1 daily; 13hr 30min; from ¥9460; ☎0985 29 5566, ⓦmiyazakicarferry.com) dock at Miyazaki Port Ferry Terminal, east of the city centre; buses to Miyazaki Station (15–20min; ¥270) wait outside the terminal buildings.

10

GETTING AROUND

By bus Nearly all local buses stop at Miyazaki Station and most also call at stops around the city's central crossroads, Depāto-mae; the minimum fare is ¥160. The Miyazaki Kōtsū one-day pass for the tourist office (see below) includes city buses. At weekends, the "One-Coin"

one-day pass (¥500) covers city buses.

By bike Bikes can be rented outside Miyazaki Station's west exit (¥500/day).

Car rental Nippon Rent-a-Car has outlets at the station (☎0985 25 0919) and the airport (☎0985 56 5007).

INFORMATION

Tourist information The main tourist office is inside Miyazaki Station (daily 9am–6pm; ☎0985 22 6469, ⓦmiyazaki-city.tourism.or.jp), and there's a desk at the airport (daily 7am–9pm; ☎0985 51 5114).

Services The Prefectural Hospital (☎0985 24 4181) is on

Takachiho-dōri, west of the central crossroads. The Prefectural Police Headquarters is on Kencho Kusunamiki-dōri (☎0985 31 0110). Miyazaki Central Post Office is on Takachiho-dōri, east of the Tachibana junction. They operate a 24hr service for express mail.

ACCOMMODATION

APA Hotel APAホテル 3-4-4 Tachibanadōri-higashi ☎0985 20 5500, ⓦapahotel.com. South of Miyazaki's central crossroads, this smart business hotel features English-style facilities, and boasts a few twin and double rooms (cheaper rooms lack windows). Buffet breakfast (an extra ¥1000) is served at the grandly named Café London. **¥9600**

Green Rich Hotel グリーンリチホテル 1-5-8 Kawara-machi ☎0985 26 7411, ⓦgr-miyazaki.com. This excellent-value business hotel is near the river, and has smart, spick-and-span rooms that are relatively spacious for the price. 🛜 **¥6340**

Guesthouse Heiwa ホテルゲストハウス平和 1041-4 Oaza ☎0985 48 1880, ⓦghouse-heiwa.webnode.jp. Cheap hostel with Japanese- and Western-style dorms,

located some way north of the centre, though this makes it pretty convenient for Miyazaki-Jingū and its surrounding sights. The owner speaks little English, but goes out of her way to make guests feel welcome. Free bicycles, washing machine and computer for guest use. Meals available if ordered in advance. 🛜 Dorms **¥2280**

Sheraton Grande シェラトングランドオーシャンリゾート On the coast about 5km north of central Miyazaki ☎0985 21 1133, ⓦstarwoodhotels.com; buses run roughly hourly from the station. Housed in a 43-storey skyscraper (its top floor devoted to a wedding chapel) in a huge, seaside country club complex, Seagaia, this is Miyazaki's top hotel. Bedrooms are very spacious and luxurious – try to bag one with an ocean view – and facilities include tennis courts and several pools. 🛜 **¥16,200**

EATING

The best choice of **restaurants** is in the streets either side of Tachibana-dōri and particularly those behind the Bon Belta department store. Local **specialities** include beef, wild boar, *ayu* (sweet fish), shiitake mushrooms from the mountains, clams, flying fish and citrus fruits. There's also good local sushi – *retasu-maki* – containing shrimp, lettuce and mayonnaise; chicken *Namban* – deep-fried, succulent chicken morsels with tartar sauce; and, in summer, *hiyajiru*, an aromatic soup of fish, tofu, cucumber and sesame, served ice-cold and then poured over hot rice. A popular local snack is cheese *manju*, consisting of a small, sweet almond butter-cake bun filled with melt-in-the-mouth cream cheese.

10

★**Gunkei** ぐんけい 8-12 Chūō-dōri ☎ 0985 28 4365, ⓦ gunkei.jp. Tender *jidori* free-range chicken (raised on their own farm), seared over coals and brought sizzling to the table is the order of the day in this great restaurant, decorated in traditional rustic style. There's no English menu, but ask for the *jidori* set (¥2820) and you won't be disappointed. Reservations strongly recommended. There's another branch in Kiten Plaza, outside Miyazaki Station's west exit (daily 5–11pm). Daily 5–11.30pm.

Hidaka Honten 日高本店 3-10-24 Tachibanadōri-nishi ☎ 0985 25 5300. This shop is the best place to sample Miyazaki's delectable cheese *manju* (see p.755). While you're at it, try their *Nanjya-kora Daifuku* – a chilled package of soft white rice-flour, filled with red-bean paste, a strawberry, a chestnut and cream cheese; it's absolutely divine. Daily 9.30am–9pm.

Ogura おぐら 3-4-24 Tachibanadōri-higashi ☎ 0985 27 7333. A diner-style restaurant offering good, cheap food, which has hardly changed since they invented chicken *Namban* (¥1010) here in 1968. They also serve burgers, fried pork cutlets, curry rice and other comfort food in generous portions. It's a little way down an alley – look for the red-and-white awning. 11am–2.30pm & 5–8pm; closed Tues.

★**Suginoko** 杉の子 2-1-4 Tachibanadōri-nishi ☎ 0985 22 5798. One of the city's most famous restaurants, at the southern end of Tachibana-dōri (entrance on the side street), serving delicious, good-value local cooking in elegant, rustic-chic surroundings. Offerings range from lunchtime curry sets (¥1000), through charcoal-grilled chicken and *hiyajiru* (¥2200) to seasonal *kaiseki* sets (¥4000). Reservations recommended, especially at lunchtime. Mon–Sat 11.30am–1.30pm & 5–9.30pm.

DRINKING

The Bar ザバー 3F, 3-7-15 Tachibanadōri-higashi ☎ 0985 71 0423, ⓦ thebarmiyazaki.info. Popular expat drinking hole, and a good base from which to organize further drinking.

As well as laying on pool, Wii games and big-screen sports, the owner is also an expert source of advice regarding the region's surf-spots. 📶 Tues–Sun 7pm–3am or later.

The Nichinan coast

South of Miyazaki, the hills close in as road and railway follow the coast down to **Aoshima**, a small island surrounded by peculiar rock formations; further along the coast, **Udo-jingū**'s main shrine nestles in a sacred cave. As you head down the **Nichinan coast** to **Cape Toi**, famed for its wild horses, there are more sandy coves and picturesque islands, as well as the castle remains and old samurai houses of **Obi**, a small, attractive town lying 6km inland. If you're planning to do any travelling in this area by **bus** (even if it's just from Aburatsu to Udo-jingū and back), you should arm yourself with a ¥1000 **day pass** from Miyazaki tourist office and you'll save a lot of money (see p.755).

Aoshima

青島

Fourteen kilometres south of Miyazaki, the tiny island of **AOSHIMA**, just 1.5km in circumference, is little more than a heap of sand capped by a dense forest of betel palms and other subtropical plants. The island lies a five-minute walk across a causeway from the neighbouring town, also known as Aoshima. The town itself has no other sights worth stopping for, though the **Aoshima Subtropical Botanic Garden** beside the causeway (daily 8.30am–5pm; free; ⓦ mppf.or.jp/aoshima), known for its palm trees and bougainvillaea, is worth a quick browse while you're waiting for onward transport.

Aoshima-jinja

青島神社

Aoshima island is at its best at low tide when you can explore the rock pools trapped on the surrounding "devil's washboard" shelf of rocks, scored into deep grooves as if by a giant's comb. After that, the only other thing to do is walk round the island – it takes all of fifteen minutes – and drop in at its small attractive shrine, **Aoshima-jinja**. Swathed in vegetation, the shrine is dedicated to Yamasachi Hiko, a god of mountain products. Each year he's honoured with a couple of lively festivals: on the last weekend in July portable shrines are paraded round the island on boats and then manhandled

---

SURFIN' MIYAZAKI

To scores of adventurous young Japanese, Miyazaki prefecture is inextricably linked to **surfing**. These are Japan's best and warmest waters, and though few foreigners get in on the action, this makes a trip here all the more appealing. The peak season runs from August to October, when most weekends will have a surfing event of some description.

There's decent surfing in the waters immediately west of **Aoshima** – protected by the island, these smaller swells are perfect for beginners. **Nagisa Store** (☎ 0985 65 1070), between Kodomonokuni Station and *Grand Hotel Qingdao*, rents boards (¥3500/day), body-board and fin sets (¥3000) and wetsuits (from ¥2000). A little further towards Miyazaki is **Kisaki-hama** (木崎浜), a decent beach popular with surfers, and a ten-minute walk from Undōkōen Station. Equipment here can be rented at **Blast Surf World** (boards from ¥4000/day, wetsuits ¥3000; ☎ 0985 58 2038), located behind the *Mos Burger* just about visible from the station exit.

Experienced surfers with their own equipment should head to the reefs and reef breaks south of Aoshima, though these can be hard to get to without a local friend. Far to the north of Miyazaki, there are similarly ferocious waters surrounding **Hyūga** (日向), just south of Nobeoka.

10

back to Aoshima, while mid-January sees men rushing semi-naked into the sea. Come warmer weather, countless souls do likewise, though armed with surfboards – Aoshima is a prime base for the surfing fraternity (see box above).

ARRIVAL AND DEPARTURE

AOSHIMA

By train You can take the JR Nichinan Line train from Miyazaki Station (roughly hourly; 30min; ¥370) to Aoshima Station, from where it's an 800m walk east to the island; the map outside the station will point the way.

By bus Buses depart from Miyazaki Station's west exit (1–3 hourly; 45min), with a stop at Depāto-mae, and drop you beside the west entrance to the botanical garden.

ACCOMMODATION

Aoshima Guesthouse Hooju 青島ゲストハウス風樹 ☎ 0801 902 1691, �🌐 hoojuaoshima.web.fc2.com. Worthy, sociable hostel on the mainland side of the island, just a few minutes' walk from the causeway. Dorms are either tatami in style or bunk-bedded, rather pretty, and perfectly comfortable. Dorms ¥2500, twins ¥6000

Udo-jingū

鵜戸神宮 • Free; five *undama* ¥100 • The shrine is only accessible by road; buses run from Miyazaki (8 daily; 1hr 30min) via Aoshima (40min), and continue to Obi (40min); or take a train to Aburatsu Station (accessible from Miyazaki, Aoshima and Obi), then a bus (20min)

Eighteen kilometres south of Aoshima, a cleft in the rock hides one of this area's most famous sights, **Udo-jingū**. The main **shrine** fills the mouth of a large, low cave halfway down the cliff face, its striking, vermilion *torii* and arched bridges vivid against the dark rock. According to legend, Udo-jingū was founded in the first century BC and marks the spot where Emperor Jimmu's father was born. The rounded boulders in front of the cave are said to represent his mother's breasts – expectant women come here to pray for an easy birth and newlyweds for a happy marriage. It's also supposed to be lucky if you land a small clay pebble (*undama*) in the hollow in the top of the nearest "breast"; women throw with their right hand, men with their left.

Obi

飫肥

An old **castle town** 45km south of Miyazaki, **OBI** is a pristine little place with a number of samurai houses and a fine collection of traditional whitewashed warehouses, many of them immaculately restored, clustered under the castle walls. Obi's heyday was under the Itō family, who were granted the fiefdom in 1588 and then spent much of their time feuding with the neighbouring Shimazu clan of Kagoshima. Only the walls of

10

their once formidable castle remain, though the main gate and lord's residence have been rebuilt in the original style. Central Obi lies in a loop of the Sakatani-gawa, with its historic core concentrated north of the main east–west highway.

Obi-jō

飫肥城 • Daily 9.30am–4.30pm • Ruins free; sights ¥200 each, or ¥610 for entry to all of them

In the old centre, you'll find a few streets of **samurai houses** and carp streams, as well as the castle, **Obi-jō**, on the low hill behind. Walk north up Ōte-mon-dōri to enter the castle via its great southern gate and follow the path round to the right to find a white-walled **history museum**, which has a small but impressive collection of Itō family heirlooms.

Matsu-no-maru

松の丸

On the hill heading up from the main entrance stands the **Matsu-no-maru**, an exact replica of the rambling Edo-period buildings where the lords once lived, including the reception rooms, women's quarters, tea-ceremony room and a lovely "cooling-off" tower, where the lord could catch the summer breezes after his steam bath.

Yoshōkan

豫章館

The rest of the castle grounds are now just grass and trees, but on the way out take a quick look at Obi's largest samurai house, the **Yoshōkan**, immediately west of Ōte-mon gate. When the Meiji reforms abolished feudal holdings in the late nineteenth century, the Itō family moved to this more modest villa, which had previously belonged to their chief retainer. Though you can't go in, the house is a lovely, airy building surrounded by a spacious garden that was designed with the backdrop of Mt Atago as "borrowed scenery".

Komura Memorial Hall

小村記念館, Komura Kinentan

On the opposite side of Ōte-mon-dōri from the Yoshōkan, the **Komura Memorial Hall** commemorates a famous Meiji-era diplomat who was born in Obi in 1855. He's best remembered for his part in concluding the 1905 peace treaty following the Russo-Japanese War; most of the museum's material, much of it in English, revolves around this period.

ARRIVAL AND DEPARTURE   OBI

By train The quickest way to reach Obi is by train from Miyazaki (roughly hourly; 1hr 10min; ¥940) via Aoshima. Obi Station lies on the east side of town, about a 15min walk across the river from the castle – staff at the ticket office can provide a sketch map. Electric bicycles can be rented outside the station (¥500/day).

By bus Buses from Miyazaki (10 daily; 2hr), Aoshima (10 daily; 1hr 30min) and Udo-jingū (10 daily; 40min) stop on the main road a 5min walk south of the castle.

EATING

Obi-ten Chaya おび天茶屋 4-2-15 Obi ☎ 0987 25 1918. A nicely rustic restaurant in a garden immediately south of the Komura Memorial Hall. They sell good-value *obi-ten* teishoku (a local speciality of minced flying fish mixed with tofu, miso and sugar, rolled into a leaf shape and deep-fried), including rice, soup and pickles, for ¥950. Daily 9am–4pm.

Kirishima National Park

On the border between Kagoshima and Miyazaki prefectures, **Kirishima National Park** is known as the "Volcano Museum" because of its diverse array of more than twenty volcanic mountains, encompassing ten crater lakes and numerous hot springs. The park's main centre is the amenity zone of **Ebino Kōgen**, a cluster of shops, a hotel and a campsite on the plateau of the same name, from where it's a short scramble up the highest peak,

Karakuni-dake (1700m). The park's easternmost peak, **Takachiho-no-mine**, however, holds greater significance, since according to legend this is where Ninigi-no-mikoto, grandson of the sun goddess Amaterasu (see box, p.744) and legendary founder of the Japanese imperial line, descended to earth. The traditional approach to Takachiho-no-mine is from the park's southern gateway, **Kirishima-jingū**, stopping first at a shrine shrouded in cryptomeria trees. The peaks are linked by a skein of **hiking** trails – it's worth scaling at least one of them for superb views over jagged craters filled with perfectly round, cobalt-blue lakes and Sakurajima puffing angrily on the southern horizon.

10

Ebino Kōgen
えびの高原

At 1200m above sea level, the views from **EBINO KŌGEN** are stunning. Temperatures here on the plateau rarely exceed 20°C in summer and dip well below freezing in winter, when the peaks boast a dusting of snow and hoarfrost and the tennis courts morph into an ice-skating rink. This is the best time to appreciate the local **onsen** – Kirishima is Japan's highest hot-spring resort – while spring and autumn provide perfect hiking weather. Despite the natural beauty, the epicentre of Ebino Kōgen consists of a large, bleak car park, surrounded by several cafés and restaurants, souvenir shops and a visitors' centre.

Karakuni-dake and around
韓国岳

If it's a clear day, the hike up to **Karakuni-dake** from Ebino Kōgen is worth tackling: the volcano's crater is nearly a kilometre in diameter and has commanding views of Sakurajima and inside the active crater of Shinmoe-dake. It's not a difficult climb, though you'll want good footwear on the loose stones. From the rim of Karakuni-dake, it's best to head southwest to Ōnami-no-ike (大波の池), Japan's largest crater lake, and then back to Ebino Kōgen by a different trail – allow about three and a half hours for the circuit, or five hours if you decide to walk all the way around the rim of Ōnami-no-ike.

The classic walk from Karakuni-dake (5hr) is south along Kirishima's magnificent volcanic peaks – Shishiko-dake (獅子戸岳; 1428m), Shinmoe-dake (新燃岳; 1421m) and Naka-dake (中岳; 1345m) – to Takachiho-gawara. However, in January 2011 **Shinmoe-dake** sprang back to life in spectacular fashion, sending 24 million tonnes of ash and pumice into the air, and the trail has been closed ever since.

Hiking the Ebino plateau

There are also more gentle ambles across the Ebino plateau. The most rewarding is a 4km walk starting from behind the visitor centre, where you can use the free hot-spring footbath to ease your aching feet. The walk wends through forests of Japanese red pine and maple, and past three beautiful, cobalt-blue **crater lakes**. If you are here in May or June, head south from the visitor centre to where thirty thousand wild azaleas give the hillsides a dusty-pink tinge.

KIRISHIMA
NATIONAL PARK

■ **ACCOMMODATION**
Ebino-Kōgen Campground	2
Ebino-kōgen-sō	1
Iwasaki Hotel	3
Sakura Sakura Onsen	4
Tozan-guchi Onsen	5

Kirishima-jingū

霧島神宮

The village of **KIRISHIMA-JINGŪ**, built on the southern slopes of Takachiho-no-mine, makes a possible alternative base to Ebino Kōgen. It's named after the beautiful shrine at its top end, set above an appealing village square that's partly enveloped in cedar woods.

Kirishima Tengu-kan

霧島天狗館 • Daily, irregular hours • ¥250 • ⓣ 0995 64 8880

The first sight of any interest in Kirishima-jingū village is **Kirishima Tengu-kan** at the top of the central square – look for the building sprouting long-nosed goblin-like creatures. These are *tengu*, supernatural mountain spirits that often appear in folk tales, nō plays and, more recently, manga and video games. Inside, some 1600 masks are on display, including a monster over 2m in length carved from local camphor wood.

Kirishima-jingū

霧島神宮 • 24hr • Free

A short walk from Kirishima Tengu-kan – head over a red-lacquer bridge, beneath the bright vermilion *torii* and up a steep flight of steps – is the shrine of **Kirishima-jingū**. A surprisingly imposing complex, it's dedicated to Ninigi-no-mikoto and his fellow gods who first set foot in Kirishima at the dawn of Japan's creation. Said to have been founded in the sixth century AD, the shrine was moved here piece by piece in the fifteenth century from Takachiho-gawara, to avoid being engulfed in a lava flow. It provides some fine views over Kagoshima Bay.

Takachiho-gawara and Takachiho-no-mine

高千穂峰 • 高千穂河原 • Visitors' Centre daily 9am–5pm • ⓣ 0995 57 2505, ⓦ www4.synapse.ne.jp/visitor

The summit of **Takachiho-no-mine** (1574m) is a good three-hour walk to the northeast of Kirishima-jingū, but rewards the effort with some fantastic views over the bay of Kagoshima. With your own transport you can at least halve the walking time by driving 7km up the road to **Takachiho-gawara**. It's then a steady climb on a well-marked path, passing the former site of the Kirishima-jingū (see above) and, in May and June, stands of flowering Kyūshū azalea, ending in a short scramble on scree to the crater rim – where a replica of Ninigi's sacred spear points skywards. Before setting off from Takachiho-gawara, you might want to take a brief look at the displays in the **visitors' centre**, which is also surrounded by several **nature trails** (30min–1hr 40min), where you might encounter wild boar and deer.

ARRIVAL AND DEPARTURE — KIRISHIMA NATIONAL PARK

By train and bus If you don't have your own transport, the best way to reach the national park is by train to Kirishima-jingū Station, in the valley 7km to the south of Kirishima-jingū village. Buses from the station (7–10 daily; 15min; ¥480, or buy a one-day bus pass – see below) coincide with train arrivals, and will drop you in the village, before heading on to Maruo and the *Iwasaki Hotel*.

Kirishima-jingū Station destinations Kagoshima (10 daily; 40–50min); Miyazaki (10 daily; 1hr 20min).

GETTING AROUND

By sightseeing bus A daily sightseeing bus does a whistlestop tour of Kirishima National Park in 3–4hr on a rather eccentric route: *Iwasaki Hotel*–Maruo–Kirishima-jingū Station–Kirishima-jingū–Takachiho-gawara–Ebino Kōgen–*Iwasaki Hotel*–Maruo–Kareigawa Station (on the Kagoshima–Kumamoto line)–Kagoshima Airport. Kirishima-jingū Station to Kareigawa Station, for example, costs ¥2150.

By Trekking Bus A better option if you want to see more of the park is to visit on a Saturday or Sunday, when a "Trekking Bus" (timed to connect with regular buses from Kirishima-jingū Station via Kirishima-jingū village to Maruo) has three departures before lunchtime from Maruo for Ebino Kōgen and Takachiho-gawara (1hr; ¥720), with two return journeys in the afternoon. A one-day bus pass (¥1100) covers the Trekking Bus and the regular bus up from Kirishima-jingū Station to Maruo.

INFORMATION

EBINO KŌGEN

Tourist information It's well worth having a look at the informative displays in the Ebino Eco Museum Centre (daily 9am–5pm; ☎0984 33 3002) on the north side of the car park, which also provides detailed trekking maps. While you're here, take a look at the 3-D model of the area – it's handy for getting the lie of the land.

KIRISHIMA-JINGŪ

Tourist information There's a small tourist office (daily 9am–5pm; ☎0995 57 1588, ⓦkirishimakankou.com) beside the big *torii* at the south end of the main square, where you can rent bicycles (¥1000 for 4hr).

Services The main square has convenience stores and a post office.

ACCOMMODATION

EBINO KŌGEN

Ebino-Kōgen Campground えびの高原キャンプ村 ☎0984 33 0800. This campsite has an onsen, tents and cheap wooden cabins by a stream among the pine forests; rates include blankets and heating. Open April–Oct and over New Year. Per person **¥1600**

Ebino-kōgen-sō えびの高原荘 ☎0984 33 0161, ⓦebinokogenso.com. A couple of minutes' walk west of the central car park, this hotel run by Miyazaki Prefecture offers comfortable Western and Japanese rooms with mountain views and a decent restaurant. Non-residents can also use the smart rotemburo here (daily 11.30am–8pm; ¥520). Call ahead for a pick-up from Kirishima-jingū Station. **¥11,000**

KIRISHIMA-JINGŪ

Tozan-guchi Onsen 登山口温泉 2459-83 Kirishimataguchi ☎0995 57 0127 or ☎0995 57 1188. Spruce little minshuku tucked just off the square – take the road heading east from the roundabout. It has a rooftop rotemburo and also doubles as a youth hostel (¥3390/person, or ¥5010 including meals), with accommodation in shared tatami rooms. Half-board per person **¥7500**

ELSEWHERE IN THE PARK

Iwasaki Hotel いわさきホテル 8km south of Ebino Kōgen visitor centre on the Maruo road, at the terminus of the public bus from Kirishima-jingū Station ☎0995 78 4888, ⓦkirishima.iwasakihotels .com. Huge, comfortable hotel, popular with tour groups, that offers spectacular views of Sakurajima and Kaimon-dake. Its other big selling point is an unusual, semi-wild rotemburo, with eight hot-spring rock pools around a fast-flowing stream, shaded by trees (open to non-residents at weekends; ¥1550). Half-board deals available (from ¥12,960/person). ⓦ **¥13,070**

★Sakura Sakura Onsen さくらさくら温泉 3km west of Kirishima-jingū, on the bus route from Kirishima-jingū Station and Kirishima-jingū village to Maruo ☎0995 57 1227, ⓦsakura-sakura.jp. This quality hotel offers Japanese-, Western-style and hybrid rooms, as well as log cabins, each with its own mud bath. It has several rotemburo, but its speciality is volcanic mud – especially popular with young women for its skin-softening effects. The stunning baths are open to non-residents (daily 10.30am–8pm; ¥700). Free pick-ups for guests from Kirishima-jingū Station. ⓦ Half-board per person **¥9400**

Kagoshima

鹿児島

KAGOSHIMA's most obvious and compelling attraction is the smouldering cone of **Sakurajima**, one of the most active volcanoes on earth (see p.768). On the other side of the bay from the city – just fifteen minutes away by ferry – it frequently billows an enormous cloud of ash into the southern Kyūshū sky. Local weather forecasts show which direction the plume is heading; if it's coming your way, ash will get in your eyes, hair and teeth, while cars end up covered in a sheet of dust. Aside from the volcano, Kagoshima contains a few sights of its own which justify at least a day's exploration. Highlight among them is **Sengan-en**, a fascinating seventeenth-century villa and formal garden with a grandstand view of Sakurajima.

Brief history

Originally known as **Satsuma**, the Kagoshima region was ruled by the powerful **Shimazu** clan for nearly seven centuries until the Meiji reforms put an end to such fiefdoms in 1871. The area has a long tradition of overseas contact and it was here that Japan's first Christian missionary, the Spanish-born Jesuit **Francis Xavier**, arrived in 1549. Welcomed by the Shimazu lords – who were primarily interested in trade and acquiring new technologies –

10

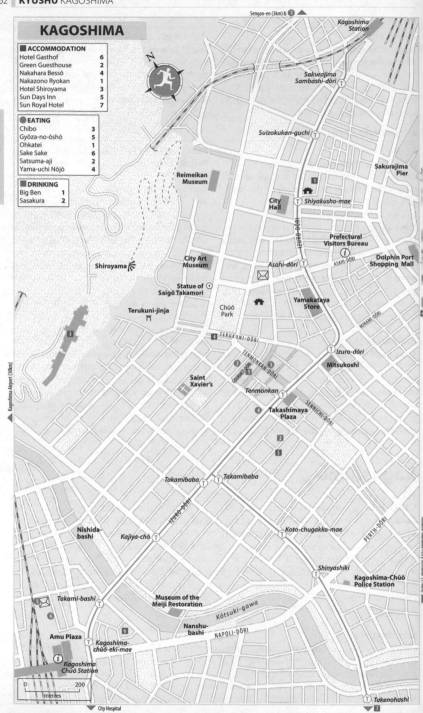

KAGOSHIMA

ACCOMMODATION
Hotel Gasthof	6
Green Guesthouse	2
Nakahara Bessō	4
Nakazono Ryokan	1
Hotel Shiroyama	3
Sun Days Inn	5
Sun Royal Hotel	7

EATING
Chibo	3
Gyōza-no-ōshō	5
Ohkatei	1
Sake Sake	6
Satsuma-aji	2
Yama-uchi Nōjō	4

DRINKING
Big Ben	1
Sasakura	2

Sengan-en (3km) &

Kagoshima Station

Sakurajima Sambashi-dōri

Suizokukan-guchi

Sakurajima Pier

Reimeikan Museum

City Hall

Shiyakusho-mae

Prefectural Visitors Bureau

Dolphin Port Shopping Mall

Shiroyama

City Art Museum

Asahi-dōri

ASAHI-DŌRI

Statue of Saigō Takamori

Terukuni-jinja

Chūō Park

Yamakataya Store

MINAMI-DŌRI

TERUKUNI-DŌRI

TENMONKAN-DŌRI

GOURMET-DŌRI

Izuro-dōri

Mitsukoshi

Saint Xavier's

Tenmonkan

SENNICHI-DŌRI

Takashimaya Plaza

Takamibaba

Takamibaba

Koto-chugakko-mae

PERTH-DŌRI

IZURO-DŌRI

Nishida-bashi

Kajiya-chō

Shinyashiki

Kagoshima-Chūō Police Station

Kagoshima Airport (50km)

Takami-bashi

Museum of the Meiji Restoration

Kōtsuki-gawa

Nanshu-bashi

NAPOLI-DŌRI

Amu Plaza

Kagoshima-chūō-eki-mae

Kagoshima Chūō Station

0   200
metres

Takenohashi

City Hospital

SAIGŌ TAKAMORI AND THE SATSUMA REBELLION

Born in Satsuma in 1827, **Saigō Takamori** made his name as one of the leading figures in the **Meiji Restoration**. Though aware of the need for Japan to modernize, he grew increasingly alarmed at the loss of traditional values and eventually left the government to set up a military academy in Kagoshima. He soon became a focus for opposition forces – mainly disaffected samurai but also peasants protesting at punitive taxes. Things came to a head in January 1877 when Saigō led an army of forty thousand against the government stronghold in Kumamoto, in what came to be known as the **Satsuma Rebellion**. After besieging the castle for nearly two months, the rebels were forced to withdraw before the sixty-thousand-strong Imperial Army. They retreated to Kagoshima where they were gradually pinned down on Shiroyama. On September 24, the imperial forces closed in and Saigō, severely wounded, asked one of his comrades to kill him. His courage, idealism and heroic death earned Saigō enormous popular support – so much so that he was officially pardoned by imperial decree in 1891.

---

he spent ten months working in Kagoshima, where he found the poorer classes particularly receptive to Christian teachings. After just a few months Xavier declared "it seems to me that we shall never find among heathens another race to equal the Japanese".

Soon after, Japan was closed to foreigners and remained so for the next two hundred years, although Satsuma was permitted to trade with China through their joint vassal state Ryūkyū (present-day Okinawa). As central control crumbled in the mid-nineteenth century, however, the far-sighted **Shimazu Nariakira** began introducing Western technology, such as spinning machines, the printing press and weapons manufacture, and it was Kagoshima that saw Japan's first gas light, steamships, electric lights, photographs and Morse code transmission. However, not all relations were cordial. In 1862 an Englishman was decapitated in Yokohama by a Shimazu retainer for crossing the road in front of the *daimyō*'s procession. When the Shimazu refused to punish the loyal samurai or pay compensation, seven **British warships** bombarded Kagoshima Bay in 1863. Fortunately there was little loss of life and the Shimazu were so impressed by this show of force that three years later they dispatched nineteen "young pioneers" to study in London – many of these young men went on to assist the new Meiji government in its mission to modernize Japan. Easily Kagoshima's most famous son, however, is **Saigō Takamori** (see box above).

Terukuni-jinja

照国神社 • 19-35 Terukuni-chō • 24hr • Free

There are a few interesting sights in the area around Chūō Park, including the delightful **Terukuni-jinja**. The greenery and mossy tree trunks surrounding this shrine enable it to blend seamlessly into Shiroyama, the mountain rearing up behind the complex. The main hall, however, is somewhat disappointing – its surrounding buildings and statues are of more interest. The first statue you'll come to is of Shimazu Nariakira (see above), to whom the shrine is dedicated; somewhat bafflingly, they've given him a prime position overlooking the car park. His half-brother Hisamitsu, just to the east, is in a far nicer spot, surrounded by a trickling stream; a former government advisor and minister, he led an excursion to Edo with a thousand retainers in 1862. Just to the south, by the car park, is Hisamitsu's son Tadayoshi (also a son-in-law of Nariakira), who was instrumental in improving Japan's relations with the UK.

City Art Museum

鹿児島市立美術館, Kagoshima Shiritsu Bijutsukan • 4-36 Shiroyama-chō • Tues–Sun 9.30am–6pm • ¥300 • ☏ 099 224 3400

Housed in a spacious modern building, the **City Art Museum** boasts a good collection of Impressionist and twentieth-century Western art, including works by Monet, Picasso and Warhol, as well as highly rated local artists such as Kuroda Seiki and Fujishima Takeji.

Outside the museum, and facing south across Chūō Park, is a bronze statue of the close-cropped, portly Saigō Takamori (see box, p.763), portraying him as an uncompromising military leader. Behind him are carp-filled moats and some bullet-pocked walls, remains of the castle, **Tsurumaru-jō**, that was destroyed in the 1877 Satsuma Rebellion.

Reimeikan

黎明館 • 7-2 Shiroyama-chō • Tues–Sun 9am–6pm • ¥310 • ☎ 099 222 5100

North of the City Art Museum, an arched stone bridge from the former castle leads up to the **Reimeikan** museum, which provides a good introduction to local history and culture. Apart from a delightful mock-up of Tenmonkan arcade as it would have looked in the 1930s, the most interesting displays cover local festivals and the southern islands' distinct traditions, showing the influence of Melanesian culture from the islands of the West Pacific.

Shiroyama

城山

Behind the Reimeikan museum, a path leads up through impressive stands of mature, subtropical trees to the top of **Shiroyama** hill. The twenty-minute climb is worth it for superb views over Kagoshima and the smouldering cone of Sakurajima.

City Aquarium

かごしま水族館, Kagoshima Suizokukan • 3-1 Honkoshin-machi • Daily 9.30am–6pm (last admission 5pm) • ¥1500 • ☎ 099 226 2233, Ⓦ ioworld.jp

A fifteen-minute walk southeast from the Reimeikan museum, the **City Aquarium** sits on a man-made island in the harbour. Thanks to the warm Kuroshio Current sweeping across from the East China Sea, the waters around Kagoshima's southern islands are rich in temperate and subtropical aquatic life, a broad range of which is on show in this well-designed installation, from Sakurajima's unique tube worm to colourful sea anemones.

Museum of the Meiji Restoration

維新ふるさと館, Ishin Furusato-kan • Daily 9am–5pm • ¥300 • Sound and light show roughly hourly 9.15am–4.30pm • ☎ 099 239 7700, Ⓦ ishinfurusatokan.info

The engaging **Museum of the Meiji Restoration** sits beside the tranquil Kōtsuki-gawa. No expense has been spared to re-create the "golden age" of Kagoshima, when Saigō Takamori (see box, p.763) and other local luminaries were instrumental in returning power to the emperor and then spearheading the Meiji reforms. The highlight is a 25-minute sound and light show in which robots – including a wild-eyed Saigō – re-enact scenes from the restoration. The show takes place in the basement theatre, which also hosts a less compelling show about the "young pioneers" who studied in London (see p.827). Upstairs, don't miss the original version of the Japanese national anthem, recorded by the Satsuma Military Band in 1870, composed two years earlier by Irish bandmaster, John William Fenton.

Sengan-en

仙巌園 • **Gardens, villa & Shōko Shūseikan** Daily 8.30am–5.30pm • Gardens & Shoko Shuseikan ¥1000, or ¥1600 including entry to the villa, plus tea and sweet • ☎ 099 247 1551, Ⓦ sengan.jp and Ⓦ facebook.com/senganenEN • **Glass factory** Tues–Sun 9am–noon & 1–5pm • Free • Ⓦ satsumakiriko.co.jp • City View tourist bus, or regular bus from Kagoshima Chūō Station or Tenmonkan (every 30min; 15–20min; ¥190)

When their base at Tsurumaru-jō was destroyed during the 1877 Satsuma Rebellion, the Shimazu lords set up residence in their garden-villa Iso Tei-en, now known as

Sengan-en, which they had built in 1658. Now run by the 32nd and 33rd generations of Shimazu, Sengan-en, 3km east of the city centre, makes for a compelling visit of several hours. As well as the gardens, house and Shōko Shūseikan history museum, there's also a glass-cutting factory where you can watch the artisans at work, a fine restaurant (see p.767) and a busy programme of events, including horseback archery, and chrysanthemum and iris festivals (check their Facebook page).

The gardens

The lovely formal **gardens** feature shapely ornamental rocks and rustic shrines. Though they're now separated from the shoreline by a road and a rail line, you can still appreciate the panorama of Kinko Bay and Sakurajima that was designed to act as "borrowed scenery": the bay taking the place of the pond that all feudal lords' gardens were meant to have, the volcano instead of an artificial hill. At the east end of the grounds, the 200-year-old **kyokusui garden** is a lawn with a stream running through the middle, where poetry composition parties are still held, under the cherry and plum blossoms of April – sitting on the banks of the stream, each contestant must come up with a poem before a floating sake cup reaches them from upstream. Nearby, behind the villa, a stepped path leads up through lush, mossy woods to a **viewpoint** with spectacular vistas of Sakurajima and the city (20–30min walk each way).

The villa

You can tour the warren-like wooden **villa** either with an English-speaking guide or with an excellent handout in English. On the way you'll pass beautiful cedarwood *fusuma*, painted with cherry blossoms and peonies, while kids can have fun looking for the eleven different varieties of *kugi kakushi* – decorative covers for nail heads in the shape of bats, giant Sakurajima radishes and the like. Round off the tour with a traditional Shimazu family sweet and a cup of green tea, while admiring the magnolia tree, pond and rocks of the beautiful inner garden.

Shōko Shūseikan and the glass factory

Just outside the main gardens entrance, Shuseikan was the first Western-style factory in Japan, constructed by Shimazu Nariakira in the 1850s. Part of it is now the **Shōko Shūseikan**, an engaging museum that celebrates the history of the Shimazu family, not least their modernizing zeal of the nineteenth century. Highlights include lovely palanquins and early examples of coloured **glassware**, Satsuma Kiriko. Shimazu Nariakira imported colouring techniques from China and blowing and cutting techniques from Venice via Tokyo to create this style of glass, with its gentle gradation between the coloured and transparent layers. Next door to Shōko Shūseikan, you're free to go into the **glass factory** to watch the artisans blowing, layering and cutting.

ARRIVAL AND DEPARTURE | KAGOSHIMA

By plane Kagoshima Airport (⌨ koj-ab.co.jp), served by flights to Seoul, Shanghai, Hong Kong and Taipei as well as domestic routes, is located some 30km north of the city, near the Kirishima National Park (see p.758). Buses leave the airport every ten or twenty minutes for Kagoshima Chūō Station and central Kagoshima's Tenmonkan crossroads (about 1hr; ¥1250), some continuing to the ports.
Destinations Fukuoka (1 daily; 50min); Nagoya (6 daily; 1hr 15min); Naha (2 daily; 1hr 25min); Osaka (18 daily; 1hr 10min); Tokyo (1–2 hourly; 1hr 35min); Yakushima (3 daily; 35min).
By train The Shinkansen line connects Kagoshima Chūō Station with Kumamoto, Hakata and Osaka; local trains use the same station (and sometimes Kagoshima Station, east of the city centre).
Destinations Fukuoka (every 30min; 1hr 20min–2hr 30min); Ibusuki (1–2 hourly; 50min–1hr 20min); Kirishima-jingū (10 daily; 40–50min); Kumamoto (every 30min; 40min–1hr 15min); Miyazaki (10 daily; 2hr–2hr 15min); Osaka (1–2 hourly; 3hr 50min–4hr 30min).
By bus Most bus services to Kagoshima stop at Kagoshima Chūō Station or the central Tenmonkan crossroads, or both; some continue to the terminal for Yakushima hydrofoils.
Destinations Chiran (9–10 daily; 1hr 20min); Fukuoka (every 30min–1hr; 4hr 30min); Kumamoto (4 daily; 3hr 20min); and Miyazaki (7 daily; 2hr 40min).

By ferry A Line (☎ 099 226 4141, ⊛ aline-ferry.com) and Marix Line (☎ 099 225 1551, ⊛ marixline.com) ferries sail to Naha, Okinawa from the Amami-Okinawa Ferry Terminal to the southeast of the city centre (4–6 weekly; 25hr; ¥14,610); "Port Liner" buses leave Kagoshima Chūō Station's east gate to coincide with departures. Ferries to Yakushima (1 daily; 4hr; ¥4900) depart from the more central Minami-Futō (South Pier; next to Dolphin Port shopping mall), while jetfoils to Ibusuki (1–2 daily; 40min; ¥2500) and Yakushima (6–7 daily; 1hr 50min–2hr 45min; ¥8800; ⊛ tykousoku.jp) use the adjacent terminal; buses run to the jetfoil terminal from Kagoshima Chūō Station's east gate via Tenmonkan (every 15min; 10min), or you can catch a City View bus (see below) to Dolphin Port.

GETTING AROUND

By tram Moving around central Kagoshima is simplified by a highly efficient two-line tram system. Both lines head westward from Kagoshima Station to Tenmonkan before splitting at Takamibaba, with the more useful Line #2 continuing to Kagoshima Chūō Station and beyond. There's a flat fare of ¥170, which you pay on exit; trams run roughly every eight minutes from 6.30am–10.30pm.

By bus The local bus system is rather complicated, with services run by five different companies. However, easily recognizable City View tourist buses (individual tickets ¥190) ply two routes around the main sights from Kagoshima Chūō Station's east gate: the Shiroyama and Iso Course (every 30min; 1hr) covers the Museum of the Meiji Restoration, the City Art Museum, Reimeikan, Shiroyama and Sengan-en, before returning via the aquarium and Tenmonkan; the Waterfront Course (7 daily; 1hr 15min) covers the aquarium and Sengan-en, before returning via Reimeikan, the City Art Museum and Tenmonkan.

Transport passes There's a ¥600 one-day pass for trams and most city buses, including the City View tourist buses. Alternatively, the Welcome Cute pass (¥1000/day or ¥1500 for 2 days) covers all of the above plus the ferry to Sakurajima (including the Yorimichi Cruise) and the Sakurajima Island View Bus (though not the Sakurajima Regular Sightseeing Bus).

Car rental Budget has offices near Kagoshima Chūō Station (☎ 099 250 0543) and at the airport (☎ 099 558 3543).

INFORMATION

Tourist office Helpful tourist offices with lots of useful publications and maps in English can be found at Kagoshima Chūō Station (daily 8am–8pm; ☎ 099 253 2500, ⊛ kagoshima-yokanavi.jp) and the downtown Prefectural Visitors Bureau on Asahi-dōri (daily 8.30am–5.15pm; ☎ 099 223 5771, ⊛ kagoshima-kankou.com).

ACCOMMODATION

★**Hotel Gasthof** ホテルガストフ 7-1 Chūō-chō ☎ 099 252 1401, ⊛ gasthof.jp. Remodelled in an eclectic mix of foreign styles, this hotel near the station is excellent value. The attention to detail is admirable – think bathrooms lined with pearlescent tiling, chunky beds and tartan frills. 📶 **¥8520**

★**Green Guesthouse** グリーンゲストハウス 5-7 Sumiyoshi-chō ☎ 099 802 4301, ⊛ green-guesthouse .com. Excellent hostel with Japanese- and Western-style dorms, an easy 10min walk from Izuro-dōri tram stop and just a hop and a skip from the ferry terminals – great if you've got an early morning departure. There's a lovely little bar downstairs, a rooftop terrace, rental bicycles and a computer for guests. For a mere ¥500 above the regular dorm price, you can sleep in a capsule-like private cabin. 📶 Dorms **¥1800**, twins **¥4600**

Nakahara Bessō 中原別荘 15-19 Higashi-Sengoku-chō ☎ 099 225 2800, ⊛ nakahara-bessou.co.jp. Nicely decorated onsen hotel in the city centre overlooking Chūō Park. The spacious, en-suite Japanese-style rooms are the best value, and, though the rates quoted below are for room-only, the meals are highly recommended. Excellent rates for singles (¥5400). 📶 **¥12,960**

Nakazono Ryokan 中薗旅館 1-18 Yasui-chō ☎ 099 226 5125, ⊛ nakazonoryokan.wix.com/nakazonoryokan. There's always service with a smile at this homely minshuku, tucked behind a temple opposite Kagoshima City Hall. The tatami rooms are clean and large enough, though facilities are mostly shared. 📶 Room-only **¥8400**

★**Hotel Shiroyama** 城山観光ホテル Shiroyama hill ☎ 099 224 2200, ⊛ shiroyama-g.co.jp. Landmark hotel set among fountains and fairy lights on the hill, with very high standards of service. Many of the luxurious, Western-style rooms and the open-air onsen enjoy great views over the city to Sakurajima. Free, regular shuttle bus to the station and Tenmonkan. 📶 **¥15,420**

Sun Days Inn サンデイズイン 9-8 Yamanokuchi-chō ☎ 099 227 5151, ⊛ sundaysinn.com. Stylish rooms, friendly staff and low prices make this nicely contemporary business hotel a real treat – try to get a room with views of Sakurajima. Coin laundry, good-value breakfast buffet (¥540 if booked in advance) and free pick-ups from the ports. **¥6300**

Sun Royal Hotel サンロイヤルホテル 1-8-10 Yojiro ☎ 099 253 2020, ⊛ sunroyal.co.jp. This luxury hotel is in a slightly inconvenient location southeast of the centre, but the meals are excellent (especially the breakfast buffet – extra cost), there's a scenic top-floor onsen and all rooms are exceedingly comfortable; ask for one with a Sakurajima view. Very good rates for singles (¥11,290). 📶 **¥20,200**

EATING

Central Kagoshima is chock-full of **restaurants**, with the classiest establishments in a tight, semi-pedestrianized area west of Tenmonkan-dōri. Its most popular **speciality foods** are *satsuma-age*, a deep-fried, slightly sweet patty of minced fish and sake, eaten with *wasabi* and soy sauce, and steaks of succulent *kurobuta* pork. The prettiest local dish is *kibinago sashimi*, in which slices of a silvery, sardine-like fish are arranged in an eye-catching flower head. *Keihan* mixes shredded chicken with carrot, egg, mushroom and spring onions over a bowl of rice in a hot, tasty broth, while *sake-zushi* consists of sushi with a drop of sake. For snacks, there's *satsuma-imo* ice cream (made with sweet potato) and *jambo mochi* – rice cakes smothered in sweet sauce and impaled on a pair of bamboo skewers.

10

Chibō 千房 15-4 Higashisengoku-chō ☎099 255 7001, ⓦchibo.com. This excellent *okonomiyaki* chain started in Kansai, but has gone down well in southern Kyūshū too. Prices are very reasonable, with the savoury pancakes starting at ¥700. Daily 11am–9.30pm.

★Gyōza-no-ōshō 餃子の王将 1-4 Chūō-chō ☎099 253 4728. Good, cheap Chinese-style food near the main station, served up by cheery staff, with an English menu. Particularly recommended are the delectable *gyōza* dumplings (¥230) and the fried rice (¥490). Noon–4pm & 5–10pm; closed Wed.

Ohkatei 桜華亭 Sengan-en. It's well worth timing your visit to Sengan-en (see p.764) to coincide with lunch at its elegant, first-floor restaurant with great views of the gardens and Sakurajima. Sets (from ¥1550) include tasty specialities such as *kibinago sashimi*, *satsuma-age* and local eels. There's also a nice little noodle café on the ground floor and, nearby, a simpler

restaurant serving curries and the like. 🛜 Daily 11am–3.30pm.

Sake Sake さけ咲 1-10 Chūō-chō ☎099 214 5885, ⓦwako-21.jp. This lively, cradle-to-grave operation near the station specializes in black, free-range Kurosatsuma chickens bred on its own farm – so fresh that they can be served as sashimi (not actually raw, but cooked very rare). The grilled chicken with mayonnaise and *suzu* (citrus) sauce (¥1200) is excellent, and the *kurobuta teppanyaki*, served on a plate of lava from Sakurajima, is also very tasty and sweet. Mon–Thurs & Sun 5pm–midnight, Fri & Sat 5pm–1am.

Satsuma-aji さつま路 6-29 Higashi-Sengoku-chō ☎099 226 0525, ⓦsatumaji.co.jp. Elegantly rustic restaurant in the heart of Kagoshima's trendiest area, serving fairly pricey but top-quality local food. Lunch sets start at ¥1600, or try *satsuma-age* (¥630), *kibinago sashimi* (¥750) or their famous *kurobuta shabu-shabu* (¥1100) from

---

KAGOSHIMA SHŌCHŪ

Kagoshima prefecture is Japan's biggest producer and consumer of **shōchū** and the Japanese are in near-unanimous agreement that Kagoshima's *shōchū* is the best in the land. There are more than 800 local varieties available, and these are usually made from **sweet potato** rather than rice, which makes for a heavier flavour and a higher alcohol content – 25 percent, rather than the national norm of 20 percent. As is the case elsewhere, one can have the hooch served straight, with soda, heated, mixed with hot water, or on the rocks. Like wine, each variety has its own specific taste – below are a few top picks to get you started. A good place to try local *shōchū* is in the city's pleasantly sleazy nightlife district, in the lanes either side of the Sennichi arcade, south of Izuro-dōri; alternatively, buy it in the Kagoshima Brand Shop at the Prefectural Visitors Bureau (see opposite).

Kaidō 海童 Served in a distinctive red bottle, this is perhaps the best low- to mid-range choice, and has a clean, crisp taste that works best on the rocks.

Kojika 小鹿 Cheap but high-quality option, whose slightly dry taste is magnified when served heated.

Kuro 黒 Popular with young and old alike, this tasty cheapie is available in pretty much every *izakaya* and convenience store across the prefecture. Best served heated.

Maō 魔王 Running Mori Izō a close second for quality, this slightly sweet variety is a favourite with Kagoshima connoisseurs.

Mori Izō 森伊蔵 The king of local *shōchū*, this high-roller favourite can cost over ¥70,000 per bottle in a Tokyo *izakaya*, but is usually available here for a fraction of the price. Have it neat, or with hot water.

Nofū 野風 A rarity in Kagoshima *shōchū* terms, in that it's made from corn rather than sweet potato. Though, being 35 percent alcohol by volume, you may not notice.

Shiranami 白波 The most famed variety in Kagoshima city itself, this is available in over a dozen different grades, including the somewhat hazardous 37 percent-alcohol Genshū variety.

10

the picture-menu. Daily 11.30am–2pm & 5.30–9pm.

Yama-uchi Nōjō 山内農場 Izuro-dōri, above Lawsons (entrance on the side street) ☎099 223 7488. Bright, brash izakaya, popular with thirty-somethings, that serves lots of local specialities: kurobuta, horsemeat and very good dried herring with sugar and mirin (¥480), which goes well with their draught Kirin lager and stout. 📶 Mon–Thurs 4pm–2am, Fri & Sat 4pm–3am, Sun 4pm–1am.

DRINKING

Big Ben ビッグベン Gourmet-dōri ☎099 226 4470, 🖰bigben1001.com. From the name, and the Union Jack outside, you'd expect a British-style pub, but in reality it's a regular-looking Japanese bar. Nevertheless, it's a hit with local expats, and also popular with locals (in part due to its imported booze) – all in all, it's a great place to meet people and the city's best venue for watching international sports. Find it on Gourmet-dōri, a narrow lane of restaurants and cafés, in the basement. Mon–Thurs & Sun 5.30pm–1/2am, Fri & Sat 5.30pm–4am.

Sasakura 酒々蔵 9-17 Yamanokuchi-chō ☎099 224 1356. There are over 150 different types of Kagoshima shōchū available in this traditionally styled izakaya, and good, inexpensive food to soak it up with, though you'll have to pay a ¥600–700 cover charge. 📶 Mon–Sat 6.30pm–2.30am, Sun 6.30pm–1.30am.

DIRECTORY

Bookshops Kinokuniya, on Amu Plaza's fourth floor, has the largest selection of English-language books and magazines.

Hospital The most central hospital with English-speaking staff is the Kagoshima City Hospital (☎099 230 7000), 1km south of Kagoshima-chūo Station near Shiritsu Byōin-mae tram stop (line #2).

Police Kagoshima-chūo Police Station, 17-26 Shinyashiki-chō ☎099 222 0110.

Post office Kagoshima Central Post Office is right next to Kagoshima Chūo Station. There's also a handy sub-office on Asahi-dōri near Chūo Park. Both have ATMs which take international bank cards.

Sakurajima

桜島

Kagoshima's most stirring sight is the volcanic cone of **SAKURAJIMA**, which grumbles away just 4km from the city centre, often pouring a column of dense black ash into the air. This is one of the world's most active volcanoes, and hiking its peak has been prohibited since 1955 – adventurous sorts should note that security cameras have been installed around the mountain. A single road (40km) circles Sakurajima at sea level, past a couple of observation points, lava fields and onsen baths – the island's smouldering cone provides tangible proof of just how their waters have been heated. Kagoshima's **Welcome Cute pass** (see p.766) can be used for getting to and around the island.

EXPLOSIVE ISLAND

Major **eruptions** of Sakurajima have been recorded from the early eighth century, but the most violent in living memory was that of 1914, during which enough lava spilled down the southeast slopes to fill the 400m-wide channel that previously separated Sakurajima from the mainland. Volcanic activity has increased since 1955, with thousands of small explosions occurring every year, and scientists now predict another major eruption within the next thirty years. During periods of high activity, the likely direction of the **ash cloud** forms part of the weather forecasts on TV – it usually heads northeast during colder months, and west (towards Kagoshima city centre) in the summer, when you may find yourself crunching granules of dust that were, just a few hours beforehand, several hundred metres below the surface of the earth, and considerably hotter. Sakurajima's prime **viewing point** is its eastern coast at night-time – if you're in luck, you may well see the faraway glow of molten lava.

Yunohira Observatory

East of the island's ferry terminal, a tortuous route heads up the volcano's west flank to the **Yunohira Observatory** (373m). This is the closest you can get to the deeply creviced summit, which in fact comprises three cones, from the highest, northerly Kita-dake (1117m), to Minami-dake (1040m), the most active, in the south. Weather permitting, you'll also be treated to sweeping views of Kagoshima Bay.

The rest of the island

10

Heading along the island's south coast, Sakurajima's brooding presence becomes more apparent as you start to see the lava fields around the **Arimura Observatory**, barren since the devastating explosion of 1914 (see box opposite). A little further on, past the narrow isthmus, look out on the left for the *torii* of Kurokami-jinja, buried in 1914. It was originally 3m tall, but now just the top crossbars protrude from a bed of ash and pumice. Along the north coast, the slopes get gentler and you'll see plenty of crops growing in the fertile volcanic soils, which produce not only the world's largest radishes – up to 40kg in weight and over 1m in diameter – but also its smallest mandarins, measuring a mere 3cm across.

ARRIVAL AND INFORMATION

SAKURAJIMA

By ferry Ferries from Kagoshima (15min; ¥160) dock at a small pier on Sakurajima's west coast. The service operates 24 hours a day, with sailings every 15min from 6am to 8.30pm; you pay at the Sakurajima end. If you fancy spending longer on the water, take the special daily sailing at 11.05am (the Yorimichi Cruise; ¥500, pay at the Kagoshima pier), which cruises around the bay for 50min, passing lava islands produced by the 1914 eruption, on its voyage from Kagoshima to Sakurajima. In Kagoshima, the pier is east of the city centre

near the aquarium; it's a stop on both City View bus routes or a 5min walk from Suizokukan-guchi tram stop.
Tourist information The visitor centre (daily 9am–5pm; ☎ 099 293 2443, ⓦ sakurajima-kinkowan-geo.jp/en) is an easy 10min walk from the Sakurajima ferry terminal, around the south side of the harbour just beyond the *Rainbow Sakurajima* hotel. Fronted by a bayside park with free hot-spring footbaths, it has English-speaking staff and exhibits and audiovisuals about the volcano.

GETTING AROUND

Sakurajima Regular Sightseeing Bus Most people get around using the Sakurajima Regular Sightseeing Bus, which loops up to Yunohira Observatory before doing a complete circuit of Sakurajima. It departs twice daily from Kagoshima Chūō Station (East Exit, bus stop E-8; 8.55am & 1.40pm; 3hr 40min; ¥2300 including return ferry tickets); you can also pick it up from Sakurajima ferry terminal (9.40am & 2.30pm; 2hr 10min; ¥1800).
Sakurajima Island View Bus Alternatively, once on the island, you can also use the Sakurajima Island View Bus, which just does the shorter loop up to the Yunohira Observatory and

back (8 daily; 1hr, including stops at Yunohira and two other lookout points; ¥120–440, or ¥500 for a day pass).
By car and bike The island is much too large to walk, but Sakurajima Rent-a-Car (☎ 099 293 2162) rents cars (¥4800 for 2hr, then ¥1000/hr) and bicycles (¥300/hr) just outside the ferry terminal. Note that if you're cycling, it's best to go clockwise around the island (around 4hr), as you will usually be on the outside of the road and thus more visible to cars. If you're only planning a short ride, you'll find the north coast far nicer than the south, where most of the traffic pours through on the way to the ferries.

ACCOMMODATION AND EATING

Rainbow Sakurajima レインボー桜島 1722-16 Yokoyama-chō ☎ 099 293 2323. This modern hotel on the seafront, less than a 10min walk south round the harbour from the ferry terminal, makes a good base for exploring the island. It offers a mix of Japanese and Western (twin-bedded) rooms and a big onsen bath with views of Kinko Bay (¥390 for non-guests; Mon, Tues & Thurs–Sun 10am–10pm, Wed 1–10pm). Sharing these bay views, its restaurant is a good lunch option for day-trippers: udon sets go for ¥880, and more expensive

specialities include local *wagyu* beef, lobster (in season) and *kurobuta* (pork from black pigs). Restaurant daily 11.30am–2pm. 🛜 **¥9980**
Sakurajima Youth Hostel 桜島ユースホステル 189 Yokoyama-chō ☎ 099 293 2150, ⓦ e-yh.net /kagoshima. This relaxed, 100-bed hostel with an onsen bath, laundry and spacious common areas is a 10min walk uphill from the ferry terminal – just follow the signs. Meals available. Dorms **¥2721**

Ibusuki and around

指宿

Japan's third-largest hot-spring resort by volume of water, the small town of **IBUSUKI** is a low-key, relaxed place, where onsen-goers clank around in their wooden sandals, wearing the different coloured *yukata* of competing ryokan. The town's main attributes are an attractive setting on a sweeping bay and a **sand bath** where you can be buried up to the neck in hot sand – a more enjoyable experience than it sounds. Ibusuki's main north–south avenue is palm-tree-lined **Hibiscus-dōri**, while **Chūō-dōri**, which counts as Ibusuki's prime shopping street, leads from the JR station to meet Hibiscus-dōri and the sea at the bay's midpoint.

Surigahama

摺ヶ浜 • Sand bath daily 8.30am–8.30pm, closed Mon–Fri noon–1pm • ¥1080, including sand bath, onsen and *yukata* rental; ¥200 to borrow a bath towel • ☎ 0993 23 3900, ⓦ sa-raku.sakura.ne.jp

Ten minutes' walk south of Chūō-dōri brings you to the southern stretch of beach known as **Surigahama**, where a clutch of shops and restaurants gathers around the famous **sand bath** (*suna-mushi*). Like much of Japan's coast, the beach is protected by concrete breakwaters, but a few stretches of black volcanic sand remain, from which wisps of scalding steam mark the presence of hot springs.

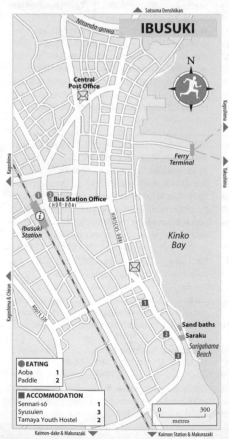

Taking a sand bath is the done thing in Ibusuki, and is best at low tide when you can be buried on the beach itself, leaving just a row of heads visible beneath snazzy sunshades; at high tide a raised bed beside the sea wall is used. You can buy tickets (and a small souvenir towel to wrap round your head) and change into a *yukata* in the modern **Saraku** (砂楽) bathhouse immediately behind the beach. You then troop down to the beach and lie down. At over 50°C, the sand temperature is much hotter than at Beppu (see p.746), and most people find it difficult to last the recommended ten minutes. All sorts of claims are made as to the sand bath's medical benefits, but if nothing else it leaves you feeling wonderfully invigorated, especially if you finish off with an onsen back at Saraku.

Satsuma Denshōkan

薩摩伝承館 • In Ryokan Ibusuki Hakusuikan, about 3km north of the station • Daily 8.30am–7pm • ¥1500 (including English audio guide) • ☎ 0993 23 0211, ⓦ satsuma -denshokan.com • Buses roughly hourly to Gatayama stop

A gorgeous double-roofed building in a Nara/Heian style, surrounded by a rippling pond, **Satsuma Denshōkan** stands in the grounds of a luxury ryokan and was built eight years ago for the owners' art and history collections. The ground floor showcases **Kinrande**, elaborate, multicoloured stoneware decorated with high-relief gold, which was produced around Kagoshima and became very popular in the West in the late nineteenth century. It all looks rather gaudy for modern tastes, and you'll probably find the first-floor displays of more restrained, early **Satsuma ware** and beautiful imperial Chinese ceramics more appealing.

Kaimon-dake

10

開聞岳 • From Ibusuki Station take the JR line to Kaimon Station (8 daily; 35min)

Though rather small at 922m, the triangular peak of **Kaimon-dake** is known locally as "Satsuma Fuji". The volcano last erupted some 15,000 years ago and some of it is now a nature park inhabited by wild Tokara ponies. The classic route up Kaimon-dake is from Kaimon Station, the start of a 5km-long path which spirals round the cone. It takes about two hours each way and the effort is rewarded with views south to the islands of Yakushima and Tanegashima, and north beyond Sakurajima to Kirishima.

ARRIVAL AND INFORMATION

IBUSUKI

By train The easiest and quickest way to reach Ibusuki is on the JR line from Kagoshima Chūō (1–2 hourly; 50min–1hr 20min; ¥1000), which features special Ibusuki-no-tamatebako trains three times a day (see box, p.701); sit on the east side of the train for sea views. Ibusuki Station is on the west side of town.

By bus Buses stop on the road outside the station, and the Kagoshima Kōtsū bus office is across the road.

By jetfoil It's also possible to arrive by jetfoil from Kagoshima (1–2 daily; 40min; ¥2500), which offers views across Kinko Bay if you manage to reserve a window seat. The jetfoils head on to Yakushima (see p.773; 1hr 15min; ¥7000).

Tourist information There's a tourist information desk inside the train station (daily 9am–6pm; ☎0993 22 4114), which rents out electric bikes (¥500/2hr).

ACCOMMODATION

Sennari-sō 千成荘 5-10-9 Yunohana ☎0993 22 3379. Good-value place 200m north of the sand bath on Hibiscus-dōri, with a home-like atmosphere, friendly staff and small but sparkling en-suite tatami rooms. Dinner and breakfast available. 🛜 **¥8840**

★**Syusuien** 秀水園 South end of Hibiscus-dōri ☎0993 22 6789, ⑩syusuien.co.jp. Excellent, very traditional ryokan with immaculate service and spacious, en-suite tatami rooms, decorated throughout with beautiful objets d'art. The public and private onsen are lovely, and the restaurant, where the private rooms are

designed like a lane of cottages, serves truly superb *kaiseki* meals (open to non-guests; from ¥5000; reservations advised). Restaurant Mon–Fri 6–8pm, Sat & Sun 11am–1pm & 6–8pm. 🛜 **¥40,000**

Tamaya Youth Hostel 圭屋ユースホステル 5-27-8 Yunohana ☎0993 22 3553, ⑩jyh.or.jp. Acceptable place to stay opposite the sand bath, about a 15min walk from the station, with Japanese- and Western-style dorms, dinner and breakfast available and a computer for guest use. 🛜 Dorms **¥3325**

EATING

Aoba 青葉 1-2-11 Minato ☎0993 22 3356. Conveniently located on the main road just north of the station, this restaurant serves a broad range of inexpensive dishes, including *kurobuta* (black pork), local eels and *kaiseki* dinners from ¥2050. 11am–2.30pm & 5.30–9.30pm;

closed Wed.

Paddle パドル 1-6-3 Minato ☎0993 24 4175. Nice *izakaya*-style venue that's just about the only non-seedy place to drink in town. They also do cheap pizzas, pastas and curries (¥700–900). 🛜 Mon–Sat 6pm–midnight.

Chiran

知覧

A small town lying in a broad valley, **CHIRAN** owes its fortune to the Shimazu lords of Kagoshima (see p.761). In the eighteenth century, the Shimazu's chief retainers, the Sata family, were permitted to build a semi-fortified village, and a number of their handsome **samurai houses** survive today. Two hundred years later, an airfield on the outskirts of Chiran became a base for kamikaze suicide bombers during World War II, now commemorated by a **museum** on site. The road to it from the town centre is lined with stone lanterns, one for each pilot.

The samurai houses

武家屋敷, Buke Yashiki • Daily 9am–5pm • ¥500 • ☎ 0993 58 7878, ⓦ chiran-bukeyashiki.jp

10

On the east side of the town centre, several **samurai houses** – known as *buke yashiki* – are scattered along an attractive lane that runs for 700m parallel to and south of the main road towards Kagoshima, behind ancient stone walls topped by neatly clipped hedges. Since many of the houses are still occupied, you can't see inside, but the main interest lies in their small but intricate **gardens**, some said to be the work of designers brought from Kyoto. Seven gardens, indicated by signs in English, are open to the public. Though each is different in its composition, they mostly use rock groupings and shrubs to represent a classic scene of mountains, valleys and waterfalls taken from Chinese landscape painting. In the best of them, such as the gardens of **Hirayama Katsumi** and **Hirayama Ryōichi**, the design also incorporates the hills behind as "borrowed scenery". Look out, too, for defensive features such as solid, screened entry gates and latrines beside the front gate – apparently, this was so that the occupant could eavesdrop on passers-by.

Hotaru-kan

ホタル館 • Daily 9am–5pm • ¥400

The main road runs roughly east–west through Chiran town centre: just after it crosses the river for the first time, five minutes' walk from the samurai houses, you'll find **Hotaru-kan**, a moving museum that commemorates the young kamikaze pilots. During the war this old wooden house was a restaurant, run by a motherly figure called Torihama Tome, who saw hundreds of young pilots pass through on their way to certain death. Many left personal possessions and messages for their families with Tome-san, some of which are now on display, alongside deeply moving pictures, letters and personal effects. Unfortunately, there are no English-language translations.

Special Attack Peace Hall

特攻平和会館, Tokko Heiwa Kaikan • 2km southwest of the town centre on the main road towards Makurazaki • Daily 9am–5pm • ¥500, or ¥600 including Museum Chiran (see opposite); audio guide ¥100 • ☎ 0993 83 2525, ⓦ chiran-tokkou.jp

The **Special Attack Peace Hall** (aka Chiran Peace Museum) marks the site of a military airfield that was established in 1941. Three years later Chiran was chosen as the main base for the "Special Attack Forces", known in the west as **kamikaze** pilots. During the battle of Okinawa (see p.783), 1036 pilots died; before leaving, they were given a last cigarette, a drink of sake and a blessing, after which they donned their "rising sun" headband and set off on the lonely, one-way mission with enough fuel to last for two hours. It seems that many never reached their target: the toll was 56 American ships sunk, 107 crippled and 300 seriously damaged.

The hall, which was established in 1975, is essentially a memorial to the pilots' undoubted courage and makes little mention of the wider context or moral argument. That aside, the photos, farewell letters and the pilots' often childish mascots are tragic mementoes of the young lives wasted. Several pilots' letters reveal that, though they knew the war was lost, they were still willing to make the ultimate sacrifice – you'll see many older Japanese people walking round in tears and it's hard not to be moved, despite the chilling overtones. Since very little is translated into English, make sure you pick up an audio guide at the ticket desk.

Museum Chiran

ミュージアム知覧, Myūjiamu Chiran • 2km southwest of the town centre on the main road towards Makurazaki • 9am–5pm; closed Wed • ¥300, or ¥600 including the Special Attack Peace Hall (see opposite) • ☎ 0993 83 4433

Beside the Peace Hall, you can visit the more cheerful **Museum Chiran**. Concentrating on local history and culture, its exhibits are beautifully displayed, with the most interesting showing the strong influence of Okinawan culture on Kagoshima's festivals and crafts.

ARRIVAL AND INFORMATION

By bus Bus services to Chiran from Kagoshima run more or less hourly (1hr 20min), stopping at the samurai houses a few minutes before Hotaru-kan (Nakagori-machi stop), and the Peace Hall a few minutes after; the last bus back to Kagoshima is usually around 6.30pm. Buses from the sand baths and the station in Ibusuki serve the same stops in the opposite direction (5 daily; 1hr 10min).

Tourist information In the expansive car parks in front of the Peace Hall, you'll find the town's information office (daily 9am–4pm; ☎ 0993 83 1120), where you can pick up handy maps and bus timetables.

EATING

Nagōmi 和 Overlooking a car park behind Hotaru-kan ☎ 0993 83 1753. One of the nicest places to eat in Chiran is this old wooden, tatami-matted house set in gardens, which offers a range of well-priced set lunches from ¥800. 11am–2pm; closed Wed.

Taki-an 高城庵 East end of the samurai houses street ☎ 0993 83 3186. In this lovely, thatched former samurai house, you can sit on the tatami mats and admire the rock and moss garden. Their speciality is soba and udon, or try the sweet *jambo-mochi* (pounded rice on bamboo skewers). Daily 10.30am–2.30pm.

Yakushima

屋久島

Craggy mountain peaks; wave after wave of dripping rainforest; towering cedar trees which predate the Roman Empire; and the all-pervasive scent of moss and flowers – if this all sounds a little like the setting for an anime, rather than real-life Japan, you'd be half-right: Miyazaki Hayao was said to have taken his inspiration from **Yakushima**'s lush forests when creating *Princess Mononoke* (see p.861). Logging companies worked the forests until the early 1970s, but now much of the island is protected within the **Yakushima National Park**, a UNESCO World Heritage Site. Climbing steeply from the sea some 60km off Cape Sata, Yakushima encompasses the eight highest mountains in Kyūshū, centred on 1935m-high **Miyanoura-dake**. It's one of the rainiest places in Japan, with an average annual rainfall of at least 4m on the coast and a staggering 8–10m in its mountainous interior. All this creates an astonishing vertical distribution of vegetation, ranging from subtropical at the coast to subarctic on the peaks, where the Yakushima gentian numbers among the island's 94 endemic plant species.

Yakushima's population of around 13,000 is confined to the coast, concentrated in the two main towns of **Miyanoura** and **Anbō**. An increasingly popular tourist destination, Yakushima now boasts a number of swish resort hotels in addition to simpler accommodation. Most people, however, come to hike and camp among the peaks, where the **Yaku-sugi** (Japanese cedars more than a thousand years old) are found. For the less adventurous, **Shiratani Unsuikyō** and **Yaku-sugi Land** forest reserves contain a few more accessible trees and can be reached by public bus. Otherwise, there are a couple of good local **museums**, seaside **onsen** on the south coast, and several **beaches**, two of which – Isso and Nakama – offer decent snorkelling. Lastly, if you're in luck, you may get to see **rocket launches** from the nearby island of Tanegashima, the centre of the Japanese space agency.

There are no dry months here, but the best time to visit is May, when the rhododendrons are at their best, or during the autumn months of October and November. June sees by far the highest rainfall, followed by a steamy July and August. Winter brings snow to the peaks, although sea-level temperatures hover around 15°C.

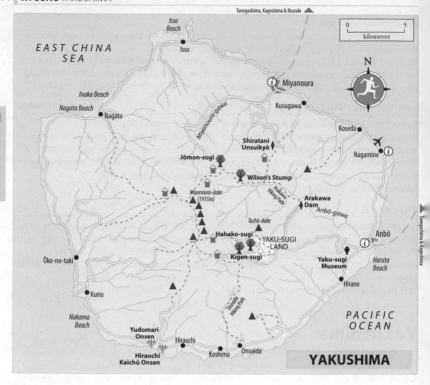

Miyanoura

宮之浦

While first impressions of **MIYANOURA**, Yakushima's main town, aren't very favourable, the place soon grows on visitors, and it's a delight to walk around the port and simply appreciate the calm atmosphere.

Yakushima Environmental and Cultural Village Centre

屋久島環境文化村センター, Yakushima Kankyō Bunkamura Sentā • Daily 9am–5pm; closed third Tues of month (not Aug) & second half of Feb • Film hourly; 25min • ¥520 • ☎ 0997 42 2900, ⓦ yakushima.or.jp

The informative **Yakushima Environmental and Cultural Village Centre** is set in a modern white building, just two minutes' walk up from the ferry pier. The exhibits are arranged in a spiral, proceeding from the ocean up through village life and the cedar forests to the mountain tops. Allow time to see the film, projected onto a huge screen, which takes you on a fabulous helicopter ride over the island.

Shiratani Unsuikyō

白谷雲水峡 • 24hr • ¥300 • Bus from Miyanoura port (4 daily; 35min)

Dank, mossy and mysterious, the forest reserve of **Shiratani Unsuikyō**, 12km south of Miyanoura, offers an easy opportunity to encounter Yaku-sugi (Japanese cedars). Two looped trails (1–3hr) and an in-and-out route (4hr; the first part of the longer trail to Jōmon-sugi – see opposite) lead through old-growth forests of laurel. Along the way the trails pass crashing waterfalls and a dozen of the ancient cedars, some of which have whole epiphytic rowan trees growing on them, producing a spectacular display in autumn.

Inland from Anbō

From Miyanoura, the main road leads southeast past the airport to the rather scruffy town of **Anbō** (安房). Here, you turn inland for a wonderful forty-minute ride into the mountains, corkscrewing up into a lost world wreathed in drifting cloud banks. Every so often there are glimpses of plunging, tree-filled valleys, the lush greens accentuated by cascading, ice-white torrents.

Yaku-sugi Museum

屋久杉自然館, Yaku-sugi Shizen-kan • Daily 9am–5pm • ¥600 • ☏ 0977 46 3113, ⊛ yakusugi-museum.com • Bus from Anbō (2 daily; 5min)

Some 2km outside Anbō on the road up to the interior, the well-designed **Yaku-sugi Museum** is full of fascinating displays about the ancient cedar trees, revealing that they're so resistant to decay and insects because of their high resin content. There's also a stump and cross section of a 1660-year-old tree and a virtual reconstruction of Wilson's Stump (see below) as it might have looked today if it hadn't been felled.

10

Yaku-sugi Land

屋久杉ランド • 24hr • ¥300 • Bus from Anbō (2 daily; 40min to Yaku-sugi Land, 1hr to Kigen-sugi)

At around 1000m above sea level, a wooden resthouse marks the entrance to **YAKU-SUGI LAND**, a forest reserve that contains four looped **walking trails** varying in length from 800m (around 30min) to 3km (around 2hr 30min). The three shortest and most popular walks wind along an attractive river valley that is home to several thousand-year-old cedar trees, their gnarled roots clinging to the rock, as well as clumps of rhododendron, and macaques and deer. For those with the time and energy, the longest course is by far the most interesting, taking you deeper and higher into the forest past another four Yaku-sugi, of which the oldest is the 2600-year-old **Hahako-sugi** ("Mother-and-child Cedar").

Near the terminus of the bus route, 6km up the paved road from Yaku-sugi Land stands **Kigen-sugi**, a grand old lady of 3000 years with 21 kinds of epiphyte living on her, including rhododendron and rowan.

Jōmon-sugi

縄文杉 • Bus to Arakawa Dam from Yaku-sugi Museum (March–Nov 4–8 daily; 35min); or bus to Shiratani Unsuikyō from Miyanoura port (4 daily; 35min)

The trees in Yaku-sugi Land are mere saplings compared with the great **Jōmon-sugi**, whose mossy, tattered trunk, 16.4m in circumference, looks more like rock face than living tissue. The tree is at least 2300 years old, though some estimates go back 7200 years, which would make it pre-date Ancient Egypt – since its centre has rotted away it's impossible to tell exactly. Growing 1300m up in the forest and five hours' hike from the nearest road, the tree was only discovered in 1968, an event which sparked moves to protect the forests and create the tourist industry that now accounts for over half the island's economy.

Jōmon-sugi stands on the north face of **Miyanoura-dake** (宮之浦岳), 2km west of **Wilson's Stump**, the remnant of a 2000-year-old Yaku-sugi named after an early twentieth-century English botanist. The tree was felled by order of Toyotomi Hideyoshi in 1586 to build a giant Buddha temple in Kyoto, and now shelters a spring and a shrine in its massive hollow interior.

There are two **trailheads** for the walk to Jōmon-sugi via Wilson's Stump, both accessible by bus: the Arakawa Dam; and the more distant Shiratani Unsuikyō (see opposite).

Onoaida and the south-coast onsen

Hirauchi Kaichū Onsen 平内海中温泉 • Low tide only • ¥100 • **Yudomari Onsen** 湯泊温泉 • 24hr, closed Tues morning for cleaning • ¥100 • Bus from Miyanoura via Anbō (roughly hourly; 1hr 20min)

On Yakushima's southern coast, the area around the tiny town of **Onoaida** (尾之間) is surrounded by orchards of tropical fruits, such as mango, papaya, lychee and orange, while bright sprays of bougainvillea and bird-of-paradise flowers decorate the villages.

10

A few kilometres west of Onoaida, **Hirauchi Kaichū Onsen** makes the perfect place to kick back with the locals in a hot rock pool overlooking the sea. You just have to get the timing right – the pool is only uncovered for an hour or two either side of low tide – though most locals and the tourist offices will be able to tell you the times each day. If the tide doesn't agree with your own schedule, head 500m west along the coast to the slightly less scenic, lukewarm rock pool of **Yudomari Onsen**.

ARRIVAL AND DEPARTURE YAKUSHIMA

By plane Yakushima's tiny airport (☎ 099 742 1200), roughly midway between Miyanoura and Anbō, is served by all buses between the two towns.
Destinations Fukuoka (1 daily; 1hr); Kagoshima (5–7 daily; 35min); Osaka (Itami; 1 daily; 1hr 35min).
By hydrofoil Toppy "jetfoils" run between Kagoshima and Yakushima (6–7 daily; 1hr 50min–2hr 45min; ¥8800; ⓦ tykousoku.jp); you can buy tickets from a travel agent or at their offices in Kagoshima (☎ 099 226 0128), Miyanoura

(☎ 099 742 2003) or Anbō (☎ 099 746 3399). Some of these services also stop at Tanegashima or Ibusuki (p.770) en route; most of them dock at Miyanoura, but one or two use Anbō port. You're not allowed to leave your seat during the voyage, so arrive early for your departure if you'd like to bag a window seat. Bear in mind that hydrofoils stop running in bad weather.
By ferry The *Ferry Yakushima 2* departs daily from Kagoshima (4hr; ¥4900); buy tickets at the terminal.

GETTING AROUND

By bus Yakushima's road system consists of one quiet highway circumnavigating the island, plus a few spurs running up into the mountains. Buses depart roughly hourly from outside the Toppy terminal on Miyanoura ferry pier for Anbō (40min; ¥810) and the *Iwasaki Hotel* in Onoaida (1hr; ¥1270). There are also buses from Miyanoura and Anbō up into the mountains. If you're planning to get around by bus, it's well worth getting hold of a bus pass (1 day ¥2000; 2 or 3 days ¥3000; 4 days ¥4000; not valid for the Arakawa Dam bus).
By car The biggest rental company, Toyota, has branches at Miyanoura port (☎ 099 742 2000) and the airport

(☎ 099 743 5180), and operates a taxi service. Make sure you keep the tank topped up since there are no petrol stations on west Yakushima between Hirauchi and Nagata; many of those on the rest of the island close in the evening and on Sundays.
By bicycle You can rent bikes (¥1000/day) at the Yakushima Kankō Center (屋久島観光センター), on the main road opposite the Miyanoura ferry terminal; and at You Shop in Anbō (ⓦ youshop-nangoku.jimdo.com). In summer, the latter opens a shop in Miyanoura and allows one-way rentals.

INFORMATION AND ACTIVITIES

Tourist information The most useful tourist office, with helpful English-speaking staff, is in the Yakushima Environmental and Cultural Village Centre (see p.774) in Miyanoura (daily 9am–5pm; ☎ 099 742 1019). You can pick up bus timetables, maps and brochures here and they can book accommodation. There are also offices at Anbō port (daily 9am–6pm; ☎ 099 746 2333) and the airport (daily 9am–6pm; ☎ 099 749 4010). The website Yakumonkey (ⓦ yakumonkey.com) has good, up-to-date information.
Services Half a dozen post offices on the island, including

in Miyanoura and Anbō, have international ATMs. The Yakushima Kankō Centre, on the main road opposite the entrance to Miyanoura ferry pier, offers a left-luggage service (¥300/bag/day).
Dive and hiking equipment There are a number of dive and hiking shops on the island that rent gear; enquire at the Miyanoura tourist office for details.
Adventure tours The Yakushima Nature Activity Centre (☎ 099 742 0944, ⓦ ynac.com) on the main drag in Miyanoura offers guided hiking, mountain biking, canyoning, kayaking, snorkelling and scuba diving.

ACCOMMODATION

Yakushima has a fair range of **accommodation**, but you still need to plan well ahead during holiday periods. Note that those hiking the interior can make use of unstaffed **mountain huts**, basic shelters without electricity or cooking facilities; ask at one of the island's tourist offices for advice.

MIYANOURA
Yakushima Youth Hostel 屋久島ユースホステル ☎ 099 749 1316, ⓦ yakushima-yh.net. Conveniently located just a 10min walk round the harbour from the ferry pier, this has simple but pleasing rooms, a seaside terrace,

and a computer, washing machine and mini-kitchen for guest use. ☎ Dorms **¥3560**
Yakusugi-sō 屋久杉荘 ☎ 099 742 0023. On the east bank of the river south of the main bridge, this gorgeous minshuku has well-appointed tatami rooms, which range

from cosy to absolutely huge, most sharing bathrooms. Free pick-up from the port, and breakfast and dinner included. 🛜 **¥15,000**

★**Yaman-kami** 山ん神 ☎099 742 0618, �🌐www5 .synapse.ne.jp/yamankami. One of the cheapest minshuku in the area, and it's quite lovely – built in a sort of chalet style, its tatami rooms are simple and have shared facilities, but are perfectly comfortable. It's on the west side of the river, backing up against the hillside; free pick-ups from the port. Room-only **¥6000**

ANBŌ

Minshuku Shiho 民宿志保 ☎099 746 3288. The best cheap option in the area – a white bungalow shaded by palm trees, it's the first building you come to on the road up from the pier, and provides spick-and-span, no-frills tatami rooms. No evening meals served. Breakfast included. **¥10,000**

★**Sankara** 8km south of Anbō ☎099 747 3488,

🌐sankarahotel-spa.com. At this appealing boutique hotel, the rooms have been designed in keeping with Yakushima's natural vibe, and all have balconies with a sea view. The attached spa is rather heavenly, while the main on-site restaurant serves local ingredients in a distinctively French style. Half-board per person **¥31,000**

ONOAIDA

Iwasaki Hotel いわさきホテル ☎099 747 3888, 🌐iwasakihotels.com. Luxury hotel in expansive grounds on a hill overlooking Onoaida, with an onsen and a four-storey replica Yaku-sugi in the atrium. The Japanese- and Western-style rooms are very spacious and comfortable, with French windows and balconies to make the most of the views. The very good, top-floor restaurant is open to non-residents (two-course lunch ¥1130, *kaiseki* dinner from ¥6000 or à la carte). Restaurant daily noon–2pm & 6–9pm. **¥25,000**

EATING AND DRINKING

MIYANOURA

Jane ジェーン Yakushima Environmental and Cultural Village Centre. Cool, friendly café with jazz on the sound system, serving flying fish sashimi on rice (¥1200), noodles, simple Western breakfasts, espresso coffees and a wide range of teas. 🛜 Daily 11am–5pm.

★**Naminohana** 波の華 5min walk south of Miyanoura's main bridge on the Shiratani Unsuikyō road, 50m beyond A Coop on the right ☎099 742 3955. This is where the locals come to eat: don't expect an English-language menu, or speedy service; do expect an exceedingly cheery atmosphere in the evenings, and

delicious meals of *kurobuta nabe* (¥1300) and flying fish (*tobi-uo*), the local speciality (¥1000 for a set) – the dish lands on your table with its wings still on, like a little fried angel. Tues–Sun 11.30am–2pm & 6–10pm, or when the last customer leaves.

ANBŌ

Rengaya れんが屋 On the road down to the harbour ☎099 746 3439. This pleasantly rustic venue specializes in venison but offers a varied menu, including *yakiniku* (meat barbecued at your table) and *tonkatsu* (pork cutlets), with set meals from around ¥1500. Daily 11am–2pm & 6–10pm.

10

Okinawa

沖縄

OKINAWA CHURAUMI AQUARIUM

Okinawa

Mention Okinawa to a mainland Japanese and you'll likely receive a wistful sigh in return. Perpetually warm weather, clear seas bursting with fish, fantastic food, gentle people, unspoiled beaches and jungles ... the list could go on. More than one hundred subtropical islands, collectively known as the Ryūkyū Shotō, stretch over 700km of ocean from Kyūshū southwest to Yonaguni-jima, within sight of Taiwan on a clear day, and provide one of Japan's favourite getaways. Getting here may be a little costly, but Okinawa's lush vegetation, vision-of-paradise beaches and superb coral reefs can charm even the most jaded traveller – if you've had your fill of shrines and temples and want to check out some of Japan's best beaches and dive sites, or simply fancy a spot of winter sun, then Okinawa is well worth a visit.

11

The largest island in the group, **Okinawa-Hontō**, usually referred to simply as Okinawa, is the region's transport hub and home to its prefectural capital, **Naha**. It's also the most heavily populated and developed of the Ryūkyū chain, thanks largely to the controversial presence of **American military bases** (see box, p.794). Okinawa-Hontō boasts a number of historical sights, many of them associated with the **Battle of Okinawa** at the end of the Pacific War (see p.783). But the island has more to offer than just battlegrounds, particularly in its northern region, where the old way of life still survives among the isolated villages.

To see the best of Japan's most distinctive prefecture, you'll have to hop on a plane or ferry and explore the dozens of **outer islands** away from Okinawa-Hontō, many of them uninhabited. One of the most accessible places to head for is **Zamami-jima**, part of the **Kerama Islands** and just a short ferry ride west of Naha, which offers great beaches and diving and has recently become a centre for whale-watching. For a real sense of escape, however, you need to go further south, to **Miyako-jima** and the **Yaeyama Islands**. The latter grouping includes mountainous **Ishigaki-jima**; **Taketomi-jima**, a tiny place with almost no traffic and a languid, end-of-the-line feel; and nearby **Iriomote-jima**, often described as Japan's last wilderness. On most of these islands, it's the scenery and watersports that provide the main attractions, but Iriomote has the added distinction of its unique wildlife population (including the elusive Iriomote lynx) and lush, almost tropical, rainforest.

With its subtropical **climate**, Okinawa stays warm throughout the year. Average annual temperatures are around 23°C, with a winter average of 17°C and a minimum of 10°C. Winter (or what passes for it) stretches between December and February, while the hot, humid summer can start as early as April, and continues into September. Temperatures at this time hover around 34°C, and the sun can be pretty intense, though the sea breezes help. The **best time to visit** is in spring or autumn (roughly

BUFFALO CART, OKINAWA

Highlights

❶ **Diving** From the soft corals and tropical fish around the Kerama Islands to the enigmatic rocks near Yonaguni-jima, Okinawa offers a wealth of outstanding diving experiences. **See p.784**

❷ **Shuri-jō** Perhaps the most distinctive of Japan's wonderful array of castles, this World Heritage-listed re-creation of the Ryūkyū kingdom's former base is Naha's crowning glory. **See p.787**

❸ **Okinawa Churaumi Aquarium** Get to grips with Okinawa's diverse sea life without the need to don diving gear at one of the world's most spectacular aquariums. **See p.798**

❹ **Zamami-jima** Just a short ferry ride from Naha, this island has some of Japan's finest beaches and offers the chance to spot whales or snorkel with turtles. **See p.799**

❺ **Taketomi-jima** Wave goodbye to the day-trippers and watch the stars come out on this tiny, beach-fringed island. **See p.811**

❻ **Iriomote-jima** Take advantage of the great kayaking and trekking opportunities on this adventure paradise, or kick back on the remote, yet serenely beautiful, beach near Funauki. **See p.813**

HIGHLIGHTS ARE MARKED ON THE MAP ON P.782

RYŪKYŪ CULTURE

On Okinawa's outer islands, you'll find evidence of the much-vaunted **Ryūkyū culture**, borne of contact with Taiwan and China, as well as the rest of Japan. The most obvious expressions of this culture are found in the islands' cuisine and in a vibrant use of colour and bold tropical patterns, while the Chinese influence is clearly visible in the region's architecture, traditional dress and the martial art of **karate** – the Ryūkyū warriors' preferred mode of protection. Ancient religious beliefs are kept alive by shamen (called *yuta*) and, in central Okinawa-Hontō, there are sumo bouts between bulls. There's also a Ryūkyū dialect, with dozens of variations between the different islands, unique musical instruments, and a distinctive musical style that has reached an international audience through bands such as Nēnēs, Diamantes and Champloose (see p.846).

If you're lucky, you'll stumble upon **local festivals**, such as tug-of-war contests or dragon-boat races, while the biggest annual event is the **Eisā festival** (on the fifteenth day of the seventh lunar month, usually late August or early September), when everyone downs tools and dances to the incessant rhythms of drums, flutes and the three-stringed *sanshin*.

11

March to early May and late September to December). The rainy season lasts from early May to early June, while typhoons can be a problem in July and August, and occasionally all the way into October.

Brief history

In the fifteenth century, the islands that now make up Okinawa were united for the first time into the **Ryūkyū kingdom**, governed from Shuri-jō in present-day Naha. This period is seen as the golden era of Ryūkyū culture. Trade with China, the rest of Japan and other Southeast Asian countries flourished, while the traditionally non-militarized kingdom maintained its independence by paying **tribute to China**. But then, in 1609, the **Shimazu** clan of Kagoshima (southern Kyūshū) invaded. The Ryūkyū kings became **vassals** to the Shimazu, who imposed punitive taxes and ruled with an iron hand for the next two hundred years, using the islands as a gateway for trade with China when such contact was theoretically outlawed by the Tokugawa Shogunate. When the Japanese feudal system was

OKINAWA

HIGHLIGHTS

1. Diving
2. Shuri-jō
3. Okinawa Churaumi Aquarium
4. Zamami-jima
5. Taketomi-jima
6. Iriomote-jima

abolished in the 1870s, the islands were simply annexed to the mainland as **Okinawa Prefecture**. Against much local opposition, the Meiji government established a military base and tried to eradicate local culture by forcing people to speak Japanese and swear allegiance to the emperor, forbidding schools to teach Ryūkyū history.

Battle of Okinawa

By the early twentieth century, Okinawa had been fairly successfully absorbed into Japan and became a key pawn in Japan's last line of defence during the **Pacific War**. Following the battle of Iwō-jima in March 1945, the American fleet advanced on Okinawa and, after an extensive preliminary bombardment, referred to locally as a "typhoon of steel", the Americans invaded on **April 1, 1945**. It took nearly three months of bitter fighting before General Ushijima, the Japanese commander, committed suicide and the island surrendered. The **Battle of Okinawa** left over 20,000 American troops dead (plus over 50,000 injured) and up to 150,000 on the Japanese side, nearly half of whom were local civilians.

American occupation

It's estimated that one third of the population of Okinawa died in the war, many in **mass suicides** that preceded the surrender, and others from disease and starvation. But the islanders' subsequent anger has been directed at the Japanese government rather than America. Most people feel Okinawa was sacrificed to save the mainland – this was the only major battle fought on Japanese soil – and that they were misled to believe they were luring the American fleet into a trap. Compounding this was the behaviour of Japanese troops, who are accused of denying locals shelter and medical treatment, and ultimately of abandoning them to the Americans.

By comparison, the American invaders were a welcome relief, despite the islanders' worst fears. They brought in much-needed food supplies – Spam was an instant hit, and a precursor of the processed luncheon meat found in pork *champurū* – and gradually helped restore the local economy. This wasn't wholly altruistic, of course, since Okinawa was ideally placed for monitoring events in Southeast Asia. As the 1950s Korean War merged into the Vietnam War, so the **American bases** became a permanent feature of the Okinawa landscape (see box, p.794).

Japanese sovereignty

Okinawa remained under **American jurisdiction** until 1972, when local protests led to the restoration of **Japanese sovereignty**. Since then, the two governments have colluded to maintain an American military presence on the island despite growing opposition, which reached a peak when three American servicemen were found guilty of raping a twelve-year-old schoolgirl in 1995; a similar incident took place in 2008, while 2016 saw demonstrations following the alleged murder of an Okinawan woman by an American military contractor.

WILDLIFE IN OKINAWA

Besides Hokkaidō, Okinawa contains Japan's largest areas of unspoiled natural environment and its greatest biodiversity. Much of this wealth of **wildlife** is underwater, spawned by the warm Kuroshio Current that sweeps up the east coast and allows coral reefs to flourish. But there are a number of endemic species on land, too, including turtles, a crested eagle and the *noguchigera* (Pryer's woodpecker), in addition to Iriomote's wildcat, the *yamaneko*. A less welcome local resident is the highly venomous **habu snake**. It measures around 2m in length, is dark green with a yellow head, and usually lurks in dense vegetation or on roadsides; it rarely ventures into urban areas. As long as you're careful – especially during spring and autumn, when the snakes are more active – you should have no problems; if you are bitten, make for the nearest hospital, where they should have antivenin.

Okinawa has, in recent times, borne witness to some curious political shifts. **Shimajiri Aiko** came to power in the 2007 local elections, winning with a focus on the local economy rather than military issues. However, the latter came to the fore in national elections two years down the line, when **Hatoyama Yukio** was elected prime minister on a pledge to remove, rather than relocate, the Futenma air base (see box, p.794) – his failure to do so saw him step down in disgrace less than a year later. In 2016, **Iha Yōichi** replaced Shimajiri as Okinawa's representative in the national Upper House, after running on an anti-American military ticket.

ARRIVAL AND DEPARTURE

By plane The vast majority of visitors arrive by plane. Most come from the Japanese mainland, though there are international flights to Naha (see p.789). Domestic airlines operate between Naha and most major Japanese cities; Naha acts as a hub for the rest of the islands, though there are direct services from the mainland to Ishigaki and Miyako. While flying can be expensive, overseas visitors can take advantage of the air passes offered by Japan Airlines (JAL) and All Nippon (ANA) (see p.38). In addition, budget carriers (see p.37) fly to the islands: Solaseed to Naha from Kagoshima, Kōbe and Miyazaki (and from Naha on to Ishigaki); Vanilla to Naha from Tokyo (often the cheapest way from the capital); Peach to Naha and Ishigaki from Osaka; and Skymark to Naha from various mainland cities including Kagoshima, Kumamoto, Miyazaki and Kōbe.

By ferry The most pleasant way to get to Okinawa is by ferry: there are sailings to Naha (see p.790) from Tokyo, Osaka and Kōbe, as well as several cities on Kyūshū.

GETTING AROUND

By plane These days, getting around between the island groups is almost entirely done by plane. Using Naha as the main hub, inter-island flights are operated by Japan Transocean Air, Ryūkyū Air Commuter and ANA Wings, with connections to all major islands.

By ferry There are services from Naha to Zamami-jima and other nearby islands, though you'll have to fly to head south to Miyako-jima or the Yaeyama Islands.

The Yaeyamas themselves are well connected by ferry services.

By bus Okinawa-Hontō has a fairly decent bus network; most smaller islands have bus services, though they can be very sparse indeed.

By car The lack of a strong bus network on the smaller islands is a good reason to rent a car: Okinawa is among the most pleasant places to drive in Japan.

DIVING IN OKINAWA

With scores of dive sites around Okinawa-Hontō – and many more around the outer islands – one of the best reasons for visiting Okinawa is to go **diving**. There are plenty of dive shops, but only a few with English-speaking instructors. A useful website is ⓦ divejapan.com, which includes links to operators, articles, dive-site maps and photos. PADI courses are available on Okinawa-Hontō from *Maeda Misaki Divers House* (see p.795) and the American-run *Reef Encounters* (ⓦ reefencounters.org). Once you have your certificate, the islands are yours for the taking. Prices vary, but equipment rental is generally ¥3000–5000, first dives are ¥8000–11,000, and second dives are usually a couple of thousand more. To rent equipment, you should know the metric readings of your height, weight and shoe size.

DIVE SITES

There are great diving opportunities every way you turn on the islands, but the following sites are particularly notable.

Zamami-jima (p.799) Expect fantastic hard corals, more reef fish than you could count in a week and plenty of turtles.

Miyako-jima (p.802) There are over fifty dive spots to choose from, though cave dives are particularly popular.

Ishigaki-jima (p.806) As well as rare blue coral reefs off Shiraho-no-umi, you can expect to swim with barracuda, butterfly fish, redfin fusiliers, spadefish and manta rays.

Iriomote-jima (p.813) There's easily accessible coral in the waters surrounding this enchanting island.

Yonaguni-jima (p.817) For the ultimate dive experience, head way out here to see sea turtles and hammerhead sharks, and to explore the enigmatic rocks that some claim are the remains of a sunken civilization.

Okinawa-Hontō

沖縄本島

Once the centre of the Ryūkyū kingdom, **Okinawa-Hontō**, or Okinawa Main Island, is a strangely ambivalent place. Locals are proud of their Ryūkyū heritage, but to some extent the island still feels like occupied territory, especially in central Okinawa-Hontō where the **American bases** have become a bizarre tourist attraction for mainland Japanese.

Fascinating though all this is, it doesn't make Okinawa-Hontō the most obvious holiday destination. But if you're drawn by the more appealing outer islands (see p.805), chances are you'll spend some time here waiting for plane or ferry connections. Okinawa-Hontō's capital city (and the former Ryūkyū capital) is **Naha**, whose prime attraction is **Shuri-jō**, its reconstructed, World Heritage-listed castle. There are also some interesting market streets and a pottery village to explore, and you might want to take advantage of the banks here – not to mention the excellent bars and restaurants – before heading off.

Southern Okinawa-Hontō saw the worst of the fighting in 1945, and the scrubby hills are littered with **war memorials**, particularly around Mabuni Hill where the final battles took place. North of Naha, the island's central district has little to recommend it, but beyond Kadena the buildings start to thin out. Here you'll find one of the better "Ryūkyū culture villages", **Ryūkyū-mura**, and the island's best beaches. The largest settlement in northern Okinawa-Hontō, **Nago** is also an appealing town for visiting the stunning Okinawa Churaumi Aquarium and exploring the scenic coastline and mountainous tip of the island, culminating in the dramatic cape of **Hedo Misaki**.

11

EAT YOUR WAY TO 100: OKINAWAN CUISINE

The Japanese have famously long average lifespans – the current **life expectancy** is just under 83 years, while 350 people in every million live to 100 years of age. These are both world-ranking toppers, yet in Okinawa those stats go through the roof; the tiny village of **Ōgimi**, on the northeast of the main island (see map, p.786), is often said to be the oldest place on earth, since it boasts over a dozen centenarians. Such figures are put down to the fact that Okinawa has particularly low incidences of heart disease, cancer and other maladies, and this in turn is attributed to the **diet** of the islanders – even more fish, tofu, grains, veggies and soy products than mainland Japan, with a fraction of the meat, sugar or dairy goods. Visiting Okinawa might just add a few weeks to your life; what follows are a few recommended culinary specialities to look out for on your way around.

Gōya champurū A stir-fry featuring egg, pork and slices of *gōya* (bitter melon), this is the most famous Okinawan dish, and when done right it's extremely tasty. Variants include *fū champurū*, which is made with tofu instead of *gōya*.

Shimahata It almost seems a crime to eat such a beautiful fish – this local one's a big fella with gorgeous red and yellow stripes. Other sea goodies to look out for (then gobble) are *irabucha*, a blue parrotfish; *gurukun*, a small fish usually served fried; and *yakōgai*, a giant turban shell.

Sōki soba The local favourite, featuring yellow wheat noodles, spring onions and bonito flakes in a clear soup, with hunks of pork rib – still on the bone, they'll give your chopstick skills a thorough examination. The quality of the pork varies substantially; in some places it's mostly fat and gristle, while in better venues (such as those listed throughout this chapter) the meat is lean and tender. Variants include *Okinawa soba* and *Yaeyama soba*.

Sukugarasu Tiny pieces of tofu topped with a salted minnow. Often served with *awamori* (see below), it should be eaten in one bite.

Taco rice OK, so this one's not so healthy. It would be, if made with the other *tako* (octopus); instead, what we have here is a bed of rice topped with taco ingredients: minced meat, cheese, veggies, tomato salsa and a little spice. As with most unhealthy food, it tastes great.

Umi budō Sold in Naha's market areas as "green caviar", this is actually a strange sort of seaweed, made up of poppable bubbles that do, indeed, resemble sturgeons' eggs. Yummy stuff, it's often served with local sashimi.

Awamori Also worth a mention is Okinawa's own variant on sake; it's anywhere from 30–50 percent alcohol, though even the "weak" stuff can give you a banging headache. Orion is the local beer of choice.

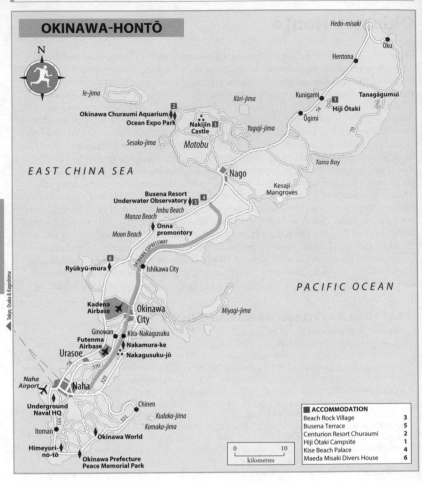

GETTING AROUND

OKINAWA-HONTŌ

By car Long and thin, Okinawa-Hontō measures just 135km from top to toe, so you can drive the whole length in a matter of hours. The best way to get around is to rent your own car or motorbike, particularly if you want to explore the northern hills.

By bus Buses head around the island from Naha, but travelling in this way will likely involve a lot of waiting for connections (see individual accounts for details).

Tours An easier alternative to bus travel or car rental is to join one of the organized bus tours out of Naha, which pack a lot into a short time at a reasonable price. The Hip Hop buses operated by Jumbo Tours (☏ 098 917 5575, ⓦ jumbotours.co.jp) are a good, foreigner-friendly choice with English-language commentary (which notably doesn't run non-stop, unlike most of the Japanese-oriented tours). They run three separate full-day tours from Naha (¥6000–8000), all bookable online.

Naha

那覇

The Okinawan capital of **NAHA** should, in fairness, be a place to get things done and be on one's way. This is the only large city in a region of Japan that leans heavily on nature – despite being capital of the Ryūkyū kingdom for over four hundred years, wartime destruction and rampant commercialization have colluded to ensure that there's precious little to see bar bland residential blocks. Despite this, and the near-constant stream of Japanese holidaymakers, Naha somehow makes a great place to kick back. A fair proportion of the locals you meet will be mainland Japanese, here to trade in a hefty chunk of their salary for a relaxed lifestyle. Foreign travellers often end up staying far longer than they planned – the weather's great, the food's terrific, beaches and bars are never far away, and busting a gut to get somewhere else just wouldn't be in the Okinawan spirit of things.

There are, of course, a few things you shouldn't miss while you're here. The beautifully reconstructed **Shuri-jō**, the old Ryūkyū kings' castle, constitutes the city's major sight and is well worth visiting; the **Tsuboya** district, a pleasing area of little workshops and dusty galleries that is famous for its pottery kilns, is fun for a wander; and there's **Naminoue beach**, a short curl of sand that would boast grand sea views were it not for the roads firing across the waves a few dozen metres offshore. Domestic tourists make a beeline for **Kokusai-dōri**, the city's main thoroughfare.

Shuri-jō and around

Perched on a hill 3km northeast of central Naha, **Shuri-jō** served as the royal residence of the Ryūkyū kings from the early fifteenth century until 1879. Elaborate ceremonies took place in the castle's opulent throne room, on occasion attended by envoys from China and, later, from Kyūshū. Very little of the original remains, but the present buildings, painstakingly restored in the early 1990s, are certainly worth seeing for their distinctive blend of Chinese and Japanese architecture.

Shuri-jō

首里城 • 1-2 Shurikinjo-chō • Daily: April–June & Oct–Nov 8.30am–7pm; July–Sept 8.30am–8pm; Dec–March 8.30am–6pm • ¥820 • Bus #1 from Kokusai-dōri or #17 from Naha Bus Terminal (every 15–20min; 30min), or a 10min walk from Shuri monorail station

The castle's main entrance is the decorative **Shurei-mon**. This outer gate is a popular spot for group photos, but the inner **Kankai-mon** is a far more impressive structure, its no-nonsense guard tower flanked by sun-baked limestone walls. Inside, there's yet another defensive wall and no fewer than three more gates – the last now housing the ticket office – before you reach the central courtyard. Pride of place goes to the **Seiden**, a double-roofed palace with an immense, colourful porch and two throne halls. From the more elaborate upper throne room, the king, surrounded by gilded dragons writhing against lustrous red and black lacquer, would review his troops or watch ceremonies in the courtyard below.

Shuri-jō Park

首里城公園

A quiet place featuring a stone-walled pond and ancient trees, **Shuri-jō Park** lies across the road from the Shuri-jō exit. The pond's pretty island pavilion once belonged to **Engaku-ji**, and was built in 1492 as the local headquarters of the Rinzai sect; it was said to have been the most impressive structure in the kingdom. Nowadays, only a few shell-pocked walls remain of the original temple, east of the pond.

Okinawa Prefectural Museum

沖縄県立博物館, Okinawa Kenritsu Hakubutsukan • 3-1-1 Omoromachi • Mon–Thurs & Sun 9am–6pm; Fri & Sat 9am–8pm • ¥410; art museum ¥310; extra for special exhibitions • 10min walk from Omoromachi monorail station • ☎ 098 941 8200, ⓦ museums.pref .okinawa.jp

Sitting on the route between Shuri-jō and central Naha, the splendid **Okinawa Prefectural Museum** is worth seeing on your way to or from the castle. Designed to make visitors feel that they're stepping onto an island, and partly open-air in nature, this modern venue provides a good overview of local history, nature and culture; a separate wing focuses on local art and puts on diverting **exhibitions** several times a year.

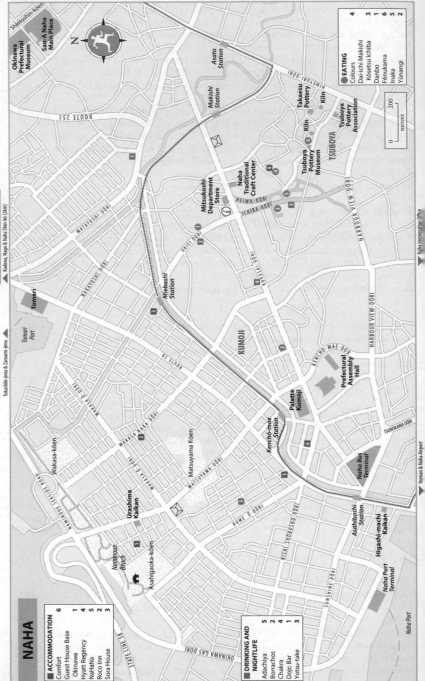

NAHA

ACCOMMODATION
Comfort	6
Guest House Base	1
Okinawa	4
Hyatt Regency	5
NaHaNa	2
Roco Inn	2
Sora House	3

DRINKING AND NIGHTLIFE
Adachiya	5
Borrachos	2
Chakra	4
Dojo Bar	1
Yotsu-take	3

EATING
Colours	4
Dai-ichi Makishi	3
Kōsetsu Ichiba	1
Danbo	6
Fēnukama	5
Inaka	2
Yunangi	

0 — 200 metres

Kokusai-dōri and around
国際通り

The busiest place in town is **Kokusai-dōri**, effectively the city's main road, even though few locals choose to hang out here; nearly 2km long, it's lined with a strange mix of tourist restaurants, souvenir stalls and army-surplus outlets selling American military leftovers. The **market** area to the south is charmingly ramshackle; within its several covered arcades you'll find some great souvenirs, as well as one of Japan's best fish markets.

Naha Traditional Craft Center

那覇市伝統工芸館, Naha-shi Dentoū Kōgeikan • 3-2-10 Makishi • Daily 10am–8pm • ¥310; craft classes ¥1540–3100 • ☎ 098 868 7866, ⓦ kogeikan.jp

If you're interested in local crafts, drop by the **Naha Traditional Craft Center** on the second floor of the Tembusu building off Kokusai-dōri, near Mitsukoshi. The entrance fee will get you into a small gallery with prime examples of fabrics, ceramics, glass and lacquerware, but more interestingly (and without paying the entrance fee) you can watch artisans fashion these objects in the adjoining workshops and studios. You can try your hand at weaving, *bingata* dyeing, glass-blowing, pottery and lacquerware, and there's also a well-stocked gift shop.

Naha Market and Dai-ichi Makishi Kōsetsu Ichiba

那覇市場, Naha Ichiba • 第一牧志公設市場, Dai-ichi Makishi Kōsetsu Ichiba • Daily 9am–8pm, closed fourth Sun of every month

Just south of Kokusai-dōri, the various covered arcades that make up **Naha Market** are great places for a wander – 1960s architecture, cheap fruit and occasionally hilarious Okinawan novelty T-shirts are all on the agenda. Among the souvenir stalls and discount outlets, these covered streets host a number of lively **markets**, of which the best is Ichiba's food market, **Dai-ichi Makishi Kōsetsu Ichiba**. The ground-floor stalls are piled high with sweet-smelling tropical fruits, every conceivable part of pig and ice-packed arrays of multicoloured fish and mysterious, spiny crabs. You'll see fishmongers deftly slicing sashimi, some of it destined for the **food stalls** upstairs (see p.791).

Tsuboya
壺屋

The pottery district of **Tsuboya** is a compact area that's been the centre of local ceramics production since 1682, when the government gathered a number of workshops together – ten are still in operation today. Traditionally, the potters here produced large jars for storing the local liquor (*awamori*) and miso paste, but nowadays they concentrate on smaller items for the tourist market, typically half-moon-shaped sake flasks and snarling *shiisā* lions.

Tsuboya Pottery Museum

壺屋焼物博物館, Tsuboya Yakimono Hakubutsukan • 1-9-32 Tsuboya • Tues–Sun 10am–6pm • ¥350; top-floor art exhibits free • ☎ 098 862 3761

To get an overview of the area's history, drop into the **Tsuboya Pottery Museum**, which is less than a hundred metres from the end of Naha Market's arcades. It's a decent enough place, though the exhibitions of earthenware can feel a little repetitive. If you exit through the back door, you'll see the remains of an ancient kiln.

ARRIVAL AND DEPARTURE   NAHA

By plane Naha Airport (那覇空港) occupies a promontory some 3km southwest of the city centre. One terminal handles flights from mainland Japan and to Okinawa's outer islands, while the adjacent building is for overseas flights; there's also the LCC terminal 1km away (see box, p.790). From the airport, you can either take a taxi (around ¥1500) or the monorail (¥300) for the short journey into central Naha, or one of several frequent local buses departing from outside the terminal buildings (¥230).

Destinations Fukuoka (17 daily; 1hr 40min); Hiroshima (daily; 1hr 40min); Ishigaki (1–3 hourly; 1hr); Kagoshima

(3 daily; 1hr 15min); Kōbe (6 daily; 1hr 50min); Kumamoto (daily; 1hr 35min); Matsuyama (daily; 1hr 35min); Miyako (1–2 hourly; 45min); Miyazaki (daily; 1hr 35min); Nagasaki (daily; 1hr 35min); Nagoya (9 daily; 2hr); Osaka (15 daily; 1hr 50min); Okayama (2 daily; 1hr 50min); Sapporo (daily; 4hr); Sendai (daily; 2hr 30min); Shizuoka (daily; 2hr 10min); Takamatsu (daily; 1hr 50min); Tokyo (1–4 hourly; 2hr 30min); Yonaguni (2 daily; 1hr 15min).

By bus Services run around the island from Naha Bus Terminal (那覇バスターミナル), just to the east of the Asahibashi monorail stop. This is also where most of the local bus tours start (see p.786).

By ferry The ferry port, Naha Shin-kō (那覇新港), lies 2km north of the city centre. Most ferries from mainland Japan dock here, while slow boats from Kagoshima pull in further south at the old Naha Port Terminal (那覇埠頭). Naha Shin-kō is on the #101 bus route (1–3 hourly; 25min; ¥230), while Naha Port is more conveniently located about a 15min walk from the bus terminal. Marix Line (T 098 868 9098, W marixline.com) and A-Line Ferry (T 098 861 1886, W aline-ferry.com) have slow boats to Kagoshima (from ¥14,500); the latter also has sailings from Kansai, alternating between Osaka and Kōbe (from ¥19,000). From the Tomari Port, on the west side of the city centre, there are sailings to Zamami-jima and other islands due west; you'll have a choice of fast (at least 2 daily; 55min; ¥3140) or slow services (10am daily; 2hr; ¥2120), though note that bad weather can see everyone lumped onto the latter.

Destinations Kagoshima (2 daily; 25hr); Osaka/Kōbe (2–3 monthly; 41hr); Zamami-jima (3 daily; 55min–2hr).

11

GETTING AROUND

By monorail The smart monorail (daily 6am–11.30pm; single-station hops ¥110, otherwise ¥230 minimum fare; W yui-rail.co.jp) is a useful way to get around, linking Naha Airport with Shuri, 13km away. You can buy tickets from the machines by the gates.

By bus There are plenty of local buses, though services can be confusing and traffic often gridlocks at peak times. There's a flat fare of ¥230 within the city, but on other buses you'll need to take a numbered ticket on entry and pay when you disembark.

By car Nippon Rent-a-Car (T 098 868 4554, W nipponrentacar.co.jp) and Toyota (T 098 857 0100, W rent.toyota.co.jp) are among the agencies with representatives in both the airport and the city centre. If you want to take a taxi, Okitō Kōtsū (T 098 946 5654) has English-speaking drivers, and you can arrange sightseeing taxi tours with English-speaking driver-guides through Okinawa-ken Kojin Taxi T 098 868 1145.

By bike and motorbike You can rent motorbikes and scooters at Helmet Shop SEA (3-15-50 Makishi; T 098 864 5116), west of Kokusai-dōri, from ¥1700 for 3hr; most hostels and some hotels also rent bikes out, though the prices vary.

INFORMATION

Tourist information Naha's tourist information service has desks in both the domestic (daily 9am–9pm; T 098 857 6884) and international (daily 10.30am–7.30pm; T 098 859 0742) terminals at the airport. Both have English-speaking staff, plentiful maps and brochures, and can help with hotel reservations. In downtown Naha, there's an office on Okiei-dōri (daily 8.30am–8pm; T 098 862 1442).

ACCOMMODATION

Naha has a good range of accommodation, especially for backpackers – there are more than a dozen hostels charging around ¥1500 for a dorm bed, making this the cheapest backpacker city in Japan. Rooms are hard to come by in the peak holiday seasons – Golden Week, August and New Year – when rates may rise by up to forty percent. Don't assume, however, that Naha is the only place on Okinawa-Hontō with accommodation, as there are some great alternatives around the island.

NAHA AIRPORT: FLYING FROM THE LCC TERMINAL

Officially, Naha airport has two terminals: one domestic, one international. However, some budget airlines – Peach and Vanilla, at the time of writing – use the separate low-cost-carrier (LCC) terminal, which is actually part of the cargo area, 1km away from the main airport. It's a pretty horrid little space, devoid of anywhere to eat or drink, and often anywhere to sit; there are no money-changing facilities available here either, which could be important if you're flying out of Japan. To get here, you'll need to catch a free shuttle bus from outside the domestic terminal; it's close enough to walk, but they won't let pedestrians through the gate. The queues for the shuttle bus can be long, and with all the confusion it's common for passengers to miss their flights. If you're flying from the LCC terminal, give yourself some extra time – you have been warned.

Comfort コンフォートホテル 1-3-11 Kumoji ☎ 098 941 7311, ⓦ choice-hotels.jp. Popular business hotel within spitting distance of the monorail. Rooms have been decorated with gentle pastel colours, and you can usually score hefty discounts from the rack rates. 🛜 **¥9000**

Guest House Base Okinawa ゲストハウス BASE OKINAWA 1-17-5 Wakasa ☎ 090 1385 9044. Your mother may have warned you about places like this, but the grungy atmosphere of this hostel suits Naha to a tee. Rooms are adequate, and you'll be so close to Nami-no-ue beach that you won't even have to don your flip-flops. 🛜 Dorms **¥1500**, singles **¥3000**, doubles **¥5000**

Hyatt Regency ハイアットリージェンシー 3-6-20 Makishi ☎ 098 866 8888, ⓦ naha.regency.hyatt.com. With an excellent location between teeming Kokusai-dōri and the relaxed Tsuboya pottery district, this is top dog in town, with luxurious rooms, thick carpets and a pool-with-a-view that's a great place to be come sundown. 🛜 **¥18,000**

NaHaNa ナハナホテル 2-1-5 Kume ☎ 098 866 0787, ⓦ nahana-hotel.jp. An appealingly retro exterior – replete with a ledge that may have been envisioned as a hover-car parking space – conceals surprisingly swish rooms, each mixing modern design with Okinawan motifs. Guests get special rates at the attached spa. 🛜 **¥14,000**

Roco Inn ロコイン 1-27-11 Matsuyama ☎ 098 869 6511, ⓦ rocoinn-okinawa.jp. Good, cheap option within walking distance of the beach, the Zamami ferries and the city centre. Both the staff service and the buffet breakfasts (¥800) are a cut above what you'd expect at this price range, while the rooms themselves are comfortable (if slightly garish) affairs. 🛜 **¥7200**

★**Sora House** 空ハウス 2-24-15 Kumoji ☎ 098 861 9939. This is the best of the city's backpacker joints, with a mix of capsule and regular dorms as well as comfy private rooms. The only real downside is that there are too few showers for guest use. 🛜 Dorms **¥1800**, doubles **¥5600**

EATING

Naha undoubtedly has Okinawa-Hontō's widest choice of restaurants, with everything from international cuisine to delectable **local dishes** (see box, p.785). One Naha speciality is *tundā-bun*: banquets once enjoyed by Ryūkyū kings, and today generally served with an accompanying show.

Colours カラーズ 3-6-5 Matsuo ☎ 098 927 6508. Appropriately colourful restaurant which has taken the taco rice theme and run with it; here you can have the minced meat, cheese and greens served in a *doria* (rice gratin; ¥480) or atop a small pizza (¥450). It's located on Naha's artiest road – huddled under the disco ball, the clientele here is an odd mix of hipsters and grannies. Mon & Wed–Sun 11.30am–8pm.

★**Dai ichi Makishi Kōsetsu Ichiba** 第一公設牧志市場 Matsuo 2-10-1. An absolute must for seafood fans, this is not one restaurant but several tiny ones, all set together atop the city's biggest and best fish market. All the Okinawan staple dishes are here, but it would be a crime not to go for the fish – choose from the menu, or for added fun pick your own sea creature from downstairs and pay an extra ¥500 to have it cooked for you. Alternatively, for ¥500 you can sit among the market stalls with a tray of ultra-fresh sashimi – you can't really lose here. Daily 10am–9pm.

Danbo 暖暮 2-16-10 Makishi ☎ 098 863 8331. No list of Naha restaurants is complete without a mention of this ramen spot, which is part of a chain whose noodles were once voted the best in Japan. It's still living off those former glories, as the staff are surly and most customers are visitors from other Asian countries, but hey – it's still good ramen. A bowl of *rekka-ramen*, their house speciality, will set you back ¥750. Daily 11am–2am.

Fēnukama 南窯 Tsuboya 1-9-29 ☎ 098 861 6404. This is Naha's best café, and a handy excuse to pop over to the Tsuboya pottery district; it is, in fact, backed by the ruins of a kiln built more than 300 years ago, as seen from a couple of the outdoor tables. Inside or out, the coffee's great (¥500); take it with a *chinbin*, a sort of local crepe (¥250). Daily 10am–6.30pm.

Inaka 田舎 Matsuo 2-9-5. This hard-to-find market den dates from just after Okinawa's handover to Japan; unfortunately, tax rises meant that prices for their tasty *sōki soba* recently increased for the first time since 1976 (Japan's stagnant economy makes such miracles possible), but at ¥390 for a bowl it's still the cheapest in the whole prefecture. If you're still in the retro mood, climb your way up any neighbouring staircase to drink amid some throwback architecture. Daily 10am–7pm.

Yūnangi ゆうなんぎい 3-3-3 Kumoji. Country-style restaurant, offering a warm welcome and serving Okinawan cuisine, including Okinawa soba, *champurū* and various pork dishes. Set meals go from around ¥1300, with free rice refills. Mon–Sat noon–3pm & 5.30–10.30pm.

DRINKING AND NIGHTLIFE

As you'd expect, with plenty of off-duty GIs and footloose young Japanese tourists and locals, Naha's **entertainment** scene is far from dull. Following orders from above, the grunts are only allowed into certain bars. The city is also a good place to catch performances of traditional **Ryūkyū court dance**; some performances are served with *tundā-bun* banquets.

BARS

Adachiya 足立屋 2-10-20 Matsuo ☎098 869 8040. Tucked into the market, this *izakaya* is a fun spot where customers are – rarely for the area – mainly locals. Drinks are super cheap, with beer from ¥300 and *awamori* for ¥200, and there's plenty of Japanese pub-grub on offer, from yakitori sticks to *hamaguri* (sake-steamed clams). The only pity is that it closes so early. Daily 6am–10pm.

Borrachos ボラチョス 1-3-31 Makishi ☎098 943 4488. Mexican bar which, it seems, only employs male staff with copious facial hair. Good Mexican beer (from ¥600) and food are on offer, and the atmosphere is as relaxed as Naha gets. Daily 5pm–midnight.

★**Dojo Bar** 道場バー 2-16-10 Makishi ☎098 911 3601, ⓦ dojobarnaha.com. Naha makes surprisingly little play of its status as the birthplace of karate, so this English-owned bar makes a nice change – paraphernalia pertaining to martial fisticuffs is dotted all over the place, and you'll often find a fair few black-belts among the customers. If you're interested in studying karate yourself, staff here will do their best to help grease the wheels, possibly over an English ale (from ¥500) or their selection of *awamori*. Daily 7pm–2am, Sat & Sun till 3am.

LIVE MUSIC AND TRADITIONAL DANCE

Chakra チャクラ 2F, 1-2-1 Makishi, Kokusai-dōri ☎098 869 0283. Owned by local music legend Kina Shoukichi, and often home to the nationally renowned Champloose collective, this is a fun place to hear some local sounds; Okinawan dancing often forms part of the performance, and guests sometimes get to join in. Entry is ¥2500. Mon, Tues & Thurs–Sun 7pm–1am.

Yotsu-take 四つ竹 2-22-1 Kume ☎098 866 3333, ⓦ yotsutake.co.jp. The best of Naha's umpteen dinner-and-dance venues. As well as watching a local court dance (40min), you can also get a *tundā-bun* – a set meal of beautifully presented royal hors d'oeuvre. Entry is ¥1620, or from ¥6500 including a meal. Shows daily 6.30pm & 8.30pm.

DIRECTORY

Hospitals and medical care Naha City Hospital, 2-31-1 Furujima (☎098 884 5111), is located next to the castle. If you need an English-speaking doctor, your best bet is the Adventist Medical Centre, 4-11-1 Kohagura, on Route 29 northeast of Naha (☎098 946 2833).

Immigration office To renew your visa, apply to the Naha Immigration Office, 1-15-15 Hikawa (☎098 832 4185),

southeast of Kokusai-dōri on Route 221.

Police 1-2-9 Izumizaki (☎098 836 0110; see p.71 for emergency numbers).

Post offices Naha Central Post Office is located on the south side of town around 500m down Naha Higashi Bypass from the Meiji Bridge. For ordinary services, you'll find smaller post offices in every district around town.

Southern Okinawa-Hontō

During the long-drawn-out Battle of Okinawa (see p.783), it was the area south of Naha that saw the worst fighting and received the heaviest bombardment. Not only were the **Underground Naval Headquarters** dug deep into the hills here, but the region's many limestone caves also provided shelter for hundreds of Japanese troops and local

---

OKINAWAN SOUVENIRS

Those in search of local **crafts** will find beautiful **bingata** textiles the most appealing. Originally reserved for court ladies, *bingata* fabrics are hand-dyed with natural pigments from hibiscus flowers and various vegetables, in simple but striking patterns. Also worth searching out are the fine **jōfu** cloths of Miyako-jima and the Yaeyama Islands, once gifted in tribute to the local monarchs. **Ceramics** are thought to have been introduced to the region from Spain and Portugal in the fifteenth century, but Ryūkyū potters concentrated on roof tiles and fairly rustic utensils. Nowadays, they churn out thousands of sake flasks and *shiisā*, the ferocious lion figures that glare down at you from every rooftop – there are plenty for sale around Naha's Tsuboya district. The exquisite local **lacquerware** has a long history in the islands, too, having been introduced over five hundred years ago from China, but the glassware you'll find is much more recent: it's said production took off in the postwar years when Okinawans set about recycling the drinks bottles of the occupying US forces. Lastly, there's plenty of cheap **food and clothing** in the covered arcades off Kokusai-dōri, hunt down some Okinawan patterned underpants, Puma T-shirts with the panther replaced by a smiling *shiisā*, and all manner of other pleasing tat.

civilians, many of whom committed suicide rather than be taken prisoner. One of these caves has been preserved as a memorial to the young Himeyuri nurses who died there, and the area is dotted with peace parks and prayer halls. It's not completely devoted to war sights, however. **Okinawa World**, over on the southeastern coast, combines 890m of extraordinary stalactite-filled caves with a tourist village dedicated to Ryūkyū culture, and there's also the lovely islet of **Komaka-jima**, which is a great spot for snorkelling.

Underground Naval Headquarters

旧海軍司令部壕, Kyū Kaigun Shireibu Gō • 236 Tomigusuku • Daily 8.30am–5pm • ¥440 • Bus #33, #46 or #101 from central Naha to Tomigusuku-jō Shi-kōen-mae stop (1–2 hourly; 25min; ¥250), then a 10min walk

For centuries, the castle of Tomigusuku-jō has stood on the low hills looking north over Naha. During the Pacific War, the spot was chosen for the headquarters of the Japanese navy, but, instead of using the old fortifications, they tunnelled 20m down into the soft limestone. The complex, consisting of Rear Admiral Ōta's command room and various operations rooms, is now preserved as the **Underground Naval Headquarters**. Inside, there are a few photos of the 1945 battle, but little else to see beyond holes gouged in the plaster walls; the cavities are said to be where Ōta and 175 of his men killed themselves with hand grenades on June 13 as the Americans closed in. Beside the tunnel entrance, there's a small museum and a monument to the four thousand Japanese troops who died in this area.

Himeyuri-no-tō

ひめゆりの塔 • 6/1-1 Ihara • Museum daily 9am–5pm • ¥310 • ⓦ www.himeyuri.or.jp • Bus #34 or #89 from Naha to Itoman (1–2 hourly; 30min; ¥580), then #82, #107 or #108 (15min; ¥350)

Heading south down the coast from the Underground Naval Headquarters, Highway 331 passes through **Itoman** town (糸満) and then cuts inland across the peninsula to **Himeyuri-no-tō**, a deeply moving war memorial dedicated to more than two hundred schoolgirls and their teachers who committed suicide here in a shallow cave.

The nearby **museum** describes how the high-school students, like many others on Okinawa, were conscripted as trainee nurses by the Japanese army in the spring of 1945. As the fighting became more desperate, the girls were sent to a field hospital, gradually retreating south from cave to cave, and were then abandoned altogether as the Japanese army disintegrated. Terrified that they would be raped and tortured by the Americans, the women and girls killed themselves rather than be captured.

Peace Memorial Park

平和祈念公園, Heiwakinen-kōen • 444 Mabuni, Itoman • Daily 9am–5.30pm (winter till 5pm) • ¥450 • ☎ 098 997 2765, ⓦ sp.heiwa-irei-okinawa.jp • Bus #82 from Itoman (9 daily; 30min; ¥470)

The final battle for Okinawa took place on **Mabuni Hill** (摩文仁の丘), on the island's southeast coast. The site is now occupied by a cemetery and park containing monuments (the "Cornerstone of Peace") to the more than 200,000 troops – both Japanese and American – and civilians who died on the islands during the war. A white tower crowns the **Peace Memorial Hall**, which contains a 12m-high lacquered Buddha.

Okinawa Prefecture Peace Memorial Museum

沖縄県立平和記念資料館, Okinawa Kenritsu Heiwa Kinen Shiryōkan • 614-1 Mabuni, Itoman • Daily 9am–5pm • ¥300 • ⓦ www.peace-museum.pref.okinawa.jp • Bus #82 from Itoman (9 daily; 30min; ¥470)

You'll learn plenty (though not the full story) about the Battle of Okinawa if you visit the **Okinawa Prefecture Peace Memorial Museum**, very close to the Peace Memorial Hall, which has full English translations throughout. This interesting museum, planned under the anti-establishment regime of Governor Ōta but completed by the more conservative Governor Inamine, doesn't shirk the uncomfortable fact that Japanese soldiers ruthlessly killed Okinawan civilians. Generally, however, the whole build-up to the war is treated in the usual euphemistic way, and the exhibition ends on an upbeat note with displays on the postwar history of Okinawa to the present day.

11

THE AMERICAN QUESTION

Twenty percent of Okinawa-Hontō and a small number of outer islands are covered by **American military bases**, employing 27,000 American military personnel. This in itself has fuelled local anger, but what rankles most is that Okinawa makes up less than one percent of the Japanese landmass, yet contains 75 percent of the country's American bases. The issue is, however, far from black and white for the islanders, since the bases provide thousands of jobs and contribute vast sums to the local economy – rather important, given that Okinawa remains the poorest of Japan's prefectures. In addition, many younger Okinawans relish the peculiar hybrid cultural atmosphere that the large number of foreigners brings to the islands.

Recent political manoeuvrings have been largely focused on **Futenma**, a large US Marine Corps air base just northeast of Naha. **Nakaima Hirokazu** was elected governor of Okinawa in 2006 on an anti-base ticket, but in 2014 he flip-flopped and approved certain elements of the plans. Although he was ousted from office later in the year, work on the Futenma site started in 2015, but partially thanks to fierce criticism from celebrities such as filmmakers Miyazaki Hayao and Oliver Stone, everything still remained in the balance at the time of writing. Regardless of what happens with Futenma, the American issue is likely to rumble on for some time.

11

Okinawa World

おきなわワールド • 1336 Tamagusuku • Daily 9am–6pm; Eisā dances 10.30am, 12.30pm, 2.30pm & 4pm; snake shows 11am, noon, 2pm, 3.30pm & 4.30pm • Day pass ¥1650; village and cave ¥1240; village and Habu Park ¥1130; craft workshops additional ¥100–200 • ☎ 098 949 7421 • Bus #83 or #54 from Naha (8 daily; 1hr; ¥580), or #82 from Itoman (9 daily; 30min; ¥320)

Okinawa World is a quirky "village" showcasing local crafts and culture, including *bingata* dyeing, *awamori* brewing and Eisā dance performances. It's built across an 890m-long cave with an impressive array of rock formations along an underground river, but the most popular attraction is the **Habu Park**, where you can learn about the Okinawan venomous snake and pose for the cameras with a python wrapped around your shoulders. You can also try your hand at the various local crafts.

Komaka-jima

コマカ島 • Bus #38 to Chinen from Naha; speedboats run 9am–5pm from the Chinen Kaiyō Leisure Centre (知念海洋レジャーセンター) in Chinen (知念村) to the island (every 30min; ¥2800 return)

If you just want to chill out, head to tiny **Komaka-jima**, 3km east of the Chinen Peninsula. An uninhabited islet surrounded by golden sands and a coral reef, it's an ideal snorkelling spot; alternatively, it's pleasant to simply muck around on a pristine, tourist-free beach. Plenty choose to camp here overnight, though be sure to bring all your own supplies if you plan to stay.

Central Okinawa-Hontō

North of Naha, traffic on Highway 58 crawls up the coast of **central Okinawa-Hontō** between a strip of *McDonald's*, *Shakey's Pizza* and used car lots on one side, and neat rows of artillery on the other. This is army country, with huge tracts of land occupied by the **American military** (see box above). Camps and bases extend along the coast as far north as the Maeda peninsula, where beach resorts take over. You can avoid the coastal strip by taking the expressway or Highway 330 up the island's less crowded centre past **Okinawa City** – this is the best way to reach the north of the island quickly. A bizarre mix of American and Japanese life, Okinawa City is the region's main urban centre, but there's little reason to stop. A short way south, though difficult to get to, **Nakamura-ke** is one of the few genuinely old buildings still standing on Okinawa-Hontō, while the nearby ruins of **Nakagusuku-jō** offer commanding views. On the district's northern fringes lies **Ryūkyū-mura**, a quieter, more interesting culture village than Okinawa World (see above).

Nakamura-ke

中村家 • 106 Ogusuku • Daily 9.30am–5.30pm • ¥500, including tea • ⓦ nakamura-ke.net • Bus #27, #80 or #127 from Naha to Okinawa City (Futenma junction), then bus #59 (hourly; 15min; ¥200) to the Nakamura-ke turn-off

A little north of Futenma air base, a road cuts east through the hills to **Kitanakagusuku** village (北中城) where, in the early fifteenth century, Nakamura Gashi served as a teacher to a local lord, Gosamaru. In the early eighteenth century, one of Gashi's descendants was appointed village leader and started building his family's large, beautifully solid residence, **Nakamura-ke**. Protected by limestone walls, a thick belt of trees and a growling *shiisā* perched on the red-tile roof, the house is typical of a wealthy landowner.

Nakagusuku-jō

中城城跡 • 503 Kitanakagusuku • Daily 8.30am–5pm (May–Sept till 6pm) • ¥400 • ☏ 098 935 5719, ⓦ nakagusuku-jo.jp

A five-minute walk west of Nakamura-ke, limestone cliffs merge into the crumbling walls of **Nakagusuku-jō**, designated a World Heritage Site in 2000. These impressive fortifications, consisting of six citadels on a spectacular promontory, were originally built in the early fifteenth century by Lord Gosamaru. However, they weren't enough to withstand his rival, Lord Amawari, who ransacked the castle in 1458 and then abandoned the site. Nowadays you can walk through the grassy, tree-filled park and scramble among the ruins to admire the views clear across the island.

11

Ryūkyū-mura

琉球村 • 1130 Yamada • Daily 8.30am–5.30pm • ¥1200 • ⓦ ryukyumura.co.jp • Bus #120 or #20 from Naha (every 15–20min; 1hr 20min; ¥1050)

Over on the west coast, **Ryūkyū-mura** preserves several old Okinawa farmhouses brought from all over the islands and reassembled here to showcase the remnants of Ryūkyū culture. Though some will find it too touristy, the village provides a hint of what Okinawa was like before the war. In addition to performances of Eisā dances and traditional music, you can see people weaving, dyeing textiles and milling sugar cane for molasses.

ACCOMMODATION   CENTRAL OKINAWA-HONTŌ

Maeda Misaki Divers House 真栄田岬ダイバーズハウス 357 Yamada, Onna village ☏ 098 965 6459, ⓦ maedamisaki.com; map p.786. A 15min walk northwest of Ryūkyū-mura, this is a great place to stay, particularly if you've come to Okinawa to dive. The building – an old youth hostel – is a bit run-down, but it's in a quiet location and offers walks along the cliffs and down to the white, sweeping curve of Moon Beach. Accommodation is in bunk beds, and they do good meals. The nearest bus stop is Kuraha, on bus route #120, from where the hostel is a 10min walk northwest. Dorms **¥2000**

ACTIVITIES

Diving and cycling The *Maeda Misaki Divers House* run diving trips, starting from ¥9500 for an introductory dive, including all equipment. Five-day PADI courses are ¥51,000, accommodation included. They also rent out bikes for ¥1500 per day.

Northern Okinawa-Hontō

North of Okinawa-Hontō's pinched waist, the scenery begins to improve as classy resort hotels line the western beaches. Bleached-white, coral-fringed Moon Beach merges into Tiger Beach, after which there's the rocky, wild Onna promontory before you rejoin the sands at Manza and up through Inbu Beach. Beyond this strip, **northern Okinawa-Hontō**'s only major settlement, **Nago**, sits at the base of the knobbly **Motobu peninsula**. A generally quiet, workaday place, there's not a lot to see in Nago, but the small city makes a good base for exploring the region's mountainous north and visiting the impressive **Okinawa Churaumi Aquarium** at the far western tip of the peninsula. The district boasts the island's most attractive scenery, particularly around **Hedo Misaki**, the northern cape, and on through sleepy **Oku** village down the rugged northeast coast. It's possible to travel up the west coast by slow local bus, but after Oku you're on your own.

Nago and around

名護

Apart from weekends, when off-duty soldiers come up from the bases, **NAGO** sees few foreigners. If the proposed relocation of the Futenma base goes ahead (see box, p.794), all this will change, but for the moment Nago is a slow-moving, fairly pleasant city – more a large town – that's best known for its huge **banyan tree** and a spectacular display of **spring cherry blossoms**. Its other draws consist of a marginally interesting local museum and nearby **Nago Castle Hill**; nothing remains of the castle, but it does boast lovely views over Nago bay.

Busena Resort Underwater Observatory

ブセナ海中公園, Busena Kaichi Kōen • 1808 Kise • Daily 9am–6pm • ¥1000

Some 10km southeast of Nago, at the tip of the promontory occupied by the *Busena Terrace* resort (see below), there's an **Underwater Observatory** owned and operated by the hotel. It's a good way to see some of the area's marine life if you're not going diving; though not a patch on Ocean Expo Park (see below), it's markedly less busy and the location is almost as spectacular.

11

ARRIVAL AND INFORMATION   NAGO

By bus Arriving by bus (including the #111 from Naha), most services stop near Nago's central crossing before terminating at the bus terminal on the main highway to the west of town. However, some stop on the seafront, notably the Express Bus from Naha Airport's bus terminal (hourly; 2hr; ¥2000), which ends up outside Nago's Lego-block City Hall, roughly 500m west of the central crossroads.

Tourist information You'll find the tourist information office (Mon–Fri 8.30am–5.30pm, Sat & Sun 10am–5pm; ☎098 053 7755) in Nago City Hall (1-1-1 Minato), which has English-language maps and pamphlets on the area. **Services** The Ryūkyū Bank, just north of the central junction, can exchange dollar and sterling cash, and there's a small post office with an ATM a couple of blocks to the west.

ACCOMMODATION

Busena Terrace ブセナテラスリゾート 1808 Kise ☎098 051 1333, ⓦterrace.co.jp; map p.786. Some way south of Nago, and still proudly displaying evidence of hosting the G8 Summit in 2000, this resort has simple but tastefully designed rooms, charming staff and impressive facilities, including six restaurants, an enormous landscaped pool and a pleasant beach. If you want to see what's going on under the waves, you can visit its

Underwater Observatory (see above). ☎ **¥44,000**
Kise Beach Palace 喜瀬ビーチパレス 115-2 Kise ☎098 052 5151, ⓦkise-beachpalace.jp; map p.786. There's some seriously good value on offer at this beachside hotel – curiously, the ocean-view rooms are often cheaper than those looking at the boring mountains, but they're all comfy and pretty sizeable. The outdoor pool, open during warmer months, rounds things off nicely. ☎ **¥7500**

Ocean Expo Park

海洋博公園, Kaiyō Haku-kōen • 424 Ishikawa • Daily 8am–7.30pm • General entry free; Oceanic Culture Museum ¥170; Tropical Dream Centre ¥690; electric bus day ticket ¥200, one ride ¥100 • ⓦoki-park.jp • Bus #111 from Naha to Nago (2hr), then #65, #66 or #70 (1hr)

Sitting on the northwestern tip of the hilly, mushroom-shaped Motobu peninsula, the **Ocean Expo Park** is up there with Okinawa's most famous attractions. The majority of visitors race to the fantastic, world-famous **aquarium** (see p.798) and head straight back to Naha, but the sprawling park boasts umpteen other attractions to help you make the most of the long trip here (and it is a long trip). These include dolphin shows, an ocean nursery, a manatee tank (if you haven't come across these creatures before, be prepared for some strange sights) and a good beach at the north end. Other minor highlights include an **Oceanic Culture Museum** (closed for renovations at the time of writing), which contains a vast collection of boats and artefacts from Southeast Asia and the South Pacific; and the **Tropical Dream Centre**, containing two thousand types of orchids and flowers. All of the above are connected by electric bus.

Okinawa Churaumi Aquarium

沖縄美ら海水族館, Okinawa Churaumi Suizokukan • Daily: Oct–Feb 8.30am–6.30pm; March–Sept 8.30am–8pm • ¥1850 • W churaumi.okinawa/en

The highlight of the park is the **Okinawa Churaumi Aquarium**, a spectacular facility showcasing the marine life of the Kuroshio Current. The main tank holds 7500 tonnes of water and is home to several whale sharks, the largest fish in the world; there are plenty of manta ray here too, and the aquarium is justly proud of the fact that four have been born here. When the place opened in 2002, the glass panel at the front was the largest in the world at a whopping 22.5m in length. Though this has since been surpassed by one in Dubai, the cinema-scope view will still hold you entranced. Most explanations are in English, and there's an informative section on sharks that dispels many myths about these extraordinary creatures.

ACCOMMODATION	OCEAN EXPO PARK

★Beach Rock Village ビーチロックビレッジ 1331 Nakijin ☎ 098 056 1126, W shimapro.com; map p.786. A little artsy gem about 15km east of the park. Accommodation here is in tents, with rates (up to a maximum of ¥7000 per person) depending upon your required level of luxury, but you can also drop by for coffee or tea, served on balconies with commanding views. They also run regular tours of the surrounding area, and host events such as movie nights or live acts. From **¥700** per person

Centurion Resort Churaumi センチュリオンリゾート 沖縄美ら海 938 Ishikawa ☎ 098 048 3631, W www .centurion-hotel.com; map p.786. This swanky hotel is ideally located for the aquarium, which is right next door. The decor in the rooms is a bit cheesy, but all of them have a sea view and there's a fantastic on-site pool to splash around in. 🛜 **¥16,000**

Hiji Ōtaki

比地大滝 • Daily sunrise–3.30pm • Trail ¥200

North of Nago, Highway 58 hugs the mountainside as the cliffs rise higher, and the only settlements are a few weather-beaten villages in sheltered coves. At the village of **Kunigami** (国頭), head inland along the road that follows the river to reach the start of the walk to **Hiji Ōtaki**, a picturesque 26m waterfall. About halfway along the 1.5km-long trail, you'll cross a 17m suspension bridge with lovely views across the river; further up and at the falls themselves there are excellent swimming spots.

ACCOMMODATION	HIJI ŌTAKI

Hiji Ōtaki Campsite 比地大滝キャンプ 781-1 Kunigami ☎ 098 041 3636; map p.786. This is a rather beautiful campsite at the beginning of the Hiji Ōtaki walking trail. It has good washing and cooking facilities, plus a small restaurant-cum-shop; it's possible to rent tents if you haven't brought your own. **¥2000** per person

Hedo-misaki

辺戸岬 • Bus #67 from Nago to Hentona (辺土名; 1–2 hourly; 1hr; ¥1050), then the special "Oku" bus to Hedo-misaki-iriguchi (4 daily; 30min; ¥550) and a 20min walk

From Kunigami, it's another 20km to Okinawa-Hontō's northern cape. The unsightly restaurant block and cigarette butts aside, this is a good spot to stretch your legs and wander over the headland's dimpled limestone rocks while the waves pound the cliffs below. On clear days, you can see northerly Yoron-tō, the first island in Kagoshima prefecture, and lumpy Iheya-jima to the west, over a churning sea where the currents sweeping around Okinawa collide.

Tanagāgumui and Kesaji mangrove forest

タナガーグムイ・慶佐次マングローブ

Route 70 snakes its way along the east coast, through forests and pineapple groves with the occasional sea view, and makes for a pleasant drive. There are few sights here, but one place to aim for is **Tanagāgumui**, a gorgeous swimming hole and small waterfall in a glade reached by a perilous scramble down a 200m clay slope. There are ropes strung down the drop to help, but you still need to be sure-footed.

Further south, just beyond Taira Bay, is the **Kesaji mangrove forest**, where a boardwalk runs alongside the river. This is a good spot to arrange a kayak trip – ask at the tourist offices in Naha (see p.790).

Kerama Islands

慶良間諸島, Kerama Shotō

The **KERAMA ISLANDS** are the closest group to Naha, lying some 30km offshore. A knot of 22 islands – though just four are inhabited – and numerous patches of sand and coral, the Keramas offer some of the most beautiful and unspoiled beaches in Okinawa and superb diving among the offshore reefs. In 2014, much of the area was designated a national park. The main island, **Zamami-jima**, is a sleepy place home to just hundreds, yet has recently become popular with international tourists thanks to the recent boom in wintertime whale-watching, as well as the demise of ferries heading from Naha to Miyako and the Yaeyamas – many are now choosing the Keramas over costly flights south. More are also now opting for **Aka-jima**, an even sleepier island, over its illustrious neighbour.

11

ARRIVAL AND DEPARTURE

KERAMA ISLANDS

By ferry The islands are served by ferry from Naha's Tomari Port. The high-speed *Queen Zamami* departs twice daily for Zamami-jima, calling at Aka-jima either on the outward or return journey (50min–1hr 15min; ¥3140 one-way, ¥5970 return; ☎ 098 868 4567); it's best to reserve tickets at least a day ahead of time. Alternatively, there's the slower *Ferry Zamami* (2hr 15min; ¥2120 one-way, ¥4030 return; ☎ 098 868 4567), which leaves Naha at 10am and returns at 2pm; this stops at Aka-jima too, and tickets almost never sell out.

In bad weather, which is quite often, everyone gets bundled onto the slow services; cancellations, when they do take place, are announced daily at 8am (boomed over the village with incredibly loud speakers), or you can simply ask at your accommodation.

By plane You may well see Kerama Airport on local maps. It does exist, on Fukaji-jima, an island connected to Geruma-jima, which is itself connected to Aka-jima; however, there have been no scheduled passenger services since 2006.

GETTING AROUND

By ferry In summer (June to mid-Sept) there are a few local services from Zamami to the uninhabited islets of Gahi-jima and Agenashiku-jima, just to the south; at these times they cost ¥1500 return, but out of season you'll have to charter your own boat. There are also year-round passenger services from Zamami to Aka-jima (4 daily; ¥300 each way).

Zamami-jima

座間味島

A whale statue greets ferries pulling in to **Zamami-jima**'s harbour, behind which lies the tiny village of **ZAMAMI** (座間味村), the only settlement of any size on the island, with seven hundred inhabitants out of a total population of one thousand. They speak their own dialect and maintain a fierce rivalry with the people of much larger Tokashiki-jima, a couple of kilometres away to the east. A fine place to get away from it all, Zamami-jima has spectacular **beaches**, both on the island itself or a short boat ride away. You can **dive** year-round, but the best time to visit is in autumn, when most of

---

WHALE-WATCHING

From late January through to April, Zamami is Okinawa's main centre for **whale-watching**. The Whale-Watching Association (☎ 098 896 4141) arranges **boat trips** from Zamami port every day at 9am and in the afternoon, depending on the weather (2hr 30min; ¥5000). Reservations are essential, and you should bring rain gear as you'll be out on the open sea. With a good pair of binoculars, you can even spot humpbacks spouting and cavorting off Zamami's northern coast. There's a special **whale observatory** about 3.5km northwest of Zamami village, which is one of several lookout points scattered around the cliffs and on the island's highest peak, **Takatsuki-yama**.

the beach bums have gone but the whale-watchers are yet to appear; the water stays warm enough for swimming and snorkelling well into December.

The beaches

Roughly 1.4km southeast of the village, over a small hill, **Furuzamami beach** (古座間味浜) boasts excellent coral and shoals of multicoloured fish. You can rent snorkels (¥500 each for goggles and fins) at the small shop, and there's also a restaurant and showers.

A similar distance west of Zamami village is **Ama beach** (阿真浜). The drop-off is quite some way out, making this beach more family-friendly than Furuzamami; when the tide's in, lucky snorkellers may be able to see sea turtles hunting for food (equipment is available from a couple of easy-to-spot places in Ama town).

GETTING AROUND   ZAMAMI-JIMA

By car Zamami Rent-a-Car (daily 9am–6pm; ☎098 987 3250) operate from the sandy lanes on the village's eastern edge, but the island's so small that it's hard to justify the expense.

By bike There are plenty of places from which to rent a bike, but the cheapest spot (¥300 for 2hr; ¥1500/day) is on the road up to *Joy Joy*. The main rental depot is in the very centre of Zamami, just along from the supermarket; they rent bikes (¥500/hr, ¥2000/day) and mopeds

(¥1500/hr, ¥4500/day).

On foot If all you want to do is see the beaches (there's little else on offer), they're both accessible in under half an hour from Zamami town – in fact, you can quite easily traverse the whole island by foot, though there are some hilly bits.

By bus A little service trundles along to both beaches (¥300), leaving infrequently from the port throughout the day, often with nobody on board.

INFORMATION AND ACTIVITIES

Tourist information As you come off the ferry in Zamami, you'll hit the tourist information office (daily 9am–5pm; ☎098 987 2277). Be sure to pick up an English map of the island from the tourist office; it features all places to sleep and eat in town. Lastly, there's some good information online (🌐zamamienglishguide.com).

Diving There are dozens of operations around Zamami, but *Joy Joy* (☎098 987 2445, 🌐keramajoyjoy.com) is recommended for its knowledgeable service. Prices tend to

be the same across the village; count on ¥3000 for a simple snorkelling trip, plus ¥1000 for equipment rental, or ¥5500 for a scuba dive including equipment and transfers.

Kayaking The Kerama Kayak Centre (☎098 868 4677), just around the corner from *Zamamia Guesthouse*, offers kayaking excursions around the Zamami area.

Boat trips Operators around Zamami offer banana boat (¥1500) or glass-bottomed-boat rides (¥2000).

ACCOMMODATION

Zamami has a reasonable selection of family-run minshuku with a few simple Japanese- and Western-style rooms. It's wise to book ahead at any time of year, and note that you may be able to score a significantly cheaper deal if you book without full board.

DOGS AND DOLPHINS

Zamami-jima has sourced much of its fame from the animal kingdom. The millions of fish enjoyed by divers (and diners at local restaurants) are an obvious draw, but dogs and whales have also made their mark. Historically, **whaling** was an important part of the local economy, but in the 1960s the whales disappeared and the industry died. Then, towards the end of the last century, the **humpbacks** started coming back to their winter breeding grounds – which the locals have been quick to exploit, though this time for tourism rather than hunting (see box, p.799). In addition, Japanese associate the Keramas with the cutesy 1988 film **I Want to See Marilyn**. Based on a true story, it tells of a romance between two dogs on neighbouring islands: Shiro on Aka-jima, and Marilyn some 3km away on Zamami-jima. They met when Shiro travelled to Zamami in his owner's boat, but the passion was such that he started swimming over every day to rendezvous with Marilyn on Zamami's Ama beach – or so the story goes. You'll pass a statue of Marilyn on your way from Zamami town to Ama beach.

Okinawa Resort 沖縄リゾート 415 Zamami ☎098 987 2736. This is possibly the friendliest place in the village, presided over by a delightful local couple who'll be more than willing to assist with diving trips. Rooms are good value, and they also have comfy chalet-style accommodation. ¥8500

Shirahama Islands Resort シラハマアイランズリゾート 32 Zamami ☎098 987 3111, ⓦzamami-shirahama .com. On the road out to Furuzamami, this is Zamami's biggest, smartest hotel. You'll chop a fair bit from the rates stipulated here if you go without meals, which are decent but not quite worth the extra fee. 🛜 ¥20,000

Zamami Campsite 座間味キャンプ ☎098 987 3259. A 20min walk east along the coast, this campsite offers several camping pitches. You can rent tents (¥500) and other equipment such as sleeping bags and BBQ sets. Camping ¥600

Zamamia Guesthouse 座間味ゲストハウス 126 Zamami ☎098 987 3626, ⓦzamamia-guesthouse .com. This new, foreign-owned option is a boon for backpackers, with decent dorms (including a female-only one) and good-value private rooms too. The lobby doubles as a burger restaurant (see below), and makes a good place to hang out over a beer. 🛜 Dorms ¥2000, twins ¥6000

EATING AND DRINKING

Small though it may be, Zamami does have a couple of half-decent places to eat, as well as a well-stocked supermarket (daily 7am–10pm). An attached shack sells *yakitori* in the evenings, and it's the done thing to grab a few sticks and a beer, then enjoy them on the harbour wall. Note that opening times can vary; those listed here should not be taken as gospel.

11

Amulet Z アミュレットZ 153 Zamami ☎098 987 2861. This new operation is surprisingly attractive for somewhere so far-flung. Their menu varies by the day (¥800–1000), but for lunch you can expect things like keema curry and avocado with raw tuna and garlic-fried shrimp. It's worth popping by for a drink in the evening – it's always the last place to shut. Mon–Sat 11.30am–2.30pm & 6pm–2am.

Cha Villa チャーヴィラ 90 Zamami ☎098 987 3737. This guesthouse is the only place in town serving coffee throughout the day; enjoy it out in the garden with a nice slab of cheesecake (¥850 all in). 🛜 Daily 9am–6pm.

★**La Toquée** ラトケ 225 Zamami ☎098 987 3558. A smart place to eat local staples like taco rice and Okinawa soba. If you're feeling more adventurous, you can also dig into plates of seared tuna with bonito flakes (¥720); in

addition, they have a good range of beer and spirits. Mon & Wed–Sun 6pm–midnight.

★**Marumiya** まるみや 432-2 Zamami ☎098 987 3166. At the back end of town, this is the most popular place with locals themselves, and it can get packed at mealtimes. They do an ¥800 lunch special, typically focusing on Japanese staples or Okinawan specialities. Mon, Tues & Thurs–Sun 11.30am–2pm & 6–11pm.

Zamamia Guesthouse 座間味ゲストハウス 126 Zamami ☎098 987 3626, ⓦzamamia-guesthouse .com. For something a little different, head to this hostel for a hearty burger (from ¥750); some of the selection on offer have Okinawan-style fillings. Drinks available too. 🛜 Daily 11.30am–2.30pm & 6–9pm.

Aka-jima

阿嘉島

Like Zamami, **Aka-jima** has some spectacular beaches on its periphery, and plentiful accommodation. Those who base themselves here tend to prefer the place to Zamami, while those who hunker down in Zamami tend to prefer it there; you can't really lose, whichever one you end up picking.

There are beaches on almost every edge of the island, with the longest stretch being **Nishi-bama** (北浜) to the northeast, almost 2km from the main town. If you really want to get away from it all, bring along a bike and cycle over the bridge to **Geruma-jima** (慶留間島), home to yet more pristine stretches of sand.

GETTING AROUND AND ACTIVITIES   AKA-JIMA

By bike and moped Aka-jima may be rather hilly, but it's a little smaller than Zamami and easy enough to get around on foot. That said, there are numerous places in which to rent bikes (¥500/hr; ¥2000/day) and mopeds (¥1500/hr; ¥4500/day), though there isn't anywhere to rent a car.

Diving There are several operators on the island, but *Seasir* (see p.802) comes highly recommended. Prices are higher than on Zamami; count on ¥8000 for a snorkelling trip, or ¥11,000 for a single scuba dive including equipment and transfers.

ACCOMMODATION

There are quite a few places to stay on Aka-jima, but even more so than on Zamami, it's best to book in advance.

Seasir シーサー 162 Aka ☎ 098 987 2973, ⓦ seasir.com. De facto choice for most of the island's divers (see p.801), this is a decent guesthouse with a range of Western- and Japanese-style rooms; rates are a bit steep but include three meals, and the rooftop Jacuzzi is a nice touch. ☎ **¥18,500**

Tatsu-no-jō 民宿辰登城 11 Aka ☎ 098 987 3557. One of the few local options which doesn't insist on meal packages, this simple minshuku sets a low-ish bar at ¥4500 per head. Rooms are simple, but there's a cool little hot tub on the second floor, and a rooftop terrace a level above that. **¥9000**

Miyako Islands

宮古列島, Miyako Rettō

One has to feel sorry for the **MIYAKO ISLANDS**. Centred around **Miyako-jima**, the main island of the chain, this small cluster boasts some of the best beaches, but they're graced by few international visitors. Long overshadowed by Zamami-jima (see p.790) and the Yaeyama group (see p.805), their appeal took another knock in 2008 with the closure of ferry services to Naha and Ishigaki, making Miyako a pricey add-on to an Okinawan tour.

Miyako-jima

宮古島

The flat, triangular-shaped island of **Miyako-jima** is roughly 35km from tip to tip – its most immediately notable aspect is field after field of sugar cane. Though essentially devoid of sights, it remains a favourite with mainland Japanese, some of whom stay for weeks or months on end, chalking off beach after beach and dive after dive. **Hirara**, the main town, lies on the island's northwest coast, from where roads fan out through the fields.

Hirara

平良

Although officially part of Miyakojima City, everyone still refers to the island's main town as **HIRARA**. Small though it may be, this is actually one of the largest Okinawan conurbations outside the mainland. Hirara has its own beach, **Painagama** (パイナガマ浜), immediately south of the harbour, but there are much better ones around the island.

Miyako Traditional Arts and Crafts Centre

宮古伝統工芸品研究センター, Miyako Dentō Kōgeihin Kenkyū Sentā • 3 Nishizato • Mon–Sat 9am–6pm • Free

It won't take long to tick off Hirara's paltry collection of sights before scooting off to the beaches, and few bother. Most appealing is the newly refurbished **Miyako Traditional Arts and Crafts Centre**, where you can watch women weaving the delicate Miyako-jōfu fabric (see box, p.792).

Sunayama beach

砂山浜, Sunayama-hama • 2.5km north of Hirara, accessed via a steep, winding path through trees and over a large sand dune

Within walking distance of Hirara and tucked into the northwestern stretch of the island is **Sunayama beach**. Some consider it the best beach of the lot – when you first catch sight of the place, it looks nothing short of heavenly. It's a good spot to come for sunset, which can often be viewed through a natural stone arch.

Ikema-jima

池間島

At the far north of Miyako-jima, a bridge connects the island with tiny **Ikema-jima**. Ikema has a lazy fishing port and more deserted beaches and good coral reefs, including the extensive Yaebishi reef, which is exposed annually during the low spring tides. You can take a glass-bottomed boat tour out there, too (50min; ¥2000). The best reason for detouring here, though, is the *Raza Cosmica Tourist Home* (see p.805).

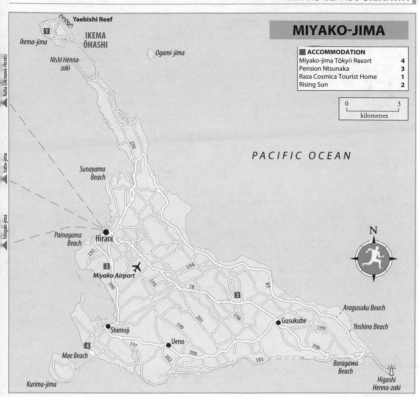

MIYAKO-JIMA

■ ACCOMMODATION
Miyako-jima Tōkyū Resort	4
Pension Ntsunaka	3
Raza Cosmica Tourist Home	1
Rising Sun	2

0   3
kilometres

PACIFIC OCEAN

The southeastern corner

Reached by a steep, winding road from Route 390, **Boragawa beach** (保良川浜) is a good spot for snorkelling and kayaking, and equipment for both is available from the attractive beachside complex that includes a refreshment hut and a fresh-water swimming pool.

At the very eastern point of the island lies beautiful **Higashi Henna-zaki** (東平安名崎), a 2km-long peninsula renowned for its wild flowers and panoramic views. Head out to the lighthouse at the very tip (daily 9am–4.30pm; ¥150), where you can climb to the top and check out the views.

Just north of the cape are the quiet beaches at **Yoshino** (吉野) and **Aragusuku** (新城), both excellent snorkelling spots with corals and a plethora of tropical fish.

Mae beach

前浜, Mae-hama

On the southwestern corner of the island, and just 10km south of Hirara, **Mae beach** is a long and remarkably pristine strip of soft white sand – it's often hailed as Japan's best beach, though some feel that it's not even the best on Miyako. Naturally, a prime chunk of it has been requisitioned by the swanky *Miyako-jima Tōkyū Resort* (see p.805).

ARRIVAL AND DEPARTURE   MIYAKO-JIMA

By plane Most flights to Miyako-jima come from Naha, though there are also a few direct services from the mainland. From Miyako Airport, there are only three buses per day into the main town of Hirara, meaning that you'll most likely have to get a taxi (¥1500), as it's too far to walk. However, if you arrange motorbike or scooter rental at the

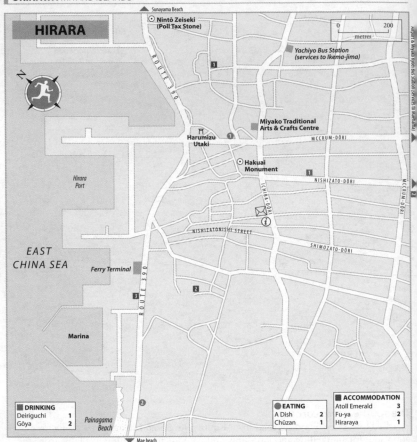

HIRARA

Sunayama Beach

⊙ Nintō Zeiseki
(Poll Tax Stone)

0 200
metres

Yachiyo Bus Station
(services to Ikema-jima)

ROUTE 390

N

Miyako Traditional
Arts & Crafts Centre

⛩ Harumizu
Utaki

MCCRUM-DŌRI

⊙ Hakuai
Monument

NISHIZATO-DŌRI

Hirara
Port

ICHIBA-DŌRI

MCCRUM-DŌRI

NISHIZATONISHI STREET

SHIMOZATO-DŌRI

EAST
CHINA SEA

Ferry Terminal

ROUTE 390

Marina

Painagama
Beach

Mae beach

airport & Miyako Kyoei Bus Station (services to Maehama)

■ DRINKING	
Deiriguchi	1
Gōya	2

● EATING	
A Dish	2
Chūzan	1

■ ACCOMMODATION	
Atoll Emerald	3
Fu-ya	2
Hiraraya	1

airport, the agents will ferry you to your hotel in Hirara for free first, before you pick up your chosen mode of transport. **Destinations** Ishigaki (2 daily; 30min); Naha (1–2 hourly; 45min); Osaka (daily; 1hr 55min); Tokyo (2 daily; 2hr 35min). **By ferry** It's important to note that there's currently no ferry service to Miyako-jima – the staff at the ferry terminal in Naha has to disappoint foreign travellers most days with this information. However, when planning your Okinawa trip it's certainly worth double-checking to see if services have resumed.

GETTING AROUND

By bus In Hirara, irregular buses for the north of the island depart from Yachiyo Bus Station, a few blocks north of the Central Post Office, while buses south to Maehama and Higashi Henna-zaki leave from Miyako Kyoei bus station on McCrum-dōri, around 1km east of the post office.

By rented vehicle The airport has car-rental stands aplenty, and given the paucity of public transport this is by far the best way of getting to the beaches. The hostels will be able to give you details about the various scooter rental places dotted around Hirara.

INFORMATION AND ACTIVITIES

Information There's a helpful information desk in the airport (daily 9am–5.30pm; ☎ 098 072 0899). **Money** An ATM accepting foreign cards is at Hirara's post office (Mon–Sat 8.45am–7pm, Sun 9am–5pm). More and more local places also accept international card payments,

but it's still advisable to come with plenty of cash. **Diving** Most hotels will be able to hook you up with a dive operator, though by far the best for English-speakers is Penguin Divers (☎ 090 8231 7161, ⓦ diving-penguin.com) in central Hirara.

ACCOMMODATION

HIRARA

Atoll Emerald ホテルアトールエメラルド 108-7 Shimozato ☎ 098 073 9800; map opposite. Right beside the ferry terminal, this upmarket option is showing its age for sure, but for now remains the classiest place in downtown Hirara, with spacious rooms, a pool (summer months only) and a smart Japanese restaurant full of kimono-clad waitresses. ¥18,000

★ **Fu-ya** 風家 109-7 Shimozato ☎ 098 075 4343; map opposite. Run by an impossibly cute family who don't seem too concerned about turning a profit – they'll pick up from the airport for ¥500, let you in on their family dinner for the same price, and their dorms are up there with the cheapest in Okinawa. Superb. Dorms ¥1350, doubles ¥6000 per person

Hiraraya ひららや 282-1 Higashinakasone ☎ 098 075 3221; map opposite. Backpacker decadence – the bunk beds at this hostel are simply huge. Service is friendly and staff can help to organize trips, but the common areas may be too smoky for some. Dorms ¥2500, doubles ¥6000

Rising Sun ホテルライジングサン 1063 Hirara-azakugai ☎ 098 079 0500, ⓦ hotel-risingsun.com; map p.803. A little south of central Hirara, this relatively new mid-ranger attained early popularity with its switched-on staff, large rooms and relaxed atmosphere. ¥11,000

AROUND THE ISLAND

Miyako-jima Tōkyū Resort 宮古島東急リゾート 914 Shimoji ☎ 098 076 2109, ⓦ miyakojima.tokyuhotels.com; map p.803. Top-class resort sitting on pretty Maehama beach, accessible by a free shuttle bus from the airport. Watersports enthusiasts won't be disappointed by the range of activities on offer. ¥35,000

★ **Pension Ntsunaka** ペンション道半 363-1 Gusukube ☎ 098 077 2577, ⓦ ntsunaka.com; map p.803. So what if this place is in the middle of nowhere? For many, that's precisely the reason to visit Miyako. An air of calm pervades this traditionally styled home, whose owner is an extremely affable chap. Shared facilities only. ¥7800

Raza Cosmica Tourist Home ラサコスミカツーリストホーム 309-1 Hiraramaezato ☎ 098 075 2020, ⓦ www.raza-cosmica.com; map p.803. There's a vaguely hippy feel to this delightful South Asian-themed adobe pension, a small, five-room affair perched above a secluded beach on Ikema-jima. Rates include an organic vegetarian breakfast, and snorkelling equipment and bikes are available. ¥14,000

11

EATING

The best place to look for restaurants in Hirara is in the tangle of streets immediately inland from the harbour, particularly on Nishizato-dōri, which runs parallel to the main road, Highway 390, but two blocks west.

A Dish アディシュ 215-3 Shimozato ☎ 098 072 7114; map opposite. The menu changes daily at this stylish and relaxed restaurant, 500m south of the ferry terminal. There's good pasta and thin-crust pizza (from ¥1000), as well as local dishes with a contemporary spin. Tues–Sat 6pm–midnight, Sun 5–11pm.

Chūzan 中山 1-10 Nishizato ☎ 098 073 1959; map opposite. Authentic *izakaya*, specializing in fish and sushi as well as what they call "ethnic" food (the Vietnamese spring rolls are quite nice). A meal shouldn't cost more than ¥1000. Daily 4pm–midnight.

DRINKING

Deiriguchi でいりぐち 224 Nishizato ☎ 098 072 8017; map opposite. This is a large, friendly bar that wouldn't look out of place in Tokyo. Arranged in booths and around the bar under a lattice of wood, customers enjoy myriad brands of *awamori*, as well as good local *izakaya* grub. Mon & Wed–Sun 5.30pm–midnight.

★ **Gōya** 郷家 570-2 Nishizato ☎ 098 074 2358; map opposite. Friendly *izakaya* and *minyō* house further east along Nishizato-dōri. Be warned – you may well end up dancing your way around the venue with the rest of the clientele, after the *sanshin* comes out at around 7.30pm. Mon–Wed & Fri–Sun 5.30pm–midnight.

Yaeyama Islands

八重山諸島, Yaeyama Shotō

Star-sand beaches to stroll along, waterfalls tumbling down emerald mountains, and not a soldier in sight … it's no wonder even Okinawans go misty-eyed when talking about the **YAEYAMA ISLANDS**. Japan fizzles out at this far-flung spray of semi-tropical islets, 430km south of Okinawa-Hontō and almost 3000km from Hokkaidō, and those lucky enough to visit are in for quite a finale. The bad news is that the Yaeyamas are no longer accessible by ferry, meaning you'll have to fly from Naha or the mainland – but it's worth it.

Most flights arrive at **Ishigaki-jima**, the most populous Yaeyama island by far. Travellers tend to base themselves here, but while Ishigaki has its charms, you'd be mad to come this far and not go that little bit further – a fifteen-minute ferry ride will take you to tiny **Taketomi-jima**, which is essentially a freeze-frame of traditional Ryūkyū life, while a little further away is **Iriomote-jima**, almost entirely cloaked with jungle and about as wild as Japan gets. Even more remote are **Hateruma-jima**, to the south, and **Yonaguni-jima**, stuck out on its own between Ishigaki and Taiwan.

Ishigaki-jima

石垣島

Yaeyama life revolves around **Ishigaki-jima**, the islands' main transport hub and population centre. Most travellers base themselves here, making use of the excellent accommodation and dining options to be found in Ishigaki, the only Yaeyama settlement large enough to warrant description as a town. The rest of the island is a predominantly rural and mountainous landscape, fringed with rocky peninsulas, stunning beaches and easily accessible reefs, while its interior is scored with the gorgeous walls of hand-stacked stone which gave Ishigaki its name. Though the main town is nice enough, it may make you wonder why you came so far to enjoy yet more urban Japan; consider basing yourself up north in beautiful **Kabira Bay** instead.

Ishigaki

石垣

ISHIGAKI is quite a nice little town; there are plenty of cool restaurants in the tight lattice of streets north of the bus and ferry terminals, as well as most of the mod cons of mainland Japan. However, apart from hosting the Yaeyamas' best range of tourist facilities, there's not too much to actually see – after your umpteenth walk through the **covered arcades**, or along the scruffy **portside**, you might start to feel a tiny bit bored. Following the airport's recent eastward relocation, and considering the island's irregular bus connections, it's perhaps best used as a first or last base if you've a late flight in or early one out.

Yaeyama Museum

八重山博物館, Yaeyama Hakubutsukan • 4-1 Tonoshiro • Tues–Sun 9am–5pm • ¥200

The small **Yaeyama Museum** lies five minutes' walk inland from Ishigaki harbour, and contains a moderately interesting collection of local artefacts, including a pile of traditional canoes, shaggy *shiisā* masks used in local festivals and a rather gruesome scroll depicting the tortures of hell.

Miyara Dunchi

宮良殿内 • 178 Okawa • Mon & Wed–Sun 9am–5pm • ¥200

Just north of Ishigaki town centre is **Miyara Dunchi**, which was built in 1819 and modelled on a traditional samurai residence; it's surrounded by a coral rock garden, designated a National Scenic Beauty. As the family still lives there, you can't enter the house itself but only look into the rooms that open onto the traditional garden.

Tōrin-ji

桃林寺 • 285 Ishigaki • Daily 9am–7pm • Free

On Ishigaki's northwestern outskirts is **Tōrin-ji**, an attractive Zen temple founded in 1614. Meditation is still practised here, though you'll be lucky to see it. Interestingly, the temple's two Deva king statues (called *niōzo*) are now worshipped as the island's protectors.

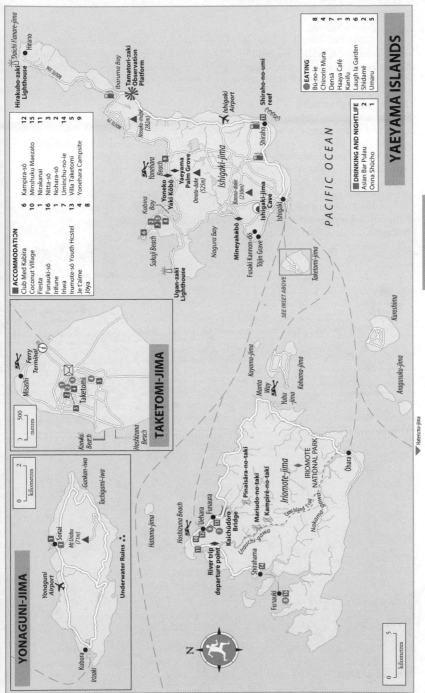

YAEYAMA ISLANDS

YONAGUNI-JIMA

TAKETOMI-JIMA

■ ACCOMMODATION

Club Med Kabira	6	Kampira-sō	12
Coconut Village	10	Minshuku Maezato	15
Fiesta	1	Nirakanai	11
Funauki-sō	16	Nitta-sō	3
Irifune	1	Nohara-sō	2
Iriwa	7	Uminchu-no-ie	14
Irumote-sō Youth Hostel	13	Villa Taketomi	5
Je t'aime	4	Yonehara Campsite	9
Joya	8		

■ DRINKING AND NIGHTLIFE

Asian Bar Pulau	2
Onna Shūcho	1

● EATING

Bū-no-ie	8
Chironin Mura	4
Densā	7
Haaya Café	1
Kanifu	3
Laugh la Garden	6
Shidamē	2
Umaru	5

PACIFIC OCEAN

11

Hirakubo-zaki
Lighthouse

Tamatori-zaki
Observation
Platform

Ibaruma Bay

Daichi Hanare-jima

Hirano

ROUTE 206

Nosoko-mahé
(282m)

ROUTE 79

Ishigaki
Airport

Shiraho-no-umi
reef

Shiraho

Ishigaki-jima

Yonehara
Beach

Yoneko
Yaki Kōbō

Kabira
Bay

Yaeyama
Palm Grove

Omoto-dake
(525m)

Banno-dake
(230m)

Ishigaki-jima
Cave

Ishigaki

Sukuji Beach

Mineyakabō

Fusaki Kannon-dō

Tōjin Grave

Nagura Bay

Ugan-zaki
Lighthouse

SEE INSET ABOVE

Taketomi-jima

Kuroshima

Aragusuku-jima

Kohama-jima

Kayama-jima

Manta
Way

Yubu-
jima

Iriomote-jima

IRIOMOTE
NATIONAL PARK

Pinaisara-no-taki

Mariudo-no-taki

Kampiré-no-taki

Kaichūdoro
Bridge

Cross Island Trail

Unauchi-gawa

Nakama-gawa

Ōhara

Funaura

Uehara

Hoshizuna Beach

Hatoma-jima

River trip
departure point

Shirahama

Funauki

N

Ferry
Terminal

Misashi

Taketomi

Konkai
Beach

Hoshizuna
Beach

500
metres

Yonaguni
Airport

Sonai

Mt Urabu
(71m)

Kubura

Irizaki

Gunkan-iwa

Tachigami-iwa

Underwater Ruins

kilometres
0   2

kilometres
0   5

kilometres
0   5

Hateruma-jima

Yonaguni-Jima (see inset top left)

Fusaki Kannon-dō

冨崎観音堂 • Fusaki • 24hr • Free

Around 2km northwest along the coast from Ishigaki town centre is the temple of **Fusaki Kannon-dō**, which was built in 1701. It boasts good views of Taketomi and Iriomote from its hillside perch, though the paths around the temple are arrestingly beautiful too – shrouded by trees, some are lined with pretty stone lanterns.

Kabira Bay and around

川平湾, Kabira-wan

Locals and tourist literature will urge you to head straight to **KABIRA BAY**, home of cultured black pearls and gorgeous emerald waters. Though it feels a bit commercial, it's still worth battling through the *omiyage* stands for the superb views of the pearl farms and surrounding islands; with the place near-silent after the tourist hordes are tucked up back in Ishigaki town, it's almost up there with the best places to stay on the island. Swimming is prohibited due to the pearl farms, but (somewhat hypocritically) you can head out on a glass-bottom boat (daily 9am–5pm every 30min; ¥1000). North of the bay is **Sukuji beach** (底地浜), one of the nicest on Ishigaki.

11

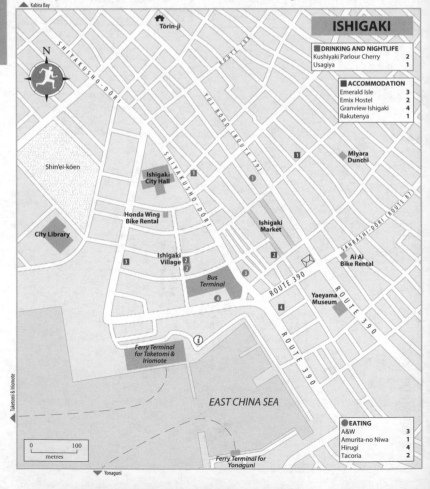

Kabira Bay

ISHIGAKI

■ **DRINKING AND NIGHTLIFE**
Kushiyaki Parlour Cherry   2
Usagiya   1

■ **ACCOMMODATION**
Emerald Isle   3
Emix Hostel   2
Granview Ishigaki   4
Rakutenya   1

Tōrin-ji

Miyara Dunchi

Shin'ei-kōen

Ishigaki City Hall

Honda Wing Bike Rental

City Library

Ishigaki Market

Ishigaki Village

Bus Terminal

Ai Ai Bike Rental

Yaeyama Museum

Ferry Terminal for Taketomi & Iriomote

Taketomi & Iriomote

EAST CHINA SEA

ROUTE 390
ROUTE 390
ROUTE 390

SHIYAKUSHO-DŌRI
YUI RŌDO (ROUTE 79)
SHIYAKUSHO-DŌRI
SANBASHI-DŌRI (ROUTE 87)
ROUTE 203

0   100
metres

● **EATING**
A&W   3
Amurita-no Niwa   1
Hirugi   4
Tacoria   2

Ferry Terminal for Yonaguni

Yonaguni

Ugan-zaki Lighthouse
御神崎灯台, Uganzaki Tōdai

On the very northwestern tip of the island is the picturesque **Ugan-zaki Lighthouse**, which commands an impressive view back across the island. Pack a picnic and enjoy it in peace here or at one of the secluded beaches nearby, which are scattered with giant shells; the sunsets are also often spectacular.

Yonehara beach and around
米原浜, Yonehara-hama

Ishigaki's most rewarding beach experience by far lies some 5km east of Kabira at **YONEHARA** (米原). Here you can wade out across a broad expanse of dead coral (make sure to wear foot protection) to the very edge of the reef, which drops off to the sea floor and is full of tropical fish. Be wary of jellyfish here, which can pack a potentially fatal sting. Snorkelling gear can be rented from shops on the main road (see p.810), and there's a good **campsite**, too (see p.810).

Yoneko Yaki Kōbō
米子焼工房 • Daily 9am–6pm • Free

If padding around the Yonehara beach area, you'll surely come across the giant, colourfully painted *shiisā* statues outside **Yoneko Yaki Kōbō**, a cottage industry factory and shop churning out the traditional Okinawan guardians.

Omoto-dake
於茂登岳

Behind Yonehara, Ishigaki's mountainous interior holds several options for **trekking**, including the hike up **Omoto-dake**; not far north of Yonehara is the turn-off to a grove of Yaeyama palms from where a trail runs up the slopes of the mountain to an observation platform.

Tamatori-zaki Observation Platform
玉取崎展望台, Tamatori-zaki Tembōdai • Infrequent buses #5 and #6 head up the east coast from Ishigaki bus terminal; they stop at the foot of the hill at the Tamatori stop, before heading on to Hirakubo-zaki

On the eastern side of the island, the views from the **Tamatori-zaki Observation Platform** are splendid, and the landscaped grounds burst with crimson hibiscus blooms; naturally, it's a favourite stop for tour buses. Further north is **Hirakubo-zaki** (平久保岬), a cape which marks the end of the line on Ishigaki-jima, punctuated by a dazzling white **lighthouse** overlooking the tiny island, Daichi Hanare-jima; it's only really worth the trek if you've got your own wheels.

Shiraho-no-umi
白保の海

One of Ishigaki's main attractions lies off the southeast shore – **Shiraho-no-umi**, a patch of reef containing some rare corals. The village of **Shiraho** (白保) has several minshuku where you can stay and arrange snorkelling boat trips at high tide (¥2000).

ARRIVAL AND DEPARTURE — ISHIGAKI-JIMA

By plane At the time of writing, the only way into the Yaeyamas is by plane. Ishigaki's sparkling new airport handles daily flights from Tokyo and a handful of other mainland cities. These include budget services with the likes of Peach from Osaka and Solaseed from Naha, as well as flights to Taipei, which can work out very handy if you're continuing on from Japan. Buses from the airport to Ishigaki run every 20min or so (40min; ¥540); it's usually worth buying one of the island passes (see p.38).

Destinations Kōbe (daily; 2hr 15min); Osaka (2 daily; 2hr 15min); Miyako (2 daily; 30min); Nagoya (daily; 2hr 40min); Naha (1–2 hourly; 1hr); Tokyo (3 daily; 3hr 15min); Yonaguni (2 daily; 30min).

By ferry The ferry terminal serving Taketomi-jima and Iriomote-jima is in the thick of things, across the road from the bus terminal; a smaller wharf serving Yonaguni-jima is

a 10min walk around the dock.
Destinations Ōhara, Iriomote-jima (every 30min; 45min); Taketomi-jima (2–3 hourly; 15min); Uehara, Iriomote-jima (hourly; 50min); Yonaguni-jima (2 weekly; 4hr 30min).

INFORMATION AND ACTIVITIES

Tourist information There's a small information booth at the airport, though more useful are the staff at Hirata Tourism (daily 7.30am–6pm; ☎098 082 6711, ⓦhirata -group.co.jp), located in the main ferry terminal. There's also good, reasonably up-to-date information about the island online at ⓦishigaki-japan.com.

Money The island's main post office (12 Okawa; daily 9am–7pm) has cash machines which accept foreign cards;

you may also have some luck at the Family Mart near the ferry terminal.

Diving There are dozens of dive operators itching to get visitors underwater; recommended are Sea Friends (☎098 082 0863, ⓦsea-friends.net) in Ishigaki and Umicoza (☎098 088 2434, ⓦumicoza.com) in Kabira.

Snorkelling Equipment can be rented out from the shops on the main road by Yonehara beach for ¥1000.

GETTING AROUND

By bus If you're planning on getting around the island by bus, it's worth investing in one of the two Free Passes, available from the driver: a one-day pass costs ¥1000, and a five-day one is ¥2000; both cover all of the island's buses, but services are not all that regular. You could also try one of the guided bus tours (¥3200 or ¥4600; Japanese only),

which visit all the island's main sights, departing from the bus terminal daily at 9am.

By car Car rental is easy to organize at the airport, or prior to arrival. Keep in mind that most of the island's petrol stations are closed on Sundays, except for those in Ishigaki; make sure you fill up before setting off around the island.

ACCOMMODATION

ISHIGAKI

★**Emerald Isle** ホテルエメラルドアイル 7-14 Misaki ☎098 082 2111, ⓦisle.okinawa; map p.808. A great new place whose quirky design lies somewhere on the spectrum between business and boutique. On one side, rooms are small and have all necessary mod cons; on the other, everything from the lobby up has been complemented with artistic flourishes. At these prices, it's a steal. ☎ **¥8300**

Emix Hostel えみっくすホステル 117 Tonoshiro ☎098 082 5236, ⓦemix-ishigaki.com; map p.808. The best of several hostels in the town centre, with relatively spacious dorms, piping-hot water in the showers, fun hosts, a paddling pool on the roof (closed in winter), and a great location in the covered arcade. Their private rooms are very good value. ☎ Dorms **¥1500**, doubles **¥5000**

Granview Ishigaki ホテルグランビュー石垣 1 Tonoshiro ☎098 082 6161, ⓦgranview.co.jp; map p.808. This is a smart hotel in a convenient location, with simple but elegantly furnished rooms. It also has a large communal bath and sauna. The official rates are fairly high; it's worth asking about discounts. Wi-fi in lobby only. ☎ **¥22,000**

Rakutenya 楽天屋 291 Ōkawa ☎098 083 8713; map p.808. English-speaking hosts Ren and Miyako have created a cosy guesthouse (actually two, next door to each other) with both tatami and Western-style rooms. Advanced booking advised. **¥7000**

KABIRA BAY

Club Med Kabira クラブメッドカビラ 1 Ishizaki ☎098 084 4600, ⓦclubmed.com; map p.807. A good resort option, with all the creature comforts one might expect – all staff speak English or French and there are excellent

facilities, including a trapeze artist on hand to teach you the ropes. Note that most guests book their rooms as part of a tour; otherwise, rates are even higher. ☎ **¥30,000**

★**Iriwa** 島宿イリワ 599 Kabira ☎098 088 2563, ⓦiriwa.org; map p.807. A fantastic addition to the area, this has swiftly become the best hostel in the Yaeyamas. The welcoming Korean–Japanese couple running the place are great sources of local information, while the accommodation – from the dorms to the private cabins – is clean and comfy. It's hard to find by yourself, so call to be picked up from the nearby Kabira Rotari bus stop, or ask the tourist office to let the owners know which bus you're taking. ☎ Dorms **¥2500**, doubles **¥8000**

Jōya 上や 920-1 Kabira ☎098 088 2717, ⓦjo-ya.jp; map p.807. Just a short walk from the bay, this ryokan has been lovingly redesigned with a mix of traditional and modern aesthetics. The shared lounge encourages guests to mingle, as does the table outside – something akin to a converted boat. ☎ **¥12,000**

SHIRAHO

Minshuku Maezato 民宿まえざと 68 Shiraho ☎098 086 8065; map p.807. The best minshuku option in the area, with amiable owners who are adept at organizing snorkelling trips. It's next to the post office; if you're coming here by bus, get off at the Shōgaku-mae stop. Rates include two meals. **¥9500**

YONEHARA BEACH

Yonehara Campsite 米原キャンプ場 446-1 Fukai; map p.807. Simple campsite with basic toilet facilities, located in the copse of trees beside the beach. Open April–Dec. **¥800**

EATING

For self-catering and local colour, check out the market in the covered arcade in Ishigaki, just north of the central Shiyakusho-dōri. Also worth mentioning are the bars and restaurants filling the new, partially open-air Ishigaki Village dining complex, which was by far the busiest place in town at the time of writing.

ISHIGAKI

A&W 245 Ōkawa ☎098 083 1234; map p.808. Many places in Ishigaki offer much the same rundown of Okinawan food, so it may come as a relief to have some good, old-fashioned Western staples. Those from outside North America may not recognize the chain, which started life as a root-beer brand and gained popularity in Okinawa as part of the military legacy. You can get free refills of the good stuff (one, in theory; infinite, in practice), so you might as well go for a small cup (¥170), as well as grub like burgers or chilli cheese curly fries (¥420). Daily 11am–10.30pm.

★Amurita-no Niwa あむりたの庭 Ōkawa 282 ⓦamuritanoniwa.com; map p.808. This smart yet laidback venue serves local dishes with a contemporary twist –the most delectable example is *Yaeyama soba* in green curry soup (¥900), though their vegan specials are certainly worth a mention. It's also good for coffee or an evening drink – they'll prove that the galaxy of Okinawan beer extends far beyond Orion. Note that it can close unpredictably, as the friendly young hosts take breaks and holidays when they feel like it. Daily 11am–midnight.

Hirugi ひるぎ 4-9 Misaki-chō ☎098 082 0732; map p.808. Colourful new venue in which you can choose all sorts of Okinawan staples from a bewildering assortment of menus – cold or hot-soup noodles, all manner of meat and fish dishes, and a fine assortment of *awamori*. Expect to pay from ¥800 for a meal, and to get annoyed by the end of it by the Barney-like Okinawan music they play non-stop. Daily 11am–2pm & 5.30–10pm.

★Tacoria タコリア 8-10 Misaki-chō ☎098 087 0768; map p.808. Is this the best taco-rice (¥850) in Okinawa? If not, it's mighty close. This superb little joint – located on the second floor of the new Ishigaki Village complex – also has non-fusion Tex-Mex fodder, including guacamole and chips (¥500), as well as soft or fried tacos (from ¥300); wash them down with a mojito. Daily 3–11pm.

KABIRA BAY

Umaru うーまる 900 Kabira ☎098 088 2841; map p.807. Small, simple joint whose *okonomiyaki*, for whatever reason, hits the spot every single time; prices are reasonable, starting at ¥650. It's just uphill from the Kabira bus stop, on the right-hand side of the road. Daily 5–10pm.

DRINKING AND NIGHTLIFE

ISHIGAKI

★Kushiyaki Parlour Cherry 串焼きパーラーチェリー 8-10 Misaki-chō ☎098 087 0872; map p.808. On the ground floor of the Ishigaki Village complex, this little venue sells grilled stick-snacks such as *yakitori* (¥140) and bacon-wrapped veggies or eggs (¥200). Yummy though these are, even more notable are the drinks on offer, which include a curated selection of highly rare cup sake – every single one's a winner – and several varieties of *shōchū* from Kyūshū island (all ¥500 each). Daily 3pm–midnight.

Usagiya うさぎや 1-1 Ishigaki ☎098 088 5014; map p.808. Every night's music night at this fun *izakaya* – performances of traditional *sanshin* music get going at 7pm (¥480 extra music charge), and songbook menus mean that, if you can read katakana (see p.869), you can join in the singalong. The food's great, with a mix of local dishes and *izakaya* staples; it's best washed down with some three-year-old *awamori*. Daily 5pm–midnight.

KABIRA BAY

Asian Bar Pulau プラウ 852-2 Kabira ☎098 088 2620; map p.807. Whatever an "Asian bar" should be, this one is very nice – strangely so, for such a remote location. Hammerhead sharks and the like cavort in the aquarium (OK, it's a television, but one can pretend), while the cheery owners dole out cocktails, locally brewed sake and more. Daily 5pm–midnight.

Taketomi-jima

竹富島

Just before six o'clock each evening, the tiny island of **Taketomi-jima** undergoes a profound, magical transformation. This is the time of the last ferry back to Ishigaki-jima – after that, you're marooned, but there are few better places to be stuck. Just over 1km wide and home to fewer than three hundred people, the island's population swells during the day with folk eager to see its traditional houses, ride on buffalo-drawn carts and search lovely sandy beaches for the famous minuscule star-shaped shells. When the day-trippers are safely back in Ishigaki, those who have chosen to stay on will have

Taketomi almost to themselves – it's possible to walk its dirt paths at night for hours on end without seeing a single soul.

A great way to get around the island is by pedalling your way over the dusty paths and roads on a bike, which is also a good way to see the local butterflies.

Taketomi

竹富

There's only one village on Taketomi – also called **TAKETOMI** – and it's a beauty. Practically all of its houses are built in traditional bungalow style with low-slung terracotta-tiled roofs, crowned with bug-eyed *shiisā*. Surrounding them are rocky walls, draped with hibiscus and bougainvillea: these are the *ishigaki* that gave a certain neighbouring island its name, yet these days they're far more prevalent on Taketomi. There aren't too many traditional sights here bar a small **museum**, but there's a lovely ocean scene around the pier on the west side of the village – this is the best spot from which to view sunset, or sit taking in the constellations at night with a can of Orion beer, and if you're in luck you'll spot some glow-worms.

Kihōin Shūshūkan

喜宝院蒐集館 • 108 Taketomi • Daily 9am–5pm • ¥300

Apart from soaking up the atmosphere, the main thing to see in Taketomi village is the **Kihōin Shūshūkan**, a small museum with an attached gift shop. There are over two thousand items on display here, including old cigarette packets, rusting samurai swords, an ornate shrine and expressive festival masks.

Beaches

The star-sand beaches, **Kondoi** (コンドイ浜) and **Hoshizuna** (星砂浜), also known as **Kaiji** (カイジ浜), are a short pedal south of Taketomi, also on the west side of the island. Swimming is possible at both, but at low tide you'll have to wade a long way out. The best snorkelling spot is at **Misashi** (ミサシ), on the northern coast, where three rocky islets and their surrounding reefs provide a home to a multitude of colourful sea life.

ARRIVAL AND INFORMATION

TAKETOMI-JIMA

By ferry Ferries from Ishigaki (¥600 one-way; 15min) run regularly (daily 7.30am–5.30pm). There are two major companies serving this route; you'll save a full ¥60 by purchasing a return ticket (enough for a can of coffee, if there are two of you), though this is slightly inconvenient since you'll only be able to return with the same company. If you've booked accommodation anywhere but the hostel and given advance warning of your arrival time, you'll be met at the terminal and taken to your room. Otherwise, it's a 10min walk from the ferry terminal to Taketomi village.

Tourist information There's a small information booth inside the ferry terminal, but more interesting is the adjacent visitor centre (ゆがふ館; daily 8am–5pm; free; ⓦ taketomijima.jp), which has displays and short films about the island's unique lifestyle. You can equip yourself with a map from the ferry terminal, or just ask around if you can't find your way – these are some of the friendliest locals in Japan.

Money There's an ATM at the post office (Mon–Fri 8.45am–5.30pm, Sat 9am–5pm), though it's a good idea to bring all necessary cash with you.

GETTING AROUND

By bike There are plenty of places in town to rent bicycles, with prices starting at ¥300/hr. Touts for the larger operations meet the ferries, and if you agree to rent a bike from them, they'll give you a free ride into town; they'll also take you back to the ferry at intervals on a pre-arranged schedule.

By suigyūsha Another way to get around is on buffalo-driven carts known as *suigyūsha* (¥1200 per person for

30min), while being serenaded by *sanshin*-plucking locals. It has to be said that these days they're commonly not locals at all, but young mainlanders on a gap year. Local or not, the experience is fun but rather cheesy, and as with rickshaws and other similar forms of transport, it's hard not to feel like a bit of a plum once you actually get moving.

ACCOMMODATION

Taketomi has some great accommodation options, almost all of which are in the village. Rates include breakfast and dinner unless otherwise mentioned.

Je t'aime ジュテーム 321-1 Taketomi ☎ 098 085 2555, ⊕ taketomi.net/jetaime. A little bit of Thailand transported to the Yaeyamas, this rickety little hostel has bunk beds in a scruffy dorm and geckos patrolling the walls. Non-smokers may not like the common room very much, since the chain-smoking owners make it reek all day as they sit around watching TV and playing video games. No meals served. ☞ Dorms **¥2800**

Nitta-sō 新田荘 347 Taketomi ☎ 098 085 2201. A good budget option for single travellers, with a range of modest tatami rooms and friendly staff; rates come down by ¥2000 if you're willing to forgo meals, and the non-meal price of ¥5800 per head makes it a good bet for single travellers. Note that the a/c is coin-operated, and at ¥100 for 30min it

can work out to be quite costly; the fans are free, though in summer it can be sweltering. **¥11,600**

★ **Nohara-sō** のはら荘 280 Taketomi ☎ 098 085 2252. A fantastic place to stay, with a very laidback atmosphere, excellent food and free snorkelling gear. Come sundown, a bottle of *awamori* is likely to appear, while the three-stringed *sanshin* comes out and an Okinawan singsong begins. ☞ **¥11,000**

Villa Taketomi ヴィラたけとみ 1493 Taketomi ☎ 098 084 5600, ⊕ www.taketomi-v.com. There's a real sense of remoteness at this cluster of en-suite pine chalets, which sit in solitude to the west of the island and are perfect for those who want to unwind. It's overpriced, for sure, though the meals are really rather good. ☞ **¥23,000**

EATING

The village offers a few eating options, but things can wind down early. A mini-market by the post office sells snacks and booze until 8pm, but don't take any of the times listed here too seriously.

Chirorin Mura ちろりん村 653 Taketomi ☎ 098 085 2007. The name of this out-of-the-way "island café" has been stylised into a vaguely South Asian-style script, which hints at the slight hippy sensibilities of the young owners. Whether you sit at the bar or in one of the hammocks outside, it's a great place to kick back over juice (including a tasty mix of *shīkuwāsā*, an Okinawan citrus and soda; ¥700), or their range of cocktails and *awamori*. Daily 10am–midnight.

Haaya Café ハーヤカフェー 379 Taketomi ☎ 098 085 2253. This café-cum-restaurant-cum-bar is the island's most urbane place to eat or drink. The coffee's good, the food's fine (including taco-rice; ¥850), and the atmosphere is a sort of modern South Sea style. It's also a good place for a drink – juices include bitter *gōya juice* (¥500), and they've plenty of *awamori* (¥500) among their range of alcoholic drinks. Daily 10am–5pm & 7–10pm.

★ **Kanifu** かにふ 494 Taketomi ☎ 098 085 2311. *Gōya champurū* (¥850), pork-and-ginger stir-fry (¥1000) and local shrimp are the stars of the show at this excellent, barn-like restaurant, while the sweet potato cheesecake (¥450) is great for dessert. Check out the cute, tropically styled bar by the outdoor seating area. Mon–Wed & Fri–Sun 11am–5pm & 6–8.30pm, Thurs 11am–5pm.

Shidamē しだめー館 361 Taketomi ☎ 098 085 2239. Relaxed spot with outdoor seating and a modest range of Okinawan staples – try the taco-rice or *sōki soba* (both ¥800), or the *maguroage keishoku* (featuring fried, breaded tuna balls; ¥700). A whole clutch of Japanese B-list celebrities have eaten here and left their signatures – look out for the giant palm-print of Hakuhō, the most successful sumo wrestler in history. Daily noon–3pm & 6–8pm.

Iriomote-jima

西表島

Brooding darkly some 20km west of Ishigaki, **Iriomote-jima** is an extraordinarily wild place for Japan. Rising sharply out of the ocean, some ninety percent of its mountainous interior is covered with dense subtropical rainforest, much of which is protected as the **Iriomote National Park**. Yaeyama rumour would have it that Iriomote often – or even perpetually – plays host to disaffected Japanese, living rough in the jungle. A more substantiated inhabitant, though equally elusive, is one of the world's rarest species, the *yamaneko*, or **Iriomote lynx**, a nocturnal animal that looks something like a scruffy house cat. The island and its surrounding waters are also home to a splendid array of flora and coral reefs rich with tropical fish. There are plenty of opportunities for snorkelling, diving, kayaking and hiking through the rainforest; at night-time, it can be quite exciting to take a walk on the empty main road, admiring the stars overhead, and listening to the distant crash of waves.

11

Although it's Okinawa's second-largest island, fewer than two thousand people live here, most of them along barely developed strips on the north and south coasts. Ferries from Ishigaki sail to two ports on the island: Ōhara (大原) in the south and **Uehara** in the north. The latter is the best place to head for, since it's closer to Iriomote's main scenic attractions and offers the widest range of accommodation, but neither is particularly visually appealing. With more time on your hands, consider heading way out west to end-of-the-line **Shirahama** (白浜), or even further on by ferry to remote **Funauki (船浮)**, which cannot be reached by road – with a real frontier feel and a truly glorious beach nearby, this is one of the most characterful towns in Japan. It's certainly worth staying at least one night on Iriomote, though it's best to opt for an accommodation deal that includes two meals (or at least breakfast) unless you're staying in one of the two main towns, since eating options are thin on the ground.

Uehara
上原

It's hard to believe that **UEHARA** is Iriomote's main settlement – it's home to mere hundreds of people, and you can traverse every single road in well under an hour. It's not terribly interesting or very attractive, but this is the main centre of affairs; if you want to kayak, hike or go diving, it's best to bite the bullet and use Uehara as a base. If you find yourself staying here and craving a little adventure, wander up any of the side streets heading uphill away from the main road. All eventually head to a charmingly bucolic plateau, full of farmyard sights and smells; if the moon's fat and the sky clear, head up at night to drink in some truly haunting beauty (and perhaps a little *awamori*).

Urauchi-gawa and the waterfalls

浦内川 • **Jungle cruise** 7 daily 9.30am–3.30pm; 1hr • ¥1800 • **Waterfall trip & hike** 6 daily 9.30am–2pm; 3hr • ¥1800 • **Waterfall & kayak tour** Daily 9.30am; 6hr • ¥8400 • **Kayak tour** Daily 10am & 1.30pm; 2hr • ¥4000 • **Waterfalls & jungle trek** Daily 10.30am; 5hr • ¥7000 • **Night tour** Daily 7pm; 2hr • ¥5000 • ☎ 098 085 6154, ⓦ urauchigawa.com • Boat and kayaking tours can be arranged at the Urauchi-gawa centre (daily 8am–5pm) • Island bus to Urauchi-gawa stop

The vast majority of visitors to Iriomote-jima come only for the day, heading straight to the **Urauchi-gawa**, a broad, almost Amazon-like river reachable by island bus. Here, they hop on one of various boat tours operated by the local visitor centre; the most popular terminate at a trail heading up to two scenic waterfalls: **Kampirē-no-taki** (カンピレーの滝) and **Mariudo-no-taki** (マリウドの滝). The touristy nature of this excursion is undeniable (almost anyone can easily negotiate the gentle 1.5km "trek" through the rainforest up to the falls), yet it's still enjoyable, and there are several more adventurous options. The truly hardy may wish to consider the 15km hike across the island from the head of the Kampirē falls to the **Nakama-gawa** (仲間川), Iriomote's second-largest waterway, and Ōhara – you'll need local advice and a guide before tackling this. It's also possible to paddle back from the falls in a **kayak**, which is a great way to view the rainforest at close quarters.

Pinaisāra-no-taki
ピナイサーラの滝

Operators in town (see p.816) can organize kayaking trips and treks up to **Pinaisāra-no-taki**, the tallest waterfall in Okinawa; the youth hostel (see p.816) can also provide details of hiking trails from **Funaura** (船浦), but even if you don't get too close, you can clearly see the cascade from the Kaichūdōro bridge that spans the bay immediately south of Funaura. At low tide, you may well find yourself dragging your kayak across the shallows to the Hinai-gawa before paddling to the start of the trek. This will give you a chance to inspect the mangrove forests closely and see armies of purple soldier crabs scuttling across the sandbanks. On the climb to the head of the falls, keep a lookout for snakes and be prepared for leeches, especially in the wet season. At the foot of the trail, you'll also pass many of the distinctive **sakishima suōnoki** trees.

SNORKELLING AND DIVING OFF IRIOMOTE

Iriomote is a **divers' paradise**; the **Manta Way**, between the island's eastern coast and Kohama-jima, is particularly famous for its shoals of manta rays, which you're most likely to see between April and June. The youth hostels and all minshuku can put you in touch with the island's several dive operations (see p.816). **Snorkelling** is particularly good at **Hoshizuna Beach** (星砂の浜), around 4km northwest of Funaura, where you'll also find a **campsite** (¥300 per person), a decent restaurant and snorkelling gear for rent – unsurprisingly, it's quite popular. If you're looking to escape the crowds, head to **Funauki** (船浮), reachable by three ferries a day (¥410) from **Shirahama** (白浜), at the far west end of the coastal road; the beach here, a short trek through the jungle, is one of the most beautiful in all of Japan and great for snorkelling, though for actual diving you'll have to get on a boat tour.

Shirahama

白浜

The road that snakes most of the way around Iriomote hits its western terminus in **Shirahama**; there is no lovelier, more relaxed place on the full 53km stretch than this. While there are no sights here as such, it won't take long to spot the **monument** to a geographical nicety: it's placed on the 123°45'6.789" line of longitude (the eagle-eyed will have seen another one on the way in from Uehara).

Funauki

船浮 • Ferries from Shirahama 5 daily; 20min • ¥950 return

An even more pleasant and chilled out place than Shirahama lies not far away: **Funauki**, a tiny village that's only reachable by ferry. The town's own focal points are a curry restaurant (see p.816) and a hilariously oversized **school**; at the time of writing, the latter boasted a fully stocked gymnasium, a whole orchestra's worth of musical equipment, seven staff, one principal... and two poor students, one of whom will have graduated by the time you read this. Pop by to say hello, and you'll make everyone's day. The real draw here, however, is **Ida beach** (イダの浜), a stretch of pristine sand reachable after a fifteen-minute walk along a jungle path; this is one of the most splendid beaches in all Japan, with one distant lighthouse the only blot on an almost entirely natural horizon. In fact, the only annoyance is that the most convenient ferry back to Shirahama misses the last island bus by ten minutes – truly ridiculous.

Yubu-jima

由布島 • Buffalo every 30min • ¥1300 per load • ⓦ yubujima.com/english

If schedules oblige you to use the Ōhara ferry terminal (which is quite often the case), and if you've got your own wheels, you may care to stop by quirky little **Yubu-jima** on the way between here and Uehara. The islet lies just offshore, and for much of the day it's basically possible to walk across with suitable footwear. A more enjoyable means of access – and useful if you don't have a pair of wellies with you – are the **buffalo** that trudge through the mud, carting wagons behind them. Once on the island, walking paths allow you to see butterflies, warthogs and flowers aplenty, as well as part-submerged mangrove forests on the land-facing side.

ARRIVAL AND DEPARTURE   IRIOMOTE-JIMA

By ferry Yaeyama Kankō and Anei Kankō both run regular high-speed ferries from Ishigaki to Uehara (50min; ¥2300 one-way, ¥4400 return) and Ōhara (40min; ¥1770 one-way, ¥3390 return). Inclement conditions (or a lack of demand) may force ferries to use Ōhara – check with your accommodation when you're on your way back to Ishigaki.

GETTING AROUND

By bus Iriomote's only main road runs along the coast from Ōhara via Funaura and Uehara to Shirahama in the west; all of these villages are linked by just four daily public buses. It's usually best to buy a pass, which will pay for itself if you take even one lengthy journey; a one-day pass costs ¥1030, and a three-day one ¥1540.

By car and bike To really explore the island, you'll need to rent a bike or car; if your accommodation can't help, they'll be able to point the way to the nearest rental spot. There are several in both Ōhara and Uehara.

INFORMATION AND ACTIVITIES

Services The island's few post offices (in the two main towns and just north of Shirahama) are usually able to accept international cards; that said, it's advisable to arrive with enough cash to cover your stay.

Diving Reef Encounters (see box, p.815), on Okinawa-Hontō, organizes excellent trips to this distant island. There are plenty of operators in the immediate environs of the Uehara ferry terminal, though none speak English; the curry restaurant in Funauki (see below) also rents out snorkelling equipment if you're hitting the beach way out that way.

Kayaking You'll find a variety of places around the Uehara ferry terminal that rent out kayaks or arrange tours.

ACCOMMODATION

UEHARA

Coconut Village ココナッツビレッジ 397-1 Uehara ☎ 098 085 6045. On the northwestern outskirts of Uehara, this modern beachside complex has small tatami and Western-style rooms (with very low beds), a restaurant and a fresh-water pool. 📶 **¥13,000**

Irumote-sō Youth Hostel いるもて荘ユースホステル 870-95 Uehara ☎ 098 085 6255. This is a great budget place with a hilltop location that makes it a little hard to walk to – no matter, since the friendly owners will pick you up from Uehara. Serves excellent meals, has bikes and scooters for rent, and organizes a daily drop-off at the Urauchi-gawa and Hoshizuna beach. The dorms are far too expensive – just pay a little extra for a private room. 📶 Dorms **¥4000**, doubles **¥4500**

★**Kanpira-sō** カンピラ荘 545 Uehara ☎ 098 085 6508, ⊛ kanpira.com. Only a minute on foot from Uehara ferry terminal (turn right at the main road and you're already there), this is a lovely place with cosy, good-value rooms, both en-suite and otherwise. Little English is spoken, but they have a wealth of pamphlets, schedules and the like. **¥6000**

WESTERN IRIOMOTE

Funauki-sō ふなうき荘 By the port, Funauki ☎ 098 085 6161. This basic minshuku is nothing special, but there's only one other choice in Funauki, and that's the same price but worse. There's a little *izakaya* just around the corner, and a real edge-of-the-world atmosphere. **¥12,000**

★**Nirakanai** ホテルニラカナイ 2-2 Uehara ☎ 098 085 7111, ⊛ nirakanai-iriomotejima.jp. The fanciest place on the island, this is a little slice of secluded paradise with snazzy, wood-floored rooms separated from the beach by nothing more than a swimming pool. It's a bit distant from everything, so you'll most likely have to rent a car if you want to eat or drink elsewhere, but they've free shuttle buses to Uehara port. **¥18,000**

Uminchu-no-ie 海人の家 1499-57 Taketomi-chō ☎ 098 085 6119. Simple Japanese-style accommodation in a large, blue municipal building at Shirahama – useful if you want to get away from what constitutes crowds on Iriomote. Rates include a breakfast of coffee and bread. **¥8000**

EATING

As with any small Okinawan island, don't take the stipulated restaurant opening times too seriously. There aren't too many eating options in Uehara; those who are not getting fed at their accommodation should note that there's also a small supermarket opposite the ferry terminal (daily 8am–8pm).

UEHARA

Densā デンサー 558 Uehara ☎ 098 085 6453. On Uehara's main "drag", though a bit hard to spot, this small eatery is often the only place serving food in the middle of the day. A decent range of Okinawan staples is on offer, including Yaeyama soba (¥500) and pork on rice (¥600). Mon, Tues & Thurs–Sun 11.30am–7pm.

Laugh la Garden ラフラガーデン 550-1 Uehara ☎ 098 085 7088. On the other side of the main road from the ferry terminal, this second-floor venue is Uehara's most reliable restaurant by far (despite the odd name and opening hours). The *gōya champurū* set meal (¥800) is big and tasty, as is the *oden*. Lastly, it's a nice drinking hole, too; there's plenty of *awamori* (from ¥400), as well as more regular Japanese tipples. Mon, Tues & Sat–Sun 6.30pm–midnight.

FUNAUKI

★**Bū-no-ie** ぶーの家 2462 Iriomote ☎ 090 6868 7184. For a Funauki restaurant run by an elderly couple, this has its marketing cap on straight – you'll see signs all the way from Shirahama ferry terminal, and it's also the only place in town renting out snorkelling equipment. They serve curry (¥800 with chicken, ¥900 with mountain boar hunted by them) and coffee (¥200 extra) in their garden-like outdoor area. Daily 9am–5pm.

Yonaguni-jima

与那国島

Some 127km west of Ishigaki and 2000km from Tokyo, **Yonaguni-jima** is the farthest west you can go and still be in Japan; on a clear day, you can see Taiwan 111km away from Yonaguni's highest point, **Mount Urabu**. It's just 11km long, so it won't take you long to tour this predominantly rural but hilly island. **SONAI** (祖納) on the north coast is the main community; ferries dock in its port, and the **airport** is a couple of kilometres west. A circuit of the island shouldn't take you more than half a day, although you'd be mad to pass up the chance to linger at some of the most deserted beaches in the Yaeyamas. Heading west from Sonai past the tiny port of **Kubura** (久部良) and out to **Irizaki** (西崎), you'll find a simple monument marking Japan's westernmost point, atop sheer cliffs.

Intriguing rock formations can be found above water on Yonaguni's east coast. **Gunkan-iwa** (軍艦岩) is said to resemble a battleship, although it actually looks more like a submarine rising to the surface. There's little debate over what the **Tachigami-iwa** (立神岩) outcrop resembles – it's worshipped by locals as a symbol of virility. On the nearby hillsides, wild Yonaguni horses roam.

11

ARRIVAL AND GETTING AROUND

YONAGUNI-JIMA

By plane Yonaguni is accessible with flights from Ishigaki (2 daily; 30min) and Naha (2 daily; 1hr). The planes are tiny and propeller-driven.

By ferry Twice-weekly ferries run from Ishigaki (4hr; ¥3740) to Kubura port, on the west side of the island.

By bike and car The best way to get around is with a rented bike or car – the latter is best arranged at the airport, while for bikes try asking at *Fiesta* (below).

ACCOMMODATION

Sonai has a handful of hotels, though not many places to eat – few places are open for more than a couple of hours a day.

Fiesta ホステルフィエスタ 1080 Yonaguni ☎098 087 2339. Occasionally lively hostel, with dorm "beds" (futons on the floor) and a few private rooms, plus cooking facilities and free coffee. ☎ Dorms **¥2000**, doubles **¥4500**

Irifune ホテル入船 59-6 Yonaguni ☎098 087 2311.

This is the classiest place in town, though that's not saying much – the rooms are overpriced for sure. However, it's run by Aratake Kihachiro, who discovered the nearby underwater ruins and runs glass-bottom boat tours, diving and fishing trips. ☎ **¥9000**

DRINKING

Onna Shūcho 女酒長 5-2 Yonaguni ☎098 087 3282. Yonaguni's best *izakaya* by a long way, a sometimes rowdy affair lassoing together the area's locals, divers and visitors.

Try their delectable *gōya tempura*, a snip at ¥500. Mon, Tues & Thurs–Sun 5pm–1am.

UNDERWATER YONAGUNI

Much more interesting than anything on Yonaguni's tiny landmass is what lies on the seabed beneath. In 1986, local divers came across what looked like a giant rock-carved staircase, or possibly part of a pyramid, 80m long, 50m wide and 20m high. Researchers have flocked to what have been described as the **underwater ruins** (海底遺跡) ever since. Some claim the rocks are part of the legendary ancient civilization of Mu, an Asian Atlantis. The weather dictates whether diving is possible here – when the wind's blowing from the south, it's too dangerous. Another diving highlight here is the sight of schools of hammerhead sharks, particularly in the winter months.

To organize a diving trip, your best bets are the hotel *Irifune* (see above), whose owner actually discovered the ruins, or *Marine Club Sou-Wes* (☎098 087 2311, ☎www.yonaguni.jp); a single dive with either company will set you back around ¥13,000, including equipment rental, while snorkeling trips are closer to ¥5000. For kayaking, try your luck at *Guesthouse Adan* (ゲスト ハウス阿檀; 186-1 Yonaguni; ☎098 087 2947).

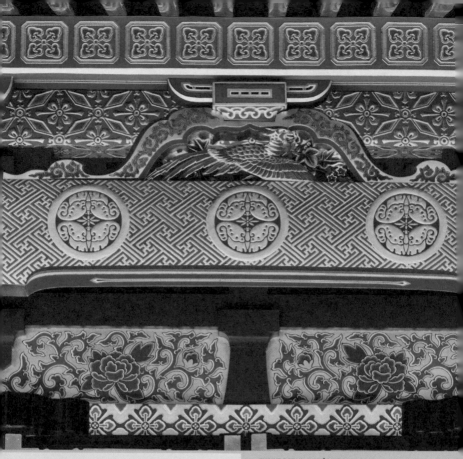

SHRINE DETAIL, NIKKŌ NATIONAL PARK

Contexts

History

Archeological evidence shows that humans settled in Japan more than 30,000 years ago; most probably migrants from mainland Asia as well as Polynesians who moved north along the east Asian coast. Living mainly by hunting, fishing and gathering, with some cultivation of plants, they spread through the Japanese archipelago. The Jōmon culture began about 10,000–15,000 years ago; in this age, the Japanese began to live in fixed communities composed of large wooden structures. The pottery they made was decorated with a rope pattern (jōmon). By about 1000 BC, these communities showed increasingly developed social structures and cultural practices.

The impetus for the change from a hunting, fishing and gathering culture to one based on **agriculture** was the arrival of large numbers of Korean immigrants to Japan, who brought with them the technologies for growing rice in irrigated fields and for making bronze implements. This process had begun at least by 400 BC, initiating what is called the **Yayoi period**, which was characterized by highly developed communities and lasted until about 300 AD. As the Yayoi communities developed socially and economically, **class divisions** appeared, and some families became rulers of small "countries". Chinese records indicate that Japan was composed of more than a hundred of these local states, which were often at war with each other.

The Kofun (Tomb) period and the arrival of Buddhism

As the ruling families of the Yayoi era became more powerful and wealthy, they began to build large **burial mounds** (*kofun*) for their deceased leaders. This took place from the fourth to the seventh centuries AD, in what is known as the Kofun, or Tomb, period. These mounds, numbering in the thousands, can be found throughout Japan. The largest, attributed to the ruler **Nintoku**, was built in the mid-fifth century and is one of the three largest tombs in the world. In this period, many **technologies** were brought from Korea that improved upon existing methods, including new techniques

THE MAJOR HISTORICAL PERIODS

Jōmon	10,000–300 BC	Azuchi-Momoyama	1573–1600
Yayoi	300 BC–300 AD	Edo (or Tokugawa)	1600–1868
Kofun	300–710	Meiji	1868–1912
Nara	710–794	Taishō	1912–1926
Heian	794–1185	Shōwa	1926–1989
Kamakura	1185–1333	Heisei	1989–present
Muromachi	1333–1573		day
(or Ashikaga)			

c.35,000 BC	c.12,000 BC	c.300 BC	c.300 AD
Humans settle in Japan.	Jōmon era begins; people live in settlements and produce distinctive pottery.	Yayoi period sees the arrival of Koreans with new technologies.	Kofun period begins. Small local kingdoms gradually unite under the Yamato court.

for irrigating rice fields, making ceramics, metalworking, weaving and writing. At the same time, political organization spread throughout Japan, fuelling the increasing power of ruling families.

During the **Tomb period**, the numerous small local kingdoms gradually merged into one nation under the rule of the **Yamato** court, in central Japan. To consolidate their power, the Yamato rulers made use of Chinese political ideas, such as court rituals and Confucian philosophy. The introduction of **Buddhism** in around 550 (see p.836) provided another opportunity for the imperial family to strengthen its position. **Prince Shōtoku**, regent during the reign of Empress Suiko, emphasized both Confucian and Buddhist principles for governance in his Seventeen-article Constitution of 604, and he is traditionally associated with the founding of the Buddhist temples Hōryū-ji near Nara and Shitennō-ji in Osaka.

However, the ruling family was still weak and had been dominated by the **Soga** clan since the mid-sixth century. The Soga's power came to an end with the **Taika** ("great change") coup d'état in 645, followed by the Taika Reforms, which decreed that all agricultural land was state property and all persons were subject to the imperial government. **Emperor Tenmu** was the key figure in establishing the power of the imperial family and the building of a strong central government. Having obtained real power through his victory in the succession dispute known as the Jinshin War (672), he staffed his government with imperial relatives and brought other clan chieftains into the government at lower ranks. The concept of a **divine emperor**, descended from the gods, was established at this time. Tenmu put Amaterasu (the Sun Goddess), the ancestral deity of the imperial clan, ahead of all other ancestral deities.

The first permanent capital city, **Fujiwara-kyō**, was established in 694, with a layout similar to the Chinese capital city of Chang'an. Further, a number of penal and administrative codes were promulgated at this time, attempting to establish a government on the Chinese model, headed by the emperor and administered by a vast bureaucracy.

Cultural awakening in the Nara period

The city of **Nara**, originally named Heijō-kyō, was established in 710 as the capital city. It, too, was laid out in a checkerboard pattern on the model of Chang'an, and was built on a grand scale, a hint of which can be seen in the recent reconstructions of the Nara imperial palace. The government continued to issue **Chinese-style law codes**, expand the bureaucracy and attempt to establish control over the provinces. **Emperor Shōmu** sought to use the increasing popularity of Buddhism as an additional means of enhancing imperial power. He ordered the construction of the Great Buddha (*daibutsu*) statue depicting the cosmic Buddha Rushana (Vairocana), who presides over the universe; Shōmu sought to establish a parallel between Rushana's rule over the universe and the emperor's rule over the officials and the people.

The Nara period saw a tremendous flowering of the **arts**, remains of which can be seen in the city today (see p.485). In addition to great works of sculpture, painting and architecture, important literary works were produced. Japan's oldest surviving historical documents were transcribed in these years – the *Kojiki* (*Record of Ancient Matters*) and the *Nihon-shoki* (*Chronicles of Japan*) – establishing the legitimacy of the imperial rulers through divine descent. Nara was the eastern terminus of the **Silk Road** trade route, and

c.550	604	672	694
Buddhism is brought to Japan and gradually spreads throughout the country.	Prince Shōtoku issues his Seventeen Articles, based on both Confucian and Buddhist ideas.	The Jinshin War establishes the power of the imperial family.	Fujiwara-kyō, in present-day Nara Prefecture, is made the first permanent capital.

many objects from as far as Persia – now deposited in the Shōsō-in, the imperial repository at Tōdai-ji – reached Japan this way. Finally, numerous advances in administrative procedures such as **taxation** and **census-taking** helped to establish the imperial government in Nara as the government of all Japan.

Beneath the surface, however, imperial rule was far from stable. The **Fujiwara** family, descendants of a clan that aided the imperial family to escape from the control of the Soga clan in the Taika coup of 645, increasingly exerted control over the imperial family by marrying their daughters to princes, such as in the case of Emperor Shōmu, whose mother and wife were both Fujiwara women. There were even two armed **rebellions** against the imperial government led by members of the Fujiwara family. Struggles both within the imperial family itself and against the Fujiwara caused several temporary relocations of the capital during this period; finally, under Emperor Kammu, a new capital city was built at **Nagaoka-kyō** (near present-day Kyoto), and the government resided there from 784 until 794.

The Heian Period and the rise of the samurai

In 794, the imperial palace moved once again, and a new capital was established at **Heian-kyō (Kyoto)**. This move served to strengthen Emperor Kammu's branch of the imperial family, weakening the other noble families at court because of the heavy cost of the move, and bringing the Buddhist clergy under stricter control. Again, the capital was laid out on the Chinese model in a checkerboard pattern, evidence of which remains to this day. The Heian Shrine, a modern replica on a smaller scale, gives some idea of the Chinese style of the original Great Hall of State. In contrast to the many relocations of the capital in the past, Kyoto was to remain the imperial capital of Japan for more than a thousand years, until 1869.

For much of the **Heian period**, the imperial court was dominated by the Fujiwara family, who continued their strategy of "marriage politics." Fujiwara Michinaga, whose villa in Uji became Byōdō-in, represented the high point of Fujiwara dominance, with four of his daughters married to emperors. However, the daughters of his son Yorimichi did not produce male heirs, so when **Go-Sanjō** ascended the throne in 1068, he was the first emperor in almost two centuries whose mother was not a Fujiwara. This competition between the imperial family and the Fujiwara continued throughout the Heian period, complicated by the increasing influence of the great Buddhist temples and the rising power of **warrior families**. These elite groups gradually usurped powers of taxation and administration, so that aspects of government began to be privatized, beginning with land. Noblemen sent as governors to the provinces formed ties with powerful local families and gradually established control over **land** that they treated as their private property and for which they paid no taxes. The great temples and shrines also held land that was tax exempt; the income from it was used to support religious activities. Finally, even the imperial family came to hold land privately. By the end of the Heian period, almost half of the land in the country was no longer public land.

The privatization of government functions was also reflected in the rise of the notorious military class of the **samurai** (see box, p.824). Chinese-style conscription, established in the mid-seventh century, proved both unnecessary and ineffective, and led the government gradually to rely on private military professionals, composed of

710	794	806	c.1000
A new capital is established at Heijō-kyō, present-day Nara.	The imperial capital is moved from Nagaoka-kyō to Heian-kyō, present-day Kyoto, which remains the capital until 1869.	The monk Kobo Daishi returns from China and founds the Shingon school of Buddhism.	Murasaki Shikibu writes The Tale of Genji – the world's first novel.

provincial elites as well as aristocrats of lower rank: two of the leading warrior families, the **Taira** (Heike) and **Minamoto** (Genji), were descendants of emperors. Despite this, while the central government itself gradually lost political power as administrative and military functions were privatized, the imperial family and the aristocrats surrounding them continued to hold symbolic and sacerdotal authority. Just as the Fujiwara clan ruled by dominating the imperial family rather than replacing it, so too would the succeeding **military governments** rule in the emperor's name.

The struggle between the Taira and the Minamoto brought the Heian period to an end. Taking part in a succession dispute within the imperial family, these two clans fought each other in the late 1150s; the Taira, led by **Taira Kiyomori**, emerged the victors. Kiyomori sought to consolidate his power by adopting the same methods that the existing elite had used, taking high court posts and using "marriage politics" to become grandfather to an infant emperor.

In the meantime, **Minamoto Yoritomo**, who had been sent into exile in eastern Japan, spent several years building a strong military force from his headquarters at Kamakura, and in a civil war lasting from 1180 to 1185, the Minamoto defeated the Taira. The tragic figure in this story is **Minamoto Yoshitsune**, Yoritomo's half brother. His skill in battle did much to enable the Minamoto victory; however, jealous of Yoshitsune's popularity and suspicious of his loyalty, Yoritomo sent soldiers out to kill him. On the run for several years, Yoshitsune was eventually betrayed and forced to commit suicide; his head was sent, preserved in sake, to his brother.

The Kamakura period and invasions by the Mongols

The **Kamakura bakufu** (shogunate) was founded by Minamoto Yoritomo in 1185. It was legitimized by the imperial court, specifically by his appointment as shogun in 1192. However, it remained separate from the imperial establishment in Kyoto not only by maintaining headquarters in Kamakura (see p.188), but by creating a highly developed civil administration and code of government.

After Yoritomo's death, the *bakufu* was dominated by the **Hōjō** clan, the family of the late shogun's wife Masako, who by all accounts was one of the dominant personalities of this era. The Hōjō served as regents to the actual shogun, who were often aristocrats brought from Kyoto. Although the Kamakura *bakufu* increased its power over Kyoto to some extent, thirteenth-century Japan was basically a "dual polity" in which the imperial government in Kyoto ruled Japan in tandem with the military government in Kamakura.

The thirteenth century was marked by two great events: Japan was **invaded** twice by forces of the **Mongol Empire**, first in 1274 and again in 1281. The Japanese managed to fight off the Mongols, with the aid of typhoons ("divine winds", or kamikaze), from Hakata Bay in northern Kyūshū, where the foreigners landed. Remains of the stone wall constructed around Hakata Bay after the first invasion as defensive fortifications can be seen to this day. Despite this victory, the invasions were a heavy blow to the *bakufu*. The basic relationship between the shogun and his vassals was the granting of land in return for service. Many vassals had been mobilized, at great expense to themselves, but after the defeat of the Mongols, there was no land available for distribution as rewards for service. This added to the economic hardships many vassals were already undergoing; the situation was ripe for revolt.

1185	1227	1274; 1281	1333
The Minamoto family destroys the Taira forces and Yoritomo founds the Kamakura *bakufu*; he is appointed shogun in 1192.	The monk Dōgen returns from China and establishes the Sōtō sect of Zen Buddhism.	Mongol forces attack Japan.	The Kamakura *bakufu* is destroyed and Emperor Go-Daigo asserts direct rule.

The Muromachi (or Ashikaga) period and a century of warfare

The insurgency was led by **Emperor Go-Daigo** and aided by **Ashikaga Takeuji** (1305–58), head of an eastern warrior family that had become disaffected with the Kamakura *bakufu* and its Hōjō leaders. Kamakura was taken in 1333, and for the next three years Go-Daigo attempted to re-establish direct rule by the imperial family. However, by favouring court nobles and officials rather than the warriors who had supported him, he alienated Takeuji, who drove him from Kyoto in 1336 and threw his support behind a rival claimant to the throne, Kōmyō. Go-Daigo fled to the mountains of Yoshino, where he set up court at **Yoshimizu Shrine**. Until the end of the fourteenth century, two lines of the imperial family each claimed legitimacy. This occasioned much warfare, although the military tactics of the time relied on small groups of mounted **archers**, so the number of combatants was relatively small.

The Ashikaga (or **Muromachi**) *bakufu* began officially in 1338 when Takeuji was appointed shogun; he was the first of fifteen Ashikaga shogun who headed the *bakufu*, until it was destroyed in 1573. The *bakufu* headquarters was in Kyoto, which suggests how closely they were dependent on the imperial court for legitimacy. In fact, the Ashikaga shoguns' control over the military families in the provinces was quite weak.

The early Ashikaga shoguns are justly famous for their love of the **arts**. The nō theatre developed under their patronage; Kinkaku-ji and Ginkaku-ji temples were originally their villas. They also established a network of Zen temples throughout Japan, in an unsuccessful attempt to use Buddhism to strengthen their political power.

This Muromachi period saw a number of important **changes** in Japanese society: military force gradually replaced the imperial court and *bakufu* as the ultimate authority in settling disputes; the population grew; the economy developed significantly and became increasingly based on capital; international trade, both official and private, expanded significantly; and farmers became more economically powerful vis-à-vis their rulers. The shogunate itself relied less on income from land holdings and more from taxes on the commerce that flourished in Kyoto.

The beginning of the end for the Ashikaga *bakufu* was the **Ōnin War** (1467–77), which had its roots in succession disputes among the Ashikaga leadership. During this drawn-out struggle, much of Kyoto was destroyed. Many of the participants were troops led by provincial governors, who fought on one side or the other to secure recognition from the shogun to legitimize their authority in the provinces. But while they were engaged in this struggle at the centre, the very provinces the governors were trying to protect were being taken over by local warriors. Other governors remained in the provinces to consolidate their control by military force without much concern for court or *bakufu* appointments. This ushered in the century of warfare, the **Warring States** period from roughly the end of the Ōnin War until the unification of Japan in the late sixteenth century.

The "states" of this era were areas of land under the control of warlords called "*daimyō*" who held this land by virtue of their military strength, although they often sought prestige and legitimacy by seeking appointment by the shogun as provincial governor or even imperial court titles. *Daimyō* established formal governments and legal systems, tried various means to expand agricultural production, took control of local resources (such as metals) and stimulated the local economy by encouraging trade.

1336	1467–77	1549	1573
Ashikaga Takeuji drives Go-Daigo from Kyoto and founds the Ashikaga *bakufu*.	The Ōnin War is fought in Kyoto, destroying much of the city.	Francis Xavier of the Society of Jesus lands in Kagoshima.	Oda Nobunaga drives the last Ashikaga shogun from Kyoto, ending the Muromachi *bakufu*.

Where they were successful, towns grew up around their castles. These ruling warlords were able to improve their military strength by creating large armies of **foot soldiers** equipped initially with pikes, and, after the Portuguese brought powerful new weapons to Japan in the 1540s, subsequently with firearms.

"State" instability caused **constant war** between them; in many cases the domains were nothing more than a coalition of alliances, not actual territory, so the *daimyō's* rule lasted only for as long as he could keep his vassals satisfied by grants of new land. To gain this land, the *daimyō* had to be perpetually engaged in warfare; this required more vassals, who in turn required more land as rewards, which led to a vicious circle from which most *daimyō* were unable to escape.

Reunification (Azuchi-Momoyama period)

The end of the **Warring States** period of political uncertainty and relentless warfare came in the late sixteenth century. First, **Oda Nobunaga** managed through military tactical skill and sheer ruthlessness to dominate first his local area to the east of Kyoto, and then to enter the capital at the head of fifty thousand troops in 1568. He established relationships with the *bakufu* and the court, and set about gaining control of central Japan. In 1573, he drove the last Ashikaga shogun out of Kyoto, thus bringing the *bakufu* of the Muromachi period to an end. He continued to expand and strengthen his hold over central and a portion of eastern Japan until he met his death by the treachery of a vassal in 1582.

Shortly afterwards, another Oda vassal, **Toyotomi Hideyoshi**, avenged Nobunaga's death, took over as leader of Nobunaga's forces and, by military might and skilful diplomacy, managed to bring all of Japan under his control by 1590. Hideyoshi sought legitimacy by supporting the imperial family and being rewarded with court rank. The

THE WAY OF THE WARRIOR

The origins of the **samurai**, Japan's warrior caste, go back to the ninth century, when the feudal lords began to maintain regular forces. Gradually, they evolved into an elite group of hereditary warriors, their lives governed by an unwritten code of behaviour and unquestioning loyalty that came to be known as *bushidō*, **the way of the warrior**.

According to *bushidō*, the samurai and his family were expected to die willingly to protect the life and honour of their feudal lord. If they failed in this duty, or were about to be taken prisoner on a battlefield, then suicide was the only fitting response. The traditional method of **ritual suicide** was disembowelment with a sword or dagger (*seppuku*), though in later years an accomplice would stand by to cut off the victim's head. The samurai creed reached full bloom in the early Tokugawa era when class distinctions were officially delineated. The samurai were deemed "the masters of the four classes" – above farmers, artisans and merchants – and they alone were permitted to carry swords. They even had the right to kill any member of the lower orders for disrespectful behaviour, real or imagined.

During the more peaceful seventeenth and eighteenth centuries, many samurai found themselves out of work as their lords were dispossessed and fiefdoms redistributed. Many became **rōnin**, or masterless samurai, whose lives were romanticized in such films as *The Seven Samurai* (see p.859).

1579	1582	1590	1600
Sen no Rikyū becomes tea master to Oda Nobunaga, establishing the core tenets of the tea ceremony.	Oda Nobunaga is assassinated by a vassal at Honnō-ji in Kyoto.	Toyotomi Hideyoshi completes the reunification of Japan.	Tokugawa Ieyasu defeats the Toyotomi forces at the Battle of Sekigahara.

political system he established, together with his social and economic policies, set the stage for the next two centuries. Politically, Hideyoshi dominated the central government, but most of Japan was ruled by local *daimyō* who served as Hideyoshi's vassals, and in turn were confirmed as the rulers of their domains. Farmers were tied to their land by means of land surveys, and their weapons confiscated. The local samurai in turn were cut off from their local bases of power and forced to move to the *daimyō*'s castle town. Hideyoshi's economic policies included **freeing production and trade** by abolishing guilds, minting coins, standardizing weights and measures and taking control of international trade.

When he died in 1598, Hideyoshi's heir, Hideyori, was still a child, allowing **Tokugawa Ieyasu**, Hideyoshi's most powerful vassal, to take control. After defeating the Toyotomi forces at the **Battle of Sekigahara** in 1600, Ieyasu asserted his authority over the other *daimyō* and was appointed shogun by the emperor in 1603. This began the Tokugawa (or Edo) *bakufu*, headquartered at Edo Castle, the present-day site of the Imperial Palace in Tokyo.

Tokugawa shogunate (Edo period)

The basis for **Tokugawa rule** was the overwhelming military strength of the Tokugawa and their allies over the other *daimyō*. As liege lord, the shogun commanded the obedience of the 260 to 280 *daimyō*, who owed their loyalty to him in return for being confirmed in their domains. As shogun, the Tokugawa drew on the authority and legitimacy of the imperial court. Further, the *bakufu* held vast territories throughout Japan under its direct control; these included not only agricultural land but also important cities such as Kyoto and Osaka, as well as ports, mines and markets. The *daimyō* were required to reside part of the year in **Edo**, thus forcing them into expensive, time-consuming journeys, and to surrender family hostages who lived in Edo permanently. The expense of these journeys, combined with the cost of maintaining a household in Edo, could cost the *daimyō* as much as one-half of their annual revenues. Further, a network of inspectors and spies was set up, and any significant rebuilding of local castles had to be reported.

Despite this successful control of the ruling elite, the Tokugawa *bakufu* never established a unified, centralized government. Its revenues came from its own lands; the *daimyō* domains were not taxed. Likewise, administrative and legal functions were not unified; each *daimyō* domain had its own administration and laws. This system of "**centralized feudalism**" lasted for more than 250 years, interrupted by only one major rebellion, at Shimabara in 1637–38 (see p.732), and numerous small-scale riots by farmers.

It is often said that Tokugawa Japan was isolated from the rest of the world, but in fact the *bakufu* maintained **trading relations** with several Asian countries, as well as the Dutch. Embassies from **Korea** and the **Netherlands** visited the shogun in Edo regularly, enhancing the government's prestige. Fearful of subversion, the shogunate outlawed Christianity, expelled the Portuguese merchants and missionaries and confined the Dutch traders to Deshima (Dejima) in Nagasaki in 1641. International trade declined from the late seventeenth century, as Japan mined less silver but produced more silk. Conversely, the demand for European scientific knowledge brought by the Dutch grew stronger.

1603	1637–38	1641	1703
Tokugawa Ieyasu is appointed shogun; the Tokugawa *bakufu* begins.	The Shimabara Rebellion, led by Japanese Catholics, takes place in Kyūshū. Christianity is outlawed until 1865.	The Dutch are confined to Deshima in Nagasaki.	The Forty-seven Rōnin Incident takes place in Edo.

Tokugawa society was dominated by the samurai class, whose main function was to serve as administrators in the *bakufu* and domain governments. In this way, the samurai were transformed from warriors into **bureaucrats**, and their study of the martial arts became more philosophical than practical. There were more samurai than administrative posts, however, so many were reduced to poverty.

A main characteristic of Tokugawa Japan was that it was a **highly urbanized society**, with more than thirty cities of over 25,000 residents; Edo itself was perhaps the largest city in the world in the eighteenth century with a population of one million. Most of these cities were castle towns, such as Himeji, Matsumoto, and Matsue. The *daimyō* lived in the castle, which was surrounded by the houses of their samurai retainers, and of the merchants and artisans who supplied their needs. The requirement that all *daimyō* travel regularly to Edo led to the construction of a nationwide network of highways, stimulated commerce in both Edo and the domains, and the creation of a national culture, including the kabuki and *bunraku* theatres and *ukiyo-e* prints.

The arrival of the Black Ships

British survey vessels and **Russian** envoys visited Japan in the early nineteenth century, but the greatest pressure came from the **US**, whose trading and whaling routes passed to the south of the country. In 1853, Commodore Matthew Perry of the US Navy arrived with a small fleet of "**black ships**", demanding that Japan open at least some ports to foreigners. Japan's ruling elite was thrown into turmoil. The shogunate was already fearful of foreign incursions following the British defeat of China in the Opium Wars. However, when the emperor demanded that the foreigners be rebuffed, it quickly became clear that Japan's military was not up to the task.

There followed a decade of jockeying for power among different factions, and for influence by the foreign envoys. The first of these was the American Townsend Harris, who managed to extract concessions in the form of the pioneering **Treaty of Commerce and Navigation** in 1858. This was followed by a flurry of similar **agreements** with other Western countries, which opened the treaty ports of Yokohama, Hakodate, Nagasaki and, later, Kōbe and Osaka to trade, forbade the Japanese to impose protective tariffs and allowed foreigners the right of residence and certain judicial rights in the enclaves.

Opponents of such shameful appeasement by the shogunate took up the slogan *sonnō jōi* (*Revere the emperor! Expel the barbarians!*). Other, less reactionary, factions could see that Japan was in no state to do this, and their only hope of remaining independent was to learn from the more powerful nations. Eventually, the great **western domains** – Satsuma, Chōshū, Tosa and Hizen, previously rivals – combined forces under the banner of the emperor to exact revenge against the Tokugawa, whom they had seen as usurpers of the throne's authority ever since the Battle of Sekigahara, two hundred and fifty years previously.

Evidence of the shift in power came in 1863, when Emperor Kōmei ordered the fourteenth shogun, **Tokugawa Iemochi**, to Kyoto to explain his conciliatory actions; it was the first visit by a shogun to the imperial capital since 1634. To add to the humiliation, Iemochi could only muster a mere three thousand retainers, compared with the three hundred thousand who had accompanied the third shogun, Tokugawa Iemitsu, to Kyoto on that earlier occasion.

1853	1858	1867	1869
Commodore Perry's ships arrive in Japan.	The US–Japan Treaty of Amity and Commerce is signed.	The Tokugawa *bakufu* comes to an end and power is returned to the emperor.	Edo, renamed Tokyo, becomes the new capital of Japan.

In 1867, the fifteenth and final shogun, Tokugawa Yoshinobu, formally applied to the emperor to have imperial power restored. The shogunate was terminated, and in December of the same year, the **Imperial Restoration** was formally proclaimed, and the 15-year-old **Mutsuhito** acceded to the throne, ushering in a period dubbed **Meiji**, or "enlightened rule." In 1869, the young emperor moved his court from Kyoto to Edo, and renamed it **Tokyo** (Eastern Capital).

Modernization and colonization in the Meiji period

The reign of **Emperor Meiji**, as Mutsuhito was posthumously known, saw vast changes in Japan. A policy of **modernization**, termed *fukoku kyōhei* ("enrich the country, strengthen the military"), was adopted. Railways were built, compulsory education and military service introduced, the solar calendar adopted, and the *daimyō* domains and the class system abolished. Such rapid changes created resistance, and in 1877, **Saigō Takamori**, a hero of the restoration, led an army of forty thousand in the **Satsuma Rebellion**, named after the area of Kyūshū in which it erupted (see p.763). His defeat demonstrated that an army of farmers trained as soldiers could overcome samurai.

In the 1880s, even more changes were imposed by the ruling oligarchy of **Meiji Restoration** leaders, who imported several thousand foreign advisers for assistance. Japan adopted a Western-style constitution in 1889, drawn up by **Itō Hirobumi** (1841–1909), who had spent time in Europe studying constitutions. The **Meiji Constitution** created a weak parliament (the Diet), the lower house of which less than two percent of the population were entitled to vote for. In effect, a small group of leaders known as the Meiji "oligarchs" dominated the government, a situation reinforced by the Imperial Rescript on Education in 1890, which enshrined almost as law loyalty to the emperor, family and state. Shintō, which emphasized emperor-worship, became the state religion, while Buddhism, associated too closely with the previous order, was disestablished. Japan's rulers also began to copy the West's **territorial ambitions**. The island of Hokkaidō, previously left pretty much to the native Ainu, was actively colonized, partly to ward off a takeover by Russia. In 1894, territorial spats with an ailing China developed into the **Sino-Japanese War** over the Chinese tributary state of Korea. The fighting lasted less than a year, with a treaty being signed in Shimonoseki in 1895 that granted Korea independence, and indemnities, economic concessions and territory to Japan, including Taiwan, then called Formosa.

This unexpected victory brought Japan into conflict with Russia, which had its eye on China's Liaodong peninsula for a naval base at Port Arthur. After cordial relations with Britain were cemented in the 1902 Anglo-Japanese Alliance, Japan declared war on Russia in 1904 and destroyed the Russian fleet in 1905. The land battles of the **Russo-Japanese War** were less decisive, but in a US-mediated treaty in 1905, Russia was forced to make some territorial concessions to Japan. In 1909, the assassination of Itō Hirobumi, the newly appointed "resident general" of Korea, provided Japan with an excuse to fully annexe the country the following year. Thus, by the beginning of the twentieth century, Japan had not only "modernized" its government and society but had become a **colonial power** as well.

1871–73	1877	1879	1889
The Iwakura Mission travels in the USA and Europe to study Western civilization.	The Satsuma Rebellion fails to overhaul the Meiji government.	The Ryūkyū Islands are incorporated into Japan as Okinawa Prefecture.	The Meiji Constitution is promulgated on February 11.

The Taishō period

The sudden death of Emperor Meiji in 1912 ushered in the relatively brief **Taishō** (Great Righteousness) **era**. This period saw much political ferment and numerous popular protests, including the nationwide Rice Riots of 1918. This period is called the age of "Taishō Democracy" because of the rise of political parties and the growing prominence of elected politicians. Universal male suffrage became law in 1925.

During **World War I**, Japan allied itself with Britain. Despite gaining more territory in Asia after the war and being one of the "Big Five" at the Paris Peace Conference and a founding member of the League of Nations in 1920, Japan was frustrated by Australia, Britain and the US in its attempts to get a declaration of racial equality inserted as part of the Charter of the League. This snub, however, didn't preclude continued friendly relations between Japan and the West. In 1921, Crown Prince Hirohito was a guest of King George V at Buckingham Palace, while the following year the Prince of Wales spent a month touring Japan.

Levelling Yokohama and much of Tokyo, and leaving over a hundred thousand dead or missing, the 1923 **Great Kantō Earthquake** was a significant blow, but the country was quickly back on its feet and celebrating the enthronement of Emperor Hirohito in 1926, who chose the name **Shōwa** (Enlightened Peace) for his reign.

The slide to war

Economic and political turmoil in the early 1930s provided the military with the opportunity it needed to seize full control. In 1931, the **Manchurian Incident** saw army officers cook up an excuse for attacking and occupying the Manchurian region of northern China. Japan installed **P'u Yi**, the last emperor of China's Qing dynasty, as the head of their puppet state, Manchukuo, and responded to Western condemnation of its actions by withdrawing from the League of Nations in 1933.

At home, the military increased its grip on power in the wake of **assassinations** in 1932 of both the prime minister and the former finance minister, and a confused, short-lived **coup** by 1400 dissident army officers in February 1936. **Rapid industrialization** also laid the foundations for some of the most famous Japanese firms of the twentieth century, including the automobile makers Mazda, Toyota and Nissan, and the electronics giant Matsushita.

In 1936, Japan joined Nazi Germany (and later Fascist Italy) in the **Anti-Comintern Pact**, and the following year launched a full-scale invasion of China. From December 1937, the infamous **Rape of Nanking** took place over a six-week period, with appalling atrocities committed by the Japanese military. As **World War II** began in Europe, Japan initially held off attacking Allied colonies in the Far East, but when France and the Netherlands fell to Germany, Japan's qualms disappeared. Sanctions were imposed by Britain and the US as Japan's army moved into Indo-China, threatening Malaya and the East Indies.

The Pacific War

On December 7, 1941, the Japanese launched a surprise attack on the US naval base at Hawaii's **Pearl Harbor**, starting the **Pacific War**. In rapid succession, the Philippines,

1894–95	1904–05	1910	1912
Japan defeats China in the Sino-Japanese War, winning control over Formosa (Taiwan).	Japan's victory in the Russo-Japanese War gives it exclusive rights in Korea.	Japan annexes Korea as a colony.	The Meiji emperor dies and the Taishō era begins.

Indonesia, Malaya and Burma fell to Japanese forces. However, the tide was stemmed in New Guinea and, in June 1942, the US Navy won a decisive victory at the **Battle of Midway** by sinking four Japanese aircraft carriers. Although Japan had launched its campaign to secure a "Greater East Asia Co-Prosperity Sphere" in which it would free its neighbours from colonization and help them develop like the West, the brutal, racist, and exploitative reality of Japanese occupation meant there was no support from these potential Southeast Asian allies. Nor was there a likelihood of military cooperation between Japan and Germany, who eyed each other suspiciously, despite their pact.

By 1944, with the US capture of the Pacific island of Saipan, Japan was heading for defeat. The country was now within range of US heavy bombers, but there was a determination to fight to the bitter end, as exemplified by suicidal "kamikaze" pilots and the defending forces on the islands of Iwo-jima and Okinawa who fought to the last man. In March 1945, Tokyo was in ashes, and a hundred thousand were dead following three days of fire bombings. The government insisted that the emperor system remain inviolate when they put down arms, but no such assurances were offered in July 1945 when the Allies called for Japan's unconditional surrender in the Potsdam Declaration. Japan failed to respond, providing the Allies with the excuse they needed to drop an **atomic bomb** on **Hiroshima** on August 6. Two days later, the USSR declared war on Japan, and the next day, August 9, the second A-bomb exploded over **Nagasaki**.

With millions homeless and starving, and the country brought to its knees, it was a breathtaking understatement for Emperor Hirohito to broadcast, on August 15, 1945, that the war had "developed not necessarily to Japan's advantage". For his subjects, gathered at wireless sets around the country, the realization of defeat was tempered by their amazement at hearing, for the first time, the voice of a living god.

The American occupation

Never having been occupied by a foreign power, Japan little knew what to expect from the arrival of the "American Shogun" **General Douglas MacArthur**, designated the Supreme Commander for the Allied Powers (SCAP). Some five hundred soldiers committed suicide, but for the rest of the population the **occupation** was a welcome relief from the privations of war and an opportunity to start again. MacArthur wasted no time in instituting **political and social reform**. The country was demilitarized, the bureaucracy purged of military supporters, and war crimes trials were held, resulting in seven hangings, including that of the ex-prime minister, Tōjō Hideki. The emperor, whose support for the new regime was seen as crucial, was spared, although he had to publicly renounce his divinity to become a symbolic head of state.

In 1946, the Americans took a week to draft a **new constitution**, which proclaimed that sovereignty resided in the Japanese people, and contained the unique provision renouncing war and "the threat or use of force as a means of settling international disputes". Land and education reforms followed.

The **peace treaty**, signed in San Francisco on September 8, 1951, resolved all issues with the Allies, except that the USSR refused to sign. The outbreak of the **Korean War** in 1950 gave a much-needed boost to Japan's economy, as the country became an important supplier to the US forces.

1914	1923	1931	1933
Japan enters World War I on the British side and captures German possessions in China.	The Great Kantō Earthquake devastates the Tokyo area.	The Manchurian Incident serves as an excuse for Japan to occupy Manchuria.	Japan withdraws from the League of Nations.

The occupation officially ended on April 28, 1952, but with the Korean War continuing and the **Treaty of Mutual Cooperation and Security** guaranteeing the US the right to maintain bases on Japanese soil, a strong American presence remained. The island of Okinawa was returned to Japan in 1972, but a large American military presence remains there to this day.

The 1960s economic miracle

In 1955, the Democratic and the (conservative) Liberal parties joined forces to form the **Liberal Democratic Party** (LDP), a coalition of factions that governed Japan uninterruptedly for close to the next forty years, creating stable political conditions for an incredible economic recovery. The term "**Japan, Inc.**" was coined to show the close cooperation that developed among government, bureaucracy and business.

In 1959, **Crown Prince Akihito** married Shōda Michiko, a commoner he had met while playing tennis at the summer resort of Karuizawa. In 1964, Japan joined the **Organization for Economic Cooperation and Development** (OECD), inaugurated the high-speed bullet train, or **Shinkansen**, and hosted the Summer Olympic Games.

During the 1960s, Japanese exports grew twice as fast as world trade, while Japan protected its home markets by subjecting imports to quotas, a mass of regulations, or outright bans. Yet **rapid industrialization** physically scarred the country, and **pollution** wrecked lives. In 1971, Tokyo's metropolitan government officially declared that the capital's residents breathed polluted air, drank contaminated water, and were "subjected to noise levels that strain the nerves."

By the 1970s, the ingrained **corruption** festering at the heart of Japanese politics was also becoming clear. The conservative LDP had continued to hold power mainly by entering into cosy financial relationships with supporters in industry and commerce. Prime Minister **Tanaka Kakuei**, a self-made politician from Niigata, had already attracted criticism for pushing through the needless construction of a Shinkansen line to his home town, when his abuse of party funds in the Upper House elections of July 1974 caused fellow LDP grandees to quit the Cabinet in protest. Tanaka rode the scandal out, but couldn't survive the bribery charges, brought in February 1976, in connection with the purchase of aircraft from America's Lockheed Corporation.

The bubble economy

As the economy continued to grow in the 1980s, Japan's huge balance of payments surplus and restrictive trade practices set it at odds with the international community, and particularly the US. The tense situation wasn't eased as cash-rich Japanese companies snapped up American firms and assets, such as the Rockefeller Center in New York, and the trade surplus with the US totalled over $30 billion. This overseas spending spree was made possible by what would later be known as the **bubble economy** – a period when low interest rates fuelled booming land prices and a runaway stock market. The **Tokyo Stock Exchange** became the largest in the world, and by late 1987 the market value of Japan's land area came to almost three times that of the United States. Weak opposition parties and a continually rising standard of living across the country allowed the LDP to hold on to power, despite factional infighting within the party.

1936	1937	1941	1945
In February, a group of army troops attempts a coup, assassinating some government officials.	A skirmish at the Marco Polo Bridge near Beijing leads to full-scale war with China.	The attack on Pearl Harbor leads to war with the USA, Britain and Australia.	Japan surrenders after atomic bombs are dropped on Hiroshima and Nagasaki.

The Heisei period

When Emperor Hirohito died in January 1989, it wasn't just the Shōwa period coming to an end: the overheated bubble economy had also reached bursting point. The new **Heisei** (Accomplished Peace) period started, and Emperor Akihito took the throne in November 1990. In 1993, Crown Prince Naruhito married Owada Masako, a high-flying career diplomat (see box, p.87). In the same year, a successful no-confidence motion led to a hasty general election, with the result that the overall balance of power passed to a **coalition** of opposition parties, who formed the first non-LDP government in 38 years. The following year, the LDP was forced to form a coalition government with their rivals, the Japan Socialist Party. Finally, after a series of party realignments, the LDP managed to regain control with the assistance of coalition partners. In the meantime, the collapse of the bubble in both the stock market and real estate led to a period of **economic stagnation** and deflation lasting more than a decade.

The government earned much ignominy for its botched response to the massive **Great Hanshin Earthquake** of January 1995, which devastated Kōbe. Offers of foreign help were initially rebuffed, and the local *yakuza* (criminal gangs) further shamed the government by organizing food supplies to the thousands of homeless. The nation's self-confidence took a further battering two months later when members of a religious cult, **Aum Shinrikyō**, killed twelve people and poisoned a further 5500 in a nerve gas attack on the Tokyo subway.

In 1996, the LDP returned to full power, under the leadership of former tough-talking trade negotiator **Hashimoto Ryūtarō**, but economic woes continued. The official announcement of recession in June 1998, coupled with the plummeting value of the yen and rising unemployment, saw the LDP take a drubbing in the July 1998 upper-house elections. Hashimoto resigned and was replaced by the genial but lacklustre **Obuchi Keizō**. A major nuclear accident in September caused pause for thought, but no cancellation of Japan's increased reliance on this form of energy.

LDP defeated

Much hope for positive change was placed on reform-minded **Koizumi Jun'ichirō**, who became prime minister in April 2001. Exports began to recover in 2003, and the stock market headed for heights last seen in the 1980s, helping Koizumi win two general elections for the LDP. However, when he stepped down as prime minister in 2006, Koizumi's reputation as a maverick reformer was undermined by the fact that he had ultimately been unable to push through many structural changes to Japan's system of government and economy. He'd also angered pacifists at home by deploying Self-Defense Force troops in **Iraq** and – much to the ire of China and South Korea – continuing to visit Tokyo's controversial **Yasukuni shrine** that honours the nation's war dead (see p.88).

Koizumi's successors didn't fare much better, and as Japan's economy was battered by the **global financial crisis of 2008**, voters signalled that they had finally had their fill of the LDP. After a nearly unbroken run of 54 years in power, the party lost almost two-thirds of its seats in the Diet's lower house in the general election of 2009. The LDP was replaced by the **Democratic Party of Japan (DPJ)**, with **Hatoyama Yukio** as

1951	1964	1966	1989
The San Francisco Peace Treaty is signed, bringing the Occupation of Japan to an end the following year.	The first Shinkansen (bullet train) service starts between Tokyo and Osaka. Japan hosts the Summer Olympics.	Japan's first commercial nuclear power plant begins operating at Tōkai, Ibaraki Prefecture.	Emperor Hirohito dies and the Heisei era begins.

prime minister. The euphoria over this major political change quickly evaporated in 2010 when a series of events dented national pride. The national airline JAL declared bankruptcy, and Toyota was forced to recall millions of its cars from around the world in the light of possible product faults. In the political arena, too, the DPJ fumbled, and following more of the usual funding scandals and the breaking of a campaign promise to close a military base on the island of Okinawa, Hatoyama was forced to resign. His replacement, **Kan Naoto** – Japan's fifth prime minister in three years – saw his party lose badly in the upper-house elections in July 2010. Voters had been turned off by Kan's call for a sales tax hike to help deal with the nation's public debt, estimated to be twice the size of Japan's US$5 trillion economy. Kan raised the ire of right-wingers a month later, when his government issued an apology to Korea on the centenary of Japan's annexation of their country (see box below) and, along with his Cabinet, refrained from visiting Yasukuni shrine.

Tōhoku earthquake

On March 11, 2011 a **magnitude nine earthquake** ripped up from the seabed, its epicentre 70km east of Tōhoku's Oshika Peninsula. The subsequent destruction wrought by one of the most powerful seismic events ever to hit Japan, and the ensuing tsunami that smashed into the coast, left the country reeling under the weight of over 15,883 confirmed deaths, 6150 injured and 2651 missing people. Entire towns were swept away, and millions more households were left without electricity and water. Wrecked highways, railways and airports hampered the immediate relief efforts, while the damaged **Fukushima nuclear plant**, 200km north of Tokyo, appeared to be heading for meltdown, necessitating the government to call a nuclear emergency and evacuate 140,000 people living within 20km of the facility.

JAPANESE–KOREAN RELATIONS

For centuries, Japan has had close links with **Korea**, and a significant number of Japan's ruling class – including the imperial family – are of Korean heritage. Despite this, relations between the two countries have frequently been far from neighbourly. Toyotomi Hideyoshi (see p.824) led two unsuccessful invasions of the peninsula in the late sixteenth century, and in 1910 Japan annexed Korea. Japan's harsh colonial rule has impacted on relations with its neighbour ever since.

The successful co-hosting of the **2002 World Cup** and a Japanese taste for South Korea's soap operas, pop music and spicy food have helped mend relations with its near neighbour. There have also been several **official apologies** for Japan's colonial rule of the peninsula. In 2015, the Abe government negotiated an agreement and reparations regarding the "comfort women" issue and pledged 1 billion yen to the care of surviving Korean sex slaves. However, in early 2017 the agreement seemed in jeopardy after the erection of commemorative "comfort women" statues in South Korea and overseas, at which the Japanese government has protested.

Relations with **North Korea** remain decidedly frosty. In 2002, after decades of denials, North Korea came clean about how it had abducted thirteen Japanese citizens in the 1970s and 1980s and forced them to train North Korean spies in Japanese language and culture. North Korea's nuclear weapons ambitions don't help either, especially as the rogue state keeps launching test missiles in Japan's direction.

2011

The Tōhoku earthquake occurs on March 11, accompanied by a massive tsunami and serious nuclear accident.

2012

The government purchases the Senkaku islands, sparking territorial disputes with China and Taiwan.

At a televised news conference three days after the quake, Prime Minister Kan acknowledged the crisis as "the toughest and the most difficult" for Japan since the end of World War II, and called on the country's stunned but typically stoical and quietly heroic population to pull together and jointly shoulder the necessary sacrifices. On top of the financial toll, estimated to be in the range of ¥25 trillion (US$300 billion), there was the immediate effect of the need to assist some 300,000 refugees and a steep decline in electricity generation, leading to rolling blackouts throughout 2011. Reflecting the anxious mood of the population, the prime minister adopted an **anti-nuclear stance**, closing down the ageing Hamaoka nuclear power plant, 200km southwest of Tokyo, and saying he would freeze plans to build new reactors. However, facing mounting public dissatisfaction at his government's handling of the crisis, he was forced to **resign**, and at the end of August 2011 was replaced by Noda Yoshihiko, the country's sixth prime minister in five years.

Recent developments

In the lower-house election held in December 2012, the LDP made a strong comeback, and the party's head, **Abe Shinzō**, became prime minister for the second time (having previously held office in 2006–7). He carried out measures to stimulate the economy and led his party to another victory in the upper-house election in July 2013. Later in September, the International Olympic Committee chose Tokyo as the site of the **2020 Olympic Games**, which was a cause for national celebrations. However, the preparations have been mired in controversy with accusations of bribery and overspending, and allegations that funds allocated for rebuilding in the devastated Tōhoku region have been diverted to the construction of Olympic facilities in Tokyo.

In 2015, Abe and the ruling party rammed through new security legislation in the Diet amending Japan's "peace" constitution and allow for the **Self-Defense Forces** to be more active on overseas missions. This sparked some of the largest political protests seen in post-war Japan. The new laws were enacted in 2016, angering China and South Korea, and bringing about claims that Abe's agenda is to remilitarize Japan. Meanwhile, the government has also followed through with attempts to restart many of the nation's ageing nuclear power plants – beginning with the Sendai nuclear power plant in Kyūshū in 2015, less than 150km away from the epicentre of the powerful 2016 Kumamoto earthquake. The latter half of 2016 saw some unexpected political developments – Emperor Akihito expressed his wish to retire due to ill-health despite the fact that abdication is not constitutionally possible. A government committee is deciding how to allow his request so that his son, Crown Prince Naruhito, can ascend the Chrysanthemum Throne. The citizens of Tokyo elected their first female governor, Koike Yuriko, an Arabic-speaking former TV announcer, and the main opposition Democratic Party of Japan elected Murata Renho as their first woman leader. Japan still faces many problems concerning the stagnant economy, an ageing population and the ongoing clean-up of the Fukushima nuclear plant, and there are some signs that Japan is set to experience more political upheavals in the near future.

2013	2016
Contaminated water from the Fukushima Daiichi nuclear power plant is found to have been leaking into the Pacific Ocean.	In April, an earthquake hits Kumamoto, causing loss of life and severe damage. Emperor Akihito announces his wish to retire.

Religion

Japan's indigenous religion is Shintō, and all Japanese belong to it by default. About half the population are also practising Buddhists and around one million are Christian. Combining religions may seem odd, but a mixture of philosophy, politics and a bit of creative interpretation has, over time, enabled this to happen.

It has helped that Shintō does not possess one all-powerful deity, sacred scriptures or a particular philosophy or moral code. Followers live their lives according to the way or mind of the **kami** (gods), who favour harmony and cooperation. In this way, Shintō tolerates its worshippers following other religions, and it's a fairly easy step to combine Shintō's nature worship with the worship of an almighty deity, such as that of Christianity, or with the philosophical moral code of Buddhism.

Religious festivals are common, and many Shintō customs are still manifest in everyday Japanese life, from marriage ceremonies to purifying building plots and new cars. Nevertheless, few Japanese today are aware of anything other than the basic tenets of either Shintō or Buddhism, and many would not consider themselves "religious" as such.

Shintō

Shintō, or "the way of the gods", only received its name in the sixth century to distinguish it from the newly arrived Buddhism. Gods are felt to be present in natural phenomena – mountains, for example, or trees, waterfalls, strangely shaped rocks and even in sounds. But Shintō is more than just a nature-worshipping faith; it is an amalgam of attitudes, ideas and ways of doing things that, over two thousand years, has become an integral part of what it is to be Japanese.

Shintō shrines

Shintō shrines are called **jinja** (*kami*-dwelling), although you will also see the suffixes *-jingū* and *-gū*. These terms, and the *torii* (see opposite), are the easiest ways to distinguish between Shintō shrines and Buddhist temples. The shrine provides a dwelling for the *kami*, who are felt to be present in the surrounding nature, and it is also a place to serve and worship them. Though there are many styles of **shrine architecture**, they are traditionally built from unpainted cypress wood with a grass-thatch roof. The best examples of such traditional architecture are the Grand Shrine of

---

STATE SHINTŌ

Throughout most of Japanese history, Shintō did not play a particularly important role in state politics. This all changed, however, after the Meiji Restoration of 1868 (see p.827), when Shintō was declared the national faith, largely to re-establish the cult of the emperor. Most Buddhist elements were removed from Shintō shrines and destroyed, and Buddhism was suppressed. **State Shintō** ushered in a period of **extreme nationalism** that lasted from around 1890 to 1945. During this period, Japan's mythological origins were taught as historical fact and people were encouraged to believe that all Japanese were descended from the imperial line. At the same time, the traditional values of *bushidō* (see box, p.824) were promoted as desirable personal qualities. After World War II, Emperor Hirohito was forced to renounce his divinity, becoming a merely titular head of state, and the State branch of Shintō was abolished, returning freedom of religion to Japan.

Ise (see p.537), Izumo Taisha (near Matsue; see p.624) and Tokyo's Meiji-jingū (see p.117). Later designs show Chinese or Korean influences, such as the use of red and white paint or other ornamentation.

The **torii** marks the gateway between the secular and the spiritual world. Traditionally, these were plain and simple wooden constructions consisting of two upright pillars and two crossbeams. Gradually, various styles, such as the distinctive red paint, evolved on the same basic design until there were over twenty different types of *torii*. Nowadays, they are also made of stone, metal and concrete, in which case they tend to remain unpainted.

Inside the compound, you often find pairs of human or animal **statues** on the approach to the shrine building: austere dignitaries in ancient court costume laden with weapons are the traditional Japanese guardians, though you'll also find lion-dogs (*koma-inu*), or large, ferocious-looking *Niō*, the wooden guardians that usually guard the gates of Buddhist temples. Others may be animal-messengers of the *kami*, such as the fox-messenger of Inari, the deity of good harvests.

Somewhere in the compound, you'll often see a **sacred tree**, denoted by a twisted straw rope, *shimenawa*, sporting zigzags of white paper tied around it. In the past, these trees were believed to be the special abode of some *kami*. Now they're just an expression of divine consciousness which, like other aspects of the surrounding nature, helps to bring people's minds out of the mundane world and enter into that of the *kami*.

Finally, you come to the **shrine building** itself. At the entrance, there's a slotted box for donations and a rope with a bell or gong at the top. Some say the bell is rung as a purification rite to ward off evil spirits, others that it's to attract the *kami*'s attention. You'll also notice another *shimenawa* delineating the *kami*'s sacred dwelling place. Inside each shrine, there's an **inner chamber** containing the *shintai* (divine body). This is a sacred object which symbolizes the presence of the *kami* and is kept under lock and key – if ever seen, it loses its religious power.

A large shrine will also comprise many other buildings, such as subordinate shrines, an oratory, ablution pavilion, offering hall, shrine office and shop, priests' living quarters, treasure house and sometimes even a platform for **sacred dances**, a nō drama stage or a sumo arena. In some cases, there will be no shrine building as such, but simply a *torii* and a straw rope around a tree or rock to indicate a *kami*'s dwelling place.

Visiting a shrine

When **visiting a shrine**, try to fulfil at least three of the four elements of worship. Of these, **purification** is perhaps the most important, as it indicates respect for the *kami*. At the ablution pavilion (a water trough near the entrance), ladle some water over your fingertips and then pour a little into your cupped hand and rinse your mouth with it; afterwards, spit the water out into the gutter below. Now purified, proceed to the shrine itself and the **offering**. This normally consists of throwing a coin in the box – a five- or fifty-yen coin (the ones with holes in the middle) is considered luckiest – though a special service warrants a larger sum wrapped in formal paper. Depending on the occasion, food, drink, material goods or even sacred dances (*kagura*, performed by female shrine attendants) or sumo contests are offered to the *kami*.

The third element is **prayer**. Pull the rope to ring the bell, step back, bow twice and clap twice. Pray quietly, then bow again. The final element of worship is the **sacred feast**, which usually only follows a special service or a festival. It sometimes takes the form of consuming the food or drink offered to the *kami* – once the *kami*'s had its symbolic share.

At the shrine shop you can buy charms (*omamori*) against all manner of ills, fortune papers (*omikuji*), which people then twist round tree branches to make them come true, and wooden votive tablets (*ema*) – write your wishes on the tablet and tie it up alongside the others.

KNOW YOUR FOLK GODS

Adding spice to the Japanese religious pot is a legion of folk gods, guardians and demons. The ones to have on your side are the **Seven Lucky Gods** (*Shichi Fuku-jin*), often seen sailing in a boat on New Year greetings cards to wish good fortune for the coming year. Of these, the best-loved are **Ebisu**, the god of prosperity, identified by his fishing rod and sea bream; **Daikoku**, the god of wealth, who carries a treasure-sack over one shoulder and a lucky hammer; the squat **Fukurokuju**, god of longevity, marked by a bald, egg-shaped head; while the jovial god of happiness, **Hotei**, sports a generous belly and a beaming smile.

Characters to avoid, on the other hand, are the **oni**, a general term for demons and ogres, though *oni* aren't always bad. **Tengu** are mischievous mountain goblins with red faces and very long noses, while **kappa** are a bit like small trolls and live under bridges. If anything goes missing while you're hiking, you can probably blame one of these, as they both like to steal things. If it's your liver that's missing, however, it will definitely be a *kappa*; he likes to extract them from people's bodies through the anus, so watch out.

All shrines have at least one annual **festival**, during which the *kami* is symbolically transferred from the inner chamber to an ornate palanquin or portable shrine, called a *mikoshi*. This is its temporary home while young men hurtle around the local area with it so that the *kami* can bless the homes of the faithful. The passion with which they run, turning it this way and that, jostling it up and down shouting "*wasshoi, wasshoi*", has to be seen to be believed, especially in rural towns where festivals are usually conducted with more gusto. All this frantic action is said to make the *kami* happy, and it is highly contagious: long after the palanquin has returned to the shrine the merriment continues with the help of copious amounts of alcohol.

Buddhism

Buddhism, which originated in India, was introduced to Japan from China and Korea in the mid-sixth century. As with many things, Japan adapted this import to suit its own culture and values. The Buddha was accepted as a *kami* and, over the years, certain religious aspects were dropped or played down, for example celibacy and the emphasis on private contemplation.

But Buddhism did not travel alone to Japan; it brought with it Chinese culture. Over the next two centuries, monks, artists and scholars went to China to study religion, art, music, literature and politics, all of which brought great advances to Japanese culture. As a result, Buddhism became embroiled in the **political struggles** of the Nara and Heian eras, when weak emperors used Buddhist and Chinese culture to enhance their own power and level of sophistication and to reduce the influence of their Shintōist rivals. Buddhist temples were often built next to Shintō shrines, and statues and regalia placed on Shintō altars to help raise the *kami* to the level of the Buddha. Eventually, some *kami* became the guardians of temples, while the Buddha was regarded as the prime spiritual being.

Up until the end of the twelfth century, Japanese Buddhism was largely restricted to a small, generally aristocratic minority. However, at this time the dominant sect, **Tendai**, split into various **new sects**, notably Jōdo, Jōdo Shinshū, Nichiren and Zen Buddhism. The first two – simple forms of the faith – enabled Buddhism to evolve from a religion of the elite to one which also appealed to the population en masse. The Nichiren sect had a more scholastic approach, while Zen's concern for ritual, form and practice attracted the samurai classes and had a great influence on Japan's traditional arts. Almost all contemporary Japanese Buddhism developed from these sects, which are still very much in existence today.

Buddhist temples and worship

As with Shintō shrines, **Buddhist temples** (called *-tera*, *-dera* or *-ji*) come in many different styles, depending on the sect and the date they were built, but the foremost architectural influences are Chinese and Korean. The temple's **main hall** (the *kon-dō* or *hon-dō*) is where you will find the principal image of the Buddha, and a table for offerings. Sometimes the entry **gate** (*San-mon*) is as imposing as the temple itself, consisting of a two-storey wooden structure with perhaps a pair of brightly coloured, fearsome guardians called *Niō*, or *Kongō Rikishi*. Despite their looks, *Niō* are actually quite good-natured – except to evil spirits.

Some temples also have a **pagoda** in their compound – they are Chinese versions of stupas, the Indian structures built to enshrine a relic of the Buddha, and were once the main focus of Buddhist worship. Depending on the temple's size, you might also see other buildings such as a study hall (*kō-dō*), scripture or treasure houses and living quarters. Zen temples are also famous for their stunningly beautiful rock and landscape gardens, which are designed to aid meditation. The most important occasion in Japan's Buddhist calendar is **Obon**, in mid-August, when spirits return to earth and families traditionally gather to welcome them back to the ancestral home. *Ohigan*, which falls on the spring and autumn equinoxes (usually March 21 and Sept 23), is again a time to visit ancestors' graves. But probably the biggest celebration is **Shōgatsu** (New Year), though it's as much a Shintō event as a Buddhist one.

Christianity

Though churches can be found even in small rural towns, Christians represent less than one percent of Japan's population. The religion arrived in Japan with the Jesuit missionary **Saint Francis Xavier** in 1549 (see p.600). Initially, the local *daimyō* were eager to convert, largely in order to acquire firearms and other advanced European technologies, while the poor were attracted to the message of equality and social programmes which helped raise their standard of living.

The port of **Nagasaki** soon became a centre of Jesuit missionary activity, from where Catholicism spread rapidly throughout Kyūshū. Converts were tolerated, but by the late sixteenth century the authorities considered that the Christian merchants' increasing stranglehold on trade, coupled with a growing influence in secular affairs, was beginning to pose a threat. **Persecution** began in 1587. Suspected Christians were forced to trample on pictures of Christ or the Virgin Mary to prove their innocence. If they refused, they were tortured, burnt at the stake or thrown into boiling sulphur; over three thousand Japanese converts were martyred between 1597 and 1660.

Following the **Battle of Shimabara** of 1637 (see box, p.732), Christianity was forbidden in Japan up until the late nineteenth century. Amazingly, the religion endured, and when foreign missionaries again appeared in Nagasaki in the mid-1860s, they were astonished to discover some twenty thousand "hidden Christians". Since then, around 250 Japanese martyrs have either been recognized as saints or beatified by the Catholic Church, including Nagasaki's 26 martyrs (see p.721).

SŌKA GAKKAI

Several **new religions** appeared in Japan during the nineteenth and twentieth centuries, many of them offshoots of Shintō or Nichiren Buddhism. The most successful has been **Sōka Gakkai** (Value Creation Society), founded in 1930 by schoolteacher Makiguchi Tsunesaburō, who emphasized the importance of educational philosophy alongside the day-to-day benefits of religion. With its proselytizing mission and broad appeal to people of all ages and classes, Sōka Gakkai International (🌐 sgi.org) now claims around twelve million members. The movement also endorses the political party New Kōmeitō (🌐 www.komei.or.jp).

Japanese arts

One of the joys of visiting Japan is experiencing the ordinary ways in which the Japanese aesthetic enters into everyday life. The presentation of food, a window display or the simplest flower arrangement can convey, beyond the walls of any museum or gallery, the essential nature of Japanese art.

Periods of aristocratic rule, military supremacy and merchant wealth have all left their mark on **Japanese arts**, building on a rich legacy of religious art, folk traditions and the assimilated cultural influences of China and Korea. More recently, the West became a model for artists seeking to join the ranks of the avant-garde. Today, Japanese artists both draw on traditional sources and take their place among international trends.

Spanning the centuries is a love of nature, respect for the highest standards of craftsmanship and the potential for finding beauty in the simplest of things. These qualities pervade the visual arts of Japan but are also reflected in aspects of the performing arts, where the actor's craft, costume and make-up combine with the stage setting to unique dramatic effect. The official designation of valued objects and individuals as **National Treasures** and **Living National Treasures** acknowledges the extent to which the arts and artists of Japan are revered.

The religious influence

Shintō and Buddhism, Japan's two core religions, have both made vital contributions to its arts. **Shintō**'s influence is extremely subtle, but apparent in the Japanese love of simplicity, understatement and a deep affinity with the natural environment. The plain wooden surfaces of Shintō shrines, for example, together with their human scale, are reflected in a native approach to architecture in which buildings strive to be in harmony with their surroundings (for more about Shintō shrines, see p.834).

Some of Japan's earliest **Buddhist sculptures** can be found at Hōryū-ji, near Nara (see p.496), and take their inspiration from Chinese and Korean sculpture of an earlier period. The temple's bronze Shaka (the Historical Buddha) Triad by Tori Bushii, a Korean–Chinese immigrant, dates back to 623 and reflects the stiff frontal poses, archaic smiles and waterfall drapery patterns of fourth-century Chinese

---

THE WAY OF THE FLOWER

Ikebana, or the art of flower arranging, has its roots in ancient Shintō rituals and Buddhist practice. The original emphasis was on creating flower displays that imitated their **natural state**. This gradually evolved into using just three leading sprays to represent heaven, earth and humankind, which are arranged to express the harmonious balance of these elements, with the use of empty space being as crucial as the sprays themselves. The container, setting and season influence the choice of materials, which can range from bare branches and withered leaves to fruits, moss and grass.

The art of *ikebana* reached its peak in the sixteenth century, largely on the coat tails of the **tea ceremony** (see box, p.54) in which the only decoration in the room is an *ikebana* display or hanging scroll. As it became more widely practised, several distinct styles evolved, broadly divided into the self-explanatory *shōka* (living flowers), the formal *rikka* (standing flowers), *moribana* (heaped flowers), and the more naturalistic *nage-ire* (thrown in). Each of these is further subdivided into different schools, dominated nowadays by Ikenobō (🌐ikenobo.jp), Ohara (🌐ohararyu.or.jp) and Sōgetsu (🌐sogetsu.or.jp). To find out more, contact Ikebana International (🌐ikebanahq.org), an umbrella organization with branches in sixty countries.

sculpture. At the same time, Hōryū-ji's standing wooden Kudara Kannon, depicting the most compassionate of the bodhisattvas, is delicately and sensitively carved to emphasize its spirituality.

During the early years of Buddhism in Japan and the periods of closest contact with China (the seventh to tenth centuries), Japanese styles of Buddhist art mimicked those current in China or from its recent past. However, a gradual process of assimilation took place in both painting and sculpture until the Kamakura period (see p.822), when the adaptation of a distinctly Japanese model can be observed in Buddhist art.

The Heian period

In 898, the Japanese stopped sending embassies to the Chinese T'ang court, ending centuries of close relations with China. Gradually, the cloistered and leisured lifestyle of the Heian-period (794–1185) aristocracy spawned a uniquely Japanese cultural identity.

Court life in Heian Japan revolved around worldly pleasures and aesthetic pastimes, and the period is renowned for its artistic and cultural innovation. *Kana*, or the phonetic syllabary, was developed and employed in the composition of one of Japan's greatest literary masterpieces, **The Tale of Genji**, or *Genji Monogatari*. Lady Murasaki's portrayal of the Heian-court nobility eloquently described the artistic pursuits which dominated their daily life – poetry competitions, the arts of painting, calligraphy and gardening and the elaborate rituals of court dress.

A new painting format, the **emaki** ("picture scroll"), also evolved during the Heian period. *Emaki* depicted romances, legends and historical tales, of which the most famous is an illustrated edition of *The Tale of Genji*, published around 1130. The painting technique used, known as *Yamato-e*, employs flat blocks of colour with a strong linear focus and a unique boldness of style. The **decorative arts** reached a similarly high level of sophistication. Inlaid lacquerware, using the *maki-e* technique (sprinkling the surface with gold or silver powder) and finely crafted bronze mirrors, employed surface designs to equally dramatic effect.

The lavishness of Heian taste is reflected in **Buddhist painting and sculpture** of this period. New sects of Buddhism gave rise to the diagrammatic mandalas, schematic depictions of the Buddhist universe, while religious sculpture became more graceful and sensual, with gilded, delicately featured deities marking the transition to an aristocratic form of Buddhist art.

Samurai culture

The establishment of the Kamakura Shogunate in 1185 (see p.822) generated an alternative artistic taste more in keeping with the simplicity, discipline and rigour of the military lifestyle. This new **realism** made itself felt in the portrait painting and picture scrolls of the **Kamakura era** (1185–1333), most graphically in the *Handbook on Hungry Ghosts*, now in Tokyo's National Museum (see p.98). Highly individualized portraits of military figures and Zen masters became popular. Kamakura sculpture similarly combined a high degree of realism with a dynamic energy. The two giant guardian figures at Nara's Tōdai-ji (see p.488), fashioned by the sculptors Unkei and Kaikei in 1203, are outstanding examples of this vigorous new style.

However, samurai culture had a more direct impact on the development of the decorative arts. By the Edo period (1600–1868), Edo and Osaka had become leading centres of **sword-making**, where swordsmiths were noted for their skill in forging and for the meticulousness of finish which they applied to the blades. Through the peaceful years of the Edo era, however, sword fittings gradually came to be more decorative than functional.

The arts of Zen

With the spread of **Zen Buddhism** in the thirteenth century, Japanese arts acquired a new focus. Meditation is at the centre of Zen practice and many Zen art forms can be seen as vehicles for inward reflection or as visualizations of the sudden and spontaneous nature of enlightenment.

Monochromatic **ink painting**, known as *suiboku-ga* or *sumi-e*, portrayed meditative landscapes and other subjects in a variety of formats including screens, hanging scrolls and hand-scrolls, with a free and expressive style of brushwork that was both speedily and skilfully rendered. *Haboku*, or "flung-ink" landscapes, took this technique to its logical extreme by building up (barely) recognizable imagery from the arbitrary patterns formed by wet ink splashed onto highly absorbent paper. **Sesshū** (1420–1506), a Zen priest, was Japan's foremost practitioner of this technique.

Zen **calligraphy** similarly can be so expressively rendered as to be almost unreadable except to the practised eye. One of the most striking examples, by the monk Ryōkan Daigu (1757–1831), is a hanging scroll with the intertwined symbols for heaven and earth. These qualities of abstraction and suggestion were also applied to the design of **Zen gardens**, while meditation techniques spawned the highly ritualized and almost mesmeric **tea ceremony** (see box, p.54).

The Momoyama and Edo periods

Japanese art was most opulent during the **Momoyama period** (1573–1600). The scale of feudal architecture created a new demand for decorative **screen paintings**, which were placed on walls, sliding doors (*fusuma*) and folding screens (*byōbu*). From the late sixteenth century, the Kyoto-based **Kanō School** of artists came to dominate official taste. Subjects were mainly drawn from nature and from history and legend, while the extensive use of gold leaf added a shimmering brightness to the dark interior spaces of the great Momoyama castles, palaces and temples. Kanō Eitoku and his grandson, Kanō Tan'yū, were the school's most famous exponents, and their works can still be seen in Kyoto's Daitoku-ji and Nijō-jō.

During the **Edo period** (1600–1868), the arts flourished under the patronage of a newly wealthy merchant class. Artists such as Tawaraya Sōtatsu and Ogata Kōrin stand out for reviving aspects of the *Yamato-e* tradition and injecting new decorative life into Japanese painting. Sōtatsu's famous golden screen paintings based on *The Tale of Genji* dramatically adapt the subject matter and style of Heian-era *emaki* to this larger format. Kōrin's most noted works include the "Irises" screens at Tokyo's Nezu Museum (see p.121).

PICTURES OF THE FLOATING WORLD

During the Edo era, the lively entertainment districts of Edo, Osaka and Kyoto, with their brothels, teahouses and kabuki theatres, provided inspiration for artists. This new genre of painting, **ukiyo-e**, or "pictures of the floating world", devoted itself to the hedonistic pastimes of the new rich. By the early eighteenth century, *ukiyo-e* were most commonly produced as hand-coloured woodblock prints which became more sophisticated in their subtle use of line and colour as mass-printing techniques developed.

Late eighteenth-century artists such as Harunobu, Utamaro and Sharaku portrayed famous beauties of the day and kabuki actors in dramatic poses. Explicitly erotic prints known as *shunga* (spring pictures) were also big sellers, as were humorous scenes of daily life (*manga*), the forerunners of today's comics. **Hokusai** (1760–1849), perhaps the most internationally famous *ukiyo-e* artist, was originally known for his *manga*, but went on to create one of the most enduring images of Japan, *The Great Wave*, as part of his series *Thirty-Six Views of Mount Fuji*. Followed by the equally popular *Fifty-Three Stages of the Tōkaidō*, by Hiroshige (1797–1858), these later landscape prints were instantly popular at a time when travel was both difficult and restricted.

MINGEI: THE FOLK CRAFT TRADITION

Japanese **folk crafts**, *mingei*, delight in the simplicity and utilitarian aspects of ordinary everyday objects. *Mingei* really is "people's art", the works of craftsmen from all regions of Japan that are revered for their natural and unpretentious qualities.

While Japanese folk crafts flourished during the Edo period, the mass production techniques of the machine age led to a fall in the quality of textiles, ceramics, lacquer and other craft forms. The art critic and philosopher **Yanagi Sōetsu** (1889–1961) worked from the 1920s to stem this tide and to preserve the craft products of the pre-industrial age. Yanagi established the **Mingei-kan**, or Japan Folk Crafts Museum, in Tokyo in 1936 (see p.122). But the revival of the *mingei* tradition also celebrated works by living artist-craftsmen, as well as regional differences in style and technique. The potters Hamada Shōji, Kawai Kanjirō and the Englishman Bernard Leach were most famously associated with the *mingei* movement, as was the woodblock artist, Munakata Shikō, and the textile designer Serizawa Kiesuke.

A wide range of **traditional handicrafts**, including pottery, lacquerware, wood, bamboo and handmade paper products, is still being produced today all over Japan. *Yūzen*-style kimono dyeing and *kumihimo* braid craft are associated with Kyoto; *shuri* weaving techniques with Okinawa; *Hakata ningyō*, or earthenware dolls, with Fukuoka; and Kumano brushes with Hiroshima.

The **decorative arts** reached new heights of elegance and craftsmanship. Varieties of Imari- and Kutani-ware **porcelain** were made in large quantities for domestic consumption and later for export. Inlaid **lacquerware** was executed in bold and simple designs. Hon'ami Kōetsu was a leading lacquer artist of the period, as well as a celebrated painter and calligrapher. One of Kōetsu's most famous lacquer works, an inkstone box in the Tokyo National Museum, reflects these combined talents, with its inlaid-lead bridge and silver calligraphy forming integral parts of the overall design.

Western influences

The period of **modernization and westernization** which followed the fall of the Tokugawa Shogunate in 1867 transformed the face of Japanese visual arts. The opening of the treaty ports furnished a new subject matter for woodblock print artists who produced marvellous portraits of Westerners in Yokohama and other ports. The opening of the first railway, the first spinning factory and many other advances were also recorded for posterity.

In the early years of the Meiji period (1868–1912), traditional Japanese and Chinese styles of painting were rejected in favour of Western styles and techniques. Artists such as Kuroda Seiki and Fujishima Takeji studied in Paris and returned to become leaders of **Western-style painting** (*Yō-ga*) in Japan. Realism, Impressionism and other Western art movements were directly transplanted to the Tokyo art scene. More conservative painters, such as Yokoyama Taikan, worked to establish *Nihon-ga*, a modern style of Japanese painting, drawing on a mixture of Chinese, Japanese and Western techniques.

Western influence on the arts expanded greatly in the Taishō period (1912–26) with **sculpture**, as well as painting, closely following current trends. In the postwar period, Japanese artists looked again to Europe and America but more selectively took their inspiration from a range of avant-garde developments in the West.

Contemporary visual art

Visual art in Japan today blends Japanese and international currents, which at best interact to create innovative new styles. A prime example of such vigorous cross-fertilization is the development of **manga** as a sophisticated, internationally popular art form in which sources of tradition can no longer be identified purely with the East or the West.

CONTEMPORARY JAPANESE WOMEN ARTISTS

Over the last decade, Japanese women artists working in the contemporary visual field have been producing diverse and exciting works that challenge both their society and international perceptions of female identity in Japan. **Yanagi Miwa** (ⓦyanagimiwa.net) has explored the roles of women in Japanese society, from elevator girls to grandmothers, in beautifully executed photographic series. **Sawada Tomoko** (ⓦbit.ly/tomoko-sawada) also looks at women's roles, usually with herself as the subject. The work of **Yamaguchi Ai** (ⓦninyu.com) is influenced by manga and anime, with references to Edo-period courtesans, and depicts young female prostitutes. **Ninagawa Mika** (ⓦninamika.com) is known for her colourful photographs of flowers and goldfish, while also branching into fashion and film. **Matsui Fuyuko** (ⓦmatsuifuyuko.com) is a *Nihon-ga* artist who skilfully uses the traditional ink-painting genre to depict disturbing gothic scenes.

The international success of artists such as **Nara Yoshitomo**, **Murakami Takashi** and **Yayoi Kusama** has shaped the world's perception of Japanese contemporary art in recent years. The works of **Matsuura Hiroyuki** and **Nishizawa Chiharu** are also much in demand at international art fairs and auctions. Matsuura, a one-time manga character model maker, now produces ambiguous but dynamic canvases that have been described as "manga as fine art". Nishizawa's work uses the elevated point of view of traditional Japanese painting, but portrays the uneasy emptiness of modern life. The Damien Hirst-influenced **Nawa Kohei** creates installations and sculptures which reject the "culture of cute" which has become symbolic of Japanese pop culture art. **Ito Zon** is known for his delicate drawings, embroideries and video works that explore nature. The mystical paintings of **Yamaguchi Akira** are rooted in traditional Asian aesthetics and display a masterful technique. Artists who deal with more political themes include **Tomiyama Taeko**, who visually explores war and issues of social justice, and **Morimura Yasumasa**, who deals with gender and identity through photography and lithograph.

Manga

The word **manga** (meaning "whimsical pictures") is attributed to the great nineteenth-century artist Hokusai. Today, it covers comics, graphic novels, cartoon strips and even creations such as the character Hello Kitty. Japan's love of images is ingrained in the culture; **ukiyo-e**, woodblock prints, many of which depict lively scenes of daily life and imaginative renditions of fables and fantasy, were as popular two centuries ago as manga is today. Indeed, Hokusai's erotic print *The Dream of the Fisherman's Wife* (1824), which depicts a naked woman being pleasured by a couple of rather randy octopuses, could be straight out of contemporary pornographic manga (*hentai*).

International reception of the medium can be clouded by the graphic sexual imagery and violence seen in some manga, compounded by the misconception that the subject matter is exclusively limited to sci-fi and fantasy. In reality, manga covers an enormous range of stories, from cooking to politics, and has many genres – for example, *manga-shi* (magazines) aimed at young people are split into *shōjo* (girls), *shōnen* (boys) and *seinen* (youth) categories.

Performing arts

The traditional theatre arts of **nō** (sometimes written Noh in English), **bunraku**, **kabuki** and **buyō** evolved in the context of broader cultural developments during different periods of Japan's history. The plays of each art form often draw on similar plots, but their presentation couldn't be more different.

Nō

The oldest – and most difficult to appreciate   type of Japanese theatre is **nō**. This form of masked drama has its roots in sacred Shintō dances, but was formalized six hundred years ago under the patronage of the Ashikaga shoguns and the aesthetic influence of Zen. The bare wooden stage with its painted backdrop of an ancient pine tree, the actors' stylized robes and the fixed expressions of the finely crafted masks create an atmosphere that is both understated and refined. The dramatic contrasts of stillness and sudden rushes of movement, and of periods of silence punctuated by sound, conjure up the essence of the Zen aesthetic.

The actor's skill lies in transcending the conventions of archaic language, mask and formalized costume to convey the dramatic tensions inherent in the play. Dance elements and musical effects aid directly in this process and draw on the folk entertainment tradition from which nō is derived.

The comic **kyōgen** interludes in a nō programme provide light relief. As in the main drama, *kyōgen* performers are all male and assume a variety of roles, some of which are completely independent of the nō play, while others comment on the development of the main story. The language used is colloquial (though of sixteenth-century origin) and, compared with the esoteric poetry of nō, far more accessible to a contemporary audience.

Kabuki

Colourful, exuberant and full of larger-than-life characters, **kabuki** is a highly stylized theatrical form which delights in flamboyant gestures and elaborate costumes, make-up and staging effects. While the language may still be incomprehensible to foreigners, the plots themselves deal with easily understood, often tragic themes of love and betrayal, commonly taken from famous historical episodes.

Kabuki originated in the early 1600s as rather **risqué dances** performed by all-female troupes. The shogun eventually banned women from taking part, because of kabuki's association with prostitution, but their replacement – young men – were also available to customers as prostitutes. In the end, kabuki actors were predominantly older men, some of whom specialize in performing female roles (*onnagata*). Kabuki developed as a more serious form of theatre in the late sixteenth century when it was cultivated chiefly by the merchant class. It gave theatrical expression to the vitality of city life and to the class tensions between samurai, merchants and peasants that inform the plots of so many plays. To learn more about kabuki, go to ⓦkabuki21.com and ⓦkabuki-bito.jp/eng.

Bunraku

Japan's puppet theatre, **bunraku**, developed out of the *jōruri* storytelling tradition, in which travelling minstrels recited popular tales of famous heroes and legends, accompanied by the *biwa* (Japanese lute) or *shamisen* (three-stringed guitar). Adapted to the stage in the early seventeenth century, *bunraku* made use of stylized **puppets**, one-half to one-third the size of humans, to enact the various roles. The great Osaka

---

THE TEZUKA EFFECT

Many of anime and manga's stylistic traits – exaggerated facial features, episodic storytelling and the cinematic quality of presentation – are credited to the seminal manga artist **Tezuka Osamu** (1928–89), creator of **Astro Boy**, or Tetsuwan Atomu, as he's known in Japan. Astro is a boy robot, with rockets for feet and a memory bank of human experiences, who forever ponders his relationship to humans; such philosophical character traits and dark, complex themes are a prominent feature throughout the genre. Tezuka is credited with jump-starting anime in the 1960s, when he turned his comic Astro Boy into a TV series. The flat, two-dimensional look of anime, which is still common today, was a result of the need to keep production budgets low, using fewer images per second.

playwright **Chikamatsu Monzaemon** (1653–1724), often referred to as "the Shakespeare of Japan", is responsible for around one hundred *bunraku* plays, many of which are still performed today.

Puppets are worked by three operators, while a chanter, using a varied vocal range, tells the story to the accompaniment of *shamisen* music. The main puppeteer is in full view of the audience and uses his left hand to manipulate the face and head, with his right controlling the puppet's right arm. One assistant operates the left arm while another moves the puppet's legs. The skill of the puppeteers – the result of lengthy apprenticeships – contributes to the high degree of **realism** in the performance, and the stylized movements can result in great drama. Indeed, kabuki actors employ some puppet-like gestures from *bunraku* to enhance and enliven their own acting techniques. To learn more about *bunraku*, go to ⓦbunraku.or.jp.

Buyō

Classical Japanese dance is known as **buyō**, and elements of this art form intersect with other traditional performing arts traditions such as nō and kabuki. Buyō originates from the folk and ritual dances of ancient Japan. It developed into a refined form of dance, to be performed on stage, around the time that kabuki began to flourish in the seventeenth century. Today, there are over two hundred schools of buyō. Dancers usually wear kimono, and as a result their graceful movements are slow and restricted. The geisha of Kyoto continue the Kamigata style of buyō, which they perform throughout the year (see box, p.438).

Contemporary theatre and dance

Contemporary Japanese theatre and dance ranges from the all-female musical revues of **Takarazuka** (see box, p.525) and serious drama, to the abstract and improvisational dance form of **butō** (or butoh), which draws on the traditions of kabuki and nō as well as contemporary American dancers such as Martha Graham. Though it remains a marginal art form in Japan, butō's haunting beauty and eccentric expression has found greater appreciation in Europe and America.

In the 1970s, **Hideki Noda** became one of the most prominent figures in Japanese contemporary theatre and has since been involved in projects ranging from new kabuki writing and working with his theatre group, Noda Map (ⓦnodamap.com), to forays into opera. Members of the **Setagaya Public Theatre** have also collaborated with foreign producers on international productions such as a stage adaptation of Haruki Murakami's collection of short stories, *The Elephant Vanishes*.

There are hundreds of other theatre groups throughout Japan creating original works. One of the most acclaimed and active both locally and abroad is **chelftisch** (ⓦchelfitsch.net), the project of **Okada Toshiki**. The work of auteur/director Tanino Kurō, a specialist in the theatre of the absurd, is also worth looking out for.

Music

The arrival of eighty Korean musicians in 453 AD and the introduction of Buddhism in the mid-sixth century are key early events in the history of Japanese music. *Gagaku* (court orchestral music) and religious music survive from this period, and Buddhist chanting, *shōmyō*, can still be heard in temples today.

Similar to a chamber orchestra, *gagaku* ensembles include as many as twenty instruments, with flutes, oboes, zithers, lutes, gongs and drums. *Gagaku* is now played only as **bugaku** (dance music) or **kangen** (instrumental music), typically at the imperial court and at larger Shintō shrines and Buddhist temples. Unlike Western classical music, themes aren't stated and repeated. Instead, the rhythms are based on breathing and the result is a form that sounds sometimes discordant, sometimes meditative.

Distinctive musical styles also developed for the principal theatrical arts: nō, *bunraku* and kabuki (see p.843). The sparse music of **nō** features solo singers, small choruses and an instrumental ensemble of *fue* (bamboo flute), two hourglass drums and a barrel drum. The **shamisen** (three-string lute) was added to the flute and drums for *bunraku*, leading to a more lively and popular musical style.

In the seventeenth and eighteenth centuries, during Japan's period of isolation from the outside world, instruments like the *koto* (a kind of zither) continued to develop a repertoire, as did the *shakuhachi* bamboo flute. The *nagauta shamisen* style for kabuki theatre also developed at this time, as did the *sankyoku*, the typical instrumental ensemble of the age – *koto, shamisen, shakuhachi* and *kokyū* (a bowed fiddle).

Min'yō (regional folk music)

Each region of Japan has its own style of **min'yō** (folk music), the most famous being the instrumental *shamisen* style from Tsugaru in Tōhoku. **Kinoshita Shin'ichi** has earned the nickname "the man with the divine hands" for his pioneering Tsugaru *shamisen* playing, which marries the traditional northern *shamisen* style of fast plucking with jazz and rock. Kinoshita played a major part in the *shin-min'yō* (new *min'yō*) wave led by singer **Ito Takio**, well known for his passionate singing style and willingness to experiment. Since the millennium, Tsugaru *shamisen* has been experiencing a boom in popularity, helped by stand-out performers the **Yoshida Brothers** (ⓦdomomusicgroup.com) and **Agatsuma Hiromitsu** (ⓦagatsuma.tv).

Traditional **drumming** from Sado-ga-shima (see box, p.285) has now become famous internationally. **Za Ondekoza** (ⓦondekoza.com), the original group of drummers, and its offshoot, **Kodō** (ⓦkodo.or.jp), are capable of playing very powerful, theatrical gigs with just the various Japanese drums (from the big *daiko* to small hand-drums).

At Japan's northern extremity is the island of Hokkaidō, home to the indigenous Ainu. Their traditional music and instruments, including the skinny string instrument the *tonkori* and the *mukkuri* ("Jew's harp"), have been taken up by **Oki Kano**, an Ainu–Japanese musician. Together with his Oki Dub Ainu Band (ⓦtonkori.com), Oki has released several toe-tapping and soulful albums and has played at international music festivals including WOMAD in the UK.

Enka

Described as *Nihonjin no kokoro*, "the soul of the Japanese", **enka** (from *enzetsu*, "public speech", and *ka*, "a song") are songs about lost love, homesickness or simply drowning

> ## BEAUTIFUL SKYLARK
>
> A musical icon and the undisputed queen of *enka* is **Misora Hibari** ("beautiful skylark"). Born Kazue Katō, she made her debut as a singer in 1946, at the tender age of 9, and became an instant hit for her ability to memorize long poems and mimic adult singers. Her powerful, sobbing *kobushi* vocal technique created a highly charged atmosphere, but she was also talented enough to cover jazz, *min'yō*, Latin, chanson and torch songs in the thousand recordings and 166 films she made before her untimely death in 1989, aged 52. See ⓦmisorahibari.com for more information on this Japanese musical legend.

the sorrows of a broken heart with sake. Over one hundred years old, and still enormously popular, *enka* originally was a form of political dissent, disseminated by song sheets. However, in the early twentieth century it became the first style to truly synthesize Western scales and Japanese modes. Shimpei Nakayama and Koga Masao were the trailblazing composers. Koga's first hit in 1931, *Kage Wo Shitaite* (*Longing For Your Memory*), remains a much-loved classic.

It's difficult to escape *enka*. Television specials pump it out, and you'll hear it in restaurants and bars. And, of course, it received a major boost with the invention of karaoke, which helped to spread the genre's popularity both with younger Japanese and foreigners.

The classic image is of *enka* queen **Misora Hibari** (see box above) decked out in a kimono, tears streaming down her face as she sobs through Koga's *Kanashii Sake* (*Sad Sake*), with typically understated backing and single-line guitar. **Miyako Harumi** is also famed for her growling attack and the song *Sayonara*. Many *enka* stars have long careers, and veterans like Kitajima Saburō are still going strong today, as are Mori Shin'ichi, Yashiro Aki, Kobayashi Sachiko, Tendo Yoshimi and Itsuki Hiroshi. More recent stars are **Hikawa Kiyoshi**, known as the prince of *enka*, and Pittsburgh native **Jero**, aka Jerome Charles White Jr, whose hip-hop attire gives a contemporary spin to the genre.

Rock and pop classics

By the late 1960s, musicians were starting to create **Japanese-language rock**. Seminal band **Happy End** were pioneers. Led by composer Hosono Haruomi (later a founding member of Yellow Magic Orchestra) and lyricist Matsumoto Takashi, the band meshed folk-rock with Japanese lyrics about love and politics. Their song *Kaze Wo Atsumete* featured on the soundtrack for the film *Lost in Translation*.

Okinawan musician **Kina Shōkichi** and his band, named after the traditional Okinawan stir-fry, **Champloose** (ⓦchamploose.co.jp), gained acclaim in the 1970s, particularly with his song *Haisai Oji-san* (*Hey, Man*), which became so famous that it is used today as a drill song for high-school baseball games. **Southern All Stars** (ⓦsas-fan.net), whose way of singing Japanese as if it were English helped them to become Japan's biggest-selling band in the late 1980s, were another influential group; they're still going strong today.

Yellow Magic Orchestra (YMO; ⓦymo.org), formed in 1978 by Hosono Haruomi, Sakamoto Ryūchi and Takahashi Yukihiro, were heavily influenced by German technopop band Kraftwerk. Having gone their own ways in the mid-1980s – Sakamoto, in particular, developed a highly successful international career, both as a soloist and as an Oscar-winning film-score composer – the trio reformed in 2007 and still play together today, having become active in the anti-nuclear movement in Japan.

The roots boom

The growing popularity of **world music** has had a significant effect in Japan. **Reggae**, for example, was considered "underground" for years, but is now part of the mainstream, as is ska, following the success of the **Tokyo Ska Paradise Orchestra** (ⓦtokyoska.net). **Latin music** has also had a big effect, propelling salsa band **Orquesta de la Luz** (ⓦlaluz.jp) to the top of the Billboard Latin chart in the early 1990s.

The Boom (ⓦtheboom.jp), led by Miyazawa Kazufumi, helped to spawn the Okinawan music boom (see box below) in 1993 with their single *Shima Uta* (*Island Songs*). In the mid-1990s, they experimented with Brazilian music, opening up a new generation's ears to the South American melodies. In 2006, Miyazawa formed a new band, **Ganga Zumba**, with Brazilians Marcos Suzano and Fernando Moura, again playing a mix of Brazilian- and Latin-inspired pop.

The most significant development of the 1980s, however, was the rise of **roots-influenced** bands and singers such as **Shang Shang Typhoon** (ⓦshangshang.jp), Rinken Band, Nenes and Daiku Tetsuhiro. Inspiration came from both within Japan (Okinawa and local popular culture) and outside (world music).

Foremost among the 1990s wave of bands plundering global music styles was **Soul Flower Union** (SFU), a seven-member outfit from Osaka led by Nakagawa Takashi. SFU also have an appealing alter ego, **Soul Flower Mononoke Summit** (SFMU), where the band blends acoustic guitars, Okinawan and *chindon* (street) music, which advertises products or shops, with drums and various brass instruments. Recent work has included gigs with the respected Irish musician and producer Donal Lunny, who is married to SFU member Itami Hideko.

THE SOUND OF THE DEEP, DEEP SOUTH

Music has been integral to **Okinawa**'s culture and social life for centuries; it's said that peasants carried their musical instruments into the rice fields, ready for a jam session after work. The **folk tradition** is very much alive: in some villages, *umui* (religious songs) are still sung at festivals to honour ancestors; work songs that reflect communal agriculture techniques can still be heard; and various kinds of group and circle dances, some performed exclusively by women, can be found in the smaller islands.

Popular entertainment is known by the general term *zo odori* (common dance), though everyone calls these songs **shima uta** (island songs). The best-known style, one no wedding would be complete without, is called *katcharsee*. Set to lively rhythms laid down by the *sanshin*, which plays both melody and rhythm, and various drums, the dance is performed with the upper body motionless and the lower body swaying sensuously, accompanied by graceful hand movements that echo similar dances in Thailand and Indonesia.

The Asian connection can be clearly seen in the history of the **sanshin**. This three-stringed lute began life in China as the long-necked *sanxian* and was introduced to Okinawa around 1392. Local materials were quickly exhausted, so that Thai snakeskin was used for the soundbox and Filipino hardwood for the shorter neck of the altered instrument, which became known as the *sanshin*. Once introduced to mainland Japan, the *sanshin* became bigger, produced a harder sound and was renamed the *shamisen*, one of the quintessential Japanese instruments.

A more recent influence on Okinawan music has come via the US military presence. Local musicians started to copy American pop styles in the 1950s, sometimes mixing in folk music. One major star whose music developed in this way was **Kina Shōkichi** who formed the band Champloose (see opposite) while still at high school, thus opening the way for a new generation of Okinawan rockers, including ex-band members **Nagama Takao**, famous for his fast-action *sanshin* playing, and **Hirayasu Takashi**.

Another legendary Okinawan musician is **Sadao China**, who records his own solo *min'yō*, as well as reggae-rock with an Okinawan flavour. As a producer, China brought the all-female group **Nenes** to international fame; the original four band members have since played with Ry Cooder and Michael Nyman among others. China has a club, *Shima Uta Live House*, in Naha, which is one of the best places in the islands to see Okinawan roots music. A good blog to find out more on the Okinawan music scene is ⓦpowerofokinawa.wordpress.com.

JAPAN'S IDOLS

In the Japanese entertainment industry, singers, models and media personalities are referred to as **idols**. They are overwhelmingly manufactured, whether they be solo or group acts, and controlled by powerful management companies. More important than any recognizable talent is the ability to attract loyal fans who are willing to buy their CDs, DVDs, calendars and other associated merchandise. Maintaining a devoted fan base is key to survival, to the extent that many idols must sign contracts barring them from romantic relationships, so as not to offend their fans and thereby destroy the illusion of intimacy. In 2016, a Japanese court ruled that this condition was a human rights violation.

Contemporary sounds

Among teenagers and young adults across Asia, it's **J-pop** (Japanese pop) that shifts the largest number of units. **Hamasaki Ayumi** (ⓦavexnet.or.jp/ayu/en) commonly known as Ayu, is J-pop's ruling empress. **SMAP**, formed in 1991, were Japan's longest-running "boy band" when they retired at the end of 2016. However, SMAP member **Kimura Takuya** is as big a star as you can get, his career apparently set to continue with major roles in film and TV dramas, as well as lucrative advertising contracts for a wide range of products. More appealing to goths, glam-rock and cyberpunk fans are the so-called **Visual kei**, bands such as Dir en Grey, X and Luna Sea.

Super **idol groups** such as **AKB48** (ⓦwww.akb48.co.jp), a singing and dancing ensemble with 136 girl members and their own theatre, plus love-balladeers **Arashi** (ⓦwww.j-storm.co.jp), a group of five young men, are incredibly popular both at home and abroad and have active fan groups. Another J-pop sensation is **Kyary Pamyu Pamyu** (ⓦkyary.asobisystem.com), a singer who has emerged from the Harajuku kawaii fashion scene. Her child-like super-sweet pop songs such as Pon Pon Pon and Fashion Monster have also found an enthusiastic international audience. She regularly tours in Europe, the Asia-Pacific and North America. Heavy-metal idol group **Babymetal** (ⓦbabymetal.com), consisting of three teenage girls in identical gothic Lolita-style outfits, have had huge success both domestically and internationally, performing at Wembley Arena in 2016.

Hip hop and **rap** have been enthusiastically adopted by musicians and spin-masters such as DJ Krush (aka Ishi Hideaki; ⓦsus81.jp/djkrush), the duo **m-flo** (ⓦm-flo.com) and rap rock band **Dragon Ash** (ⓦdragonash.co.jp). Techno DJs **Ken Ishii** and **Ishino Takkyu** (of Denki Groove fame) and electronica outfits such as **Ryukyu Underground** (ⓦryukyu-underground.wwma.net), who mix up the sounds of Okinawa with dub beats and the occasional lounge-style tempo, have found audiences outside Japan, too.

Indie bands and singers have a strong local following. The singer known as **UA** (ⓦuauaua.jp) has a unique style – part jazz, part avant-garde – and is one of Japan's most interesting contemporary singer-songwriters. **Ringo Sheena**'s 2003 *Karuki, Zamen, Kuri no Hana* (*Chlorine, Semen, Chestnut Flowers*) is an impressive concept album embracing everything from big-band swing to traditional *koto, shamisen* and flute music. Sheena has since gone on to form the band Tokyo Jihen, before going solo again to score the music for the period drama film *Sakuran*. She's also collaborated with explosive jazz combo **Soil & "Pimp" Sessions** (ⓦjvcmusic.co.jp/soilpimp), which is gaining international attention.

If you want to hear work by some of the artists mentioned above, check out the *Rough Guide to the Music of Japan* (available from World Music Network; ⓦworldmusic.net), which offers a fine introduction to the nation's music scene, covering both traditional and contemporary classics.

The environment

In the words of one of Japan's leading environmental activists, Yamashita Hirofumi, "Japan's postwar development has had a disastrous impact on the natural environment." In the wake of the March 2011 nuclear accident, this statement is truer than ever. There is now increased public debate over Japan's future energy use, and much concern over the damage which nuclear radiation has caused both humans and the environment. This has gone hand in hand with a growing awareness of the need to safeguard spectacular areas of unspoilt natural beauty that remain, and to ensure that neither the government nor big business can exploit these areas. Japan also stands guilty of over-packaging products and wasteful use of disposable chopsticks, but at the same time, levels of recycling of items such as plastic, paper and metal cans are admirably high.

Fauna and flora

Generally speaking, the fauna and flora of the Japanese archipelago can be divided into three categories: the Southeast Asiatic tropical zone, the Korean and Chinese temperate zone and the Siberian subarctic zone.

The **Southeast Asiatic tropical zone** extends from Taiwan up into the Ryūkyū island chain (Okinawa). Wildlife typically associated with this zone includes the fruit bat, crested serpent eagle, variable lizard and butterflies of the Danaidae family. Animals that belong to the **Korean and Chinese temperate zone** inhabit the deciduous forests of Honshū, Shikoku and Kyūshū, the most common of which are the raccoon dog, sika deer and mandarin duck. If you're lucky, you'll see the rarer yellow marten, badger and flying squirrel, while in the seas around central Honshū you may also spot sea lions and fur seals. The **Siberian subarctic zone** covers the coniferous forests of Hokkaidō, inhabited by the brown bear, rabbit-like pika, hazel grouse, common lizard, arctic hare and nine-spined stickleback, among other species.

LAST CHANCE TO SEE ...

According to the Mammalogical Society of Japan (Ⓦmammalogy.jp), over half of the country's **endangered animals** are close to extinction. Examples include the Iriomote lynx, endemic to Iriomote-jima (see p.813), of which probably fewer than a hundred remain, the short-tailed albatross and the Japanese otter of Shikoku, both of which were once thought to be extinct.

Conservation efforts come in the form of breeding and feeding programmes, habitat improvement and research projects. In an example of Russo–Japanese cooperation, researchers from both countries attached transmitters to fourteen sea eagles and tracked them by satellite to discover their migratory routes and feeding grounds. Unfortunately, however, many such **conservation programmes** fall far short of their goals, largely due to an ineffective government system.

One programme that has been successful has been that to protect the **red-crowned** or **Japanese crane** (tanchō in Japanese). This magnificent, tall-standing bird, highly celebrated in Japan for its grace and beauty and as a symbol of longevity, has benefited from volunteer-based feeding programmes and other conservation measures in its home territory of eastern Hokkaidō (see p.341).

In addition, the archipelago contains a number of **endemic species** such as the Japanese macaque, Japanese dormouse, copper pheasant, giant salamander, Pryer's woodpecker and Amami spiny mouse, all of which are now relatively rare. Japan is also home to a number of "living fossils", animals whose characteristics differ from more developed species, such as the critically endangered Amami rabbit and Iriomote wild cat (both native to the Ryūkyū Islands), the frilled shark and the horseshoe crab of Sagami Bay, off Kamakura.

You don't need to get off the beaten track to encounter wildlife in Japan. In urban areas **raccoon dogs** (*tanuki*) come out at night to forage for food. These dogs are an integral part of Japanese folklore and are believed to have supernatural powers and cause all sorts of mischief; they are always depicted as big-bellied, with huge testicles and a bottle of sake. Foxes, too, are widespread and were believed to possess people – fox (or *inari*) shrines are found across the country.

Monkeys are also common in some areas, such as Wakinosawa and Shiga Kōgen, while **wild boar** occasionally make an appearance in outer urban areas, though fortunately these forbidding-looking creatures avoid human contact and are generally heard but not seen. Kites, cranes, herons, cormorants and migratory seagulls can often be seen around lakes and rivers, while the steamy summer brings an onslaught of insects, none more so than the **cicada** (*semi*), whose singing provides a constant background thrum.

Marine life

Japan's seas and rivers contain roughly three thousand species of fish. The waters around the Ryūkyū Islands are home to subtropical anemone fish, parrot fish, wrass and spiny lobster as well as numerous species of shark, turtle and whale. The ocean south of Shikoku and Honshū teems with life, from loggerhead turtles and butterfly fish to dugongs and porpoises, while the colder waters around Hokkaidō bring with them some of the larger whale species – humpback, grey and blue whale – from the Bering Sea and north Pacific.

Ocean currents play a crucial role in this diversity. Warm water flowing round Taiwan and up through the Ryūkyū island chain splits into two on reaching the island of

---

THE NATIONAL PARKS

In the early twentieth century, the growing popularity of recreational activities such as mountaineering provided the spur for the creation of Japan's **national parks** (*kokuritsu-kōen*), the first of which were created in 1934 and are now under the control of the **Ministry of Environment** (W www.env.go.jp). There are 33 national parks, covering around 5.6 percent of Japan's land mass, and 57 quasi-national parks (*kokutei-kōen*; 3.6 percent), which between them receive over 900 million visitors each year. In addition, prefectural natural parks cover a further 5.2 percent of Japan. While for the most part national parks are thought of in terms of recreation, their establishment has been a lifesaver for ecological preservation. Below are details of some of the most important.

Aso-Kujū National Park, Kyūshū (see p.739). Includes the world's largest volcano crater (90km in circumference), part of which is still active.

Chichibu-Tama National Park, Honshū (see box, p.199). Only three hours west of Tokyo, this is a haven for city dwellers. Its forested hills, gorges and valleys give rise to the Tama River that flows through Tokyo.

Iriomote National Park, Okinawa (see p.813). Features lush, virgin jungle, cascading waterfalls, mangroves, white beaches and Japan's largest coral reef, with spectacular underwater life. The dense jungle, which has served to resist human encroachment, is home to the rare Iriomote wild cat.

Shiretoko National Park, Hokkaidō (see p.335). Another UNESCO World Heritage Site, and utterly wild; it's home to brown bears, Blakiston's fish-owls and Steller's sea eagles.

Kyūshū. The branch flowing north into the Sea of Japan, between Japan and China, is known as the Tsushima-shio, while the Kuro-shio or "Black current" follows the more easterly route. Bearing down from the north, hitting Hokkaidō's northern and eastern shores, comes the cold, nutrient-rich Oya-shio or Kuril current. Where it meets the Kuro-shio off northeastern Honshū, abundant plankton and the mingling of cold- and warm-water species create one of the richest fishing grounds in the entire world.

Forests

Forests of beech, silver fir, broad-leaved evergreens and mangroves once carpeted Japan. However, development during the postwar economic boom – in particular, the massive increase in construction and the rampant building of golf courses – led to the decimation of many of these natural forests. While nearly 67 percent of Japan is still forested, about half of this comprises commercial plantations of quick-growing Japanese cedar and cypress. Not only do these contain a fraction of the biodiversity found in natural forests, but when cheaper timber flooded in from Southeast Asia, Canada and South America in the 1970s and local demand slumped, a large proportion of Japan's domestic plantations were left unused and untended.

As a result, Japan has come precariously close to losing some of its most spectacular areas of natural forest. The old-growth **beech forests** – stands of ancient trees, but not necessarily untouched virgin forest – of the Shirakami Mountains in northwest Honshū, for example, came under direct threat in the 1980s from a government proposal to build a logging road right through them. Citizens' groups, together with the Nature Conservation Society of Japan (NCSJ), mounted a huge campaign to demonstrate the forest's immeasurable ecological and national value. The government reconsidered the plan and the forest is now designated a UNESCO World Heritage Site.

Environmental issues

Japan is forging ahead with measures to improve its environmental performance. The gradual shift from heavy to hi-tech industry has led to apparently cleaner rivers and air; anecdotal evidence points to an increase in birdlife and statistics show that Mount Fuji is visible more often these days from Tokyo. However, although there have been successes down the years, there remains a litany of **environmental issues** blotting Japan's ecological scorecard.

Waste and recycling

In 2009, Japan's Ministry of Environment announced plans to reduce the country's **total waste** from a staggering 52 million tonnes a year (as measured in 2007) to about 50 million tonnes in 2012, and to raise the waste **recycling rate** from 20 to 25 percent. This reduction in waste generation was intended to be achieved through raising awareness and promoting a charging system for waste disposal services.

Unfortunately, **illegal dumping** in the countryside has increased since people now have to pay for the disposal of large items. However, the Home Appliance Law, in effect since 2001, is reported to have resulted in an 85 percent recycling rate by 2012 for white goods such as refrigerators and air-conditioning units. Despite such moves, working out exactly what to do with all the waste still remains a logistical nightmare. Burning it releases poisonous dioxins, while using garbage for land reclamation and landfill has also resulted in significant contamination in some areas.

One positive sign has been the **Mottainai campaign** (ⓦ mottainai.info/english), launched in 2005. The campaign, backed by the Mainichi newspapers and the Itochu Corporation, aims to cut all types of waste by reducing consumption and encouraging greater levels of recycling through education and awareness-raising activities.

Nuclear power

With hardly any natural resources of its own, Japan has long been reliant on **fossil fuel** imports to meet its energy needs. Government tax incentives and subsidies supporting the use of solar power mean that Japan is now a world leader in photovoltaic production. It is also beginning to develop wind power, biomass and other **renewable energies**.

However, the main area of investment has been in **nuclear power**. Up until March 11, 2011 the country was meeting around a third of its electricity needs from 55 nuclear reactors, with a plan to increase this to sixty percent by 2050. The Tōhoku earthquake and the **ongoing crisis** at the Fukushima 1 nuclear power plant confirmed the worst fears environmentalists and the public had about this strategy. The electricity companies have been conducting stress tests on all remaining nuclear power plants to evaluate their safety margins. The Fukushima plant is still undergoing delicate and dangerous shutdown operations, but there have been a number of worrying accidents during the clean-up operation, including the discovery that huge amounts of contaminated water have been leaking into the ocean.

Polls show that the majority of Japanese people are anti-nuclear and distrust government information on radiation, with more than fifty percent wanting nuclear power plants scrapped or the number of them reduced. There have been calls from politicians, civil society groups and former prime ministers for a **new energy policy** with less reliance on nuclear power and more development of renewable energy. However, current Prime Minister Abe and his government have included nuclear power in their basic energy policy, arguing that it is still important for "energy security". They intend to restart more reactors once safety aspects have been confirmed. In 2015, the Sendai nuclear power plant in Kagoshima Prefecture, in Kyūshū, was restarted despite citizen protests. In 2016, the Takahama nuclear power plant in Fukui Prefecture went online but experienced problems and was eventually shut down by a court injunction. Later in the year, one unit of the Ikata nuclear power plant in Shikoku came online and the government announced plans for more restarts in 2017 and 2018.

In the meantime, there remains the question of what to do with the growing stockpiles of **nuclear waste**, environmental contamination caused by radiation and Japan's increased carbon dioxide emissions from restarting coal power plants in order to meet energy needs.

Pollution

The Minamata tragedy of the 1950s, in which a Kyūshū community suffered the devastating effects of organic mercury poisoning, was a landmark case that brought to public attention the hazards of industrial pollution. Half a century later, **chemical pollution** – from agriculture and domestic use, as well as the industrial sector – remains a serious problem; one of the issues raised in the Oscar-winning documentary *The Cove* is about the off-the-scale toxicity levels of some types of seafood.

Citizens' movements have been active in tackling issues related to **air pollution** from factories, power plants and national highways, helping victims to win important lawsuits or reach out-of-court settlements against local authorities and industrial corporations. In November 2000, for example, the Nagoya District Court ordered the state and ten enterprises to pay a total of nearly 300 million yen in compensation to pollution victims and ordered that emissions along a stretch of national highway should be substantially reduced. The government subsequently imposed stricter emission limits and is gradually replacing its own transport fleets with "green" vehicles as well as working towards phasing out diesel buses and trucks in general.

A related issue is the widespread habit of drivers to keep their **engines running** – for the air-conditioning or heating – even when parked or in long traffic queues. You'll often see taxis parked up, for example, engine running and the driver sound asleep inside. Despite a number of public awareness campaigns, the message is slow getting

NUCLEAR RADIATION IN JAPAN

Apart from the exclusion zone surrounding the Fukushima nuclear power plant, Japan has been declared **safe** for both citizens and visitors. However, many environmental and human rights groups still have major concerns about the levels and extent of the **radioactive contamination** from the nuclear accident. Agriculture and fishing industries were affected by the disaster. Although the government is still conducting checks on food and water, citizen groups are also conducting their own monitoring activities all over Japan. Below are some resources for checking the latest radiation levels.

Citizens' Nuclear Information Center (🕸 cnic.jp) Information gathered by a network of citizens, scientists and activists.

Nuclear Regulation Authority (🕸 radioactivity.nsr.go.jp) Government website with monitoring information of environmental radioactivity levels.

Safecast (🕸 blog.safecast.org) Citizen group that collects radiation measurements from all over Japan and aims to strengthen the global information network.

across and, though some prefectures have even introduced "anti-idling" laws, there is little enforcement.

Whaling

The Japanese have traditionally caught whales for oil and meat, and the country continues to catch hundreds of these mammals every year, despite an international ban, exploiting a loophole which allows a quota for "scientific research". Japan argues that the research provides essential data on populations, feeding habits and distribution to allow the mammals to be properly monitored. Indeed, the government now claims that populations of minke, humpback and some other whale species have recovered sufficiently to support managed **commercial whaling**. In 2005, the national whaling fleet began hunting endangered fin whale for the first time and the following year added the vulnerable humpback to its quota, which now stands at a total of nearly 1300 whales a year.

All the major political parties support whaling, and it is often presented as a matter of **national pride** to preserve Japanese cultural identity in the face of Western, particularly American, imperialism. Opponents of whaling, on the other hand, accuse Japan of buying the votes of developing countries in order to overturn the 1986 ban imposed by the International Whaling Commission (IWC).

Ironically, less than thirty percent of the Japanese public are in favour of whaling; some surveys put the figure as low as ten percent. Consumption of **whale meat**, or *kujira*, has declined markedly since 1986, and the only way the government can now get rid of the meat its scientific fleet brings home is to sell it at highly subsidized prices. Even then, as revealed by Morikawa Jun in his book *Whaling in Japan: Power, Politics and Diplomacy*, a third of this meat remains unsold.

Japan's continued whaling has been an international public relations disaster. In recent years, the environmental rights organization **Sea Shepherd Conservation Society** (🕸 seashepherd.org) has disrupted Japanese whaling with violent clashes in the Southern Ocean, which has been documented in the Animal Planet series *Whale Wars*. In 2014, Australia won a case against Japan in the International Court of Justice, which ruled that Japanese research whaling in the Southern Ocean must stop because it was not being carried out for legitimate scientific research. However, Japan ignored the ruling and resumed whaling in 2016.

Scientists have also begun voicing their concerns over the high levels of toxins found in dolphin and whale meat available in Japanese stores. At the same time, interest in whale-watching has been on the increase, and it is becoming abundantly clear that there's more money to be made from whales through tourism than from killing them. For more information on whaling, see the **Whale and Dolphin Conservation Society** website (🕸 uk.whales.org).

Overfishing

To offset problems caused by **overfishing**, the Japanese fishing fleet has been cut by a quarter in recent years and increasingly strict quotas are being imposed. This has not, however, stopped the import of fish into Japan from developing countries which, for their own economic reasons, are less concerned about protecting fish stocks.

Of particular concern is the **bluefin tuna** (*hon-maguro*), which is prized for sashimi and sushi, particularly the *toro* (the fatty belly meat). It's estimated that Japan consumes around eighty percent of the world's total bluefin tuna catch. At the same time, bluefin populations are decreasing at an alarming rate in the face of increasing demand worldwide. Conservationists argue that curbing Japanese consumption is a key to preventing total collapse. Japan's case was not helped when it admitted to exceeding its 6000-tonne-quota of southern bluefin (which inhabit the southern hemisphere) by around 1800 tonnes in 2005. The **Commission for the Conservation of Southern Bluefin Tuna** (ⓦccsbt.org) says the figure is probably much higher if you also include fish caught by other countries over and above their quotas and sold in Japan. As a punishment, Japan's quota was halved to 3000 tonnes a year. However, overfishing has continued, and it was reported that Japan caught more than 13,000 tonnes in 2011. In 2016 it was estimated that Pacific bluefin tuna stocks had been depleted by 97 percent.

At the consumer's end, the rocketing price of bluefin tuna should put the brakes on consumption. Conservation bodies have started to mount awareness campaigns, encouraging people to opt for yellowfin tuna and other environmentally sustainable species instead.

Sustainable forestry

Japan has long been the world's largest consumer of **tropical timber**, and the activities of Japanese paper and timber companies in the old-growth and primary forests (those subjected to only minimal human disturbance) of neighbouring countries is a huge concern for environmentalists worldwide. Much of the timber is now imported in the form of plywood, which is used in the construction industry to make moulds for pouring concrete and incinerated after it's been used a couple of times. Since the early 1990s, rainforest protection groups in Japan and abroad have campaigned relentlessly to persuade construction companies and local authorities to reduce their use of tropical wood. There have been some successes, but activists note that the exploitation of developing countries continues.

Excessive packaging and **disposable wooden chopsticks** (*waribashi*) are other incredibly wasteful uses of resources. While "my chopsticks" awareness drives are having some impact in getting people to carry their own chopsticks with them, Japan still gets through a staggering 130 million *waribashi* daily, accounting for over 400,000 cubic metres of timber a year.

The role of Japanese companies in the Australian **woodchip industry** has also caused much criticism, both at home and abroad. One such company operates a wood-chipping mill that is fed by old-growth eucalyptus trees at a rate of several football fields a day under a twenty-year licence granted by the Australian government. Various Australian environmental groups, including Chipstop (ⓦchipstop.savetheforests.org.au) and The Wilderness Society (ⓦwilderness.org.au), have joined forces with the Japan Tropical Forest Action Network (JATAN; ⓦjatan.org) to petition the Australian government and the Japanese paper industry to use woodchips from sustainable sources instead. Again, the campaign seems to be paying off: due to public pressure, Japanese companies are increasingly sourcing woodchips from sustainable forests.

Film

Japan got its first taste of cinema at Kōbe's Shinko Club in 1896 – and since then, as in many other creative endeavours, the country has excelled at making films, producing many internationally recognized directors including Kurosawa Akira, Ozu Yasujirō, Itami Jūzō, Kitano Takeshi and Miyazaki Hayao.

Pre-World War II

From the advent of **cinema** in Japan, theatrical embellishments were considered a vital part of the experience; one theatre had a mock-up of a valley in front of the screen, complete with fish-filled ponds, rocks and fan-generated breeze, to increase the sense of realism. Additionally, the story and dialogue were acted out to the audience by a *benshi* (narrator). Thus when "talkies" arrived in Japan they were less of a sensation, because sound had long been part of the film experience.

The **1930s** were the boom years for early Japanese cinema, with some five hundred features being churned out a year, second only in production to the United States. One of the era's top directors, though he didn't gain international recognition until the mid-1950s, was **Mizoguchi Kenji** (1898–1956). His initial speciality was melodramas based in Meiji-period Japan, but he is best known in the West for his later lyrical medieval samurai dramas, such as *Ugetsu Monogatari* (1954). During the 1920s and 1930s, however, Mizoguchi also turned his hand to detective, expressionist, war, ghost and comedy films. As Japan fell deeper into the ugliness of nationalism and war, Mizoguchi embraced traditional concepts of stylized beauty in films such as 1939's *The Story of the Last Chrysanthemums* (*Zangiku Monogatari*). Also honing his reputation during the pre-World War II period was director **Ozu Yasujirō**, whose *Tokyo Story* (see p.859) from 1954 is a classic.

The 1950s and 1960s

World War II and its immediate aftermath put the dampers on Japan's cinematic ambitions, but in 1950, the local industry produced **Kurosawa Akira**'s brilliant *Rashōmon* (see p.858), which subsequently won a Golden Lion at the following year's Venice Film Festival and an honorary Oscar. A string of Kurosawa-directed classics followed, including *The Seven Samurai* (*Schichinin no Samurai* 1954; see p.859), *Throne of Blood* (*Kumonosu-jō*; 1957) based on *Macbeth*; *Yōjimbō* (1961; see p.859); and *Ran* (1985; see p.858).

The 1950s also saw the birth of one of Japan's best-known cinema icons, **Godzilla** – or *Gojira* as he was known on initial release in 1954. Despite the monster being killed off in the grand finale, the film's success led to an American release, with added footage, in 1956, under the title *Godzilla, King of the Monsters*. Over the next four decades, in 28 movies, Godzilla survived to do battle with, among others, King Kong, giant shrimps, cockroaches, moths and a smog monster.

Highly romanticized, violent **yakuza** flicks were also popular in the 1960s. These *ninkyō eiga* (chivalry films) often played like modern-day samurai sagas, the tough, fair *yakuza* being driven by a code of loyalty or honour. One of the major actors to emerge from these films is Takakura Ken, who has since starred in Western films including Ridley Scott's *Black Rain*. Try to check out the cult classics *Branded to Kill* (*Koroshi no Rakuin*) and *Tokyo Drifter* (*Tokyo Nagaremono*) by maverick director **Suzuki Seijun**, whose visual style and nihilistic cool was an inspiration to Kitano Takeshi and Quentin Tarantino among others.

The 1970s and 1980s

In 1976, *In the Realm of the Senses* (see p.858) by rebel film-maker **Ōshima Nagisa** created an international stir with its explicit sex scenes and violent content. Ōshima fought against Japan's censors, who demanded cuts, but ultimately lost. This was all the more galling for the director, whose film gathered critical plaudits abroad, but remained unseen in its full version at home, because at the same time major Japanese studios were making money from increasingly violent films and soft-core porn, called *roman poruno*.

By the **late 1970s**, Japanese cinema was in the doldrums. Entrance fees at the cinema were the highest in the world (they're still relatively expensive), leaving the public less willing to sample offbeat local films when they could see sure-fire Hollywood hits instead. Ōshima turned in the prisoner-of-war drama *Merry Christmas Mr Lawrence* in 1983 and the decidedly quirky *Max Mon Amour* (1986), in which Charlotte Rampling takes a chimp as a lover, before retiring from directing to build his reputation as a TV pundit. Instead of investing money at home, Japanese companies, like Sony, went on a spending spree in Hollywood, buying up major American studios and film rights, thus securing access to lucrative video releases.

Flying the flag for the local industry was **Itami Jūzō**, an actor who turned director with the mildly satirical *The Funeral* (see p.859) in 1984. His follow-up, *Tampopo* (1986; see p.859), a comedy set against the background of Japan's gourmet boom, was an international hit, as was his *A Taxing Woman* (*Marusa no Onna*) in 1988. The female star of Itami's films, which poke gentle fun at Japanese behaviour and society, was his wife, the comic actress Miyamoto Nobuko.

Anime

Japanese animation is known as **anime**, and it encompasses movies, television series and straight-to-video releases. It was developed from the early twentieth century and is considered to have a distinctive style, particularly in regards to its aesthetics and production. Around sixty percent of anime is based on previously published manga, while others, like *Pokémon*, are inspired by video games. Anime has been a staple of Japanese TV since the 1960s, with some series such as *Astro Boy* (see box, p.843) becoming popular overseas. However, it was the critical international success of **Ōtomo Katsuhiro**'s feature-length film *Akira* and the rise of **Studio Ghibli**, purveyors of some of the most successful anime of all time, including *Howl's Moving Castle* and the Oscar-winning *Spirited Away*, that has ignited the current global interest in all things anime.

The 1990s and 2000s

Itami Jūzō's 1992 satire *The Gentle Art of Japanese Extortion* (*Minbō-no-Onna*), which sent up the *yakuza*, led to the director suffering a knife attack by mob thugs. Undaunted, he recovered and went on to direct more challenging comedies, such as *Daibyōnin* (1993), about the way cancer is treated in Japanese hospitals, and *Sūpā-no-Onna* (1995), which revealed the shady practices of supermarkets. Itami committed suicide in 1997, prior to the publication of an exposé of his love life in a scandal magazine, leaving the field clear for **Kitano Takeshi** (see box, p.859) to emerge as Japan's new cinema darling.

Kurosawa Akira, referred to respectfully as "Sensei" (teacher) by all in the industry, received an Honorary Award at the Oscars in 1990, the same year as he teamed up with George Lucas and Steven Spielberg to make the semi-autobiographical *Yume* (*Dreams*). His anti-war film *Rhapsody in August* (*Hachigatsu-no-Kyōshikyoku*; 1991), however, attracted criticism abroad for its somewhat one-sided treatment of the subject. Kurosawa's final film before his death, aged 88, on September 6, 1998, was the low-key drama *Mādadayo* (1993) about an elderly academic.

TORA-SAN

Although hardly known outside of Japan, the country's most beloved – and financially successful – series of films are those featuring **Tora-san**, or Kuruma Torajirō, a loveable itinerant peddler from Tokyo's Shitamachi. The series began with *Otoko wa Tsurai yo* (*It's Tough Being a Man*) in 1969, and the lead character was played by Atsumi Kiyoshi in 48 films up until the actor's death in 1996. The format of the films is invariably the same, with Tora-san chasing after his latest love, or "Madonna", in various scenic areas of Japan, before returning to his exasperated family.

Meanwhile, the prolific **Kurosawa Kiyoshi** had begun to make waves with quirky genre pictures, such as *The Excitement of the Do-Re-Mi-Fa Girls* (1985), *The Serpent Path* (1998) and its sequel *Eyes of the Spider* (1998). **Tsukamoto Shin'ya** had an art-house hit with the sci-fi horror film *Tetsuo* about a man turning into a machine, a story inspired by the acclaimed anime *Akira* (see p.860). A much bigger hit, with both local and international audiences, was *Shall We Dance?*, a charming comedy-drama about ballroom dancing, which swept up all thirteen of Japan's Academy Awards in 1996.

While Kitano continues to be one of Japan's most internationally popular film-makers, other directors are coming to the fore. Master of the gleeful splatterfest is the prolific **Miike Takashi**, who has jumped around from the stylized gangster violence of *Ichi the Killer* (see p.860) to the sci-fi action of his *Dead or Alive* trilogy, via the musical horror comedy of *The Happiness of the Katakuris*. In 2009 his *Yatterman*, based on a popular cartoon series from the 1970s, was a local hit. After Miike's 2013 splatterfest *Shield of Straw* flopped, he filmed an historical biopic about a Japanese doctor in war-torn Kenya called *The Lion Standing in the Wind* (2015).

Reinterpreting the horror genre has been **Nakata Hideo**, whose *Ring* (1998) and paranormal chiller *Dark Water* (2002) were both remade in English in Hollywood before Nakata himself went west in 2005 to direct his English-language debut *The Ring Two*, a new sequel to the Hollywood version of *Ring*. Fans will want to compare it to Nakata's original – and different – Japanese sequel *Ring 2* (1999). This trend of English-language remakes and new versions has continued with **Takashi Shimizu**'s *Ju-on: The Grudge* (2000) and *Ju-on: The Grudge Two* (2003).

A decade into the new millennium, the film industry seemed to be thriving. In his 80s, **Suzuki Seijun** made a wonderful and surprising comeback in 2006 with the fairy-tale musical *Princess Racoon*. In 2007, *The Mourning Forest* scooped up the Grand Prix at Cannes for director **Kawase Naomi**, a decade after her debut film *Moe no Suzaku* had scored a prize at the same festival. Also scoring at Cannes and other awards ceremonies was Kurosawa Kiyoshi's satirical drama *Tokyo Sonata* (see p.860). And, in 2009, **Takita Yōjirō**'s *Departures* (see p.860) took top honours as best foreign-language film at the Oscars.

The 2010s

After the March 2011 earthquake and tsunami, there were fewer major successes for Japanese films, both at home and abroad. In 2012, a considerable number of films released were based on manga and even video games. In 2013, **Kore-eda Hirokazu**'s family drama *Like Father, Like Son* won the Prix du Jury at Cannes, making it the first Japanese film to win an award since Kawase's film in 2007, and showing that some film-makers who debuted and were successful in the 1990s are still prominent. Kawase's most recent film, *Sweet Bean* (2015), about an elderly leprosy patient, was well received at home and abroad. However, a new generation of film-makers is beginning to break through and there are some standouts – Kusano Natsuka's *Antonym* (2015) and Ohsaki Akira's *Obon Brothers* (2015) are two. Fukada Koji's dark family

ANIME ON THE BIG SCREEN

In 1958, Toei produced Japan's first full-length, full-colour animated feature *Hakujaden* (released as *Tale of the White Panda* in the US) and went on to make a series of increasingly sophisticated films, culminating in *Little Norse Prince* (*Taiyō no Ōji Horusu no Daibōken*) in 1968. This was the directorial debut of Takahata Isao who, in 1985, teamed up with Miyazaki Hayao to form **Studio Ghibli** (ⓦghibli.jp), the most successful of Japanese animation companies.

During the 1960s, TV anime came to the fore with **Tezuka Osamu**'s *Tetsuwan Atomu* series, more popularly known as *Astro Boy*, a success both at home and abroad. Tezuka's *Kimba the White Lion* and Tatsuo Yoshida's *Mach Go Go Go* (*Speed Racer* in the US) were other hit TV series from this era, while in the 1970s it was space-based adventures, such as *Space Battleship Yamato* (*Star Blazers*) and *Kagaku Ninja tai Gatchaman* (*Battle of the Planets*), that had kids glued to the gogglebox.

By the 1980s, ambitious artists were pushing the boundaries of the genre into cinema-scale works with higher production values such as Ōtomo Katsuhiro's dark sci-fi fantasy **Akira** (see p.860). Miyazaki Hayao was also making his name, initially with his ecological man vs nature fantasy adventure *Nausicaä of the Valley of Wind* (1984), then with Studio Ghibli smashes such as *My Neighbour Totoro* (see p.860), *Princess Mononoke* (see p.860) and the Oscar-winning **Spirited Away** (see p.860). In 2013, Miyazaki announced his retirement. His last feature-length film, *The Wind Rises*, is based on the story of the man who designed the Zero fighter planes in World War II, and attracted controversy due to its anti-war message.

Among other cinema anime directors to watch out for are: **Kon Satoshi**, whose films include the Hitchcockian psychological drama *Perfect Blue* (1997), *Tokyo Godfathers* (see p.860), and *Paprika* (2006), a visually splendid tale about the search for a stolen device that allows physical access to people's dreams; **Oshii Mamoru**, who has the seminal *Ghost in the Shell* (see p.860) and *The Sky Crawlers* (2008) to his credit; and **Hosoda Mamoru**, whose *The Girl Who Leapt Through Time* (*Toki o Kakeru Shōjo;* 2006) and *Summer Wars* (2009) have both garnered rave reviews. For an in-depth look at the medium, read *The Rough Guide to Anime*.

More recently, **Shinkai Makoto**, the director of the 2016 mega-hit *Your Name*, has been touted as "The New Miyazaki".

drama *Harmonium* won a Prix du Certain Regard at Cannes in 2016, and he is being hailed as a major new talent in Japanese film. However, the obstacles to Japan's cinema industry are certainly not a lack of creativity or drive. Many film-makers are becoming increasingly vocal about the lack of government support for the feature film industry, compared to countries such as France or South Korea, and emphasize the cultural value of supporting a viable film production environment.

FILM RECOMMENDATIONS

JAPANESE CLASSICS

Black Rain (Imamura Shōhei; 1989). Not to be confused with the US *yakuza* flick, this serious drama traces the strains put on family life in a country village after the atomic bomb is dropped on Hiroshima.

Godzilla, King of the Monsters (Honda Ishirō & Terry O Morse; 1956). Originally released two years earlier in Japan as *Gojira*, the film about a giant mutant lizard, born after a US hydrogen bomb test in the Bikini Atoll, was such a hit that previously cut scenes were added for the American market. Raymond Burr plays the journalist telling in flashback the event that led to Godzilla running amok in Tokyo.

In the Realm of the Senses (*Ai no Koriida*; Ōshima Nagisa; 1976). Based on the true story of servant girl Sada

Abe and her intensely violent sexual relationship with her master Kichi – who ends up dead and minus his penis.

Kagemusha (Kurosawa Akira; 1980). Nominated for an Academy Award and co-winner of the Grand Prix at Cannes, Kurosawa showed he was still on form with this sweeping historical epic in which a poor criminal is recruited to impersonate a powerful warlord who has inconveniently died mid-campaign.

Ran (Kurosawa Akira; 1985). This much-lauded, loose adaptation of *King Lear* is a real epic, with thousands of extras and giant battle scenes. The daughters become sons, although the Regan and Goneril characters survive in the form of the gleefully vengeful wives Lady Kaede and Lady Sue.

★**Rashōmon** (Kurosawa Akira; 1950). The film that established Kurosawa's reputation in the West. A notorious bandit, the wife he perhaps rapes, the man he perhaps murders and the woodcutter who perhaps witnesses the events each tell their different story of what happened in the woods. Fascinatingly open-ended narrative and a memorable performance by Mifune Toshirō as the restless bandit make this a must-see film.

The Seven Samurai (*Shichinin no Samurai*; Kurosawa Akira; 1954). A small village in sixteenth-century Japan is fed up with being raided each year by bandits, so it hires a band of samurai warriors for protection. Kurosawa's entertaining period drama was later remade in Hollywood as *The Magnificent Seven*.

Tokyo Story (*Tōkyō Monogatari*; Ozu Yasujirō; 1954). An elderly couple travel to Tokyo to visit their children and grandchildren. The only person who has any time for them is Noriko, the widow of their son who was killed in the war. On their return, the mother falls ill and dies. Ozu's themes of loneliness and the breakdown of tradition are grim, but his simple approach and the sincerity of the acting make the film a genuine classic.

Twenty-Four Eyes (*Nijūshi no Hitomi*; Kinoshita Keisuke; 1954). This four-hankie weepy is one of Japan's most-loved films. Events leading up to, during and after World War II are seen through the eyes of a first-grade female teacher (a luminous performance by Takamine Hideko), on the island of Shōdo-shima. The twelve cute children in Ōishi-san's class make up the 24 eyes.

When a Woman Ascends the Stairs (*Onna ga Kaidan o Agaru Toki*; Naruse Mikio; 1960). Naruse ranks alongside Kurosawa and Ozu as one of Japan's great film directors. This film, about an ageing hostess in a Ginza bar, is from the latter end of his career and has a splendid central performance by Takamine Hideko.

Yōjimbō (Kurosawa Akira; 1961). Mifune Toshiro stars in one of Kurosawa's best-known samurai sagas as a *rōnin* who arrives in a dusty town, is greeted by a dog carrying a human hand and discovers he's walked in on a bloody feud.

ITAMI JŪZŌ AND KITANO TAKESHI

The Funeral (*Osōshiki*; Itami Jūzō; 1984). Itami's directorial debut is a wry comedy about a grieving family bumbling their way through the obscure conventions of a proper Japanese funeral. The young couple learn the "rules" by watching a video, and the Buddhist priest turns up in a white Rolls-Royce.

★**Hanabi** (Kitano Takeshi; 1997). Venice Festival winner with Kitano directing himself as a detective pushed to breaking point by a stakeout that goes wrong, a seriously ill wife and outstanding loans to the *yakuza*. Kitano also painted the artwork that appears in the film.

Sonatine (Kitano Takeshi; 1993). One of Kitano's most accomplished films. He plays a tired gangster, hightailing it to the sunny isles of Okinawa and getting mixed up in mob feuds, before it all turns nasty on the beach.

★**Tampopo** (Itami Jūzō; 1985). Tampopo, the proprietress of a noodle bar, is taught how to prepare the perfect ramen, in this comedy about Japan's gourmet boom. From the old woman squishing fruit in a supermarket to the gangster and his moll passing a raw egg sexily between their mouths, this is a film packed with memorable scenes.

★**Zatoichi** (Kitano Takeshi; 2003). A classic of Japanese TV remade with an assured, modern touch by Kitano, who also stars as the eponymous hero, a blind master swordsman with whom you really don't want to tangle. The film's finale has the cast doing a tap-dancing number in *geta* (wooden sandals).

CONTEMPORARY JAPANESE CINEMA

★**Campaign** (*Senkyo*; Sōda Kazuhiro; 2007) and **Campaign 2** (*Senkyo 2*; Sōda Kazuhiro; 2013). Fly-on-the-wall-style documentary following Yamauchi-san, a novice LDP candidate on the campaign trail during the Kawasaki municipal elections. The follow-up catches him as an independent candidate standing in local elections less than a month after the 2011 disaster; he was the only candidate

---

BEAT TAKESHI

Comedian, actor, director, writer, painter and video-game designer – is there anything that **Kitano Takeshi** (⊕ kitanotakeshi.com) can't do? Known locally as Beat Takeshi after his old comedy double act, the Two Beats, Kitano, who was born in Tokyo in 1947, first came to international attention for his role as a brutal camp sergeant in Ōshima's *Merry Christmas Mr Lawrence*. His directorial debut *Violent Cop* (1989) saw him star as a police officer in the *Dirty Harry* mould. His next film, *Boiling Point (3-4 x 10 Gatsu)*, was an equally bloody outing, but it was his more reflective and comic *Sonatine* (see above), about a gang war in sunny Okinawa, that had foreign critics hailing him as Japan's Quentin Tarantino.

Kitano survived a near-fatal **motorbike accident** in 1994, and triumphed with *Hanabi* (see above), which scooped up a Golden Lion at the Venice Festival in 1997. In 2003, he directed the popular *Zatoichi* (see above), playing the blind swordsman of the title with bleached-blonde hair. Kitano has won acclaim with *yakuza* film *Outrage* (2010) and its sequel, *Outrage Beyond* (2012), as well as a dark comedy in the same genre, *Ryuzo and the Seven Henchmen* (2015). More recently, he appeared in the live action remake of *Ghost in the Shell* (2017).

mentioning the nuclear issue. Both films are a brilliant insight on Japanese politics and society.

Departures (*Okuribito*; Takita Yōjirō; 2008). Oscar-winning drama about an out-of-work cellist who winds up working at a funeral parlour in his home town in Yamagata prefecture. Because of the nature of this taboo profession, he at first keeps his new job secret from his family and friends.

Fake (Mori Tatsuya; 2016). Follows disgraced "modern-day Japanese Beethoven" after he is exposed for not being deaf and unable to read music. An intriguing exploration of celebrity and public apology.

From Ashes to Honey (Kamanaka Hitomi; 2010). Third in a trilogy on anti-nuclear activism in Japan. Kamanaka follows the residents of Iwaijima, in the Inland Sea, as they try to stop the construction of a nuclear power plant.

Harmonium (*Fuchi ni Tatsu*; Fukada Koji; 2016). Suspenseful and devastating drama starring Asano Tadamobu as an ex-con who manipulates and finally destroys a family. The harmonium of the title refers to the church-going wife, her non-harmonious marriage and her daughter's reluctance to learn to play the harmonium.

Ichi the Killer (Miike Takashi; 2001). Stand by for graphic depictions of bodies sliced in half in this *yakuza* tale, set in Tokyo's Kabukichō, as told by the *enfant terrible* of Japanese cinema. Not for the squeamish.

The Long Excuse (*Nagai Iiwake*: Nishikawa Miwa; 2016). Exploring themes of bereavement and empathy, Nishikawa's clever and darkly comedic film (based on her novel) is about a popular writer whose wife dies in an accident, and his inability to mourn her death appropriately.

The Mourning Forest (*Mogari no Mori*; Kawase Naomi; 2007). This Cannes film festival prize-winner is a moving tale of a caretaker at a retirement home and one of the residents, both struggling with bereavement, who make a road trip into the forests around Nara.

Nobody Knows (Kore-eda Hirokazu; 2004). Tragic story of four children trying to survive after being abandoned by their mother. Wonderful performance by the child actors, which earned Yagira Yaya a best actor award at Cannes in 2004.

Nuclear Nation (Funahashi Atsushi; 2012). Documenting a year in the life of nuclear refugees, this film shows the anger and struggles of an entire town in Fukushima who were displaced after the 2011 disasters.

Osaka Story (*Ōsaka Monogatari*; Nakata Toichi; 1994). Nakata Toichi ticks off many difficult contemporary issues in this documentary, which follows the homecoming of a gay, Korean–Japanese film student to his Osaka-based family. His staunchly Korean father expects him to take over the business and get married, but the son has other ideas.

Our Little Sister (*Umimachi Diary*; Kore-eda Hirokazu; 2015). Based on Yoshida Akimi's manga series of the same name, this emotionally complicated and somewhat sentimental family drama focuses on the lives of four sisters after their estranged father's death and how they rebuild their relationships.

Ring (Nakata Hideo; 1998). Remade in Hollywood, this is the original and far superior spine-chiller about a videotape that kills everyone who sees it exactly one week after viewing.

Shall We Dance? (Suo Masayuki; 1996). At turns touching and hilarious, *Shall We Dance?* features Yakusho Kōji playing a quietly frustrated middle-aged salaryman whose spark returns when he takes up ballroom dancing, though he must keep it secret from his family and work colleagues to avoid social stigma.

Tokyo Sonata (Kurosawa Kiyoshi; 2008). When a father decides not to tell his family he's lost his job as a salaryman it has all kinds of repercussions. A bleak, satirical drama reflective of contemporary Japanese society.

ESSENTIAL ANIME

Akira (Ōtomo Katsuhiro; 1988). Dynamic action sequences drive forward this nihilistic sci-fi fantasy about biker gangs, terrorists, government plots and a telekinetic teenager mutating in Tokyo, 2019.

Ghost in the Shell (*Kokaku Kidōtai*; Oshii Mamoru's; 1995). A sophisticated sci-fi thriller that's director Mamoru Oshii's finest work, together with its sequel *Innocence* and the fascinating TV series it spawned.

In This Corner of the World (*Kono Sekai no Katasumi ni*; Katabuchi Sunao; 2016). Set in World War II Hiroshima, this award-winning anime is the story of a feisty young woman and her experiences before and after the atomic bombing. The emphasis here is less on victimhood and more on the injustices and deprivations of war.

My Neighbour Totoro (*Tonari no Totoro*; Miyazaki Hayao; 1988). Charming kids' fable set in 1950s Japan about two little girls with a sick mother who make friends with the mythical creatures of the forest, including the giant cuddly character of the title.

Only Yesterday (*Omohide Poroporo*; Takahata Isao; 1988). Beautifully realized film about a woman, on a life-changing vacation in the countryside, recalling the childhood episodes that shaped her personality.

★**Princess Mononoke** (*Mononoke Hime*; Miyazaki Hayao; 1997). Exciting period drama set in medieval Japan has an ecological message about saving the earth's resources.

Spirited Away (*Sen to Chihiro no Kamikaskushi*; Miyazaki Hayao; 2001). Oscar-winning Japanese *Alice in Wonderland*-style adventure. When her parents take a wrong turn into a mysteriously deserted theme park, Chihiro finds she has to negotiate her way around the strange creatures she meets at a huge bathhouse before finding a way home.

★**Tokyo Godfathers** (Kon Satoshi; 2003). This heart-warming Christmas fairy tale of redemption for three tramps and the baby they discover in the trash is pure anime magic.

Your Name (*Kimi no Na wa*; Shinkai Makoto; 2016). Record-breaking box-office hit from the up-and-coming Shinkai Makoto (touted as Miyazaki Hayao's successor) about two high-school students who switch bodies and genders overnight. The usual comedic incidents ensue, but it's also a touching time-travelling love story.

FOREIGN FILMS FEATURING JAPAN

Black Rain (Ridley Scott; 1989). Gruff Michael Douglas and younger sidekick Andy Garcia team up with stoic Osaka policeman, played by Takakura Ken, to deal with the *yakuza*.

The Great Happiness Space (Jake Clennell; 2006). This riveting documentary on an Osaka host club has brutally honest interviews with the male hosts and their female customers.

The Last Samurai (Edward Zwick; 2003). Tom Cruise, Billy Connolly and some of Japan's top acting talent star in this tale of a US Civil War vet who comes to train the Emperor Meiji's troops in modern warfare, but finds much to learn himself in the samurai code of honour.

Letters from Iwo-jima (Clint Eastwood; 2006). Experience the bloody battle for the island of Iwo-jima at the end of World War II from the point of view of two Japanese soldiers played by Watanabe Ken and Ninomiya Kazunari.

Lost in Translation (Sofia Coppola; 2003). Memorable performances from Bill Murray and Scarlett Johansson in this stylish comedy-drama set in and around Shinjuku's *Park Hyatt* hotel. Brilliantly captures the urban experience for foreigners in Tokyo.

Memoirs of a Geisha (Rob Marshall; 2005). Epic-scale film which gallops through Arthur Golden's bestselling tale of the trials and tribulations of apprentice geisha Sayuri, played here by Chinese actor Zhang Ziyi, wearing uncommonly blue contact lenses. Gong Li chews up the scenery as her arch-rival, and Watanabe Ken, Hollywood's pin-up Japanese actor *de jour*, also puts in an appearance as Sayuri's saviour, the Chairman.

Ramen Girl (Robert Allen Ackerman; 2009). One of Brittany Murphy's last films where she does a charming job of learning to cook ramen at a neighbourhood Tokyo restaurant with no Japanese language skills. Heavily references the classic *Tampopo*.

Shugendo Now (Jean-Marc Abela; 2010). Poetic documentary on modern mountain ascetics in Japan as they perform shamanistic rituals and Tantric Buddhism. Shows the extraordinary contrast between urban life and ancient spirituality in Japan.

Books

The one thing the world is not short of is books about Japan; the following selection includes ones that provide a deeper understanding of what is lazily assumed to be one of the world's most enigmatic countries. As throughout this Guide, for Japanese names we have given the family name first. This may not always be the order in which it is printed on the English translation.

USEFUL CONTACTS

The following publishers specialize in English-language books on Japan, as well as translations of Japanese works: Kodansha (ⓦwww.kodanshausa.com); Charles E. Tuttle (ⓦtuttlepublishing.com); Stonebridge Press (ⓦstonebridge.com); and Vertical (ⓦvertical-inc.com), which publishes not only great manga titles but also a series of fiction and non-fiction titles by lesser-known (outside of Japan) talents.

HISTORY

Ian Buruma *Inventing Japan*. Focusing on the period 1853 to 1964, during which Japan went from a feudal, isolated state to a powerhouse of the modern world economy. Buruma's *The Wages of Guilt* also skilfully explains how and why Germany and Japan have come to terms so differently with their roles in World War II.

★**John Dougill** *In Search of Japan's Hidden Christians*. Part historical narrative, part travelogue, the fascinating and largely unknown history of Japan's hidden Christians is told in an engaging way. The in-depth research reveals some surprising stories of survival and belief.

John Dower *Embracing Defeat: Japan in the Aftermath of World War II*. Accessible look by a Pulitzer prizewinner at the impact of the American occupation on Japan. First-person accounts and snappy writing bring the book alive.

Karl Friday *Japan Emerging: Premodern History to 1850*. Incorporating the latest scholarship on premodern Japan, this textbook is both comprehensive and highly readable.

Andrew Gordon *A Modern History of Japan: From Tokugawa Times to the Present*. An excellent overview of two centuries of history covering modernization and militarism, as well as the postwar economic "miracle".

John Hersey *Hiroshima*. Classic account of the devastation and suffering wrought by the first A-bomb to be used in war.

John Man *Ninja: 1000 Years of the Shadow Warrior*. An investigation into the world of ninja, the "shadow warriors" or assassins with stealth and spy skills. Man traces their origins to China, while dispelling pop culture stereotypes and revealing how their legendary tactics were utilized during World War II.

Giles Milton *Samurai William*. Will Adams was one of a handful of shipwrecked sailors who arrived in Japan in 1600 and went on to become adviser to the shogun and the only foreigner ever to be made a samurai. Milton tells the tale with gusto.

★**William Tsutsui** *A Companion to Japanese History*. An authoritative and in-depth text which includes the latest research and current debates on Japanese history from early civilization to popular culture, with both Japanese and Western viewpoints.

BUSINESS, ECONOMICS AND POLITICS

★**Alex Kerr** *Dogs and Demons*. A scathing and thought-provoking attack on Japan's economic, environmental and social policies of the past decades, by someone who first came to Japan as a child in the 1960s and has been fascinated by it ever since. Also worth reading is his earlier book *Lost Japan*.

Laura J Kriska *Accidental Office Lady*. Kriska's account of her two years working in Japan as a trainee for Honda in the late 1980s is particularly good for its perspective on gender in Japanese corporate life.

Miyamoto Masao *Straitjacket Society*. As the subtitle hints, this "insider's irreverent view of bureaucratic Japan" is quite an eye-opener. Unsurprisingly, Miyamoto was fired from the Ministry of Health and Welfare, but his book sold over 400,000 copies.

★**Niall Murtagh** *The Blue-eyed Salaryman*. Anyone who has ever worked for a Japanese company will find much to identify with in this honest, witty account by an Irish computer programmer, who became a salaryman for Mitsubishi.

★**Karel Van Wolferen** *The Enigma of Japanese Power*. A weighty, thought-provoking tome, but one worth wading through. This is the standard text on the triad of Japan's bureaucracy, politicians and business.

TRADITIONAL ARTS, ARCHITECTURE AND GARDENS

★ **Liza Dalby** *Geisha*. In the 1970s, anthropologist Dalby immersed herself in the fast-dissolving life of the geisha. This is the fascinating account of her experience and those of her teachers and fellow pupils. *Kimono*, her history of that most Japanese of garments, is also worth reading.

Itoh Teiji *The Gardens of Japan*. Splendid photos of all Japan's great historical gardens, including many not generally open to the public, as well as contemporary examples.

Thomas F. Judge and **Tomita Hiroyuki** *Edo Craftsmen*. Beautifully produced portraits of some of Shitamachi's traditional craftsmen, who can still be found working in the backstreets of Tokyo. A timely insight into a disappearing world.

Alex Kerr and **Kathy Arlyn Sokol** *Another Kyoto*. The intricate heritage of Kyoto's architectural and artistic traditions, with fascinating anecdotes and illustrated examples.

Matsui Kesako *Kabuki, a Mirror of Japan*. A fascinating look at ten of the most renowned and popular kabuki plays, and how they relate to larger patterns of cultural development in Japan since the late seventeenth century.

Nakagawa Takeshi *The Japanese House*. Comprehensively illustrated book, which takes the reader step by step through the various elements of the traditional Japanese home, and is the essential manual on vernacular architecture.

Joan Stanley-Baker *Japanese Art*. Highly readable introduction to the broad range of Japan's artistic traditions (though excluding theatre and music), tracing their development from prehistoric to modern times.

CULTURE AND SOCIETY

Jake Adelstein *Tokyo Vice*. With forensic thoroughness and gallows humour, Adelstein documents his unsentimental education in crime reporting for the *Yomiuri Shimbun*, Japan's top-selling newspaper. A movie version of the book, starring Daniel Radcliffe, is in development.

★ **Anne Allison** *Precarious Japan*. A sobering look at modern Japanese society immediately before and after the 2011 disaster. Anthropologist Allison provides some fascinating insights into the many social ills which plague daily life and the stories of those who are effecting change.

Ruth Benedict *The Chrysanthemum and the Sword*. This classic study of the hierarchical order of Japanese society, first published in 1946, remains relevant (and controversial) for its conclusions on the psychology of a nation that had just suffered defeat in World War II.

★ **Lucy Birmingham and David McNeill** *Strong in the Rain*. Tokyo-based journalists ponder their experiences in the aftermath of the 2011 disaster and closely follow the lives of six survivors who showed great courage and determination. A moving and well-written account.

Ian Buruma *A Japanese Mirror* and *The Missionary and the Libertine*. The first book is an intelligent, erudite examination of Japan's popular culture, while *The Missionary and the Libertine* collects together a range of essays on everthing from Pearl Harbor to the film director Ōshima Nagisa.

Veronica Chambers *Kickboxing Geishas*. Based on interviews with a broad cross section of women, from Hokkaidō DJs to top executives, Chambers argues that modern Japanese women are not the submissive characters so often portrayed in the media, but in fact a strong force for change. A sympathetic and insightful book.

Kittredge Cherry *Womansword*. The thirtieth anniversary edition of this highly readable book shows how much, and also how little, has changed in the gendered vocabulary used to talk about Japanese women.

Edward Fowler *San'ya Blues*. Fowler's experiences living and working among the casual labourers of Tokyo's San'ya district make fascinating reading. He reveals the dark underbelly of Japan's economic miracle and blows apart a few myths and misconceptions on the way.

Paul Murphy *True Crime Japan*. Journalist Murphy smashes some stereotypes about Japanese people in his account of the chilling, farcical and extraordinary stories of the thieves, rascals, killers and dopeheads he witnessed in the Kafkaesque but functional Japanese justice system.

Roger Pulvers *If There Were No Japan*. Arriving in Japan in 1967 unable to speak the language, Pulvers has since published dozens of books, as well as written and directed many plays, in Japanese. This memoir includes frank analysis of modern Japan, as well as reminiscences on friendships with some of Japan's most creative people.

Saga Junichi *Confessions of a Yakuza*. This life story of a former *yakuza* boss, beautifully retold by a doctor whose clinic he just happened to walk into, gives a rare insight into a secret world. Saga also wrote the award-winning *Memories of Silk and Straw*, a collection of reminiscences about village life in premodern Japan.

★ **David Suzuki** and **Oiwa Keibo** *The Japan We Never Knew*. Canadian scientist and writer Suzuki teamed up with half-Japanese anthropologist Oiwa to tour the country and interview an extraordinary range of people, from the Ainu of Hokkaidō to descendants of the "untouchable" caste, the Burakumin. The result is an excellent riposte to the idea of a monocultural, conformist Japan.

Tendo Shoko *Yakuza Moon*. The daughter of a *yakuza*, Tendo lived her teens in a blur of violence, sex and drugs. By age 15, she was in a detention centre and then gradually pulled her life together to write this searing account of life in the underclass of Japanese society.

POP CULTURE

Ban Toshio *The Tezuka Osamu Story: A Life in Manga and Anime*. Fittingly, the life story of the "God of Manga" and pioneer of anime is told here in graphic form by one of Tezuka's closest friends and collaborators.

Patrick Galbraith *The Otoku Encyclopedia*. This is the insider's guide to *otaku* (geek or nerd) culture in Japan. It looks at the history of fandom of manga and anime and the associated cultural practices of maid cafés and cosplay.

★**Hector Garcia** *A Geek in Japan*. An encyclopedic overview of "Cool Japan". This cultural guide has everything from tea ceremonies to TV Drama, covered in an engaging and visual style.

★**Roland Kelts** *Japanamerica*. Highly accessible, personalized account of how Japanese pop culture – and in particular manga and anime – has become such a huge success in the US. Kelts, half Japanese, half American and living in both countries, makes many intelligent observations and digs up some fascinating tales.

Frederik L. Schodt *Dreamland Japan: Writings on Modern Manga*. A series of entertaining and informative essays on the art of Japanese comic books, profiling the top publications, artists, animated films and English-language manga.

FOOD AND DRINK

Shirley Booth *Food of Japan*. More than a series of recipes, this nicely illustrated book gives lots of background detail and history on Japanese food.

John Gauntner *Sake Confidential*. This is a fun basic guide to expanding your knowledge and developing a more sophisticated understanding of sake. Gauntner unpacks the secrets of Japan's favourite tipple with the intention of making it more accessible and more enjoyable.

★**Nancy Singleton Hachisu** *Japanese Farm Food*. Recipes and life experiences from an American expat living in an 80-year-old farmhouse in rural Japan. Beautiful photography and healthy food.

Kurihara Harumi *Harumi's Japanese Cooking*. An easy-to-follow guide from Japan's Martha Stewart, with a down-to-earth approach to preparing typical dishes that Japanese eat at home.

★**Barak Kushner** *Slurp! A Social and Culinary History of Ramen*. A fun and informative history of Japan's favourite noodle soup, looking at its political identity (is it Chinese or Japanese food?) and its place in popular culture.

★**Jane Lawson** *Zenbu Zen*. The author spends a year in Kyoto soaking up the seasons and the food culture. Sumptuous photos, recipes and observations on life in the ancient capital.

Robb Satterwhite *What's What in Japanese Restaurants*. Written by a Tokyo-based epicure, this handy guide covers all the types of Japanese food and drink you're likely to encounter, and the menus annotated with Japanese characters are particularly useful.

TRAVEL WRITING

Isabella Bird *Unbeaten Tracks in Japan*. After a brief stop in Meiji-era Tokyo, intrepid Victorian adventurer Bird is determined to reach parts of Japan unexplored, as yet, by tourists. She heads north to Hokkaidō, taking the time to make acute, vivid observations along the way.

★**Alan Booth** *The Roads to Sata* and *Looking for the Lost*. Two classics by one of the most insightful and entertaining modern writers on Japan, whose talents were tragically

---

JAPAN THROUGH AN AMERICAN'S EYES

Donald Richie wrote intelligently about Japanese culture since he first arrived in the country in 1947 to work as a typist for the US occupying forces, until his death in 2013. Richie is best known as a scholar of Japanese cinema, but among his forty-odd books it's his essay collections – **Public People, Private People; A Lateral View; Partial Views** – that set a standard to which other expat commentators can only aspire. *Public People* is a series of sketches of famous and unknown Japanese, including profiles of novelist Mishima Yukio and the actor Mifune Toshirō. In *A Lateral View* and *Partial Views*, Richie tackles Tokyo style, avant-garde theatre, pachinko, the Japanese kiss and the Zen rock garden at Kyoto's Ryōan-ji, among many other things.

His subtle, elegiac travelogue *The Inland Sea*, first published in 1971, captures the timeless beauty of the island-studded waterway and is a must read. In *Tokyo*, Richie captures the essence of the city he lived in for more than fifty years. Naturally, he also served as editor on *Lafcadio Hearn's Japan*, which includes sections from the classic *Glimpses of Unfamiliar Japan*, among Hearn's other works (see box, p.620). For an overview of the immense Richie *oeuvre*, dip into *The Donald Richie Reader: 50 Years of Writing on Japan* or his *Japan Journals 1947–2004*.

cut short by his death in 1993. The first book sees Booth, an avid long-distance walker, hike (with the aid of many a beer) from the far north of Hokkaidō to the southern tip of Kyūshū, while *Looking for the Lost*, a trio of walking tales, is by turns hilarious and heartbreakingly poignant.

Josie Drew *A Ride in the Neon Sun*. At nearly seven hundred pages, this isn't a book to pop in your panniers, but full of useful tips for anyone planning to tour Japan by bike. Drew has subsequently put out an equally entertaining sequel, *The Sun in My Eyes*.

★**Will Ferguson** *Hokkaido Highway Blues*. Humorist Ferguson decides to hitch from one end of Japan to the other, with the aim of travelling with the Japanese, not among them. He succeeds (despite everyone telling him – even those who stop to pick him up – that Japanese never stop for hitch-hikers), and in the process turns out a great

book of travel writing about the country. Funny and ultimately moving.

Pico Iyer *The Lady and the Monk*. Devoted to a year Iyer spent studying Zen Buddhism and dallying with a married woman in Kyoto, who subsequently became his life partner. It's a rose-tinted, dreamy view of Japan, which he has since followed up, in a more realistic way, with his excellent and thought-provoking *The Global Soul*.

Karin Muller *Japanland*. Documentary film-maker and travel writer Muller heads to Japan in search of *wa* – the Japanese concept of harmony. The interesting cast of characters she meets in the year she spends there – part of the time living just south of Tokyo, the other travelling, including to Kyoto, Shikoku and northern Honshū – is what makes this book rise above similar efforts.

GUIDES AND REFERENCE BOOKS

John Dougill and **Joseph Cali** *Shinto Shrines: A Guide to the Sacred Sites of Japan's Ancient Religion*. An interesting introduction to the history and philosophy of Japan's native religion. This detailed and practical guide profiles more than sixty major Shintō shrines, many of which are World Heritage Sites.

Ed Readicker-Henderson *The Traveller's Guide to Japanese Pilgrimages*. A practical guide to Japan's top three

pilgrim routes: Hiei-zan (near Kyoto); the 33 Kannon of Saigoku (a broad sweep from the Kii peninsula to Lake Biwa); and following the steps of Kōbō Daishi round Shikoku's 88 temples.

Marc Treib and **Ron Herman** *A Guide to the Gardens of Kyoto*. Handy, pocket-sized guide to more than fifty of the city's gardens, with concise historical details and step-by-step descriptions of each garden.

CLASSIC LITERATURE

★**Kawabata Yasunari** *Snow Country*, *The Izu Dancer* and other titles. Japan's first Nobel prizewinner for fiction writes intense tales of passion – usually about a sophisticated urban man falling for a simple country girl.

★**Murasaki Shikibu** *The Tale of Genji*. Claimed as the world's first novel, this lyrical epic about the lives and loves of a nobleman was spun by a lady of the Heian court around 1000 AD.

Sōseki Natsume *Botchan*, *Kokoro* and *I am a Cat*. In his comic novel *Botchan*, Sōseki draws on his own experiences as an English teacher in early twentieth-century Matsuyama. The three volumes of *I am a Cat* see the humorist adopting a wry feline point of view on the

world. *Kokoro* – about an ageing *sensei* (teacher) trying to come to terms with the modern era – is considered his best book.

Sei Shōnagon *The Pillow Book*. Fascinating insight into the daily life and artful thoughts of a tenth-century noblewoman.

Tanizaki Jun'ichirō *Some Prefer Nettles* and *The Makioka Sisters*. One of the great stylists of Japanese prose, Tanizaki's finest book is often considered to be *Some Prefer Nettles*, about a romantic liaison between a Japanese man and a Eurasian woman. However, there's an epic sweep to *The Makioka Sisters*, which documents the decline of a wealthy merchant family in Osaka.

CONTEMPORARY FICTION

Kawakami Hiromi *Manazuru*. A haunting, almost surreal story where the main character tries to forget her loss by visiting places where her memories are the strongest, notably the seaside town of Manazuru.

Mishima Yukio *After the Banquet*, *Confessions of Mask*, *Forbidden Colours* and *The Sea of Fertility*. Novelist Mishima sealed his notoriety by committing ritual suicide after leading a failed military coup in 1970. He left behind a highly respectable, if at times melodramatic, body of literature, including some of Japan's finest postwar novels.

Mizumura Minae *A True Novel*. A wonderful reworking

of *Wuthering Heights* in the context of postwar Japan and the high economic growth period. The heroine straddles East and West and suffers many trials and tribulations through her doomed romance with an angry young man.

★**Murakami Ryū** *Almost Transparent Blue*, *Sixty-nine* and *Coin Locker Babies*. Murakami burst onto Japan's literary scene in the mid-1980s with *Almost Transparent Blue*, a tale of student life mixing reality and fantasy. *Sixty-nine* is his semi-autobiographical account of a 17-year-old stirred by rebellion. *Coin Locker Babies* is his most ambitious work – a revenger's tragedy about the lives of two boys dumped in adjacent coin lockers as babies.

Ōe Kenzaburō *Nip the Buds*. Winner of Japan's second Nobel prize for literature in 1994. *Nip the Buds*, his first full-length novel, published in 1958, is a tale of lost innocence concerning fifteen schoolboys evacuated in wartime to a remote mountain village and left to fend for themselves when a threatening plague frightens away the villagers.

Shiba Ryōtarō *Clouds Above The Hill*. This best-selling epic novel of the modernization of Japan and the Russo-Japanese War has only recently been translated into English. The four-volume set is enthralling reading and shows the hope and vision of the Meiji reformers.

Tsujihara Noboru *Jasmine*. Nicely written adventure and suspense novel which explores the relationships between a Japanese man and a Chinese woman, linking the Tiananmen Massacre of 1989 to the 1995 Kōbe earthquake and the touchy issue of Sino–Japanese relations.

JAPAN IN FOREIGN FICTION

Ellis Avery *The Teahouse Fire*. Set in the tea ceremony world of Kyoto in the late nineteenth century, this elegantly written novel is told through the eyes of a young American woman who is orphaned and then adopted by a family of tea masters. A fascinating portrait of women's lives and the political upheavals of Meiji Japan.

Alan Brown *Audrey Hepburn's Neck*. Beneath this rib-tickling, acutely observed tale of a young guy from the sticks adrift in big-city Tokyo, Brown weaves several important themes, including the continuing impact of World War II and the confused relationships between the Japanese and *gaijin*.

William Gibson *Idoru*. Love in the age of the computer chip. Cyberpunk novelist Gibson's sci-fi vision of Tokyo's hi-tech future – a world of non-intrusive DNA checks at airports and computerized pop icons (the *idoru* of the title) – rings disturbingly true.

Arthur Golden *Memoirs of a Geisha*. Rags to riches potboiler following the progress of Chiyo from her humble beginnings in a Japanese fishing village through training as a geisha in Kyoto to moving to New York.

Mo Hayder *Tokyo*. Disturbing crime thriller set in 1990s Tokyo and Nanking during the Japanese invasion in 1937, weaving a frightening story around war atrocities, the *yakuza* and foreign women bar hostesses. Also recently re-published as *The Devil of Nanking*.

★**Barry Lancet** *Japantown*. Thriller set in San Francisco and Tokyo that follows an antique-dealer as he sets out to solve the murder of a Japanese family. Lots of detailed cultural references and interesting plot twists make this a fun and informative read.

★**David Mitchell** *Ghostwritten, number9dream* and *The Thousand Autumns of Jacob De Zoet*. Mitchell lived in Japan for several years, a fact that is reflected in three of his novels. *Ghostwritten* is a dazzling collection of interlocked short stories, a couple of which are based in Japan. *number9dream* conjures up a postmodern Japan of computer hackers, video games, gangsters and violence. His latest, *The Thousand Autumns of Jacob De Zoet*, is a fascinating historical novel focusing on life on Nagasaki's island enclave of Dejima – the only place Europeans were allowed to live in Japan during the Tokugawa era.

HARUKI MURAKAMI

One of Japan's most entertaining and translated contemporary writers, **Haruki Murakami** has been hailed as a postwar successor to the great novelists Mishima, Kawabata and Tanizaki, and talked of as a future Nobel laureate.

Many of Murakami's books are set in Tokyo, drawing on his time studying at Waseda University in the early 1970s and running a jazz bar, a place that became a haunt for literary types and, no doubt, provided inspiration for his jazz-bar-running hero in the bittersweet novella *South of the Border, West of the Sun*. A good introduction to Murakami is **Norwegian Wood**, a book in two volumes about the tender coming-of-age love story of two students, which has sold over five million copies.

Considered among his best works are **The Wind-Up Bird Chronicle**, a hefty yet dazzling cocktail of mystery, war reportage and philosophy, and the surreal **Kafka on the Shore**, a murder story in which cats talk to people and fish rain from the sky. His 2011 mega-opus is *1Q84*, a complex tale of cults and assassins set in 1984 that unravels over more than 1000 pages. His most recent novels are *Colorless Tsukuru Tazaki and His Years of Pilgrimage*, set in Nagoya and Finland, and most recently *Murder of a Knight Commander*.

For a wonderful insight into what makes this publicity-shy author tick, read his brief memoir about running marathons and writing, **What I Talk About When I Talk About Running**.

Japanese

Picking up a few words of Japanese is not difficult. Pronunciation is simple and standard and there are few exceptions to the straightforward grammar rules. With a just a little effort, you should be able to read the words spelled out in *hiragana* and *katakana*, Japanese phonetic characters, even if you can't understand them. And any time spent learning Japanese will be amply rewarded by delighted locals, who'll always politely comment on your fine linguistic ability.

That said, it does take a very great effort to master Japanese. The primary stumbling block is the thousands of **kanji** characters (Chinese ideograms) that need to be memorized, most of which have at least two pronunciations, depending on the sentence and their combination with other characters. Also tricky are the language's multiple levels of **politeness**, married with different sets of words used by men and women, as well as different **dialects** involving whole new vocabularies.

Japanese characters

Japanese is written in a combination of three systems. To be able to read a newspaper, you'll need to know around two thousand *kanji* – even more difficult than it sounds, since what each one means varies with its context.

The easier writing systems to pick up are the phonetic syllabaries, **hiragana** and **katakana**. Both have 46 regular characters (see box, p.870) and can be learned within a couple of weeks. *Hiragana* is used for Japanese words, while *katakana*, with the squarer characters, is used mainly for "loan words" borrowed from other languages (especially English) and technical names. **Rōmaji** (see p.870), the roman script used to spell out Japanese words, is also used in advertisements and magazines.

The first five letters in *hiragana* and *katakana* (**a, i, u, e, o**) are the vowel sounds (see p.870). The remainder are a combination of a consonant and a vowel (eg **ka, ki, ku, ke, ko**), with the exception of **n**, the only consonant that exists on its own. While *hiragana* provides an exact phonetic reading of all Japanese words, *katakana* does not do the same for foreign loan words. Often words are abbreviated, hence television becomes *terebi* and sexual harassment *sekuhara*. Sometimes, they become almost unrecognizable, as with *kakuteru* (cocktail).

Traditionally, Japanese is written in vertical columns and read right to left. However, the Western way of writing from left to right, horizontally from top to bottom is increasingly common. In the media and on signs you'll see a mixture of the two ways of writing.

Grammar

In Japanese, **verbs** do not change according to the person or number, so that *ikimasu* can mean "I go", "he/she/it goes", or "we/they go". **Pronouns** are usually omitted, since it's generally clear from the context who or what the speaker is referring to. There are no **definite articles**, and **nouns** stay the same whether they refer to singular or plural words.

Compared to English grammar, Japanese **sentences** are structured back to front. An English-speaker would say "I am going to Tokyo" which in Japanese would translate directly as "Tokyo to going". Placing the sound "*ka*" at the end of a phrase indicates a **question**, hence *Tokyo e ikimasu-ka* means "Are you going to Tokyo?" There are also levels of **politeness** to contend with, which alter the way the verb is conjugated, and sometimes change the word entirely. Stick to the polite -*masu* form of verbs which we use in this chapter and you should be fine.

Japanese: A Rough Guide Phrasebook includes essential phrases and expressions and a dictionary section and menu reader. The phonetic translations in the phrasebook are rendered slightly differently from the standard way *rōmaji* is written in this book, as an aid to pronunciation.

Pronunciation

Japanese words in this book have been transliterated into the standard Hepburn system of romanization, called **rōmaji**. Pronunciation is as follows:

a as in cat	**ai** as in Thai
i as in macaroni, or **ee**	**ei** as in weight
u as in put, or **oo**	**ie** as in two separate sounds, **ee-eh**
e as in bed; e is always pronounced, even at the end of a word	**ue** as in two separate sounds, **oo-eh**
	g, a hard sound as in girl
o as in not	**s** as in mass (never z)
ae as in the two separate sounds, **ah-eh**	**y** as in yet

A bar (macron) over a vowel or "ii" means that the vowel sound is twice as long as a vowel without a bar. Only where words are well known in English, such as Tokyo, Kyoto, judo and shogun, have we not used a bar to indicate long vowel sounds. Sometimes, vowel sounds are shortened or softened; for example, the verb *desu* sounds more like *des* when pronounced, and *sukiyaki* like *skiyaki*. Some syllables are also softened or hardened by the addition of a small ° or " above the character; for example, **ka** (か) becomes **ga** (が) and **ba** (ば) becomes **pa** (ぱ). Likewise a smaller-case ya, yu or yo following a character alters its sound, such as **kya** (きゃ) and **kyu** (きゅ). All syllables are evenly stressed and pronounced in full. For example, Nagano is Na-ga-no, not Na-GA-no.

Wherever there's a double consonant (eg *tetsudatte*), pause for a moment before saying it. It's somewhat like a glottal stop, and, as always, the best way to learn it is to listen out for it. When you see "**tch**" (eg *matcha*), pronounce it as ch as in chair.

USEFUL WORDS AND PHRASES

BASICS

yes	hai	はい
no	iie/chigaimasu	いいえ／違います
ok	daijōbu/ōkē	大丈夫／オーケー
please (offering something)	dōzo	どうぞ
please (asking for something)	onegai shimasu	お願いします
Excuse me	sumimasen/shitsurei shimasu	すみません／失礼します
I'm sorry	gomen nasai/sumimasen	ごめんなさい／すみません
Thanks (informal)	dōmo	どうも
Thank you	arigatō	ありがとう
Thank you very much	dōmo arigatō gozaimasu	どうもありがとうございます
What?	nani?	ない／何
When?	itsu?	いつ
Where?	doko?	どこ
Who?	dare?	だれ
this	kore	これ
that	sore	それ
that (over there)	are	あれ
How many?	ikutsu?	いくつ
How much?	ikura?	いくら

JAPANESE SCRIPT IN THE GUIDE

To help you find your way around, in the Guide we've included **Japanese script** for all places covered, as well as sights, hotels, restaurants, cafés, bars and shops where there is no prominent English sign. Where the English name for a point of interest is very different from its Japanese name, we've also provided the *rōmaji* (see opposite), so you can pronounce the Japanese.

I don't want/need (x)	Watashi wa (x) ga hoshii desu	私は(x)が欲しいです
I don't want (x)	Watashi wa (x) ga irimasen	私は(x)がいりません
Is it possible…?	…koto ga dekimasu ka	。。。ことができますか
It is not possible	…koto ga dekimasen	。。。ことができません
Is it…?	…desu ka	。。。ですか
Can you please help me?	Tetsudatte kuremasen ka	手伝ってくれませんか
I don't speak Japanese	Nihongo ga hanasemasen	日本語は話せません
I don't read Japanese	Nihongo ga yomemasen	日本語は読めません
Can you speak English?	Eigo ga dekimasu ka	英語ができますか
Is there someone who can interpret?	Tsūyaku wa imasu ka	通訳はいますか
Could you please speak more slowly?	Motto yukkuri hanashite kuremasen ka	もっとゆっくり話して くれませんか
Please say that again	Mō ichido yutte kuremasen ka	もう一度言ってくれませんか
I understand/I see	Wakarimasu/Naruhodo	わかります／なるほど
I don't understand	Wakarimasen	分かりません
What does this mean?	Kore wa dō iyu imi desu ka	これはどういう意味ですか
How do you say (x) in Japanese?	Nihongo de (x) o nan-to iimasu ka	日本語で(x) を何と言いますか
What's this called?	Kore wa nan-to iimasu ka	これは何と言いますか
How do you pronounce this character?	Kono kanji wa nan-to yomimasu ka	この漢字は何と読みますか
Please write in English/Japanese	Eigo/Nihongo de kaite kudasai	英語／日本語で書いてください

PERSONAL PRONOUNS

I	watashi	私
I (familiar, men only)	boku/ore	僕/俺
you	anata	あなた
you (familiar)	kimi	君
he	kare	彼
she	kanojo	彼女
we	watashi-tachi	私たち
you (plural)	anata-tachi	あなたたち
they (male/female)	karera/kanojo-tachi	彼ら／彼女たち
they (objects)	sorera	それら

GREETINGS AND BASIC COURTESIES

Hello/Good day	Konnichiwa	今日は
Good morning	Ohayō gozaimasu	おはようございます
Good evening	Konbanwa	今晩は
Good night (when leaving)	Osaki ni	お先に
Good night (when going to bed)	Oyasuminasai	おやすみなさい
How are you?	O-genki desu ka	お元気ですか
I'm fine (informal)	Genki desu	元気です
I'm fine, thanks	Okagesama de	おかげさまで
How do you do/Nice to meet you	Hajimemashite	はじめまして
Don't mention it/You're welcome	Dō itashimashite	どういたしまして

I'm sorry	Gomen nasai	ごめんなさい
Just a minute please	Chotto matte kudasai	ちょっと待ってください
Goodbye	Sayonara/sayōnara	さよなら/さようなら
Goodbye (informal)	Dewa mata/Jā ne	では又/じゃあね

CHITCHAT

What's your name?	Shitsurei desu ga o-namae wa	失礼ですがお名前は
My name is (x)	Watashi no namae wa (x) desu	私の名前は(x)です
Where are you from?	O-kuni wa doko desu ka	お国はどこですか
Britain	Eikoku/Igirisu	英国／イギリス
Ireland	Airurando	アイルランド
America	Amerika	アメリカ
Australia	Ōsutoraria	オーストラリア
Canada	Kanada	カナダ
France	Furansu	フランス
Germany	Doitsu	ドイツ
New Zealand	Nyū Jiirando	ニュージーランド
Japan	Nihon	日本
Outside Japan	Gaikoku	外国
How old are you?	O-ikutsu desu ka	おいくつですか
I am (age)	(age) sai desu	(age)才です/ (age)歳です
Are you married?	Kekkon shite imasu ka	結婚していますか
I am married/not married	Kekkon shite imasu/imasen	結婚しています／いません

KATAKANA AND HIRAGANA

Katakana and *hiragana* are two phonetic syllabaries represented by the characters shown below. *Katakana*, the characters in the first table, are generally used for writing foreign "loan words". The characters in the bottom table, *hiragana*, are generally used for Japanese words, in combination with, or as substitutes for, *kanji*.

KATAKANA

a	ア	i	イ	u	ウ	e	エ	o	オ
ka	カ	ki	キ	ku	ク	ke	ケ	ko	コ
sa	サ	shi	シ	su	ス	se	セ	so	ソ
ta	タ	chi	チ	tsu	ツ	te	テ	to	ト
na	ナ	ni	ニ	nu	ヌ	ne	ネ	no	ノ
ha	ハ	hi	ヒ	fu	フ	he	ヘ	ho	ホ
ma	マ	mi	ミ	mu	ム	me	メ	mo	モ
ya	ヤ			yu	ユ			yo	ヨ
ra	ラ	ri	リ	ru	ル	re	レ	ro	ロ
wa	ワ							wo	ヲ
n	ン								

HIRAGANA

a	あ	i	い	u	う	e	え	o	お
ka	か	ki	き	ku	く	ke	け	ko	こ
sa	さ	shi	し	su	す	se	せ	so	そ
ta	た	chi	ち	tsu	つ	te	て	to	と
na	な	ni	に	nu	ぬ	ne	ね	no	の
ha	は	hi	ひ	fu	ふ	he	へ	ho	ほ
ma	ま	mi	み	mu	む	me	め	mo	も
ya	や			yu	ゆ			yo	よ
ra	ら	ri	り	ru	る	re	れ	ro	ろ
wa	わ							wo	を
n	ん								

Do you like…?	…suki desu ka	。。。好きですか
I do like	…suki desu	。。。好きです
I don't like	…suki dewa arimasen	。。。好きではありません
What's your job?	O-shigoto wa nan desu ka	お仕事は何ですか
I'm a student	Gakusei desu	学生です
I'm a teacher	Sensei desu	先生です
I work for a company	Kaisha-in desu	会社員です
I'm a tourist	Kankō kyaku desu	観光客です
Really?	Hontō/Hontō ni	本当/本当に
That's a shame	Zannen desu	残念です
It can't be helped (formal/informal)	Shikata ga nai/shō ga nai	仕方がない／しょうがない

NUMBERS

There are special ways of **counting** different things in Japanese. The most common first translation is used when counting time and quantities and measurements, with added qualifiers such as minutes (*pun/fun*) or yen (*en*). The second translations are sometimes used for counting objects. From ten, there is only one set of numbers. For zero, four and seven, alternatives to the first translation are used in some circumstances.

zero	zero/rei		ない／何	ない／何
one	ichi	hitotsu	一	ひとつ
two	ni	futatsu	二	ふたつ
three	san	mittsu	三	みっつ
four	yon/shi	yottsu	四	よっつ
five	go	itsutsu	五	いつつ
six	roku	muttsu	六	むっつ
seven	shichi/nana	nanatsu	七	ななつ
eight	hachi	yattsu	八	やっつ
nine	kyū	kokonotsu	九	ここのつ
ten	jū	tō	十	とう
eleven	jū-ichi		十一	
twelve	jū-ni		十二	
twenty	ni-jū		二十	
twenty-one	ni-jū-ichi		二十一	
thirty	san-jū		三十	
one hundred	hyaku		百	
two hundred	ni-hyaku		二百	
thousand	sen		千	
ten thousand	ichi-man		一万	
one hundred thousand	jū-man		十万	
one million	hyaku-man		百万	
one hundred million	ichi-oku		一億	

TIME AND DATES

now	ima	今
today	kyō	今日
morning	asa	朝
evening	yūgata	夕方
night	yoru/ban	夜/晩
tomorrow	ashita	明日
the day after tomorrow	asatte	あさって
yesterday	kinō	昨日
week	shū	週
month	gatsu/tsuki/getsu	月
year	nen/toshi	年

Monday	Getsuyōbi	月曜日
Tuesday	Kayōbi	火曜日
Wednesday	Suiyōbi	水曜日
Thursday	Mokuyōbi	木曜日
Friday	Kin'yōbi	金曜日
Saturday	Doyōbi	土曜日
Sunday	Nichiyōbi	日曜日
What time is it?	Ima nan-ji desu ka	今何時ですか
It's 10 o'clock	Jū-ji desu	十時です
...10.20	Jū-ji ni-juppun	十時二十分
...10.30	Jū-ji han	十時半
...10.50	Jū-ichi-ji juppun mae	十一時十分前
AM	gozen	午前
PM	gogo	午後
January	Ichigatsu	一月
February	Nigatsu	二月
March	Sangatsu	三月
April	Shigatsu	四月
May	Gogatsu	五月
June	Rokugatsu	六月
July	Shichigatsu	七月
August	Hachigatsu	八月
September	Kugatsu	九月
October	Jūgatsu	十月
November	Jūichigatsu	十一月
December	Jūnigatsu	十二月
1st (day)	tsuitachi	一日
2nd (day)	futsuka	二日
3rd (day)	mikka	三日
4th (day)	yokka	四日
5th (day)	itsuka	五日
6th (day)	muika	六日
7th (day)	nanoka	七日
8th (day)	yōka	八日
9th (day)	kokonoka	九日
10th (day)	tōka	十日
11th (day)	jū-ichi-nichi	十一日
12th (day)	jū-ni-nichi	十二日
20th (day)	hatsuka	二十日
21st (day)	ni-jū-ichi nichi	二十一日
30th (day)	san-jū-nichi	三十日

GETTING AROUND

aeroplane	hikōki	飛行機
airport	kūkō	空港
bus	basu	バス
long-distance bus	chōkyori basu	長距離バス
bus stop	basu tei	バス停
train	densha	電車
station	eki	駅
subway	chikatetsu	地下鉄
ferry	ferii	フェリー
left-luggage office	azukarijo	預かり所
coin locker	koin rokkā	コインロッカー

ticket office	kippu uriba	切符売り場
ticket	kippu	切符
one-way	kata-michi	片道
return	ōfuku	往復
non-smoking seat	kin'en seki	禁煙席
window seat	mado-gawa no seki	窓側の席
platform	hōmu/purattofōmu	ホーム/プラットフォーム
bicycle	jitensha	自転車
taxi	takushii	タクシー
map	chizu	地図
Where is (x)?	(x) wa doko desu ka	(x)はどこですか
straight ahead	massugu	まっすぐ
in front of	mae	前
right	migi	右
left	hidari	左
north	kita	北
south	minami	南
east	higashi	東
west	nishi	西
entrance	iriguchi	入口
exit	deguchi/-guchi	出口／－口
highway	kaidō	街道
street	tōri/dōri/michi	通り／道

PLACES

temple	otera/-dera/-ji/-in	お寺／－寺／－院
shrine	jinja/jingū/-gū/-taisha	神社／神宮／－宮／－大社
castle	shiro/-jō	城
park	kōen	公園
river	kawa/gawa	川
bridge	hashi/-bashi	橋
museum	hakubutsukan	博物館
art museum	bijutsukan	美術館
garden	niwa/teien/-en	庭／庭園／－園
island	shima/-jima/-tō	島
slope	saka/-zaka	坂
hill	oka	丘
mountain	yama/-san/-take	山／岳
hot spring spa	onsen	温泉
lake	-ko	湖
bay	-wan	湾
peninsula	hantō	半島
cape	misaki/saki	岬
sea	umi/kai/nada	海／灘
gorge	kyō	峡
plateau	kōgen	高原
prefecture	-ken/-fu	県／府
ward	-ku	区
shop	mise/-ten/-ya	店／屋

ACCOMMODATION

hotel	hoteru	ホテル
traditional-style inn	ryokan	旅館
guesthouse	minshuku	民宿

youth hostel	yūsu hosuteru	ユースホステル
single room	shinguru rūmu	シングルルーム
double room	daburu rūmu	ダブルルーム
twin room	tsuin rūmu	ツインルーム
dormitory	kyōdō/ōbeya	共同／大部屋
Japanese-style room	washitsu	和室
Western-style room	yōshitsu	洋室
Western-style bed	beddo	ベッド
bath	o-furo	お風呂
Do you have any vacancies?	Kūshitsu wa arimasu ka	空室はありますか
I'd like to make a reservation	Yoyaku o shitai no desu ga	予約をしたいのですが
I have a reservation	Yoyaku shimashita	予約しました
I don't have a reservation	Yoyaku shimasen deshita	予約しませんでした
How much is it per person?	Hitori ikura desu ka	一人いくらですか
Does that include meals?	Shokuji wa tsuite imasu ka	食事はついていますか
I would like to stay one night / two nights	Hitoban/futaban tomaritai no desu ga	一晩／二晩泊まりたいのです/が
I would like to see the room	Heya o misete kudasaimasen ka	部屋を見せてくださいませんか
key	kagi	鍵
passport	pasupōto	パスポート

SHOPPING, MONEY AND BANKS

shop	mise/-ten/-ya	店／屋
How much is it?	Kore wa ikura desu ka	これはいくらですか
It's too expensive	Taka-sugimasu	高すぎます
Is there anything cheaper?	Mō sukoshi yasui mono wa arimasu ka	もう少し安いものはありますか
Do you accept credit cards?	Kurejitto kādo ga tsukaemasu ka	クレジットカードが使えますか
I'm just looking	Miru dake desu	見るだけです
gift/souvenir	omiyage	お土産
foreign exchange	ryogae	両替
bank	ginkō	銀行

INTERNET, POST AND TELEPHONES

internet	intānetto	インターネット
post office	yūbinkyoku	郵便局
envelope	fūtō	封筒
letter	tegami	手紙
postcard	hagaki/ehagaki	葉書/絵葉書
stamp	kitte	切手
airmail	kōkūbin	航空便
telephone	denwa	電話
international telephone call	kokusai-denwa	国際電話
reverse charge/collect call	korekuto-kōru	コレクトコール
mobile phone	keitai-denwa/keitai	携帯電話/携帯
fax	fakkusu	ファックス
telephone card	terefon kādo	テレフォンカード
I would like to call (place)	(place) e denwa o kaketai no desu	(place)へ電話をかけたいのです
I would like to send a fax to (place)	(place) e fakkusu shitai no desu	(place)へファックスしたいのです

HEALTH

hospital	byōin	病院
pharmacy	yakkyoku	薬局
medicine	kusuri	薬
doctor	isha/o-isha-san	医者/お医者さん

dentist	haisha	歯医者
diarrhoea	geri	下痢
fever	netsu	熱
food poisoning	shoku chūdoku	食中毒
I'm ill	byōki desu	病気です
I've got a cold/flu	kaze o hikimashita	風邪を引きました
I'm allergic to (x)	(x) arerugii desu	(x) アレルギーです
antibiotics	kōsei busshitsu	抗生物質
antiseptic	shōdoku	消毒

FOOD AND DRINK

PLACES TO EAT AND DRINK

bar	nomiya	飲み屋
standing-only bar	tachinomiya	立ち飲み屋
café/coffee shop	kissaten	喫茶店
cafeteria	shokudō	食堂
pub	pabu	パブ
pub-style restaurant	izakaya	居酒屋
restaurant	resutoran	レストラン
restaurant specializing in charcoal-grilled foods	robatayaki	炉端焼
street food stall	yatai	屋台

ORDERING

breakfast	asa-gohan	朝ご飯
lunch	hiru-gohan	昼ご飯
dinner	ban-gohan/yushoku	晩ご飯/夕食
boxed meal	bentō	弁当
chopsticks	hashi	はし
fork	fōku	フォーク
knife	naifu	ナイフ
spoon	supūn	スプーン
set meal	teishoku	定食
daily special set meal	higawari-teishoku	日替り定食
menu	menyū	メニュー
Do you have an English menu?	eigo no menyū ga arimasu ka	英語のメニューがありますか
How much is that?	ikura desu ka	いくらですか
I would like (a)...	(a) ...o onegai shimasu	(a)をお願いします
May I have the bill?	okanjō o onegai shimasu	お勘定をお願いします

STAPLE FOODS

oil	abura	油
butter	batā	バター
rice	gohan	ご飯
pepper	koshō	こしょう
fermented soybean paste	miso	味噌
garlic	ninniku	にんにく
dried seaweed	nori	のり
bread	pan	パン
sugar	satō	砂糖
salt	shio	塩
soy sauce	shōyu	しょうゆ
egg	tamago	卵
bean curd tofu	tōfu	豆腐

FISH AND SEAFOOD DISHES

horse mackerel	aji	あじ
abalone	awabi	あわび
sweet fish	ayu	あゆ
yellowtail	buri	ぶり
sushi topped with fish, egg and vegetables	chirashi-zushi	ちらし寿司
prawn	ebi	えび
blowfish	fugu	ふぐ
squid	ika	いか
lobster	ise-ebi	伊勢海老
shellfish	kai	貝
oyster	kaki	かき
crab	kani	かに
tuna	maguro	まぐろ
sushi rolled in crisp seaweed	maki-zushi	まき寿司
bite-size portion of sushi rice with topping	nigiri-zushi	にぎり寿司
herring	nishin	にしん
fish	sakana	魚
raw fish	sashimi	さしみ
sushi	sushi	寿司
sea bream	tai	たい
octopus	tako	たこ/タコ
cod	tara	たら
eel	unagi	うなぎ
sea urchin	uni	うに

FRUIT

banana	banana	バナナ
grapes	budō	ぶどう
grapefruit	gurēpufurūtsu	グレープフルーツ
strawberry	ichigo	いちご
persimmon	kaki	柿
fruit	kudamono	果物
melon	meron	メロン
tangerine	mikan	みかん
peach	momo	桃
pear	nashi	なし
orange	orenji	オレンジ
pineapple	painappuru	パイナップル
lemon	remon	レモン
apple	ringo	りんご
watermelon	suika	すいか
Japanese plum	ume	うめ

VEGETABLES

radish	daikon	大根
cauliflower	karifurawā	カリフラワー
mushroom	kinoko	きのこ
sweetcorn	kōn	コーン
beans	mame	豆
beansprouts	moyashi	もやし
aubergine	nasu	なす

leek	negi	ねぎ
carrot	ninjin	にんじん
green pepper	piiman	ピーマン
potato	poteto/jagaimo	ポテト、じゃがいも
salad	sarada	サラダ
onion	tamanegi	たまねぎ
tomato	tomato	トマト
green horseradish	wasabi	わさび
vegetables	yasai	野菜

MEAT AND MEAT DISHES

pork	butaniku	豚肉
beef	gyūniku	牛肉
skewers of food dipped in breadcrumbs and deep-fried	kushiage	串揚げ
stew including meat (or seafood), vegetables and noodles	nabe	鍋
meat	niku	肉
lamb	ramu	ラム
thin beef slices cooked in broth	shabu-shabu	しゃぶしゃぶ
thin beef slices braised in a sauce	sukiyaki	すきやき
breaded, deep-fried slice of pork	tonkatsu	とんかつ
chicken	toriniku	鶏肉
grilled meat	yakiniku	焼肉
chicken, grilled on skewers	yakitori	焼き鳥

VEGETARIAN AND NOODLE DISHES

Chinese-style dumplings	gyōza	ぎょうざ
soba in a hot soup	kake-soba	かけそば
stewed chunks of vegetables and fish on skewers	oden	おでん
Chinese-style noodles	rāmen	ラーメン
Buddhist-style vegetarian cuisine	shōjin-ryōri	精進料理
thin buckwheat noodles	soba	そば
thick wheat noodles	udon	うどん
fried noodles	yakisoba/yakiudon	焼そば／焼うどん
cold soba served with a dipping sauce	zaru-soba/mori-soba	ざるそば／もりそば

OTHER DISHES

fried rice	chāhan	チャーハン
Chinese food	Chūka-/Chūgoku-ryōri	中華／中国料理
rice topped with fish, meat or vegetable	donburi	どんぶり
French food	Furansu-ryōri	フランス料理
Italian food	Itaria-ryōri	イタリア料理
Japanese haute cuisine	kaiseki ryōri	懐石料理
Korean food	Kankoku-ryōri	韓国料理
curry served with rice	karē raisu	カレーライス
pounded rice cakes	mochi	もち
"no-nationality" food	mukokuseki-ryōri	無国籍料理
fermented soybeans	nattō	納豆
savoury pancakes	okonomiyaki	お好み焼き

rice triangles wrapped in crisp seaweed	onigiri	おにぎり
Thai food	Tai-ryōri	タイ料理
octopus in balls of batter	takoyaki	たこ焼き
lightly battered seafood and vegetables	tempura	天ぷら
meat, vegetable and fish cooked in soy sauce and sweet sake	teriyaki	照り焼き
Japanese-style food	washoku	和食
Western-style food	yōshoku	洋食

DRINKS

beer	biiru	ビール
fruit juice	jūsu	ジュース
black tea	kōcha	紅茶
coffee	kōhii	コーヒー
powdered green tea	matcha	抹茶
milk	miruku	ミルク
water	mizu	水
whisky and water	mizu-wari	水割り
sake (rice wine)	sake/nihon-shu	酒／日本酒
green tea	sencha	煎茶
distilled liquor	shōchū	焼酎
whisky	uisukii	ウイスキー
Oolong tea	ūron-cha	ウーロン茶
wine	wain	ワイン

Glossary

aikido A form of self-defence recognized as a sport.

ANA All Nippon Airways.

anime Japanese animation.

banzai Traditional cheer, meaning "10,000 years".

basho Sumo tournament.

benten or **benzai-ten** One of the most popular folk-goddesses, usually associated with water.

bentō Lunch box of rice, fish, vegetables and pickles.

bodhisattva or **bosatsu** A Buddhist intermediary who has forsaken nirvana to work for the salvation of all humanity.

bunraku Traditional puppet theatre.

Butō or **Butoh** Highly expressive contemporary performance art.

cha-no-yu, chadō or **sadō** The tea ceremony. Ritual tea drinking raised to an art form.

-chō or **-machi** Subdivision of a city, smaller than a -ku.

-chōme Area of the city consisting of a few blocks.

daimyō Feudal lords.

Dainichi Nyorai or **Rushana Butsu** The Cosmic Buddha in whom all Buddhas are unified.

-dake Mountain peak, usually volcanic.

DPJ Democratic Party of Japan.

Edo Pre-1868 name for Tokyo.

ema Small wooden boards found at shrines, on which people write their wishes or thanks.

fusuma Paper-covered sliding doors, more substantial than shōji, used to separate rooms or for cupboards.

futon Padded quilt used for bedding.

gagaku Traditional Japanese music used for court ceremonies and religious rites.

gaikokujin or **gaijin** Foreigner.

geisha Traditional female entertainer accomplished in the arts.

genkan Foyer or entrance hall of a house, ryokan and so forth, for changing from outdoor shoes into slippers.

genki Lively and/or healthy, friendly.

geta Traditional wooden sandals.

haiku Seventeen-syllable verse form, arranged in three lines of five, seven and five syllables.

hanami "Flower-viewing"; most commonly associated with spring outings to admire the cherry blossom.

hashi Chopsticks.

-hashi or **-bashi** Bridge.

hiragana Phonetic script used for writing Japanese in combination with kanji.

ijinkan Western-style brick and clapboard houses.

ikebana Traditional art of flower arranging.

Inari Shintō god of harvests, often represented by his fox-messenger.

JAL Japan Airlines.

-ji Buddhist temple.

jigoku The word for Buddhist "hell", also applied to volcanic mud pools and steam vents.

-jinja or **-jingū** Shintō shrine.

Jizō Buddhist protector of children, travellers and the dead.

JNTO Japan National Tourist Organization.

-jō Castle.

JR Japan Railways.

kabuki Popular theatre of the Edo period.

kami Shintō deities residing in trees, rocks and other natural phenomena.

Kamikaze The "Divine Wind" which saved Japan from the Mongol invaders (see p.822). During World War II the name was applied to Japan's suicide bombers.

kanji Japanese script derived from Chinese characters.

Kannon Buddhist goddess of mercy. A bodhisattva who appears in many different forms.

katakana Phonetic script used mainly for writing foreign words in Japanese.

-kawa or **-gawa** River.

-ken Prefecture. The principal administrative region, similar to a state or county.

kendo Japan's oldest martial art, using wooden staves, with its roots in samurai training exercises.

kimono Literally "clothes", though usually referring to women's traditional dress.

-ko Lake.

kōban Neighbourhood police box.

kōen or **gyoen** Public park.

kōgen Plateau, or highlands.

konbini Convenience store.

-ku Principal administrative division of the city, usually translated as "ward".

kura Traditional storehouse built with thick mud walls as protection against fire, for keeping produce and family treasures.

kyōgen Short, satirical plays, providing comic interludes in nō drama.

LDP Liberal Democratic Party.

-machi Town or area of a city.

maiko Apprentice geisha.

manga Japanese comics.

matcha Powdered green tea used in the tea ceremony.

matsuri Festival.

Meiji Period named after Emperor Meiji (1868–1912), meaning "enlightened rule".

Meiji Restoration End of the Tokugawa Shogunate, when power was fully restored to the emperor.

mikoshi Portable shrine used in festivals.

minshuku Family-run lodgings which are cheaper than ryokan.

mon Gate, usually to a castle, temple or palace.

mura Village.

netsuke Small, intricately carved toggles for fastening the cords of cloth bags.

ningyō Japanese doll.

nō Highly stylized dance-drama, using masks and elaborate costumes.

noren Split curtain hanging in shop and restaurant doorways to indicate they're open.

notemburo Outdoor hot-spring pool, usually in natural surroundings.

obi Wide sash worn with kimono.

odori Traditional dances performed in the streets during the summer Obon festival.

onsen Hot spring, generally developed for bathing.

pachinko Vertical pinball machines.

pond-garden Classic form of garden design focused around a pond.

rōmaji System of transliterating Japanese words using the roman alphabet.

rōnin Masterless samurai.

rotemburo Outdoor hot-spring pool, often in the grounds of a ryokan.

ryokan Traditional Japanese inn.

salarymen Office workers who keep Japan's companies and ministries ticking over.

samurai Warrior class who were retainers of the *daimyō*.

SDF (Self-Defence Forces) Japan's army, navy and airforce.

sensei Teacher.

sentō Neighbourhood public bath.

seppuku Ritual suicide by disembowelment, also referred to as *harakiri*.

Shaka Nyorai The Historical Buddha, Sakyamuni.

shamisen Traditional, three-stringed instrument played with a plectrum.

-shima or **-jima** Island.

Shinkansen Bullet train.

Shintō Japan's indigenous animist religion.

Shitamachi Old working-class districts of east Tokyo.

shogun Japan's military rulers before 1868, nominally subordinate to the emperor.

shōji Paper-covered sliding screens used to divide rooms or cover windows.

shōjin ryōri Buddhist cuisine

shukubō Temple lodgings.

sumi-e Ink paintings, traditionally using black ink.

sumo A form of heavyweight wrestling which evolved from ancient Shintō divination rites.

taiko Drums.

tatami Rice-straw matting, the traditional covering for floors.

tokonoma Alcove in a room where flowers or a scroll are displayed.

torii Gate to a Shintō shrine.

ukiyo-e Colourful woodblock prints.

waka Thirty-one-syllable poem, arranged in five lines of five, seven, five, seven and seven syllables.

washi Traditional handmade paper.

Yakushi Nyorai The Buddha in charge of physical and spiritual healing.

yakuza Professional criminal gangs, somewhat akin to the Mafia.

yamabushi Ascetic mountain priests.

yokozuna Champion sumo wrestler.

yukata Cotton kimono usually worn in summer, and after a bath.

Small print and index

ABOUT THE AUTHORS

Paul Gray has been travelling in and writing about Asia for over twenty years. He is co-author of *The Rough Guide to Thailand* and *The Rough Guide to Ireland*, and has edited and contributed to many other guidebooks, including an update of his native Northeast for *The Rough Guide to England*.

Sally McLaren has been writing about Japan for local and international media since 1997, and has worked on four editions of the *Rough Guide to Japan*. She's travelled all over the country but especially loves Kansai for its great food culture, fabulous onsen and ancient festivals.

Tamatha Roman (ⓦfreshcoffeestains.com) has been wandering the world for many years as an English teacher and a journalist for various travel publications, including Rough Guides and Metropolis Japan. She lived in Japan for eight years, hitchhiking across the country and exploring abandoned theme parks in her free time. She currently resides in Boston.

Simon Scott first moved to Japan in 1999 and feels a strong connection to Shikoku, having spent his formative years in Japan living in the shadow of the giant Seto Ohashi bridge, the main gateway to the island. Eventually he traded in the quiet life of sunny Okayama for the bright lights of Tokyo's frantic Shinjuku distict, where he now lives and works as a freelance journalist and travel writer.

Greg Ward (ⓦgregward.info) has been writing Rough Guides for over twenty years. He's the sole author of guides to *Southwest USA*, *Brittany & Normandy*, *Blues CDs*, *US History* and *the Titanic*, and the joint author of others including *Provence*, *Spain* and *Australia*. Travelling the length and breadth of Honshū for this edition of Japan, however, was an absolute career highlight.

Martin Zatko started travelling in early 2002, and hasn't really stopped since. Finding that food, shelter and coffee cost money, he started writing guidebooks for a living, and has now written or contributed to almost thirty Rough Guides, including those to *Korea*, *Seoul*, *China*, *Beijing*, *Vietnam*, *Myanmar*, *Turkey*, *Morocco* and *Europe*. A big fan of noodles in general, he finds that Tokyo suits him down to the ground, and that the city's unique blend of tame chaos simply never gets boring.

Rough Guide credits

Editors: Tim Locke, Claire Saunders, Georgia Stephens
Senior editor: Edward Aves
Layout: Jessica Subramanian
Cartography: Swati Handoo
Picture editor: Phoebe Lowndes
Proofreader: Jan McCann
Japanese proofreader: Rebecca Hallett
Managing editor: Andy Turner

Assistant editor: Payal Sharotri
Production: Jimmy Lao
Cover photo research: Sarah Stewart Richardson
Editorial assistant: Aimee White
Senior DTP coordinator: Dan May
Programme manager: Gareth Lowe
Publishing director: Georgina Dee

Publishing information

This seventh edition published September 2017 by
Rough Guides Ltd

Distribution

UK, Ireland and Europe
Apa Publications (UK) Ltd; sales@roughguides.com
United States and Canada
Ingram Publisher Services; ips@ingramcontent.com
Australia and New Zealand
Woodslane; info@woodslane.com.au
Southeast Asia
Apa Publications (SN) Pte; sales@roughguides.com
Worldwide
Apa Publications (UK) Ltd; sales@roughguides.com
Special sales, content licensing and co-publishing
Rough Guides can be purchased in bulk quantities
at discounted prices. We can create special editions,
personalized jackets and corporate imprints tailored to
your needs. sales@roughguides.com
roughguides.com
Printed in China

Help us update

We've gone to a lot of effort to ensure that the seventh
edition of **The Rough Guide to Japan** is accurate and up-
to-date. However, things change – places get "discovered",
opening hours are notoriously fickle, restaurants and
rooms raise prices or lower standards. If you feel we've got
it wrong or left something out, we'd like to know, and if
you can remember the address, the price, the hours, the
phone number, so much the better.

Please send your comments with the subject line
"**Rough Guide Japan Update**" to mail@uk.roughguides
.com. We'll credit all contributions and send a copy of the
next edition (or any other Rough Guide if you prefer) for
the very best emails.

A ROUGH GUIDE TO ROUGH GUIDES

Published in 1982, the first Rough Guide – to Greece – was a student scheme that became a
publishing phenomenon. Mark Ellingham, a recent graduate in English from Bristol University,
had been travelling in Greece the previous summer and couldn't find the right guidebook.
With a small group of friends he wrote his own guide, combining a contemporary, journalistic
style with a thoroughly practical approach to travellers' needs.

The immediate success of the book spawned a series that rapidly covered dozens of
destinations. And, in addition to impecunious backpackers, Rough Guides soon acquired a
much broader readership that relished the guides' wit and inquisitiveness as much as their
enthusiastic, critical approach and value-for-money ethos. These days, Rough Guides include
recommendations from budget to luxury and cover more than 120 destinations around the
globe, from Amsterdam to Zanzibar, all regularly updated by our team of roaming writers.

Browse all our latest guides, read inspirational features and book your trip at **roughguides.com**.

Acknowledgements

Paul Gray Heartfelt thanks to Hiroaki Ono and Masayuki Fuchigami in Yufuin; Zoushiki-san in Miyazaki; Tomoko Takae and Takenori Yokoyama in Kagoshima; Anson Lan and Tatsuro Sato in Kumamoto; Mutsumi Yamaguchi, Miyuri Tsuru, Yoshihisa and Misono Tsuruta and Hanneke Morre in Arita; Junji Mamitsuka, Director of the Dejima Restoration Office, and Yuki Taniguchi in Nagasaki; Toshihiro Mori in Fukuoka; Hollie Mantle at JNTO; James Mundy at Inside Japan; Professor Nicole Rousmaniere and Ai Fukunaga at the British Museum; Simon Richmond, Jan Dodd, Mike Barraclough and Junko-san; Claire, Ed and Andy at Rough Guides.

Sally McLaren A big ōkini to the many people in Kansai who kindly helped me, especially Aria at the Osaka Convention and Tourism Bureau, Brad and the Kumano Tourism Bureau, Kyoko in Himeji, Kiku and her team in Toba and Hanae at the Iga-Ueno TIC. Many thanks also to JNTO and Inside Japan for your generous cooperation; Stone Bridge Press, Sekai Bunkasha, Tuttle and the Japan Publishing Industry Foundation for Culture. To friends in Kansai – your help and support is always appreciated. Many thanks to Ed, Andy, Claire at Rough Guides. Finally, thanks to Albie for love and support.

Tamatha Roman I'd like to thank the "strangers" that helped me during my research: the drivers who picked me up and the Couchsurfing hosts that brought me into their homes. To my family for putting up with my restlessness and never saying no. To Robbie, my lifeline, for pushing me to write. To my friends (Dani, Liz, Erin and Mari) and colleagues in Japan who made my life there endlessly fulfilling.

Simon Scott Thanks to the talented Masumi Kamozaki for her invaluable assistance and support with research, fact-checking and translation; Kevin "Gomyo" Seperic for his spiritual inspiration and insights about Shikoku's 88-temple pilgrimage; Keizo Kubota from the *Mori no Kuni Hotel* in the beautiful Nametoko Gorge. Matt from *Sen Guesthouse* in Dogo; James Mundy from InsideAsia Tours. And all the many others who helped and inspired me on my journey, especially the innumerable Shikoku locals who were so often willing to help a tired traveller without asking for anything in return.

Greg Ward Thanks above all to my wife Samantha Cook, for sharing a totally memorable adventure. Thanks too to Hollie Mantle at the JNTO, to Noriko Kobayashi and Chiko Shimomiya in Onomichi, and to the many other people who helped along the way. And thanks to my editor Tim Locke for all his hard work, and to Ed Aves and Andy Turner at Rough Guides.

Martin Zatko would like to thank the TCVB, the JNTO and the Freshroom team for their kind assistance with his research trip, and Claire Saunders for her careful editing work. He would also like to thank housemate Pierre Terron for his sterling company in distant Akatsuka; German Serina and Swiss Reto for the karaoke nights, convenience store runs and rooftop drinks; Thomas Clinard and Yoko Yagi for their cameo appearances; Ayano Tamaki for the 2003 time-warp; Rena and Mey for the Godzilla nights in Shinjuku; Nakameguro for barely changing a jot; David Carruth for the loan of his apartment during the write-up; Hyeri Yang for the retro nights during that time; and Y's for all the tsukemen, plus the near-death experience.

Readers' updates

Thanks to all the readers who have taken the time to write in with comments and suggestions (and apologies if we've inadvertently omitted or misspelt anyone's name):

Gordon Barrett; Helen Bonser; Martin Cooper; Francoise Dubosclard; David Eves; David and Joyce Graves; Claire Gulvin; Tomoko Hanawa; Sanne Hiddinga; Mariette Huisjes; Torbjörn Johansson; Mauricio Karam; Tim Laslavic; Neil Masters; Vicky Miller; millanakkeeran1; Philippe Parée; Chris Price; Pilar Restrepo; Klas Rönnbäck; Peter Rooke; "Skocianski"; Florian Spath; Midori Tabata; Mark Thomas; Ian Thomson; Peter Thomson; Yuki Tokui; David A. Valinsky; Jef Wouters; Kembo Yukinor.

Photo credits

All photos © Rough Guides, except the following:
(Key: t-top; c-centre; b-bottom; l-left; r-right)

Index

Maps are marked in grey

Map symbols

The symbols below are used on maps throughout the book

International boundary		Point of interest		Spring
State/province boundary		Parking		Waterfall
Chapter division boundary		Post office		Mountain refugee
Motorway		Information centre		Mountain peak
Main road		Internet access		Campground
Minor road		Hospital		Tree
Pedestrianized road		Embassy		Gorge
Steps		Cave		Ferris wheel
R line		Viewpoint/lookout		Pagoda
Shinkansen line		Observation platform		Buddhist temple
Other rail line		Museum		Shrine
Monorail		Archeological site		Lighthouse
Tram		Castle		Ruins
Cable car		Statue		Church (town maps)
Funicular		Port		Market
Coastline		Scuba diving		Cemetery
Ferry		Observatory		Building
Footpath		Bridge		Stadium
Subway		Boat		Park/forest
Bus stop		Gate/park entrance		Beach
International airport		Domestic airport/airfield		

Listings key

- ■ Accommodation
- ● Eating
- ■ Drinking and nightlife
- ● Shopping

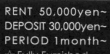

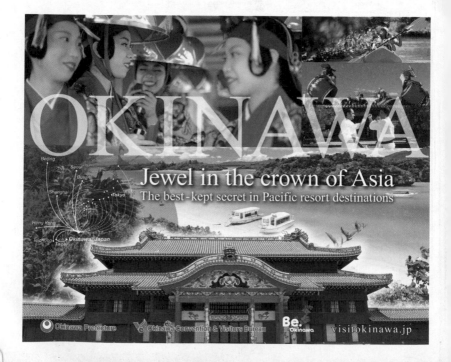

JAL MOMENTS

Welcoming you aboard with authentic
Japanese hospitality and making your every moment
with us an unforgettable experience. JAL.

Fly into tomorrow.

 JAPAN AIRLINES oneworld

 Pass the time with us smoothly and effortlessly.
JAL International Economy Class, JAL SKY WIDER.
Visit our website www.uk.jal.com